THE NEW CAMBRIDGE HISTORY OF

ISLAM

*

VOLUME 4

Islamic Cultures and Societies to the End of the Eighteenth Century

Robert Irwin's authoritative introduction to the fourth volume of *The New Cambridge History of Islam* offers a panoramic vision of Islamic culture from its origins to around 1800. The chapter, which highlights key developments and introduces some of Islam's most famous protagonists, paves the way for an extraordinarily varied collection of essays. The themes treated include religion and law, conversion, Islam's relationship with the natural world, governance and politics, caliphs and kings, philosophy, science, medicine, language, art, architecture, literature, music and even cookery. What emerges from this rich collection, written by an international team of experts, is the diversity and dynamism of the societies which created this flourishing civilisation. Volume 4 of *The New Cambridge History of Islam* serves as a thematic companion to the three preceding, politically oriented volumes, and in coverage extends across the pre-modern Islamic world.

Robert Irwin is senior research associate of the history department, School of Oriental and African Studies, University of London. His previous publications include *For lust of knowing: The Orientalists and their enemies* (2006), *Night and horses and the desert: An anthology of classical Arabic literature* (1999) and *The Arabian Nights: A Companion* (1994).

THE NEW CAMBRIDGE HISTORY OF

ISLAM

The New Cambridge History of Islam offers a comprehensive history of Islamic civilisation, tracing its development from its beginnings in seventh-century Arabia to its wide and varied presence in the globalised world of today. Under the leadership of the Prophet Muḥammad the Muslim community coalesced from a scattered, desert population and, following his death, emerged from Arabia to conquer an empire which, by the early eighth century, stretched from India in the east to Spain in the west. By the eighteenth century, despite political fragmentation, the Muslim world extended from West Africa to South-East Asia. Today Muslims are also found in significant numbers in Europe and the Americas, and make up about one-fifth of the world's population.

To reflect this geographical distribution and the cultural, social and religious diversity of the peoples of the Muslim world, *The New Cambridge History of Islam* is divided into six volumes. Four cover historical developments, and two are devoted to themes that cut across geographical and chronological divisions – themes ranging from social, political and economic relations to the arts, literature and learning. Each volume begins with a panoramic introduction setting the scene for the ensuing chapters and examining relationships with adjacent civilisations. Two of the volumes – one historical, the other thematic – are dedicated to the developments of the last two centuries, and show how Muslims, united for so many years in their allegiance to an overarching and distinct tradition, have sought to come to terms with the emergence of Western hegemony and the transition to modernity.

The time is right for this new synthesis reflecting developments in scholarship over the last generation. *The New Cambridge History of Islam* is an ambitious enterprise directed and written by a team combining established authorities and innovative younger scholars. It will be the standard reference for students, scholars and all those with enquiring minds for years to come.

General editor

MICHAEL COOK, CLASS OF 1943 UNIVERSITY PROFESSOR OF NEAR EASTERN STUDIES, PRINCETON UNIVERSITY

VOLUME 1
The Formation of the Islamic World
Sixth to Eleventh Centuries
EDITED BY CHASE F. ROBINSON

VOLUME 2
The Western Islamic World
Eleventh to Eighteenth Centuries
EDITED BY MARIBEL FIERRO

VOLUME 3
The Eastern Islamic World
Eleventh to Eighteenth Centuries
EDITED BY DAVID O. MORGAN AND ANTHONY REID

VOLUME 4
Islamic Cultures and Societies to the End of the Eighteenth Century
EDITED BY ROBERT IRWIN

VOLUME 5
The Islamic World in the Age of Western Dominance
EDITED BY FRANCIS ROBINSON

VOLUME 6
Muslims and Modernity
Culture and Society since 1800
EDITED BY ROBERT W. HEFNER

Grants made from an award to the General Editor by the Andrew W. Mellon Foundation, and from the National Endowment for the Humanities RZ-50616-06, contributed to the development of *The New Cambridge History of Islam*. In particular the grants funded the salary of William M. Blair, who served as Editorial Assistant from 2004 to 2008.

THE NEW CAMBRIDGE HISTORY OF ISLAM

*

VOLUME 4

Islamic Cultures and Societies to the End of the Eighteenth Century

*

Edited by
ROBERT IRWIN

CAMBRIDGE
UNIVERSITY PRESS

CAMBRIDGE UNIVERSITY PRESS
Cambridge, New York, Melbourne, Madrid, Cape Town, Singapore,
São Paulo, Delhi, Mexico City

Cambridge University Press
The Edinburgh Building, Cambridge CB2 8RU, UK

Published in the United States of America by Cambridge University Press, New York

www.cambridge.org
Information on this title: www.cambridge.org/9780521838245

First published 2010
Reprinted 2013

Printed and bound in the United Kingdom by the MPG Books Group

A catalogue record for this publication is available from the British Library

ISBN 978-0-521-83824-5 Volume 4 Hardback
ISBN 978-0-521-51536-8 Set of 6 Hardback Volumes

Contents

Figures

Illustrations

Dynastic tables

Contributors

SAÏD AMIR ARJOMAND is Distinguished Service Professor of Sociology at the State University of New York at Stony Brook and is the founder and president (1996–2002, 2005–8) of the Association for the Study of Persianate Societies. His books include *The shadow of God and the Hidden Imam: Religion, political organization and societal change in Shi'ite Iran from the beginning to 1890* (Chicago, 1984), *The turban for the crown: The Islamic Revolution in Iran* (Oxford, 1988) and *Rethinking civilizational analysis* (London, 2004; ed. with Edward Tiryakian).

ÇİĞDEM BALİM HARDING is the Director of Graduate Studies and Director of Language Instruction at the Department of Near Eastern Languages and Cultures, Indiana University. She is the Middle East Regional Editor of the journal *Women's Studies International Forum* (Elsevier Publications). Her previous publications include, as co-author, *Meskhetian Turks: An introduction to their history, culture, and US resettlement experience* (Washington, DC, 2006), as co-editor, *The balance of truth: Essays in honour of Geoffrey Lewis* (Istanbul, 2000) and *Turkey: Political, social and economic challenges in the 1990s* (Leiden, 1995).

JONATHAN BERKEY, Professor of History at Davidson College in North Carolina, is the author of several books on medieval Islamic history, most recently *The formation of Islam: Religion and society in the Near East, 600–1800* (Cambridge, 2003).

MICHAEL BONNER is Professor of Medieval Islamic History in the Department of Near Eastern Studies, University of Michigan. He received his Ph.D. in the Department of Near Eastern Studies, Princeton University, in 1987. His recent publications include *Jihad in Islamic history: Doctrines and practices* (Princeton, 2006), and *Poverty and charity in Middle Eastern contexts*, co-edited with Amy Singer and Mine Ener (Albany, 2003). He has been a Helmut S. Stern Fellow at the University of Michigan Institute for the Humanities, and has held the position of Professeur Invité at the Institut d'Études de l'Islam et des Sociétés du Monde Musulman, École des Hautes Études en Sciences Sociales, and of Chaire de l'Institut du Monde Arabe, also in Paris. He was Director of the University of Michigan Center for Middle Eastern and North African Studies in 1997–2000 and 2001–3, and Acting Chair of the Department of Near Eastern Studies in 2007–8.

JONATHAN BLOOM holds both the Norma Jean Calderwood University Professorship of Islamic and Asian Art at Boston College and the Hamad bin Khalifa Endowed Chair of

Islamic Art at Virginia Commonwealth University. Among his most recent publications are *Arts of the city victorious: Islamic art and architecture in Fatimid North Africa and Egypt* (New Haven and London, 2007) and *Paper before print: The history and impact of paper in the Islamic world* (New Haven, 2001). He is also the co-editor of the three-volume *Grove Encyclopedia of Islamic art and architecture* (Oxford, 2009).

JULIA BRAY is Professor of Medieval Arabic Literature at the University of Paris 8–Saint Denis. Her previous publications include, as editor, *'Abbasid belles-lettres* (Cambridge, 1990) and *Writing and representation in medieval Islam* (London and New York, 2006).

SONJA BRENTJES is Senior Researcher in a Project of Excellence of the Government of Andalusia at the Department of Philosophy and Logic, University of Seville. She has taught and done research in several European countries and the USA, and is currently on a visiting professorship to Sabanci University, Turkey. She has studied mathematics, Arabic and Near Eastern history and has focused on the history of mathematics, institutions and cartography in Islamic societies as well as the transmission of knowledge between different cultures in Asia, Europe and North Africa. Her previous publications include 'Euclid's *Elements*, courtly patronage and princely education' (*Iranian Studies* 41 (2008)) and 'Patronage of the mathematical sciences in Islamic societies: structure and rhetoric, identities and outcomes' (in Eleanor Robson and Jackie Stendall (eds.), *The Oxford handbook of the history of mathematics* (Oxford, 2008)).

RICHARD W. BULLIET is Professor of History at Columbia University in New York City. His publications include *The patricians of Nishapur* (Cambridge, MA, 1972), *The camel and the wheel* (Cambridge, MA, 1975), *Conversion to Islam in the medieval period* (Cambridge, MA, 1979), *Islam: The view from the edge* (New York, 1994), *The case for Islamo-Christian civilization* (New York, 2004), *Hunters, herders, and hamburgers* (New York, 2005), and *Cotton, climate, and camels in early Islamic Iran* (New York, 2009).

MICHAEL COOPERSON is Professor of Arabic at the University of California, Los Angeles. He is the author of *Classical Arabic biography* (Cambridge, 2000) and *al-Ma'mun* (Oxford, 2005), a co-author of *Interpreting the self* (Berkeley, 2001), and the translator of Abdelfattah Kilito's *The author and his doubles* (Syracuse, 2001).

FARHAD DAFTARY is Associate Director and Head of the Department of Academic Research and Publications at the Institute of Ismaili Studies, London. He is a consulting editor of *Encyclopaedia Iranica*, co-editor of *Encyclopaedia Islamica*, as well as the general editor of the Ismaili Heritage Series and the Ismaili Texts and Translations Series. An authority on Ismaili history, Dr Daftary's publications include *The Ismāʿīlīs: Their history and doctrines* (Cambridge, 1990; 2nd edn, 2007), *The Assassin legends* (London, 1994), *A short history of the Ismailis* (Edinburgh, 1998), *Ismaili literature: A bibliography of sources and studies* (London, 2004), *Ismailis in medieval Muslim societies* (London, 2005) and (with Z. Hirji) *The Ismailis: An illustrated history* (London, 2008). Dr Daftary's books have been translated into Arabic, Persian, Turkish, Urdu and numerous European languages.

DICK DAVIS is Professor of Persian and Chair of the Department of Near Eastern Languages and Cultures at Ohio State University. His publications include a number of translations of major works of Persian literature, including Ferdowsi's *Shahnameh*, Gorgani's *Vis and Ramin* and Attar's *Conference of the birds* (with Afkham Darbandi, winner of the AIIS Translation Prize) as well as scholarly works on medieval Persian literature.

SURAIYA N. FAROQHI teaches Ottoman history at Bilgi University, Istanbul. Her publications include *Approaching Ottoman history: An introduction to the sources* (Cambridge, 1999) and *The Ottoman empire and the world around it* (London, 2004). A collection of her articles was published in *Stories of Ottoman men and women: establishing status, establishing control* (Istanbul, 2002). *Artisans of empire: crafts and craftspeople under the Ottomans* is in the course of publication (London, 2009).

SHAMSUR RAHMAN FARUQI, Urdu critic, literary theorist, poet, fiction writer and translator, is best known for his *Early Urdu literary culture and history* (New Delhi, 2001), a four-volume study, in Urdu, of the eighteenth-century Urdu poet Mir Taqi Mir (1723–1810), and an ongoing study, in Urdu, of the Urdu oral romance called *Dastan-e Amir Hamza*. Three of the projected four volumes have been published. More recently, his voluminous historical-cultural novel in Urdu called *Ka'i Chand The Sar-e Asman* was published to wide acclaim in both India and Pakistan. A retired civil servant, Faruqi lives in Allahabad, India.

LI GUO received his Ph.D. from Yale University (1994) and is currently Associate Professor at the University of Notre Dame, Indiana. He is the author of *Early Mamluk Syrian historiography: al-Yūnīnī's Dhayl Mirʾāt al-zamān* (Leiden, 1994) and *Commerce, culture, and community in a Red Sea port in the thirteenth century: The Arabic documents from Quseir* (Leiden, 2004).

GOTTFRIED HAGEN is Associate Professor of Turkish Studies in the Department of Near Eastern Studies at the University of Michigan. He received his MA in Islamic Studies from the University of Heidelberg (1989) and his Ph.D. in Turkish Studies from Free University in Berlin (1996). He is the author of *Ein osmanischer Geograph bei der Arbeit: Entstehung und Gedankenwelt von Kātib Čelebis Ǧihānnümā* (Berlin, 2003), as well as numerous articles on Ottoman and Islamic geography, cartography, historiography and religious literature.

WAEL B. HALLAQ is a James McGill Professor of Islamic Law, teaching at the Institute of Islamic Studies, McGill University. He is author of over sixty scholarly articles and several books, including *Ibn Taymiyya against the Greek logicians* (Oxford, 1993), *A history of Islamic legal theories* (Cambridge, 1997), *Authority, continuity and change in Islamic law* (Cambridge, 2001), *The origins and evolution of Islamic law* (Cambridge, 2005), *An introduction to Islamic law* (Cambridge, 2009) and *Sharīʿa: Theory, practice, transformations* (Cambridge, 2009).

S. NOMANUL HAQ is on the faculty of the School of Humanities and the Social Sciences at the Lahore University of Management Sciences and is General Editor of the Oxford University Press monograph series Studies in Islamic Philosophy. Until recently he remained Scholar-in-Residence at the American Institute of Pakistan. His first book,

Names, natures, and things: The alchemist Jābir ibn Ḥayyān and his Kitāb al-aḥjār *(Book of stones)* (Boston, 1994), was a textual study of an enigmatic medieval Arabic alchemical school. Since then he has published widely in multiple fields of the history of Islamic philosophy and of science, religion, cultural studies and Persian and Urdu literature.

ROBERT IRWIN is Senior Research Associate of the History Department, School of Oriental and African Studies, London University. His previous publications include *For lust of knowing: The Orientalists and their enemies* (London, 2006), *Night and horses and the desert: An anthology of classical Arabic literature* (Harmondsworth, 1999) and *The Arabian Nights: A Companion* (London, 1994).

HUGH KENNEDY is Professor of Arabic at the School of Oriental and African Studies, University of London. He is the author of numerous books on Islamic history, including *The Prophet and the age of the caliphates* (London, 1986; new edn Harlow, 2004), *The court of the caliphs* (London, 2004) and *The great Arab conquests* (London, 2007).

ALEXANDER KNYSH is Professor of Islamic Studies at the University of Michigan at Ann Arbor. He has published extensively (in English, Russian and Arabic) on Islamic intellectual and political history and various manifestations of Islamic religiosity in local contexts from Yemen to the Caucasus. Recent English publications include *Islamic mysticism: A short history* (Leiden, 2000), *al-Qushayri's Epistle on Sufism* (Reading, 2007) and *Islam in historical perspective* (Reading, 2009).

BRUCE LAWRENCE is Nancy and Jeffrey Marcus Humanities Professor of Religion and Professor of Islamic Studies at Duke University. He is currently the Director of the Duke Islamic Studies Center. His publications include *Muslim networks from Hajj to hip hop*, co-edited with Miriam Cooke (Chapel Hill, 2005), *Messages to the world: The statements of Osama bin Laden* (London and New York, 2006) and *The Qur'an: A biography* (London, 2007).

MANUELA MARÍN is a Research Professor at the Consejo Superior de Investigaciones Científicas (Madrid). She is the author of *Mujeres en al-Andalus* (Madrid, 2000), and of 'Disciplining wives: a historical reading of Qur'an 4:34' (*Studia Islamica*, 97 (2003)).

MARCUS MILWRIGHT is Associate Professor of Islamic Art and Archaeology in the Department of History in Art, University of Victoria, Canada. He is the author of *The fortress of the raven: Karak in the middle Islamic period (1100–1650)* (Leiden, 2008) and is preparing a book on Islamic archaeology for the New Edinburgh Islamic Surveys series.

ROBERT G. MORRISON is Associate Professor of Religion at Bowdoin College. He is the author of *Islam and science: The intellectual career of Niẓām al-Dīn al-Nīsābūrī* (London and New York, 2007). He has also published articles on astronomy texts in Judaeo-Arabic and on the astronomy of Quṭb al-Dīn al-Shīrāzī.

FRANCIS ROBINSON is Professor of the History of South Asia in the Department of History, Royal Holloway, University of London. His publications include *Islam and Muslim history in South Asia* (Delhi, 2000), *The 'ulamā' of Farangī Maḥall and Islamic culture in South Asia* (Delhi, 2001), *Islam, South Asia and the West* (Delhi, 2007) and *The Mughal emperors and the Islamic dynasties of India, Iran and Central Asia 1206–1925* (London, 2007).

WARREN C. SCHULTZ is Associate Professor of History and departmental chair at DePaul University in Chicago. He is the author of 'The monetary history of Egypt, 642–1517' in *The Cambridge history of Egypt*, vol. I (1998), as well as several articles on Mamlūk monetary history.

AMNON SHILOAH is Emeritus Professor of the Department of Musicology, Hebrew University of Jerusalem. His research interests involve history and theory of Arab and Jewish Near Eastern musical tradition and medieval writings. His magnum opus includes the two volumes of *The theory of music in Arabic writings* published in the RISM series (Munich, 1979–2003), and two volumes of essays published in Ashgate's Variorum collected studies series. The French translation of his book *Music in the world of Islam* won the 2003 Grand prix de l'Académie Charles Cros: Littérature musicale.

RICHARD C. TAYLOR of the Philosophy Department at Marquette University works in Arabic philosophy, its Greek sources and its Latin influences. He has written on the *Liber de Causis*, Averroes and other related topics. He has a complete English translation of Averroes' *Long Commentary on the 'De Anima'* of Aristotle forthcoming.

DAVID WAINES is Emeritus Professor of Islamic Studies at the Department of Religious Studies, Lancaster University. His recent publications include *Introduction to Islam* (2nd edn, Cambridge, 2003) and *Patterns of everyday life* (Aldershot, 2002).

DAVID J. WASSERSTEIN is Professor of History and Eugene Greener Jr. Professor of Jewish Studies at Vanderbilt University. He is the author of *The rise and fall of the party: Kings, politics and society in Islamic Spain, 1002–1086* (Princeton, 1985), *The caliphate in the West: An Islamic political institution in the Iberian Peninsula* (Oxford, 1993) and (with the late Abraham Wasserstein) *The legend of the Septuagint, from Classical Antiquity to today* (Cambridge, 2006).

ANDREW M. WATSON is Professor Emeritus of Economics at the University of Toronto. His research includes many projects on the economic and agricultural history of medieval Europe and the Islamic world. Among his publications is *Agricultural innovation in the early Islamic world: The diffusion of crops and agricultural techniques, 700–1100* (Cambridge, 1983; repr. 2008, also published in Arabic by the Institute for the History of Arab Science, University of Aleppo, and in Spanish by the University of Granada).

Note on transliteration

The transliteration of Arabic and Persian words is based on the conventions used by the *Encyclopaedia of Islam*, second edition, with the following modifications. For the Arabic letter *jīm*, *j* is used (not *d̲j̲*). For the Arabic letter *qāf*, *q* is used (not *ḳ*). Digraphs such as *th*, *dh*, *kh* and *sh* are not underlined.

Words and terms in other languages are transliterated by chapter contributors according to systems which are standard for those languages.

Place-names, many of which are familiar, appear either in widely accepted Anglicised versions (e.g. Cairo), or in most cases without diacritical points (e.g. Baghdad, not Baghdād).

Abbreviations

AI	*Annales Islamologiques*
BAR	British Archaeological Reports
BGA	*Bibliotheca geographorum arabicorum*, 8 vols., Leiden, 1870–1938
BSOAS	*Bulletin of the School of Oriental and African Studies*
DLB:ALC	*Dictionary of literary biography*, vol. CCCXI: *Arabic literary culture, 500–925*, ed. M. Cooperson and S. M. Toorawa, Detroit, 2005
EAL	*Encylopedia of Arabic literature*, ed. J. S. Meisami and P. Starkey, 2 vols., London and New York, 1998
EI2	*Encyclopaedia of Islam*, 2nd edn, Leiden, 1960–2009
IJMES	*International Journal of Middle East Studies*
ILS	*Islamic Law and Society*
JAOS	*Journal of the American Oriental Society*
JESHO	*Journal of the Economic and Social History of the Orient*
JNES	*Journal of Near Eastern Studies*
JRAS	*Journal of the Royal Asiatic Society*
JSAI	*Jerusalem Studies in Arabic and Islam*
SI	*Studia Islamica*
ZDMG	*Zeitschrift der Deutschen Morgenländischen Gesellschaft*
ZGAIW	*Zeitschrift für Geschichte der Arabisch-Islamischen Wissenschaften*

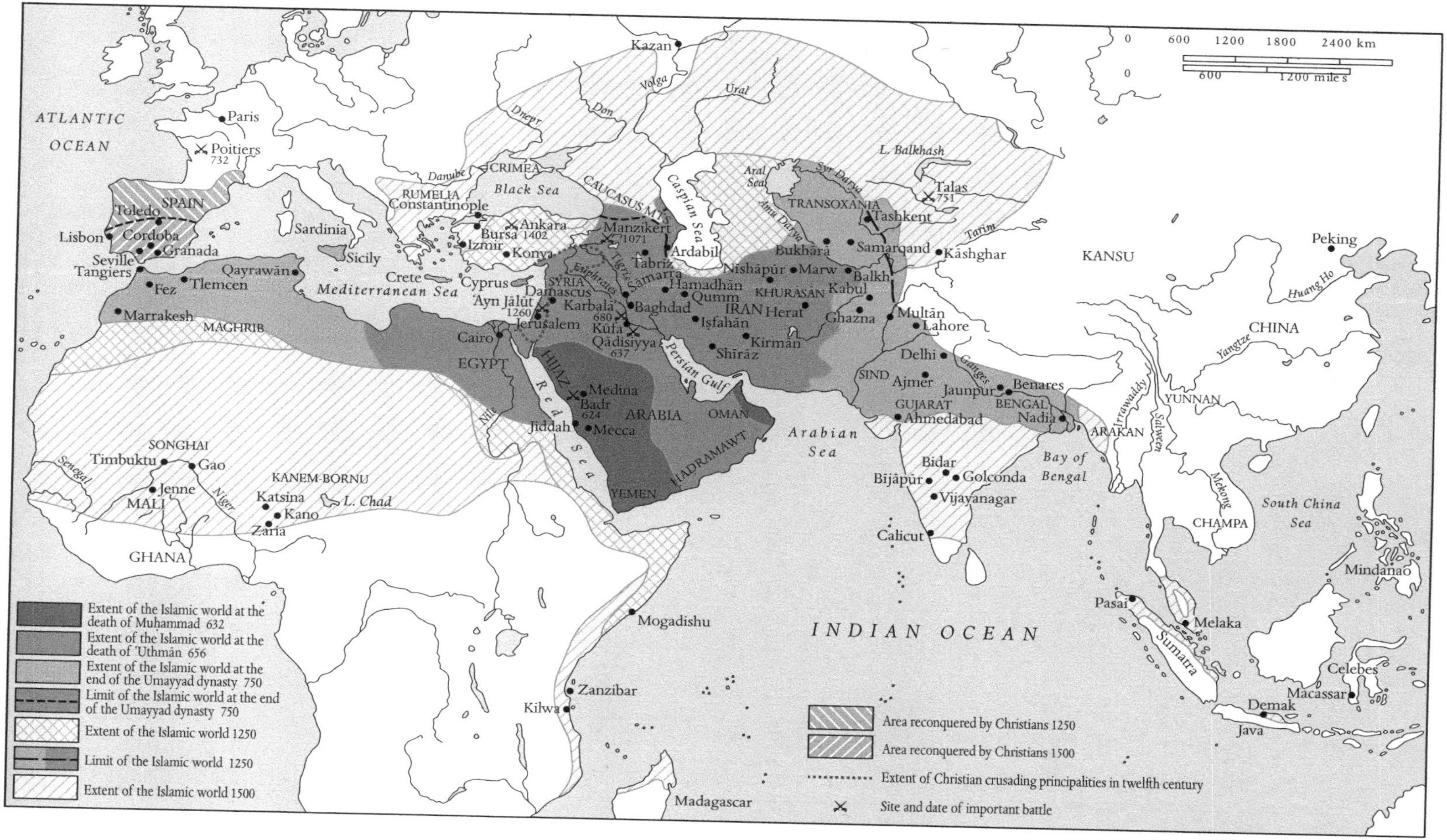

0 600 1200 1800 2400 km
0 600 1200 miles
ATLANTIC OCEAN
Paris
Poitiers 732
SPAIN
Toledo
Lisbon
Cordoba
Granada
Seville
Tangiers
Fez
Tlemcen
Qayrawān
Marrakesh
MAGHRIB
Sardinia
Sicily
Crete
Mediterranean Sea
Cyprus
RUMELIA
Constantinople
Danube
CRIMEA
Black Sea
Dnepr
Don
Volga
Kazan
Ural
Ankara
Bursa 1402
Izmir
Konya
CAUCASUS MTS
Manzikert 1071
Tabriz
Ardabil
Caspian Sea
Aral Sea
Amu Darya
Syr Darya
TRANSOXANIA
Tashkent
Samarqand
Bukhārā
L. Balkhash
Talas 751
Kāshghar
Tarim
SYRIA
Damascus
'Ayn Jālūt 1260
Jerusalem
Euphrates
Tigris
Samarra
Karbalā' 680
Kūfa
Qādisiyya 637
Baghdad
Hamadhān
Qumm
Iṣfahān
Shīrāz
Kirmān
IRAN
Herat
KHURĀSĀN
Nīshāpūr
Marw
Balkh
Kabul
Ghazna
Multān
Lahore
Delhi
Ganges
SIND
Ajmer
Jaunpur
Benares
BENGAL
GUJARAT
Ahmedabad
Nadia
ARAKAN
Bay of Bengal
Bidar
Golconda
Bījāpūr
Vijayanagar
Calicut
Arabian Sea
Persian Gulf
Cairo
EGYPT
Nile
HIJAZ
Red Sea
Medina
Badr 624
ARABIA
OMAN
Jiddah
Mecca
HADRAMAWT
YEMEN
SONGHAI
Timbuktu
Gao
Senegal
Jenne
MALI
Niger
KANEM-BORNU
Katsina
Kano
Zaria
L. Chad
GHANA
Mogadishu
Zanzibar
Kilwa
Madagascar
INDIAN OCEAN
KANSU
Peking
Huang Ho
CHINA
Yangtze
YUNNAN
Irrawaddy
Salween
Mekong
CHAMPA
South China Sea
Mindanao
Pasai
Melaka
Sumatra
Celebes
Macassar
Demak
Java
Extent of the Islamic world at the death of Muḥammad 632
Extent of the Islamic world at the death of 'Uthmān 656
Extent of the Islamic world at the end of the Umayyad dynasty 750
Limit of the Islamic world at the end of the Umayyad dynasty 750
Extent of the Islamic world 1250
Limit of the Islamic world 1250
Extent of the Islamic world 1500
Area reconquered by Christians 1250
Area reconquered by Christians 1500
Extent of Christian crusading principalities in twelfth century
Site and date of important battle

Introduction

ROBERT IRWIN

The miniature *Humāy and Humāyūn in a garden* was painted in the bright colours of the world when it was younger. It was produced in Herat around 833/1430 by an anonymous artist, and it is most likely that it was originally bound in an anthology of verse and pictures. The depiction of a night scene was rare in Islamic art. It is curious to note that artists in western Europe were similarly experimenting with night scenes some decades later. In the frescoes in San Francesco of Arezzo, painted in the 1450s, Piero della Francesca showed Constantine asleep in his tent at night and, later in the same century, a French illuminated manuscript of *Le livre du cueur d'amours espris* featured three even more remarkable nocturnes. However, whereas the Western artists concerned themselves with the realistic registration of the fall of candlelight and shadow, as well as the muting of colours and the disappearance of detail in nocturnal obscurity, the Persian miniaturist presents us with a night scene in which we (and apparently the figures in the miniature) have perfect night vision. Instead of trying to reproduce the real world, the artist was using conventionalised images of people, plants, trees, lamps and architecture in order to fill the picture plane in a decorative and, indeed, ravishing way.

Although a painting of this kind is therefore not a window on the world in the ordinary sense, nevertheless study of such a work tells us a great deal about the culture that produced it. The painting, which celebrates an aristocratic way of life and sensibility, was aimed at an aristocratic clientele. (Hardly anything that can be called popular art survives from this period.) There had long been an Arab literary and visual cult of the garden in the Islamic world. Medieval visitors to the Alhambra in Granada were at least as impressed by the gardens as they were by the palace; and *rawḍiyyāt*, or poetry devoted to gardens, was a recognised genre of Arabic poetry. If anything, the cult of the garden intensified in the Turco-Persian culture of the late medieval and early modern period. Persian painters depicted the garden as an earthly paradise and the privileged dwelling place of princes. Depictions of battles and enthronements were certainly not unknown, but artists usually preferred to celebrate the world of an idle and tranquil aristocracy among whom a code of decorum concealed any passions that may have been felt. Poetry competed with the Qur'ān as a guide to conduct. The culture of the aristocracies of ninth/fifteenth-century Herat, Samarqand, Istanbul, Cairo and Granada was highly literary, and the arts of the book were correspondingly highly valued. The range of calligraphies displayed in *Humāy and Humāyūn* would have been as impressive to the cognoscenti as the representation of the figures in the garden. As for the style of the painting, it is unmistakably Persian and, as such, has evolved from the earlier (Byzantine influenced) Arab tradition of the art of the book. Nevertheless, there are also a number of stylistic features that derive from Chinese art. No history of the culture of this period can afford to neglect the massive influence of China on the visual arts, economy and technology of the Islamic world. Finally, the anthology form, for which this sort of painting was produced, was a leading feature of Islamic culture. Some of the greatest figures in the literary world, such as Abū al-Faraj al-Iṣfahānī or Ibn ʿAbd Rabbih, were famous not for what they composed themselves but for their diligent compilations of other men's flowers. Such anthologies had the effect of canonising and prolonging the cultural conventions and sensibilities of past centuries.

Although *Humāy and Humāyūn in a garden* is unmistakably a work of Islamic art, it is extremely difficult to articulate why it is classified as such. The subject matter is not obviously religious (though the poem by Khwājū al-Kirmānī that it illustrated was an allegory of the soul's quest for God disguised as a princely romance).[1] Moreover, the depiction of human figures might be deemed to be in violation of the Qur'ān's ban on the fashioning of images. It is also difficult to identify what, if anything, it has in common with the literary and plastic creations of the Islamic world in the first century of its existence (the frescoes found in Umayyad desert palaces, for example). 'Islamic art' is a term of convenience, although a potentially misleading one. 'Islamic art' or 'Islamic literature' or 'Islamic science' and, above all, 'Islamic civilisation' could even be held to be merely labels for all the stuff produced in the areas dominated by Muslim rulers or populations. However, there is more to it than that, for

1 On this painting and its literary subject matter, see Teresa Fitzherbert, 'Khwāju Kirmānī (689–753/1290–1352): An eminence grise of fourteenth century Persian painting', *Iran*, 29 (1991); Thomas W. Lenz and Glen D. Lowry (eds.), *Timur and the princely vision: Persian art and culture in the fifteenth century* (Washington, 1989), pp. 117, 236; Eleanor Sims, Boris Marshak and Ernst Grube, *Peerless images: Persian painting and its sources* (New Haven and London, 2002), pp. 82–3.

'Islamic civilisation' is a shorthand term for quite a different set of realities. Ludwig Wittgenstein, when he came in *Philosophical investigations* to confront the problem of how to define 'game', denied that there was any single feature that games had in common. Instead 'we see a complicated network of similarities overlapping and criss-crossing: sometimes overall similarities, sometimes similarities of detail'. Wittgenstein went on to characterise these similarities as 'family resemblances' and to argue that 'games' formed a 'family'.[2] In much the same way, there has not been one Islamic civilisation, but many different Islamic civilisations at various times and in various places. These Islamic civilisations have various features in common and constitute a 'family'. Some of the things many of these civilisations shared derived from the religion that they had in common, but this was not always the case. Thus, although the employment of slaves in the army and the higher ranks of the administration was a fairly pervasive feature of Islamic societies, there is nothing strictly Islamic about it; the employment of such slaves (*mamlūks* or *ghulāms*) does not derive from any injunctions in the Qurʾān. Similarly, although the *qaṣīda* form of verse is common to all the Islamic literatures, there is nothing specifically religious about it – and the same point can be made about the proliferation of the arabesque and *muqarnas* in the artistic vocabulary of the Islamic lands from Andalusia to Sumatra. Much of what we recognise as forming part of Islamic culture derived from local cultures and past non-Islamic histories, rather than being something that was imposed by Arab Muslim conquerors.

Some sources of belief and behaviour in the Muslim world

To return to Herat, in the ninth/fifteenth century this city was one of the leading centres of a high culture that was Sunnī Muslim and Persianate in most of its leading features. It is important to bear in mind that prior to the sixteenth century Iran was overwhelmingly Sunnī Muslim, while Shīʿism was largely restricted to certain remote regions of Lebanon, eastern Turkey and Yemen. While Turks and Circassians tended to predominate in the political and military elites of the Islamic heartlands, the style of their culture was Persian (notwithstanding the saying, popular in the Arab world, 'He who learns Persian loses half his religion'). Several of the Ottoman sultans wrote poetry in Persian. The Mamlūk sultan of Egypt and Syria, Qaṅṣawh al-Ghawrī knew Persian, and he commissioned a translation of Firdawsī's *Shāhnāma* into Turkish so that those of his *amīrs* who only knew Turkish could see what

2 Ludwig Wittgenstein, *Philosophical investigations* (Oxford, 1953), pp. 31–4.

they were missing.[3] In Herat the poet and minister of state ʿAlī Shīr Nawāʾī more or less single-handedly set about creating a Chaghatay Turkish literature that was based on Persian models. In the visual arts what has come to be known as the International Tīmūrid style (which was characterised above all by floral chinoiserie motifs) prevailed in Ottoman Turkey, Mughal India and the territories in between. Merinid Morocco and Naṣrid Andalusia were relatively untouched by this Persianate culture. Even so, it has been suggested that certain features of the palaces of the Alhambra – their polychrome, *muqarnas* and *chahārbāgh*-type gardens – derive ultimately from Persian prototypes.

In the ninth/fifteenth century Islamic science had reached an unprecedented level of sophistication. (Muslim innovations in mathematics, astronomy and the other exact sciences did not come to an end in the sixth/twelfth century when Europeans stopped translating Arabic treatises on the subject.) Many of the most important advances, for example work on geometric solutions for quadratic equations by ʿUmar al-Khayyām (d. 526/1131) and on plane and spherical trigonometry by Naṣīr al-Dīn al-Ṭūsī (d. 672/1273f.), were made in the eastern Islamic lands. Astronomy enjoyed a cult status under the Tīmūrids (as it had earlier under the Ilkhānids of Iran and the Rasūlid sultans of Yemen). Ulugh Beg, the Tīmūrid ruler of Transoxania and Khurāsān in the years 850–3/1447–9, presided over a team of astronomers and mathematicians of whom the most prominent was al-Kāshī (d. 832/1429), who worked on decimal fractions and the approximation of pi, among much else. It would take European mathematicians another two centuries to arrive at the discoveries that had already been made by Ulugh Beg's team in Samarqand.

Despite the efflorescence of a courtly Persianate culture, older Arabic genres and conventions fed into that culture. The Arabic verse form the *qaṣīda* or ode, which had been first developed in pre-Islamic Arabia, was taken up by Persian poets (and eventually also by poets writing in Hebrew, Turkish, Urdu, Swahili and other languages). The ideal types of the *nadīm* (the cultured cup-companion) and the *ẓarīf* (the refined dandy), though first codified in the ʿAbbāsid period, still provided models of conduct for courtiers and literati throughout the Islamic world. Arabic also remained the chief medium of scholarship, and religious topics in particular were studied and debated in Arabic. Arabic encyclopaedias and other compendia provided the Islamic world with an enormous common pool of knowledge. In 833/1429

3 Esin Atil, *Renaissance of Islam: Art of the Mamluks* (Washington, 1981), pp. 264–5; Esin Atil, 'Mamluk painting in the late fifteenth century', *Muqarnas*, 2 (1984); Doris Behrens-Abouseif, 'Sultan al-Ghawrī and the arts', *Mamluk Studies Review*, 6 (2002), p. 77.

Shāh Rukh, the Tīmūrid ruler of Khurāsān, sent an embassy to Egypt to request that the Mamlūk sultan Barsbāy send him a copy of the commentary on al-Bukhārī's *Ṣaḥīḥ* (a collection of sayings of the Prophet) by the renowned Egyptian scholar Ibn Ḥajar, as well as the *Kitāb al-sulūk*, a chronicle by the hardly less famous historian al-Maqrīzī. The fame (or in some cases notoriety) of Muslim scholars could span continents. In the eighth/fourteenth and ninth/fifteenth centuries the suspect orthodoxy of the seventh/thirteenth-century Andalusian Sufi Ibn al-ʿArabī (who was accused of monism among other things) was debated not just in Andalusia and North Africa, but also in Egypt, Yemen and Khurāsān, and later also in eleventh/seventeenth-century Java.[4] (Sufi adherents of the doctrines of Ibn al-ʿArabī had a leading role as missionaries in South-East Asia.) The cohesion of the Muslim communities was strengthened by the common practice of pious scholars of travelling in order to listen to and memorise *ḥadīths* (orally transmitted reports of the sayings of the Prophet and his Companions) from as wide a range of authorities as possible. Sufis also travelled widely, and travel features prominently in the formative part of the careers of such prominent Sufis as al-Ḥallāj, al-Ghazālī and Ibn al-ʿArabī. The shared code of law (the *sharīʿa*) and curriculum of higher education throughout the Muslim world made it relatively easy for scholars, statesmen and others to find employment in lands distant from their place of birth. Ibn Baṭṭūṭa, Ibn Khaldūn and Ibn ʿArabshāh were among the many famous Muslims who did so. The case of Ibn Baṭṭūṭa is particularly striking. In the early eighth/fourteenth century he travelled everywhere in the Muslim world from Mali to the Maldives and, wherever he went, he encountered urban institutions that he was already familiar with from his youth in Tangiers, including the mosque, the *ḥammām*, the *madrasa* (teaching college) and the *sūq* (market). Moreover, his path criss-crossed with those of other roaming Muslim traders, scholars and job-seekers.

Besides the scholars and the Sufis, many ordinary Muslims went on the *ḥajj* (and in Spain and North Africa in particular the practice gave rise to the literary genre of the *riḥla*, a narrative of the pilgrimage). The *ḥajj* and the consequent mingling of peoples from all over the world at Mecca and Medina facilitated the exchange of ideas and information. Most Muslims went on the *ḥajj* in order to fulfil a religious duty, but a few seem to have done so in order to find brides, and many others made use of the commercial opportunities afforded by their pilgrimage. The economic prosperity of Damascus, in particular, was

4 Alexander D. Knysh, *Ibn ʿArabī in the later Islamic tradition: The making of a polemical image in medieval Islam* (Albany, 1999).

dependent on the success of the *ḥajj*. The coming together and dispersal of Muslims on the *ḥajj* had the effect of spreading information about religious and cultural developments throughout the Islamic world. Moreover, Islam was the language of trade throughout the greater part of the known world. This was particularly the case in the Indian Ocean and across the landmass of Asia. Because of this, many Chinese, who wished to establish themselves in international commerce, found it advantageous to convert to Islam. The family of styles and techniques that has come to be known as 'Islamic art' owed much of its continuing evolution to the transmission, via international commerce, of designs on textiles and ceramics made for long-distance export.

Muslims were the heirs to a set of overlapping and competing legendary, semi-legendary and historical versions of the past. Firdawsī's Persian verse epic the *Shāhnāma* (written in the early fifth/eleventh century) combined the legends of pre-Islamic Iran to produce a celebration of Iranian identity. His saga also offered reflections on the rights and duties of princes, as well as models for princes, most notably a (fancifully Iranicised) Emperor Alexander. Fantasies about Alexander and his tutor Aristotle also figured largely in the Arabic literary version of Classical Antiquity in which the Greek sages appeared in Muslim garb. The legacy of Pythagoras, Aristotle, Plato and later authors of romances was evident in such things as the vast body of alchemical and related literature conventionally ascribed to the ninth-century alchemist Jābir ibn Ḥayyān, as well the *Rasā'il*, a tenth-century encyclopaedia put together by the Brethren of Purity in Baṣra. Ibn Sīnā (d. 428/1037) and Ibn Rushd (d. 595/1198) provided what were largely rational commentaries and elaborations on the philosophy of Aristotle, but the genuine legacy of Aristotle competed with that of the much more popular bogus Aristotle, who was supposed to have written the *Sirr al-asrār* (Secret of secrets), a rather chaotic compendium in the mirrors-for-princes genre, with a great deal of additional material of an occult or folkloristic nature. A rather different aspect of the Greek legacy was also evident in the popular Arabic genre of stories of lovers parted and reunited which followed the conventions of late Hellenistic romances. Islamic art and architecture, like Byzantine architecture, was heir to the visual culture of the Hellenistic world. The quintessentially Islamic arabesque evolved from the earlier Greek deployment of vine-leaf motifs in decoration. The arabesque, together with the Corinthian capitals of the columns in the Umayyad palace of Madīnat al-Zahrā' outside Cordoba and the classical images on twelfth-century Artuqid coinage all attested in their different ways to the continued vitality of the visual legacy of Classical Antiquity.

The poetry of the *jāhilī* or pre-Islamic poets in the Arabian Peninsula and stories about the context of the composition of that poetry constituted a third sort of quasi-legendary prehistory with which the cultured Muslim was supposed to be familiar. Arab *jāhilī* values, such as *ṣabr* (patience) and *muruwwa* (manliness), continued to be adopted and espoused by much later sultans and warlords, including the famous Saladin. The extraordinarily high status of poetry, the backward-looking nature of most of that poetry and the esteem in which the poetic genres of *fakhr* (boasting) and *hijā'* (satire) were held were all part of the *jāhilī* heritage that survived under Islam. Yet a fourth type of past was anonymously manufactured in later centuries in the form of the Turkish and Arab popular epic, celebrating the exploits of historical or legendary figures, including ʿAntar, Sayyid Baṭṭāl and the Mamlūk sultan al-Ẓāhir Baybars among many others. (It is worth noting that popular epics tended to place as much stress on the value of cunning as on military prowess and derring-do.)[5] Again, from the seventh/thirteenth century onwards, after the Mongols had established an empire that stretched from China to the Euphrates, the traditional practices of Chinggis Khān and his Mongols constituted yet another code of conduct (one can think of it as the Chinggisid *sunna*) for many in Iran, Khurāsān and elsewhere who nevertheless chose to describe themselves as Muslims.[6]

Ideals of Islam and their implementation

All these various 'histories' offered potential role models and ideals of life. However, by far the most important ideal of life was that provided by the Prophet Muḥammad and members of his immediate family. The life story of the Prophet and accounts of the preaching of Islam and early Islamic conquests constituted the core history that gave the Islamic community its identity, and this history was transmitted and authenticated by the religious scholars, the *ʿulamā'*.

The semi-legendary and secular versions of the Muslim world's pre-history and history had to be reconciled with or refuted by the orthodox version of

5 On these epics and the role of the cunning man in them see in particular Malcolm Lyons, *The Arabian epic: Heroic and oral story-telling*, 3 vols. (Cambridge, 1995).

6 David O. Morgan, 'The great *Yāsa* of Chingiz Khān and Mongol law in the Ilkhanate', *BSOAS*, 49 (1986); Robert Irwin, 'What the partridge told the eagle: A neglected Arabic source on Chengīz Khan and the early history of the Mongols', in Reuven Amitai-Preiss and David O. Morgan (eds.), *The Mongol empire and its legacy* (Leiden, 1999); R. D. McChesney, *Central Asia: Foundations of change*, Leon B. Poullada Memorial Lecture Series (Princeton, 1996), pp. 122–3, 127–41.

Islamic history, and the ideals of life of pious Muslims. The orthodox version was based on the Qurʾān, *ḥadīth* and the *sīra* (biography of the Prophet). Islam's history and the religious sciences, orally transmitted from generation to generation, played the leading role in sustaining Islamic norms. Such Islamic norms constituted the *sunna*, both law and code of conduct, as established by precedent. However, it should be remembered that substantial Shīʿite communities did not accept this *sunna*. The Shīʿa tended to transmit different traditions, many of which referred back to the chain of imams, who were members of the Prophet's family by descent from Muḥammad and ʿAlī, the Prophet's cousin. Moreover, Shīʿa tended to place greater stress on the power to interpret those traditions by *mujtahids*, scholarly religious authorities who were deemed to be able to exercise independent judgement in these matters. Shīʿa also tended to place less emphasis on consensus than the Sunnīs did, and esoteric texts and secret doctrines loomed larger in their heritage. All the same, despite the Sunnī stress on the transmission of traditions in providing a basis for both a Muslim society and a virtuous life at the individual level, the Sunnī tradition was something that had to be elaborated, rather than merely inherited. Its evolution, like that of Shīʿism, was shaped to a large degree by the demands and expectations of the peoples that the Muslims conquered. Religious codes were slowly elaborated to answer any of the questions that might be raised about conduct or belief and, to some extent, rival Sunnī and Shīʿite communities established their identities by defining their beliefs and practices in opposition to one another. Moreover, within Sunnism itself, as the leading *madhhabs* (law schools) developed in rivalry to one another, a similar process of self-definition occurred.[7]

The Ḥanbalī *madhhab*, which tended to take particularly rigorous positions on points of Islamic law and conduct, played a leading role in defeating a school of thought known as Muʿtazilism. Muʿtazilism, in a narrow sense, refers to the doctrine that the Qurʾān was created, as opposed to coexisting eternally in time with God. In practice, the term referred to a wider body of vaguely secularist and rationalist opinion. The ʿAbbāsid caliph al-Maʾmūn (r. 198–218/813–33) adopted the createdness of the Qurʾān as official doctrine, and he persecuted Ḥanbalī opponents of the Muʿtazila. He also presided over a translation and scientific research programme centred on his library

7 On the formation of a Sunnī identity see, among much else, Patricia Crone and Martin Hinds, *God's caliph: Religious authority in the first centuries of Islam* (Cambridge, 1986); Richard W. Bulliet, *Islam: The view from the edge* (New York, 1994); Christopher Melchert, *The formation of the Sunni schools of law, 9th–10th centuries CE* (Leiden, 1997).

in Baghdad known as the Bayt al-Ḥikma (House of Wisdom).[8] By the 240s/850s Muʿtazilism was no longer in favour at court and the Muʿtazila were suffering persecution. The Bayt al-Ḥikma declined into obscurity around the same time. However, the full fruits of the early ninth-century intellectual debate and translation activity (much of it from Greek) only became fully apparent in the tenth and eleventh centuries, by which time the ʿAbbāsid caliphate was not much more than a political fiction.

The period from approximately 340/950 to 440/1050 was arguably the golden age of Islamic Arab intellectual culture (as well as of Persians writing in Arabic). The thinkers and writers of first rank who flourished in this period included the historian and belletrist al-Masʿūdī (*c.* 283–345/*c.* 896–956), the poet al-Mutanabbī (*c.* 303–54/*c.* 915–65), the philosopher Ibn Sīnā (d. 428/1037), the scientist Ibn al-Haytham (d. *c.* 431/1039), the scientist, historian and geographer al-Bīrūnī (362–*c.* 442/973–*c.* 1050), the jurist and political thinker al-Māwardī (364–450/974–1058), the poet al-Maʿarrī (363–449/973–1058) and the belletrist and heresiographer Ibn Ḥazm (384–456/994–1064). It was also during this period that the somewhat mysterious Brethren of Purity (Ikhwān al-Ṣafāʾ) compiled their encyclopedia of all the sciences. Furthermore, the beginnings of high Islamic culture in the Persian language can be dated to this period, with the composition of the *Shāhnāma* by Firdawsī (d. *c.* 411/1020). The explosion of knowledge and debate in this period owed something to the increased use of paper. This had a role in sustaining not just literature, but also commerce, technology and art. During this period philosophy, as well as many forms of freethinking and outright defences of hedonism, flourished. Esoteric ideas added to the ferment, and the fourth/eleventh century has been characterised as that of a *revolution manquée* when Ismāʿīlīs seemed to be in a position to take over the heartlands of Islam, though in the event they were unable to convert their hopes into reality.[9] In the long run, the entry of Turkish tribesmen in large numbers into the heartlands and the enlistment of those Turks in the Sunnī cause, as well as the Sunnī institution of the *madrasa*, played crucial roles in reversing the tide of Shīʿite fortunes.

In Cairo the Fāṭimid caliph al-Ḥākim (r. 386–411/996–1021), the head of the Shīʿite Ismāʿīlī regime, had founded the Dār al-ʿIlm (House of Knowledge).

8 L. E. Goodman, 'The translation of Greek materials into Arabic', in M. J. L. Young, J. D. Latham and R. B. Serjeant (eds.), *The Cambridge history of Arabic literature*, vol. III: *Religion, learning and science in the ʿAbbasid period* (Cambridge, 1990), pp. 477–97; Dmitri Gutas, *Greek thought, Arabic culture: The Graeco-Arabic translation movement in Baghdad and early ʿAbbasid society (2nd–4th/8th–10th centuries)* (London, 1998).

9 Bernard Lewis, *The Arabs in history*, 3rd edn (London, 1956), p. 139.

According to the fifteenth-century Egyptian historian al-Maqrīzī 'people from all walks of life visited the House; some came to read books, others to copy them, and yet others to study'. However, the House of Knowledge was not a centre for the disinterested dissemination of knowledge; it also served as a centre for Ismāʿīlī indoctrination and propaganda. This was an age when institutions of higher education were set up in order to serve competing religious ideologies. The *madrasa*, or teaching college, which specialised in teaching the Sunnī religious sciences, originated in third/tenth-century Khurāsān. The institution of the *madrasa* had the effect of consolidating the position of the four chief *madhhabs*, or schools of Sunnī religious law (Shāfiʿī, Ḥanbalī, Ḥanafī and Mālikī). The institution also facilitated the channelling of patronage from the politicians and wealthy merchants to religious scholars. As the institution of the *madrasa* spread westwards, it was used in sixth/twelfth-century Syria by the Zangid princes to combat Shīʿism. Later, after Saladin overthrew the Fāṭimid caliphate in Egypt and established his own rule, the foundation of *madrasas* in Egypt played a crucial role in the Sunnī intellectual recolonisation of Egypt. Thereafter political Shīʿism was on the defensive in Egypt, Syria, Iran and elsewhere, and would remain so until the triumph of the Shīʿite Ṣafavid movement in Iran at the end of the ninth/fifteenth century.

The Umayyad caliphate of Cordoba, which had been fighting a losing struggle against the Christian *reconquista*, was overthrown by rebel soldiers in 1031. Though its demise and the departure of past magnificence were repetitiously mourned in verse and prose, the breakup of the caliphate preceded the culturally fertile rivalries of the *ṭāʾifa* ('party') dynasties, which divided up what was left of the territory of Muslim Spain. Just as Umayyad Cordoba had sought to recreate in the west the lost glories of Umayyad Damascus, so the *ṭāʾifa* kings, through literary and artistic patronage, sought to recreate the lost glories of the Cordoban caliphate (and later, in the fourteenth and fifteenth centuries, the Naṣrid kingdom of Granada would have similarly nostalgic aspirations). In Syria and Egypt under the Ayyūbids and Mamlūks, the period from the end of the twelfth century to the opening of the sixteenth proved to be a golden age for Sunnī *ʿulamāʾ* culture. Much of that culture took the form of vast encyclopaedias, literary anthologies and histories that were largely compiled from the works of earlier chroniclers. From the mid-thirteenth century onwards cultural life in these lands was enriched by the presence of refugees who had fled west to escape the Mongol occupation of Iran and Iraq. Ibn Taymiyya, the rigorist Ḥanbalī jurist and polemicist, and Ibn Dāniyāl, the author of pornographic scripts for shadow plays, provide contrasting examples of such refugees. More generally, as Ibn Khaldūn, writing around 803/1400 was to note, Cairo and its numerous *madrasas* and Sufi foundations proved a magnet for wandering scholars in search of patronage. He was one of them himself. The *ʿulamāʾ* were the main recipients of the literary and intellectual patronage dispensed by the Kurdish, Turkish and Circassian politico-military elite.[10]

Self-sufficiency and stagnation

From approximately the sixth/thirteenth century until the end of the twelfth/eighteenth, the governing and military elite in much of the heartlands of the Islamic world drew heavily upon specially educated men who were of slave origin. Thus the Mamlūk regime regularly renewed itself with military slaves recruited from the Russian steppes and the Caucasus; the Ottoman sultans relied on prisoners of war, as well as those who had been press-ganged by the *devşirme* (a levy of young men imposed on Christian villages); and the Ṣafavid shahs were served by elite slaves who were mostly of Georgian, Circassian or Armenian origin. These slave elites were not just the audience for cultural products, dispensing patronage and constituting an educated readership. They were often themselves the originators of culture. The Mamlūk historian Baybars al-Manṣūrī and the Janissary engineer and architect Sinān may serve as examples.

There was an unmistakable decline in the vitality and productivity of *ʿulamāʾ* culture in Egypt and Syria after the Ottoman conquest in 922/1516f. (even though the region seems to have benefited economically from the increased security provided by Ottoman garrisons and policing). Selīm the Grim, the conqueror of the Mamlūk lands, rounded up leading scholars and Sufis, as well as artists and artisans, and sent them to Istanbul. From the tenth/sixteenth century onwards Istanbul and cities to the east in Ṣafavid Iran and Mughal India were the high centres of Muslim civilisation. In India syncretistic and pantheistic versions of Sufism flourished (much of it influenced by Ibn al-ʿArabī). Those kinds of Sufism were usually looked on with favour by the Mughal court, and they facilitated Muslim coexistence with the Hindu majority. However, Shaykh Aḥmad Sirhindī (d. 1034/1624), a Naqshbandī Sufi, spearheaded a reaction against what he perceived as lax and potentially heterodox forms of Islam. The *mujaddidī* (revivalist) form of Islam pioneered by Sirhindī and those Naqshbandīs who followed him was to exercise an enormous influence not just in Muslim India but throughout the Islamic world, particularly in the twelfth/eighteenth and thirteenth/nineteenth

10 Robert Irwin, 'Mamluk literature', *Mamlūk Studies Review*, 7 (2003).

centuries.[11] In Iran the triumph of the Shīʿite Ṣafavid movement was followed by the persecution of traditional forms of Sufism. However, a great deal of traditional Sufi thinking (of Ibn al-ʿArabī and others) was included in the newer style of philosophical and gnostic mysticism (*ʿirfān*), of which Mīr Dāmād and Mullā Ṣadrā were the leading figures in the eleventh/seventeenth century.

Elsewhere, however, the international networks of the great Sufi orders were now exercising unprecedented influence at all levels of society. The Naqshbandī order, for example, attracted adherents in India, Inner Asia, South-East Asia, the Caucasus and the Middle East. Naqshbandīs had previously been prominent at the Tīmūrid courts of Samarqand and Bukhārā. Naqshbandī missionaries went out to convert the Kazakhs to Islam in the ninth/sixteenth century, and were also active in Malaya and Java. Naqshbandīs were also prominent in the cultural formation of the Ottoman elite, where they competed for influence with members of the Mevlevī Sufi order. Naqshbandī teachings also had a role in the development of fundamentalist Wahhābī doctrine in the Arabian Peninsula.[12] Other orders, among them the Chishtīs, the Kubrawīs and the Shādhilīs, played a hardly less notable role in the continuing evolution of the civilisations of Islam. Sufism's success on the edges of the Muslim world in areas such as Central Asia and South-East Asia may have been due in part to the readiness of some Sufis to make accommodations with cultic beliefs and practices that derived from Shamanism, Hinduism, Buddhism and other local faiths. Islam at its fringes was not hard edged.

In the late tenth/seventeenth century Jean Chardin, a French jeweller who visited Shāh ʿAbbās II's Iṣfahān to trade, classified Persian trades and crafts according to whether what was produced was superior or inferior to that produced in Europe. It is striking that the list of manufactured items in which the Persians excelled is a long one, while the list of crafts in which the Persians lagged behind Europe is quite short. Chardin admired Persian textiles, ceramics, wirework, metalwork in general, tanning, wood-turning, gunsmithing, firework manufacture, stone-cutting, dyeing, barbering and tailoring. He

11 On Indian Sufism and on reform movements see Richard Maxwell Eaton, *The Sufis of Bijapur 1300–1700: Social roles of Sufis in medieval India* (Princeton, 1982); Francis Robinson, *The ʿulama of Farangi Mahall and Islamic culture in South Asia* (Delhi, 2001); Francis Robinson, 'Islam and Muslim society in South Asia', in Francis Robinson, *Islam and Muslim society in South Asia* (New Delhi, 2000).

12 K. A. Nizami, 'The Naqshabandiyyah order', in Seyyed Hossein Nasr (ed.), *Islamic spirituality: Manifestations* (London, 1991).

did not think much of their glass, paper, trunks, bookbinding or goldsmithing.[13] Until approximately the second half of the eighteenth century Islamic commerce and technology was not crucially dependent on relations with Europe. The seaborne commerce of the Indian Ocean and the Red Sea was dominated not by the fleets of the East India Company and similar European enterprises, but by Indian Muslim shipping. Most of the Ottoman empire's long-distance commerce was still conducted within its own frontiers. It has been estimated that, even as late as the end of the twelfth/eighteenth century, only 14.6 per cent of the Ottoman province of Egypt's trade was with Europe, whereas more than twice that was with lands to the east.

The striking economic self-sufficiency of the Islamic world was mirrored by the heartland's cultural self-sufficiency. When Antoine Galland, in his preface to the *Bibliothèque orientale* (1697), asked himself why oriental peoples (particularly Arabs, Persians and Turks) took so little interest in Western literature, his answer was that their own literature was so rich that they felt no need to explore beyond it. Although this literature was rich, it is worth noting how much of what was being read, recited, copied and debated had either been produced centuries before or, at the very least, was cast in the retrospective mode. Islamic cultures remained largely shaped by their awareness of the past, as Muslim analyses of the present or blueprints for the future were remarkably rare (though there is an interesting body of literature produced by Ottoman statesmen and intellectuals analysing what they perceived to be the causes of the empire's decay).[14] It is hard – probably impossible – to point to historians of the first rank who wrote in Arabic in between the Algerian al-Maqqarī (*c.* 986–1041/*c.* 1577–1632) and the Egyptian al-Jabartī (1167–1241/1753–1825). All the same, it is clear from the number and provenance of manuscripts of chronicles surviving from the intervening period that there was widening taste for reading history. The readership was no longer drawn overwhelmingly from princes, state servants and the *ʿulamāʾ*.

The return to the past was one of the factors behind the impetus for reform that swept through the Islamic lands from the twelfth/eighteenth century onwards – though of course that sense of need for reform was given extra urgency by the appearance of the British in India and then the French in Egypt.

13 Jean Chardin, *Voyages du Chevalier Chardin en Perse et autres lieux d'Orient*, ed. L. Langlès (Paris, 1811), vol. IV, pp. 88–187 (chaps. 17, 'Des arts mécaniques et métiers', and 18, 'Des manufactures').

14 Bernard Lewis, 'Ottoman observers of Ottoman decline', *Islamic Studies*, 1 (1962); repr. in Bernard Lewis, *Islam in history: Ideas, people and events in the Middle East*, 2nd edn (Chicago and La Salle, IL, 1993).

For most reformers, reform meant not the embrace of some cloudy future, but rather the return to the practices of early Islam. The blueprint for an ideal society had been spelt out in fantastic detail in the lives of the Prophet and the imams, and in the bemusingly numerous *ḥadīths* transmitted by communities of Muslim scholars across the centuries. Reform then meant shedding past accretions and rooting out abuses rather than devising innovations. Some of the impetus for this sort of return to what were held to be the earliest and best practices came from reformed Sufi groups – especially Naqshbandīs, especially in India. Shāh Walī Allāh of Delhi (d. 1176/1762), preaching in the tradition of Sirhindī, taught that only a return to strict conformity to the *sharīʿa* could arrest the political decline of Islam in India and elsewhere. But Ḥanbalī rigorists also played a role in Muslim revivalism. From the 1150s/1740s onwards Wahhābī fundamentalists fought to impose a purer form of Islam on the Arabian Peninsula. In the nineteenth century similar movements would spring up in Africa, South-East Asia and on the frontiers of China. In the twelfth/eighteenth century Bukhārā, Khiva, Delhi and Timbuktu were at least as important centres of religious thought and revival as Cairo and Istanbul.

Just as it is hard to trace the descent of ninth/fifteenth-century Persian painting from works produced in the first century of Islam, it is also hard to find much in common between Qājār paintings of the late twelfth/eighteenth century and the Tīmūrid miniatures from which they descend. It is evident from comparing the two sorts of work that there has been a vast shift in sensibility and taste. During the intervening Ṣafavid period, the *Shāhnāma* and Persian epic poetry more generally had ceased to dominate the literary and visual culture in quite the way they had done formerly. Genre and portraiture had replaced the stock medieval scenes. Moreover, the change in sensibility (not to mention technologies) is quite unmistakable. The palette has darkened. Books illustrated with miniatures are now relatively rare. In Iran life-size painting on canvas or wood has become the fashion. Where once the artist struggled to assimilate Chinese elements, now many of his visual ideas come ultimately from Europe. Artists now sought to produce real portraits of sitters rather than to paint idealised moon-faced types. They also rendered light and shadow more realistically. However, only an imperceptive fool would mistake a Qājār (or a Mughal) painting for a work of Western art and, most often, those 'Western' influences came not directly from the West, but were filtered via Indian Mughal art. Mughal and Qājār painters took what they wanted from the West. Like any culture, the Islamic cultural framework made some things possible and others impossible. It filtered and reinterpreted

1. The Persian prince Humāy meeting the Chinese princess Humāyūn in a garden, *c.* 1450, Islamic School. Musée des Arts Decoratifs, Paris, France / Giraudon / The Bridgeman Art Library

what it had received from the Hellenistic, Chinese and Turco-Mongol cultures.

The Islamic world in 1800 was still in all sorts of ways effectively self-sufficient. However, it would be perverse to ignore the fact that, by 1800, its various cultures and economies were weak in relation to those of the West and vulnerable to penetration by it. The problems included a widespread reluctance among the Muslims to innovate, and the preferred recourse to the sacred past for solutions. There were also perhaps certain weaknesses in civil society, including the absence of a developed *Widerstandrecht* (a formulated right of resistance to unjust authority). Muslim commerce suffered from a lack of access to the Americas, as well as from long-standing problems arising from the shortage of such natural resources as wood, copper and coal in the heartlands of Islam. Al-Jabartī, the witness of French triumphs in Egypt in the 1210s/1790s, affected to be amused by their technology, and judged that their balloons were mere toys for children. Yet at the same time it is clear that he was more fascinated by French ways of doing things than he dared to admit. After witnessing scientific experiments conducted by Bonaparte's savants he declared: 'These are things which minds like ours cannot comprehend.'[15] In Egypt and elsewhere self-sufficiency was giving way to self-doubt.

15 ʿAbd al-Raḥmān al-Jabartī, *ʿAjāʾib al-āthār fiʾl-tarājim waʾl-akhbār*, 3 vols. (Bulaq, 1297/1878–80), vol. III, pp. 32, 36; ed. and trans. Thomas Philipp and Guido Schwald as *ʿAbd al-Raḥmān al-Jabartī's history of Egypt*, 3 vols. (Stuttgart, 1994) vol. III, pp. 51, 57.

PART I

*

RELIGION AND LAW

I

Islam

JONATHAN BERKEY

Islam, like any major religion, is a complex phenomenon. Diverse, at times even contradictory, it resists summary and categorical description. The religion was born among the inhabitants of the Arabian Peninsula in the early seventh century CE. Yet Islam as we know it is the product of many peoples and cultures: the Arabs, but also converts from among the Jewish, Christian and Zoroastrian communities of the Near East. By 1800 Islam had expanded into south-eastern Europe, central, south and South-East Asia, and sub-Saharan Africa. Indeed, Islam formed what many have called the first global civilisation. Its ecumenical reach finds inspiration in a famous verse from the Qurʾān: 'Thus we have appointed you a middle nation, that you may be witnesses to mankind' (Q 2:143). As a historical matter, however, Islam is best understood as an expression of the larger tradition of Near Eastern monotheism. It is distinct from its older cousins, Judaism and Christianity, but its origins and early development owe much to them.

The historical relationship of Islam and Christianity is especially fraught. From the beginning, Muslims were aware of Christianity. Several of their core beliefs were constructed as a response to or reaction against Christian doctrine. The Muslim state took shape in the context of an existential struggle against the Byzantine empire, which understood itself to be the defender of the Church. Over the ensuing centuries the competition between Christianity and Islam took ever sharper forms. In the Middle East, at least, most of those who eventually converted to Islam did so from Christianity, a fact that underlies the intense competition between the two religions. The competition only worsened, and grew more violent, with the rise of the Crusading movement in the late fifth/eleventh and sixth/twelfth centuries. Despite all this, there is much that binds the two religious traditions together. Both Muslims and Christians worship the God of Abraham who created the world and gave it purpose. For all that they differ, the Muslim and Christian traditions share much more in the way of belief and practice than either one does with any of the other major religious traditions – Hinduism, say, or Buddhism. And for all that they have found themselves locked in conflict over the last millennium and a half, both Christianity and Islam arguably constitute twin foundations of a single civilisation.[1]

At least until recently, Islam's relationship with Judaism was less highly charged than that with Christianity. Fewer Jews than Christians lived in those lands Islam inherited, and with few (but important) early exceptions Jews did not pose a political threat to the Muslim state. In terms of doctrine and practice, Judaism and Islam are even more closely related than either one is to Christianity. Both, for example, insist upon the radical oneness of God, and reject the Trinitarian speculations of Christian theology. Both Islam and Judaism have developed broad and comprehensive systems of laws, laws which regulate believers' behaviour, especially in the domestic and commercial spheres, and which, far more than is the case with Christianity, define their adherents' religious identities. Religious authority in the fully developed Islamic tradition came to reside in a class of religious scholars (the *ʿulamāʾ*) who resemble the Jewish rabbinate far more than the Christian clergy. Muslim roots in Jewish belief and practice go back to the very beginning. Suggestions by some Western historians that, for several generations, Islam in fact constituted a Judaising movement rather than a distinct religion have not been widely accepted, but the controversy sparked by this argument has highlighted the close early ties between the two traditions.[2]

Islam in Arabia

Islam begins with a religious message preached by a man named Muḥammad ibn ʿAbd Allāh in Mecca, in the western part of the Arabian Peninsula known as the Ḥijāz, in the early years of the seventh century of the Common Era. The religious milieu into which Muḥammad was born some time around the year 570 is somewhat obscure, in part because we have almost nothing in the way of direct literary evidence from the period and place in question. Later Muslim narratives describe the Arabs as worshipping numerous deities, including the three so-called 'daughters of Allāh' whose worship was prominent in Mecca. As that appellation suggests, the creator God Allāh was also known to the Arabs – Muḥammad's own father bore the name of ʿAbd Allāh, or 'servant of Allāh' – although he did not figure prominently in the Meccans' worship.

1 Richard Bulliet, *The case for Islamo-Christian civilization* (New York, 2004).
2 Michael Cook and Patricia Crone, *Hagarism: The making of the Islamic world* (Cambridge, 1977).

More importantly, both Judaism and Christianity had reached the Arabian Peninsula in the centuries before the coming of Islam. (Other Near Eastern religions such as Zoroastrianism and Manichaeism may have been known there as well, although the evidence for their presence is more attenuated.) Christianity had probably been introduced by missionaries from several churches, including Monophysites from Ethiopia and Nestorians from Iraq, as well as representatives of the Orthodox Church affiliated with the Byzantine state. There are some suggestions that the association of Christianity with the Byzantine empire limited its appeal to the pre-Islamic Arabs, who resisted efforts by external powers to extend their political authority over the Peninsula. There are also suggestions that Christianity was known to the Arabs in somewhat garbled form: the Qur'ān, for instance, at one point seems to suggest that the Trinity is composed of God, Jesus and his mother Mary (Q 5:116). Judaism was probably better known by and more firmly established among its adherents in the region, whether they were the descendants of Jews who had fled persecution by the Romans or native Arabs who had embraced the Jewish faith. There is no sign of an organised Jewish presence among the Arabs of Mecca, but half or more of the population of the nearby agricultural community of Yathrib were Jews. More generally, the Arabs were familiar with tales of the prophets and other biblical figures: they had somehow absorbed, that is, the narrative foundations of Near Eastern monotheism, although not always in a form directly dependent on the accounts known in the Jewish and Christian scriptures. The Qur'ān itself makes this clear by alluding to biblical figures without always providing the full narratives identifying them – by assuming, in other words, that its audience already knew their stories.

Muḥammad began to call his fellow Arabs to the worship of a single true God as a result of a transforming spiritual encounter. Around the age of forty, he first began to hear a voice which called him to (in the words of what was probably the very first revelation): 'Recite! In the name of your Lord who created – created mankind from a clot of blood.' Over the next two decades Muḥammad continued to receive these revelations – sometimes at unexpected moments, sometimes in response to particular crises. After Muḥammad's death, the verses he had been commanded to recite were collected by his followers and assembled as the *qur'ān* (lit. 'the recitation') we have today. The revelations identified Muḥammad as a prophet in line with those who had come before to the Jews and Christians. He is a 'prophet' (*nabī*, lit. a 'warner' or 'spokesman'; cf. Heb. *navi*), a 'clear warner' (*nadhīr mubīn*), a 'bearer of good news' (*bashīr*), and above all a 'messenger' (*rasūl*) bringing a new law to his people. A story told by the later Muslim tradition reflects its understanding of Muḥammad's connection to the earlier 'prophets' – to Abraham, Moses, Jesus and the rest. In this tale, a pious Christian living in Mecca who had 'read the scriptures and learned from those that followed the Torah and the Gospel' reassured the frightened Muḥammad that the words he was hearing were authentic revelations from God, and that he was indeed 'the prophet of this people', the Arabs.[3] Indeed, at first there was little sense that the revelations demanded the establishment of a new religion. The worshipper of Allāh was simply a *mu'min*, a 'believer'. Muḥammad, in other words, saw himself as *restoring* the worship of the one true God: he saw himself as a prophet operating within the tradition of Near Eastern monotheism.

The central religious message of the Qur'ān concerns God. God is portrayed in the Qur'ān in transcendent terms reminiscent of Jewish and Christian belief. He is 'the Lord of the worlds' (Q 1:2), 'the light of the heavens and the earth' (Q 24:35), who created the world through the simple statement of his will: 'Be!' (Q 6:73). He is the 'owner of the Day of Judgement' (Q 1:4), that inescapable day 'when the heavens are split apart, and the planets are dispersed, and the oceans are poured out, and the graves are overturned, and a soul will learn what it has sent ahead and what it has held back' (Q 82:1–5), that day when all humans will be called to account for their actions. God is the judge, but he is also 'merciful' and 'compassionate', cares deeply for his creation and 'accepts repentance from his servants' (Q 42:25). Above all, he is alone: 'Allāh! There is no god but he, the living, the eternal' (Q 2:255), to whom belong 'the last and the first' (Q 92:13).

For several years Muḥammad preached this message to a small group of followers in Mecca. Eventually the radical monotheism of the Qur'ānic revelations forced a confrontation with the dominant social group there, the merchants belonging to the tribe of Quraysh, to which Muḥammad himself belonged and whose members enjoyed a kind of aristocratic status in the surrounding region. They worried that the worship of Allāh to which Muḥammad called the Arabs would undermine the cults associated with the Kaʿba, the ancient shrine in Mecca which Quraysh controlled. These cults drew worshippers from all over Arabia, and the commercial fairs associated with them formed the foundation of Quraysh's wealth. The confrontation grew worse, and finally Muḥammad and his followers were forced to flee, an

3 Ibn Iṣḥāq, *Ṣīrat rasūl allāh*, trans. Alfred Guillaume as *The life of Muḥammad* (Oxford, 1955), p. 107.

event known as the *hijra*. They sought refuge in the oasis settlement of Yathrib, where Muḥammad may have hoped that the Jews would recognise him as a prophet of God.

This event would prove critical to the future trajectory of the new religion that would emerge from Muḥammad's revelations – indeed, it is from the *hijra*, and not the birth of Muḥammad or the beginning of the revelations, that Muslims date their calendar. In Yathrib (or Medina, as it came to be known, for *madīnat al-nabī*, 'city of the Prophet') Muḥammad was both spiritual leader and the dominant political figure. His political authority was never absolute. In pre-Islamic Arabia there was no tradition of standing government, and in some ways Muḥammad functioned as little more than the temporary leader of a grand confederation of Arab tribes. The tradition preserves a document – actually a collection of several distinct agreements between Muḥammad and the various tribes and social groups living in Yathrib – known as the 'Constitution of Medina'. The document identifies Muḥammad as the 'apostle of God', but describes his political role principally as a simple arbiter of disputes.[4] Nonetheless, from the moment of the *hijra* Islam expressed itself both as what we would call a 'religion' and as a political authority – that is, as a 'state'. As later Muslims would put it, *al-islām dawla wa-dīn*: 'Islam is both a state and a religion'. This fact is fundamental both to the character of the emerging Islamic tradition and to much of its subsequent tension with both Christianity and Judaism. The relationship of both post-exilic Judaism and early Christianity to political authority was more contingent: in Judaism because there were few Jewish states after the suppression of the Maccabean kingdom; in Christianity because the new religion grew up in opposition to the Roman empire for its first three centuries. In Islam a certain tension would ultimately develop between religious and political authority, as we shall see. But they were two sides of the same coin; more precisely, legitimate political authority was always construed in explicitly religious terms. And that was a consequence of the establishment in Medina of a political community (*umma*) headed by a man who also claimed to be the messenger of God.

Another consequence of the *hijra* and the establishment of the *umma* was that the Islamic tradition began to take firmer and fuller shape. There has been considerable controversy of late about this – that is, about the moment at which 'Islam' became a distinct religion, one which its adherents understood to be different from, and in competition with, the older Near Eastern monotheisms. The controversy revolves around the degree to which Muslim

4 Ibid., pp. 232–3.

literary accounts of Muslim origins, which date at the earliest to a period a century or more after the events they describe, can be trusted.[5] There were certainly many things about 'Islam' as it came to be known in later centuries that were missing from the stage in this formative period. Nonetheless, taken at face value, the Qur'ān and the dominant Muslim narratives of Islamic origins provide evidence of a religious community that, during the decade that Muḥammad lived at Medina, came to see itself as distinct, a community not just of 'believers' but of *Muslims*.

Several of the fundamental cultic aspects of Muslim religious life now took clearer form, chief among them prayer (*ṣalāt*). The Qur'ān consistently speaks of prayer as the fundamental act of worship in Islam. The word *islām* means submission, and prayer is the ritual act by which a believer expresses his acknowledgement of God and of God's sovereignty. A very early revelation enjoined Muḥammad to 'pray to your Lord' (Q 108:2). Prayer was not new: Abraham, Moses and many others appearing in the Qur'ān all worshipped God through prayer. But a distinctively Muslim form of prayer began to emerge. The precise guidelines that Muslims now follow in their ritual prayer – for example, the requirement that Muslims pray at five specified times each day – probably crystallised slightly later, in the century or so after Muḥammad's death, but their essential elements were already in place during the Prophet's lifetime. The Qur'ān states that 'prayer is enjoined on the believers at fixed times' (Q 4.103), although it is a little imprecise as to what those times are. Prayer as described in the Qur'ān involved ritual purification, the glorification of God, prostration of the worshipper, reciting God's word – all components of the ritual *ṣalāt* now universally practised among Muslims.

Prayer was an act of individual submission, but also a collective experience. According to one famous story, the Prophet stated that the prayer of an individual in a group was worth twenty-five prayers of a solitary man.[6] When the body of Muslims assembled, the Prophet himself normally served as *imām*, or prayer leader. Already in Muḥammad's day the community was called to prayer through a public pronouncement. The Muslim tradition records that Muḥammad at first considered the use of a horn or wooden clappers to summon the faithful, in imitation of, respectively, Jewish and eastern Christian practice, but that shortly after the *hijra* he settled on a verbal

5 For a brief survey of the problem see Jonathan P. Berkey, *The formation of Islam: Religion and society in the Near East, 600–1800* (Cambridge, 2003), pp. 57–60.

6 al-Bukhārī, *Ṣaḥīḥ*, 'Kitāb al-adhān', *bāb* 30, 31.

call to prayer shouted out from the roof of a mosque.[7] This development was symptomatic of the emergence of a distinctive Islamic tradition. More decisive was the contemporaneous shifting of the *qibla*, the direction faced by the assembled worshippers. At first, and for about eighteen months after the *hijra*, Muḥammad and his Companions faced the holy city of Jerusalem when they prayed. But then the Qurʾān intervened to show them a new path: 'We shall turn you to a *qibla* you prefer. So turn your face to the sacred mosque [i.e. the Kaʿba in Mecca].' The Qurʾān spelled out precisely the larger implications of this shift: 'And even if you brought every sign to those who have [previously] been given the scripture, they would not follow your *qibla*, nor should you follow their *qibla*' (Q 2:144–5).

A similar transformation revalorised the practice of fasting. Fasting was a common element in the Near Eastern religious traditions, and some pre-Islamic Arabs may have embraced it as an act of piety. Muḥammad insisted that his followers should fast, at first apparently with the Jews on the day of ʿĀshūrāʾ, the tenth day of the month of Muḥarram, which corresponded with the Jewish Day of Atonement. But then, in the second year of the *hijra*, a revelation again provided new guidance. Now Muḥammad's followers were instructed to fast during the month of Ramaḍān, 'in which the Qurʾān was revealed as a guide for the people'. During this month they were allowed to 'eat and drink, until the white thread is distinguished for you from the black thread at dawn' (Q 2:185, 187). Here too the evolving Muslim practice was grounded in, but increasingly distinct from, that of the earlier monotheistic communities.

The differentiation of Islam from the other Near Eastern religions was paralleled by another development: the growing mistrust of the Jews and Christians expressed in the Qurʾān. The Muslim holy book conveys mixed messages concerning those known as the 'people of scripture', those communities that had previously received revelations from God. Those earlier revelations were certainly genuine. 'We have revealed the Torah, in which is guidance and light', says the Qurʾān, and 'after them [i.e. the Jews], we sent Jesus son of Mary, confirming the previous [scripture], the Torah, and we gave him the Gospel, in which is guidance and light' (Q 5:44, 46). All revelation, in fact, is God's: 'Say: We believe in God, and what is revealed to us and what was revealed to Abraham and Ishmael and Isaac and Jacob and the Tribes, and that which Moses and Jesus received, and what the prophets received from their Lord. We do not distinguish between them, and we have surrendered to

7 Ibn Iṣḥāq, *Life of Muḥammad*, pp. 235–6.

Him' (Q 2:136). At several places the Qur'ān indicates that Jews and Christians, or at least some of them, continue to stand in God's favour. 'Those who believe, and the Jews and the Christians and the Sabians[†] and whoever believes in God and in the last day and does good deeds – they will have their reward with their Lord, and they shall neither fear nor grieve' (Q 2:62; cf. 5:69).

But increasingly the Qur'ān also spoke critically of Jews and Christians. Islam's underlying historical vision suggests that the new revelation was sent in response to the unfaithfulness of the earlier recipients of God's grace. A dominant motif in the Qur'ānic accounts of the previous religions concerns the contumacy of the Israelites. 'We made a covenant with the Children of Israel, and we sent to them messengers. And when a messenger came to them with that which their souls did not desire, some of them they rejected, and some of them they killed' (Q 5:70). Jesus had predicted the coming of an Arabian prophet, but had been ignored (Q 61:6). Christians faced condemnation on theological grounds, too. The Qur'ān dismissed the doctrine of the incarnation as incompatible with God's essential oneness.

> O people of the book, do not go beyond the bounds in your religion, and do not say anything of God except the truth. Truly, the Messiah Jesus son of Mary was an apostle of God and his word, which he conveyed to Mary, and a spirit from him. So believe in God and his apostles, and do not say [that God is] three. Stop – it is better for you. Surely God is one God. He is exalted beyond having a son. (Q 4.171)

Behind the Qur'ān's growing stridency lay the political realities faced by the Prophet in Medina. The presence of Jews there may have suggested to Muḥammad that the oasis might prove to be a congenial refuge from the persecution he faced in Mecca. In fact, relations between the Jewish tribes and Muḥammad quickly broke down. Faced with their reluctance to accept his political authority and (according to the later Muslim sources) their conspiring with his enemies among Quraysh, Muḥammad first ordered the expulsion of two of the principal Jewish tribes, and then the execution of the male members of a third. These events are certainly disturbing, but they reflect first and foremost the political obstacle that the Jews and their allies among Quraysh posed to Muḥammad's position. Hence, as the Qur'ān says: 'You will find that those who are most strident in their enmity to those who believe are the Jews and the polytheists.' The Christians, who at this point posed a more

† The identity of this group is unclear, and the name has been claimed by several different communities.

remote political challenge since the seats of Christian power were far removed from Medina, emerged more favourably: 'And you will find that those who are closest in friendship to those who believe are those who call themselves Christians' (Q 5:82).

In the end, Muḥammad was successful – successful, that is, in overcoming the opposition of both Jews and polytheists. In the ten years between the *hijra* and Muḥammad's death in 11/632, virtually all the Arabs of the Peninsula were brought into the *umma*: that is, they were brought to make the act of *islām*, acknowledging at once the existence and sovereignty of God and the leadership of Muḥammad. Among other things this meant paying *zakāt*, which served not simply as an 'alms-tax' but also as a public recognition of submission to Islam and membership in the *umma*. So the Qur'ān urged Muslims to resist their polytheist enemies, but 'if they repent and take up prayer and pay the *zakāt*, then they are your brethren' (Q 9:11). Even Quraysh eventually joined the parade. Faced with a demonstration of the overwhelming power the *umma* had amassed, they too became Muslims. For the first time in history the Arabs were united under a single state.

The political success of Muḥammad in uniting the Arabs had profound consequences for Islam. Most significantly, it confirmed the connection between the Arabs as a people and the new religion. As Muḥammad and the Qur'ān grew more sceptical of Jews and Christians they turned increasingly to an Arab past, grounding Islam in a specifically Arab identity. Abraham and his son Ishmael, recognised as the ancestors of the Arabs, played a special role in this. Abraham, according to the Qur'ān, 'was not a Jew or a Christian, but rather a monotheist[††] who had submitted to God [*ḥanīf muslim*]' (Q 3:67). That Abraham and Ishmael were identified as the builders of the Kaʿba made it possible to incorporate veneration of that structure and pilgrimage to it into Muslim ritual:

> And when we made the house a place of gathering for the people and a sanctuary; and take Abraham's station as a place of prayer. And we made a covenant with Abraham and Ishmael [saying]: 'Purify my house for those who go around it and those who stay there, in bowing and prostration.' … And when Abraham and Ishmael raised the foundations of the house [they said]: 'Our Lord, accept this from us.' (Q 2:125, 127)

Muḥammad's desire to perform the ancient ceremonies of the *ḥajj* was a central factor in the submission of Quraysh, and his performance of the

†† The Arabic term *ḥanīf* is of uncertain meaning, but generally indicates an individual who had embraced monotheism before the coming of Islam.

pilgrimage in the final year of his life served as a model for later Muslims. These factors, even more than the simple fact that the Qur'ān was revealed in Arabic, would bind Arab and Muslim identities closely together once the new religion moved out of its Arabian homeland.

Despite his success, Muḥammad's sudden and unexpected death in 11/632 came as a devastating blow. The community he had assembled faced several critical challenges, and might easily have collapsed. That it did not do so testifies to the strength of the religious vision that lay at its base. And the manner in which the community survived – the choices they made, and their resolution of the challenges they faced – decisively shaped the contours of the emerging Islamic tradition.

Within hours of Muḥammad's death the community faced schism. Significantly, the divisive issue was leadership. There was no question of anyone succeeding Muḥammad as a messenger of God: the Sunnī tradition has insisted that with Muḥammad's passing the book of prophecy closed; that he was, in the Qur'ān's words, the 'seal of the prophets' (Q 33:40). But his authority, especially over political affairs, was another matter. If the community were to survive, it would have to have a leader. According to the later Sunnī sources Muḥammad's followers among the native Medinans (the *anṣār*, or 'helpers') contemplated naming one of their own as leader of the community. This was unacceptable to Muḥammad's Companions from among those who had accompanied the Prophet on the *hijra* (the *muhājirūn*). This was a small but powerful group whose status within the community derived from their early conversion to Islam and their closeness to Muḥammad, and also from the fact that most of them belonged to the aristocratic tribe of Quraysh. The principal Sunnī account describes a confrontation between the *anṣār* and several of Muḥammad's Qurashī Companions in which the latter persuaded the Medinan Muslims to accept the leadership of the Prophet's close friend and father-in-law, Abū Bakr. In this way the unity of the *umma* was preserved.

Abū Bakr thus became the first 'successor' (*khalīfa*) of Muḥammad. Under his leadership the *umma* survived another dangerous threat. Some of the Arab tribes living at considerable distance from Medina decided that, with Muḥammad's death, they were freed of their obligations to his community. As a mark of their independence they refused to send in their *zakāt*. Abū Bakr and the Muslim leadership rejected their claim, and fought them in what came to be known as the wars of the *ridda* ('apostasy'). Abū Bakr's victory over the rebels did more than preserve the Muslim state as the dominant political power in the Peninsula. It also confirmed the link between Islam and the Arabs, by helping to establish the expectation that, unless they had previously converted to Judaism or Christianity, all Arabs would from now on be Muslim. Moreover, it lay behind what eventually became a principle of Islamic law: that apostasy from Islam is unacceptable.

The events of these years between the *hijra* and the period just after Muḥammad's death are critical to an understanding of what Islam became. Later Muslims understood the actions of Muḥammad and his close Companions to constitute models for correct Muslim practice. Since the sources on which the narratives are based are all relatively late, it is possible that they are not completely reliable: they may project backwards onto the earliest years of Islam values and practices that emerged only later. But whether or not they are historical, the narratives are normative. The religious tradition they portray would develop further, but it is recognisably 'Islam'. At its heart lay the submission of the individual to the will of a single, creator God; the acknowledgement of the unique historical role of his messenger, Muḥammad; the organic relationship with, but growing estrangement from, the other Near Eastern monotheisms; the expression of faith through a precise array of religious obligations, including prayer, pilgrimage and the payment of a tax to support the community's work; the conviction that the Muslim community itself constituted the instrument of God's will, and hence the recognition that the political order was a matter of deep religious concern; the special role of the Arabs in the historical formation of that community; and the privileged claim of Arabs of the Quraysh tribe with demonstrable affinity for and devotion to the Prophet and his mission to the leadership of that community.

Classical Islam

Despite its roots in Arabia, classical Islam took shape in a much larger world. This was the result of Muslim Arabs' sudden and unexpected conquest of North Africa and much of south-west Asia in the century following Muḥammad's death. These conquests brought the Muslim Arabs face to face with large communities of Jews, Christians, Zoroastrians and others. For some time the Arabs remained aloof from the peoples of the lands they conquered, ruling over them but expecting little besides their submission and payment of taxes. The non-Muslim residents of the *dār al-islām*, those territories brought by conquest under Muslim rule, came to be known as *dhimmīs*, who held a pact of protection with the Muslim state which guaranteed their freedom to worship in exchange for their political submission. By and large the *dhimmīs* were left alone. Indeed, conversion to Islam by non-Arabs was at first discouraged. The concern was in part fiscal: if the conquered peoples embraced the new faith, they would be exempt from the special taxes imposed on non-Muslims. But there is a universalist message at least implicit in the Qurʾān, especially in that verse about the Muslims serving as 'witnesses to mankind', and over time that imperative came to the fore. There were reports that Muḥammad himself, shortly before his death, had urged the rulers of lands beyond Arabia to embrace the new faith.[8] Eventually and inevitably, many of the conquered peoples converted to Islam. The timing of the process is obscure, although it probably peaked some time between the late second/eighth and the end of the following century.[9] The conversion of large numbers of non-Arabs changed forever the nature of the Muslim *umma*. Within two centuries the radically enlarged and transformed Muslim community had defined much more precisely the fundamental doctrines, practices and institutions of the new faith.

The mature tradition of Islam took shape against the tumultuous political history of this formative period, which can be summarised quickly. Abū Bakr died after only two years as caliph. He was replaced first by another close friend of Muḥammad, ʿUmar ibn al-Khaṭṭāb, and then by ʿUthmān ibn ʿAffān. After ʿUthmān's murder most Muslims recognised the Prophet's cousin and son-in-law, ʿAlī ibn Abī Ṭālib, as the fourth caliph. ʿAlī, however, failed to punish ʿUthmān's murderers, and the dead caliph's relatives demanded vengeance. A civil war ensued, at the end of which ʿAlī was dead and ʿUthmān's relative Muʿāwiya ibn Abī Sufyān had claimed the throne. Despite considerable resistance Muʿāwiya and his family (the Umayyads) established a dynastic claim to the caliphate which they held until the middle of the second/eighth century. At that point they were overthrown by a rebellion on behalf of another prominent Muslim family belonging to the tribe of Quraysh, and more closely related than the Umayyads to Muḥammad, the ʿAbbāsids. Having established a new capital, Baghdad, the ʿAbbāsids ruled as caliphs until the middle of the seventh/thirteenth century, when the invading Mongols destroyed the city. By the fourth/tenth century, however, ʿAbbāsid rule was largely formal. Real power had passed to a variety of local regimes. By that point the contours of classical Islam were in place.

The most contested religious issue was leadership. The account of Abū Bakr's selection as caliph told by later Sunnī Muslims provided a model for who the leader should be and how he should be chosen. He should be the

8 Ibid., pp. 652f.
9 Richard Bulliet, *Conversion to Islam in the medieval period* (Cambridge, MA, 1979).

most worthy man available (Abū Bakr was recognised for his piety, his early conversion to Islam and his close relationship with Muḥammad); he should be from Muḥammad's tribe of Quraysh ('we [the emigrants from Quraysh] are the commanders', Abū Bakr is said to have told the Medinan Muslims, 'while you are the helpers'[10]); and he should be chosen through a process of *shūrā* (consultation, as took place between the leaders of the *muhājirūn* and the *anṣār*), at the end of which there should be a public proclamation of fealty (*bayʿa*) to the new caliph. But that model is in fact a retrospective projection of the later, fully developed political theory of the Sunnī jurists. At the time there were no widely accepted standards either for the criteria of leadership or for the character of the ruler's authority, or even for how he was to be selected. Sectarian divisions in Islam tend to cluster around these questions, and sectarian identities emerged gradually in response to disagreements over how to answer them.

The most immediate problem was establishing guidelines for the selection of a new ruler. The early caliphs were chosen because of their close connections to the Prophet, but the Umayyads and then the ʿAbbāsids founded dynasties. They did so in the face of considerable opposition. Some objected to the very idea of dynastic rule. For example, the earliest Muslim sectarian group, who came to be known as the Khārijites, insisted that the imam's office should be filled by whoever was the most pious and competent, regardless of descent. The Khārijites went further, and held that impious or incompetent rulers can and should be deposed. As a sectarian movement Khārijism never amounted to much in most of the Islamic world (outside North Africa and some peripheral parts of the Arabian Peninsula, where Khārijites have remained active down to the present day). But early Islamic history is littered with rebellions against the reigning caliphs, inspired by Khārijite thought. A much more serious movement of opposition formed around the group known as the Shīʿa. These were the 'party of ʿAlī' (*shīʿat ʿalī*), and in their view only ʿAlī ibn Abī Ṭālib and his descendants (and thus through his wife Fāṭima, Muḥammad's daughter, the Prophet's descendants as well) could legitimately rule. It took well over a century for a distinctive Shīʿite sectarian movement to crystallise, but from the late seventh century the peace of the *umma* was disturbed by rebellions on behalf of various descendants of ʿAlī. The dominant political theory of the Muslim jurists crystallised against the background of

10 Muḥammad ibn Jarīr al-Ṭabarī, *Ta'rīkh al-rusul wa'l-mulūk*, ed. M. J. de Goeje *et al.*, 15 vols. in 3 series (Leiden, 1879–1901), series I, p. 1840; trans. as *The history of al-Ṭabarī*, vol. X: *The conquest of Arabia*, trans. Fred Donner (Albany, 1993), p. 5.

conflicts resulting from these movements of opposition to Umayyad and ʿAbbāsid rule. Those conflicts produced considerable anxiety, and so the dominant Muslim tradition (what came to be known as Sunnism) embraced political quietism, urging the acceptance of established rulers and making every effort to legitimise the status quo. The Sunnī jurists never grew comfortable with the idea of dynastic rule, but they tacitly accepted it, at least in the case of the ʿAbbāsids, as long as the caliph was a descendant of Quraysh.

A more complex issue concerned the nature of the ruler's authority. From the beginning the caliphs were recognised as having executive authority over the administration and defence of the *umma*. But it seems that the early caliphs played an active role in the religious life of the community as well. Indeed, there was a widespread conviction that the *umma* required an authoritative guide (imam) at its head. The Shīʿa took this idea to the extreme. For them, the imam – that is, the rightful imam, the descendants of ʿAlī who never actually ruled – was the absolute and authoritative arbiter of all matters political and religious, the only individual endowed by God with correct knowledge of his will. In the first century or two of the Islamic era, however, the idea that the caliph was an authoritative guide on religious questions as well as the recognised executive of political affairs was widely shared in the Muslim community. The caliph as imam was expected to lead prayers, for example, and to deliver a sermon at noon on Fridays to the assembled male congregation, as Muḥammad had done before his death. The sources frequently credit ʿUmar with making important decisions concerning legal questions, such as setting the punishment for adultery, or matters concerning the cult, such as defining precise rules for prayer and establishing the pilgrimage to Mecca as a religious obligation. His successor ʿUthmān was (according to the dominant Sunnī narrative, although there are others that contradict it) responsible for collecting what became the received version of the Qurʾān, assembling its verses into *sūras* (chapters) and arranging them in the order that has prevailed to this day – an action which angered many Muslims who recited the revelations in a different order, and which may have contributed to ʿUthmān's assassination. The Umayyad caliphs, too, claimed authority as imams over religious questions, not only appointing *qāḍīs* but sometimes serving as judges themselves, and settling points of law involving not simply public administration but matters as diverse as marriage and the manumission of slaves. Later Muslims chastised the Umayyads for taking for themselves the title *khalīfat allāh* ('successor [or viceroy] of God'), a title implying a good deal of religious authority, rather than Abū Bakr's more modest *khalīfat rasūl allāh* ('successor of the messenger of God'). At the time, however, this seems to have raised little opposition.[11]

Under the ʿAbbāsids a different vision of leadership and of the proper distribution of political and religious authority took shape. The roots of this development lay in a movement of pious opposition which emerged under the later Umayyads. These Muslims insisted on putting Islam rather than Arab ethnicity or the interests of one particular family at the centre of the *umma*'s identity. They objected to many things about the Umayyads, including their alleged indulgence in a profligate lifestyle. At its heart, however, the objections of the pious focused on what they saw as the Umayyads' increasingly arbitrary rule, which they likened to that of pre-Islamic monarchs. In religious terms, they accused the caliphs of usurping a sovereignty that properly belonged to God.

The rise of this pious opposition was connected to broader developments in the religious sphere. Increasingly, Muslims focused on the person of Muḥammad, or rather on their memories of him. That is, they answered questions of a religious nature – what does it mean to be Muslim? and how should a Muslim behave? – by asking what Muḥammad himself had said, and how he had acted. Supply met demand, and reports about the Prophet's words and deeds circulated more and more widely among the pious. Along with the Qurʾān, these reports, known as *ḥadīth*, formed the foundations of a new edifice of religious scholarship, the construction of which was under way by the middle of the second/eighth century. This literature, which included commentaries on the Qurʾān (*tafsīr*) as well as discussions of legal matters ranging from taxes to holy war, was the product of an increasingly self-conscious group of religious scholars. These scholars, known collectively as the *ʿulamāʾ*, saw themselves as defenders of Muḥammad's memory and of the religion he inspired.

Some sort of collision between the *ʿulamāʾ* and the authority of the caliph was inevitable. At first the ʿAbbāsids embraced the idea that the holder of the executive office of the caliph served as the community's authoritative guide as well. Indeed, their claim to religious authority is implicit in the regnal names they took for themselves – *al-manṣūr* ('the one granted victory [by God]'), *al-mahdī* ('the divinely guided'), *al-hādī* ('the one who guides [to God]') – titles which had a messianic aura. Eventually, however, a de facto separation of political and religious authority emerged.

11 On the religious authority of the early caliphs see Patricia Crone and Martin Hinds, *God's caliph: Religious authority in the first centuries of Islam* (Cambridge, 1986).

The process of separation was never complete, but two famous incidents illustrate the gradual circumscription of caliphal authority. The first involved the second ʿAbbāsid caliph, Abū Jaʿfar al-Manṣūr (r. 136–58/754–75). His vizier Ibn al-Muqaffaʿ, a convert from a family that had served the Sasanian emperors, saw the office of caliph through the lens of pre-Islamic Persian political traditions which stressed the absolute, almost divine, authority of the ruler. To bring order to the increasingly diverse practice of Muslim courts, he urged the caliph to use his authority to codify Islamic law. Such a move would have tacitly eliminated the *ʿulamāʾ*'s role in determining what was properly Muslim. In the end al-Manṣūr rejected Ibn al-Muqaffaʿ's advice, and indeed had his vizier executed. Several decades later al-Maʾmūn (r. 198–218/813–33) also sought to confirm the caliph's authority over matters of religious concern. The test came in an episode known as the *miḥna*, sometimes translated as 'inquisition'. For reasons that are still debated, al-Maʾmūn sought to impose on the *ʿulamāʾ* a controversial theological doctrine associated with a group known as the Muʿtazila: that the Qurʾān is created, not, like God, eternal. Most of the *ʿulamāʾ* subscribed to the opposite view, and in the end they prevailed. A later caliph, al-Mutawakkil (r. 232–47/847–61), brought the *miḥna* to an end, and in so doing effectively acknowledged the *ʿulamāʾ*'s authority over matters of religious concern.

The separation of political and religious authority in Sunnī Islam is not really analogous to the Western doctrine of the separation of Church and state. The office of the caliph – or the imam, as the jurists preferred to call him – was always conceived in religious terms. Sovereignty, after all, belonged to God. So, for example, the Sunnī jurists considered acknowledging the authority of a single imam ruling over the *umma* a religious obligation of the community. The jurists identified the implementation of the *sharīʿa*, the religious law, as one of the imam's fundamental duties, and the *qāḍī*s of the religious courts were always appointed by, and derived their authority from, the ruler. The caliph was expected to lead the community in the Friday noon prayer, delivering the required sermon (*khuṭba*), and to accompany the annual pilgrimage to Mecca – although increasingly the caliphs would delegate these responsibilities to others. Nor was the process of separation ever complete. Even after the failure of the *miḥna* subsequent caliphs continued to intervene in disputes over religious doctrine. In the early fifth/eleventh century, for instance, the caliph al-Qādir (r. 381–422/991–1031) issued a public statement which embraced a variety of political and theological doctrines and which stands as one of the fullest statements of Sunnī Muslim faith. Nonetheless, the articulation of religious doctrine, and especially of legal principles and judgments, was increasingly left to the collective authority of the *ʿulamāʾ*. In this respect, while the imam was the 'successor of the messenger of God', the *ʿulamāʾ* could also claim to be, in the words of a famous tradition, the 'heirs of the prophet'.

One of the fullest descriptions of the office and responsibility of the Sunnī caliph was written by a jurist named al-Māwardī in the mid-fifth/eleventh century. Al-Māwardī's vision is not normative – other jurists' accounts differed on details – but it will serve as a model for the classical Muslim understanding of the office and responsibility of the ruler. The imam is to be of the tribe of Quraysh, of legally responsible age and physically and mentally fit. He is to have a just character, and sufficient knowledge of the law to exercise independent judgement on legal matters. He must have sufficient courage to undertake the defence of the Muslim community. His responsibilities demand action: he is to defend the community and protect its faith from unlawful innovation, enforce the *sharīʿa* either personally or through jurists he selects, receive legitimate taxes and booty taken in war and use them in proper legal fashion for the benefit of the *umma*.[12]

There is a certain irony here, since by this point the actual power of the caliphs had been considerably circumscribed. Already under the early ʿAbbāsids, the caliphs delegated much of the administration of government to their viziers and other bureaucrats. By the late third/ninth century caliphal authority was severely and, as it turned out, permanently shrunken. In many parts of the Islamic empire local dynasts took power. Sometimes these were governors of the caliphs who established autonomous regimes; sometimes they were local potentates or military strongmen who seized power for themselves. Even in the capital, Baghdad, the caliphs' authority was from the mid-fourth/tenth century restricted by a dynasty of Persian Shīʿite military leaders (*amīrs*) known as the Būyids. With several important exceptions, however, most of these local rulers paid at least lip service to acknowledging the suzerainty of the caliph in Baghdad – for example, by seeking a formal investiture of authority from the caliph. In doing so they demonstrated the power of the ideal of the unity of the *umma* under a single caliph for Sunnī Muslims.

For all the importance of disputes over the imamate and the principle of uniting under a single imam, it was the *ʿulamāʾ* who really defined the classical

12 ʿAlī ibn Muḥammad al-Māwardī, *al-Aḥkām al-sulṭāniyya*, trans. Wafaa H. Wahba as *The ordinances of government* (Reading, 1996); Patricia Crone, *God's rule: Government and Islam* (New York, 2004), pp. 219–43.

Muslim tradition during the two or three centuries following Muḥammad's death. Indeed, the emergence of the *ʿulamāʾ* as a distinctive and self-conscious group was probably the most important development in Islam in this period. Islam, like Judaism, is very much a religion of learning, and it was the arbiters of that learning, the *ʿulamāʾ*, who would to a large degree define what Islam became.

The word *ʿulamāʾ* means 'those who know', and that which they knew was *ʿilm*, 'knowledge'. It is not easy to separate the various disciplines of the Islamic religious sciences. In the first place, there is considerable intersection between them: inquiry into the community's history, for example, and Qurʾānic exegesis and the study of the Prophet's sayings all overlapped. Moreover, the chronology of their emergence is still a matter of debate. But starting with the Qurʾān and the *ḥadīth*, the scholars gradually built up an intricate and interlocking web of knowledge and speculation about God and his expectations for his community. Once established, this body of knowledge, embedded in a vast array of texts and commentaries on those texts, played a remarkable role as a unifying force in Islamic history. Students studied the same basic texts, and not just the Qurʾān and *ḥadīth*, in the disparate parts of the Muslim world. The journey in search of knowledge – to learn *ḥadīth* from a famous traditionist, or to study a work of religious scholarship with its author – became one of the most highly valued expressions of Muslim piety.

The Muslim religious sciences begin, naturally, with the Qurʾān. The Qurʾān, however, is not an easy book to read or to understand. In the first place, it is not a sustained narrative. The verses of the holy book were revealed sporadically over the course of twenty years, and the order in which they were assembled by ʿUthmān was in some ways arbitrary. Consequently, stories about Abraham or Moses, for example, or discussions of topics such as fighting or the rights of women, are scattered throughout the text. Moreover, the language of the holy book is difficult, to say the least. Its syntax is often puzzling, and the vocabulary, to later speakers of Arabic, is frequently obscure. As time moved away from the historical setting of the revelations, Muslims increasingly needed help understanding their scripture.

These problems gave rise to several basic disciplines of the Islamic religious sciences, among them *tafsīr* (exposition), or Qurʾānic exegesis. Since the meaning of Qurʾānic verses depended in large degree on the circumstances in which they were revealed, much of the science of *tafsīr* was historical. So, for example, the Qurʾān told believers that 'once the sacred months are past, [you should] slay the polytheists wherever you find them' (Q 9:5). But what was the specific crisis to which that injunction was addressed? Were there clues in the historical circumstances that would serve to limit the injunction's force or, conversely, to lend it a more general application? An even more basic need was determining the meaning of the holy text's Arabic words and phrases. To meet that need scholars began to construct a grammar of the Arabic language, and to compile a record of the meaning of old and obscure Arabic words. The latter project in particular required the preservation of and commentary on the oldest Arabic texts, including compilations of the poetry that had been the premier art form of the pre-Islamic Arabs. Significantly, many of the earliest grammarians and students of Arabic literature were of non-Arab background. Their contribution to the study of Arabic linguistics reminds us both of how important the Arabic language was for all Muslims, given the status of the Qur'ān as God's revealed word, and also of how the composition of the *umma* was gradually changing through the conversion of the non-Arab peoples of the Middle East.

The other major textual source of Islamic religious knowledge is the *ḥadīth*. Gradually, during the first two centuries of Islamic history, many Muslims came to regard the practice of Muḥammad and his Companions, known as *sunna*, as normative.[†††] The *sunna* was known through the stories told about what the earliest Muslims had said and done – that is, through *ḥadīth*. So powerful did the attraction of the *sunna* become that in many ways the *ḥadīth* eclipsed the Qur'ān as a source of normative guidance. The classic illustration of this development concerns the issue of adultery. The Qur'ān is fairly clear on the matter: 'The adulteress and the adulterer – flog each of them with a hundred stripes' (Q 24:2). But *ḥadīth* told a different story, in which Muḥammad and his Companions had approved of the stoning of adulterers, at least those who were legally competent married adults, and the weight of Prophetic example carried the day with the Muslim jurists. Examples such as this gave rise to a more general proposition, that 'the *sunna* is the judge of the Qur'ān, not the Qur'ān of the *sunna*'.[13]

Given the normative force of *sunna*, it was not long before *ḥadīth* began to be fabricated. This was an easy thing to do, since Muslims now lived so widely dispersed across the Middle East and North Africa, and since at first the *ḥadīth* circulated only orally, passed on by word of mouth from person to person. The early Muslim scholars were aware of this problem. Gradually they

††† The appellation 'Sunnī' of course is related to the word *sunna*. The connection should not obscure the fact that Shīʿa also recognise the force of *sunna*. Shīʿite *sunna* differs, however, in identifying the words and deeds of their imams as normative as well.

13 Ignaz Goldziher, *Muslim studies*, ed. S. M. Stern, trans. C. R. Barber and S. M. Stern, 2 vols. (Chicago and London, 1971), vol. II, p. 31.

developed criteria for distinguishing authentic *ḥadīth* from false. These criteria stressed the need to identify as secure and uninterrupted as possible a chain of individual transmitters through whom the stories could be traced back to Muḥammad and his Companions – although of course these 'chains of authority' (*asānīd*, sing. *isnād*) could be fabricated as well. By the late second/eighth century, if not before, scholars had begun the process of collecting and writing down the *ḥadīth*, and thus giving the corpus of Prophetic traditions a more-or-less definitive form. One of the earliest comprehensive collections of *ḥadīth* is found in a compilation by a Medinan jurist named Mālik ibn Anas (d. 179/796). More influential were two by Muḥammad ibn Ismāʿīl al-Bukhārī (d. 256/870) and Muslim ibn Ḥajjāj (d. 261/875), who sorted through tens of thousands of *ḥadīth* and selected for inclusion only those whose chains of authority they considered reliable.

The importance of the *ḥadīth* in the religious life of Muslims can hardly be overstated. Most importantly, they formed one of the foundations of Islamic jurisprudence (*fiqh*), which was crystallising at the same time as (and as part of the process by which) the body of *ḥadīth* was stabilised. The amount of actual legislation in the Qur'ān is quite limited; the *ḥadīth*, by contrast, provide instruction for an enormous range of problems, from matters of personal etiquette to correct commercial practice to prayer. The traditions also include historical accounts of the life of Muḥammad and the earliest Muslim community. Consequently they were of great interest to scholars in a variety of fields. In addition, the *ḥadīth* played an important role in the popular religious experience. The public recitation of the major collections of traditions, particularly those of al-Bukhārī and Muslim, became a standard feature of the celebrations associated with religious holidays, especially the month-long fast during Ramaḍān. In addition to the major compilations, scholars frequently put together collections of forty *ḥadīth* selected for their special importance, or their focus on a single topic, and the recitation and memorisation of these shorter anthologies became a staple of popular piety.

As vast as the range of topics covered by the *ḥadīth* was, they were not sufficient in themselves to support a comprehensive system of law. The articulation of Islamic law, the *sharīʿa*, was the work of the jurists (*fuqahāʾ*, sing. *faqīh*) of the classical period. Chief among them was Muḥammad ibn Idrīs al-Shāfiʿī (d. 204/820), the premier theorist of Islamic jurisprudence. Over time the jurisprudential methods espoused by al-Shāfiʿī and other jurists crystallised as 'schools' (*madhāhib*, sing. *madhhab*) of law – not institutions, but traditions of legal thought. Originally there were many of these schools, but by the early medieval period only four remained as living traditions, each named for an eponymous scholar who stood at the head of the tradition: the Ḥanafī, Mālikī, Shāfiʿī and Ḥanbalī schools. Adherence to one school precluded affiliation with another, but the adherents of each school recognised the others as legitimate. In terms of substantive law, the differences between the schools were minor. Shīʿa of course have their own jurisprudential traditions, which have sometimes been identified as a fifth school, called the Jaʿfarī (named for Jaʿfar al-Ṣādiq, the sixth Shīʿite imam and a scholar widely respected, even by Sunnīs), although the major issues dividing Sunnī and Shīʿa are historical and political rather than legal.

The system of jurisprudence developed by al-Shāfiʿī and other jurists was built upon a series of four 'foundations' (*uṣūl*): the Qurʾān; the *sunna* as reflected in *ḥadīth*; human reason (usually meaning *qiyās*, 'analogy'); and the 'consensus' (*ijmāʿ*) of the scholarly community. The different schools employed these sources in varying combinations, but patterns in and conflicts over their use highlight some of the basic principles and characteristics of the Sunnī tradition. The jurists viewed the *sharīʿa* as God's law, the fullest revelation of his will for humanity. Consequently, they were generally sceptical of the free application of human reason in constructing the law. Indeed, the jurisprudential traditions developed in part as a reaction against the unfettered use of reason (*raʾy*) in the courts of the early community. The Ḥanbalīs, at least in theory, reject human reasoning entirely, in favour of strict adherence to the precepts of the Qurʾān and *sunna*. More commonly the jurists accepted reason as a source of law, but limited it to analogy, a jurisprudential tool they may have borrowed from Jewish law. So, for example, while the Qurʾān forbids drinking wine, it says nothing about beer. But analogy suggests that beer, too, is forbidden: after all, the problem with wine is that it inebriates, a quality shared by all alcoholic beverages. The human element, however, is also apparent in the last but in many ways most important of the foundations: consensus – that is, the consensus of the jurists. While it may be God's law, Islamic law is in the final analysis what the jurists say it is. The importance of the principle of consensus is reflected in a well-known *ḥadīth*, in which the Prophet is alleged to have said: 'My community will never agree upon an error.'

There is a conservative streak to most legal systems, and Islamic law is no exception. So, for example, if *sunna* was normative, its opposite was *bidʿa*, 'innovation'. According to a well-known dictum, also ascribed to Muḥammad, 'every new thing is an innovation, and every innovation is an error, and every error leads to hell'.[14] More controversial was a doctrine that gained ground

14 Ibn al-Ḥājj, *Madkhal al-sharʿ al-sharīf*, 4 vols. (Cairo, 1929), vol. I, p. 79.

among some jurists from about the fourth/tenth century, according to which at some point the 'gates of independent reasoning (*ijtihād*)' had closed, and future jurists must practise *taqlīd*, 'imitation' of those who had gone before. This doctrine was less widely accepted, and had less comprehensive application, than Western scholars of Islam once thought. *Ijtihād* is a nuanced legal concept. It can mean very different things, and many legal scholars insisted upon its continuing necessity. The kind of *ijtihād* that is the subject of this doctrine was a particular kind of independent reasoning: the fresh and unfettered construction of a jurisprudential system from the 'foundations' alone. The doctrine was never universally embraced by the Sunnī jurists, although in later centuries they did increasingly stress the importance of *taqlīd*, and of adhering to the established rulings of the different schools of law.[15]

Despite their conservative nature, legal systems need to create channels for growth and response to new circumstances, and again Islamic law conforms to the rule. The normative power of the Prophetic *sunna* cast a cloud over the idea of innovation, at least in theory: if Muḥammad had not done something, why should later Muslims? But in practice some innovations had to be accepted. Many jurists recognised this, and stipulated that not all *bidʿas* were forbidden. Depending on their nature and their conformity to general principles of the faith, some might be praiseworthy, or even required.[16] One of the principal mechanisms by which the jurists accepted new things or responded to new problems was the *fatwā*. A *fatwā* is a legal opinion, issued by a legal scholar (in which capacity he is known as a *muftī*), in response to some question: is something, especially some practice, acceptable according to Islamic law or not? *Fatwās* had no binding authority; their force reflected simply the reputation of the jurist issuing the ruling. Consequently there was plenty of room for disagreement among jurists and, as a result, evolution in the practical application of legal principles. Indeed, it was one of the hallmarks of classical Islamic law that it was never codified. Ibn al-Muqaffaʿ's abortive appeal to the caliph to assert his authority was the last major attempt to codify Islamic law until the modernising reforms of the thirteenth/nineteenth century.

15 On the subject of *ijtihād* the most rigorous work is that of Wael Hallaq, esp. 'Was the gate of *ijtihad* closed?', *IJMES*, 16 (1984); *A history of Islamic legal theories* (Cambridge, 1997); and *Authority, continuity, and change in Islamic law* (Cambridge, 2001). But see also Sherman Jackson, *Islamic law and the state: The constitutional jurisprudence of Shihab al-Din al-Qarafi* (Leiden, 1996), esp. pp. xxv–xxxv.

16 For a particularly clear and interesting example of this see N. J. G. Kaptein, *Muḥammad's birthday festival: Early history in the central Muslim lands and development in the Muslim west until the 10th/16th century* (Leiden, 1993).

At least in theory, the *sharīʿa* touched on virtually all matters of concern to Muslims. It is for this reason that Islam is often described less as a 'religion' than as a comprehensive way of life. In this respect it resembles Judaism much more than it does Christianity. So, for example, the jurists developed a broad range of guidelines covering commercial life. Sales, loans, business partnerships, contracts – all this and more was regulated by the *sharīʿa*, and such topics took up significant portions of the legal treatises. Commercial law also demonstrates, however, how flexible and accommodating Islamic legal practice could be. The lawyers went to some lengths to ensure that their legal rulings were consonant with the custom (*ʿurf*) of the marketplace. Where conflicts arose – as, for example, over interest on loans, which the Qurʾān explicitly forbids but which is essential to a functioning market – the jurists developed certain 'tricks' (*ḥiyal*) which allowed Muslims to conform to the letter of Islamic law while accommodating the demands of business life. The jurists appear to have been swayed not only by custom and business necessity, but also by other legal systems: for example, they probably borrowed from Jewish law a flexible model of business partnerships which facilitated a flourishing commercial life in the classical Islamic Near East.[17]

The comprehensiveness of Islamic law and its centrality to what it means to be a Muslim highlight the similarities between Islam and Judaism. By contrast, theology serves to differentiate Islam from Christianity. Almost from the beginning, Christians embraced doctrines – Jesus as the son of God, Christ as the pre-existing Logos, the doctrine of the Trinity – which required complex theological explanation and justification. The complexity of Christian theology is evident even in one of the tradition's basic statements of faith, the Nicene Creed. Set against such doctrines, Islamic faith seems remarkably simple. At the heart of Muslim faith is the austere statement known as the 'witnessing' (*shahāda*): 'There is no god but God, and Muḥammad is his prophet.' The first of the five 'pillars' of Islam, the *shahāda* figures prominently in the formal Muslim prayer (*ṣalāt*), and in spontaneous expressions of Muslim piety. Its simple message resonates with the stark monotheism of the Qurʾān, which is emphatic in its rejection of Christian doctrines it sees as compromising God's oneness: 'Those who say that God is the third of three are unbelievers' (Q 5:73).

Eventually Muslims developed a more sophisticated theology. That they did so was perhaps inevitable, given the diverse religious composition of the Middle East and the religious competition that diversity engendered.

17 Abraham L. Udovitch, *Partnership and profit in medieval Islam* (Princeton, 1970).

If Christians had elaborate theological doctrines, then it was necessary for Muslims to develop them too. Muslim theology has always had an apologetic character. It is known as *ʿilm al-kalām*, 'the science of speech', *kalām* implying 'argument'. There were plenty of opportunities for the exchange of arguments and ideas across the religious divides. Muslims for the most part did not live in hermetic isolation from the adherents of other religions, some of whom on occasion served the Muslim state. Under the ʿAbbāsids Muslim, Jewish and Christian apologists sometimes gathered for spirited theological debates. And the influence was not a one-way street: the impact of Qurʾānic language has been detected in Christian monastic writings from Syria, while the Byzantine movement of iconoclasm may have been inspired by the Muslim prohibition on pictorial representation.[18]

But the central issues of Islamic theology grew out of specifically Muslim concerns, most of them raised by a thoughtful reading of the Qurʾān. Those issues included the nature of the Qurʾān itself, and whether it was created by God or co-eternal with him – the question that lay behind the *miḥna* imposed by al-Maʾmūn. The Qurʾān's emphasis on God's omniscience and omnipotence raised doubts as to whether or not human beings could be held responsible for their own actions – essentially a question about the relationship of God and justice. How far did God's mercy run? Do major sins mark a reversion to a state of unbelief? And finally there was the question of the nature of God himself, and the connection between God and the divine 'attributes' (*ṣifāt*) associated with the various names by which God is known in the Qurʾān: the 'merciful', the 'all-seeing', the 'all-knowing', the 'just', the 'generous' and so on. How did these separate attributes comport with God's fundamental unity and permanence? Did God, for example, really 'see'?

The theologians saw themselves as defenders of the doctrines of Muslim faith. So, for example, the great historian and polymath Ibn Khaldūn (d. 808/1406) defined *ʿilm al-kalām* as the 'science that involves arguing with logical proofs in defense of the articles of faith and refuting innovators who deviate in their dogmas from the early Muslims and Muslim orthodoxy'.[19] At first their principal opponents were those whose rational scepticism challenged beliefs grounded in simple faith. These included philosophers, such as those who

18 Sidney H. Griffith, 'The view of Islam from the monasteries of Palestine in the early ʿAbbāsid period: Theodore Abū Qurrah and the *Summa Theologiae Arabica*', *Islam and Christian–Muslim Relations*, 7 (1996); Patricia Crone, 'Islam, Judeo-Christianity and Byzantine iconoclasm', *JSAI*, 2 (1980).

19 Ibn Khaldūn, *The muqaddimah*, trans. Franz Rosenthal, 3 vols. (Princeton, 1967), vol. III, p. 34.

participated in the translation movement which, under the patronage of the early ʿAbbāsid caliphs, made many of the classics of Greek philosophy and science available in Arabic. For a time philosophical scepticism was rife in intellectual circles, and many perceived in 'free thinkers' a serious threat to Islam. The school of theologians known as the Muʿtazila saw themselves as a bulwark against such disbelief, and referred to themselves as 'the people of justice and unity' – i.e. those who insisted on God's inherent justice and who defended the principle of divine oneness. Hence, for example, their conviction that God's acts are just, and that they could only be just. Hence too their insistence that Qurʾānic statements about God's 'sight' and similar attributes, or *ḥadīth* about how the believers will 'see' God in the next life, should be interpreted metaphorically, and not understood to suggest that God in some sense has a body. The Qurʾān, in their view, was created, not co-eternal with God. If the latter were the case, they argued, would that not amount to associating something with God – in effect, undermining the principle of divine unity?

The problem was that making this case involved the use of rational arguments grounded in philosophical logic – in other words, employing the intellectual tools of the rational sceptics – as Ibn Khaldūn's definition of theology implies. And so the theologians were also challenged from the opposite end of the intellectual spectrum: from traditionalists who demanded the uncritical acceptance of Qurʾānic statements and doctrines grounded in *ḥadīth*, whether or not they made rational sense. Muslims, according to the traditionalists, had to accept such doctrines *bi-lā kayf*, without asking 'how'. So, for example, if the Qurʾān speaks of God sitting on a throne (Q 7:54; 20:5), then a Muslim must accept that God sits on a throne, without worrying about the anthropomorphism such a statement might imply. The traditionalists did not so much resolve the ethical dilemma of monotheism – the tension between an all-powerful God and the reality of evil – as simply ignore it, with the affirmation that God commands everything, and that what he does is good not because he is good, but because he does it. Such views, associated especially with Aḥmad ibn Ḥanbal, hero of the traditionalist resistance to the *miḥna* and founder of the Ḥanbalī school of law, were enormously popular in the third/ninth and fourth/tenth centuries.

Kalām as a discipline survived the opposition of the traditionalists, but by and large their views of God and of God's relation to the world prevailed. This development can be traced in part to Abu 'l-Ḥasan al-Ashʿarī (d. 324/935f.), a theologian who began his career as a Muʿtazilite but who later embraced traditionalist positions on matters such as God's attributes. What al-Ashʿarī then did was to use the tools of *kalām* in defence of traditionalist propositions about God. Not everyone was satisfied, and many strict traditionalists remained hostile to any application of the tools of rational thinking to matters of faith. Nonetheless, theology survived. Al-Ashʿarī is regarded as the founder of a school of theological thought that bears his name, and many of the most famous later Muslim theologians, including al-Juwaynī (d. 478/1085), al-Ghazālī (d. 505/1111) and Fakhr al-Dīn al-Rāzī (d. 606/1209) were Ashʿarīs. Its major rival was a school of theology closely associated with the Ḥanafī *madhhab* known as Māturīdism. Māturīdīs embraced positions closer to Muʿtazilite rationalism on matters such as God's attributes and humans' responsibility for their actions. On the other hand, some later Ashʿarīs moved away from the strict positions of the school's founder, and it was primarily among them that the tools of systematic theology flourished within the Sunnī tradition, despite the persistent opposition of the traditionalists.[20]

The finer points of theology, of course, meant little to most people's experience of Islam. For the vast majority of Muslims Islam meant first and foremost the encounter with God in worship. The elements of worship were already in place during the Prophet's lifetime, but in the classical period they took definitive shape. The central act of worship was prayer. The importance of prayer is evident from the considerable space accorded to it in most collections of *ḥadīth*. *Islām* literally means 'submission' or 'surrendering', and the prostration of the worshipper during the *ṣalāt* symbolised the submission of his soul to God. The sources record a number of stories, most of them fanciful, explaining why the number of daily prayers was fixed at five. The most colourful attributes the number to a protracted negotiation between Muḥammad and God during the Prophet's legendary ascension to heaven from the Temple Mount in Jerusalem. It has been suggested that the number five may have been borrowed from Zoroastrian practice. In any case, for many Muslims the experience of Islam focused principally on the daily *ṣalāt*.

Prayer was not the only form of ritual engagement, however. Of particular importance was the gathering of the Muslim congregation at noon on Fridays. This gathering involved performing the *ṣalāt*, but to it was added the pronouncement of a sermon (*khuṭba*). Muḥammad himself had preached to his community, and at first, following his practice, the caliphs or their official representatives delivered the sermon. As defined by the evolving tradition, the *khuṭba* consisted less of a free-ranging homily than the formulaic

20 For a general survey of the history of Muslim theology see Tilman Nagel, *The history of Islamic theology from Muhammad to the present* (Princeton, 2000).

pronouncement of prayers and blessings upon the Prophet and his family and on the Muslim community. At its heart, however, the *khuṭba* and its setting had a political purpose. It became customary to mention the name of the ruler as a marker of his authority; to omit his name, or to mention that of some rival, constituted an act of rebellion. More generally, the regular gathering of the community (or at least of its male members) at one time and place served as a reminder of the *umma*'s unity and political significance.

Islam largely rejected the hierarchical structure of Christian worship. Where Muslims gathered together for prayer they would be led by an *imām* ('one who stands in front' – the same word the jurists used to refer to the ruler of the community), but the *imām* could be any individual with the requisite knowledge. Neither he nor the preacher (*khaṭīb*) was distinguished from the body of worshippers by anything like the Christian practice of ordination or consecration. Consequently, prayer could take place anywhere, and any place that served for worship constituted a *masjid*, a 'place of prostration', from which the English term 'mosque' derives. Nonetheless, from the beginning Muslim rulers and others established structures designed especially for worship. In particular, a large 'gathering mosque' (*masjid jāmiʿ*) constituted one of the defining features of Islamic cities. In theory each city or settlement would have one congregational mosque, since the entire community was expected to gather there on Fridays for prayers and the *khuṭba*, although eventually the growing numbers of Muslims meant that large towns might boast several such mosques. These congregational mosques include some of the most famous structures in the Muslim world, including the Prophet's Mosque in Medina, the Umayyad Mosque in Damascus, al-Aqṣā in Jerusalem and the great mosque in Cordoba, Spain, which, after the *reconquista*, became a Christian cathedral.

For most Muslims, then, Islam *was* prayer, at least as far as the religious experience was concerned. For others, however, prayer constituted only the first step in a larger project of submitting their wills to that of God. In such individuals lie the origins of the pietistic tradition which later would be called Sufism. The historical roots of Sufism are obscure, but the tradition grew out of a cluster of concerns and developments characteristic of Islam in the classical period. First and foremost was the desire to break free from the distractions of this world in order to focus on the promise of the next, and on the love of God himself. So, for example, Rābiʿa of Baṣra (d. *c.* 185/801), the archetypal early Muslim ascetic, embraced her poverty and focused on the absolute and exclusive love of God. 'O God,' she is reported to have prayed, 'my whole occupation and all my desire in this world of all worldly things, is to remember Thee, and in the world to come, of all things of the world to come, is to meet Thee.'[21] Muslim asceticism, unlike the Christian variety, was never categorical in its renunciation of the world. Monasticism, according to the Qur'ān, was a Christian innovation which God 'did not prescribe for them' (Q 57:27). But Muslims were moved by the Qur'ānic admonition that the life of this world was mere 'play and amusement' (Q 6:32), and by stories about the indifference of Muḥammad and some of his Companions to wealth. It is possible, too, that Muslim pietists were influenced by the well-developed tradition of asceticism among the 'holy men' who were so central to the experience of Late Antique Christianity. The very term 'Sufi' probably derives from the word *ṣūf*, 'wool', and may refer to coarse woollen garments embraced by ascetics in the hot Middle Eastern climate – a practice for which there is certainly Christian precedent.

The pietistic tradition that became Sufism thus was grounded in an ascetic impulse which Muslims shared with other Middle Eastern faith traditions. But there were other, more specifically Muslim, concerns involved as well. Accounts of the earliest Sufis are encrusted with legend, but suggest that they were connected to the pious opposition that arose in reaction to the perceived excesses of the Umayyad caliphs. The name of al-Ḥasan al-Baṣrī (d. 110/728), for example, a pious preacher who chastised the Umayyads for their worldliness, often appears in Sufi chains of authority. Other early figures claimed by the Sufi tradition were deeply involved in waging *jihād*, particularly along the Byzantine frontier.[22] Ascetic piety, in other words, did not preclude an active – even violent – commitment to the faith. Eventually, in many parts of the world, including South Asia and Africa, Sufis were instrumental in efforts to convert non-Muslims to Islam.

By the end of the classical period the Sufi tradition moved beyond its ascetic and pietistic roots to embrace a mystical approach to God. The beginnings of this development lie in the doctrine of divine love expressed by Rābiʿa and others. It is possible that mystical doctrines in other religions – Christianity, but also South Asian traditions – may have influenced Sufi Islam. For example, the doctrine of the 'annihilation' (*fanā'*) of the soul in its contemplation of the divine, as expressed by Sufis such as Abū Yazīd al-Bisṭāmī (d. 261/874) and Junayd (d. 298/910), recalls certain aspects of Hindu or Buddhist monism. As in other religions, Sufi mysticism was built around various theories of esoteric

21 R. A. Nicholson, *Muslim saints and mystics* (Boston, 1976), p. 47.
22 Michael Bonner, *Aristocratic violence and holy war: Studies in the* jihād *and the Arab–Byzantine frontier* (New Haven, 1996), pp. 130–545.

knowledge – special ways, that is, in which the mystic came to 'know' God. The resulting theological speculation raised concerns with many of the *'ulamā'*. Perhaps the most controversial Sufi was the Persian mystic al-Ḥallāj (d. 309/922). His enthusiastic and apparently outrageous utterances – for example, 'anā 'l-ḥaqq' ('I am the truth', *al-ḥaqq* being one name for God) – contributed to his gruesome execution for heresy at the orders of the 'Abbāsid caliph. But it was not only exuberant and theologically dubious outbursts that angered and worried the *'ulamā'*. The mystical path is inherently individualistic and antinomian, and therefore worrisome to a religious tradition such as Islam, focused so heavily on social experience and communal identity. 'Prayer is unbelief, once one knows,' al-Ḥallāj is said to have cryptically remarked. If the mystical experience could undermine so fundamental a practice as prayer, what might it do to the larger legal scaffolding that regulated Muslim life?[23]

In the fourth/tenth century the Islamic tradition confronted an existential crisis. For much of the early Islamic period the distinction between Sunnī and Shī'ite Islam was not always clear. But in the fourth/tenth century the sectarian division became extremely sharp. In part this resulted from the fact that, in the mid-third/ninth century, the principal line of Shī'ite imams came to an end when (according to the Shī'a) the twelfth imam went into protective hiding. The disappearance of the locus of authority for these Shī'a (who came to be known as Twelvers) forced them to define their own tradition more precisely. Even more significant was the rise in various places of regimes that in one way or another embraced Shī'ism. These included the Ismā'īlī Fāṭimid state in North Africa and Egypt, which represented a line of imams different from those recognised by the Twelvers, and which made a concerted (although unsuccessful) effort to convince Sunnī Muslims throughout the Muslim world to recognise their leadership. The Shī'ite Būyid regime in Iraq and Iran did not, oddly, challenge the nominal authority of the 'Abbāsid caliphs, but they did patronise Twelver Shī'ite scholars, and so helped Twelver (or Imāmī) Shī'ism to take definitive shape.

And so, in the fourth/tenth century, the Islamic tradition generally could have moved in a very different direction. In the end, however, the Shī'ite moment passed. The Fāṭimids were never able to convince many to embrace their cause, not even in Egypt. And by the mid-fifth/eleventh century the Būyids were overwhelmed by a new and militantly Sunnī political power.

23 On al-Ḥallāj see Louis Massignon, *The passion of al-Hallaj: Mystic and martyr of Islam*, trans. H. Mason, 4 vols. (Princeton, 1982).

That set the stage for the further development of the Islamic tradition through the medieval and early modern periods.

Developments in medieval and early modern Islam

The dominant political development of the medieval period was the rise of a series of Turkish regimes. The 'Turks' who ruled them were a disparate group, but mostly had roots in nomadic peoples from Central Asia who spoke various Turkic languages. They entered the Islamic world beginning in the third / ninth century, first as slave-soldiers purchased and trained by the ʿAbbāsid caliphs. Later whole tribes of nomadic and recently converted Turks moved out of Central Asia and into the central Islamic world. By and large these regimes recognised the lingering authority of the ʿAbbāsid caliphs, but wielded effective power themselves as *sulṭāns* from the various cities in which they established themselves. Among the most important were the Saljūqs, who defeated the Būyids and ruled over Iraq and Iran in the fifth / eleventh and sixth / twelfth centuries; a series of Turkish and Afghan regimes which dominated north Indian politics from the sixth / twelfth and seventh / thirteenth centuries, culminating with the Turco-Mongol regime of the Mughals; the Mamlūks, a dynasty of slave-soldiers who ruled over Egypt and Syria from the middle of the seventh / thirteenth to the beginning of the tenth / sixteenth centuries; and finally the Ottomans, who from meagre origins on the Byzantine frontier in the seventh / thirteenth century built the largest and greatest of the medieval Turkish empires, one which in fact lasted into the twentieth century.

These regimes had an indirect but significant impact on the Islamic religious tradition. In the first place, they were responsible for another round of expansion in the territories known as the *dār al-islām*. The Saljūqs defeated the Byzantine emperor at the battle of Manzikert in eastern Anatolia in 463 / 1071. In the aftermath Anatolia was overrun by Turkish tribes, who established Muslim regimes in the peninsula and precipitated its Islamisation. From that process emerged the Ottomans, who carried the battle and the tide of conversion into south-eastern Europe. One result was the emergence in the Balkan Peninsula of Muslim communities, such as the Bosnians, which have remained down to the present day. A similar development took place to the east. Islam had been present in India since at least the late first / early eighth century, but the medieval Muslim regimes there encouraged further conversion, as a result of which the Muslim population of South Asia today stands at about 25 percent. The significance of this expansion in the *dār al-islām* was accentuated by contrary developments at the other end of the Islamic world.

The ninth/fifteenth century saw the end of the process known as the *reconquista*, whereby the Iberian Peninsula passed out of Muslim hands. Soon Spain's Muslims (as well as its Jews) were either forcibly converted to Christianity or expelled. With the exception of the Balkans, the demographic growth of Islam in the medieval and early modern periods occurred not in Europe but elsewhere, particularly in South, South-East and Central Asia.

Religious developments in medieval Islam took place against a background of new and threatening challenges. The rise of the Shīʿite regimes in the fourth/tenth century had already sharpened sectarian identities and tensions. But even greater dangers loomed. In the late fifth/eleventh and sixth/twelfth centuries a splinter movement within Ismāʿīlī Shīʿism waged a violent insurrection against the Sunnī status quo in scattered parts of Iran, Iraq and Syria. The Assassins, as they were known, had little chance of success, but the spectre raised by their campaign of targeted killing prompted widespread panic (and, in response, violent suppression of Ismāʿīlī communities in the cities of the region).[24] Then, in 490/1097, the first Crusaders appeared in Syria. Their violent challenge to the status quo – later Crusader accounts describe their conquest of Jerusalem that year as an especially bloody affair – left the Muslims in the region bewildered. Before long, however, the Muslims came to see the Crusaders in a larger context: that they, along with the Normans who overwhelmed Muslim Sicily and the Spanish and French warriors who led the *reconquista* in the west, represented a broad and existential threat from a newly militant and confident Christian Europe.[25]

In the first half of the seventh/thirteenth century an even greater threat appeared: the Mongols. Most of the tribesmen belonging to the Mongol confederation that conquered Iran and penetrated as far as Syria were pagan. In 656/1258 they destroyed the city of Baghdad, and slaughtered the last ʿAbbāsid caliph to reign there. Muslims at the time understood the Mongols to pose a mortal threat to Islam. The Mamlūks, who defeated the Mongols in Syria and so checked their advance, earned the gratitude of many Muslims for having 'saved' Islam. (They also saved what was left of the ʿAbbāsid caliphate: a series of refugees from Baghdad who claimed to be members of the ʿAbbāsid family, whom the Mamlūks installed as caliphs but whose authority was not widely recognised in the Muslim world.) By the late

24 See Marshall G. S. Hodgson, *The order of Assassins: The struggle of the early Nizārī Ismāʿīlīs against the Islamic world* (The Hague, 1955).

25 On the impact of the Crusades on Islam see Emmanuel Sivan, *L'Islam et la croisade: Idéologie et propagande dans les réactions musulmanes aux croisades* (Paris, 1968); and Carole Hillenbrand, *The Crusades: Islamic perspectives* (Chicago, 1999).

seventh/thirteenth century, however, the Mongols in the Middle East had converted to Islam, and established regimes in Iran and the area north of the Caucasus essentially similar to others in the region. They included that of one of the greatest medieval Muslim warriors, Tīmūr Lang, known to Western legend as Tamerlane.

The various and apparently nefarious challenges – from Shīʿa, Crusaders, Mongols and others – prompted multiple movements in response. Some of the earliest and most militant appeared in the west – significantly, perhaps, since it was there that Muslims, faced by the *reconquista*, found themselves in long-term retreat. Both the Almoravids and their successors, the Almohads, came to power in part as a result of political tensions among the Berber population of the Maghrib. But both also cast themselves as movements of religious reform, campaigning against moral laxity and what they perceived to be unlawful innovations. Having been invited by the weakened Spanish Muslim princes to assist them in their struggle against the Christians, the Almoravids and especially the Almohads sought to suppress the liberal and tolerant cultural atmosphere that, in the third/ninth and fourth/tenth centuries, had made Muslim Spain a cosmopolitan and religiously pluralist society.[26] Their religious militancy made life uncomfortable for non-Muslims as well, and many Christians and Jews living under their rule fled. Among them was the famous Jewish theologian and philosopher Maimonides, who ended up in the comparatively tolerant society of Cairo, where he served the Jewish community as a judge and the famous Muslim warrior Ṣalāḥ al-Dīn al-Ayyūbī, better known in the West as Saladin, as personal physician.

The Almohads were unusual for their xenophobia, but a growing suspicion of non-Muslims was a widespread and understandable response to persistent external threats. In Syria and the central Muslim world the appearance of the Crusaders sparked renewed interest in *jihād*. Several medieval scholars produced treatises collecting *ḥadīth* on the subject, or extolling the virtues of waging war on Islam's behalf. The jurists recognised *jihād* as what they called a *farḍ kifāya*, an obligation not on individual Muslims but on the community as a whole. But when Islam itself was threatened, they said, *jihād* became a *farḍ ʿayn*, an individual responsibility incumbent on all Muslims. (It is striking that the 1998 *fatwā* by a group of Muslim radicals including Osama bin Ladin cites several Crusader-era jurists in support of the proposition that Muslims today

26 On the cultural florescence of early medieval Spain and its suppression see Maria Rosa Menocal, *The ornament of the world: How Muslims, Jews, and Christians created a culture of tolerance in medieval Spain* (New York, 2002).

are enjoined *individually* to fight against the Americans.) The targets of the new *jihād* spirit were Islam's external enemies, Christian Europeans and pagan Mongols, whom envoys of the Pope approached about an alliance against the Muslims. (Xenophobia often has deep roots.) But inevitably the *dhimmīs*, especially Christians, came under a cloud of suspicion, since they shared a religion with some of the most dangerous enemies. There are indications that their life grew more difficult in this period, as restrictions on their activities, including public celebrations of their faith, were enforced more rigorously.

Internally, too, Muslim society experienced a sort of 'circling of the wagons' in the face of the new medieval challenges. The period has sometimes been called one of a 'Sunnī revival', and indeed the Turkish military regimes were by and large enthusiastically Sunnī. What the period really witnessed, however, was a process of homogenising religious life, circumscribing the parameters of permitted thought and behaviour and giving greater force to the 'consensus' (*ijmāʿ*) of the jurists and the scholarly elite. The public creedal statement issued by the caliph al-Qādir in the fifth/eleventh century (see p. 34 above) constituted an early benchmark. The statement reflects the consensus of traditionalist scholars about what 'Islam' was, and by and large they defined it through a series of negations: to be a Sunnī Muslim meant to reject Christianity, to reject Khārijite intolerance and Shīʿite sectarianism, to reject Muʿtazilism and speculative theology more generally. Another aspect of the homogenising trend was a reinvigorated opposition to innovation (*bidʿa*). This constituted one of the dominant themes of medieval Islamic religious discourse, and formed the subject of numerous polemical treatises composed between the sixth/twelfth and tenth/sixteenth centuries; interestingly, many of them were written by scholars originally from the Maghrib. This is not to suggest that innovation stopped; simply that many of the *ʿulamāʾ* rejected the *idea* of innovations as a matter of principle. The charged atmosphere of the time is reflected in the language of polemical discourse, in which a scholar might argue that waging war against innovating Muslims was 'preferable to doing so against the infidels of the House of War, as the damage [that they inflict on Islam] is more severe'.[27]

Like other areas of religious experience, the practice of Islamic law, which was so central to Muslim identity, underwent a degree of regularisation. By the medieval period most of the earlier schools of law had ceased to exist as

27 Berkey, *Formation of Islam*, pp. 189–202; Jonathan Berkey, 'Tradition, innovation and the social construction of knowledge in the medieval Islamic Near East', *Past and Present*, 146 (1995).

living traditions, and only the four surviving *madhāhib* – the Ḥanafīs, the Mālikīs, the Shāfiʿīs and the Ḥanbalīs – were recognised as legitimate. In some cases the *madhāhib* became vehicles for the expression or advancement of other interests. The Ḥanbalīs in particular often constituted not just a school of law but a broad-based community dedicated to traditionalist Islam, and Ḥanbalī crowds in Baghdad sometimes rioted against Shīʿism or speculative theology of which they disapproved.[28] But the differences of jurisprudence and positive law separating one school from the next were relatively minor, and adherents of one school generally recognised the others as orthodox expressions of Sunnī Islam. Although *ijtihād* did not disappear entirely, the force of accepted opinion within the *madhāhib* increasingly circumscribed the judgments most individual jurists could make. The doctrine of *taqlīd* required that jurists accept not only the jurisprudence but the substantive judgments of their predecessors.

New institutional forms reinforced the regularisation of religious life. Chief among them was the *madrasa*. The *madrasa* first appeared in eastern Iran in the fourth/tenth or fifth/eleventh century, but by the seventh/thirteenth and eighth/fourteenth had become a ubiquitous presence in Islamic cities in the Middle East and South Asia. The medieval *madrasa* bore little resemblance to the similarly named religious schools allegedly breeding Islamic militants which have come to light in the early twenty-first century. The *madrasa* was principally an institution dedicated to instruction in *fiqh* (Islamic jurisprudence) according to one or more of the surviving *madhāhib*. The institutions themselves had little impact on instruction or the curriculum. The transmission of religious knowledge depended on the informal ties established between teachers and students, just as it had in the centuries before the *madrasa* made its appearance. One did not 'enrol' in a *madrasa*; one attended classes given by a particular teacher which happened to meet in one (although those classes might also take place elsewhere: in a mosque or a home, for example). Similarly, one did not 'graduate' from an institution; instead, one received an *ijāza*, a 'licence' to teach or to transmit a particular text issued by the master with whom one had studied. But the spread of *madrasa*s did have an enormous impact on the networks of scholars through whom religious knowledge was transmitted and by whom Islam was defined. The *madrasas*' endowments created paid professorships which for the first time provided

28 See George Makdisi, *Ibn ʿAqīl et la résurgence de l'Islam traditionaliste au XIe siècle (Ve siècle de l'Hégire)* (Damascus, 1963); on Shāfiʿīs and Ḥanafīs as political factions in medieval Nīshāpūr see Richard W. Bulliet, *The patricians of Nishapur: A study in medieval Islamic social history* (Cambridge, MA, 1972).

regular compensation for the *ʿulamāʾ*'s activities. This helped to clarify the social and professional identity of the learned elite. And the number of these schools, and consequently the number of scholars they supported, was considerable. By the ninth/fifteenth century, for example, Cairo probably had well over one hundred such institutions. All this helped to establish the *ʿulamāʾ*, the class of religious scholars, as a formidable and influential component of medieval Islamic urban society.[29]

A similar and equally ubiquitous institution was the Sufi 'convent' (known by several terms: *khānqāh*, *ribāṭ*, *zāwiya* and others). Like the *madrasa*, a typical *khānqāh* might provide lodging and meals, and possibly stipends, to support the mystics who lived and worshipped in it. There are certain parallels between the Sufi convents and Christian monasteries, but there are also important differences. In particular, the *khānqāh*, unlike the monastery, was principally an urban institution. More importantly, its residents did not in most cases permanently isolate themselves from the surrounding society. Sufis often married and had families, and worked in 'normal' professions. But the spread of *khānqāhs* did reflect the regularisation of the mystical life. It is significant that the functions of *madrasas* and *khānqāhs* overlapped. Architecturally there was little to distinguish them, and the activities they supported were often one and the same: Sufis living in *khānqāhs* might take classes in *ḥadīth* or Islamic jurisprudence, while students in *madrasas* might engage in Sufi rituals.

The spread of Sufi convents reflects one of the most important developments of the medieval period: the integration of Sufism into mainstream Muslim religious life. By the late classical period Sufi mysticism had evolved in directions many *ʿulamāʾ* considered subversive. Much of their opposition, however, dissipated in the ensuing centuries. This was due in part to scholars such as Abū Ḥāmid al-Ghazālī (d. 505/1111) and Ibn ʿAṭāʾ Allāh al-Iskandarī (d. 709/1309), who embraced Sufism, sometimes despite initial misgivings, and saw Sufi practice as a means to cultivate a more sincere and transformative piety. The acceptance of Sufism was eased by the routinisation of Sufi practice. By the fourth/tenth and early fifth/eleventh centuries some mystics had begun

29 The literature on the *madrasa*, religious education and the medieval *ʿulamāʾ* is enormous. The interested reader should start with George Makdisi, *The rise of colleges: Institutions of learning in Islam and the West* (Edinburgh, 1981); Carl Petry, *The civilian elite of Cairo in the later Middle Ages* (Princeton, 1981); Jonathan Berkey, *The transmission of knowledge in medieval Cairo: A social history of Islamic education* (Princeton, 1992); Michael Chamberlain, *Knowledge and social practice in medieval Damascus, 1190–1350* (Cambridge, 1994); and Daphna Ephrat, *A learned society in transition: The Sunnī ʿulamāʾ of eleventh-century Baghdad* (Albany, 2000).

to develop rules to guide adepts, and so to discipline and routinise the tradition. At some point Sufis began to speak of spiritual discipline as a form of *jihād* or 'struggle' – what many jurists themselves came to recognise as the 'greater *jihād*', distinct from and more important than the 'lesser *jihād*' of holy war.[30] This process was carried further by the crystallisation of the 'brotherhoods' or 'orders' (*ṭuruq*, sing. *ṭarīqa*). By joining an order an adept would subject himself to a certain discipline, and also to the authority of a master (shaykh) who would guide him on his spiritual path. By the late medieval period affiliation with at least one *ṭarīqa* was common if not universal among the *ʿulamāʾ*. Even those scholars who continued to fault some mystics for offensive practices or beliefs, such as Ibn Taymiyya, were themselves often members of Sufi *ṭarīqas*.

The new forms and institutions of religious life transformed the relationship between the religious and political elites. Ever since the *miḥna* the *ʿulamāʾ* had prized their hard-won independence from political authority. In the absence of any formal institutional structure such as a Church, and with the *ʿulamāʾ*'s own authority only loosely organised around the principle of consensus, the Muslim state had been unable to exercise direct and consistent control over the religious establishment. But the new institutional structures changed that equation. Mosques, *madrasas* and *khānqāhs* were generally constructed and endowed by individuals, as acts of charitable donation, rather than by the state. But most of those with the means to establish such an institution belonged to the political elites. This nurtured an increasingly symbiotic relationship between the *ʿulamāʾ* and their political benefactors.

For the *ʿulamāʾ* the benefits were tangible and obvious. The institutions and their endowments supported them and their activities directly and materially. This did not make them subservient to the state and the political elites, but it is striking that medieval rulers increasingly drew on the *ʿulamāʾ* for political assistance. The ruling elites most responsible for confronting the Crusaders in Syria and Palestine, for example, relied heavily on the *ʿulamāʾ* to mobilise resistance to the European Christian invaders. Rulers such as Nūr al-Dīn ibn Zangī and his more famous successor, Saladin, commissioned scholars to compose treatises extolling the virtues of *jihād*, or lauding the splendours of the city of Jerusalem, as a way of cultivating enthusiasm among the Muslim population for military campaigns against the Crusaders. *ʿUlamāʾ* might accompany troops into battle, reciting *ḥadīth* about the military struggles of Muḥammad and the early Muslims.

30 David Cook, *Understanding jihad* (Berkeley, 2005), pp. 32–48.

In the later medieval period the relationship between state and religious establishment grew closer. Rulers did not attempt to return to pre-*miḥna* days, or make extravagant claims about their authority to establish religious doctrine or determine legal practice. But over time the *ʿulamāʾ* did increasingly become susceptible to political manipulation and control. In Cairo, for instance, the Mamlūk sultans acquired or usurped the right to appoint professors in the leading *madrasas*. The shaykh of one of the leading *khānqāhs* in Cairo acquired the title of *shaykh al-shuyūkh* ('master of masters'), an office which he held by royal appointment, and in which official capacity he exercised some sort of supervisory responsibilities for all the Sufis of Egypt. In the late ninth/fifteenth century a dispute broke out among the Sufis of Cairo concerning some controversial lyrics by a Sufi poet named Ibn al-Fāriḍ (d. 632/1235). The theological issues at stake led to dissension among the mystics, but the enormous popularity of Ibn al-Fāriḍ and his poetry gave the dispute a political dimension, and the matter was only resolved when the reigning sultan intervened to affirm the opinions of those who viewed Ibn al-Fāriḍ's verse as perfectly orthodox.[31]

By the early modern period, with the rise of more centralised states, the authority exercised by rulers over the religious establishment became even more pronounced. The Ṣafavids of Iran present a rather unusual case. The Ṣafavids were in origin one of a number of heterodox Sufi sects active among the nomadic Turkmen populations of eastern Anatolia in the eighth/fourteenth and ninth/fifteenth centuries. Gradually they drifted towards Shīʿism, and under the leadership of their *pīr* Ismāʿīl (d. 930/1524) they conquered Iran, establishing a dynasty that lasted into the twelfth/eighteenth century. As rulers the Ṣafavids began a campaign to convert the Iranian population, up to this point overwhelmingly Sunnī, to Twelver Shīʿism. To accomplish this the Ṣafavid shahs created a Shīʿite clerical establishment through recruiting Shīʿite scholars from centres of Shīʿite learning elsewhere in the Muslim world, and through the establishment of Shīʿite mosques and schools. The Ṣafavids then entrusted to the clerics the conversion of the country, authorising them to pursue a campaign of (sometimes forced) conversion in the towns and villages of Iran. All of this made the Shīʿite *ʿulamāʾ* of Iran particularly dependent on the patronage of the rulers.

To the west, the Ottomans present another example of growing state control over the religious establishment. The Ottoman example had greater

31 T. Emil Homerin, *From Arab poet to Muslim saint: Ibn al-Fāriḍ, his verse, and his shrine* (Columbia, SC, 1994), pp. 55–75.

long-term significance, both because they were Sunnīs and because the Ottomans at one point or another controlled virtually the whole of the Middle East outside Iran, and so left their imprint on a much wider field. In the Ottoman empire the *ʿulamāʾ* were for the first time organised in a formal, institutional hierarchy; along with the military and the bureaucracy, the religious establishment (which the Ottomans referred to as the *ʿilmiyye*) served as one of the foundations of the political structure. The leading *qāḍīs*, preachers, professors in the *madrasas* and other important religious and legal figures became in fact employees of the state. Ottoman *qāḍīs* not only served as appointed judges in religious courts, but undertook a variety of administrative responsibilities on behalf of the state in the territories under their jurisdiction. At the top of the religious hierarchy stood the *şeyhülislam*, a scholar appointed by the sultan who supervised the entire religious institution.[32]

The authority of the Ottoman government over the religious institution was also extended by the use of the title caliph. The Ottomans had occasionally invoked the title since the early ninth/fifteenth century. At first they claimed it simply as an honorific, as something due to them by virtue of the extent of their power. By the tenth/sixteenth century, however, after the disappearance of the rump ʿAbbāsid caliphate of Cairo, some Ottoman jurists employed the term in a new, juridical sense, to indicate that the ruler had the right, not to create law, but to rationalise and homogenise the law by choosing from among the disparate rulings and interpretations included within the consensus of the *ʿulamāʾ*. These claims foreshadowed later, thirteenth/nineteenth-century efforts by the Ottoman sultans to produce a definitive code of Islamic law.[33]

Against these homogenising tendencies must be set the persistent diversity and complexity of the Islamic tradition. The *ʿulamāʾ*'s reinvigorated campaign against innovations proved incapable of stamping them out – indeed, the very vigour of that campaign points to the stubborn popularity of religious practices of which the *ʿulamāʾ* disapproved. These practices were many and varied, but they shared certain common characteristics. They were often associated with Sufi celebrations. Others reflect a remarkable syncretism, with Muslims,

32 R. C. Repp, 'The altered state of the ulema', in Thomas Naff and Roger Owen (eds.), *Studies in eighteenth-century Islamic history* (Carbondale, 1977); R. C. Repp, *The müfti of Istanbul: A study in the development of the Ottoman learned hierarchy* (London, 1986); Madeleine Zilfi, *The politics of piety: The Ottoman ulema in the postclassical age (1600–1800)* (Minneapolis, 1988).

33 On the Ottoman use of the title caliph see Colin Imber, *Ebu's-suʿud: The Islamic legal tradition* (Stanford, 1997).

Jews and Christians participating in each other's festive holidays – Egyptian Muslims, for example, participating in Coptic Easter festivities, or purchasing amulets inscribed with Hebrew letters. Most of the practices of which the *'ulamā'* disapproved concerned matters of personal hope or daily survival rather than issues of law or theology. Many of them sought to invoke the spiritual power (*baraka*) of some revered individual, living or dead, or to claim his intercession (*shafā'a*) – perhaps with some temporal ruler, or perhaps with God. Hence the popularity throughout the Islamic world of pilgrimage (*ziyāra*, 'visiting', as opposed to the formal *ḥajj*) to local shrines or to the tombs of pious scholars or 'saints'.[34]

Sufism, too, despite its integration into the Islamic mainstream, remained a source of ideas and practices that rankled some in the religious establishment. Sufi mystical speculation continued to flirt with theologically troublesome ideas, particularly those that tended to reduce the sharp distinction between God and his creation. Such, for example, was the doctrine of *waḥdat al-wujūd*, or the 'oneness of being', articulated by the Andalusian mystic Ibn al-'Arabī (d. 638/1240). Ibn al-'Arabī's ideas were in fact fantastically complex, and so resist easy classification, but they did prove remarkably popular. Their influence can be seen in the Persian poetry of the Anatolian mystic Jalāl al-Dīn Rūmī (d. 672/1273). Such ideas percolated more widely through the population via a variety of ritual practices which gave practical expression to them. So, for example, Rūmī and the dervishes who followed him developed a mode of enthusiastic communion with the divine through music and dance. Critics worried not only about the theological dubiousness of Ibn al-'Arabī's doctrines and Rūmī's poetry, but about the disruptive potential and erotic undertones of music, dance and other forms of ecstatic worship adopted by some Sufis. Mystical excess and enthusiasm threatened the established religious order in other ways too. The inherent individualism and anarchism of the mystical path pushed some to adopt a sceptical attitude towards *sharī'a*-based orthopraxy. In a famous couplet Rūmī himself gave expression to a kind of antinomianism which challenged the very foundations of religious identity: 'What is to be done, O Muslims? For I do not recognize myself./ I am neither Christian, nor Jew, nor Zoroastrian, nor Muslim.'[35]

34 On the *ziyāra* see Christopher S. Taylor, *In the vicinity of the righteous:* Ziyāra *and the veneration of Muslim saints in late medieval Egypt* (Leiden, 1999); Joseph Meri, *The cult of saints among Muslims and Jews in medieval Syria* (Oxford, 2002). On the phenomenon of 'popular religion' generally, see Berkey, *Formation of Islam*, pp. 248–57.

35 R. A. Nicholson, *Selected poems from the Dīvāni Shamsi Tabrīz* (Cambridge, 1898), p. 125.

There were in fact plentiful channels through which Muslims outside the ranks of the leading *ʿulamāʾ* could influence the general experience of Islam. The *khuṭba* delivered on Fridays in congregational mosques necessarily retained a formal – even official – character, but many other opportunities presented themselves for pious and interested individuals to preach to gatherings of Muslims. Popular preachers and raconteurs of religious tales held sway in mosques, homes, the street and other informal settings, delivering homilies to men and women both. Concerned jurists worried about the suitability of the religious messages they preached, but the depth of their concerns and the frequency of their complaints suggest that for many Muslims these itinerant or poorly educated preachers constituted the principal source of religious instruction and guidance.[36] The example of popular preachers serves as a reminder that, despite the growing regularisation of religious life, and despite too the ever-closer alliance of *ʿulamāʾ* and the Sunnī state in the late medieval and early modern period, the Islamic tradition remained creative and flexible. Opposition to *bidʿa* notwithstanding, innovations took root, and often the *ʿulamāʾ* themselves were persuaded by the force of their popularity to accept them as legitimate expressions of Muslim piety. The *ziyāra* is a case in point. So too is the celebration of the Prophet's birthday, which dates only from the early Middle Ages. Some scholars worried, no doubt with good reason, that the festivities bore too close a resemblance to Christmas. But ultimately the holiday became, with *ʿulamāʾ* approval, one of the most popular in the Muslim calendar.[37]

Because of these underlying tensions – between the leading *ʿulamāʾ* and more popular preachers and shaykhs, between the growing control exercised by political authorities and the persistent independence of the religious establishment – Islam never lost its capacity for renewal. Western complaints about Islam's supposed need for a 'reformation' miss the dynamism and capacity for reinventing itself at the religion's heart.[38] On the cusp of the modern period this dynamism was fully at work. In the twelfth/eighteenth century the powerful and centralised states that had dominated political life since the tenth/sixteenth century – the Ottoman, Ṣafavid and Mughal empires – weakened (and, in the case of the Ṣafavids, disappeared).

36 Jonathan P. Berkey, *Popular preaching and religious authority in the medieval Islamic Near East* (Seattle, 2001).
37 See Kaptein, *Muḥammad's birthday festival.*
38 John Voll, 'Renewal and reform in Islamic history: *Tajdid* and *islah*', in John L. Esposito (ed.), *Voices of resurgent Islam* (New York, 1983); Nehemiah Levtzion and John Voll (eds.), *Eighteenth-century renewal and reform in Islam* (Syracuse, 1987).

Simultaneously, various movements of reform and renewal set the stage for important developments in the modern world. Most notable among them was that associated with a cantankerous Arabian scholar, Muḥammad ibn ʿAbd al-Wahhāb, in Arabia, inspired in part by the writings of Ibn Taymiyya, and another driven by one of the leading Muslim scholars of India, Shāh Walī Allāh of Delhi.

The movements led by these religious reformers and their successors have produced disparate results, but they have also shared certain common characteristics. They have tended to combine a fierce commitment to the principle of restoring an idealised Muslim past associated with Muḥammad and his Companions with the recognition that changed conditions require the full exercise of all tools, including in some cases that of unfettered *ijtihād*, to reconstruct a reformed Islam capable of meeting the new challenges of the modern world. They have also tended to look to political forces to help implement the necessary reforms, and to capitalise on a revitalised spirit of *jihād* in the Muslim community to defend it against its external enemies. After the twelfth/eighteenth century the power of those external enemies – principally the Western powers – proved to be overwhelming. Muslims throughout the world have had no choice but to confront the challenges posed to them by the West. Their efforts to do so have been shaped in part by movements of renewal and reform which have been both modern in their application and firmly grounded in an authentic and evolving Muslim tradition.

2
Sufism

ALEXANDER KNYSH

Introduction

The ascetic and mystical element that was implicit in Islam since its very inception grew steadily during the first Islamic centuries (the seventh–ninth centuries CE), which witnessed the appearance of the first Muslim 'devotees' (*'ubbād*; *nussāk*) in Mesopotamia, Syria and Iran. By the sixth/twelfth century they had formed the first ascetic communities, which spread across the Muslim world and gradually transformed into the institution called *ṭarīqa* – the mystical 'brotherhood' or 'order'. Each *ṭarīqa* had a distinct spiritual pedigree stretching back to the Prophet Muḥammad, its own devotional practices, educational philosophy, headquarters and dormitories as well as its semi-independent economic basis in the form of a pious endowment (either real estate or tracts of land). Between the thirteenth and sixteenth centuries CE Islamic mysticism (Sufism) became an important part of the Muslim devotional life and social order. Its literature and authorities, its networks of *ṭarīqa* institutions and its distinctive lifestyles and practices became a spiritual and intellectual glue that held together the culturally and ethnically diverse societies of Islamdom. Unlike Christian mysticism, which was marginalised by the secularising and rationalistic tendencies in western European societies, Sufism retained its pervasive influence on the spiritual and intellectual life of Muslims until the beginning of the twentieth century. At that point Sufi rituals, values and doctrines came under sharp criticism from such dissimilar religio-political factions as Islamic reformers and modernists, liberal nationalists and, somewhat later, Muslim socialists. They accused Sufis of deliberately cultivating 'idle superstitions', of stubbornly resisting the imposition of 'progressive' and 'activist' social and intellectual attitudes and of exploiting the Muslim masses to their advantage. Parallel to these ideological attacks, in many countries of the Middle East the economic foundations of Sufi organisations were undermined by agrarian reforms, secularisation of education and new forms of taxation instituted by Westernised nationalist governments. The extent of Sufism's decline in the first half of the twentieth century varied from one country to another. On the whole, however, by the 1950s Sufism had lost much of its former appeal in the eyes of Muslims, and its erstwhile institutional grandeur was reduced to low-key lodges staffed by Sufi masters with little influence outside their immediate coterie of followers. At that point it seemed that in most Middle Eastern and South Asian societies the very survival of the centuries-old Sufi tradition and lifestyle was in question. However, not only has Sufism survived, it has been making a steady comeback of late.[1] Alongside traditional Sufi practices and doctrines there emerged the so-called 'neo-Sufi' movement whose followers seek to bring Sufi values in tune with the spiritual and intellectual needs of modern men and women.

This chapter provides a brief historical overview of Sufism's evolution from a simple world-renouncing piety to the highly sophisticated doctrines and rituals practised primarily, albeit not exclusively, within the institutional framework of the Sufi *ṭarīqa*.

The name and the beginnings

Normative Sufi literature routinely portrays the Prophet and some of his ascetically minded Companions as 'Sufis' (*al-ṣūfiyya*) *avant la lettre*. However, the term does not seem to have gained wide currency until the first half of the third/ninth century, when it came to denote Muslim ascetics and recluses in Iraq, Syria and, possibly, Egypt. More than just fulfilling their religious duties, they paid close attention to the underlying motives of their actions, and sought to endow them with a deeper spiritual meaning. This goal was achieved through a thorough meditation on the meaning of the Qurʾānic revelation, introspection, imitation of the Prophet's pious ways, voluntary poverty and self-mortification. Strenuous spiritual self-exertion was occasionally accompanied by voluntary military service (*jihād*) along the Muslim–Byzantine frontier, where many renowned early devotees flocked in search of 'pure life' and martyrdom 'in the path of God'. Acts of penitence and self-abnegation, which their practitioners justified by references to certain Qurʾānic verses and the Prophet's normative utterances,[2] were, in part, a

1 A. Knysh, 'The *tariqa* on a Landcruiser: The resurgence of Sufism in Yemen', *Middle East Journal*, 55, 3 (2001).

2 M. Smith, *Studies in early mysticism in the Near and Middle East*, 2nd edn (Oxford, 1995), pp. 125–52; cf. A. Arberry, *Sufism: An account of the mystics of Islam* (London, 1950), pp. 15–30.

reaction against the Islamic state's newly acquired wealth and complacency as well as the 'impious' pastimes of the Umayyad rulers and their officials. For many pious Muslims these 'innovations' were incompatible with the simple and frugal life of the first Muslim community at Medina. While some religio-political factions, such as the Khārijites and the early Shīʿa, tried to topple the 'illegitimate' government by force of arms, others opted for a passive protest by withdrawing from the corrupt society and engaging in supererogatory acts of worship. Even though their meticulous scrupulousness in food and social intercourse were sometimes interpreted as a challenge to secular and military authorities, they were usually left alone as long as they did not agitate against the state. As an outward sign of their pietistic flight from the 'corrupt' world, some early devotees adopted a distinct dress code – a rough woollen habit, which set them apart from the 'worldlings' who preferred more expensive and comfortable silk or cotton. Wittingly or not, the early Muslim devotees thereby came to resemble Christian monks and ascetics, who also donned hair shirts as a sign of penitence and contempt for worldly luxuries.[3] In view of its strong Christian connotations some early Muslim authorities sometimes frowned upon this custom. In spite of their protests, wearing a woollen robe (*taṣawwuf*) was adopted by some piety-minded elements in Syria and Iraq under the early ʿAbbāsids. By the end of the second/eighth century, in the central lands of Islam the nickname *ṣūfiyya* ('wool-people' or 'wool-wearers'; sing. *ṣūfī*) had become a self-designation of many individuals given to an ascetic life and mystical contemplation.

Basic assumptions and goals

While many early Muslims were committed to personal purity, moral uprightness and strict compliance with the letter of the divine law, there were some who made asceticism and pious meditation their primary vocation. These 'proto-Sufis' strove to win God's pleasure through self-imposed deprivations (especially abstinence from food and sex), self-effacing humility, supererogatory prayers, night vigils and meditation on the deeper implications of the Qurʾānic revelation. In their passionate desire for intimacy with God they drew inspiration from selected Qurʾānic verses that stressed God's immanent and immediate presence in this world (e.g. Q 2:115; 2:186; 50:16). They found

3 A. Vööbus, *Syriac and Arabic documents regarding legislation relevant to Syrian asceticism* (Stockholm, 1960); cf. J. van Ess, *Theologie und Gesellschaft im 2. und 3 Jahrhundert Hidschra*, 6 vols. (Berlin and New York, 1991–5), vol. II (1992), pp. 88, 94, 610 etc.

similar ideas in the Prophetic traditions (*ḥadīth*), some of which encouraged the faithful to 'serve God as if they see Him', to count themselves among the dead, to be content with the little that they have over against the abundance that may distract them from the worship of their Lord and to constantly think of God.[4] In meditating on such scriptural passages, and in imitating the pious behaviour ascribed to the first Muslim heroes, the forerunners of the Sufi movement developed a comprehensive set of values and a code of behaviour that can be defined as 'world-renouncing' and 'other-worldly oriented'. It may have had an implicit political intent, as some early ascetics consciously abandoned gainful professions, avoided any contact with state authorities or even refused to inherit in protest against the perceived injustices and corruption of the Umayyad regime.[5] Many disenchanted devotees found solace in the more benign aspect of divine majesty, and gradually started to speak of love between God and his servants, citing relevant Qurʾānic verses such as Q 5:54. With time the initial world-renouncing impulse was augmented by the idea of mystical intimacy between the worshipper–lover and his divine beloved. Celebrated in poems and utterances of exceptional beauty and verve, it was counterbalanced by the worshipper's self-doubt and fear of divine retribution for the slightest slippage in thought or action (*ghafla*). Particularly popular with the early ascetics and mystics was the idea of a primordial covenant between God and the 'disembodied' human race prior to the creation of individual human beings endowed with sinful and restive bodies. Basing themselves on the Qurʾān (Q 7:172) the proto-Sufis argued that during this covenant the human souls bore testimony to God's absolute sovereignty and promised him their undivided devotion. However, once the human souls were given their sinful bodies and found themselves in the corrupt world of false idols and appearances, they forgot their promise and succumbed to the drives and passions of the moment. The goal of God's faithful servant, therefore, consists in 'recapturing the rapture' of the day of the covenant in order to return to the state of primordial purity and faithfulness that characterised the human souls before their actual creation.[6] To this end the mystic had to contend not only with the corrupting influences of the world, but also with his own base self (*nafs*) – the seat of egotistic lusts and passions. These general

4 Wakīʿ ibn al-Jarrāḥ, *Kitāb al-zuhd*, ed. ʿAbd al-Raḥmān al-Faryawānī, 2nd edn, 2 vols. (Riyadh, 1994), vol. I, p. 234.

5 B. Reinert, *Die Lehre vom tawakkul in der klassischen Sufik* (Berlin, 1968), p. 188; van Ess, *Theologie*, vol. I, pp. 228–9.

6 G. Böwering, *The mystical vision of existence in classical Islam* (Berlin, 1980), pp. 145–65.

tenets manifested themselves in the lives and intellectual legacy of those whom later Sufi literature portrayed, anachronistically, as the first Sufis.

The archetypal 'Sufis': al-Ḥasan al-Baṣrī and his followers

The fame of the early preacher and scholar of Baṣra al-Ḥasan al-Baṣrī (21–110/642–728) rests on the unique uprightness of his personality, which made a deep impression on his contemporaries. He was, above all, famous for his fiery sermons in which he warned his fellow citizens against committing sins and urged them to prepare themselves for the Last Judgement by leading pure and frugal lives, as he did himself. Al-Ḥasan invited his audience to abandon attachment to earthly possessions, which are of no use to either the living or the dead. He judged sins strictly, and considered the sinner to be fully responsible for his actions. Respectful of caliphal authority, despite its real or perceived 'transgressions', he reserved the right to criticise it for what he saw as its violation of the divinely ordained order of things. Al-Ḥasan's brotherly feeling towards his contemporaries and his self-abnegating altruism (*īthār*) were appropriated by later Sufis and formed the foundation of the code of spiritual chivalry (*futuwwa*) which was embraced by Sufi associations in the subsequent epochs.

Whether or not al-Ḥasan was indeed the founding father of the Sufi movement, as he was portrayed in later Sufi literature, his passionate preaching of high moral and ethical standards won him numerous followers from a wide variety of backgrounds – professional Qur'ān reciters and Qur'ān copyists, pious warriors *(nussāk mujāhidūn*), small-time traders, weavers and scribes. They embraced his spirited rejection of worldly delights and luxury, and his criticism of social injustices, oppressive rulers and their unscrupulous retainers. Their actions and utterances exhibit their constant fear of divine retribution for the slightest moral lapse and their exaggerated sense of sin, which they sought to alleviate through constant penance, mortification of the flesh, permanent contrition and mourning.[7] This self-effacing, God-fearing attitude often found an outward expression in constant weeping, which earned many early ascetics the name of 'weepers' (*bakkā'ūn)*. Already at that stage some of them were aware that their exemplary piety, moral uprightness and spiritual fervour placed them above the herd of ordinary believers, who were unable to overcome their simplest passions of the moment, not to

7 Wakīʿ ibn al-Jarrāḥ, *Kitāb al-zuhd*, vol. I, pp. 248–63.

mention the complex moral dilemmas faced by God's elect folk. Hence the idea of 'friendship with', or 'proximity to', God (*walāya*), which the early ascetics and mystics traced back to several Qur'ānic phrases suggesting the existence of a category of God's servants enjoying his special favour in this and future life (e.g. Q 10:62; 18:65). It is in this narrow circle of early Muslim ascetics that we witness the emergence of an elitist charismatic piety, which was gradually translated into superior moral authority and, eventually, into a substantial social force. At that early stage, however, its social ramifications were rather limited. It was confined to a narrow circle of religious *virtuosi*, whose search for personal salvation through constant meditation on their sins and extraordinary ascetic feats was too individualistic to win them a broad popular following. Nevertheless, the arduous sermonising and exemplary uprightness of al-Ḥasan and his disciples secured them relatively wide renown among the population of Baṣra and Kūfa. From there the practice of wearing wool, and the style of piety that it symbolised, spread to Syria and Baghdad, eventually giving the name to the ascetic and mystical movement that gained momentum in the mid-third/ninth century (see chart 2.1). Most of its representatives, including such important ones as ʿAbd al-Wāḥid ibn Zayd (d. *c.* 133/750) and the famous female mystic Rābiʿa al-ʿAdawiyya (d. 185/801), are usually portrayed as spiritual descendants of al-Ḥasan al-Baṣrī. The former is said to be the founder of the first Sufi 'cloister' (*duwayra*) on the island of ʿAbbādān at the mouth of the Shaṭṭ al-ʿArab, while Rābiʿa distinguished herself as an ardent proponent of 'pure' and 'disinterested' love of God – to the exclusion of all other religious emotions, including the love of the Prophet – and is commonly regarded as the founder of 'love mysticism' in Islam.

The nascent Sufi movement was internally diverse, and displayed a variety of devotional styles: the 'erotic mysticism' of Rābiʿa al-ʿAdawiyya existed side by side with the stern piety of Ibrāhīm ibn Adham (d. 161/777) – an otherworldly recluse who renounced not only what was prohibited by Islamic law but also much that it permitted. He, in turn, was distinct from both Ibn al-Mubārak (d. 181/797) – an inner-worldly 'warrior monk' from the Byzantine–Muslim frontier – or Fuḍayl ibn ʿIyāḍ (d. 187/803) – a moderate world-renouncer and vocal critic of the rulers and scholarly 'establishment' of his time, whom he accused of departing from the exemplary custom of the Prophet and his first followers. Finally, in Shaqīq al-Balkhī (d. 195/810), a Khurāsānī ascetic who was killed in action fighting against the 'pagan Turks', we find a curious hybrid of Ibrāhīm ibn Adham and Ibn al-Mubārak – both a holy warrior and an extreme ascetic who strove to avoid the corrupting influence of the world by completely withdrawing from it.

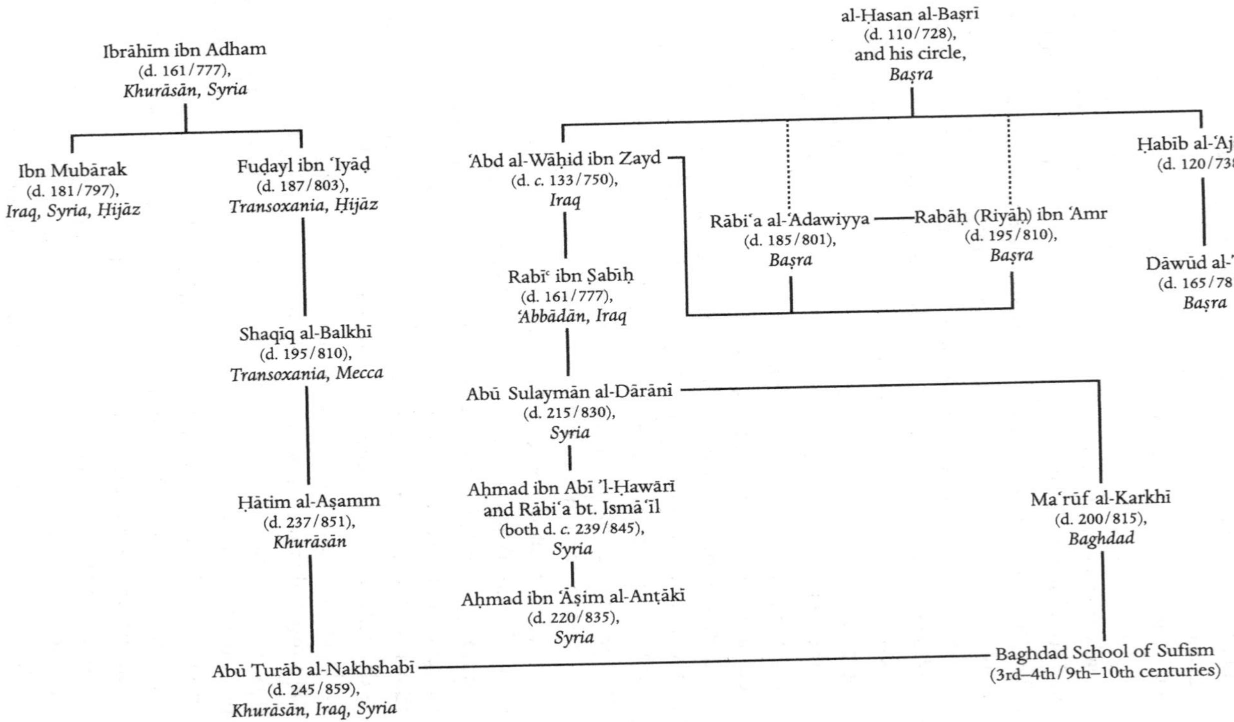

Chart 2.1 al-Ḥasan al-Baṣrī and the first Muslim ascetics and mystics

Shaqīq is often described as the earliest exponent, if not the founder, of *tawakkul* – a doctrine of complete trust in, and total reliance on, God, which entailed absolute fatalism and the abandonment of any gainful employment.[8] He is also credited with early theorising about various levels – or 'dwelling stations' (*manāzil*) – of spiritual attainment, and can thus be viewed as one of the founders of the 'science of the mystical path' (*'ilm al-ṭarīq*). The reason why individuals of so widely disparate temperaments and convictions ended up in the same classificatory category of 'early Sufis' should be sought in the underlying ideological agendas of the creators of the Sufi tradition, which will be discussed further on.

Some regional manifestations

In the eastern lands of the caliphate the ascendancy of Baghdad-style Sufism was delayed by almost a century by the presence of local ascetic groups, notably the Karrāmiyya of Khurāsān and Transoxania and the Malāmatiyya of Nīshāpūr, whose leaders resisted the imposition of the 'foreign' style of ascetic piety. We know relatively little about the values and practices of these groups, which were suppressed by, or incorporated into, the Sufi movement under the Saljūqs.[9]

In the western provinces of the caliphate we find a few ascetics who studied under al-Ḥasan al-Baṣrī or his disciples, and who taught his ideas to their own students. The most notable of them were Abū Sulaymān al-Dārānī (d. 215/830) in Syria and Dhū 'l-Nūn al-Miṣrī (d. 245/860) in Egypt. The former emphasised complete reliance on God and unquestioning contentment with his will (*riḍā*). Any distraction from God, including marriage, was, for al-Dārānī, unacceptable. The amount of one's knowledge of God was in direct proportion to one's pious deeds, which al-Dārānī described as an internal *jihād* and which he valued more than the 'external' warfare against an 'infidel' enemy. In Egypt the most distinguished representative of the local ascetic and mystical movement was Dhū 'l-Nūn al-Miṣrī, a Nubian whose involuntary stay in Baghdad on charges of heresy had a profound impact on the local ascetics and mystics. His poetic utterances brim with the erotic symbolism that was to become so prominent in later Sufi poetry. They depict God as the mystic's intimate friend (*anīs*) and beloved (*ḥabīb*). God, in turn, grants his faithful lover a special,

8 Reinert, *Die Lehre*, pp. 172–5.

9 J. Chabbi, 'Réflexions sur le soufisme iranien primitif', *Journal Asiatique*, 266, 1–2 (1978); B. Radtke, 'Theologen und Mystiker in Hurasan und Transoxanien', *ZDMG*, 136, 1 (1986).

intuitive knowledge of himself, which Dhū 'l-Nūn called 'gnosis' (*maʿrifa*). This esoteric knowledge sets its possessors, God's elect friends (*awliyāʾ*), apart from the generality of the believers.

The activities and teachings of ascetics and mystics who resided in the caliphate's provinces indicate that the primeval ascetic and mystical movement was not confined to Iraq. However, it was in Iraq – more precisely, in Baghdad – that it came to fruition as a free-standing and distinct trend within Islam.

The formation of the Baghdadi tradition

The ascetic and mystical school of Baghdad – the capital of the ʿAbbāsid empire established shortly after the fall of the Umayyads – inherited the ideas and practices of the early Muslim devotees residing in the first Muslim cities of Iraq: Baṣra and Kūfa. However, the beginnings of the Baghdad school proper are associated with a few individuals who came to serve as the principal source of identity to its later followers. One of them was Maʿrūf al-Karkhī (d. 200/815), who studied under some prominent members of al-Ḥasan al-Baṣrī's inner circle (see chart 2.2). He established himself as an eloquent preacher who admonished his audience to practise abstention and contentment with God's decree from the pulpit of his own mosque in the Karkh quarter of Baghdad. Al-Karkhī took little interest in theological speculation, and enjoined deeds, not words. Legends describe his numerous miracles, and emphasise in particular the efficacy of his prayers. After his death his tomb on the Tigris became a site of pious visits and supplicatory prayers. Equally important for the self-identity of the Baghdad school of Sufism is Bishr ibn al-Ḥārith (al-Ḥāfī, 'the Barefoot', d. 227/842). He started his career as a jurist and *ḥadīth* collector, but later relinquished his studies and embarked on the life of a pauper, because he realised that formal religious knowledge was irrelevant to the all-important goal of salvation. We find a similar career trajectory in the case of another founding father of the Baghdadi school, a learned merchant named Sarī al-Saqaṭī (d. 253/867). His transformation from well-to-do merchant and *ḥadīth* collector to indigent Sufi occurred under the influence of Maʿruf al-Karkhī's passionate sermons. Like Bishr, he considered the collection of Prophetic reports, especially when it became a profession, to be 'no provision for the Hereafter'. Of the practical virtues required of every believer he emphasised fortitude in adversity, humility, trust in God and absolute sincerity (*ikhlāṣ*), and warned against complacency, vainglory and hypocrisy (*riyāʾ*). In this he was in agreement with another prominent ascetic scholar of

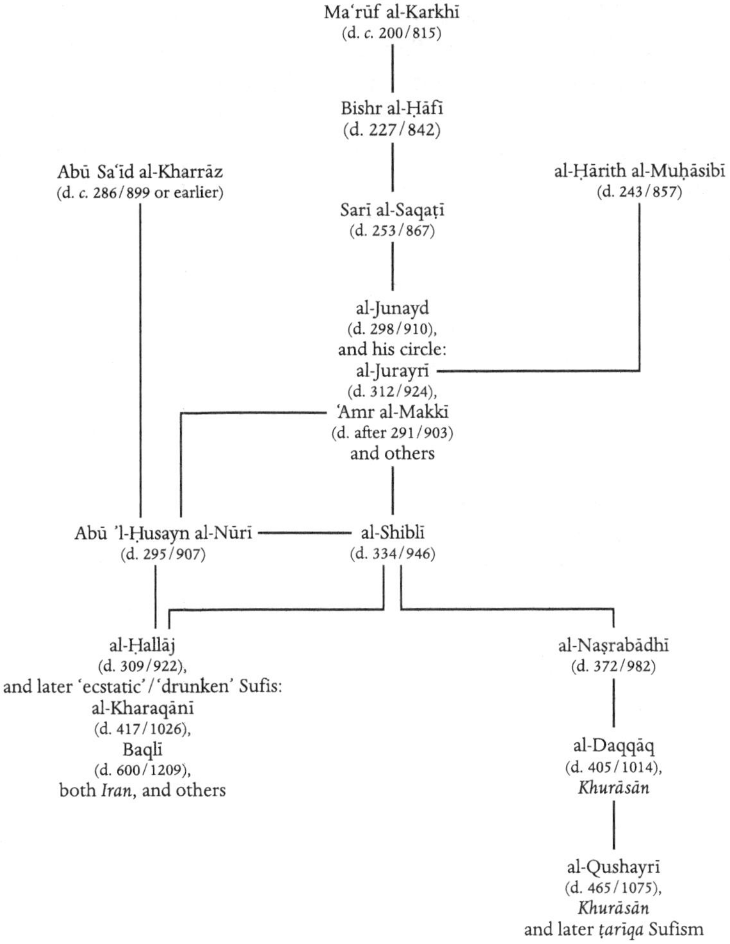

Chart 2.2 Sufism of the Baghdad school

that age, al-Ḥārith al-Muḥāsibī (d. 243/857). Unlike the individuals just mentioned, al-Muḥāsibī was a prolific writer, whose written legacy reflects his intense and occasionally tortuous quest for truth, purity of thought and deed and, eventually, salvation. His emphasis on introspection as a means of bringing out the true motives of one's behaviour earned him the nickname 'al-Muḥāsibī', or 'one who takes account of oneself'. By scrupulously examining the genuine motives of one's actions, argued al-Muḥāsibī, one can detect and eliminate the traces of *riyā'* that may adhere to them. Although al-Muḥāsibī's 'theorising' about mystical experience and theological issues was spurned by some of his Sufi contemporaries, there is little doubt that it contributed in significant ways to the formation of 'Sufi science' (*ʿilm al-taṣawwuf*). Moreover, the paternal nephew and successor of Sarī al-Saqaṭī as the doyen of the Baghdadi Sufis, Abu 'l-Qāsim al-Junayd (d. 298/910), cultivated a close friendship with al-Muḥāsibī and was influenced by his ideas.

Later Sufi literature portrays al-Junayd as the greatest representative of Baghdad Sufism, who embodied the 'sober' strain within it, as opposed to the 'intoxicated' one of Abū Yazīd al-Bisṭāmī, al-Ḥallāj, al-Shiblī and their like. Like al-Muḥāsibī, al-Junayd combined scholarly pursuits with 'mystical science', and presented himself as either a scholar or a Sufi, or both. He was convinced that the most daring aspects of 'Sufi science' should be protected from outsiders who had not tasted it themselves. Hence his 'profoundly subtle, meditated language' that 'formed the nucleus of all subsequent elaboration'.[10] A popular spiritual master, he wrote numerous epistles to his disciples as well as short treatises on mystical themes. Couched in recondite imagery and arcane terminology, his teaching reiterates the theme, first clearly reasoned by him, that, since all things have their origin in God, they are to be reabsorbed, after their dispersion in the empirical universe (*tafrīq*), into him (*jamʿ*). On the level of personal experience, this dynamic of the divine reabsorption/dispersion is reflected in the state of 'passing away' of the human self (*fanāʾ*) in the contemplation of the oneness of God, followed by its return to the multiplicity of the world and life in God (*baqāʾ*). As a result of this experiential 'journey' the mystic acquires a new, superior awareness of both God and his creation that cannot be obtained by means of either traditional or speculative cognition. Unlike the 'intoxicated' Sufis, who considered *fanāʾ* to be the ultimate goal of the mystic, al-Junayd viewed it as an intermediate (and imperfect) stage of spiritual attainment. On the social plane, al-Junayd preached responsibility and advised his followers against violating social conventions and public decorum. The accomplished mystic should keep his unitive experiences to himself, and share them only with those who have themselves 'tasted' them. He is said to have disavowed his erstwhile disciple al-Ḥallāj for making public his ecstatic encounters with the divine reality. Al-Junayd's eminence as a great, if not the greatest, master of the 'classical age' of Sufism is attested by the fact that he figures in the spiritual pedigree of practically every Sufi brotherhood. His awesome stature

10 Arberry, *Sufism*, pp. 56–7.

sometimes overshadows some of his contemporaries, whose contribution to the growth of the Sufi teaching was at least as important as his.

One such contemporary was Abū Saʿīd al-Kharrāz (d. *c.* 286/899), who was probably the first Sufi – along with al-Tirmidhī al-Ḥakīm (d. 310/910) – to discuss the relationship between the prophets (*anbiyāʾ*) and the (Sufi) 'friends of God' (*awliyāʾ*). Al-Kharrāz argued that the prophetic missions of the former and the 'sainthood' (*wilāya*) of the latter represent two distinctive if complementary types of relationship between God and his creatures. Whereas the *anbiyāʾ* are entrusted by God with spreading and enforcing the divine law, the *awliyāʾ* are absorbed in the contemplation of divine beauty and majesty and become oblivious of the world around them. The two thus represent respectively the outward (*ẓāhir*) and the inward (*bāṭin*) aspects of the divine revelation, and their missions are equally valid in the eyes of God.[11]

Several individuals in al-Junayd's entourage form a distinct group due to their shared single-minded focus on love of God. One of them was Abu 'l-Ḥusayn al-Nūrī (d. 295/907), an associate of both al-Junayd and al-Kharrāz. Unlike his teachers, he shunned any theoretical discussion of the nature of mystical experience, and defined Sufism as 'the abandonment of all pleasures of the carnal soul'. In expressing his intense passion for the divine beloved al-Nūrī frequently availed himself of erotic imagery, which drew upon him the ire of some learned members of the caliph's entourage, who charged him and his followers with blasphemy, and even attempted to have them executed. Characteristically, in that episode al-Junayd is said to have avoided arrest by claiming to be a mere 'jurist' (*faqīh*).

A similar ecstatic type of mysticism was espoused by al-Shiblī, whose unbridled longing for God expressed itself in bizarre behaviour and scandalous public utterances. He indulged in all manner of eccentricities: burning precious aromatic substances under the tail of his donkey, tearing up expensive garments, tossing gold coins into the crowds and speaking openly of his identity with the divine, etc.[12] Faced with the prospect of prosecution on charges of heresy, he affected madness.

Our description of the Baghdad school would be incomplete without a mention of al-Ḥallāj, whose ecstatic mysticism bears a close resemblance to that of al-Nūrī and al-Shiblī, but who, unlike them, paid with his life for his intoxication with divine love. His trial and public execution in Baghdad in 309/

11 P. Nwyia, *Exégèse coranique et langage mystique* (Paris, 1970), pp. 237–42.

12 R. Nicholson (ed.), *The* Kitāb al-lumaʿ fi 'l-taṣawwuf *of Abū Naṣr ... al-Sarrāj* (Leiden and London, 1914), pp. 398–406.

922 on charges of 'heresy' demonstrated the dramatic conflict between the spirit of communal solidarity promoted by Sunnī *'ulamā'* and the individualistic, at times asocial aspirations of lovelorn mystics – a conflict al-Junayd and his 'sober' followers were so anxious to overcome. Al-Ḥallāj's trial took place against the background of political intrigues and struggle for power at the caliph's court in Baghdad, into which he was drawn, perhaps unwittingly. His public preaching of loving union between man and God was construed by some religious and state officials as rabble-rousing and sedition. On the other hand, his behaviour violated the code of prudence and secrecy advocated by the leaders of the capital's Sufi community, who followed in the footsteps of al-Junayd. Finally, al-Ḥallāj was also accused of public miracle-working (*ifshā' al-karāmāt*) with a view to attracting the masses to his message. This too contradicted the ethos of 'sober' Sufism, which required that mystics conceal supernatural powers granted to them by God. All this – and perhaps also jealousy of his popularity – led to his disavowal and condemnation by his fellow Sufis, including al-Junayd and al-Shiblī. While the theme of the union of the mystic lover with the divine beloved was not unique to al-Ḥallāj, his public preaching of it and his attempt to achieve it through voluntary martyrdom were unprecedented and scandalous. Al-Ḥallāj thus came to exemplify the 'intoxicated' brand of mysticism associated, apart from him, with such Persian mystics as Abū Yazīd al-Bisṭāmī (d. 261/875), Ibn Khafīf (d. 371/982), Muḥammad al-Dastānī (d. 417/1026), al-Kharaqānī (d. 425/1033) and Rūzbihān al-Baqlī (d. 606/1209).[13]

The age of al-Junayd and al-Ḥallāj was rich in charismatic and mystical talent. Among their contemporaries Sahl al-Tustarī of Baṣra (d. 283/896) deserves special mention. He and his followers represented a distinct strain of Sufi piety that assigned a special role to the practice of 'recollection' of God (*dhikr*) with a view to 'imprinting' his name in the enunciator's heart. After the mystic has completely internalised *dhikr*, God begins to effect his own recollection in the heart of his faithful servant. This leads to a loving union between the mystic and his Creator. Al-Tustarī's mystical commentary on the Qur'ān, which seeks to bring out its hidden, inner meanings, represents one of the earliest samples of Sufi exegesis.[14]

As mentioned, the Sufism of Iraq was not the only ascetic and mystical movement within the confines of the caliphate. In the eastern provinces of the 'Abbāsid empire it had to compete with its local versions, such as the

13 A. Knysh, *Islamic mysticism: A short history* (Leiden, 2000), pp. 68–82.
14 Böwering, *The mystical vision*.

Malāmatiyya and the Karrāmiyya. The eventual ascendancy of Baghdad Sufism has not yet found a satisfactory explanation. One reason for its success may lie in 'the efficacy of its powerful synthesis of individualist and communalist tendencies', which allowed it to 'disenfranchise' its rivals 'by sapping them of their spiritual thrust and absorbing their institutional features'.[15] One can also point out the role of powers-that-be in deliberately promoting Baghdadī Sufism over its rivals, which eventually disappeared from the historical scene. According to this view, the rulers of the age found the loosely structured, urban, middle-class Sufism to be more 'manageable' than the lower-class and largely rural Karrāmiyya or the secretive and independent Malāmatiyya.[16] Finally, the fortunes of all these ascetic and mystical movements may have been influenced by the fierce factional struggle between the Shāfiʿī–Ashʿarī and the Ḥanafī–Māturidī parties in Khurāsān, which helped to propel Sufism – associated with the former – to the forefront and to push its opponents to the fringes of local societies.[17] Another possible reason is that in the aftermath of the execution of al-Ḥallāj many Baghdadi Sufis migrated to the eastern lands of the caliphate, where they aggressively disseminated the teachings and practices of their school among local communities. This process was accompanied by the emergence in Khurāsān and Transoxania of a considerable body of apologetic Sufi literature which we shall discuss in the next section.

The systematisation of the Sufi tradition

The fourth/tenth and fifth/eleventh centuries witnessed a rapid growth of Sufi lore. It was classified and committed to writing by the Sufi writers who can be considered as the master architects of 'Sufi science' (see chart 2.3). They discussed such issues as the exemplary behaviour of the great Sufi masters of old, Sufi terminology, the nature of saintly miracles, the rules of companionship in Sufi communities, Sufi ritual practices etc. Such discussions were accompanied by references to the authority of Sufism's 'founding fathers', including those whose lives almost surely pre-dated its emergence as an independent trend of piety in Islam. The Sufi writers pursued a clear apologetic agenda – to demonstrate the consistency of Sufi teachings and practices with the Sunnī creed as laid down by the creators of Islamic legal theory and

15 A. Karamustafa, *God's unruly friends* (Salt Lake City, 1994), p. 31.
16 Chabbi, 'Réflexions', *passim*.
17 Knysh, *Islamic mysticism*, p. 99.

Abū Naṣr al-Sarrāj (d. 378/988), *Khurāsān and Baghdad*	*Kitāb al-luma'*, the first extant Sufi manual
Abū Bakr al-Kalābādhī (d. after 380/990), *Transoxania*	*Kitāb al-ta'arruf li-'ilm al-taṣawwuf*, a compendium of the Sufi teachings of the Baghdad School.
Abū 'Abd al-Raḥmān al-Sulamī (d. 412/1021), *Khurāsān*	numerous treatises on various aspects of 'Sufi science'; the first extant collection of Sufi biographies and the first Sufi *tafsīr*
Abū Nu'aym al-Iṣbahānī (d. 430/1038), *Khurāsān*	*Ḥilyat al-awliyā'*, massive collection of 'Sufi' biographies that includes those of the pious individuals of early Islam who are normally not considered Sufis
'Abd al-Karīm al-Qushayrī (d. 465/1072), *Khurāsān*	*al-Risāla fī 'ilm al-taṣawwuf*, classical manual of 'Sufi science' still in use among Sufis
al-Hujwīrī (d. after 465/1073), *Afghanistan, India*	*Kashf al-maḥjūb*, the earliest known Sufi treatise in Persian
'Abd Allāh al-Anṣārī (d. 481/1089), *Afghanistan*	numerous Sufi treatises and a massive collection of Sufi biographies in Persian
Muḥammad al-Ghazālī (d. 505/1111), *Khurāsān, Baghdad, Syria*	*Iḥyā' 'ulūm al-dīn*, a definitive synthesis of ascetic and mystical ideas and ethos based on earlier Sufi literature

Chart 2.3 The systematisation of the Sufi tradition

theology. By availing themselves of quotations from the Qur'ān and the *sunna* they endeavoured to prove that Sufism had been part of Islam from its inception, and that the Sufis were true heirs to the Prophet and his closest Companions. In what follows we shall provide a brief survey of normative Sufi literature of the period.

The earliest surviving Sufi treatise, *Kitāb al-luma' fī 'l-taṣawwuf* (The book of the essentials of Sufism), is the work of Abū Naṣr al-Sarrāj of Khurāsān (d. 378/988). He associated with the major members of al-Junayd's circle in Baghdad and the followers of al-Tustarī in Baṣra. Al-Sarrāj's goal was to demonstrate the pre-eminence of Sufis over all other men of religion, since they alone were able to live up to the high standards of personal piety and worship enjoined by the Muslim scripture. They thus constituted the spiritual 'elite' (*al-khāṣṣa*) of the Muslim community to whom its ordinary members should turn for guidance. Within this Sufi elite al-Sarrāj identified three categories: the beginners; the accomplished Sufi masters; and the 'cream of the cream' (*khāṣṣ al-khawāṣṣ*) of Sufism, or 'the people of the true realities' (*ahl al-ḥaqā'iq*). Al-Sarrāj's work represents an early attempt to categorise mystical experiences by placing them in the prefabricated conceptual pigeonholes corresponding to the three levels of spiritual attainment outlined above. It also tried to demarcate the limits of Sufi 'orthodoxy' and to cleanse Sufism of perceived errors and excesses.

The work of Abū Ṭālib al-Makkī, *Qūt al-qulūb* (Nourishment for the hearts), presents the teachings of the Baṣran school of piety associated with al-Tustarī and his followers known as the Sālimiyya. It is reminiscent of a standard manual of religious jurisprudence in which meticulous discussions of the mainstream Islamic rituals and articles of the Islamic creed are interspersed with quintessential Sufi themes, such as the 'states' and 'stations' of the mystical path, the permissibility and nature of gainful employment, pious self-scrutiny etc. Like al-Sarrāj, Abū Ṭālib confidently states that the Sufi teachings and practices reflect the authentic custom of the Prophet and his Companions, 'transmitted by al-Ḥasan al-Baṣrī and maintained scrupulously intact by relays of [Sufi] teachers and disciples'.[18] Abū Ṭālib's work was highly influential. It formed the foundation of the celebrated *Iḥyā' 'ulūm al-dīn* (Revivification of religious sciences) of Abū Ḥāmid al-Ghazālī (d. 505/1111).

Another famous Sufi author of the age, Abū Bakr al-Kalābādhī (d. 380/990 or 385/994) of Bukhārā, produced the Sufi manual *Kitāb al-ta'arruf li-madhhab ahl al-taṣawwuf* (Introduction to the teaching of the Sufis). Despite the fact that it originated in a region located far from Iraq, its author exhibits an intimate knowledge of Iraqi Sufism and its major exponents. Like other advocates of Sufism, he saw his main task in demonstrating Sufism's compliance with the principles of Sunnī Islam, as represented by both Ḥanafī and Shāfi'ī schools of theology and law. Quoting the Sufi authorities of the Baghdad school, al-Kalābādhī meticulously described the principal 'stations' of the mystical path: repentance, abstinence, patience, poverty, humility, fear, pious scrupulousness in word and deed, trust in God, contentment with one's earthly portion, recollection of God's name, intimacy and nearness to God, love of God etc.[19]

The most influential expositions of 'Sufi science' were composed by the Khurāsānī Sufis Abū 'Abd al-Raḥmān al-Sulamī (d. 412/1021) and 'Abd al-Karīm al-Qushayrī (d. 465/1072). The former also provided the earliest extant

18 Arberry, *Sufism*, p. 68.

19 Muḥammad ibn Ibrāhīm al-Kalābādhī, *The doctrine of the Sufis:* Kitāb al-ta'arruf li-madhhab ahl al-taṣawwuf *by Muḥammad Ibn Ibrāhīm al-Kalābādhī*, trans. A. Arberry (Cambridge and New York, 1977) (repr.).

biographical account of earlier Sufi masters, entitled *Ṭabaqāt al-ṣūfiyya* (Generations of the Sufis), and a collection of Sufi exegetical dicta.[20] Unlike his predecessors, al-Sulamī was intimately familiar and sympathetic with the Malāmatiyya ascetic and mystical tradition of Khurāsān and included references to its teachings in his Sufi tracts. Al-Sulamī's intellectual legacy became the foundation of all subsequent Sufi literature, including the celebrated *al-Risāla al-Qushayriyya* (Qushayrī's epistle [on Sufism]) by al-Qushayrī – acknowledged as the most widely read and influential treatise on 'Sufi science' that is still being studied in Sufi circles. After providing an account of Sufi lives – with obvious edifying intention – al-Qushayrī presented the major concepts and terms of the Sufism of his age, followed by a detailed account of various Sufi practices, including listening to music during 'spiritual concerts' (*samāʿ*), miracles of saints, rules of companionship and travel and, finally, 'spiritual advice' to Sufi novices (*murīdūn*). Several other Sufi works were written around that time, including *Ḥilyat al-awliyā'* (Ornament of the friends of God) – a massive collection of Sufi biographies by Abū Nuʿaym al-Iṣbahānī (d. 430/1038); *Kashf al-maḥjūb* (The unveiling of the veiled) – the first Sufi manual in Persian; and the numerous Sufi treatises of the Ḥanbalī Sufi ʿAbd Allāh al-Anṣārī (d. 481/1089) of Herat. Given the diversity of intellectual backgrounds and scholarly affiliations of these Sufis, their writings display a surprising uniformity in that they refer to basically the same concepts, terms, anecdotes, authorities and practices. This indicates that by the first half of the fifth/eleventh century the Baghdadi/Iraqi Sufi tradition had already stabilised and spread as far as Central Asia and the Caucasus.[21] These writings constitute a concerted effort on the part of their authors to bring Sufism into the fold of Sunnī Islam by demonstrating its complete consistency with the teachings and practices of Islam's 'pious ancestors' (*al-salaf*). This tendency was brought to fruition in the life and work of the celebrated Sunnī theologian Abū Ḥāmid al-Ghazālī (d. 505/1111).

The maturity of 'Sufi science': al-Ghazālī the conciliator

A naturally gifted man, al-Ghazālī, originally from Iran, established himself as the leading Sunnī theologian and jurist of his day. After serving as a professor at

20 G. Böwering (ed.), *The minor Qur'ān commentary of Abū ʿAbd al-Raḥmān ... al-Sulamī (d. 412/1021)* (Beirut, 1995).
21 See e.g. A. K. Alikberov, *Epokha klassicheskogo islama na Kavkaze* (Moscow, 2003).

the prestigious Niẓāmiyya religious college (*madrasa*) in Baghdad, he was suddenly afflicted with a nervous illness (488/1095) and withdrew from public life into an eleven-year spiritual retreat during which he composed a succession of books including his greatest masterpiece, *Iḥyā' ʿulūm al-dīn* (The revivification of religious sciences), and his autobiography, *al-Munqidh min al-ḍalāl* (Deliverance from error). The latter provides a poignant account of his difficult quest for truth and serenity. Upon examining the most influential systems of thought current in his epoch (speculative theology, the messianic teachings of Ismāʿīlism and Hellenistic philosophy) al-Ghazālī arrived at the idea of the superiority of mystical 'unveiling' over all other types of cognition. He argued that Sufi morals and spiritual discipline were indispensable in delivering the believer from doubt and self-conceit and in instilling in him intellectual serenity, which, in turn, would lead him to salvation.[22] The concrete ways to achieve this serenity and salvation are detailed in the *Iḥyā'* – a synthesis and amplification of the ascetic and mystical concepts and ethos outlined in the classical Sufi works enumerated above (see chart 2.3). This book was intended to serve as a comprehensive guide for the devout Muslim to every aspect of religious life from daily worship to the purification of the heart and advancement along the mystical path. Addressed to the general audience, it highlighted the practical moral and ethical aspects of Sufism, which al-Ghazālī presented as being in perfect harmony with the precepts of mainstream Sunnī Islam. The more esoteric aspects of his thought came to the fore in his *Mishkāt al-anwār* (Niche for the lights) – an extended commentary on the 'Light verse' of the Qur'ān (Q 24:35) in which al-Ghazālī identified the God of the Qur'ān with the light of truth and existence, revealing his kinship with the controversial philosophy of Ibn Sīnā.[23] Al-Ghazālī's 'illuminationist' metaphysics and mystical psychology received further elaboration in the work of later thinkers, especially Shihāb al-Dīn Yaḥyā al-Suhrawardī (d. 597/1191) and Ibn al-ʿArabī (d. 638/1240).

Al-Ghazālī undoubtedly performed a great service for devout Muslims of every level of education by presenting obedience to the prescriptions of the *sharīʿa* as a sure and meaningful way to salvation. His Sufi lodge (*khānqāh*) at Ṭūs (near present-day Mashhad), where he retired towards the end of his life and where he and his disciples lived together, can be seen as an attempt to implement his pious precepts in real life. To what extent al-Ghazālī can be considered the ultimate 'conciliator' between mainstream Sunnism and

22 W. M. Watt, *Faith and practice of al-Ghazali* (London, 1953), *passim*.

23 H. Landolt, 'al-Ghazali and Religionswissenschaft', *Asiatische Studien*, 55, 1 (1991), p. 54; cf. M. Hodgson, *The venture of Islam*, 3 vols. (Chicago, 1974), vol. II, p. 314; P. Heath, *Allegory and philosophy in Avicenna (Ibn Sina)* (Philadelphia, 1992), *passim*.

Sufism is difficult to ascertain. His relative success in this regard may be attributed more to his imposing reputation as a Sunnī scholar 'who commanded the respect of all but the narrowest of the orthodox'[24] rather than to his innovative interpretation of the Sufi tradition. Nevertheless, there is little doubt that his enthusiastic advocacy for Sufi morals and ethics were of critical importance in making Sufism a respectable option for both Sunnī *'ulamā'* and the masses.

Al-Ghazālī's versatility aptly reflects the complexity and sophistication of Islamic culture, in which Sufism was playing an increasingly important role. He was instrumental in fusing elements of various Islamic teachings and practices into a comprehensive world-view that formed the ideological foundation of the nascent Sufi 'orders'.

Sufism as literature

Although the goals of poetic expression and mystical experience would seem to be quite distinct (self-assertion as opposed to self-annihilation in the divine, or a silent contemplation of God as opposed to a creative verbalisation of personal sentiment), under certain conditions they may become complementary, if not identical. Their affinity springs from their common use of symbol and parable as a means to convey subtle experiences that elude conceptualisation in a rational discourse, which by its very nature requires lucidity and a rigid, invariable relation between the signifier and the signified. In the same way as poetical vision cannot be captured by a cut-and-dried rational discourse, mystical experience avoids being reduced to a sum total of concrete and non-contradictory statements. Both poetry and mystical experience carry emotional, rather than factual, content; both depend, in great part, on a stream of subtle associations for their effect. It is therefore little wonder that mystical experience is often bound intimately with poetic expression. Both the poetry and the experience are couched in the formative symbols of the poet-mystic's religious tradition and shaped by the totality of his personal predisposition and intellectual environment.

This being the case, it is only natural, then, for mystical experience to be bound intimately with poetic inspiration and, consequently, poetic expression. It is with these general considerations in mind that we should approach the work of Sufism's greatest poets, Farīd al-Dīn 'Aṭṭār (d. between 586/1190 and 627/1230), Jalāl al-Dīn Rūmī (d. 672/1273) and Jāmī (d. 898/1492).

24 Arberry, *Sufism*, p. 83.

Farīd al-Dīn ʿAṭṭār of Nīshāpūr is often seen as the greatest mystical poet of Iran after Jalāl al-Dīn Rūmī, who learned much from him. The genre of his most important writings is the couplet-poem (*mathnawī*), which was to become a trademark of Persian mystical poetry from then on. ʿAṭṭār's *mathnawī* usually tell a single frame-story which, in the course of the narrative, is embellished by numerous incidental stories and by various narrative vignettes.[25] His more esoteric poems are inward-looking and visionary in character; they show little interest in the events of the external world. Here a few principal ideas are pursued with intensity and great emotion, and couched in intricate parables. Among such recurring ideas are: the ecstatic annihilation of the mystic in God (*fanāʾ*); the underlying unity of all being (there is nothing other than God, and all things are derived from and return to him); the knowledge of the mystic's own self which gives him the key to the vital mysteries of God and of the universe; the indispensability of the Sufi master (shaykh) for the spiritual progress of his disciple (*murīd*) etc. ʿAṭṭār's works are full of allusions to Sufi gnosis (*maʿrifa*), which the author presents as superior to all other types of cognition. He avails himself freely of the sayings and stories of earlier Sufi masters, among whom he is particularly fascinated by al-Ḥallāj.

Of ʿAṭṭār's prose writing special mention should be made of his *Tadhkirat al-awliyāʾ* (Memorial of the saints) – a collection of anecdotes about, and sayings of, the great Muslim mystics before his time. Here ʿAṭṭār's literary propensities take precedence over his concern for historical accuracy: he freely embellishes the dry, factual accounts of the older Sufi biographers with fanciful details, marvels and legends. While such additions definitely make ʿAṭṭār's Sufi biographies unreliable as sources of historical data, they tell us a great deal about the author's intellectual preferences and religious views as well as his vision of the ideal Sufi master.[26]

The family of Jalāl al-Dīn Rūmī, whom his followers often call 'Our Master' (*mawlānā*), migrated from Balkh (present-day Afghanistan) to Konya (Anatolia) on the eve of the Mongol invasions. A turning-point in his life was the arrival in Konya in 642/1244 of a wandering dervish nicknamed Shams-i Tabrīz – 'a wildly unpredictable man who defied all conventions and preached the self-sufficiency of each individual in his search for the divine'.[27] In Shams-i Tabrīz, Rūmī found his muse and symbol of ultimate

25 Hodgson, *The venture of Islam*, vol. II, p. 305.

26 Farīd al-Dīn ʿAṭṭār, *Muslim saints and mystics: Episodes from the* Tadhkirat al-awliyāʾ *by Farīd al-Dīn ʿAṭṭār*, trans. A. Arberry (London and New York, 1990) (repr.).

27 Hodgson, *The venture of Islam*, vol. II, p. 245.

beauty in which he discovered the genuine meaning of his life. Rūmī's love for Shams-i Tabrīz transformed him from an ordinary mortal into a divinely inspired poet of great stature. Upon Shams's tragic death Rūmī suffered a deep psychological crisis, which he tried to overcome by composing poems and participating in Sufi concerts and dances in the hope of finding his friend in his own soul. The real history of the Sufi order founded by Rūmī (which came to be known as the Mawlawiyya (or Mevleviyya) – after Rūmī's honorific title) began with his son Sulṭān Walad (Veled; d. 712/1312), whose able leadership secured it high prestige and wide acceptance among the Muslims of Anatolia. Although originally recruited from among the craftsmen, the order gradually won over many members of the Anatolian upper class. The distinctive feature of the Mawlawiyya is the pre-eminent role that its leaders assigned to music and dancing. With time they were regularised, culminating in the famous 'whirling dance' ceremony. The Mawlawī dancing rituals reflect the joyous and highly emotional world outlook characteristic of the founder and his poetry.

Rūmī saw himself as neither a philosopher nor a poet in the usual meaning of these words. Rather, he comes across as a passionate lover of God, unconcerned about societal conventions and religious stereotypes. At the same time, he drew heavily on the Sufi tradition systematised by earlier Sufi writers. He viewed all creatures as being irresistibly drawn to their maker in the same way as trees rise from the dark soil and extend their branches and leaves towards the sun. Their aspiration reaches its climax in their mystical annihilation in the divine essence (*fanā'*), which, however, is never complete. As the flame of a candle continues to exist despite being outshone by the radiance of the sun, so does the mystic retain his individuality in the overpowering presence of his Lord. In this state he is both human and divine, and may be tempted to declare his complete identification with God. Due to the intensely personal and 'ecstatic' character of Rūmī's poetic work, it found practically no successful imitators in later Persian poetry. In Rūmī we find a paragon of Sufi artistic creativity, who harmoniously combined mystical experience with poetic inspiration.

'Abd al-Raḥmān Jāmī came from the district of Jām near Herat in present-day Afghanistan. As a youth he developed a deep passion for mysticism and decided to embark on the mystical path. His first spiritual director was Sa'd al-Dīn Muḥammad Kāshghārī, a foremost disciple of and the organisational successor to the founder of the Naqshbandiyya, Bahā' al-Dīn Naqshband (d. 791/1389). Later on, Jāmī made friends with another influential Naqshbandī leader, 'Ubayd Allāh Aḥrār (d. 896/1490), whom he admired and whom he mentioned frequently in his poetical works.[28] He spent most of his life in Herat under the patronage of the Tīmūrid sultan Ḥusayn Bāyqarā, dividing his time between religious studies, poetry and mystical meditation.

Jāmī's written legacy in Persian and Arabic includes a giant biographical history of Sufism, *Nafaḥāt al-uns* (The breaths of divine intimacy), which draws on ʿAṭṭār's *Tadhkirat al-awliyāʾ* and the works of earlier Sufi biographers. Jāmī's Arabic treatises on various difficult aspects of Sufi philosophy are masterpieces of lucidity and concision. They reveal his deep indebtedness to Ibn al-ʿArabī and his philosophically minded followers, whose recondite mystical ideas and terminology he sought to make accessible to a less sophisticated audience. His writings intricately mingle mystical poetry with didactic, biographical and metaphysical narratives, providing a helpful summation of various strands of Sufism in his age.

Sufism as metaphysics: the impact of Ibn al-ʿArabī

As mentioned, Jāmī was profoundly influenced by Ibn al-ʿArabī (d. 638/1240). In this he was not alone – there was hardly a mystical thinker in that age or later who was not. Although Ibn al-ʿArabī spent the first half of his life in al-Andalus and the Maghrib, his talents came to full bloom in the east, where he composed most of his famous works – especially his controversial masterpieces *Fuṣūṣ al-ḥikam* (Bezels of wisdom) and *al-Futūḥāt al-makkiyya* (Meccan revelations) – and trained his most consequential disciple, Ṣadr al-Dīn al-Qunawī (d. 673/1274), who spread his ideas among the Persian-speaking scholars of Anatolia and beyond.[29]

Ibn al-ʿArabī's legacy consists, in his own estimation, of some 250–300 works, although some modern scholars credit him with twice this number of writings.[30] Nowhere in these works did Ibn al-ʿArabī provide a succinct and final account of his basic tenets. On the contrary, he seems to have been deliberately elusive in presenting his principal ideas, and took great care to offset them with numerous disclaimers. In conveying to the reader his personal mystical insights, Ibn al-ʿArabī made skilful use of 'symbolic images that evoke emergent associations rather than fixed propositions'.[31] Although familiar with the syllogistic reasoning

28 N. Heer (ed.), *The precious pearl: al-Jāmī's* al-Durrah al-fākhirah (Albany, 1979), pp. 1–2.

29 H. Corbin, *Creative imagination in the Sufism of Ibn ʿArabī* (Princeton, 1969), pp. 69–71, 224; W. Chittick, 'Ibn ʿArabī and his school', in S. H. Nasr (ed.), *Islamic spirituality: Manifestations* (New York, 1991); W. Chittick, 'Rūmī and *waḥdat al-wujūd*', in A. Banani, R. Hovannisian *et al.* (eds.), *Poetry and mysticism in Islam* (Cambridge, 1994).

30 O. Yahia, *Histoire et classification de l'oeuvre d'Ibn ʿArabī*, 2 vols. (Damascus, 1964).

31 Hodgson, *The venture of Islam*, vol. II, p. 224.

of Muslim philosophers (*falāsifa*), he always emphasised that their method fell short of capturing the dizzying dynamic of oneness/plurality that characterises the relationship between God and human beings, human beings and the universe. To capture this complex dynamic Ibn al-ʿArabī availed himself of shocking antinomies and breathtaking paradoxes meant to awaken his readers to what he regarded as the real state of the universe, namely, the underlying oneness of all its elements. Oftentimes his discourses strike us as a mishmash of seemingly disparate themes and motifs operating on parallel discursive levels from exegesis to poetry and mythology to jurisprudence and speculative theology. Ibn al-ʿArabī explored such controversial themes as the status of prophecy vis-à-vis sainthood; the concept of the perfect man; the relations between the human 'microcosm' and its cosmic counterpart; the ever-changing divine self-manifestation in the events and phenomena of the empirical universe; the different modes of the divine will; and the allegoric aspects of the scripture. He addressed these issues in ways that were 'never really repeated or adequately imitated by any subsequent Islamic author'.[32] The goal of this deliberately devious discourse was to 'carry the reader outside the work itself into the life and cosmos which it is attempting to interpret'.[33] His recondite narratives were 'meant to function as a sort of spiritual mirror, reflecting and revealing the inner intentions, assumptions and predilections of each reader … with profound clarity'.[34] It is, therefore, hardly surprising that each Islamic century produced new interpretations of his ideas.

This is not the place to detail Ibn al-ʿArabī's complex metaphysical doctrine. Suffice it to say that he viewed the world as a product of God's self-reflection that urged his unique and indivisible essence to reveal itself in the things and phenomena of the material universe as in a mirror. This idea scandalised many medieval *ʿulamāʾ*, who accused him of admitting the substantial identity of God and the world:

> a concept that contravened the doctrine of divine transcendence so central to Islamic theology. In Ibn ʿArabī's system, God was not the absolutely otherworldly and impregnable entity of mainstream Muslim theologians. Consequently, many of the latter condemned him as the founder of the heretical doctrine of oneness of being (*waḥdat al-wujūd*) understood as pantheism pure and simple.[35]

32 J. Morris, 'How to study the *Futūḥāt*', in S. Hirtenstein and M. Tiernan (eds.), *Muḥyiddīn Ibn ʿArabī: A commemorative volume* (Brisbane, 1993).

33 Hodgson, *The venture of Islam*, vol. II, p. 315.

34 Morris, 'How to study the *Futūḥāt*', p. 73.

35 A. Knysh, *Ibn ʿArabī in the later Islamic tradition: The making of a polemical image in medieval Islam* (Albany, 1999), p. 14.

Major intellectual and practical trends in later Sufism

Al-Ghazālī and Ibn al-ʿArabī's complex synthesis of Sufi moral and ethical teaching, theosophy, Neoplatonic metaphysics, gnosticism and mainstream Sunnism aptly captures the astounding diversity of post-classical Sufism. This diversity allowed it to effectively meet the intellectual and spiritual needs of a broad variety of potential constituencies – from a pious merchant or craftsman in the bazaar to a refined scholar at the ruler's court. Contrary to a commonly held assumption, such philosophical and metaphysical systems were not 'foreign implants' grafted onto the pristine body of classical Sufism. Rather, they were a natural outgrowth of certain tendencies inherent in Sufism from its outset. Early Sufi masters had viewed God as the only real agent in this world, to whose will and action man should submit unconditionally. In the fifth–sixth/eleventh–twelfth centuries this idea evolved – probably not without the influence of Avicennan ontology – into a vision of God not just as the only agent but also the only essence possessing real and unconditional existence. This vision, which may loosely be defined as 'monistic', was rebuffed by the great Ḥanbalī scholar Ibn Taymiyya (d. 728/1328), who condemned its followers as heretical 'unificationists' (*al-ittiḥādiyya*) bent on undermining divine transcendence and blurring the all-important borderline between God and his creatures. A fierce polemic between the champions of Ibn al-ʿArabī and his detractors ensued that has not yet quite subsided. It has divided Muslim divines into two warring factions, one of which praised Ibn al-ʿArabī as the greatest 'saint' (*walī*) and divine 'gnostic' (*ʿārif*) of all ages, while the other condemned him as a dangerous heretic who undermined the very foundations of Islamic faith.[36]

In addition to monistic metaphysics, the post-Ghazālian period of Sufism's history witnessed the institutionalisation of a number of distinctively Sufi rituals and meditation techniques, including retreat (*khalwa*), collective recollection of God (*dhikr*) and ritualised 'listening' to music and mystical poetry (*samāʿ*). These practices served as a means to intensify the relationship between the mystics and God, and to open the former to the outpourings of divine grace. During *samāʿ* sessions music was played and mystical poetry recited in order to induce in the audience a state of ecstasy (*wajd*) which often resulted in a spontaneous dance or frantic rhythmical movements. Thanks to *samāʿ* mystics could achieve changed states of consciousness, during

36 Ibid., p. 272.

which they had visionary or cognitive experiences known as 'unveilings' (*mukāshafāt*).

The 'sober' strain of Sufi piety which drew its inspiration from al-Junayd and his circle tried to purge Sufism of ecstatic, uncontrollable elements and re-emphasise its moral and ethical aspects as the surest way to God. It found an eloquent exponent in the famous Baghdad preacher ʿAbd al-Qādir al-Jīlānī (d. 561/1166) – a typical representative of community-oriented mysticism. This sober, socially responsible brand of mystical piety received a further authoritative articulation in the influential Sufi manual entitled *ʿAwārif al-maʿārif* (Gifts of divine knowledge) of Shihāb al-Dīn ʿUmar al-Suhrawardī of Baghdad (d. 635/1234). A Persian translation and adaptation of this seminal work, which was made in the ninth/fifteenth century, has served as a standard textbook for Persian-speaking mystics ever since.

The rise and spread of the *ṭarīqas*

From the sixth/twelfth century onward mystical life was increasingly cultivated in Sufi associations or orders (*ṭuruq*; sing. *ṭarīqa*), some of which have survived down to the present. Taking their origin in relatively small lodges (*zāwiya*; *khānqāh*), Sufi institutions gradually acquired freestanding complexes of buildings where their members engaged in collective and individual worship undisturbed by the hustle and bustle of everyday life. The conduct of the members of such Sufi communities was governed by fixed rules enforced by a hierarchical Sufi leadership. While in the fourth–fifth/tenth–eleventh centuries the teacher–disciple relationship was relatively informal, with the disciple (*murīd*) being free to study under several different masters (*shuyūkh*; sing. *shaykh*), in the Sufi orders it was formalised and strictly regimented. The head of a Sufi *ṭarīqa* was capable of supporting his – often numerous – disciples from the endowments and pious donations provided by the rulers, blessing-seeking nobility, wealthy merchants and members of the military elite. In return, he demanded undivided loyalty of his adherents. The training technique of an individual Sufi master came to be known as his 'way' or 'method' (*ṭarīq*). Metonymically it came to be applied to the entire Sufi community which he had founded, and which usually assumed his name. The headship of some orders was hereditary; in others the successor was elected from a pool of eligible candidates. After the novice had completed his training under the guidance of a Sufi master, he obtained from him a licence (*ijāza*) to instruct his own disciples in accordance with the master's spiritual 'method'. His new status as an independent Sufi was symbolised by the ritual bestowal – either public or private – of a Sufi robe (*khirqa*) upon the graduate. In addition to the *khirqa* or the patched cloak (*muraqqaʿ*), the typical Sufi outfit also included a prayer rug (*sajjāda*), a rosary (*misbaḥa*) and a beggar's bowl (*kashkūl*). With time, each Sufi order acquired a distinctive dress-code and colours that set them apart from the members of other Sufi communities.[37]

The major early *ṭarīqas* – the Qādiriyya, Rifāʿiyya, Suhrawardiyya, Chishtiyya, Kubrawiyya, Naqshbandiyya and Shādhiliyya – were formed in the seventh–ninth/thirteenth–fifteenth centuries (see charts 2.4, 2.5 and 2.6). Each of them had its own character and was initially associated with a particular geographical region. Thus the Qādiriyya, which originated in Baghdad, gradually spread across the entire Muslim world – from the Maghrib to India and Indonesia and as far as China. Likewise, the Naqshbandiyya, founded in Central Asia, thrived in India, where it became probably the most influential and well-organised Sufi community. Later on it extended its reach to the Caucasus, the Volga basin, the Arab lands and even North Africa. The Shādhiliyya emerged in the Maghrib, thrived in Egypt and then spread to Yemen and Indonesia. Despite their international outreach, these and other orders were, for the most part, decentralised, and their regional branches had little in common except for a shared initiatic line and set of litanies, *dhikr* formulas and ritual requirements, all of which were usually traced back to the eponymous founder. The political and social roles of the *ṭuruq* varied dramatically in time and space, and were usually determined by the personalities of their leaders and the concrete historical circumstances of their existence. It is very difficult, therefore, to make any generalisations about any given Sufi order. Nevertheless, such generalisations abound in both popular imagination and literary sources. Thus, the Qādiriyya is famous for its emphasis on the role of its founder, who is believed to maintain his guiding and protective presence among his followers in all epochs and locations. Apart from this belief, however, its regional branches had little in common. The 'loud', energetic *dhikr* and exotic dance of Qādirī dervishes are often contrasted with the 'silent' *dhikr* and restraint of the Naqshbandiyya, which is considered to be more 'sober' and '*sharīʿa*-abiding'. The Rifāʿiyya with its 'howling' *dhikr* and spectacular public performances that involve walking on live coals, eating glass and the piercing of the flesh by its *murīds* (to demonstrate the spiritual power of their masters) is viewed as 'ecstatic' and 'libertine'. Similar generalisations are often made about the orders' stance vis-à-vis the powers-that-be – the Naqshbandiyya being regarded as prone to

37 See e.g. John Brown, *The darvishes or oriental mysticism*, ed. H. A. Rose (London, 1968).

cooperate with or manipulate them, in contrast to the more standoffish and independent attitude of the Chishtiyya and the Shādhiliyya. However, as mentioned, a single order could behave differently under different leaders and in different historical conditions.[38] Each order derived its distinct identity from the following defining rules and characteristics:

1. The order's 'spiritual chain' (*silsila*), which was traced back from its contemporary head to the Prophet Muḥammad. It may have thirty to forty 'rungs'. This 'chain' served as the major source of legitimacy for the *ṭarīqa* leader and of pride and self-identity for his followers.
2. The conditions and rituals for admission into the order. Some orders took men and women, some only men. The novice (*murīd*) owed the shaykh unconditional obedience and was required to seek his advice and instruction on all matters of worship and personal life. Initiation rituals differed from one order to another, but were, as a rule, reminiscent of those practised in artisan guilds, with which the orders were often closely connected.
3. Instructions about the performance and formulas of *dhikr*, which were peculiar to every *ṭarīqa*, and which also gave it a distinct identity. They stipulate the regulation of breathing, the rhythm and frequency with which these formulas must be recited, allow or disallow use of music and dance etc.
4. Instructions regarding the terms and conditions of retreat or seclusion (*khalwa*), the voluntary withdrawal from communal life by the order's members to devote themselves to pious meditation, self-reflection and *dhikr*.
5. Rules of fellowship and communal life, which regulated relations among the members of a given Sufi community and between the shaykh and his followers.

Unlike the sophisticated metaphysical theories discussed above, which were confined to the Sufi intellectual elite, or even deliberately concealed by them from the rank and file, knowledge of the normative literature of the order was required of all its literate members. The illiterate ones learned them in the course of oral instruction by the shaykh of the order or his deputies.

Sufism and the cult of saints

Already during their lifetimes some prominent Sufi masters and heads of Sufi orders were treated as 'God's (elect) friends' or 'saints' (*awliyāʾ*) by both their

38 Knysh, *Islamic mysticism*, chaps. 8 and 9.

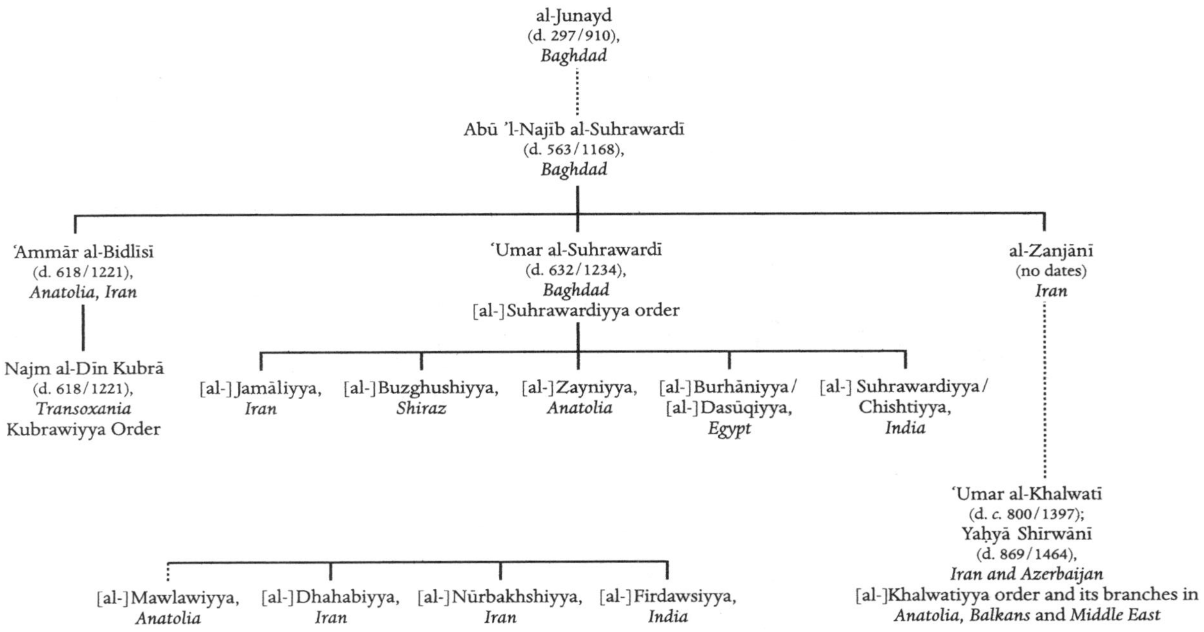

Chart 2.4 Sufi orders (al-Suhrawardiyya, al-Kubrawiyya and al-Khalwatiyya)

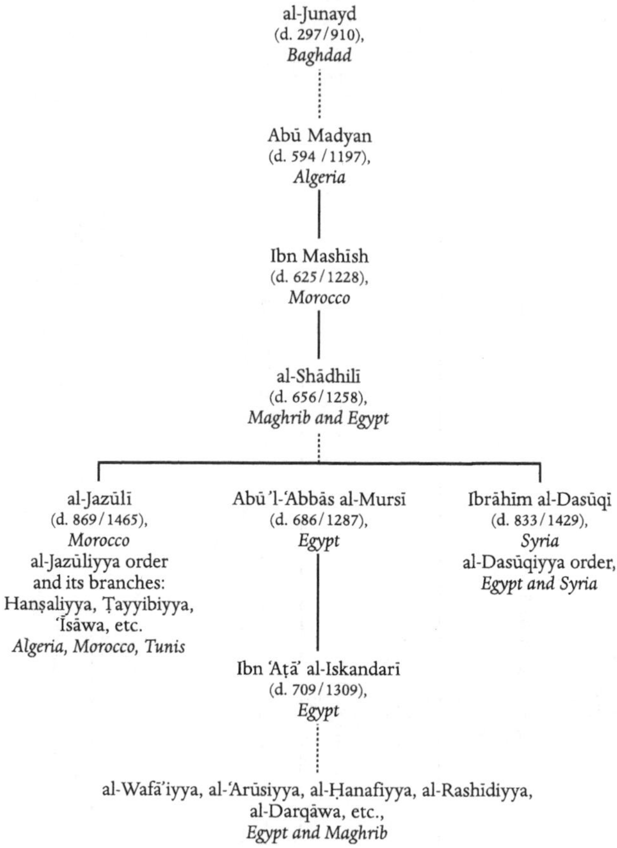

Chart 2.5 The Madaniyya/Shādhiliyya of the Maghrib and Egypt

followers and the local populations not directly affiliated with any Sufi community. Their elevated spiritual status and lack of self-centred impulses were seen by the populace as signs of their special standing in the eyes of God. Due to their intimate knowledge of human psychology, which they acquired through training their disciples, and their special position in society, they often assumed the role of arbitrators in conflicts between different social and kinship groups and between rulers and their subjects. Their mediatory functions further elevated their stature in the eyes of the masses, who came to credit them with supernatural knowledge and perspicacity and, eventually, the ability to work miracles (*karāmāt*). The revered status of the *awliyāʾ* usually did not cease after their death – their tombs often became objects of pious

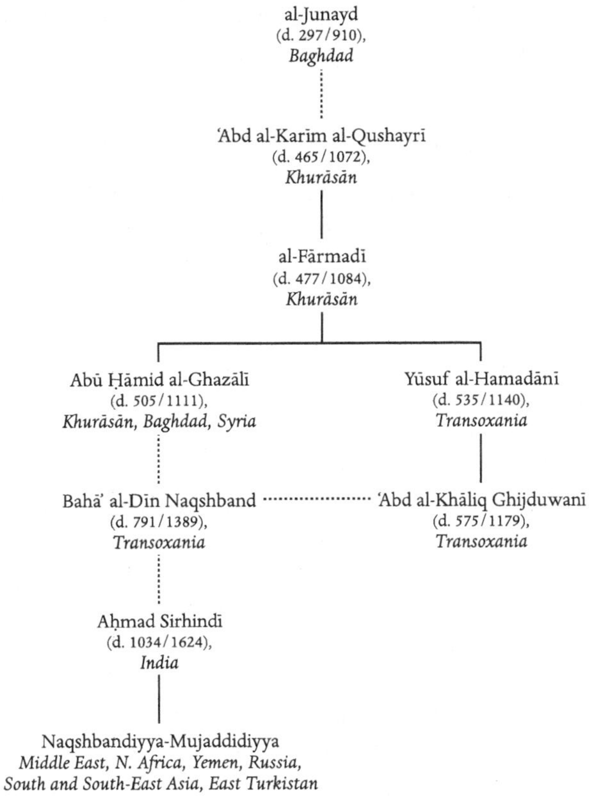

Chart 2.6 The Naqshbandiyya

visits, and even annual pilgrimages (*ziyārāt*) accompanied by special ritual activities. Visitors brought votive gifts to Sufi shrines and asked the Sufi masters buried therein for blessing and intercession. Legends were circulated about their miraculous interference in the lives of their followers during their lifetimes and after their deaths. These were written down in numerous hagiographical collections that became part of Sufi literature. Devotional activities associated with Sufi shrines were condemned by some puritanically minded scholars, such as Ibn Taymiyya, Ibn 'Abd al-Wahhāb (d. 1206/1791), al-Shawkānī (d. 1255/1839) and, later, by thirteenth/nineteenth-century Muslim reformers, as a gross violation of the doctrine of divine oneness, which, according to them, forbade seeking the assistance of anyone or anything other than God. It should, however, be pointed out that not all 'saints' were necessarily Sufis, and that some Sufi orders occasionally discouraged worship at saints' tombs.

Sufi institutions in regional contexts

After examining the rise and subsequent evolution of the first major Sufi brotherhoods, it would be helpful to consider their respective roles in various geographical areas of the Muslim world over the last seven centuries.

The Maghrib

Here Sufi lodges and military outposts became an essential part of the local religious and social landscape, both in towns and in the countryside. The fundamentals of 'Sufi science' were often taught in local religious colleges (*madrasas*) and, conversely, Islamic theology and jurisprudence became part of the curricula of local Sufi lodges, the *zāwiyas* and *ribāṭs*. In many areas of the Maghrib Sufi *zāwiyas* and, from the eighth/fourteenth century, Sufi orders became an important factor of social and political life. Their leaders were favourably positioned to secure social cohesion of local communities in times of political anarchy and breakdown of the central power, when the sovereignty of the state was often confined to a few urban centres, leaving the rest of the country at the mercy of tribal chiefs and local strongmen. Under such circumstances Sufi leaders often acted as mediators between warring parties and tribes, and frequently stepped in to protect the local agricultural population from their depredations.[39]

Throughout the Middle Ages, and into the modern epoch, relations between the Maghribī brotherhoods and the country's rulers were ambivalent, and at times tense. While the latter welcomed the consolidating and stabilising role of Sufi leaders and therefore lavishly endowed Sufi *zāwiyas* and *ribāṭs*, they were suspicious of their autonomous tendencies. Such suspicions were not always groundless, as some popular Sufi leaders were prone to entertain their own political ambitions. The most dramatic example of a Sufi bid for political power is the attempt of the Sufi leadership of the Shādhilī *zāwiya* at Dilāʾ to wrest power from the Saʿdid dynasty of Morocco in the eleventh/seventeenth century. The leaders of the Shādhiliyya exercised a particularly pervasive influence upon the social and political life of the Maghrib. Of its numerous offshoots, one should mention the powerful and influential *ṭarīqa* founded by the charismatic recluse Muḥammad al-Jazūlī

39 B. G. Martin, *Muslim brotherhoods in nineteenth-century Africa* (Cambridge, 1976), pp. 1–8.

(d. *c.* 869/1465).[40] His popularity was such that his followers came to see him as the awaited messiah (*mahdī*). Apprehensive of al-Jazūlī's charismatic personality and influence on the masses, the local governor had him poisoned. This caused a popular revolt of his numerous disciples that continued until 890/1485.

Al-Jazūlī's popularity sprang, among other things, from his abolition of a formal Sufi novitiate. Those who wanted to join his *ṭarīqa*, the Jazūliyya, had simply to declare their allegiance to its founder and his successors. Thanks to this 'streamlined' admission procedure and simplicity of rituals the ranks of the Jazūliyya soon swelled, although its followers never formed a centralised Sufi order.[41] The Jazūliyya gave rise to several popular brotherhoods, including the Hanṣaliyya and the Ṭayyibiyya, which enjoyed substantial followings in the territories of present-day Algeria and Morocco.

The early thirteenth/nineteenth century witnessed an attempt to breathe new life into Maghribī Sufism. A movement for Sufi revival was led by a popular shaykh of the Shādhilī order named al-Darqāwī (d. 1239/1823), who attacked various popular 'superstitions' that had adhered to Sufism in the course of its long history and preached humility and detachment from the affairs of this world. Nevertheless, some of his followers adopted an activist stance and participated in several Berber rebellions against the ruling dynasty.[42]

In addition to the Shādhiliyya and the Jazūliyya, the Qādiriyya too enjoyed wide popularity among the Maghribī populations both in towns and in the countryside. Like other Maghribī orders, it usually did not constitute a cohesive, centralised movement. Rather, one can define it as a spiritual and devotional tradition current among some local communities.[43] A few branches of the Khalwatiyya order, especially the Raḥmāniyya, gained prominence in the territories of present-day Tunisia and Algeria from the end of the twelfth/eighteenth century. The teachings of these orders were synthesised by Shaykh Aḥmad al-Tijānī (d. 1230/1815), the founder of the popular Tijāniyya *ṭarīqa* that was active in Morocco, the Western Sahara and the Sudan. A follower of both the Shādhiliyya and the Khalwatiyya, al-Tijānī adopted the ritual practices of both orders.[44] As with the Jazūliyya, he imposed no special penances or spiritual exercises upon his followers, emphasising above all his role as the

40 V. Cornell, *Realm of the saint* (Austin, 1998), pp. 155–71.

41 J. S. Trimingham, *Sufi orders in Islam*, 2nd edn (Oxford, 1998), pp. 84–5.

42 Ibid., p. 85.

43 Martin, *Muslim brotherhoods*, pp. 15–67.

44 J. M. Abun-Nasr, *The Tijāniyya: A Sufi order in the modern world* (Oxford, 1965).

supreme saint of his age (*al-quṭb*) and as the intercessor par excellence between God and man. Although al-Tijānī himself belonged to several orders, he strictly prohibited his followers from joining any other local Sufi institutions. He encouraged a quiet *dhikr* and looked down upon visits of saints' tombs in search of blessing (*baraka*). Acting through a network of 'emissaries' (*muqaddamūn*), he managed to spread his initiatic line across the Maghrib. Under his successors it penetrated into western and central Sudan, where it gained a following primarily among the Fulbe and Tokolor.

The brotherhoods that combined shamanistic and animistic practices with *ṭarīqa* ideology and organisation constitute a special group. The most prominent among them was the controversial ʿĪsāwā, founded by Muḥammad ibn ʿĪsā al-Mukhtār (d. 931/1524), an ascetic of Shādhilī–Jazūlī persuasion (see chart 2.5). His followers practised spectacular *dhikr* and faith-healing sessions that were often accompanied by trances and communication with the spirits of local folklore. Similar practices were cultivated by the related Moroccan order named the Ḥamdūshiyya, which originated in the eleventh/seventeenth century.

An important movement for revival of Sufism in various areas of Africa, including the Maghrib, is associated with Aḥmad ibn Idrīs (d. 1253/1837), a native of Morocco, who spent most of his life in Egypt and the Ḥijāz.[45] His principal legacy was his numerous students, who converted Sufism into a powerful instrument of mass mobilisation and instituted several popular religio-political movements in north-eastern and eastern Africa, including the Sanūsiyya of Cyrenaica and the Central Sahara, the Khatmiyya (Mīrghāniyya) of the Sudan, Egypt, Yemen, Ethiopia and Eritrea, as well as the Rashīdiyya–Ṣāliḥiyya and the Dandarawiyya, which were active in Egypt, Somalia and South-East Asia (Malaysia). These and other orders laid the foundations of Sufism's triumph in Africa in the thirteenth/nineteenth century, which is sometimes referred to as Africa's 'Sufi century'.

Sufism in sub-Saharan Africa exhibited many common features with that of the Maghrib. In fact, it is sometimes hard to draw a crisp geographical borderline between these regions, since many Maghribī shaykhs proselytised among the populations of sub-Saharan Africa. In many cases the same brotherhood had branches in both areas; most of the sub-Saharan African orders derived their genealogy from a Maghribī order. The Qādiriyya enjoyed considerable success in the Western Sahara, from present-day Mauritania to eastern Mali, where it was promoted by the scholars of the Arabic-speaking Kunta tribe in the late

45 R. O'Fahey, *The enigmatic saint: Aḥmad ibn Idrīs and the Idrīsī tradition* (Evanston, IL, 1990).

twelfth/eighteenth–early thirteenth/nineteenth centuries. The leader of one of the Kunta branches, Sīdī al-Mukhtār al-Kabīr (d. 1226/1811), who combined personal charisma with political and commercial acumen, established a major centre of dissemination of the Qādiriyya. It is from the sub-order that he established, the Mukhtāriyya, that most of the Qādirī groups in West Africa derive their affiliation. The Qādirī–Tijānī rivalry dominated the spiritual and intellectual landscape of West Africa in the nineteenth and twentieth centuries CE.

Sufism in the Ottoman lands

In Anatolia, the Balkans and the Arab provinces of the Ottoman empire we find a wide variety of Sufi orders. One of them, the Khalwatiyya, owes its name to Muḥammad ibn Nūr, who had earned the sobriquet 'al-Khalwatī' because of his habit of spending time in spiritual retreat (*khalwa*). However, its real founder was Yaḥyā al-Shīrwānī of Shamākha (present-day Azerbaijan), who died in Baku in 869/1464 (see chart 2.4). Yaḥyā is the author of the *Wird al-sattār* – the favourite prayer book of most of the Khalwatī branches. Yaḥyā's deputies (*khalīfas*) ʿUmar Rūshanī and Yūsuf al-Shīrwānī spread the order's teachings in Anatolia and Khurāsān. Their disciples Demirdāsh al-Muḥammadī (d. 929/1524) and Ibrāhīm Gulshānī (940/1533) founded their own orders, al-Demirdāshiyya and al-Gulshāniyya respectively, both with their centres in Cairo. Two branches of the latter order gained some renown: al-Sezāʾiyya, founded by Ḥasan Sezāʾi (d. 1151/1738 in Edirne) and al-Ḥāletiyya, founded by Ḥasan Ḥāleti ʿAlī Aʿlā (d. 1329/1911 in Edirne). Among the *khalīfas* succeeding Yūsuf al-Shīrwānī the most notable were Shams al-Dīn Aḥmad Sīvāsī (d. 1006/1597 in Sīvās) and ʿAbd al-Aḥad Nūrī Sīvāsī (d. 1061/1650 in Istanbul) who established their own sub-orders, the Shamsiyya and the Sīvāsiyya.

Initially, the order spread in Anatolia, mainly in the Amasya region, which was then governed by the future Ottoman sultan Bāyazīd II. Here, the most notable shaykh of the order was Jamāl al-Dīn al-Aqsarāʾī, known as Çelebī Efendī, who died around 903/1497 near Damascus. This branch of the Khalwatiyya was named al-Jamāliyya after him. After the death of his successor, Yūsuf Sünbül Sinān al-Dīn (d. 936/1529 in Istanbul), it was renamed al-Sünbüliyya. During the rule of Bayazīd II (886–918/1481–1512) the order's centre migrated to Istanbul. It achieved prominence under Süleymān the Magnificent (r. 926–74/1520–66) and Selīm II (r. 974–82/1566–74), when many high-ranking officials in the Ottoman administration were affiliates of the order and favoured it over its rivals. Through their good offices it received substantial donations in cash and property, which allowed it to recruit more members.

Over time new branches of the Khalwatiyya, which are too numerous to be listed here, appeared in Ottoman Anatolia. The most important of them, the Shaʿbāniyya, was established by Shaʿbān Walī al-Qastamūnī, who, after a period of study at Istanbul, settled in Kastamonu, where he died in 976/1568. His lieutenant Shaykh Shujāʿ (d. 996/1588) had influence on the mystically minded sultan Murād III (r. 982–1003/1574–95) and his courtiers. The Shaʿbāniyya gained fresh impetus under the leadership of ʿAlī Qarābāsh Walī (d. 1097/1685), who established the popular Qarābāshiyya branch of the Shaʿbāniyya-Khalwatiyya, which was active in central Anatolia (Kastamonu and Ankara) and in Istanbul. His teachings had a long-lasting impact on the fortunes of the Khalwatiyya, not just in Anatolia, but also in the Arab provinces of the Ottoman empire, where it contributed to the revival of the Khalwatī tradition at the end of the twelfth/eighteenth century.[46] Qarābāsh Walī's pupil Nasūḥī Meḥmed (d. 1130/1718 in Istanbul) established his own *ṭarīqa*, al-Nasūḥiyya, which in turn gave birth to the Cherkeshiyya, named after Cherkeshī Muṣṭafā (d. 1229/1813). Cherkeshī, a native of the town of Cherkesh, south-west of Kastamonu, introduced several innovations aimed at lightening the ritual and spiritual obligations of the order's followers and expanding its popular base. In the first half of the twelfth/eighteenth century a new branch of the Qarābāshiyya emerged under the leadership of Muṣṭafā Kamāl al-Dīn al-Bakrī (d. 1162/1749), called al-Bakriyya after him. Al-Bakrī's foremost lieutenant and successor in Egypt, Muḥammad ibn Sālim al-Ḥifnī (d. 1181/1767 in Cairo), presided over a spectacular blossoming of the Khalwatiyya in Egypt in the thirteenth/nineteenth century.[47]

On the doctrinal plane, many Khalwatī masters adhered to the teachings of Ibn al-ʿArabī and his followers, especially the concept of the oneness of being (*waḥdat al-wujūd*). Others advised caution and insisted that it can be applied only to certain levels of existence. Muṣṭafā al-Bakrī rejected Ibn al-ʿArabī's monistic tendencies altogether,[48] stressing the unbridgeable chasm between God and his creatures. He and his followers derived the teachings of the order from al-Junayd – the epitome of 'moderate' Sufism. On the practical level, special emphasis was placed on voluntary hunger (*jūʿ*), silence (*ṣamt*), vigil (*sahar*), seclusion (*iʿtizāl*), recollection (*dhikr*), meditation (*fikr*), permanent

46 F. de Jong, 'Muṣṭafā Kamāl al-Bakrī (1688–1749): Revival and reform of the Khalwatiyya tradition', in N. Levtzion and J. O. Voll (eds.), *Eighteenth-century renewal and reform in Islam* (Syracuse, NY, 1987).

47 F. de Jong, *Ṭuruq and ṭuruq-linked institutions in nineteenth-century Egypt* (Leiden, 1978).

48 E. Bannerth, 'La Khalwatiyya en Égypte', *Mélanges de l'Institut Dominicain d'Études Orientales*, 8 (1964–6).

ritual cleanness and tying (*rabṭ*) one's heart to that of the master. The hallmark of the Khalwatiyya and its numerous subdivisions is the periodic retreat (*khalwa*) that it required of every member.

Apart from the Khalwatiyya, we find several other popular orders in the Turkic-speaking territories stretching from Anatolia to eastern Turkistan. If we were to identify a typical Turkic order, the Yasawiyya of Transoxania and Turkistan would fit the bill. From the sixth/twelfth century onward this loosely structured initiatic line was active in disseminating Islam among the Turkic peoples of the steppe and the Mongol rulers of the Golden Horde. Its founder, Aḥmad Yasawī, or Yasevī (d. 562/1162), was probably a disciple of the great charismatic leader Abū Yūsuf Hamadānī (d. 534/1140), who in turn traced his spiritual genealogy back to Abū Yazīd al-Bisṭāmī. Yasawī's poetic collection in a Turkic vernacular, *Ḥikmet* (Wisdom), became the ideological foundation of his loosely structured order. Passages from the *Ḥikmet* were chanted during Yasawī assemblies, which were often accompanied by frantic dances and ecstatic behaviour.[49] Emissaries and disciples of Aḥmad Yasawī spread his teachings in the regions of Syr Darya, Volga, Khwārazm and as far as eastern Turkistan. The expansion of the Yasawiyya went hand in hand with the Islamisation of the Central Asian steppes.[50] After the tenth/sixteenth century the Central Asian Yasawiyya gradually lost its influence to the powerful Naqshbandiyya order, with which it was closely associated.

As early as the seventh/thirteenth century we find references to the 'wandering dervishes' (*qalandariyya*) who were to become part of the social landscape of Central Asia and Anatolia. The Qalandars were individualistic drifters who did not form permanent communities. However, they donned distinctive garments and followed the unwritten rules that set them apart from ordinary, affiliated Sufis. By the tenth/sixteenth century the Qalandarī groups had disappeared from Anatolia, yet they survived in Central Asia and eastern Turkistan until the beginning of the twentieth century CE.[51]

Although the Qalandariyya spread primarily in the eastern lands of Islam,[52] it first asserted itself as a recognisable trend within Sufism in Damascus and Damietta (Egypt) in the early decades of the seventh/thirteenth century. Its

49 T. Zarcone, 'Le Turkestan chinois', in A. Popovic and G. Veinstein (eds.), *Les voies d'Allah: Les ordres soufis dans le monde musulman* (Paris, 1996), p. 270.

50 D. DeWeese, *Islamization and native religion of the Golden Horde: Baba Tükles and conversion to Islam in historical and epic tradition* (University Park, PA, 1994).

51 Zarcone, 'Le Turkestan', pp. 268–70.

52 J. Baldick, 'Les Qalenderis', in A. Popovic and G. Veinstein (eds.), *Les voies d'Allah*, pp. 500–1.

founder, Jamāl al-Dīn Sāwī, or Sāvī (d. *c.* 630/1223), bequeathed to his followers such distinctive practices as shaving the hair, beard, moustache and eyebrows, avoidance of gainful employment and itinerancy. After his successful career as a conventional Sufi master, Jamāl al-Dīn grew disgusted with the trappings of institutionalised Sufism, abandoned his comfortable position as head of a Sufi lodge, gave up his property and began to roam the land in the company of forty dervishes. Despite the individualistic and anti-establishment message preached by Jamāl al-Dīn, his disciples soon formed a community of wandering dervishes. He himself was forced to make concessions to the exigencies of everyday life in order to sustain the nascent Qalandarī community. Contrary to his original teaching, which demanded that his followers survive on wild weeds and fruit and go around naked with only leaves to cover the loins, Jamāl al-Dīn issued a dispensation that allowed them to accept alms and wear heavy woollen garments to cover their private parts.[53]

Jamāl al-Dīn and his followers professed a deep contempt for formal learning, the conventions of social life and worship and for secular and religious authorities. They despised precious metals and valuable objects, but worshipped beautiful faces, which they considered to be manifestations of divine beauty in a human guise. In Anatolia Jamāl al-Dīn's followers came to be known as 'the wearers of sack-cloth' (*jawlaqiyya*). The movement consisted of a congeries of small localised groups that were found, apart from Anatolia, in Iran and India. An extreme version of Qalandarī piety was pursued by the Ḥaydariyya brotherhood, which flourished in the eastern Ottoman domains in the ninth/fifteenth and tenth/sixteenth centuries. Its members 'covered themselves with sacks, coarse felt, or sheep-skins' and wore 'iron rings on their ears, necks, wrists, and genitals'.[54] They took a dim view of official religion and deliberately flouted the conventions of social conduct. Ottoman scholars routinely accused the Ḥaydarīs of such vices as paedophilia, the smoking of cannabis and drunkenness.[55]

Closely related to the Qalandariyya is the Bayramiyya, which was founded in the ninth/fifteenth century in Ankara by Ḥājjī Bayram (d. 833/1429), who claimed to be the restorer of the Malāmatī tradition of Khurāsān. In line with the precepts of the original Malāmatiyya he prohibited his followers from engaging in a public *dhikr* and ostentatiously displaying their piety. A splinter group of the Bayramiyya, led by ʿUmar (Ömer) the Cutler (Sikkīnī; d. 880/

53 Karamustafa, *God's unruly friends*, pp. 43–4.
54 Ibid., p. 68.
55 Baldick, 'Les Qalenderis', p. 501.

1476) refused to recognise the authority of Ḥājjī Bayram's successor, Aq Shams al-Dīn, and formed an independent branch known as Malāmatiyya–Bayramiyya. This split was probably caused by the rivalry between two groups of Ḥājjī Bayram's disciples; however, later sources cast their disagreement in doctrinal terms. While followers of Aq Shams al-Dīn adopted a mainline Sufi doctrine that stressed the unbridgeable gap between God and his creatures, the Bayramiyya embraced al-Ḥallāj's idea that God can manifest himself in the personalities of some saintly individuals, especially in the leaders of the Malāmatiyya. This concept scandalised many Sunnī *ʿulamāʾ* of the Ottoman state, who interpreted it as an implicit denial of the finality of the divine dispensation and the blurring of the all-important line between what is permitted and what is prohibited under the Islamic law. As a result, the Bayramiyya was subjected to persecutions which forced it underground and made its followers conceal their true beliefs from the uninitiated masses, including the ruling class, whom they regarded as mere 'animals' undeserving of the subtle truths of the Malāmatī teaching.[56]

Until the first quarter of the tenth/sixteenth century the Malāmatiyya–Bayramiyya was confined to Central Anatolia. It was introduced to the Balkans by one Aḥmad the Cameleer (d. 952/1545) and became especially deep-rooted in Bosnia, where it adopted an anti-government stance by refusing to recognise the legitimacy of the incumbent Ottoman sultan. However, after more than a century of persecution, some branches of the Malāmatiyya finally abandoned their original antinomian beliefs and adopted a moderate doctrinal position that stressed the primacy of the *sharīʿa*. This transformation attracted to the Malāmatiyya some members of the Ottoman ruling elite, who were instrumental in consolidating its orthodox credentials.

The history of the Bektāshiyya begins with the arrival in Anatolia from Khurāsān of its semi-legendary founder Ḥājjī Bektāsh in the middle of the seventh/thirteenth century. Little is known about his background except that he had some association with the *bābās* – the itinerant preachers who spread Islam in Anatolia among the recently immigrated Turkic nomadic and semi-nomadic tribes;[57] Ḥājjī Bektāsh may have been a follower of Bābā Ilyās and Bābā Isḥāq, who led a popular revolt that shook the Saljūq state

56 T. Zarcone, 'Muhammad Nūr al-ʿArabī et la confrèrie Malāmiyya', in Popovic and Veinstein (eds.), *Les voies d'Allah*, p. 480.

57 I. Mélikoff, 'L'ordre des Bektachis et les groupes relevant de Hadji Bektach', in A. Popovic and G. Veinstein (eds.), *Bektachiyya: Études sur l'ordre mystique des Bektachis et les groupes relevant de Hadji Bektach* (Istanbul, 1995), p. 3; cf. S. Faroqhi, 'The Bektashis: A report on current research', in ibid., pp. 9, 13–15.

in 638/1240. When the rebel army was demolished by the Saljūqs in the same year, Ḥājjī Bektāsh was one of the few survivors, and began to propagate his version of Islam – a mixture of Sufism, Shīʿism and the semi-pagan beliefs[58] of the Turkic tribesmen of Anatolia. While Ḥājjī Bektāsh provided the movement with his name, its true organisational founder was Bālim Sulṭān, who was appointed as head of the chief Bektāshī lodge (*tekke*) by the Ottoman sultan Bayazīd II in 907/1501. Around that time or later, the order split into two factions. One faction, the Ṣofiyān, was associated with the presumed descendants of Ḥājjī Bektāsh, called Çelebī, who occupied the order's main lodge between Qirshehir and Qayṣerī. The other faction, known as Bābāgān, was ruled by the so-called *dede-bābā* ('grand master'), who was elected from among eligible celibate Bektāshī preachers (*bābās*). Members of this faction derived their genealogy from Bālim Sulṭān.[59] The Ottoman administration was concerned first and foremost with the Ṣofiyān–Çelebī faction that controlled most of the order's *zāwiyas* and all but ignored the Bābāgān, who are practically absent from official records.[60] They were particularly active in the provinces, for example Albania, which was home to many prominent members of the order.[61] The majority of *zāwiyas* were run by local Çelebī families, who, by and large, acknowledged the tutelage of the chief *zāwiya* of Ḥājjī Bektāsh. The headship of all such *zāwiyas* was for the most part hereditary, although the new incumbent had to secure the approval of the Ottoman administration and the shaykh of the chief *zāwiya*. This centralised control was essential to prevent the local branches of the order from being 'hijacked' by 'extremist' religious groups, which were lumped together under the blanket name of 'Qizilbāsh' or 'Ghulāt'. These groups operated in the countryside and were notorious for their heterodoxy (e.g. they held ʿAlī, the Prophet's cousin, to be a manifestation of God).[62] A typical Bektāshī *tekke* consisted of the lodge proper with an oratory, bakery, women's quarters, kitchen and a hostel for travellers and visitors. The *tekkes* and *zāwiyas* were supported through pious endowments, usually tracts of land. For the most part such endowments were barely enough to provide for the needs of the *tekke*'s inhabitants

58 Mélikoff, 'L'ordre', p. 4.

59 J. Birge, *The Bektashi order of dervishes* (London, 1937), pp. 56–8; N. Clayer, 'La Bektachiyya', in Popovic and Veinstein (eds.), *Les voies d'Allah*, pp. 468–9.

60 Faroqhi, 'The Bektashis', p. 19.

61 Clayer, 'La Bektachiyya', p. 470.

62 Mélikoff, 'L'ordre', p. 6.

and their visitors, although several wealthy lodges exported large quantities of grain.[63]

The order's political importance was determined by its close links to the Janissary Corps, whose warriors regarded Ḥājjī Bektāsh as their patron saint. When the sultan Maḥmūd II decided to disband the Janissaries in 1241/1826, many of the Bektāshī centres were closed and their property confiscated by the Ottoman chancery or given to other orders, primarily the Naqshbandiyya.[64]

The origin of many Bektāshī beliefs and practices remains moot. Their most salient feature is their syncretism. Christian elements are evident in the initiation rituals of the order (e.g. the distribution of cheese, wine and bread) and in its practices (e.g. a confession of sins before the spiritual leader). Other beliefs seem to go back to 'extreme' Shīʿism, such as the veneration of ʿAlī and his progeny, as well as to the secret belief that ʿAlī, Muḥammad and God form a trinity. One can also point out an affinity between Bektāshī teachings and the secret cabbalistic speculations of the heretical Ḥurūfiyya sect and other 'extremist' groups of the Qizilbāsh Turcomans which deified their leaders.[65] Finally, the Bektāshiyya combined some pre-Islamic Turkic cults which it inherited from its first Turcoman followers with standard Sufi teachings, such as the concept of the Sufi path as a means towards self-perfection and entering into the presence of God.

Mughal India

The following brotherhoods have been particularly prominent in India: Chishtiyya, Suhrawardiyya, Qādiriyya, Shaṭṭāriyya, Naqshbandiyya, Kubrawiyya, Firdawsiyya and ʿAydarūsiyya. In the course of their development they produced numerous semi-independent sub-orders. While such *ṭarīqas* as the Chishtiyya and the Naqshbandiyya were spread out all over the country, there were also regional, localised brotherhoods. Thus, the Suhrawardiyya was active mainly in the Punjab and Sind; the followers of the Shaṭṭāriyya concentrated in Mandu, Gwalior and Ahmedabad; the Firdawsiyya was, for the most part, confined to Bihar; the ʿAydarūsiyya recruited its adherents in Gujarat and the Deccan, etc.

The Chishtiyya and the Suhrawardiyya were the first *ṭarīqas* to reach India. Introduced by Khwāja Muʿīn al-Dīn Ḥasan Chishtī (d. 634/1236), the Chishtī

63 S. Faroqhi, *Der Bektaschi-Orden in Anatolien* (Vienna, 1981), pp. 53–5.
64 Faroqhi, 'The Bektashis', p. 21; Clayer, 'La Bektachiyya', p. 469.
65 Mélikoff, 'L'ordre', pp. 4–5; Faroqhi, 'The Bektashis', pp. 23–6.

order thrived under the leadership of Niẓām al-Dīn Awliyāʾ of Delhi (d. 725/1325), who gave it all-India status. His numerous disciples set up Chishtī centres all over the country.[66] The Suhrawardiyya was introduced into India by Shaykh Bahāʾ al-Dīn Zakariyyāʾ (d. 661/1262). A native of Kot Karor (near Multān), he studied under Shihāb al-Dīn al-Suhrawardī of Baghdad, who later sent him as his deputy (*khalīfa*) to Multān (see chart 2.4). On arrival, Bahāʾ al-Dīn managed to establish a magnificent *khānqāh*, which gradually evolved into a major centre of Sufism in medieval India. Unlike contemporary Chishtī Sufis, who were eager to mingle with the masses, Bahāʾ al-Dīn kept aloof from the populace and cultivated friendship with men of quality. Thanks to their donations his *khānqāh* accumulated great wealth, which Bahāʾ al-Dīn used to buy off the Mongol armies that threatened to invade Multān. The Suhrawardiyya reached its acme under Shaykh Rukn al-Dīn Abu ʾl-Fatḥ (d. 735/1334) and Sayyid Jalāl al-Dīn Makhdūm-i Jahāniyān (d. 788/1386).

Though both the Suhrawardiyya and the Chishtiyya looked to Shihāb al-Dīn al-Suhrawardī's *ʿAwārif al-maʿārif* as their guide, they differed in their organisation of communal life and relations with the state. While the first Chishtī masters refused to accept donations from the government and relied exclusively on pious gifts of private individuals, their Suhrawardī counterparts pointedly cultivated friendship with the ruling class, and benefited from its largesse.[67]

The Firdawsiyya *ṭarīqa*, which traced its genealogy back to the Kubrawiyya of Central Asia, was introduced into India by Shaykh Badr al-Dīn of Samarqand (see chart 2.4). Initially its leaders were based in Delhi, but later moved to Bihar, where the order enjoyed great popularity under Shaykh Sharaf al-Dīn Yaḥyā Manērī (d. 782/1371), a diligent *ḥadīth* collector and a sophisticated exponent of Sufi teachings. The Qādiriyya was established in India by Sayyid Muḥammad Makhdūm Gīlānī (d. 923/1517) and flourished under such masters as Dāwūd Kirmānī (d. 982/1574), Shāh Qumays Gīlānī (d. 998/1584), Miyān Mīr (d. 1045/1635) and Mullā Shāh (d. 1072/1661).

The Shaṭṭāriyya was introduced into India by Shāh ʿAbd Allāh (d. 890/1485), a descendant of Shihāb al-Dīn al-Suhrawardī. On reaching India Shāh ʿAbd Allāh acquired a throng of devoted disciples, whereupon he settled at Mandu and established the first Shaṭṭārī *khānqāh*. Under his disciples his *ṭarīqa* spread to Bengal, Djawnpur and in northern India. Under Shaykh Muḥammad

66 C. Ernst, *Eternal garden: Mysticism, history, and politics at a South Asian Sufi center* (Albany, 1992).

67 A. Schimmel, *Mystical dimensions of Islam* (Chapel Hill, NC, 1975) pp. 342, 352.

Ghawth of Gwalior (d. 970/1562) the *ṭarīqa* received a compact organisation and a distinctive ideological direction. A prolific writer and eloquent preacher, he sought to establish good relations with the Hindus by hosting them in his *khānqāh* and cultivating bulls and cows. The Shaṭṭāriyya maintained friendly relations with secular rulers and played an active role in local politics. Muḥammad Ghawth helped Bābur in his conquest of Gwalior, and he and his elder brother Shaykh Bahlūl were on friendly terms with Bābur's successor, Humāyūn (r. 937–63/1530–56), whom they instructed in the intricacies of Sufi teachings. Emperors Akbar and Jahāngīr built imposing shrines over the tombs of some popular Shaṭṭārī masters. However, after the death of Muḥammad Ghawth the influence of the Shaṭṭāriyya was overshadowed by its principal rivals, the Qādiriyya and Naqshbandiyya.

In the tenth/sixteenth century the Naqshbandī *ṭarīqa* was introduced into India by Khwāja Baqī Bi-ʾllāh (d. 1012/1603). It reached its high water mark under his chief disciple, Shaykh Aḥmad Sirhindī (d. 1034/1624), who expanded the order so successfully that, according to one observer, his disciples reached every town and city in India (see chart 2.6). For about two centuries it was the most influential and popular *ṭarīqa* in India, and many of the eminent figures of the time, such as Shāh Walī Allāh, Mīrzā Maẓhar Jān-i Jānān, Shāh Ghulām ʿAlī and others, belonged to it. A member of the Naqshbandiyya, Khwāja Mīr Nāṣir (d. 1172/1758) founded a new branch of the order called Ṭarīqa-yi Muḥammadī. Another prominent Naqshbandī teacher, Sayyid Aḥmad Barēlwī (d. 1247/1831) instituted a new order known as Ṭarīqa-yi Nubuwwat. It encouraged its followers to emulate the Prophet's behaviour. Under Shāh Ghulām ʿAlī the Indian branch of the Naqshbandī order, which had come to be known as the Mujaddidiyya, spread across the entire Muslim world.

The heyday of the Indian *ṭarīqas* was during the Mughal period. Contemporary sources mention about two thousand Sufi *ribāṭs* and *khānqāhs* in Delhi and its surroundings during the ninth/fifteenth century. They experienced a gradual decline under British rule. Indian *ṭarīqas* have a number of distinguishing features. First, except for the Naqshbandiyya, most of them embraced Ibn al-ʿArabī's doctrine of the oneness of being (*waḥdat al-wujūd*). To counter what they regarded as dangerous social implications of this doctrine, some Naqshbandī leaders introduced the doctrine of the 'oneness of witnessing' (*waḥdat al-shuhūd*), which denied that the monistic experiences of the mystic necessarily reflect the real state of affairs in the universe, and held that a strict distinction must be asserted between God and his creatures. Second, except for the early Chishtī masters, the leaders of all other *ṭarīqas* were eager to maintain close relations with the rulers in an effort to influence state politics as a means of gaining access to state support. Third, while the Naqshbandiyya required that its followers engage in rigorous self-negating exercises aimed at subduing their ego, flesh and base instincts, the Chishtiyya and Suhrawardiyya were more concerned with inculcating in their followers the awareness of the underlying unity of all existence and, consequently, tranquillity in the face of adversity and hardship. Fourth, whereas the Chishtiyya disseminated its teachings by word of mouth, the Naqshbandiyya relied on epistles (*maktūbāt*) to propagate its tenets among its actual and potential followers. The Qādiriyya, on the other hand, made extensive use of poetry to popularise its ideas. Fifth, the Chishtiyya encouraged communal living in special dormitories (*jamāʿat-khāna*), while other *ṭarīqas* constructed *khānqāhs* and hospices with provision for individual accommodation. Sixth, the Chishtiyya looked upon concern for social welfare and helping the needy as a means to achieving spiritual progress and to obtaining the pleasure of God; other *ṭarīqas*, particularly the Naqshbandiyya, believed in rigorous individual discipline and arduous ascetic exercises to reach God. Seventh, the Indian *ṭarīqas* practised different types of *dhikr*. The Naqshbandiyya insisted on the silent '*dhikr* of the heart', whereas the Qādiriyya practised both the loud (*dhikr-i jahr*) and the quiet ones (*dhikr-i khāfī*). Eighth, the Shaṭṭāriyya sought to internalise mystical discipline and tried to develop a synthesis of Hindu and Muslim mysticism, whereas the Naqshbandiyya rejected any compromise with Hinduism. Ninth, each Indian Sufi was expected initially to belong to a single *ṭarīqa*, and to structure his spiritual life according to its principles. Later on, Indian *murīds* started to join several brotherhoods and spiritual lines at once, a practice that undermined the stability of Sufi institutions. As multiple membership became common among Indian Sufis, attempts were made at reconciling conflicting points of different Sufi teachings and practices. Thus Amīr Abu 'l-ʿUlā Akbarābādī tried to combine the doctrines and practical teachings of the Chishtiyya and the Naqshbandiyya, while Shāh Walī Allāh of Delhi viewed the difference between *waḥdat al-wujūd* and *waḥdat al-shuhūd* as merely a difference of perspectives that refer to the same underlying truth. Finally, almost every Indian *ṭarīqa* had one central book on which its ideology was based: the *Fawāʾid al-fuʾād* for the Chishtiyya; the *Maktūbāt-i imām rabbānī* for the Naqshbandiyya; the *Jawāhir-i khamsa* for the Shaṭṭāriyya; the *Maktūbāt* of Sharaf al-Dīn Manērī for the Firdawsiyya, etc.

Indonesia and Iran

The first concrete evidence of Sufism's presence in Indonesia is found in the sources from the late tenth/sixteenth century – at least three centuries after the introduction of Islam into this area. This and the following century witnessed a rapid dissemination of Sufi ideas and practices among the local populations, especially in the flourishing Muslim sultanate of Aceh (Atjeh) in northern Sumatra. Here we find the first prominent exponent of Sufism in the Indonesian Archipelago, Ḥamza Fanṣūrī, who was active in the second half of tenth/sixteenth century. An adherent of the doctrine of *waḥdat al-wujūd* and of seven levels of existence, as expounded by Ibn al-ʿArabī and his follower ʿAbd al-Karīm al-Jīlī (d. 832/1428), Fanṣūrī is famous for his mystical poems of great lyrical power and mystical treatises that describe the four stages of the mystical path (*sharīʿa, ṭarīqa, ḥaqīqa* and *maʿrifa*), the nature of existence (*wujūd*), divine attributes and mystical rapture. Commentaries on some of Ḥamza Fanṣūrī's works were written by his disciple Shams al-Dīn al-Samatrāʾī (d. 1039/1630), who served as religious adviser and spiritual director to the powerful sultan Iskandar Muda of Aceh, whom he inducted into the Naqshbandiyya brotherhood. On the death of Iskandar Muda in 1046/1636 and the accession of Iskandar II, Shams al-Dīn al-Samatrāʾī lost his position to the Indo-Arab scholar Nūr al-Dīn al-Ranīrī (d. 1068/1658). An ardent adherent of the Indian Sufi reformer Aḥmad Sirhindī, al-Ranīrī vigorously attacked both al-Samatrāʾī and his teacher, Ḥamza Fanṣūrī, on account of their espousal of Ibn al-ʿArabī's doctrine of the oneness of being (*waḥdat al-wujūd*). Citing the dangerous social and political implications of this doctrine, al-Ranīrī ordered Shams al-Dīn's writings to be burned. From the eleventh/seventeenth century onwards the orders in Indonesia developed under the influence of some Arabian teachers, especially the Medinan scholars Aḥmad Qushāshī (d. 1071/1660), Ibrāhīm al-Kūrānī (d. 1102/1691) and ʿAbd al-Karīm al-Sammān (d. 1189/1775). They had multiple Sufi affiliations, which they passed on to their students from the Indonesian Archipelago. One of such students was ʿAbd al-Raʾūf al-Singkīlī (d. late eleventh/seventeenth century), who spent nineteen years in the Ḥijāz. Upon his return to the sultanate of Aceh he became a vigorous propagator of the teachings of the Shaṭṭāriyya order. His best-known work, *ʿUmdat al-muḥtājīn* (The support of those in need), describes the methods of *dhikr*, the formulas of Sufi litanies (*rawātib*) and breath-control techniques during mystical concerts. On the doctrinal plane, ʿAbd al-Raʾūf was a moderate follower of Ibn al-ʿArabī and his commentators (especially ʿAbd al-Karīm al-Jīlī), whose concepts of seven stages of existence and of the perfect man (*al-insān al-kāmil*) he discussed in his works written in both Malay and Arabic.

Indonesian Sufism was initially restricted to court circles, where the teachings of Ibn al-ʿArabī and his school, especially the concept of the perfect man, were used by the rulers to legitimise their power. Only around the twelfth/eighteenth century did the *ṭarīqas* begin to win adherents among the common people. Although for the most part apolitical, in the thirteenth/nineteenth century the *ṭarīqas* sometimes provided the organisational networks for anti-colonial rebellions. As a result of this they were much feared by the Dutch colonial administration.

Of numerous Iranian Sufi orders one should mention the Kubrawiyya and the Niʿmatullāhiyya. The former flourished in Central Asia and Khurāsān, only to be displaced by the powerful Naqshbandiyya around the eleventh/ seventeenth century. Of the numerous branches of the Niʿmatullāhiyya only the Nūrbakhshiyya and the Dhahabiyya enjoyed a substantial following. The Niʿmatullāhiyya, which started as a Sunnī order, embraced Shīʿite Islam under the Ṣafavids. In the twelfth/eighteenth century it was singled out for persecution by the Shīʿite religious establishment, probably on account of its 'extreme' doctrines of a messianic slant. It experienced a revival under the Qājār rulers of Iran (thirteenth/late eighteenth–early nineteenth centuries), whereupon it split into a congeries of mutually hostile sub-orders.[68]

Conclusion

Even a cursory and incomplete review of Sufism's evolution across time and space shows that it has been inextricably entwined with the overall development of Islamic devotional practices, theology, literature, aesthetics and institutions. Discussing Sufism in isolation from these religious, social and cultural contexts will result in serious distortions. Sufism's cardinal ideas, practices and values have been continually reinterpreted, rearticulated and readjusted in accordance with the changing historical circumstances of its adherents. Any attempt to posit an immutable and unchanging essence of Islamic mysticism ignores the astounding diversity of religious and intellectual attitudes that falls under the rubric of 'Sufism'.

68 S. Bashir, *Messianic hopes and mystical visions: The Nūrbakhshiya between medieval and modern Islam* (Columbia, SC, 2003); M. van den Bos, *Mystic regimes: Sufism and state in Iran* (Leiden, 2002).

3

Varieties of Islam

FARHAD DAFTARY

The Prophet Muḥammad laid the foundations of a new religion which was propagated as the seal of the great monotheistic religions of the Abrahamic tradition. However, the unified and nascent Muslim community (*umma*) of the Prophet's time soon divided into numerous rival factions, as Muslims disagreed on a number of fundamental issues. Modern scholarship has indeed shown that at least during the first three centuries of their history, marking the formative period of Islam, Muslims lived in an intellectually dynamic and fluid milieu characterised by a multiplicity of communities of interpretation, schools of thought and a diversity of views on a range of religio-political issues. The early Muslims were confronted by many gaps in their religious knowledge and understanding of Islam, which revolved around major issues such as the attributes of God, the nature of authority and definitions of believers and sinners. It was during this formative period that different groups and movements began to formulate their doctrinal positions and gradually acquired their distinctive identities and designations. In terms of theological perspectives, diversity in early Islam ranged from the stances of those, later designated as Sunnīs, who endorsed the historical caliphate and the authority–power structure that had actually emerged in the Muslim community, to various religio-political communities, notably the Shīʿa and the Khārijites, who aspired towards the establishment of new orders and leadership structures.

The Sunnī Muslims of medieval times, or rather their religious scholars (*ʿulamāʾ*), however, produced a picture that is at variance with the findings of modern scholarship on the subject. According to this perspective, endorsed by earlier generations of orientalists, Islam from early on represented a monolithic community with a well-defined doctrinal basis from which different groups deviated over time. Thus, Sunnī Islam was portrayed by its proponents as the true interpretation of Islam, while all non-Sunnī Muslim communities, especially the Shīʿa among them, who had 'deviated' from the right path, were accused of heresy (*ilḥād*), innovation (*bidʿa*) or even unbelief (*kufr*).

As a result, the orientalists, too, studying Islam mainly on the basis of Sunnī sources, endorsed the normativeness of Sunnism and distinguished it from Shīʿism, or any other non-Sunnī interpretation of Islam, with the aid of terms such as 'orthodoxy' and 'heterodoxy' – terms grounded in their Christian experience and categorically inapplicable to an Islamic context.

The Shīʿa, too, have elaborated their own paradigmatic model of 'true Islam', based on a particular interpretation of early Islamic history and a distinctive conception of religious authority vested in the Prophet's family (*ahl al-bayt*). The Shīʿa, whose medieval scholars, similarly to the Sunnī *ʿulamāʾ*, did not generally allow for doctrinal evolution, also disagreed among themselves regarding the identity of the legitimate spiritual leaders (imams) of the community. As a result, the Shīʿa themselves in the course of their history subdivided into a number of major communities, notably the Imāmī Ithnā ʿAsharīs or Twelvers, the Ismāʿīlīs and the Zaydīs, as well as several minor groupings. There were also those Shīʿite communities, such as the Kaysāniyya, who did not survive even though they occupied important positions in early Shīʿism. At any rate, it is to be noted that each Shīʿite community has possessed a distinct self-image and perception of its earlier history, rationalising its own claims and legitimising its leadership and the authority of its line of imams to the exclusion of other communities.

In such a milieu of pluralism and diversity of communal interpretations, abundantly recorded in the heresiographical tradition of the Muslims, obviously general consensus could not be attained on designating any one interpretation of Islam as 'true Islam', as different regimes too lent their support to particular doctrinal positions that were legitimised in different states by the *ʿulamāʾ*. It is important to emphasise that many of the original and fundamental disagreements among Sunnīs, Shīʿa and other Muslims will probably never be satisfactorily explained and resolved, mainly because of a lack of reliable sources, especially from the earliest centuries of Islamic history. As is well known, almost no written records have survived from the formative period of Islam, while the later writings of the historians, theologians, heresiographers and other Muslim authors display variegated 'sectarian' biases. It is within such a frame that this chapter concentrates mainly on Shīʿism and its divisions.

Origins and early history of Shīʿism

The origins of Islam's divisions into Sunnism and Shīʿism may be broadly traced to the crisis of succession to the Prophet Muḥammad, who died after a brief illness in 11/632. As the 'seal of the prophets' (*khātim al-anbiyāʾ*) Muḥammad could not be succeeded by another prophet (*nabī*), but a successor was needed to assume his functions as leader of the Islamic community and state. According to the Sunnī view a successor had not been designated, and in the event this choice was resolved by a group of Muslim notables who chose Abū Bakr as 'successor to the Messenger of God' (*khalīfat rasūl Allāh*). The Muslims had now also founded the distinctive Islamic institution of the caliphate (*khilāfa*). Abū Bakr and his next two successors, ʿUmar and ʿUthmān, belonging to the influential Meccan tribe of Quraysh, were among the early converts to Islam and the Prophet's Companions (*ṣaḥāba*). Only the fourth of the 'rightly guided' (*rāshidūn*) caliphs, ʿAlī ibn Abī Ṭālib (r. 35–40/656–61), who occupies a unique position in the annals of Shīʿism, belonged to the Prophet's own clan of Banū Hāshim within the Quraysh. ʿAlī was also closely associated with the Prophet, being his cousin and son-in-law, bound by marriage to the Prophet's daughter Fāṭima.

It is the fundamental belief of the Shīʿa of all branches that the Prophet himself had designated ʿAlī as his successor, a designation (*naṣṣ*) instituted through divine command and revealed by the Prophet at Ghadīr Khumm shortly before his death. In addition to the *ḥadīth* of Ghadīr Khumm, which was proclaimed publicly in Kūfa by ʿAlī, the Shīʿa have also interpreted certain Qurʾānic verses in support of ʿAlī's designation. ʿAlī himself was firmly convinced of the legitimacy of his own claim to succeed Muḥammad, based on his close kinship and association with him, his intimate knowledge of Islam and his early merits in the cause of Islam. Indeed, ʿAlī made it plain in his speeches and letters that he considered the Prophet's family (*ahl al-bayt*) to be entitled to the leadership of the Muslims.[1] The partisans of ʿAlī also held a particular conception of religious authority that set them apart from other Muslims. They believed that a full understanding of Islam, including its inner dimension, necessitated the continuing presence of a religiously authoritative guide – or imam, as the Shīʿa have traditionally preferred to call their spiritual leader. And for the Shīʿa the *ahl al-bayt* provided the sole authoritative channel for elucidating the teachings of Islam.

Pro-ʿAlī sentiments and broad Shīʿite tendencies persisted in ʿAlī's lifetime, and were strongly revived during the caliphate of ʿUthmān (r. 23–35/644–56), a period of strife in the community. ʿAlī succeeded to the caliphate in turbulent circumstances following ʿUthmān's murder, marking the first civil war in Islam. Centred in Kūfa, the partisans of ʿAlī now became generally designated as *shīʿat ʿAlī*, 'party of ʿAlī', or simply as the Shīʿa. They also referred to themselves by

1 W. Madelung has produced an exhaustive analysis of the existing historiography on the subject in his *The succession to Muḥammad: A study of the early caliphate* (Cambridge, 1997).

terms with more precise religious connotations such as the *shīʿat ahl al-bayt*, or its equivalent the *shīʿat āl Muḥammad*, 'party of the Prophet's household', as against the *shīʿat ʿUthmān*, the partisans of the murdered caliph, who were opposed to ʿAlī. The Umayyad Muʿāwiya, the powerful governor of Syria and leader of the pro-ʿUthmān party, found the call for avenging ʿUthmān's murder a suitable pretext for seizing the caliphate.

The early Shīʿa survived ʿAlī's murder in 40/661 and numerous subsequent tragic events. After ʿAlī, his partisans in Kūfa recognised his eldest son, al-Ḥasan, as his successor to the caliphate. A few months later, under obscure circumstances, al-Ḥasan declined to assume the role, and Muʿāwiya was speedily recognised as the new caliph. Following his peace treaty with Muʿāwiya, al-Ḥasan retired to Medina and abstained from any political activity. However, the Shīʿa continued to regard him as their imam after ʿAlī. On al-Ḥasan's death in 49/669, the Kūfan Shīʿa revived their aspirations for restoring the caliphate to the Prophet's family and invited al-Ḥasan's younger brother al-Ḥusayn, their new imam, to rise against the oppressive rule of the Umayyads. In the aftermath of Muʿāwiya's death and the succession of his son Yazīd, al-Ḥusayn finally responded to these summons and set out for Kūfa. On 10 Muḥarram 61/10 October 680 al-Ḥusayn and his small band of relatives and companions were brutally massacred at Karbalāʾ, near Kūfa, where they were intercepted by an Umayyad army. The martyrdom of the Prophet's grandson infused a new religious fervour in the Shīʿa, and contributed significantly to the consolidation of Shīʿite ethos and identity. Thenceforth the passion motif and the call for repentance and martyrdom became integral aspects of Shīʿite spirituality. Later, the Shīʿa began to commemorate the martyrdom of al-Ḥusayn annually on 10 Muḥarram (ʿĀshūrāʾ) with special ceremonies and passion plays (*taʿziya*).

During its first half-century Shīʿism remained unified, and maintained an almost exclusively Arab membership, with limited appeal to non-Arab Muslims. These features changed with the next important event in the history of Shīʿism: the movement of al-Mukhtār ibn Abī ʿUbayd al-Thaqafī, who launched his own Shīʿite campaign with a general call to avenge al-Ḥusayn's murder. Al-Mukhtār claimed to be acting on behalf of ʿAlī's only surviving son, Muḥammad ibn al-Ḥanafiyya, whose mother was a woman of the Banū Ḥanīfa; he was half-brother to al-Ḥasan and al-Ḥusayn, ʿAlī's sons by Fāṭima. Ibn al-Ḥanafiyya, who declined to assume the leadership of the movement and remained in Medina, was proclaimed by al-Mukhtār as the imam and *mahdī*, 'the divinely guided one', the messianic saviour-imam and restorer of true Islam who would establish justice on earth and deliver the oppressed from tyranny. The concept of the *mahdī* was a very important doctrinal innovation, and proved particularly appealing to the *mawālī* – the Aramean, Persian and other non-Arab converts to Islam, who under the Umayyads were treated as second-class Muslims. As a large and underprivileged social class, the *mawālī* provided a major recruiting-ground for any movement opposed to the exclusively Arab hegemony of the Umayyads. They became particularly drawn to al-Mukhtār's movement and Shīʿism, calling themselves the *shīʿat al-mahdī* ('party of the *mahdī*'). Al-Mukhtār readily won control of Kūfa in an open revolt in 66/685. The Shīʿa now took revenge for al-Ḥusayn, killing those involved in the massacre at Karbalāʾ. However, al-Mukhtār's success was short-lived. In 67/687 he was defeated and killed together with thousands of his *mawālī* supporters. But the movement founded by al-Mukhtār survived his demise.

The sixty-odd years between the revolt of al-Mukhtār and the ʿAbbāsid revolution mark the second phase of early Shīʿism. During this period different Shīʿite groups, consisting of both Arabs and *mawālī*, came to coexist, each one having its own imams and propounding its own doctrines. Furthermore, the Shīʿite imams now hailed not only from the major branches of the extended ʿAlid family, namely the Ḥanafids (descendants of Ibn al-Ḥanafiyya), the Ḥusaynids (descendants of al-Ḥusayn ibn ʿAlī) and, later, the Ḥasanids (descendants of al-Ḥasan ibn ʿAlī), but also from other branches of the Banū Hāshim including the descendants of the Prophet's uncles Abū Ṭālib and al-ʿAbbās. This is because the Prophet's family, whose sanctity was supreme for the Shīʿa, was then still defined broadly in its old Arabian tribal sense. It was after the ʿAbbāsid revolution that the Shīʿa came to define the *ahl al-bayt* more precisely to include only the Fāṭimid ʿAlids, covering both the Ḥusaynids and the Ḥasanids. In this fluid and often confusing setting, Shīʿism developed in terms of two main branches or trends, the Kaysāniyya and the Imāmiyya, each with its own internal divisions; and, later, another Shīʿite movement led to the foundation of the Zaydiyya. There were also those Shīʿite *ghulāt*, individual theorists with small groups of followers, who existed in the midst or on the fringes of the major Shīʿite communities.

A radical branch, in terms of both doctrine and policy, evolved out of al-Mukhtār's movement and accounted for the bulk of the Shīʿa until shortly after the ʿAbbāsid revolution. This branch, breaking away from the religiously moderate attitudes of the early Kūfan Shīʿa, was generally designated as the Kaysāniyya by the heresiographers who were responsible for coining the names of numerous early Muslim communities. The Kaysāniyya, named after the chief of al-Mukhtār's guard, Abū ʿAmra Kaysān, and comprising a number of interrelated groups recognising various Ḥanafid ʿAlids and other Hāshimites as their imams, drew mainly on the support of the *mawālī* in southern Iraq, Persia and elsewhere, though many Arabs were also among them. Heirs to a variety of pre-Islamic traditions, the *mawālī* played an important role in transforming Shīʿism from an Arab party of limited size and doctrinal basis to a dynamic movement.

On Ibn al-Ḥanafiyya's death in 81/700, the Kaysāniyya split into several groups commonly designated as sects (*firaq*) by the heresiographers. In the ideas expounded by these Kaysānī groups we have the first Shīʿite statements of the eschatological doctrines of *ghayba*, the absence or occultation of an imam whose life has been miraculously prolonged and who is due to reappear as the *mahdī*, and *rajʿa*, the return of a messianic personality from the dead, or from occultation, some time before the Day of Resurrection (*qiyāma*). The closely related concept of the *mahdī* had now more specifically acquired an eschatological meaning as the messianic deliverer in Islam, with the implication that no further imams would succeed the *mahdī* during his occultation. Be that as it may, the majority of the Kaysāniyya recognised Ibn al-Ḥanafiyya's son Abū Hāshim as their next imam. These Kaysānīs, known as the Hāshimiyya, accounted for the bulk of the contemporary Shīʿa. On Abū Hāshim's death in 98/716 the majority of the Hāshimiyya recognised the ʿAbbāsid Muḥammad ibn ʿAlī ibn ʿAbd Allāh ibn al-ʿAbbās as their new imam. They held that Abū Hāshim had personally appointed his ʿAbbāsid relative as his successor to the imamate. This party continued to be known as the Hāshimiyya and later also as the ʿAbbāsiyya; it served as the main instrument of the ʿAbbāsid movement.

The Kaysāniyya elaborated some of the doctrines that came to distinguish the radical wing of early Shīʿism, which was also characterised by messianic aspirations. For instance, they condemned the three caliphs who preceded ʿAlī as usurpers. Many of the Kaysānī doctrines were propounded by the so-called *ghāliya* or *ghulāt* (sing. *ghālī*), 'exaggerators'. The *ghulāt* were accused retrospectively by the more moderate Shīʿa of later times of exaggeration (*ghuluww*) in religious matters and with respect to their imams. In addition to attributing superhuman qualities to imams, the early *ghulāt* speculated freely on a range of wider issues, such as the soul, death and afterlife. Many of the *ghulāt* thought of the soul in terms of the doctrine of metempsychosis or transmigration of souls (*tanāsukh*), involving the passing of the individual soul (*nafs* or *rūḥ*) from one body to another.

In the mean time there had appeared another major branch or faction of Shīʿism, later designated as the Imāmiyya, the common heritage of the

Twelver and Ismāʿīlī Shīʿa. The Imāmiyya, who like other Shīʿa of the Umayyad period were based in Kūfa, adopted a quiescent policy in the political field while doctrinally subscribing to some of the views of the Kaysāniyya, such as the condemnation of the caliphs before ʿAlī. The Imāmiyya traced the imamate through al-Ḥusayn ibn ʿAlī's sole surviving son, ʿAlī ibn al-Ḥusayn Zayn al-ʿĀbidīn, who gradually came to be held in great esteem in the pious circles of Medina. It was after ʿAlī ibn al-Ḥusayn (d. *c*. 95/714) that the Imāmiyya began to gain some importance under his son and successor Abū Jaʿfar Muḥammad ibn ʿAlī, known as al-Bāqir. Imām al-Bāqir engaged in active Shīʿite teachings in the course of his imamate of some twenty years. Above all, he seems to have concerned himself with the religious rank and spiritual authority of the imams. He is also credited with introducing the principle of *taqiyya*, the precautionary dissimulation of one's true religious belief and practice that was to protect the imam and his followers under adverse circumstances. This principle was later adopted by the Twelver and Ismāʿīlī Shīʿa. It should also be added that the teaching of ʿAbd Allāh ibn al-ʿAbbās (d. 68/687), the Prophet Muḥammad and ʿAlī's cousin, had a significant impact on early Imāmī religious and legal doctrine.

On al-Bāqir's death around 114/732, the majority of his partisans recognised his eldest son Abū ʿAbd Allāh Jaʿfar, later called al-Ṣādiq (the Trustworthy), as their new imam. In the earlier years of al-Ṣādiq's long and eventful imamate, the movement of his uncle Zayd ibn ʿAlī, al-Bāqir's half-brother, was launched with some success, leading to the formation of the Zaydiyya. Zayd visited Kūfa and was surrounded by the Shīʿa, who urged him to lead a rising. Zayd's revolt proved abortive, however, and he and many of his followers were killed in 122/740. Few details are available on the ideas propagated by Zayd and his original followers. According to some later, unreliable, reports, Zayd was an associate of Wāṣil ibn ʿAṭāʾ (d. 131/748), a reputed founder of the theological school of the Muʿtazila. However, modern scholarship has shown that the doctrinal positions of the early Shīʿa and the Muʿtazila were rather incompatible during the second/eighth century. It was only in the latter part of the third/ninth century that both Zaydism and Imāmī Shīʿism came to be influenced by Muʿtazilism.[2]

Meanwhile, the ʿAbbāsids had learned important lessons from all the abortive Shīʿite revolts against the Umayyads. Consequently, they paid particular attention to developing the organisation of their own movement,

2 See W. Madelung, *Der* Imam *al-Qāsim ibn Ibrāhīm und die Glaubenslehre der Zaiditen* (Berlin, 1965), esp. pp. 7–43, which is the best modern study on the subject.

establishing secret headquarters in Kūfa but concentrating their activities in Khurāsān. The ʿAbbāsid *daʿwa* was cleverly preached in the name of *al-riḍā min āl Muḥammad*, an enigmatic phrase which spoke of an unidentified person belonging to the Prophet's family. This slogan aimed to maximise support from the Shīʿa of different groups who commonly supported the leadership of the *ahl al-bayt*.

However, the ʿAbbāsid victory in 132/749 proved a source of disillusionment for the Shīʿa, who had all along expected an ʿAlid, rather than an ʿAbbāsid, to succeed to the caliphate. The animosity between the ʿAbbāsids and the ʿAlids was accentuated when, soon after their accession, the ʿAbbāsids began to persecute many of their former Shīʿite supporters and the ʿAlids, and, subsequently, became the spokesmen of a Sunnī interpretation of Islam. The ʿAbbāsids' breach with their Shīʿite roots was finally completed when the third caliph of the dynasty, Muḥammad al-Mahdī (r. 158–69/775–85), declared that the Prophet had actually appointed his uncle al-ʿAbbās, rather than ʿAlī, as his successor. With these developments, the remaining Kaysānī Shīʿa sought to align themselves with alternative movements. In Khurāsān and other eastern regions many of these alienated Shīʿa attached themselves to groups generically termed the Khurramiyya (or Khurramdīniyya), espousing a variety of anti-ʿAbbāsid and anti-Arab ideas. In Iraq, however, they rallied to the side of Imām Jaʿfar al-Ṣādiq or Muḥammad ibn ʿAbd Allāh al-Nafs al-Zakiyya, then the main ʿAlid claimants to the imamate of the Shīʿa. With the demise of the Ḥasanid movement of al-Nafs al-Zakiyya in 145/762f., Imām al-Ṣādiq emerged as the main rallying-point for Shīʿa of diverse backgrounds – other than the Zaydīs, who were following their own imams.

Meanwhile, Jaʿfar al-Ṣādiq had gradually acquired a widespread reputation as a religious scholar. He was a reporter of *ḥadīth*, and later cited as such in the chain of authorities (*isnād*) accepted by Sunnīs as well. He also taught *fiqh* (jurisprudence) and has been credited with founding, after the work of his father, the Imāmī Shīʿite *madhhab* (school of religious law), named Jaʿfarī after him. Imām al-Ṣādiq was accepted as a teaching authority not only by his Shīʿite partisans but by a wider circle that included many other piety-minded Muslims. In time he acquired a noteworthy group of scholars around himself, comprising some of the most eminent jurist-traditionists and theologians of the time, such as Hishām ibn al-Ḥakam (d. 179/795), the foremost representative of Imāmī scholastic theology (*kalām*). Indeed, the Imāmiyya now came to possess a distinctive body of ritual as well as theological and legal doctrines. Like his father, Imām al-Ṣādiq attracted a few *ghulāt* thinkers to his circle of associates, but kept the speculations of the more extremist elements of his following within bounds by imposing a certain doctrinal discipline. The foremost radical theorist in al-Ṣādiq's following was Abu 'l-Khaṭṭāb al-Asadī (d. 138/755), who acquired many followers of his own, the Khaṭṭābiyya.

As a result of the intellectual activities of Imām al-Ṣādiq and his circle of associates, and building on the teachings of Imām al-Bāqir, the basic conception of the doctrine of the imamate had become defined in its outline. This doctrine, expressed in numerous *ḥadīth*s reported mainly from Jaʿfar al-Ṣādiq, is preserved in the earliest corpus of Imāmī *ḥadīth* compiled by Abū Jaʿfar Muḥammad al-Kulaynī (d. 329/940), and retained by the Ismāʿīlīs in their foremost legal compendium produced by al-Qāḍī Abū Ḥanīfa al-Nuʿmān ibn Muḥammad (d. 363/974).[3] The Imāmī Shīʿite doctrine of the imamate, which was essentially retained by the later Ithnā ʿAsharīs and the Ismāʿīlīs, was founded on a belief in the permanent need of mankind for a divinely guided and infallible (*maʿṣūm*) imam who, after the Prophet Muḥammad, would act as the authoritative teacher and guide of men in their spiritual affairs. Although the imam, who can practise *taqiyya* when necessary, is entitled to temporal leadership as much as religious authority, his mandate does not depend on having temporal authority. The doctrine further taught that the Prophet himself had designated ʿAlī ibn Abī Ṭālib as his legatee (*waṣī*) and successor, by an explicit *naṣṣ* under divine command. However, the majority of the Companions disregarded the Prophet's testament. After ʿAlī, the imamate was to be transmitted from father to son by *naṣṣ*, among the descendants of ʿAlī and Fāṭima; and after al-Ḥusayn it would continue in the Ḥusaynid line until the end of time. This ʿAlid imam, the sole legitimate imam at any time, is in possession of special knowledge (*ʿilm*), and has perfect understanding of all aspects and meanings of the Qurʾān and the message of Islam. Indeed, the world cannot exist for a moment without such an imam, who is the proof of God (*ḥujjat Allāh*) on earth. The imam's existence is so essential that recognition of and obedience to him were made the absolute duty of every believer.

Having established a solid doctrinal basis for Imāmī Shīʿism, Jaʿfar ibn Muḥammad al-Ṣādiq, the last of the early Shīʿite imams recognised by both the Ismāʿīlīs and the Ithnā ʿAsharīs (Twelvers), counted as the fifth one for the former and the sixth for the latter, died in 148/765. The dispute over his succession caused historic divisions in Imāmī Shīʿism leading to the eventual formation of independent Ithnā ʿAsharī and Ismāʿīlī communities.

3 These *ḥadīth*s are contained in the *Kitāb al-ḥujja*, the first book in Abū Jaʿfar Muḥammad ibn Yaʿqūb al-Kulaynī's *al-Uṣūl min al-kāfī*, ed. ʿA. A. al-Ghaffārī, 2 vols. (Tehran, 1388/1968), vol. I, pp. 168–548, and in the *Kitāb al-walāya* in al-Qāḍī al-Nuʿmān's *Daʿāʾim al-Islām*, ed. A. A. A. Fyzee, 2 vols. (Cairo, 1951–61), vol. I, pp. 14–98.

Later Imāmī Ithnā ʿAsharīs or Twelvers

On Imām Jaʿfar al-Ṣādiq's death in 148/765 his succession was simultaneously claimed by three of his sons, ʿAbd Allāh al-Afṭaḥ, Mūsā al-Kāẓim and Muḥammad al-Dībāj, while a group of the Imāmiyya denied his death and awaited his return as the *mahdī*. As we shall see, there were also those proto-Ismāʿīlī Imāmīs who now recognised the imamate of al-Ṣādiq's second son Ismāʿīl or the latter's son Muḥammad. At any rate, the Imāmiyya now split into six groups, one of which eventually acquired the designation of the Ithnā ʿAshariyya or Twelvers, recognising a line of twelve imams.

The majority of al-Ṣādiq's followers initially recognised his eldest surviving son ʿAbd Allāh al-Afṭaḥ as his successor. When ʿAbd Allāh died a few months later in 149/766, they turned to his younger brother Mūsā al-Kāẓim, who already had a following of his own. Those Imāmī Shīʿa who continued to recognise ʿAbd Allāh as the rightful imam before Mūsā became known as Afṭaḥiyya (or Faṭḥiyya); they constituted an important Imāmī sect in Kūfa until the fourth/tenth century. Mūsā al-Kāẓim, later counted as the seventh imam of the Twelvers, who excluded ʿAbd Allāh from the list of their imams, soon received the allegiance of the majority of the Imāmī Shīʿa, including the most renowned scholars in al-Ṣādiq's entourage. In spite of refraining from all political activity, Mūsā was not spared the persecutions of the ʿAbbāsids. He was arrested several times and imprisoned on the caliph Hārūn al-Rashīd's orders. In 183/799, on his death in a Baghdad prison – perhaps due to poisoning, as the Twelvers claim in the case of almost all their imams – many of his partisans considered him as their seventh and last imam, who would return as the *mahdī*. These Imāmīs formed another sizeable group in Kūfa known as the Wāqifa. However, another group of Mūsā al-Kāẓim's following acknowledged his son ʿAlī al-Riḍā as their new imam, later counted as the eighth in line of the Twelver imams. The caliph al-Maʾmūn attempted to achieve reconciliation between the ʿAbbāsids and ʿAlids by appointing ʿAlī al-Riḍā as his heir apparent in 201/816, also giving the imam a daughter in marriage. This attempt proved futile when ʿAlī died two years later in Khurāsān, where he had joined the entourage of al-Maʾmūn. A new city near Ṭūs, called Mashhad (martyr's place), grew around ʿAlī al-Riḍā's tomb and became the most important Shīʿite shrine in Persia. Imām al-Riḍā's Shīʿa traced the imamate for three more generations in his progeny down to their eleventh imam, al-Ḥasan al-ʿAskarī, with minor schisms. These imams, too, were brought to Baghdad or Sāmarrāʾ (the new ʿAbbāsid capital), and watched closely by the ʿAbbāsids.

On al-Ḥasan al-ʿAskarī's death in 260/873f. his Imāmī partisans experienced a crisis of succession, and subdivided into numerous splinter groups.[4] Many believed that the deceased imam had left no male progeny, and recognised al-Ḥasan himself as the *mahdī*. Others acknowledged al-Ḥasan's brother Jaʿfar as their new imam, on the basis of different arguments. However, the main body, later designated as the Ithnā ʿAshariyya, eventually held that a son named Muḥammad had been born to al-Ḥasan al-ʿAskarī in 255/869 and that the child had remained hidden. They further held that Muḥammad had succeeded his father to the imamate while remaining in concealment. Identified as the *mahdī* or *qāʾim*, Muḥammad was expected to reappear in glory before the final Day of Judgement to rule the world in justice.

According to Ithnā ʿAsharī tradition Muḥammad al-Mahdī's occultation fell into two periods. During his initial 'lesser occultation' (*al-ghayba al-ṣughrā*), covering 260–329/873–941, the imam remained in regular contact with four successive agents, called variously the gate (*bāb*), emissary (*safīr*) or deputy (*nāʾib*), who acted as intermediaries between him and his community. But in the 'greater occultation' (*al-ghayba al-kubrā*), initiated in 329/941 and still continuing, the hidden imam has chosen not to have any representative living on earth and participating in the affairs of the world. Enjoying miraculously prolonged life, his titles include the 'lord of the age' (*ṣāḥib al-zamān*) and the 'expected imam' (*al-imām al-muntaẓar*), among others. Twelver Shīʿite scholars have written extensively on the eschatological doctrines of occultation (*ghayba*) of their twelfth imam and the conditions that would prevail before his return (*rajʿa*) or parousia (*ẓuhūr*). By the first half of the fourth/tenth century, when the line of the twelve imams had been identified, those Shīʿa believing in that series of imams became known as the Ithnā ʿAshariyya, and they were distinguished from all earlier Imāmī groups.

In the first period of their religious history the Imāmī (Ithnā ʿAsharī) Shīʿa benefited from the direct guidance and teachings of their imams. It was in the second period, from the occultation of the twelfth imam until the Mongol age, that Twelver scholars emerged as influential guardians and transmitters of the teachings of the imams, compiling collections of Imāmī *ḥadīth* and formulating the law. This period coincided with the rise of the Būyids, or Buwayhids, to power in Persia and Iraq, as overlords of the ʿAbbāsids. The Būyids were originally Zaydī Shīʿa from Daylam, but now they supported Muʿtazilism and

4 Abū Muḥammad al-Ḥasan ibn Mūsā al-Nawbakhtī, *Kitāb firaq al-Shīʿa*, ed. H. Ritter (Istanbul, 1931), pp. 79–94; Saʿd ibn ʿAbd Allāh al-Ashʿarī al-Qummī, *Kitāb al-maqālāt waʾl-firaq*, ed. M. J. Mashkūr (Tehran, 1963), pp. 102–16.

Shīʿism without allegiance to any of its specific branches. The earliest comprehensive collections of Twelver traditions of the imams, which were first transmitted in Kūfa and elsewhere, were compiled in Qumm, in Persia. By the late third/ninth century, when these activities were well under way, Qumm had already served for more than a century as a chief centre of Imāmī Shīʿite learning. The earliest and most authoritative of the Imāmī *ḥadīth* collections is the *Kitāb al-kāfī* by al-Kulaynī (d. 329/940), which also came to be recognised as the first of the four Imāmī canonical collections, *al-kutub al-arbaʿa* (the four books), dealing with theology and jurisprudence. The traditionist school of Qumm, which rejected all forms of *kalām* theology based on extensive use of independent reasoning and instead relied on the traditions of the Prophet and the imams, reached its peak in the works of Ibn Bābawayh, also known as Shaykh al-Ṣadūq (d. 381/991). He produced the second major compilation of Imāmī *ḥadīth* called *Man lā yaḥḍuruhu'l-faqīh* (He who has no legal scholar in his proximity). Ibn Bābawayh was strongly opposed to the Muʿtazila and their *kalām* methodology, preferring to base his own doctrine on the use of *ḥadīths* with a minimum of reasoning.

In the course of the fourth/tenth century, the Shīʿite century of Islam with Būyids, Fāṭimids, Qarāmiṭa and others in power, the school of Qumm was overshadowed by the rise of a rival school of Imāmī theology in Baghdad which adhered to the rationalist theology (*kalām*) of the Muʿtazila and also produced the principles of Imāmī jurisprudence (*uṣūl al-fiqh*) based on a legal methodology opposed to unqualified adherence to tradition.[5] It may be recalled at this juncture that members of the influential Banū Nawbakht Twelver family in Baghdad, notably Abū Sahl Ismāʿīl (d. 311/923) and his nephew al-Ḥasan ibn Mūsā (d. between 300 and 310/912 and 922), had already pioneered the amalgamation of the Muʿtazilite theology with Imāmī doctrine. The first leader of the Baghdad school was Muḥammad ibn Muḥammad al-Ḥārithī, known as Shaykh al-Mufīd (d. 413/1022), who criticised the creed of Ibn Bābawayh, his teacher. He argued for the methodology of religious disputation and *kalām*, and espoused the Muʿtazilite acceptance of human free will and denial of predestination, also rejecting anthropomorphism. On the other hand, the Baghdad school rejected those Muʿtazilite doctrines that were in conflict with the basic Imāmī beliefs related to the imamate. Thus, refuting the Muʿtazilite dogma of the unconditional punishment of the Muslim sinner, it allowed for the intercession (*shafāʿa*) of the imams for the

5 W. Madelung, 'Imamism and Muʿtazilite theology', in T. Fahd (ed.), *Le Shîʿisme imâmite* (Paris, 1970), pp. 13–28.

sinners of their community to save them from punishment, also condemning the adversaries of the imams as infidels and maintaining that the imamate was, like prophecy, a rational necessity.

Shaykh al-Mufīd was succeeded as chief authority of the Baghdad school by his student Sharīf al-Murtaḍā ʿAlam al-Hudā (d. 436/1044), a descendant of Mūsā al-Kāẓim and also head (*naqīb*) of the ʿAlid family. He went further than al-Mufīd and insisted, like the Muʿtazila, that the basic truths of religion are to be established by reason (*ʿaql*) alone. Even the traditions were to be subjected to the test of reason rather than being accepted uncritically. It is to be noted here that al-Murtaḍā's younger brother Sharīf al-Raḍī (d. 405/1015) is responsible for having compiled the *Nahj al-balāgha* (Peak of eloquence), an anthology of the letters and sermons of ʿAlī ibn Abī Ṭālib, which serves as one of the most venerated books of the Twelvers.

Muḥammad ibn al-Ḥasan al-Ṭūsī (d. 460/1067), known as Shaykh al-Ṭāʾifa, another member of the Baghdad school who studied with both Shaykh al-Mufīd and Sharīf al-Murtaḍā, became the most authoritative early systematiser of Twelver law. His two main works, *al-Istibṣār* (Consideration) and the *Tahdhīb al-aḥkām* (Appeal of decisions), are included among the 'four books' of the Twelvers. Al-Ṭūsī also partially rehabilitated the school of Qumm and its reliance on traditions. He argued that although many of the traditions of the Imāmī traditionists were of the *āḥād* (singly transmitted) category and therefore unacceptable on rational grounds, they were nevertheless to be sanctioned for having been universally used by the Imāmī community in the presence of the imams themselves. It was also during this period that the earliest Imāmī bio-bibliographical works (*kutub al-rijāl*), listing trustworthy authorities and transmitters of *ḥadīth*, were compiled by Shaykh al-Ṭūsī himself, as well as others such as Aḥmad ibn ʿAlī al-Najāshī (d. 450/1058).

In the mean time Twelver Shīʿite communities had appeared in numerous parts of Persia and Transoxania. Shīʿism received a serious blow when the Sunnī Saljūqs succeeded the Shīʿite Būyids. But the situation of the Twelver Shīʿa improved when the Mongols established their rule in south-west Asia. By then a number of local dynasties in Iraq and Syria adhered to Twelver Shīʿism and encouraged the work of their *ʿulamāʾ*, such as the ʿUqaylids of Iraq and the Ḥamdānids and Mirdāsids of Syria. With the collapse of the Qarmaṭī state of Baḥrayn, a number of Twelver communities and dynasties had also begun to gain prominence in eastern Arabia and in other locations around the Persian Gulf. Foremost among these local dynasties were the Mazyadids, who had their capital at Ḥilla on the banks of the Euphrates. Indeed, from the opening decade of the sixth/twelfth century Ḥilla was established as an important centre of Shīʿite activity, and it later superseded Qumm and Baghdad as the main centre of Imāmī scholarship. Meanwhile, Sharīf al-Murtaḍā's basic approach to *kalām*, holding that reason alone was the sole source of the fundamentals of religion, had become widely accepted in Twelver circles. The same approach was later adopted, without any significant revision, by the then chief exponents of Imāmī *kalām*, Khwāja Naṣīr al-Dīn al-Ṭūsī (d. 672/1273f.) and his disciple al-Ḥasan ibn Yūsuf Ibn al-Muṭahhar al-Ḥillī (d. 726/1325), who in fact represented the last school of original thought in Twelver theology. Subsequently, with a few exceptions, Twelver Shīʿite scholars mainly produced commentaries on, or restatements of, the earlier teachings. Indeed, with the Mongol invasions and Naṣīr al-Dīn al-Ṭūsī a third period was initiated in Twelver Shīʿism, which lasted until the establishment of the Ṣafavid dynasty. In this period the influence of al-Ṭūsī in both theology and philosophy was a key factor, while close relations developed between Twelver theology and the Sufism of Ibn al-ʿArabī (d. 638/1240).

Ibn al-Muṭahhar al-Ḥillī, known as ʿAllāma al-Ḥillī, was a major scholar from Ḥilla. A prolific writer and author of numerous legal treatises, ʿAllāma al-Ḥillī had lasting influence on the development and theoretical foundations of Twelver jurisprudence. Following in the tradition of the Baghdad school, he provided a theoretical foundation for *ijtihād*, the principle of legal ruling by the jurist through reasoning (*ʿaql*). In his *Mabādiʾ al-wuṣūl ilā ʿilm al-uṣūl* (Points of departure for attaining knowledge of the principles) ʿAllāma al-Ḥillī expounds the principles of *ijtihād*, exercised by *mujtahids*, who, he argues, are fallible by comparison to infallible imams. The *mujtahid* can, therefore, revise his decision. *Ijtihād* also allowed for *ikhtilāf*, or differences of opinions among *mujtahids*. Al-Ḥillī's acceptance of *ijtihād* represents a crucial step towards the enhancement of the authority of the jurists (*fuqahāʾ*) in Twelver Shīʿism. *Ijtihād* also gained importance within the Zaydī Shīʿite communities, but it was rejected by the Ismāʿīlīs.

Meanwhile, Shīʿite tendencies had been spreading in Persia and Central Asia since the seventh/thirteenth century, creating a more favourable milieu in many predominantly Sunnī regions for the activities of the Shīʿa (both Twelvers and Ismāʿīlīs) as well as a number of other movements with Shīʿite inclinations. In this connection particular reference should be made to the Ḥurūfī movement founded by the Shīʿite Sufi Faḍl Allāh Astarābādī (d. 796/1394), whose doctrines were later adopted by the Bektāshī dervishes of Anatolia; and the Nuqṭawīs who split off from the Ḥurūfiyya under the initial leadership of Maḥmūd-i Pasīkhānī (d. 831/1427). There were also the Twelver-related Mushaʿshaʿ of Khūzistān, founded by Ibn Falāḥ (d. *c.* 866/

1461), who claimed Mahdism. The Mushaʿshaʿ ruled over parts of Iraq, and under their persecutionary policies Ḥilla lost its prominence as a centre of Twelver learning to Jabal ʿĀmil in Lebanon. These movements normally entertained messianic aspirations for the deliverance of oppressed and underprivileged groups. Instead of propagating any particular form of Shīʿism, however, a new syncretic type of popular Shīʿism was now arising in post-Mongol Central Asia, Persia and Anatolia, which culminated in early Ṣafavid Shīʿism. Marshall Hodgson designated this as '*ṭarīqah* Shīʿism', as it was transmitted mainly through a number of Sufi orders then being formed.[6] The Sufi orders in question remained outwardly Sunnī, following one of the Sunnī *madhhabs*, while being particularly devoted to ʿAlī and the *ahl al-bayt*. It was under such circumstances that close relations developed between Twelver Shīʿism and Sufism, and also between Nizārī Ismāʿīlism and Sufism in Persia. The most important Twelver Shīʿite mystic of the eighth/fourteenth century, who developed his own rapport between Twelver Shīʿism and Sufism, was Sayyid Ḥaydar Āmulī (d. 787/1385), who was influenced by the teachings of Ibn al-ʿArabī.

A fourth and final period may be identified in the development of Twelver Shīʿism, from the establishment of Ṣafavid rule to the present. Among the Sufi orders that contributed to the spread of ʿAlid loyalism and Shīʿism in predominantly Sunnī Persia, the most direct part was played by the Ṣafawiyya *ṭarīqa*, founded by Shaykh Ṣafī al-Dīn (d. 735/1334), a Sunnī of the Shāfiʿī *madhhab*. The Ṣafawī order spread rapidly throughout Azerbaijan, eastern Anatolia and other regions, acquiring influence over several Turcoman tribes. With Shaykh Ṣafī's fourth successor, Junayd (d. 864/1460), the order was transformed into a revolutionary movement. Junayd's son and successor Shaykh Ḥaydar (d. 893/1488) was responsible for instructing his soldier-Sufi followers to adopt the scarlet headgear of twelve gores commemorating the twelve imams, for which they were dubbed the Qizilbāsh, a Turkish term meaning redhead.

The eclectic Shīʿism of the Qizilbāsh Turcomans became more clearly manifested when the youthful Ismāʿīl became the shaykh of the Ṣafawī order. Ismāʿīl represented himself to his Qizilbāsh followers as the representative of the hidden imam, or even the awaited *mahdī* himself, also claiming divinity. With the help of his Qizilbāsh forces Ismāʿīl speedily seized Azerbaijan from the Aq Qoyunlu dynasty and entered their capital, Tabrīz, in 907/1501. He now proclaimed himself shah (king), and at the same time

6 Marshall G. S. Hodgson, *The venture of Islam: Conscience and history in a world civilization*, 3 vols. (Chicago, 1974), vol. II, pp. 493ff.

declared Twelver Shīʿism the official religion of his newly founded Ṣafavid state. Shāh Ismāʿīl brought all of Persia under his control during the ensuing decade, and his dynasty ruled until 1135/1722.

The Ṣafavids originally adhered to an eclectic type of Shīʿism which was gradually disciplined and brought into conformity with the tenets of 'orthodox' Twelver Shīʿism. In order to enhance their legitimacy, Shāh Ismāʿīl and his immediate successors claimed variously to represent the hidden *mahdī*, in addition to fabricating an ʿAlid genealogy for their dynasty, tracing their ancestry to Imām Mūsā al-Kāẓim. Shīʿism was, in fact, imposed on the subjects of the Ṣafavid empire rather gradually, while the Ṣafavids from early on strove to eliminate any major religio-political challenge to their supremacy. As a result, under Shāh Ismāʿīl (r. 907–30/1501–24) and his son and successor Ṭahmāsp (r. 930–84/1524–76) the Ṣafavids articulated a religious policy for the elimination of all millenarian and extremist movements, persecution of Sufi orders and popular dervish groups and suppression of Sunnism while actively propagating Twelver Shīʿism. As Persia did not have an established class of religious scholars, however, the Ṣafavids were obliged for quite some time to invite scholars from the Arab centres of Twelver scholarship, notably Najaf, Baḥrayn and Jabal ʿĀmil, to instruct their subjects. Foremost among these Arab Shīʿite *ʿulamāʾ* mention should be made of Shaykh ʿAlī al-Karakī al-ʿĀmilī (d. 940/1534), known as the Muḥaqqiq al-Thānī, who adhered to the Ḥilla school of Imāmī *kalām* with its recognition of *ijtihād* for the qualified scholars, combined with *taqlīd*, or authorisation of the majority who emulated the *mujtahid*.

Meanwhile, the Ṣafavids encouraged the training of a class of Imāmī legal scholars who would propagate the established doctrines of Twelver Shīʿism. The training of the Twelver scholars was further facilitated through the foundation of a number of religious colleges. By the time of Shāh ʿAbbās I (r. 995–1038/1587–1629), the greatest member of the dynasty, who established his capital at Iṣfahān, the Ṣafavids' claim to any divine authority or to representing the *mahdī* were rapidly fading, while the Qizilbāsh had lost their influence and the Sufi orders had disappeared almost completely from Persia. On the other hand, Twelver Shīʿite rituals and practices, such as regular visiting (*ziyāra*) of the tombs of the imams and their relatives in the *ʿatabāt* – Najaf, Karbalāʾ and other shrine cities of Iraq, as well as in Mashhad and Qumm in Persia – had gained wide currency.

The Ṣafavid period witnessed a renaissance of Islamic sciences and Shīʿite scholarship. Foremost among the intellectual achievements of the period should be noted the original contributions of a number of Shīʿite scholars belonging to the so-called 'school of Iṣfahān'. These scholars integrated a variety of philosophical, theological and gnostic traditions within a Shīʿite perspective into a metaphysical synthesis known as *al-ḥikma al-ilāhiyya* (Pers. *ḥikmat-i ilāhī*), divine wisdom or theosophy. The founder of this school was Muḥammad Bāqir Astarābādī (d. 1040/1630), known as Mīr Dāmād, a Shīʿite theologian, philosopher and poet who was also the *shaykh al-Islām* (chief religious authority) of Iṣfahān.

The most important representative of the school of Iṣfahān in theosophical Shīʿism was, however, Mīr Dāmād's principal student, Ṣadr al-Dīn Muḥammad Shīrāzī (d. 1050/1640), better known as Mullā Ṣadrā. He produced his own synthesis of four major schools of Islamic thought: *kalām* theology; Peripatetic philosophy (*al-ḥikma al-mashshāʾiyya*); the illuminationist philosophy of Shihāb al-Dīn Yaḥyā al-Suhrawardī (*al-ḥikma al-ishrāqiyya*); and gnostic–mystical traditions (*ʿirfān*), particularly the Sufism of Ibn al-ʿArabī. Similar to the 'philosophical Ismāʿīlism' expounded by the Iranian Ismāʿīlī *dāʿīs* of the Fāṭimid times, the members of the school of Iṣfahān, too, elaborated an original intellectual perspective in philosophical Shīʿism. Mullā Ṣadrā trained eminent students, such as Mullā Muḥsin Fayḍ Kāshānī (d. 1091/1680) and ʿAbd al-Razzāq Lāhījī (d. 1072/1661), who passed down the traditions of the school of Iṣfahān in later centuries in both Persia and India.

The Twelver *ʿulamāʾ*, and especially the jurists among them, played an increasingly prominent role in the affairs of the Ṣafavid kingdom. This trend reached its climax under the last Ṣafavids with Muḥammad Bāqir Majlisī (d. 1111/1699), who held the highest clerical offices and consolidated the influence of the Imāmī hierocracy. The author of an encyclopaedic *ḥadīth* collection, *Biḥār al-anwār* (Seas of lights), Majlisī, like many other jurists, was opposed to philosophers and Sufis. However, the *ʿulamāʾ* also disagreed among themselves on certain theological and juristic issues, and became particularly divided into two opposing camps, generally designated as Akhbārī and Uṣūlī, on the role of reason in religious matters. From early on, traditionist and rationalist trends had existed within Twelver Shīʿism. The original predominance of the Imāmīs adhering to the traditionist Akhbārī position was superseded by the scholars of the school of Baghdad who established the rationalist Uṣūlī doctrine on a solid foundation by adopting Muʿtazilī *kalām* principles. However, by the early eleventh/seventeenth century Mullā Muḥammad Amīn Astarābādī (d. 1033/1624) had articulated the traditionist position afresh and, in effect, became the founder of the later Akhbārī school that sought to establish Shīʿite jurisprudence on the basis of traditions (*akhbār*) rather than the rationalistic principles (*uṣūl*) of jurisprudence used in *ijtihād*. Indeed, he attacked the very idea of *ijtihād* and branded the Uṣūlī *mujtahids* as enemies of religion. Criticising the innovations of the schools of Baghdad and Ḥilla in *uṣūl al-fiqh* and theology, Astarābādī recognised the *akhbār* of the imams as the most important source of law, required also for correct understanding of the Qurʾān and the Prophetic traditions.

The Akhbārī school flourished for almost two centuries in Persia and the shrine cities of Iraq; its teachings were adopted by many eminent Twelver scholars such as Muḥammad Taqī Majlisī (d. 1070/1660) and Muḥammad al-Ḥurr al-ʿĀmilī (d. 1104/1693), who compiled another vast collection of the *akhbār* of the imams. In the second half of the twelfth/eighteenth century, when Twelver Shīʿism was already widespread in Persia, the Uṣūlī doctrine found a new champion in Muḥammad Bāqir Bihbahānī (d. 1208/1793), who defended *ijtihād* and successfully led the fight against the Akhbārīs. He went so far as to brand the Akhbārīs as infidels. Thereafter the Akhbārīs rapidly lost their position to the Uṣūlīs, who emerged as the prevailing school of jurisprudence in Twelver Shīʿism. The re-establishment of the Uṣūlī school was to lead to unprecedented enhancements in the authority of the *ʿulamāʾ* under the Qājār monarchs of Persia and in modern times.

Meanwhile, Twelver Shīʿism had also spread in southern Lebanon and certain regions of India. Twelver *mujtahids*, who were often of Persian origin, were particularly active in India after the disintegration of the first Muslim state, the Bahmanid kingdom in the Deccan, and the appearance of five independent successor Shīʿite states, which were under the influence of the Ṣafavids. The ʿĀdil-Shāhīs of Bījāpūr (r. 895–1097/1490–1686) were the first Muslim dynasty in India to adopt Twelver Shīʿism (in 908/1503) as the religious doctrine of their state. Later, Shāh Ṭāhir al-Ḥusaynī, a scholar and a Muḥammad-Shāhī Nizārī Ismāʿīlī imam, converted Burhān Niẓām Shāh, who in 944/1537 proclaimed Twelver Shīʿism as the official faith of the Niẓām-Shāhī state. Sultan Qulī (r. 901–50/1496–1543), the founder of the Quṭb-Shāhī dynasty of Golconda, also adopted Twelver Shīʿism. In India too the Imāmī *ʿulamāʾ* encountered the hostility of the Sunnīs. Nūr Allāh Shūshtārī, another eminent Twelver theologian-jurist who emigrated from Persia to India and enjoyed some popularity at the Mughal court, was executed in 1019/1610 at the instigation of the Sunnī *ʿulamāʾ* and on Emperor Jahāngīr's orders. However, Shīʿite communities survived even in the Mughal empire, especially in the region of Hyderabad. Twelver Shīʿism also spread to northern India and was adopted in the kingdom of Awadh (1722–1856) with its capital at Lucknow.

The Ismāʿīlīs, Qarāmiṭa and Druzes

Representing the second most important Shīʿite community, the Ismāʿīlīs have had their own complex history. Imām Jaʿfar al-Ṣādiq had originally designated his second son, Ismāʿīl, the eponym of the Ismāʿīliyya, as his successor to the imamate by the rule of *naṣṣ*. According to the Ismāʿīlī religious tradition Ismāʿīl survived his father and succeeded him in due course, while most non-Ismāʿīlī sources relate that he predeceased his father. At any rate, Ismāʿīl was not present in Medina or Kūfa at the time of Imām al-Ṣādiq's death in 148/765, when three of his brothers claimed the succession. As noted above, this confusing succession dispute split the Imāmiyya into several groups, two of which may be identified as proto-Ismāʿīlīs or the earliest Ismāʿīlīs. One group denied the death of Ismāʿīl ibn Jaʿfar in his father's lifetime. Dubbed *al-ismāʿīliyya al-khāliṣa* (the 'pure Ismāʿīliyya'), these Imāmī Shīʿites awaited Ismāʿīl's return as the *mahdī*.[7] The second proto-Ismāʿīlī group, known as the Mubārakiyya, derived from Ismāʿīl's epithet al-Mubārak (the blessed one), affirmed Ismāʿīl's death during the lifetime of his father and recognised his son Muḥammad as their imam. Before long, Muḥammad ibn Ismāʿīl, the seventh imam of the Ismāʿīlīs, went into hiding, marking the initiation of the *dawr al-satr* (period of concealment) in early Ismāʿīlī history, which lasted until the emergence of the Ismāʿīlī imams as Fāṭimid caliphs.

It is certain that for almost a century after Muḥammad ibn Ismāʿīl (d. *c.* 179/795) a group of leaders worked secretly for the creation of a unified, revolutionary movement against the ʿAbbāsids. These leaders did not openly claim the imamate for three generations. ʿAbd Allāh, the first of these leaders, had in fact organised his campaign around the central doctrine of the majority of the earliest Ismāʿīlīs, acknowledging Muḥammad ibn Ismāʿīl as the awaited *mahdī*. This was perceived as a tactic to safeguard the leaders of the movement against ʿAbbāsid persecution. At any rate, ʿAbd Allāh eventually found refuge in Salamiyya, which served as the secret headquarters of the early Ismāʿīlī movement. The Ismāʿīlīs now referred to their movement simply as *al-daʿwa* (the mission) or *al-daʿwa al-hādiya* (the rightly guiding mission).

The efforts of ʿAbd Allāh and his successors began to bear fruit in the 260s/870s when numerous *dāʿīs* appeared in southern Iraq and other regions. In 261/874 Ḥamdān Qarmaṭ was converted to Ismāʿīlism in the Sawād of Kūfa. Ḥamdān and his chief assistant ʿAbdān organised the *daʿwa* in southern Iraq

7 al-Nawbakhtī, *Firaq al-Shīʿa*, pp. 57–61; al-Qummī, *Kitāb al-maqālāt*, pp. 80–1, 83.

and adjacent regions. The Ismāʿīlīs of southern Iraq became generally known as the Qarāmiṭa, after their first local leader. The *daʿwa* in Yemen was initiated by Ibn Ḥawshab (d. 302/914), later known as Manṣūr al-Yaman. By 280/893 the *dāʿī* Abū ʿAbd Allāh al-Shīʿī (d. 298/911) was already active among the Kutāma Berbers in the Maghrib. Meanwhile, Abū Saʿīd al-Jannābī was dispatched to Baḥrayn, in eastern Arabia, where he rapidly won converts from among the Bedouin and the Persian emigrants. It was also in the 260s/870s that the *daʿwa* was taken to al-Jibāl, the west-central and north-western parts of Persia, where the *dāʿīs* adopted a new policy, targeting the elite and the ruling classes. The same policy was later adopted successfully, at least temporarily, by the *dāʿīs* of Khurāsān and Transoxania.

In 286/899, soon after the future Fāṭimid caliph ʿAbd Allāh al-Mahdī had succeeded to the central leadership of the *daʿwa* in Salamiyya, Ismāʿīlism was rent by a major schism. ʿAbd Allāh now felt secure enough to claim the imamate openly for himself and his predecessors, the same individuals who had organised and led the early Ismāʿīlī *daʿwa*. Later he explained that, as a form of *taqiyya*, the central leaders of the *daʿwa* had adopted different pseudonyms, also assuming the rank of *ḥujja* (proof or full representative) of the absent Muḥammad ibn Ismāʿīl. ʿAbd Allāh further explained that the earlier propagation of the return of Muḥammad ibn Ismāʿīl as the *mahdī* was itself another dissimulating measure.[8] ʿAbd Allāh al-Mahdī's reform split the then unified Ismāʿīlī movement into two rival branches. One faction remained loyal to the central leadership and acknowledged continuity in the Ismāʿīlī imamate, recognising ʿAbd Allāh al-Mahdī and his ʿAlid ancestors as their imams, which in due course became the official Fāṭimid Ismāʿīlī doctrine. On the other hand, a dissident faction, originally led by Ḥamdān Qarmaṭ and ʿAbdān, rejected the reform and maintained their belief in the Mahdism of Muḥammad ibn Ismāʿīl. Thenceforth the term Qarāmiṭa came to be applied more specifically to the dissident Ismāʿīlīs who did not acknowledge ʿAbd Allāh al-Mahdī and his successors in the Fāṭimid dynasty as their imams. The dissident Qarāmiṭa, who lacked central leadership, soon acquired their most important stronghold in Baḥrayn, where a Qarmaṭī state had been founded in the same eventful year, 286/899, by Abū Saʿīd al-Jannābī. Soon after these events ʿAbd Allāh left Salamiyya and embarked on a a historic journey which ended several years later in North Africa, where he founded the Fāṭimid caliphate.

8 See the letter of the first Fāṭimid caliph addressed to the Yemenī Ismāʿīlīs, in Ḥusayn F. al-Hamdānī, *On the genealogy of Fatimid caliphs* (Cairo, 1958), text pp. 10–12.

The early Ismāʿīlīs elaborated the basic framework of a system of religious thought which was further developed or modified in the Fāṭimid period, while the Qarāmiṭa followed a separate doctrinal course. Central to the Ismāʿīlī system of thought was a fundamental distinction between the exoteric (*ẓāhir*) and the esoteric (*bāṭin*) aspects of the sacred scriptures and religious commandments and prohibitions. They further held that the *ẓāhir*, the religious laws enunciated by prophets, underwent periodical changes, while the *bāṭin*, containing the spiritual truths (*ḥaqāʾiq*), remained eternal. These truths, representing the message common to Judaism, Christianity and Islam, were explained through the methodology of *taʾwīl* (esoteric interpretation), which often relied on the mystical significance of letters and numbers.

The esoteric truths (*ḥaqāʾiq*) formed a system of thought for the Ismāʿīlīs, representing a distinct world-view. The two main components of this system were a cyclical history of revelations or prophetic eras and a cosmological doctrine represented through the language of myth. Their cyclical conception, applied to Judaeo-Christian as well as several other pre-Islamic religions, was developed in terms of eras of different prophets recognised in the Qurʾān. Accordingly, they held that the religious history of humankind proceeded through seven prophetic eras (*dawrs*) of various durations, each inaugurated by a speaker or enunciator (*nāṭiq*) of a divinely revealed message which in its exoteric (*ẓāhir*) aspect contained a religious law (*sharīʿa*). The *nāṭiqs* of the first six eras were Adam, Noah, Abraham, Moses, Jesus and Muḥammad. As the seventh imam of the era of Islam, Muḥammad ibn Ismāʿīl was initially expected to return as the *mahdī* (or *qāʾim*) as well as the *nāṭiq* of the seventh eschatological era when, instead of promulgating a new law, he would fully divulge the esoteric truths of all the preceding revelations. Recognising continuity in the imamate, the advent of the seventh era lost its earlier messianic appeal for the Fāṭimid Ismāʿīlīs, for whom the final eschatological age was postponed indefinitely. On the other hand, the Qarāmiṭa of Baḥrayn and elsewhere continued to consider Muḥammad ibn Ismāʿīl as their *mahdī* who, on his reappearance as the seventh *nāṭiq*, was expected to initiate the final age.

The Fāṭimid period represents the 'golden age' of Ismāʿīlism, when the Ismāʿīlīs possessed a state of their own and Ismāʿīlī scholarship and literature attained their summit.[9] The foundation of the Fāṭimid caliphate in 297/909 in

9 The Fāṭimid era of Ismāʿīlī history is one of the best-documented periods in Islamic history: see P. E. Walker, *Exploring an Islamic empire: Fatimid history and its sources* (London, 2002).

Ifrīqiya in North Africa indeed marked the crowning success of the early Ismāʿīlīs. The religio-political *daʿwa* of the Ismāʿīliyya had finally led to the establishment of a state (*dawla*) headed by the Ismāʿīlī imam, ʿAbd Allāh al-Mahdī (r. 297–322/909–34). In line with their universal claims, the Fāṭimid caliph-imams did not abandon their *daʿwa* activities on assuming power, as they aimed to extend their rule over the entire Muslim community. And they concerned themselves with the propagation of the Ismāʿīlī *daʿwa*, especially after the transference of the seat of the Fāṭimid state in 362/973 to Egypt, where Cairo was founded as their new capital city. The religio-political messages of the *daʿwa* were disseminated by networks of *dāʿī*s within the Fāṭimid dominions as well as in other regions referred to as the *jazāʾir* (sing. *jazīra*, 'island').

It was during the Fāṭimid period that the Ismāʿīlī *dāʿī*s, who were at the same time the scholars and authors of their community, produced what were to become the classical texts of Ismāʿīlī literature, dealing with a multitude of exoteric and esoteric subjects as well as *taʾwīl*, which became the hallmark of Ismāʿīlī thought.[10] The *dāʿī*s of the Iranian lands set about in the course of the fourth/tenth century to amalgamate Ismāʿīlī Shīʿite theology (*kalām*), revolving around the doctrine of the imamate, with ideas drawn from Neoplatonism and other philosophical traditions into complex metaphysical systems of thought. This led to the development of a unique intellectual tradition of 'philosophical theology' within Ismāʿīlism. The major proponents of this tradition were the *dāʿī*s Muḥammad ibn Aḥmad al-Nasafī (d. 332/943), Abū Ḥātim al-Rāzī (d. 322/934), Abū Yaʿqūb al-Sijistānī (d. after 361/971) and Ḥamīd al-Dīn al-Kirmānī (d. after 411/1020). Nāṣir-i Khusraw (d. after 462/1070), who spread the *daʿwa* in Badakhshān, was the last major member of this Iranian school of Ismāʿīlism. Neoplatonic philosophy also influenced the cosmology elaborated by the Ismāʿīlī-affiliated Ikhwān al-Ṣafāʾ (the 'Sincere Brethren'), a group of anonymous authors in Baṣra, who produced an encyclopaedic work of fifty-two epistles, *Rasāʾil Ikhwān al-Ṣafāʾ*, on a variety of sciences during the fourth/tenth century.

The Sunnī polemicists always accused the Ismāʿīlīs of ignoring the *sharīʿa*, supposedly because of their emphasis on its hidden meaning, and hence they were commonly referred to as the Bāṭiniyya (Esotericists). However, the Fāṭimids from early on concerned themselves with legal matters and the precepts of Imāmī Shīʿite law. The promulgation of an Ismāʿīlī *madhhab* resulted mainly from the efforts of al-Qāḍī Abū Ḥanīfa al-Nuʿmān ibn

10 See I. K. Poonawala, *Biobibliography of Ismāʿīlī literature* (Malibu, 1977), pp. 31–132.

Muḥammad (d. 363/974), the foremost Ismāʿīlī jurist who was officially commissioned to prepare legal compendia. He codified Ismāʿīlī law by systematically collecting the firmly established *ḥadīths* transmitted from the *ahl al-bayt*, drawing on existing collections. Al-Nuʿmān's efforts culminated in his *Daʿāʾim al-Islām*, which served as the official code of the Fāṭimid state. The authority of the infallible ʿAlid imam and his teachings became a principal source of Ismāʿīlī law. The *Daʿāʾim al-Islām* has continued to be used by Ṭayyibī Ismāʿīlīs as their main authority in legal matters, while the Nizārī Ismāʿīlīs continue to be guided in their legal affairs by their living imams.

The Fāṭimid caliph-imam al-Ḥākim's reign (386–411/996–1021) witnessed the opening phase of what was to become known as the Druze religion. A number of *dāʿīs* who had come to Cairo from Persia and Central Asia, notably al-Akhram (d. 408/1018), Ḥamza and al-Darazī, began to propagate certain extremist ideas regarding al-Ḥākim and his imamate. Drawing on the traditions of the Shīʿite *ghulāt* and eschatological expectations of the early Ismāʿīlīs, these *dāʿīs* founded a new religious movement, and proclaimed the end of the era of Islam and the abrogation of its *sharīʿa*. By 408/1017 (the opening year of the Druze era) Ḥamza and al-Darazī were also publicly declaring al-Ḥākim's divinity. It was after al-Darazī that the adherents of this movement later became known as Daraziyya or Durūz; hence their general designation as Druzes.

The Fāṭimid *daʿwa* organisation in Cairo launched a campaign against the new doctrine. The *dāʿī* al-Kirmānī was invited to Cairo to refute officially the new doctrine from a theological perspective. He composed a number of treatises reiterating the Ismāʿīlī Shīʿite doctrine of the imamate and rejecting the idea of al-Ḥākim's divinity. Nonetheless, the Druze movement acquired momentum and popular appeal; and when al-Ḥākim disappeared mysteriously during one of his nocturnal outings in 411/1021, the Druze leaders interpreted this as a voluntary act initiating al-Ḥākim's *ghayba* (occultation). In the same year Ḥamza went into hiding; he was succeeded as the leader of the movement by Bahāʾ al-Dīn al-Muqtanā. With the subsequent persecution of the Druzes in Fāṭimid Egypt, the movement found its greatest success in Syria, where a number of Druze *dāʿīs* had been active.

The Druzes eventually developed their own body of theological doctrine. In particular, the extant letters and other writings of al-Muqtanā and Ḥamza have been collected into a canon, arranged in six books and designated as the *Rasāʾil al-ḥikma* (Epistles of wisdom), which has served as the sacred scripture of the Druzes. A highly closed and secretive community, and observing *taqiyya* very strictly, the Druzes who call themselves the Muwaḥḥidūn

(Unitarians) possess elaborate doctrines of Neoplatonic cosmology, eschatology and metempsychosis (*tanāsukh*). Considering al-Ḥākim as the last *maqām* (locus) of the Creator, the Druzes await his reappearance (*rajʿa*) together with Ḥamza, who is considered an imam. Druze teachings effectively represent a new religion falling outside Ismāʿīlism. Under the Ottomans the Druzes of Syria and Lebanon were ruled by their own *amīrs*, especially those belonging to the Maʿnid and Shihābid dynasties, who remained in power until the end of the twelfth/eighteenth century.

Meanwhile, the Qarāmiṭa had survived in Baḥrayn and in other communities scattered in Iraq, Yemen, Persia and Central Asia. All the Qarāmiṭa were still awaiting the reappearance of Muḥammad ibn Ismāʿīl as the *mahdī* and final *nāṭiq*, though some Qarmaṭī leaders themselves claimed Mahdism. After Abū Saʿīd al-Jannābī (d. 300/913), several of his sons rose to leadership of the Qarmaṭī state of Baḥrayn, where communal and egalitarian principles played an important role. Under his youngest son, Abū Ṭāhir Sulaymān (r. 311–32/923–44), the Qarāmiṭa became infamous for their anti-ʿAbbāsid raids into Iraq and their pillaging of the Meccan pilgrim caravans. Abū Ṭāhir's ravaging activities culminated in his attack on Mecca during the pilgrimage season in 317/930, when the Qarāmiṭa committed numerous abominations, and dislodged the Black Stone (*al-ḥajar al-aswad*) from the corner of the Kaʿba and carried it to al-Aḥsāʾ, their capital in Baḥrayn. This sacrilegious act, presumably committed in preparation for the coming of the *mahdī*, shocked the entire Muslim world and provided a unique opportunity for Sunnī polemicists to condemn the whole Ismāʿīlī movement as a conspiracy to destroy Islam. The Qarāmiṭa eventually returned the Black Stone in 339/950 – for a large ransom paid by the ʿAbbāsids and not, as alleged by anti-Ismāʿīlī sources, at the instigation of the Fāṭimid caliph. By the time the Qarmaṭī state of Baḥrayn was finally uprooted in 470/1077 by the local tribal chieftains, other Qarmaṭī groups in Persia, Iraq and elsewhere had either disintegrated or switched their allegiance to the Ismāʿīlī *daʿwa* of the Fāṭimids.

In the mean time, Ismāʿīlī *daʿwa* activities, especially outside the Fāṭimid dominions, reached their peak in the long reign of al-Mustanṣir (427–87/1036–94), even after the Sunnī Saljūqs replaced the Shīʿite Būyids as overlords of the ʿAbbāsids in 447/1055. The Fāṭimid *dāʿīs* won many converts in Iraq, Persia and Central Asia as well as Yemen, where the Ṣulayḥids ruled as vassals of the Fāṭimids from 439/1047 until 532/1138. On al-Mustanṣir's death in 487/1094 the unified Ismāʿīlī *daʿwa* split into two rival factions, as his son and original heir-designate Nizār (d. 488/1095) was deprived of his succession rights by the all-powerful Fāṭimid vizier al-Afḍal, who installed Nizār's younger brother on the Fāṭimid throne with the title al-Mustaʿlī biʾllāh (r. 487–95/1094–1101). The imamate of al-Mustaʿlī was also recognised by the Ismāʿīlī communities of Egypt, Yemen and western India. These Mustaʿlī Ismāʿīlīs traced the imamate in the progeny of al-Mustaʿlī. On the other hand, the Ismāʿīlīs of Persia supported the succession rights of Nizār and his descendants. The two factions were later designated as the Nizāriyya and the Mustaʿliyya.

The power of the Fāṭimid caliphate declined rapidly during its final decades. The Mustaʿlī Ismāʿīlīs themselves split into Ḥāfiẓī and Ṭayyibī branches on the assassination of al-Mustaʿlī's son and successor al-Āmir in 524/1130. Al-Āmir's successor on the Fāṭimid throne, al-Ḥāfiẓ, and the later Fāṭimid caliphs were recognised as imams by the *daʿwa* headquarters in Cairo and the Mustaʿlī Ismāʿīlīs of Egypt, Syria and a portion of the community in Yemen. These Mustaʿlī Ismāʿīlīs, known as the Ḥāfiẓiyya, did not long survive the downfall of the Fāṭimid dynasty in 567/1171. On the other hand, the Mustaʿlī community of Ṣulayḥid Yemen recognised the imamate of al-Āmir's infant son al-Ṭayyib and became known as the Ṭayyibiyya. According to the Ṭayyibīs the disappearance of al-Ṭayyib soon after his father's death in 524/1130 initiated another era of *satr* (concealment) during which the Ṭayyibī imams have all remained hidden (*mastūr*); the current *satr* will continue until the appearance of an imam from al-Ṭayyib's progeny. Meanwhile, the affairs of the Ṭayyibī *daʿwa* were led by *dāʿī*s with absolute authority, known as *dāʿī muṭlaq*. Around 997/1589 the Ṭayyibīs were divided over the question of the succession to their *dāʿī* into Dāʾūdī and Sulaymānī factions. The Dāʾūdīs, accounting for the bulk of the Ṭayyibī Ismāʿīlīs, were mainly converts of Hindu origin, and were known as Bohras in India, while Yemen remained the stronghold of the Sulaymānīs.

The Nizārī Ismāʿīlīs have had their own complex history. By the time of the Nizārī–Mustaʿlī schism of 487/1094, Ḥasan-i Ṣabbāḥ (d. 518/1124), who preached the Ismāʿīlī *daʿwa* within the Saljūq dominions in Persia, had emerged as the leader of the Persian Ismāʿīlīs. His acquisition of the fortress of Alamūt in 483/1090 had, in fact, signalled the foundation of what would become the Nizārī Ismāʿīlī state. In the dispute over the succession to al-Mustanṣir, Ḥasan supported Nizār's cause, and severed his relations with the Fāṭimid regime. Ḥasan then also founded the independent Nizārī Ismāʿīlī *daʿwa* on behalf of the Nizārī imam, who remained inaccessible. At the same time, *dāʿī*s dispatched from Alamūt organised an expanding Nizārī community in Syria.

From early on the Nizārī Ismāʿīlīs were preoccupied with survival in an extremely hostile environment. Nevertheless, they did maintain a sophisticated intellectual outlook and a literary tradition, elaborating their teachings in response to changed circumstances. Ḥasan-i Ṣabbāḥ himself is credited with restating in a more rigorous form the old Shīʿite doctrine of *taʿlīm*, or authoritative teaching by the imam of the time. Emphasising the autonomous teaching authority of each imam in his own time, this became the central doctrine of the Nizārīs who were thenceforth known as the Taʿlīmiyya. The intellectual challenge posed to the Sunnī establishment by the doctrine of *taʿlīm*, which also refuted the legitimacy of the ʿAbbāsid caliph as the spiritual spokesman of all Muslims, called forth the reaction of the Sunnī establishment. Many Sunnī scholars, led by Abū Ḥāmid al-Ghazālī (d. 505/1111), sought to refute this Ismāʿīlī doctrine.

The fourth lord of Alamūt, Ḥasan II (r. 557–61/1162–6) to whom the Nizārīs refer with the expression *ʿalā dhikrihi'l-salām* (on his mention be peace), declared the *qiyāma* (day of resurrection) in 559/1164, initiating a new phase in the religious history of the Nizārī community. Relying extensively on Ismāʿīlī *ta'wīl* and earlier traditions, Ḥasan II interpreted the *qiyāma* symbolically and spiritually. Ḥasan II was also recognised as an imam, a descendant of Nizār; and thereafter the Nizārī imamate continued in his line of descent.

The surrender of the Alamūt fortress to the all-conquering Mongols in 654/1256 sealed the fate of the Nizārī state. The Mongols massacred large numbers of Nizārīs, also destroying their fortresses in Persia. In Syria, where the Nizārīs attained the peak of their power and fame under their most eminent *dāʿī*, Rāshid al-Dīn Sinān (d. 589/1193), the sectarians attracted the attention of the Crusaders, who made them famous in Europe as the Assassins (derived from *ḥashīshiyyīn* – a local term of abuse). Medieval Europeans also disseminated a number of legends about the secret practices of the Nizārīs. By 671/1273 the Syrian Nizārī fortresses had all fallen into Mamlūk hands, but the Nizārīs were permitted to remain in their traditional abodes there as subjects of Mamlūks and Ottomans.

In the post-Alamūt period of their history the Nizārī Ismāʿīlī communities, scattered from Syria to Persia, Central Asia and South Asia, elaborated a diversity of religious and literary traditions in different languages. They also resorted to *taqiyya* practices under different external guises, especially Sufism. Indeed, by the ninth/fifteenth century a type of coalescence had developed between Persian Sufism and Nizārī Ismāʿīlism. An obscure dispute over the succession to Imām Shams al-Dīn Muḥammad (d. *c.* 710/1310) split the line of the Nizārī imams and their followers into the Qāsim-Shāhī and Muḥammad-Shāhī branches. The Muḥammad-Shāhī Nizārī imams transferred their seat to India in the tenth/sixteenth century, and by the end of the twelfth/eighteenth this line had become discontinued. By the end of the eleventh/seventeenth century the Qāsim-Shāhī Nizārī *da'wa* had been particularly successful in Afghanistan, Central Asia and the Indian subcontinent. In South Asia the converts became known as Khojas, who developed their own distinctive tradition of Nizārī Ismā'īlism, known as Satpanth (the 'true path'), as well as a devotional literature, the *ginān*s. The Qāsim-Shāhī Nizārī imams and communities have survived to the present time, and their last four imams have enjoyed prominence under their hereditary title of the Aga Khan.

The Zaydīs

Representing another major Shī'ite community, the general influence and geographical distribution of the Zaydiyya, named after their fourth imam, Zayd ibn 'Alī Zayn al-'Ābidīn, have been more restricted than those of the Twelvers and the Ismā'īlīs.[11] The Zaydī branch of Shī'ism developed out of Zayd ibn 'Alī's abortive revolt in 122/740. The movement was initially led by Zayd's son Yaḥyā, who escaped from Kūfa to Khurāsān and concentrated his activities in that eastern region. Counted as one of the Zaydī imams, Yaḥyā was eventually tracked down by the Umayyads and killed in 125/743. The Zaydīs were later led by another of Zayd's sons, 'Īsā (d. 166/783), and others recognised as their imams. In early 'Abbāsid times groups of Zaydīs participated in a number of abortive 'Alid revolts in the Ḥijāz and elsewhere. By the middle of the third/ninth century the Zaydīs had shifted their attention away from Kūfa and concentrated their activities in regions removed from the centres of 'Abbāsid power, namely the Caspian region in northern Persia and Yemen, where two Zaydī states were soon founded.

The early Zaydīs essentially retained the politically militant and religiously moderate attitude prevailing among the early Kūfan Shī'a. However, the Zaydiyya elaborated a doctrine of the imamate that clearly distinguished them from Imāmī Shī'ism and its two subsequent branches, the Ithnā 'Ashariyya and the Ismā'īliyya. The Zaydīs did not recognise a hereditary line of imams, nor did they attach any significance to the principle of the *naṣṣ*. Initially they accepted any member of the *ahl al-bayt* as an imam, though later their imams were restricted to the Fāṭimid 'Alids. According to Zaydī doctrine, if an imam wished to be recognised he would have to assert his claims publicly in a rising (*khurūj*) – sword in hand if necessary – in addition to having

11 Our discussion of the Zaydiyya is based on Madelung's *Der Imam al-Qāsim* and his numerous other studies.

the required religious knowledge (*ʿilm*). Many Zaydī imams were learned scholars and authors; and, in contrast to the Twelvers and the Ismāʿīlīs, the Zaydīs also excluded under-age males from the imamate. They also rejected the eschatological idea of a concealed *mahdī* and his expected return. As a result, messianic tendencies remained rather weak in Zaydī Shīʿism. Their emphasis on activism also made the observance of *taqiyya* alien to Zaydī teachings. The Zaydīs did, however, develop a doctrine of *hijra*, the obligation to emigrate from land dominated by unjust, non-Zaydī rulers.

During the second/eighth century the Zaydīs were doctrinally divided into two main groups, the Batriyya and the Jārūdiyya. Representing the moderate faction of the early Zaydiyya, the Batriyya upheld the caliphates of Abū Bakr and ʿUmar. They held that though ʿAlī was the most excellent (*al-afḍal*) of Muslims to succeed the Prophet, the caliphates of his less excellent predecessors (*al-mafḍūl*) were nevertheless valid, because ʿAlī had pledged allegiance to them. In the case of ʿUthmān the matter was more complicated; the Batriyya either abstained from judgement or repudiated him for the last six years of his rule.The Batriyya, by contrast to the Jārūdiyya, did not ascribe any particular religious knowledge to the *ahl al-bayt*, or to the ʿAlids, and accepted the knowledge transmitted in the Muslim community. They were closely affiliated to the Kūfan traditionist school and, with the latter's absorption into Sunnism in the third/ninth century, the Batriyya Zaydī tradition also disappeared. Thereafter the views of the Jārūdiyya on the imamate prevailed in Zaydī Shīʿism. The Jārūdiyya adopted the more radical doctrinal views of the Imāmiyya.

By the fourth/tenth century Zaydī doctrine, influenced by Jārūdī and Muʿtazilite elements, had been largely formulated. The Zaydīs were less concerned than Imāmī Shīʿa to condemn the early caliphs and the Muslim community at large. They held that ʿAlī, al-Ḥasan and al-Ḥusayn had been imams by designation (*naṣṣ*) of the Prophet. However, the designation had been unclear and obscure (*khafī* or *ghayr jalī*), and its intended meaning could be understood only through investigation. After al-Ḥusayn ibn ʿAlī the imamate could be claimed by any qualified descendant of al-Ḥasan and al-Ḥusayn who was prepared to launch an armed uprising (*khurūj*) against the illegitimate rulers and issue a formal summons (*daʿwa*) for gaining the allegiance of the people. Religious knowledge, ability to render independent ruling (*ijtihād*) and piety were emphasised as the qualifications of the imam, in addition to his ʿAlid descent. The imams were not generally considered as divinely protected from error and sin (*maʿṣūm*), with the exception of the first three imams. The list of the Zaydī imams has never been completely fixed, though many of them are unanimously accepted. There were, indeed, periods without any Zaydī imam; and in practice at times there was more than one. Due to high requirements in terms of religious learning the Zaydīs often backed ʿAlid pretenders and rulers as summoners (*dāʿīs*) or imams with restricted status (*muḥtasibūn* or *muqtaṣida*), rather than as full imams (*sābiqūn*).

In theology, the Kūfan Zaydiyya, like the early Imāmiyya, were predestinarian and opposed to the Muʿtazila, but later developed close relations with this rationalist school of *kalām*. By the fourth/tenth century the Zaydīs had adopted practically all the principal Muʿtazilite tenets, including one rejected by the Twelvers and the Ismāʿīlīs: the unconditional punishment of the unrepentant sinner. In law, the Zaydīs initially relied on the teachings of Zayd ibn ʿAlī himself and other ʿAlid authorities. By the end of the third/ninth century, however, four legal schools (*madhhabs*) had emerged on the basis of the teachings of different Zaydī scholars, including Imām al-Qāsim ibn Ibrāhīm al-Rassī (d. 246/860), founder of the school later prevalent in Yemen as well as among a faction of the Caspian Zaydīs.

Zaydī doctrines were first effectively disseminated in Persia by some local followers of al-Rassī, who lived and taught on the Jabal al-Rass near Medina. As a result, al-Rassī's legal and theological teachings, which were partially in agreement with Muʿtazilite tenets, were spread in western Ṭabaristān (today's Māzandarān) in the Caspian region, known in medieval times as Daylam. In 250/864 the Ḥasanid al-Ḥasan ibn Zayd led the local Daylamīs in a revolt against the region's Ṭāhirid governor, who ruled on behalf of the ʿAbbāsids and established the first Zaydī ʿAlid state in Ṭabaristān with its capital at Āmul. On his death in 270/884 he was succeeded by his brother Muḥammad ibn Zayd. The two ʿAlid brothers, who adopted the regnal title al-Dāʿī ila'l-Ḥaqq and were not generally recognised as full imams, supported Zaydī doctrine and Muʿtazilite theology. The first period of Zaydī rule in Ṭabaristān ended in 287/900 when Muḥammad ibn Zayd was killed in battle against the Sāmānids, who restored their rule – and Sunnism – to Daylam.

In 301/914 Zaydī ʿAlid rule was restored in Ṭabaristān by the Ḥusaynid al-Ḥasan ibn ʿAlī al-Uṭrūsh, known as al-Nāṣir li'l-Ḥaqq. He reigned until his death in 304/917, and was succeeded by his vizier, the Ḥasanid al-Ḥasan ibn al-Qāsim, also known as al-Dāʿī ila'l-Ḥaqq. Al-Ḥasan had an eventful career and was eventually killed in 316/928 by Mardāvīj ibn Ziyār (d. 323/935), the founder of the Ziyārid dynasty of northern Persia. At the same time Ṭabaristān was invaded by the Sāmānids, who once again ended Zaydī rule there. Al-Nāṣir had converted many Daylamīs and Gīlīs, and was generally recognised as an imam; it was also in his armies that the Būyids of Daylam had first risen to prominence. A learned scholar with numerous works on theology and law, al-Nāṣir's teaching differed somewhat from that of al-Rassī; in particular, in ritual and law he was close to the Kūfan Zaydī tradition and to Imāmī doctrines. In fact, al-Nāṣir founded his own doctrinal school of Zaydī Shīʿism, known as the Nāṣiriyya, in distinction from the older school of the Qāsimiyya prevalent in Daylam and later in Yemen. As a result, the Daylamī Zaydīs were thenceforth divided into two rival factions: the Qāsimiyya, concentrated in western Ṭabaristān and Rūyān; and the Nāṣiriyya, in eastern Gīlān and the interior of Daylam. There was much antagonism between the two Zaydī communities, which often supported different imams, *dāʿī*s or *amīr*s. Matters were further complicated by ethnic differences and the close ties existing between the Qāsimiyya and the Zaydīs of Yemen. Prolonged Zaydī sectarian hostilities ceased in Daylam when around the middle of the fourth/tenth century Abū ʿAbd Allāh Muḥammad al-Mahdī li-Dīn Allāh (d. 360/970), an imam of the Qāsimiyya, declared both doctrinal schools equally valid because they were based on the *ijtihād* of legitimate imams. This ruling became generally accepted by the Caspian Zaydīs, who nevertheless remained divided in terms of their adherence to the two schools.

In the mean time, after the collapse of the second Zaydī state of Ṭabaristān in 316/928 under Sāmānid attacks, other ʿAlid rulers had appeared in the Caspian provinces. In 320/932 Hawsam, and later Lāhījān in Gīlān, became the seats of the Zaydī ʿAlid dynasty of the Thāʾirids, who reigned as *amīr*s without claiming the Zaydī imamate, as well as other ʿAlid rulers supporting the Nāṣiriyya school. At the same time, a number of ʿAlids recognised as Zaydī imams by the Qāsimiyya were active in Daylamān, with their seat at Langā. The Zaydī imams belonging to the Qāsimiyya branch espoused the theological doctrines of the Baṣran school of Muʿtazilism. In the course of the sixth/twelfth century the Caspian Zaydīs lost much of their prominence to the Nizārī Ismāʿīlīs, who had then successfully established themselves in Daylamān with their seat at Alamūt. Subsequently, the Zaydīs, now restricted mainly to eastern Gīlān, were further weakened due to incessant factional quarrels among different ʿAlid pretenders. However, minor ʿAlid dynasties and Zaydī communities survived in Gīlān and Daylamān until the tenth/sixteenth century when the Zaydīs of the Caspian provinces converted to Twelver Shīʿism under Ṣafavid rule over Persia. Thereafter Zaydī Shīʿism was confined to Yemen.

In Yemen, Zaydī rule and imamate were founded in 284/897 by Imām Yaḥyā ibn al-Ḥusayn al-Hādī ila'l-Ḥaqq (d. 298/911), a Ḥasanid ʿAlid and grandson of al-Qāsim ibn Ibrāhīm al-Rassī. With the help of the local tribes he established himself in Ṣaʿda, in northern Yemen, which remained the stronghold of Zaydī Shīʿism, *daʿwa* and learning in Yemen. Concerning the imamate, he adopted the radical Shīʿite and Jārūdī position, condemning Abū Bakr and ʿUmar as usurpers of ʿAlī's rights. In his theology al-Hādī essentially supported the contemporary doctrine of the Muʿtazilite school of Baghdad, while in law his teaching was based on that of his grandfather Imām al-Rassī with more specifically Shīʿite views, which were further elaborated by his sons, Muḥammad al-Murtaḍā (d. 310/922) and Aḥmad al-Nāṣir li-Dīn Allāh (d. 322/934), who were consecutively recognised as imams. Al-Hādī's legal teachings, collected and further elaborated later, provided the foundation of the Hādawiyya legal school, which became authoritative in parts of the Caspian Zaydī community while serving as the only recognised school in Yemen.

The descendants of Imām al-Hādī, after his two sons, quarrelled among themselves and failed to be acknowledged as imams, undermining Zaydī rule in Yemen. In the fifth/eleventh century the Yemenī Zaydīs experienced further problems due to two schismatic movements in their community. Earlier, in 389/999, the Zaydī imamate of the Rassid line had been reinstated in Yemen by al-Manṣūr bi'llāh al-Qāsim al-ʿIyānī (d. 393/1003), another descendant of Imām al-Rassī. However, al-Manṣūr's son and successor al-Ḥusayn al-Mahdī li-Dīn Allāh, also recognised as an imam, made the unusual Zaydī claim of being the Shīʿite *mahdī*; when he was killed in battle in 404/1013 his partisans did, in fact, deny his death and awaited his return. These Zaydīs became known as the Ḥusayniyya. Led by the descendants of al-Mahdī, the Ḥusayniyya Zaydīs had numerous confrontations with the Ismāʿīlī Ṣulayḥids who ruled over parts of Yemen as vassals of the Fāṭimids. Later in the fifth/eleventh century another splinter Zaydī sect, known as the Muṭarrifiyya, appeared in Yemen. Its founder, Muṭarrif ibn Shihāb (d. after 459/1067), interpreted the Zaydī teachings of the earlier authorities and imams in an arbitrary fashion. As a result, serious discrepancies arose between the Muṭarrifiyya views and the teachings of the contemporary Yemenī Zaydī imams, as well as those of the Caspian Qāsimiyya Zaydīs who espoused Baṣran Muʿtazilite doctrines. The Muṭarrifiyya were also inclined towards pietism and asceticism, and founded numerous *hijras* or 'abodes of emigration', where they engaged in worship and ascetic practices. The Ḥusayniyya and Muṭarrifiyya sects disappeared by the ninth/fifteenth century.

The Zaydī imamate and its fortunes were briefly restored in Yemen by Aḥmad ibn Sulaymān al-Mutawakkil (532–66/1138–71), who favoured the unity of the Zaydiyya and recognised the Zaydī teachings of the Caspian authorities. As a result, numerous Zaydī texts of Caspian provenance were brought to

Yemen. At the same time, certain Yemenī imams were now acknowledged by the Caspian Zaydīs. A key role was played in these unifying developments by Shams al-Dīn Jaʿfar ibn Abī Yaḥyā (d. 573/1177), a Zaydī jurist and scholar, who founded a school holding that the Zaydī imams of the Caspian region were equal in authority to those in Yemen.

The Zaydī imamate prevailed in Yemen even after the occupation of southern Arabia by the Sunnī Ayyūbids in 569/1174, though the power of the imams was now considerably restricted. The Yemenī Zaydīs were at times obliged to develop better relations with the Sunnīs by modifiying some of their own doctrines. For instance, Imām al-Muʾayyad biʾllāh Yaḥyā ibn Ḥamza (729–47/1329–46) praised the early caliphs as the Companions of the Prophet deserving respect equal to that due to ʿAlī. In later centuries, too, especially as the Zaydī imams extended their rule to the predominantly Sunnī lowlands of Yemen, the Zaydīs attempted to achieve a certain doctrinal rapport with their Sunnī subjects. In particular, they favoured the neo-Sunnī school that emerged out of the teachings of Sayyid Muḥammad ibn Ibrāhīm al-Wazīr (d. 840/1436). On the other hand, the Yemenī Zaydīs maintained their traditional hostility towards the Sufis, even though a Zaydī school of Sufism was founded in Yemen in the eighth/fourteenth century. They also had prolonged conflicts with the Yemenī Ismāʿīlīs, and wrote numerous polemical treatises refuting their doctrines.

The final phase of the Zaydī imamate in Yemen started with al-Manṣūr biʾllāh al-Qāsim ibn Muḥammad (1006–29/1597–1620), the founder of the Qāsimī dynasty of imams who ruled over much of Yemen until modern times. A warrior-imam, al-Manṣūr reaffirmed the Jārūdī position of the Zaydīs on the imamate and pointed to certain divergencies between the Zaydī and Muʿtazilite views; he also fought against the Ottoman occupation of Yemen (945–1045/1538–1636). However, it was his son and successor, al-Muʾayyad biʾllāh Muḥammad (1029–54/1620–44), who expelled the Ottomans from Yemen in 1045/1636. Thereafter Ṣanʿāʾ served as the capital of an independent Zaydī state and imamate for more than two centuries until 1289/1872, when Yemen once again became an Ottoman province. The later Qāsimī Zaydī imams ruled over Yemen on a purely dynastic basis (until 1382/1962), though still claiming the title of imam.

The Nuṣayrīs or ʿAlawīs

A Shīʿite community with syncretic doctrines, the Nuṣayriyya, who were initially also called the Namīriyya, retained the traditions of the early Shīʿite *ghulāt*. The origins of the Nuṣayrīs may be traced to a certain Imāmī *ghālī*, Muḥammad ibn Nuṣayr al-Namīrī (d. 270/883), who was a supporter of the tenth and eleventh Twelver imams and also enjoyed some favour at the ʿAbbāsid court in Baghdad. Ibn Nuṣayr was particularly close to the eleventh imam, al-Ḥasan al-ʿAskarī (d. 260/873f.) and, according to Nuṣayrī tradition, was entrusted with a new revelation by him. Not much more is known about the eponymous founder of the Nuṣayriyya other than that he deified the imams and professed metempsychosis (*tanāsukh*), which has an important function in Nuṣayrī cosmogony. After Ibn Nuṣayr, the sect founded by him continued to grow under other leaders such as Muḥammad ibn Jundab and ʿAbd Allāh al-Junbulānī al-Jannān (d. 287/900), who was of Persian origin and was possibly responsible for incorporating the Persian festivals of the spring and autumn equinoxes, Nawrūz and Mihragān, into Nuṣayrī rituals, celebrated as the days when the divinity of ʿAlī is manifested in the sun.

Abū ʿAbd Allāh al-Ḥusayn ibn Ḥamdān al-Khaṣībī (d. *c*. 346/957), who initially led the sect in the Baghdad Shīʿite suburb of Karkh and was also a poet at the Būyid court, was the person responsible for propagating the Nuṣayrī doctrines in northern Syria, the permanent stronghold of the community. The author of numerous works, he dedicated his *Kitāb al-hidāya al-kubrā* (Book of the great guidance) to Sayf al-Dawla (r. 333–56/944–67), the Shīʿite Ḥamdānid *amīr* of Aleppo. In 423/1032 al-Khaṣībī's grandson and student Abū Saʿīd Maymūn ibn al-Qāsim al-Ṭabarānī (d. 426/1034f.) left Aleppo for Lādhiqiyya (Laodicea) in the northern coastal region of Syria, then still under Byzantine domination. Al-Ṭabarānī became the real founder of the Nuṣayrī community and teachings; his numerous writings account for the bulk of the Nuṣayrī sacred scriptures. As a result of the efforts of al-Ṭabarānī and his disciples, the rural inhabitants of the Syrian coastal mountain range converted to Nuṣayrism.

The later medieval history of the Nuṣayrīs is rather obscure. They had encounters with the Frankish Crusaders who established themselves in the northern part of the Jabal Anṣāriyya (today known as Jabal al-ʿAlawiyyīn), the heartland of the community. They also had prolonged conflicts with the Nizārī Ismāʿīlīs, who by the middle of the sixth/twelfth century had acquired a network of fortresses in the same area. In 584/1188, following Saladin's capture of Lādhiqiyya and a number of fortresses in the region, Jabal Anṣāriyya was incorporated into the Ayyūbid sultanate. By 622/1225 the Nuṣayrīs had appealed for help to some Bedouin tribes of the Jabal Sinjār to repel Ismāʿīlī attacks. Thereupon, a number of these tribes settled in the Jabal Anṣāriyya and later evolved into the Nuṣayrī tribes of the Ḥaddādiyya, Matāwira and others. In Mamlūk times both Baybars and Qalāwūn unsuccessfully attempted to convert the Nuṣayrīs to Sunnī Islam. Soon afterwards the famous Ḥanbalī jurist Ibn Taymiyya (d. 728/1328) issued a *fatwā* against the Nuṣayrīs, describing them as more heretical than even idolaters, and authorising *jihād* against them. The Mamlūks also made efforts to destroy Nuṣayrī books and confiscate their properties. Under the Ottomans, however, the Nuṣayrīs were recognised as a distinct group with their own judicial practices. Intent on emphasising their Shīʿite roots, in the 1340s/1920s the Nuṣayrīs, situated in Syria, Lebanon and south-eastern Turkey, changed their name to ʿAlawīs.

The Nuṣayrīs or ʿAlawīs are a secretive community, observing *taqiyya* and guarding their literature and doctrines closely. Even within the community the Nuṣayrī teachings are accessible only to the initiated members (*khāṣṣa*), as distinct from the uninitiated masses (*ʿāmma*); women are excluded from the process. At the basis of the Nuṣayrī complex religious system of thought is a cosmogony. Nuṣayrīs also believe in metempsychosis (*tanāsukh*) and incarnation (*ḥulūl*) of the divine essence (*maʿnā*) in certain historical and mythical figures as well as the imams. The Nuṣayrī religion indeed draws on pre-Islamic, Christian and Islamic traditions (both Sunnī and Shīʿite). They also resort to allegorical interpretation (*ta'wīl*) of the Qur'ān. Central in this system of thought is the deification and exclusiveness of ʿAlī ibn Abī Ṭālib. Aspects of Nuṣayrī teachings are to be found in the *Kitāb al-haft wa'l-aẓilla* (Book of the heptad and the shadows), a Mufaḍḍalī-Nuṣayrī text preserved by the Ismāʿīlīs, who recruited converts from the Nuṣayrī community in the sixth/twelfth century.

Espousing a cyclical view of history, the Nuṣayrīs hold that the deity has been manifested in seven eras (*akwār* or *adwār*), each time in the form of a trinity. In each case, two entities or persons emanate from the divine essence (*maʿnā*), namely *ism*, the Name (or *ḥijāb*, the Veil), and *bāb*, the Gate. In each era the *maʿnā* is veiled by the presence of *ism* or *ḥijāb*, representing the prophets from Adam to Muḥammad. Each prophet is, in turn, accompanied by a *bāb*, the gate through which the believer may contemplate the mystery of divinity. In the seventh and final era, that of Islam, the divine trinity is represented by ʿAlī as *maʿnā*, Muḥammad as *ism* or *ḥijāb* and Salmān al-Fārisī as *bāb*. In Nuṣayrī thought this trinity is designated symbolically by *'ayn–mīm–sīn'*, standing for the first letters of the names ʿAlī, Muḥammad and Salmān and functioning as the primary initiatory expression of the Nuṣayrīs. Later the deity was manifested in the imams and their disciples. For instance, Ibn Nuṣayr himself is regarded as the *bāb* of the eleventh Ithnā ʿAsharī imam, al-Ḥasan al-ʿAskarī, whose secret revelation was preserved exclusively for the Nuṣayrīs. The syncretic nature of the Nuṣayrī religion is also reflected in the

Nuṣayrī calendar of festivals rooted in different local, Persian, Christian and Islamic traditions, which are often interpreted allegorically.

The Khārijites

Representing one of the earliest schismatic movements in Islam, the original Khārijites (Khawārij) may be identified as those who seceded from ʿAlī's army in protest against his arbitration agreement with Muʿāwiya after the battle of Ṣiffīn in 37/657. They were initially also called the Ḥarūriyya, after the locality (Ḥarūrāʾ) near Kūfa to which the first seceders had retreated, as well as the Shurāt (sing. Shārī, 'the vendor'), signifying those who sold their souls for the cause of God. Seriously opposed to both Sunnī and Shīʿite Islam, to ʿUthmān and Muʿāwiya as well as ʿAlī, the Khārijites organised a rapidly spreading movement, comprised of numerous branches and sects, that many times in the later history of Islam challenged any form of dynastic rule. Only the Ibāḍiyya (or Abāḍiyya), the most moderate branch of the Khārijites, as well as their literature, have survived, and Ibāḍī communities are still to be found in Oman, East Africa and southern Algeria. The heresiographers with their biases provide the main source of information on non-Ibāḍī Khārijites.

The Khārijites did not have a uniform body of doctrine. But they were uncompromising in their application of the Islamic theocratic principle holding that 'judgement belongs to God alone' (*lā ḥukma illā li'llāḥ*), after which they were also called the Muḥakkima. Even caliphs or imams must observe this principle as embodied in the Qur'ān. If they deviate in any sense from the right conduct, they must repent or be removed, if necessary by force, notwithstanding their previous meritorious behaviour and services to Islam. The unjust imam, who has thus lost his legitimacy, and his partisans are all considered infidels. Any Muslim who fails to dissociate himself (*barāʾa*) openly from them shares their state of infidelity. Similarly, Muslims who do not declare their solidarity (*walāya*) with the just imams, such as Abū Bakr, ʿUmar and imams recognised by the Khārijites, are infidels. In their view both ʿUthmān and ʿAlī became infidels, though they had initially ruled legitimately; ʿUthmān during the first six years of his caliphate and ʿAlī until his acceptance of the arbitration. Their emphasis on right conduct, which would guarantee the believer's salvation, led to continuous factionalism within the Khārijite movement. According to general Khārijite doctrine the establishment of the imamate is obligatory on the community, and the imam is to be elected. Any qualified Muslim could be elected as the legitimate imam deserving of the title commander of the faithful (*amīr al-muʾminīn*). The imam's qualifications were related to his religious merit rather than any legitimist principles or hereditary attributes. Among these qualifications, special emphasis was placed on his moral austerity as well as his duty to 'command right and prohibit wrong'; he was also expected to lead the *jihād* against the non-Khārijite Muslims.

The Khārijites were originally concentrated in Kūfa, where they survived until early ʿAbbāsid times. However, they soon established their stronghold in Baṣra, where they organised numerous revolts. Khārijite activities assumed serious dimensions after the second civil war in Islam, following Yazīd's death in 64/683, and also spread to Persia and the eastern regions. Meanwhile, the Islamic egalitarianism of the Khawārij had drawn the *mawālī* to their movement. In the event, large numbers of the Azāriqa, a major Khārijite sect in Baṣra, sought refuge in Persia and became active in Fārs, Kirmān and other provinces there. Named after their leader, Nāfiʿ ibn al-Azraq al-Ḥanafī, the Azāriqa represented the most radical sect of the Khawārij. They subscribed to the principle of *istiʿrāḍ* (religious murder) and held the killing of the women and children of non-Khārijite Muslims licit, also considering as polytheists (*mushrikūn*) even those Khārijites who did not join them. Meanwhile, the Najdiyya Khārijites, who repudiated some of the more radical views of the Azāriqa, were mainly active in Arabia. The Khārijites who refused to join them were considered only as hypocrites (*munāfiqūn*); thus they were not to be killed. Unlike the Azāriqa, who condemned *taqiyya*, the Najdiyya also permitted this practice. The ʿAjārida, a sub-sect of the Najdiyya with its own numerous groups, were active in Khurāsān and other regions of the eastern Iranian world. By the end of the third/ninth century the Khārijites as an insurrectional movement had practically disappeared from Persia and Iraq. Thenceforth Khārijism survived in its moderate forms in the remoter corners of the Islamic world, notably in North Africa and eastern Arabia.

The moderate wing of Khārijism was represented by the Ṣufriyya, who have not survived, and the Ibāḍiyya, with its own internal divisions. In contrast to the Azāriqa, the Ibāḍiyya considered other Muslims as well as the sinners of their own community as 'infidels by ingratitude' (*kuffār niʿma*) rather than polytheists (*mushrikūn*); therefore they rejected their murder. It was also licit to intermarry with them. The practice of *istiʿrāḍ* was, however, authorised by Abū Yazīd Makhlad ibn Kaydād (d. 336/947), one of the imams of the Nukkārī sub-sect of the Ibāḍiyya who was also involved in a long, drawn-out conflict with the Fāṭimid rulers of North Africa. Earlier the Fāṭimids had uprooted the Ibāḍī imamate and principality of the Rustamids of Tāhert in the Maghrib. However, the success of Ibāḍī Khārijism among the Berbers of North Africa proved lasting.

The Ibāḍiyya were also less involved than other Khārijite communities in armed rebellions. The Ibāḍīs produced eminent scholars and played an important role in the elaboration of religious scholarship in early Islam. All this contributed to the survival of the Ibāḍī Khārijites in the Muslim world. Since the middle of the second/eighth century the Ibāḍī Khārijites have had another imamate and stronghold in eastern Arabia, and they have ruled intermittently over various parts of Oman. Many members of the Yaʿrubid and Āl Bū Saʿīd dynasties of Oman and East Africa were, in fact, acknowledged as Ibāḍī imams. After Saʿīd ibn Aḥmad (d. *c.* 1226/1811), however, the Bū Saʿīdī sultans of Oman styled themselves sayyids rather than imams.

4

Islamic law: history and transformation

WAEL B. HALLAQ

Introduction

If we must refer to the *sharīʿa* as 'Islamic law', then we must do so with considerable caution. The latter expression bears a connotation that combines modern notions of law with a particular brand of modern politics, both of which were largely – if not entirely – absent from the original landscape of the *sharīʿa* we are considering here. Throughout the last three or four centuries European modernity has produced legal systems and legal doctrines that are almost exclusively the preserve of the equally modern nation-state. Intrinsic to its behaviour, the modern state is systemically and systematically geared towards the transformation and homogenisation of both the social order and the national citizen, features that have a direct bearing on law. To accomplish these goals the state engages in *systemic* surveillance, discipline and punishment. Its educational and cultural institutions, among others, are designed to manufacture the citizen who is respectful of law, submissive to notions of order and discipline, industrious and economically productive. Without the law and its tools of surveillance and punishment, no state apparatus can exist. Ergo the centrality, in the definition and concept of the state, of the element of violence, and of the state's exclusive right to threaten its use.

Now, this vision of the law perforce permeates our notions of what it, as a species, represents. Yet one would immediately misrepresent both the *modus vivendi* and *modus operandi* of the *sharīʿa* should such modern assumptions be allowed to partake in its definition. The misrepresentation may further be aggravated by the fundamental modern separation between law and morality, which the *sharīʿa* 'lacked' and which has for long been deemed one of its shortcomings.[1] To this important point I shall return in due course.

1 On the modern splits into fact/value and moral/legal in the context of *sharīʿa* see Wael Hallaq, 'Groundwork of the moral law: A new look at the Qurʾān and the genesis of *sharīʿa*', *Islamic Law and Society*, 17, 1 (forthcoming, 2010), esp. section II.

The differences, noted above, between the law of the modern state and the *sharīʿa* suggest that, prior to the dawn of modernity, the *sharīʿa* coexisted with a body politic far weaker than the modern state, lacking the characteristics of the latter, including corporate identity, a public welfare apparatus, a universal administrative and bureaucratic control, surveillance and law making. With the encroachments of modernity on the Muslim world during the nineteenth and twentieth centuries, the *sharīʿa* was first gradually absorbed and later largely destroyed by the modern Muslim nation-states, leaving remnants of it (mainly in the sphere of personal status) to be remoulded in a fashion that served those states' imperatives, mainly in the cause of social engineering.[2] The new states and societies that have now emerged in the Muslim world lack nearly all the fundamental attributes that characterised the weaker pre-modern states and traditional societies in which the *sharīʿa* had operated and, indeed, taken as a premise for its functioning. Not only such aspects of it as family law, but even criminal law, have been dramatically refashioned and appropriated by the modern state for political gain, particularly for garnering the much-coveted mantle of political legitimacy. This appropriation was concomitant with a structural transformation in the meaning of *sharīʿa*, now regarded as a body of texts and as an uncompromising deontology almost entirely severed from the anthropological and sociological backgrounds that sustained its functioning throughout a millennium before the rise of modernity. This is to say that one of the chief effects of this transformation was the subjection of the *sharīʿa* to a process of 'entexting', a process that began in British India and continued unrelentingly under the nationalist regimes after independence.[3] Stripped of its traditional anthropological, sociological and institutional underpinnings (which defined how traditional substantive law was modulated and applied in social contexts, and in turn how these contexts allowed this law to assume the existence of a moral community), the *sharīʿa* has become an entexted and codified law, existing within modern-state legal structures and without the traditional checks and balances that the moral community had afforded.

Yet another modern transformation, intimated above, occurred through the introduction of a line of separation between law and morality.[4] Since the *sharīʿa* was seen as having failed to distinguish conceptually between the two

2 For a detailed analysis see Wael B. Hallaq, *Sharia: Theory, practice, transformations* (Cambridge, 2009), chap. 16.

3 On the processes and significance of 'entexting' the *sharīʿa* see Wael B. Hallaq, 'What is Sharia?', *Yearbook of Islamic and Middle Eastern Law, 2005–2006*, vol. XII (Leiden, 2007).

4 Hallaq, 'Groundwork of the moral law', section II.

and to separate them in practice, the legislatures of the modern Muslim nation-states as well as individual legal thinkers and reform-minded Muslims followed colonialist policies and orientalist understanding in enhancing the segregation of the two spheres. Among the consequences of this segregation has been the rise of the modern distinction between *ʿibādāt* and *muʿāmalāt*, the former referring to worship and ritual belonging to the 'domain of God' and the latter referring to the 'properly' legal transactions between and among social individuals. Known and acknowledged by jurists for centuries, the distinction now acquired an entirely new meaning deriving from the European separation between the private and public spheres. Belief in God became a private matter, having almost nothing to do with the state and its positive law, both of which regulate the social sphere. For the first time in history, the *sharīʿa* in many modern Muslim countries was made to conform to the maxim 'give to God what is to God, and to Caesar what is to Caesar'.

The modern segregation of the 'ritual' from the 'legal' has been a function of overlooking the moral force of the law, a failure to appreciate both the *legal* ramifications of *ʿibādāt* rituals and the *moral* ramifications of those 'strictly legal' provisions of *muʿāmalāt*. While this fluid interchangeability between the moral and the legal could never obtain in modern law, it was the cornerstone of *sharīʿa* and its functioning in the social order; which is to say that the failure, if not deliberate, was necessary and inevitable in a process in which the modern state, by its very nature, had to assume the role of an amoral lawgiver.

But the traditional *technical* separation between *ʿibādāt* and *muʿāmalāt* had an entirely different function, one that in fact underscored the importance of the moral for that which we now regard as strictly legal. Traditionally, *fiqh* books (containing both substantive and procedural law) begin their exposition with five chapters or 'books' (*kutub*; sing. *kitāb*), reflecting, in strict order, four out of the five pillars of Islam,[5] the *arkān*, on which fundamental religious beliefs rested. These books discuss (a) ritual purification (*ṭahāra*), which was preparatory and a prerequisite for (b) performance of prayer (*ṣalāt*); (c) payment of alms-tax (*zakāt*); (d) performance of pilgrimage (*ḥajj*); and (e) fasting (*ṣawm*). The priority of these 'ritualistic' books in the overall corpus of the law is reflected in their universal placement at the beginning, a long-standing tradition that no jurist appears to have violated. Furthermore, they often

5 The fifth, which is in fact first in order, is the *shahāda* (testimony) or double *shahāda*, namely, that 'there is no god but God and that Muḥammad is the messenger of God'. This double *shahāda* did not receive coverage in legal works, as its implications were strictly theological. For more on these implications see Wael B. Hallaq, 'Fashioning the moral subject: Sharia's technologies of the self', unpublished MS.

occupy as much as one-quarter to one-third of the entire body of these treatises.[6] Their placement was not merely of symbolic importance; it had a function that made this ritualistic grouping a logical and functional antecedent. The function was subliminal, programmatic and deeply psychological,[7] fashioning the moral subject and laying the foundations for achieving willing obedience to the law that followed – that is, the regulations affecting, among much else, persons and property. The legal treatises, depending on the school and the jurist, continue their exposition with either contractual and pecuniary subjects (such as sales, agency, pledge, partnerships, rent etc.) or family law (marriage, various forms of marital dissolution, custody, maintenance, inheritance etc.). Following these rules one usually finds sections dealing with offences against life and limb, some regulated by the Qurʾān (*ḥudūd*), and others by principles of retaliation or monetary compensation (*qiṣāṣ*). The last sections of legal works usually treat adjudication and rules of evidence and procedure, and often include an exposition of *jihād* (law of war and peace), although in some schools or juristic writings this section appears earlier in the treatise. It bears repeating that, whatever the arrangement of books within the treatises, the materials dedicated to the elaboration of so-called rituals always come first, having universal precedence over all else.

If *sharīʿa* is divine guidance, then this guidance had to be as much imbued with morality as legality, which is to say that all capable Muslim individuals (*mukallafs*) were required to do what is right (as opposed to what is strictly legal). Accordingly, the *sharīʿa* came to organise human acts into various categories, ranging from the moral to the legal, without however making such distinctions in either a conscious or typological manner. In fact, there are no words in Arabic, the lingua franca of the law, for the contrastive modern notions of moral/legal. Thus, conforming to any of five norms, all acts are regarded as *sharʿī* (i.e. subject to the regulation of the *sharīʿa* and therefore pronounced as law, in its jural-cum-moral sense). The norm or category of the forbidden (*ḥarām*) entails punishment upon commission of an act deemed prohibited, while that of the obligatory (*wājib*) demands punishment upon omission of an act whose performance is decreed legally necessary. Breach of contract or committing adultery, not to mention uprooting trees or hunting within the Meccan sanctuary, are just some of the infractions falling within the

6 However, the Mālikīs add to these five a chapter on *jihād*, discussed by the other schools usually towards the end of their books. For the Mālikīs see Jamāl al-Dīn ibn ʿUmar ibn al-Ḥājib, *Jāmiʿ al-ummahāt*, ed. Abū Abd al-Raḥmān al-Akhḍarī (Damascus and Beirut, 1421/2000), pp. 243ff.

7 On the function of these books see Hallaq, 'Fashioning the moral subject'.

ḥarām category, while prayer and payment of pecuniary debts are instances of the *wājib*. Both categories require punishment upon non-compliance, while the diametrical, ungraded opposition of punishable/non-punishable deprives the individual of any freedom of action or choice. The distinctly punitive outlook embedded in these two categories initially led several modern scholars to the notion, now a century old, that the *sharīʿa* qualifies and acts as 'law' only when rules belonging to these two categories are involved ('law' here is, of course, essentially assumed to be a *positive* system of rules). The three remaining categories – the recommended (*mandūb*), the neutral (*mubāḥ*) and the disapproved (*makrūh*) – do not, in the view of this scholarship, constitute law proper, as they do not possess any *truly* coercive or punitive content. In other words they are said to be unenforceable, since commission of the disapproved and non-commission of the recommended do not entail punishment in any real sense. Instead, their omission and commission, respectively, entail a reward, assumed to await the individual in the hereafter. Similarly, the category of the neutral prescribes neither permission nor prohibition, leaving the choice entirely up to the preferences of the individual. The neutral, it must be stressed, is a strictly legal category rather than an area in which the *sharīʿa* failed, or did not care, to regulate human acts. Put differently, categorising an act as neutral is both a deliberate choice and a conscious commitment not to assign particular values to particular acts.

The punitive character of the obligatory and forbidden and the absence of this quality from the other three categories conflate any distinction between the moral and strictly legal, for the distinction was never perceived as integral to the law.[8] Indeed, the categories of the recommended and the disapproved do entail punitive consequences, where applicable, though these are not of the earthly kind. That they are entirely theological and eschatological does not consign them a place outside the law. Divine punishment is horrendous and eternally painful, to an extent and quality that cannot even be imagined by the human mind. But for the petty, and not so petty, wrongdoers, God is forgiving and merciful. Not only can many bad deeds be forgiven, but good deeds are rewarded manifold and have, in their overall weight, an offsetting effect against bad deeds. The reward is thus exponential. Doing good and performing beneficial deeds increases one's credit, meticulously noted in a believer's transcendental ledger. Thus, to do good is by definition to be 'near God' (*qurba*) in this life and in the hereafter, to be loved and in receipt of His grace and bounty. The pronouncement 'there is no god but God' ultimately

8 Ibid.

epitomises, but does not mask, the totality of these relationships with the Creator, in their threat and promise.[9] That *sharīʿa* norms engendered *willing obedience*, where the inner sources of the self willingly generate actions that are at once moral and legal, is perhaps the most striking difference between what we call Islamic law and the law of the modern state.

It is with these caveats in mind that we now turn to discuss the *sharīʿa*'s history and some of the salient ways of its functioning.

Formation

By the end of the sixth century CE Mecca and its northern neighbour, Yathrib, had known a long history of settlement and were largely a part of the cultural continuum that had dominated the Near East since the time of the Sumerians. True, the two cities were not direct participants in the imperial cultures that prevailed elsewhere in the Near East, but they were tied to them in more ways than one. Prior to the Arab expansion in the name of Islam, Arabian society had developed the same types of institutions and forms of culture that were established in the societies to the south and north, a development that would later facilitate the Arab conquest of this region.

Through intensive contacts with the Lakhmids and Ghassānids and with their Arab predecessors who dominated the Fertile Crescent for a century or more before the rise of Islam, the Arabs of the Peninsula maintained forms of culture that were their own, but which represented a regional variation on the cultures of the north. The Bedouin themselves participated in these cultural forms, but the sedentary and agricultural settlements of the Ḥijāz were even more dynamic participants in the commercial and religious activities of the Near East. Through trade, missionary activities and connections with northern tribes (and hence constant shifting of demographic boundaries) the inhabitants of the Ḥijāz knew Syria and Mesopotamia quite as well as the inhabitants of the latter knew the Ḥijāz. When the new Muslim state began its expansion to the north, north-west and north-east it did not enter these territories empty-handed, desperately in search of new cultural forms or an identity. Rather, the conquering Arabs, led by a sophisticated leadership hailing from commercial and sedentary Medina and Mecca, were very much products of the same culture that dominated what was to become their subject territories.[10]

9 Ibid.

10 For a detailed discussion of the place of Arabia in Near Eastern culture see Wael B. Hallaq, *The origins and evolution of Islamic law* (Cambridge, 2005), pp. 8–28.

The earliest military campaigns and conquests, although not systematic, were geared towards major centres. The Muslim armies consisted primarily of tribal nomads and semi-nomads who, rather than take up residence in the newly won cities of the Fertile Crescent, Egypt and Iran, for the most part inhabited garrison towns (*amṣār*) as a separate class of conquerors. Kūfa and Baṣra in southern Iraq and Fusṭāṭ in Egypt constituted the chief settlements at the early stage of the conquests.

It did not escape the Muslim political leaders of Medina, the capital, or their military representatives in the garrison towns, that their warriors needed to learn the principles of the new order, its new ethic and world-view. Tribal Bedouins to the core, most soldiers found alien the military organisation to which they were subjected, and by which their freedom was constrained. Even more alien to them must have been the new ideas of Islam, its mode of operation and its generally non-tribal conception, if not organisation. ʿUmar I (r. 13–23/634–44) quickly realised that it was not sufficient to appease the largely Bedouin contingents in his armies through allocations of booty. Thus, in each garrison town, and in every locale where there happened to be a Muslim population, a mosque was erected.[11] This place of worship was to serve several functions for the emerging Muslim community, but at the outset it was limited mainly to bringing together the Muslims residing in the garrison town for the Friday prayer and sermon – both intended, among other things, to imbue the Bedouin with religious values. The sermon, which played an important role in the propagation of the new Islamic ethic, included extensive passages from the Qurʾān and other messages that were relevant, in the emerging religious ethos, to the living experience of the Muslim community in the garrisons.

To each of these towns ʿUmar I appointed a military commander-cum-administrator who also functioned as propagator of the new religious ideas that were gradually but steadily taking hold. The commander also led the Friday prayer, distributed booty pensions and commanded military campaigns. His duties also involved the resolution and arbitration of conflicts that arose between and among the tribesmen inhabiting the garrison town. ʿUmar was also quick to deploy Qurʾān teachers who enhanced the religious values propagated by the commanders and their assistants.[12]

11 R. G. Hoyland, *Seeing Islam as others saw it: A survey and evaluation of Christian, Jewish and Zoroastrian writings on early Islam* (Princeton, 1997), pp. 561ff., 567–73, 639.

12 Abū Isḥāq Ibrāhīm al-Shīrāzī, *Ṭabaqāt al-fuqahāʾ*, ed. I. ʿAbbās (Beirut, 1970), pp. 44, 51; M. Ibn Ḥibbān, *Kitāb al-thiqāt* (Hyderabad, 1968), pp. 149, 157.

In the spirit of the Qur'ān, and in accordance with what he deemed to have been the intended mission of the Prophet (to which he himself had contributed significantly), ʿUmar I promulgated a number of ordinances and regulations pertaining to state administration, family, crime and ritual. He regulated, among other things, punishment for adultery and theft, declared temporary marriage (*mutʿa*) illegal and granted rights to concubines who bore the children of their masters. Similarly, he upheld Abū Bakr's (r. 11–13/632–4) promulgations, such as enforcing the prohibition on alcohol and fixing the penalty for its consumption.[13] He is also reported to have insisted forcefully on adherence to the Qur'ān in matters of ritual and worship – a policy that culminated in a set of practices and beliefs that were instrumental in shaping the new Muslim identity, and that later became, as we saw, integral to the law. Combined with the public policies of the new order, the Qur'ān's injunctions represented a significant modification to the customary laws prevailing among the peninsular Arabs, laws that contained indigenous tribal elements and, to a considerable extent, legal provisions that had been applied in the urban cultures of the Near East – including the cities of the Ḥijāz – for over a millennium.

From the very beginning of the conquests the military commander – or, more frequently, his assistant – functioned, among other things, in the capacity of *qāḍī*, whose duties entailed far more provincial administration than law and whose involvement in the latter did not go beyond the experience of having served as arbitrators (*ḥakams*). These arbitrators were men deemed to possess sufficient experience, wisdom and charisma and to whom tribesmen resorted for the adjudication of disputes. Although their verdicts were not binding in the strict legal sense, disputants normally conformed to their findings. Their appointments as *qāḍīs* were neither general in jurisdiction nor intended to regulate and supervise the affairs of the conquered provinces; rather, they were confined to the garrison towns where the conquering Arab armies resided with their families and other members of their tribes.[14] The policy of the central power in Medina, and later in Damascus, was clear on this matter from the outset: the conquered communities were to regulate their own affairs exactly as they had been doing prior to the advent of Islam, a situation that continued to obtain until the thirteenth/nineteenth century.

With the passage of time, when the occupying populations permanently settled in the garrison towns, their life acquired its own complexity, giving rise

13 ʿAbd al-Ghanī ibn ʿAbd al-Wāḥid al-Jammāʿīlī, *al-ʿUmda fī al-aḥkām*, ed. M. ʿAṭā' (Beirut, 1986), p. 463.
14 Abū Zurʿa al-Dimashqī, *Tārīkh*, ed. S. Allāh al-Qawjānī, 2 vols. (n.p., 1970), vol. I, p. 202.

to problems that called for a much wider range – and technically more complex set – of laws. During this initial stage of legal development, the *qāḍīs* were instrumental. Despite the lack of organised legal education they were expected, if not required, at least to have a degree of religious knowledge. At the time this meant possessing a reasonable knowledge of the legal stipulations of the Qurʾān plus knowledge of the rudimentary socio-religious values the new religion had developed. This would be coupled with a proficient knowledge of customary law – an element taken for granted, then and for centuries thereafter.

The early *qāḍīs* did not apply Qurʾānic law systematically, although there was a growing tendency to do so from the beginning. The application of Islamic content to the daily life of the community came after the articulation of a certain ethic, depending on the particular sphere of life or the case at hand. In matters of inheritance, for instance, where the Qurʾān offered clear and detailed provisions, the proto-*qāḍīs* seem to have applied these provisions as early as the caliphates of Abū Bakr and ʿUmar I. Government policy insisted on a faithful adherence to the Qurʾānic stipulations on inheritance (although we do not know the extent to which these rules were applied in areas distant from the centres of government power). On the other hand, many areas of life were either lightly touched by Qurʾānic legislation or not at all. Even such Qurʾānic prohibitions as those pertaining to wine drinking were not immediately enforced, and remained largely inoperative at least for several decades after the death of the Prophet.

It was the second generation of Muslims, those raised during the second half of the first/seventh century, who came under a more systematic influence of Qurʾānic teachings and religious instruction. Unlike their parents, who had become Muslims at a later stage in their lives, often under coercion (by virtue of the apostasy wars), they, together with the children of non-Arab converts, imbibed from infancy the rudimentary religious morality and values. By the time they reached the age of majority they were frequent mosque-goers (i.e. regular consumers of religious preaching and religious acculturation), and were involved in various activities relating to the conquests and building of a religious empire. It was therefore the learned elite of this generation – which flourished roughly between 60/680 and 90/708 – who embarked upon promoting a religious ethos that permeated – indeed, impregnated – so much of Muslim life and society. A useful gauge of the upsurge of a religious ethos is the *qāḍīs*ʾ interest in religious narrative, including stories and biographical anecdotes about the Prophet. Already in the 60s/680s, if not earlier, some *qāḍīs* had started propounding Prophetic material, the precise nature of which is still unclear to us.

That legal authority during the better part of the first Islamic century was not exclusively Prophetic is clear. It must be remembered that by the time Muḥammad died his authority as Prophet was anchored in the Qurʾānic event and in the fact that he was God's spokesman – the one through whom this event materialised. To his followers he was and remained nothing more than a human being, devoid of any divine attributes (unlike Christ, for instance). But by the time of his death, when his mission had already met with great success, he was the most important figure the Arabs knew. Nonetheless, these Arabs also knew of the central role that ʿUmar I, Abū Bakr and a number of other Companions had played in helping the Prophet, even in contributing to the success of the new religion. Like him they were charismatic men who commanded the respect of the faithful. Inasmuch as Muḥammad's authority derived from the fact that he upheld the Qurʾānic Truth and never swerved from it, these men derived their own authority as privileged Companions and, in some cases, caliphs from the same fact, namely, their upholding of the Qurʾānic Truth. This is not to say that caliphal authority was necessarily or entirely derivative from that of the Prophet; in fact, it ran parallel to it. Muḥammad was the messenger through whom the Qurʾānic Truth was revealed; the caliphs were the defenders of this Truth and the ones who were to implement its decrees.

The caliphs – until at least the middle of the second/eighth century – tended to see themselves as God's *direct* agents in the mission to implement His statutes, commands and laws. Throughout the entirety of the first Islamic century they adjudicated many issues that required authority-statement solutions, without invoking Prophetic authority. As late as the 90s/710s, and for some decades thereafter, they and most other *qāḍīs* appear to have relied on three sources of authority in framing their rulings: the Qurʾān; the *sunan* (including 'caliphal law'); and what we will call here considered opinion (*raʾy*). The *qāḍīs*' practice of writing letters seeking caliphal opinion on difficult cases confronting them in their courts was evidently a common one. So were caliphal letters to the *qāḍīs*, most of which appear to have been solicited, although some were written on the sole initiative of the caliph himself or – presumably – in his name, by his immediate advisers.

Yet much of caliphal legal authority rested on precedent, generally accepted custom and the practice of earlier caliphs, of the Prophet's close Companions and, naturally, of the Prophet himself. Like their *qāḍīs*, caliphs adhered to the same sources of legal guidance. And when no precedent was to be found, considered opinion adjudged. In short, the sources of authority that governed the emerging Islamic law were three: the Qurʾān, the *sunan* and considered opinion.

Sunna (pl. *sunan*) is an ancient Arab concept, meaning an exemplary mode of conduct, and the verb *sanna* has the connotation of 'setting or fashioning a mode of conduct as an example that others would follow'. Many caliphal practices came to constitute *sunan* since they were viewed as commendable. When caliphs and proto-*qāḍīs* referred to *sunan* they were speaking of actions and norms that were regarded as ethically binding but which may have referred to various types of conduct.

During the first decades of Islam it became customary to refer to the Prophet's biography and the events in which he was involved as his *sīra*, which constituted a normative, exemplary model, overlapping with notions of Prophetic model behaviour, namely, *sunna*. The Qur'ān itself explicitly and repeatedly enjoins believers to obey the Prophet and to emulate his actions. That the Prophet was associated with a *sunna* very soon after, if not upon or before, his death cannot be doubted. Yet it stood as one among many *sunan*, however increasingly important it was coming to be. In the hundreds of biographical notices devoted to the early *qāḍīs* by Muslim historians, it is striking that Prophetic *sunna* surfaces relatively infrequently – certainly no more frequently than those of Abū Bakr and 'Umar I.

During the 60s/680s a number of *qāḍīs*, among others, began to transmit Prophetic material, technically referred to by the later sources as *ḥadīth*. This activity of transmission is significant because it marks the beginning of a trend in which the *sunna* of the Prophet received special attention, independent of other *sunan*. This very attention constituted an unprecedented and fundamental transformation. It was both the result of a marked growth in the Prophet's authority and the cause of further epistemic and pedagogical developments. The developments were epistemic because the need to know what the Prophet said or did became increasingly crucial for determining what the law was. In addition to the fact that Prophetic *sunna* – like other *sunan* — was already central to the Muslims' perception of model behaviour and good conduct, it was gradually realised that this *sunna* had an added advantage in that it constituted part of Qur'ānic hermeneutics: to know how the Qur'ān was relevant to a particular case, and how it was to be interpreted, Prophetic verbal and practical discourse, often emulated by the Companions, was needed. And they were pedagogical because, in order to maintain a record of what the Prophet said or did, approved or disapproved, certain sources had to be mined; this information, once collected, needed in turn to be imparted to others as part of the age-old oral tradition of the Arabs, now imbued with a heavy religious element.

The Muslim leadership, caliphs included, was acting within a social fabric inherited from tribal Arab society in which forging social consensus before reaching decisions or taking actions was a normative practice. This is one of the most significant facts about the early Muslim polity and society. In the spirit of this social consensus, people sought to conform to the group and to avoid deviating from its will or normative ways, as embodied in a cumulative history of past action and specific manners of conduct. What their fathers had done or said was as important as, if not more important than, what their living peers might say or do. When an important decision was to be taken, a precedent – a *sunna* – was nearly always sought. The caliph, with all his authority and might, *first looked for precedent.* What he was looking for was nothing short of a relevant *sunna* that represented the established way of dealing with any problem at hand. It should not then be surprising that the Prophet's own practice was largely rooted in certain practices, mostly those deemed to have fallen within the province of *sunan*.[15]

Apart from this repertoire of *sunan* and the superior Qur'ān, the *qāḍīs* and caliphs also heavily relied on considered opinion (*ra'y*), which was, during the entire first Islamic century and part of the next, a major source of legal reasoning and thus of judicial rulings. While some cases of *ra'y* involved personal opinion and individual discretion, this legal source overlapped with the concept of *sunan*. In a case occurring around 65/684, for instance, a judge was asked about the value of criminal damages for causing the loss of any of the hand's five fingers, and in particular whether or not they are of equal value. He replied: 'I have not heard from any one of the people of *ra'y* that any of the fingers is better than the other.'[16] Here, 'the people of *ra'y*' are persons whose judgement and wisdom is to be trusted and, more importantly, emulated. *Ra'y*, or considered opinion, comes very close to the notion of *sunna*, from which *ra'y* cannot in fact be separated.

From the very beginning *ra'y* stood as the technical and terminological counterpart of *'ilm*, which referred to matters whose settlement could be based on established norms that one could invoke from the past. *'Ilm*, in other words, reflected knowledge of past experience – what we might call an authority-statement. *Ra'y*, on the other hand, required the application of new norms or procedures, with or without reference to past experience or model behaviour. While both might apply to social, personal, legal and

15 A well-studied example is that of 'surplus of property'. The Prophet is said to have spent the surplus of his personal revenue on the acquisition of equipment for warlike projects, whereas the pre-Islamic Arabs used to spend theirs on charitable and social purposes. 'Umar I adopted this practice as a Prophetic *sunna*. See M. M. Bravmann, *The spiritual background of early Islam* (Leiden, 1972), pp. 129, 175–7, 229ff.

16 M. ibn Khalaf Wakī', *Akhbār al-quḍāt*, 3 vols. (Beirut, n.d.), vol. I, p. 299.

quasi-legal matters, they remained distinct from each other. Yet, with the gradual metamorphosis of the content of historical, secular experience into a Prophetic and religious narrative, authority-statements became gradually less secular, acquiring an increasingly religious meaning. This metamorphosis is evidenced in the absorption of pre-Islamic customary and other practices into caliphal and Prophetic *sunan*: the latter would emerge more than two centuries later as the exclusive body of authority-statements.

Yet, inasmuch as *ra'y* was at times dependent on *ʿilm*, so was *ijtihād*, a concept akin to *ra'y*. *Ijtihād*, from the very beginning, signified an intellectual quality supplementing *ʿilm*, namely, the knowledge of traditional practice and the ability to deduce from it, through *ra'y*, a solution.[17] It is no coincidence therefore that the combination *ijtihād al-ra'y* was of frequent use, signalling the exertion of *ra'y* on the basis of *ʿilm*, or knowledge of the authoritative past.

Technically, *ʿilm*, *ra'y* and *ijtihād* were interconnected and at times overlapping. So were the concepts of *ra'y* and derivatives of *ijmāʿ* (consensus), a concept that was to acquire central importance in later legal thought. The notion of consensus met *ra'y* when the latter emanated from a group or from a collective tribal agreement. The consensual opinion of a group (*ijtamaʿa ra'yuhum ʿalā* ...) not only provided an authoritative basis for action, but also for the creation of *sunna*. A new *sunna* might thus be introduced by a caliph on the basis of a unanimous resolution formed by a (usually influential) group of people. Other forms of consensus might reflect the common, unanimous practice of a community, originally of a tribe and later of a garrison town or a city.

If there was a consensus to be reckoned with, it was that of learned men who populated the Muslim cities and what once began as garrison towns. These men, flourishing between 80 and 120 AH (*c.* 700 and 740 CE), were private individuals whose motive for engaging in the study of law was largely a matter of piety. While it is true that a number of these did serve as *qāḍīs*, their study of the law was not necessarily associated with this office or with the benefits or patronage accruing therefrom. Instead, they were driven above all by a profoundly religious commitment to study, and this, among other things, meant the articulation of a law that would in time come to deal with all aspects of social reality.

Intense personal study of religious narratives was largely a private endeavour, but it overlapped and mutually complemented the scholarly activity in the specialised circles of learning (*ḥalqas*), usually held in the mosques. Some *ḥalqas* were exclusively concerned with Qur'ānic interpretation, while others

17 Ibid., vol. I, pp. 186–8.

were occupied with Prophetic narrative (to emerge later as Prophetic *sunna*). A number of *ḥalqas*, however, were of an exclusively juristic nature, led by and attracting the most distinguished legal specialists in the lands of Islam. The scholars of the legal circles were acknowledged as having excelled in law, but not yet in jurisprudence as a theoretical study – a discipline that was to develop much later. Some of them possessed a special mastery of Qurʾānic law, especially inheritance, while others were known for their outstanding competence in ritual law or in *sunan*.

The activities of the legal specialists initiated what was to become a fundamental feature of Islamic law: that legal knowledge as an *epistemic* quality was to be the final arbiter in law making. They made of piety a field of knowledge, for piety dictated behaviour in keeping with the Qurʾān and the good example of the predecessors' *sunan*. Considered opinion was part of this piety, since it more often than not took into consideration the Qurʾān and the exemplary models that came so highly recommended. Yet adherence to these legal sources was not a conscious methodological act: the Qurʾān, the *sunan* and *raʾy* had so thoroughly permeated the ethos according to which judges operated and legally minded scholars lived that they had become paradigmatic.

Those who made it their concern to study, articulate and impart legal knowledge acquired both a special social status and a position of privileged epistemic authority. Whether Arab or non-Arab, rich or poor, white or black, scholars emerged as distinguished leaders, men of integrity and rectitude by virtue of their knowledge, and their knowledge alone. This epistemic authority became a defining feature of Islamic law, rightly giving it the modern epithet 'jurists' law'.

The emergence of legal specialists was one development that got under way once Muslims began engaging in religious discussions, story-telling and instruction in mosques. Another, concomitant, development was the gradual specialisation of the *qāḍī*'s office, a specialisation dictated by the fact that the Arab conquerors' expansion and settlement in the new territories brought with it an unprecedented volume of litigation, including legally complex cases usually associated with sedentary styles of life. By the end of the first/seventh century, and the beginning of the next, judges were relieved of certain non-legal functions, such as policing. At the same time, their legal knowledge was enhanced by the contributions of the legal specialists, some of whom were themselves judges. These specialists, moreover, began to be seen as essential to the courtroom, whence an early doctrine began to surface: a judge must consult the legal specialists, the *fuqahāʾ*, especially if he is not one of them.

Another development, which had started during the 60s/680s and continued long thereafter, was the emergence of Prophetic authority as a legal source independent of other narratives and model practices. The logic of the Prophet's centricity emerged soon after his death, but its most obvious manifestation occurred during the second half of the second century (770–810 CE) and thereafter, when his authority became exclusive. The central phenomenon associated with this process was, however, the proliferation of formal *ḥadīth* which came to compete with the practice-based, local *sunan* – what we call here sunnaic practice. The competition was thus between a formal and nearly universal conception of the Prophetic model and those local practices that had their own view of the nature of Prophetic *sunna*. With the emergence of a mobile class of traditionists, whose main occupation was the collection and reproduction of Prophetic narrative, the formal, literary transmission of *ḥadīth* quickly gained the upper hand over sunnaic practice. The traditionists were not necessarily jurists or judges, and their impulse was derived more from religious ethic than from the demands and realities of legal practice; nevertheless, at the end of the day, their *ḥadīth* project proved victorious, leaving behind as distant second the local conceptions of Prophetic *sunna* – a *sunna* that did not have the overwhelmingly personal connection to the Prophet claimed by the traditionist version. That many local jurists participated in the traditionist project to the detriment of their own sunnaic practice is eloquent testimony to the power of the newly emerging *ḥadīth*.

During the first two centuries AH (seventh–eighth CE) the concept of sunnaic practice could hardly be distinguished from consensus, since the sanctioning authority of the former resided in the overwhelming agreement of the legal specialists who collectively upheld this practice. As an expression of sunnaic practice, consensus was seen as binding and determinative of *ḥadīth*. It was not conceived merely as 'the agreement of recognised jurists during a particular age', a definition that became standard in later legal theory. Rather, consensus during this early period strongly implied the agreement of scholars based on continuous practice which was, in turn, based on the consensus of the Companions. It should be stressed here that the latter was viewed as essential to the process of foregrounding later doctrine in Prophetic authority, since the consensus of the Companions, *ipso facto*, was an attestation of Prophetic practice and intent. The Companions, after all, could not have unanimously approved a matter that the Prophet had rejected or prohibited. Nor, in the conception of early jurists, could they have pronounced impermissible what the Prophet had declared lawful.

From the very beginning until the end of the second/eighth century (and for decades thereafter) the legists employed *ra'y* in their reasoning. Whether based on knowledge of sunnaic practice or not, *ra'y* encompassed a variety of inferential methods that ranged from discretionary and loose reasoning to arguments of a strictly logical type, such as analogy or the *argumentum a fortiori*. In a gradual process of terminological change that began around the middle of the second/eighth century, *ra'y* appears to have been broken down into three categories of argument, all of which had originally been offshoots of the core notion. The most general of these categories was *ijtihād*, which term, during the first/seventh and most of the second/eighth century, appeared frequently in conjunction with *ra'y*, namely, as *ijtihād al-ra'y*, which meant the exertion of mental energy for the sake of arriving, through reasoning, at a considered opinion. Later, when the term *ra'y* was dropped from the combination, *ijtihād* came to stand alone for this same meaning, but this terminological transformation was short-lived.

The second category of arguments to emerge out of *ra'y* was *qiyās*, signifying disciplined and systematic reasoning on the basis of the revealed texts, the Qur'ān and *ḥadīth*. In addition to analogy, its archetypal form, *qiyās* encompassed the *a fortiori* argument in both of its forms – the *a maiore ad minus* and the *a minore ad maius* – as well as syllogistic, relational and *reductio ad absurdum* arguments.[18]

Yet another argument under the heading of *ra'y* was *istiḥsān*, commonly translated as 'juristic preference'. We have no adequate definition of this reasoning method from the period before al-Shāfiʿī, most of our knowledge of it being derived either from al-Shāfiʿī's polemics against it (hardly trustworthy) or late Ḥanafī theoretical reconstructions of it (which involved an ideological remapping of legal history). It seems, however, safe to characterise the second/eighth-century meaning of *istiḥsān* as a mode of reasoning that yields reasonable results – unlike strictly logical inference such as *qiyās*, which may lead to undue hardships or impractical solutions. But it was also employed as a method of achieving equity, driven by reasonableness, fairness and commonsense. Yet, like *ra'y*, which acquired a negative connotation because it included personal opinions that lacked formal grounding in the revealed texts, *istiḥsān* too was rejected. Unlike *ra'y*, however, it survived in the later Ḥanafī and Ḥanbalī schools as a secondary method of reasoning, though not without ingenious ways of theoretical rehabilitation.[19]

18 Mālik ibn Anas, *al-Muwaṭṭa'* (Beirut, 1414/1993), pp. 737–9. For a more detailed discussion on how these arguments developed in later legal theory see Wael B. Hallaq, *A history of Islamic legal theories: An introduction to Sunnī* uṣūl al-fiqh (Cambridge, 1997), pp. 96–9.

19 Hallaq, *History*, pp. 107–13. See also G. Makdisi, 'Ibn Taymīya's autograph manuscript on *istiḥsān*: Materials for the study of Islamic legal thought', in G. Makdisi (ed.), *Arabic and Islamic studies in honor of H. A. R. Gibb* (Cambridge, MA, 1965).

One jurist whose writings exemplify the transition from what we may call the pre-*ḥadīth* to the *ḥadīth* period was al-Shāfiʿī, a champion of Prophetic *ḥadīth* as an exclusive substitute for sunnaic practice. His writings manifest a stage of development in which *ra'y* meets with the first major attack in an offensive that ultimately led to its ouster (terminologically and to a certain extent substantively) from Islamic jurisprudence. Categorically labelling *ra'y* as arbitrary, he excluded it, along with *istiḥsān*, from the domain of reasoning altogether. *Ḥadīth*, on the other hand, reflected, for him, divine authority, leaving no room for human judgement except as a method of inference, which he interchangeably called *qiyās/ijtihād*.

Al-Shāfiʿī appears to have been the first jurist consciously to articulate the theoretical notion that Islamic revelation provides a full and comprehensive evaluation of human acts. The admittance of *qiyās* (*ijtihād*) into his jurisprudence was due to his recognition of the fact that divine intent is not completely fulfilled by the revealed texts themselves, since these latter do not afford a direct answer to every eventuality. But to al-Shāfiʿī, acknowledging the permissibility of *qiyās* does not bestow on it a status independent of revelation. If anything, without revelation's sanction of the use of this method it would not have been allowed, and when it is permitted to operate it is because *qiyās* is the only method that can bring out the meaning and intention of revelation regarding a particular eventuality. *Qiyās* does not itself generate rules or legal norms; it merely discovers them from, or brings them out of, the language of revealed texts. This theory was to become the basis of all later legal theories, elaborated under the rubric of *uṣūl al-fiqh*.

Judiciary

These developments in legal thought were accompanied by other emerging institutions in the law, notably, the *qāḍī* and his court. By the close of the second century (*c.* 800–815 CE) the structure and make-up of the court had taken final shape. All the basic personnel and logistical features had been introduced by this point, so that any enlargement or diminution of these elements were merely a function of the nature and needs of the *qāḍī*'s jurisdiction. Thus, for example, a *qāḍī* might have had one, two or more scribes, depending on the size of his court and the demands placed on it, but the scribe's function itself was by then integral to the proceedings, whatever their magnitude. The same went for all other court officials and functions.

The court's personnel consisted of a judge and any number of assistants (*aʿwān*) who performed a variety of tasks. One of these was the court chamberlain (*jilwāz*), whose function it was to maintain order in the court, including supervising the queue of litigants and calling upon various persons to appear before the judge. Some courts whose jurisdiction included regions inhabited by various ethnic and linguistic groups were also staffed by an interpreter or a dragoman. Furthermore, witness examiners appear as a fully established fixture of the court. They were appointed by *qāḍīs* to enquire into the rectitude of witnesses who either testified to the claims of litigants or attested to the legal records, contracts and all sorts of transactions passing through the court. The court's prestige and authority were also enhanced by the presence in it of men learned in the law. These, we have seen, were the legal specialists who, mostly out of piety, made the study and understanding (lit. *fiqh*) of religious law their primary private concern, and it was this knowledge that lent them what I have elsewhere called epistemic authority.[20] The sources are frequently unclear as to whether or not these specialists were always physically present in the court, but we know that from the beginning of the second century (*c.* 720 CE) judges were encouraged to seek the counsel of these learned men and that, by the 120s/740s, they often did.[21] It is fairly certain that the legal specialists were regularly consulted on difficult cases and points of law, although evidence of their *permanent* physical presence in the court is meagre.

The practice of consulting trained jurists was therefore normative, although it was not required by any official political authority. At least this was the case in the east. In Andalusia, on the other hand, soliciting the opinions of legal specialists – properly called the *mushāwars* – was mandatory. There it became something of a formal matter, insisted upon by both the legal profession and the political sovereign. Thus, generally speaking, an Andalusian judge's decision was considered invalid without the prior approval of the *mushāwars*.

The courts also included a number of other assistants, including those whose function it was to search out and apprehend persons charged with a felony or to bring in defendants against whom a plaintiff had presented the court with a claim. They were also sent out by the judge to look for witnesses who might have seen, for example, an illegal act being committed. Some of these assistants specialised in 'public calling', thus acquiring the technical title *munādīs*. These *munādīs* usually appeared in markets and public spaces and spoke out loud on court-related matters. They 'called' on certain individuals, sought either as witnesses or as defendants, to appear before the judge.

20 Hallaq, *Authority*, pp. ix, 166–235.
21 Wakīʿ, *Akhbār*, vol. II, p. 423, vol. III, p. 86.

Occasionally they were used as a means of communicating the judge's messages to the public.

The judge's assistants also included a number of *umanāʾ al-ḥukm* (lit. trustees of the court) whose tasks involved the safekeeping of confidential information, property and even cash. One category of these officials was responsible for the court's treasury, known as the *tābūt al-quḍāt* (the judge's security chest). Its location was in the state treasury but the key to it usually remained with the judge and/or his trustee placed in charge of it. We know that all sorts of monies were kept in it, especially those belonging to heirless deceased persons, to orphans and to absentees.[22]

Another trustee, the *qassām*, was responsible for dividing cash and property among heirs or disputed objects among litigants. This official was usually hired for his technical skills and knowledge of arithmetic. Last, but by no means least, a major official of the court was the judge's scribe, who usually sat immediately to the right or left of the judge, recorded the statements, rebuttals and depositions of the litigants and, moreover, drew up legal documents on the basis of court records for those who needed the attestation of the judge to one matter or another. His appointment to the court appears to have been the first to be made when a new judge assumed office, and he was required to be of just character, to know the law and to be skilled in the art of writing.[23]

The scribe's function was closely linked with the rise of the institution of the *dīwān*, which represented the totality of the records (*sijillāt*) written by the scribe, kept by the judge and normally filed in a bookcase termed a *qimaṭr*.[24] The *dīwān* usually contained records of actions and claims made by two parties in the presence of the judge, who usually signed them before witnesses in order for them to be complete and confirmed. It also contained: (a) copies of contracts, pledges, acknowledgements, gifts, donations and written obligations as well as other written instruments; (b) a list of court witnesses; (c) a register of trustees over *waqf* properties, orphans' affairs and divorcées' alimonies; (d) a register of bequests;[25, 26] (e) copies of letters sent to, and

22 M. ibn Yūsuf al-Kindī, *Akhbār quḍāt Miṣr*, ed. R. Guest (Cairo, n.d.), p. 405.

23 Wael B. Hallaq, 'The *qāḍī*'s *dīwān (sijill)* before the Ottomans', *BSOAS*, 61, 3 (1998), p. 423.

24 Wakīʿ, *Akhbār*, vol. II, p. 159. Taqī al-Dīn ibn al-Najjār, *Muntahā al-irādāt*, ed. ʿAbd al-Mughnī ʿAbd al-Khāliq, 2 vols. (Cairo, 1381/1962), vol. II, p. 582.

25 Kindī, *Akhbār*, p. 379; Aḥmad ibn ʿAlī al-Qalqashandī, *Ṣubḥ al-aʿshā fī ṣināʿat al-inshāʾ*, 14 vols. (Beirut, 1987), vol. X, p. 284.

26 Wakīʿ, *Akhbār*, vol. II, p. 136; Kindī, *Akhbār*, pp. 319, 379; Ibn Māza al-Ḥusām al-Shahīd, *Sharḥ adab al-qāḍī lil-Khaṣṣāf* (Beirut, 1994), pp. 57–62; on written obligations see Michael Thung, 'Written obligations from the 2nd/8th to the 4th century', *ILS*, 3, 1 (1996).

received from, other judges, including any relevant legal documents attached to such letters;[27] and (f) several other types of registers, such as a record of prisoners' names and the terms of their imprisonment, a list of guarantors and a list of legally empowered agents, including the terms of each agency and the lawsuits involved.[28]

The *dīwān* was acknowledged to be the backbone of legal transactions and the means by which the judge could review his decisions as well as all cases and transactions passing through his court. It was also essential for reviewing the work of earlier judges, especially that of the immediate predecessor. Such a review was usually prompted either by complaints against the outgoing judge or by reasonable suspicion on the part of the new judge of abuse, corruption or one form or another of miscarriage of justice that might be associated with his predecessor. It was access to the *dīwāns* that allowed judicial review in Islam to take on a meaningful role – a role that was, to some limited extent, equivalent to the practice of appeal in Western judicial systems.

By the beginning of the third/ninth century the judge's functions were defined once and for all, and litigation in all its aspects became his main concern. For in addition to arbitrating disputes, deciding cases and executing verdicts,[29] he supervised the performance of all his assistants – the scribe, the witness examiner, the chamberlain, the trustees and the *munādī*. His functions, however, did not exclude other normative duties performed by *qāḍīs* in earlier periods. Thus, directly or indirectly, he: (1) supervised charitable trusts (*awqāf*), their material condition, their maintenance and the performance of those who managed them;[30] (2) acted as guardian for orphans, administering their financial affairs and caring for their general well-being;[31] (3) took care of the property of absentees, as well as that of anyone who died heirless;[32] (4) heard petitions for conversion from other religions to Islam, and signed witnessed documents to this effect for the benefit of the new Muslims;[33] (5) attended to public works; and (6) often led Friday prayers and prayers at funerals, and announced the appearance of the new moon, signalling the end of the fast of Ramaḍān.

27 Kindī, *Akhbār*, p. 410; Abū Naṣr al-Samarqandī, *Rusūm al-quḍāt*, ed. M. Jāsim al-Ḥadīthī (Baghdad, 1985), p. 46.
28 Qalqashandī, *Ṣubḥ al-aʿshā*, vol. X, pp. 274, 291–2; Samarqandī, *Rusūm al-quḍāt*, pp. 34, 39ff.; Hallaq, '*Qāḍī*'s *dīwān*', pp. 421, 428–9.
29 Wakīʿ, *Akhbār*, vol. II, p. 415, vol. III, pp. 89, 135.
30 Kindī, *Akhbār*, pp. 383, 424, 444, 450.
31 Wakīʿ, *Akhbār*, vol. II, p. 58; Kindī, *Akhbār*, p. 444.
32 Wakīʿ, *Akhbār*, vol. II, p. 58; Kindī, *Akhbār*, p. 444.
33 Wakīʿ, *Akhbār*, vol. II, p. 65.

Some time after the middle of the second/eighth century there appeared a new set of tribunals that stood at the margins of the *sharīʿa* courts. These were the *maẓālim* (lit. 'boards of grievances'), generally instated by governors and viziers, theoretically on behalf of the caliph, and presumably for the purpose of correcting wrongs committed by state officials. Theoretically, too, they were sanctioned by the powers assigned to the ruler to establish justice and equity according to the religious law (*siyāsa sharʿiyya*). In reality, however, they at times represented his absolutist governance and interference in the *sharīʿa*, however marginal this may have been given that the jurisdiction of these tribunals was both limited and sporadic.

These tribunals tended to apply a wide range of procedural laws – wider, at any rate, than those procedures adopted by the *sharīʿa* court judges. They seem to have adopted a far less stringent procedure – admitting, for instance, coercion and summary judgments. Their penalties, furthermore, exceeded the prescribed laws of the *sharīʿa*. They thus applied penal sanctions in civil cases, or combined civil and criminal punishments in one and the same case. Yet the *maẓālim* tribunals functioned less as an encroachment on the *sharīʿa* courts than as a supplement to their jurisdiction. Characterised as courts of equity, where the sovereign showed himself to be conducting justice, the *maẓālim* tribunals operated within four main spheres: (1) they prosecuted injustices committed in the performance of public services, such as unfair or oppressive collection of taxes, or non-payment of salaries by government agencies; (2) they dealt with claims against government employees who transgressed the boundaries of their duties and who committed wrongs against the public, such as unlawful appropriation of private property; (3) they heard complaints against *sharīʿa* judges that dealt mainly with questions of conduct, including abuses of office and corruption (the *maẓālim* tribunals did not arrogate to themselves the power to hear appeals against *sharīʿa* court decisions, which as we have seen were to all intents and purposes final);[34] and (4) they enforced *sharīʿa* court decisions that the *qāḍī* was unable to carry out.

The schools

By the beginning of the third/ninth century the *sharīʿa* courts and a corpus of positive law had fully developed. Legal theory and the doctrinal legal schools, however, were to emerge much later, reaching their apex in the middle of the

34 For a discussion of successor review see D. Powers, 'On judicial review in Islamic law', *Law and Society Review*, 26 (1992).

fourth/tenth century. Considerations of space preclude a discussion of legal theory,[35] but permit brief remarks about the schools and their formation.

We saw that the early interest in law and legal studies evolved in the environment of the scholarly circles, where men learned in the Qur'ān, the *sunna* and the general principles of Islam began discussions, among other things, of quasi-legal and often strictly legal issues. By the early part of the second century (*c.* 720–40 CE) such learned men had already assumed the role of teachers whose circles often encompassed students interested specifically in *fiqh*, the discipline of substantive law. However, by that time no obvious methodology of law and legal reasoning had yet evolved, and one teacher's lecture could not always be distinguished, methodologically, from another's. Even the body of legal doctrine they taught was not yet complete, as can be attested from each teacher's particular interests, which were often limited to a narrow section of legal doctrine (e.g. inheritance, ritual).

By the middle of the second/eighth century not only had law become more comprehensive in coverage (though still not as comprehensive as it would become half a century later), but also the jurists had begun to develop their own legal assumptions and methodology. Teaching and debates within scholarly circles must have sharpened methodological awareness, which in turn led jurists to defend their own, individual conceptions of the law. On adopting a particular method, each jurist gathered around him a certain following who learned their jurisprudence and method from him. Yet it was rare that a student or a young jurist would restrict himself to one circle or one teacher; in fact, it was not uncommon for aspiring jurists to attend more than one circle in the same city, and even perhaps several circles, each headed by a different professor. During the second half of the century aspiring jurists not only made the round of the circles within one city, but travelled from one region to another in search of distinguished teachers.

Prominent teachers attracted students who 'took *fiqh*' from them. A judge who had studied law under a teacher was likely to apply that teacher's doctrine in his court – although, again, loyalty was not exclusive to a single doctrine. And if a student acquired a reputation as a qualified jurist, he might 'sit' (*jalasa*) as a professor in his own turn, transmitting to his students the legal knowledge he had gained from his teachers, but seldom without his own reconstruction of this

35 On the post-Shāfiʿī emergence of legal theory see Wael B. Hallaq, 'Was al-Shafiʿi the master architect of Islamic jurisprudence?', *IJMES*, 25 (1993). For a sketch of legal theory as it had stood around the middle of the fourth/tenth century see Hallaq, *Origins*, pp. 122–49. For later formulations of this theory see B. Weiss, *The search for God's law* (Salt Lake City, 1992); Hallaq, *History*.

knowledge. The legal doctrine that Abū Ḥanīfa taught to his students was largely a transmission from his own teachers, notably Ḥammād (d. 120/737). The same is true of Mālik, al-Awzāʿī, al-Shāfiʿī and many others. None of these, however, despite the fact that they were held up as school founders, constructed their own doctrine in its entirety. Rather, all of them were as much indebted to their teachers as these latter had been indebted to their own. In sum, by the middle of the third/ninth century numerous jurists had established themselves as leaders in their field and acquired personal followings through the scholarly circles in which they debated legal issues, taught jurisprudence to students and issued *fatwās* (responsa).

The absence of loyalty to the doctrines of leading jurists thus meant that no normative personal schools had yet existed. Where the latter existed, they did so in a narrow sense. Only when a leading jurist attracted a loyal following of jurists who exclusively applied his doctrine in courts of law or taught it to students, or issued *fatwās* in accordance with it, can we say that a personal school of his existed. This was indeed the case with a number of prominent jurists, including Abū Ḥanīfa, Ibn Abī Laylā, Abū Yūsuf, al-Shaybānī, Mālik, al-Awzāʿī, al-Thawrī and al-Shāfiʿī. All these had loyal followers, but they also had many more students who did not adhere exclusively to their respective doctrines.

Yet even when such personal schools had loyal followers, they did not truly represent what Islamic law knew as 'the *madhhab*', the doctrinal school, which possessed several characteristics lacking in the personal schools. First, the personal school, when fulfilling the condition of exclusive loyalty, comprised the positive legal doctrine of a single leading jurist and, at times, his doctrine as transmitted by one of his students. The doctrinal school, on the other hand, possessed a cumulative doctrine of substantive law in which the legal opinions of the leading jurist, now the supposed 'founder' of the school, were at best, *primi inter pares*, and at least equal to the rest of the opinions and doctrines held by various other jurists, also considered leaders *within* the school. In other words, the doctrinal school was a collective, authoritative entity, whereas the personal school remained limited to the individual doctrine of a single jurist.

Second, the doctrinal school was as much a methodological entity as a substantive, doctrinal one. In other words, what distinguished a particular doctrinal school from another was largely its legal methodology and the positive principles it adopted – as a composite school – in dealing with its own law. Methodological awareness on this level was not yet a feature of the personal schools, although it was on the increase from the middle of the second/eighth century.

Third, a doctrinal school was defined by its substantive boundaries, namely, by a certain body of legal doctrine and methodological principles that clearly identified the outer limits of the school as a collective entity. The personal schools, on the other hand, had no such well-defined boundaries, and departure from these boundaries in favour of other legal doctrines and principles was a common practice.

Fourth, and issuing from the third, was loyalty; for departure from its substantive law and methodological principles amounted to abandoning the school, a major event in the life (and biography) of a jurist. For whereas in the personal schools doctrinal loyalty was almost unknown, in the later doctrinal schools it was a defining feature of both the school itself and the careers of its members.

A central feature of the doctrinal school – in fact a fifth characteristic distinguishing it from the personal school – was the creation of an axis of authority around which an entire methodology of law was constructed. This axis was the figure of what came to be known as the founder, the leading jurist, in whose name the cumulative, collective principles of the school were propounded. Of all the leaders of the personal schools – and they were many – only four were raised to the level of 'founder' of a doctrinal school: Abū Ḥanīfa, Mālik, al-Shāfiʿī and Ibn Ḥanbal, to list them in chronological order. The rest, perhaps with the possible exception of the Ẓāhirite school, did not advance to this stage, with the result that they, as personal schools, were of relatively short duration.

The so-called founder, the eponym of the school, thus became the axis of authority construction: as bearer of this authority he was called the imam, and characterised as the absolute *mujtahid* who presumably forged for the school its methodology on the basis of which the positive legal principles and substantive law were constructed. The legal knowledge of the absolute *mujtahid* was presumed to be all-encompassing and thus wholly creative. The school was named after him, and he was purported to have been its originator. His knowledge included mastery of legal theory (*uṣūl al-fiqh*), Qur'ānic exegesis, *ḥadīth* and its criticism, legal language, the theory of abrogation, substantive law, arithmetic and the all-important science of juristic disagreement.

All these disciplines were necessary for the imam because he was thought to be the only one in the school who could engage directly with the revealed texts – from which, presumably, he derived the foundational structure of the school's substantive law. The imam's doctrine therefore constituted the only purely juristic manifestation of the legal potentiality of revealed language.

Without it, in other words, revelation would have remained just that, revelation, lacking any articulation as law.

The *madhhab*, therefore, was mainly a body of authoritative legal doctrine existing alongside individual jurists who participated in the elaboration of, or adhered to, that doctrine in accordance with an established methodology attributed exclusively to the eponym. The latter thus became, in this system, the absolute and independent *mujtahid*, while all subsequent *mujtahids* and jurists, however great their contributions, remained attached by their loyalty to the tradition of the *madhhab* that was symbolised by the figure of the founder. What made a *madhhab* (as a doctrinal school) a *madhhab* was therefore this feature of authoritative doctrine whose ultimate font is presumed to have been the absolute *mujtahid*-founder, not the mere congregation of jurists around the name of a titular eponym. This congregation would have been meaningless without the polarising presence of an authoritative, substantive and methodological doctrine constructed in the name of a founder, who was regarded as an axis of authority.

Devolving as it did upon the individual jurists who were active in the scholarly circles, legal authority never resided in the state, and this too was a prime factor in the rise of the *madhhab*. Whereas law in other imperial systems and complex civilisations was often 'state'-based, in Islam the ruling powers had virtually nothing to do with the production and promulgation of law. Therefore the need arose to anchor law in a system of authority that was not political. Yet the early scholarly circles, which consisted of little more than legal scholars and interested students, lacked the ability to produce a unified legal doctrine that would provide an axis of legal authority. The personal schools managed to afford the first step towards providing such an axis, since the application (in courts and *fatwās*) and the teaching of a single, unified doctrine – that is, the doctrine of the leading jurist around whom a personal school had formed – permitted a measure of doctrinal unity. But since the personal schools, though vast in number, were only slightly more effective than the even more numerous scholarly circles, a more significant, polarising axis of authority was still needed.

The second/eighth-century community of jurists fashioned and administered law in the name of the ruling dynasty. This community was – juristically speaking – largely independent, and possessed the power to serve as the ruler's link to the masses, aiding him in his bid to acquire legitimacy. As long as the ruler benefited from this legitimising agency, the legal community benefited from financial support and at the same time easily acquired independence. Accordingly, rallying around a single juristic doctrine was certainly one way in which a personal school could acquire a mass following and thus attract political/financial support. Such support was not limited to direct financial favours bestowed by the ruling elite, but extended to prestigious judicial appointments that guaranteed not only handsome pay but also political and social influence. These considerations alone – not to mention others – would be enough to explain the importance of such rallying around outstanding figures. The construction of the figure of an absolute *mujtahid* who represented the culmination of doctrinal developments within the school was a way to anchor law in a source of authority that constituted an alternative to the authority of the body politic. Whereas in other cultures the ruling dynasty promulgated the law, enforced it and constituted the locus of legal authority, in Islam it was the doctrinal *madhhab* that produced law and afforded its axis of authority. This is to say that legal authority resided in the collective, juristic doctrinal enterprise of the school, not in the body politic or in the doctrine of a single jurist.

The legists served the rulers as an effective tool for reaching the masses, from whose ranks they emerged and whose interests they represented. It was one of the salient features of the pre-modern Islamic body politic (as well as those of Europe and Far Eastern dynasties) that it lacked control over the infrastructures of the civil populations it ruled. Jurists and judges thus emerged as the civic leaders who, though themselves products of the masses, found themselves, by the nature of their profession, involved in the day-to-day running of the masses' affairs. The legists were often called upon to express the will and aspirations of those belonging to the non-elite classes. They not only interceded on their behalf at the higher reaches of power, but also represented for the masses the ideal of piety, rectitude and fine education. Their very profession as Guardians of Religion, experts in religious law and exemplars of a virtuous Muslim lifestyle made them not only the most genuine representatives of the masses but also the true 'heirs of the Prophet', as a Prophetic *ḥadīth* came to attest.[36] Therefore the government fulfilled its dire need for legitimisation through the powerful legal profession. At the same time, however, the latter clearly depended on royal and government patronage, the single most important contributor to their financial well-being. They were often paid handsome salaries when appointed to the judgeship, in addition to generous grants received in their capacity as private scholars. Thus, inasmuch as the legists depended on the financial favours of

36 Abū ʿUmar Yūsuf ibn ʿAbd al-Barr, *Jāmiʿ bayān al-ʿilm wa-faḍlihi*, 2 vols. (Beirut, n.d.), vol. I, p. 34.

those holding political power, these latter depended on the legists for realising their aims. Put differently, the more the political elite complied with the imperatives of the law, the more legitimising support it received from the legists. And the more these latter cooperated with the former, the more material and political support they received. This dialectic of mutual dependence between the political and the legal was to dominate the entirety of Islamic history until the dawn of modernity, which ushered in the nation-state which appropriated law making and in the process marginalised and finally obliterated the traditional legal class altogether.[37]

Practice and legal change

One of the most remarkable features of Islamic civilisation as a whole, and of the *sharīʿa* in particular, is the successful synthesis it struck between the ethical, legal and religious principles, on the one hand, and the demands of worldly reality, on the other. From a legal perspective, the primary locus of this synthesis was the *sharīʿa* court, the default and unrivalled court of Islamic societies – until, that is, Muslims began to react to modernity. Although much conflict resolution and other transactions occurred on the periphery and outside of the court, the latter, represented by its single *qāḍī*, formed the axis around which these out-of-court transactions took place and conflicts were resolved. The highly informal setting of the court allowed much strictly non-legal negotiation to take place, where social values, family and tribal connections and social status were brought to bear on the cases at hand. Emphasis was placed on amicable settlement (*ṣulḥ*), normatively requested by the *qāḍī* before any court proceedings began. The *qāḍī* himself often presided over 'sessions' in which the disputants met, but his function and capacity as *qāḍī* was not exercised. It was his prestige – as a judge, scholar and man of social status – that was brought to bear on the dispute, and it was his skill of forging consensus (essential to any such role) that permitted a satisfactory solution.

Once amicable settlement failed, the case would normally be introduced to the court, although – in comparison with Western courts of law – the proceedings would remain largely informal and subject to the discretion of the judge. This is not to say, however, as Max Weber and his followers once

37 For a detailed discussion of the relationship between law and politics see M. Q. Zaman, *Religion and politics under the early* ʿAbbāsids*: The emergence of the proto-Sunni elite* (Leiden, 1997).

mistakenly thought, that the *qāḍī* dispensed primitive 'palm-tree justice',[38] since the latter was, at the end of the day, bound by both an articulate system of procedure and a highly developed corpus of substantive law. But these very procedures and laws bestowed on him a wide margin of discretion that, in turn, afforded him and his court the flexibility that is comparatively absent in the highly formal tribunals of the modern state. This flexibility and informality was the hallmark of the Islamic court. It manifested itself in the carrying out of the court's business, from start to finish. Anyone apart from minors and madmen could 'approach the court' (an expression absent in the language of *sharīʿa*, but indicative of the formal and stratified distance between the common-law magistrate, on the one hand, and the litigating parties and their council, on the other). Similarly, plaintiffs and defendants, as well as others, could speak as they knew best (or not). No decorum specific to the court was maintained, but the *qāḍī* and his bailiffs usually encouraged, and politely demanded, proper and seemly behaviour. It was not uncommon for some defendants or others to be loud and disorderly (on occasion even insulting towards the judge), but such situations never required the penalties involved in the Western concept, where one can be declared 'in contempt of the court'. The *qāḍī*, in other words, was not, in his court, a wielder of discipline and punishment, representing the coercive powers of the state. Rather, he engaged with the disputants directly, informally and without mediation, since lawyers and council were never known in the courts of Islam. In such an engagement no one was required to conform to a particular manner of conduct, beyond what is socially acceptable. The *qāḍī* heard the parties, who might have hailed from the ranks of peasants or princes, the illiterate or the learned. In such a setting, much non-legal material was presented before the court, but the *qāḍī* normatively considered it his duty to sort out for himself the 'legal facts' relevant to the dispute.

To these legal facts the *qāḍī* applied *fiqh*, the substantive law of the *sharīʿa*. This stage involved the sociological channelling of *fiqh*, namely, the transference of the latter, with all of its worldly potentialities, from the textual world of the professional jurist to the world of social practice. The court, then, constituted the juncture where theory met practice, where the formal legal conception was reduced to a positivist fit within a concrete – perhaps unique – social reality dominated by the localised imperatives of the moral community.

38 D. Powers, '*Kadijustiz* or qāḍī-justice? A paternity dispute from fourteenth-century Morocco', *ILS*, 1, 3 (1994), repr. in D. Powers, *Law, society, and culture in the Maghrib, 1300–1500* (Cambridge, 2002).

By the point when it was applied in the *qāḍī*'s court, *fiqh* would have already undergone a long and complex process. The *qāḍī*'s reference might have been the long compendium (*mabsūṭ*), but it might just as well have been the abridgement (*mukhtaṣar*) he studied in the college of law (*madrasa*), where he acquired knowledge of it by memorising and understanding the legal text. The *mukhtaṣar* is by necessity adroitly exiguous, dense and often exhibiting an elliptic economy of words. Often impenetrable, it elicits the commentary of the professor, without whose expert intervention the text would remain inaccessible to the student. Something of a medium-size or a thin volume, the *mukhtaṣar* represents a condensation of the *fiqh* corpus as expounded in the *shurūḥ* or *mabsūṭāt* – multi-voluminous works of exquisite but enormous detail.

Defying the human capacity to retain information by rote, the *shurūḥ* and *mabsūṭāt* were abridged in a manner that allowed the student to recall mentally – through citing from the *mukhtaṣar* a clause or a sentence – a principle plus a host of cases and examples illustrating the law applicable to a particular case. The student's memorisation of the abridgement was integral to the process of commentary received from the professor in the study-circle (*ḥalqa*). The oral commentary in the *ḥalqa* reflected the contents of the *shurūḥ* and the *mabsūṭāt*, but did not necessarily duplicate them. Examples of a casuistic nature were constantly introduced to illustrate positive legal principles, but the source of these examples might have been either a long text or the professor's own legal practice. For it was quite common, if not the norm, that a professor of law was also a *muftī* or a judge, and when he engaged in the role of a teacher he would bring his experience as *muftī* and judge to the *ḥalqa*, where it would be brought to bear upon his students' course of study. Also common was the scholarly companionship (*ṣuḥba*) between student and teacher: a student might sit in a judge's court as an apprentice or as a witness or scribe, and when the *qāḍī* finished his hearings, he might well open the *ḥalqa* for *iftā*ʾ or teaching, and the same student/apprentice/witness/scribe will continue his learning in the transformed *ḥalqa*.

From the early fourth/tenth century every school adopted a *mukhtaṣar*, not only as a standard pedagogical text, but also as an authoritative summary of its substantive and procedural law.[39] The utility of these *mukhtaṣar*s could at times last up to a century or two before needing to be replaced by another abridgement, but such a substitution never meant that the older *mukhtaṣar*s became obsolete. In fact, the process of replacement itself was gradual, slow

39 M. Fadel, 'The social logic of *taqlīd* and the rise of the *mukhtaṣar*', *ILS*, 3, 2 (1996).

and, strictly speaking, never complete, for while new *mukhtaṣars* did become standard and 'canonical', the old ones, as a rule, never totally faded away.

This continuing relevance of the *mukhtaṣar* was typical of all other legal genres, beginning with those basic works written down on the authority of the founding masters during the second/eighth century and ending with the magisterial compendia of the last great jurists of the thirteenth/nineteenth. Yet it is a salient feature of Islamic legal history that legal works – the basis of legal practice in the law courts, in *iftāʾ* and document drafting (*shurūṭ*) – were constantly updated, rewritten and modified in a number of ways. No work was identical to another, and significant differences could indeed be observed between and among successive works of the same genre and in the same school. For the past century, and until quite recently, Western scholarship viewed this cumulative textual activity as a hair-splitting exercise, where the piling of commentary upon commentary yielded nothing of substance worth studying.[40] More recent scholars, however, have come to appreciate the output of Muslim legal scholarship, and indeed took delight in studying its rich and varied scholarly texture; yet their verdict remained that the juristic tradition, with all its massive corpus of texts, commentaries and super-commentaries, represented no more than 'intellectual play', having little, if anything, to do with their society and its problems.[41] This brand of scholarship is clearly associated with the academic but predominantly political doctrine espousing the *sharīʿa*'s stagnation – a doctrine that justifies and rationalises the latter's eradication as part of the colonising and modernising project.[42] Thus far there has been no serious research to show that such stagnation ever existed. In fact, the latest scholarship has demonstrated a diametrically opposing thesis, namely, that Islamic legal discourse constituted the vehicle through which legal change – as a response to changing social reality – was modulated.

It must be stressed that legal change during the pre-modern period was characterised by two qualities, the first of which was its imperceptible nature. No sudden mutability was required, no ruptures, violent or otherwise, but rather a piecemeal modification of particular aspects of the law, and only when general and wide-ranging circumstances (*mā taʿummu bi-hi al-balwā*) demanded such modifications. The change, therefore, was always eminently organic, naturally arising, as it were, from the adaptive experiences of the past

40 See, e.g., N. J. Coulson, *A history of Islamic law* (Edinburgh, 1964), esp. at p. 84.
41 See, e.g., N. Calder, 'Law', in S. H. Nasr and O. Leaman (eds.), *History of Islamic philosophy*, (London, 1996).
42 Wael B. Hallaq, 'The quest for origins or doctrine? Islamic legal studies as colonialist discourse', *UCLA Journal of Islamic and Near Eastern Law*, 2, 1 (2002–3).

and, most importantly, from within the legal subculture of a particular region. (After the third/ninth century the main regions that developed legal subcultures were Transoxania, Iran, Iraq, Syria, Egypt, western North Africa and Andalusia. By that time the Ḥijāz and the Yemen had become legally marginal.) The second quality lay in the fact that a modern notion of change (which tends to signify qualitative leaps and at times epistemically violent ruptures from the past) was clearly absent from the conceptual world and discourse of the jurists. The famous dictum that 'the *fatwā* changes with the changing of times and places' certainly did not mirror the presence in traditional Islamic law of this modern notion of change, but instead stated a working principle of accommodation and malleability. Change, however it was understood, was both evolutionary and organic.

How, then, did the juristic works reflect and serve as a vehicle of imperceptible and piecemeal change? During the late first/seventh and second/eighth centuries legal issues arising from the discussions and debates of the legal specialists (all of which issues were integral to the emerging Muslim communities) found their way into the legal treatises written on the authority of Abū Ḥanīfa, Abū Yūsuf, al-Shaybānī and al-Shāfiʿī, among others. This mode of 'textualising' socio-legal experiences and discourses continued to operate for many centuries but, with the crystallisation of law and legal institutions, this process of textualisation was effected through well-defined channels and mechanisms. By far the most important of these was the *fatwā*. Although laypersons addressed the *muftī* with a wide variety of questions, the legally significant – and thus important – *fatwā*s usually originated in the law courts where, upon finding a case difficult to adjudicate, the judge would solicit a solution from a *muftī*. Finding it at times too difficult to answer, the latter would redirect the question to a higher *muftī*, one who possessed scholarly credentials superior to his own. Note that the ultimate authority remained within the class of *muftī*s, whose counsel to the court, we saw earlier, was highly recommended (and, in Andalusia, required).

Originating in the world of legal practice, the *fatwā*s (not, notably, court decisions) were collected and published, particularly those among them that contained new law or represented new legal elaborations on older problems that continued to be of recurrent relevance. The collected *fatwā*s usually underwent a significant editorial process in which irrelevant facts and personal details (proper names, names of places, dates, immaterial facts etc.) were omitted. Moreover, they were abridged with a view to abstracting their contents into strictly legal formulas, usually of the hypothetical type: 'If X does Y under a set of conditions P, then L (legal norm) follows.'

Whether abstracted and edited or not, these *fatwā* collections became part of the authoritative legal literature. In Ḥanafī law, for example, they formed the third tier of legal doctrine, reflecting the contributions made by jurists who flourished after the first school masters, Abū Ḥanīfa, Abū Yūsuf, al-Shaybānī and al-Ḥasan ibn Ziyād. The first and second tiers mainly belonged to the first three. In sheer size and in the daily reality of legal practice, however, the third tier was the most dominant, as it reflected the multiple accretions and successive modifications over the 'basic doctrine' of the first masters.

As part of their integration into the authoritative body of legal doctrine, the *fatwās*, once abstracted, were incorporated into the work of the author–jurist, the *muṣannif*. The latter can be said to have provided the world of *sharīʿa* with the fully developed and comprehensive accounts of the law, with all of its juristic disagreements (*ikhtilāf*), dialectical subject matter and authoritative opinion. The author–jurist's activity extended from writing the short *risāla* to compiling the long work, be it the *mabsūṭ* (lit. extended) or *sharḥ* (commentary). It was mainly these two types of discourse that afforded the author–jurist the framework (and full opportunity) to articulate a modified body of law, one that reflected both the evolving social conditions and the state of the art in the law as a technical discipline. His subject matter was multi-layered, comprising the fundamental and foundational principles of the law – principles overlaid by the technical contributions of successive generations of jurists, ranging from the founders' disciples down to his immediate predecessors. His main source for elaborating the basic law and foundational principles was the *fatwā* literature, which intimately reflected legal practice within the courts and outside them, as well as the general practical concerns of the community. Each generation of these long works maintained the general principles of positive and procedural law while simultaneously incorporating all current and relevant subject matter, whether found in older or newer works. Cases that had gone out of circulation were discarded, whereas new legal opinions dealing with evolving conditions, especially those of relevance to communal issues (*mā taʿummu bi-hi al-balwā*) were incorporated.[43]

These long works, or abridged versions thereof, constituted the jurisprudential basis of legal practice and adjudication. Thus the movement was at once circular and dialectical, one that may aptly be described as a 'dialectical wheel': society's legal disputes ended up before the courts of law; judges encountered hard cases which they took to the *muftī* for an expert opinion (though the *muftī* was approached by laypersons too); the *muftī* provided solutions to these hard

43 Hallaq, *Authority*, pp. 166–235.

cases, thereby preparing them for integration into the positive law of his school; students usually copied, collected, edited, abridged and finally 'published' such *fatwās*; the author–jurist, the author of the school's authoritative *fiqh* work, incorporated most of these *fatwās* into his compendium. This he did while (1) strictly maintaining the body of principles governing his school's positive legal corpus; (2) weeding out opinions that had fallen out of circulation; and, conversely, (3) retaining opinions that continued to be relevant to legal practice. The product of this juristic activity was the *fiqh* work that continued to gauge and be gauged by legal practice. In sum, while legal practice was guided by *fiqh* discourse, the latter was shaped and modified by the former. Dialectically, one issued from, yet also fed, the other.

Modernity and the eclipse of the *sharīʿa*

By every indication the *sharīʿa* served Muslim societies well for centuries. However, from the eleventh/seventeenth century onwards India had progressively fallen under British rule, Indonesia under Dutch rule and, by the beginning of the thirteenth/nineteenth, Russian armies had subjected the Ottoman empire to crushing defeats that were later exacerbated by onerous debts to Britain. Much the same was also true of Qājār Iran as well as of other Muslim principalities and dynasties.

Under colonialist pressures the *sharīʿa* underwent significant changes, so that by the end of the thirteenth/nineteenth century it had been reduced to the area of family law. Some of the first *sharīʿa* spheres to disappear were commercial and criminal laws, both replaced by European regulations that were necessary for efficient economic exploitation of the Muslim colonies and of other lands that otherwise came under European influence. Local Muslim governments, aware of their military incompetence, realised the need to update their armies and to build a more centralised rule along lines that Europe had by then already developed. This was the beginning of a modernisation process that required building a state system in the modern image – which meant not only centralisation, but also a bureaucratic machinery that could subordinate all legal and educational institutions to the imperatives of a homogenising policy. In the Ottoman empire this translated, as a first step, into a central administration of *waqfs*, for which a special government ministry was established. The *waqfs*' importance stemmed from the fact that they often were rich charitable endowments that sustained legal education. Under the Ottomans these foundations, whose *madrasas* produced the *qāḍīs* running the empire's legal and administrative systems, were centred in Istanbul. Until 1242/1826 the *waqfs* operated independently, with each *waqf* having its finances administered by a private supervisor. But in that year, and for decades thereafter, *waqf* income increasingly went to the public treasury, to be redistributed with diminishing returns back to the *waqfs* themselves. While this policy enriched the central treasury, it had the effect of depleting these *waqfs*, thereby weakening the professional legal class.

Sharīʿa's position in the Ottoman empire was further eroded when, after the middle of the century, new modern, secular schools began to appear, and a modern school of law was established in 1293/1876. Not only were new, Western-inspired codes introduced in lieu of *sharīʿa* laws, but a hierarchical system of secular courts (called Niẓāmiyya) came to supplement, and then gradually replace, most religious courts. By the end of the thirteenth/nineteenth century these latter adjudicated matters of personal status, which included child custody, paternity, inheritance, gifts and, to a limited extent, *waqf*.

The creation of secular schools began to attract the younger generations, who found in them greater opportunity – and the potential for superior pay – than in the increasingly depleted institutions teaching the *sharīʿa*. Thus, *ʿulamāʾ* families, often in positions of power, would direct their children to study in the new schools in preparation for careers in the newly created secular courts and bureaucracy, since their new educational backgrounds equipped them to pursue such careers better than others. This professional transformation signalled the end of a *sharīʿa*-trained and *sharīʿa*-minded class that had until then exercised exclusive control over the law.

The transposition of Islamic law from the fairly independent and non-formal terrain of the jurists to that of the highly formalised and centralised agency of the state found manifestation in the compendium entitled *Majallat al-aḥkām al-ʿadliyya*. Between 1870 and 1877 (1287–95 AH) the sixteen books making up the *Majalla* (containing 1,851 articles in the Turkish language) were published, all dealing with civil law and procedure (to the exclusion of marriage and divorce). One of the aims of the *Majalla* was to provide, in the manner of a code, a clear and systematic statement of the law for the benefit of *both* the *sharīʿa* and Niẓāmiyya courts, a statement that was geared to a professional elite that had lost touch with Arabicate juristic hermeneutics. Yet the source of this codification was the *corpus juris* of the Ḥanafī school, particularly those opinions within it that seemed to its drafters to offer – especially in their reconstituted form – a modernised version of Islamic law thought to 'suit the present conditions'.[44] The opinions chosen did not

44 S. Onar, 'The Majalla', in M. Khadduri and H. J. Liebesny (eds.), *Law in the Middle East* (Washington, 1955), p. 295.

necessarily reflect the authoritative doctrines in the Ḥanafī school, nor were they, strictly speaking, all exclusively Ḥanafī, for some were imported from the other schools if they had been approved by the later Ḥanafites.[45]

The *Majalla* was to be implemented in the new Niẓāmiyya courts, whose staff were increasingly being trained in non-*fiqh* law. And since no juristic opinion was truly binding on any judge without the sovereign's intervention, the *Majalla*, after its complete publication, was promulgated as a sultanic code (a momentous act sanctioning, once and for all, the supreme authority of the state). But it was soon to have a fierce rival in the 1880 Code of Civil Procedure, modelled after the French example. Procedure was steadily and rapidly gaining greater importance towards the close of the century, it being increasingly seen, in the manner of all modern legal systems, as the backbone of the law. The highly formalised and complex procedural processes represented a large domain in which the *sharīʿa* was almost totally replaced.

It was obvious to the reformers, and even to their opponents, that the venture of the *Majalla* was a last-ditch effort to salvage the *sharīʿa* as a law in force, in part intended to keep at bay the flood of legal Westernisation. The systematic substitution of Turkish for Arabic as the language of instruction in the newly established modern schools was in part a phenomenon integral to the intentional spreading of nationalist feelings that were harnessed as a tool to keep the empire from disintegrating into various ethnic groupings. The *sharīʿa* faced the challenge not only of adapting to the rapidly changing economic and material conditions brought about by modernity, but also to a linguistic decentring whereby the new institutions and the legal personnel that staffed them literally communicated in a language that was not the language of the traditional law.[46]

Thus the *sharīʿa*'s rival was not only the modern state, but the nationalism that the state had so efficiently harnessed.[47] The *Majalla* was thus as much an attempted linguistic (i.e. nationalist) remedy as it was a legal one (although its production also created another dialectic by which, on the one hand, knowledge of the Arabicate tradition – so central to the law – was weakened, while on the other, the chances of success in closing the gap between any

45 J. N. D. Anderson, 'Law reform in Egypt: 1850–1950', in P. M. Holt (ed.), *Political and social change in modern Egypt* (London, 1968), p. 217.

46 On the global movement of using language as a means of constructing nationalism see the insightful analysis in B. Anderson, *Imagined communities: Reflections on the origin and spread of nationalism*, 2nd edn (London and New York, 2006), pp. 67–82.

47 On nationalism as the secularised religion of the state see T. Asad, *Formations of the secular* (Stanford, 2003), pp. 187–94.

Majalla-like effort and the demands of the economic and political orders were greatly reduced). Ultimately, however, the *Majalla* was less about such linguistic-nationalist matters than it was about a discreet political assertion of *legal* power. It said once and for all that, like the now-centralised *sharīʿa* courts themselves, the *fiqh* from now on was not the province of the jurists but rather that of the state.

Similar processes of codification occurred in British India. It was not until the appointment of Warren Hastings as governor of Bengal in 1772 that a serious British legal redesign of India got under way.[48] The appointment ushered in the so-called Hastings Plan, to be implemented first in Bengal. The plan conceived a multi-tiered system that required exclusively British administrators at the top, seconded by a tier of British judges who would consult with local *qāḍīs* and *muftīs* (*mulavis*) with regard to issues governed by Islamic law. On the lowest rung of judicial administration stood the run-of-the-mill Muslim judges who administered law in the civil courts of Bengal, Madras and Bombay. The plan also rested on the assumption that local customs and norms could be incorporated into a British institutional structure of justice that was regulated by 'universal' jural ideals.

In order to deal with what was seen by the British as an uncontrollable mass of individual juristic opinion, the Oxford classicist and foremost orientalist Sir William Jones (1746–94) proposed to Hastings the creation of codes, or what he termed a 'complete digest of Hindu and Mussulman law'.[49] The justification for the creation of such an alien system within Islamic (and Hindu) law was articulated in a language that problematised this law by casting it as unsystematic, inconsistent and arbitrary. The challenge thus represented itself in the question of how to understand and legally manage native society in an economically efficient manner, which in part shaped Jones's ambition of constructing a system that offered 'a complete check on the native interpreters of the several codes'.[50]

It was not long before Hastings commissioned the translation of Marghīnānī's *Hidāya* (a Ḥanafī classical work) into Persian, a version that Charles Hamilton in turn used for his own translation (1791) into English. A year later Jones himself translated *al-Sirājiyya*, this time directly from the

48 W. Menski, *Hindu law: Beyond tradition and modernity* (Oxford, 2003), pp. 164ff.
49 B. Cohn, *Colonialism and its forms of knowledge: The British in India* (Princeton, 1996), p. 69.
50 Cited in ibid. See also M. R. Anderson, 'Legal scholarship and the politics of Islam in British India', in R. S. Khare (ed.), *Perspectives on Islamic law, justice, and society* (Lanham, MD, 1999), p. 74.

Arabic.[51] This treatise on inheritance was adopted in translation to compensate for the silence of the *Hidāya* on this important branch of the law.[52] The immediate purpose of these translations was to make Islamic law directly accessible to British judges, who deeply mistrusted the native *mulavis* advising them on points of law.[53]

The choice of the *Hidāya* was not fortuitous. The text was composed by one of the most esteemed jurists in the Ḥanafī school, to which the great majority of India's Sunnī Muslims adhered. To cite it, the British thought, was to reduce the likelihood of juristic disagreement, the source of the much-detested legal pluralism. Furthermore, it was concise enough to qualify as a code. In fact, it was the briefest authoritative manual of Ḥanafī law that could serve in such a manner. And it is precisely here where the usefulness of this text lay. Its brevity reflected the authoritative doctrine of the Ḥanafī school as Marghīnānī, the distinguished Transoxanian author–jurist, saw it. It did not, however, sum up the general doctrine of the school, much less its range, especially in South Asia; as all such authoritative texts do, it stated only what Marghīnānī considered, in his *own age and region* (sixth/twelfth-century Farghāna and, more widely, Transoxania), to be the commonly practised and accepted doctrines of the school (common acceptance and practice of a doctrine being constitutive of epistemic and juristic authority).[54] Furthermore, it did not constitute the law, but the interpretive basis on which the law might be applied in a particular time and place. For in so far as application of the law was concerned it was the commentary, rather than the *Hidāya* itself, that was the practical judicial desideratum. In and by itself it was therefore far less important than the British appeared to assume, since their formal use of it qualitatively differed from its nativist, heuristic use as a peg for commentarial and practice-based jurisprudence.

The translation of the *Hidāya* amounted in effect to its codification, for by severing it from its Arabicate interpretive and commentarial tradition, it ceased to function in the way it had done until then. Thus, the 'codification' of the *Hidāya* (and through it, of the Islamic law of personal status, broadly speaking) served at

51 William Jones, *al-Sirajiyah or the Mahomedan law of inheritance* (Calcutta, 1861).

52 The *Hidaya* does deal with bequests, however. See Burhān al-Dīn ʿAlī ibn Abī Bakr al-Marghīnānī, *al-Hidāya: Sharḥ bidāyat al-mubtadī*, 4 vols. (Cairo, 1980 (repr.)), vol. IV, pp. 231ff. On omissions from the translated text and on its later uses in colonial education, see John Strawson, 'Islamic law and English texts', *Law and Critique*, 6, 1 (1995), pp. 27–8.

53 Anderson, 'Legal scholarship', 74; D. H. Kolff, 'The Indian and the British law machines: Some remarks on law and society in British India', in W. J. Mommsen and J. A. De Moor (eds.), *European expansion and law: The encounter of European and indigenous law in 19th- and 20th-century Africa and Asia* (Oxford, 1992), pp. 213–14.

54 Hallaq, *Authority*, pp. 155–64.

least four purposes. First, it accomplished what the British had aimed to do for so long – namely, to curb the judicial 'discretion' of the *qāḍī* and, more specifically, the *mulavis* and *muftīs* who assisted the courts. Thus, by making the text of the law available to the British judges, these Muslim legists were eliminated as jural middlemen, leaving the British with the sole power and prerogative to adjudicate in the name of Islamic law. Second – a further step towards totalistic control – the act of translation-cum-codification represented a replacement of the native system's interpretive mechanisms by those of English law. Thus the seemingly innocuous adoption of the translation amounted in effect to what might be termed a policy of 'demolish and replace'. Third, by casting Arabic-Islamic juristic texts in a fixed form, in English, the law ceased to be related organically to the Arabicate juristic and hermeneutical tradition of Islam. And fourth, the new legal texts served to silence customary law, which was not only multifarious but essential to the functioning of Islamic law. This removal of custom from the domain of 'official' law was intended, first, to streamline (or homogenise) the otherwise complex jural forms with which the British had to deal, and second, to deprive Islamic law of one of its mainstays: the communal and customary laws that were entwined with the *sharīʿa* on the level of application. Thus the *very act* of translation uprooted Islamic law from its interpretive-juristic soil and at the same time from the native social matrix in which it was embedded, and on which its successful operation depended. It is instructive that the same process, this time of Turkification, occurred in the Ottoman empire towards the end of the thirteenth/nineteenth century and thereafter, producing similar results in severing the *sharīʿa* from its interpretive tradition.

By the early years of the thirteenth/nineteenth century the courts of India had begun to depend heavily on these translations, which not only made less sense when shorn of their sociological and native hermeneutical contexts, but were also replete with inaccuracies and plain juristic–linguistic errors. This court practice, so-called Anglo-Muhammadan law, was the legal system that the British created, or caused to be created, in their Indian colony. The designation refers less to the fact that it was the British who determined a particular application of the law in an Islamic judicial and juristic context, and much more to the fact that it was a heavily distorted English legal perspective on Islamic law that was administered to Muslim individuals. It may even be argued that Anglo-Muhammadan law at times involved the forceful application of English law as Islamic law[55] – exemplified only in part by *Abul Fata* v

55 M. B. Hooker, *Legal pluralism: An introduction to colonial and neo-colonial laws* (Oxford, 1975), p. 96.

Russomoy Dhur Chowdhury (1894), wherein the Privy Council deliberately ignored Ameer Ali's opinion regarding the law of *waqf*, and instead decided the matter on the basis of the English law of trust. (It was not until two decades later that this ruling was reversed in the 1913 Mussalman Waqf Validating Act.) Yet no systematic importation of raw English regulations was involved in the creation of this hybridity; rather, what was mostly implicated was the imposition of English jural principles grounded in the colonisers' highly subjective notions of 'justice, equity and good conscience' – notions that were bound to alter the shape of Islamic *fiqh* itself.

Furthermore, the Anglo-Muhammadan law was no less affected by the British perceptions of governance, themselves heavily derived from the intractable connections between law and the modern state. For instance, both Governors Hastings and Cornwallis (1786–93) rejected, as did their British counterparts elsewhere,[56] the entire tenor of the *sharīʿa* law of homicide (*dimāʾ*) on the grounds that this law granted private, extrajudicial privileges to the victim's next of kin, who were empowered to mete or not mete out punishment (ranging from retaliation, to payment of blood-money, to pardon) as they saw fit. This right, they held, was the exclusive preserve of the state, which, by definition, had the 'legitimate' right to exercise violence.[57] Reflecting an entrenched state culture of monopoly over violence, Cornwallis further argued that too often criminals escaped punishment under the rule of Islamic law, a situation that would not be allowed to obtain under what he must have seen as an efficient state discipline.[58] His voice echoed Hastings' complaint that Islamic law was irregular, lacking in efficacy and 'founded on the most lenient principles and on an abhorrence of bloodshed'.[59] (Ironically, these colonial perceptions of Islamic law have been diametrically reversed during the last three or four decades.)

A salient systemic change effected by the creation of Anglo-Muhammadan law was the rigidification of Islamic law, a symptom of the attempt to remould Islamic law in the image of the concision, clarity, accessibility and blind-justice tendency of European jural conceptions. Yet another rigidifying process was the conversion of the *sharīʿa* court into a body that operated on the doctrine of

56 See, e.g., Y. Alon, 'The tribal system in the face of the state-formation process: Mandatory Transjordan, 1921–46', *IJMES*, 37 (2005).
57 M. van Creveld, *The rise and decline of the state* (Cambridge, 2000), pp. 155–70.
58 R. Singha, *A despotism of law: Crime and justice in early colonial India* (Delhi, 1998), pp. 2, 49–75.
59 N. Dirks, *The scandal of empire: India and the creation of imperial Britain* (Cambridge, MA, 2006), p. 221.

stare decisis, the obligation of courts to follow the uncontroversial previous judicial decisions of higher courts.

This system could have evolved in Islam, but for a good reason did not. The *sharīʿa* assigned legal expertise and, more importantly, epistemic authority to the *muftī* and author–jurist,[60] not to the *qāḍī*, who, while possessing more or less the same amount of legal knowledge as did his British counterpart, was deemed – qua *qāḍī*[61] – insufficiently qualified to 'make' law. Ijtihādic hermeneutics was the very feature that distinguished Islamic law from modern codified legal systems, a feature that permitted this law to reign supreme in, and accommodate, as varied and diverse cultures, subcultures, local moralities and customary practices as those that flourished in Java, Malabar, Khurāsān, Madagascar, Syria and Morocco. But in so far as judicial practice was concerned, the bindingness of a ruling according to the specifically British doctrine of precedent deprived the *qāḍī* of the formerly wider array of opinions to choose from in the light of the facts presented in the case. Once a determination of law in a specific case was made binding, as would happen in a British court, the otherwise unceasing hermeneutical activities of the Muslim *muftī*-cum-author–jurist were rendered pointless; indeed, he would subsequently disappear from the legal as well as the intellectual life of the jural community.

The doctrine of *stare decisis* also stimulated far-reaching changes in the way the courts worked. The product of an intensive book-keeping culture, the logic of *stare decisis* required the maintenance of a systematic recording of law reports, an activity which began in some parts of India during the early decades of the thirteenth/nineteenth century and which was systematised for the whole colony in the Indian Law Reports Act of 1875. A by-product of this process – one of whose attributes was an unwavering emphasis upon the physical act of recording data – was a fundamental change in the Islamic law of evidence, where oral testimony based on integrity, morality and rectitude was paradigmatic. Long before the 1875 Act the British began the practice of recording testimony, which, once committed to the court record, also acquired a fixed form. But this was an interim development, for the British introduced further reforms in 1861 and 1872, whereby the English law of procedure fully supplanted both its Islamic and Anglo-Muhammadan counterparts.

Anglo-Muhammadan law, however, was an interim colonialist solution that mediated the British domination of India until the uprising of 1857. The 1860s

60 Two juristic roles discussed in detail in Hallaq, *Authority*, pp. 166–235.

61 On the epistemic authority of the *qāḍī* qua *qāḍī* see ibid., pp. 168–74.

and 1870s witnessed the abolition of slavery, as well as of the Islamic laws of procedure, criminal law and evidence. All these were superseded by British laws enacted by statute. By the end of the century, and with the exception of family law and certain elements of property transactions, all indigenous laws had been supplanted by British law. But all this was introduced piecemeal, answering, in an ad hoc and generally incremental manner, the growing anxiety of the British to exercise control over their Indian subjects, especially after the rebellion of 1857. In this picture, Anglo-Muhammadan law represented no more than a middle stage permitting the solidification of the colonialist hold over economic, political and legal power.

The process through which legal power was transferred to the hands of the modern state continued unabated under the new and now independent nationalist regimes throughout the Muslim world. What was left for the *sharīʿa* to regulate, as we have said, was personal status, including such areas as inheritance, child custody and gifts. While the popular Muslim imagination, even today, appears to hold these remnants of the *sharīʿa* to be an authentic and genuine expression of *fiqhī* family law, the fact of the matter is that even this sphere of law underwent structural and foundational changes that ultimately resulted in severing it from both the substance of classical *fiqh* and the methodology by which *fiqh* had operated. This severance was effected through various devices that included both administrative and interpretive techniques. Attributed to nebulous origins in Islamic tradition and history, these modern devices were cultivated and augmented to yield results that had never been entertained before.

The first of these devices was the adoption of the principle of necessity – marginal in traditional law, but now given a much wider scope to justify a utilitarian approach to the promulgation of laws. Simply put, that which is deemed necessary becomes justifiable as a matter of law. The second device was procedural, which is to say that, without changing certain parts of Islamic substantive law, it was possible through this device to exclude particular claims from judicial enforcement, thus in effect leaving *fiqhī* law mere ink on dusty paper. The third device, one of the most effective methods by which new positive law was created from the virtual dispersal-cum-restructuring of *fiqh*, consisted of an eclectic approach that operated on two levels: *takhayyur* and *talfiq* (lit. 'selection' and 'amalgamation'). The former involved the incorporation not only of weak and discredited opinions from the school, but also of opinions held by other schools not followed in the country adopting them. The options opened up by this device seemed boundless, since not only could Twelver Shīʿite opinions be absorbed by the codes of

Sunnī countries, but also those of the long defunct Ẓāhirite school. *Talfīq* involved an even more daring technique. While *takhayyur* required the plucking of opinions, for a single code, from various schools, *talfīq* amounted to combining elements of one opinion from various quarters within and without the school. The product thereof was entirely new, because the opinions now combined had originally belonged to altogether different and perhaps incongruent premises.[62] The fourth device was the so-called neo-*ijtihād*, an interpretive approach that is largely free of what we have here called Arabicate hermeneutics. In a sense, the second device of *takhayyur*-cum-*talfīq* rests on this general approach, since the act of combining different, if not divergent, elements of one opinion entails a measure of interpretive freedom. The fifth and final device, much like the first, represented a new application of the old but restricted principle that any law that does not contradict the *sharīʿa* may be deemed lawful.

In their entirety, therefore, these devices did the bidding of the state in absorbing the Islamic legal tradition into its well-defined structures of codification. In the so-called reform process, many of the rights of women and children were expanded and improved, but many others resulted in privations. Partha Chatterjee's characterisation in the context of nationalism may be aptly applied to the modern state's legal engineering, which 'conferred upon women the honor of a new social responsibility and by associating the task of female emancipation with the historical goal of sovereign nationhood, bound them to a narrow, and yet entirely legitimate, subordination'.[63]

62 See H. Liebesny, *Law of the Near and Middle East* (Albany, 1975), p. 138; Hallaq, *History*, pp. 210, 261.

63 Partha Chatterjee, 'Colonialism, nationalism, and colonized women: The contest in India', *American Ethnologist*, 16, 4 (1989), pp. 629–32. For a detailed account of legal modernisation and the concomitant production of a new patriarchy see Hallaq, *Sharia: Theory, practice, transformations*.

5

Conversion and the *ahl al-dhimma*

DAVID J. WASSERSTEIN

The problem

The word *islām* means 'submission', 'submitting', and conversion to Islam involves nothing more, at base, than submitting oneself to God. It has consequences – legal, fiscal and especially social – in different contexts, but its religious aspect consists of just the formal recognition of the one God and of Muḥammad as His messenger. Reciting the formula *lā ilāha illā Allāh, Muḥammad rasūl Allāh* is enough. The act of coming to Islam is thus very simple. The worldwide spread of a faith that at first was exclusively that of the inhabitants of the Arabian Peninsula was, however, much more complex as Islam came for centuries also to mean an empire created and at first largely ruled over by Arabs and a culture dominated by Islam: 'civilization and Islam went together'.[1]

Between 632 and about 1500 the great majority of the people between the Atlantic and India, and many beyond, converted to Islam. Who did it, when, where, how and above all why? What was the meaning of conversion, for converts and for those around them, their new co-religionists and their former ones? Can we measure the degree or rate of conversion in different societies and areas of the Islamic world? Did it happen all at once or over a longer period of time? Was it voluntary or did converts change their faith under compulsion? What happened to those left behind, those who did not undergo conversion?

We have less direct evidence and source material for this most important of the transformations brought by Muḥammad than for many others, such as the Arabicisation in language of the lands between the Atlantic and the Persian Gulf. Description and explanation are accordingly not easy. Variety of many

1 The phrase comes from Natalie Zemon Davis, *Trickster travels: A sixteenth-century Muslim between worlds* (New York, 2006), p. 149.

sorts, in different times and places, increases our difficulty further. And in large parts of the early conquests, Islamisation was intimately tied up with two other processes, linguistic and ethnic acculturation to the Arab rulers, without, however, being coterminous with them.

Reasons for conversion

Motives for conversion appear at first sight easy to classify: heading the list should be acceptance of the message brought by Muḥammad. When we read the biography of the Prophet himself, and occasionally also accounts of later generations, this is indeed what we find: someone hears a statement about Islam that dramatically dismisses his commitment to his earlier faith and brings him over to Islam, a simpler version of the road to Damascus and one travelled by very many over the centuries. Al-Ṭufayl ibn ʿAmr al-Dawsī came to the Prophet, and 'the apostle explained Islam to me and recited the Quran to me. By God I never heard anything finer nor anything more just. So I became a Muslim and bore true witness.' Then he went home and told his father and his wife about his new religion, and each of them in turn said, 'All right, then my religion is your religion.'[2] Charismatic, if also laconic, conversions of this sort are among the most commonly reported in the sources, but there must be doubt both as to their authenticity and as to their numbers. The bareness of the account in most cases provides little explanatory support for those outside the circle of the faithful.

Doubt also attends autobiographical accounts by converts. These, still more than other autobiographies, tend to the self-serving, and, like many texts of interreligious polemic, have more the character of set-piece literary constructs than of genuine spiritual journeying. The *Ifḥām al-Yahūd* of Samaw'al al-Maghribī, of the sixth/twelfth century, is a good case in point. Its very title, 'Silencing the Jews', reveals that it is at least as much concerned with apologetic polemic and missionising among its author's former co-religionists as with describing the spiritual life of its author. So too in the case of another ex-Jew from north Africa, ʿAbd al-Ḥaqq al-Islāmī, author of a work entitled 'The sword stretched out in refutation of the rabbis of the Jews'.[3]

2 Ibn Isḥāq, *The life of Muhammad* (Sīrat Rasūl Allāh), trans. with introduction and notes Alfred Guillaume (Oxford, 1955), pp. 175–7.

3 ʿAbd al-Ḥaqq al-Islâmî, *al-Sayf al-mamdûd fî al-radd ʿalà aḥbâr al-yahûd (Espada extendida para refutar a los sabios judíos)*, ed., trans. and with notes and introd. Esperanza Alfonso (Madrid, 1998).

Conversion as part of larger social processes offers additional motives for our understanding. While we can still see the individual moving over to Islam, he (or she) appears now as an anonymous face in a crowd, choreographed by such motivations as the desire to preserve or improve socio-economic position or to change cultural identity. A major source of converts in the early Umayyad period following the initial conquests was prisoners of war, enslaved and then manumitted and converted to the faith of their new rulers.[4] Under the later Umayyads converts came especially from fugitive peasants, escaping taxes in their villages for the safety and anonymity of the large garrison cities and converting along the way. Papyri from Egypt as well as literary sources portray them as converting purely in order to evade taxation. Governors would be instructed to send them back home, and to collect the taxes.[5] Conversion to the faith of the rulers did not, however, in this early period mean adoption into the ranks of the rulers. As Crone remarks, 'the Arabs were not always willing to share their God with gentile converts'.[6] At a higher social level things could be handled differently, and a number of non-Muslim rulers in Khurāsān and the eastern Iranian region in the reigns of al-Mahdī (158–69/775–85) and al-Ma'mūn (198–218/813–33), wishing to maintain their status and to retain their positions in the new dispensation, were able to surrender their thrones to the caliph and receive them back by converting and becoming clients (*mawālī*) of Islam.[7] In similar fashion, several marcher lords in northern Spain, between Islamic and Christian areas of control, like the Banū Qasī, converted to Islam and continued to dominate border territories, intermarrying with both Christian and Muslim families as circumstances and opportunity permitted.

All of these, despite the great numbers involved, are individual conversions. We also find mass conversions, as for example among the Berbers of North Africa, with entire tribes accepting Islam as part of the process of conquest in the course of the seventh century.[8] Similar phenomena of mass conversion are found among other tribes and nomads, especially among the Turks who

4 Patricia Crone, *Slaves on horses: The evolution of the Islamic polity* (Cambridge, 1980), pp. 49–51.

5 Gladys Frantz-Murphy, 'Conversion in early Islamic Egypt: The economic factor', in *Documents de l'Islam médiéval: Nouvelles perspectives de recherche, actes de la table ronde, Paris, 3–5 mars 1988* (Paris, 1991). For other examples of conversion due to economic distress see Milka Levy-Rubin, 'New evidence relating to the process of Islamization in Palestine in the early Muslim period: The case of Samaria', *JESHO*, 43 (2000).

6 Crone, *Slaves on horses*, p. 49; also pp. 40–53.

7 Ibid., pp. 76–7.

8 See Michael Brett, 'The spread of Islam in Egypt and north Africa', in Michael Brett (ed.), *Northern Africa: Islam and modernization* (London, 1973); also Henri Teissier, 'La

entered the Islamic world during the early Middle Ages, both those who came as mercenaries and those who came as conquerors, and later on in Central Asia. What the real religious meaning of such conversion can have been for the individual is difficult to say. However, as with similar mass religious transformations in England at about the same time (and also in Iceland and Kiev somewhat later), the new faith struck deep roots fairly fast. Berber rebellions in North Africa and al-Andalus after the first generation or so do not take anti-Islamic form, but opt rather for variety within the fold of Islam – in this not very different from Berber behaviour centuries earlier with respect to Christianity.

How to convert

How did they convert? At the start, as we have seen, conversion could be very informal. Later on things became more ordered. We know a little about this, especially as we have, in several legal formularies from al-Andalus, the texts of documents 'for the conversion' of various types of individual – a Christian man, a Jewish woman, a Majūsī etc. The texts differ slightly, to take account of the varying backgrounds of the converts and the different faiths and beliefs (as understood by Muslim lawyers) that they are required explicitly to renounce as they become Muslims. The Christian attests that 'the Masīḥ Jesus son of Mary, may God bless him and give him peace, is His servant, His envoy, His word and His breath that He sent unto Mary', the Jew, that 'Moses and Ezra together with the other prophets are His servants and envoys'.[9] These documents lay jargonised legal stress on the voluntary aspect of the convert's abandonment of his former faith and his adoption of Islam ('being of sound mind and good health, enjoying full possession of his mental faculties and legal capacity'[10]). This was a necessity for the validity of the conversion as a formal act in an organised society (and something we find also in medieval Christendom).

desaparición de la antigua iglesia de África', in Henri Teissier and Ramón Lourido Díaz (eds.), *El Cristianismo en el norte de Africa* (n.p., 1993); Elizabeth Savage, 'Conversion or metamorphosis: the Christian population after the Islamic conquest', in Mark Horton and Thomas Wiedemann (eds.), *North Africa from Antiquity to Islam: Papers of a conference held at Bristol, October 1994* (Bristol, 1994).

9 See Pedro Chalmeta, 'Le passage à l'Islam dans al-Andalus au Xe siècle', in *Actas del XII Congreso de la UEAI (Malaga, 1984)* (Madrid, 1986), p. 163; M. Abumalham, 'La conversión según formularios notariales andalusíes: valoración de la legalidad de la conversión de Maimonídes', *Miscelánea de estudios árabes y hebraicos*, 34 (1985), p. 72.

10 See the references in the preceding note.

These are forms and come from legal minds and a later period, when things had settled down, not from the inchoate early period of the conquests. Too great a concern with these, for all their importance, can obscure the larger picture. In the case of mass conversions of Berber tribes, we can scarcely imagine entire tribes queuing up, whether to sign off on legal documents – illiterates signing documents drawn up in a non-literate society, in a script and a language which they did not know – or to affirm orally the oneness of God and the status of His Messenger. Similarly, at another extreme, the picture drawn by the Spanish scholar Mikel de Epalza, of Andalusī Christians becoming Muslims by default as a result of the absence in al-Andalus of duly ordained bishops or priests, should be rejected as too rigid in its view of Christian canon law in practice, of Islamic notions of conversion and of individual realities on the ground.[11] What both do suggest, rather, is the delineation of conditions in which Islam could grow with some ease, encouraged by its status, socially and politically, and by the practical impossibility of apostasy, a capital crime under Islamic law.

Rates of conversion

How fast did the overall process occur? Did it progress at the same rate everywhere? Some significant moments can be observed. In Egypt economic motives, taxation of non-Muslims and the attractions of employment that required conversion began the process, and the repression of tax revolts in 238/852 and after gave additional impetus to large-scale conversion. Under the Mamlūks, too, in 700/1301 and again in 755/1354, anti-Christian rioting persuaded large numbers of Christians to convert, and at various dates, for example under the Fāṭimid caliph al-Ḥākim (r. 386–411/996–1021), confiscation of Church properties helped to impoverish the Christian community and drive Christians into Islam.[12] In al-Andalus the failure of the so-called martyrs of Cordoba in the mid-third/ninth century to arouse Christian reaction to

11 M. de Epalza, 'Mozarabs: An emblematic Christian minority in Islamic al-Andalus', in Salma Khadra Jayyusi (ed.), *The legacy of Muslim Spain*, Handbuch der Orientalistik 1, 12 (Leiden, 1992).

12 For Egypt see Frantz-Murphy, 'Conversion'; Yaakov Lev, 'Persecutions and conversion to Islam in eleventh century Egypt', *Asian and African Studies*, 22 (1988); Donald P. Little, 'Coptic converts to Islam during the Baḥrī Mamlūk period', in Michael Gervers and Ramzi Jibran Bikhazi (eds.), *Conversion and continuity: Indigenous Christian communities in Islamic lands, eighth to eighteenth centuries*, Papers in Medieval Studies 9 (Toronto, 1990). See now also Tamer el-Leithy, 'Coptic culture and conversion in medieval Cairo, 1293–1524 AD', Ph.D. thesis, Princeton University (2005).

Muslim rule gave added impetus to conversion, and by the fourth/tenth century we find Christians going over to Arabic and giving up Latin even for religious purposes. However, while Muslims were probably a majority in al-Andalus by the fifth/eleventh century, we cannot point to any decisive events there that precipitated conversion en masse.[13] In the sixth/twelfth century the Almohads dealt terrible blows to the remaining Christian communities in al-Andalus, as well as in North Africa. But by that time Christians, to say nothing of Jews and other non-Muslims, all over the Islamic world were greatly reduced, and they faced broader social pressures inducing them to convert.

Some apparently significant moments may be less significant than they appear: the Sufi shaykh Ibrāhīm ibn Shahriyār al-Kāzarūnī (352–426/963–1035), from south-western Iran, was a grandson of Zoroastrian converts. He himself worked hard to proselytise for Islam among the Zoroastrians, though with little success. He also wanted to build the first Friday mosque in Kāzarūn, but every time his followers started to build it the structure was destroyed by the local Zoroastrians. Throughout 370/981 the shaykh had to pray outside in the fields. Finally, he saw the Prophet in a dream, working at building a mosque himself. From that time on, the building of the mosque went ahead successfully, the Zoroastrians ceased their interference and even gradually came over to Islam, and the shaykh eventually made a total of 24,000 converts.

Morony has seen this story as evidence of the presence of larger numbers of rural than of urban Zoroastrians in the region. Yavari, by contrast, prefers to see the story as recalling the struggles of the Prophet against his contemporaries in Mecca and his success in finally setting up a community in Medina.[14] Yavari stresses that we should not look for historical data in a story like this. It comes from a hagiographical context. The literary and the historiographical contexts of such stories are what give them their meaning.[15]

In the absence of much direct evidence for conversion, questions about the rate of conversion seemed for long impossible to answer. However, in 1979,

13 The best work on this topic is still E. P. Colbert, *The martyrs of Cordoba, 850–859: A study of the sources* (Washington, DC, 1962); see also Jessica A. Coope, 'Religious and cultural conversion to Islam in ninth-century Umayyad Córdoba', *Journal of World History*, 4 (1993).

14 See David W. Damrel, 'Some aspects of Sufis, miracles and conversion in 16th century Central Asia', *Journal of Central Asian Studies*, 5 (1994), p. 7, for a similar point.

15 See Michael Morony, 'The age of conversions: A reassessment', in Gervers and Bikhazi (eds.), *Conversion and continuity*, pp. 137, 144; Neguin Yavari, 'The conversion stories of Shaykh Abū Isḥāq Kāzarūnī', in Guyda Armstrong and Ian N. Wood (eds.), *Christianizing peoples and converting individuals*, International medieval research 7 (Turnhout, 2000), pp. 242–6.

Richard Bulliet suggested a possible avenue to advance on this issue.[16] He proposed using the huge, repetitive, and hence quantifiable, resources of the medieval Arabic biographical dictionaries. Noting that their contents offered a random and hence representative cross-section of their populations, that they rarely mentioned non-Islamic names in genealogies, that these seemed to occur at the earliest point in the genealogies, and that they were often succeeded by names carrying Islamic significance, he suggested that we could see here the generation of conversion in multiple individual cases. Analysis of the material by geography and by period – with all the difficulties that these threw up – could show us how fast people who converted in different areas did so. Bulliet's theory has much to commend it, not least the fact that it appears to conform to our general impressions, based on other, largely anecdotal, sources, of how things were. His analysis shows, for example, that Iran probably had a Muslim majority as much as a century earlier than Syria. And for problematic areas, such as al-Andalus, where the body of relevant information is too small to carry statistically persuasive force, the conclusions to which the information points nevertheless agree with what might be expected from a comparison with other areas at comparable periods in the development of their Islamisation.

Bulliet's use of methods of statistical analysis and models borrowed from the hard and social sciences, as well as his dependence on graphs for the exposition of much of his argument, made his hypothesis difficult for many Islamicists to accept, sometimes even to understand – it seems to remain impossible for some to understand Bulliet's explanation that all of his quantified assertions concern only the portion of a total population that actually, over time, converted to Islam (not least because the biographical dictionaries cover only Muslims). Thus if only 80 per cent converted, a suggestion about 70 per cent of the conversion having taken place would refer only to some 56 per cent of the population (70 per cent of 80 per cent = 56 per cent – in fact things are a little more complex than this) and not to 70 per cent of the population as a whole. We know very little about medieval population sizes, and we can know next to nothing about such matters as the size of the unconverted parts of any population.[17] The distinction escaped many readers of the book, and helped to demonstrate the continuing difficulty of using such non-humanistic techniques in this field.

16 Richard W. Bulliet, *Conversion to Islam in the medieval period: An essay in quantitative history* (Cambridge, MA, 1979).

17 David Ayalon, 'Regarding population estimates in the countries of medieval Islam', *JESHO*, 28 (1985).

Bulliet's analysis did not take into account two further elements of possible difficulty: first, the huge numbers of converts, mentioned above, resulting from the conquests, the enslavement of prisoners of war and their subsequent manumission and Islamisation; and second, the flight of the peasants to evade taxation. The great numbers and the population movements involved in both, while they do not necessarily invalidate the conclusions he offered, nevertheless need to be taken into account in any reckoning of the early period of conversion.

A further difficulty with Bulliet's hypothesis is that, more than is the case with historical analysis generally, it does not lend itself to any form of external testing or verification. It depends critically, for example, on the assumption that, overall, the genealogies given in the biographical dictionaries are both authentic and correct. Such an assumption is untestable for any but isolated cases, and it can also be challenged more broadly. The degree to which such a challenge can be faced down is debatable.

The reconstruction by region and by period that Bulliet's theory provided also permitted him to attempt a broad co-relation between observed rates of conversion and other developments. Two in particular deserve notice: first, the rise and relative strength in different areas of the various Islamic law schools; and second, the rise of independent or semi-independent dynasties in different regions of the early Islamic world.

Why should particular law schools win so many adherents in one place, only to see others dominate elsewhere? Bulliet argued that the varying success of different schools – the Ḥanafīs as against the Shāfiʿīs, for example, in Iran – reflected the particular stages that Islamisation had reached in different places. Similarly, in the case of the emergence of local dynasties, such as the Ṭāhirids in Iran (205–59/821–73) or the Ṭūlūnids in Egypt (254–92/868–905), he was able to argue that they reflected the development of conversion to a point where there was no fear of non-Islamic rule returning, with the added implication that the caliphate was now far less necessary as a focal institution for a unitary Islamic state. Again, however, in the absence of other evidence, his hypothesis here as earlier remains attractive – even plausible – rather than wholly convincing.

Bulliet's hypothesis was of importance in at least two ways. It transformed the medieval Arabic biographical dictionaries into a new type (for Islamic studies) of historical source; and it offered answers to problems going far beyond those of conversion and Islamisation alone. It did so for the critical early period of mass conversion in the heartlands of what, as a result of just such conversion, became the Islamic world – as distinct from merely an empire ruled by Muslims. At the same time, Bulliet's innovativeness turned out to be also a limitation: biographical dictionaries either do not exist or cannot for extraneous reasons be used for other periods and areas; parallel sources seem to be absent; and, not least because of the change in the size and character of Islamic societies wrought by conversion, the historical problems that Bulliet sought to use his approach to solve are largely absent there too.

Conversion outside the heartlands

In consequence, despite the exciting character of this marriage of modern quantitative analysis (and marketing strategies) with repetitive medieval Arabic texts, study of the underlying problem has turned in two directions since 1979. On the one hand, there has been a return to smaller-scale case studies of conversion – incidents or individuals or places. On the other, there have been more attempts to study later areas of Islamic growth, beyond the lands of the early conquests, where Islam has expanded largely without conquest, such as sub-Saharan Africa and Central and South-East Asia.[18] Here scholars have offered a variety of models to account for the penetration and growth of Islam.

In the absence of conquest in many of these areas, conversion had social but no legal implications; further, in non-literate societies documentation of conversion was impracticable and offered no benefit. Penetration and conversion were generally peaceful, resulting from cultural and economic contact between different groups, and encouraged by the simplicity and adaptability of Islam. Islamisation was accordingly less clear-cut and could be less definitive than in the earlier conquests. At the same time, it overlapped very often with the expansion of political Islam, and the two can sometimes scarcely be distinguished from each other. In these areas legend abounds and patterns are more varied.

Africa

In Africa Berbers brought Islam across the Sahara, and it was carried southwards from one group to another by traders. They established economic

18 See the articles collected in Nehemia Levtzion (ed.), *Conversion to Islam* (New York and London, 1979); Gervers and Bikhazi (eds.), *Conversion and continuity*; Mercedes García-Arenal (ed.), *Conversions islamiques: Identités religieuses en Islam méditerranéen* (Paris, 2001); and, for a comparative perspective, Christopher Lamb and M. Darrol Bryant (eds.), *Religious conversion: Contemporary practices and controversies* (London, 1999).

networks whose importance was recognised by rulers and was supported by them. Not only did they establish trading links, they also made themselves visible by building mosques (often in very distinctive local styles), created links with other Islamic centres and developed local traditions of Islamic scholarship. Lineages of Muslim scholar-traders in such places as Gao (in Mali), Timbuktu and elsewhere offered a focus for other Muslims from outside and attracted interest from locals for religious and cultural as well as economic reasons.[19] The economic benefits brought by the traders gave them easy access to rulers; rulers fostered such contact in order the better to control the traders and benefit from their activity; Islam represented a high culture through association with which a chief might win prestige; the prayers and amulets that Muslims could offer protected chiefs against droughts or plots; the moral and legal structures of Islam offered a convenient standard both for individual behaviour and for generalised trading rules.

Nonetheless, the advance of Islam was fitful. Sometimes only the ruling elite would convert. In Malal, beyond upper Senegal, the prayers and sacrifices of the local priests could not end a drought. A Muslim promised to pray for relief if the king accepted Islam. He taught the king some prayers and passages from the Qurʾān, and the next Friday the king and the Muslim prayed together. At dawn rain began to fall abundantly. The king destroyed the local idols, expelled the sorcerers and converted, together with his family and the nobility. However the common people, we are told, remained pagans.[20]

Paganism could even return. The empire of Mali, whose ruler Mansā Mūsā travelled in great magnificence through Egypt on the *ḥajj* to Mecca in the eighth/fourteenth century, went into a decline in the following century. It lost direct contact with Muslim centres, Muslim traders abandoned the capital and, though Muslims still served the ruler, there was a slide back towards paganism.[21]

The role of teachers, as in the case from Malal just mentioned, reflects the importance of traders and scholars, often the same individuals, in bringing Islam to new areas, in East as in West Africa. In East Africa Muslim traders settled on the coast of Ethiopia as early as the second/eighth century, and by

19 Elias N. Saad, *Social history of Timbuktu: The role of Muslim scholars and notables 1400–1900* (Cambridge, 1983).

20 Nehemia Levtzion, 'Patterns of Islamization in West Africa', in Daniel F. McCall and Norman R. Bennett (eds.), *Aspects of West African Islam*, Boston University Papers on Africa 5 (Boston, 1971), p. 33, quoting al-Bakrī (fifth/eleventh century).

21 Ibid., p. 35.

the third/ninth Muslim communities along the routes inland were growing into small states. Harar, the most important of these, became a centre for learning as well as trade, and Islam gradually attracted converts from among the ruling classes of the nomadic tribes of the region, though without ever succeeding in eliminating the Christianity of Ethiopia.

India

More Muslims live east of Karachi than west of it. Islam came to the Indian subcontinent early, with Muslim armies reaching Sind (now in Pakistan) in the same year as the conquest of Spain, 92/711. However, it was not until the time of the Ghaznavids and the Ghūrids, from the late fourth/tenth to the seventh/thirteenth centuries, that large advances were made. The Ghūrids in particular won huge areas of northern India, laying the foundations for the later vast spread of Islam there.

Richard Eaton identifies a problem with our understanding of conversion in India.[22] He argues that the three theories traditionally held to explain conversion in India do not work, principally because the areas of massive conversion, East Bengal and West Punjab, were paradoxically those that saw less political penetration by Islam. Where political Islam penetrated most strongly, he points out, conversion was less thoroughgoing. Foreign rule, by Turco-Iranian invaders between the seventh/thirteenth and the twelfth/eighteenth centuries, did not bring massive conversion in its wake. Economic disabilities, or employment possibilities, what he labels 'political patronage', also do not explain mass conversion. Accordingly, he has little time for the great rulers of subcontinental Islam as agents of conversion. As for the notion that conversion offered an escape from the caste system of Hinduism, it is rarely referred to in the sources, it does not seem generally to have had a liberating, equalising effect in India and, most importantly, East Bengal and West Punjab were in any case not properly integrated into the Hindu caste system at the time of the massive conversions to Islam, so that this claim has little relevance here.

In place of these theories Eaton offers a new and highly attractive theory, which he sums up in the words accretion and reform.[23] He suggests that

22 Richard Eaton, 'Approaches to the study of conversion to Islam in India', in Richard C. Martin (ed.), *Approaches to Islam in religious studies* (Tucson, 1985).

23 Ibid.; Richard Eaton, 'Who are the Bengal Muslims? Conversion and Islamization in Bengal', in Richard Eaton, *Essays on Islam and Indian history* (New Delhi, 2000), repr. in Rowena Robinson and Sathianathan Clarke (eds.), *Religious conversion in India: Modes, motivations, and meanings* (New Delhi, 2003).

people living in a pre-literate society on the ecological and political frontier of an expanding agrarian society were the more easily absorbed into that society's religious ideology. Both East Bengal and West Punjab were fringe areas, on the socio-ecological frontier of Hindu agrarian society and the political frontier of Islamic society. Eaton sees agents of change in Muslim *qāḍīs*, who could offer judgment for Muslims and non-Muslims alike, in the appeal of a written and hence unchanging Qur'ān to a pre-literate society, and to some degree also in Sufis. But Sufis were far from being the missionaries that they have been seen as in the past. Rather, he points out, after their deaths Sufis could work miracles: their shrines and their descendants possessed *baraka*. In the Punjab from the seventh/thirteenth century we find huge Sufi shrines for Jāṭs who were migrating into the area. The many hundreds of shrines to different Sufi saints all over India served to present the Islamic God in a locally accessible idiom.

That idiom was expressed in various ways. Islamic names, for example, in our sources increased among the Sials in the Punjab from 10 per cent in the early ninth/fifteenth century to 56 per cent in the mid-eleventh/seventeenth, and reached 100 per cent in the early thirteenth/nineteenth. The progression is slow, as he notes, but it is definite. Similar changes can be observed in the growth in the use of names for God denoting Islamic attributes of the divine and in the building of mosques.

Islam in India is a religion of the plough, as it is also part of the machinery of agrarianisation, taming the wilderness, clearing the jungle, establishing markets and introducing a cash economy. Thus a poet in the late tenth/sixteenth century writes:[24]

> From the South came the harvesters,
> Five hundred of them came under one organizer.
> From the West came Zafar Mian,
> Together with twenty two thousand men.
> Sulaimani beads in their hands,
> They chanted the names of their *pir* and the Prophet.
> Having cleared the forest,
> They established markets.
> Hundreds and hundreds of foreigners
> Ate and entered the forest.
> Hearing the sound of the axe,
> The tiger became apprehensive and ran away, roaring.

24 Mukundaram, *Caṇḍī-Mangala*, cited in Eaton, 'Who are the Bengal Muslims?', p. 267 (*Religious conversion*, pp. 85–6).

Political change and new forms of transport, improving contact with Mecca, especially from the twelfth / eighteenth century onwards, led to greater integration into the broader world of Islam. The increased awareness of the normative unity of Islam led to Eaton's second stage, that of reform. This was expressed in a greater literalness in understanding of the Qur'ān and, above all, in more social exclusiveness at the local level. The result, Eaton suggests, was the demand for a separate Muslim state when the British withdrew in 1947, and, curiously, the adoption of Arab culture as a kind of supra-national model of Islam in the Indian context.

Eaton's theory explains religious change in social terms, describing Islam in India as appealing to non-literate, non-agricultural populations, not part of the Hindu caste system. The gradual accretion, in the first stage of his model, of elements of Islamic social behaviour and the initial syncretism with neighbouring cultures and religions share much with what happens elsewhere, particularly in South-East Asia.

South-East Asia

Islam seems to have reached different parts of South-East Asia between the end of the seventh / thirteenth and the eleventh / seventeenth centuries. This is one of the most poorly documented periods in the history of the region.[25] The bulk of the sources are late and legendary, and concerned with just a single place in this vast area of 13,000 islands. They tend to relate the introduction of Islam in a particular locality as the sudden conversion, occasionally with miraculous intervention by the Prophet, of the ruler and the ruling elite. The mass of the populace has little more than walk-on parts in these stories, whose aim seems to be rather to legitimise an existing dynasty's adoption of Islam than to provide historical information.[26] Thus in North Sumatra around 696 / 1297 a local ruler saw the Prophet in a dream, discovered on awakening that he was circumcised, and found himself reciting the *shahāda* and all thirty sections of the Qur'ān, even though he had never been taught any of it and did not know a word of Arabic. Following the arrival of a ship bearing a Muslim shaykh 'the whole population willingly recited the profession of faith, in all sincerity and with belief in their hearts'.[27]

25 M. C. Ricklefs, *A history of modern Indonesia since c. 1200*, 3rd edn (Basingstoke, 2001), p. 3, says: 'The spread of Islam is one of the most significant processes of Indonesian history, but also one of the most obscure.'

26 Russell Jones, 'Ten conversion myths from Indonesia', in Levtzion (ed.), *Conversion*.

27 Ibid., pp. 134–5.

Islam was, however, present even in northern Sumatra earlier than 696/1297, for we have the tombstone of another ruler there dated 608/1211. What is not clear in most places is whether the conversion of the ruler and the elite really did involve the conversion of the mass of the population. An apothecary from Lisbon, Tomé Pires, who spent three years in Malacca between 1512 and 1515, reports that there were still some non-Muslim rulers in Sumatra in his time, though the majority were already Muslims. He also reports local people converting to Islam.[28] Is this an indication of wider social transformation?

In the absence of evidence, history is re-modelled and simplified in later literature. In the thirteenth/nineteenth century Pakubuwana VI, a Javanese king exiled by the Dutch, composed a poem, the *Babad jaka tingkir* (Story of a youth), in which he described the Islamisation of the island and the building of a monumental mosque in Demak in the early tenth/sixteenth century:[29]

> Now at that time in Java's land
> All had become Moslem
> There was none who did resist
> All the mountain hermits
> The ascetics and acolytes, the devotees and disciples
> Many converted to the Faith.
>
> And the royal Buddhist and Saivite monks, the Hindu priests
> Were exchanged for *fuqaha* lawyers
> Great and mighty pundits
> Excellent *ulama*
> ...
> Why! Even of the foreign kings
> Who were to Java vassal
> Many had become Moslem

The agents of Islamisation in Indonesia are still unclear. International trade appears to be a necessary element in this, for it brought the islands into contact with the world of Islam. But trade seems to have been there for a long time before conversion took off, so trade in itself is not the explanation. In different places Muslim merchants, both visitors and settlers, intermarriage with locals, converted rulers and local elites, learned mystics and Sufis and holy men too

28 Ricklefs, *History*, p. 4.
29 Translated in Nancy K. Florida, *Writing the past, inscribing the future: History as prophecy in colonial Java* (Durham, NC, and London, 1995), p. 155.

are all plausible agents of diffusion, but we do not have the evidence to be sure, so scholarly hypotheses abound.

Turks and Mongols

The Turks of Central Asia had experience of Islam very early. Turkish slaves had been bought by Islamic rulers, trained as soldiers and converted to Islam as early as the middle of the third/ninth century.[30] Other Turks later conquered and Islamised Anatolia.[31] Soldiery of Turkish background, whether imported individually as slaves or invading in groups as conquerors, came to rule large parts of the eastern Islamic world from the fourth/tenth century for nearly a millennium. Other Turks and Mongols, who invaded the Iranian region and came close to taking over the whole of the Islamic world, converted to Islam in Central Asia.

The reasons for the change of faith appear to have been mixtures of *raison d'état* and spiritual conversion. Some of the stories that we have about the conversions of individual rulers are clearly pious or political legends – thus the father of Berke Khān, who succeeded as ruler of the Golden Horde in 655/1257, is said to have given him as a baby to a Muslim midwife to cut his navel-string and give him milk (another version of the story has the baby Berke already born as a Muslim, refuse his mother's milk and wait until a Muslim midwife gave him her milk) – others may well be true.[32] Michal Biran has recently argued that the conversion of Tarmashirin Khān in around 730/1330 (he reigned from 731/1331 to 735/1334) generated no legends because he was not the first Muslim ruler in his dynasty and because he was a relative failure during his brief reign, but above all because he (and his descendants) would

30 Crone, *Slaves on horses*; David Ayalon, 'The military reforms of Caliph al-Muʿtaṣim: Their background and consequences', in David Ayalon, *Islam and the abode of war: Military slaves and Islamic adversaries* (Aldershot, 1994), Item I. For possible exceptions see David Ayalon, 'On the eunuchs in Islam', *JSAI*, 1 (1979), p. 69 (repr. in *Outsiders in the lands of Islam: Mamluks, Mongols and eunuchs* (London, 1980), Item III). For the possibility that some eunuchs were actually born Muslims see David Ayalon, 'The Mamluk novice, on his youthfulness and his original religion', *Revue des Études Islamiques*, 54 (1986), esp. p. 6 (repr. in *Islam and the abode of war*, Item V).

31 For this process see especially Speros Vryonis, Jr., *The decline of medieval Hellenism in Asia Minor and the process of Islamization from the eleventh through the fifteenth century* (Berkeley, Los Angeles and London, 1971); also V. L. Ménage, 'The Islamization of Anatolia', in Levtzion (ed.), *Conversion*.

32 For an exhaustive study of one conversion narrative, that of the *khan* Özbek, and its echoes through six centuries, see Devin DeWeese, *Islamization and native religion in the Golden Horde: Baba Tükles and conversion to Islam in historical and epic tradition* (University Park, PA, 1994).

have represented an inconvenience to Tamerlane (Tīmūr Lang, r. 771–807/1370–1405) a generation later as he built his own legitimising ideology.[33]

We know still too little about the conversion of the Mongols, but it seems clear that the rulers and the ruling elite converted separately from the masses of the tribesmen. Sufis, especially extremist ones, such as howling dervishes, are believed to have played a role in attracting many of the tribesmen to Islam, but it has recently been shown both that the reason that used to be assumed for their success – their similarity to the shamans of Mongol tradition – is mistaken and that such Sufis played little or no role in the conversion of the rulers.[34] These latter were influenced by Sufis, but the Sufis in question were of much more moderate bent, and probably enjoyed the favour of the Muslims in the royal administrative and bureaucratic elite. Nonetheless, the conversion of the rulers may have been motivated by the need to follow their subjects, who were converting ahead of them. One recent study suggests that most of the Mongol soldiers in Persia had probably converted by 694/1295, when Ghāzān Khān converted in order to secure their loyalty. According to this view the conversion of Tegüder a decade earlier had been too early for the Mongol elite, still pagan, and he was deposed and executed as a result.[35]

What came after

Conversion to the faith of Islam has many motives, and it is usually hazardous to assign any individual or group acceptance of Islam exclusively to one motive. Those who converted may not themselves have had too clear an understanding of why they were doing it, or even of what they were doing. That included not only a change of religious label, but also a gradual and

33 For these legends see István Vásáry, '"History and legend" in Berke Khan's conversion to Islam', in D. Sinor (ed.), *Aspects of Altaic civilization, III: Proceedings of the thirtieth meeting of the permanent International Altaistic Conference, Bloomington, 1987*, Uralic and Altaic series 145 (Bloomington, 1990); Michal Biran, 'The Chaghadaids and Islam: The conversion of Tarmashirin Khan (1331–34)', *JAOS*, 122 (2002).

34 See, e.g., Reuven Amitai-Preiss, 'Sufis and shamans: Some remarks on the Islamization of the Mongols in the Ilkhanate', *JESHO*, 42 (1999); Reuven Amitai-Preiss, 'Ghazan, Islam and Mongol tradition: A view from the Mamlūk sultanate', *BSOAS*, 59 (1996); also Jean Richard, 'La conversion de Berke et les débuts de l'islamisation de la Horde d'Or', *Revue des Études Islamiques*, 35 (1967).

35 Angus Stewart, 'The assassination of king Het'um II: the conversion of the Ilkhans and the Armenians', *JRAS* (2005) (who stresses that we should not see the struggle between Armenia and its Muslim neighbours in simplistic terms of Christian versus Muslim, even or especially at this early stage of the Mongols' conversion); Charles Melville, '*Pādshāh-i Islām*: The conversion of Sultan Maḥmūd Ghāzān Khān', *Pembroke Papers*, 1 (1990); Reuven Amitai, 'The conversion of Tegüder Ilkhan to Islam', *JSAI*, 25 (2001).

comprehensive reordering of much in the individual's life and in the collective social environment. In Africa what Pouwels labels a 'reorientation' of religious belief and practice in the direction of Islam may have amounted to little more than an adjustment of daily life incorporating new, Islamic practices and, eventually but not universally, the phasing out of the old. In India and South-East Asia 'creeping orthopraxy' is something similar writ large. The immense variety of Islam – or of Islams – in the world are a product of the encounter of different Muslims and their versions of Islam at different times and under very varied circumstances with the immense variety of local contexts. Something in the processes, or the methods, has changed in the modern period, with the universal reach of modern technologies, but the pilgrimage to Mecca in earlier times, if slower, was nevertheless an efficient channel for the diffusion of Islamic norms. Today the growth of Islam continues apace, in Europe and the Americas, in Asia and in Africa. Recent projections suggest that France may have a Muslim majority by the middle of this century, and the Ivory Coast went from under 10 per cent Muslim at the time of independence from France in 1960 to well over 70 per cent Muslim within a generation.

Free will or compulsion

One feature that has characterised the preaching of Islam and conversion to that faith over the last fourteen centuries is the general absence, other than in the cases of conversion of an entire state or group for political reasons, of compulsion. Justified by a sentence in the Qurʾān (Q 2:256), 'there is no compulsion in religion' (*lā ikrāha fī al-dīn*), the prohibition thus implied has been largely honoured. Exceptions have been few and scattered: Jews and Christians under the mad Fāṭimid caliph al-Ḥākim in Egypt in the early fifth/eleventh century (they were allowed to return to their original faiths following his death); Jews and Christians under the Almohads in al-Andalus and North Africa in the sixth/twelfth century (the effect was to reduce these communities to near disappearance); Jews in Istanbul as a result of the activity of Shabbetai Sevi (the descendants of these converts formed a separate sub-sect, the Dönme, surviving to this day); Jews in Yemen on several occasions, notably in the eleventh/seventeenth century following the appearance of a false messiah (they were later permitted to resume their Judaism);[36] Jews in

36 See P. S. van Koningsveld, J. Sadan and Q. al-Samarrai, *Yemenite authorities and Jewish messianism: Ahmad ibn Nasir al-Zaydi's account of the Sabbathian movement in seventeenth-century Yemen and its aftermath* (Leiden, 1990).

Mashhad in Iran in the thirteenth/nineteenth century (these Jews maintained a Marrano-style existence, intermarrying only among themselves, until the middle of the twentieth century, when they managed to leave the country and return to Judaism). Other cases include the forcible Islamisation of *dhimmī* boys taken away from their families by the Ottomans under the *devşirme* system and impressed into the military, much as the Mamlūks, slave-soldiers imported into the Middle East between the seventh/thirteenth and twelfth/eighteenth centuries, were Islamised as part of their education as soldiers and often as a ruling class there. Anatolia, during the period when the Ottomans and others were taking it over from the Byzantines, offers a further model of forcible Islamisation, this time much more in tune with popular images. Here we find examples of Greeks and Armenians being offered the choice between Islam and the sword, with many choosing the former.[37]

What stands out in these accounts is not just that occasionally the forced converts were allowed to return to their original faiths – though Islamic legal schools offer contrasting views on the permissibility of this – but rather the overall attitude to compulsion, especially by comparison with Christianity. In general, and with some notable exceptions, Islamic societies have exhibited a surprising degree of indifference to the existence of Jewish and Christian minorities in their midst. If they have not encouraged them – and indeed, have by their actions and attitudes sought rather to wear them down – they have virtually never sought to extirpate these faiths or to compel their followers to go over to Islam.

The *ahl al-dhimma*

Definitions

Not everyone converted to Islam. Especially in the former Christian-ruled areas, where Arabic and, later, Turkish came to dominate, communities of Jews and Christians remained.[38] Their survival reflects not so much tolerance (an anachronistic concept for classical and medieval Islam) as Qurʾānic recognition that, though degraded forms of religious truth, both Judaism and

37 See Vryonis, *Decline*, pp. 177–8, 240–2; see also Cemal Kafadar, *Between two worlds: The construction of the Ottoman state* (Berkeley, 1995); Selim Deringil, '"There is no compulsion in religion": On conversion and apostasy in the late Ottoman empire: 1839–1856', *Comparative Studies in Society and History*, 42 (2000).

38 For the argument that few Jews converted, while most Christians did, see David J. Wasserstein, 'Islamisation and the conversion of the Jews', in García-Arenal, *Conversions islamiques*.

Christianity were true religions. Possessed of holy texts (though their contents were no longer necessarily all authentic or properly preserved), Jews and Christians were *ahl al-kitāb*, People(s) of the Book, and, as such, *ahl al-dhimma*, people with a contract of protection under the rule of Islam.[39] By the same token, others – polytheists and idolaters – enjoyed no such protection, and must be offered simply Islam or the sword. But reality trumped this theory: entire populations could not be exterminated, even if they persisted in their failure to acknowledge the truth of Muḥammad and his message. Zoroastrians were neither Christians nor Jews, and possessed no holy book – but in the reality of the Islamic conquests they were soon identified with the otherwise obscure Majūs mentioned in the Qur'ān, and by the third/ninth century this faith without one had patched together a set of scriptures from pre-Islamic Zoroastrian religious writings to make them people of a book too. India offered a greater difficulty. Islamic conquests in the subcontinent as early as the second/eighth century brought vast numbers of Hindus under Islamic rule. Zoroastrians could somehow be found a place under the umbrella of monotheism, but there was not enough space there for the glorious richness of the Hindu pantheon. Reality again, however, in the form of the vast size of the Hindu subject population, pointed the way to a solution, and Hindus were recognised as *ahl al-dhimma* (though not as *ahl al-kitāb*) from an early date.[40]

Legal status

Christians and Jews enjoyed definite and clear legal status under Islamic rule. They were governed by a complex of rules derived from the Qur'ān and from a document known as the Pact of ʿUmar (*ʿahd ʿUmar*), with much variation according to time and place. The Pact of ʿUmar itself is associated with the caliph ʿUmar I (r. 13–23/634–44), but it is probably rather less old, and a link with ʿUmar II (r. 99–101/718–20) seems more likely.[41] It lays down, in the form of a letter addressed to ʿUmar by the Christian inhabitants of an unnamed place in Syria, how they are to behave, and what their rights and obligations are. The document appears first only hundreds of years after the conquests, but its contents offer the

39 For the arguments about the texts see Hava Lazarus-Yafeh, *Intertwined worlds: Medieval Islam and Bible criticism* (Princeton, 1992); Camilla Adang, *Muslim writers on Judaism and the Hebrew Bible from Ibn Rabban to Ibn Hazm* (Leiden, 1996).

40 Yohanan Friedmann, *Tolerance and coercion in Islam: Interfaith relations in the Muslim tradition* (Cambridge, 2003), p. 85.

41 See Mark R. Cohen, 'What was the Pact of ʿUmar? A literary-historical study', *JSAI*, 23 (1999); Albrecht Noth, 'Abgrenzungsprobleme zwischen Muslimen und Nicht-Muslimen: Die "Bedingungen ʿUmars (*aš-šurūṭ al-ʿumariyya*)" unter einem anderen Aspekt gelesen', *JSAI*, 9 (1987).

paradigm for *dhimmī* status over the whole of the Islamic world before the modern period. In particular, it establishes the *dhimmī* communities as distinct corporations within the Islamic *umma*, with the communities having responsibility for their members' actions, and standing to lose those rights if they misbehave or go beyond what Islamic law and society allowed them.

Rooted as it was in the Qur'ān and related documents, the *dhimma* offered Christians and Jews security in return for loyalty, and broad religious freedom in return for acceptance of second-class status. They were liable for a poll-tax, the *jizya*; could not make too public practice of their faiths; could not, in theory at least, build new or very high houses of worship; their testimony in court was not worth as much as that of a Muslim. Occasionally they were forced to wear distinctive clothing or even marks on their dress, and were, again in theory, supposed not to occupy posts that gave them authority over Muslims.

The aim of the restrictions contained in the Pact of ʿUmar is far from clear. Was it to force second-class status on non-Muslims and provide through the *jizya* an additional source of income for the state? Was it to enforce separation of non-Muslims from Muslims? Was it, through the burdens it imposed, to encourage conversion? At different times each of these arguments has appeared persuasive to scholarship, but if the Pact of ʿUmar is early then certain of its provisions, in particular the undertaking not to teach *dhimmī* children the Qur'ān or to use Arab names, wear the appearance of attempts simply to maintain separation between rulers and ruled.

With time the restrictions were enforced with varying degrees of severity in different periods and places, and came to be used for all of the aims just mentioned. How the poll-tax should be collected offered jurists much opportunity for discussion: while some maintained that it should be collected just like any other tax, there were those who insisted that it should be collected directly from the individual *dhimmī* taxpayer, in such a way as to humiliate him. The economic weight of the tax varied according to the wealth of the individual, but it seems rarely to have been so high as to encourage conversion as a way out of paying it.[42] The *jizya* was probably the one universally applied part of the prescriptions of the *dhimma*.

42 For medieval prescriptions and some medieval and modern examples see Norman Stillman, *The Jews of Arab lands: A history and source book* (Philadelphia, 1979), pp. 159–61, 180, 251, 368–9. Aviva Klein-Franke, 'Collecting the *jizya* (poll-tax) in the Yemen', in Tudor Parfitt (ed.), *Israel and Ishmael: Studies in Muslim–Jewish relations* (Richmond, 2000) is a rare study of the collection of the *jizya* in practice, though it deals with the modern period. See also above for examples of conversion resulting from economic distress, possibly related to the *jizya*.

Distinctive clothing was selectively enforced.[43] The caliph al-Mutawakkil in 236/850, under popular pressure, tried to enforce the wearing of distinctive signs by *dhimmīs*. In al-Andalus in the fifth/eleventh and sixth/twelfth centuries special signs may have been required, and the Almohads in al-Andalus and North Africa in the sixth/twelfth century used the requirement of special clothing for Christians and Jews as one means to encourage conversion. (It is thought that the medieval Christian European Jew-badge may have its origins in the Almohad prescriptions.) In Egypt under the Mamlūks in 700/1301, and again in 755/1354, sumptuary laws attempted to force *dhimmīs* to wear special colours, and an Irish visitor to Cairo in 1323, Simon Semeonis, offers testimony to the wearing of special colours by the different minorities there.[44] But the nature of such laws is to be selective, and their repetition shows that they quickly fell into desuetude.

Churches and synagogues existed all over the medieval Islamic world, encountering occasional hostility from Muslim zealots, being closed and even destroyed, in riots or by legal means, on the ground that they had not been in existence at the birth of Islam, but they were generally rebuilt very soon.[45] Most importantly, the Islamic empire could not have survived at the start without *dhimmī* administrators, and for many centuries even Egypt was run by Coptic civil servants. Jews and Christians served Muslim rulers as viziers, as advisers and as doctors from al-Andalus in the west eastwards to Iran – and if several came to bad ends because of their *dhimmī* identity, Muslim viziers, whether Muslim-born or converts, do not seem to have had much greater success in avoiding such fates.[46]

Boundaries

Islamic law defined some of the boundaries of *dhimmī* life: *dhimmīs* could convert to Islam, occasionally to each other's faiths, but Muslims might not apostatise to Christianity or Judaism, under pain of death.[47] *Dhimmī* men were

43 For the distinctive signs see Stillman, *Jews*, p. 167 (from al-Ṭabarī); I. Lichtenstadter, 'The distinctive dress of non-Muslims in Islamic countries', *Historia Judaica*, 5, 1 (1943).

44 Simon Semeonis, *Itinerarium Symonis Semeonis ab Hybernia ad Terram Sanctam*, ed. Mario Esposito, Scriptores Latini Hiberniae 4 (Dublin, 1960), pp. 58–9, sec. 34; in the same section Simon reports what may have been an episode of forced conversion.

45 Seth Ward, 'Ibn al-Rifʿa on the churches and synagogues of Cairo', *Medieval Encounters*, 5 (1999).

46 See, e.g., for doctors, Doris Behrens-Abouseif, *Fatḥ Allāh and Abū Zakariyya: Physicians under the Mamluks* (Cairo, 1987); and more generally Bernard Lewis, 'An ode against the Jews', in Bernard Lewis, *Islam in history: Ideas, men and events in the Middle East* (London, 1973).

47 The regulations, with the variations in the attitudes of the different legal schools, are conveniently assembled in Antoine Fattal, *Le statut légal des non-musulmans en pays d'Islam* (Beirut, 1958); also S. A. Rahman, *Punishment of apostasy in Islam*, 2nd edn (Lahore, 1978).

forbidden to marry Muslim women, but Muslim men were permitted to marry *dhimmī* women, any offspring being Muslim. Conversion was thus a one-way street (we hear occasionally of people uttering the formula of conversion in the heat of family arguments and the like, and being unable to undo the change thus made[48]), while interreligious marriage served likewise to increase the proportion of Muslims in the population.

Other boundaries were constructed by the *dhimmīs* themselves. Beyond religion as a marker of communal ascription, Christians and Jews with varying success used language and script, combined with culture, in ways that marked them off from their neighbours. While they too went over to Arabic or New Persian, in the case of Arabic they created communally identifiable forms of that language, and in the Persian case Jews used the Hebrew script to write the language (preserving in the manuscripts valuable evidence of early stages of New Persian).[49] For Christians, linguistic adaptation was often a first step towards Islamisation and, in the Arab world, Arabisation (we cannot know, in fact, much about the relative chronology of these processes on a large scale). For Jews too, though much more slowly, linguistic acculturation was a step in the direction of fuller assimilation, but it never created – beyond some starry-eyed secularists in the modern period – the notion of a Jewish Arab to parallel that of Christian Arab which had existed since before Islam.

Dhimmīs enjoyed communal autonomy and generally governed themselves by their own laws, but they were not cut off from the broader society.[50] As we have seen, *dhimmīs* could serve government – though tenure was never very secure. More importantly, they were not confined to any particular occupations: other than activities such as the law and the military, the *dhimmī* was as free as the Muslim to take up any profession or trade. The Cairo Geniza offers numerous cases of *dhimmīs* and Muslims engaging together in business or in

48 For a probable example of this see David Wasserstein, 'A *fatwā* on conversion in Islamic Spain', *Studies in Muslim–Jewish Relations*, 1 (1993); a modern case is described in Nissim Rejwan, *The Last Jews in Baghdad: Remembering a lost homeland* (Austin, 2004), p. 10.

49 Geoffrey Khan, 'Judaeo-Arabic and Judaeo-Persian', in Martin Goodman (ed.), *The Oxford handbook of Jewish studies* (Oxford, 2002); David J. Wasserstein, 'The language situation in al-Andalus', in A. Jones and R. Hitchcock (eds.), *Studies on the* Muwaššaḥ *and the* Kharja (Reading, 1991) (repr. in M. Fierro and J. Samsó (eds.), *The formation of al-Andalus*, part 2: *Language, religion, culture and the sciences* (Aldershot, 1998), pp. 3–17); David J. Wasserstein, 'Langues et frontières entre juifs et musulmans en al-Andalus', in Maribel Fierro (ed.), *Judíos y musulmanes en al-Andalus y el Magreb: Contactos intelectuales* (Madrid, 2002).

50 See Mark R. Cohen, *Jewish self-government in medieval Egypt: The origins of the office of head of the Jews, ca. 1065–1126* (Princeton, 1980).

different trades.[51] *Dhimmī* physicians treated both *dhimmī* and Muslim patients, though occasionally Muslims spoke out against the potential danger of a *dhimmī* doctor killing his Muslim patients. One anecdote in an anti-*dhimmī* treatise of the eighth/fourteenth century has Maimonides warning his patron the Qāḍī al-Fāḍil, 'Let me advise you not to receive any medical treatment from a Jew, because with us, whoever desecrates the Sabbath – his blood is licit for us,' with the result that the *qāḍī* banned Jews from practising as doctors.[52]

Cultural life

The degree of security and of religious freedom enjoyed by Christians and Jews varied, reflecting external circumstance, but there was enough to make possible, for the Jews, a remarkable cultural renaissance under Arab Islam. The conquests of Islam brought most of the Jews in the world under one rule; they gave the Jews greatly improved status – second-class status, it is true, but that was far better than what they had had before, especially under Christian rule; the adoption, apparently quite rapid, of a Jewish form of Arabic, written in Hebrew letters, gave them a common language everywhere, while it also opened up for them a window onto the fast-developing Arabic-language culture of their neighbours. By the beginning of the fourth/tenth century Arabic had penetrated sufficiently to make an Arabic translation of the scriptures a necessity. It was made by the polymathic and productive Saʿadya Gaon (880–942), born in Egypt but active especially in Bagdad.[53]

Depending on the new culture of the Muslims, using a common language with them and acquainted with their literature and cultural concerns, Jews under Islam took their literary genres and forms, many of their subjects, their poetical forms and metres, the very pattern of their linguistic behaviour, from those of Arabic.[54] The result was in effect a subset of Islamic-Arabic culture (the only significant genre that is absent from Jewish writing on Arabic models is historiography, for reasons having to do with Jewish history itself). The

51 S. D. Goitein, *A Mediterranean society: The Jewish communities of the Arab world as portrayed in the documents of the Cairo Geniza*, 6 vols. (Berkeley and Los Angeles, 1967–93), esp. vol. I, *passim*; A. L. Udovitch, *Partnership and profit in medieval Islam* (Princeton, 1970).

52 The anecdote is found in al-Wāsiṭī's *Radd ʿalā ahl al-dhimma*, trans by Richard Gottheil in *JAOS*, 41 (1921), pp. 396–7, quoted in Stillman, *Jews*, p. 276.

53 For Saʿadya see still Henry Malter, *Saadia Gaon, his life and works* (Philadelphia, 1942); for the broader situation now Robert Brody, *The geonim of Babylonia and the shaping of medieval Jewish culture* (New Haven, 1998).

54 Rina Drory, *Models and contacts: Arabic literature and its impact on medieval Jewish culture* (Leiden, 2000).

great centres of Jewish cultural life under Islamic rule were in what became the Arab world – Baghdad, Cairo, Qayrawān, al-Andalus, Morocco, Yemen – and their rise and fall tended to approximate to the rise and fall of these centres of Islamic Arabic cultural life.[55] The greatest of these centres was in al-Andalus, between the fourth/tenth and sixth/twelfth centuries, and was brought to an end by the persecutions of the Almohads, which are said to have destroyed many of the Jewish communities both in al-Andalus and in Morocco, converting many to Islam and sending others into exile.[56]

Among these exiles was Moses Maimonides, the most fertile and significant of Jewish minds in the Middle Ages. Born in Cordoba, he spent some time in Morocco before making his home in Egypt, where he worked as a doctor at the court of Saladin and became leader of the Jewish community in that country.[57] Several generations of his descendants inherited his mantle, but Egypt never attained the significance in Jewish life that it had enjoyed in the ancient world, and with the decline of the great Arab cultural centres by the seventh/thirteenth century Jewish culture in the Islamic world went into a decline too.

Christians and their cultures flourished intermittently, until the sixth/twelfth century or so, but the overall trend was downwards: in North Africa Christianity had more or less disappeared by the sixth/twelfth century, if not before;[58] in al-Andalus but for the *reconquista* it would probably not have lasted much longer.[59] Further east, Christianity declined to something like its present proportions of the populations in Egypt and Syria under the pressures of the Mamlūks and in Iraq under the later ʿAbbāsids. In Egypt and Iraq Christians are now around 10 per cent of the population, in Israel and the Palestinian

55 For Baghdad see now Brody, *Geonim*; for Cairo, Goitein, *A Mediterranean society*; Elinoar Bareket, *Fustat on the Nile: The Jewish elite in medieval Egypt* (Leiden, 1999); for Qayrawān, Menahem Ben-Sasson, *The emergence of the local Jewish community in the Muslim world: Qayrawan, 800–1057*, 2nd edn (Jerusalem, 1997) (in Hebrew); for al-Andalus, still Eliyahu Ashtor, *The Jews of Moslem Spain*, 3 vols. (Philadelphia, 1973–84, repr. in 2 vols., 1992); for Morocco, H. Z. (J. W.) Hirschberg, *A history of the Jews in North Africa*, 2 vols. (Leiden, 1974–81); for Yemen, Reuben Ahroni, *Yemenite Jewry: Origins, culture and literature* (Bloomington, 1986).

56 The significance of the Almohads in the decline of the Christian and especially the Jewish communities is debated: see A. S. Halkin, 'On the history of apostasy under the Almohads', in *The Joshua Starr memorial volume: Studies in history and philology*, Jewish Social Studies Publications 5 (New York, 1953) (in Hebrew); David Corcos, 'The attitude of the Almohads towards the Jews', *Zion*, 32 (1967), repr. in David Corcos, *Studies in the history of the Jews of Morocco* (Jerusalem, 1976), (in Hebrew).

57 See now Herbert Davidson, *Moses Maimonides: The man and his works* (Oxford, 2005).

58 See Teissier, 'Desaparición'.

59 David J. Wasserstein, 'The Christians of al-Andalus: Some awkward thoughts', *Hispania Sacra*, 64, 110 (2002).

territories far lower, about 3–4 per cent. In all these areas the move to Arabic was early and rapid.[60] In Egypt Coptic Christianity took till the sixth/twelfth century to go over to Arabic and, in that language, even enjoyed a small literary revival in the seventh/thirteenth century, represented especially by Ibn al-Rāhib and several members of the family of Ibn al-ʿAssāl.[61] But for Christians, more than for Jews, domination by Arab Islam meant in the end Arabicisation in tongue and Arabisation in ethnic identity, with Islamisation, or emigration, just a step away.

60 For a revival of Christian culture in Arabic in early Islam see the articles collected in Sidney Griffith, *Arabic Christianity in the monasteries of ninth-century Palestine* (Aldershot, 1992).

61 For the Banū al-ʿAssāl see A. S. Atiya, 'Ibn al-ʿAssāl', *EI2*, vol. III, pp. 721–2; for Ibn al-Rāhib see A. Y. Sidarus, *Ibn al-Rahibs Leben und Werk: Ein koptisch-arabischer Enzyklopädist des 7./13. Jahrhunderts* (Berlin, 1975).

6

Muslim societies and the natural world

RICHARD W. BULLIET

Introduction

There have been as many ways of comprehending the natural world as there have been human societies. Indeed there have been more, for most societies nurture divergent and contending views. With respect to societies oriented towards Islamic belief and practice, it might seem reasonable to begin by asking how the Qur'ān depicts the natural world. But the status of the Qur'ān as the word of God does not mean that Muslim societies have necessarily built their views of the world around them upon a foundation of divine revelation. Rather, each society – recognising here that the very word 'society' comprehends a multiplicity of individual outlooks – has woven a tissue of comprehension from disparate and sometimes incompatible sources, not always giving priority to religious belief.

In attempting to bring a sense of order and chronological development to the great complexity of the subject, this chapter divides into three sections. The first, 'The pastoral order', deals with the Muslim community prior to 183/800, when it was still primarily Arab in ethnicity. The second, covering the Middle East, North Africa and Spain during the ʿAbbāsid caliphate down to 596/1200, is entitled 'The Hellenistic inheritance'. The third deals with regions at greater remove from the historical Muslim heartland and extends down to 1214/1800. It is entitled 'Legacies and syntheses'.

The pastoral order

Disagreement about the origin of the Qur'ān will never disappear. Virtually all Muslims hold the conviction that it contains the word of God as delivered to and through Muḥammad between approximately 611 and 10/632. Among non-Muslim scholars, an older view accepts this chronology but sees Muḥammad as the book's conscious or unconscious author. This point of view has led to much discussion of the 'sources' of the Qur'ān in Jewish and Christian scriptural or oral tradition. A more recent view, propounded mostly by non-Muslim scholars, maintains that the text of the Qur'ān accumulated gradually during the first two centuries of Arab rule inaugurated by the eighty years of conquest that began around 12/634. This hypothesis focuses on Iraq as the place where the text achieved its canonical form in the late second/eighth century. Corollary to this view is the notion that the *ḥadīth*, or sayings of the Prophet, and the *sīra*, or 'biography' of the Prophet, both of which contain extensive lore about the purported circumstances under which specific verses were 'revealed', took form at roughly the same time.

These fundamental differences of opinion are irresolvable given the current state of evidence; but the first of them, belief in the Qur'ān as God's revealed word, has been the operative reality in the development of all Muslim societies. Moreover, all three approaches converge on the notion that the contents of the Qur'ān were intended, either by divine will or the artifice of fiction, to be comprehensible to an Arab society of nomadic tribes interspersed with clusters of farmers and other settled folk living in western Arabia in the early seventh century CE. As a consequence, the natural milieu of second/eighth-century Iraq – a land of agriculture, cities, broad rivers and complex division of labour – is little in evidence. Similarly missing in the portions of the Qur'ān that parallel the Bible are the lengthy biblical narratives describing the rise and fall of the kingdoms of Israel and Judah, with their implication that kingship is a natural basis for social order, as well as references to temple rituals, priests and the study and expounding of religious law. In short, to the extent that Jewish and Christian 'sources' are thought by some to underlie the Qur'ānic text, the text itself contains little that is inconsistent with life in a remote Arabian locale with no tradition of kingship or political dependence on the nearby agricultural societies in Ethiopia, Yemen, Iraq or Palestine. The natural world evoked in the Qur'ān is consistent with the pastoral order of western Arabia, as verses drawn virtually at random amply testify:

> Consider the winds that scatter the dust far and wide,
> and those that carry the burden [of heavy clouds],
> and those that speed along with gentle ease,
> and those that apportion [the gift of life] at [God's] behest! Q 51:1–4[1]

1 Translations are from *The message of the Qur'ān*, trans. Muḥammad Asad (Gibraltar, 1980).

When the sun is shrouded in darkness,
and when the stars lose their light,
and when the mountains are made to vanish,
and when she-camels big with young, about to give birth, are left untended,
and when all beasts are gathered together,
and when all human beings are coupled [with their deeds],
and when the girl-child that was buried alive is made to ask for what
crime she had been slain,
and when the scrolls [of men's deeds] are unfolded,
and when heaven is laid bare,
and when the blazing fire [of hell] is kindled bright,
and when paradise is brought into view:
[on that Day] every human being will come to know what he has
prepared [for himself]. Q 81:1–14

Art thou not aware that before God prostrate themselves all [things and beings] that are in the heavens and all that are on earth – the sun, and the moon, and the stars, and the mountains, and the trees, and the beasts? Q 22:18

The term 'pastoral order' as used here denotes a society in which the herding of animals plays a more important role than the growing of crops; the landscape is typified by natural features such as mountains and trees, as opposed to croplands, villages or cities; and social organisation focuses on the individual and the kin-group rather than on categories derived from complex social roles, such as rulers, priests, artisans, traders and farmers. On the other hand, the term does not imply that every person lives as a nomad in the desert, or even that most people do; for societies frequently idealise the natural world in terms of bygone landscapes and lifestyles. Evocations of life on family farms or in agricultural villages, for example, still convey an ideal of peace and simplicity for Americans and Europeans whose families left the farm for the big city several generations ago.

But even if the pastoral order of western Arabia as evoked in the Qur'ān was more an atavistic ideal than a day-to-day reality in first/seventh-century Mecca, or (more improbably) was fictively recreated in second/eighth-century Iraq for the purpose of fabricating a foundation myth for an empire originating in western Arabia, the imagery of the pastoral order conveyed in hundreds of verses became a constant of later Islamic belief and practice in all of the lands the faith ultimately spread to. God's creation encompasses angels, *jinn*, humans and beasts. The sun and the clouds above, the mountains on the horizon, the trees that provide occasional verdure, the herds of animals: these dominate the natural landscape of the Qur'ān. Gardens and streams of running water are delights of paradise, not the day-to-day reality of the believer. And paradise itself will be the reward of the pious when the God who created the natural world sees fit to bring it to an end.

Reinforcement of this view of nature came by way of the most memorable non-religious cultural phenomenon of the first two Islamic centuries: Arabic poetry. Though scholars sometimes evince scepticism about the pre-Islamic dates ascribed to some of the poems preserved from the first Islamic centuries, there is no doubt about the esteem in which those early poets were held, or about their works becoming models for Arabic poetic composition. Through them the desert setting and the pastoral way of life abstractly evoked in the Qur'ān gained precision and vivid expression in the most widely memorised and deeply honoured odes. This extract from a pre-Islamic ode (*qaṣīda*) by Imru' al-Qays is representative:

Early in the morning, while the birds were still nesting, I mounted my steed.
Well-bred was he, long-bodied, outstripping the wild beasts in speed,
Swift to attack, to flee, to turn, yet firm as a rock swept down by the torrent,
Bay-coloured, and so smooth the saddle slips from him, as the rain from a smooth stone,
Thin but full of life, fire boils within him like the snorting of a boiling kettle;
He continues at full gallop when other horses are dragging their feet in the dust for weariness.
A boy would be blown from his back, and even the strong rider loses his garments.
Fast is my steed as a top when a child has spun it well.
He has the flanks of a buck, the legs of an ostrich, and the gallop of a wolf.
From behind, his thick tail hides the space between his thighs, and almost sweeps the ground.
When he stands before the house, his back looks like the huge grinding-stone there.
The blood of many leaders of herds is in him, thick as the juice of henna in combed white hair.
As I rode him we saw a flock of wild sheep, the ewes like maidens in long-trailing robes;
They turned for flight, but already he had passed the leaders before they could scatter.
He outran a bull and a cow and killed them both, and they were made ready for cooking;
Yet he did not even sweat so as to need washing.[2]

It may legitimately be questioned whether the Arabs who made up the great preponderance of Muslim society down to the year 183/800 universally

2 *The hanged poems*, trans. F. E. Johnson, in Charles F. Horne (ed.), *Ancient Arabia*, Sacred Books of the East 5 (New York, 1917).

took their cues about the natural world from the Qur'ān, particularly during the early Umayyad period when tribal identities became highly politicised. But the appeal of Arabic poetry was felt by the pious Arab Muslim, the Christian Arab and the tribesperson who knew little about the Qur'ān alike. It also set the Arabs apart from the scattering of non-Arab Muslims who began to grow numerous in Iraq and Iran after 132/750. Yet daily life in the military encampments that in some places – Baṣra and Kūfa in Iraq, Fusṭāṭ in Egypt, Qayrawān in Tunisia – had turned into genuine cities by the end of the period was far from the pastoral ideal. For some, chafing under the density of urban life, the classic odes generated nostalgia for an idealised nomadic past. Yet for others, most of all the large numbers of Arabs from the farming villages of Yemen, life in and around the city spelled opportunity. Thus it would be short-sighted to see the fading of the pastoral order and the rise of a new conception of the natural world in the third/ninth century solely in terms of non-Arabs coming to outnumber Arabs in the Muslim society. The Arabs themselves adapted to changed circumstances, acquired new tastes and entertained questions about the nature of the world around them.

The Hellenistic inheritance

'Hellenism' is the term used to designate the culture of intellectual, religious and political syncretism that emerged around the Mediterranean Sea and in hinterlands as far inland as Armenia and Iran during the millennium that preceded the Arab conquests. Deriving from the word Hellene, meaning Greek, the term overstates the importance of Greek culture per se in the cultural amalgam; but it correctly identifies the Greek language as the most important medium of intellectual discourse, even when other languages prevailed in everyday speech: Aramaic in Syria, Palestine and Iraq; Latin and Berber in North Africa; Coptic in Egypt; and varieties of Middle Persian in Iran. The hallmark of Hellenism was an openness to the wide variety of ideas and religious beliefs found within the vast swath of territory conquered by Alexander the Great in the fourth century BCE – essentially all the lands between the Nile and the Indus rivers – and later extended into western Europe and North Africa by the Romans, who were deeply imbued with the new syncretistic world-view. Chaldean astronomy from southern Iraq; Egyptian temple worship; Greek philosophy and drama, as much from Ionia in what is today western Turkey as from Greece proper; Iranian models of imperial government; and a variety of monotheistic cults from Palestine, Syria and Iraq claimed and received attention in the intellectual and spiritual marketplace even as more localised traditions, particularly those transmitted in the dying cuneiform and hieroglyphic writing systems of Iraq and Egypt respectively, faded away.

Views of the natural world diverged widely during the Hellenistic period, and only certain of them made their way into Muslim discourses on nature as religious conversion brought increasing ethnic diversity to Muslim society from the third/ninth century onward. Astrology, for example, which rested on the notion that the heavenly macrocosm could provide a trained observer with a blueprint for the microcosm of a person's individual life, made the transition despite the absence of firm support in Qurʾānic verse. The same was true of oneiromancy, or interpretation of dreams as indicators for waking life. However, most other kinds of divination did not. The historical record gives little indication that Muslims of the third/ninth through sixth/twelfth centuries sought knowledge of the future through watching the flight of birds, as was done in Greece and Rome, or examining water in magical bowls or the livers of slaughtered animals, as was done in Hellenistic Iraq. Very possibly the Qurʾānic verses that raise suspicions about diviners played a role in bringing these practices to an end: 'Say: "I seek refuge with the Sustainer of the rising dawn … from the evil of those that blow upon knots"' (Q 113:1, 4).

To understand how Islam affected this selective transmission of the Hellenistic legacy, it is useful to distinguish religious views on the nature of the divine, and on the connection of divinity with nature, from non-religious teachings. The Qurʾān condemned polytheism in no uncertain terms, leaving little room for the survival of cults such as those of the Iranian god Mithra or the Egyptian goddess Isis that were popular in the Roman empire. Thus the religious outlooks that passed across the divide between Hellenism and Islam were almost entirely predicated on monotheism, making it impossible to associate natural phenomena such as storms or the sun with specific gods. Manichaeism was a signal exception. Though it preached a dualistic interpretation of the natural world as a realm of competition between Good and Evil, it did manage to survive for some time underground, despite the imprecations of Muslim preachers who condemned its doctrines.

Non-religious materials made their way into Muslim discourse more easily, but there, too, selectivity was apparent. Greek poetry and drama, for example, seem not to have appealed to Muslim audiences, possibly because of too-frequent mention of the Olympian gods. More importantly with respect to the natural world, the Greek tradition of portraying the unclothed human body with a high degree of realism clashed with the Arab tribal tradition of wearing form-concealing clothing, as well as with the emergence during the

Umayyad period of a Muslim aversion to making visual representations of human beings in general.

However, these gaps in the transmission of Hellenistic approaches to nature shrink in significance beside the vast corpus of lore that was translated into Arabic from Greek (often via Syriac), and to a lesser degree Middle Persian and Sanskrit, during the ʿAbbāsid period. From Aristotle to Galen, a cornucopia of systematic observations and experiments dealing with the natural world became available to Muslim philosophers and physicians who built upon the corpus of Hellenistic knowledge to advance this legacy further. Muslim geographers similarly drew upon Persian and Greek ideas in composing their descriptions, and later their cartographic depictions, of the physical world. Hellenistic astronomical, botanical, zoological and geological lore was greatly augmented by the observations of Muslims interested in natural science. And in the industrial realm, Muslim chemists and engineers pioneered basic processes and devices on the basis of Hellenistic understandings of materials, mechanics and mathematics. In sum, the Hellenistic inheritance that ʿAbbāsid Muslim society received from the preceding cultural traditions of the lands conquered two centuries earlier by the Arabs was not just understood, but powerfully advanced by the efforts of Muslim thinkers of many ethnicities.

Nevertheless, the distinction made here between the religious and non-religious elements of this inheritance belies the fact that religious thinkers in the non-Muslim communities, both before Islam and during the early Islamic centuries, were more inclined to integrate non-religious philosophical and scientific matter into their religious writings than were most of the Muslim religious scholars, or *ʿulamāʾ*, who by the late third/ninth century became increasingly active in elaborating Islamic theology, law and religious practice.

In each of the Muslim cities that flourished during the third/ninth and fourth/tenth centuries thousands of (male) children and adolescents studied the Qurʾān and the *ḥadīth*, or sayings of Muḥammad, as a normal part of their education and socialisation into Muslim society. But only handfuls studied astronomy, philosophy or medicine. In similar fashion, proficiency in Arabic (and from the fourth/tenth century Persian) poetry and belles-lettres was a widely esteemed attainment; but only a few of these litterateurs turned their attention to the natural world by composing works on geography, zoology and the like. Moreover, those who did were most likely to write in a literary vein. The lists of 'wonders' (Ar. *ʿajāʾib* – weather anomalies, mutant animals, urban legends, historical peculiarities etc.) that are so frequently encountered in the works of Muslim writers owe more to the Hellenistic style of diverting the reader – the first 'Seven Wonders of the World' list was devised by a Greek writer from Lebanon in the second century BCE – than to Aristotle's practice of systematic observation.

Thus the Middle Eastern Muslim societies of the third/ninth through sixth/twelfth centuries inherited a vast amount of lore about the natural world. Though translation, which was avidly encouraged by the ʿAbbāsid caliphs of the third/ninth century, made major texts available in Arabic, the process of conversion, which progressed quite rapidly in Iran and Iraq during that century, played an equally important role. Sometimes learned people converted to Islam and shared their knowledge with their new community; at other times converts brought with them an interest in such knowledge and thus became patrons or readers of learned works.

Economic developments must also be considered. Some regions, most notably Iran, experienced rapid urbanisation accompanied by a boom in trade and manufactures. Growing markets favoured the cultivation of a broad range of new crops, including citrus trees, rice, cotton and sugar cane. Though not entirely unknown in the pre-Islamic period, the rapid spread of these crops created new landscapes and caused farmers to experiment with new farming techniques, as evidenced by agricultural manuals written during this period.

Compared with the preceding pastoral order, therefore, the accommodation of the Hellenistic inheritance, with the accompanying burgeoning of the economy, greatly multiplied the approaches to the natural world available to Muslim communities. In 183/800 these communities still constituted, outside Arabia proper, a minority population in largely non-Muslim lands; but by 596/1200 they had become so numerically dominant as to characterise the culture of the entire Middle East and North Africa. This chronology of conversion reinforces the fact that Islam should not always be considered the sole or dominant perspective from which people viewed the natural world. The various perspectives of the Hellenistic era that selectively and gradually made their way into Muslim discourse were already present within the non-Muslim communities with which Muslims could not help but interact. Thus it is necessary to guard against the idea that once a text on medicine or astronomy became translated into Arabic, the ideas contained in the text became extensions of Islamic thought. There is no denying the great intellectual flowering represented by the philosophical and scientific writings of this period. But it is more credible to see this as the consequence of an unprecedented bringing together of different peoples in a single religious community than as something that was intrinsic to the religion of Islam at that time.

Legacies and syntheses

From the fifth/eleventh through the eighth/fourteenth centuries major portions of the Hellenistic legacy passed to Christian Europe via translations from Arabic into Latin. This period of cultural borrowing, which triggered a profound intellectual revival in Europe, has prompted some historians to regard philosophers such as al-Fārābī (d. 338/950), Ibn Sīnā or Avicenna (d. 428/1037) and Ibn Rushd or Averroes (d. 594/1198), and scientists such as al-Khwārizmī (d. 235/850) and Ibn al-Haytham (d. 431/1040) as key figures in an 'Islamic civilisation'. They further portray the Muslim society of the Middle East, North Africa and Andalusia between 183/800 and 802/1400 as an incomparable manifestation of Muslim intellectual creativity. By this light, earlier and later Muslim societies, as well as Muslim societies in other geographical areas, appear deficient, and this has led to questions about why Islam 'stagnated' or 'declined'. Interpreting all of the intellectual achievements of the period as aspects of the religion of Islam deflects attention from the cultural affinities that criss-crossed the Mediterranean Sea and its hinterlands for centuries before the appearance of Islam. It also forms a barrier to appreciating the richness and variety of those Muslim societies that were not involved in receiving and retransmitting the Hellenistic heritage.

Key to this interpretation is the portrayal of the Arab conquests as creating an unbridgeable gulf between an 'Islamic civilisation' and a non-Muslim European civilisation variously called 'Christendom' or 'the West'. Religious difference thereby becomes the single most important factor in societal relations, despite the fact that the millennium that preceded Islam's confrontation with Christianity had witnessed the coexistence of myriad religious communities within an intricately interconnected Hellenistic cultural zone. Since Islam, Christianity and Judaism share many elements of the same scriptural tradition, the power and endurance of the view that the rise of Islam severed the multitudinous cultural links within this zone cannot credibly be ascribed to religious difference. Rather, it arose (and persists to the present day) from an assumption of eternal enmity between Christianity and Islam stemming from the Arab takeover of the largely Christian lands of Syria, Palestine, Egypt and Tunisia.

Looking at the situation in less warlike terms, it can be observed that the geographical zone in which the Hellenistic culture evolved was bounded by the frozen north, the Atlantic Ocean and a series of regions marked by pastoral nomadism. These regions stretched from the northern borderlands of the Sahara desert from the Atlantic to the Red Sea, through the heart of the

Arabian Peninsula, to the nearly waterless southern reaches of Iran. The arc of pastoral lands then turned northward to encompass wide stretches of Afghanistan before merging into the deserts and steppe-lands of Central Asia. In the Hellenistic period the Greek word 'ecumene', from the root *oikos* meaning 'house', denoted the settled and largely agricultural lands situated within these boundaries. Trans-Saharan, Central Asian and riverine trade routes – the Nile and the rivers of Ukraine and Russia – connected the ecumene with lands beyond this pastoral belt; but travelling merchants do not embody a culture in the way that continuous agricultural settlement does.

As had happened with earlier empires, the rise of the Islamic empire, or caliphate, created new foci for interconnections within the ecumene: first the caliphal capitals of Damascus and Baghdad, and then a series of other major cities from Cordoba in Spain, to Qayrawān in Tunisia, to Cairo in Egypt, to Iṣfahān, Rayy and Nīshāpūr in Iran. But Islam did not permanently or fundamentally alter the interconnectedness of the region, which was manifested anew with the transmission of the Hellenistic legacy from Muslim lands to Christian Europe.

Islam, of course, expanded far beyond this ecumene, partly through the efforts of traders. From the fourth/tenth century onward it found devotees among both pastoralists and settled peoples in lands far removed from the Hellenistic cultural zone. But for the most part, with the exception of astronomy and the related fields of astrology and calendar making, the Hellenistic legacy did not travel to these new frontiers. The works of Aristotle and Galen were not translated into Chinese or Sanskrit, nor did the Muslim societies of China, India, South-East Asia and sub-Saharan Africa produce Muslim philosophers and scientists of the quality of Ibn Sīnā and Ibn Rushd. Instead, the Muslim communities that took form in these more distant lands went through their own processes of amalgamation with pre-existing cultural traditions of different sorts.

The Turkic peoples of Central Asia devised myths of conversion to Islam that often hinged on dreams or images of a sacred tree growing from the body of the ruler. One the one hand, this reflects the practice of revering trees growing from, or near to, the tombs of saintly Muslims; and on the other, it gave an Islamic form to a pre-existing world-view, often referred to as shamanistic, in which spirits inhabit natural features.

In many areas Sufism, a form of organised mysticism, proved a more important factor in shaping the outlook of the new Muslim communities than formal Islamic learning. In northern India, for example, a tenth/sixteenth-century Sufi poet named Manjhan wrote a long romance that treated metaphorically the Sufi's love of God. It begins:

God, giver of love, the treasure-house of joy
Creator of the two worlds in the one sound Om,
my mind has no light worthy of you,
with which to sing your praise, O Lord!
King of the three worlds and the four ages,
the world glorifies you from beginning to end …

Listen now while I tell of the man:
separated from him, the Maker became manifest.
When the Lord took on flesh, he entered creation.
The entire universe is of His Essence.
His radiance shone through all things.
This lamp of creation was named Muhammad!
For him, the Deity fashioned the universe,
and love's trumpet sounded in the triple worlds.
His name is Muhammad, king of three worlds.
He was the inspiration for creation.[3]

Here the portrayal of the natural world, and of the role of Muḥammad in its creation, is clearly Hindu in inspiration and incompatible with both the Qur'ānic and the Hellenistic views of the world. Yet the poem served as a means of accommodating Islam to a pre-existing cultural tradition, just as translations of Greek texts had done seven centuries earlier in Baghdad.

In the Sudan and many other Muslim areas influenced by the culture of sub-Saharan Africa, '*zār* cults' preserved a view of the natural world in which an irresponsible spirit (*zār*) could take possession of a person, and even induce illness if a proper ceremony of propitiation was not performed. Women are the primary participants in *zār* cult dances and rituals, which are also performed in Christian Ethiopia.

Another example of Muslims accommodating pre-existing views of nature comes from the Gayo highlands district of northern Sumatra in Indonesia. There a ritual specialist known as the Lord of the Fields negotiates with spirits, ancestors and pests for a good rice harvest. The Lord of the Fields recites 'Qur'ānic verses', which are actually spells in the local Acehnese language that begin with the Arabic formula 'In the name of God'. In an interview, a Lord of the Fields used the following myth to explain the spiritual connection between rice and Islam:

> The prophet Adam and Eve had a child, Tuan [Lady] Fatima. They lived on leaves from trees and rarely had enough to eat. Tuan Fatima wanted to marry

3 Manjhan, *Madhumalati: An Indian Sufi romance*, trans. Aditya Behl and Simon Weightman (Oxford, 2000), pp. 1, 5.

> the prophet Muhammad. She talked to him but without touching him, without intercourse – there was a barrier between them; he had seen her but not yet married her. But merely from that contact there was a spark between them, and she became pregnant by him without intercourse. She had a daughter, Maimunah.
>
> God sent word to Muhammad by way of an angel that he should cut the child's throat, cut her up into little pieces ... and scatter the pieces into the field. The pieces became rice seeds, and grew to become rice plants.[4]

This story so diverges from the Qur'ān, which explicitly condemns female infanticide, and so offends Muslim morality in its intimation of incest between Fāṭima and Muḥammad, that most Muslims find it positively horrifying. Members of the Gayo community who are well educated in Islam share this distaste. But it represents a familiar effort to translate pre-existing attitudes towards the natural world into a Muslim frame of reference. The rice plant had a spirit before Islam became known, and the people who adopted the new religion wanted to preserve this concept.

Further examples are not needed to make the point that Muslim communities in different parts of the globe have repeatedly dealt with cultural legacies and their understandings of the natural world by linking them in some way to Islam. As with the Hellenistic legacy, only certain elements entered into Muslim discourse; and many of these passed away in time, or are passing away now, just as the Hellenistic legacy meant less in the twelfth/eighteenth century, by which time few *ʿulamāʾ* interested themselves in the natural sciences, than it had in the fifth/eleventh. In addition, it is obvious that new environments affected local Muslim views of the natural world in more material ways: different landscapes, building materials, climates, plant and animal life, and the like. What is striking is the ease with which Islam adapted to so many cultural traditions.

Conclusion

While there is certainly a Qurʾānic view of the natural world that affects all Muslim societies to some degree, there has not been a general Islamic view since the end of the second Islamic century (eighth century CE). However, this historical fact has not deterred thinkers from postulating that such a general view exists. Persistent rationalist arguments for regarding the philosophical and scientific exuberance of the ʿAbbāsid period as normative for

4 John R. Bowen, *Muslims through discourse* (Princeton, 1993), pp. 202–3.

Islam, when it was actually the product of accommodating the Hellenistic legacy, effectively marginalise the syntheses of Islamic belief and practice with non-Islamic cultural legacies in other parts of the world. A competing pietistic view, by which normative Islam is identified strictly with the putative religious practices of Muḥammad's own time and place, delegitimises not just the Asian and African Muslim syntheses, but also the rationalistic interpretations of the Qur'ān and the world that arose from the Hellenistic legacy.

These and other efforts to find a definitive interpretation of the natural world that is consonant with, or derived from, the data supplied by the Qur'ān and *ḥadīth* parallel similar efforts in other religious traditions. In the twentieth century religious scholars pored over the Bible, the Qur'ān, the Rig Veda and other seminal religious texts to find evidence of atomic theory or astrophysics. Today other scholars search the same texts for proof that vegetarianism is a religiously preferred lifestyle. It is in the nature of religious traditions that this should occur, for people of faith expect their beliefs to be congruent with their views of the natural world. It is not surprising, therefore, that Muslim societies in different parts of the world evolved disparate views of nature.

PART II

*

SOCIETIES, POLITICS AND ECONOMICS

7

Legitimacy and political organisation: caliphs, kings and regimes

SAÏD AMIR ARJOMAND

Although the Qur'ān frequently enjoins obedience to God and His Prophet, in verses generally recognised as belonging to the period of Medina, and formulates a powerful concept, *jihād*, for the revolutionary struggle against the Meccan oligarchy to establish Islam, it says nothing about the form of government under the Prophet or after his death. There is, however, an implicit model of dynastic rule in the house of the earlier prophets who were also explicitly designated as kings, most notably the houses of Abraham, David and 'Umrān (Moses and Aaron). The fact that no male offspring survived Muḥammad precluded the institutionalisation of that model, which was, however, espoused by 'Alī as the leading descendants of Hāshim, and after his assassination by his son al-Ḥasan, seconded by his cousin 'Abd Allāh ibn al-'Abbās.[1]

Our oldest historical document, the so-called 'Constitution of Medina', did provide a basis for the organisation of authority in the nascent Islamic polity. It in fact consists of a number of pacts with the Jews of Medina that mark the foundation of a 'single community' (*umma wāḥida*) under God, which was unified in matters of common defence and undivided peace, recognised Muḥammad as His Messenger, and invested him with judiciary authority. Nevertheless, as with the Qur'ān itself, no provisions were made regarding the form of government. Muḥammad's political activities centred on the organisation of *jihād*. It culminated in the march on Mecca and the defeat of the Arab confederates of the Meccan oligarchy, which was followed by the voluntary submission of most of the remaining tribes and the unification of Arabia. Muḥammad died shortly afterwards. Immediately after his death Abū Bakr and 'Umar were clearly apprehensive that the caliphate and prophethood would be reunited in the same family, the Banū Hāshim, and blocked 'Alī's

1 Wilferd Madelung, *The succession to Muḥammad: A study of the early caliphate* (Cambridge, 1996), pp. 311–13.

succession. The haphazard manner in which they themselves succeeded the Prophet in turn and were followed by ʿUthmān and finally ʿAlī, and the civil war that began with the murder of ʿUthmān and did not end until the murder of ʿAlī, are ample proof that Muḥammad had not settled the issue of succession before his death. *A fortiori*, he left no blueprint for the organisation of government, while his rule had extended beyond Medina to the whole of Arabia, and, within a decade, over a vast empire of conquest that had come into being with the defeat of the Byzantine and Persian armies. As a consequence, by the end of the first civil war in 40/661 the Muslim state looks like a huge army of Arab tribal contingents, mostly settled in a few garrison cities, with only the most rudimentary civil bureaucracy.

The establishment of the caliphate and the political organisation of the Arab empire

The term *khalīfa* appears in a number of passages in the Qurʾān, and can mean 'successor' or 'deputy', though with considerable ambiguity. As the succession of Abū Bakr is the most intensely contested issue in Islamic history and its accounts are heavily doctored, we may dismiss his designation of *khalīfat rasūl allāh* (deputy of the messenger of God) as anachronistic, though the report that ʿUmar was the first caliph to assume the title of *amīr al-muʾminīn* (commander of the faithful) is quite probable. The Shīʿite doctrine has preserved ʿAlī's conception of the imam as the *khalīfat allāh* (deputy of God); there is a coin of ʿUmar bearing that expression, which is also amply attested for ʿUthmān and for Muʿāwiya, who claimed to continue his rule, and became the designation of the caliphs of the Umayyad dynasty (41–132/661–750) established by him.[2]

By the final phase of the first civil war (35–40/656–61) the dispute over the legitimacy of the ruler had shaped the conception of Islam as a religion and separated the Muslim community dominating a vast empire of conquest into the followers of 'the religion (*dīn*) of ʿAlī' and 'the religion of Muʿāwiya'. This lack of differentiation in the authority of God's caliph as the ruler of the Arab empire gave all subsequent socio-political movements a religious, sectarian character and, conversely, all religio-cultural trends a pronounced political colouring.

2 Patricia Crone and Martin Hinds, *God's caliph: Religious authority in the first centuries of Islam* (Cambridge, 1986), pp. 6–42.

A distinct form of authority was, however, taking institutional shape under the early caliphate with the creation of a new administrative and fiscal bureaucracy, and a new class of secretaries as carriers of its broader culture. The first Muslim administrators of the conquered lands – notably Ziyād ibn Abīhi, ʿAlī's governor of Fārs, who joined Muʿāwiya and was recognised as his half-brother – became acquainted with the administrative tradition of the empires, but it took decades for the bureaucratic class that carried out the fiscal and administrative tasks for the Muslim ruler to appropriate the normative order of universal monarchy by translating Persian works on statecraft into Arabic. This normative order was binding on both Muslim and non-Muslim subjects of the caliphate. ʿAbd Allāh ibn al-Muqaffaʿ, the late Umayyad bureaucrat who perished in the ʿAbbāsid revolutionary power struggle, translated the most important maxims of Persian statecraft in his collections of aphorisms, and transmitted those of Indian statecraft in his translation of political animal fables, *Kalīla wa Dimna*, from the Pahlavi. The imported Persian literature on statecraft was easily absorbed into the public law of the caliphate and Muslim monarchies, and shaped the medieval Muslim conception of government. It included the testaments of important Persian kings to their heirs, most notably that known as the covenant (*ʿahd*) of Ardashīr, including an ordinance (*āyīn*) that purported to record the act of foundation of order: regulation of the hours of the day, domestic life, dietary and sumptuary regulations, and above all the institution of the social order in the form of the four castes. Ardashīr's foundation of the social order was sometimes projected back to the mythical king and founding figure, Jamshīd, who, according to one tradition, 'categorized (*ṣannafa*) men into four strata (*ṭabaqāt*): a stratum of soldiers (*muqātila*), a stratum of religious scholars (*fuqahāʾ*), a stratum of secretaries (*kuttāb*), artisans (*ṣunnāʿ*) and cultivators (*ḥarrāthīn*), and he took a stratum of them as servants (*khadam*)'.[3]

Ibn al-Muqaffaʿ's aphorisms and maxims from the early Persian statecraft literature, especially the covenant of Ardashīr, offered a model for what was lacking in the Qurʾān and the Constitution of Medina: a constitution that regulated the relationship between the ruler and his subjects (*raʿiyya*), his viziers and counsellors.

There was no large-scale conversion to Islam, except for the prisoners of war who formed the nucleus of a new social class of *mawālī* (clients) attached to Arab commanders or Arab tribes. The privileged status of the Arab Muslims

3 Cited in L. Marlow, *Hierarchy and egalitarianism in Islamic thought* (Cambridge, 1997), pp. 78–9, *apud* Ṭabarī.

made the Umayyad polity very much an Arab empire. Except for Syria, where the Byzantine cities of Damascus and Ḥimṣ were occupied, the conquering Muslim armies were settled in new garrison cities (*amṣār*), notably Kūfa and Baṣra in Iraq, Fusṭāṭ in Egypt, Marw in Khurāsān and Qayrawān in North Africa. These became centres of government and administration over extensive conquered agrarian hinterlands. Voluntary conversion to Islam was the slow work either of Muslim Qurʾān readers (*qurrāʾ*), story tellers (*quṣṣāṣ*) and later scholars, or of heterodox Islamic movements such as the Khārijites (Khawārij), while the converts acquired the legal status of the *mawālī*. The governors and military commanders were all Arabs, the fiscal agents in charge of the bureau (*dīwān*) that levied the land tax (*kharāj*), nearly always *mawālī*.

The Islamicisation of political ideas within the Arab empire, and eventually of the empire itself, owed much to the contested interpretation of Islam by the rebels and oppositional movements. The Khawārij were the first to challenge the unconditional legitimacy of the caliph as the deputy of God, arguing that the caliph would forfeit his legitimacy by wrongdoing, as ʿUthmān and ʿAlī had done, and advocated God's government and the election and deposing of imams by a radically egalitarian community of believers. The imamate was thus opened to the non-Arab *mawālī*, but no constitutional mechanism was devised for the deposing of the imam. All other rebellions and social movements appealed either to the Book of God and the *sunna* (of the Prophet) or to the charismatic leadership of a rightly guided (*mahdī*) imam from the House of the Prophet, or to both. (On the extreme fringe, the *mahdī* was to be the apocalyptic riser, *qāʾim*, of the end of time.)

The pattern of controlled conversion first broke down early in the second/eighth century with the Murjiʾite movement in Khurāsān and Transoxania, which demanded the equality of Arabs and the *mawālī* on the basis of Islam, and introduced the element of consent in the election of the imam who was to be *al-riḍā* (the agreed upon). Their great rebellion in Khurāsān stimulated the rival mobilisation by the Hāshimite movement on behalf of an indeterminate imam who was 'the agreed upon from the House of the Prophet', as well as its *mahdī* and its *qāʾim*. With the ʿAbbāsid – or, more accurately speaking, Hāshimite – revolution, the Arab empire was transformed into an Islamic polity. As Wellhausen remarked over a century ago, 'the ʿAbbasids called their government the *dawla*, *i.e.*, the new era. The revolution effected at this time was indeed prodigious.'[4] The term *dawla* meant divinely ordained 'turn in

4 Julius Wellhausen, *The Arab kingdom and its fall*, trans. M. G. Weir (Beirut, 1963 [1902]), p. 556.

power' or 'empire' in the sense of the Book of Daniel, and was soon backed by astronomical theories that calculated its precise beginning and duration, and acquired the meaning of 'the state'. The Khurāsānian *mawālī* who had brought the ʿAbbāsids to power were thus called *abnāʾ al-dawla* (sons of the state).

The Umayyad empire, militarily exhausted by overextension from Transoxania and Sind to Andalusia, managed to suppress the rebellion of Zayd ibn ʿAlī in 122/740 and the great Berber rebellion of 122–5/740–3, but broke down with the crisis of succession that followed the death of the caliph Hishām in 125/743. It succumbed to the Hāshimite revolution on behalf of the House of the Prophet, leaving it to the ʿAbbāsids to suppress or neutralise rival claimants from the Hāshimites among the descendants of Abū Ṭālib, al-Ḥasan, al-Ḥusayn and Zayd, as well as the Khawārij, and to inherit the caliphate and the empire in 132/750. (In the third/ninth century, however, the Zaydīs managed to establish independent imamates in the Yemen and the Caspian region in northern Iran, as did the Khawārij in North Africa.) The ʿAbbāsid revolution inaugurated an era of caliphal absolutism that lasted over a century. The bureaucracy became more centralised and the army included the non-Arab *mawālī*, especially from Khurāsān, on a massive scale, becoming much less dependent on Arab tribal contingents. The caliph appointed the judges, and represented Islam by having the Friday sermon delivered in his name, having his name on coins and continuing the *jihād* against Byzantium.

The evolution of the theory of the imamate was the result of prolonged debate between the ʿAbbāsids and their ʿAlid rivals, mediated by other trends, notably *ḥadīth* traditionalism and Muʿtazilite rationalism. While his obscure ʿAbbāsid cousins gained control of the clandestine Hāshimite revolutionary movement and established a new dynasty of caliphs, the scion of the Ḥusaynid branch of the ʿAlids, Jaʿfar al-Ṣādiq, was completing his father's organisation of sundry partisans of ʿAlī (*shīʿat ʿAlī*) into a sect which became known as the Imāmiyya on account of his formulation of its distinctive core theory of the imamate. According to that theory the imam was appointed by God, and was the charismatic leader of the believers and their divinely inspired and infallible teacher in religion from the descendants of ʿAlī, whose succession was valid upon explicit designation (*naṣṣ*) of the previous imam.

During al-Maʾmūn's brief reconciliation with the ʿAlids and his appointment of ʿAli ibn Mūsā as his successor with the significant title of al-Riḍā (the agreed upon), the Imamī idea of divinely sanctioned legitimacy was partially appropriated by the ʿAbbāsid regime, and the legend 'God's caliph' reappeared on the coins. Although the earliest Muʿtazila had participated in the rebellion of the Ḥasanid *mahdī* of the House of the Prophet, known as the *nafs al-zakiyya* (pure soul), in 145/762, considered non-Arabs eligible for the imamate and remained vigorous advocates of a political ethic that made the imam accountable, they were integrated now into the ʿAbbāsid regime as a school of thought under the same caliph, al-Maʾmūn, and played a major role in the cultural elaboration of Islam. As such, they contributed significantly to the development of the idea of imamate. Al-Jāḥiẓ (d. 255/868), representing the Baṣran Muʿtazila, for instance, refuted the Imāmī and Zaydī theories of the imamate, and put forward his own rudimentary and syncretic theory that rehabilitated ʿUthmān alongside legitimising the transfer of the imamate to the ʿAbbāsids. The theory was, however, barely abstracted from partisan historical reconstruction. It argued for the election of the imam and, incidentally, allowed for his deposition by 'the elite' (*khawāṣṣ*), but without specifying any constitutional procedure.[5]

Ḥadīth traditionalism, the movement led by the pious collectors and scholars of the sayings and deeds of the Prophet (*ḥadīth*) who eventually defined the Muslim community as Sunnī or 'the people of the *sunna*' (*ahl al-sunna*) and equated the latter term with the reliable *ḥadīth* as the normative foundation of Islam second to the Qurʾān, had been growing throughout the first two centuries of Islam and began to capture the legal field in the third. In the third/ninth century, however, the traditionalists did not show the same hostility to Persian statecraft that they displayed towards Shīʿite sectarianism, which they branded as divisive and heterodox, or towards the incipient philosophical movement following the translations of the works of Greek philosophy and science, which they rejected as foreign. On the contrary, the absorption of Perso-Indian political ideas is evident in the opening chapter on sovereignty (*sulṭān*) in *ʿUyūn al-akhbār* by the traditionalist *qāḍī* Ibn Qutayba (d. 276/889f.), which reproduced many of the political aphorisms taken from Ibn al-Muqaffaʿ, and the more contemporary *Kitāb al-tāj* (Book of the crown), and quotes very extensively from the Persian and Indian books on statecraft and ethics. One of the key aphorisms was a variant of what was later called 'the circle of justice': 'There is no sovereignty without men, and no men without wealth, and no wealth without cultivation, and no cultivation except through justice and good policy (*siyāsa*).' (Some variants, especially those in Persian from the fifth/eleventh century, omitted the word 'good' in order to read *siyāsa(t)* as punishment in line with the Indo-Persian sense of the term.) These aphorisms were treated as traditions (*akhbār*) relating to 'the ruler, his exemplary manner (*sīra*) and his policy'.[6] Ibn Qutayba thus accepted the normative

5 Charles Pellat, 'L'Imamat dans la doctrine de Jāḥiẓ', *SI*, 15 (1961).
6 Ibn Qutayba, *ʿUyūn al-akhbār*, ed. Y. ʿA. Tawil, 4 vols. (Beirut, 1986), vol. I, pp. 53, 63.

status given to the traditions and exemplary lives of the ancient kings analogously to those of the prophets. Under the later impact of the Shāfiʿī and Ḥanbalī schools of law the normative *sīra* came to mean the exemplary life of the Prophet and, alongside the normative *sunna* (tradition), was exclusively appropriated for the Prophet. But in this period these terms were applied to the normative sayings and deeds of the ancient kings as well. In fact, the customs and traditions of the ancient kings were given a similar normative status by the use of identical vocabulary. The title of *Taʾrīkh al-rusul waʾl-mulūk* (History of the prophets and the kings) recording them is attested several times, one of the latest being the great universal history by Abū Jaʿfar Muḥammad ibn Jarīr al-Ṭabarī in the early fourth/tenth century.

Furthermore, the conception of the polity in the Persian statecraft literature remained definitive. The polity was defined in terms of the ruler and his subjects without any meaningful reference to the *umma* (community of believers), a term which was to become a fundamental point of reference for the religion of Islam, but not for the development of political ethic and public law. It is rarely used in the literature on ethics and statecraft, which instead conceived of political community as the subjects of the ruler on the ancient Mesopotamian model of the flock (*raʿiyya*) and its shepherd. When opening the book on taxation for the commander of the faithful, the caliph Hārūn al-Rashīd, his chief justice Abū Yūsuf mentions the word *umma* once, but only to equate it with the *raʿiyya*. Every other notion comes from the Persian theory of kingship based on justice. Distinctive Persian institutions, too, are the subject of legal discussion. These include the intelligence service and, above all, the ruler's court and keystone of his justice, the *maẓālim*, where he heard the complaints of the subjects. A generation later, in a covenant of succession to his own son, ʿAbd Allāh, which was widely circulated with the caliph al-Maʾmūn's endorsement, the powerful governor of the east, Ṭāhir the Ambidextrous, bypassing the caliphate, derives the authority to rule from God directly: 'Know that power belongs to God alone; He bestows it upon whom He wills, and takes it away from whom He wills ... Know that you have been placed in your governorship as a custodian of valuables, a watchman, and a shepherd; the people in your realm are only called your flock (*raʿiyyatuka*) because you are their shepherd.'[7]

The third/ninth century also witnessed the reception of Greek political science under the ʿAbbāsid caliphate. Abū Yūsuf ibn Isḥāq al-Kindī

7 C. E. Bosworth, 'An early Arabic mirror for princes: Ṭāhir Dhūʾl-Yamīnain's epistle to his son, ʿAbdallāh (206/821)', *JNES*, 29, 1 (1970), pp. 34, 37–8.

(d. 252/866) divided philosophy (*ḥikma* or wisdom) into the theoretical and practical, and the latter into the governance of the soul (ethics), of the household (economics) and of the city (political science). This division was accepted, sometimes with slight modification, by Muslim writers of all persuasions down to the modern period. The promotion of Greek political science, however, was primarily the work of Abū Naṣr al-Fārābī (d. 339/950), who considered it the most important branch of philosophy; at one time he went so far as to take the position that there was no happiness apart from political/civic happiness. His work is therefore singly the most important channel of transmission of Greek political science into the Islamic civilisation. Al-Fārābī used 'civic politics' (*al-siyāsa al-madaniyya*) synonymously with 'governance' (*tadbīr*) and 'rulership' (*riyāsa*), and equated the term with the 'royal craft' (*al-mihna al-mulkiyya*), the art (*ṣināʿa*) of political science. The goal of political science was the health of the city, as the goal of the medical craft was bodily heath. The royal craft brought order to the civic community by establishing a hierarchy among the classes of citizens and their respective activities.

The Imāmī Shīʿa were considered moderate because they did not insist on the armed uprising of their imam, and in fact did not expect him to reappear until the end of time as the *qāʾim* (riser) and the *mahdī* (the rightly guided one). It was otherwise with the Ismāʿīlī sect, which began as a clandestine revolutionary movement in Iraq and the Yemen during the last quarter of the third/ninth century and was organised on the basis of the belief that their imam, Muḥammad ibn Ismāʿīl, a grandson of Jaʿfar al-Ṣādiq, had not died and was the Qāʾim-Mahdī. The director of the mission, the Proof (*ḥujja*) of the hidden imam, moved to Syria and sent out missionaries to the rest of the Muslim world. In 297/909 the missionary who had been active on the *mahdī*'s behalf in North Africa established the caliphate of ʿAbd Allāh al-Mahdī, a descendant of Fāṭima and ʿAlī. The *mahdī* as the founder of the Fāṭimid dynasty was in due course succeeded by his son, Muḥammad, who took the title al-Qāʾim. The Fāṭimid caliph al-Muʿizz conquered Cairo in 359/969, and extended the North African empire to Egypt and Syria for two more centuries until it was overthrown by Saladin in 566/1171. Although the majority of the population of their empire remained Sunnī, the Fāṭimid caliphs established a powerful department of mission, and sent out missionaries to overthrow the ʿAbbāsid caliphate and the Saljūq sultanate, and systematically developed terrorism in the form of assassination of major political figures by self-sacrificers (*fidāʾī*) as a tool of revolutionary struggle.

Emergence of the sultanate and patrimonial monarchies under the caliphate

Political developments of the second half of the third/ninth and fourth/tenth centuries are important for understanding the elaboration of the theory of the two powers that legitimised monarchy as the divinely sanctioned supplement to prophethood, as well as the later emergence of a juristic theory that reconciled monarchy with the caliphate, normatively subordinating the former to the latter. The era of caliphal absolutism in Baghdad ended with the murder of the caliph al-Mutawakkil in 247/861 by Turkish military slaves (sing. *mamlūk*; *ghulām*) recruited by his predecessor as palace guards to offset the power of al-Maʾmūn's army of Khurāsānian *mawālī*. Independent royal dynasties were established in Iran and Egypt in the latter part of the century, with the rulers minting their own coins and having the Friday sermon delivered in their names. The term *sulṭān*, a substantive used in the Qurʾān to mean 'authority', and subsequently commonly used to mean 'government', was applied to a person and acquired the meaning of 'ruler'. The Shīʿite Būyids (Buwayhids), who had established an independent dynasty in Iran, captured Baghdad itself in the mid-fourth/tenth century, and effectively ruled in Iraq alongside the caliph, becoming the first of a series of secular independent rulers to assume the title of *sulṭān*, and of *shāhanshāh* in Iran. They were also the first monarchs to claim the transfer from the ʿAbbāsids to their dynasty of *dawla*, the divinely ordained turn in power, and used the term for their dynastic state. This dramatic bifurcation of sovereignty into caliphate and sultanate was the expression of the autonomy of the political order in the form of monarchy from the caliphate that had in fact existed for decades. It roughly coincided with the formative period of Islamic law and the consolidation of the normative autonomy of the *sharīʿa*. This meant that from the fourth/tenth century onward the constitutional order of the caliphate had two normatively autonomous components: monarchy and the *sharīʿa*. This duality is reflected in the medieval literature on statecraft and kingship as a theory of the two powers: prophecy and kingship.

Naṣīḥat al-mulūk (Advice to kings), an early fourth/tenth-century book on statecraft written in Arabic under the Sāmānid kings, states that 'God has put kings as his deputies in his cities and as trustees of his servants and executors of his commandments among his creatures'. This assertion is backed by the key Qurʾānic justification of kingship alongside prophethood: 'Say God, possessor of kingship, you give kingship to whomever you will, and take away kingship from whomever you will' (Q 3:26), the verse used to justify the advent of the

Būyid dynastic state (*dawla*), and further supplemented by a number of other verses in which God appoints the prophets of Israel as both kings and prophets. The core idea of the Persian theory of kingship, 'the Sultan is the Shadow of God on Earth', is reported as a maxim (and not yet a *ḥadīth*), supported by other maxims attributed to Ardashīr: 'Religion and kingship are twins, there is no consolidation for the one except through its companion, as religion is the foundation of kingship, and kingship becomes its guardian. Kingship needs its foundation, and religion needs its guardians.'[8]

A collection of old aphorisms on statecraft and political ethics in Persian attributed the saying that the king is the shadow of God to the Sasanian vizier Buzurgmihr, while affirming that 'kingship (*pādshāhi*) ... is the deputyship (*khilāfat*) of God Most High on Earth. If the kings do not contradict divine command and the Prophetic prescriptions, and if justice and equity are exercised in kingship ... its degree will be equal to the rank of prophecy.'[9] The same notion was epitomised in the statecraft maxim versified alongside many others by Firdawsī early in the fifth/eleventh century: 'Kingship and prophecy are two jewels on the same ring.' Somewhat later in that century the Ghaznavid secretary and historian Abū al-Faḍl Bayhaqī, after a preparatory discussion of Ardashīr as the greatest king and Muḥammad as the greatest prophet, offers a concise statement on what he calls the two powers: 'Know that God Most High has given one power (*quwwat*) to the prophets and another power to the kings; and He has made it incumbent on the people of the earth to follow these two powers and thus to know God's straight path.'[10] Last but not least we have a clear statement of the theory in the opening paragraph of the second part of another *Naṣīḥat al-mulūk*, which was already attributed to the great al-Ghazālī in the sixth/twelfth century: 'Know and understand that God Most High chose two categories of mankind, placing them above others: the prophets and the kings (*mulūk*). He sent the prophets to His creatures to lead them to Him. As for the kings (*pādshāhān*), He chose them to protect men from one another and made the prosperity of human life dependent on them ... As you hear in the traditions, "the ruler is the shadow of God on earth."' The Sasanian maxim 'religion and kingship are twins' is then confirmed, and the author, dispensing with imamate and caliphate altogether, makes royal charisma (*farr-i īzadī*), confirmed by the justice of

8 Pseudo-Māwardī, *Naṣīḥat al-mulūk* (Baghdad, 1986), pp. 62–3, 108.
9 *Tuḥfat al-mulūk* (Tehran, 2003), pp. 71, 92.
10 Abu 'l-Faḍl Bayhaqī, *Tārīkh-i Bayhaqī*, ed. M. Dānishpazhūh, 2 vols. (Tehran, 1376/1997), vol. I, p. 154.

the ruler, the independent basis of political authority. Monarchy was, however, necessary for the maintenance of the *sharʿī* order.

The autonomous political order thus defined as monarchy had its own ethico-legal sphere. The term used in the translations of the Greek political science, *siyāsa(t)*, came to mean the craft of government or policy, and generally acquired the sense of statecraft. It comprised both discretionary rules and maxims of policy and punishment, and the more explicit rules of administration that had a ceremonial and legal character and were variously termed *āyīn* (ordinance), *ādāb* (manners (of rulership and administration)), *dastūr* (regulation), *marsūm* (customary norm) and, above all, *qānūn* (regulation, law). With these regulations, backed by the political ethics in the literature of advice to rulers (mirrors for princes), statecraft provided an independent basis for the normative regulation of government under monarchy. Government, however, was necessary for the prevalence of divine guidance and law, and al-Ghazālī would therefore adduce the maxim 'religion and kingship are twins' to establish that without statecraft – or, to use his precise words, 'government of the people through monarchy' (*siyāsat al-khalq bi'l-salṭana*) – though it was not one of the religious sciences, religion would not be complete.[11]

It should be noted that in the Persian literature on statecraft *siyāsa(t)* came to mean both statecraft and punishment, thus conjoining the two functions of government and administration of penal law, and as such travelled westward to Mamlūk Egypt and the Ottoman empire, and eastward to the Delhi sultanate and the Mughal empire. In the Ottoman empire the term was used almost exclusively with reference to penal codes.

Max Weber applied to medieval Muslim kingdoms his well-known ideal type of patrimonialism as a form of political organisation in which authority is personal and the administration of the kingdom is an extension of the management of the household of the ruler, and analysed the use of military slaves by Muslim patrimonial rulers.[12] Weber's type fits the system of delegated authority that developed with the appearance of independent monarchies, even though a variety of political regimes in the Muslim world can be subsumed under it.

A very early tract on public law in Persian, which should be dated from the late Sāmānid period, *Ādāb-i salṭanat wa wizārat* (Rules of kingship and

11 al-Ghazālī, *Iḥyā' ʿulūm al-dīn*, 5 vols. (Cairo, n. d. [1965]), vol. I, p. 17.
12 Max Weber, *Economy and society*, ed. G. Roth and C. Wittich, 2 vols. (Berkeley, 1978), vol. II, pp. 1015–20.

vizierate), after adducing two fundamental *ḥadīth* on the political ethic, 'You are all shepherds, each responsible for his flock' and 'One hour of justice by a ruler is worth more than seventy years of worship', describes the functions of the highest officials of the patrimonial monarchy and ranks them in this order: (1) the vizier; (2) the *amīr-i dād* (lord of justice), corresponding to the caliph's *ṣāḥib/nāẓir al-maẓālim*, charged with the administration of justice as the cornerstone of monarchy; (3) *wakīl-i dar* (deputy at the gate); (4) *amīr-i ḥājib* (lord chamberlain); (5) *ʿāriḍ* (army inspector); and (6) *ṣāḥib-i barīd* (postmaster) in charge of the intelligence service.[13] The Sāmānids were more successful than the third/ninth-century ʿAbbāsid caliphs in recruiting and controlling their slave generals and, in his famous treatise on government, Niẓām al-Mulk discussed their example at length and drew lessons from it,[14] which he may have applied in practice in organising his own *mamlūk* corps. Nevertheless, some of the freed slave generals established their own rule with the disintegration of the Sāmānid and Saljūq empires, notably Sebüktegin, who established the Ghaznavid dynasty and whose son, Sultan Maḥmūd, conquered northern India in the early fifth/eleventh century. The slave generals of the Ghūrids established the Delhi sultanate in the early seventh/thirteenth century.

Two Iranian philosophers who sought to synthesise Greek political science and Persian statecraft in this period are of particular interest. Abu 'l-Ḥasan al-ʿĀmirī al-Nīshābūrī (d. 381/991) diverged from al-Fārābī to allow for a more harmonious reconciliation of Islam and philosophy. Al-ʿĀmirī considered prophecy and kingship the two institutions fundamental for the preservation of the world, and even sought to reconcile religious jurisprudence and statecraft based on political science in view of the overlap between the religious and political spheres. The key to this reconciliation is the idea of rational religion, rationality being the quality taken to establish the superiority of Islam over other religions. Al-ʿĀmirī's reading of Islam as rational religion is analogically extended by his compatriot, ʿAlī ibn Muskūya (Miskawayh) (d. 421/1030), to the conception of Persian, Indian, Greek and Roman political ethics and norms of statecraft as the 'eternal wisdom' (*jāwīdān khirad*). In line with his idea of natural, civic religion, Islam is conceived as rational/natural religion which is therefore universal. Ibn Muskūya, writing towards the end of the fourth/tenth century, thus relativised the traditions of the Prophet, among

13 Charles Schefer, *Chrestomathie persane*, 2 vols. (Paris, 1883), vol. I, pp. 11–13, 19–20.
14 Niẓām al-Mulk, *Siyar al-mulūk (Siyāsatnāma)*, ed. Hubert Dark (Tehran, 1355/1976), pp. 141–58.

which he included the 'shadow of God' maxim as a *ḥadīth*, by subsuming them under 'the Arab wisdom', alongside the Persian, the Indian and the Greek. He is an exception, however, and other authors continued to privilege the words of God and His Prophet over the wisdom of the other nations, and thus remain in line with their colleagues in Islamic jurisprudence.

In the latter part of the sixth/twelfth century Shihāb al-Dīn Yaḥyā al-Suhrawardī (d. 587/1191) extended al-ʿĀmirī's theory of the two powers along Neoplatonic, emanationist lines. The salvational function of the prophets is shared by the Persian kings (and he extends the same compliment to the Greek sages and those of other ancient religions). Calling the light of wisdom emanating from the Great Luminous Being the *kayān khurra*, he saw the ancient kings as possessors of royal authority, saving wisdom and auspicious fortune. In the *Farāʾid al-sulūk*, a book on ethics and statecraft written a generation later (in 610/1213), we read that the kings should be obeyed like the prophets because of the 'divine effulgence (*farr-i īzadī*) ... which emanates from their chest to their countenance and is called in Persian the *khurra-yi kayānī*'.[15] As we shall see, the idea influenced the construction of the Mughal imperial ideology under Akbar.

Meanwhile, another type of patrimonial regime was developing with the formation of nomadic Turkic states in the fifth/eleventh century, namely the Qarakhānid kingdom in Central Asia and the Saljūq empire in Iran, Iraq, Syria and Anatolia. According to this conception the kingdom was the patrimonial property of the whole family of the *khān*, and was divided into appanages upon his death. The Turkic conception of kingship as a divine gift to the founder of the state also linked it to the establishment of the law (*törü*), but as the Saljūqs adopted the Persian conception of kingship and championed the Sunnī restoration under the caliphate, the impact of the Turkic conception of the law had to wait for the Mongol invasion two centuries later. The problem of succession, however, resulted in the disintegration of the Saljūq nomadic empire, as it did with the Tīmūrid empire in the ninth/fifteenth century.

In considering the character of medieval Muslim regimes, note should be taken of Marshall Hodgson's rejection of Weber's ideal types of patrimonialism and sultanism (which was defined too narrowly to capture illegitimate domination of the Turkish guards of the caliphs). In their place Hodgson offers two ideal types of his own: 'the *aʿyān–amīr* system' in the Saljūq period; and 'the military patronage state' of the post-Mongol era. The first describes the regime that emerged with the development of the *iqṭāʿ* system of land tenure

15 *Farāʾid al-sulūk*, ed. N. Wiṣālī and G. Afrasiyābī (Tehran, 1368/1989), pp. 49–50.

and in which the social power of the notables (*aʿyān*) in towns and villages was subordinated to the domination of the military elite (*amīrs*) commanding the garrisons. It was characterised by a considerable degree of social and geographical 'cosmopolitan' mobility assured by the *sharīʿa*. According to Hodgson the system represented a stalemate between agrarian and mercantile power. With the weakening of bureaucracy and the decentralisation of land assignments that resulted from the increase in the size of the *iqṭāʿ* and amalgamation of fiscal revenue collection and prebendal grants for military and administrative service, the system developed in a military direction.[16] In fact, in interaction with the above-mentioned absence of primogeniture and indivisibility in nomadic kingdoms, the power of women in Turkic royal families created a novel political regime. The appanage of a young Saljūq prince was in practice governed by his tutor (*atabeg/atābak*) whom his widowed mother tended to marry. The regime of the *atabegs* of Fārs survived the collapse of the Saljūq empire and the Mongol invasion, but most *atabeg* domains disintegrated towards the end of the seventh/twelfth century, with some cases of seizure of power by Saljūq *mamlūks*. The *aʿyān–amīr* system thus changed into an extremely decentralised system in the latter part of the sixth/twelfth and early seventh/thirteenth centuries.

Meanwhile, a very different pattern had developed in Andalusia, where an Umayyad caliphate had been established after the ʿAbbāsid revolution and by the fifth/eleventh century disintegrated into a system of *mulūk al-ṭawāʾif* (*reyes de taifas* or *ṭāʾifa* kingdoms) which Ibn Rushd (Averroes) had explained in terms of the typology of regimes taken from Greek political science. His approach was developed by another thinker from the Maghrib, ʿAbd al-Raḥmān ibn Khaldūn (d. 808/1406), who put forward an original typology of government based on the generation of Muslim historical experience in the epochal *Muqaddima* (Introduction) to his universal history, *Kitāb al-ʿibar*. He distinguished the caliphate from kingship (*mulk*), offering an entirely sociological explanation of the latter as a natural system of authority based on group solidarity (*ʿaṣabiyya*). He then theorised the historical experience of the rise of the Fāṭimids and of the Almoravid and Almohad dynasties in the fifth/eleventh and sixth/twelfth centuries in the Maghrib within the framework of the cycle of rise and fall of tribal dynasties. Each cycle began as a revolution carried out by a tribal confederation whose group solidarity was decisively reinforced by religion under the leadership of religious

16 Marshall G. S. Hodgson, *The venture of Islam*, 3 vols. (Chicago, 1974), vol. II, pp. 64–74, 93–4.

reformers. Be that as it may, the subsequent dynasties in the Maghrib retained the designations of caliph and commander of the faithful as a heritage of these religious revolutions, and the king of Morocco is considered the commander of the faithful to this day.

Attempts had been made even before the Būyid sultanate to create a tradition of administration under the vizierate of the ʿAbbāsid caliphate, notably in *Kitāb al-wuzarāʾ waʾl-kuttāb* (Book of viziers and secretaries) by Muḥammad ibn ʿAbdūs al-Jahshiyārī (d. 331/942). The great vizier of the Saljūq sultans, Niẓām al-Mulk Ṭūsī, who built his famous Niẓāmiyya colleges to promote Islamic learning and is therefore considered the chief architect of 'the Sunnī restoration', personally took an important step to integrate the tradition of vizierate into the dual theory of power. In his classic book on statecraft, *Siyar al-mulūk* (Ways of kings) or *Siyāsatnāma* (Book of statecraft), Niẓām al-Mulk, after discussing the legitimacy of monarchy and the principles of its government and political organisation, proceeded to legitimise the authority of the vizier as well, adducing traditions of both the kings and the prophets: 'Every king who has attained greatness … has had good viziers, as have had the great prophets.' Great kings such as Khusrau I, Anūshīrwān and the Ghaznavid sultan Maḥmūd appointed great viziers and 'the *sunnat* [custom or tradition] of the prophets and the *sīra* [manner, way] of the kings have thus become well-known tales'.[17] Niẓām al-Mulk's project of creating an administrative tradition of the secretaries alongside the legal tradition of the *ʿulamāʾ* gave birth to a new genre in Persian literature: the history of the viziers, modelled on the earlier Arabic books on the traditions of the viziers (*akhbār al-wuzarāʾ*). In the following century a major concern of the authors who followed his example was the legitimisation of administrative authority in terms of the traditions of the kings, on the one hand, and of the prophet and his caliphs, on the other. To justify a tradition of vizierate on the basis of the tradition of kings, one such author equated the turban of the vizier with the crown to signify the delegation of royal authority to him, and saw it as adorning the head of 'the lord of vizierate and the *muftī* of the seat of the *sharīʿat*'. The norms of giving gifts to the king, for instance, are said to amount to 'an approved tradition (*sunnat*)' with respect to which the viziers have made 'the law of their predecessors (*qānūn-i aslāf*) their own regulation (*dastūr*)'. What is more interesting from our point of view is that Qurʾānic verses and traditions from the Prophet and his Companions are cited very frequently and

17 Niẓām al-Mulk, *Siyar al-mulūk*, p. 234.

given normative priority over the maxims of statecraft and poetry. Of some fifty-five verses cited, Q 3:26: 'You give the kingdom to whom you will' occurs most frequently (four times). Perhaps the most pertinent of the cited traditions is the saying of the Prophet: 'For him who institutes a good tradition (*man sanna sunna ḥasana*), there is a reward, and a reward for whoever acts according to it.' The goal of this solid traditional backing is, however, to justify and elaborate an autonomous administrative tradition with whose foundation he credits Niẓām al-Mulk.[18]

To conclude this section, the core conception of the theory of the two divinely sanctioned powers was that God had chosen two classes of mankind above the rest: the prophets to guide mankind to salvation; and the kings to preserve order as the prerequisite for the pursuit of salvation. This allowed for the legal pluralism of the Islamic empire. A just ruler made the pursuit of salvation possible for his subjects through the Islamic *sharīʿa* or the Christian *sharīʿa*, or the Jewish *sharīʿa*, or those of the Zoroastrians, Sabians and other honorary 'Peoples of the Book'.

The juristic theory of the caliphate and imamate

The Sunnī theory of the caliphate, also termed imamate, was formulated during the ʿAbbāsid–Būyid joint rule and in contradistinction to the Imāmī theory on almost all its major points. It censored the term 'God's caliph' and substituted for it 'the deputy of the messenger of God' (*khalīfat rasūl allāh*), which highlighted the post-Būyid, post-sultanic religious character of the caliph's differentiated authority. The Sunnī jurists adopted the Muʿtazilite position that the imam–caliph should be elected, as against the Imāmī argument for appointment by designation. The idea of election was sustained by the legal fiction of the *bayʿa* (oath of allegiance) as an act of investiture constitutive of a binding contract, ideally concluded by 'the people of loosening and binding' (*ahl al-ḥall wa'l-ʿaqd*) on behalf of the community (*jamāʿa*), but for most jurists following al-Ghazālī also valid even when concluded by a single potentate.

By this time the appropriation of Islamic law by the people of *ḥadīth* and their professionalisation into the estate of *ʿulamāʾ* (the learned) was far advanced. With this momentous differentiation of religious authority and its extension over the ethico-legal order that was identified as the *sharīʿa* (divine

18 Muḥammad ibn Muḥammad ibn Ḥasan Iṣfahānī, *Dastūr al-wizāra*, ed. R. Anzābi-nizhād (Tehran, 1364/1985), pp. 29, 40, 67, 246–8.

path), the jurists of the century-old Ḥanbalī and Shāfiʿī schools of law became the carriers of a new political theory. To shore up the position against the Būyid sultans in Iraq and the Fāṭimids in North Africa, Egypt and Syria, the ʿAbbāsid caliph al-Qādir and his son al-Qāʾim embarked on a policy of defining Islam and becoming dispensers of Islamic legitimacy to the sultans and kings who had an independent power base and were already claiming independent divine sanction for their rule. This meant identifying the caliphate increasingly with the differentiated religious authority of the *ʿulamāʾ* as officially representative of Islam. The result was the publication of two works with the identical title of *Aḥkām al-sulṭāniyya* (Governmental ordinances) and with very similar content that claimed political ethics and public law as a branch of Islamic jurisprudence distinct from the statecraft literature of the secretaries and from the more recent political science of the philosophers. This claim, however, was far from exclusive, and its major proponents, ʿAlī ibn Muḥammad al-Māwardī (d. 450/1058) and Abū Ḥāmid Muḥammad al-Ghazālī (d. 505/1111) in the second half of the fifth/eleventh century, had no hesitation in supplementing their Islamic jurisprudence with writing on statecraft and ethical advice (*naṣīḥa*[*t*]) for kings.

It is sociologically misleading to presume that major sectarian differences reflected in various theories of the imamate formulated dialectically in the latter part of the fourth/tenth century and throughout the fifth/eleventh were a source of different conceptions of government and its legitimacy. Such a presumption, common in the conventional wisdom and among contemporary Muslim clerics, would make it impossible to understand the prominence of Imāmī Shīʿite viziers and jurists in the long century of ʿAbbāsid–Būyid co-dominion in Iraq, or in the last century of the ʿAbbāsid caliphate, including the remarkable attempt by the caliph al-Nāṣir li-Dīn Allāh (r. 576–622/1180–1225) to revive the caliphate as a real social and political force. The Imāmīs had been prominent in the government of the ʿAbbāsid caliphs even before the Būyid seizure of power.

There is in fact a fundamental similarity between the attitudes of medieval Sunnī and Imāmī jurists towards political order in relation to the *sharīʿa*. The bifurcation of political authority into caliphate and sultanate after the Būyid seizure of Baghdad resulted in a distinct mode of justification of political authority in terms of the necessity of maintenance of public order through the enforcement of the *sharīʿa*. This mode of derivation of 'the necessity of the imamate' is common to the Sunnī and Shīʿite jurists of the Būyid period alike; in both cases, it results in the severing of the link between the necessity of upholding the Islamic norms and the legitimacy or qualification of the ruler.

The legal rationale of the respective positions was basically the same, although the Sunnī and the Shīʿite jurists adduced different traditions and used different arguments to support it. This identical legal logic consisted in the following: both groups derived the necessity of imamate from the necessity of the upholding of the *sharīʿa* and observing the Islamic norms.

This similarity is already evident in the fourth/tenth century:

> All the *ʿūlamāʾ* have agreed unanimously that the Friday prayers, the two festivals (*ʿīds*) ... warfare against the infidels, the pilgrimage, and the sacrifices are incumbent upon every *amīr* whether he be upright or an evildoer; that it is lawful to pay them the land tax ... to pray in the cathedral mosques they build and to walk on the bridges which they construct. Similarly, buying and selling and other kinds of trade, agriculture and all crafts, in every period and no matter under what *amīr*, are lawful in conformity with the Book and the Sunna. The oppression of the oppressor and the tyranny of the tyrant do not harm a man who preserves his religion and adheres to the Sunna of his prophet ... in the same way that if a man, under a just Imam, makes a sale contrary to the Book and the Sunna, the justice of his Imam will be of no avail to him.[19]

Thus the Ḥanbalite Ibn Baṭṭa (d. 387/997). His Imāmī Shīʿite contemporary, the Shaykh al-Mufīd (d. 413/1022), similarly argued in the *Irshād* that 'it is impossible for the duty-bound believers (*mukallafūn*) to be without an authority (*sulṭān*) whose presence draws them closer to righteousness and keeps them away from corruption ... who would carry out the laws, protect the land of Islam, and assemble the people to hold the Friday prayer and the two festivals (*ʿīds*)'.[20] This was offered as the rational proof for the necessity of 'the existence of an infallible imam in every age', including this one of the 'longer occultation'!

The major difference between the two positions is that the just imam of the Shīʿa was in occultation. This difference, paradoxically, enhanced the similarity of the two attitudes. The logic of al-Mufīd's position is the same as that of Ibn Baṭṭa: there must be public authority to make the laws of Islam effective.

Writing 'on the necessity of the imamate' in the same vein, the Sunnī jurist ʿAbd al-Qāhir al-Baghdādī (d. 428/1037) notes the agreement among the Sunnīs, the Shīʿa and the Muʿtazila that the imamate is compulsory 'and that it is essential for the Muslims to have an Imam to execute their ordinances,

19 Bernard Lewis (ed. and trans.), *Islam from the Prophet Muhammad to the capture of Constantinople*, 2 vols. (New York, 1974), vol. I, p. 171.

20 Muḥammad ibn Muḥammad ibn Nuʿmān al-Mufīd, *al-Irshād li'l-shaykh al-Mufīd* (Qumm, n.d.), p. 347.

enforce legal penalties, direct their armies [and] marry off their widows'.[21] It is interesting to note that al-Baghdādī required *ijtihād* for the imam, reporting that the Shīʿa require infallibility (*ʿiṣma*). The stipulation of *ijtihād* was to maintain a strong link between the imamate and the *sharīʿa*. This was just the link to snap.

In *al-Aḥkām al-sulṭaniyya* al-Māwardī insisted on this condition, however unrealistically, to ensure the Islamic legitimacy of the caliph as the imam, while transmitting this legitimisation to the office-holders of the state, the governors and the *qāḍīs*, who were duly invested with the authority (*wilāya*) of the caliph. But he had to acknowledge the presence of the elephant in the room, and accommodated monarchy (*salṭana*) under the caliphate as 'emirate by seizure' (*imārat al-istīlāʾ*). The caliph could *ex post facto* legitimise the authority of such an *amīr* or sultan on the condition that the latter enforces the ordinances of the *sharīʿa*, if necessary, by accepting knowledgeable representatives of the caliph. Once more, the justification is in terms of the necessity of the maintenance of the *sharʿī* order. Perhaps to compensate for this acknowledgement, however, al-Māwardī, who authored a separate book on 'government of kingdom' that conceived of political community as the subjects, suggests that the caliph should apply himself to the government (*siyāsa*) of the *umma* and defence of the *milla* (religion). Furthermore, the reigning caliph could institute a binding contract, called a 'covenant' (*ʿahd*) on the model of ancient kings, investing a successor-designate with authority as the *walī al-ʿahd*. It is interesting to note that the conception of public interest (*maṣlaḥa ʿāmma*) is introduced in connection with the possibility of consecutive designation of his successors by the caliph.[22]

A generation later the Imam al-Ḥaramayn Juwaynī, who like Māwardī subscribed to Shāfiʿite jurisprudence and Ashʿarite theology, but unlike the latter dedicated his book *Ghiyāth al-umam* (Saving of the nations) to Niẓām al-Mulk instead of the ʿAbbāsid caliph, argued for the incumbency of the maintenance of the *sharʿī* order even when the imam was patently incompetent, as was the case with the ʿAbbāsid caliph in his time, and shifted the responsibility for maintenance of the *sharʿī* order entirely to the *ʿulamāʾ* under the aegis of any effective ruler who could establish peace and order in the realm.

Perhaps the most forceful, and certainly the most famous, Sunnī statements on the necessity of imamate as the source of public authority come to us from

21 Quoted in H. A. R. Gibb, 'Constitutional organization', in M. Khadduri and H. J. Liebesney (eds.), *Law in the Middle East* (Washington, DC, 1955), p. 7.

22 E. I. J. Rosenthal, *Political thought in Medieval Islam* (Cambridge, 1958), pp. 32–7; Hanna Mikhail, *Politics and revelation: Māwardī and after* (Edinburgh, 1995), pp. 40–5.

Juwaynī's student, al-Ghazālī, who was a younger protégé of Niẓām al-Mulk. Al-Ghazālī was frank enough to admit that the imamate had to be conceded to a person who lacked not only *ijtihād* but also many of the other qualifications required by Islamic jurisprudence. However,

> The concessions which we hereby make are not voluntary, but necessity may render lawful even that which is forbidden. We know that it is forbidden to eat carrion, but it would be worse to die of hunger. If anyone does not consent to this, and holds the opinion that the Imamate is dead in our time, because the necessary qualifications are lacking … then we would ask him 'Which is the better part, to declare that the kadis are revoked, that all delegations of authority (*wilāyat*) are invalid, that marriages cannot be legally contracted, that all acts of government are everywhere null and void, and thus to allow that the entire population is living in sin – or is it better to recognize that the Imamate exists in fact, and therefore that transactions and administrative actions are valid, given the actual circumstances and the necessities of these times?'[23]

To say, in this manner, that the necessity of the imamate was established was a tortuous and tortured way of saying that there had to be authority and public order for Muslims to live under the law of God.

The separation of considerations of legitimacy of the imamate from the observance of the *sharīʿa* and validity of legal transactions by Shaykh al-Mufīd opened the way for the endorsement of political theory by the Imāmī Shīʿa alongside the Sunnīs, and the Shīʿite vizier Abu 'l-Qāsim al-Maghribī (d. 418/1027) published a concise *Kitāb fi'l-siyāsa* (Book on government), dividing the government into three kinds: the ruler's government of his self; his elite (*khāṣṣa*); and his subjects (*raʿiyya*). To ensure that the Shīʿite participation would have full legal sanction he commissioned a lecture on 'working with government' (*ʿamal maʿ al-sulṭān*) by his spiritual mentor and the leading Imāmī jurist of Baghdad, the Sharīf al-Murtaḍā (d. 436/1044), who had accepted the office of the judge of the *maẓālim* from the caliph, and was a legal consultant to the Būyid ruler who employed al-Māwardī in the same capacity. Al-Murtaḍā was emphatic in justifying the exercise of public authority (*wilāya*) to ensure the prevalence of Islamic normative order in the absence of the imam, irrespective of the qualities and legitimacy of the ruler. Working for a just ruler was obviously permissible; but al-Murtaḍā went much further, and argued that it was not only permissible but commendable, and under some circumstances even obligatory, to accept office and exercise public

23 Quoted in Gibb, 'Constitutional organization', pp. 19–20.

authority on behalf of a tyrannical ruler. His position was made definitive for Shīʿism in the 'canonical' treatise of his student, the Shaykh al-Ṭāʾifa al-Ṭūsī (d. 460/1067), the *Nihāya*.

The Muʿtazilite doctrine that the imamate was necessary as a divine grace for the maintenance of the revealed laws was also adopted by the Shīʿite theologians of the Būyid period. Their Sunnī opponents saw a contradiction between this doctrine and that of the occultation of the imam. The Shaykh al-Ṭāʾifa tried to meet the objections of his Sunnī opponents, and to establish occultation on rational grounds from two principles: the incumbency of grace upon God, which entails the necessity of the imamate; and the necessity of certainty of the imam's infallibility. This last point is particularly interesting from our point of view. The sinfulness and fallibility of the actual political leaders, who are considered imams by the Sunnīs, is said to establish, with certainty, 'that the Infallible Imam is absent and hidden from [men's] views'.[24]

The differentiation and mutual articulation of the caliphate and the sultanate became clearer in the second half of the sixth/twelfth century. While the religious aspect of the holy offices of the caliphate continued to be emphasised by the Ḥanbalite Ibn al-Jawzī, who considered obedience to the caliph al-Mustaḍīʾ (r. 566–75/1170–80) an integral part of the faith, the Saljūq sultans forcefully maintained that the function of the caliph as the imam of the community of believers (*umma*) was restricted to the religious sphere. The caliph's position thus became similar to that of the pope in Western Christendom.

Islamic royalism and the military-patronage state

The juristic mode of reconciliation of monarchy and the ethico-legal order based on the *sharīʿa*, as the two normative orders of the late ʿAbbāsid era, survived the overthrow of the caliphate in 556/1258 with only a minor modification prefigured in the Saljūq period. The fundamental distinction between the political order and the *sharʿī* order did not disappear but was accommodated within the framework of the post-caliphal sultanism in a distinctive type of regime that could be called 'Islamic royalism'. According to this the ruler (*sulṭān*) maintained both the political and the *sharʿī* order, and was therefore the shadow of God on earth and the 'king of Islam'.

24 S. A. Arjomand, *The shadow of God and the hidden imam: Religion, political organization and societal change in Shiʿite Iran from the beginning to 1890* (Chicago, 1984), p. 44, *apud Kitāb al-ghayba*.

The locutions *pādshāh-i Islām*, *malik-i Islām* and *sulṭān-i Islām* must have been current in the Saljūq era, and al-Ghazālī used them in his didactic works and letters addressed to the Saljūq sultan Sanjar. Writing in support of the *khʷārazmshāh*'s serious challenge to the suzerainty of the ʿAbbāsid caliph in the latter part of the sixth/twelfth century, the Shāfiʿite jurist and philosopher Fakhr al-Dīn al-Rāzī used the philosophical division of practical philosophy into ethics, economics and civic politics to offer a synthesis of Perso-Indian statecraft and Greek political science, but only to proceed to establish the total independence of his royal patron from the caliph. The *khwārazmshāh*, 'the king of Islam', who led the 'army of Islam' as an instrument of its expansion among the infidels in Central Asia, was God's immediate deputy. Al-Rāzī maintained that the order of the world is impossible without the existence of 'the king (*pādshāh*) who is God's caliph'. 'The king', he further affirmed, 'is the shadow of God and the deputy of the Prophet.'[25]

Meanwhile, the spread of Sufism was also giving a new meaning to the representation of God by the ruler without the mediation of divine law. Thus in 618/1221 Najm al-Dīn Rāzī would declare: 'Monarchy (*salṭanat*) is the caliphate and lieutenancy (*niyābat*) of God; the Prophet said "the ruler is the shadow of God", which signifies the Caliphate.' He further takes the monarch's being the shadow and deputy of God to entitle him to spiritual as well as temporal sovereignty.[26]

The ʿAbbāsid caliphate was thus made redundant even before its overthrow. After its extinction the kings' claim to being God's deputy gained universal acceptance, and the kings added caliph as well as sultan to their titles. Monarchy was thenceforth derived independently from God. The ruler maintained order in the world; he was therefore God's caliph or representative on earth. The one exception to this new Islamic royalism was the Mamlūk kingdom in Egypt and Syria, where the ʿAbbāsid caliphate, as we shall see, did have an afterlife.

In their normative hermeneutics, post-Mongol books on ethics often alternated between the Qurʾānic verses and the traditions of the Prophet, on the one hand, and the Persian and Greek wisdom and the tradition of kings, on the other. The impact of traditionalism after the Sunnī restoration by the Saljūqs was not confined to Islamic jurisprudence, but also gave prominence to Qurʾānic verses and to *ḥadīth* in works on political ethics. This is evident in

25 Fakhr al-Dīn al-Rāzī, *Jāmiʿ al-ʿulūm*, ed. M. Malek al-Kottb (Bombay, 1905), pp. 62, 204–6.
26 Charles-Henri de Fouchécour, *Moralia: Les notions morales dans la littérature persane du 3e/9e au 7e/13e siècle* (Paris, 1986), p. 430; *apud Mirṣād al-ʿibād*.

the Persian literature on ethics and statecraft that flourished at the courts of the later Ghaznavids and the Ghūrids who succeeded them, notably in the preface to the Persian translation/adaptation of *Kalīla wa Dimna* by the Ghaznavid official Naṣr Allāh Munshī. This Perso-Islamicate political ethic and thought was disseminated by the sultans of Delhi in India in the seventh/thirteenth century with such works as the *Jawāmiʿ al-ḥikāyāt* of Sadīd al-Dīn Muḥammad ʿAwfī and the *Ādāb al-ḥarb wa'l-shajāʿa* (The manners of warfare and bravery) of Muḥammad ibn Manṣūr Mubārakshāh, known as Fakhr-i mudabbir, both of which were eventually dedicated to Sultan Īltutmish (d. 633/1235–6) of Delhi. A remarkable feature of this last book is its extensive coverage of military organisation and warfare; there, too, supportive traditions abound, and traditional precedents are sought, wherever possible, in the practice of the early prophets, beginning with Adam and the rightly guided caliphs, while other nations and practices are also duly incorporated. This Islamic justification of military organisation can be understood in the light of the continued importance of and legitimisatory function of *jihād* for the sultanate of Delhi, where the Muslims were a small ruling minority dominating a large Hindu population.

Kingship, according to the official and historian of the Delhi sultanate, Ḍiyāʾ al-Dīn Baranī, is 'the lieutenancy of the divinity and deputyship [caliphate] of God'. Baranī saw the caliphate as a mere phase in the history of kingship. The *sharʿī* order was to be maintained by kings who had military power, or their successors. Another point of departure for him was the theory of dual power, but he was much more frank than earlier jurists about admitting the possibility of a serious clash between monarchy and the *sharʿī* order. Yes, religion and kingship were united in Muḥammad, but this was the Prophet's miracle, impossible for ordinary mortals to achieve. 'Prophecy is the perfection of religiosity, and kingship is the perfection of the world – and the two perfections are opposite and contradictory to each other.' That is why Sultan Maḥmūd, the archetypal 'king of Islam', is made to declare to his children that 'rulership is impossible without practicing the tradition and customs of the Persian kings. And all the *ʿulamāʾ* of the *umma* know that the tradition and customs of the Persian rulers are contrary to the Mohammadan traditions and to Mohammad's manner of life.' The central paradox of Islamic royalism is that, in order to protect and promote Islam, the kings of Islam have to commit what is forbidden by the sacred law. He repeats twice al-Ghazālī's famous statement that eating carrion is forbidden by the sacred law but justifiable under necessity (an allusion to Q 2:173).[27]

27 Zia-ud-Din Barani, *Fatāwā-i jahāndārī (Rulings on temporal government)*, ed. A. S. Khan (Lahore, 1972), pp. 140, 142.

In Iran, meanwhile, the *Gulistān* of Shaykh Muṣliḥ al-Dīn Saʿdī, singly the most influential medieval book on ethics (incidentally, written in the year of the overthrow of the ʿAbbāsid caliphate), begins with a chapter 'On the tradition of kings' (*dar sīrat-i pādshāhān*) and similarly combines the Qurʾānic verses and the traditions of the Prophet eclectically with Persian and Greek wisdom and the tradition of kings, albeit with his distinctive and exceptional genius for highlighting the paradoxes and moral ambiguities in statecraft and political ethic. Naṣīr al-Dīn al-Ṭūsī was more systematic than most in ranking the scriptural and wisdom sources as the fundamentals of ethics. His *Akhlāq-i muḥtashamī* (Muḥtashamian ethics) is a collection of Qurʾānic verses, traditions and maxims from wisdom literature arranged in order of priority in each of the forty topical chapters and translated into simple Persian. Some revealed verses are also integrated into the maxims of wisdom. This work is also very interesting for demonstrating, as does the reception of al-Ṭūsī's greater classic, that there is absolutely no sectarian difference between the Shīʿite and Sunnī conceptions of statecraft and political ethic. The normative hermeneutic is identical in both cases. As an Ismāʿīlī at the time, al-Ṭūsī simply extended the tradition of the Prophet to include those of ʿAlid imams and, at the lower level of normativity, the wisdom of the Greeks and the Persians to include a few directives from the Fāṭimid caliphs and Ismāʿīlī missionaries.

Statements of Greek practical philosophy in Persian also continued in the era of Turko-Mongolian domination. The most important such statement was Naṣīr al-Dīn al-Ṭūsī's *Akhlāq-i nāṣirī* (Nāṣirian ethics), which consists of a free translation of Ibn Muskūya's *Tahdhīb al-akhlāq* (The purification of ethics), itself an Arabic rendering of Aristotle's *Ethics*, supplemented by a section on civic politics. This last section includes some of the writings of al-Fārābī, as well as the older aphorisms of Ibn al-Muqaffaʿ. It also incorporates the political ethic of patrimonial kingship under 'royal government' (*siyāsat-i mulk*), which begins with the consideration of the tradition (*sīrat*) of the kings. To establish the authority of the head of the household, al-Ṭūsī produces the much-quoted *ḥadīth* 'You are all shepherds, each responsible for his flock (*raʿiyyat* = subjects).'[28]

Al-Ṭūsī had many imitators, and his book on ethics was highly influential in the great Muslim empires of the early modern era. It provided the model for *Akhlāq-i Jalālī* (Dawānī's ethics) by the *qāḍī* of Fārs, Jalāl al-Dīn Dawānī

28 Naṣīr al-Dīn Ṭūsī, *Akhlāq-i Nāṣirī*, ed. M. Mīnuwī and ʿA.-R. Ḥaydarī (Tehran, 1356/1976), pp. 208, 300.

(d. 908/1502f.), and *Akhlāq-i ʿalāʾī* (ʿAlāʾiyan ethics) by the Ottoman *qāḍī* of Damascus, ʿAlī Celebī Qinalizāda (d. 979/1572). The book itself was used widely in the Indian colleges, and was regularly read to the Mughal emperor Akbar. Unlike his contemporary Aristotelian Thomas Aquinas, however, al-Ṭūsī and the Muslim philosophers were unfortunate in that the only work of Aristotle that was not translated into Arabic was his *Politics*. They therefore mistook Plato's *Republic* as the natural extension of Aristotle's *Ethics*, with the consequent loss of many key Aristotelian political concepts that shaped Western political thought.

The bureaucratic class, secretaries of the chanceries who were the bearers of the culture of ethics and statecraft, also dealt with the civic society and institutions of the kingdoms and provided us with a picture of the social hierarchy and stratification in terms of status by arranging different modes of address appropriate for different ranks within the civilian population. This picture could be very detailed, but it basically followed the Sasanian division of society into 'men of the sword', 'men of the pen' and 'men of affairs', with the cultivators appearing indirectly and often collectively as 'the subjects' (*raʿāyā*). This conception of social hierarchy remained deeply rooted, but a dichotomy of the military elite (*ʿaskarī*) and the subjects (*raʿāyā*), which corresponded to the division of society into a dominant Turco-Mongolian estate and the non-military Persian or Tajik state comprising both the urban strata and the peasantry, was superimposed on it.

As for the Imāmī Shīʿa, the position of the Būyid doctors was reaffirmed in the Mongol period. Al-Ṭūsī's student, the ʿAllāma al-Ḥillī (d. 726/1325), stated:

> Let it not be said [as our opponents say] that the Imamate is only a divine mercy (*lutf*) when the Imam manifestly has power so that the benefit of the Imamate can be had from him ... For we say that ... the benefit is there even if the Imam is concealed, because the possibility of his advent at any time is a mercy with regard to the believer who is duty-bound by the Law.[29]

This passage can be read to mean that the divine grace is symbolised by the hidden imam, the imam in complete occultation, and consists in the revelation of the law. Thus the doctrine of occultation in effect severs the link between the imamate as legitimate rule and the necessity of the enforcement of the *sharīʿa*. As we have seen, the Sunnī and Imāmī Shīʿite jurists alike argued that the imamate was necessary because there had to be public authority for the

29 Ibn al-Muṭahhar al-Ḥillī, 'The ʿAllāma al-Ḥillī on the imamate and *ijtihād*', ed. and trans. John Cooper, in S. A. Arjomand (ed.), *Authority and political culture in Shiʿism* (Albany, 1988), p. 241.

law of God to prevail. If considering the actual ruler as imam could be, as al-Ghazālī suggested, like eating carrion out of necessity, was it not more convenient to consign the imam to occultation until the end of time?

Upon his conversion to Islam in 694/1295, which was followed by the mass conversion of his army, the Mongol ruler of Iran, Ghāzān Khān, called himself 'the king of Islam', thus adopting Islamic royalism as the type of regime that was to prevail in the eastern part of the Muslim world. It became polity for the Turco-Mongolian empires from 657/1258 to 906/1500. The Mongol invasion, however, had also brought in a new, Turkic, notion of public law, which was gradually absorbed within the framework of Islamic monarchy. The Turkic notion of divinely granted sovereignty (*kut*), as attested in the seventh-century Orkhon inscriptions and the fifth/eleventh-century mirror for a Qarakhānid prince, *Kutadgu bilig* (Wisdom of royal glory), was inseparably tied to that of law (*törü*): a *kagan* blessed by divine fortune established a state and his law at the same time. Chinggis Khān thus established the great *yāsā* alongside his universal empire. The notion of divinely granted sovereignty was reinforced by the prevalent astrological theories that calculated the turn in power (*dawla*) in terms of auspicious conjunctions of planets, and world conquerors, both Chinggis Khān and Tīmūr assumed their place alongside Alexander as *ṣāḥib qirān* (lord of (auspicious) conjunction), thus bestowing legitimacy upon the imperial dynasties they had respectively established. When the Mongol rulers of Iran adopted Islam, the *yāsā* was assimilated to the *qānūn* and the *sharīʿa* simultaneously. But it gradually ceded its religious character to the *sharīʿa*, and became the law of the state with regard to the Turco-Mongolian ruling estate. Under Tīmūr (d. 807/1405) the *yāsā*, in addition to being the special law of the Turco-Mongolian ruling caste, coexisted in a broader sense with the *sharīʿa*, as the sacred law and the state law. Tīmūr's son and most important successor, Shāh Rukh, reportedly abolished the Chinggis-Khānid regulations, though this was at any rate reversed by his son, Ulugh Beg, in Samarqand, where the *yāsā* survived under the Uzbeks in the tenth/sixteenth century.

In elaborating his model of the 'military-patronage state' with reference to the Ilkhānid and Tīmūrid dynasties, Hodgson noted the character of the *yāsā* as the law of the military estate, of which the civilian population took no cognisance, but also noted the increased importance of 'dynastic law' as the sum total of the royal decrees as long as the dynasty remained in power.[30] The nomadic tribal confederations that established these empires transformed themselves into permanent ruling castes after conquest, and remained rigidly separate

30 Hodgson, *The venture of Islam*, vol. II, pp. 406–10.

from the civilian population, to which they cultivated the ties of patronage by holding courts and founding endowments. Holding enormous undifferentiated land grants (*suyūrghāl*), which did not distinguish between fiscal and prebendal elements, they became the landlords of the peasant masses. The royal decrees (*yarlīgh*, *farmān*) created a written body of state law, while the *yāsā* as the law of the military estate, enforced by a special prosecutor, *yārghūchī*, introduced a new element of legal pluralism. *Yārghū* appears to have been extended to the viziers and high officials, and a special department (*dīwān*) dealing with cases of peculation, treason and disputes among local rulers under an *amīr-i yārghū* is mentioned in the sources.

In Egypt and Syria, meanwhile, a different type of regime had already taken shape: the Mamlūk sultanate. The *mamlūk* generals of the last Ayyūbids who were in control of Egypt in 658/1260 defeated the Mongol army at ʿAyn Jālūt in Syria, and one of them, Baybars, who had seized power by murdering the victor of ʿAyn Jālūt, established an alleged survivor of the ʿAbbāsid family as caliph in Cairo in 659/1261. The shadow ʿAbbāsid caliphate persisted in Cairo until the Ottoman conquest in 923/1517, and made the Mamlūk sultanate distinct from other post-Mongol Muslim monarchies.

Following the argument of the preceding section, we can say that the caliph as a powerless commander of the faithful and a political cipher served as a symbol of the separation of the religious and political spheres even better than the hidden imam of the Imāmī Shīʿa. This is clear in a decree of investiture in which the Cairo caliph prefaces the conferment of divinely granted sultanate by first justifying the office of caliphate (in the same vein as the Sunnī and Shīʿite jurists of Baghdad had done) as the precondition for the prevalence of the *sharʿī* order. In other words, it was a precondition for the legal validity, 'according to the four official schools of law', of marriages contracted and transactions carried out by Muslims, and for the appointment of the *qāḍī*s and officials.[31]

The Islamic policy of Baybars in fact had three elements. He was a *mamlūk* convert to Islam, and his sponsor at the gathering that elected him had based his title on regicide according to the custom of the Turks. As his subjects clearly did not know this alleged custom of the Turks, Baybars was badly in need of Islamic legitimacy, and the ʿAbbāsid caliph's primary function was to provide it. The function of conferring legitimacy on the Mamlūk sultan by the caliph also meant the endorsement of the Mamlūk sultan's claim to champion

31 Ahmad ibn ʿAlī al-Qalqashandī, *Ṣubḥ al-aʿshā fī ṣināʿat al-inshāʾ*, 14 vols. (Beirut, 1987), vol. X, p. 56.

Islam in the *jihād* against the Mongols and the Crusaders on behalf of the entire community of believers. This proved an asset in Mamlūk foreign policy, as some post-Mongol regimes that wished to enhance their Islamic credentials, such as the Tughluq-shāhs in Delhi and the Muẓaffarids in Fārs in the eighth/fourteenth century, would on occasion strike coins in the name of the Cairo caliph. (At one time, coins of the Delhi sultanate bore his name even three years after his death!) Needless to say, however, the policy of championship of holy war against the Mongols and the Franks in the seventh/thirteenth century did not depend on the caliph but was vigorously voiced by the spokesmen of the Mamlūk regime.

Baybars' Islamic policy also had a third element. He was not foolish enough to give the caliph exclusive purchase over the *sharʿī* order. On the contrary, he promoted the more obvious identification of Islam with the estate of the *ʿulamāʾ* as its official representatives, and enhanced the *de jure* legal pluralism under Islam by the institution of four chief justices for the four official schools of law in Cairo in 663/1265. The same system was established in Damascus in the same year. The four *qāḍīs* also performed the function of conferring legitimacy on the sultan by countersigning the caliph's decree of investiture as witnesses and taking part alongside him in the crowning ceremony, while the division of the clerical estate enhanced the sultan's control. Nevertheless, given the relatively small number of the Mamlūk elite and the surprising barring of their offspring from military careers, the Mamlūk sultans and *amīrs* were in fact more dependent on the good will of the *ʿulamāʾ*, and contributed, through extensive endowments (*awqāf*), to the development of the civic and religious institutions under the control of the latter state on a much larger scale than the ruling elite of the Turco-Mongolian monarchies of the east. For this reason the Mamlūk regime could also be called a 'military-patronage state'.

The most distinctive feature of the Mamlūk regime, however, consists in its being the first lasting Muslim polity under a system of collective rule. Young *mamlūks* were military slaves purchased and trained by the Mamlūk *amīrs*, who became their masters (*ustādh*), and, upon emancipation, entered the military household of the *amīr* as comrades (*khushdāshiyya*) at his service. The *amīrs* elected the sultan among themselves. Hereditary succession did occur after the charismatic warlords Baybars and Qalāwūn, but was never officially justified. Furthermore, when succession did become hereditary in the dynasty of Qalāwūn, most of the sultans were puppets of the heads of the Mamlūk households. In contrast to the Turco-Mongolian nomadic empires the Mamlūk state was remarkably centralised, with the *iqṭāʿ* land assignments not usually including revenue collection prerogatives and remaining under tight central control and rarely being inherited, and a bureaucracy heavily manned by religious minorities, especially the Copts – a fact that presumably facilitated their large-scale conversion in the eighth/fourteenth century. The *iqṭāʿ* sytem sustained the tripartite Mamlūk military system. The largest went to the *amīrs* with *mamlūk* retinues, the smallest were shared by the obsolescent *ḥalqa* (circle) troops, surviving units of Ayyūbid bodyguards, while the royal Mamlūks were maintained from the crown land, whose size increased dramatically with the cadastral survey and redistribution in 715/1315f. The other special features of the Mamlūk regime included the office of regent (*nāʾib al-salṭana*), who represented the sultan, especially in his court of justice (*dār al-ʿadl*), and whose position gained in importance as the Mamlūk sultan ceased *jihād* expeditions to Syria, but eventually declined somewhat with the takeover of the function of hearing petitions at the court of justice by the *ḥājib* (chamberlain). The title was also borne by the governors who represented the sultan in the Syrian region. The office of *atābak*, inherited from the Ayyūbids, was also transformed into that of the senior Mamlūk *amīr*.[32]

While both *ḥadīth* traditionalism and Greek political science were exercising considerable influence on the literature on political ethics in Iran and the Delhi sultanate, the extinction of the caliphate had a strong impact on the development of juristic theory under the Mamlūks. In his tract on public law, *Taḥrīr al-aḥkām fī tadbīr ahl al-islām* (Treatise on the ordinances concerning the management of Muslims), the Shāfiʿite judge of Damascus Badr al-Dīn ibn Jamāʿa (d. 733/1333) completely blurred the distinction between the imamate, the caliphate and the sultanate by deliberately alternate synonymous pairing of imam and sultan and, less frequently, the caliphate and the sultanate as the source of all legitimate authority and validity of all judicial, administrative and military appointments. He added compulsion to election as a legitimate mode of establishing the imamate and introduced a corresponding notion of '*bayʿa* [made valid] by compulsion' (*qahriyya*), thus legitimising the imamate (not just the 'emirate') by seizure in terms of 'the public interest and unity of the Muslims'.[33] In his three chapters on the imamate he absorbed virtually all the major maxims of Persian statecraft and wisdom without any disparagement of their normative status, and proceeded to sanction the validity of the *iqṭāʿ* land grants as practised under the Mamlūk sultanate. It is

32 P. M. Holt, 'The structure of government in the early Mamluk sultanate', in P. M. Holt (ed.), *The eastern Mediterranean lands in the period of the Crusades* (Warminster, 1977).

33 Badr al-Dīn Ibn Jamāʿa, 'Handbuch des islamischen Staats- und Verwaltungsrechtes von Badr-ad-dīn Ibn Ǧamāʿa', ed. Hans Kofler, *Islamica*, 6, 4 (1934), pp. 356–7.

interesting to note, however, that some current practices are not sanctioned. Ibn Jamāʿa does not allow any levies on the commerce of the Muslims (but only on that of the infidels), and likewise restricts the fiscal authority of non-Muslim officials to the official minorities.

The irrelevance of the caliphate under the Mamlūk regime resulted in an even greater shift in the juristic political theory of public law with the appearance in Damascus of *Kitāb al-siyāsa al-sharʿīyya* (Book of *sharʿī* statecraft) by Ibn Jamāʿa's Ḥanbalī contemporary, Taqī al-Dīn ibn Taymiyya (d. 728/1328). While rejecting the requirement that the Muslim community should have only a single imam, plausible though contrary to fact during the ʿAbbāsid caliphate, Ibn Taymiyya rested Islamic unity on the solidarity of the community (*jamāʿa*) and its adherence to the practice of the pious ancestors (*salaf*). The rulers and their appointees were typically referred to as 'authorities' (*wulāt*), and their duty, never defined with reference to the *umma*, was 'the improvement of the subjects' (*iṣlāḥ al-raʿiyya*), as expressed in the subtitle of the treatise on public law. Imamate and caliphate were not at all necessary as long as the rulers sought the advice of the *ʿulamāʾ*, enforced the divine commandments and maintained the *sharʿī* order. While recognising public law as 'governmental custom' (*ʿāda sulṭāniyya*) Ibn Taymiyya, unlike al-Māwardī and al-Ghazālī, did not try his hand at the ethics and advice genre, but rather sought to integrate it into Islamic jurisprudence. Government and exercise of authority could be brought in line with the general principles of jurisprudence, as their ultimate purpose was enjoining good and forbidding evil, while the rules of the *sharīʿa* applied more flexibly when required by public interest (*maṣlaḥa*). Thus, in contrast to the theory of Islamic monarchy under the 'king of Islam', Ibn Taymiyya's juristic theory subordinated monarchy to the *sharʿī* order. As such, it can be considered a programme for Islamic or *sharīʿa*-based government, but it did not reflect the public law of the Mamlūk or any other regime.

Malay sultanates

The Persian theory of kingship and dynastic state (*dawla*) travelled to Malaysia via northern India and Gujarat in the early ninth/fifteenth century. The Hindu–Buddhist kings of Melaka adopted the title of *syah* (*shāh*) two generations before that of sultan, which appears with the adoption of Islam as the religion of the royal house by Sultan Muẓaffar Shāh (r. 1444–59), who codified the laws of Melaka, adding certain provisions of the *sharīʿa* to customary law. There was a basic continuity in the conception of government as *kerajaan* (being in the condition of having a raja), and the conception of *dawlat* as divinely sanctioned state was distinctively coupled with *derhaka*, or treason towards the raja, as tantamount to sin against God.[34] Nevertheless, the conception of the ruler became recognisably Perso-Islamicate. With the Persian theory of kingship also came the maxim of the two powers, 'kingship and prophecy are two jewels on the same ring'. Our earliest source explains that 'the just Raja is joined with the Prophet of God like two jewels in one ring. Moreover, the Raja is as it were the deputy of God.'[35] Sultans of Melaka, and following them other Malay sultans, styled themselves as 'caliph' and 'shadow of God on earth' on their coins, which indicates their adoption of the model of Islamic royalism.[36] As the factor second to royal patronage in the spread of Islam was Sufism, the ruler could also claim spiritual perfection, and represented Islam without the rivalry of the clerical estate, the *'ulamā'*, the *qāḍīs* usually being relatives of the sultan, and sometimes a descendant of Sufi shaykhs.

The Malay sultanate was, however, very different from the types of political regime that developed elsewhere in the Muslim world. The enormous Chinese-propelled growth of maritime trade by the beginning of the ninth/fifteenth century, to which the Portuguese and Dutch were to contribute a century later, set the stage for the emergence of cosmopolitan city-states oriented to overseas trade rather than agricultural production in the hinterland, where important state functions could be given to foreign merchants. State formation in these new multi-ethnic mercantile cities was the work of the class of *orang kaya* (lit. rich man) who constituted the consultative council (*mesyuarat* (*mashwarat*) *bicara*) of nobles, one of whom would often be the sultan. The four highest officials of the state were the *bendahara* (grand treasurer and at times prime minister), the *tumenggung* (police chief), the *laksamana* (admiral) and the *syahbandar* (*shāhbandar*) (port master; a Persian term that had travelled through the coastal regions of India). Melaka was the first such city-state to adopt Islam and, with it, superimpose the imported conception of Muslim monarchy on the model the anthropologist Clifford Geertz calls *negara*, or the theatre-state, in the direction of Islamic royalism. However, the sultan was chosen in consultation with the *orang kaya*, and there was constant rivalry between the sultan and the *bendahara* in the manipulation

34 Barbara Watson Andaya and Leonard Y. Andaya, *A history of Malaysia*, 2nd edn (Honolulu, 2001), p. 47.

35 *Sĕjarah Mĕlayu or Malay annals*, trans. and annotated C. C. Brown, new introd. R. Roolvink (Kuala Lumpur, 1970), p. 111.

36 A. C. Milner, 'Islam and Malay kingship', *JRAS*, 1 (1981), p. 52.

of consensus (*muafakat*) of the *orang kaya* in the consultative council. The sultanate of Melaka, which was multiplied throughout South-East Asia after the conquest of the city by the Portuguese in 1511, can thus be considered, alongside the contemporary Mamlūk sultanate in Syria and Egypt, the second major type of Muslim regime characterised by collective rule.

As compared to the rest of the Muslim world, trade rather than agriculture was the main source of the sultan's revenue. Maritime and commercial matters were covered fairly extensively in the oldest law code, and there is an extant mid-seventeenth-century port law of Kedah that promulgated the public law administered by the *syahbandar*.[37] The sultan was the first merchant of his domains, and a committee of merchants assessed the value of the cargo in the presence of the police chief, the *tumenggung*, who immediately levied the customs duties. The *Sĕjarah Mĕlayu* declared: 'Where there is a dynastic state (*dawlat*), there is gold.'[38] Melaka basically consisted of four colonies (sing. *kampong*) for the Gujaratis (the most important), the Keling (Tamils), the Javanese (with the largest population) and the Chinese, each under the administration of a colony *syahbandar*, who probably had military functions and armed his clients, as did the merchants themselves. The legal system of the Malay sultanate was dualistic. A very clear and basic distinction is made between the law of the land (*ḥukum negeri*) and the law of God (*ḥukum Allāh*)[39] and is systematically followed throughout, with the (law of) *qānūn* (*ḥukum qānūn*) as a synonym for the former. The rules of either law are stipulated where appropriate, but in cases when the two vary, provisions of both the *qānūn* and the *sharīʿa* are stated side by side, suggesting that the judge could enforce either. The *qāḍī* enforced the code in his court, but his was not the most important court, and the *bendahara* had his own court, as did the *syahbandar*, who dealt with maritime and commercial cases.

Johor, where the royal family of Melaka moved after its fall to the Portuguese in 1511 and ruled until 1722, was the immediate successor state, but the sultanates of Pahang and Sumatra also affiliated with it, as did the rulers of Perak. Further east, Islam was spread in Maluku (possible derivation from *muluk*) by the sultans of Ternate in the sixteenth century, who acted as

37 R. O. Winstedt, 'Kedah laws', *Journal of the Malayan Branch of the Royal Asiatic Society*, 6 (1928), pp. 2–7, 15–26.

38 Quoted in Leonard Andaya, 'The structure of power in seventeenth-century Johor', in Anthony Reid and Lance Castles (eds.), *Pre-colonial state systems in Southeast Asia* (Kuala Lumpur, 1975), p. 3 (translation modified to conform to the usage of the term *dawla*[*t*] in this chapter).

39 Liaw Yock Fang (ed.), *Undang undang Melaka: The laws of Melaka* (The Hague, 1976), pp. 68–9.

religious teachers of their people and heads of Islamic institutions and bore the titles 'shadow of God on the earth' and 'the perfect man'. The great majority of the population, however, remained unconverted. The sultan appointed a brother or relative as the *kali* (*qāḍī*) and, as Islam grew, created two new posts which bore the title of *hukm*, whose incumbents conducted judicial hearing 'by reason and custom'.[40] The Malay sultanate was transplanted even as far away as Cotabato in the southern Philippines, where a certain *sarip* (*sharīf*) Kabungsuwan, claiming descent from the fallen Melakan royal family through his mother, established a sultanate and applied elements of Shāfiʿī law alongside the customary law, which were compiled together into a code of law in the mid-eighteenth century.[41]

The Malay sultanate regime, classically combining Muslim royalism and mercantile collective rule in Melaka and Johor, could develop in either direction along the continuum. Until their conquest by the Dutch in 1621 the tiny Banda islands represented the one exceptional extreme of rule by a kingless oligarchy of *orang kaya*. Transformation in the opposite direction of autocracy is represented by the cases of Aceh, Banten and East Java in the seventeenth century. The exemplary case is perhaps the rise of autocracy in Aceh, a prosperous mercantile city-state in the sixteenth century consisting of five ethnic colonies. Under Sultan ʿAlāʾ al-Dīn Riʿāyat Shāh, al-Sayyid al-Mukammil (1589–1604), a title indicative of his claim to be the spiritual guide of his people and the 'perfect man' of the Sufis, and his protégé Iskandar Muda (Young Alexander) (1607–36), we witness the destruction of the oligarchy and centralisation of power, creation of palace guards and establishment of a royal trade monopoly.[42]

As is typical with the advice literature on monarchy, the *Tāj al-salāṭīn* (The crown of rulers), compiled from a Persian source for the autocratic sultan of Aceh in 1603, opens its preface with 'Say God, possessor of kingship, you give kingship to whomever you will, and take away kingship from whomever you will' (Q 3:26). The core of *Bustān al-salāṭīn* (The garden of rulers), written in the mid-seventeenth century, is a 'History of the prophets and kings' that begins with a chapter on the prophets from Adam to Muḥammad, followed by one on the Persian kings until the time of ʿUmar. There follow chapters on the

40 Leonard Y. Andaya, *The world of Maluku: Eastern Indonesia in the early modern period* (Honolulu, 1993), pp. 62, 70.

41 Thomas McKenna, *Muslim rulers and rebels: Everyday politics and armed separation in the southern Philippines* (Berkeley and Los Angeles, 1998), pp. 48–68.

42 Anthony Reid, 'Trade and state power in the 16th and 17th century Southeast Asia', in *Proceedings of the Seventh IAHA Conference* (Bangkok, 1977).

kings of other nations, the last three being on the Muslim rulers of Delhi, the rulers of Melaka and Pahang, and finally, the rulers of Aceh. It is interesting to note that the Malay sultans typically claimed descent from Iskandar Dhu'l-Qarnayn (Alexander the Great), whose name was taken by the first raja of Melaka who assumed the title of shah, and by many others, including the above-mentioned autocrat of Aceh, Iskandar Muda. Alexander was a convenient figure, as he was considered both a prophet and a Persian king, and royal descent from him was through other Persian kings, notably Khusrau Anūshīrwān, the Just.

Centralised autocracy in South-East Asia was unstable, however. In Aceh the mercantile oligarchy made its comeback and perfected a variant of collective rule under reigning queens (1641–99), beginning with Queen Tāj al-ʿālam (1641–75). The type also emerged elsewhere, generating in Sumatra the symbol of female good governance of the ideal queen, somewhat generically called Ratu Sinuhun in Palembang. Also close to the centre of our typological continuum was the sultanate of Perak in the eighteenth century. The sultan was the deputy (*khalīfa*) of God on earth, and one of them, Raja Iskandar, was typically said to be 'blessed with good fortune (*tuah*), *dawlat* [divinely ordained sovereignty], wisdom and nobility ... who governed according to the laws of Allah and of *ʿādat* [customary law], protecting his people'. At the same time sultans were selected from the royal offspring (*anak raja*) by the oligarchs, whose consultative council had 300 members, according to Dutch reports. The idea of the ruler as the shepherd of the flock finds an interesting maritime supplement, and he is said to be the captain (*nākhudā*) of the ship of state, and his ministers his crew. Unlike Melaka and Johor, however, Perak was not a mercantile city-state oriented to overseas trade, but was more dependent on the hinterland, and therefore on the inland territorial chiefs (*orang besar*). The chiefs were accordingly urged alongside the ministers to 'support their Raja and consider the welfare of the *rakyat* [subjects]'.[43]

The patrimonial-bureaucratic empires

The Ottomans combined the Persianate and Turco-Mongolian traditions of kingship with the law. Like his predecessors Meḥmed II was the 'king (*pādishāh*) of Islam', and had added 'God's caliph' to his titles in accordance with Muslim royalism long before becoming 'the Conqueror' with the

43 Cited from various sources by Barbara Watson Andaya, 'The nature of the state in eighteenth century Perak', in Reid and Castles (eds.), *Pre-colonial state systems*, pp. 23–4, 28.

overthrow of the Byzantine empire. By the beginning of the ninth/fifteenth century the legitimacy of the Ottoman kings was enhanced by their conquest of Christian lands, and they were presented as holy warriors, the term celebrating this status, *ghāzī*, being anachronistically projected onto the early eighth/fourteenth-century Ottoman raiders (*akıncı*). Meḥmed II enhanced his legitimacy as the leader of the holy war (*ghazā*) by assuming the title commander of the faithful. The Turkish tradition, however, came to prominence with the proclamation of his law upon the conquest of Constantinople in 857/1453. Under the early Ottomans the *yāsā* had gradually lost its Mongol connotations in the ninth/fifteenth century and, in the forms *yasāgh* and *yasāgh-nāme*, came to common use as code of law, especially of penal law, being used as a synonym for *siyāsat-nāme*, and was thus assimilated to the *qānūn*.

Meḥmed the Conqueror's *reʿāyā qānūn-nāme* was the first step in the lasting institutionalisation of the dynastic law of the Ottomans. It was greatly enlarged through the inclusion of subsequent royal decree-laws (*qānūn-ḥukm*) and published by Bāyazīd II as *Kitāb-i qawānīn-i ʿurfiyya-yi ʿUthmāniyya* (Book of Ottoman customary laws) in 907/1501, revised further under Selīm I (r. 918–26/1512–20) as *Qānūn-nāma-yi ʿUthmānī* (Ottoman law code) and then reissued with further addition of minor decree-laws as the Law of the Ottoman Dynasty (*Qānūn-i ʿUthmānī*) by Süleymān the Lawgiver (*qānūnī*) (r. 926–74/1520–66). This marked the culmination of the age of law. The Ottoman law was periodically revised and updated, and was also referred to as the law code (*qānūn-nāme*) of the illustrious Conqueror and Süleymān.[44] The distinctive Ottoman judicial organisation was that the *qāḍīs* administered both the *sharīʿa* and the state law (*qānūn*). Justice as the cornerstone of government by the *pādishāh*, symbolised by a 'tower of justice (*ʿadālet*)' at the Ottoman court, was also institutionalised in tandem. The *maẓālim* court was organised as the royal court (*dīwān-i humāyūn*), receiving thousands of petitions from the subjects every month, which were recorded in a registry of complaints, and periodically issuing 'decrees of justice' (*ʿadālet-nāme*). Süleymān's justice decree of 1565, for example, regulated the relations between state officials and the subjects, threatening officials guilty of maladministration and fiscal exaction with the direst of punishments.

With the rise of the Ottoman empire, the social stratification system of the Turco-Mongolian empires to the east underwent considerable change, as did

44 H. Inalcik, 'Suleiman the Lawgiver and Ottoman law', *Archivum Ottomanicum*, 1 (1969), esp. p. 125.

the system of *mamlūk* recruitment to the west. The caste boundaries between the military estate and the civilian bureaucracy were broken, and the officials of the bureaucracy and of the judiciary were absorbed into the *ʿaskerī* estate that came to comprise everyone working for the state as against the subjects, the *reʿāyā*. Two high judicial offices were created for the *qāḍī ʿaskers* of Anatolia and Rome (Rumeli, as the former Byzantine lands were called) who dealt with the legal affairs of the *ʿaskerī* estate.

'Men of the sword' (*sayfī*), as the military component of the enlarged *ʿaskerī* estate, were of two different kinds. The first was a landowning cavalry (*sipāhī*), each of whom had to arm himself and one or two men with the income from a modest land assignment (*tīmār*), representing an extraordinary refinement of the *iqṭāʿ* system made possible by the detailed cadastral surveys compiled by the Ottomans upon conquest. The second component was the corps of new soldiers (*yeni çeri* or Janissary) of royal slaves that was a unique and enduring institutionalisation of the *mamlūk* system of military organisation extended to administration. The conquest of the Christian lands in Europe enabled the Ottomans to transform the recruitment of military slaves into the centralized *devşirme* system of levies of boys to be trained as the sultan's slaves that formed the military and administrative backbone of the empire from the ninth/fifteenth century onward. In a remarkable transformation of patrimonialism, the Ottomans preserved the centrality of the palace as the household of the ruler by training the royal slaves and sons of the nobility for 'inner' (*enderūn*) palace service, and after a graduation ceremony (*çikma*), where they could be joined by other members of the *ʿaskerī* estate with the requisite rank, were assigned to 'outer' (*bīrūn*) service and appointed to district and provincial governorships, thus introducing a strong element of bureaucratic rationalisation while still treating administration of the empire as the extension of the household of the sultan and allowing high officials to maintain their own households of large personal retinues.

In 907/1501, the year Bayazīd II reissued the Code of Ottoman Law, a millenarian Shīʿite revolution was launched by a charismatic youth of fourteen, Ismāʿīl, at the head of the Ṣafavid Sufi order in Anatolia and Iran, making an unmistakable bid for world domination. The revolution succeeded in Iran but was suppressed in Anatolia by Selīm I at the beginning of his reign. Like all revolutions Shāh Ismāʿīl's produced a large body of exiles, consisting of Iranian Sunnī notables who fled east and west, and set in motion an interaction between Shīʿite and Sunnī Islam whose consequences for the development of public law were as momentous as those in the medieval development of the theory of imamate surveyed in the earlier sections of this chapter. To stop the expansion of the Ṣafavid empire the Uzbeks in the east and the Ottomans in the west solicited the help of these Sunnī jurists to act as defenders of Islamic orthodoxy against the rampant new heresy. On both sides, prominent jurists supplied the rulers with *fatwās* making the shedding of the blood of the Ṣafavid Turkish troops, the Qizilbāsh, lawful – indeed, obligatory.

In the east, the rise of the Ṣafavids and their chiliastic disregard of the *sharīʿa* provoked one of Dawānī's students, the Shāfiʿite jurist Faḍlallāh Rūzbihān Khunjī (d. 927/1521), to produce a remarkable book on public law. Unlike the Ottoman code, it was not an actual code of law but, like Ibn Taymiyya's and with the same sense of crisis, a programme for reform in the face of the perceived threat, emanating from the Ṣafavid uprising, to the survival of the *sharīʿa*. After a few years in hiding and exile, Khunjī called upon the Uzbek Muḥammad Khān Shibānī to be the renewer (*mujaddid*) of the tenth century (beginning in 1494 CE). In *Mihmān-nāma-yi Bukhārā*, written in 916/1509, the Khān was addressed as 'the Imam of the Age (*imām al-zamān*) and the Deputy of the Merciful (*khalīfat al-raḥmān*)'. Muḥammad Khān was not to be the renewer of the tenth century, however, and fell in the battle of Marw a year later; Shāh Ismāʿīl made his skull into a drinking-cup. Khunjī had to wait four more years for ʿUbayd Allāh Khān to emerge from the struggle for succession and adopt the cause of orthodox restoration, prompting him to write a programme for *sharīʿa*-based government as a law book for him in 920/1514 entitled *Sulūk al-mulūk* (The manner of kings).

The programmatic nature of his treatise, 'an exposition of the [prescribed] acts of the Imam and the ruler', is explicit: 'If the ruler of Islam, who has secured his domination through seizure of power because he lacked some of the conditions for the Imamate, wants to obtain the sovereignty (*salṭanat*) of Islam and kingship by right, he must carry out the very acts that are necessary for the Imam.' Having enumerated three legally valid (but unrealistic) ways of establishing the imamate, he follows Ibn Jamāʿa in endorsing the one that is relevant to his time:

> The fourth manner in which the establishment of kingship (*pādshāhī*) and the Imamate is caused is through domination and power (*shawkat*). The *ʿulamāʾ* have said that when the Imam dies and a person takes charge of the Imamate without a *bayʿa* and without anyone having made him Caliph, and subjugates the people by power and force of the army, his Imamate is established without a *bayʿa*, whether or not he is from the Quraysh, whether or not he is an Arab, a Persian or a Turk, whether or not he has the qualifications, even if he is corrupt and ignorant ... [He] is [nevertheless] called the Sultan, and the titles of Imam and Caliph can be given to him. And God knows best ... The

> *ʿulamāʾ* have said that obedience to the Imam and the Sultan in whatever they command and forbid is incumbent, be he just or tyrannical (*jāʾir*), so long as [what he commands] is not contrary to the *sharīʿa* ... He is called the Caliph and the Imam and the Commander of the Faithful and the Deputy (*khalīfa*) of the Messenger of God, but it is not permissible to call him the Deputy of God.[45]

Khunjī's response to Ismāʿīl's 'heretical' – i.e. mahdistic – charismatic authority on behalf of the Uzbeks was the proclamation of the Khān as the 'deputy of the merciful' and the 'imam of the age'. Luṭfī Pāshā, Süleymān's grand vizier (946–8/1539–41), did the same for the Ottoman sultan. Pushing Ibn Jamāʿa's argument for the legitimacy of imamate by compulsion to the extreme in a tract written in Persian and translated into Arabic, Luṭfī Pāshā dismissed descent from the Quraysh as irrelevant and, claiming to prove his argument on the basis of traditions rather than rationally, he calls Sultan Süleymān, son of Salīm Khān son of Bāyezīd Khān, the just imam of the age who maintains the congregational prayer and the *ʿīd* festivals, who is also the caliph and invested with authority (*walī*) by God.[46] The theory of the Ottoman caliphate was endorsed by Süleymān's great *shaykh al-islām* (chief *muftī*), Abu 'l-Suʿūd, who considered his royal patron 'the shadow of God over all people' and the 'possessor of the supreme Imamate', and used the sultan's authority as imam and caliph to justify legislation by decree-law in civil matters.[47]

Notable among the learned jurists who participated in Selīm I's campaign against the Qizilbāsh was Kemāl Pāshāzāda (d. 940/1534), who was later appointed the *shaykh al-islām* (932–40/1526–34). Kemāl Pāshāzāda issued injunctions declaring the Qizilbāsh infidels, their territory the land of war, and the waging of holy war (*jihād*) against them the individually incumbent duty of every Muslim, assigning the task of a more detailed refutation of the Ṣafavid claims to his student, Abu 'l-Suʿūd Muḥammad ibn Muḥyī al-Dīn ʿImādi. Abu 'l-Suʿūd Efendi, who was from the Kurdish region under Ṣafavid domination, enumerated the deviations of the Qizilbāsh from orthodoxy, refuting Shāh Ismāʿīl's claim to descent from ʿAlī and the Ṣafavid claim to being a Shīʿite sect, and considered fighting against the Qizilbāsh the most important duty of the Muslim.[48] He later rose to prominence, holding the

45 Faḍlallāh Rūzbihān Khunjī, *Sulūk al-mulūk* (Hyderabad, 1966), pp. 39, 47–8.

46 H. A. R. Gibb, 'Luṭfī Paşa on the Ottoman caliphate', *Oriens*, 15 (1962), pp. 287–95.

47 Colin Imber, 'Ideals and legitimation in early Ottoman history', in M. Kunt and C. Woodhead (eds.), *Süleyman the Magnificent and his age* (London, 1995), pp. 152–3.

48 E. Eberhard, *Osmanische Polemik gegen die Safawiden im 16. Jahrhundert nach arabischen Handschriften* (Freiburg im Breisgau, 1970), pp. 164–7.

office of *shaykh al-islām* (952–82/1545–74), and was a chief architect of the Ottoman judicial organisation. The construction of the imposing Ottoman judicial system by these two chief *muftīs* was in part a reaction to the heterodox Ṣafavid revolution. It included appointment of *muftīs* (jurisconsults) in addition to judges, all ranked hierarchically under the *shaykh al-islām* of Istanbul, and went hand in hand with the exclusive establishment of the Ḥanafī rite in Anatolia and the building by Abu 'l-Suʿūd of mosques in villages to force the population to pray according to the official rite.

There was also a consistent effort to rationalise the two components of Muslim monarchy, the religious and the temporal, into an integrated system of authority. Luṭfī Pāshā wrote a concise practical manual on the craft of vizierate, called *Āṣif-nāma* after Solomon's legendary vizier, Āṣif, and financial administration grew in importance and became more specialised, beginning the differentiation and rationalisation of tax-farming into the Ottoman *iltizām* system. Süleymān allowed a group of determined *madrasa*-trained clerical bureaucrats to reconcile the *qānūn* and the *sharīʿa*. Foremost among the group from the side of the religious hierarchy was the above-mentioned Abu 'l-Suʿūd Efendi, and from the side of the bureaucracy, the chancellor (*nişānci*) Muṣṭafā Jalālzāda (941–63/1534–56). In drafting decree-laws and administrative directives Jalālzāda was mindful of the *sharīʿa* and sought to make them consistent with it. The section of the law code of Meḥmed the Conqueror on administrative organisation had introduced a rational bureaucratic distinction between rank and office, allowing the lateral movement of the holders of high judicial, financial and secretarial offices to become provincial governors alongside those in the two branches of the military elite. Judge Qinalizāda, in the above-mentioned *Akhlāq-i ʿalāʾī*, considered the Ottoman *qānūn* as a set of dynastic laws supportive of the *sharīʿa* and derived, with clerical advice, from principles of Islamic jurisprudence. His student, ʿĀlī Pāsha (d. 1009/1600), like him a clerical bureaucrat and a beneficiary of the lateral movement allowed by the Conqueror's code, expressed great faith in imperial law (*qānūn-i pādshāhī*), maintaining that 'the chancellors should be the jurisconsults (*muftīs*) of imperial law'. He also remained convinced of its compatibility and need for articulation with the *sharīʿa*. This '*qānūn*-consciousness' can be taken as a distinct form of Ottoman constitutionalism that prevailed in the tenth/sixteenth century.[49]

The success of this attempt should not be exaggerated. Abu 'l-Suʿūd's promotion of the sultan as the imam was useful for his judicial reforms but

49 Cornell H. Fleischer, *Bureaucrat and intellectual in the Ottoman empire: The historian Mustafa Âli (1541–1600)* (Princeton, 1986), chap. 6; quotation at p. 228.

receded from the public domain, while in the increasing size of the bureaucracy and its specialisation made more rigid the lines dividing the 'men of the pen' in general, and the *ʿulamāʾ* in particular, from the military-administrative elite of the empire, resulting in growing tension between the religious and temporal elements in Ottoman constitutionalism in the seventeenth century. The *qānūn*-consciousness was transformed into a nostalgia for the Ottoman golden age and bemoaning of the decline in advice literature (*naṣīḥat-nāmas*), while the religious hierarchy demonstrated its opposition to state law by prevailing upon the sultan in 1107/1696 to issue a decree-law forbidding the mentioning of the *qānūn* and the *sharīʿa* side by side.

Meanwhile, the development of religious authority in Iran proceeded along a path unique in Islamic history. The consolidation of the Ṣafavid revolution required the routinisation of the charisma of Shāh Ismāʿīl as an invincible war hero who claimed divine incarnation and mahdihood into a stable structure of authority. Monarchy and hierocracy were the super- and subordinate components of this structure of authority. There was in fact a radical change in the conception of kingship. Popular Sufism, which became increasingly tinged with the Shīʿite expectation of the manifestation of the *mahdī* in the mid-ninth/fifteenth century, infused a sacral element into the idea of kingship as temporal rule. Ismāʿīl's father (and grandfather) had sought the 'unification of dervishhood and kingship' (*jamʿ-i darwīshī wa shāhī* (i.e. material and spiritual monarchy)).[50] The popular Sufi conception of unified material and spiritual monarchy was institutionalised under Shāh Ismāʿīl and reconciled with Imāmī Shīʿism by his successors, who claimed to be the lieutenants of the hidden Imam. The Shīʿite conception of ʿAlī as the *walī allāh* (friend of God) was key in the fusion the Sufi notion of *wilāyat* (friendship of God) and the juristic meaning of the term as 'authority'; the Ṣafavids conjoined both senses by claiming descent from the seventh imam, Mūsā al-Kāẓim, and accordingly by calling themselves the house of *wilāyat*. In a decree issued in 917/1511 Shāh Ismāʿīl claims divine sanction for his sovereignty (*salṭanat*) and caliphate (*khilāfat*) by citing the Qurʾān (Q 2:118 and 38:25), and refers to the Ṣafavid house as the 'dynasty of spiritual authority (*wilāyat*) and Imamate'.[51] With the assumption of the title of shah at the outset, the Ṣafavids relied primarily on the traditional legitimacy of Persianate kingship. However, a sacral element

50 Khwānd-Amīr, *Ḥabīb al-siyar*, ed. M. Dabīr-Siyāqī, 4 vols. (Tehran, 1362/1983), vol. IV, p. 426. Note below the author's own transplantation of this conception to the Mughal empire at the end of his life.

51 A.-H. Navāʾi, *Shāh Ismāʿīl Safavī: Asnād wa mukātibāt-i tārīkhī* (Tehran, 1347/1969), pp. 101–3.

was superimposed on it as a residue of the Sufi–Shīʿite charismatic leadership of Ismāʿīl. A decree of appointment issued by the last Ṣafavid shah, Sulṭān-Ḥusayn (1105–35/1694–1722) is quite explicit in distinguishing the two elements: 'As the perfect being of our fortunate majesty derives from the light of Prophecy and Authority (*wilāyat*), obeying [our] command is more incumbent upon the God-fearing than that of other kings of kings.'[52] This new sacral idea of kingship was, however, inconsistent with the logic of Shīʿism, and collapsed with the Ṣafavid empire in 1135/1722, making for the return of the traditional idea of monarchy as temporal rule necessary for the prevalence of religion and the *sharʿī* order. The routinisation of the charismatic war hero into the hereditary charisma of the Ṣafavid lineage as the family and lieutenants of the Shīʿite holy imams, together with the Persian idea of kingship as monarchy over an undivided empire, was of great importance for solving the succession problem of nomadic patrimonialism that had resulted in the disintegration of the Tīmūrid and successor empires, though the absence of primogeniture still required the killing or blinding of the princes of the royal household.

The declaration of Imāmī Shīʿism as the national religion of Iran by Shāh Ismāʿīl also resulted in an unprecedented differentiation of religious and political authority. The architect of the new hierocratic system of authority under the Ṣafavids was Shaykh ʿAlī al-Karakī (d. 940/1534), a Syrian who responded to Ismāʿīl's invitation to migrate to Iran. With the development of jurisprudence in the medieval period there had been a tendency to transfer some of the specific functions of the imam, such as his authority to marry women without guardians, to the jurists. The most significant of these was the transfer of the imam's function of holding the Friday congregational prayer by some jurists. Glossing the ʿAllāma al-Ḥillī's statement that the holding of the congregational prayer required 'the just ruler (*al-sulṭān al-ʿādil*) or whoever he orders to do so', al-Karakī states: 'According to our Consensus, the incumbency of the congregational prayer is conditional upon the just ruler who is the infallible Imam, *or his deputy in general*, or his deputy for the congregational prayer.' The presumption of consensus here hides what is in fact a striking departure from the earlier statements of the theory of the imamate. He again conveniently claims consensus for the holding of the congregational prayer being conditional upon the presence of the imam *or his deputy*. The reason in both cases is that 'the secure jurist who has all the qualifications for issuing opinions is appointed (*manṣūb*) by the Imam; therefore his ordinances (*aḥkām*)

52 M. Dhabīḥī and M. Sutūda (eds.), *Az Āstārā tā Astarābād*, 7 vols. (Tehran, n.d.[1976]), vol. VI, p. 504.

are effective, and helping him to implement the *ḥudūd* and to adjudicate among the people is incumbent'. The idea of 'appointment' is linked to that of being a 'deputy in general' by claiming that the imam has 'indeed appointed a deputy in a general matter, as in the saying of [the sixth imam Jaʿfar] al-Ṣādiq reported by ʿUmar b. Ḥanẓala: "I have indeed appointed him an authority [*ḥākiman*] upon you."' An additional proof of this appointment is the decree of the hidden imam to the Shīʿa which sets 'the reporters of our Traditions' as 'my proofs upon you, as I am the proof of God upon them'.[53]

Al-Karakī thus developed the notion of the 'general deputyship/vicegerency' (*niyāba ʿāmma*) of the imam during the occultation, and, as the foremost Shīʿite jurist of 'the *mujtahid* of the age', claimed it for himself.

The Turcoman adepts of the Ṣafavid order, who were known as Qizilbāsh (redheads) on account of the headgear devised for them by Ismāʿīl's father, were divided according to their clans, and a number of new Qizilbāsh clans were formed during the uprising. The Qizilbāsh troops remained divided into these clans and maintained by undifferentiated land grants (*tuyūl*) and, despite their factionalism, were the military mainstay of the Ṣafavid regime in the sixteenth century. They remained members of the now exclusively military Ṣafavid Sufi order, and as such venerated the shah as their 'perfect spiritual guide' (*murshid-i kāmil*). In a major feat of centralisation, Shāh ʿAbbas the Great in the first decade of the seventeenth century was able to subdue the factionalism of the Qizilbāsh troops, halving their number to some 30,000 and greatly reducing the dependence of the state on them by creating a new corps of some 12,000 musketeers and, more importantly, a slave corps initially consisting of some 4,000 recruited from Georgia, which increased until its size settled around 10,000 by mid-century. His two successors, Ṣafī (r. 1037–52/1629–42) and ʿAbbās II (r. 1052–77/1642–66), continued the policy of centralisation by converting the inner provinces in their entirety into crown land (*khāṣṣa*) and putting them under the administration of the commanders of the royal slave corps.

The question not addressed by al-Karakī in the tenth/sixteenth century was the relationship between the newly legitimised, impersonal hierocratic authority and the old personal and patrimonial authority of the king. It could be addressed only awkwardly within the framework of jurisprudence, and required the distinct literary genre on ethics and statecraft that had been developed to express the normative order of monarchy. The revival of

53 ʿAlī ibn al-Ḥusayn al-Karakī al-Muḥaqqiq al-Thānī, *Jāmiʿ al-maqāṣid fī sharḥ al-qawāʿid*, 15 vols. so far (Beirut, 1991–), vol. II, pp. 371–9.

philosophy in seventeenth-century Iṣfahān as the new capital of the Ṣafavid empire made this new genre readily available as practical philosophy (*ḥikmat-i ʿamalī*), with Naṣīr al-Dīn Ṭūsī's *Akhlāq-i nāṣirī* serving as the model treatise. In *Gawhar-i murād,* ʿAbd al-Razzāq Lāhījī considered prophecy and kingship as the two sources of authority. The functions of the prophet and the ruler were unified only in the Prophet Muḥammad, and not in other prophets, who always needed kings.[54] Lāhījī's younger contemporary, Mullā Muḥammad Bāqir Sabzawārī, the *shaykh al-islām* of Iṣfahān under ʿAbbās II, went a step further in reconciling practical philosophy with Shīʿism. He recognised the differentiation between 'the office (*manṣab*) of prophecy' and 'the office of monarchy (*salṭanat*)', and was explicit in his reconciliation of kingship and the Shīʿite theory of imamate. In his massive and widely circulated treatise on political philosophy, Sabzawārī stated that the lawgiver is indeed the Prophet, and 'the just ruler ... is called Imam and God's Caliph'. However, when the real (*aṣlī*) imam is in occultation, 'the people inevitably need a king to live with justice and follow the custom and tradition (*sīrat wa sunnat*) of the real Imam'.[55] Such a king is his royal patron, the king of kings and shadow of God, ʿAbbās. This justification was in line with the Ṣafavids' coupling of their royal legitimacy with their charisma of lineage as the lieutenants and alleged descendants of the immaculate imams. This was somewhat inconsistent with the logic of Shīʿism and, after the disappearance of the Ṣafavid dynastic vested interest in maintaining it, it gave way to a more consistently dualistic theory.

However, in contrast to the Ottoman empire, there was no development in the public law of monarchy, and Sabzawārī in the second half of the seventeenth century was content to reproduce medieval Persian ideas on statecraft and political ethics within the framework of practical philosophy, while administration and taxation were regulated by the decrees of the rulers. The idea of hierocratic authority, by contrast, increasingly disengaged itself from the personal, patrimonial matrix. With al-Karakī's powerful legal fiction of general vicegerency, the jurists could consider themselves invested, *ex ante* and in perpetuity, by the hidden imam, thus possessing impersonal, official authority. In practice, the institutionalisation of hierocratic authority could not proceed as simply as in al-Karakī's legal arguments, and was contested by the clerical notables (*sayyids*) who controlled landed estates and held important offices, most notably that of the *ṣadr* who controlled the religious endowments; and their contestation did not take long to appear at the theoretical

54 ʿAbd al-Razzāq Lāhījī, *Gawhar-i murād* (Tehran, 1377/1958), pp. 293–5.
55 Muḥammad Bāqir Sabzawārī, *Rawḍat al-anwār-i ʿabbāsī* (Tehran 1377/1998), pp. 52, 65–7.

level either, and Akhbārī traditionalism in fact slowly gained the upper hand over jurisprudential rationalism in the seventeenth and eighteenth centuries. More significantly, the enforcement of the *sharīʿa* through the state was never effectively institutionalised, as it was in the Ottoman empire, and the office of the *qāḍī* in fact declined with the rise of an independent hierocracy.[56] Nevertheless, on the foundations laid by al-Karakī, an independent hierocracy would stand after the collapse of the Ṣafavid empire in the eighteenth century, and would generate the dual structure of authority distinctive of Iran in the Qājār period.

From the very beginning of his reign (1785–96) the founder of the Qājār monarchy, Āqā Muḥammad Khān, turned for help with consolidating his power to the Shīʿite *mujtahids* who were leading the Uṣūlī movement in jurisprudence against Akhbārī traditionalism. Around 1200/1787 a leading *mujtahid*, Mīrzā Abu ʾl-Qāsim Qummī, composed the *Irshād-nāma* for him, maintaining that 'the rank of kingship is by divine decree' and explaining the meaning of the term 'shadow of God'. However, his statement of the theory of the two powers transferred the fulfilment of the prophetic function to the hierocracy, while stressing the mutual interdependence of the king and his *ʿulamāʾ*: 'As God Most High has established kings for the protection of the world of men ... the *ʿulamāʾ* need them; and as He established the *ʿulamāʾ* for the protection of the religion of men ... the king and other than the king need them.' Here, the hierocracy as the guardians of the prophetic heritage is put in the place given to the prophets (whose heritage it guards) in the more conventional formulations of the idea of the two powers in the medieval statecraft literature. A more clearly traditional statement of the idea of duality was offered by the royal librarian who served the second Qājār monarch: '[God] has chosen two classes among mankind and given them the crown of sovereignty and the ring of superiority. The first are the prophets ... The second class consists of the rulers of the earth and the just kings ... After the rank of prophecy, there shall be no position higher than kingship.'[57]

State formation in the Delhi sultanate was mostly the work of Turkish military slaves, except for the Khaljīs (689–720/1290–1320), and the later Afghan dynasty of the Lodīs (855–932/1451–1526). All the Delhi sultanate, however, drew upon the Persianate conception of kingship. At the end of the ninth/fifteenth century the Iranian immigrants also played the leading role

56 Arjomand, *The shadow of God*, chap. 5.

57 Quoted in S. A. Arjomand, 'Political ethic and public law in the early Qajar period', in Robert M. Gleave (ed.), *Religion and society in Qajar Iran* (London, 2005), p. 24.

in state formation in the Deccan. Early in the century Fīrūz Shāh Bahmanī (r. 800–25/1397–1422) would reportedly send empty ships to the Persian Gulf to bring back Iranian soldiers, administrators, traders and artists. One such imported soldier who rose to prominence, Yūsuf ʿĀdil Khān (r. 895–916/1490–1510) founded the dynasty of 'just kings', the ʿĀdilshāhī sultanate of Bījāpūr and, emboldened by the news of the rise of Shāh Ismāʿīl in Iran, declared Shīʿism the official religion of his kingdom. Babūr (r. 932–7/1526–30) took a large number of Tīmūrid officials with him to India, and almost half of the noblemen who accompanied Humāyūn after his restoration were Iranians. Iranians were the single largest group (as compared to the Turanians and the Hindus) under Akbar, and their prominence increased under the vizierate of the father and brother of Nūr-i Jahān, the favourite Persian queen of Jahāngīr (r. 1014–37/1605–27). They remained conspicuous throughout the seventeenth century, making up a quarter of Aurangzeb's (r. 1069–1118/1658–1707) nobility.[58] The Persianate theory of kingship as universal monarchy had its most lasting impact in India on the creation of the Mughal empire. As Tīmūrids the Mughal emperors claimed divine sanction and legitimacy, as their dynasty had been founded by the great *ṣāhib qirān*, and Shāhjahān (r. 1037–68/1627–58) was even called the second *ṣāhib qirān*, and some echoes of the Turkish conception of the law persisted, but the nomadic patrimonial rule of succession that Bābur had been reluctant to give up (and proved disastrous for Humāyūn) died with him, leaving the field to the idea of *pādshāhī* as monarchy over an undivided empire.

Persian books on statecraft travelled with Bābur from Kabul and Herat to India upon its conquest. The Tīmūrid chief *qāḍī* of Herat, Ikhtiyār al-Dīn Ḥusayn al-Ḥusaynī, met Bābur after the conquest of India and retitled a book on the rules of vizierate *Akhlāq-i Humāyūnī* (Royal ethics) and dedicated it to him. Following Naṣīr al-Dīn al-Ṭūsī, he assimilated *sharīʿa* to *nomos*, said to work only through a just king. 'Excellent politics', required for the establishment of the imamate of the king, is the pattern of governance of a king who, as the shadow of God, allows each class of men to achieve perfection according to its competence within the social hierarchy. The aged Tīmūrid bureaucrat and historian Khwāndamīr took the more Sufi-tinged conception of kingship made definitive by the Ṣafavid revolution with him to India, and expressed it in a book commissioned by Bābur before his death but dedicated to his successor, Humāyūn, as 'the unifier of the real and the apparent sovereignty

58 Sanjay Subrahmanyam, 'Iranians abroad: Intra-Asian elite migration and early modern state formation', *Journal of Asian Studies*, 51, 2 (1992), pp. 342–7.

(*jāmiʿ-i salṭanat-i haqīqī wa majāzī*)'. Humāyūn himself devised a ceremony with the king like the sun representing the centre of the world while his officials were divided into twelve orders according to the signs of the zodiac to represent the rays of light shining to the corners of the empire.[59]

Abu 'l-Faḍl ʿAllāmī, the learned vizier of Akbar (r. 963–1014/1556–1605), was the architect of his imperial ideology. The key imperial concept was, needless to say, kingship (*pādshāhī*), a gift of God that was not bestowed easily and had thousands of prerequisites. 'Kingship is a radiance (*furūgh*) from the Incomparable Dispenser of justice [God] and a ray of the sun, illuminator of the universe ... The contemporary language calls it *farr-i īzadī* [divine effulgence], and the tongue of the antiquity calls it *kiyān Khurra*.' This enabled him to push the Persian idea of kingship beyond the limits of 'Islamic royalism' to its logical conclusion as universal (i.e. imperial) monarchy. Akbar was indeed not merely the 'king of Islam' but 'the emperor (*shāhanshāh*) of mankind', as predestined by the first manifestation of his divine origins, the divine ray of light that impregnated his legendary Mongolian grandmother, Alanquwa.[60] Needless to say, this universalistic extension of the divine mandate of the Mughal emperors in no way diluted their Islamic credentials. The coins issued in Akbar's royal camp (*urdū*) referred to it as the 'seat of the caliphate (*dār al-khilāfa*)'. Jahāngīr and Shāhjahān were called God's caliph by their high-ranking *qāḍīs*, as was Aurangzeb, who was also called the commander of the faithful.

As a pantheistic mystic and son of Akbar's spiritual guide, Abu 'l-Faḍl called his royal patron the 'perfect man', and may have helped him with the creation of a special Sufi order of 'divine unity' (*tawḥid-i ilāhī*), for the officials of which, not unlike the Ṣafavid order for the Qizilbāsh *amīrs*, the emperor himself was to be the supreme spiritual guide. But spiritual guidance of the entire people, who looked up to him because of his exalted rank, was also one of the king's duties. As a keen student of all religions Abu 'l-Faḍl would not hesitate to stipulate religious tolerance as a prerequisite for one who wishes to attain the exalted dignity of kingship. Tolerance is almost certainly what he meant by the ambiguous concept of *ṣulḥ-i kull* (peace for all), where 'thousands find rest in the love of the king, and sectarian differences do not raise the dust of strife'.[61]

59 Khwānd-Amīr, *Qānūn-i Humāyūnī*, included in *Maʿāthir al-mulūk*, ed. Mīr Hāshim Muḥaddith (Tehran, 1372/1993), pp. 247–334.

60 J. F. Richards, 'The formation of imperial authority under Akbar and Jahangir', in Muzaffar Alam and Sanjay Subrahmanyam (eds.), *The Mughal state 1526–1750* (Delhi, 1998), p. 144.

61 Saiyid Athar Abbas Rizvi, *Religious and intellectual history of the Muslims in Akbar's reign, with special reference to Abu'l Fazl, 1556–1605* (New Delhi, 1975), pp. 354–7, 364 (translations slightly modified).

Sher Shāh Sūr (r. 947–52/1540–5), who had dislodged Humāyūn, came to power with a platform of justice for the subjects, installed the *amīr-i dād* as the chief judge of his court of complaints (*maẓālim*), thus following the Delhi sultan's importation of that Sāmānid office as *dādbeg*. The office remained important after the Mughal restoration, though the title was changed slightly to *mīr ʿadl*. Jahāngīr installed a gold chain in his palace, in imitation of Anūshirwān's legendary 'chain of justice', to assure his constant accessibility to his subjects with pleas and petitions against oppression. The didactic *Akhlāq-i Jahāngīrī* (Jahāngīrian ethics) by Qāḍī Nūr al-Dīn Khāqānī, versified into a quatrain an old maxim of statecraft that had, incidentally, been cited by the leading Imāmī jurist in a *fatwā* that justified the overthrow of the ʿAbbāsid caliphate by Hülegü:

> Consider justice and equity, not infidelity (*kufr*) nor religion (*dīn*),
> That which is at work in the maintenance of the kingdom.
> Justice without religion is better for the order of the world
> Than the oppression of the pious (*dīndār*) king.[62]

In presenting the massive constitution of Akbar's empire, *Āʾīn-i Akbarī* (The Akbarian constitution), Abu 'l-Faḍl offers the rationale of its division into three parts: 'I shall explain the regulations (*āyīn*) of the household (*manzil*), the army (*sipāh*) and the kingdom (*mulk*) since these three constitute the work of a ruler.'[63] The Mughal emperors maintained the distinctively Turco-Mongolian feature of their mobile court and spent a considerable time outside their capitals, with the government bureaucracy, treasury and the royal court of appeals moving with the royal camp (*urdū*), which constituted a huge moving city. The household regulations included the personal guidance of the officials by Akbar through initiation into the above-mentioned order. This was continued by Jahāngīr, and was indeed expanded to include the entire body of high office-holders, who were treated as the emperor's disciples and given the imperial image and seal to wear. As in the Ottoman empire, provincial administration was absorbed into the military organisation, as was much of central administration. The highest office-holders, the *manṣabdārs*, were appointed on the basis of their personal devotion and loyalty to the ruler, as indicated by the adoption of the ethos of *mamlūk* tradition of corporate

62 Muzaffar Alam, *The languages of political Islam: India, 1200–1800* (London and Chicago, 2004), p. 73 (translation modified).
63 Quoted in Stephen P. Blake, 'The patrimonial-bureaucratic empire of the Mughals', *Journal of Asian Studies*, 39, 1 (1979), p. 82 (translation slightly modified).

military slavery, which referred to any officer as 'slave' (*banda*) of the ruler, and by the patrimonial ethos of being *khānazād* (born to the household), both of which were shared by the Ṣafavids and the Ottomans. A quarter or more of the state revenue came from the crown lands, and the *manṣabdār*, the lesser cavalrymen and civil and judicial officials were given land assignments (*jāgīrs*) for the maintenance of a specific number of men, horses and cavalry, or as prebends. The *jāgīrs*, treasury and other property of the *manṣabdārs* escheated to the state on their death, though it could be reassigned to a son. Other grants to landholders (*zamīndārs*), whose proportion greatly increased with the expansion of the Mughal empire into Bengal and the Deccan, were however much harder to control centrally.

Abu 'l-Faḍl also organised the Mughal chancery and supplied a model epistolary manual for it. As the Mughal imperial administration expanded, administrative manuals (*dastūr al-ʿamals*) multiplied under Jahānshāh, and its intelligence service for reporting local events and developments to the emperor became more elaborate. Finally, there was an attempt to rationalise the judicial system alongside bureaucracy, and in 1075/1664 Aurangzeb ʿĀlamgīr (world-conqueror) ordered Shaykh Niẓām of Burhānpūr to compile a book of legal opinions for use by the judges of the empire, and at least twenty-eight jurists working under four section heads produced the practically oriented *Fatāwā-yi ʿĀlamgīrī* (Rulings of the world conqueror), which included a comprehensive treatment of the law of *waqf* in fourteen chapters.

The Ottoman, Ṣafavid and Mughal empires are usually put together as early modern Muslim empires, and Hodgson characterised them as 'gunpowder empires'. This characterisation exaggerates the importance of military technology and fails to capture the most salient features of these imperial regimes. A more sociological approach typifies them as 'historical bureaucratic empires'.[64] Along this line, anticipated by Weber's posthumously published notes,[65] we have adopted 'patrimonial-bureaucratic empire' as the type that captures the common features of the Ottoman, Ṣafavid and Mughal political regimes. Despite the development of bureaucracy and its specialisation and technical rationalisation, the early modern Muslim empires shared a fundamental feature of earlier patrimonialism: they remained systems of personal authority through delegation, with the royal court – the household of the ruler – at its centre. Our survey of the imperial regimes in this section has been informed by this model, though it has also shown major differences among

64 S. N. Eisenstadt, *Political system of empires* (New York, 1969).
65 Weber, *Economy and society*, vol. II, pp. 1028–44.

the three species of this general type. Many of these differences stem from variations in the Islamicate cultural heritage. We may conclude, however, with one major difference regarding the importance of bureaucracy and degree of centralisation of authority which is linked to the social structure. The Ṣafavid empire fits the 'patrimonial-bureaucratic type' only in the seventeenth and first quarter of the eighteenth century, and even then the size of the central bureaucracy was quite modest in comparison to the Ottoman and Mughal empires (as was the royal palace in Iṣfahān), and rested largely on the ad hoc creation of a royal slave corps with the conquest of Georgia. Unlike the Ottoman and the Mughal empires, the great majority of whose subjects were sedentary cultivators, the tribal population of Iran remained large – and probably increased when the Ottomans stopped the westward migration from the steppes and pushed back some of its Anatolian nomadic population into Iran. ʿAbbās I's impressive feat of centralisation eventually foundered because of the large size of the nomadic population and its military importance. With the collapse of the Ṣafavid empire in 1135/1722 its army and bureaucracy disintegrated, and when the Qājārs came to power with confederate tribal military forces at the end of the eighteenth century their government had only a handful of scribes and tax officials and was entirely patrimonial. However, in the Ottoman and Mughal empires too, centralisation was somewhat precarious, as demonstrated by the seventeenth century with the Jelālī rebellions and the rise of the local warlords (*āqā*, *derre-beğ*) in the Ottoman empire, and with rebellions of the *zamīndārs* in the seventeenth and the transformation of Mughal rule beyond the core of the empire into nominal suzerainty in the eighteenth century.

In conclusion, it should be pointed out that the characterisation of these imperial regimes as 'Oriental despotism', skilfully theorised by Montesquieu and widely spread by the modern constitutionalist movement in the Muslim world itself, is misleading. Imperial monarchies were undoubtedly autocratic, but they were not systems of total power without law. Autocracy was bound by the public law of the empire/dynasty, and subject to limitation by the *sharīʿa* as the law of God. The striking weakness of mechanisms of constitutional controls through checks and balances should not obscure the fact that the *sharʿī* ethico-legal order created a considerable sphere of civic autonomy for commercial and civic activities. Although the subject is beyond the scope of this chapter, the growth of educational and charitable institutions, in particular, made possible by the *sharīʿa*'s (civil) law of *waqf* under the 'military-patronage system', continued and was generally accelerated under the 'patrimonial-bureaucratic empires'.

8

The city and the nomad

HUGH KENNEDY

Cities

The 'Islamic city' has been an important focus of historical discussion for at least a century; scholars have drawn attention to the importance of cities in Islamic society, the vast size of certain cities in the medieval Muslim world and the importance of merchants, not only as generators of wealth but as religious leaders, intellectuals and exemplars of good and worthy citizens.[1] All this is in implied contrast with the societies of north-west Europe, in which, it is argued, elite power was based in the countryside and the rural estate and where cities were comparatively small and merchants regarded with suspicion and contempt by the upper reaches of both secular and religious hierarchies.[2]

The built environment of the Islamic city also appears to have certain definable characteristics. The most obvious of these was the apparent absence of formal planning, the narrow winding streets, the closed-off residential quarters. The main arteries of such a Muslim city were narrow and sometimes stepped because they were not designed for wheeled vehicles. Medieval Muslim society almost disinvented the wheel: it was the pack animal and the human porter that shifted goods, not the cart.[3] This meant that there was no need for wide, well-engineered streets of the sort that Roman towns had required. The closed residential quarters were a result of the Muslim concern with the privacy and sanctity of domestic family life, which had to be protected from prying eyes. With this went the development of a typical

1 For a general introduction see A. Hourani and S. M. Stern, *The Islamic city: A colloquium* (Oxford, 1970); P. Wheatley, *The places where men pray together* (Chicago, 2001).
2 S. D. Goitein, 'The rise of the Near Eastern bourgeoisie', *Cahiers d'histoire mondiale*, 3 (1956–7).
3 R. Bulliet, *The camel and the wheel* (Cambridge, MA, 1975).

urban core, the markets grouped around the mosque, with the high-status trades such as textiles and jewellery closest to the centre.[4]

The Islamic city, in short, holds an immense attraction for historians of Islamic culture, primarily because it appears to present a particularly and distinctively Islamic contribution to civilisation.

It has become a commonplace to note that Islam began as an urban religion. The Prophet Muḥammad was no nomad, but came from the commercial city of Mecca, a genuinely urban community which had become rich on international trade. Revisionist historians have cast doubts on the viability – and indeed the very existence – of Meccan trade, arguing that so remote and impoverished an area could never have been the centre of the sort of commercial networks reported in the early Muslim sources.[5] Recent research, however, has pointed to the existence of gold and silver mines in the Ḥijāz at this period and suggests that the wealth derived from mining precious ores might have been the generator of the economic expansion of Mecca.

When he left his native city, the Prophet settled in another city, Yathrib, which became known as *al-madīna* (the city) par excellence. It was from this city that Muḥammad and his successors, the *rāshidūn* caliphs, exercised their authority. In the aftermath of the Muslim conquests new cities were founded to provide places for the soldiers of the Muslim armies and their families to settle. These new towns, the *amṣār*, became the paradigmatic early Muslim cities. The most famous were Kūfa, in central Iraq, Baṣra in southern Iraq and Fusṭāṭ (Old Cairo) in Egypt. The *amṣār* were not simply army cantonments. They were part of a deliberate strategy by the early Muslim elite to settle and control the largely nomad and tribal men who formed the bulk of the Muslim armies. Above all, they were the centres at which the *ʿaṭāʾ*, the pension, was paid in cash to the troops and their families. The presence of so many people in receipt of regular incomes naturally attracted merchants and other suppliers of goods and services, and the settlements became fully fledged cities with the multiplicity of functions normally associated with an urban environment. The characteristic architectural forms of the commercial centre seem to have appeared very early: *funduq*s, lodging and commercial premises in the markets, are recorded in the second/eighth century. In the descriptions of the fourth/tenth-century geographers many towns clearly had bazaars or *sūq*s with shops in rows, separate streets for each trade, *funduq*s and

4 H. Kennedy, 'From *polis* to *madina*: Urban change in Late Antique and early Islamic Syria', *Past and Present*, 106 (1985).
5 P. Crone, *Meccan trade and the rise of Islam* (Princeton, 1986).

khans for visitors, *ḥammāms* for all and gates that could be shut at night. The 'classic' form of the Islamic urban markets developed in the first three centuries of Islam. It took longer for the religious and official architecture to reach maturity.

Despite the fact that they were founded by government initiative, these early *amṣār* showed little evidence of formal planning; men tended to settle in distinct areas with their fellow tribesmen, and gradually replaced their tents or huts with more permanent structures on the same sites. Only the main mosque and the *dār al-imāra* (government house) at the centre showed evidence of formal or monumental architecture.

Other new towns followed in the Umayyad period as Muslims began to settle in other provinces. In Fārs, Shīrāz was founded to replace Iṣṭakhr and other cities of Sasanian origin as the main centre of government. In al-Jazīra Mosul developed into a thriving Muslim city; in Ifrīqiya (Tunisia) Qayrawān was built to provide a base for Arab soldiers from the east at the same time.

In other areas the new Muslim rulers based themselves in existing cities, although these often expanded to provide new quarters for the new arrivals. Damascus was the capital of the Umayyad caliphate. The imprint of the new state was made clear with the construction of a new mosque on the site of the cathedral and a *dār al-imāra* nearby. The city also expanded a bit to the south and west of the old walls, but urban growth seems to have been modest for the capital city of an empire which stretched from the Atlantic to the Indus. Aleppo, which emerged as the leading city in northern Syria in the first two centuries of Muslim rule, was also an ancient city which acquired new suburbs *extra muros* while remaining centred on its historic core. In the far west and the far east Muslim rule was exercised from existing urban centres, Cordoba in al-Andalus and Marw in Khurāsān: both these cities expanded beyond the previous walled area, Cordoba in the fourth/tenth century, Marw in the second/eighth.

The reasons for this massive expansion of the larger cities are complex. There is no evidence that new technologies or new crops were developed which allowed people to gather together in larger and more intensive settlements. Bulliet has argued that towns in Iran expanded as a result of conversion to Islam.[6] When men converted to the new religion they abandoned their old village communities, where they were ostracised, and moved to cities to be with other Muslims. This may have been the case in some areas, but it is unlikely to be the whole explanation. Cities attracted people because they

6 R. Bulliet, *Islam: The view from the edge* (New York, 1994).

offered economic opportunities. The Muslim city was where the court, the administration and the army were based, and this was where money was spent and earned.

Cities also expanded because they became the centres of expanding industries. Textile manufacture was the most important industry in the Muslim Middle East and probably the largest provider of employment in most towns. Textiles were also a major generator to trade links; the Arab geographers constantly refer to the different sorts of textiles produced in different areas. In the era before artificial fibres, different areas specialised in different crops – linen from Egypt, silk from Armenia – depending on climate and agriculture. This was a society in which rich and elegant woven fabrics were very highly prized. Fine robes formed what was almost an alternative currency, and rulers constantly used them to reward followers and demonstrate rank. The ʿAbbāsid court of the second/eighth and third/ninth centuries was a massive purchaser and consumer of fabrics from Armenia in the north and Khūzistān in the south. In both areas this demand stimulated manufacture, urban life and trade and transport. Sometimes these fabrics were woven at state-run *ṭirāz* workshops, but many were probably purchased from independent artisans. Large numbers of men must have been engaged in transporting the finished products, and this had a major impact on local economies, stimulating growth. The decline in urban life in Khūzistān from the fourth/tenth century onwards may well have been a result of the collapse of the ʿAbbāsid caliphate and the disappearance of the most important customer for their manufactured goods.

The new Muslim government shaped the distribution of cities in many ways. In the lands of the old Sasanian empire we can observe how cities that became the centres of government tended to thrive and often expand very greatly. Other small provincial towns gradually declined and lost their urban status. Thus Nīshāpūr vastly increased in size after the Ṭāhirids adopted it as the seat of government in the third/ninth century, and the scattered settlements of the Iṣfahān oasis were brought into a single urban nucleus by a governor in the second half of the second/eighth century while the other settlements of the oasis were reduced to village status. In Fārs the Islamic new town of Shīrāz flourished and expanded while older centres such as Iṣṭakhr and Bishāpūr lost their urban character.

The greatest city founded in the early Islamic period was of course Baghdad, begun by al-Manṣūr in 145/762.[7] Here, where the courses of the Tigris and Euphrates come closest together, he built a new city which was to

7 J. Lassner, *The topography of Baghdad in the early Middle Ages* (Detroit, 1970).

be the centre of his government. He and his engineers constructed the official core, the heavily fortified Round City with the mosque and palace at its centre. The caliph also entrusted his most loyal servants, notably the *ḥājib* al-Rabīʿ ibn Yūnus, with laying out the mosques and *sūqs*. The units of the army were given plots of land to build houses on outside the walls of the Round City, and a few years later the caliph's son and heir, al-Mahdī, constructed a new quarter for his own supporters on the east bank of the Tigris.

Baghdad was founded as an administrative capital, but the presence of the court and the army meant that it soon became a major commercial city as suppliers of goods and services crowded in to take advantage of the markets. Because it stood at the head of what was still the richest area of agricultural land in the world, the alluvial lands of the Sawād of southern Iraq, and because it lay at the centre of a network of waterways, the growth of the city was not constrained by problems of food supply, and the population may well have reached half a million by the beginning of the third / ninth century. Very little of this growth was planned in any formal sense, though some markets were laid out by government officials and speculators. In one sense the development of the city was a gigantic property speculation, designed to enrich the new elite of soldiers and officials who were granted land, but it also became a vibrant and successful city in its own right. When the capital was moved to Sāmarrāʾ in the 220s / 830s, Baghdad showed that it could still flourish without the presence of the government apparatus.

Sāmarrāʾ was founded for much the same reasons as Baghdad: to house the new, largely Turkish, army recruited by the caliph al-Muʿtaṣim and to reward the supporters of his regime.[8] The city was further expanded by al-Mutawakkil, who erected what was essentially another new palace quarter at the northern end of the site. The ruins of Sāmarrāʾ can still be seen today, stretched out along the east bank of the Tigris. This was a measure of the lack of success of the city, which dwindled almost to nothingness when the government left to return to Baghdad in 279 / 892. The failure of Sāmarrāʾ was due to a number of factors: the gravelly plateau on which it was built prevented the development of the systems of canals which made Baghdad look almost Venetian; the distance from the Euphrates meant that grain could not easily be imported from the steppes of al-Jazīra, while the Sawād was further away down the swift-flowing course of the Middle Tigris. Vast amounts of money were spent by the caliphs in attempts to bring water to

8 C. F. Robinson, *A medieval Islamic city reconsidered: An interdisciplinary approach to Samarra* (Oxford, 2001); T. Leisten, *Excavation of Samarra, volume I: Architecture* (Mainz, 2003).

the city, but without effect. The contrasting fates of Sāmarrā' and Baghdad help us to understand something of the role of Muslim governments in the creating of new cities: they could provide a nucleus of attraction, but the long-term viability of any city depended on more general geographical and economic factors. The mute ruins of Madīnat al-Zahrā', Sulṭāniyya and Fatehpur Sikri all show the consequences of failure; the bustle of Cairo and Iṣfahān the long-lasting effects of success.

The model of Baghdad had a lasting influence on the formation of new capitals in the Muslim world. In Egypt the original *miṣr* at Fusṭāṭ was supplemented by a series of military settlements, which culminated in the Fāṭimid capital of Cairo, laid out in a large walled rectangle to the north of the existing cities, another example of an official city, dominated by palaces and the mosque (Azhar).[9] After the collapse of Fāṭimid rule Cairo, like Baghdad, continued to thrive as an economic and cultural centre. It also remained the capital of the Mamlūk sultanate, perhaps the most powerful and stable state in the later medieval Islamic world. Mamlūk sultans and *amīrs* spent vast sums on creating religious institutions and monuments for themselves in the heart of the city.

In much of the medieval world cities were defined and limited by city walls. In the early Islamic Middle East, however, city walls were in many cases dispensed with so that settlement could develop without the restrictions imposed by a fortified perimeter. The new *amṣār* at Kūfa, Baṣra and Fusṭāṭ seem to have been unwalled, at least in their early formative period. In existing fortified cities the Muslims and other immigrants usually settled in open areas outside the walls. In Marw[10] the city expanded to the west in the lands irrigated by the Majān canal, and it was here that Abū Muslim constructed his famous *dār al-imāra*. This new elite quarter was unfortified while the great rectangular enclosure of the old city with its ancient citadel and massive mud-brick ramparts became gradually depopulated or given over to industrial use. In Nīshāpūr the old fortress was abandoned as the mosques and markets were constructed well outside the protection of its walls. In Aleppo the settlements of the Arabs and the palaces of the Ḥamdānids lay outside the walls to the south of the city. In Cordoba in the fourth/tenth century the new residential areas spread far beyond the walls to the west. This apparent disregard for physical security was reflected in the fact that sieges of towns were rare and that military dominance was usually secured in battles between

9 S. J. Staffa, *Conquest and fusion: The social evolution of Cairo AD 642–1850* (Leiden, 1977).
10 G. Herrmann, *The monuments of Merv* (London, 1999).

field armies in open terrain: military leaders were often reluctant to cramp their armies inside fortifications.

With the coming of the Saljūqs in the late fifth/eleventh century we can begin to see the development of the urban citadel as a prominent feature of the townscape of the Islamic city. Wherever possible these citadels were built on high ground overlooking the city, and were protected by thick walls and massive towers. In Marw a citadel was constructed and the new quarters surrounded by a wall in the late fifth/eleventh century. At the same time Damascus acquired a citadel for the first time, and this was rebuilt and added to throughout the sixth/twelfth and seventh/thirteenth centuries. Cairo had to wait until the late sixth/twelfth century to be endowed with a citadel by Saladin, greatly strengthened by al-Malik al-ʿĀdil and, as at Marw, this was accompanied by the building of walls to enclose previously open areas of settlement. In al-Andalus at the same time the skylines of the developing cities of Granada and Badajoz were dominated by their citadels. These new-style citadels usually enclosed a place for the governor or ruler and barracks or places for the military to pitch their tents, and the emergence of the fortified *enceinte* reflects the status of the *amīr* and his *ʿaskar* (army) or *shiḥna* (police force), ruling the city but in many ways separate from the citizens and their lives. In Damascus a palace of modest size occupied part of the area; in Granada the citadel expanded in the eighth/fourteenth century to enclose the palace-city known as the Alhambra.

The period from the sixth/twelfth to the ninth/fifteenth centuries might be described as the classic period of the Islamic city, a period which, thanks to the works of Lapidus and others, has come to appear normative for all other Islamic cities. This was not a period of great urban planning projects. Even in Tīmūr's Samarqand, where massive buildings were undertaken, there was no grand design for the city. The Mamlūks in Cairo and Damascus were great builders of mosques and mausolea, but they did not attempt to reshape the urban environment with squares and avenues. Instead, this middle period saw the development of a number of different types of monumental structure with which the elite sought to establish their imprint on the city. There were mosques of course. In this case the patrons constructed small neighbourhood mosques or added to and embellished more established ones, with new minarets or *miḥrāb*s. Urban space *intra muros*, for all cities were now walled, meant that land was at a premium; architects had to use all their ingenuity to contrive great buildings. *Madrasa*s were another characteristic of the city, showing its learning and preserving the traditions of the scholars who had come before and who formed the intellectual and religious capital of the city.

Finally there were the mausolea where the great dead lay, often attached to *madrasas* or mosques.

From the tenth/sixteenth century much of the Muslim world was ruled by three great empires: the Ottoman, the Ṣafavid and the Mughal. All three were great builders. In Istanbul the urban scene was transformed by the creation of great complexes such as the Süleymāniye in which the mosque was surrounded by a large court and a number of service buildings, libraries and hospitals which virtually created a city within the city. The street plan, however, evolved naturally from the Roman and Byzantine plan which underlay it. In Iṣfahān, by contrast, the Ṣafavid Shah ʿAbbās I and his successors laid out a city on a scale which had had no parallels since Fāṭimid Cairo, six centuries before. A vast new *maydān* (square) was laid out at the edge of the old walled city, with a congregational mosque, a smaller mosque and the entrance to the palace quarter, where elegant pavilions stood in beautiful gardens. There was also a broad, straight street, the Chahār Bāgh, running through gardens to the river, which was itself crossed by elegant bridges. The whole project was on a scale and regular planning which had no equal in the Muslim world, but the contemporary Uzbek rulers of Samarqand completed a third *madrasa* which transformed the open space of the Registan into one of the great urban spaces of the Muslim world.

The best surviving urban layout from the Mughal empire is the largely deserted city of Fatehpur Sikri. This was built slightly before Iṣfahān, between 874/1470 and 994/1585 at the command of the emperor Akbar. Unlike Iṣfahān, this was not a royal quarter added to a thriving existing city, but a largely new creation whose original focus was the shrine of Salīm Chishtī (883–980/1479–1572) a Sufi saint who is said to have predicted the birth of Akbar's sons. The site was along a ridge overlooking a lake, and the city was divided into two zones: an official quarter comprising the great mosque with its vast courtyard; and the palace. The palace had a number of courts, each more secluded than the last, from the public Dīvāni Am to the sequestered harem. Outside the official quarter, and orientated at a different angle, were the commercial buildings that served the complex, a long bazaar with a central dome, a caravanserai and a mint or factory. The whole was enclosed by stone walls 11 kilometres long, beyond which lay gardens and residences for the nobility. Fatehpur Sikri never throve as a city. As at Sāmarrāʾ, the departure of the ruler, in 994/1585, spelled the end of its prosperity; but, again like Sāmarrāʾ, the failure of the city to develop a self-sustaining urban life has preserved the vision of urban development down to the present day.

The expansion of Islam also brought the expansion of urban life in areas where cities had been virtually non-existent before. With the exceptions of Volubilis and Ceuta, Morocco at the time of the Islamic conquest seems to have been almost deurbanised. The first real cities to develop were Fez, from the late second/eighth century, which was a dynastic and government centre and home to refugees from al-Andalus, and Sijilmāsa, a trading emporium in the south on the fringes of the Sahara. Urbanism received a major boost with the founding of Marrakesh in the 460s/1070s when the Almoravid rulers sought to settle their Ṣanhāja nomad followers north of the Atlas Mountains. Under the Almohads who succeeded them, Marrakesh became the capital of a large empire, and a centre of learning. Meanwhile the Almohads founded Rabāṭ as a military base for expeditions against the Christians of al-Andalus. The nomads who supported the Almoravids and the village dwellers who sustained the Almohads both used and created cities to exercise their power.

Saharan trade led to the creation of cities on the fringes of the Muslim world. Along the Niger river, Muslim merchants created cities such as Jenne and Timbuktu, and made them seats of learning.

The 'Islamic city' has become something of an academic cliché, a useful tool of argument but difficult to define. What was distinctive about this city? The most obvious features were certain distinctive public buildings. The mosque, especially in the early days of Islam, was both place of worship and community centre for the Muslim population of a town, providing housing for teachers and their classes and the court of the *qāḍī*. From the fifth/eleventh century *madrasas* and mausolea began to appear in the city, and by the late Middle Ages urban centres from Delhi to Timbuktu were dominated by the domes and minarets of these buildings. The commercial centres of Islamic cities were also distinctive, the long narrow *sūqs* of the Arabic-speaking world and the characteristic crossroad bazaar (*chārsū*) of the eastern Iranian world marked them out. Islamic cities were also distinguished by the separation of commercial and residential areas: there was no tradition of living above the shop, and the *sūqs* were usually closed and deserted at night. Most Islamic cities too shared the tradition of secluded residential quarters, sometimes gated, with narrow cul-de-sac lanes leading to blank-walled houses which looked inward on their courtyards; it was very different from the public, sometimes ostentatious, housing of the western city.

At first sight, the hand of government rested lightly on the Islamic city. There might be grand urban projects such as the Ṣafavid development at Iṣfahān and the Mughal city of Fatehpur Sikri, but little attempt was made to plan commercial and residential areas. However, the role of government was crucial to the functioning of the city. The Islamic world inherited and maintained a system of public finances, a system with no parallel in the west, where public taxation had collapsed with the Roman empire. Governments collected money and paid salaries in cash. Where the government and its employees lived, there was an active market and people flocked to provide goods and services for the salarymen. More than anything else, the fiscal role of the state ensured the continued vitality of urban life in the Islamic Middle East when it effectively disappeared in north-west Europe and the Byzantine empire. This fiscal structure was itself part of the *dīn*, part of the faith of the Muslims, and perhaps it was in this way that the Islamic city really was a product of the religious environment in which it flourished.

Nomads

If there is one feature of the human geography of the Muslim world in the pre-modern period which distinguishes it from that of western Europe, India or China it is surely the presence of large numbers of nomadic or transhumant peoples. The impact of the nomads has been enormous – sometimes destructive, sometimes leading to the formation of major states and empires. This impact can be seen in their establishment and support of important states, their influence on political systems and patterns and their dominance of the battlefield.

Nomads and transhumants can be grouped together because they move their dwellings and live in tents. They are also, practically without exception, dependent on animals – sheep, goats, camels and horses – for their survival. Despite these common characteristics, different groups have very different historical roles.

True nomads have traditionally lived in three major geographical areas: the deserts of Arabia and Syria, the steppes of Central Asia and the Sahara desert in Africa. Each of these populations created major states in the Muslim world. The first Muslim conquests were successful because of the military experience and abilities of the Arab nomads of the Arabian Peninsula; the steppes of Central Asia provided the manpower for the Saljūq and Mongol imperial armies; and the Sahara nomads created the short-lived but extensive empire of the Almoravids. These nomad populations can be grouped according to the animals they lived off, the camels and sheep in the Arabian and Syrian deserts, camels in the Sahara and horses of the Central Asian steppes. In the deserts of Syria and Arabia there is a further distinction between breeders of sheep, who need access to water and markets and so have to keep near settled lands, and breeders of camels, who can roam wider in the inner desert. Many tribes, of course, raised both.

Nomad populations formed the military manpower of many Islamic states in the pre-modern period. The most extensive and spectacular were the Mongols, only partly Muslim, whose imperialism was based on the support of the horse nomads of the central Asian steppes. The early Saljūqs too were dependent on their nomad followers, though in a development repeated elsewhere, the nomads were soon marginalised and replaced by professional *ghulām* soldiers, often of Turkish stock but paid and recruited as regular troops. The remaining nomads, generally known in the sources as Turkmen, were allowed to roam in the steppe lands of Iran and Anatolia and came to form a dangerous political challenge as the power of the Saljūq rulers waned in the sixth/twelfth century: it was an army of Turkmen like this who captured and humiliated Sultan Sanjar, the last great Saljūq ruler, near Marw in 553/1157.

Transhumants were the dominant pastoral people in a wide swath of territory which ran around the edge of the Fertile Crescent from the Taurus mountains of south-eastern Anatolia, along the Zagros ranges which divide the Iranian Plateau from Iraq and south to the mountains of Fārs along the eastern shores of the Gulf. There were also transhumant groups in the mountains of Azerbaijan and the steppes at the south-east corner of the Caspian. Transhumants followed established roads from the winter pastures in the plains to the high summer grazing lands. They lived in tents but their chiefs sometimes built bridges to help them pass the most rapid streams so that the tribesmen could pay their respects to the tomb towers of their dead leaders en route. The transhumants were mostly Kurdish speaking in the early Islamic period, but by the end of the fifth/eleventh century they had been joined – and in some cases replaced – by Turkish speakers.

Transhumants usually existed on the margins of mainstream politics, and there are no examples of transhumant people creating major empires. They did, however, create small states at times of general political fragmentation. One such was in the fourth/tenth century after the breakup of the ʿAbbāsid caliphate when dynasties such as the Marwānids of Mayyāfāriqīn in south eastern Anatolia and the Ḥasanūyids and ʿAnnāzids of the Zagros were based on transhumant Kurdish tribes. The rulers may have exercised power from their small-town capitals or strategic fortresses but the manpower of their armies lay in their pastoral followers.

The Ilkhānid empire, the Mongol successor state in Iran, was also transhumant on a larger scale. The *khāns* would spend the summer months in the high pastures of Azerbaijan, around Ujjān and Tabrīz. In the winter they would either move north to the low-lying Qarabāgh steppes of the south-west corner of the Caspian Sea, or through the Zagros passes to Iraq. If the rulers were feeling more adventurous, they might travel up the Euphrates to ravage the lands of northern Syria. It is clear that the political geography of the Ilkhānid state and the ambitions of its rulers were almost entirely guided by the needs of their pastoral, transhumant followers.

Both nomads and transhumants were grouped in tribes. The definition of the tribe, which has numerous descriptive terms in Arabic, is complex. In the literature and lore of the Middle East the tribes have a clearly defined self-image: they purport to be the descendants of a common ancestor. There is supposed to be, in fact, a biological rationale for their existence as a group. In reality, however, the position was much more complex. Some tribes clearly were part of extended kinship structures, others were little more than genealogical fictions created to define groups of pastoralists who acted together in a common purpose. The tribes of pre-Islamic Arabia, who form the archetype of later Islamic tribal groups, were central to the success of the early Muslim conquests. In the second/eighth century their genealogies were elaborated and written up in prodigious detail, with thousands of names supposedly arranged in their correct places. This erudition certainly gave a spurious clarity to the question of nomad descent.

The large tribes of pre-Islamic Arabia seldom came together as a group. For the purposes of everyday life the much smaller tenting group was the normal unit for moving and decision making. Perhaps paradoxically, the Muslim conquests brought members of tribes together as never before. Settlement in the *amṣār*, designed in part to reduce the influence of tribes and tribal leaders, actually had the opposite effect: members of, say, Tamīm (a tribe from north-east Arabia which settled in Iraq in large numbers), who had never previously worked or lived together now found themselves living together in close proximity and competing for government resources with rival tribes. Tribal solidarities and rivalries were built up and became a significant factor in the politics of the Umayyad and early ʿAbbāsid caliphates.

Nomad societies have very different attitudes to the ownership and use of wealth from those of their settled neighbours. Among nomads it is, of course, moveable property, especially livestock, that forms the true valuable property. Some leaders may have larger and more beautiful tents than their fellow tribesmen, but these are a sign of status rather than disposable assets. Many nomads in the Arabian and Syrian deserts also own agricultural lands and even urban properties in the areas on the fringes of the desert. The income from such properties may boost their status among their fellows to some extent and give them political leverage, but it can never be the foundation of their wealth. In the fourth/tenth and early fifth/eleventh centuries, when the influence of nomads in the Fertile Crescent reached a high point, the leaders who founded the small states of the time used the income from urban properties and subsidies from settled powers to establish the leadership within their tribes without which they could never have created lasting polities.

The livestock of the nomad constitute his true wealth, and such wealth creates its own limitations. A large flock brings prestige and the resources to entertain on a grand scale, but it is also self-limiting. Any number of *dīnārs* can be stored up in a palace vault, but flocks cannot be extended exponentially: there will not be enough grazing for them; if they are entrusted to other shepherds to take them away to new pastures, they will be impossible to control and will inevitably disperse and disappear.

Attitudes to land ownership were very different in many nomad societies from those held among settled peoples. Among the settled peoples of the Middle East, land was the major source of wealth. The urban bureaucratic and military elites sometimes owned it and took rents; more often they held the rights to collect government taxes on the land, the *iqṭāʿ*, *suyūrghāl* or any of the numerous other terms used to describe this. Whether held in direct ownership, or as *iqṭāʿ*, the land needed to be surveyed and recorded; farmers needed to be settled on it and encouraged to stay, for land without workers was valueless. Landholders were encouraged to care for and develop their properties. In some areas, Iraq and al-Jazīra in Umayyad times, Syria in Mamlūk times, the government and its representatives invested in improving the land and the agricultural base.

For the 'pure' nomad, land represents grazing opportunities. Grazing was the essential fuel of the nomad life and the most important desideratum of nomad armies. The grazing had no boundaries save those imposed by natural conditions, and artificial borders were merely obstacles. So too were the inhabitants, with their inconvenient habits of putting up buildings and walls and digging ditches across the land. For the nomad the land was more use unpeopled.

Of course this contrast is in a sense artificial and the differences far too sharply drawn to be realistic. In many Middle Eastern societies, as has already been noted, nomad chiefs owned landed estates, and no doubt cultivated and improved them like everyone else. The clearest examples of the different priorities of nomads and settled peoples come from Iran and Turkistan after the Mongol invasions. The mass slaughter of the inhabitants of the settled lands and the destruction of irrigation systems should be seen, in part at least, as a reflection of the need for pasture, a rational use of resources. The differing attitudes are clearly reflected in texts on good government, such as the *Siyāsatnāma* of Niẓām al-Mulk in which care of the peasants, to persuade them to stay and make the land productive, is urged on the Saljūq rulers. Even clearer is Rashīd al-Dīn's life of Ghāzān Khān, essentially a mirror for princes, which purports to describe Ghāzān's efforts to force and persuade his nomad followers to adopt a more constructive and sustainable attitude to landholding.

High status in such a nomad society depends not on numbers of beasts but on various forms of social capital, above all on the ability to entertain and reward. The generosity of nomads is often commented on by travellers, and the feeding and lodging of strangers is one of the hallmarks of Bedouin society. The obligations of hospitality were widely recognised in the society and, to an extent, formalised in custom. Hospitality has an essential function in the exercise of leadership: a reputation for generosity brings guests from far and wide to a man's tent, and guests bring with them information. They bring news of raids, alliances and, probably most important of all, news of grazing opportunities. The man who entertains the most guests is the man who is best informed and able to make the best decisions for his followers.

Leadership in many nomad societies is very different from monarchy as it developed among the settled peoples of the Islamic world. Leadership among many tribes is both hereditary and elective. Chiefs are usually chosen from a ruling kin, an extended family which embraces brothers and first cousins – and sometimes a more extended group than that. Son may succeed father, but there is no presumption in favour of hereditary succession and, even in the case of hereditary succession, there is no natural preference for primogeniture.

Within this kin, the most able individual is selected by the kin itself and the wider group. The qualities they are looking for will certainly include courage in battle and ability as a military leader, but wider social skills are also important. These will include being a good and fair arbitrator and settler of disputes, and being able to make wise decisions about economic choices: where to find good grazing, which markets to visit. The chosen leader has to work in cooperation with the other members of the kin. The more prominent members of his family will expect that their advice will be heeded and that they will have a share of both the responsibilities and the rewards of power.

The chief has no coercive power to enforce his authority: it can only be exercised by consent and the pressure of popular opinion. In the case of criminal or other individuals who transgress the boundaries of tribal custom, it will be this popular opinion that forces the individual to conform or leave. The leader has no power to force his followers into battle if they have no confidence in his military abilities.

This means that in most nomad societies the powers of the leader are severely circumscribed, and rulership is based on consent; but not all nomad societies are the same. Among the Mongols of Central Asia a different form of leadership can be seen. Chinggis Khān became supreme because of his abilities as a conqueror, which meant that men were eager to follow him. However, unlike an Arab Bedouin chief, he demanded and received absolute obedience; those who hesitated or wavered were brutally punished, and Chinggis can be seen as the nomad chief as absolute ruler.

The nomad model of more or less consensual rulership exercised by a ruling kin was extremely influential in many areas and periods of Islamic history. The Umayyads and early ʿAbbāsids were certainly not nomadic, but both dynasties shared power among the ruling kin. It was not until the third/ninth century that the ʿAbbāsids ceased to rely on the extended family as one of the mainstays of the dynasty and turned instead to professional soldiers and administrators. The early days of Saljūq rule in Iran saw tension between the idea of power sharing among the ruling kin espoused by Qutulmush when he challenged Alp Arslān's right to succeed in 455/1063. It was also a protest against the more authoritarian and statist policy of Alp Arslān who began the recruitment of *ghilmān* to provide an alternative power base. The rebellion was supported by many Turkmen. In the aftermath the Turkmen were encouraged to move to Anatolia and engage the Byzantines, while Alp Arslān continued to recruit *ghilmān* and establish a monarchy based on a professional army. It is a classic example of a dynasty brought to power by nomads in one generation and then breaking with its supporters in the next.

The military superiority of nomads and soldiers of nomad stock was a fact of life through much of Islamic history. It was above all their ability as horsemen that assured this mastery. The armies of the early Islamic conquests had largely fought on foot, though they had used horses and camels to reach the battlefield. From the third/ninth centuries, however, horsemen, usually of Turkish origin, came to form the core of most Muslim armies. It was at this time too that the mounted archer became the key elite soldier. The demands of firing arrows from a swiftly moving horse mean that it can only be achieved by men who have been practising it from childhood. The triumph of the mounted archer may have been assisted by the adoption of stirrups in the Middle East in around 81/700. The young Turkish nomad, who could often ride before he could walk, was best placed to take advantage of this technology.

From the third/ninth to the tenth/sixteenth centuries the Turkish horseman was master of the battlefield. Mongol warriors comprised the most effective armies that had ever been seen in the Muslim east. Early Fāṭimid rule in North Africa and Egypt was sustained by the Kutāma Berber nomads of North Africa, although these were largely replaced by Turks during the course of the fifth/eleventh century. In al-Andalus, the Ṣanhāja Berbers who supported the Almoravids were able to defeat the Christian forces at the battle of Zallāqa (479/1086).

The military dominance of the nomads faltered in the early tenth/sixteenth century. This can be seen most clearly in the struggle between the Ottomans and the Ṣafavids in eastern Anatolia. The Ṣafavid forces were largely recruited among the Turkmen Qizilbāsh of eastern Anatolia and they fought as they had always done, as nomad warriors with sword and bow. The Ottoman army was altogether more organised. In the crucial battle of Chaldiran in 920/1514 Ottoman professionalism and Ottoman cannon completely defeated the Ṣafavid forces. Three years later the Ottoman mastery of artillery may have played a part in the defeat of the Egyptian Mamlūks.

The use of gunpowder weapons gave an important advantage to the settled peoples. The traditional bows of the nomads could be made in camp from materials (bone, glue) that were essentially animal by-products, swords could also be easily purchased. The production of cannon and handguns, on the other hand, needed resources of iron and fuel, not to speak of expertise, which were simply impossible in the nomad camp.

It could be argued that the nomad domination of the battlefields of the Middle East lasted from the introduction of stirrups and mounted archery in the second/eighth and third/ninth centuries to the arrival of effective gunpowder weapons in the tenth/sixteenth. In fact, of course, it was not as clear-cut as that. The introduction of firearms did not always mean that they were used effectively and to good purpose. The Ṣafavid empire, which certainly had firearms technology, was defeated and brought down in 1135/1722 by the Ghilzai Afghans, who were still essentially nomads. As late as the thirteenth/nineteenth century the Tekke Turkmen of the Marw oasis were able to raid the settled lands of Iran with virtual impunity, looting property and capturing unfortunate Persian villagers. In the Syrian desert and Arabia, Bedouin were still a threat to the fringes of the Ottoman empire (and the Ḥijāz railway) until the first decades of the twentieth century.

9

Rural life and economy until 1800

ANDREW M. WATSON

Diversity

The lives of sedentary people in the Islamic countryside unfolded in a multi-faceted context. Natural, technological, economic, political, cultural and religious factors all bore on rural life, and were in turn affected by it.

The natural world provided a backdrop of topography, soils, climate and water, while technologies offered tools, irrigation devices, plants, animals and rotations. Economic factors such as population densities, urbanisation, monetisation of the economy and long-distance trade further conditioned the activities of agriculturists, as did the policies of governments concerning security, land tenure, inheritance, water rights, taxation and the construction and maintenance of irrigation works. Cultural biases showed in preferences for different modes of settlement and production, as well as in diets, and both political and cultural elements were informed by religious teachings. None of these was a constant.

Not surprisingly there was much variation in agricultural activities over time and space. To give just one example, Vincent Lagardère has identified seven types of agricultural undertakings in Islamic Spain, each the product of a particular situation. These are as follows: (1) the *munya*, an aristocratic estate generally located near large cities, and as much pleasure garden as farm, where year-round irrigation supported orchards and intensive cultivation; (2) the *raḥal*, a small aristocratic estate, probably resulting from the distribution of confiscated lands to people of high rank, generally located further from cities and containing irrigated land, which was heavily cropped, and rain-fed land, mainly given over to olive trees and vines; (3) the *janna*, or small irrigated orchard and market garden, often located near towns and owned by town-dwellers, typically operated for pleasure and profit by the owners and their families, sometimes with the help of hired labour; (4) the *qarya*, usually a village of around ten to thirty families, who generally owned their farmlands but might be the sharecroppers of a great person, producing a wide range of crops on both irrigated and un-irrigated lands; (5) the *ḍayʿa*, a large estate with a single owner, which with the help of sharecroppers or hired labourers produced both crops and animals; (6) the *majshar*, a privately owned estate devoted to the production of livestock in hilly and mountainous areas unsuited to crop production; and (7) other communities specialised in the raising of animals in marshy or well-watered areas along river basins.[1]

If one looks beyond Spain to other parts of the early Islamic world one encounters still more variation, but this is strikingly limited in scope. Two types of settlement inherited from Antiquity are notably absent from the above list for Spain, but were found elsewhere. One of these is the larger farms along river valleys, where seasonal irrigation allowed the production of crops for subsistence and for sale, the labour being most often provided by sharecroppers. The other, found in many regions, is a community practising mixed, but hardly integrated, farming: most of its members grew crops, but they also entrusted flocks to shepherds for grazing on near or more distant pastures.

These appear to complete the list of early Islamic modes of production. That these same types repeat themselves all over the early Islamic world; that they appear to have been the only types of agricultural undertakings in early Islamic times; and that they persisted well into modern times, by which time several new types of undertakings had appeared, calls for an explanation.

Uniformity

This would suggest that the repetition of the same patterns over vast spaces and long periods of time was the result of several inherited or emerging commonalities: similarities in the natural environments in which agriculture was practised; the region's common heritage of agricultural technologies developed in the ancient world; the changes wrought all over this world by its Arab conquerors; and finally, during the first four centuries of Islam, the massive diffusion from east to west of crops, farming techniques and irrigation technologies, which further unified agricultural practice.

The physical environment of the early Islamic world, though extremely varied, allowed agriculture in very limited areas. Normally, dry farming could be successful only where rainfall was above 250 millimetres per year; typically, annual rainfall in cultivated areas was between 300 and 400 millimetres, but in

1 Vincent Lagardère, *Campagnes et paysans d'al-Andalus, VIIIe–XVe siècles* (Paris, 1993), *passim*.

a few places it was as high as 700 millimetres. Nearly all the rain fell in the autumn, winter and early spring, allowing only a single agricultural season. The hot, dry summer was almost dead. Where rainfall was adequate, topography might not be: crops could be grown only on plains and on the slopes of hills and mountains that had retained enough soil to permit terracing; uncultivable areas, in the plains and on mountain slopes, might be used for seasonal grazing of animals. If irrigation water was available, this could be used to increase the productivity of rain-fed areas and to support agriculture in areas with inadequate rainfall: along river valleys, around oases and in places where wells or underground canals gave access to ground water.

To exploit the possibilities of this difficult environment a common body of agricultural knowledge and practice had emerged in ancient times, and was inherited by the conquering Arabs. Uniformity was particularly striking in the Mediterranean basin, where Phoenicians, Greeks, Romans and finally Byzantines had diffused tools, crops and practices over wide areas, so that by the seventh century CE there could be found almost everywhere the same ways of coping with environmental challenges. Generally, rain-fed lands were planted with drought-resistant permanent crops, such as olive trees, fig trees and vines, or they were sown bi-annually with winter grains, mostly wheat, barley and millets, as well as winter pulses such as chickpeas, lentils, peas and broad beans. In alternate years cultivated lands were fallowed to replenish moisture and fertility. On irrigated lands a wider range of crops was grown, including fruits, vegetables and, in warmer areas, date palms. Biennial fallowing was usually suppressed in favour of annual cropping on irrigated land; sometimes, but rarely, two crops were produced in one year. Depending on the region and the type of undertaking, some large animals might be raised, commonly sheep, goats, cattle, camels, horses, mules and donkeys. But in general the production of animals and the growing of crops were two distinct activities, carried out by different people on different types of land. There was no trace of the integrated (or mixed) farming of medieval Europe, in which the same land and labour were used to produce both crops and large animals.

In the valleys of the Tigris and Euphrates, as well as in the Indus Valley, some differences from Mediterranean practices are noteworthy in pre-Islamic times: most particularly in irrigation, which in some places allowed a summer season, and in range of crops, which included some plants, such as sorghum and rice, diffused out of India. But to a remarkable degree, even in these distant regions, a 'Mediterranean' mode of agriculture prevailed.

In the regions they conquered the Arabs were in many ways a unifying force. Their armies and the settlers who came in their wake brought the

Arabic language, which was the language of Islam and was almost everywhere to become the language of government, of learning and, in many places, of vernacular discourse, thus encouraging the development of a common culture throughout *dār al-islām*. And they brought a new religion. Though the Qur'ān seems to have a low regard for sedentary rural people and their work, Islam offered teachings and developed legal traditions which bore on agriculture in important ways. Islam forbade the eating of pork and the drinking of wine, proscriptions which banished pigs from the farmyards of Muslims and greatly reduced – but did not eliminate – their making and drinking of wine. Legal traditions included laws of inheritance which decreed how estates, including agricultural properties, should be divided among heirs; there might be a great many inheritors, resulting in the extreme fragmentation of farms or else their continued exploitation as a single property jointly owned, but poorly managed, by many absentee landlords. There developed a complex and bewildering body of tax laws explaining how different categories of rural people, lands, crops and animals should be taxed. There were also rules concerning rights over irrigation water, including the proscription of its sale; these rights undoubtedly encouraged investment in irrigation. And there were teachings and laws concerning the ownership of land, which, depending on circumstances and jurist, was seen to belong to God, to the state, to the Muslim community, to institutions and to individuals. Although in time different schools of law emerged with somewhat different rules concerning taxation and the ownership of land, and although realities increasingly diverged from the teachings of jurists, at least in the early centuries Islamic law contributed significantly to the uniformity of rural life across the Islamic world.

Further homogenisation of agriculture occurred in the first four centuries of Islam through the widespread diffusion of old and new technologies. The principal direction of flow was from the eastern part of the caliphate – the Sind and the valleys of the Tigris and Euphrates – to the Mediterranean basin. These were regions that in earlier times had had little contact but which, as a result of the Arab conquests, were brought under a single rule. Over the length and breadth of this world there was much travel by pilgrims, scholars, merchants, fighters and settlers, who carried the agricultural knowledge and food preferences of their homelands to new places. Among the crops diffused westwards were rice, sorghum, sugar cane, cotton, various citrus trees (Seville oranges, lemons, limes and shaddocks), bananas, plantains, watermelons, spinach, aubergines, colocasia, mango trees and coconut palms. With the exception of mango trees and coconut palms, which could be grown only in tropical or semi-tropical zones, these new crops were diffused to all regions of the early Islamic world and many became economically important. One irrigation technology was also carried westward: the *qanāt* or *kārīz*, an underground canal which brought water, often over long distances, from aquifers at the base of mountains to fields, villages and towns. At the same time, two water-lifting devices, which had been known to the Romans but were little used until the labour shortages of the fifth and sixth centuries, were widely diffused through the early Islamic world. These were the noria or water-wheel, which was driven by the flow of streams and rivers, and the *sāqiya* or chain of pots, powered by animals.

Thus similarities in physical environment, commonalities in agricultural heritage, the imprint of the Arab conquerors and of Islam and, finally, a massive diffusion of agricultural technologies from east to west: these seem to account for the limited variety of agricultural forms found throughout the early Islamic world.

Only later, when Islam moved outwards into new areas, or when new forms were introduced by invaders or migrants coming from outside, or when new modes of production slowly evolved within the Islamic world in response to new conditions, did greater variation appear. Just three examples out of many will be given here to illustrate the growing complexity of agriculture in later times; several other cases will be treated later in this chapter. As Islam spread into sub-Saharan Africa, it came to embrace quasi-sedentary communities whose members burned stretches of the savannah for shifting cultivation. In some of the lands of the Balkans conquered by the Ottomans, for instance on the plains of Wallachia, another mode of exploitation appeared: this closely resembled the medieval European manor, which may well be its origin, with share-cropping tenants who cultivated their own holdings, performed labour services on the owner's demesne and grazed animals on common pasture lands. Finally, in parts of Central Asia there is evidence in the fifteenth and sixteenth centuries of what Jürgen Paul has called a *communité villageoise*, a seemingly more ancient type of settlement in which villagers collectively controlled the construction and maintenance of irrigation works, the distribution of water and, apparently, the allocation and reallocation of farmlands which individual cultivators were not allowed to alienate. Whether such communities were introduced by conquerors or migrants coming from outside or evolved within the Islamic world is not clear, but the principle of collective management suggests a nomadic origin.[2]

2 Jürgen Paul, 'Le village en Asie centrale aux XVe et XVIe siècles', *Cahiers du Monde Russe et Soviétique*, 32 (1991).

Interfaces: cities and nomads

Rural people in the Islamic world had crucial relations with two non-agricultural elements of society: city-dwellers and nomadic pastoralists. Together, these involvements were in large measure – though certainly not entirely – responsible for the rhythm of growth and decay that periodised the region's agricultural history.

Between the cities and the countryside there was a flow, in both directions, of money, services and goods. Funds moved from agriculturists to cities in the form of taxes, rents and other dues, which were the main support for the bureaucracy, the military and a land-owning rentier class. There was a return flow of money to the countryside, as landowners and urban moneylenders provided loans to allow farmers to buy inputs, to tide them over till harvest time and to get them through years of bad harvests; the frequent inability of borrowers to repay on time was one factor leading to the build-up of great estates. Funds might also flow from the cities as governments took an interest in the construction and repair of large irrigation works, though often the labour needed for such work was provided by corvées. The city – more precisely the government – was also the main source of whatever protection could be given to rural dwellers against invaders, marauders and Bedouin. In the other direction, the countryside sent to the city some of its excess of labour to seek seasonal or long-term employment in households, services and industry. Trade saw the cities exporting some industrial goods to the countryside, most notably textiles and tools, while the agricultural surplus of crops and animals was, in large measure, sold to the cities. Indeed, the cities depended almost entirely upon the countryside for their food supplies and for many of their industrial raw materials; and as cities grew they drew into their orbits ever larger hinterlands where agriculture became increasingly specialised and intensive. When hinterlands could not increase their surpluses at prices that were economic, the growth of cities was blocked – unless long-distance trade could offer alternative sources of supply. Thus although city-dwellers and agriculturists are often seen as opposing worlds in Islamic belief, the former favoured over the latter by the Prophet and his religion, in fact they lived in a close symbiotic relationship. The spectacular rise of cities in the early centuries of Islam was possible only because of a corresponding development of agriculture.

Contacts between sedentary rural people and nomadic pastoralists – often referred to as Bedouin – were perhaps more limited. Indeed, to some extent the worlds of these two peoples who shared the countryside seem diametrically opposed. They had different modes of production, different cultures, different values, different dress and different diets. At the margins they competed for land. Yet for this very reason there were periodic shiftings of people and land between these two ways of life. As Bedouin populations rose or the yield of their pastures fell, or as the protection of sedentary agriculture became lax, they might extend their pastures onto cultivated lands. When sedentary agriculture was contracting, for whatever reason, farmers might become nomads. Those who could most easily make the switch were those already engaged in animal production; they had the necessary skills and they often lived in regions where farming was most at risk. Conversely, there were periods when settled communities, usually with government support, might take over fertile pasture lands or Bedouin might be settled on these lands; typically, Bedouin settlements would be of the *majshar* type, producing mainly animals which grazed on common pastures, or else they would consist of small villages where crops were grown and animals entrusted to herders for transhumant grazing.

Even when the balance between sedentarism and nomadism was stable the frontiers between these two opposing worlds were porous, allowing for a peaceful flow of goods in both directions. Bedouin typically sold a part of their surplus production of animals, milk products, hides and wool to settled rural communities, most particularly to those that did not produce large animals, and especially at the times of the great annual feasts when large numbers of sheep would be slaughtered. And Bedouin obtained a good part of their grain supplies from sedentary farmers. In many parts of the Islamic world these exchanges were effected in rural markets, which as yet have been little studied. These gathered weekly or monthly on sites lying at convenient distances from a number of villages and near to the nomads' pasturelands. Through the week the markets in a region might rotate from one site to another, so that on most or all days of the week there was an operating market.

Vulnerabilities

Partly because of the dependency of farmers on city-dwellers and Bedouin, and partly for very different reasons, farming was an uncertain, risky undertaking, and in many regions agriculture itself was fragile. Rural prosperity depended on the behaviour of various elements in the cities: on the ability and willingness of rulers to tax fairly, to maintain the larger irrigation works and to provide protection to settled communities, their lands and their trade; on the interest in their estates or the neglect of these on the part of landowners living in the cities; on the size of markets, near and distant, which varied as urban populations waxed or waned and as trade routes opened or closed. Rural producers were also at the mercy of urban rulers, bureaucrats and merchants who might unscrupulously manipulate grain supplies and prices. On the interface with the Bedouin other vulnerabilities appeared. In fact, the Bedouin were an ever-present threat in most regions, particularly in the many places where settlement was discontinuous or bordered on nomadic grazing lands. Even in the best of times such communities could not easily be protected against Bedouin *razzias*, transhumance or longer-term incursions. The trade routes on which agriculturists depended might be even more difficult to defend.

To complete the list of rural vulnerabilities, it is important to note that farmers were also subject to the vagaries of nature and they were, moreover, in many times and places, the victims of their own excesses. Nature might strike in many ways. There were great year-to-year fluctuations in rainfall, river flows and temperatures; and there could be harsh winds, hailstorms, infestations of rodents and insects and attacks of plant and animal diseases. Perhaps for these reasons the Qurʾān views good harvests as a gift of God rather than the fruit of human labour endowed with agricultural skills developed over eight or more millennia. And certainly there were many years when harvests failed over smaller or larger areas. Michael Dols has stated that between 661 and 1500 there are records of 186 major famines in the Islamic world, a figure he thinks is 'far too low' owing to the incompleteness of the sources. Famines could cause high death rates in the cities, and also in the countryside where, even in good times, peasants often lived barely above the subsistence level. When starvation was followed by disease, as often happened, mortality rose still further.[3]

Finally, the activities of agriculturists themselves might in the long term damage agriculture. Over-cultivation could deplete soils of their fertility; over-irrigation could lower water tables or lead to salinisation of soil, especially in Iraq; and over-grazing degraded the vegetation of pasture lands, often leaving little that animals would eat. Furthermore, over-cultivation, over-grazing and deforestation left land more vulnerable to erosion by rainfall, winds and floods, and in not a few places the soil cover on which agriculture depended was lost. Whether these human activities also caused climate

3 Michael Dols, 'Famine in the Islamic world', in Joseph Strayer (ed.), *Dictionary of the Middle Ages*, 13 vols. (New York, 1982–9), vol. V, pp. 1–3.

changes affecting agriculture, or whether there was any change in climate for other reasons, are questions that cannot yet be answered.

In any case, these dependencies of agriculture – on urban dwellers, Bedouin, natural phenomena and the practices of farmers themselves – are responsible for short-term fluctuations in rural prosperity. And they are also in large measure responsible for the longer-term cycles of agricultural progress and decline.

Periodisation: ups and downs

In this necessarily very brief treatment of agricultural history over a vast expanse of the earth's surface and over a very long stretch of time it will not be possible to describe in detail, let alone attempt to explain, the long-term fluctuations in rural fortunes. Only the most cursory overview can be offered.

Once the disruptions caused by the Arab conquests were over, the early centuries of Islam were nearly everywhere a time of sustained agricultural progress, in which the area of sedentary agriculture expanded and the productivity of most categories of agricultural land and labour rose. Backed by policies of the Umayyad and ʿAbbāsid caliphates, local pastoralists and conquering Arabs in many regions were persuaded to become sedentary farmers. Thus, for instance, in several parts of Ifrīqiya and the Maghrib nomadic Berbers and other transhumant tribes began constructing huts to replace tents and cultivating fields at the expense of grazing. According to recently published archaeological evidence a large region in the central Euphrates Valley, which on the eve of Islam was virtually uninhabited, had 103 villages by the early ninth century.[4] In this process of sedentarisation the widespread construction of irrigation works – canals, embankments, weirs, dams, dykes, reservoirs, terraces and water-lifting machines – was often critical. These brought more water to more land over more months of the year, and quite often perennial irrigation was achieved. One outstanding example of many is the large-scale water-engineering projects undertaken by the governor of Iraq, al-Ḥajjāj ibn Yūsuf (d. 714) in the region of Wāsiṭ, which he founded. Similarly, Ziyād ibn Abīhi (d. 680), the governor of two other new cities, Baṣra and Kūfa, each surrounded by newly irrigated hinterlands, ordered the construction of two large canals connecting Baṣra with the Shaṭṭ al-ʿArab. Still other important irrigation and land-reclamation works in the Sawād were undertaken by private developers.

4 Sophie Berthier *et al.*, *Peuplement rural et aménagements hydroagricoles dans la moyenne vallée de l'Euphrate, fin VIIe–XIXe siècle* (Damascus, 2001), *passim*.

The new crops also played an important role. Some, such as sorghum and watermelons, were relatively drought-tolerant and thus encouraged the advance of agriculture into drier areas. Many other new crops were either permanent crops – such as citrus and banana trees – or were summer crops; both required heavy irrigation during the summer months and thus went hand-in-hand with progress in irrigation. Together, the traditional and new crops permitted new rotations in which land could be cropped two or more times a year without fallowing; the greater flexibility of rotations allowed farmers to take special advantage of micro-climates and local soils.

The gains in productivity achieved in these ways are bound up with general economic development, demographic growth and the spread of the money economy into the countryside. More particularly, they are linked, as both cause and effect, to the impressive rise of cities.

But in many places growth was not to last. As early as the ninth century, when agriculture was still prospering in most of the Islamic world, settlement retreated from the western fringes of the desert in the Ḥijāz, in Transjordania and in much of Syria. In the eastern part of this desert, along the middle Euphrates, there was a dramatic decline of settlement as many communities were abandoned. The causes of this early decline are obscure: possibly it is due to climate change, or perhaps settlement had pushed into regions where rainfall and river flows were too low and too variable for viable agriculture, or perhaps the slow decentralisation and decline of the powers of the caliphate left the government unable to protect sedentary agriculture in these regions. Whatever the explanation, the eleventh century saw new threats to agriculture, as nomadic invaders overran large areas in the eastern and western parts of the Islamic world. In the west, the Banū Hilāl, a nomadic people from northern Arabia, devastated agriculture in Cyrenaica and Tripolitania, and then, in 1052, moved on to Ifrīqiya and the western Maghrib, where they destroyed most inland settlements and forced a retreat of sedentary agriculture back to coastal regions; the littoral towns were obliged to turn to Sicily for a large part of their grain supplies. In the eastern part of the caliphate the Saljūq Turks, another nomadic people, established an empire based in Persia in 1040; after raiding Anatolia repeatedly in the early part of the century they fought the Byzantines, and won a decisive victory in 1071. This was followed by a massive movement into Anatolia of nomadic Turcomans, who were largely unsympathetic to sedentary agriculture. In the century that followed the frequent battles with Byzantines and Crusaders prevented agricultural recovery in most of Anatolia.

The subsequent history of the rural economy in the Islamic world is the tale of periods of recovery, and even advance, followed by further decay, in which regional variation became more evident. In general, agriculture continued to suffer from the successive waves of invaders who, with almost monotonous regularity, overran different parts of the Islamic world: the Crusaders, Ayyūbids, Mongols, Tīmūrids and Ottomans in the east, and the Almoravids and Almohads in the west. Like the Banū Hilāl and the Saljūqs, these later conquerors were mostly nomadic or semi-nomadic peoples, more familiar with grazing and extensive grain cultivation than with the intensive, irrigated agriculture that had developed so brilliantly in the early Islamic world. In the course of their conquests they often destroyed settlements and irrigation works, and their victories were usually followed by large-scale immigration of nomads into the conquered areas. The usually short-lived regimes they established often showed little interest in promoting agriculture. Particularly devastating were the conquests of the Mongols in thirteenth-century West Asia: these were followed by massive slaughters of city-dwellers and rural folk alike, neglect or destruction of irrigation works and widespread abandonment of cultivated land, triggering what I. P. Petrushevsky has called a 'colossal economic decline'.[5] Recovery was thwarted by the Black Death, which, through the second half of the fourteenth century, reduced population by perhaps one-third in territories formerly ruled by the Mongols (and indeed all over West Asia, North Africa and al-Andalus), making intensive agriculture, in most places, unnecessary and uneconomic.

To be sure, after the initial damage of the conquests some of the conquerors were able to create governments that were sufficiently strong and stable to support agriculture; and in fact the strength and stability of their governments depended in considerable measure on prosperity in the countryside. One such example is Spain under its Berber conquerors, the Almoravids and the Almohads, where not only did intensive agriculture flourish in many places but agricultural science was advanced on botanical gardens and experimental farms, and scholars wrote extensively on the emerging science of agriculture. Other examples are Egypt under the Baḥrī Mamlūks (1240–1382), Iran during the rule of Ghāzān Khān (1295–1304), Yemen in the time of the Rasūlid kings (early thirteenth century–1428), the Ottoman empire from 1470 until the end of the rule of Süleymān the Magnificent in 1566, and Iran during the reign of

5 I. P. Petrushevsky, 'The socio-economic condition of Iran under the Īl-Khāns', in *The Cambridge history of Iran*, 7 vols. in 8 (London and New York, 1968–91), vol. V; J. A. Boyle (ed.), *The Saljuq and Mongol periods*, p. 483.

Shāh ʿAbbās I (1571–1629). In general, these were periods when governments were sufficiently strong to provide the support needed by agriculture and sedentarisation of nomads was encouraged; they were also usually times when trade flourished and money supplies were relatively abundant, factors which may have contributed to the strength of governments. Agricultural revival in the early modern era may also have been fed by new crops arriving in the Islamic world following the voyages of discovery: from China came sweet oranges and from the New World were brought maize, potatoes, sweet potatoes, capsicum peppers, tomatoes, tobacco, New World cotton and haricot, runner and lima beans. Although maize (fed at first to animals and later to human beings) spread quickly through the early modern Islamic world, the other crops seem to have been diffused more slowly; they may nevertheless have given some new strength to agriculture, even in its periods of decay.

Recovery from invasions, regressive policies and epidemics grew increasingly difficult as new landholding and taxation arrangements became more widespread and more pernicious. The earliest of these was tax-farming. Adopted in the ʿAbbāsid caliphate in the ninth century, the delegation of tax collection to provincial governors allowed them to collect, and largely keep, the taxes from their jurisdictions. Collection in some regions was soon decentralised further as individuals were allowed to buy the taxation rights over smaller or larger areas of the provinces; rates of taxation tended to rise and become more arbitrary in such areas, and peasants had little recourse. The second of these harmful institutions was the *iqṭāʿ*, introduced by the Būyids and the Saljūqs in the eleventh century and widely adopted in later centuries. This was a benefice granted to high-ranking officers; in return for military service, the holder obtained the right to collect and retain taxes over considerable areas of agricultural land. Originally granted for a period of years or for a lifetime, the *iqṭāʿ* thus encouraged short-term maximisation of revenue with little reinvestment in land or irrigation works. In some regions it became hereditary and the holder began to assume 'feudal' rights over lands and people in his benefice, thus obscuring the locus of land ownership and sometimes extinguishing individual property rights. Finally, the institution of the *waqf* had further damaging effects on agricultural production. By the tenth century this had become a means of granting lands in perpetuity to charitable institutions, such as mosques, schools and caravanserais. Typically, the recipient had little agricultural knowledge and little interest in managing the lands received; and as an institution's endowments grew in size its holdings became increasingly scattered and difficult to supervise. Many *waqf* lands also escaped taxation. Because they were in principle inalienable, the progressive accumulation of such endowments was difficult to stop: by later Ottoman times it has been estimated that the dead hand of the *waqf* had touched three-quarters of the empire's agricultural land. Thus all three arrangements tended to undermine enlightened management of lands by peasants or owners; by eroding state revenues they also weakened the ability of the state to govern and hence to promote agriculture. As these institutions spread, further decline seemed inevitable. Recovery, when it occurred, was usually incomplete and often short-lived.

Indeed, from the early or mid-seventeenth century onwards the general trend was downwards: rural areas were slowly depopulated, trade faltered, and agricultural output and productivity fell. Only with the arrival of the colonial powers did matters change, but then the change did not always benefit peasants or landowners.

Trade

Probably the most powerful engine of agricultural progress was trade. It led to the specialisation of land use in those activities for which land was better suited. It also encouraged specialisation of the labour force, which thereby improved its skills. The pressure to increase productivity occurred not only on the lands shifted to commercial production but also on the reduced areas available for subsistence agriculture. Where these latter became insufficient for a community's needs, it would start buying part of its sustenance from other villages; these would then try to increase their productivity. If land or labour was scarce, the ripples could travel far.

It is probable that in the Islamic world, at all times and in all places, there were few rural communities that did not trade. In the panoply of types of agricultural undertakings described by Vincent Lagardère and outlined above, probably none was near to self-sufficiency. They all traded, most on a considerable scale; indeed, without trade they could not have survived, and the modes of agricultural production would have been very different and less productive. The *munya* and *janna* were clearly involved in production of fruits and vegetables for sale in urban markets, and their inhabitants must have bought meat, and probably grains, from elsewhere. The *raḥal* appears to have produced few or no large animals, and its inhabitants must have procured small amounts of meat – and perhaps wool, skins and milk products – from other estates. The *majshar* and other communities raising animals seem to have produced no crops at all, and must have obtained these from others.

Although the inhabitants of the *ḍayʿa* and the *qarya* may have been more self-sufficient than those on other types of undertakings, almost certainly they too depended, to varying degrees, on markets. Trade occurred not only at the rural markets described above, where settled communities could trade with one another and with Bedouin, but also at markets on the outskirts of towns, where agriculturists, Bedouin and city-dwellers could all exchange their products.

Specialisation of the rural labour force seems to have been carried further by the fact that household industries in the countryside – both usufacture and market-oriented industries – appear to have been negligible. While rural areas did have some non-household industries, such as mining, and considerable amounts of raw and spun silk were indeed produced in rural households, the overwhelming part of industrial production seems to have occurred in cities. As far as one can tell from the sources, even the production of textiles, pottery and baskets, as well as much of the processing of foods, was carried out mainly in urban workshops. Rural dwellers, therefore, seem to have depended on the cities for most of their tools, cloth, pots and much else. This division of industrial labour in turn put pressure on rural dwellers to produce still greater agricultural surpluses: in order to buy industrial products, in addition to a part of their food supplies, they had to sell more.

As cities grew in the period from 700 to 1100, sometimes reaching unprecedented sizes for their regions, rural specialisation increased. Thus in Ifrīqiya in the early eleventh century, the expanding hinterland of the capital, Qayrawān, encompassed what Claudette Vanacker has called a 'juxtaposition of specialised zones'. The region of Faḥṣ al-Darrāra sent grains and fruits to the capital; the lands between Qayrawān and Sfax produced olives; the area north of Gafsa specialised in animal production; the oasis of Tozeur exported northwards (according to al-Bakrī) a thousand camel-loads of dates almost every day; a number of areas sent saffron for the city's textile industry; and other localities provided pistachios, figs, silk cocoons and flowers. These and other specialisations were held in place by the ability of the zones to trade with one another and with the capital.[6]

Some regions of agricultural specialisation traded not only with nearby cities but with more distant markets. Where conditions permitted, such longer-distance trade could lead to much larger areas of agricultural land

6 Claudette Vanacker, 'Géographie économique de l'Afrique du Nord selon les auteurs arabes, du XIe siècle au milieu du XIIe siècle', *Annales: Économies, Sociétés, Civilisations*, 28 (1973).

being given over to near monoculture. Thus, for instance, although cotton was grown widely over almost all the Islamic world from 800 onwards, certain zones of intense specialisation appeared: a wide stretch of land in the highlands of Syria reaching from Aleppo south to Ḥamā; a southern extension of this zone around the lake of al-Ḥūla, where 200 villages were said to be given over to cotton production; the lower Tigris and its dependent canals around Baṣra; and the area in the upper Euphrates Valley around Nahr Ḥabūr. Equally concentrated production of sugar cane could be found from the tenth century onwards in the Sind, in Khūzistān, on much of the Levantine coastal plain, in the Jordan Valley, along the Nile and in its Delta, and in the Sūs in southern Morocco. The cotton and sugar produced in these regions were exported in many directions, sometimes to very distant markets. As trans-Mediterranean trade opened up from 1100 onwards, cotton bought by European merchants in the eastern Mediterranean supplied a growing textile industry in northern Italy and later in Germany; and sugar of various types began appearing in Barcelona, Marseilles and the northern Italian cities, whence some of it made its way to markets in north-western Europe.

Whether the specialisation in land use induced by such extensive trade led to changes in the mode of production is not clear from the sources, which have little to say on the subject. It seems, however, that large and small units, using family, tenant and wage labour, could all successfully compete in the production of speciality crops for sale. Quite possibly, in the absence of agricultural slaves and colonial overlords, there were no economies of scale to be derived from large-scale production of the plantation type. We do learn, however, that in fourteenth-century Egypt the Banū Fuḍayl family planted 2500 *feddans* of sugar cane every year. In both Egypt and Syria Mamlūk *amīrs*, viziers, princes and even sultans were deeply involved in the production of sugar cane on their estates. As they paid little or nothing in taxes they had an advantage over other producers, whom they partially displaced; and on the sultan's estates this advantage was increased as tenants became liable to corvée on lands he exploited directly. Mamlūk producers came to exercise greater control over the industry through vertical integration: many acquired their own sugar presses and refineries. Carrying this process one stage further, the Sultan Barsbāy (1422–38) attempted to establish a state monopoly over both the production of cane and the manufacture of sugar. Perhaps indeed we can see here the beginnings of a plantation mode of production.

While incorporation into the emerging world economy undoubtedly increased incomes from agricultural activities, these gains came at a price. Not only were the rewards unevenly distributed, so that the returns to labour in some cases hardly changed, or even fell, but dependence on overseas markets also created new vulnerabilities for peasants, landowners and merchants. All found themselves at the mercy of events in distant places over which they and their rulers had no control: trade cycles, wars, changes in taste and competition from other sources of supply could all adversely affect markets and prices, and sometimes markets simply dried up. In the fifteenth century the Spanish and Portuguese introduced sugar cane into the islands of Madeira, the Canaries, Santiago and São Tomé; and by the sixteenth sugar from these islands was flooding onto European and Arab markets. By then, too, the voyages of discovery had opened sea routes to continents with vast tropical and semi-tropical regions, where sugar cane, rice, cotton, bananas and other crops of tropical origin could be grown more cheaply. By the end of the seventeenth century these crops had largely disappeared from the Mediterranean basin, where they had once been so important, as well as from some parts of West Asia. In the eighteenth century the British shifted their source of raw silk from Iran to India. By the end of that century coffee production – long the exclusive domain of Yemen – had spread to India, South-East Asia, the Indonesian archipelago and Central and South America.

Where European trading companies still sought agricultural products from Islamic regions, as they did from Islamic parts of West Africa, India, South-East Asia and the Indonesian archipelago, there was every danger that they would try to maximise profits by monopolising first the export and then the production of the goods: they could then buy more cheaply and sell at higher prices, thus capturing monopoly profits from both production and trade. To establish and enforce their monopolies they usually found that political control was needed, and regions exporting key agricultural products to Europe became prime targets for colonial rule.

Thus, in the early modern period, as the world economy tightened, agriculturists in many parts of the Islamic world had a foretaste of new vulnerabilities. In the nineteenth and early twentieth centuries there was worse to come.

10

Demography and migration

SURAIYA N. FAROQHI

Estimating medieval population figures

A number of suggestions have been made for estimating urban populations for periods from which no direct data are extant, some being more convincing than others. Thus it is problematic to assume that the floor space of a given city's principal mosque indicates the size of the relevant settlement, or at least of its adult male population, unless a written source tells us that such a relationship did in fact exist. Patrons may well have financed a huge building due to considerations of 'magnificence' or political rivalry, or else they may have wished to provide for villagers who came to the city on market days and attended communal prayers on this occasion. None of these considerations was connected to the actual number of inhabitants. Another measure of pre-modern urban populations, namely the quantities of grain needed to feed a given city, can only convey a very rough notion: rich people may have fed grain to their animals, thus augmenting the demand, or else others may have had supplementary sources of food in their gardens and thus needed less than the statistical minimum of grain required to keep body and soul together. But even so, where information on grain consumption is available it does provide an idea of urban population size.

As to the number of public baths (*ḥammāms*) in a good-sized city, which has also been suggested as a measure of population, it is probably a better criterion; for baths were supposed to make money, and thus probably were built only if the owners anticipated an appreciable number of customers. But the construction of such facilities indicates merely the geographical expansion of the city; certainly this latter feature will often, but by no means always, be consonant with population growth. Something similar can be said about the progressive removal of tanneries away from the city centre, also cited as a sign of urban growth: due to the smells the latter tended to give off, it is indeed probable that they were moved as soon as houses appeared in the vicinity. But once again we do not know for sure whether the expansion of the built-up area involved an increase of the urban population, or whether it was only a concomitant of lower habitation densities.

A similar argument can be made in the case of new pious foundations such as mosques and dervish lodges, whose dissemination has been observed and analysed, among other places, in Ottoman Arab cities such as Aleppo, Damascus and Cairo.[1] After all, new mosques and other buildings may have been constructed on the urban perimeter because land was cheaper there than in the centre of the city, while the connection to population increase could once again have been quite tenuous. Or else the city centre already contained numerous pious foundations, so that additional land was simply not available at any cost. We can also assume that sometimes new immigrants arriving, for instance, after a major epidemic wanted or were obliged to live apart from the established population: in this case they might sponsor new pious foundations even though the total number of urbanites did not substantially increase.

But on the other hand, there is not much sense in quibbling and hyper-criticism: especially if several phenomena of the kind described here coincided, there is a strong case for assuming that urban population really did increase. Admittedly all these methods of estimation only apply to towns, while rural populations of the pre-Ottoman period remain almost completely unknown.

Attempts to trace the broad outlines of population growth in the pre-Ottoman centuries of Middle Eastern history can therefore only involve the direction of change. We can discern losses due to the Black Death and other pandemics, or else gains in a given town or region due to substantial immigration. By contrast, any attempt to establish absolute numbers, incidentally one of the major aims of historical demography, has led to estimates so divergent that – at least in the eyes of the present author – they are best ignored.[2] Even more problematic, or so it seems to me, are estimations of trends based not on conclusions derived from primary written sources or archaeological observations but rather from assumptions connected with the world-view of a particular historian. One of the best-known cases of this type is the belief that the population of Egypt and Syria, at one time prosperous core provinces of the Roman empire, declined constantly until about the thirteenth/nineteenth century.[3] Judgements based on overall considerations of this kind may at first glance seem to a have a higher scientific status due to

1 André Raymond, *Grandes villes arabes à l'époque ottomane* (Paris, 1985), pp. 206–14.
2 Bassim Musallam, *Sex and society in Islam* (Cambridge, 1983), pp. 111–12.
3 Ibid., p. 110.

the generality inherent in them; yet such reasoning can also lower the status of countervailing empirical evidence, and thus lead us badly astray.

There is no doubt that population plummeted during certain periods throughout the entire Mediterranean world; this applied particularly to the later 700s/1300s and the entire ninth/fifteenth century, when the plague was at its most virulent. But that the same trend continued unabated in the tenth/sixteenth century and beyond should, at the very least, be considered 'not proven'. Even the claims of contemporaries that the 'decline of the times' involved – among other matters – a decreasing population are not always to be taken at face value: even in early modern Europe it was often and quite mistakenly claimed that the population of the period was smaller than that of Roman times. By contrast, some indirect evidence has been unearthed indicating that in Egypt during the later tenth/sixteenth century population may in fact have picked up again. Thus sugar cultivation, which had been given up in the ninth/fifteenth century, probably because the labour force had become too small, revived somewhat during the late 900s/1500s and early 1000s/1600s.[4]

Whether the interventions of men and women had an impact upon population size is also difficult to ascertain. Many Muslim jurists were willing to tolerate birth control, albeit in certain cases with reluctance, provided that the family lived in straitened circumstances and the man first gained the consent of his wife. Moreover, fairly accurate information on the relevant techniques was available not only in specialised treatises, accessible only to a limited number of specialist scholars, but also in legal texts studied by a much larger number of readers. We may assume that during times of crisis birth control was practised by a certain number of couples at least in the towns of Syria and Egypt, from where most of the literature on contraception apparently originated. But once again we have no numeric data at our disposal; and a great deal of caution is required when drawing inferences from purely qualitative information.

Migrations: Arabs in the Mashriq and in Spain, Berbers in al-Andalus[5]

While our sources contain plenty of evidence concerning migrations that occurred throughout the first/seventh to ninth/fifteenth centuries, this information is almost never quantitative; moreover, the few figures recorded in

4 Nelly Hanna, *Making big money in 1600: The life and times of Isma'il Abu Taqiyya, Egyptian merchant* (Syracuse, 1998), pp. 90–1.

5 The term Mashriq stands for Syria, Egypt and Iraq, and Maghrib for North Africa to the west of Egypt. The Muslim regions of Spain and Portugal are described by the term al-Andalus.

chronicles should be regarded with extreme caution. The Arab conquests immediately following the acceptance of Islam, by both sedentary people and nomads originally inhabiting the Ḥijāz, resulted in far-flung migrations. However, the conquests themselves were made by more or less professional armies, and not by entire tribes on the march; immigration by the nomads' families normally took place after military action had been completed. While on campaign fighters from the same tribe were typically grouped together. Yet the leaders from this milieu commanding their fellow tribesmen occupied rather lowly places in the military hierarchy, higher-echelon commanders typically being chosen from among the urban population. As a result it was difficult for tribal leaders to break away from the Muslim army on the occasion of some dispute or other, and the early Islamic conquests should not be viewed as tribal actions.[6]

On the contrary, the early caliphs evidently regarded settlement and the abandonment of a nomadic lifestyle as a guarantee of loyalty to the cause of Islam, and established the Bedouin who had immigrated into Iraq after the Muslim conquest in army camps that soon mutated into cities. While the same policy was also applied in Syria it was of less importance there because many tribesmen preferred to settle in the numerous towns and cities that had flourished in this area since Antiquity and through early Byzantine times. A major aim of founding new camp-towns such Kūfa, Baṣra or Ramla must have been the control of the former Byzantine and Sasanid subjects living in these areas. But in addition, the settling of many former nomads in urban settings was probably intended as a means of controlling those tribes that as desert-dwellers were considered especially prone to rebellion.[7]

Other groups of Arabs settled along the Mediterranean coasts of North Africa and passed on into Spain, Arab troops entering the Visigoth kingdom in 92/711. In the following two years the country was rapidly conquered as far as Saragossa and Toledo. Barcelona and Narbonne in today's Mediterranean France soon followed suit, and in 114/732 an Arab expedition was defeated on the banks of the Loire, near Tours and Poitiers, by Charles Martel, the grandfather of Charlemagne. By 185/801, when the latter's son Louis conquered Catalonia, the Umayyad caliphate of the west (138–422/756–1031) controlled virtually the entire Peninsula.[8]

6 Fred McGraw Donner, *The early Islamic conquests* (Princeton, 1981), pp. 221–2.
7 Ibid., pp. 262–7.
8 E. Lévi-Provençal, 'al-Andalus', *EI2*, vol. I; Charles Julian Bishko, 'The Spanish and Portuguese reconquest', in Kenneth Setton (gen. ed.), *A history of the Crusades* (Madison, 1969–89), vol. III: Harry Hazard (ed.), *The fourteenth and fifteenth centuries*.

The Islamic conquest led to the immigration into what is today Spain and Portugal of both Berbers from western North Africa (Maghrib) and of Arabs who themselves had arrived in the Maghrib only a few generations earlier. However the bulk of Spanish Muslims probably were descended from converts, although throughout the Islamic period it was a source of pride if a family could point to Arab ancestry. Bilingualism in Arabic and the locally spoken Romance languages was common. However, the Berbers, once established in al-Andalus, soon were Arabised linguistically. Berber immigration occurred not only during the original conquest but also as a result of successive takeovers on the part of Berber dynasties during the fifth/eleventh and sixth/twelfth centuries; for the Almoravids and Almohads, as they are known in Western historiography, brought along their own mercenaries. In addition, slave traders supplied wealthy households with black people from Africa, and also the so-called Ṣaqāliba, who were of Slavic or Germanic background. By 390/1000 these different ethnic groups had organised themselves politically; and when the Umayyad caliphate entered a period of crisis during that very period, the ethno-political factions of Andalusians, Berbers and Ṣaqāliba set up a multitude of small states that lasted until the Almoravid takeover of the late fifth/eleventh century.

In the Middle Ages, when the Peninsula was also home to a substantial Jewish population, it was generally assumed that Catholic rulers might have Muslim and Jewish subjects. However, in 897/1492, with the fall of Naṣrid Granada to Isabella and Ferdinand, the rulers of Castile and Aragon, this policy changed radically. Jews and Muslims were now required to accept baptism if they wished to remain. Moreover, the activities of the Inquisition, which, through an elaborate apparatus of spies, attempted to find out whether the recently baptised secretly adhered to their former religions, made life extremely difficult and dangerous for ex-Muslims and former Jews. As a result Jewish refugees, either directly or by detours, made their way to the Ottoman empire, where the sultans settled them in the capital and particularly in Salonika. Muslim communities with a Christian veneer (Moriscos) continued to exist in Spain throughout the tenth/sixteenth century, although there was much piecemeal emigration to North Africa, particularly after a failed uprising in the region of Granada (976–7/1568–70). Moreover, probably around 300,000 people became refugees when all Moriscos were driven out of Spain between 1018/1609 and 1023/1614.[9]

9 Antonio Dominguez Ortiz and Bernard Vincent, *Historia de los Moriscos: Vida y tragedia de una minoría* (Madrid, 1978), pp. 17–35; Mercedes Garcia Arenal, *La diaspora des Andalousiens* (Paris, 2003).

In North Africa: the mass migrations of the Banū Hilāl

Throughout the history of al-Andalus, nomads were never of any significance. But they did migrate into North Africa on a large enough scale that regions in which Berber languages had previously been spoken were largely Arabised. At the same time nomadism was diffused, especially in Ifrīqiya. This process has been described by the historian Ibn Khaldūn (732–808/1332–1406), who had been born in Tunis and educated there; he thus knew the affected areas at first hand. According to Ibn Khaldūn, in the mid-fifth/eleventh century the ʿAbbāsid caliph in Baghdad had been recognised by a ruler governing the central part of North Africa, and this move resulted in an act of revenge by the ʿAbbāsid's major rival, the Fāṭimid caliph of Egypt al-Mustanṣir. The latter sent the tribesmen known as the Banū Hilāl, who up to this time had been nomadising in Upper Egypt and causing trouble to his own government, to the territories west of the Nile, where the immigrants appropriated resources for themselves and their half-starved families by pillaging the countryside and finally also the towns. The major city of Qayrawān was taken and plundered (449/1057). The Banū Hilāl retained a dominant position for about a century, until the arrival of the Almohads in the mid-500s/1100s, when the tribesmen were forced to pay allegiance to these sultans, who had their centre in Morocco; the latter attempted to neutralise the nomads by incorporating them into their own armies. Yet an attempt to transplant the Banū Hilāl to Spain, where they were to have fought the Christian princes, was thwarted by the resistance of the tribesmen themselves. It has been assumed that the Bedouin of the Maghrib are for the most part descendants of the Banū Hilāl.[10]

Turkish migrants

Another major consequence of caliphal rule was the entry of Turks into the Middle East, and also into India. Both nomads and sedentary people, Turkish inhabitants of Central Asia first encountered Islam during the Arab conquest of Transoxania, and especially following the battle of Talas (133/751); this spate of warfare first brought Arab settlers into the region, and may have prevented a rival Chinese takeover. But the massive entry of Turks into the Islamic world was due to the recruitment of slave-soldiers (*mamlūks*) and also of free

10 H. R. Idris, '[Banū] Hilāl', *EI2*, vol. III, p. 385; Xavier de Planhol, *Les fondements géographiques de l'histoire de l'Islam* (Paris, 1968), pp. 140–62.

mercenaries into the caliphs' armies during the third/ninth and fourth/tenth centuries; some of these men came from the Khazar principality to the north of the Caucasus, whose rulers had converted to Judaism.[11] Mercenaries were paid by assigning them the right to collect taxes in a given place (*iqṭāʿ*); for their special benefit these grants, previously revocable at the ruler's will, became hereditary concessions of the usufruct of important stretches of land. Although even under the new dispensation the caliphs in principle retained the right of confiscation and redistribution, exercising it in practice might induce the mercenaries, now in a position of power, to rebel and even to murder the ruler who had thus offended them.

Turkish mercenaries and slave guards became even more widespread as the example of the ʿAbbāsid caliphs was followed by more localised dynasties such as the Sāmānids, who ruled much of Iran in the fourth/tenth century. Other commanders of Turkish background who transformed military command into political power included Aḥmad ibn Ṭūlūn, who made himself ruler of Egypt. Moreover, the Ghaznavid dynasty, which formed the most important polity after the decline of ʿAbbāsid power, was inaugurated in the late 300s/900s by a Turkish military slave named Sebüktegin. While its centre was located in what is today Afghanistan, the empire founded by Sebüktegin and expanded by his son Maḥmūd extended far into India, and thus Ghaznavid rule first brought Turks into the subcontinent.

Moreover, once, in the fifth/eleventh century, Turkish military men were established at the core of most Middle Eastern states, it became possible for compact tribes to enter the region from Central Asia, without the previous acculturation that most soldiers had gone through before they could obtain positions of power. The resulting cultural conflict had political repercussions: thus certain Turkish tribesmen considered that the succession to the sultanate should go to the oldest living member of the dynasty (seniorate) and not to a crown prince the previous ruler had designated during his lifetime, as inherent in the Iranian tradition of absolute rule that, for instance, the Ghaznavids had adopted. The immigration of such unassimilated tribes into an Islamic empire could thus become a source of major instability.

Differences of opinion between the officials of settled government and recently arrived tribesmen became politically relevant once the latter were sufficiently numerous for a given ruler to try to use them as his power base.

11 C. E. Bosworth, 'Barbarian incursions: The coming of the Turks into the Islamic world', in D. S. Richards (ed.), *Islamic civilisation 950–1150: A colloquium published under the auspices of the Near Eastern History Group Oxford* (Oxford, 1973).

Moreover, new immigrants from Central Asia frequently replaced those earlier arrivals that had already adapted to the political structures of the Islamic Middle East. Thus the Great Saljūq dynasty, which governed the central Islamic lands in the fifth/eleventh and sixth/twelfth centuries, faced the same problem as the Ghaznavids had done before them: the sultans had to figure out a way of reconciling the political assumptions of their tribal backers with Islamic and Iranian traditions of settled rule. In this case the challenge was particularly urgent. Tribal protest on the part of the Ghuzz/Oğuz, who had migrated into Iran in large numbers, in 548/1153–6 led to the capture of Sultan Sanjar, the last major representative of the Great Saljūq dynasty, and also to the terrible sack of Nīshāpūr and the demise of Sanjar's empire.

However, a secondary branch of the defunct dynasty continued to play an important role. Because it was established in previously Byzantine Anatolia, where it flourished during the sixth/twelfth and early seventh/thirteenth centuries, its representatives were known as the Saljūq sultans of Rūm. After the emperor Romanos Diogenes had been defeated by the Great Saljūq ruler Alp Arslān near the eastern Anatolian town of Malazgırt (463/1071) state formation in Anatolia and concomitant Turkish settlement followed rapidly. While there had been substantial incursions into Byzantine territory even before this event, Turkish immigration now became a mass phenomenon, first in the aftermath of Malazgırt and a century later, following the equally serious Byzantine defeat at Myriokephalon (572/1176). Raids and counter-raids were undertaken by both sides in large numbers. During the late fifth/eleventh and throughout the sixth/twelfth century, the Comnene emperors built and repaired numerous Anatolian forts in order to consolidate the territories they had – more or less briefly – regained. However, it is not so clear how many of these fortified places were indeed inhabited over lengthy periods of time.[12] Further Turkish settlement occurred after 659/1261, when Constantinople had been regained from the occupying Crusaders (600–59/1204–61) and Anatolia was no longer at the centre of Byzantine preoccupations.

Most of the newly arriving Turks were probably Muslims by the time they came to Anatolia, although remnants of nature cults lingered on for quite a while. Fully trained religious scholars being rare among the nomads, the latter relied on 'fathers' (*bābās*) who from the viewpoint of formally schooled Muslims might appear somewhat heterodox. But there were exceptions.

12 Clive Foss, 'The defenses of Asia Minor against the Turks', repr. in Clive Foss, *Cities, fortresses and villages of Asia Minor* (Aldershot, 1996), V.

Thus apparently the Gagauz, Orthodox in religion and today a Turkish ethnic minority in Romania and Ukraine, have taken their name from a Saljūq prince named Kay Kāvūs, who went over to the Byzantines and was sent north with his followers to the borderlands of what was, at the time, still imperial territory.[13]

As so many immigrants into Anatolia were nomads the Saljūq administration was concerned about the political threat that they might pose, and therefore also dispatched them to distant places – in other words, to the Byzantine frontier. But an urban element was also present: Islamic scholars from as far afield as today's Afghanistan felt the attraction of the Rūm Saljūq establishment in Konya, an important centre of courtly and religious culture. Thus the famous mystical poet Mawlānā Jalāl al-Dīn Rūmī, who later was to give his name to the Mawlawī order of dervishes, arrived from Balkh along with his father, a well-known scholar. A son-in-law of Ibn al-ʿArabī (560–638/1165–1240), the famous mystic of Spanish origin, also resided in Konya and gathered adherents for his master. Other Anatolian towns that Saljūq rulers developed through sometimes spectacular pious foundations included Sıvas and Kayseri; communications and thus the arrival of foreign traders in the sultan's domains were facilitated by the construction of numerous caravanserais. Nor did the closely connected processes of Turkish immigration and Islamisation come to an end when the Saljūqs of Rūm were defeated by the Mongols in the mid-seventh/thirteenth century. The Christian population of Anatolia appears to have converted to Islam in fairly large numbers from the sixth/twelfth century onwards; this process was largely completed by the time the first surviving Ottoman records were prepared in the middle of the ninth/fifteenth century.[14]

Mamlūks in Egypt and Syria

As we have seen, Islamic rulers from Spain to northern India often used military slaves in large numbers; this kind of recruitment always involved immigration, usually over long distances, as the enslavement of subjects of a Muslim ruler was forbidden by religious law. Wherever this system flourished it was not rare for a successful freedman commander of soldiers to make himself ruler. But what was remarkable about the regime of the Mamlūks in

13 Speros Vryonis, *The decline of medieval Hellenism in Asia Minor and the process of Islamization from the eleventh through the fifteenth century* (Berkeley, Los Angeles and London, 1971), p. 192.
14 Ibid., pp. 383–91.

Egypt and Syria (*c.* 648–922/1250–1517) was the fact that the typical succession was not from father to son. Rather, the most active and long-lived sultans were former military slaves who had won support among the principal Mamlūks.

As young men sold to a well-established and often powerful personage (*amīr, beg*) the Mamlūks lived in the households of their owners or else, particularly if they belonged to the reigning sultan, in barracks. There they were inducted into Islam and learned the military arts; those with linguistic talent also studied Arabic. After manumission an ambitious warrior might himself gather a household by raising slave boys as soldiers and ultimately enter the competition for the sultanate.

For its perpetuation this system depended on a steady stream of military slaves, in this instance from north of the Black Sea and the Caucasus region. In spite of papal prohibitions Genoese dealers played a crucial role in this trade. Demand was increased by the fact that the newcomers were accustomed to colder climates and often succumbed to infections against which they had not gained any immunity: losses due to the factional struggles inherent in this system also must have taken their toll. Ethnically these slaves were quite diverse, but they adopted Turkish as their lingua franca and throughout the existence of the Mamlūk sultanate used Turkish personal names; in addition, dignitaries were distinguished by Arabic titles.

Although high achievers in horsemanship, the Mamlūks did not build a navy or place any great emphasis on the deployment of firearms; this weakness – among other matters – allowed the Ottoman ruler Selīm I (r. 918–26/1512–20) to overthrow the sultan of Egypt and Syria in a single campaign (922–3/1516–17). Under Ottoman rule Mamlūks disappeared from Syria. However, military slaves continued to be imported into Egypt throughout the period under consideration and from the same regions as before, but now through the agency of Ottoman slave traders. Marrying either women from their own milieu or else Egyptians, the new arrivals formed a ruling group that developed institutions of dominance so different from their medieval predecessors that specialists nowadays play down the continuities between 'independent' and 'Ottoman' Mamlūk regimes.[15]

Certain commanders built elaborate households that competed for power on the local level, and while an independent sultanate was no longer an option, the most successful heads of such units obtained key positions in

15 David Ayalon, 'Studies in al-Jabarti I: Notes on the transformation of Mamluk society in Egypt under the Ottomans', *JESHO*, 3 (1960); Jane Hathaway, *The politics of households in Ottoman Egypt: The rise of the Qazdağlıs* (Cambridge, 1997).

local administration as well as in the military. By the late twelfth/eighteenth century Mamlūk heads of households, by using their newly acquired military slaves, had penetrated and ultimately evicted the Ottoman garrison troops, which originally had been stationed in Egypt in order to control them. By the same token, the ties of powerful twelfth/eighteenth-century *begs* to their overlords in Istanbul had worn rather thin. In the long run the Mamlūk system in its different avatars led to a substantial immigration of Circassians and other people from north of the Black Sea into Egypt.

The Mongol invasions

From the population historian's point of view, however, the migrations with the most dramatic consequences were doubtless those of the Mongols and other soldiers incorporated into the armies of the latter, who were often of Turkish ethnicity. For previous immigrants, even if they plundered and destroyed cities, as the Ghuzz had done in Nīshāpūr (548/1153), ultimately were prepared to collect taxes from town and countryside and govern with the help of established urban elites.[16] However, this was not true of the Mongols, at least not of the first wave that overran the Middle East – apart from Egypt – during the seventh/thirteenth century. Mongol troops were virtually invincible due to their superior discipline and coordination; to maintain this advantage, their leaders did not hesitate to engage in methodical mass murder on a scale not previously seen in Middle Eastern warfare. The aim was to strike terror into the hearts of potential opponents, eliminate alternative elites and in some cases also free land for the extensive breeding of livestock. The figures of the dead and enslaved relayed in contemporary chronicles may not be overly reliable. But as both partisans and opponents of the Mongols insisted on the enormous scale of bloodshed the reality of such methodical killing, which incidentally also was practised during the Mongol conquest of China, is not itself in doubt.[17]

Moreover, when entering Iran in the 620s/1220s these pastoralists and their commanders apparently regarded the elaborate underground irrigation systems (*qanāts*) that were a precondition for agriculture in this arid territory as a needless impediment to the pastoral life. In the first decades of Mongol

16 Carl F. Petry, *The civilian elite of Cairo in the later Middle Ages* (Princeton, 1981), pp. 61–2; Richard Bulliet, *The patricians of Nishapur* (Cambridge, MA, 1972), pp. 76–9.

17 I. P. Petrushevsky, 'The socio-economic condition of Iran under the Īl-khāns', in J. A. Boyle (ed.), *The Cambridge history of Iran*, vol. V: *The Saljuq and Mongol periods* (Cambridge, 1968).

(Ilkhānid) domination in Iran the underground water channels were often destroyed. Attempts on the part of Ghāzān Khān (r. 695–704/1295–1304) and his vizier, the historian and patron of scholars Rashīd al-Dīn, to reverse this policy and give – limited – protection to the taxpaying peasantry were only moderately successful. For by this time petty provincial bosses, even though they owed their positions to the Mongols, were often refractory to directions from the centre. Agricultural recovery was also impeded by the fact that taxes came to be completely unpredictable; it was common for the same tax to be demanded more than once a year, or for several years in advance. Peasants in Iran were regarded as serfs and considered bound to the soil; but the extreme conditions under which they were forced to live resulted in both flight and localised rebellions suppressed with much bloodshed. As a result even Ghāzān Khān and Rashīd al-Dīn were not able to increase rural revenues to a level even approximating that of the years before 617/1220.

The conquests of Tīmūr (*c.* 736–807/1336–1405) took place in a different socio-political context: while he apparently aimed at resurrecting the Mongol empire, this ruler was soon convinced that steppe territories brought in less income than agricultural lands and cities. In Tīmūr's own territories there was thus no attempt to eliminate the settled population, although at least in Iran the irregularity and brutality of rural taxation once again resulted in major setbacks. But in areas belonging to his opponents Tīmūr used methods that resembled those of his seventh/thirteenth-century Chinggisid predecessors, including the systematic devastation of the Don–Volga region, the sack of Delhi and, albeit on a more limited scale, that of the Ottoman town of Sıvas.[18]

Small-scale but significant: the migrations of specialists

In spite of great differences between city-dwellers, villagers and nomads, between languages both spoken and written, between ordinary servants, military slaves and free men, between royal courts and urban quarters, Islamic civilisation had certain common traits that bound together regions as diverse as northern India and Spain. Several factors favoured unity, but in the present context what counts are the migrations of traders, artists, literary men and religious scholars.

The activities of merchants trading over long distances out of Egypt during the fifth/eleventh and sixth/twelfth centuries are relatively well documented

18 Beatrice Manz, *The rise and rule of Tamerlane* (Cambridge, 1989).

due to the papers found in the Cairo Geniza.[19] These texts were written by Jews and thus highlight the activities of Jewish merchants. But partnerships between Muslims and Jews were common enough to permit the conclusion that many of the activities documented in the Geniza were also undertaken by Muslims. We thus find traders who travelled with their goods and sedentary merchants who entrusted their wares to others: given the frequent cooperation between Muslims and Jews, the relevant contracts were mostly concluded according to Islamic law. Merchants who left some of their records in the Cairo Geniza occasionally travelled to Byzantium, the Italian ports or Marseilles; but normally they circulated within the Islamic world. Before the 440s/1050s – that is, roughly before the disruptions connected with the invasion of the Banū Hilāl – Tunisia and Sicily formed the hub of Mediterranean trade; from here trans-shipment to Spain usually took place. Numerous boat connections also linked Egypt to Syrian ports; caravans criss-crossed Africa north of the Sahara.

In addition there was the trade through the Red Sea and the Indian Ocean, which was to remain a mainstay of Cairo's merchants well into the twelfth/eighteenth century.[20] For throughout the long period covered by this chapter, Cairo was a major entrepôt for South Asian goods: merchants travelling to India typically returned to this city and there sold their goods to traders arriving from the entire Mediterranean region. Some of the Cairo merchants engaged in the Indian trade might form such close links to the subcontinent that they even acquired workshops in the latter location. Moreover, in the Fāṭimid period there emerged a coterie of ship-owners, first known as al-Kārim, who minimised the risks inherent in Red Sea traffic by sailing in convoy. In the Mamlūk period this group, now known as Kārimī, mutated into a conglomerate of potent merchant families closely linked by intermarriage, who down to the early 800s/1400s all but monopolised trade with India.

Contacts with China were more intermittent; yet the Moroccan world traveller Ibn Baṭṭūṭa (703–70/1304–68 or 779/1377) states that he encountered flourishing Muslim communities on the Chinese coast.[21] The first traders from

19 S. D. Goitein, *A Mediterranean society: The Jewish communities of the Arab world as portrayed in the documents of the Cairo Geniza*, 6 vols. (Berkeley and Los Angeles, 1967–93), vol. I: *Economic foundations* (Berkeley, 1967), pp. 70–4, 148–61, 209–14.

20 S. D. Goitein, 'Letters and documents on the India trade in medieval times' and 'The beginnings of the Karim merchants and the nature of their organization', both in S. D. Goitein, *Studies in Islamic history and institutions* (Leiden, 1966).

21 Ross Dunn, *The adventures of Ibn Battuta: A Muslim traveler of the 14th century* (Berkeley and Los Angeles, 1986), pp. 241–65. Whether Ibn Baṭṭūṭa actually visited China or collected his information elsewhere is not of any great relevance in our context.

the Islamic world had already reached China in the second/eighth century; and between the fourth/tenth and seventh/thirteenth centuries emperors of the Sung dynasty encouraged both the trade of indigenous Chinese with India and the settlement of foreign Muslims in their domains. Moreover, Chinese engaged in international trade often converted to Islam. Once the Mongols had taken over the Sung empire they continued these policies if anything more energetically; the advantages of Islamic traders only ended with the Ming dynasty's takeover after 769/1368. At the time of Ibn Baṭṭūṭa's visit Muslim trading communities, which might or might not contain immigrants, could be found in many inland cities of China as well.

Artists were another group whose members travelled widely and often settled in places far from the localities where they had been born. Our information concerns mainly painters of miniatures, as from the ninth/fifteenth century onwards it was common to record the names and places of origin of the masters who had illustrated a given volume. Miniature painting often being a courtly art, painters might not find employment in their places of residence once a given patron had died or was no longer in a position to sponsor them.[22] Conversely, if a centre of miniature painting was captured by an invader the new ruler might carry off the artists he found on site to continue their work in his own capital. Thus the Ottoman sultan Selīm I brought a number of masters from Tabrīz to Istanbul, after he had occupied the former residence of his defeated rival Shāh Ismāʿīl I (r. 907–30/1501–24). Registers of court artists still recorded the presence of the Iranians and that of their descendants quite a few years after the sultan's death.[23] Yet only a few years earlier, after the Tīmūrid regime of Ḥusayn Bāyqarā had been overthrown by the Uzbeks, quite a few painters had sought refuge at the court of the young Shāh Ismāʿīl I. It is thus quite possible that some of these artists were obliged to travel the enormous distance, overland, from Herat to Istanbul.

But the greatest patrons of miniature painting were the Indian courts, first in the sultanate of Delhi and from the tenth/sixteenth century onwards the Mughal emperors. In the Indian context paintings in books were also sponsored with relative frequency by non-royal patrons. This created opportunities for artists from Iran, who either travelled themselves or else received Indian students who thus visited the Ṣafavid empire for lengthy periods of time. Where the imperial court was concerned, Humāyūn (r., with an interruption,

22 Norah M. Titley, *Persian miniature painting and its influence on the art of Turkey and India: The British Library collections* (Austin, 1983–4).
23 İsmail Hakkı Uzunçarşılı, 'Osmanlı sarayında Ehl-i Hiref (Sanatkârlar) Defteri', *Belgeler*, 11, 15 (1986).

937–63/1530–56), son of the Mughal conqueror Bābur, encouraged Iranian artists, whose work he had come to admire when as a political exile he spent time at the court of the shah. By contrast, a ninth/fifteenth-century ruler of Kashmir sent artists and artisans to Iran for the completion of their training.[24]

Among the men of religion, some Sufis were great travellers, including Ibn al-ʿArabī, who spent his life criss-crossing al-Andalus, Morocco, Tunisia, Anatolia and Syria, to say nothing of two pilgrimages to Mecca.[25] Systematic research has been undertaken on the civilian elite in Cairo during the later Mamlūk period: the data are best for the domains controlled by these sultans themselves, in other words the Nile Valley and Syria.[26] Syrian scholars who had gained a reputation in their home country might receive invitations to lecture in Cairo. A respectable number of scholars and other notable immigrants from Iran were also on record, probably at least in part due to the political instability of the latter region. The sources are not so ample on scholars and other highly qualified people from the Ottoman empire who made careers in Cairo; most of them probably were not under as much pressure to emigrate as their Iranian colleagues. In some cases they also may not as yet have possessed the training necessary to succeed in Cairo's highly competitive environment. Yet incidental evidence, for instance on the Sufi, religious scholar and – possibly – political rebel Bedr el-Dīn of Simavna (760–819/1358–1416), who first studied in Cairo and then became tutor to a Mamlūk prince, shows that Ottoman scholars were not completely absent either.[27]

The Ottoman administration as a collector of data

When passing into the Ottoman realm, with its relatively extensive records of taxpayers, we enter the proto-statistical age. The sultans' conquest of Anatolia and the Balkans during the 700s/1300s and 800s/1400s and of geographical Syria, Egypt, Iraq and Cyprus after about 905/1500 has in many cases provided us, for the first time in Middle Eastern history, with reasonably well-kept registers covering entire provinces (*taḥrīr*). These lists of taxpayers and settlements both urban and rural, of which samples survive for the 800s/1400s but

24 Titley, *Persian miniature painting*, p. 211.
25 Ahmed Ateş, 'Ibn al ʿArabī', *EI2*, vol. III, p. 707.
26 Petry, *The civilian elite*, pp. 39–83.
27 Hans Joachim Kissling, 'Badr al-Dīn b. Ḳāḍī Samāwnā', *EI2*, vol. I, p. 869.

which become abundant in the tenth/sixteenth century, were intended to facilitate the collection of a whole array of dues in money and in kind. The taxes collected, often corresponding to those recorded in Ilkhānid Iran, were then distributed as revocable revenue grants to military men and administrators, while a significant share was retained by the ruler himself.

In an ideal world these records should have been regularly brought up to date. Not that this principle was always adhered to, and many registers must have been lost; yet they do survive in their hundreds for Anatolia, the Balkans and geographical Syria. Summary registers (*ijmāl*), based on the detailed listings prepared on site, sometimes provided supplementary information: remarkably enough, for purposes that we may surmise were 'proto-statistical', they enumerated tax-exempt servitors of the Ottoman administration and also employees of sultanic pious foundations, who strictly speaking did not have a place in tax registers.

When tax-farming became a major mode of revenue collection in the early 1000s/late 1500s–early 1600s the costly preparation of *taḥrīrs* was given up except in newly conquered provinces. In areas where non-Muslim populations remained numerous, especially in south-eastern Europe, records concerning the poll-tax (*jizye*) have been used as sources for demographic history. But the particular problems posed by *jizye* records have not all been solved as yet. Muslim populations can only be accessed through the records of a tax known as the *'avāriḍ*, which started out as an irregular wartime levy but by the 1000s/1600s was collected annually. In some regions taxpayers were recorded individually, and this makes the relevant registers appear rather like latter-day *taḥrīrs*; but this was by no means the case everywhere, so that on quite a few regions we lack data for the period between the early 1000s/late 1500s and the early fourteenth/later nineteenth century.

To arrive at estimates of the total population on the basis of taxation records we need to know something about average household size, which is usually not the case. By convention it is often assumed that there were five people to a household. In addition, where the population of large areas, but not of individual cities, is concerned, numerous observations concerning age pyramids – admittedly of later periods – allow us to say that males over roughly fifteen years of age – who alone were obliged to pay taxes – generally made up between one-quarter and one-third of the total population.[28] Thus multiplying the taxpayers by quotients of three and four gives us the relevant upper and

28 Leila Erder, 'The measurement of pre-industrial population changes: The Ottoman empire from the 15th to the 17th century', *Middle Eastern Studies*, 11 (1975).

lower limits; and often the estimate based on a household multiplier of five results in figures situated within these boundaries. It is generally considered that, when dealing with cities, the estimated number of taxpayers should be increased by 20 per cent to account for tax-exempt garrison soldiers and other servitors of the sultan.[29] In major centres such as Cairo or Istanbul, average household size may have been larger due to the presence of numerous upper-class families served by large numbers of slaves.

These data have been generated and interpreted in numerous monographs on individual towns and provinces of the Ottoman realm. But attempts to systematically map population and estimate the totals for large areas are still few and far between. The only published population map of Ottoman south-eastern Europe – excluding Istanbul – dates from the late 1360s/1940s: on the basis of summary registers compiled about 937/1520, it shows the Islamisation of much of the eastern Balkans – which, however, were thinly populated at this time.[30] By contrast, the western half was more densely settled, and it was here that the Christian population was concentrated. Many Balkan towns, especially the more important ones, had Muslim majorities; and in the two largest centres Christians were but a small minority. In Edirne, the Ottoman capital between the late 700s/1300s and the reign of Meḥmed the Conqueror (r. 848–50/1444–6 and 855–86/1451–81), Muslims numbered about three-quarters of the total, while in Salonika, at this time apparently the largest Balkan city outside Istanbul, over half the population was Jewish. The Jews must have been recent arrivals who had come to the Ottoman lands after their expulsion from Spain in 897/1492.

Unfortunately this map does not reflect the major event in the demographic history of this time, namely the resettlement of Istanbul by immigrants, both forced and – more or less – voluntary. Subjects of the sultans, especially those from newly conquered provinces, were drafted for relocation in the new capital. Refugees also arrived from outside the Ottoman borders; apart from the Jews we also encounter Muslims who received a separate mosque in the Istanbul port of Galata.

In recent publications we find a number of detailed maps showing the distributions of settlement in several Anatolian provinces; unfortunately they

29 Ömer Lütfi Barkan, 'Essai sur les données statistiques des registres de recensement dans l'Empire ottoman aux XVe et XVIe siècles', *Journal of the Economic and Social History of the Levant*, 1 (1958).

30 Ömer Lütfi Barkan, 'XVI. Asrın Başında Rumeli'de Nüfusun Yayılış Tarzını Gösterir Harita', *İstanbul Üniversitesi İktisat Fakültesi Mecmuası*, 11 (1949–50).

contain no data on population size.[31] Nor have any attempts at synthesising population data been undertaken for Anatolia and Syria; this is doubtless connected to the fact that today's historians are more sceptical about the accuracy of the *taḥrīrs* than was true of Barkan and other scholars of his generation. Today interest focuses on the possibility of calculating total agricultural production on the basis of the data concerning rural taxes also included in the *taḥrīr* and on the always problematic relationship between population data and estimated crops.[32] In this context, handling data for limited regions, a few districts or sub-provinces at a time has usually been preferred.

No Ottoman population data are available for Egypt and the provinces of western North Africa; by contrast, they are relatively abundant for 'geographical Syria' – in other words, the region between Aleppo in the north and al-ʿArīsh in the south. It appears that Aleppo, the third city of the Ottoman empire after Istanbul and Cairo, after an early period of crisis recorded by the *taḥrīrs* grew during the later tenth/sixteenth and also the eleventh/seventeenth centuries: a growth rate of about 40 per cent has been assumed as the city increased from approximately 80,000 in 944/1537f. to 115,000 shortly before 1094/1683. While the core of the city remained fairly stable, growth was concentrated in the suburbs.[33] In the case of Damascus it has been suggested that the construction of major Ottoman monuments on the outskirts of the Mamlūk city indicated increasing urbanisation of previously semi-rural territories; it has also been proposed that the city had about 52,000 inhabitants in the early tenth/sixteenth century and grew to 90,000 by 1214/1800.[34] Certainly the countryside of northern Syria experienced fairly serious fluctuations in population, including a significant decline in the twelfth/

31 For the data used by Barkan and his collaborators, now published, see İsmet Binark *et al.* (eds.), *438 Numaralı Muhâsebe-i Vilâyet-i Anadolu Defteri (937/1530)*, 2 vols. (Ankara, 1994); İsmet Binark *et al.* (eds.), *166 Numaralı Muhâsebe-i Vilâyet-i Anadolu Defteri (937/1530)*, 2 vols. (Ankara, 1995); İsmet Binark *et al.* (eds.), *387 Numaralı Muhâsebe-i Vilâyet-i Karaman ve Rum Defteri (937/1530)*, 2 vols. (Ankara, 1996); Ahmet Özkılınç *et al.* (eds.), *998 Numaralı Muhâsebe-i Vilâyet-i Diyâr-i Bekr ve 'Arab ve Zü'l-kadriyye Defteri (937/1530)*, 2 vols. (Ankara, 1999). For a critical evaluation see Heath Lowry, 'The Ottoman *Tahrir Defterleri* as a source for social and economic history: Pitfalls and limitations', in Heath Lowry, *Studies in defterology: Ottoman society in the fifteenth and sixteenth centuries* (Istanbul, 1992).

32 Huri İslamoğlu-İnan, *State and peasant in the Ottoman empire: Agrarian power relations and regional economic development in Ottoman Anatolia during the sixteenth century* (Leiden, 1994); Nenad Moačanin, *Town and country on the Middle Danube, 1526–1690* (Leiden, 2005).

33 André Raymond, 'The population of Aleppo in the sixteenth and seventeenth centuries according to Ottoman census documents', *IJMES*, 16 (1984).

34 André Raymond, 'The Ottoman conquest and the development of the great Arab towns', *International Journal of Turkish Studies*, 1 (1979–80); Antoine Abdel Nour, *Introduction à l'histoire urbaine de la Syrie ottomane (XVIe–XVIIIe siècle)* (Beirut, 1982), pp. 72–4.

eighteenth century; but Aleppo and Damascus received so many immigrants from rural areas that even major losses due to plague and other epidemics were soon compensated.[35]

Making sense of *taḥrīr* data

Ever since the 1380s/1960s the delicate balance between population and food resources has been a subject of debate.[36] In this context certain scholars have tried to determine whether the growth of population documented in the *taḥrīrs* of the 900s/1500s led to population pressure, in other words to a decline of per capita grain supplies to the point where holdings were subdivided into non-viable parts and poor-quality lands ploughed up. Michael Cook has concluded that at least in certain parts of Anatolia, such pressure did occur. By contrast, Huri İslamoğlu-İnan has strongly disagreed, pointing to the extra gains from rural industries that might flourish, especially if the population was increasing fast.

The next question is whether this pressure may, as Mustafa Akdağ had suggested, have made it difficult for young men to find the wherewithal for marriage, unattached young males being prime candidates for migration to the cities and enrolment in the sultan's armies. Emphasising the 'pull' rather than the 'push' factors, Halil Inalcik has proposed instead that it was military change rather than rural population pressure that resulted in many young men leaving their villages to join the sultans' armies. For around 1009/1600, with the declining importance of cavalry in battle, the sultans had begun to hire musket-wielding mercenaries for single campaigns only.[37] Last but not least, there is always the possibility that some increases were not 'real' at all, but merely due to the higher quality of late tenth/sixteenth-century counts as opposed to their predecessors from the early 900s/1500s.

Debate also has focused upon the question whether in areas other than those studied by Cook and İslamoğlu-İnan, and indeed in Anatolia as a whole, population pressure was or could have been an issue. A clear-cut answer is

35 Abdel Nour, *Introduction*, *passim*.

36 Mustafa Akdağ, *Celâlî İsyanları (1550–1603)* (Ankara, 1963); Michael A. Cook, *Population pressure in rural Anatolia 1450–1600* (London and New York, 1972); Oktay Özel, 'Population changes in Anatolia during the 16th and 17th centuries', *IJMES*, 36 (2004); Mehmet Öz, 'Population fall in seventeenth century Anatolia: Some findings for the districts of Canik and Bozok', *Archivum Ottomanicum*, 22 (2004).

37 Halil Inalcik, 'Military and fiscal transformation in the Ottoman empire, 1600–1700', *Archivum Ottomanicum*, 6 (1980); Karen Barkey, *Bandits and bureaucrats: The Ottoman route to state centralization* (Ithaca and London, 1994).

impossible. But if we keep in mind that certain potentially fertile lands such as the Çukurova in southern Anatolia were still heavily forested in the late tenth/sixteenth century, it is difficult to assume overall population pressure, whatever the situation may have been in certain regions close to the major cities and trade routes. In the same way it is worth noting that so many people who were settled in Cyprus by the sultan's orders after the Ottoman conquest (978–9/1570–1) quickly returned to the Anatolian mainland; while conditions peculiar to Cyprus may partly explain this phenomenon, it is hardly an argument in favour of population pressure.[38]

In spite of numerous conflicts over tax collection and a spate of climatic disasters, the Ottoman world knew no peasant uprisings of the type encountered in both early modern Europe and China. This absence has also formed the subject of some debate. The high level of legitimacy enjoyed by the sultans as champions of Islam may have had a part to play. Moreover, in spite of needing the permission of local administrators before they could legally move, in practice many young men found it easy to escape from whatever tensions were being generated in village life around 1009/1600.[39] Migration into the towns might be a solution of sorts, and, as we have seen, joining the sultans' armies also functioned as a safety valve. Given the distances covered by Ottoman armies and the likelihood that some mercenaries might detach themselves from their units somewhere along the road, this movement of military men into border provinces also can be viewed as a type of migration.

These debates are of special relevance for our understanding of Ottoman social structure: for while peasant uprisings were conspicuous by their absence, the early eleventh/late sixteenth and early seventeenth centuries saw a series of major mercenary revolts that laid waste large sections of Anatolia. Had these rebels been pushed out of the villages by population pressure, as an indirect and unintended consequence of military change, or for some other reason? The debate will probably continue for some time to come.

38 Ronald Jennings, *Christians and Muslims in Ottoman Cyprus and the Mediterranean world* (New York, 1993), pp. 212–39; Şenol Çelik, 'Türk fethi sonrasında Kıbrıs Adasına yönelik iskân çalışmaları', in Zehra Toska (ed.), *Kaf Dağının ötesine varmak, Festschrift in honor of Günay Kut: Essays presented by her colleagues and students*, 3 vols. (Cambridge, MA, 2003), vol. I/*Journal of Turkish Studies* 27, 1–3.

39 İslamoğlu-İnan, *State and peasant*, pp. 155–6; Suraiya Faroqhi, 'Political tensions in the Anatolian countryside around 1600: An attempt at interpretation', in J. L. Bacqué-Grammont, Barbara Flemming, Macit Gökberk and İlber Ortaylı (eds.), *Türkische Miszellen: Robert Anhegger Festschrift, Armağanı, Mélanges* (Istanbul, 1987).

Anatolian nomads in the course of settlement

Rainfall agriculture is possible throughout the Ottoman Balkans and present-day Turkey, even though the core of central Anatolia is marginal for today's farmers. Thus, unlike Iraq or Iran no elaborate irrigation arrangements were necessary whose neglect or destruction might render the affected area unfit for cultivation on a long-term basis. This situation also explains in part why Anatolian and Balkan nomads of the 900s/1500s showed a certain propensity to settle down, or at least this is the impression conveyed by the *taḥrīrs*.[40] Some scepticism certainly is in order, for Ottoman officials saw themselves as governing an empire of settled folk. Thus quite possibly certain districts of 'peasants' we encounter in the tax registers of the later 900s/1500s may have been the products of administrative convenience and wishful thinking rather than resulting from real processes of settlement. But even so, the population growth of the tenth/sixteenth century must have pushed many Anatolian and Balkan nomads into village life and, by the same token, the percentage of people who could not evade registration must have been higher than had been true in an earlier, less settled age.

In the early 1100s/late 1600s the Ottoman central government was hard pressed for revenue due to a lengthy war against the Habsburgs (1094–1110/1683–99). In consequence the authorities made their first concerted efforts to actually force nomads to settle. Officials had by now realised that on the margins of the Syrian deserts agriculture was in retreat because villagers were not being protected against the raids of desert nomads.[41] The official plan was that mainly Turkish-speaking tribesmen were to be settled in south-eastern Anatolia and what is today northern Iraq; these people would hopefully retain their warlike qualities and form a barrier against incursions from the desert.[42] But, even though an effort was made to obtain the support of the leaders of the tribal units involved, the project failed, in part because many sites chosen for settlement were important militarily but not very suitable for farming. Moreover, the former nomads were not given any funds to tide them over the first few years. Yet the latter are invariably difficult because throughout the world in such situations, animals are lost before agricultural yields are sufficient for subsistence. As a result the ex-nomads soon abandoned their

40 De Planhol, *Les fondements géographiques*, pp. 225–41.

41 Wolf Dieter Hütteroth and Kamal Abdulfattah, *Historical geography of Palestine, Transjordan and southern Syria in the late 16th century* (Erlangen, 1977).

42 Cengiz Orhonlu, *Osmanlı İmparatorluğunda aşiretleri iskân teşebbüsü (1691–1696)* (Istanbul, 1963).

villages and now, without sufficient sheep and camels, they became more dangerous to the farming population. However, during the twelfth/eighteenth century the Ottoman central administration did not give up, and campaigns to settle nomads were frequently undertaken.[43]

Migrations under state control

Nomads chose their routes themselves, and that was a major reason why they were regarded as such problematic subjects by Ottoman officialdom. On the other hand, there were migrations actually commanded by sultans and their bureaucrats; in the 800s/1400s and earlier 900s/1500s the aim was usually to populate newly conquered regions or cities with loyal subjects – Muslims, but also non-Muslims on occasion – or else to neutralise local elites by settling them in regions where they had no sources of power independent from their government grants.[44] As we have seen, artists or artisans in newly conquered regions, such as Tabrīz (920/1514) or Egypt (922/1517) were sometimes ordered to move to Istanbul and serve the court. These settlers were considered to have been banished (*sürgün*) and thus apparently suffered a loss in status, though otherwise they retained the rights of free men and women. Istanbul was thus settled by Anatolians drafted by local authorities who had been ordered to provide pre-established quotas of recruits, or else by inhabitants of newly conquered towns to the north of the Black Sea.[45] In the villages surrounding the capital prisoners of war were settled, who for a while retained certain characteristics of their former slave status.[46] The last major project of this kind was undertaken after the conquest of Cyprus from the Venetians (978–9/1570–1); it was officially considered a failure, and later conquests such as Crete were not settled under state supervision.

Sürgün were expected to remain in the places to which they had been assigned; but there were also state-controlled migrations of artisans who were

43 Yusuf Halaçoğlu, *XVIII. Yüzyılda Osmanlı İmparatorluğunun iskân siyaseti ve aşiretlerin yerleştirilmesi* (Ankara, 1988).

44 Ömer Lütfi Barkan, 'Osmanlı İmparatorluğunda bir iskân ve kolonizasyon metodu olarak sürgünler', *İstanbul Üniversitesi İktisat Fakültesi Mecmuası*, 11, 1–4 (1949–50), 13, 1–4 (1951–2), 15, 1–4 (1953–4).

45 Halil Inalcik, 'The policy of Mehmed II toward the Greek population of Istanbul and the Byzantine buildings of the city', *Dumbarton Oaks Papers*, 23 (1969–70); Nicoară Beldiceanu, 'La conquête des cités marchandes de Kilia et de Cetatea Albă par Bāyezīd II', repr. in Nicoară Beldiceanu, *Le monde ottoman des Balkans (1402–1566): Institutions, société, économie* (London, 1976), VI.

46 Stefan Yerasimos, '15. yüzyılın sonunda Haslar Kazası', in Tülay Artan (ed.), *18. yüzyıl kadı sicilleri ışığında Eyüp'te sosyal yaşam* (Istanbul, 1998), pp. 82–102.

meant to work on state projects for a limited period of time, and return to their provinces of origin once the latter had been completed. This manner of recruitment was practised throughout the early modern period, but has been studied mostly for the great palace- and mosque-building projects of the tenth/sixteenth century.[47] Judges and provincial administrators were required to locate the most skilful craftsmen and convey them to Istanbul or to the relevant provincial construction site, sometimes under guard. At least in Istanbul during slack periods these men probably found work with private employers as well; some of them may have been migrant workers to begin with. How many of these craftsmen stayed on in the capital once their work was finished remains unknown. A great deal must have depended on the number of projects under way and also the workmen already available in Istanbul.

However, some of the major Ottoman artists of the tenth/sixteenth and early eleventh/seventeenth centuries had not started their careers as apprentices in provincial towns, but had been drafted into the sultans' service through the so-called 'levy of boys' (*devşirme*). This was a forcible recruitment of Christian village youths into the Janissary corps and, for those who showed extraordinary promise, into the service of the rulers' palace. This procedure must count as a special case of migration as many of the boys concerned moved over considerable distances; and at some point in their careers quite a few of them came to be stationed in Istanbul.

Some successful recruits were also active in the artistic and technical sectors. Thus Sinān (*c.* 895–996/1490–1588), later the architect who built the Süleymāniye and Selīmiye mosque complexes in Istanbul and Edirne, began his career as a Janissary officer and military engineer.[48] Meḥmed Ağa, the architect of the mosque complex of Sultan Aḥmed I (r. 1012–26/1603–17) had entered the palace as a page and held a military command in Syria before specialising in architecture. Globally speaking, the artists and craftsmen recruited by the Ottoman sultans formed only one example of the numerous movements of this kind that occurred throughout the Islamic world. But due to the strongly centralised character of the Ottoman state, recruitment was

47 Ömer Lütfi Barkan, *Süleymaniye Cami ve İmareti inşaatı*, 2 vols. (Ankara, 1972–9); Gülru Necipoğlu, *Architecture, ceremonial and power: The Topkapı Palace in the fifteenth and sixteenth centuries* (Cambridge, MA, and London, 1991), pp. 232–4; Suraiya Faroqhi, 'Under state control: Sixteenth and seventeenth-century Ottoman craftsmen on their way to Istanbul', in Suraiya Faroqhi, *Stories of Ottoman men and women: Establishing status, establishing control* (Istanbul, 2002).

48 Gülru Necipoğlu, *The age of Sinan: Architectural culture in the Ottoman empire* (London, 2005), pp. 127–52.

more systematic than elsewhere; moreover, we know more about the movements of artists and artisans due to the survival of the central archives.

The plague and harvest failures

Some information is available concerning the demographic effects of the plague in Syria and Egypt during the Mamlūk period.[49] In these regions apparently the pneumonic variety was frequent, while the contrary seems to have applied in the western European setting; as a result the long-term consequences were more serious, as due to the extremely high mortality it became difficult for the affected populations to reproduce themselves between epidemics. As a contributing cause, the flea most likely to cause contagion in the Egyptian setting feeds on grain husks and similar debris. Moreover, overtaxed peasants often took the opportunity to flee their villages and take refuge in the cities. Thus the abandonment of cultivation in many rural areas might lead to major scarcities in spite of a diminished number of consumers. Higher population densities in the cities also made for a greater incidence of contagion; and there survives a good deal of evidence that people fled those cities that were worst affected. Remarkably, given the standard advice of Muslim men of religion to not flee from a place where the plague had broken out, some scholars of this time openly advocated flight.[50]

For the plagues of Cairo during the late eighth/fourteenth and throughout the ninth/fifteenth centuries we possess some official data relayed by contemporary chroniclers; however, they concern only those people with taxable estates, and exclude inmates of a major urban hospital as well as the corpses found in the public thoroughfares. These figures show that children and slaves, especially the females among the latter, were worst affected. Some chroniclers of the time have preceded modern historians in using these figures as the basis of an estimate of total mortality. In addition, Ibn Taghrībirdī, the author of an important chronicle, counted the coffins prayed over in one of Cairo's oratories and then multiplied that number by that of all known oratories in the city. This latter method was sometimes also used by government officials who probably wanted to estimate future revenue shortfalls.[51]

As in other parts of the early modern world, the plague was a major determinant of population size in the Ottoman realm; this was particularly

49 Michael Dols, *The Black Death in the Middle East* (Princeton, 1977), pp. 143–235.
50 Ibid., p. 175.
51 Ibid., pp. 175–83.

true of Istanbul. In the tenth/sixteenth and early eleventh/seventeenth centuries the denizens of the Ottoman empire must have suffered losses comparable to those that afflicted populations in the western Mediterranean region; however, evidence on this period is sparse. But after the 1070s/1660s major epidemics disappeared from Spain, France and Italy, apart from the murderous epidemic in Marseilles (1132/1720), which incidentally had been brought in by a ship arriving from an infected port of the eastern Mediterranean. However, until the beginning of the thirteenth/nineteenth century plague epidemics remained a major problem in the eastern regions of Anatolia and also in Epirus, today the borderland between Greece and Albania. In Istanbul apparently the local rodents had become infected to such an extent that plague became endemic: throughout the twelfth/eighteenth century epidemics in Alexandria were often initiated by ships arriving from the Ottoman capital. By contrast, epidemics in Izmir were often caused by bacilli arriving with the silk caravans from western Iran, as these had to pass through a territory where there were also sizeable populations of infected rodents.[52]

Where reactions to the plague were concerned, the social disorganisation so often witnessed in Christian countries during major epidemics was much less dramatic in the Ottoman lands. In these territories Muslims generally obeyed the religious command to not leave the region in which they found themselves at the time a plague broke out. The corollary was an injunction to not enter places where the infection was known to be raging; and Meḥmed the Conqueror is known to have followed this advice when on campaign.[53] Visits to the sick and attendance at funerals continued as in the case of other illnesses. However, in the late ninth/sixteenth century it was claimed, with what degree of justification remains unknown, that the plague had never affected the sultans' palace; if true, this fortunate situation may have been linked to the custom of immediately sending all sick palace inmates to a hospital located a good distance away from the main buildings.[54]

Wealthy non-Muslims and Europeans resident in Ottoman port towns normally left the urban perimeter and stayed in rural villas for the duration of the plague. Those who had to remain typically locked themselves in and

52 Daniel Panzac, *La peste dans l'empire Ottoman, 1700–1850* (Louvain, 1985).
53 Heath Lowry, 'Pushing the stone uphill: The impact of bubonic plague on Ottoman urban society in the fifteenth and sixteenth centuries', *Osmanlı Araştırmaları: The Journal of Ottoman Studies*, 23 (2004), p. 129.
54 Andreas Tietze (ed.), *Mustafâ 'Âlî's counsel for sultans of 1581*, 2 vols. (Vienna, 1979–82), vol. I, p. 38.

carefully fumigated all parcels received from the outside; these measures were considered relatively effective.[55] Moreover, Muslims also migrated to summer pastures or else to gardens outside the towns during the summer season, quite independently of any epidemics. This latter custom pushed down the level of congestion, and may well have served to limit infection. From the twelfth/ eighteenth century onwards certain upper-class Muslims, particularly the *begs* of Tunis, also convinced themselves that quarantines could be an effective protection, and began to enforce them in their respective domains.

As to harvest failures and the famines and mortalities that must have resulted from them, our information is very sparse and needs to be teased out of a variety of disparate sources. However, we do know that the harvest failures of the 990s/1590s, well documented in many parts of Mediterranean Europe, also occurred in Anatolia and Syria. The reason was a succession of serious droughts demonstrated by dendrochronological evidence; these catastrophes may have contributed to the abandonment of many central Anatolian villages, along with the better-known mercenary rebellions of that period.[56] In the coastlands of the Black Sea, where over the centuries the grain supply for Istanbul was purchased at artificially low prices imposed by the Ottoman state, few resources probably remained for agricultural investment. But whether this situation was the root cause of the scarcities that plagued Istanbul during the early 1200s/late 1700s or whether these were mainly caused by wartime disruption as yet remains unknown. Further work on records of the late twelfth/eighteenth and early thirteenth/nineteenth centuries probably will elucidate at least some of these problems in the not-too-distant future.

55 Panzac, *La peste*, pp. 312–27.
56 Peter I. Kuniholm, 'Archaeological evidence and non-evidence for climatic change', *Philosophical Transactions of the Royal Society*, A330 (1990).

11

The mechanisms of commerce

WARREN C. SCHULTZ

Introduction†

In the field of English-language scholarship on Islamic history in the 1960s, when the first *Cambridge history of Islam* was planned and executed, economic history was usually taken to mean the consideration of topics related to agriculture, taxation and trade – both international and local.[1] The editors of the *CHI* certainly thought economic history was important. In the context of setting the stage for the rest of the work, P. M. Holt wrote the following in the introduction:

> In the space of nearly two hundred years that have elapsed since Gibbon wrote, the Renaissance, the Reformation and the Enlightenment have themselves passed into history, and new forces have emerged in the development of European society … At the same time, the methods of historical study have continued to evolve. The source-materials available for research have immensely increased, and the range of techniques at the historian's disposal has been extended. The aims of the historian have changed in response to both of these factors. Where the pioneers in the field sought primarily to construct, from the best sources they could find, the essential framework of political history, and to chronicle as accurately as possible the acts of rulers, historians today are more conscious of the need to evaluate their materials – a critique all the more important in Islamic history since the control supplied by archives is so largely deficient. They seek to penetrate the dynastic screen, to trace the real sites and shifts of power in the capitals and the camps, and to identify, not merely the leaders or figure-heads, but the ethnic, religious, social or economic groups of anonymous individuals who supported constituted authority or promoted subversion. It is no longer possible, therefore,

† Support for research for this chapter was provided by the College of Liberal Arts and Sciences, DePaul University.

1 P. M. Holt *et al.* (eds.), *The Cambridge history of Islam*, 2 vols. (Cambridge, 1970): henceforth *CHI*.

> to segregate the political history of Islam from its social and economic history – *although in the latter field especially materials are notably sparse over wide regions and long periods*.[2] (emphasis added)

There were two important topics identified here. The first was that economic aspects of life in the pre-modern Islamic world were recognised as important and were therefore included in the work. The second was that economic history in particular was bedevilled by a paucity of sources.

Despite this endorsement of the need to incorporate economic aspects into the wider narratives of Islamic history, the subsequent chapters of *CHI* that addressed regional narrative histories were relatively barren of economic themes, with the exception of the chapter on Egypt and Syria.[3] This was probably due in part, of course, to the realities imposed by the second theme – the problem of lack of sources outside Egypt. Moreover, when economic themes were mentioned they were usually in the context of international trade, a brief discussion of agriculture or taxation, or the citing of a particularly well-known coin reform. Not surprisingly, given the wider goals of the *CHI*, there was little development of focused questions such as how economic transactions were actually conducted.[4] Thus, the main contribution to economic history in the *CHI*, the thematic chapter by Claude Cahen entitled 'Economy, society, institutions', was an essay written in broad strokes, addressing in turn each of the three terms of its title.[5] Two important emphases emerged from this chapter, however, and while the first addressed an issue that was perhaps of greater concern at the time – refuting the conception of the Islamic world's economic practices as hide-bound and unchanging – the second, an important reminder of the gap that often existed between normative theory and actual practice when it came to economic realities, is just as pertinent today as when Cahen wrote it. The chapter did not, however, contain any in-depth discussions of commercial activities.

It is this question of how commercial activities were conducted – by what means was business transacted – that is the subject of this chapter on the mechanisms of commerce, concentrating on developments since the publication of the *CHI*. What is meant by the phrase 'mechanisms of commerce'?

2 P. M. Holt, 'Introduction', in ibid., vol. IA, p. xvii.
3 Bernard Lewis, 'Egypt and Syria', in ibid., vol. IA, pp. 175–230.
4 The holistic approach sought by the work was also emphasised by Holt: 'The aim of these volumes is to present the history of Islam as a cultural whole. It is hoped that in a single, concise work the reader will be able to follow all the main threads: political, theological, philosophical, economic, military, artistic': ibid., vol. IA, p. ix.
5 Claude Cahen, 'Economy, society, institutions', in ibid., vol. IIB, pp. 511–38, 900–1.

By this I mean the mechanisms – numismatic, financial, legal – that made it possible to conduct economic transactions. The chapter asks: What were these mechanisms of commerce and did they change over time? How do we know about them? What do we need to know about them in order to understand them? The fact that it is possible to ask these questions and provide at least partial answers tells us that the state of the economic history of the Islamic world has advanced considerably since the *CHI* was published. Not only have many new sources of information been brought to light, historians have also engaged in thorough discussions of the theoretical approaches to how that information could be used and understood.

Background

This relative paucity of economic history in the *CHI* was reflective of the state of the field up to that time. While specialised studies were emerging (see below), economic issues had not yet emerged as significant features in any of the era's standard surveys. If anything, there was a nod towards the importance of merchants and the existence of long-distance trade. Occasionally, events such as the Umayyad caliph ʿAbd al-Malik's revolutionary coin reforms of the seventh century would be mentioned. Some important numismatic work had occurred in the publication of catalogues and corpora, but for the most part coins remained in their own little corner of academia. Few scholars had attempted to break down the barriers between those fields of study.[6]

In general, political or intellectual history was dominant, as the following brief survey reveals. C. Brockelmann, in his *History of the Islamic peoples*, mentioned economic matters in passing only, which was more than could be said of von Grunebaum in his *Medieval Islam*.[7] The German *Handbuch der Orientalistik* also only rarely mentioned trade and commerce, but then its format as a handbook did not allow for extended thematic discussions.[8] Four

6 An exception is W. Popper, who included some numismatic evidence in his *Egypt and Syria under the Circassian sultans 1382–1468 AD: Systematic notes to Ibn Taghri Birdi's chronicles of Egypt*, University of California Publications in Semitic Philology 15–16 (Berkeley, 1955–7).

7 C. Brockelmann, *History of the Islamic peoples*, trans. M. Perlmann and J. Carmichael (New York, 1960 [1939]); G. E. von Grunebaum, *Medieval Islam: Study in cultural orientation*, 2nd edn (Chicago, 1953 [1946]).

8 *Handbuch der Orientalistik* (Leiden, 1911–), vol. VI, parts 1–3: B. Spuler, *Die Chalifenzeit* (Leiden, 1952), trans. and adapted by F. R. C. Bagley as *The age of the caliphs* (Leiden, 1969); B. Spuler, *Die Mongolenzeit* (Leiden, 1953), trans. and adapted by F. R. C. Bagley as *The Mongol period* (Leiden, 1969); and H. J. Kissling *et al.*, *Neuzeit* (Leiden, 1959), trans. and adapted by F. R. C. Bagley as *The last great Muslim empires* (Leiden, 1969).

years after the appearance of the *CHI*, M. G. H. Hodgson's *The venture of Islam* was published.[9] Hodgson was aware of the importance of trade, and acknowledged its existence in passages scattered throughout the three volumes. Yet economic history was clearly not a major concern of this work. The only mention of a monetary event in the first two volumes, for example, was that of ʿAbd al-Malik's reforms, and then it was only discussed from an art-historical perspective – how the design choices for the coins reflected Muslim power with regard to Byzantium – and not in the context of the economic or administrative repercussions of this development.[10]

1974 also saw the publication of the second edition of *The legacy of Islam*, and this book made a step forward in terms of bringing economic history to a wider audience.[11] In speaking of the differences between this edition and the 1931 original edition, C. E. Bosworth's foreword specifically mentioned chapter 5, 'Economic developments', by M. A. Cook, as an example of the 'interaction between Islam and the outside world, above all, between Islam and the western Christian world as mediated through the Mediterranean basin' as one of the new contributions.[12] There had been no economic chapter in the first edition. Cook's chapter was divided into three sections: the first addresses the agricultural contributions of Islamic peoples to southern Europe; the second and longest section was on mercantile connections between Islam and Europe; and the third contains an extended warning (echoing Cahen in the *CHI*) not to accept uncritically dubious assertions of Muslim economic backwardness or decay. The chapter as a whole was concerned with sweeping matters: questions of agricultural and commercial legacy, particularly vis-à-vis Europe. It stressed the role of rulers in the redistribution of Mediterranean economies, rulers often indifferent to the interests of mercantile classes.[13] Yet most importantly, it had a strong subtheme of questioning assumptions, and it made two very important points that are still relevant today, whether or not one is concerned with questions of 'development' (or lack thereof) of the Islamic world.[14] The first concerned the state of our knowledge: 'The lack of Muslim inventions may reflect more on the state of our knowledge than it does on the inventiveness

9 M. G. H. Hodgson, *The venture of Islam*, 3 vols. (Chicago, 1974).
10 Ibid., vol. I, pp. 226 and 246.
11 Joseph Schacht and C. E. Bosworth, *The legacy of Islam*, 2nd edn (Oxford, 1974).
12 Ibid., p. v.
13 Ibid., p. 225.
14 The discussion is found in ibid. on pp. 240–1. For an example of contemporary assertions of decay see C. Issawi, *The economic history of the Middle East, 1800–1914: A book of readings* (Chicago, 1966), p. 3.

of the Muslims.' Any gap could just as easily be due to the limited nature of both the sources and our knowledge of the sources. 'The second caveat is that one should not accept uncritically the views often advanced *on other grounds* [emphasis added] for supposing the economic history of the Islamic world to have been of a particularly backward character.' It is worth restating the obvious that there is no neat symmetry between cultural and economic trajectories.[15] Thus in this chapter the reader was presented with an overview of the then current debates and foci of interest, but not an examination of the nuts and bolts of trade.

Three major works published in this era that did make significant contributions to an understanding of the economic history of the Islamic world must be highlighted.[16] The first was a collected-studies volume published in 1970 which addressed the economic history of the Middle East.[17] Part I of this volume contained ten valuable studies by leading scholars on economic topics from the Middle Ages, ending in 1500. Several of these studies, such as the contribution on monetary aspects of Islamic history by Ehrenkreutz, and the combined contribution 'From England to Egypt, 1350–1500' by Lopez, Miskimin and Udovitch, continue to shape inquiries to this day.[18]

The next work was Udovitch's *Partnership and profit in medieval Islam*, also published in 1970.[19] In this important book, Udovitch carefully examined jurisprudence (*fiqh*) manuals of the second/eighth and third/ninth centuries to establish the legal frameworks devised by the *ʿulamāʾ* to regulate trade and commerce. In the absence of commercial documents from Islamic populations, Udovitch provided a detailed exploration of the rules governing the many types of commercial partnerships within the Ḥanafī, Mālikī and Shāfiʿī schools of law. He also devoted attention to the commenda (*muḍāraba* in Ḥanafī texts, *muqāraḍa* in the other two *madhhabs*), an agreement wherein one partner provides the capital and the other conducts the actual business for an agreed-upon share of the profits. This split was ordinarily two-thirds profit to the capital provider, and one-third to the other partner. Udovitch was well aware of the gap between

15 A point recently reiterated by Robert Irwin in his *The Alhambra* (London, 2005), p. 19.
16 Noticeably missing from this discussion is the work of E. Ashtor. For reasons of space I am unable to address his work here.
17 M. A. Cook (ed.), *Studies in the economic history of the Middle East from the rise of Islam to the present day* (London, 1970).
18 A. Ehrenkreutz, 'Monetary aspects of medieval Near Eastern economic history', in ibid., pp. 37–50; R. Lopez, H. Miskimin and A. Udovitch, 'England to Egypt, 1350–1500: Long-term trends and long-distance trade', in ibid., pp. 91–128. Cf. S. J. Borsch, 'Thirty years after Lopez, Miskimin, and Udovitch', *Mamluk Studies Review*, 8, 2 (2004).
19 A. L. Udovitch, *Partnership and profit in medieval Islam* (Princeton, 1970).

these legal texts and actual practice, but argued convincingly that in the matter of pecuniary transactions there is reason to accept that the practices described reflected reality in many cases.[20] This would seem to be the case especially for the legal devices known as *ḥiyal*, which were designed to bring unlawful actions into apparent conformity with the law.[21]

But by far the most important contribution of this era was S. D. Goitein's seminal *A Mediterranean society*, vol. I, *The economic foundations*, published in 1967.[22] Using the documents of the Geniza, a storehouse of texts preserved by a Jewish community in old Cairo, Goitein presented a detailed description and analysis of the commercial practices undertaken by that community. Chapter 3 of this book, 'The world of commerce and finance', provided the first thorough discussion of the mechanisms of commerce of the medieval Islamic world in modern scholarship, and remains a necessary foundation stone for any serious economic analysis of the Mediterranean region and beyond. Drawing upon examples of wills, contracts, partnership contracts, bills of sale etc., this book not only provides an insight into the economic life of the Jews of Fusṭāṭ, but their relations, commercial and otherwise, with their Muslim neighbours. Goitein's analyses were based on documents from every-day life and business, informed by his awareness of what the juridical thinkers wrote. The Geniza also contained documents dealing with both local and long-distance trade. In addition to partnership and commenda texts relating to trade, there survive letters of credit (*suftajas*), which helped trade by minimising the necessity of transporting quantities of cash.[23] Goitein also carefully analysed how merchants worked in an era where many different coins circulated. The Geniza documents mentioned a wide variety of coinages. They show that merchants specified which coins to use or accept, and how coins sometimes circulated in sealed purses of set values. In his analysis Goitein took great care to illustrate how these different coinages were treated and exchanged. His example should be followed by all.[24]

20 Cf. J. A. Wakin, *The function of documents in Islamic law: The chapter on sales from Ṭaḥāwī's* Kitāb al-shurūṭ al-kabīr (Albany, 1972); and R. Brunschvig, 'Conceptions monétaires chez les juristes musulmans (VIIIe–XIIIe siècles)', *Arabica*, 14 (1967).

21 See Udovitch's discussions of *ḥiyal* in *Partnership and profit*, pp. 11–12 and 63–4. Cf. J. Schacht, 'Ḥiyal', *EI2*, vol III, pp. 510–13; M. Bernard, 'Muʿāmalat', *EI2*, vol. VII, pp. 255–7.

22 S. D. Goitein, *A Mediterranean society: The Jewish communities of the Arab world as portrayed in the documents of the Cairo Geniza*, 6 vols. (Berkeley and London, 1967–93), vol. I: *Economic foundations* (Berkeley, 1967).

23 Not all *suftajas* were for large amounts. See ibid., vol. I, pp. 242–7.

24 Cf. the glossary of S. Tsugitaka's *State and rural society in medieval Islam: Sultans,* muqṭaʿs *and* fallāḥūn (Leiden, 1997), where the entry for *dīnār* (p. 244) reads 'Unit of gold coin. 1 dinar was equal to 14 dirhams of silver during the Buwayhid period, around 38 dirhams

The case of Egypt

While the Geniza contained documents from across the Mediterranean world, and from the Indian Ocean basin as well, the majority of its documents were Egyptian in origin. In the remainder of this chapter my examples will be drawn from Egypt. Part of this is reflective of sources. One of the major changes in the intellectual milieu since 1970 has been the discovery and publication of many more sources for economic history. The study of these sources has enabled archive-based historians to publish documents and literary texts that have economic foci writ large. In addition, archaeologists have discovered local archives of individuals which make it much easier to explore economic questions. Moreover, as is discussed below, advances in numismatic scholarship have placed monetary historians on much firmer ground for many regions and eras of Islamic history. This is certainly seen, for example, in the area of the Indian Ocean-based studies, where research on the economic history of the region has increased substantially.[25] This is also the case for the Ottoman empire, which has seen an explosion of scholarship on economic history.[26] Similarly for Yemen, where recent work has advanced knowledge far beyond what was possible in 1970.[27]

Even with these and other welcome developments, however, Egypt has seen its share of newly available sources and retains its status as the most source-rich region for this area of inquiry. This remains the case even though we know of events such as that which took place in 791/1389, when the state

during the Ayyūbid period, and 20 dirhams in the first half of the Mamlūk period.' This definition ignores the fact that the *dīnārs* and *dirhams* of these dynasties differed radically from one another.

25 Contemporary to the *CHI* was D. S. Richards (ed.), *Islam and the trade of Asia: A colloquium* (Oxford, 1970). The scholarship since is wide-ranging and plentiful: K. N. Chaudhuri's *Trade and civilization in the Indian Ocean: An economic history from the rise of Islam to 1750* (Cambridge, 1985); K. N. Chaudhuri, *Asia before Europe: Economy and civilization of the Indian Ocean from the rise of Islam to 1750* (Cambridge, 1990); J. F. Richards (ed.), *The imperial monetary system of Mughal India* (Oxford, 1987); and S. Goron and J. P. Goenka, *The coins of the Indian sultanates* (New Delhi, 2001).

26 See H. Inalcik and D. Quataert, *An economic and social history of the Ottoman empire*, 2 vols. (Cambridge, 1994), vol. I: *1300–1600* and vol. II: *1600–1914*. For the monetary history of the Ottomans see Şevket Pamuk, *A monetary history of the Ottoman empire* (Cambridge, 2000). On numismatic topics see the five-volume series on the Akçe by S. Sreckovic, all published by the author: *Akçes*, vol. I: *Orhan Gazi–Murad II, 699–848 AH* (Belgrade, 1999); *Akçes*, vol. II: *Mehmed II Fatih–Selim I Yavuz, 848–926 AH* (Belgrade, 2000); *Akçes*, vol. III: *Suleyman I Kanuni, 926–974 AH* (Belgrade, 2003); *Akçes*, vol. IV: *Selim II Sarı–Murad III, 974–1003 AH* (Belgrade, 2005); and *Akçes*, vol. V: *Mehmed III–Mustafa I, 1003–1032 AH* (Belgrade, 2007); and S. Sreckovic, *Ottoman mints and coins* (Belgrade, 2002).

27 D. M. Varisco, *Medieval agriculture and Islamic science: The almanac of a Yemeni sultan* (Seattle, 1994). R. E. Margariti, *Aden and the Indian Ocean trade: 150 years in the life of a medieval Arabian port* (Chapel Hill, 2007).

archives were sold by the recently deposed Sultan Barqūq on his way out of town.[28] But there are pockets of archival-like documentary caches which survived. Notable among them are the papyri records from the early Islamic centuries;[29] the primarily Circassian-era Mamlūk *waqf* documents;[30] the Ḥaram al-Sharīf documents;[31] the Ottoman-era court documents, utilised decades apart by Rabie and Hanna;[32] the Quseir documents;[33] and the excavations of Qasr Ibrīm, which revealed a cache of 122 Arabic and Turkish documents dating from the Ottoman era.[34]

But there is more at work in my choice of Egyptian examples than their abundance or my familiarity with them. The key issue here is whether one assumes that there is an Islamic commerce, or whether there are Islamic commerces. Cahen and Cook argued that one could not support assertions of Islamic commerce as conservative and never changing. Part of accepting their conclusions is being cognisant of changes and differing practice with regard to time and place. Without a thorough examination of practices encountered within the parameters of chronology and geography it cannot be assumed that what was in effect in one place at one time was true for all places and all times. Asserting this does not ignore the overarching 'highway of coherence' of religious and juridical thought that linked the Islamic world.[35] Far from it. Within that highway of coherence one must be aware of variance, for local conditions mattered. The legal structures provided by the various Islamic schools of law contained differences, and it is known that certain schools were

28 F. Bauden, 'The recovery of Mamluk chancery documents from an unsuspected place', in M. Winter and A. Levanoni (eds.), *The Mamluks in Egyptian and Syrian politics and society* (Leiden, 2003), p. 74.

29 See the works of G. Frantz-Murphy in the bibliography to this chapter.

30 C. F. Petry, 'A Geniza for Mamluk studies? Charitable trust (*waqf*) documents as a source for economic and social history', *Mamluk Studies Review*, 2 (1998). For a close study of the monetary information found in a *waqf* document see Gilles P. Hennequin, '*Waqf* et monnaie dans l'Égypte mamluke', *JESHO*, 38 (1995).

31 D. P. Little, *A catalogue of the Islamic documents from al-Ḥaram aš-Šarīf in Jerusalem* (Beirut, 1984). An example of how these materials may be used for economic and social history is Y. Rapoport's *Marriage, money and divorce in medieval Islamic society* (Cambridge, 2005).

32 H. Rabie, *The financial system of Egypt AH 564–741/AD 1169–1341* (London, 1972); N. Hanna, *Making big money in 1600: The life and times of Ismaʿil Abū Taqiyya, Egyptian merchant* (Syracuse, 1998).

33 L. Guo, *Commerce, culture, and community in a Red Sea port in the thirteenth century: The Arabic documents from Quseir* (Leiden, 2004). Cf. the review by M. A. Friedman in *JAOS*, 126 (2006), pp. 401–9.

34 M. Hinds and H. Sakkout, *Arabic documents from the Ottoman period from Qasr Ibrīm* (London, 1986); and M. Hinds and V. Menage, *Qasr Ibrīm in the Ottoman period: Turkish and further Arabic documents* (London, 1991).

35 The term is B. Musallim's from his 'The ordering of Muslim societies', in F. Robinson (ed.), *The Cambridge illustrated history of Islam* (Cambridge, 1996), p. 164.

more influential than others in certain times and places. It is also known, for example, that local practices, some of them relating to indigenous minorities or to pre-Islamic practices, had an influence. In the case of Egypt one need only mention the importance of the Coptic calendar, to give but one example, on the agricultural (and therefore also the tax) calendar of Egypt, as seen in the works of al-Nābulusī or Ibn Mammātī.[36] These local factors specific to Egypt were not relevant to other areas of the Islamic world. It is incumbent upon scholars working in those areas to establish the local conditions that shaped the topics of their inquiry.

In short, given the state of the field of economic history of the Muslim world, the first task to accomplish is to gain an awareness of the various economic parameters in place within any geographical and temporal framework. For that reason I will focus on Egypt. Only then may comparison with regions outside that area be conducted on a firm foundation.[37] By focusing on Egypt, however, I am not assuming that it is representative of the wider Islamic world, although it may be. That remains to be established.

Mechanisms of commerce

Money

At the heart of many commercial transactions is money. It is of course possible to use many different materials as money, as well as to conduct trade by barter and avoid money entirely. The historian al-Maqrīzī stated that in his childhood he saw the people of Alexandria using bread as a means of exchange.[38] Many of the eleventh/seventeenth–twelfth/eighteenth-century bills of sale found at Qasr Ibrīm mention tracts of land exchanged for measures of cotton.[39] For the most part, however, money for the periods under examination here meant coins. Thus it is imperative for scholars interested in the economic history of any part of the Muslim world to be familiar with the coinage systems in place at that time and place, as great variance is observed. *Dīnār* and *dirham*, while by far the most commonly encountered terms for gold and silver coins

36 Ibn al-Nābulusī, *Ta'rīkh al-fayyūm wa-bilādih*, ed. B. Moritz (Cairo, 1898); Ibn Mammātī, *Kitāb qawāwīn al-dawāwīn*, ed. A. S. Atiya (Cairo, 1943). Cf. R. C. Cooper, 'Ibn Mammātī's rules for the ministries: Translation with commentary of the *Qawāwīn al-dawāwīn*', Ph.D. thesis, University of California, Berkeley (1973).

37 There is a need to develop detailed case studies first, so that the comparative may follow. See Richard Evans, *In defense of history* (New York, 2000), p. 18.

38 Al-Maqrīzī, *Ighāthat al-umma*, ed. M. M. Ziyāda and J. M. al-Shayyāl (Cairo, 1940), p. 69.

39 Hinds and Sakkout, *Arabic documents*, document nos. 3, 28, 31. Cf. no. 14, where land was exchanged for a combination of 24 measures of cotton and 1.5 piastres.

respectively, are not the only ones found in the source materials. It should also be emphasised that the coins that went by those names often varied considerably, and the failure to take that into account can cause confusion.[40] Moreover, despite the fact that there were many legal discussions of *dīnārs* and *dirhams*, modern scholars have pointed out that the market price of these coins 'rarely corresponded with these definitions'.[41]

Coins are bits of metal used as money. These coins were prepared by hand. Using basic metallurgical techniques, workers would prepare coin flans (blank disks of metal) for striking between two incuse-carved dies which would transfer the words and images of those dies to the two sides of the flan.[42] As is the case with other economic topics, it is easier to study Islamic coins today than four decades ago. This is particularly true for Egypt, where several studies have addressed its monetary history, the most recent overview appearing in 1998.[43] Since then, however, two major studies addressing understudied dynastic periods of Egyptian numismatics, the Ikhshīdid and the Fāṭimid, have appeared.[44] Another major development is the publication of sylloges. A sylloge presents images and descriptions of all the coins of a certain collection, subject to defined parameters of mint and time, and is usually organised by mint series. Sylloges are thought by many to be the next generation in numismatic scholarship after dynastic corpora and institutional catalogues. They support a general movement in this scholarship from questions of identification and attribution towards more intensive analysis of monetary developments. In order to support this sort of research, more published specimens of coins are needed so that scholars may assemble data sets of sufficient size to allow for die studies, metrological studies etc. While the field of classical numismatics is awash with sylloges presenting collections of Greek or Roman coins found in many different cabinets, until recently the field of

40 G. C. Miles, 'Dīnār', *EI2*, vol. II, pp. 297–9; G. C. Miles, 'Dirham', *EI2*, vol. II, pp. 319–20.

41 Cahen, 'Economy, society, institutions', p. 526; M. L. Bates, 'Dirham', *Dictionary of the Middle Ages* (New York, 1984), vol. IV, p. 216.

42 See D. Sellwood, 'Medieval minting techniques', *British Numismatic Journal*, 31 (1982); C. Toll, 'Minting techniques according to Arabic literary sources', *Oriental Suecana*, 19–20 (1970–1); H. W. Brown, 'The medieval mint of Cairo: Some aspects of mint organisation and administration', in N. J. Mayhew, and P. Spufford (eds.), *Later medieval mints: Organisation, administration, and technique*, BAR International Series 389 (1988); and C. Cahen, 'La frappe des monnais en Égypte au VIe/XIIIe siècle d'après le *Minhâj* d'al-Makhzûmî', in L. L. Orlin (ed.), *Michigan Oriental studies in honor of George C. Miles* (Ann Arbor, 1976).

43 W. C. Schultz, 'The monetary history of Egypt, 642–1517', in C. F. Petry (ed.), *The Cambridge history of Egypt*, vol. I: *Islamic Egypt, 640–1517* (Cambridge, 1998).

44 J. L. Bacharach, *Islamic history through coins: An analysis and catalogue of tenth-century Ikshidid coinage* (Cairo, 2006); N. D. Nicol, *A corpus of Fāṭimid coins* (Trieste, 2006).

Islamic numismatics was a relative latecomer to the publication of sylloges. To date, three institutions have begun publishing their Islamic collections in sylloge format, and another is starting the process.[45]

Along with the increased availability of numismatic information, another significant development over the past decades has been a lively debate about the way coins circulated and were valued. Simply put, there is a spectrum of belief, ranging from one end, which assumes the existence of a governing authority to control the monetary activity within its domains, to the other, which, without direct evidence of such control, argues that a different monetary marketplace existed. Central to this debate is the question of how a coin was valued in the marketplace.[46] A coin is money, and money is defined by its functions, usually three: a store of value; a unit of value; and a medium of exchange. This is where terminology such as 'unit of account' comes into play.[47] A coin is valued in terms of how it measures against a scale of value divided by regular units. Thus in the current European Community there are one hundred 'cent' units of account per larger euro unit. But this begs the question. If a coin is valued by a unit of value, what determines that value? For the periods under consideration here, the answer has two components.

The first component is based upon what the coin is made of. This is called the intrinsic value of the coin, and by this is meant the value of the metal used in the coin. In general, coins in the pre-modern Islamic era were made of gold, silver or copper alloys. For the precious metals of gold and silver, the more metal the more value. The second component is determining what that coin was worth in the marketplace. This is called extrinsic value. Standard monetary theory holds that extrinsic value is added to the coin by the cost of minting and the profit paid to the issuing authority, this latter known as the seignorage. Thus a coin would circulate above the value of its bullion content at the combined value of its intrinsic and extrinsic values. In order for this to

45 The three institutions that have published sylloges to date are Forschungstelle für Islamische Numismatik, Tübingen, with its Sylloge Numorum Arabicorum Tübingen (6 vols. to date); the Ashmolean Museum with its Sylloge of Islamic Coins in the Ashmolean Museum (4 vols. to date); and the Orientalischen Münzkabinett in Jena (1 vol. to date). Full citations in the bibliography. The Israel Museum is currently preparing the first sylloge of its Islamic coin collection, devoted to the Mamlūk Egyptian coinage.

46 For an overview of this debate see Schultz, 'The monetary history of Egypt', pp. 318–24. The works of Gilles P. Hennequin are crucial to this question.

47 For a description of the function of monies of account see Peter Spufford, 'Appendix: Coinage and currency', in the *Cambridge economic history of Europe*, vol. III: M. M. Postan, E. F. Rich and Edward Miller (eds.), *Economic organization and policies in the Middle Ages*, (Cambridge, 1963).

work, however, the issuing authority must have influence over the monetary marketplace, perhaps by insisting that only its coins be used, accepting only its coins as payment for legal obligations or requiring all foreign coins to be taken to the mint for melting and reissue. This assumes, therefore, that the issuing authority controls the monetary marketplace. If it does, then surely its coins would circulate above their intrinsic value.

The alternative view does not question the validity of these basic monetary principalities, only their applicability. When the available numismatic evidence and the documentary evidence indicates that coins of multiple types, metals, ages and weights were in circulation, as was the case in the Geniza and the following example, then it is doubtful that the issuing authority could regulate the coinages in use in its territory. The only opportunity to recoup the cost of minting, for example, would be when bullion or old coin was taken to the mint. In this situation it is imperative that scholars know and specify which coins were being used and what they were worth in terms of the other available coins. The sources often do. The documents excavated from Qasr Ibrīm in upper Egypt dating from 1030/1620–1173/1759, for example, mention no less than five different gold coin types, and three different for silver in use, and that is only from the Arabic documents.[48] The seventh/thirteenth-century Quseir documents not only provide additional examples of multiple coins in use, but also illustrate that the personal preferences of merchants and traders could affect which coins were desired for use. Thus we read that one merchant preferred Egyptian *dīnārs* to Meccan. Another document beseeched an agent to accept payment only in silver.[49] This last document also mentions that two different types of *dirhams* with different values were in circulation:

> Do not pay me in golden [*dīnārs*]: change them to silver dirhams. The exchange rate in Qina and Qūs is 37 [*dirhams* per *dīnār*] and [if it is] the *Yūsufī* (?or *tawfīqī*?) [*dirham*] then it is 19 and a quarter dirhams [per *dīnār*]. O God, O God! Send me the cash in [silver] dirhams [only].[50]

As an aside, Guo was uncertain whether the un-pointed adjective specifying the second (and evidently higher-quality silver) *dirham* was *yūsufī* or *tawfīqī* and left it to specialists to consider. As the common names for coins were

48 Hinds and Sakkout, *Arabic documents*, pp. 103–6, documents 45, dated 1718, and 57, dated 1742. These two documents of sale specify that the *qurūsh* (piastres) cited were worth 30 *nisf fiḍḍas*. Each of these was a distinct type of silver coin. In this case, texts indicate that this exchange rate was evidently stable for more than two decades. See also Hinds and Menage, *Qasr Ibrīm*, pp. 107–11.

49 Guo, *Commerce, culture, and community*, document no. 1, pp. 135–8, and no. 13, pp. 163–8.

50 Ibid., document no. 13 and the discussion on p. 57.

frequently derived from some element of the issuing ruler's name, the better choice here would be *yūsufī*, after Saladin's personal name (*ism*). This would fit what is known about Egyptian silver coins in that as an alternative to the common bad-quality 'black' silver coins then in circulation, Saladin issued better-quality silver coins in the late sixth/twelfth century.[51]

In the face of these variables, other assertions should be re-examined. One has to do with coin hoards, those accumulations of coins often found *in situ* during an archaeological dig, or surfacing in the market as an integral whole. Classical numismatic terminology establishes a continuum of hoard finds, with one end held down by 'currency' hoards and the other by 'savings' hoards. 'A currency hoard is a sum of money put together by drawing all its coins from circulation on a single occasion, whereas a saving hoard is formed by gradually adding coins to a hoard over a period of several years; the difference in the way the coins were collected will affect the internal composition of the hoard.'[52] To this distinction some scholars add the category of 'jewellers'' hoards, meaning in this case collections of coins, usually segregated by metal, which were awaiting melting by the jeweller in question. These distinctions are useful, but must be treated carefully. If, for example, coins were not governed by a tightly controlled system of currency, it would be wrong to assume at first glance that a hoard with coins dating from a span of many years is automatically a savings hoard. Such a label draws away from the distinct possibility that older coins were still in circulation long after their minting. I am not saying that this is always the case. Rather, it should always be investigated for the particular time and place under consideration. If there is evidence that coins were tightly regulated in the marketplace then these classical labels may be used with confidence. Without that evidence, however, it is not so simple.

A second area in which initial assumptions must be revisited has to do with coinages made from copper and copper alloys. Due to the low intrinsic value of copper, at least compared to silver and gold, it is usually assumed that such coins are fiat money. That is to say, that their value is controlled by the state at an amount higher than their intrinsic metallic content, usually by means of controlling the number in circulation. A corollary of this is that such coins are usually assumed to be of local currency only. How, after all, could an issuing authority guarantee value outside the area it controlled? But what if archaeological finds indicate that copper coins from Egypt circulated far from the cities

51 See P. Balog, *The coinage of the Ayyūbids* (London, 1980), pp. 29 and 36–7.

52 A. Burnett, *Coins* (London, 1991), p. 51. Cf. J. Casey, *Understanding ancient coins: An introduction for archaeologists and historians* (London, 1986), esp. chap. 5; and P. Grierson, *Numismatics* (Oxford, 1975), pp. 130–6.

of their minting? In the case of the Mamlūk provinces of Jerusalem and Kerak, where there were no mints, Mamlūk copper coins from Cairo and Damascus show up in large numbers in archaeological digs. Clearly they were in use, and people valued them. How does the assumption of 'fiat' valued money hold up in that case? These are questions that need attention. Moreover, if coins were not subject to defined periods of use (the meaning of the term currency), but continued in circulation as long as they had value, this may explain why the Mamlūk ninth/fifteenth-century chronicles consistently refer to copper in circulation while we have little evidence to suggest that it was minted in large quantities after the 790s/1390s.[53]

A third repercussion of an environment of this type is that coins were subject to supply and demand pressures not just of coins but of bullion. Perhaps the most famous example of this from Mamlūk times was the pilgrimage of the Malian ruler Mansā Mūsā in 724/1324f. His entourage spent so much gold dust and bullion in the markets of Cairo that the value of gold dropped in relation to silver. This change was only temporary, however, as normal exchange rates soon reappeared.[54]

An example of money of account: the *dīnār jayshī*

Perhaps the most well-known example of a money of account is the *dīnār jayshī* (lit. 'army dinar'). It was never an actual coin. As such, it is worth emphasising that while it was not tangible it was still real. It was used in Egypt to measure the value of the annual revenues of income-producing agricultural units (villages etc.), especially for the purpose of assigning income via *iqṭā*ʿs to military officers and men. These units produced agricultural goods, and those goods were the basis of the benefit paid to those holding the *iqṭā*ʿs. The *dīnār jayshī* was thus apparently a unit of account designed to straddle the difference between revenue in kind (*ghalla*) and in cash (*ʿayn*). It was said to have been established by the eunuch Qaraqūsh and implemented during the cadastral land survey (*rawk*) ordered by Saladin in 565/1169. It is usually said to have been equivalent in value to one *ardabb* – a measure of volume associated with grain – of wheat and barley. That amount of grain was itself equivalent to

53 See J. L. Bacharach, 'Circassian monetary policy: Copper', *JESHO*, 19 (1976); and B. Shoshan, 'From silver to copper: Monetary changes in fifteenth century Egypt', *SI*, 56 (1982).

54 W. C. Schultz, 'Mansa Musa's gold in Mamluk Cairo: A reappraisal of a world civilizations anecdote', in J. Pfeiffer, S. Quinn and E. Tucker (eds.), *Post-Mongol Central Asia and the Middle East: Studies in history and historiography in honor of Professor John E. Woods* (Wiesbaden, 2006).

one-quarter of a gold *dīnār*. While that basic narrative is well known, the *dīnār jayshī* has caused many a scholar to scratch his head in confusion.[55] Two recent studies by Sato and Borsch, however, have revisited this unit of account in attempts to better understand it and trace its changing value over time. Sato argued that the *dīnār jayshī* existed at different values at the same time, and that soldiers of lower ranks were assigned revenue payments at lower rates than higher-ranking *amīrs*.[56] Borsch rejected this conclusion, arguing that determinations of revenue made by the careful *rawk* of 715/1315 were made in the *dīnār jayshī* prior to distribution of revenue allotments (*ʿibras*) to individuals, and thus were consistent in their initial value. Any change in value in distribution was done after the *ʿibras* were set.[57] In Borsch's words:

> Thus, we know that the dinar jayshi was not a fictitious accounting device, nor was it always used as a malleable measure of value by the bureaucracy. The picture that emerges is one of a money of account that was subject to dual usage. As a measure of land value, it was employed as a unit of the *ardabb*. As a means of payment, it was manipulated by the bureaucracy for salary allocations. The first type of usage, for surveys, strove for accuracy and simplicity; the second for bureaucratic machination and control of payment flows. Viewed from this perspective, [the] superficially confusing role of the dinar jayshi becomes logically clear.[58]

Borsch also demonstrated how the *dīnār jayshī* was used and valued up to the disruptions caused by the Black Death. At that point the revenue levels established by the 715/1315 cadastral survey were rendered useless by peasant deaths and abandoned lands, and the value of the *dīnār jayshī*, set as it was by that survey, was no longer reliable.

Nevertheless the *dīnār jayshī* remains not yet fully understood. As R. S. Cooper pointed out, the earliest known value of the *dīnār jayshī* cited in Ibn Mammātī (d. 607/1209), that of one *ardabb* of wheat and barley, and equivalent to one-quarter of a *dīnār*, is in fact not reliable on textual grounds.[59]

55 See the comments by L. A. Mayer, 'Some problems of Mamluk coinage', in *Transactions of the International Numismatic Congress* (London, 1938); and H. A. R. Gibb, 'The armies of Saladin', in his *Studies on the civilization of Islam* (Boston, 1962), p. 76.

56 T. Sato, *State and rural society in Medieval Islam: Sulṭāns,* muqṭaʿ*as and* fallāḥūn (Leiden, 1997), pp. 153–6.

57 S. J. Borsch, *The Black Death in Egypt and England: A comparative study* (Austin, 2005), pp. 68–71.

58 Ibid., p. 70.

59 R. C. Cooper, 'A note on the dinar jayshi', *JESHO*, 16 (1973), pp. 317–18. Similar discussions are found in Cooper's review of H. Rabie's *The financial system of Egypt*, found in *Journal of Semitic Studies* (1973), p. 186, and in his thesis, 'Ibn Mammātī's rules for the ministries', pp. 364–8.

Moreover, that same passage of Ibn Mammātī indicates that the *dīnār jayshī*'s value in specie (as opposed to the set measure of wheat and barley) could and did change. Ibn Mammātī mentioned values of one-quarter, one-third and even as much as two-thirds of a gold *dīnār* for one *dīnār jayshī*. Thus within a few decades of its initial use the *dīnār jayshī* was being exchanged at different values. We are thus left with the distinct possibility that this unit of account was subject to the same pressures affecting value as those units of account based on actual coins, that is to say issues of supply, demand and the values of both the agricultural goods themselves and the coins in use at the time. As Borsch pointed out, there is every reason to think that agricultural revenue was carefully studied over the course of the 715/1315 survey, and that *ʿibras* were set in terms of a consistently valued *dīnār jayshī*. But as the time from that *rawk* increased, and as facts on the ground inevitably changed, it is also intriguing to consider the possible existence of an alternative marketplace where *ʿibra* – the right to agricultural revenue as stated in terms of the *dīnār jayshī*, which was based upon goods – may have been exchanged for ready cash at various rates of exchange. One can well imagine that the reluctance of an individual to take value in crops may have led to the acceptance of a lesser value in specie.

As an aside, this possible post-bureaucratic use of the *dīnār jayshī* may help us understand one of the ways by which agricultural wealth was transformed into monetary wealth. As is well known, the role of agriculture across the central regions of the eastern hemisphere, but especially in regions such as Egypt and India, always produced more wealth, in total, than trade or other mercantile activities.[60] But agricultural produce in kind does not turn into cash by itself. Someone has to buy it, with money from somewhere. Despite the significant recent work done on the rural economy of Egypt we still do not fully understand how grain was turned into coin.[61] The possibility that rights to agricultural produce, which is what receiving payment in the form of *dīnārs jayshī* implies, were sold for cash in a secondary market may be one such avenue of transformation. But this is speculation, and must await further study.

Finally, some confusion exists about units of value smaller than the existing *dirhams* and *mithqāls*. One such unit of account was the *qīrāṭ*.[62] While a *qīrāṭ* was also a unit of weight (see below), from the context of Ibn Mammātī and al-Nābulusī it clearly meant the fraction 1/24th, and was used for measuring

60 See Hodgson, *Venture of Islam*, vol. I, pp. 124ff.
61 See the works of Sato and Frantz-Murphy in the bibliography to this chapter.
62 E. von Zambaur, 'Ḳīrāṭ', *EI*, vol. IV, pp. 1023–4.

smaller units of both land and money.[63] There is no numismatic evidence, however, that there was ever a specific coin minted in Egypt to the value of a *qīrāṭ*. Thus when one encounters a document such as Quseir no. 31, where a quantity of wheat was cited as being worth 'two *dīnārs* minus two *qīrāṭs*', these two *qīrāṭs* , equivalent to one-twelfth the value of a *dīnār*, are clearly an accounting value.[64] Presumably the seller of this amount, if having received two *dīnārs*' worth of gold from the buyer, would have needed to return this one-twelfth of a *dīnār*'s worth of gold in fragments of broken gold or the equivalent value in some other means of exchange.

Weights and measures

As is clear from the above, weight mattered, especially for coins.[65] Regardless of whether the situation studied was one of consistently struck coins or not, weighing was a necessary means to determine value. It could even be used instead of counting, especially when large amounts were involved, as was the case of the ransom of King Louis IX paid to the Ayyūbids when the monarch was captured during his assault on Egypt in 646–7/1248–9.[66] When multiple coins of varying weights were in circulation, however, weighing is a necessity rather than a convenience, as such coins could not pass by tale (count), but only by weight.

The act of weighing requires three necessary components. The first is an apparatus to do the weighing. The second is a set of weights, meaning, in this sense, a set of objects of known weight used as a standard against which others are compared. The third component is a system of units of defined value which orders and is reflected by the actual weights. Taken together, the study of these phenomena fall under the subject heading of metrology. Similar to the situation of coins, the metrology of the Islamic world before 1800 is a complex topic.[67] Systems and units of measurement varied tremendously

63 In the Qasr Ibrīm documents it is frequently encountered in the meaning of 1/24th of a parcel of land.

64 Guo, *Commerce, culture, and community*, pp. 212–18.

65 For reasons of space I restrict my comments here to the smaller weight units associated with coinage. The subject of units of measurement for commercial goods is a wider topic, and the same comments about the need for an awareness of the various systems in place hold true. For an introduction to these larger units see E. Ashtor, 'Makāyīl and Mawāzīn', *EI2*, vol. VI, pp. 117–21.

66 See Jean de Joinville, 'The life of St Louis', in M. R. B. Shaw, *Chronicles of the Crusades* (London, 1963), p. 258.

67 Ashtor, 'Makāyil and Mawāzīn'; E. Ashtor, 'Levantine weights and standard parcels: A contribution to the metrology of the later Middle Ages', *BSOAS*, 45 (1982); W. Hinz, *Islamische Masse und Gewichte* (Leiden, 1955); J. Walker and D. R. Hill, 'Sanadjāt', *EI2*, vol. X, p. 3.

across time and region, and source material has survived in differing amounts from those periods and places.[68] While it once was possible to assert the existence of 'unalterable quantities' in Islamic metrology, that is no longer the case.[69] One assumes consistency at one's peril.

In terms of the first component, the apparatus for weighing, the Islamic world had access to both double-pan scales (*mīzān*) and to steelyards (*qarasṭūn*).[70] The knowledge existed to make these with great accuracy. Al-Khāzinī (*fl.* sixth/twelfth century) wrote of a scale approaching 1/60,000 in precision.[71] Techniques to measure specific gravity were known, which enabled the purity of gold and silver alloys to be determined. Fraudulent methods of manipulating scales were also known and described. Most of what we know about these instruments and their use is from analytical treatises such as al-Khāzinī's, however. Very few artifactual remnants of scales have survived.[72] Thus it is especially useful when documents such as Quseir nos. 2 and 16 are found, for the first mentions the difference observed between two scales, and the second contains a warning not to trust a particular scale. Together they corroborate aspects of what is known from the normative sources.[73]

Such instruments, however, could only establish the weight of one object (or substance) in relation to another object. They relied upon balance to establish equivalencies between the object (or substance) being weighed and an object of known weight. Thus, in order to know the weights of coins it is necessary to know the second component of weighing in place at the time, the weights that were used. While theoretical treatises exist, we are lucky that surviving weights

68 Many scholars have discussed these differences. Ashtor ('Makāyil and Mawāzīn') noted the differences between the metrological systems found in the Arabic- and Persian-speaking spheres of the early Islamic world. J. Kolbas has argued that there were four different *mithqāl*-standards influencing the Mongol coinage minted in the Islamic world. See her 'Mongol money: The role of Tabriz from Chingiz Khan to Uljaytu: 616 to 709 H/1220 to 1309 AD', Ph.D. thesis, New York University (1992), pp. 8–10.

69 Von Zambaur, 'Ḳīrāṭ'. Note as well the cautionary words of G. C. Miles ('Dirham') about earlier efforts to define traditional units in modern metric grams. These efforts have 'resulted in various figures, most of them probably erroneous'.

70 E. Wiedemann, 'al-Mīzān', *EI2*, vol. VII, pp. 195–204. For the steelyard see K. Jaouiche, 'al-Ḳarasṭūn', *EI2*, vol. IV, p. 629.

71 J. Vernet, 'al-Khāzinī', *EI2*, vol. IV, p. 1186.

72 L Holland, author of *Weights and weight-like objects from Caesarea Maritima* (Hadera, 2009), estimates the survival rate of scale parts as compared to weight objects as less than one per several hundred. Personal communication with the author.

73 See Guo, *Commerce, culture, and community*, documents 2, 16. For a documentary reference to a scale, see the Mamlūk inheritance deed that lists a scale accompanied by four Roman bronze coins (possibly used as weights?), see K. J. al-'Asali, *Wathā'iq maqdasiyya ta'rīkhiyya*, 2 vols. (Beirut, 1985), vol. II, no. 635.

are well attested for Egypt for most Islamic periods.[74] The overwhelming majority of these objects were made of glass.[75] They exist in great quantities from the early Islamic period of Umayyad and ʿAbbāsid rule, and again from the Fāṭimid period, with good representation as well from the Ayyūbid and Mamlūk eras. While it has been argued by some that these glass objects served as money, it is highly unlikely that they did so in any official capacity.[76] These objects are extremely valuable to us as source material for the actual weight values of Egyptian ponderal units.[77] Since most of the surviving examples do not have legends which tell us the weight unit for which they were used, it is necessary to study them alongside what is known about the final component of weighing, an agreed-upon system of weight values.

In Islamic Egypt the terminology of weight units often overlapped with the terminology for coins and units of account, resulting in much confusion. In a nutshell, the *dirham* was a basic unit of weight, although how much a *dirham* weighed could vary according to what was weighed. The evidence suggests, for example, that the *dirham* unit for weighing small amounts of substances such as plant extracts etc. was slightly heavier than the *dirham* unit applied to silver coins.[78] For the Mamlūk period, for example, I have argued that the *dirham* weight unit for silver coins was slightly less than 3 grams. Heavier than the *dirham* was the *mithqāl*, a unit of slightly more than 4 grams often used to weigh gold as well as other precious commodities such as gems. Multiple units of the *dirham* existed, such as the *ūqiyya* of 12 *dirhams*, and the *raṭl* of 144 *dirhams*.[79] The overwhelming majority of surviving glass weights, however,

74 See P. Balog, *Umayyad, ʿAbbāsid, and Ṭūlūnid glass weights and vessel stamps* (New York, 1976); G. C. Miles, 'On the varieties and accuracy of eighth century Arab coin weights', *Eretz Israel*, 7 (1963). It is also possible to derive metrological information from European sources. See, for example, J- C. Hocquet, 'Methodologie de l'histoire des poids et mesures le commerce maritime entre Alexandrie et Venise durant le Haut Moyen Age', in *Mercati e mercanti nell'alto medioevo: L'area euroasiatica e l'area mediterranea* (Spoleto, 1993).

75 There are some Egyptian metallic weights, however. See P. Balog, 'Islamic bronze weights from Egypt', *JESHO*, 13 (1970), esp. pp. 237–41. In nearby Syria, however, the surviving weights are almost always metallic: see L. Holland, 'Islamic bronze weights from Caesarea Maritima', *American Numismatic Society Museum Notes*, 31 (1986).

76 For an overview of these controversies see Walker and Hill, 'Sanadjāt'; and the discussion in Schultz, 'The monetary history of Egypt', p. 330.

77 Bates has pointed out that glass weights 'are a better indication of the weight standards for gold and silver and copper coins than anything we can obtain from the coins themselves'. See his 'Coins and money in the Arabic papyri', in Y. Ragheb (ed.), *Documents de l'Islam médiéval: Nouvelles perspectives de recherche* (Cairo, 1991), p. 55.

78 See W. C. Schultz, 'Mamluk metrology and the numismatic evidence', *al-Masāq* 15, 1 (2003).

79 In Syria, however, the *ūqiyya* was apparently made up of 50 *dirhams*, according to al-Maqrīzī. See Adel Allouche, *Mamluk economics: A study and translation of al-Maqrīzī's* Ighāthah (Salt Lake City, 1994), p. 90.

are lighter in weight than these larger multiples. When the weights of these specimens are plotted on a frequency table, which graphs these individual objects on a vertical axis of number and a horizontal axis of weight, the resulting graphs suggest what the desired weight values were for these units.[80] For the Fāṭimid, Ayyūbid and Mamlūk glass weights, for example, such graphs produce clear clusters around 1.50, 3.00 and 6.00 grams, strongly suggesting their use as half-*dirham*, *dirham* and double-*dirham* weights. For the Mamlūk period clusters also exist at slightly less than 4.25 and 8.50 grams, indicating possible use as *mithqāl* and double-*mithqāl* weights. These clusters are much smaller, however, which poses some problems. If they are indeed *mithqāl* weights, why do so few survive? This is especially problematic since for the first 167 years of Mamlūk rule in Egypt gold coinage was struck with a wide variance in weight.[81]

Moving back in time, frequency-table analysis has suggested another possible mystery. In 2007 a digital catalogue was published of the glass weights and other glass objects of the Gayer-Anderson Museum in Cairo.[82] When the more than 700 Fāṭimid glass weights were plotted, two clusters appeared outside the expected and found clusters around the *dirham* values. These were a small cluster of eleven objects around 1.90 grams, and a larger cluster of twenty-seven around 3.80 grams. While these clusters are smaller than those found around the *dirham*-associated values (fifty-four fall in the 2.90–2.99 gram interval, for example), they are more than another non-*dirham* affiliated cluster. In addition, the majority of these specimens bear the name of al-Hakim. When the non-al-Hakim specimens were plotted, only five objects fell into those clusters. The significance of this development is unknown, but suggests that further investigation is needed.

Finally, two comments are needed. First, it must be stated that there were smaller weight units in use, although we do not have surviving specimens of these smaller units except in multiples. Such is the case of the *qīrāṭ* used for weight. We have multiple-*qīrāṭ* weights which survive from the early Islamic

80 G. F. Hill, 'The frequency table', *Numismatic Chronicle*, 5, 4 (1924). Frequency tables are not without their limitations or their abuses. Nevertheless, they are quite useful for revealing basic metrological tendencies and developments.

81 See W. C. Schultz, 'Medieval coins and monies of account: The case of large-flan Mamluk dinars', *al-ʿUṣūr al-Wusṭá: The Bulletin of the Middle East Medievalists*, 12, 2 (October 2000).

82 J. L. Bacharach, R. al-Nabarawy, S. Anwar and A. Yousef, *A complete catalog (sylloge) of the glass weights, vessel stamps, and ring weights in the Gayer-Anderson Museum, Cairo (Mathaf Bayt al-Kritliyya)*, available at http://www.numismatics.org/dpubs/islamic/ga/. The findings presented here are discussed in my forthcoming review of this digital sylloge.

period in Egypt.[83] Second, while we have no surviving accounts of how these weights were made, we do have some information on how they were regulated. Manuals written for market inspectors often have a section describing how the market inspector (*muḥtasib*) should examine and certify weights in use by merchants. These mention, for example, checking for nicks or abrasions on weights and looking suspiciously upon merchants who have multiple sets of weights without good cause, thus showing an awareness of the possibility of fraud.[84]

Legal and commercial instruments

At the time Udovitch's *Partnership and profit* appeared there were no known examples of commenda or proprietary partnerships from Islamic sources in Egypt. The only known examples of such documents were from the Geniza.[85] It was thus impossible in 1970 to ask whether the legal strictures described in the third/ninth century, for example, continued to be used beyond the seventh/thirteenth century, which was when the Geniza documents of economic import became less numerous. A recent work, however, makes it possible to begin to address this question. In her 1998 book *Making big money in 1600* Nelly Hanna analysed the life and career of an Egyptian merchant named Ismaʿil Abu Taqiyya from around 990/1580 to 1034/1625.[86] An extremely wealthy and successful merchant, this individual left no record in the chronicles or biographical dictionaries of his age, yet left a considerable trail of legal documents preserved in the court records of Ottoman-era Cairo. He apparently never left Egypt, yet ran a commercial practice which stretched from West Africa to the north-east Mediterranean and to the Red and Arabian Seas. To run his network of commercial interests, as Hanna points out, he used legal structures far older than himself. In particular, he showed an affinity for the *ʿaqd shirka* (partnership contract), a direct legal descendant of the *sharikat al-ʿaqd* described in the earlier manuals analysed by Udovitch. Abu

83 See Balog, *Umayyad, ʿAbbāsid and Ṭūlūnid glass weights*, pp. 25–7.

84 See R. P. Buckley, 'The book of the Islamic market inspector', *Journal of Semitic Studies Supplement*, 9 (1999), pp. 44–5; Ibn al-Ukhuwwa, *The Maʿālim al-qurba fī aḥkām al-ḥisba*, ed. Reuben Levy (London, 1938), pp. 83–6 of the Arabic edition, pp. 26–9 of the summary translation.

85 Udovitch, *Partnership and profit*, pp. 8–9, citing A. Grohman, *Einführung und Chrestomathie zur Arabischen Papyruskunde*, 2 vols. (Prague, 1954), vol. I. For the examples of the Geniza documents see Goitein, *A Mediterranean society*, vol. I, pp. 87–92 and appendix C.

86 Hanna, *Making big money in 1600*. See esp. chap. 3, 'The structures of trade', pp. 43–69. For an overview of eighth-century Cairene merchants see A. Raymond, *Artisans et commerçants au Caire au XVIIIe siècle* (Damascus, 1973).

Taqiyya did not, however, make much use of the commenda. (When he did, the term used was *muḍāraba*, suggesting a Ḥanafī influence.) While Hanna did not provide texts of these documents or a detailed analysis of them, she identified them, thus providing clear signposting for further study. Such a study could provide insight into how the legal strictures of the *fiqh* materials translated into actual documentation. Moreover, Abu Taqiyya showed a willingness to use the different schools of law in his partnership contracts, and it would be a useful exercise indeed to check which transactions were registered with which judge to see what patterns, if any, emerge.

More evidence about the use of various commercial partnerships has also recently emerged from the Geniza. At the time of his death Goitein left unfinished what he called his 'India book', a collection of Geniza documents having to do with the India trade. This book was recently brought to publication by M. A. Friedman as *India traders of the Middle Ages: Documents from the Cairo Geniza*. This collection contains one poorly preserved commenda document (I, 30), and some of the letters included mention commendas and other partnerships and provide evidence of their actual use.[87]

Conclusion

This chapter has surveyed developments in the study of the mechanisms of commerce in the Muslim world before 1800. While there is no doubt that our knowledge of some aspects of these topics has expanded considerably since the publication of the *CHI* it is also true that even for Egypt, about which we probably know more than any other region of the Islamic world pre-1800, there is still much to be done. Documents discovered need to be edited. Edited documents need to be examined in the light of the theoretical issues raised here and studied for what they reveal about economic issues. Most importantly, scholars need to be trained to do this type of research and supported when they do so. The current situation for researchers interested in matters economic is similar to that encountered by the nautical archaeologist George Bass, who faced difficulties finding experts to consult on what he was bringing up from the fifth/eleventh-century 'glass-wreck' of the southwest Anatolian coast. As Bass wrote in the introduction of the first volume devoted to these archaeological findings:

87 S. D. Goitien and M. A. Friedman, *India traders of the Middle Ages: Documents from the Cairo Geniza* (Leiden, 2008), documents I, 22; I, 30; III, 4–6.

> To put our ship into an accurate historical context, to avoid misinterpretation of its artefacts and food remains, and to find more contemporary literary references to daily life in Medieval Islam, I purposely gave a series of lectures on the shipwreck at a university with one of the world's great departments of medieval Islamic Studies. I wrote in advance to ask if I might meet with some of the faculty or students who could help us avoid publishing utter nonsense … The chairman of the department answered 'I have to confess we are all rank laymen in the field, staff and students alike, and really quite unable, unfortunately, to hold an intelligent discussion on the subject … If there is anything we can do to help we shall of course be glad to do so, but our field lies mainly in language, literature, religion and history, and I do not know if this would be of any use to you.' No one from the department attended my lectures. Be tolerant, then, of mistakes made by those of us who wrote parts of this volume and the volumes that follow, but who were not formally trained in medieval Islamic literature, religion, and history.[88]

The only way we will learn more about the mechanisms of commerce throughout the wide Islamic world is by making use not only of the contributions of the traditional fields of language, literature, religion and history, but by moving beyond the normative emphasis often found (in the first three in particular) to develop the skills necessary to utilise the material artefacts and texts of daily life.

88 G. F. Bass, S. Matthews, J. R. Steffy and F. H. van Doorninck, Jr (eds.), *Serçe Limanı: An eleventh-century shipwreck*, vol. I: *The ship and its anchorage, crew, and passengers*, Ed Rachal Foundation Nautical Archaeology Series (College Station, TX, 2004).

12

Women, gender and sexuality

MANUELA MARÍN

Women and gender

The history of women in Islamic societies has made steady progress over the last few decades, following the spectacular growth of the field in other historiographical arenas. Particularly, although not exclusively, Ottomanists have contributed to the increase in publications on women's history, thanks to the richness of Ottoman archives. For other periods of Islamic history the lack of archival evidence has not hindered the completion of some good studies based upon other sources: literary works, chronicles, biographical dictionaries or juridical writings.[1] To some extent these different sources are complementary. While archival documents illuminate the lives of ordinary individuals making an appearance in court, other texts inform us about societal attitudes, normative rulings and transgressions. Biographical accounts, although normally restricted to specific social groups, such as urban elites or sovereign families, have the added value of charting women's lives across a longer period of time, which is usually impossible from research into archival documents. In a challenge to the traditional view of women in classical Islam as unknown, hidden and passive members of society, research based upon all these sources increasingly demonstrates the crucial role played by gender and gendered attitudes and norms.

Women, however, were not an absolute category, permeating all social levels – although Muslim authors gladly accepted this assumption. Against the mere fact of being a woman (undoubtedly a second-class member of the community, presided over by Muslim free males), historical research has to consider many other factors. Differences among women, according to their social or economic situation, their ethnic origins, their personal status – free or

1 See the essays collected in M. Marín and R. Deguilhem (eds.), *Writing the feminine: Women in Arab sources* (London, 2002).

slaves, single or married – and their residential lifestyles – urban, peasant or nomadic – have to be taken into account before making sweeping generalisations. Muslim women were not only defined by their religious affiliation, although this fact deeply influenced their lives. For the majority of women living in Muslim societies religion was just a factor to be considered in conjunction with many others, and social rank was predominant among them. As an example, Muslim women who were members of elite households were expected to follow seclusion rules that did not apply to their lower-class counterparts. Second, personal status affected women's lives in ways similar to men's but in a strikingly different manner. For a woman, being a slave, for example, meant that her owner had the legal right of using her sexually – and of giving her the added status of *umm al-walad*, that is, 'the mother of the child', when she became the mother of her master's acknowledged child, one among all the other legitimate inheritors of their father. Women, in urban or rural locations, populated a complex map of social and economic relationships, amalgamated kinship ties, and were used as markers of political and moral boundaries.

Women's visibility in public spaces was subjected to strict social regulations. Moralists such as Ibn ʿAbdūn in sixth/twelfth-century Seville or Ibn al-Ḥājj in eighth/fourteenth-century Cairo strongly disapproved of the appearance of women in markets, cemeteries, streets and other public spaces.[2] Women of elite families were kept out of the sight of unrelated males, and when necessity called them from their homes they had to be veiled. Family honour and prestige were at stake if free Muslim women could be seen and spoken about by men who were not their relatives, and women's seclusion became a mark of status for elite households.[3] When Ibn Bāq (d. 763/1362) wrote his manual on the economic obligations of husbands towards their wives, he observed that cork shoes (the kind of shoes used for walking in the streets) were not needed by high-class women, who scarcely used them.[4] Gender segregation was the crucial mark of the upper echelons of society, and

2 See H. Lutfi, 'Manners and customs of fourteenth-century Cairene women: Female anarchy versus male *sharʿī* order in Muslim prescriptive treatises', in N. R. Keddie and B. Baron (eds.), *Women in Middle Eastern history: Shifting boundaries in sex and gender* (New Haven, 1991); and V. Aguilar and M. Marín, 'Las mujeres en el espacio urbano de al-Andalus', in Julio Navarro Palazón (ed.), *Casas y palacios de al-Andalus* (Barcelona, 1995).

3 See F. Rosenthal, 'Male and female: Described and compared', in J. W. Wright and Everett K. Rowson (eds.), *Homoeroticism in classical Arabic literature* (New York, 1997); and L. Peirce, *Morality tales: Law and gender in the Ottoman court of Aintab* (Berkeley and Los Angeles, 2003), p. 156.

4 M. Marín, *Mujeres en al-Ándalus* (Madrid, 2000), p. 202.

transgression of this rule would imply a loss of honour for the male members of the family. By virtue of their seclusion, elite women guaranteed the purity of their family's honour; not even their names could be known by strangers. An efficient way of shaming men was to name their womenfolk in satirical poems, as attested by a well-known anecdote in which the poet Ibn Shuhayd (d. 399/1008) frightened a lady, who was going with her retinue to the Cordoba main mosque, by his presence at the gate; she left immediately, being afraid that Ibn Shuhayd would name her in a poem and dishonour her family. The poem Ibn Shuhayd wrote about the encounter is preserved, and nothing in it has the least hint of impropriety for the modern reader, but its hidden meaning – visual contact with a forbidden woman – was clearly understood as a menacing weapon by the parties involved.[5]

Restrictions on elite women's presence in public spaces did not mean that they were totally cut off from social relationships. On the contrary, a complex web of personal contacts was established around them. Slaves, eunuchs, servants and women of other social status made sure that wealthy and powerful secluded women kept in touch with the world outside their homes, and influenced events in the political and social arenas. However, beyond the scope of urban, high-class households, the public presence of women is attested to by the very censorship condemning it, as in other historical testimonials. Prohibitions for women to be out in the streets are significant, as they show how common this behaviour was in places such as Cairo or Damascus. In 653/1264 al-Muʿizz Aybak forbade women to go out from their homes, and in Ramaḍān of 690/1291 the governor of Damascus, Sanjar al-Shujāʿī, forbade men and women to circulate at night in the city.[6] In the month of Rajab of 825/1422 the governor of Cairo, Ṣadr al-Dīn Aḥmad ibn al-ʿAjamī, forbade women to stay in shops waiting for the ceremonial exit of the pilgrimage to Mecca, something that they had previously used to do, spending the night in the market stalls.[7]

Mosques, public baths, markets and cemeteries were places frequented by women, but their visits to public spaces, in particular baths and mosques, were limited to ensure that they did not come in contact with men. Visiting the tombs of relatives, or of saints and pious men in the great cemetery of al-Qarāfa, was a favourite outing for Cairene women, who also participated in religious festivals,

5 J. T. Monroe, 'The striptease that was blamed on Abu Bakr's naughty son: Was Father being shamed, or was the poet having fun? (Ibn Quzmān's *zajal* no. 133)', in Wright and Rowson (eds.), *Homoeroticism*, pp. 107–8.

6 M. Chapoutot-Ramadi, 'Femmes dans la ville mamlūke', *JESHO*, 38 (1995), p. 148.

7 A. ʿAbd ar-Rāziq, *La femme au temps des mamlouks en Egypte* (Cairo, 1973), p. 35.

such as Aḥmad al-Badawī's birthday in Ṭanṭa.[8] A more profane location for the free mingling of men and women was along the shores of the Nile, and on the river itself, where boats carried a mixed company for pleasure trips. The space surrounding rivers, such as the Nile in Cairo or the Guadalquivir in Seville, developed into areas of transgression, where social norms of segregation were suspended, to the great scandal of moralists.

The law court was perhaps the locale where the public presence of women was unquestionably admitted. Court registers, when preserved, and literary documents of many kinds, are full of instances of women who conducted lawsuits in defence of their interests. In the Ottoman registers of the Imperial Council, which was a kind of supreme court, women's petitions are frequently noted as complaints against corrupt judges, trustees of religious endowments and other high officials in their places of residence.[9] In fact, it is thanks to the gender-blind character of the Islamic legal system that we now have such detailed information about the social, economic and family problems affecting women.

Disapproval or condemnation of women's visibility in public spaces was elevated to the category of a social and religious ideal, at least for the upper classes of society. In these circles a two-faced image of women was created and developed by the learned members of the community, reflecting and adopting male anxieties about women's sexuality. As in other non-Muslim cultures – a case in point is the Christian Mediterranean space – 'good' women were characterised by their obedience, religiosity, modesty and chastity.[10] These were the virtues expected from the women in well-to-do families, whose honour had to be protected from outside dangers. But the other side of the coin was the potential threat that these same women posed, as active, sexually uncontrolled agents who could undermine the genealogical purity of the patrilineal family.[11] A continuous literary output, very similar in fact to

8 A. Schimmel, 'Eros – heavenly and not so heavenly – in Sufi literature and life', in A. L. al-Sayyid-Marsot (ed.), *Society and the sexes in medieval Islam* (Malibu, 1979), p. 120.

9 F. Zarinebaf-Shahr, 'Women, law, and imperial justice in Ottoman Istanbul in the late seventeenth century', in Amira El Azhary Sonbol (ed.), *Women, the family, and divorce laws in Islamic history* (Syracuse, 1996).

10 H. Lutfi, 'al-Sakhāwī's *Kitāb al-nisā'* as a source for the social and economic history of Muslim women during the fifteenth century AD', *The Muslim World*, 21 (1981), p. 110. See also N. El Cheikh, 'In search of the ideal spouse', *JESHO*, 45 (2002). A similar paradigm appears in the Jewish culture of the Middle East: see R. Lamdan, *A separate people: Jewish women in Palestine, Syria and Egypt in the sixteenth century* (Leiden, 2000), pp. 13–14.

11 S. H. Oberhelman, 'Hierarchies of gender, ideology, and power, in ancient and medieval Greek and Arabic dream literature', in Wright and Rowson (eds.), *Homoeroticism*, p. 67.

contemporary misogynist attitudes in the Western world, underlined the capacity of women for deceiving men, using as authoritative references texts from the Qur'ān and the Prophetic tradition.[12] The 'tricks of women' genre is well represented by the work of the ninth/fifteenth century Ibn al-Batanūnī, the *Kitāb al-ʿUnwān fī makāyīd al-niswān*.[13]

Fear of the 'disorder' (*fitna*) created by unrestricted women can be detected in apocalyptic traditions linking the upside-down reality of the last Hour with the abomination of women circulating freely in the urban landscape and asserting their own sexual personality.[14] Veiling and seclusion were thus considered to be the guardians of the social and religious order, and trangressions against this ideal could only result in punishment for the community. When, in 841/1438, Egypt suffered from plague and famine, the Mamlūk sultan Barsbāy asked the religious scholars (*ʿulamāʾ*) about the causes of these misfortunes. Their answer was unanimous: the presence of women in the streets was the first reason for God's punishment on the Egyptian realm. Immediately, the sultan issued a decree ordering women to stay at home.[15]

Beyond the images created and sustained by the male learned elite, women occupied crucial spaces in the social scene. We have just seen how their public presence, although heavily conditioned by moral censorship, is consistently documented both by its denunciation and the decrees forbidding it. More problematic was women's access to positions allowing them to preside over men. Women were excluded from judgeship and from directing the communal prayer in the mosque (although there is an instance of a woman who, in 615/1218, delivered the funeral sermon for Saladin's brother, al-ʿĀdil).[16]

12 F. Malti-Douglas, *Woman's body, woman's word: Gender and discourse in Arabo-Islamic writing* (Princeton, 1991), pp. 49ff.; on Prophetic tradition demeaning to women see K. Abou El Fadl, *Speaking in God's name: Islamic law, authority and women* (Oxford, 2001), pp. 209–63.

13 Malti-Douglas, *Woman's body, woman's word*, p. 54. See also the reflections of R. Irwin, 'ʿAlī al-Baghdādī and the joy of Mamluk sex', in Hugh Kennedy (ed.), *The historiography of Islamic Egypt (c. 950–1800)* (Leiden, 2001), p. 56, on ʿAlī al-Baghdādī's *Kitab al-Zahr al-Anīq*; for Irwin the book, although belonging to the same medieval genre, reflects the admiration of its author for the cunning and quick-wittedness of women. A. M. Eddé ('Images de femmes en Syrie à l'époque ayyoubide', in Patrick Henriet and Anne-Marie Legras (eds.), *Au cloître et dans le monde: Femmes, hommes et sociétés (IXe–XVe siècle): Mélanges en l'honneur de Paulette L'Hermite-Leclercq* (Paris, 2000), pp. 71–6) has located, in Arab chronicles from Syria, the stereotype of the witch, a threatening image for masculine sexuality.

14 W. Saleh, 'The woman as a locus of apocalyptic anxiety in medieval Sunni Islam', in Angelika Neuwirth, Birgit Embaló, Sebastian Gunther and Maher Jarrar (eds.), *Myths, historical archetypes and symbolic figures in Arabic literature* (Beirut, 1999), pp. 142–3.

15 Lutfi, 'Manners and customs', p. 101.

16 Eddé, 'Images de femmes', p. 69.

Intervention of women in political affairs was severely disapproved of, and their actual assumption of power a scandal which would bring all kinds of disasters to the community. However, the variety of cultural traditions and of historical situations within Islamic history allowed different women – and in very different positions – to share a certain degree of political power with men. In the Maghrib, one of the arguments used by the Almohads against their predecessors, the Almoravids, was that after 500/1106f. women of the Almoravid royal family had taken over the affairs of the state.[17] Historical evidence points indeed to a greater presence of women in the political scene under the Almoravids, who were of Berber origins.[18] But no woman in the Almoravid ruling family took the unprecedented step of exercising political power by herself – the most distinguished woman in the family, Zaynab al-Nafzāwīya, financed the career of her husband, Yūsuf ibn Tāshfīn (d. 500/1106), and became his most trusted adviser.

Two women's names have attracted the attention of contemporary scholarship, as they were rulers in their own right, and their names were even mentioned in the Friday sermon: the Yemenite Arwā (d. 532/1138) and the Egyptian Shajar al-Durr (d. 655/1257).[19] The only common fact linking these women's biographies is their exceptionality as feminine rulers; otherwise, their careers and circumstances could not be more dissimilar. The long reign of Arwā, who received the title Sayyida Ḥurra ('the noble free woman') was closely associated with the Fāṭimid dynasty and the propagation of Ismāʿīlī doctrines, and she reigned in Yemen after marrying the Ṣulayḥid Aḥmad al-Mukarram, who soon retired from public life and then died, leaving Arwā in charge of public affairs. Shajar al-Durr, for her part, was originally a slave, married to one of the last Ayyūbids, al-Ṣāliḥ Ayyūb. Her short reign was the prelude to the Mamlūk takeover, and although she controlled the army and the treasury for a while, she found it impossible to perform other duties expected of Muslim sovereigns, such as presiding over public ceremonies and military parades. She was finally murdered in obscure circumstances.

Exceptional as they are, the figures of these two women should not overshadow other more usual exercises of political power by women. Regency for a minor son or grandson was a not infrequent possibility, as happened in

17 Marín, *Mujeres en al-Ándalus*, p. 243.

18 It has been proposed by some historians and anthropologists that women enjoyed a greater autonomy in a Berber environment. Incidentally, Almohads were, like Almoravids, of Berber origins, although from a different tribal network.

19 See the works by F. Daftary, M. Chapoutot-Ramadi, L. al-Imad and G. Schregle cited in the chapter bibliography.

the case of the renowned Ḍayfa Khātūn (d. 640/1243) in Ayyūbid Aleppo.[20] Several women who were mothers of Mamlūk sultans are described by Arab chroniclers as having great influence over their sons in the conduct of political affairs, such as the mother of Baraka Khān, or Khawand Ashlūn, who was the mother of al-Nāṣir Muḥammad ibn Qalāwūn.[21] In the Maghrib another 'Sayyida Ḥurra', this time called ʿĀʾisha bint ʿAlī, succeeded in installing her son-in-law as governor of Tetuan in 944/1537, while herself exercising de facto governorship until 949/1542, when she was expelled from the city. She then took up residence in her birthplace of Xauen and spent the rest of her life there, devoting herself to pious activities until her death in 969/1562.[22] But it was perhaps under Ottoman rule that women acquired a more significant role as mothers of sovereigns and princes, over whose households they presided. As the *wālide sulṭān* (an official title consecrating her position) the mother of the reigning Ottoman monarch became a political entity of first importance.[23]

Arab and Turkish chronicles did not approve of the role played by women in the dynastic policies of the Mamlūks and Ottomans, and, not suprisingly, they identified the pre-eminence of women with decadence and corruption in political and social affairs.[24] The traditional view required an explanation for the unusual entry of women into the political arena, and this was more often than not the seductive powers of women over their royal husbands, whose will they were able to dominate by all kinds of means, including magic arts.[25] In all the cases presented here, however, the common factor is that the political agency of women was necessarily linked to the presence of a man: brother, husband or son. In the great imperial dynasties, such as the Mamlūks and the Ottomans, women could became – and in fact did become, under the Ottomans – powerful figures in the inner circles of the palace; always, however, as necessary elements in the family politics of the dynasty.

20 See Y. Tabbaa, 'Ḍayfa Khātūn, regent queen and architectural patron', in D. Fairchild Ruggles (ed.), *Women, patronage and self-representation in Islamic societies* (Albany, 2000). On the limits of Arab historical sources for recovering women's activities in the context of royal families see M. J. Viguera, 'A borrowed space: Andalusi and Maghribi women in chronicles', in Marín and Deguilhem (eds.), *Writing the feminine*.

21 'Abd ar-Rāziq, *La femme au temps des mamlouks*, p. 27.

22 C. de La Véronne, 'Sida el-Ḥorra, la noble dame', *Hespéris*, 48 (1956).

23 L. Peirce, *The imperial harem: Women and sovereignty in the Ottoman empire* (Oxford and New York, 1993).

24 They are sometimes followed in this interpretation by modern scholarship (see Irwin, 'ʿAlī al-Baghdādī', p. 48).

25 Peirce, *The imperial harem*, p. 63.

At all levels of society family was indeed the privileged space for women's lives, as both the religious and the social ideal consider women primarily as wives and mothers. The classical orientalist view of the patriarchical Muslim family as following the 'oriental despot model' in which the paterfamilias exercised an absolute power over the members of the household has been challenged by recent research. On the one hand, multiple relationships were created within the family, developing a variety of hierarchies among men and women, age groups and slave / free members of the household. On the other, the main characteristic of the Muslim family was the fact that these relationships were governed by a set of legal rules, giving every individual, male or female, rights and obligations. Thus marriage contracts, divorce or repudiation, polygamy and economic autonomy, all questions deeply affecting women's lives, were under the provisions of Muslim law, and the access of women to courts, as already pointed out, facilitated the role of the judicial agents as mediators in family conflicts.[26]

The protection of the law did not apply equally to all women. Those living in cities or towns with a judge – or, even better, belonging to the middle and upper classes – were more likely to be shielded from infringements of their rights. In rural or tribal contexts it seems that customary law, often damaging to women's interests, could prevail over Islamic norms, as is shown in the case of the twelfth / eighteenth-century Moroccan scholar al-Kīkī, active in the mountains of the Middle High Atlas. Al-Kīkī wrote a juridical opinion (*fatwā*) trying to convince his fellow tribesmen that they were behaving unfairly towards their women, who, contrary to the requirements of Islamic law, were obliged to donate their lawful properties to their male relatives.[27]

Central to the rights of married women was the establishment of a marriage contract. As an indispensable condition for the validity of a marriage, this document could prevent harmful actions on the part of the husband towards the psychological and economic well-being of his wife. Several clauses in the contract established the amount of the dowry to be paid to the bride (usually divided in two parts: one paid when the contract was signed; and the second delayed in anticipation of a divorce or of widowhood), the length of absence accorded to the husband from the marital home, conditions for the residence of the married couple etc. Of significant relevance was the clause by which the husband renounced marriage to a second woman or the taking

26 N. Hanna, 'Marriage among merchant families in seventeenth-century Cairo', in Sonbol (ed.), *Women, the family, and divorce laws*.

27 Muḥammad ibn ʿAbd Allāh al-Kīkī, *Mawāhib dhī l-jalāl fī nawāzil al-bilād al-sāʾiba min al-jibāl*, ed. Aḥmad Tawfīq (Beirut, 1997).

of a concubine. Contract marriages in eleventh/seventeenth-century Cairo include clauses allowing a woman who was a peddler to continue her trade after marriage, or another stipulating that her husband would permit her to go to the public bath, to visit and be visited by friends and relatives, and to perform the pilgrimage to Mecca. Physical mistreatment could be foreseen as a cause for divorce and so be written into the marriage contract.[28]

Polygamy and unilateral divorce by the husband were the more serious threats to married women's welfare. It would seem, however, that polygamy, outside the sovereign families and other exceptional cases, was not as frequent as divorce and remarriage. Research based upon Ottoman archives from ʿAintab in the tenth/sixteenth century and Bursa in the eleventh/seventeenth agree that polygamy was either non-existent or at a very low incidence level, and the same conclusion has been reached in the case of the elite group of Ottoman scholars in the twelfth/eighteenth century.[29] The Mamlūk elites, on the other hand, are described as very prone to polygamy, although the lack of archival evidence means that research has to rely on biographical and literary documents describing only selected social groups.[30] In the case of the ruling families, polygamy was such a common trait that the monogamous marriage of the Mamlūk sultan Ināl al-Ajrūd and Zaynab was considered a unique case among their peers.[31]

Repudiation and divorce affected women's position in other ways. Islamic law accords to husbands the unilateral right of divorcing their wives, a right slightly tempered by the condition of paying them the delayed part of the dowry and providing for their sustenance and that of minor children (*nafaqa*). The legal conditions for repudiation and divorce varied from one juridical school to another, and it is noteworthy that in eleventh/seventeenth century-Jerusalem the majority of divorce cases were brought before the Shāfiʿī judge, probably because this particular school is less rigorous than others in its attitude to women.[32] Similarly, and notwithstanding the fact that the Ḥanafī juridical school was the 'official' school of the Ottoman empire, Ḥanafī jurists

28 Hanna, 'Marriage among merchant families'; A. Abdal-Rehim, 'The family and gender laws in Egypt', in Sonbol (ed.), *Women, the family and divorce laws*.

29 Peirce, *Morality tales*, p. 150; H. Gerber, 'Social and economic position of women in an Ottoman city, Bursa, 1600–1700', *IJMES*, 12 (1980); M. Zilfi, 'Elite circulation in the Ottoman empire: Great mollas of the eighteenth century', *JESHO*, 26 (1983).

30 Lutfi, 'al-Sakhāwī's *Kitāb al-nisāʾ*', p. 123; ʿAbd ar-Rāziq, *La femme au temps des mamlouks*, p. 164.

31 Lutfi, 'al-Sakhāwī's *Kitāb al-nisāʾ*', p. 115.

32 D. Ze'evi, 'Women in 17th-century Jerusalem: Western and indigenous perspectives', *IJMES*, 27 (1995), p. 165.

would advise deserted wives to go to judges of the other orthodox schools of law, because their own did not allow divorce in these cases unless two witnesses could confirm that the absent husband had died or that he had been missing for fifteen years.[33] In al-Andalus and the Maghrib, according to the Mālikīs, physical mistreatment of a woman by her husband was reason enough for her to apply for a divorce, and the court would then initiate an enquiry in the neighbourhood and among friends and relatives, to check the facts given by the plaintiff.[34]

Besides the non-fulfilment of the clauses in the marriage contract (as might have happened in the examples just mentioned), women could initiate the proceedings for divorce for personal reasons, just as their husbands could repudiate them. In such cases wives were obliged to 'compensate' their husbands economically, either by renouncing the payment of the delayed part of the dowry or by handing over part of their property.[35] This is the divorce called *khulʿ*, which was obviously more easily obtained by wealthy women, who were able to bargain for their freedom. But even women from the lower classes of society chose *khulʿ* as an option, as attested in twelfth/eighteenth-century Istanbul, as the only way out of their marriages. The counterpart of this legal possibility is documented in the same city, where cases are recorded of men forcing their wives to initiate a divorce *khulʿ* to avoid paying them the delayed part of their dowries.[36]

Conflict in a marriage might not always end in a divorce or a repudiation. Before this drastic step was taken relatives and friends could intervene as mediators, and the court could nominate two arbiters, one from the family of the wife and another from the husband's family. From the fifth/eleventh century, in what is today's Tunisia, there existed an institution called *dār al-thiqa* ('the house of trust'), where a couple in a difficult situation could stay under supervision in the hope of resolving their problems, or where mistreated women could take refuge from their husbands.[37] Mutual agreements of divorce between wife and husband were also possible. An Andalusī document dated 751/1350 attests to the 'incompatibility of character' between

33 R. C. Jennings, 'Women in early 17th century Ottoman judicial records: The sharia court of Anatolian Kayseri', *JESHO*, 18 (1975), p. 93.

34 Marín, *Mujeres en al-Ándalus*, pp. 455–9.

35 Peirce, *Morality tales*, p. 232, underlines how women in ʿAintab were obliged to pay in order to retain custody of their children, although this was contrary to *sharīʿa* and reflected the customary law of the city.

36 Zarinebaf-Shahr, 'Women, law, and imperial justice', p. 92.

37 D. and A. Largueche, *Marginales en terre d'Islam* (Tunis, 1992), p. 91.

the judge and poet Abu 'l-Barakāt al-Balafīqī and his wife, ʿĀʾisha bint Abī ʿAbd Allāh ibn al-Maghīlī, and their agreement put an end to their marriage.[38]

It was usual for women to marry at an early age,[39] and not infrequently to much older men. Widowhood was therefore a common occurrence in many women's lives; together with the high possibility of being divorced or repudiated, this made remarriage a frequent possibility. A woman in a good economic position could make her own choice for a second or third marriage, while her first marriage was generally arranged by her family. The choice of a husband was in any case very much conditioned by the social provenance of the bride. Families of high social standing did not allow their daughters to marry commoners, and economic parity between the parties was also considered necessary. Marriage alliances were common among the learned elite of the Islamic cities, and cases of disciples marrying their masters' daughters or sisters are frequently mentioned in biographical sources. Scholarly networks in this way acquired a genealogical character, in which women figured as the ineluctable link between families.[40] Exceptions to the rule, religiously sanctioned, of the 'equality' between wife and husband can, however, be found in specific cases. Thus the Ottoman ruling family developed the policy of marrying the royal princesses to high officials of the court, usually of slave origin, in order to cement the network of personal loyalties around the sovereign.[41] On their side, Mamlūks often married the daughters, sisters and widows of their masters.[42]

In well-off households, female slaves and concubines played an important role in the matrimonial strategies and reproduction of the family. Slaves could change their status; in ninth/fifteenth-century Bursa young slave girls were frequently manumitted by their female owners and married off.[43] But the fate of slave women belonging to the male head of the family could be very different if they became mothers to their owner's children. Children by these slaves were as legitimate as the offspring of a legal marriage, and they had the same rights to their father's estate. But it was not in the interests of a

38 S. Gibert, 'Abū l-Barakāt al-Balafīqī, qāḍī, historiador y poeta', *al-Andalus*, 28 (1963), p. 408.

39 A. Giladi, 'Gender differences in child rearing and education: Some preliminary observations with reference to medieval Muslim thought', *al-Qanṭara*, 16 (1995), p. 303.

40 M. Marín, 'Parentesco simbólico y matrimonio entre los ulemas andalusíes', *al-Qanṭara*, 16 (1995).

41 Peirce, *The imperial harem*, pp. 65–77.

42 M. A. Fay, 'The ties that bound: Women and households in eighteenth-century Egypt', in Sonbol (ed.), *Women, the family, and divorce laws*, pp. 164–5.

43 S. Faroqhi, *Stories of Ottoman men and women: Establishing status, establishing control* (Istanbul, 2002), p. 148.

well-to-do family to duplicate the number of heirs, and disperse possessions – especially real estate. Thus male owners of slave women, with whom they had the right to have sexual relations, used to practice *coitus interruptus* with them, something that theoretically at least they could not do with their legitimate wives, unless they so agreed (only Shāfiʿī jurists did not consider the wife's permission necessary).[44] Contraception was admitted as a social practice, and religious writers and jurists permitted it, on the assumption that no human initiative would impede God's will to create a human being. Among the reasons for practising contraception, the great thinker al-Ghazālī (d. 505/1111) cited keeping the family to a reasonable size, and preserving women's beauty; this, however, was a decision to be taken by a man, not by a woman, and seems to relate to slave women rather than to free and legitimate wives. The uncertainties of *coitus interruptus* as a contraceptive method were also taken into account, and in the eighth/fourteenth century the Damascene jurist Ibn Qayyim al-Jawziyya reported that some of his trusted friends had told him that although they had been practising withdrawal, their wives had become pregnant.[45] For women, to become a mother and, more significantly, the mother of a son, was to acquire the full status of mature adulthood, and within the family hierarchy, a fundamental step towards a rise in status over younger and childless women.

It was also through their family connections that women acquired, for the most part, their own properties – either as dowries or as shares in estates. The amount of the dowry reflected the social position of both families, as well as the personal situation of the bride (a virgin, a divorcée or a widow, with or without children, could receive different amounts of money as dowry).[46] Although the dowry was the personal possession of the bride, it was not infrequent for her family to use it – or at least part of it – to buy her trousseau, including household linens and wares. The delayed part of the dowry, as we have seen, could never be paid if a wife renounced her rights in order to obtain what some jurists called 'conjugal harmony'. Similarly, as women's shares in estates were normally parts of a property and not its entirety, they were under pressure from their menfolk to sell off their portions. In eleventh/seventeenth-century Kayseri women sold properties at a rate of three times more than men, because it was common for women, on the death of their

44 B. Musallam, *Sex and society in Islam: Birth control before the nineteenth century* (Cambridge, 1983), p. 28.

45 Ibid., pp. 19–22.

46 A. Zomeño, *Dote y matrimonio en al-Andalus y el norte de África: Estudios sobre la jurisprudencia islámica medieval* (Madrid, 2000).

parents, to sell their shares in the estates to their brothers.[47] On the whole, however, the quantity and quality of data about women defending their property rights before judges across the centuries are proof of the continuous implementation of women's right to property, even if they attest to the precariousness of their position.

Muslim jurists from the formative period of Islam, such as Mālik ibn Anas, carefully defined the kind of goods normally belonging to women, such as household wares, cooking utensils, clothing and house linen, and jewels.[48] Similarly, research on Damascene inventories from 1099–1130/1687–1717 has shown that women and men did not own the same things. Women, for example, possessed practically no books, weapons or riding animals; but they owned gold, jewellery and clothing. It is noteworthy that cooking utensils were owned by both men and women, but the former possessed heavy objects in copper, while the latter owned lighter things, made from ceramics, glass or porcelain.[49] Similar conclusions have been reached for women living in tenth/sixteenth-century Üsküdar and ʿAintab, and in Ottoman Algiers.[50]

Although the tendency to sell their real-estate properties is well attested, women could and did own houses, gardens and vineyards. Regional differences in the kind of properties owned by women have been observed. In central Anatolian towns, for example, it was more common for women to possess orchards and fields (especially after the tenth/sixteenth century) than in a city such as Aleppo.[51] In Naṣrid Granada women appear in archival documents as proprietors of shares in houses, small plots of land and shops.[52] Moreover, in the Ottoman realm the eleventh/seventeenth century witnessed an increase in female proprietors of land, following changes to the rules governing tenure of state-owned lands.[53] Women's ownership of real

47 Zarinebaf-Shahr, 'Women, law, and imperial justice', p. 90; Jennings, 'Women in early 17th century Ottoman judicial records', pp. 69–71.

48 Marín, *Mujeres en al-Ándalus*, p. 315.

49 C. Establet and J.-P. Pascual, 'Women in Damascene families around 1700', *JESHO*, 45 (2002).

50 Y. J. Seng, 'Invisible women: Residents of early sixteenth-century Istanbul', in G. R. G. Hambly (ed.), *Women in the medieval Islamic world: Power, patronage, and piety* (Basingstoke and New York, 1998), p. 262; Peirce, *Morality tales*, pp. 221–6; ʿĀʾisha Ghaṭṭās, 'Mumtalakāt al-marʾa fī mujtamaʿ madīnat al-Jazāʾir khilāl al-ʿahd al-ʿuthmānī', in Dalenda Largueche (ed.), *Historie des femmes au Maghreb: Culture matérielle et vie quotidienne* (Tunis, 2000).

51 Faroqhi, *Stories of Ottoman men and women*, pp. 152–4.

52 Marín, *Mujeres en al-Ándalus*, pp. 328–9.

53 Faroqhi, *Stories of Ottoman men and women*, pp. 152–4; Ze'evi, 'Women in 17th-century Jerusalem', p. 167.

estate, however threatened by male relatives, was protected by law and custom, but management and control of these properties were frequently in the hands of men – husbands or brothers. This would also explain why women were ready to sell their properties and obtain money, a commodity easier to control and manage than land, and exchangeable for jewels, clothing and other similar goods.

As money owners, women tended to act as their families' 'bankers', granting loans to their relatives, especially their husbands. Loaning money seems to have been a very common activity among well-to-do women in different times and places, such as in Bursa, Kayseri, Jerusalem or Istanbul, where they charged high rates of interest (10–20 per cent).[54] Some women invested in commercial enterprises, as happened in Ottoman Cairo and Bursa.[55] Class played a crucial role in acquiring and maintaining women's wealth, as can be observed particularly in the case of the Egyptian Mamlūks. Women from the most important Mamlūk families could own enormous fortunes, and they also served as custodians of property, keeping it in the family after the death of their husbands.[56]

Rich women gave away a substantial part of their wealth in the form of gifts and donations made to relatives, but also as contributions to the community's welfare. Charitable endowments (*waqf*, pl. *awqāf*; in the Muslim west *ḥubs*, pl. *aḥbās*) were a characteristic feature of social life in Islamic societies. Their creation and development did not evolve from any Qur'ānic injunction, but *waqf* soon acquired religious legitimacy. Founders of *awqāf* contributed to the Islamic ideals of justice and redistribution of wealth, and in doing so acquired individual religious merit (*ajr*). Because women were economically independent under Muslim law, they were also able to establish *awqāf*, and in this way charitable endowment presented a non-gendered opportunity for them to take part in social and religious affairs.

Obviously the wealthier a woman was, the greater her capacity for donating properties to be established as pious foundations. Thus women belonging to royal families appear predominantly as founders of rich *awqāf*, established in favour of mosques, hospitals or schools. In Ayyūbid Damascus women's

54 Zarinebaf-Shahr, 'Women, law, and imperial justice', p. 91.

55 A. L. al-Sayyid Marsot, 'Entrepreneurial women in Egypt', in Mai Yamani (ed.), *Feminism and Islam: Legal and literary perspectives* (Reading, 1996); Gerber, 'Social and economic position of women'.

56 C. F. Petry, 'Class solidarity versus gender gain: Women as custodians of property in later medieval Egypt', in Keddie and Baron (eds.), *Women in Middle Eastern history*, pp. 124–6.

support for *madrasas* and Sufi hospices was significant. Of the twenty-eight Ayyūbid patrons recorded as founders of this kind of institution only fifteen were men.[57] The case of Ḍayfa Khātūn in seventh/thirteenth-century Aleppo has attracted the attention of contemporary research. The Madrasat al-Firdaws, which she financed, is still preserved as the centre of one of Aleppo's quarters,[58] as is the case with several Sufi convents, *madrasas* and funerary monuments endowed by women in Mamlūk Cairo.[59] But it was perhaps under the Ottomans that royal women left a more remarkable legacy on the urban landscape through their funding of monumental mosques and *madrasas* in the most important cities of the empire. Mihrimah Sultan, daughter of Süleymān (r. 926–74/1520–66) was the founder of one of the most renowned mosque complexes in Istanbul, and hers was not the only example; generation after generation of Ottoman royal ladies added their own contribution to the establishment of charitable endowments, some of them of an innovative character, such as public kitchens (*imaret*) where food was distributed to the poor.[60] The charitable careers of these women were linked to their places in the sultanic household and to their own position as wives and mothers. Modern research has identified a hierarchy of female patronage, related to the women's status as mothers of princes. Before the reign of Süleymān royal women financed building only in the provinces, where they resided as mothers to sons appointed as governors by the reigning sultan. After Süleymān's time, and due in part to his own special relationship with his favourite concubine, Hürrem, older women in the imperial harem took over the task of establishing charitable endowments in Istanbul, in a process paralleling the growing political influence of the queen mother (*wālide sulṭān*).[61]

Specific endowments providing for destitute or helpless women were established by wealthy women, such as the Egyptian Fāṭima (ninth/fifteenth century), who founded a convent (*zāwiya*) for widows, where she herself resided.[62] In Ottoman Üsküdar several women in the tenth/sixteenth century established foundations for house loans, which were of course open to both

57 R. S. Humphreys, 'Women as patrons of religious architecture in Ayyubid Damascus', *Muqarnas*, 11 (1994).
58 Tabbaa, 'Ḍayfa Khātūn'.
59 Petry, 'Class solidarity versus gender gain', pp. 132–6; 'Abd ar-Rāziq, *La femme au temps des mamlouks*, pp. 20ff.
60 Seng, 'Invisible women', p. 245.
61 L. Peirce, 'Gender and sexual propriety in Ottoman royal women's patronage', in Ruggles (ed.), *Women, patronage and self-representation*.
62 Lutfi, 'al-Sakhāwī's *Kitāb al-nisā*'', p. 119.

men and women.[63] This practical approach to charity can be recognised in other aspects of the beneficence exercised by women. Examples extend from the activities of a royal concubine such as the Ottoman Kösem (who financed annual distributions of clothes and food for the poor, or water supplies for pilgrims) to women of more modest means who offered their help to poor brides, allowing them to acquire trousseaus or to hire jewels for their wedding ceremonies.

Women from the lower classes participated in economic activity through their paid work and their unsalaried domestic production. Wage labour was more common in cities, where women could work in a great variety of jobs. Legally women were the sole owners of their earnings, but their rights in this respect were not always respected by their male relatives. Husbands could even forbid their wives to work outside the home. In eighth/fourteenth-century Ifrīqiya a hairdresser took the precaution of inserting a clause into her marriage contract guaranteeing her right to continue working; after the marriage, however, the husband tried to forbid her to work.[64] In spite of these encroachments on their participation in the world of labour, information abounds about women working as wet-nurses, midwives, servants, spinners, cooks, hairdressers, schoolteachers, bath attendants etc.[65] Restrictions on the public appearance of high-class women favoured the activity of female peddlers, who acted as links between rich households. Hairdressers (*māshiṭa*) specialising in wedding celebrations were very much sought after, and some of them earned high incomes.[66] Generally speaking, women occupied a gendered sector of the work space, as most of the tasks they performed were centred on the domestic area or answered needs caused by gender segregation. High-skilled professional women were not common, although in particular circumstances we find cases such as the Banū Zuhr family, famous Andalusī physicians. The daughter of one of them, Umm ʿAmr bint Abī Marwān (d. after 580/1184) was a renowned medical practitioner, who treated the women of the ruling Almohad dynasty, and who was even consulted by her male colleagues.[67]

Domestic production of goods was a general practice, giving women the advantage of not risking their reputations by mingling freely with men in the

63 Seng, 'Invisible women', p. 245.
64 M. Shatzmiller, 'Women and wage labour in the medieval Islamic west: Legal issues in an economic context', *JESHO*, 40 (1997), p. 189.
65 Lutfi, 'Manners and customs', p. 106.
66 ʿAbd ar-Rāziq, *La femme au temps des mamlouks*, p. 44.
67 Marín, *Mujeres en al-Ándalus*, pp. 296–7.

streets or the markets. Spinning and other textile-related tasks were the preferred activities in this domain, with regional specialities such as silk spinning in eleventh/seventeenth-century Bursa, where in 1089/1678, of a total of 300 silk-spinning implements, as many as 150 were owned and/or operated by women.[68] Embroiderers were present in the Sevillian market, where they had a special place to sell their handiwork. In Ottoman times embroidery was a highly sophisticated art, and it was cultivated not only by women in the royal palace, but also by many others who made a living from it.[69] Less well documented are other areas of domestic production, among which food preparation and conservation was probably one of the most important tasks performed by women.

Beyond this 'legitimate' work space lies the area of dishonourable professions: singers, dancers, prostitutes, public mourners, charms makers, procuresses etc.[70] Singing, like wine-drinking, was often associated with prostitution and, in fact, singers paid taxes as prostitutes did in various historical periods. In Ayyūbid and Mamlūk times the state earned significant amounts from these taxes. While some rulers discontinued them, others, such as the Ayyūbid al-Muʿaẓẓam ʿĪsā in 615/1218, restored them, justifying his decision on the grounds that he had to pay his army.[71] Similar oscillations are documented during the Mamlūk period, when prostitutes were obliged to inscribe their names in a general register, and to pay taxes to the controller of prostitution – who could be also a woman. But Mamlūk rulers such as Baybars I or al-Nāṣir Muḥammad ibn Qalāwūn directed their policy of redressing public morality against prostitutes, who were forbidden to work, jailed or, in some cases, obliged to marry. Notwithstanding these bouts of repression, prostitution and other related activities flourished uninterruptedly, sometimes under cover of other economic activities, such as the slave traffic.[72]

The world of learning and of religious knowledge was, in principle, open to Muslim women. In an autobiographical note Ibn Ḥazm (d. 456/1064) explained how during his childhood the women of his family taught him

68 Gerber, 'Social and economic position of women', p. 237; Faroqhi, *Stories of Ottoman men and women*, p. 202.

69 Peirce, *Morality tales*, p. 223.

70 On the religiously based disapproval of the mourner see El Cheikh, 'Mourning and the role of the *nāʾiḥa*', in Cristina de la Puente (ed.), *Identidades marginales*, Estudios Onomástico-Biográficos de al-Andalus 13 (Madrid, 2003).

71 L. Pouzet, *Damas au VIIe/VIIIe siècle: Vie et structures religeuses dans une métropole islamique* (Beirut, 1991), p. 326.

72 M. Zilfi, 'Servants, slaves, and the domestic order the Ottoman Middle East', *Hawwa*, 2 (2004), p. 6.

the Qur'ān, classical Arabic poetry and calligraphy. As a member of an aristocratic household in fifth/eleventh-century Cordoba, Ibn Ḥazm identified the areas of learning women of this social standing might be familiar with: the sacred Qur'ānic text, the culturally praised and memorised archive of Arabic poetry and the art of writing for religious and secular purposes, such as copying the Qur'ān or classical poetry.

For the most part, however, it was considered dangerous for women to write,[73] because they could use this skill for unlawful communication with men. It was only in the context of scholarly or high-class families that women were allowed to introduce themselves into the world of specialised learning, taking advantage of the fact that they could be taught by the male members of their families. Fathers, brothers or husbands were the natural masters of intelligent women, who might aspire to high levels of knowledge, and who eventually became famous teachers or transmitters of knowledge in their own right. These are usually the kinds of women who are featured in special sections of biographical dictionaries, texts which confirm the written register of high Muslim culture throughout the ages.[74] Women were taught by their relatives or by unrelated male teachers; in the latter case it was customary that a curtain separated the master from his disciples.[75] Gender segregation in public spaces hindered the presence of women in the *madrasas*, the most important institution of high learning in the Muslim world from the fifth/eleventh century onwards. Significantly, women could and did found *madrasas*, as we have seen above, but they could not attend their courses or be teachers there. Thus women were removed from the master-and-disciple network dominating the world of learning, and only in exceptional cases did they appear as masters of some renown. This happened mainly in the specialised field of *ḥadīth* (the Prophet's tradition), for which old age was a premium, in so far as the older the transmitter, the fewer the links in a chain of transmission. Moreover, senior women, in a post-sexual phase of their lives, were not subjected to strict gender segregation, and therefore they could teach freely to male disciples.[76] But it has to be noted that in spite of their

73 Giladi, 'Gender differences in child rearing'.

74 See a detailed study of the place of women in this kind of work, in R. Roded, *Women in Islamic biographical collections: from Ibn Sa'd to* Who's who (London, 1994).

75 Eddé, 'Images de femmes', p. 68; M. L. Ávila, 'Las "mujeres sabias" en al-Andalus', in María Jesús Viguera (ed.), *La mujer en al-Andalus: Reflejos históricos de su actividad y categorías sociales* (Madrid and Seville, 1989), pp. 139–84; M. L. Ávila, 'Women in Andalusi biographical sources', in Marín and Deguilhem (eds.), *Writing the feminine*.

76 J. P. Berkey, 'Women and Islamic education in the Mamluk period', in Keddie and Baron (eds.), *Women in Middle Eastern history*, pp. 151–3.

contribution to the field of *ḥadīth* women were rarely if at all authors of books on this or other scholarly matters.[77]

Secular culture, poetry and music were cultivated by women, particularly but not exclusively by slaves who had received a careful training in artistic performances. Best known are female poets from al-Andalus, where several names emerge from obscurity, such as the sixth/twelfth-century Ḥafṣa bint al-Ḥājj al-Rakūnīya and Nazhūn bint al-Qalāʿī. The former frequented aristocratic circles and is known for her love of poetry, while the latter is described as a *mājina*, that is, a poet of transgressive, and even obscene, character.[78]

It has been asserted that religion and religious practices were the privileged field for women's agency. Personal piety opened up to women a unique space for the development of individual accomplishments, and in fact, from the earliest Islamic times women figure in the annals of Muslim sainthood.[79] Biographies or short notices on female saints (*ṣāliḥāt*) appear, although sparsely, in hagiographical dictionaries, a genre particularly rich in North African regions. An analysis of these biographies yields interesting results, as women appear to the eyes of different authors as perfectly integrated in the world of sainthood.[80] The most celebrated mystic Muḥyī al-Dīn ibn al-ʿArabī (d. 638/1240) counted several women among his spiritual masters; two of them, Fāṭima bint Ibn al-Muthannā and Shams Umm al-Fuqarāʾ, were described by Muḥyī al-Dīn with warm expressions of admiration.[81] The influence of Ibn al-ʿArabī in Sufi thought can be appreciated also in the mystical interpretation of sexual relationships, which were equated to the union of God and the human being. Erotic images in Sufi poetry and literature undoubtedly contributed to the consideration of women as partners of men in the search for a higher spiritual life.

The development and spread of religious and mystical brotherhoods (*ṭarīqa*, pl. *ṭuruq*) offered other and to some extent more institutionalised ways of performing devotional acts. In Cairo and Damascus Sufi convents (*ribāṭ*, *zāwiya*) were established for women, who could live there, improving their knowledge of religion and leading a pious and ascetic life. These institutions were governed by a mistress of the convent (*shaykhat*

77 Lutfi, 'al-Sakhāwī's *Kitāb al-nisāʾ*', p. 120.

78 T. Garulo, *Dīwān de las poetisas de al-Andalus* (Madrid, 1986), pp. 71–85, 110–18.

79 A. Schimmel, *My soul is a woman: The feminine in Islam*, trans. Susan H. Ray (New York, 1999); M. Chodkiewicz, 'La sainteté féminine dans l'hagiographie islamique', in Denise Aigle (ed.), *Saints orientaux* (Paris, 1995).

80 N. Amri, 'Les *ṣāliḥāt* du Ve au IXe siècle/XIe–XVe siècle dans la mémoire maghrébine de la sainteté à travers quatre documents hagiographiques', *al-Qanṭara*, 21 (2000).

81 C. Addas, *Ibn ʿArabī ou la quête du soufre rouge* (Paris, 1989), pp. 113–14.

al-ribāṭ/al-zāwiya). In the Maghrib the Ribāṭ Shākir was frequented by women of saintly reputation, among them Munayya bint Maymūn (d. 595/1198), who performed miracles similar to those attributed to men.[82]

In conclusion, in hierarchical societies such as pre-modern Islamic society, women were assimilated with children and slaves. All three categories were in need of protection and guidance from men – or at least this was the socially accepted ideal, sanctioned by religious norms. It is clear, however, that women occupied areas of significant interest in the social arena, and that they were empowered by the legal rules to govern important areas of their own lives.

Sexuality

A long-lived Western tradition characterises Islamic societies by an unbridled sensuality and a self-indulgent allowance of fleshly pleasures. The sultanic harem, with its alluring images of countless women ready to be enjoyed by their owner and master, figures prominently in this tradition, initiated by Medieval Christian polemicists depicting the Prophet of Islam as a lustful man of licentious proclivities. More recently, a noticeable shift of emphasis presents the Islamic approach to sexuality in a different way: in contrast to Christianity, Islam is a sex-positive religion, lacking the repressive aspects of Western historical cultures towards sexuality.[83] Both the traditional and contemporary interpretations are, however, essentially identical, as they observe Islamic sexualities from their own problematic relationship with sex: condemnation of a supposedly uncontrolled lewdness is just the other side of the coin of an unreserved approval of Islamic sexual mores.

There is, however, a difference of approach to sexuality in Christianity and Islam that has influenced Western as well as Muslim interpretations.[84] While for the former sex was at best an unavoidable fact of life, and celibacy the higher ideal of existence on this earth, for the latter sexual relationships were a social and individual issue to be regulated and controlled, but never discarded or suppressed. Muslim moralists and religious thinkers openly admitted the existence of sexual desire in both women and men. The model of the

82 Amri, 'Les *ṣāliḥāt*', p. 497.

83 F. Rosenthal, 'Fiction and reality: Sources for the role of sex in medieval Muslim society', in al-Sayyid-Marsot (ed.), *Society and the sexes*, p. 4. A good representative of the contemporary interpretation is L. López-Baralt, *Un Kāma-sūtra español* (Madrid, 1992), pp. 207–22.

84 In this sense it is instructive to compare the contrasting views of G. H. Bousquet, *L'Ethique sexuelle de l'Islam* (Paris, 1966) and A. Bouhdiba, *La sexualité en Islam* (Paris, 1975).

Prophet's life, with his numerous marriages and his enjoyment of sex, undoubtedly played a crucial part in this religiously approved attitude. At the same time, however, the disturbing potential of sex, and especially its capacity of blurring the purity of genealogical descent, demanded clear and decisive control over how and with whom sexual relationships could be conducted.[85] From almost the beginning of Islamic history, the socially accepted order precluded free and honest women from any contact with unrelated men, and established a sexual hierarchy presided over by men, whose public honour was subject, however, to their women's behaviour.

The social tension between what was expected from men and women (in the first case, to act as a predator towards unrelated females; in the second, to resist the predatory efforts of the unrelated males) was not exclusive to Islamic societies, and can easily be recognised in other geographical or chronological areas. Muslim ideology dealt with the problem in a characteristic way, establishing legal limits and boundaries to sexual relationships. Licit and illicit acts became, in Islamic societies, markers for sexual activity, and so it was that illegal sex could be chastened, and legal sex was not only approved but also religiously sanctioned. As long as the purity of male lineage was not threatened, women and men could enjoy sex in legally established marriages.[86]

Literary expressions of transgressive sexual behaviour are common in classical Arabic literature, where there exists a powerful tradition of eroticism.[87] Sexual misconduct and illicit acts appear complaisantly described in much of this literature, although these were practices that were deemed socially unacceptable. Anecdotal compilations such as that of al-Tīfāshī (d. 651/1253) coexist with literary discussions on the merits of maidens and young men, penned by authors such as Shihāb al-Dīn al-Ḥijāzī (d. 875/1471) and Abu 'l-Tuqā al-Badrī (d. 894/1489).[88] Although taking erotic texts as testimonials of social indulgence towards irregular sexual activity would be misleading, their very existence and popularity proves that there was a welcome market for them.

85 J. P. Berkey, 'Circumcision circumscribed: Female excision and cultural accommodation in the medieval Near East', *IJMES*, 28 (1996), p. 32.

86 L. Peirce, 'Seniority, sexuality, and social order: The vocabulary of gender in early modern Ottoman Society', in Madeline C. Zilfi (ed.), *Women in the Ottoman empire: Middle Eastern women in the early modern era* (Leiden, 1997), pp. 184–5.

87 J. C. Bürgel, 'Love, lust, and longing: Eroticism in early Islam as reflected in literary sources', in al-Sayyid-Marsot (ed.), *Society and the sexes*, p. 85; L. Declich, 'L'erotologia arabe: Profilo bibliografico', *Rivista degli Studi Orientali*, 68 (1994); Malti-Douglas, *Woman's body, woman's word*, p. 47; López-Baralt, *Un Kāma-sūtra*, pp. 241–61.

88 See on the last two authors Rosenthal, 'Male and female'.

A frequent character in some of the anecdotes included in a book like that of al-Tīfāshī is the married noblewoman who escapes secretly from her home to pursue an illicit love affair. This narrative scheme reflects the social anxiety created around women's bodies, and helps to understand the reactive relationship between women's alleged misconduct and the loss of honour it caused to the men of their families. In high-class social circles, fear of sexual dishonour led to the establishment of severe rules segregating women from men, and to the marriage of girls at an early age, in order to keep their virginity intact for intended husbands. As a logical consequence of this obsession with women's bodies as depositories of men's honour, not even women's names could be known to outsiders. As we have seen above, naming women – or hinting at their names and personalities – in satirical poems became thus a powerful weapon in the hands of enemies, who could bring scandal and shame on their foes by these simple means.

Legal sexual relationships (*nikāḥ*) discriminated between women, who were only allowed to have sex with their husbands, and men, who had licit access to both their wives and their female slaves. Religious regulations also conditioned the nature of physical contact between women and men: heterosexual anal intercourse was severely condemned by moralists such as Ibn al-Ḥājj (d. 737/1336), and by Sunnī schools of jurisprudence, with the exception of the Mālikīs, who allowed it if the wife consented.[89] Men's sexual satisfaction was a priority in a society where males dominated the social and sexual hierarchy, but women's needs in this respect were also acknowledged. One of the reasons jurists and moralists disapproved of practising *coitus interruptus* with one's wife was precisely the dissatisfaction it caused to women. The Andalusī polymath Ibn al-Khaṭīb (d. 776/1375), following a trend already present in the Prophetic tradition, advised men, in one of his medical treatises, to take care of women's sexual desires and needs; in the early ninth/fifteenth century another medical author, al-Azraqī, specifically linked his encouragement of foreplay to a woman's sexual passion.[90] However, the aforementioned Ibn al-Ḥājj bitterly reproached his Egyptian contemporaries for having very unsatisfactory sexual relationships with their wives, who were approached without preparation or had to submit to anal intercourse.[91]

89 Monroe, 'The striptease', pp. 116–17; J. A. Bellamy, 'Sex and society in Islamic popular literature', in al-Sayyid-Marsot (ed.), *Society and the sexes*, p. 36; Lutfi, 'Manners and customs', p. 107.

90 Marín, *Mujeres en al-Ándalus*, pp. 662–3; Berkey, 'Circumcision circumscribed', p. 32.

91 Lutfi, 'Manners and customs', p. 107.

Female excision, practised in some parts of the Muslim world, as in Egypt, did not contribute to women's sexual satisfaction either.[92]

Legally, the most important illicit sexual act was *zinā'*, a term describing vaginal intercourse between a man and a woman who was not his wife or his concubine. Any child born from an adulterous relationship was illegitimate.[93] The penalty for adulterers was death by stoning, although it was necessary to prove the charges with four witnesses or by the confession of the guilty parties. But in 911/1513 a famous Cairene case of adultery ended by the hanging of the lovers, surprised in bed by the woman's husband. In this case the penalty was the personal decision of the Mamlūk sultan; the judges had previously recommended forgiveness if the sinners repented.[94] Ottoman imperial law slightly modified the Qur'ānic-inspired regulations, and in tenth/sixteenth-century courts less than four witnesses were needed to prove an adulterous relationship.[95]

Crossing religious boundaries aggravated the transgression of sexual regulations. Ibn ʿAbdūn, in sixth/twelfth-century Seville, advised Muslim women against entering churches – populated, in his opinion, by libertine and dissolute Christian priests. In 687/1288, in Damascus, a Christian man who was drinking wine with a Muslim woman during Ramaḍān was condemned to death; as stated above, prostitution and alcohol shared physical as well as imagined premises, and the woman in this situation was probably a prostitute. In Damascus, brothels (*mawāḍīʿ al-zinā'*) and taverns were contiguous.[96] Hiring women for prostitution was not exclusive to brothels, but could be done in other urban spaces, such as jails for women, slave markets, cemeteries etc.

Homoeroticism has been identified as an inherent characteristic of Muslim societies; and the amount and quality of homoerotic classical Arabic poetry could be offered as a proof for this assertion. A work by the philologist and biographer al-Ṣafadī (d. 764/1363), *Lawʿat al-shākī*, evokes a homoerotic love affair, following the major themes in this literary tradition, such as gazing at

92 Berkey, 'Circumcision circumscribed'.

93 N. J. Coulson, 'Regulation of sexual behavior under traditional Islamic law', in al-Sayyid-Marsot (ed.), *Society and the sexes*, p. 68; E. K. Rowson, 'The categorization of gender and sexual irregularity in medieval Arabic vice lists', in Julia Epstein and Kristina Straub (eds.), *Body guards: The cultural politics of gender ambiguity* (New York, 1991), p. 55.

94 C. F. Petry, 'Royal justice in Mamlūk Cairo: Contrasting motives of two sulṭāns', in *Saber religioso y poder político en el Islam* (Madrid, 1994), pp. 207–9.

95 Peirce, *Morality tales*, p. 133.

96 Marín, *Mujeres en al-Ándalus*, p. 666; Pouzet, *Damas au VIIe/VIIIe siècle*, pp. 321, 365.

the beautiful face of the beloved.[97] Love for handsome boys was, as in Greece, part of the accepted cultural view in secular high-class circles, and no shame was involved in admiring good-looking ephebes. Sex segregation left unmarried sexually active men with no alternative but to solicit sex from boys, their own slave-girls and prostitutes. In all these options men kept their sexual superiority as penetrators of women and boys. On the other hand, and in contrast to Christian views on the matter, to be sexually attracted by one's own sex was not considered by Muslim thinkers as unnatural or abnormal. Homosexual inclinations escaped condemnation, as long as homosexual acts are not practised; in this case, sinners had to expect the penalty for *zinā*ʾ.[98]

Socially, a man's reputation was not besmirched for being an active homosexual, but a passive one was considered to be a pervert, and his inclination to be penetrated a serious illness.[99] But among certain groups, such as the Mamlūk military caste or the Sufi communities, homoerotic liaisons and homosexual attachments were fairly common.[100] The great Egyptian historian al-Maqrīzī suggests that conjugal ties were weakened by the frequence of homosexuality among Mamlūks, and that wives took to wearing men's clothing to attract their husbands.[101]

While male homosexuality is well documented, lesbianism rarely attracted the attention of Muslim authors, who approached this sexual activity with great reluctance – with the exception of erotic literature, in which some vignettes on lesbians can be found, as in the *Nuzhat al-albāb* (The pleasure of the hearts), the treatise written by al-Tīfāshī. Lesbian sexual acts were of course severely condemned,[102] but homoerotic attachment between women did not threaten the genealogical capital of families, and they were usually kept in the private domain of households. Thus lesbianism escaped, to some extent, the social control of sexuality. Significantly, in the opinion of al-Samawʾal ibn Yaḥyā al-Maghribī (d. 570/1174), a Jew converted to Islam, lesbianism was more frequent among elegant and cultivated women who could read and recite poetry.[103]

97 L. A. Giffen, *Theory of profane love among the Arabs* (London and New York, 1972), pp. 124–32. On the work by al-Ṣafadī see E. K. Rowson, 'Two homoerotic narratives from Mamlūk literature: al-Ṣafadī's *Lawʿat al-shākī* and Ibn Dāniyāl's *al-Mutayyam*', in Wright and Rowson (eds.), *Homoeroticism*.

98 Monroe, 'The striptease', pp, 116–17; Rowson, 'The categorization of gender', p. 65.

99 Rowson, 'The categorization of gender', p. 64.

100 Schimmel, 'Eros'.

101 Cited by ʿAbd ar-Rāziq, *La femme au temps des mamlouks*, p. 183.

102 G. H. A. Juynboll, 'Siḥāḳ', *EI2*, vol. IX, pp. 565–7.

103 Marín, *Mujeres en al-Ándalus*, p. 679.

One of the main worries of moralists was to establish clear and impenetrable boundaries between women and men. The sexually ambiguous character of the hermaphrodite and the effeminate (*mukhannath*) greatly disturbed the ideal social order of a two-sexed community, and lengthy juridical discussions are preserved debating the place of the hermaphrodite in society.[104] But while hermaphroditism was a biological fact, transvestism was a personal choice, and the *mukhannath*, in contrast to the hermaphrodite, found a place, however despised, in society. Frequently associated with marginality, transvestites would work as actors and, more commonly, as pimps.[105]

As we have seen, far from freely celebrating all kind of sexual pleasures, medieval Islamic cultures were deeply concerned about the necessity to control sex, to ensure the purity of genealogical descent and to prevent disorder in societal norms. Apocalyptic traditions linked the upheaval of the last times to the existence of powerful and assertive women, who would behave in an immoral way; the spread of homosexuality is another sign of the approach of the apocalypse.[106] Acknowledging, however, the importance of sexual relationships in human life, Islam promoted marriage as the ideal situation for Muslim men and women, and did not consider celibacy as a religiously superior position. Social and religious control of sexuality was not, of course, total, and women and men developed their own individualities in ways that did not always conform to the orthodoxy.

104 P. Sanders, 'Gendering the ungendered body: Hermaphrodites in medieval Islamic law', in Keddie and Baron (eds.), *Women in Middle Eastern history*.

105 Y. Lev, 'Aspects of the Egyptian society in the Fatimid period', in U. Vermeulen and J. Van Steenbergen (eds.), *Egypt and Syria in the Fatimid, Ayyubid and Mamluk eras*, 5 vols. (Leuven, 2001), vol. III, p. 9.

106 Saleh, 'The woman as a locus of apocalyptic anxiety', pp. 134–5.

PART III

*

LITERATURE

13

Arabic literature

JULIA BRAY

Formative cultures and identities

The pre-Islamic poet

Ask if you are uninformed about my people when the horses return from the
  inflicting of wounds!
We halt in the [most] fearsome spot of every protected grazing-ground and
  mountain pass and no territory close to us can be ravaged,
On prancing mares and noble stallions, lean-bellied, strongly-built, with
  prominent withers, brisk and energetic.
When we halt in the very heart of a tribe's territory it receives no respite from
  fierce, constant warfare.
When war girds herself, we arise like full-grown camels in the wide enclosure
On lean-flanked, tight-bellied [horses] that kick up dust on the tousled [braves],
  fair of face.[1]

This is how Bishr ibn Abī Khāzim, who lived towards the end of the sixth century CE, describes his tribe and, by extension, himself. Arabic poetry as the vehicle of heroic themes, one of its primary roles through all succeeding periods, was the invention of pre-Islamic poets such as Bishr. It expressed the ideals of tribal society to tribal audiences, but may also have reflected wider political ambitions, boasting to the Byzantines and Sasanians of the fighting qualities of the Arabs who skirmished with each other on their borders.[2] Verse as early as that of Bishr is already both highly wrought and freighted with ethical symbolism, and its conventional motifs are more than merely descriptive. Bishr's syntax is abrupt, but it unfolds an argument: men are aggressive physical beings; because they compete for resources, war is ceaseless; war pits

1 Bishr ibn Abī Khāzim, trans. in J. E. Montgomery, *The vagaries of the* qaṣīdah: *The tradition and practice of early Arabic poetry*, E. J. W. Gibb Memorial Trust (n.p., 1997), pp. 170–1.
2 Montgomery, *Vagaries*, pp. 217–18.

like against like and breeds virtue in both winners and worthy foes ('the tousled [braves], fair of face'); it is the tribe, the 'people', that makes the individual.

The pre-Islamic and early Islamic poetry that Muslim scholars started collecting in the second/eighth century from tribesmen, and sometimes restoring or brazenly inventing, was a remnant of what had once existed, but enough survives to show differences of manner and sensibility, of milieu and of sophistication.[3] In spite of many lacunae, it increasingly seems possible to identify thought systems and trace conceptual shifts in this earliest Arabic literature.[4] But what the scholars who created the corpus strove to extract from it was rather a timeless quintessence of Arabic linguistic purity, of heroic Bedouinity and Arab virtues, and themes unique to the Arabs: a classical ideal. This ideal, shaped by cultural competition with the conquered peoples of the Islamic empire, became the key element in defining Arab culture as a programme for the future. Yet few of the scholars who championed Arabic were tribal Arabs, or even of Arab descent, and the same was true of the poets, patrons and educated people who chose an Arab – or, more properly, Arabic-literate – cultural identity during the first three or four centuries of Islam. The great majority were *mawālī* (sing. *mawlā*), foreign converts.

The early Islamic bureaucrat

What were the cultural choices that could be made during this period, and how free were individuals to make them? Just as eloquent of a sense of identity derived from the group is the following passage, separated from Bishr by the century or so that saw the coming of Islam, the Arab conquests and the establishment of a dynastic caliphate. ʿAbd al-Ḥamīd ibn Yaḥyā *al-kātib* ('the Secretary', *c.* 66–132/685–750) was a high-ranking *mawlā* bureaucrat; he served in Syria and then, for twenty years, with the governor of Azerbaijan and Armenia, who became the last Umayyad caliph, Marwān II (r. 127–32/744–50). This is ʿAbd al-Ḥamīd's picture of the ideal functionary:

> A scribe and administrator (*kātib*) should be lenient in due season and know when to be firm, bold or reticent as appropriate. Probity, justice and equity should be his preference … Your colleagues, who guard your back for you in time of need, should be more to you than your own children and brothers … When you work for a man, study his character, and once you have ascertained his good and bad points, use your subtlest ploys and most flattering

[3] Ibid., p. 39.
[4] Recent scholarship is discussed by Montgomery in ibid., *passim*.

> devices to influence him to do good according to his capacity and turn him away from evil inclinations. A groom who knows his business will, as you are aware, make a point of studying his beast's disposition. If it is over-lively, he will ride it without urging it on; if it places its feet wrongly, he will correct it; he will not let it have its head if it is a bolter ... A *kātib*, by virtue of his knowledge of things and of men (*adab*), his noble calling, his subtlety in dealing with those with whom he has converse or argument and those whose violence [*saṭwa*; the word applies both to a horse's refractoriness and to an unprovoked attack] he perceives or apprehends, should be better able gently to cajole a colleague [or: a superior] and set him straight than the rider of a brute beast which cannot return an answer and knows not right from wrong.[5]

The group addressed by ʿAbd al-Ḥamīd in his *al-Risāla ilā al-kuttāb* (Epistle to the secretaries) is one whose way of life and view of itself seem the very opposite of the Arab warrior's; most *kātibs* were *mawālī*, and it is assumed that they carried on the culture of the old imperial bureaucracies with little change. Since the reforms of ʿAbd al-Malik, however, they had been required to write in Arabic. In the same epistle ʿAbd al-Ḥamīd urges his fellow-scribes to learn Arabic poetry; and by writing Arabic epistles he himself helped to found Arabic prose literature. He tells scribes to learn non-Arab as well as Arab lore, and to study the Muslim religion: in other words, they are to make themselves the bearers of all available cultural traditions. His aim is cultural reciprocity, for his writings have two sets of recipients: *mawlā* bureaucrats and Arab rulers. His *al-Risāla ʿan Marwān ilā ibnihi ʿAbd Allāh* (Epistle to the crown prince), composed at the request of Marwān II, is the first manifesto of the duties of a Muslim ruler, and like the 'Epistle to the secretaries' recycles Graeco-Persian political wisdom. Was it directly informed by Aristotle's pseudepigraphic advice to Alexander, as has been suggested?[6]

ʿAbd al-Ḥamīd's literary world, like that of Bishr, promotes a group identity in which the individual achieves the highest virtue by loyalty to his peers. (Although he puts professional ties above those of family, in his own case the two went together by marriage, as would often be the case with *kātibs* in centuries to come.) He and Bishr both still belong to the world of Late Antiquity. The distance between them can be measured in terms of stylistic contrast, in their images of horses and horsemanship. But both live in a world of ever-present danger; violence always threatens. Even the most admirable

5 A. Z. Ṣafwat (ed.), *Jamharat rasāʾil al-ʿArab fī ʿuṣūr al-ʿarabiyya al-zāhira*, 4 vols. (Cairo, 1937), vol. II, pp. 456–8.

6 References in W. al-Qāḍī, 'ʿAbd al-Ḥamīd ibn Yaḥyā al-Kātib', *EAL*, vol. I, pp. 13–14; W. al-Qāḍī, 'Sālim Abū al-ʿAlāʾ', *EAL*, vol. II, pp. 681–2.

kātibs could not guard against all forms of ill-will, and ʿAbd al-Ḥamīd died violently when the ʿAbbāsids ousted the Umayyads.

Cultural exchange and cultural nostalgia

Under the ʿAbbāsids cultural exchange intensified and its patrons multiplied. For the most part it was a process of deliberate choice, not unconscious osmosis. Its agents were elite bureaucrats, courtiers and their protégés. Contact with high politics was dangerous: where tribal poets had often died fighting, many ʿAbbāsid poets and *kātibs* died in the torture chamber.

An example is Ibn al-Muqaffaʿ, a *kātib* whose career began in Umayyad service and continued into the reign of the second ʿAbbāsid caliph, al-Manṣūr (136–58/754–75), who had him executed in around 137/755. He was a translator from Middle Persian of Iranian political history, of Graeco-Persian, Iranian and Indian wisdom literature, including the political animal fables *Kalīla wa-Dimna*, and author of an 'Epistle on the entourage of the caliph' (*Risāla fī al-ṣaḥāba*) which proposes radical solutions, never to be adopted, to the problems of establishing a stable and united ʿAbbāsid caliphate. Like ʿAbd al-Ḥamīd, he is thought to have been an early transmitter of Aristotelianism.[7] Admired as a master stylist, he imported so many genres into Arabic as to be regarded as the main founder of Arabic prose literature, yet he was a Persian and a late convert to Islam, a paradox of the kind that underlies much of the new literature.

His contemporary the blind poet Bashshār ibn Burd (*c.* 95–167/714–84) also started his career under Umayyad patronage, and ended it under that of the caliph al-Mahdī (r. 158–69/775–85), who imprisoned and murdered him.[8] He too was of Persian origin, and in some of his poems he boasted of this and disparaged the Arabs – an attitude stigmatised as *shuʿūbiyya* (ethnic particularism) – or used Zoroastrian imagery, which smacked of diabolism to some of his listeners. Nevertheless, he not only came to be regarded as the first truly 'modern' poet – the moderns (*muḥdathūn*) were defined by their conscious use of rhetorical figures and logical argumentation (*badīʿ*) – but his Arabic linguistic purity was held to be comparable to that of the 'ancients' (*qudamāʾ*). This was a deliberately vague term for pre-Islamic poets, whose utterances were, increasingly, held to be the spontaneous expression, in the language of the Qurʾān, of a virtuous, although pagan, lifestyle. In fact, the Arabic of pre-Islamic poetry was not identical with Qurʾānic Arabic, and some

7 References in F. de Blois, 'Ibn al-Muqaffaʿ', *EAL*, vol. I, pp. 352–3.

8 See H. Kennedy, *The court of the caliphs: The rise and fall of Islam's greatest dynasty* (London, 2004), chap. 5, 'Poetry and power at the early Abbasid court', pp. 118–20.

pre-Islamic poets, as was well known, were Jews or Christians. But the bold notion that, as Arabic was the tongue of the Qurʾān and the Arabs the people chosen to receive it, so pre-Islamic Arabia as a whole must be morally transfigured, had become necessary in order to enable Arabs – politically dominant, but a numerical and cultural minority – to proclaim their possession of a culture as authoritative as that of the majority populations. The pre-Islamic Arabs' dearth of historical records also made their poetry and the lore surrounding it the crucial witness to an Arab historical identity.

So poetry became in many respects the most conservative Arabic literary form, in part in order to maintain continuity with a venerable past, but partly too because in aristocratic Arab circles it kept and even increased the function it had had since before Islam as a public weapon. A poet's praise (*madīḥ*) or ridicule (*hijāʾ*) could still make or unmake his patron's reputation (it was imprudent *hijāʾ* that caused Bashshār's downfall). Verse designed for ceremonial recitation – on the occasion of a caliph's accession, for example, or of a victory – continued to be cast broadly in the mould of the pre-Islamic *qaṣīda* (multi-thematic poem, often translated as 'ode'), and the three greatest names in ʿAbbāsid poetry are those of poets whose main output consisted of ceremonial verse: Abū Tammām (*c.* 189–232/805–45); his pupil al-Buḥturī (206–84/821–97), who both wrote poems to caliphs, viziers and other leading statesmen; and al-Mutanabbī (*c.* 303–54/915–65), who praised the glamorous Ḥamdānid prince of Aleppo, Sayf al-Dawla (r. 333–56/944–67), as the champion of Islam against Byzantium before embarking on a career as an embittered freelance. The *dīwāns* (collected works) of these three,[9] especially Abū Tammām and al-Mutanabbī, attracted commentaries as bulky as those of the pre-Islamic poets whose diction and imagery they echo, as al-Mutanabbī does those of Abū Tammām: if Abū Tammām is neoclassical, then al-Mutanabbī is neo-neoclassical. Abū Tammām reinforced his classical aura by composing an anthology of Bedouin verse, *al-Ḥamāsa* (Valour),[10] which was at least as widely admired as his own poetry: his readers found in it everything they expected of the noble Arab of the desert, and indeed the pieces were artfully selected from antiquarian sources and tailored to this end. Abū Tammām's Bedouins have little in common with the real Arab tribesmen of his day, seldom encountered by most of his readers. He also trumpeted the triumphs of Islam over heretics and rebels, and one of his most famous poems

9 Bibliographies in J. S. Meisami, 'Abū Tammām', *EAL*, vol. I, pp. 47–9; J. S. Meisami, 'al-Buḥturī', *EAL*, vol. I, pp. 161–2; J. S. Meisami, 'al-Mutanabbī', *EAL*, vol. II, pp. 558–60.

10 Studied in detail in S. P. Stetkevych, *Abū Tammām and the poetics of the ʿAbbāsid age* (Leiden, 1991), part 3.

is his *qaṣīda* celebrating al-Muʿtaṣim's (r. 218–27/833–42) victory over the Byzantines at Amorium in 223/838, which casts the caliph's soldiers – of many races, some of them mercenaries and some slaves, and not all of them Muslims – in the role of the Prophet Muḥammad's Arab holy warriors, and mocks the Christians as pagans.[11] Yet Abū Tammām himself, it was said, was the son of a Syrian Christian innkeeper; and his verse, for all its Arab neoclassicism, was steeped in conceits derived from philosophy.

This yoking of opposites triggered a long-running critical debate which bore fruit a century later, when poetic criticism (*naqd al-shiʿr*) moved out of the salon into the study and became a substantial discipline. Al-Āmidī (d. 371/987), whose *al-Muwāzana bayna shiʿr Abī Tammām wa-al-Buḥturī* (Weighing of the poetry of Abū Tammām against that of al-Buḥturī) was a key work in this transition, put a new twist on what by this time were lapsed anti-*shuʿūbī* themes when, in an echo of the debate between Aristotelian logicians and Arabic grammarians about the structure of human thought, he pinpointed what he found disturbing about Abū Tammām's poetic thought: it was not language-specific. Rather, Abū Tammām tries to impose universal logic on the Arab system of poetic truth, which is destructive, because poetry, especially Arabic poetry, is culture-specific. This sophisticated analysis had its roots in the ideal of Bedouin culture that Abū Tammām's ever-popular *Ḥamāsa* had itself helped to promote, and unfolded against the political and social backdrop of the Persian Būyid takeover of the ʿAbbāsid caliphate.

Thus the way in which an ethnic factor could stimulate cultural change could be a matter of individual attitude: it has been argued that for Bashshār and other *shuʿūbīs* it was personal resentment of their inferiority as *mawālī* that spurred them to excel at Arabic. It could also be a matter of intellectual allegiance, as in the case of Abū Tammām's poetry and al-Āmidī's criticism. But equally, specialised knowledge of languages and ideas could be made to serve a public programme. At first, with ʿAbd al-Ḥamīd and Ibn al-Muqaffaʿ, the foreign ideas brought into Arabic were those of a professional elite with a pragmatic and high-handed approach to cultural fusion. On the model of their own experience, without condescending to argue their case, they present fusion as something to be applied at once, at all levels of behaviour, for both moral and practical benefit. This is what ʿAbd al-Ḥamīd calls *adab*. *Adab* would become a central notion in Arabic culture, the link between

11 Bibliography of this much-discussed poem in J. Bray, 'al-Muʿtaṣim's "bridge of toil" and Abū Tammām's Amorium *qaṣīda*', in G. R. Hawting *et al.*, (eds.), *Studies in Islamic and Middle Eastern texts and traditions in memory of Norman Calder*, *Journal of Semitic Studies* Supplement 12 (Oxford, 2000).

literature and living, a professional and social tool and at the same time an imaginative ideal. It would weather political and social changes for centuries to come. It has been called 'Islamic humanism' by some modern scholars, for Greek thought often feeds into it directly or indirectly, it frequently praises man's rational capacity (*ʿaql*), and makes human experience the framework of its discourse.

Shuʿūbiyya was a shorter-lived phenomenon. Its effects were out of proportion to its duration: it stimulated its opponents, thinkers who, like the *shuʿūbīs* themselves, were usually non-Arabs, but who favoured Arabic (rather than Arab) particularism, to debate openly what the choice of an Arabic cultural identity might imply, and to set their own examples of the directions they wished the new culture to take. From one end to the other of the Arabic-speaking Islamic world, founding agendas were laid down in the third/ninth and fourth/tenth centuries; some of the key works, by the easterners al-Jāḥiẓ and Ibn Qutayba and the Andalusian Ibn ʿAbd Rabbih, will be touched upon shortly.

In the eastern Islamic world *shuʿūbiyya* was deflected by the re-emergence of Persian as a literary language in the fourth/tenth century. In al-Andalus it makes its appearance when Arabic showed no sign of being displaced, and there is disagreement about its social and political significance. The sole extant Andalusian *shuʿūbī* tract is the short 'Epistle' of Ibn García/Gharsiya, a Muslim of Basque extraction, composed in the second half of the fifth/eleventh century, which complains of the arrogance of privileged Arab settlers. Of the several refutations to which it gave rise, that of Abū Yaḥyā ibn Masʿada, dating from perhaps a century later, contains one of the most lyrical affirmations of the virtue of the pre-Islamic Arabs to be found in either eastern or western Arabic literature.[12]

Patronage and loyalties

Alignments of identification can seem arbitrary when they are caught up in polemic. The secretaries' loyalty to the ʿAbbāsid regime was never in doubt, but they became targets of anti-*shuʿūbiyya* because of their harping on Persian and Hellenistic wisdom and on their own privileged position as intermediaries between the ruler and the ruled, and as such as agents of divine providence. This proved extremely annoying to other *mawālī* equally loyal to the ʿAbbāsids but employed by them in other capacities, especially if they were committed, as *kātibs* rarely were, to serious religious enquiry. So, in his

12 S. Enderwitz, 'al-Shuʿūbiyya', *EI2*, vol. IX, pp. 513–16.

irritation with the scribes, Ibn Qutayba[13] the *qāḍī* and *ḥadīth* scholar (213–76/828–89), author, among other works, of *al-Maʿārif* (General knowledge) and *ʿUyūn al-akhbār* (The [anthology of] choicest narratives (Arab and foreign)) and of a handbook for bureaucrats, *Adab al-kātib* (The conduct of the scribe), three of the founding texts of second-generation ʿAbbāsid *adab*, geared to a wide middlebrow readership, for all his mistrust of his nimble and ironical predecessor, al-Jāḥiẓ (*c*. 160–255/776–868), sometimes seems to be saying the same as al-Jāḥiẓ,[14] whose huge *Kitāb al-bayān wa-al-tabyīn* (Book of eloquence and exposition) and *Kitāb al-ḥayawān* (Book of living creatures) are cornerstones of Muʿtazilite rationalism and of *adab* aimed at an intellectual elite. Al-Jāḥiẓ mocks the scribes' glib cosmopolitanism, Ibn Qutayba their glib rationalism[15] – both signs of their lack of understanding of the Arab intellectual foundations of Islam, of which al-Jāḥiẓ and Ibn Qutayba were self-appointed champions. Yet al-Jāḥiẓ, occasional propagandist of the caliph and friend to very highly placed statesmen, and Ibn Qutayba, a legal functionary with powerful protectors, were allies of the elite and therefore of its supporting bureaucracy, and both were ready to absorb into their own intellectual systems whatever foreign elements they found congenial: both, in fact, accepted the scribal synthesis, along with the notion of *adab* as a pragmatic, meliorist broadening of horizons.

Not dissimilarly, court poets occupied debatable ground. If Bashshār was not the only poet to meet a gruesome end, after taunting his patrons in a bid to raise his own standing, nor was he the last to flirt in verse with naughtiness – or even heresy – in order to thrill these same patrons: the complicity between poets and patrons was necessarily a game of risk. The stakes included monetary reward, sometimes in the form of an administrative sinecure: Abū Tammām died as *ṣāḥib al-barīd* (postmaster and intelligencer) of Mosul. Fame for the poet was inextricable from image-building for the patron, but there is no simple formula for calculating the exchange of benefits. Patrons could not make poets write to a programme, and since many poets did not wish to discard the moral authority that was a traditional part of their role, patrons and protégés rarely made wholly common cause. Exceptional was the ceremonial that the Ismāʿīlī Fāṭimids used in their new capital, Cairo; its cosmological symbolism was repeated in their architecture, their public appearances and also in the poetry written for them, as if it were a natural

13 Bibliography of editions, translations and studies, in J. E. Lowry, 'Ibn Qutaybah', *DLB:ALC*.
14 Bibliography of editions, translations and studies in J. E. Montgomery, 'al-Jāḥiẓ', *DLB:ALC*.
15 References in Enderwitz, 'al-Shuʿūbiyya'.

emanation of the sacred caliphs, though of course it was the creation of the teams of thinkers and artists in their service, just like the themes of dynastic and regnal propaganda devised by poets for the Umayyads and ʿAbbāsids.[16] But poets chose their patrons, not the other way about. Thus the political rivalries of the Fāṭimids' final years exposed the historian and court poet ʿUmāra al-Yamanī (515–69/1121–74) to conflicts of loyalty, which are reflected both in his poetry and in his autobiography, *al-Nukat al-ʿaṣriyya fī akhbār al-wuzarāʾ al-miṣriyya* (Tales of our times: particulars of Egypt's viziers). When Saladin seized power (567/1171) ʿUmāra courted the new order, but did not show enough enthusiasm, and Saladin had him strangled.[17]

Female literary identities

Choices of alignment were subject to varied pressures and constraints. Political positioning – or even personal likes and dislikes – was one factor, but not always the most important: the legal capacity of an individual was the starting-point. Bashshār had been free, legally, to choose his own, contentious identity, but many others were not, because they were slaves who had a limited legal scope and whose original identity had been deleted and replaced with an Arab one. The group of the greatest social and literary significance to whom this applies was female; its period of greatest importance was the first two ʿAbbāsid centuries.

The female slave musicians (*qayna*, pl. *qiyān* or *jāriya*, pl. *jawārī*) of the early ʿAbbāsid court were the successors of the slaves skilled in Persian or Byzantine music who had been part of the luxury culture of the pre-Islamic Arabs, either as court musicians to the Ghassānid and Lakhmid phylarchs or as performers in taverns. They are mentioned in early poetry, and the careers of the most famous are sketched in the *Kitāb al-aghānī* (Book of songs) of Abū al-Faraj al-Iṣfahānī (284–*c.* 363/897–*c.* 972). Pre-Islamic *qiyān* set various kinds of male tribal poetry to music, but were not themselves poets,[18] and their role contrasts with that of free, female tribal poets, who composed elegies (*marāthī*) for slain male relatives. In early Islamic times *qiyān* went on to play a major part, for which the *Kitāb al-aghānī* is again our authority, in the flowering in Medina and Mecca of a feminised Arabic culture which followed

16 Overview in J. S. Meisami, '*Madīḥ, madḥ*', *EAL*, vol. II, pp. 482–4.
17 P. Smoor, 'ʿUmāra's poetical views of Shāwar, Ḍirgham, Shīrkūh and Ṣalāḥ al-Dīn as viziers of the Fatimid caliphs', in F. Daftary and J. W. Meri (eds.), *Culture and memory in medieval Islam: Essays in honour of Wilferd Madelung* (London and New York, 2003).
18 The standard study remains N. D. al-Asad, *al-Qiyān wa al-ghināʾ fī al-ʿaṣr al-jāhilī*, 3rd edn (Beirut, 1988 [1960]).

the Arab conquests, when cash and slaves flowed into the Peninsula and a new, leisured Arab aristocracy set about the pursuit of pleasure. Those inhabitants of the Ḥijāz who had not gone off to fight seem to have devoted themselves at this time either, according to legal sources, to laying the foundations of Islamic law or, according to *adab* works such as the *Kitāb al-aghānī*, to developing new kinds of love poetry. These were typified, on the one hand, by the witty dialogues and love-letters of the aristocratic ʿUmar ibn Abī Rabīʿa (23–93 or 103/644–712 or 721) and his imitators, who wooed aristocratic ladies, and, on the other, by the melancholy ʿUdhrī manner (named after the tribe of ʿUdhra), which favoured chastity, despair and faithfulness unto death between pairs of Bedouin lovers, of whom the archetypal couple, Majnūn ('the madman') and Laylā,[19] may have been entirely legendary. (Later, the foul-mouthed Bashshār was famous for his love poetry in this 'courtly' tradition.) Musical and literary salons (*majlis*, pl. *majālis*) flourished, often presided over by women, either slave musicians or Arab aristocrats inviting the poetic praises of their admirers. The supporting role in this feminised culture of 'effeminate' men (*mukhannathūn*) is stressed in the anecdotal literature.[20] ʿAbbāsid depictions of this bohemian interlude like to show the merry-makers and 'effeminates' getting the better of attempts by the nascent legalists to shut them down, and this must have been more than a fictional victory, since Arabia retained its reputation for musical training and was one of the sources that supplied women slave musicians to the early ʿAbbāsid court, where some became caliphal concubines, with a marked effect on court politics and on the dynasty's reproductive strategies.[21]

It appears that ʿAbbāsid *qiyān/jawārī* had no memory of the cultures to which they or their parents had belonged before enslavement. Instead, they had an encyclopaedic knowledge of Arabic poetry, which enabled them to catch allusions, cap quotations and improvise in verse, and of course to set poetry to music, and generally match or exceed the learning and intelligence of their clientele. (The learned Tawaddud of the *Thousand and one nights* is easily recognisable as an ʿAbbāsid *jāriya*.) The *jāriya*, therefore, was the most flattering of cultural trophies, having no culture of her own but embodying that of her masters and being at the same time a luxury sexual commodity, much sought after in well-to-do circles as well as in aristocratic families and at court. In both romantic and satirical writing ʿAbbāsid *jawārī* are treated as if

19 Their legend was greatly developed in Persian literature and painting.
20 See E. R. Rowson, 'The effeminates of early Medina', *JAOS*, 111 (1991).
21 See Kennedy, *The court of the caliphs*, chap. 7, 'The harem'.

they were the agents of a significant feminisation of elite society.[22] This is probably more of a literary theme than a reality; but in the course of the fourth/tenth century their audience seems to have widened, and they popularised notions of courtliness to a cross-section of the urban population. A sequence of vignettes of singers in Baghdad dating from the 360s/970s and retailed by al-Tawḥīdī (on whom see pp. 398, 401 below) suggests that important shifts were taking place. *Qiyān* who sang to the public were not only numbered in hundreds, but a sizeable proportion of them were free women; 'boys [like] moons' were beginning to equal them in popularity; and above all, they were much admired by several leading Sufis.[23] The poetry they sang to them was ordinary love poetry (*ghazal*), but Sufis, themselves an emergent group on the larger social scene, would soon start to quote *ghazal* and secular love theory as a system of metaphor for divine love, before starting to write their own, spiritual verse, which continued to use its conventions. The women and boy singers of fourth/tenth-century Baghdad seem to have opened the way to the fusion effected by Sufism between *adab*, a delicacy of human feeling forged in elite circles, and a religious sensibility which drew on traditionalist opposition to elite intellectual purism in matters of belief. Al-Sarrāj's (*c.* 417–500/1026–1106) *Maṣāriʿ al-ʿushshāq* (Calamities of lovers) is a forerunner of these trends, whose development would be pursued over several centuries.

A significant part of the defining work of ʿAbbāsid *adab*, the *Kitāb al-aghānī*,[24] is devoted to the lives and compositions of the great *jawārī* up until the second half of the third/ninth century. Abū al-Faraj al-Iṣfahānī also collected the poetry of ʿAbbāsid slave poetesses in a separate book, *al-Imāʾ al-shawāʿir* (Slavewomen poets). The women's artistic integrity and sense of professional purpose come through clearly in his biographies, which highlight the splendours but also give glimpses of the miseries of their situation. Original material with similar qualities is found in the *Kitāb al-diyārāt* (Book of monasteries) of al-Shābushtī (d. *c.* 399/1008; see pp. 396, 397 below). Earlier, the greed and heartlessness of *qiyān* in their role of courtesans had been

22 See J. Bray, 'Men, women and slaves in Abbasid society', in L. Brubaker and J. M. H. Smith (eds.), *Gender in the early medieval world: East and West, 300–900* (Cambridge, 2004).

23 Near-identical passages in al-Tawḥīdī, *al-Imtāʿ wa-al-muʾānasa*, ed. A. Amīn and A. al-Zayn, 2nd edn, 3 vols. in 1 (Cairo, 1953), vol. II, pp. 165–83 and al-Tawḥīdī (attrib.), *al-Risāla al-Baghdādiyya*, ed. ʿA. al-Shāljī (Beirut, 1400/1980), pp. 244–67.

24 Editions and bibliography in H. Kilpatrick, *Making the Great book of songs: Compilation and the author's craft in Abū l-Faraj al-Iṣbahānī's* Kitāb al-aghānī (London and New York, 2003).

satirised by al-Jāḥiẓ in his mischievous *Risālat al-qiyān* (Epistle on singing-girls) and by al-Washshā' (d. 325/937) in chapter 20 of his *Kitāb al-muwashshā* (Book of brocade), a pessimistic meditation on modern love coupled with a guide to fashionable clothes and manners (*ẓarf*). To al-Tanūkhī (327–84/939–94), on the contrary, in chapter 13 of his *al-Faraj ba'd al-shidda* (Deliverance from evil), *jawārī* are romantic and usually self-sacrificing heroines who save their lovers from their own foolishness and are rewarded with their lifelong devotion, or even marriage. They are ubiquitous in the literature of the period, and continue to fascinate later writers, who retell the classic stories about them. But the Andalusian Ibn Ḥazm (384–456/994–1064), genealogist, jurist and heresiographer, but also theorist of love and champion of the home-grown culture of Islamic Spain, does not retell old stories in his *Ṭawq al-ḥamāma* (Ring of the dove). Instead, he shows slave musicians simply as women whom he or his friends had known and loved in the family quarters of their own aristocratic households. His account of his unconsummated adolescent affair with one such girl, and of the quiet, random unhappiness of her subsequent fate, displays an understanding of how female destinies are plotted against the different rhythm of male lives comparable to that of his Japanese contemporary Murasaki.

No chronicles of *qiyān* of later periods have come to light, although the profession did not disappear. A few passages by the leading local songwriter of his day, Ibn al-Ṭaḥḥān, afford a glimpse of female and male musicians at work in Fāṭimid Egypt in the 1050s.[25] For al-Andalus, and more particularly Seville, some contemporary detail of the training, licensing and sale of women slave musicians can be gleaned from a treatise on music by Aḥmad ibn Yūsuf al-Tīfāshī (580–651/1184–1253).[26] By this time al-Andalus was exporting to eager audiences in the east its music, and the home-grown lyrical poetic genres that went with it, the multirhymed, stanzaic *muwashshaḥ* and the vernacular Arabic *zajal*. Before this, for the first century and a half of its existence, Muslim Spain had looked to the east for its high culture, and it was musicians from the east, including women slaves, who had helped implant, in a region that felt itself to be intellectually marginal and was largely ignored by easterners, *adab*, love poetry and the makings of the sentimental code that Ibn Ḥazm sets out in the *Ṭawq al-ḥamāma*.

25 Quoted in al-Asad, *al-Qiyān*, pp. 265–7.

26 D. Reynolds, 'Music', in M. R. Menocal *et al.* (eds.), *The Cambridge history of Arabic literature*, vol. V: *The literature of al-Andalus* (Cambridge, 2000), pp. 65–7, 70–1; C. Pellat, 'Ḳayna', *EI2*, vol. IV, pp. 820–4.

The role of marginal figures

Divorced from their own backgrounds, brought up as Muslims, and often absorbed into their owners' families as concubine mothers, ʿAbbāsid *jawārī* contrast with the dynasties of non-Muslim men of learning of the same period who for several generations kept their own religion and, still more distinctively, made a family business of their knowledge of foreign sciences – medicine, philosophy and mathematics – and the foreign languages that were the key to them. Despite their small numbers, their effect on Arabic culture was pervasive. By the fourth/tenth century the new terminology and ways of thinking that the originally elite translation movement introduced had not only enriched educated vocabulary but forced all literate and thinking Muslims to re-examine their beliefs about the place of rationality (*ʿaql*) in different systems of authority, human and divine.

Medicine in particular, being in wide demand, made a deep impression in educated circles, and figures prominently in both prose and poetic *adab*.[27] Physicians, who were also courtiers and part of the *dramatis personae* of the caliph's entourage, impressed themselves on the ʿAbbāsid imaginations in a similar way to *jawārī*. The medical historian Ibn Abī Uṣaybiʿa (*c.* 590–668/1194–1270), who belonged to a dynasty of Muslim physicians in service under the Ayyūbids and Mamlūks, quotes vivid vignettes of the Nestorian Bakhtīshūʿ (or Bukhtīshūʿ) family of Baghdad, for example a scene where Bukhtīshūʿ ibn Jibrāʾīl (the fourth of eight generations of court physicians) coaxes the little prince al-Muʿtazz, whose lack of appetite is causing his father, the caliph al-Mutawakkil (232–47/847–61), great anxiety, to eat two apples – 'just for me' – and drink some syrup – 'just for me' – by bribing him with his beautiful coat, which the prince has been fingering longingly.[28] The al-Ṣābiʾ family were pagans from Ḥarrān in northern Syria; eleven generations of them have been counted, the last member dying in 619/1222. The earlier generations were scientists, mathematicians, translators and physicians. Several of them went on to write chronicles of the ʿAbbāsid caliphate; that of the physician Thābit ibn Sinān ibn Thābit ibn Qurra (d. 363/973–4) is quoted by later historians – notably the moral philosopher Miskawayh (*c.* 320–421/932–1030) and Ibn Abī Uṣaybiʿa – for its dramatic personal accounts of events such as the fall and

27 J. Bray, 'The physical world and the writer's eye: al-Tanūkhī and medicine', in J. Bray (ed.), *Writing and representation in medieval Islam: Muslim horizons* (London and New York, 2006).

28 Ibn Abī Uṣaybiʿa, *ʿUyūn al-anbāʾ fī ṭabaqāt al-aṭibbāʾ*, ed. N. Riḍā (Beirut, n.d.[1965]), p. 206.

torture of the vizier Ibn Muqla, a fine *adīb* but a foolish politician. Two other members of the al-Ṣābi' family were distinguished *kātibs* in the service of the Būyids of Baghdad: Ibrāhīm ibn Hilāl (313–84/925–94), famous for his epistles in rhymed prose (*saj*ʿ), and his grandson, Hilāl ibn al-Muḥassin (359–448/969–1056), the first member of the family to convert to Islam, who composed an elegiac account of 'The rules and regulations of the 'Abbāsid court' (*Rusūm dār al-khilāfa*) as it had been before the advent of the Būyids. An example of how, as time went on, successive pasts assumed classical status for readers of Arabic, its title is a pun on the opening motif of the classical *qaṣīda*, the 'traces of the abandoned encampment' (*rusūm dār*) of the poet's beloved.[29]

When not at court, the Bukhtīshūʿs were active in Nestorian ecclesiastical politics.[30] But in the Arabic literary landscape Christians do not appear in such humdrum roles. Rather, they provide local colour and opportunities for escapism, for example as innkeepers in the wine-poems (*khamriyyāt*) of Abū Nuwās (*c.* 140–98/755–813) – a role in which Jews and Zoroastrians sometimes appear too – and as objects of homosexual desire, notably altar boys (with a change of decor, young Turkish slave boys may also fill the role of love objects).[31] Monasteries in the neighbourhood of cities, which sold wine in the setting of orchards and gardens, are the scene of picnics, drinking-parties and amorous encounters. A whole literary genre arose out of these practices, of which only the incomplete *Kitāb al-diyārāt* of al-Shābushtī remains. He was an Egyptian in the service of the Fāṭimid caliph al-ʿAzīz (r. 365–86/975–96), but although most of the convents he describes are in Iraq and Syria, and the poems and literary anecdotes quoted mainly concern caliphs, aristocrats, courtiers and singing-women of the great 'Abbāsid century, it is clear that townspeople still went on pleasure outings to monasteries in his own day.

Monasteries also served as madhouses (the commonest term is the Persian (*bī*)*māristān*); these too were the object of outings, and so became the backdrop to another, long-lasting literary theme, that of the wise madman, who is usually either a mystic out of tune with the world or a lover deranged by separation from the beloved, itself a metaphor for the mystic's condition. Al-Sarrāj's *Maṣāriʿ al-ʿushshāq* is an early witness to this theme.

The literary stereotyping of the picturesque non-Muslim and of the alienated Muslim can be seen as approaches to connected though not identical

29 Personal communication from J. S. Meisami.

30 R. Le Coz, *Les médecins nestoriens au moyen âge: Les maîtres des Arabes* (Paris, 2004), chaps. 6 and 12.

31 See T. Bauer, *Liebe und Liebesdichtung in der arabischen Welt des 9. und 10. Jahrhunderts* (Wiesbaden, 1998) for a comprehensive thematic survey of motifs.

problems. Orthodoxy and heresy, hanging sometimes on hair's-breadth distinctions, recurrently divided the Muslim community in controversy or worse, and it must sometimes have seemed, in a happy literary solution seldom achieved in life, that only the simplicity of the madman could reconcile dogmatic differences. Parts of the *ʿUqalāʾ al-majānīn* (Wise madmen) of al-Nīsābūrī (d. 406/1015), the first surviving work on the theme, seem to suggest as much.

If the heretic within the community posed one sort of problem, the unbeliever without posed another. In societies where, until probably the beginning of the fifth/eleventh century, the majority populations were non-Muslim, and in a culture and literature that owed much to non-Muslims and non-Arabs, the question of who was an insider and who an outsider was an uneasy one, and remained so for a long time. Thus the classic pre-Islamic and early Islamic wine poets had been Christians: ʿAdī ibn Zayd (d. *c.* 600), credited with inventing the free-standing wine-song, and al-Aʿshā Maymūn (d. *c.* 7/629) and al-Akhṭal (*c.* 20–92/640–710), composers of great *qaṣīdas*.[32] But in the *khamriyyāt* of Abū Nuwās and the *diyārāt* poets Christians no longer spoke for themselves, but were reduced to erotic props. The wine-song had been simultaneously appropriated and made transgressive by Muslim poets, and would be made doubly so when Sufis such as Ibn al-Fāriḍ (d. 632/1235) adopted *khamriyya* along with *ghazal* as ways of conveying mystical experience. Yet, despite being pushed to the margins of literary vision, Christians and other outsiders continued to colonise Muslim culture, and today's outsider was often tomorrow's fellow-Muslim, like Ṣāʿid ibn Makhlad, one of al-Shābushtī's heroes, who in around 265/878 converted to Islam in order to accept high office, while his brother ʿAbdūn remained a monk at Dayr Qunnā.[33] Monasteries long remained a training-ground for *kātibs*, and *kātibs* were often also *adībs*.[34] But the process by which monastery-trained Christians became part of the Muslim literary mainstream is not yet understood; nor are the reasons why, outside religious genres, Christian Arabic culture found literary expression only in Muslim formats. The most striking example is *Daʿwat al-aṭibbāʾ* (The physicians' dinner party) of the Nestorian physician, and later monk, Ibn Buṭlān (d. 458/1066). It is a comic masterpiece which echoes

32 See references in P. F. Kennedy, *The wine song in classical Arabic poetry: Abū Nuwās and the literary tradition* (Oxford, 1997), pp. 5–6.

33 Al-Shābushtī, *Kitāb al-diyārāt*, ed. G. ʿAwwād, 3rd edn (Beirut, 1986), pp. 270–3.

34 H. Kilpatrick, 'Monasteries through Muslim eyes: The *diyārāt* books', in D. Thomas (ed.), *Christians at the heart of Islamic rule: Church life and scholarship in ʿAbbasid Iraq* (Leiden and Boston, 2003), p. 36.

the *Deipnosophists* of Athenaeus but is in the vanguard of mid-ʿAbbāsid experimental prose: a picaresque narrative full of intertextual parody, which has been bracketed with the *maqāmāt* (see pp. 409–10 below). A 'Priests' dinner party' (*Daʿwat al-qusūs*) with similar characteristics is also attributed to him. Ibn Buṭlān's other writings are in the fields of medical controversy and Christian theology;[35] we cannot reconstruct how he made the jump from these kinds of writings to fashionable literary *adab*.

The eloquent madman is an extreme reminder of split identities. He is not merely a fictional symbol; in the guise of the eccentric loner, at odds with society, he is also the biographical template of a number of major authors. For uneasy or uneasily perceived identities underlie much Arabic literary production, despite the apparent consensuality of its formats and much of its subject matter (see pp. 400, 402–9 below). Unease could arise from the antagonism felt by those who had to make their own way in the world towards those who had family and social advantages, such as the essayist Abū Ḥayyān al-Tawḥīdī (*c.* 315–411/927–1023), who was bitterly jealous of the easy praise (as he saw it) won by the Būyid vizier al-Ṣāḥib Ibn ʿAbbād (326–85/938–95), a scholar and brilliant patron of letters, and full of the aristocratic airs that came from belonging to an Iranian *kātib* family. Al-Tawḥīdī punished him for failing to recognise his own genius by lampooning him in *Akhlāq al-wazīrayn* (The characters of the two viziers).[36]

Equally, antagonism could be felt by haves towards have-nots. (Ibn) al-Qifṭī (568–646/1172–1248), member of a Syro-Egyptian *kātib* dynasty, the languidly omnicompetent minister of the Ayyūbid princes of Aleppo, who professed to scorn office routine and leave his beloved library only in emergencies, was idolised by Yāqūt (575–626/1179–1229), a self-taught former slave of Byzantine birth and the greatest Arabic literary biographer of his age. Al-Qifṭī helped Yāqūt when he arrived penniless in Aleppo after fleeing from the Mongols, who had overtaken him on his commercial-cum-scholarly travels in the east; in return, Yāqūt memorialised him in his own lifetime in a biography constructed from his own, surprisingly candid, family reminiscences and from his official epistles and praise poems, which are full of interesting historical detail and up-to-date literary devices. Yāqūt chose his materials well: they are difficult but rewarding to read, and give a strong impression of al-Qifṭī's geniality and

35 References and bibliography in P. F. Kennedy, 'The *maqāmāt* as a nexus of interests: Reflections on Abdelfattah Kilito's *Les séances*', in Bray (ed.), *Writing and representation*, pp. 171–8, and Le Coz, *Les médecins nestoriens*, pp. 200–2, 325.

36 See J. L. Kraemer, *Humanism in the renaissance of Islam: The cultural revival during the Buyid age* (Leiden, 1986), chap. 3, 'Profiles: scholars, patrons, and potentates'.

charm.[37] In one of only three works to survive from his vast and varied œuvre, the rather sloppily constructed biographical dictionary, *Inbāh al-ruwāt ʿalā anbāh al-nuḥāt* (Notable grammarians brought to the attention of transmitters [of the subject]), whose shortcomings he blames on the inconsiderate death of a collaborator, al-Qifṭī repays Yāqūt's gratitude by sneering at him as a paid copyist, trader, ex-slave and autodidact. Indeed, he belittles most of his contemporaries, not in the fashionable circumlocutory *sajʿ* of which Yāqūt's portrait shows him to have been a master, but in brutally unadorned prose; his anger is what makes him (like al-Tawḥīdī) so readable.

Yāqūt's *Irshād al-arīb ilā maʿrifat al-adīb/Muʿjam al-udabāʾ* (Guidance for the discerning in recognising men of *adab* or Dictionary of men of *adab*) is infinitely more scholarly and remains a standard reference work, although its literary genius is largely overlooked. Wherever possible Yāqūt quotes his contemporaries' own words and works, or, in the case of men of letters of earlier centuries, the testimony of writers who knew them. Yet each bio-bibliographical entry is shaped with great art, both as an individual portrait and as an element in Yāqūt's argument about what *adab* is. As depicted by Yāqūt, with their defiant virtuosity and provocative behaviour towards princes and aristocrats, several of his contemporaries, outsiders like himself, recall early *shuʿūbīs*; examples are the two eccentrics, Abū Nizār al-Ḥasan ibn Ṣāfī, 'prince of grammarians' (who came of slave parentage), and the aged 'Sniffy' (Shumaym, nickname of ʿAlī ibn al-Ḥasan ibn ʿAntar of Ḥilla). Yāqūt makes fun of their vanity but sees something heroic in their absurdity. Although they are misfits, in their independence and love of literature they are true *adībs*, and in the pages of this encyclopaedia composed by a misfit they take their place as equal heirs in a great tradition.[38]

The greatest outsider of all, the philosopher-poet and prose writer Abū al-ʿAlāʾ al-Maʿarrī (363–449/973–1058), blind, celibate, a vegetarian and a recluse in his home town of Maʿarrat al-Nuʿmān in Syria, who described himself as a captive of his infirmity and solitude, his soul a prisoner in his body, was too heterodox to meet with the approval of Yāqūt, who also hints that his isolation was relative since he had an extensive, well-placed and highly literate family which did not neglect him. He nevertheless devotes one of his longest

37 Yāqūt, *Irshād al-arīb ilā maʿrifat al-adīb*, ed. I. ʿAbbās, 7 vols. (Beirut, 1993), vol. V, pp. 2022–36.

38 Translations in J. Bray, 'Yāqūt's interviewing technique: "Sniffy"', in C. F. Robinson (ed.), *Texts, documents and artefacts: Islamic studies in honour of D. S. Richards* (Leiden and Boston, 2003).

biographical entries to him, quoting a number of his epistles.[39] Al-Maʿarrī himself, in spite of ostentatiously shunning the world, felt fully part of the fellowship of *adab* past and present, receiving disciples and employing some of his extraordinary talents in writing commentaries on the poetry of Abū Tammām, al-Buḥturī and al-Mutanabbī.[40]

A sense of belonging: the evolving sociology of adab

Who were the founders and propagators of literary ideals that could command loyalty across wounding divides and inspire a sense of belonging? The values of *adab*, whether moral or aesthetic, came to be so widely shared with the passing of time as to appear almost a set of natural features of the human landscape. The Egyptian al-Nuwayrī (667–732/1279–1332), a senior civil servant for the first part of his career, prefaces the twenty-odd volumes of history which form the bulk of his *Nihāyat al-arab fī funūn al-adab* (The heart's desire concerning the kinds of *adab*) with four books of cosmology and natural science, at the centre of which is the section on man, his institutions and *adab*. *Adab* thus forms a hinge between the structure of the universe and the ways in which man has played out his destiny; or, in another perspective, cosmology is the warp and history the weft of *adab*. Al-Ibshīhī's (790–*c*. 850/1388–*c*. 1446) *al-Mustaṭraf fī kull fann mustaẓraf* (The extreme of every kind of elegance), also from Mamlūk Egypt, is far less stately: 'elegance' is found in vernacular proverbs, including 'women's proverbs', and in poetry both contemporary and colloquial (chapter 72). Chapters on *adab*, bracketed with piety, preface the whole; the topics of subsequent chapters, such as *sulṭān* (rulership), are those of classical *adab* monographs or anthologies, and their contents are well-worn. This is familiar and comforting territory for al-Ibshīhī's readers, who cannot have been intellectuals; the little encyclopaedia guides them pleasantly through the ages of man and his activities to holy dying and the grave.

Yet the base of *adab* – its intellectual and no less its social base – had originally been narrow. Under the early ʿAbbāsids writers seem to have depended on intermittent patronage or on regular employment in government: *kātibs* were often *adībs*, and so too were the court companions (*nadīm*, pl. *nudamāʾ* or *jalīs*, pl. *julasāʾ*) whose job was to help a ruler or grandee relax after the day's business. Princely recreation included drinking and joking, but was on the whole an intellectually strenuous and strictly organised business, according to the testimony of al-Ṣūlī (d. *c*. 335/946), a scholar whose

39 Yāqūt, *Irshād*, vol. I, pp. 295–356.
40 G. J. H. van Gelder, 'Abū al-ʿAlāʾ al-Maʿarrī', *EAL*, vol. I, pp. 24–5.

works include collections of biographical anecdotes about al-Buḥturī (*Akhbār al-Buḥturī*) and Abū Tammām (*Akhbār Abī Tammām*) and an edition of the latter's *dīwān*, and who served three caliphs as one of a team of no longer very sprightly *julasā'*. His memoirs of the reigns of al-Rāḍī (322–9/934–40) and al-Muttaqī (329–33/940–4) convey vividly the incongruous decorum of literary soirées conducted against a backdrop of fear of deposition or murder.[41]

Despite the fact that almost anyone with pretensions to learning in any field also dabbled in *adab* (as they usually also did in *ḥadīth*), it does not seem to have been common for serious experts in *adab* (unlike *ḥadīth* experts) to support themselves by trade. One of the first to do so was the Baghdad bookseller Ibn Abī Ṭāhir Ṭayfūr (d. 280/893); the cheapness of paper and an expanding reading public afforded him a new economic opening. At the end of the next century Ibn al-Nadīm, the author of *al-Fihrist* (The index), a guide to contemporary books, authors and fields of human knowledge, was also a Baghdad bookseller. He appears to have been well connected and self-assured. Nevertheless, because of its associations with court culture, a certain snobbery clung to *adab*, unlike religious learning, and made self-supporting *adībs* socially vulnerable: Ibn al-Nadīm's contemporary al-Tawḥīdī smarted at having to earn his living as a copyist, and Yāqūt met with scorn as well as respect for combining bibliophilia with bookselling.

Adībs *as spectators of power*

The *kātibs* and court companions who were more typical bearers of *adab* than such independent figures as Ibn Abī Ṭāhir Ṭayfūr were of varied origins. Thanks to the ubiquitous passion for poetry and music, members of great families, even descendants of caliphs, could become court entertainers if their fortunes dwindled. The profession tended to run in families. A number of *nadīm* clans are prominent over several generations as intimate observers of the caliphs and transmitters of court literature: the al-Mawṣilīs, Ibn Ḥamdūns, Ibn al-Munajjims and al-Yazīdīs. It is in part from *nadīms* that the great writers of the third/ninth and fourth/tenth centuries, whether or not they themselves served at court, derived the vivid sense of personality, of the commanding gesture, the fateful choice, of splendour and pity, and sometimes comedy, that they attach to the great Umayyad and ʿAbbāsid caliphs, their consorts, lovers and ministers: images that were repeated in chronicles and literary compilations for centuries to come.

41 al-Ṣūlī, *Akhbār al-Rāḍī wa-al-Muttaqī*, ed. J. Heyworth-Dunne (Cairo, 1935), pp. 8–20.

This vision of Muslim sovereignty was to play the same role as pre-Islamic poetry in forging a lasting cultural bond. Its images passed into popular literature and folklore via the *Thousand and one nights* and the anthologies of such authors as the Egyptians al-Qalyūbī (d. 1069/1659) and al-Atlīdī (or al-Itlīdī, d. *c.* 1100/1689); but well before this, almost within their own lifetimes, the imagination of great scholars had coined for the thoughtful reader potent images of rulers as flawed vessels of history. A centrepiece of al-Masʿūdī's (*c.* 283–345/896–956) *Murūj al-dhahab* (Meadows of gold) is the tragi-comedy of the destinies of the sons of Hārūn al-Rashīd (d. 193/809), shot through, in his episodic telling of the tale, with ironic omens and leitmotifs, while the last section of Miskawayh's *Tajārib al-umam* (Experiences of the nations), a sustained narrative all the more suspenseful for the complexity of the threads it twists together, plots the malice, imbecility, futility and pity of the scramble for power triggered by the decay of the ʿAbbāsid caliphate. Some dynasties produced exceptional literary talents: many ʿAbbāsids; the Ḥamdānid poet Abū Firās (320–57/932–68), cousin of Sayf al-Dawla; the Fāṭimid prince and poet Tamīm ibn al-Muʿizz (337–74/948–84), to name a few; but those writers and poets who stood close to the throne or wielded power in their own right merely made use of the emblems of sovereignty which had already been created by men of letters.

Men of letters were, then, intimate spectators, in fact or in imagination, of the human drama bound up in the exercise of power, and they saw themselves as the guides and often collaborators of the elite, urging them to espouse justice and wisdom. This is an aspect of *adab* that finds heightened expression in books of 'counsel for princes' (*naṣīḥat al-mulūk*) or mirrors for princes. Sometimes these were composed for the use of a specific prince, for example al-Thaʿālibī's (350–429/961–1038) *Ādāb al-mulūk* (Conduct of princes), written in the far east of Iran and addressed to the young *khwārazmshāh* al-Maʾmūn II before his murder in 408/1017. Sometimes they were more oblique offerings, inviting a wider audience to reflect on the meaning of kingship and the duties of the rulers and the ruled.

The sense that possessed men of *adab* of addressing an elite as the spokesmen of a common moral endeavour is voiced clearly by Ibn ʿAbd Rabbih (246–328/860–940), the first writer to give coherent shape in Islamic Spain to the materials of eastern *adab*. A poet and courtier of *mawlā* descent, his ambition was to be a missionary of *adab* to his own people. His *al-ʿIqd* (The necklace, later dubbed *al-ʿIqd al-farīd* (The unique necklace): it consists of twenty-five chapters, each named for a jewel), is a thematic anthology of what he considers to be the fundamentals of the human condition, and it is the history of the Arabs, from pagan tribes to the ʿAbbāsid caliphate, that illustrates its truths and tragedies. Ibn ʿAbd Rabbih had thought hard about the most pressing intellectual issues raised by the previous generation of eastern Arabic writers: about rationality and the power of language, questions discussed by al-Jāḥiẓ, especially in his *Kitāb al-bayān wa-al-tabyīn*, and about *adab* and the role of books, rather than the traditional oral study-circle, as the key to self-cultivation, a theme dear to Ibn Qutayba, as also to Ibn Abī Ṭāhir Ṭayfūr. The *ʿIqd* is prefaced by a definition of *adab*, which is open to the experiences of all ages and nations, as 'a goodly tree with lofty branches, growing in good soil and bearing ripe fruits; whoso eats of these is heir to prophecy'. *Adab* is human experience standing in the light of reason (*ʿaql*), which God calls 'the dearest to Me of My creation, which I give to those creatures I love best'.[42] These ideas structure both Ibn ʿAbd Rabbih's prefaces and the materials he quotes within chapters. The *ʿIqd* was completed under ʿAbd al-Raḥmān III (r. 300–50 / 912–61) in the heyday of Umayyad Cordoba, and it is perhaps for this reason that the topics of sovereignty, *sulṭān* and how to approach the sovereign play an important part in it.

Some seventy years later, when many petty kingdoms were emerging from the wreck of the Cordoba caliphate, Ibn ʿAbd al-Barr al-Namarī (368–463 / 978–1070) composed an anthology called *Bahjat al-majālis wa-uns al-mujālis* (The glory of salons and the civility of those who take part in them). This too contains a substantial section on maxims concerning *sulṭān*. The rest of Ibn ʿAbd al-Barr's output was devoted to religious topics, and for him *adab* is a repository of wisdom rather than reason, but like Ibn ʿAbd Rabbih he claims a divine origin for it, and especially for the wisdom embodied in poetry: 'Every piece of wisdom not sent down as scripture or given to a prophet to deliver, God has held in store for the tongues of poets to utter.'[43]

If Ibn ʿAbd al-Barr succeeded in transforming *adab* into piety, less than a century later the Andalusian Sufi Abū Bakr al-Ṭurṭūshī (451–520 / 1059–1126), whose wanderings finally led him to settle in Fāṭimid Egypt, transformed piety into highly wrought *adab* in his *Sirāj al-mulūk* (Lantern for princes). As Ibn Khaldūn (d. 808 / 1406) remarked, the *Sirāj* is sermon-like rather than

42 Trans. J. Bray in 'ʿAbbasid myth and the human act: Ibn ʿAbd Rabbih and others', in P. F. Kennedy (ed.), *On fiction and* adab *in medieval Arabic literature* (Wiesbaden, 2005), pp. 14–15.

43 Ibn ʿAbd al-Barr al-Namarī, *Bahjat al-majālis wa-uns al-mujālis*, ed. M. M. al-Khūlī, 3 vols. (Beirut, n.d.), vol. I, p. 38.

analytical:[44] this was indeed an age of great literary sermons, which reduced huge audiences to tears; the best documented are those of the Baghdadī Ibn al-Jawzī (*c.* 511–97/1116–1201), *ḥadīth* scholar, historian, *adīb* and champion of a revived ʿAbbāsid caliphate. Al-Ṭurṭūshī contributed to a tradition that married piety to splendour of language and to activism; his targets included the Fāṭimid vizier al-Maʾmūn al-Baṭāʾiḥī, to whom he presented the *Sirāj*, and the Almoravid Yūsuf ibn Tāshfīn (453–500/1061–1107), and he counted Ibn Tūmart (d. 524/1130), the founder of the Almohad dynasty, among his pupils. The *Sirāj* is full of references to recent history and historical figures from al-Andalus to Iran, all enveloped in an air of enchantment: it has the great vizier Niẓām al-Mulk (d. 485/1092), himself in real life the author of a Persian mirror for princes, *Siyāsatnāma*, tell his master, the Saljūq sultan Malikshāh: 'Your armies will fight for you with swords two cubits long … but I have made for you an army called the Army of the Night. When your armies sleep at night, the Armies of the Night arise in ranks before their Lord, and weep, and pray, and raise their hands in supplication to God for you and your soldiers.'[45] Here, as in many similar works, *adab* and piety combine to turn history into myth and transform both into folklore.

Adab *and personal networks*

As well as a sense of moral community, often elitist, personal connections, often clannish, begin to be displayed in *adab* works from the fourth/tenth century. Many of Abū al-Faraj al-Iṣfahānī's informants for his *Kitāb al-aghānī* belong to a circle of intimate acquaintances, some of them family members,[46] while in his pupil al-Tanūkhī's collection of stories with providentially happy endings, *al-Faraj baʿd al-shidda*, material belonging to the common literary stock was taught to al-Tanūkhī by family and friends and is applied to his and their personal experiences. Miskawayh's history of the chaotic prelude to his own times relies on eyewitnesses connected with his own circles, and, in a new departure, authors of the period begin to memorialise not the great figures of the past but their own contemporaries: al-Tanūkhī's *Nishwār al-muḥāḍara* (Table-talk of a Mesopotamian judge) consists entirely of personal, oral reminiscences by contemporaries of his father, and, a little later, al-Thaʿālibī's *Yatīmat al-dahr fī maḥāsin ahl al-ʿaṣr* (Unique pearl of all time concerning the excellences of the people of this age) is the first large-scale

44 Ibn Khaldūn, *Muqaddima*, quoted in editor's introduction to al-Ṭurṭūshī, *Sirāj al-mulūk*, ed. M. F. Abū Bakr, 2 vols. (Cairo, 1414/1994), vol. I, p. 37.
45 Al-Ṭurṭūshī, *Sirāj*, vol. II, chap. 48, p. 515.
46 Kilpatrick, *Making the Great book of songs*, pp. 14–15.

anthology of contemporary written *adab*, a substantial proportion of it composed by people personally known to al-Thaʿālibī or his friends.[47]

The *Yatīma* provided a lasting model. Its region-by-region structure is copied in, for example, Ibn Maʿṣūm's (1052–1107/1642–1705) *Sulāfat al-ʿaṣr fī maḥāsin al-shuʿarāʾ bi-kull miṣr*) (Choicest pressings [of the grape]/The best of this age, concerning the excellences of poets of every region). Its immediate successors were *Dumyat al-qaṣr wa-ʿuṣrat ahl al-ʿaṣr* (The fair maid of the palace and haven of the people of this age) by al-Bākharzī (*c.* 418–67/1027–75), who met al-Thaʿālibī as a child, and the vast *Kharīdat al-qaṣr wa-jarīdat al-ʿaṣr* (Unpierced pearl/damsel of the palace and tally of the age) of ʿImād al-Dīn al-Iṣfahānī (519–97/1125–1201), also well known as one of Saladin's aides and chroniclers.[48] (The echoing titles, early examples of an enduring fashion, are deliberate *hommages* to al-Thaʿālibī and to each other.) The *Yatīma*, *Dumya* and *Kharīda* all aim to give the widest possible conspectus, for caliphal Baghdad is no longer the focus as it almost automatically was in earlier works. Tiny scraps are deemed worthy of recording and are tracked down by word of mouth, providing the sole record of many amateurs and obscure jobbing wordsmiths; but since the compilers moved in high political circles, many of their sources are statesmen with a literary bent, and they record many pieces given in the *majālis* of grandees or recited in public on ceremonial occasions; al-Bākharzī notes exact dates and places of performance.

The linguistic map of adab

Not least striking is what is omitted: al-Thaʿālibī and al-Bākharzī, natives of the Iranian east, both knew Persian, yet neither discusses contemporary New Persian writing. Similarly Ibn Maʿṣūm, who lived in Mughal India and died in Shīrāz: in his short section on the poets of contemporary Persia he quotes a mere handful of Persian verses; all the rest is Arabic. As this last example suggests, membership of the great tradition of Arabic *adab* long remained a mark of distinction, even in Muslim societies where Arabic had ceased to be the main language of high culture and where the local literatures had developed on very different lines.

47 Partial prosopography in E. K. Rowson and S. Bonebakker, *Notes on two poetic anthologies: T̲aʿālibī's* Tatimma *and Bākharzī's* Dumya (Los Angeles, 1984).

48 Bibliographies in G. J. H. van Gelder, 'Ibn Maʿṣūm', *EAL*, vol. I, p. 349; E. K. Rowson, 'al-Bākharzī, ʿAlī ibn al-Ḥasan', *EAL*, vol. I, p. 129; E. K. Rowson, 'al-Thaʿālibī', *EAL*, vol. II, pp. 764–5; C. Hillenbrand, 'ʿImād al-Dīn al-Iṣfahānī', *EAL*, vol. I, pp. 392–3.

Transitions and reorientations

A new learning: scope and formats

In 463/1071 the funeral took place in Baghdad of al-Khaṭīb al-Baghdādī, preacher, teacher and historian of renown, and a figure representative of the new directions being taken by Arabic culture. As an *adīb* he wrote on the comic and grotesque topic of misers, following the lead of al-Jāḥiẓ's *Kitāb al-bukhalāʾ* (Book of misers) two centuries before, and his *Kitāb al-ṭufayliyyīn* (Book of spongers) is in keeping with the fashion for low-life themes set in the previous century by such eminences as the vizier al-Ṣāḥib Ibn ʿAbbād; but he was, above all, a *ḥadīth* scholar. It was as such that the crowds who followed his bier to the grave acclaimed him, in this period of Sunnī assertiveness and sharpened sectarian identities, and as such that he wrote the collective biography of the city of Baghdad, the *Taʾrīkh Baghdād* (History of Baghdad), an alphabetical portrait gallery of intellectual notables great and small which focuses above all on their role in the transmission of tradition. Yet he had a poor memory and relied on written notes, whereas *ḥadīth* had always been viewed as an art of memory; and he broke with his affiliation to the arch-traditionists, the Ḥanbalīs, and became a Shāfiʿī and Ashʿarī. Despite his obsession with Baghdad, much of his career was spent in Syria, where he found himself in danger of his life from the law, Yāqūt tells us, because of a love affair with a Shīʿī youth. It was there too that in 456/1064 he taught *adab* and gave discreet charity to a student who was to become al-Khaṭīb al-Tibrīzī (421–502/1030–1109), the great commentator of the pre-Islamic poets and of Abū Tammām, al-Mutanabbī and Abū al-ʿAlāʾ al-Maʿarrī.[49]

The span of al-Khaṭīb al-Baghdādī's career saw teaching and learning and formats of writing begin to settle into formalised patterns. This had less to do with the spread of *madrasas* and institutional provision for scholarship in the latter part of his life than with the maturing of intellectual specialisations which had begun in the second half of the previous century. The trend towards tightening terminology and the style of discussion to fit with the subject in hand – an example is al-Āmidī's poetic criticism (see p. 388 above) – gave rise to disciplinary decorum, to an academic approach which was to be one of the features of the new *adab*. The way had been paved for it by such developments as the elegant, learning-made-easy manuals which al-Thaʿālibī had excelled at producing: these, despite their nonchalant appearance, rested on

49 Yāqūt, *Irshād*, vol. I, pp. 392–3.

hard thought – a critical systematisation of areas of literary competence – translated into textbook formats for easy reference and assimilation.

The academicisation of knowledge, including *adab*, effected a synthesis between two previously competing modes of cultural authority, the oral and the written. From an early date oral and written composition (e.g. of poetry) and transmission (e.g. of *ḥadīth*) had coexisted, and the oral had in theory been preferred as not only more reliable but more authentic. Orality had the incidental advantage of inclusiveness: it enabled the unlettered or merely unlearned, and the blind, such as Bashshār and Abū al-ʿAlāʾ al-Maʿarrī, to leave their mark. But the imprint of orality, supposedly the mode *par excellence* of poetry since pre-Islamic times, is perceptible above all in the formats of ʿAbbāsid prose, in which the two basic, stylised components of oral information-seeking are ubiquitous across genres: the chain of informants, as it is called in English, or 'prop' (*isnād*): 'I was told by X, who said: I was told by Y, who said: I was told by Z', and the 'text' (*matn*) or 'item of information' (*khabar*, pl. *akhbār*), e.g. 'The Prophet said: the slave who gives his master good counsel and worships God well will receive a double reward' (a *ḥadīth* not without political applications); or 'In Baghdad there was once a rich young man who inherited a fortune from his father, but fell in love with a *jāriya* and spent so much on her that he ruined himself' (the beginning of a love story from al-Tanūkhī's *al-Faraj baʿd al-shidda*).[50] Such oral formulae are the building-blocks of prose *adab*. They can be organised into illustrative or argumentative patterns, as in Ibn ʿAbd Rabbih's *ʿIqd*, yet still accommodate ongoing research, as with Abū al-Faraj al-Iṣfahānī's unfinished *Kitāb al-aghānī*, or revision, as with al-Tanūkhī's *al-Faraj baʿd al-shidda*, which like many compositions went through several emendations after 'publication'. They shape not only literary formats, so that texts made up of a mosaic of *akhbār* are overwhelmingly commoner than uninterrupted narratives, but also concepts of authorship. When a prose author sets out a topic, he almost always quotes, adding perhaps some comments in his own voice. Only the epistolographer or essayist, or the poet, makes his own voice the vehicle of his composition.

*Isnād*s acquired minute scholarly rigour in the *adab* of the fourth/tenth century. They encoded processes of research, whether among people or books, enabling readers to identify knowledge economies on the basis of prosopographical links, to gauge the reliability of information and anticipate the register of a *khabar*: serious, ironic, pious or sentimental. For later writers

50 al-Tanūkhī, *al-Faraj baʿd al-shidda*, ed. ʿA. al-Shāljī, 5 vols. (Beirut, 1398/1978), vol. IV, p. 316.

al-Khaṭīb al-Baghdādī's *Ta'rīkh Baghdād* was a prime source for the knowledge economies of his time, and as such was quarried freely by Yāqūt, and by Ibn al-Jawzī for his *al-Muntaẓam* (Well-ordered history), and it is the voices of his informants that for later generations embody the spirit of Būyid Baghdad, whose *adab* and scholarship afforded a second golden age after that of the great ʿAbbāsids.

The self-conception of the new learning

For all their admiration of their predecessors, the bearers of the new learning felt themselves to be their worthy successors. In the scholarship of this period *isnāds* may consist of two tiers: a first, sometimes symbolic, sequence of classical tradents; and a second string of contemporary scholars, for whom the networks of their own world of knowledge are of equal importance with a *khabar's* classical pedigree. Such tiered *isnāds* are found in al-Sarrāj's *Maṣāriʿ al-ʿushshāq*.

If one of the characteristics of the new learning is its careful academic discipline, this often contrasts with its performative aspects. Orality finds new outlets in ever larger public lectures and ever more crowded and emotional preaching sessions and recitations of *ḥadīth*. Writing provides the script for such performances, and the oral and written modes are so little in conflict that *adībs* and other intellectuals often seem, in their biographies, to be performing parts written for them: in Yāqūt's gallery of eccentrics the full panoply of literary media, oral and written *sajʿ*, preaching and epistolography, poetry prepared or improvised, gesture and slapstick, is deployed to show the elements that make up a personality. Generic decorum has become so well established that it affords individuals opportunities of expressing socially suspect aspects of their personalities and passing them off as literary poses, particularly through the medium of love poetry and wine poetry. Because the Arabic poet always writes as 'I', the identity of the poetic 'I' can always be disclaimed as fictional and autobiographical intentions repudiated.

Verse proliferated, especially semi-amateur occasional verse. Whether stilted or accomplished, minor verse should not be dismissed as insignificant. For all its ambivalence it was the medium of emotional, and sometimes spiritual, autobiography. People turned to poetry naturally to express themselves, as they did not to prose. Such is the function of al-Khaṭīb al-Baghdādī's homoerotic poetry, which Yāqūt quotes at the end of his biography.[51] No less

51 Yāqūt, *Irshād*, vol. I, pp. 393–5. On the role of such poetry in later biography see K. El-Rouayheb, 'The love of boys in Arabic poetry of the early Ottoman period, 1500–1800', *Middle Eastern Literatures*, 8 (2005).

importantly, verse underpinned literary expectations and literary development, for the enterprise of *adab* increasingly assumed that every *adīb* would have had some experience of composing poetry, and that his or her mind would be trained in the associations and logic of poetic thought.

Consequently, the poetic system imparted its particularities to Arabic prose. In its long journey from pre-Islamic Arabia to the courts of Muslim rulers, always maintaining the majesty of the *qaṣīda* but branching out on the way into new genres – love and wine poetry and descriptive verse (*waṣf*) are some of the most prominent – and into non-classical forms, such as the *muwashshaḥ* and *zajal*, Arabic poetry preserved and intensified the feature that marked it out from surrounding literatures and gave it a particular potency: its non-narrativity. Arabic poetry does not tell a story; it explores states of mind and feeling. Its diction is concentrated and allusive. So too is that of Arabic prose. Although it may often seem that prose gives free rein, in compulsive anecdotage, to the story-telling urge denied in poetry, the *khabar* formula tends to fragment narrative and to defer resolution indefinitely. Every *khabar* supposes a back-story, and is weighted with explicit or latent cross-reference to prototypes and variants, much as is the poetic system of themes and motifs.

The ambivalence of the poetic 'I' is also present in the prose *khabar*. Very few *akhbār* carry a specific ideological imprint. The message that an author wishes a *khabar* to convey emerges only when he has combined it with other *akhbār* according to the rules of his own intellectual syntax. Just as poetic confession can be passed off as a pose or metaphor, so the syntax of individual works of *adab* can be disregarded, and *adab* as a whole treated as neutral ground.

The maqāma

These developments explain how al-Hamadhānī (358–98/968–1008), nicknamed Badīʿ al-Zamān ('The Marvel of the Age'), could invent a new literary genre, the *maqāma* (pl. *maqāmāt*), which he launched in the princely courts of his native Iran with such success that, a hundred years later, al-Ḥarīrī (446–516/1054–1122) repatriated it to Iraq, where the new learning which al-Hamadhānī had invited his audiences to treat as a game was acquiring institutional contours.

The Hamadhānian *maqāma*[52] is a well-prepared but improvisatory slapstick performance, always 'reported', in a derisory *isnād*, by the same, solitary

52 The meaning of the word is disputed. For full bibliographies of al-Hamadhānī and al-Ḥarīrī see J. Hämeen-Anttila, *Maqāma: A history of a genre* (Wiesbaden, 2002); for critical approaches see Kennedy, 'The *maqāmāt* as a nexus of interests'.

narrator. Its anti-hero is a sponger, beggar and trickster of no fixed appearance or personality, with whom the autobiographical narrator finds himself thrown together for no good reason. As fellow adventurers or antagonists, the couple slither through every genre and register of *adab*; each of their encounters is futile in a different way, and a bathetic poetic flourish underlines its mock resolution. The pair are doomed to meet again and again, the narrator usually failing to recognise the hero until the last minute – though sometimes, unaccountably, they part company, and the worthy narrator takes on the shiftiness of the anti-hero. The more crude and ludicrous the situation, the more perfectly judged is the *sajʿ* employed as its vehicle. On one level the *maqāma* is an *exercice de style*: story types, protagonists, register and narrative development are wilfully mismatched. But disconcertingly, the Hamadhānian *maqāma* can also be the showcase for a robust realism. Comedy had reached comparable heights in al-Jāḥiẓ's *Kitāb al-bukhalāʾ*, but even al-Jāḥiẓ had not made his readers quite so uncomfortable about deciding whether they were dupes or accomplices, and whether the protagonists' antics meant anything or nothing at all.

Al-Ḥarīrī's collection of fifty *maqāmāt* is to all appearances vastly more literary; indeed, he designed it to be read as an educational exercise. It is elaborately intertextual: al-Hamadhānī is a constant, but oblique term of reference, and there are many others. It retains the autobiographical formula, but has none of al-Hamadhānī's boisterousness. Al-Ḥarīrī's playfulness is invested not in the psychological puzzles and trick storylines that he borrows from al-Hamadhānī, but rather in the chameleon concept of *adab* itself. The staid narrator, the anti-hero and the perplexed spectators all lay claim to *adab* as a proof of their own moral worth and ability to discern it in others. Like the poetic 'I', *adab* endlessly switches hosts; those who lay claim to it may be liars, but *adab* itself is always authentic.

Al-Ḥarīrī's *maqāmāt* are closely attuned to contemporary conceptions of *adab*, of life, and of their interpenetration. Autobiographical passages in, for example, al-Bākharzī's *Dumya*, ʿImād al-Dīn al-Iṣfahānī's writings and Yāqūt's portraits of contemporaries make clear the extent to which *adīb*s viewed and described their own lives through an optic little less literarised than al-Ḥarīrī's.

Modernity

As important in the reorientation of *adab* as the crystallisation of the new learning was a factor without which, for many, the new learning was devoid of meaning: the advent of new schools of thought such as the 'Oriental philosophy' of Ibn Sīnā (d. 428/1037) and the illuminationist school of Shihāb al-Dīn

Yaḥyā al-Suhrawardī (549–87/1153–91). These theosophies stimulated their followers to enquire into all the branches of knowledge necessary to an understanding of man's place in the cosmos. One path of understanding was Sufism, and Sufism now became a frequent ingredient of an *adīb*'s makeup. Conversely, the great Sufi poets such as Ibn al-ʿArabī (560–638/1165–1240) and Ibn al-Fāriḍ (576–632/1181–1235) exploited all the resources of literary learning and were remarkable for their mastery of academic *adab*.

The *adībs* of the post-classical period often sought to become polymaths – poets, mathematicians, metaphysicians and physicians – in order to create a coherent intellectual universe in keeping with the underlying unity of the cosmos and its aesthetic splendour, into which the teachings of the Sufi theosophers gave them insights that had previously formed no part either of science or of *adab*. An example of the striving for completeness is the *Kashkūl* (Begging-bowl/Provision bag) of Bahāʾ al-Dīn al-ʿĀmilī (953–1030/1547–1621), a Shīʿī from Syria who settled in Ṣafavid Persia. Much of the poetry quoted in this anthology, which contains both Arabic and Persian – including Indo-Persian – material, is recent or contemporary: no less than their Būyid, Ayyūbid or Mamlūk predecessors, writers of this period are aware of their own modernity; they have mastered the classical literary heritage but are not in thrall to it.

The range of purely literary expertise that an *adīb* was now expected to possess was very extensive indeed, and the supercommentary becomes a characteristic form not just of works of scholarship such as ʿAbd al-Qādir al-Baghdādī's (1030–93/1631–82) *Khizānat al-adab* (Treasury of *adab*), an explication, with much additional matter, of the 956 poetic passages cited by al-Astarābādhī (d. *c.* 688/1289) in his commentary on Ibn al-Ḥājib's (d. 646/1249) exhaustive treatise on syntax, *al-Kāfiya*,[53] but also of what are, on one level, original works, such as the *Tazyīn al-Aswāq* (Embellishment of *The market*) attributed to the blind physician and theosopher Daʾūd al-Anṭākī (d. *c.* 1008/1599), a work on mystical love and love poetry, which is a debate with al-Biqāʿī's (d. 885/1480) *Aswāq al-ashwāq fī Maṣāriʿ al-ʿushshāq* (*The calamities of lovers* [put on] The market of desire), which in turn takes as its point of departure al-Sarrāj's *Maṣāriʿ al-ʿushshāq*, and engages with a huge range of sources, recent and classical, from the east and west of the Arabo-Islamic world.[54]

53 M. G. Carter, ''Abd al-Qādir ibn ʿUmar al-Baghdādī', *EAL*, vol. I, pp. 15–16; M. G. Carter, 'al-Astarābādhī', *EAL*, vol. I, pp. 110–11; and M. G. Carter, 'Ibn al-Ḥājib', *EAL*, vol. I, p. 328.

54 L. A. Giffen, 'al-Anṭākī, Dāʾūd ibn ʿUmar', *EAL*, vol. I, p. 92; and L. A. Giffen, 'al-Biqāʿī, Ibrāhīm ibn ʿUmar, al-Shāfiʿī', *EAL*, vol. I, p. 152, and references.

The new sociology of adab

Changes in the way *adab* was acquired and put to use during the Ottoman period are documented in two genres in particular: the literary travelogue (*riḥla*)-cum-autobiography, of which examples have survived from across the Arabic-speaking world;[55] and the poetic correspondence, of which the Syrian Darwīsh Muḥammad al-Ṭāluwī's (d. 1014/1606) *Sāniḥāt Dumā al-qaṣr fī muṭāraḥāt banī al-ʿaṣr* (Poetical correspondence with contemporaries, inspired by *Dumyat al-qaṣr*) is a personal anthology. The title echoes al-Bākharzī's *Dumya*, but the core of the work consists of poetic letters of self-introduction (*muṭāraḥat*). These were a means for younger *adībs* to attract the attention of seniors with teaching or other posts in their gift, a sign of the institutionalisation of *adab* and of the hierarchisation of the fellowship of letters.

The ever-greater mastery of an ever-expanding body of high culture, and intense competition to reap its social and professional fruits, were one, widely attested, aspect of modernity in *adab*. But there is also evidence of divergent trends, attested above all in Mamlūk and Ottoman Egypt. One such was a broadening of the range of what was considered readable in polite society to include a semi-colloquial literature, of which the best-studied examples are Ibn Sūdūn's (*c.* 810–68/1407–64) comic occasional poems, and the late eleventh/seventeenth-century al-Shirbīnī's anti-pastoral *Hazz al-quḥūf fī sharḥ qaṣīd Abī Shādūf* (The nodding noddles: a gloss on the odes of Abū Shādūf/the irrigator), which is also a skit on the genre of the learned poetic commentary.[56] Another trend was a widening of the urban readership: the growth of a culture of reading for relaxation rather than improvement has been traced among the bourgeoisie of early modern Cairo.[57] It has been argued that among the urban merchant classes there had long been functionally literate but not highly educated readers who enjoyed books written in non-vernacular but not over-correct, 'middle' Arabic, and that the *Thousand and one nights*, and the heroic romances (*sīras*), belong to this intermediate register.[58]

55 Preliminary survey in H. Toelle and K. Zakharia, *À la découverte de la littérature arabe du VIe siècle à nos jours* (Paris, 2003), pp. 190–2.

56 G.J. van Gelder, '*The nodding noddles* or *Jolting the yokels*: A composition for marginal voices by al-Shirbīnī (fl. 1687)', in R. Ostle (ed.), *Marginal voices in literature and society: Individual and society in the Mediterranean Muslim world* (Strasbourg, 2000).

57 N. Hanna, *In praise of books: A cultural history of Cairo's middle class, sixteenth to the eighteenth century* (Cairo, 2004).

58 A. Chraïbi, 'Classification des traditions narratives arabes par "conte-type": Application à l'étude de quelques rôles de poète', *Bulletin d'Études Orientales*, 50 (1998), pp. 31–9, 42–3.

The social basis of early modern *adab* is of course more complex than analyses based simply on the economic standing of its readers can suggest; and above all, the position of writers still awaits systematic investigation within the wider framework of an exploration of the formation of identities. Ibn Sūdūn was the son of a Mamlūk slave-soldier, and as such neither a Mamlūk nor an Egyptian; *adab* afforded him a niche in society and a bare living.[59] Al-Ṭāluwī's father had been a Turk in Ottoman service and his mother a Syrian noble-woman; socially he fell between two stools, and trained in youth as an artisan; again, it was *adab* that offered him wider opportunities. From the beginnings of Islamic Arabic literature, poetry and letters had afforded a means of self-betterment; this much did not change over the centuries. State and social organisation did change, however, as did the languages and literatures with which Arabic had to compete; yet *adab*, which had followed Arab conquest or settlement even to remote and impermanent footholds, imposed itself every-where as an essential component of an Islamic society. Much of what was involved in this process remains to be discovered.

59 A. Vrolijk, 'The better self of a dirty old man: Personal sentiments in the poetry of 'Alī ibn Sūdūn (1407–1464)', in Ostle (ed.), *Marginal voices in literature and society.*

14
Persian literature

DICK DAVIS

Literature in New Persian, a language based on Middle Persian but containing a large admixture of Arabic loan words, and written in a modified form of the Arabic script, began to be composed in eastern Iran in the late third/ninth century (some two centuries after the Arab conquest), and by the mid- to late fourth/tenth century boasted a flourishing school of writers centred on the Sāmānid court in Khurāsān. As with a number of literatures that have grown up in the shadow of prestigious external cultures, a great deal of energy in the early years was given to translation, a process which both exemplifies and facilitates the adoption of originally foreign literary criteria and models. Although the surviving translations from Arabic are in prose (the most famous of these is al-Ṭabarī's *Ta'rīkh* (History), translated and in places extensively modified by Bal'amī), the influence of Arabic poetic models on Persian prosody was also clearly extensive. Virtually the whole Persian vocabulary concerned with prosody is Arabic, and all but two of the numerous metres used in Persian verse are Arabic in origin. Most telling of all in this regard is the fact that the few surviving examples of pre-Islamic Persian verse indicate that it was written in accentual metres, whereas poetry in New Persian was written using the quantitative metres of the Arabic *'arūḍ* system. Such a radical shift in the basic metrical structure of verse implies the presence of massive culture intimidation and assimilation.

However, alongside Arabic literary production as a significant model, elements derived from pre-Islamic Persian literature are also discernible in New Persian works. Two significant long narrative poems from the fifth/eleventh century, Firdawsī's *Shāhnāma* (completed *c.* 400/1010) and Gurgānī's *Wīs wa Rāmīn* (*c.* 442/1050), provide evidence, extending beyond their almost exclusively pre-Islamic subject matter, of pre-Islamic Persian models. The metre of the *Shāhnāma* (*mutaqārib*), which became the standard metre for epic in Persian, is one of the two Persian metres not derived from Arabic, and is probably a quantitative adaptation of a pre-Islamic Persian accentual metre;

the rhetoric of *Wīs wa Rāmīn*, a romance which is almost certainly Parthian in origin, has much in common with the so-called 'Asiatic' rhetoric of Greek and Latin literature in Late Antiquity, and in all likelihood reproduces Parthian and Sasanian rhetorical strategies. Evidence of the presence of pre-Islamic Persian models is less clear in the case of non-narrative poetry, but as the rhetoric of the earliest lyric poets (e.g. Rūdakī) is close to that of *Wīs wa Rāmīn* (e.g. in the common stock of images) it is likely that here too there are rhetorical survivals from pre-Islamic Iran.

The literary energy of medieval Persian societies was largely devoted to verse, but significant and influential prose works were also written, chiefly in the four genres of histories (both universal and local); mirrors for princes; works of ethical and religious edification; and popular prose romances. Apart from Balʿamī's translation of al-Ṭabarī mentioned above, the most important early history is that of Bayhaqī (fifth/eleventh century); subsequent significant histories include the *Tārīkh-i Sīstān* (fifth/eleventh century, the *Tārīkh-i jahān gushā* (History of the world conqueror) of Juwaynī (d. 681/1283) and the *Jāmiʿ al-tawārīkh* (Compendium of chronicles) of Rashīd al-Dīn (d. 718/1318). The two most memorable mirrors for princes are the *Qābūsnāma* of Kay Kāvūs ibn Iskandar (fifth/eleventh century), and the *Siyāsatnāma* (Book of statecraft) of Niẓām al-Mulk (d. 485/1092). The very popular Indian *Fables of Bidpāī* was originally considered to be an allegorical mirror for princes (it is characterised as such in the *Shāhnāma*); this work appeared in various guises in Persian, most notably as the *Kalīla wa Dimna* of Naṣr Allāh (*c.* 538/1144).

Histories and mirrors for princes were written chiefly by authors familiar with court life, and for a cultivated court audience. Works of ethical (often specifically Sufi) edification, such as the *Kashf al-maḥjūb* (Revelation of the hidden) (*c.* 442/1050) appear to have been aimed at largely artisan and middle-class Sufi circles, and their sympathisers. The most famous ethical prose work of Persian literature is Saʿdī's *Gulistān* (656/1258), a collection of anecdotes (which include gnomic verses) arranged into eight books according to their subject matter. Prose romances were clearly written for more varied audiences, and they often include many details drawn from both urban and rural middle- and lower-class life. A romance like the *Dārābnāma* of Ṭarsūsī can be presumed to have had written literary antecedents (Ṭarsūsī's work shows evidence of influence from Hellenistic narratives), and its intended audience was presumably literate. However, the rhetoric of a work such as the anonymous *Samak-i ʿayyār* suggests that at least some parts of the text are derived from oral performances intended originally for illiterate or only marginally literate audiences. The *Safarnāma* (travel narrative) of Nāṣir-i Khusraw

(d. *c.* 465/1072) is the first significant work in what was later to become a flourishing minor prose genre.

The earliest prose works, notably the early histories, were written in a direct, largely paratactic style (one that was, incidentally, to have a major influence on twentieth-century Persian prose), whose main if not sole purpose was clearly the conveying of information. This style dropped out of favour fairly quickly, and was replaced by a more rhetorically self-conscious manner, much given to increasingly elaborate periphrases (notable examples of an extreme periphrastic style are to be found in the Tīmūrid and especially Ṣafavid histories). The tradition of rhymed and rhythmic prose, deriving from Arabic models (most obviously the Qurʾān), was at first used chiefly for devotional works like Anṣārī's (d. 412/1021) *Ṭabaqāt al-ṣūfiyya* (History of the Sufis), or ethical works such as the *Gulistān*, but in time left its mark, in varying degrees, on works in most prose genres.

The development of Persian verse has traditionally been divided according to three historically successive styles: the Khurāsānī; the ʿIrāqī; and the Hindī (Indian). Although there is considerable continuity between the styles, they are nevertheless a useful way of broadly characterising prevailing poetic practice at any given time. As its name indicates, the Khurāsānī style originated in Khurāsān (north-eastern Iran, extending at this time as far north as Bukhārā and Samarqand); it was first significantly practised by the poets associated with the Sāmānid court (261–395/875–1005), and remained the predominant style into the sixth/twelfth century. It typically aims for dignity and immediacy of emotional effect, and shows a predilection for relatively simple rhetorical devices (e.g. anaphora, which it employs extensively). Most of the imagery of the Khurāsānī style belongs to a common stock, whose ubiquity suggests that, even at the opening of the period, it was an already well-established inheritance from previous literary traditions, although some of the poets whose work is characterised as being in the Khurāsānī style (e.g. Gurgānī) can occasionally also use startlingly arresting and (perhaps) original imagery.

The Khurāsānī style saw the emergence of the predominant genres of Persian poetry: these include the short poem or epigram, generally in the four-line *rubāʿī* form, or as a *qatiʿ* (i.e. fragment, a form often used for satire and invective); the medium-length *qaṣīda* and the related *ghazal*; and the long narrative, which could be epic, romance, a didactic/mystical work or some combination of the three. Narratives are always written in the couplet (*mathnawī*) form; the other forms employ monorhyme. Stanzaic forms exist in Persian but are rare. An interesting gender distinction is apparent between long, narrative poems, and shorter forms such as the *ghazal*. Narrative poems that deal with erotic themes are virtually always concerned with heterosexual relationships; *ghazals*, and many epigrams, often celebrate homosexual pederastic relationships, and the fall-back assumption for short medieval erotic poems, if a specific gender is not indicated, is that they are addressed to boys. The cause for this distinction is unclear, though it may be connected with the apparently differing historical traditions from which the genres emerged. Many poets wrote both pederastic and heterosexual poems, and personal sexual preferences were probably much less significant than expectations defined by genre.

The first recorded (in the *Tārīkh-i Sīstān*) poem in New Persian is a *qaṣīda* by Muḥammad Vaṣīf in praise of the Ṣaffārid ruler Yaʿqūb ibn al-Layth, written around 257/870 CE. As its name indicates, the *qaṣīda* form was adopted from Arabic, and the rhetoric of the typical Persian *qaṣīda* is heavily dependent on Arab models. As Bausani has written of Rūdakī (d. 329/940), 'We are in the presence of ... a linguistic Iranization of Arabic conceptual traditions and lyric elements.'[1] The *qaṣīda* is typically, though not exclusively, a praise poem written for a court personage: J. T. P. De Bruijn has shrewdly observed that the *qaṣīda* functioned in Persian courts more or less as the formal court portrait functioned in European courts.[2] The two factors of praise and the court indicate the direction the rhetoric of Persian poetry was to take well into the modern period. Unless the intent is satirical, virtually all short and medium-length poems in Persian adopt the courtier–patron relationship as the implicit model guiding the treatment of the poem's subject. The great majority of such poems address a 'you', or refer to a 'he/she', who is hyperbolically idealised by the speaker, and who correspondingly humbles himself before his subject. The stylistic conventions that resulted were not only applied to the patron–courtier relationship from which they may be presumed to have arisen, but also to other subject matter, such as carnal love or religious devotion. The rhetorical strategies of poems dealing with these three subjects, which are by far the commonest concerns addressed in non-narrative Persian verse, are virtually indistinguishable. The fact that the poetry developed in court settings gave it a strong predilection for imagery drawn from luxurious substances and objects associated with the court (precious metals, jewels, rich fabrics and so forth), and also encouraged a leisurely connoisseurship in its audience, which gradually came to prize an intricate intertextuality that

1 A. Bausani, *Storia della letteratura persiana* (Milan, 1960), p. 310.
2 J. T. P. De Bruijn, *Persian Sufi poetry: An introduction to the mystical use of classical poems* (London, 1997), p. 30.

presupposed a wide knowledge of the poetic tradition, as well as the cultivation of more and more outré rhetorical effects.

The *qaṣīda* was typically divided into three unequal sections: an introduction; a transitional passage; and hyperbolic praise of a patron. The traditional introduction of the Arabic *qaṣīda*, descriptive of the deserted campsite of the poet's beloved, involved two elements which were independently developed by Persian poets: the description of a natural scene; and the evocation of erotic longing. The former was often linked, either explicitly or implicitly, by Persian poets to pre-Islamic Persian solar festivals (especially the spring festival of Nawrūz, but also sometimes the autumn festival of Mihragān), which enabled them to provide detailed descriptions of either spring or autumn landscapes (often in the form of a garden explicitly compared to the patron's court). The erotic topos was similarly elaborated, and, as well as longing for an absent beloved, could include delight in the beloved's presence, and taxonomic descriptions of the beloved's beauty. The chief lyric form of Persian poetry, the *ghazal*, would seem to have developed as a result of this introductory section being treated as an independent unit. What can be considered as 'proto-*ghazals*' can be found in the work of the Sāmānid poets (e.g. Rūdakī and Shahīd) but it is not until the Ghaznavid period that the genre emerges fully fledged, most clearly in the work of Sanā'ī (d. 536/1141). The epigrammatic forms of *rubā'ī* and *qati'* generally employ a similar rhetoric to that of the *ghazal*. The largely stock nature of this rhetoric has meant that the ascription of specific poems to specific authors can prove difficult (unless, as is the case with many *ghazals*, the poem is 'signed' by the inclusion of the poet's name at the end of the poem), and this has been particularly the case with epigrams, a number of which are ascribed in the manuscript sources to different poets, apparently sometimes merely because the sentiments expressed in them are associated with those poets. It is virtually certain, for example, that many of the sceptical and anacreontic *rubā'iyāt* attributed to 'Umar al-Khayyām (439–526/1048–1131) are not in fact by him.

The Khurāsānī style is dominated, in aesthetic achievement as well as in sheer bulk, by a number of narrative *mathnawī*s, both as epic and romance. The major epic is the *Shāhnāma* of Firdawsī (329–*c.* 411/940–1020), which recounts the pre-Islamic myths and romanticised history of Iran, from the creation of the world until the Arab conquest of the seventh century CE. In a number of ways the *Shāhnāma* can seem closer to Indian epics such as the *Mahabharata* and the *Ramayana* than to, say, the *Iliad*. These include: its great length (*c.* 50,000 lines); its multiplicity of characters and generations; the uncertainty of the manuscript tradition; and, connected with this last point, the existence of an ancient and still-living folk tradition which continues both to feed the poem and feed off it, producing new versions of familiar stories. However, there are also strong similarities to western epics; for example, a staple theme of western epic is a conflict between the poem's king and its chief hero (the *Iliad* begins with such a conflict, between Agamemnon and Achilles). This is also a major theme of the *Shāhnāma*, one repeated over a number of generations and involving a number of feuding kings and heroes. In its lengthy examination of the problems of authority, kingship and heroism the poem often foregrounds ethical concerns; two distinct kinds of hero are portrayed: those who devote themselves to righteousness (and who are often martyred, e.g. Siyāvash); and those who can be considered as 'trickster heroes' (e.g. Rostam, whose patronymic, Dastān, indeed means 'trickery'). Epics, usually with a figure from Rostam's family either as protagonist or as a major hero, continued to be written in imitation of Firdawsī's poem throughout the medieval period, although none approached the stature of the *Shāhnāma*.

The most significant romance of the Khurāsānī style is the above-mentioned *Wīs wa Rāmīn* by Gurgānī (fifth/eleventh century). The poem is notable for its frank pleasure in carnality, which is presented in and for itself (there is no suggestion that carnal love either represents or is a poor substitute for divine love, as became usual in later romances), as well as for its attractively vivid imagery. This poem and two others which are roughly contemporary with it, and which also utilise pre-Islamic material ('Ayyuqī's *Warqa wa Gulshāh*, and the fragmentary *Wāmiq wa 'adhrā* by 'Unṣurī), show some similarities to Greek romances of the Hellenistic period, and it is likely that they draw on plot motifs and tropes common to Greek and Persian cultures in the early years of the common era.

The Khurāsānī period also saw the appearance of the mystical *mathnawī*, most notably in the work of Sanā'ī, whose *Ḥadīqat al-ḥaqīqa* (Garden of the truth) is the first significant example of the form. In Sanā'ī's work a number of short mystical/Sufi anecdotes are strung together by a linking didactic commentary. Although Sanā'ī's rhetoric is relatively austere compared to that of his successors, one paradoxical feature of Persian mystical verse that was to become more pronounced in subsequent centuries is already discernible: the recommendation, by means of allegorical tales the details of which emphatically celebrate the sensual world, that the audience renounce the sensual world.

Although not all the poets associated with the Khurāsānī style lived in Khurāsān (Gurgānī claimed to have written *Wīs wa Rāmīn* in Iṣfahān,

Qaṭrān-i Tabrīzī (d. 465/1072) was from Azerbaijan; his provincial – i.e. non-Khurāsāni – Persian was patronisingly referred to by Nāṣir-i Khusraw in his *Safarnāma*), there was nevertheless a broad identification of the style with the geographical area that gave it its name. The ʿIrāqī style, which dominated Persian verse from the mid-sixth/twelfth to the ninth/fifteenth centuries, was associated chiefly with the south and west of Iran (sometimes known as ʿIrāq-i ʿAjam – ʿIrāq of the Persians – hence the name), especially with Fārs and its capital Shīrāz, but poets writing according to its criteria worked all over Iran, and beyond the country's borders. ʿIrāqī style is both more lush and more cerebral than Khurāsānī, and delights in decoration, wordplay and conspicuous euphony. Many of the tropes current during the period of the Khurāsānī style had become conventional, and in its elaborate use of such conventions ʿIrāqī poetry became consciously self-referential; at its most sophisticated it presupposed a high level of literary awareness in its audiences. The five influential *mathnawī*s (a collection of didactic tales, three love romances and a historical romance) of the Azerbaijanī poet Niẓāmī (536–606/1141–1209) can be regarded as transitional between the two styles. Niẓāmī's work may be seen as an attempt to blend the achievements of his most notable predecessors in the *mathnawī* form, in that he took the plots of three of his poems from Firdawsī's *Shāhnāma*, and his rhetoric largely from Gurgānī, while their often broadly Sufi ethos owes something to Sanāʾī. The complex balance of sensual and allegorical/spiritual concerns evident in his romances, together with the fluency and richness of their rhetoric, have made them the most highly regarded examples of the genre in Persian.

Sufism is the overt subject matter of the *mathnawī*s of Niẓāmī's contemporary ʿAṭṭār (d. *c.* 627/1230), the best known of which is the *Manṭiq al-ṭayr* (Conference of the birds), an allegorical frame story dealing with the spiritual life. The major Sufi *mathnawī* is the *Mathnawī-yi maʿnawī* of Jalāl al-Dīn Rūmī (d. 672/1273), which abandons ʿAṭṭār's frame structure, and reverts to the more heterogeneous juxtapositions of Sanāʾī. Although Rūmī acknowledged the influence of both Sanāʾī and ʿAṭṭār, his voice is among the most distinctive in Persian poetry; he is, for example, virtually the only Persian poet before the sixteenth century who regularly and with apparent gusto goes beyond the stock vehicles (broadly, nature and the precious objects associated with court life) for his imagery.

In conjunction with the elaboration of verse rhetoric, and what one might call the 'Sufification' of its subject matter, a further development is also apparent: a gradual shift of emphasis from the public to the private world. This is noticeable both in the increasing popularity of the romance, as against the epic, and also in the emergence of the *ghazal*, as against the *qaṣīda*, as the most significant monorhymed form. Whereas, broadly, the actions (and public consequences) of epic protagonists are emphasised by epic poets, the feelings of romance characters are emphasised, and they are often characterised as very unheroic feelings at that. Similarly, the *qaṣīda* presupposes a largely public context and audience, and normally culminates in praise of a politically significant figure, whereas the *ghazal* offers itself as a quasi-private communing, albeit in highly conventional terms. The placing of the poet's name as the culminating moment of the *ghazal*, whereas the *qaṣīda* typically moves towards the celebration of the poem's politically significant dedicatee, is emblematic of the shift. The *ghazals* of Saʿdī (d. 691/1292) are renowned for their limpidity and elegance, while those of his successor and fellow-townsman Ḥāfiẓ (d. 792/1390) have been extravagantly admired for the sophistication and ambiguity with which they combine erotic and mystical motifs. A contemporary of Ḥāfiẓ, Jahān Khātūn, the daughter of a ruler of Shīrāz, is the only medieval female poet whose *dīwān* (complete short poems) has come down to us (although she was preceded by the fourth/tenth–fifth/eleventh-century Rābiʿa Quzdārī, and the sixth/twelfth-century Mahsatī; a number of poems by both these female poets, as well as a few by others, have survived).

The period in which the ʿIrāqī style flourished was one of particularly violent social and political upheaval in Iran. The style emerged around the time of the Saljūq conquest, and was predominant during the conquests by Chinggis Khān and Tīmūr Lang. The turning away from public life, which is evident in genres favoured by the style, and its cultivation of Sufism and otherworldly concerns, can plausibly be linked to the period's intermittent social and political chaos. The Mongol invasion destroyed centres of Sunnī orthodoxy, including its symbolic centre, the Baghdad caliphate, and the resulting religious heterodoxy clearly favoured the growth of Sufism. A related phenomenon, particularly noticeable in poets associated with Shīrāz (Saʿdī, Ḥāfiẓ, the scabrous ʿUbayd-i Zākānī), is the recommendation to cultivate a private life of hedonism away from centres of power, together with a sharp eye for the hypocrisy of those in positions of either secular or religious authority. Like the growth of Sufism, which it seems superficially to contradict, the often vigorous advocacy of religious scepticism by such authors can be related to the period's social and religious uncertainties. One of the distinctive qualities of Ḥāfiẓ, for example, is his ability to suggest both Sufi and religiously sceptical presuppositions simultaneously.

The time of the Mongol invasions also coincides with the internationalisation of Persian as a literary medium. Saʿdī boasted that his works were famous beyond the confines of Iran, and whether or not this was strictly true in his own lifetime it was certainly true very shortly afterwards, and the writings of his contemporary Rūmī in Turkey, and of the slightly younger Amīr Khusraw in India, attest to a flourishing Persian literary culture in both countries. Persian literary models and criteria remained a source of inspiration in Turkey for centuries to come, but no literature regarded as major in Persian was produced there subsequent to Rūmī's spectacular example; in the Mughal empire, however, literary production in Persian was extensive, and by the late tenth/sixteenth and eleventh/seventeenth centuries it is arguable that more poetry in Persian was being written in India than in Iran itself. From being an expression of local irredentist ambitions, as it had been in the early Khurāsānī period, Persian literature had become an international, and internationally emulated, enterprise.

Literature in the ninth/fifteenth century is dominated by the prolifically fluent figure of Jāmī (d. 898/1492), who consciously attempted to surpass his predecessors in most literary genres; thus his prosimetrum *Bahāristān* is an attempt to outdo Saʿdī's *Gulistān*, and his seven *mathanawīs* were written in emulation of Niẓāmī's five. The Sufi and allegorical structure of his narratives tends to eclipse almost entirely the relative realism, freshness and psychological acuity that had been Niẓāmī's legacy from Gurgānī. His two best-known *mathnawīs*, *Yūsef wa Zulaykhā* and *Salāmān wa Absāl*, both use the figure of a beautiful young man whom an older woman attempts, unsuccessfully, to seduce, and while it is true that the texts superficially keep to the heterosexual preoccupations established for *mathnawīs* in previous generations, their florid descriptions of the chaste young protagonists' physical beauty suggest a homoerotic subtext, together with a strongly implied horror of female sexuality. The romance, which in Gurgānī's hands had celebrated heterosexual carnal love on its own terms, became a vehicle for spiritual didacticism exhibiting a profound suspicion of the value of heterosexual activity, and of female sexuality per se.

With the coming to power of the Shīʿite Ṣafavid dynasty in 906/1501 Persian society changed radically, and important elements of the metaphysical and theological preconceptions that had lain behind almost all Persian literary production for the previous six hundred years (often explicitly, often merely as a foil, but always there nevertheless) were relegated to a minor and quasi-heretical status. A poetry less given over to mystical speculation might have survived such theological changes relatively unchanged, but Persian poetry had by this time invested deeply in the spiritual, or at least the mystical, as its natural domain, and a rewriting of the Persian world's spiritual boundaries had an inevitably cautionary effect on literary production. A further significant development is that painting had been increasing in prestige throughout the Tīmūrid period, and the princes of the early Ṣafavid court tended to give their patronage to painters rather than to poets, with the result that many Persian poets emigrated to the now flourishing Persian literary culture of India. These spiritual and social changes meant that while literary activity did not, as earlier scholars have often implied, become relatively worthless in Iran during the Ṣafavid period, it certainly faltered.

In Jāmī's works, and even occasionally in those of Ḥāfiẓ, hints of a new aesthetic can be found, and these coalesced during the Ṣafavid period to form the Hindi / Indian style. This style tends to value rhetorical complexity for its own sake, and the poems written in it often deal with subjects previously considered unlikely to be productive of interesting poetry. It also makes originality of imagery a conscious and widely accepted criterion in Persian poetry for the first time; if conventional tropes were used the poet was now expected to give them some new and preferably startling twist. The style is broadly comparable to that of the Gongorist poets and the Marinisti in Europe, with which it is roughly contemporary. A number of poets produced notable work in the Indian style, in both Iran and India; its undoubted master is Ṣā'ib (d. 1087 / 1676), a major poet by any criteria, who deploys the rhetorical resources of the style with great facility and charm, and whose works would probably be read and studied much more had he not belonged to a period traditionally seen as lacking in significant literary production.

15

Turkish literature

ÇİĞDEM BALİM HARDING

Introduction

The language(s) and literatures of Turkic peoples, spread over a large geography on the Silk Route, have been written with a variety of scripts over the centuries. After they were introduced to Islam traditional Turkic (mostly oral) literature and its forms and themes continued, while new literary forms and lexicons were adopted from the Persian/Arabic Islamic traditions. The two traditions did not exclude one another. At times they could have the same audience, and sometimes the authors created in both traditions. The written evidence of the pre-Islamic literary tradition of the Turkic peoples, who were latecomers to Islam, dates to the eighth century CE: the Orkhun inscriptions in today's Mongolia. This is followed by manuscripts of Buddhist and Manichaean religious literatures, which developed in the Tarim basin up to the thirteenth century and were written in Uighur, Manichaean, Brahmin and other scripts. Other information about Turkic literary forms and themes of their literatures before Islam comes from Persian and Arabic sources as well as Turkic sources in later centuries.

Upon becoming Muslims Turkic-speaking peoples began to write with the Arabic script, as had other cultures that accepted Islam. Central Asia and eastern Iran (Bukhārā, Samarqand, Herat, Kāshghar) became centres of learning, and Islamic schools (*madrasas*) educated them in Arabic and in the sciences of Islam, such as *tafsīr* (exegesis or commentary of the Qur'ān), *ḥadīth* (oral traditions relating to the words and deeds of the Prophet) and *fiqh* (Islamic jurisprudence, which deals with the observance of rituals and social legislation). The learned sections of the society studied Arabic and Persian literature and literary forms as a part of their Islamic training, because by the time Turkic-speaking peoples came onto the Islamic literary scene, Islamic Persian literature had a past of at least two centuries.

The beginnings

The first Islamic Turkic literary works, written in Arabic and Uighur scripts, were developed in eastern Turkistan under the Qarakhānid dynasty (third–seventh/ninth–thirteenth centuries), which was the first Turkic dynasty to accept Islam as an official religion. The language used in the texts from this period is close to old Uighur, with some Persian and Arabic lexical influence. *Kutadgu bilig* (The wisdom of royal glory), the first noteworthy example of Islamic Turkic literature, appeared around 461/1069. Written by an aristocrat from Balāsāghūn named Yūsuf Khāṣṣ Ḥājib, this work is a poem in rhymed couplets, of 6,645 lines divided into 85 chapters. The work is similar to other Islamic works known as 'mirrors for princes'. The author gives advice on morals and on administration through dialogues between statesmen, and tries to answer the question of how one serves God better. The book advises service and obedience not only to God but also to the established political authority. *Kutadgu bilig* thus reflects the contemporary political debate between those who, influenced by heterodox and Hellenistic ideas, questioned the traditional order, and the orthodox Sufis, who tried to maintain it. The newly Muslim Turkic-speaking peoples found themselves participating in this debate.

Meanwhile, the Turkic literature of the peoples continued in its traditional forms and themes. *Dīwān lughāt al-Turk*, a dictionary of the Turkic languages compiled by Maḥmūd al-Kāshgharī in 464–6/1072–4, gives information about the literatures and languages of the Turks together with examples. It also contains an example of a poem written in the *ʿarūḍ* metre for the first time – as opposed to the syllabic metre of Turkic poetry. In the work, al-Kāshgharī displays a strong sense of Turkic identity and attempts to refute negative Arab and Iranian discourses about Turkic-speaking peoples. He seeks to prove that Turkic and Arabic languages are on an equal footing.

From these beginnings the Turkic peoples moved on to create their unique literary synthesis. An early example is Adīb Aḥmad Yuknakī's didactic work, *ʿAtabet al-ḥaḳāīḳ* (Threshold of the truth), of the sixth/twelfth century. It is composed of 121 stanzas, which combine the Turkic linguistic form and proverbial style with Islamic content. Yuknakī's readers must have accepted that they were Turks and Muslims, and were comfortable using Turkic to express Islamic ideas. This also is a book of wisdom giving moral advice but, unlike *Kutadgu bilig*, it is written more for the masses and is more personal rather than courtly in nature.

The development of regional literatures

From the seventh/thirteenth century onwards various regional written languages and literatures begin to appear among the Turkic-speaking peoples. Following the linguistic variation between Eastern and Western Turkic languages in Central Asia, literature in Eastern Turkic comprises (1) literature in Khwārazmian Turkic, which developed after the seventh/thirteenth century as an extension of Qarakhānid Turkic; it carried the linguistic influences of Oghuz and Qipchak Turkic, and was used as a literary language in the Golden Horde; and (2) literature in Chaghatay Turkic between the ninth/fifteenth and eleventh/seventeenth centuries, and which had its heyday during the Tīmūrid empire (771–913/1370–1507). Although Chaghatay was based on Qarakhānid and Khwārazmian linguistic traditions, it contained local lexical and syntactic elements. In the west we see (1) the Qipchak Turkic language, documented by *Codex cumanicus* (eighth/fourteenth century) which contains Turkic texts, grammar, Latin, Persian and Turkic word lists, a Turkic–German dictionary compiled by Christian missionaries and translations, dictionaries and grammars composed in Egypt and Syria under the Mamlūk dynasty (648–922/1250–1517); and (2) Oghuz Turkic, which is represented by Anatolian Turkish from the fifth/eleventh century onwards and which later developed into Ottoman Turkish. Oghuz Turkic is also represented, from the ninth/fifteenth century onwards, by the Azerbaijanī literary language, which developed as distinct from Ottoman Turkish; and by the Turkmen literary language, which developed from the eighth/fourteenth century onwards, although it was later subject to strong Chaghatay influence.

Eastern Turkic literatures

The Eastern Turkic language (Qarakhānid) developed into a literary language in Turkistan, Khwārazm and the Golden Horde. We have manuscripts of prose, and poetry of religious nature by various authors. The Sufi poetry of this period reached its best as plays on words with a multiplicity of meanings and images. The forms were a series of quatrains (*rubāʿī*), similar to the Turkic *koshuğ* form with an aaba/ccdc rhyme scheme. However, Sufi poets mostly used the *ghazal* form and the *ʿarūḍ* quantitative metre, as opposed to the traditional Turkic accentual metres (counting syllables). Turkic oral style and genres remained similar to earlier periods, and Persian and Arabic lexical borrowings were not used extensively. Oral tales, which are widespread among the Turks even today, relied on concrete images from real life and were expressed with short, concrete phrases. On the other hand, *ghazals* referred to Islamic figures and important religious places, and made use of romantic classical epics / tales such as *Farhād wa Shīrīn*, *Laylā wa Majnūn* etc.

Mīr ʿAlī Shīr Nawāʾī (844–906 / 1441–1501) is the central poet of the Central Asian Islamic tradition. He composed thousands of *ghazals* and more than a dozen other major literary works. Known as the founder of Chaghatay literary language, he was a key figure in the Tīmūrid cultural life of Herat and Samarqand. The Tīmūrid ruler Zaher ud-Dīn Bābur (888–937 / 1483–1530) wrote his memoirs, *Bāburnāma* (The book of Bābur), a well-known book widely translated into other languages.

Western Turkic literatures

In the west, Mamlūk Turkish literature is generally known as Qipchak literature because the Volga Delta was populated largely by nomadic Qipchak Turks, who as slaves provided the manpower of the Mamlūk armies in Egypt and Syria. Translations from Arabic and Persian as well as history writing are among the most important works that the Mamlūks left behind. During their rule of Egypt and Syria Mamlūks played a crucial role in enabling the preservation and dissemination of important works of Turkic literature. For example, two of the oldest and most important works of Islamic Turkish literature, the *Kutadgu bilig* and the *Dīwān lughāt al-Turk*, both mentioned above, were preserved in Mamlūk libraries. After the fall of the Mamlūk sultanate in 923 / 1517 the libraries were moved to Istanbul, which had great impact on the literary scene of the Ottoman empire.

As for Anatolia, the first written examples of literature appear after 463 / 1071 following the settlement of the Oghuz tribes there. The literary works we come across are representatives of mystical (Sufi) literature; folk literature of a religious mystical nature; and early examples of classical literature (*dīwān*). The Saljūq state of Anatolia (469–706 / 1077–1307) used Arabic and Persian as state languages, Persian as the language of literature, and spoke Turkic the rest of the time. It is therefore important that after Shams al-Dīn Meḥmed Beg of Karaman captured Konya from the Saljūqs, he issued a decree in 675 / 1277 that only Turkish should be used at home and at court.

During the Mongol invasions migration from Persia and Turkistan to Anatolia intensified. Scholars, Sufis and dervishes of various sects came to Anatolia. Jalāl al-Dīn Rūmī (d. 672 / 1273) settled in Konya, and introduced not only the conventions of classical Islamic literature, but also those of the classical Sufi literature of the Mawlawī (Mevlevi) order. Some of his poetry contains sections in Turkish. Among the other settlers were the Sufis who wrote in Turkic, such as Ḥājjī Bektāsh Walī (seventh / thirteenth century) from

Khurāsān, who laid the foundations of the Bektāshī literature. This order was later embraced by the Ottoman Janissary corps. During this period, *nefes* (poetry sung to the musical accompaniment of the *sāz*, a musical instrument), became very popular among all peoples, as did the religious epics, which had originated as oral epics during the period when the Turks conquered Anatolia (late fifth/eleventh century). Alongside this folk literature we increasingly see a new type of literature, incorporating *ʿarūḍ* and the forms of classical Islamic literature. The main representatives are Sulṭān Walad (623–712/1226–1312), the son of Rūmī, whose works are in Persian but contain couplets in Turkish; Gülşehrī (d. after 717/1317), ʿĀşıq Paşa (670–733/1272–1333) and the Ḥurūfī poet Nesīmī (d. 820/1417f.), whose Turkish *dīwān* played a major role in the development of Azerī poetry. Yūnus Emre (d. *c.* 720/1320), whose posthumously collected *dīwān* is the first one written in Anatolian Turkish, is well loved to this day. Works attributed to Yūnus are seen as the best examples of 'mystical folk literature' in Turkish. Qaygusuz Abdāl (eighth–ninth/fourteenth–fifteenth centuries) is another important representative of this genre. He wrote both in syllabic metre and in *ʿarūḍ*, using both Turkic and Islamic poetic forms. The *mawlid* of Süleymān Çelebi (d. 832/1429), which narrates the Prophet's birth, *miʿrāj* and death, in Turkish, is still recited as a vital part of Muslim prayers at home and at mosques in Turkey.

During the early eighth/fourteenth century, following the decline of the Saljūq state in Anatolia, centres of the *begliks* such as Konya, Kütahya and Antalya became centres of literary activity. Since the rulers spoke and encouraged Turkic, the poets and writers produced in Turkic with confidence. When the Ottomans became dominant among the *begliks*, the centre of literary activity moved with them, and finally ended up in Istanbul. Hence the Turkic literature that was produced in the Ottoman empire is referred to as Ottoman Turkish literature.

An important characteristic of the eighth/fourteenth and ninth/fifteenth centuries was the intensive translation movement from Arabic and Persian texts. In order to bring Islamic culture to a wider audience, works in every field of Islamic learning and practice were translated into simple and clear Turkish. These were works about the basic principles of worship and conduct within the family and the community; interlinear translations of the Qurʾān and of *tafsīr*, stories of prophets, legends of saints etc.; encyclopaedic manuals on medicine and drugs, on geography, astronomy and interpretation of dreams; music treatises and dictionaries were also translated. Love stories in *mathnawī* format were translated, as were mystical *mathnawīs*, but these were not so much translated as adapted by Turkish writers, who added their own phrases and commentaries, and made 'improvements'. The translations were usually longer than the originals. Among the well-known works translated were *Khusraw wa Shīrīn* by Niẓāmī (b. 535 or 540/1141 or 1146) and the *Shāhnāma* of Firdawsī (d. 411/1020).

Also during the ninth/fifteenth century twelve heroic stories of the Oghuz tribes in eastern Anatolia and Azerbaijan dating from the sixth/twelfth century were collected and written down as the *Kitāb-ı Dede Korkut* (Book of Dede Korkud). The Ottomans admired the art and literature of the Tīmūrid court deeply. At the cultural centres of Samarqand and Herat the Uighur alphabet was used side-by-side with Arabic script in literary texts, and just like the Central Asian Turkish court, the Ottoman sultan Murād II (r. 824–48, 850–5/1421–44, 1446–51) kept secretaries at his court in Edirne capable of composing *fermāns* (firman: royal mandate or decree) in the Uighur alphabet. Even in later days the Ottoman *fermāns* were composed in Chaghatay and written down in both Arabic and Uighur scripts. Ottoman poets and intellectuals took great interest in Chaghatay and Persian literature. Many went to Central Asia even as late as the eleventh/seventeenth century to get a good education, and scholars and scientists from these lands were highly respected by the Ottomans.

Maturation of regional literatures

From the tenth/sixteenth century onwards we witness distinct literary languages and literary works. Chaghatay in its middle or late Chaghatay form continued as the major literary language in the east. However, it began to be strongly influenced by local traditions and regional spoken varieties of Turkic in eastern Turkistan, in the khanate of Qāzān, and among the Turkmens. Chaghatay was later called Turkī in eastern Turkistan, the Volga region and the Crimea. Oghuz in Anatolia developed into Ottoman Turkish, and as a literary language it was used in a variety of styles and forms. Meanwhile, a literary Azerbaijanī language developed; Qipchak Turkic vanished as a major literary language, and smaller languages such as Karaim and Armeno-Qipchak developed written forms.

Eastern Turkish literatures

Well-known examples of Turkic literature in Central Asia in the eleventh/seventeenth century are works by ruler and literary figure Abū al-Ghāzī Bahādūr Khān, two genealogies with mythological elements: *Shajare-i Tarākime* (1070/1659), the genealogical tree of the Turkmen, and *Shajare-i*

Türk (1076/1665), the genealogical tree of the Turks. This latter work is a history of the Shaybānid dynasty and was completed by his son.

During the twelfth/eighteenth century in Central Asia Turkic poets followed the classical tradition established by the Chaghatay poets, but with increasing regional influence. By the end of the twelfth/eighteenth and during the thirteenth/nineteenth century eastern Turkistan had local poets with local followings. From the second half of the thirteenth/nineteenth century written regional languages began to emerge, eventually replacing Chaghatay. For example, the Tatars developed a written norm which was closer to spoken Qāzān Tatar, and until the fourteenth/twentieth century Ottoman, Azerbaijanī, Uzbek and Tatar written languages and literatures dominated the region.

Western Turkic literatures

In the west, Ottoman literature of the ninth–tenth/fifteenth–sixteenth centuries reflected the self-confidence of the Ottomans as a world power. The literary language became full of idioms and word play; the poets were comfortable and self-confident in their use of the language both in poetry and prose. The *qaṣīda* or ode became fashionable, and every poet of significance had to compose *qaṣīdas* for the sultan and high dignitaries. An early Anatolian poet is the Ḥurūfī Nesīmī (d. *c.* 820/1417). Nawā'ī (844–906/1441–1501) and Mihrī Khātūn (d. 917/1506), the best-known female Ottoman poet, are contemporaries.

Among the well-known names are Bākī (d. 1008/1600) and Fuḍūlī (d. 963/1556). Bākī's *qaṣīdas* for Süleymān and his successors, Murād III (d. 1003/1595) and Meḥmed III (d. 1011/1603), are well known. His *dīwān* reflects his intelligence and his skill in handling poetic form and content. Fuḍūlī, a poet from Baghdad, wrote in Azerī Turkish, but is regarded as both an Ottoman and an Azerī poet. This is not controversial since the two dialects were very close at the time. Sultan Süleymān the Magnificent (d. 973/1566) himself wrote quite successful poetry. Lāmiʿī Çelebi (877–938/1472–1532), a scholar and a poet, is also well known for his translations of major Persian narrative poems into Turkish.

In the tenth/sixteenth century *mathnawī* was still a very popular genre. An increasing number of poets wrote love tales as well as on mystical and religious subjects using this form. Azerī poet Niẓāmī's (d. 606/1209) *khamse* (collection of five *mathnawīs*) was seen as an example to be followed by the Ottoman poets. The poets of the time are known for their use of Sufi terminology to express personal emotions. For example, the famous *mathnawī*

Dāstān-i Leylī vü Mejnūn (The epic of Layla and Majnūn) of Fuḍūlī has a mystical atmosphere, even though it is a story of platonic but worldly love. In the tenth/sixteenth century the Ottomans came into closer contact with the Western world, and the impressions of this contact were reflected in the diaries of Ottoman slaves and soldiers who escaped captivity in the West.

In time, although they did not abandon the traditional and classical topics, Ottoman poets moved towards more worldly pursuits. The themes of their poetry became more and more representative of real life, and their subjects were chosen from their immediate vicinity and from among their human contemporaries. Some researchers call this the 'localisation movement' (*mahallīleşme*), which continued well into the eleventh/seventeenth and twelfth/eighteenth centuries and found its best voice in Nedīm (d. 1143/1730). The most interesting feature of the period is the popularity of public performance. Although the tradition of the storyteller who recited religious–heroic stories in public was not new, now tales of unusual events happening to characters taken from everyday life were told. Also, the court always had storytellers but in this period they were educated persons, sometimes the sultan's personal courtiers. The eleventh/seventeenth century is the period when local colour dominates Ottoman literature. Poets are plentiful and very productive. There are hundreds of *dīwāns* left from this period in the libraries. While Nefʿī (d. 1044/1635) makes a name for himself with his *qaṣīdas* (poems of praise) Nābī (d. 1124/1712) excels with his lyrics filled with popular sayings and verses commemorating important occasions. Mystical poetry was also plentiful, and *mathnawī* poets created works on many topics; meanwhile, the folk minstrel Karajaoğlan (d. 1090/1680) sang his love poems, still enjoyed today, in traditional Turkic forms. The language of the prose shows a large variety, from adorned language to simple, almost everyday spoken expression, and biographies and literary histories were favourite genres. Perhaps the most famous of all prose writers is Evliyā Çelebi (1019–92/1611–82) with his ten volumes of travel diaries of the Ottoman lands, the *Seyāḥatnāme*. Reality is mixed with exaggeration and myth, but they reflect the incredible landscape, variety of the peoples of the Ottoman empire and their customs. The learned Kātib Çelebi (Ḥājjī Khalīfa, 1017–67/1609–57) is another important figure who wrote books on history, geography, society and literature. In the eleventh/seventeenth century traditional Turkish theatre, *orta oyunu* (folk theatre accompanied by music) as well as the performances of the shadow-play or *Karagöz* became very popular.

During the twelfth/eighteenth century Ottoman *dīwān* poets used the Turkic syllabic metre as well as the *ʿarūḍ*. Famous poets such as Nedīm and

Şeykh Ghālib (1170–1219/1757–99) were among these. Nedīm's *ghazal*s and *şarkī*s (poems which can be composed into songs) are a symbol of the period known in Ottoman history as the Tulip Era. His subjects were original, and language reflected his rich imagination. Ghālib's *mathnawī Hüsn-ü aşk* (Beauty and love), allegorical in nature, is one of the most important works of Turkish literature. In prose, the *sefāret-nāme* (embassy memoirs) such as the *Fransa sefāret-nāmesi* (French embassy memoirs) of Yirmisekiz Çelebi Meḥmed Efendi, described foreign lands; the *sūr-nāme*s were written to celebrate the festivals held by the sultans; and more poets wrote biographies than ever before.

The introduction of printing

Throughout the centuries discussed here, Turkic folk literature continued in its variety of traditional formats and was enjoyed by everyone. These forms include poetry, epics and tales, legends, proverbs, riddles, sung poems etc. Certain items of folk tradition were also a part of the written tradition, such as epics of all kinds. It should also be remembered that in the Ottoman empire many languages were spoken, but until the nineteenth century only some were written: Ottoman Turkish, Arabic, Persian, Greek, Armenian and Hebrew. Turkish-speaking Greek Orthodox (Qaraman) and Armenians read especially Turkish folk literature written in Greek or Armenian characters and contributed to the literary scene.

The development of the printing-press in the twelfth/eighteenth century needs special mention. The printing-press had been introduced into the empire during the reign of Bāyazīd II (r. 886–918/1481–1512) by non-Muslim subjects – Christians (Armenians and Greeks), and Jews after their expulsion from Spain in 897/1492. Non-Muslim minorities were allowed to publish works in their own languages, but printing in Arabic letters was not permitted for the Muslims. The first books, primarily grammars and dictionaries and phrase-books in Turkish, were printed in western European countries, and, since no Turkish press existed, they were imported. The reasons for abstention from printing, which had an enormous negative impact on the future of the empire, included religious conservatism and protection of the social and economic interests of the professions of calligraphers, illustrators, binders etc., the people who produced the books. Although the first book only appeared in 1141/1729, the first printing-press was established in 1140/1727, by İbrāhīm Müteferriqa (d. 1157/1745), a diplomat and literary figure who managed to convince the court of the benefits of printing. Sultan Aḥmed III authorised him to print books only on practical subjects such as medicine, crafts and geographical guides, but nothing religious in nature. However, printing did not take off immediately, and printed books were not popular. The printing-press, after changing hands, closed down in 1211/1797. In its sixty-four years of existence it had printed only twenty-four books, the last book appearing in 1209/1794. During the same period – the late 1190/1780s and early 1200/1790s – the French Embassy Press published four books. Later on, several printing-presses were opened and these were more successful. The first newspaper, *Taqvīm-i vekāyi*, was published by the Taqvīmhāne-i Āmire in 1246/1831, followed by its French version, *Le Moniteur ottoman.*

16

Urdu literature

SHAMSUR RAHMAN FARUQI

In 1111/1700 there came to Delhi a man whose *takhallus̤* (pen name) was Walī; his real name is a matter of dispute. Walī was born in 1075/1665 or 1077/1667, and almost certainly died in 1119–20/1707–8. The first account of his advent in Delhi is from the *tadhkira* (biographical dictionary of poets) *Nikāt al-shuʿarāʾ* (Finer points concerning the poets, *c.* 1165/1752) by Muḥammad Taqī Mīr (1135–1225/1723–1810), the second from *Makhzan-i nikāt* (*c.* 1169/1756), another *tadhkira*, by Qāʾim Chāndpūrī (1137–1209/1724f.–95). This is what they say about Walī:

> [Walī] is from Aurangābād. It is said that he came to Delhi too and presented himself before Miyān Shāh Gulshan and recited [before him] some verses of his own. Miyān Ṣāḥib observed, 'There are all those Persian themes lying unused; bring them into use in your own Rēkhta;[1] who is there to challenge you if you do this?'[2]

> In the forty-fourth regnal year of King ʿĀlamgīr, he [Walī] came to Jahānābād,[3] accompanied by … Abu al-Maʿālī … He used occasionally to compose a verse in Persian, praising Abu al-Maʿālī's beauty. On arrival here [in Delhi], when he had the auspicious occasion to present himself before Ḥaḍrat Shaykh Saʿd al-Lah Gulshan, may his grave be hallowed, he commanded him to compose poetry in Rēkhta, and by way of education, gave away to him the following opening verse that he composed:

> Were I to set down on paper
> The praises of the beloved's beauty,
> I would spontaneously
> Convert the paper into the White Hand
> Of Moses.

1 This was one of the many names used for Urdu at that time. The word *Urdū* came into use as a language name much later.

2 Muḥammad Taqī Mīr, *Nikāt al-shuʿarāʾ*, ed. Maḥmud Ilāhī (New Delhi 1972 [1752]), p. 91.

3 One of the popular names for Delhi at that time.

> In sum, it was due to the fortunate presaging by the saint's tongue that ... he wrote Rēkhta with such expressive power and grace that most of the Masters of that time began deliberately to compose verses in Rēkhta.[4]

Ignoring the inconsistency between the two accounts, it only needs to be pointed out that both stress the Delhi origin of Walī's poetry, which became so popular that master poets in Delhi began to compose in Walī's mode: but for the Delhi saint's advice to him, Walī would have remained an occasional poet in Persian, or a negligible poet in Rēkhta. Although the two accounts do not match and were recorded much after the event, Walī undeniably transformed Urdu poetry. Ghulām Hamadānī Muṣḥafī (1163–1239/1750–1824) reported an eyewitness account of Shāh Ḥātim (1110–97/1699–1783), a major Delhi poet:

> One day he [Shāh Ḥātim] mentioned to this faqir that in the second regnal year of him who rests in Paradise [Emperor Muḥammad Shāh, r. 1719–48] Walī's *dīwān* arrived in Shāhjahānābād,[5] and its verses became current on the tongues of young and old.[6]

Historians of Urdu literature, while crediting Walī with having revolutionised Urdu poetry, have maintained that it became possible only because Walī came to Delhi and learned his literary *savoir faire* from a Delhi-based master. The interpretation that Walī's role in the development of Urdu poetry was in fact Delhi-inspired has been challenged by some scholars, but seems still to occupy its authoritative position.

There was very little Urdu literature in the north before Walī. Masʿūd Saʿd Salmān of Lahore (437–514/1046–1121) is reputed to have produced a *dīwān* in Hindi or Hindvī. It no longer exists. Amīr Khusraw of Delhi (650–725/1253–1325) reports having 'presented to friends a few quires of [my] Hindvī verse too'.[7] Nothing of those verses exists now. Urdu literature in the north never really began before the eleventh/seventeenth century, and did not take off until the advent of Walī. Khusraw's poetics and literary theory must have influenced Urdu poets, but his Hindvī poetry did no such thing.

After Khusraw there are only two prominent names: Muḥammad Afḍal (d. 1034/1625), who left a longish poem called *Bikat kahānī* (A dire tale), and

4 Qā'im Chāndpūrī, *Makhzan-i nikāt*, ed. Iqtidā Ḥasan (Lahore, n.d. [*c.* 1756]), pp. 21–3.
5 Another popular name for Delhi at that time.
6 Ghulām Hamadānī Muṣḥafī, *Tadhkira-yi Hindī*, ed. ʿAbd al-Haq (Aurangabad, 1933 [1794–5]), p. 80.
7 Amīr Yamīn al-Dīn Khusraw, *Dībācha-i ghurrat al-kamāl*, ed. Wazīr Ḥasan ʿĀbidī (Lahore, 1975 [1294]), p. 63.

Mīr Ja'far Zatallī (1068?–1125/1658?–1713), long neglected by literary historians for his savage, pornographic satires. Afḍal wrote almost entirely in the *rēkhta* mode. Rēkhta was the name of the language then also known as Hindī, Hindvī, Gujrī and Dakanī, and later known as Urdu. It was also a genre, a macaronic verse where Hindi/Hindvī or Rēkhta (language) was freely mixed with Persian in different proportions. Zatallī wrote some of his poetry and one small piece of prose in plain Hindi. The rest is in the *rēkhta* mode and genre.

Around 1133/1720 Delhi seems suddenly to have been full of Urdu poets: Shāh Mubārak Ābrū (1094/7–1145/1683/5–1733), Sharaf al-Dīn Maḍmūn (d. 1146/1734f.), Ṣadr al-Dīn Fā'iz (1101–50/1690–1737f.), Aḥsan al-Lāh Aḥsan (d. 1150/1737f.), Muḥammad Shākir Nājī (1101?–57/60?/1690?–1744/7?), Mīrzā Maẓhar Jān-i Jānān (1110–95/1699–1781) and Shāh Ḥātim (1110–97/1699–1783), to mention only the most prominent. Some of them had been exclusively or mainly Persian poets, and had switched to Urdu later. The inference is inescapable that while the soil must have been extremely rich, it was Walī who provided the seed through his *dīwān*, which reached Delhi in 1720.

The Urdu literary environment in Delhi benefited by the presence of Sirāj al-Dīn 'Alī Khān-i Ārzū (1100–69/1689–1756) who was a Persian poet, linguist, critic and lexicographer. For Urdu poets he was a literary philosopher and mentor. Even senior Urdu poets such as Ābrū gathered around him for instruction. Prose made an appearance in the Delhi area with Faḍl-i 'Alī Faḍlī, who prepared the first version of his *Karbal kathā* (The story of Karbalā), a religious text, around 1143–5/1731–2.

The questions why there was almost no Urdu literature in the north before the twelfth/eighteenth century, and why and when the language came to be called 'Urdu' have not engaged much attention. The latter question was first discussed, somewhat inadequately, by Grahame Bailey (1872–1942).[8] A little later Maḥmūd Shērānī (1888–1945) made extensive observations on the fact that the word 'Urdu' as a language name was of recent use, but did not go into the historical and linguistic implications of the phenomenon.[9] John Gilchrist (1759–1841) was almost the first to observe that '*Rekhtu* [Rēkhta]' was a 'mixed dialect, also called *Oordoo* or the polished language of the Court'[10] and thus provide a clue to the origin of the name: *urdū* means 'royal court or camp', and the language began to be called *zabān-i urdū-i mu'allā* or 'the language of

8 T. Grahame Bailey, *Studies in North Indian languages* (London, 1938), pp. 1, 3, 6.

9 Ḥāfiẓ Maḥmūd Shērānī, *Maqālāt-i Shērānī*, ed. Maẓhar Maḥmūd Shērānī, 7 vols. (Lahore, 1966–76), vol. I, pp. 10–44.

10 Dr John B. Gilchrist, *A grammar of the Hindoostanee language, or part third of volume first, of a system of Hindoostanee philology* (Calcutta, 1796), p. 261.

the Exalted Court' some time in the late 1770s after Emperor Shāh 'Ālam (r. 1759–1806) returned to Delhi in 1772 and took up residence in the Red Fort. There is evidence to suggest that the term *zabān-i urdū-i muʿallā* was previously used for Persian.[11]

Persian may have delayed Urdu's emergence as a literary language in the north. Urdu literature originated in early ninth/fifteenth-century Gujarat and Deccan through the Sufis, who interacted with the people in the local language, variously called Dihlavī, Hindī, Hindvī, Gujrī or Dakanī. In and around Delhi at about that time Persian seems to have been very nearly the koine, if not the lingua franca. So the Sufis there used Persian almost as a local language.

Literary activity on a viable scale began in Gujarat with the Sufi poetry of Shaykh Bahā' al-Dīn Bājan (790–911/1388–1506), who composed meditative, song-like poems in a genre called *jikrī* apparently from *dhikr* (remembering, speaking (of God)). He was followed by a host of Sufi – and then some non-Sufi – poets, including Shaykh Khūb Muḥammad Chishtī (945–1022/1539–1614) whose long poem-sequence *Khūb tarang* (Waves or exuberant imaginings of Khūb/Excellent waves, 985/1578) is a great poem as well as a Sufi tract. Space permits naming only some of the major Urdu poets from Gujarat up to 1800: Qāḍī Maḥmūd Daryā'ī (822–940/1419–1534), Shaykh 'Alī Muḥammad Jīv Gāmdhanī (d. 972/1565), 'Ālam Gujrātī (*fl.* 1080s/1670s), Amīn Gujrātī (*fl.* 1100s/1690s), Rājā Rām (late eleventh/seventeenth century), and 'Abd al-Walī 'Uzlat (1103–88/1692/3–1775), who was only the second poet from Gujarat after Walī to have his work recognised in the north.

The language of these poets was originally called Dihlavī. The name changed to Gujrī, and remained so until about the first half of the twelfth/eighteenth century, when the name Hindī seems to have supervened. Themes were mostly Sufistic–didactic, with occasional sections praising Gujarat and the Sufi masters. One exception was Khūb Muḥammad Chishtī, who wrote a verse tract on Persian and Sanskrit prosody called *Chhand chhandān* (Metre and metres) and another on figures of speech called *Bhāo bhēd* (Discernment of meaning). The first is an attempt to synthesise Sanskrit and Persian prosody. The other defines the figures of speech in Persian and Gujrī, followed by examples from Gujrī. It is likely that Chishtī's ideas influenced the Deccanī king Muḥammad Qulī Quṭb Shāh (r. 1580–1611), who was the first Urdu poet to put together an Urdu *dīwān* of his own.

11 Sirāj al-Dīn 'Alī Khān Ārzū, *Muthmir*, ed. Raiḥāna Khātūn (Karachi, 1991 [*c.* 1747]), p. 32.

During its Dakanī–Gujrī phase the language shows an abundance of Sanskritic words drawn from modern North or South Indian languages, many of which are no longer recognisable as Urdu; old Urdu words based on Arabic and Persian, many of which are now obsolete; and a generous sprinkling of Persian and Arabic words. There is a comparative lack of idioms and proverbs, which form a significant component of the Delhi register until the nineteenth century. The syntax is clearly Urdu. As the language passes into its Hindī/Rēkhta mode, it gradually becomes closer to the Delhi register of the early eighteenth century, shedding more words derived from neighbouring dialects such as Braj Bhāshā.

Dihlavī/Hindī/Hindvī may have travelled south with the great exodus from Delhi forced by Muḥammad Tughlaq in 1327. Sayyid Muḥammad Gēsū Darāz (721–825/1321–1422) accompanied his father to the Deccan in 1327. He returned to Delhi in 1337, but went back in 1398 to settle in Gulbarga in modern Karnataka. Though Hindvī literary works originally attributed to him are now known to be of later date, he must have used Dihlavī/Hindī for his discourses, and there was plenty of literary activity in the Deccan from his successors and followers. His presence, and also that of numerous secular and religious notables who settled in the south, must have caused the language to spread through the territories that now form parts of Andhra Pradesh, Karnataka and Maharashtra. Some speakers of the language must also have come from Gujarat, because native South India-born writers too have described their language as Gujrī. One example is the work of the Sufi Shāh Burhān al-Dīn Jānam (d. 990?/1582?).

The first known Urdu literary product from the Deccan is a long *mathnavī* of more than 4,000 lines. It does not show any Sufi influences. Only one manuscript exists, and the poem has been internally dated between 1421 and 1434. The manuscript is incomplete, so the poem must have been longer. It has no name and has been labelled *Kadam Rāo Padam Rāo* after its chief characters. The author's name has been determined as Fakhr-i Dīn Niẓāmī. He is not a better poet than Bājan, but he wrote his poem in a regular Persian metre, while Bājan almost exclusively employed indigenous, folky metres. Although according to Sayyida Ja'far 'the idioms and proverbs used by Niẓāmī are with some changes still well understood and spoken in the rural Deccan',[12] *Kadam Rāo Padam Rāo* is extremely hard to follow because Niẓāmī's language is full of words derived from many South Indian languages, and also Sanskrit.

12 Gyān Chand and Sayyida Ja'far, *Tārīkh-i adab-i Urdū, sattarah saw tak*, 5 vols. (New Delhi, 1998), vol. I, p. 14.

Jamīl Jālibī even finds traces of Panjābī, Sarāikī and Sindhī in *Kadam Rāo Padam Rāo*, and says that, despite this medley of languages, the syntax of the poem is clearly Urdu.[13] Sayyida Ja'far believes that it could not have been the first poem of its kind.[14] The poet's handling of both metre and theme has a maturity that only experience of similar poetry engenders.

Shāh Mirān jī Shams al-Ushshāq (809–903/1407–98) came to India in the 1450s and somewhat unwillingly adopted Dakanī for imparting Sufi thought and instruction to the people. The twelfth/sixteenth and thirteenth/seventeenth centuries saw the rise and the apogee of Urdu literature in the Deccan. The breakup (1483–1518) of the Bahmanid empire into five kingdoms apparently benefited literary growth by creating more centres of patronage and economic development. At least three kings stand out as poets. The non-*ghazal* poetry of Muḥammad Qulī Quṭb Shāh is marked by a lively interest in local customs and festivals. His *ghazals* are often lightly erotic and full of the *jouissance* and ecstasy of love. Ibrāhīm 'Ādil Shāh II (r. 1580–1626) was passionately interested in music, and compiled *Kitāb-i nawras* (The book of nine essences/The newly matured book, before 1008/1600), a collection of songs and poems to be set to music. 'Alī 'Ādil Shāh Shāhī (r. 1638–74) left a fine *dīwān* of Urdu *ghazals*.

Mirān jī's son Shāh Burhān al-Dīn Jānam wrote abstract Sufi tracts in prose and verse. Ḥasan Shawqī's (947?–1042/1541?–1633) *ghazal* influenced Walī, perhaps because of its sensuousness. Jānam's son Amīn al-Dīn 'Alī A'lā (1007?–1085/1599?–1675) wrote better prose than his father on Sufi themes. Shaykh Aḥmad Gujarātī (b. *c*. 945/1539) came to Hyderabad at the invitation of Muḥammad Qulī Quṭb Shāh and wrote *Yūsuf Zulaikhā*, a long romantic *mathnavī*, during 987–96/1580–5. He devoted many verses to discussion on what good poetry is, and how he trained and educated himself before embarking upon a poetic career.

Mullā Waj'hī (or sometimes Wajīhī, d. *c*. 1069/1659 or 1081/1671) celebrated Muḥammad Qulī Quṭb Shāh's love affair in a long *mathnavī* called *Quṭb Mushtarī* (Quṭb and Mushtarī, 1017/1609), which rivals the king's work in depicting erotic themes and moments. He followed this up nearly half a century later with *Sab ras* (The essence of all, 1065–7/1655–6), one of the most enduring prose allegories in Urdu literature. Waj'hī also made interesting points of literary theory in *Quṭb Mushtarī*.

13 Jamīl Jālibi, *Tārīkh-i adab-i Urdū*, 3 vols. (Delhi, 1977–2007), vol. I, pp. 25, 38.

14 Chand and Ja'far, *Tārīkh*, p. 14.

Mullā Nuṣratī Bījāpūrī's (1008–84/1600–74) *ʿAlī nāma* (ʿAlī's book, *c.* 1080/1670), is a long *mathnavī* that contains a *qaṣīda* at the head of each section. It celebrates the military campaigns of ʿAlī ʿĀdil Shāh II, and is the most powerful *razm* poem in Urdu, just as Ḥasan Shawqī created in *Mēzbānī nāma* (The book of hospitality, *c.* 1040s/1630s) the best *bazm* poem in the language.[15] Nuṣratī also produced a *mathnavī* called *Gulshan-i ʿishq* (Love's garden, 1068/1658). To Nuṣratī should also go the credit of introducing perhaps the most far-reaching concept in Urdu literary theory: a distinction between *maʿnī* (meaning) and *maḍmūn* (theme). This enabled poets to look for new themes and construct literary utterances that meant more than they seemed to say. The influence of Sanskrit literary thought on this development cannot be ruled out.

Hāshimī Bījāpūrī (d. 1108/1697) wrote a long love *mathnavī* to which he gave the plain name of *Mathnavī-i ʿishqīya* (A love *mathnavī*), with a delightful double plot involving the king of Kashmir and the great Persian poet Saʿdī (609?–91/1213?–92). Hāshimī's greatest claim to fame is in the fact that in his *ghazals* the speaker is almost invariably female; she is beautiful and seductive in her own right, but she is the lover, and her beloved is male. This is not uncommon in *ghazals* up to the late eleventh/seventeenth century, but Hāshimī uses the device with an erotic panache and verve which suggests that he in some way adopted the female voice as his own rather than just observing a convention.

The Dakanī impulse was played out by the mid-twelfth/eighteenth century. The cultural authority of the Delhi register of language, and of the Persianate (or, in modern parlance, the *sabk-i hindī* or 'Indian style') mode introduced by Walī are the two main reasons for this. Mawlānā Bāqar Āgāh (1158–1220/1745–1806), the last great figure in pre-modern Dakanī Urdu, wrote in both modes, and lamented that while the Delhi poet Sawdā (1117–95/1706–81) was known from 'Hind to Karnatak', the greatness of Nuṣratī was not recognised.[16] Lachhmī Narāʾin Shafīq Awrangābādī (1158–1222/1745–1808) wrote that he was obliged, against his inclination, to leave Persian in favour of Rēkhta because of the latter's great popularity.[17] The

15 *Razm*, (lit. 'combat') in literary terms means a descripton of battles and conquests; *bazm* (lit. '(colourful) assembly') in literary terms means a description of wine-drinking, dancing, singing, love.

16 Mawlānā Bāqar Āgāh, 'Preface to Gulzār-i 'Ishq' (1794) in 'Alīm Ṣabā Navīdī (ed.), *Mawlānā Bāqar Āgāh kē adabī navādir* (Madras, 1994), pp. 144–5. Karnataka (Karnatak in Urdu) was the medieval name of modern-day Tamil Nadu.

17 Lachhmī Nara'in Shafīq Awrangābādī, *Chamanistān-i shuʿarā*', ed. and trans. 'Aṭā Kākvī (Patna, 1968 [1762]), p. 9.

poetry of Sirāj Awrangābādī (1126?–77/1714?–63/4), who never took a step northward and wrote like the poets of Delhi, only better, proves Shafiq's point.

If Walī took Delhi by storm, Delhi took the rest of the Urdu world by storm, and very soon became the chief seat of Urdu literature. Only a hint can be given here of the main things that happened.

The distinction between meaning and theme (*maʿnī* and *maḍmūn*) was exploited further. The search for new, even outré themes (*maḍmun āfirīnī*, that is, creating new themes), and verbal structures with multiple meanings (*maʿnī bandī*, or depicting meanings) became important in poetry. Wordplay and sophisticated or playful double entendre or *īhām* became extremely popular. Here again, the influence of Sanskrit poetics cannot be ruled out. Marginal genres such as *rubāʿī*, *qitʿa*, *marsiya* and verse chronogram were refined. New genres such as the *shahr āshōb* (poems lamenting the decline of order, and of professional classes or the world turning upside down), and *wāsōkht* (the lover's complaint) were introduced. Autobiographical poems or poems depicting personal experiences were popular. Humour, satire, scurrilous and adversarial poems achieved stunning heights. Themes of homosexuality or boy love became common, more so in some poets than in others. There had been no humour, satire or homosexuality in Gujrī or Dakanī.

Creative language became bolder and more colourful. The *ghazal* became more inward-looking and also more aware of the world. Prose began to be employed for literary discourse, Qurʾānic translation, history and romance. This prose was without verbose embellishments, much like the prose later propagated at the College of Fort William. Mention must be made here of Shāh Murād al-Lāh Sambhalī's partial translation and commentary on the Qurʾān called *Tafsīr-i Murādiyya* (1184/1771), *Qissa wa aḥwāl-i Ruhēla* (The story and circumstances of the Rohillas, 1189/1776) by Rustam ʿAlī Bijnorī, and the unfinished though still voluminous *ʿAjāʾib al-qiṣaṣ* (The most wonderful of all tales, 1206/1792) by Shāh ʿĀlam. The names of two other historians, Harī Har Parshād Sambhalī and Bindrāban Mathrāvī, also appear; but nothing else is known of them.

The new Urdu literary community in Delhi was extremely self-aware. *Tadhkiras*, initially in Persian, and then from 1801 in Urdu also, were written in large numbers. They included as many contemporary poets as possible, with the occasional polemical or critical comment and literary or biographical anecdote thrown in. While Sufis, noblemen and royalty continued to be active in poetry, the entry to the poets' ranks of women and professionals from non-elite classes was the new phenomenon. Hindus, who had previously concentrated on Persian, now turned to Urdu. The first great Hindu names in Urdu poetry date from this time, Sarb Sukh Dīvāna (1139?–1202/1727?–88/9) being the most notable among them. The society became more conscious of poetry as a worthwhile activity.

The first female poet with a *dīwān* of her own was Māh Laqā Chandā (1181–1235/1768–1820), a 'nautch girl' of great beauty and wealth in Hyderabad. Another notable female poet was Gunnā Begam (d. 1186/1773), who was the daughter of a famous Iranian poet and was married to ʿImād al-Mulk, one-time prime minister to Emperor Aḥmad Shāh. Ḥayāt al-Nisā Bēgam, a daughter of Shāh ʿĀlam, was also a poet. Europeans appear on the literary scene in the last years of the twelfth/eighteenth century.

With so many newcomers and with so little in the history to provide models, it was natural that aspirants should turn to the knowledgeable for advice. The institution of *ustād* and *shāgird* (master and pupil) thus came into existence, and was well in place by the 1760s in Delhi and elsewhere. Chandā had Shēr Muḥammad Khān Īmān, a Delhi poet, as her *ustād*.

Muḥammad Taqī Mīr (1135–1125/1723–1810) was perhaps the greatest Urdu poet, and certainly the greatest of the twelfth/eighteenth century. His poetry has the same fullness and variety that marked his century, though his reputation seems to have rested generally on unauthenticated anecdotes presenting him as a self-regarding, curmudgeonly individual. There are moods of extreme sadness in his poetry, but there are also the joys of love and life, Sufistic ideas presented with unsurpassable grace and puissance, satire, humour (which could be bawdy or directed against himself), and a miraculous feel for words.

Mīr went to Lucknow in 1196/1782, and spent his life there in reasonable comfort. Mīrzā Muḥammad Rafiʿ Sawdā and Sayyid Muḥammad Mīr Sōz (1132–1213/1720f.–98f.) had preceded him there. According to an anecdote Mīr declared that there were only two full poets, himself and Sawdā, and one half-poet, Sayyid Khwāja Mīr Dard (1134–99/1722–85). When asked about Sōz he scowled, 'Okay, so let the number of poets be two-and-three quarters.' The story, if true, reflects not so much Mīr's egotism as a critical judgement: Sawdā was an excellent poet, equally at home in all the genres of Urdu poetry. Dard was excellent too, but he had nothing to offer in *qaṣīda* and *mathnavī*, two of the triumvirate of the genres, so he was only half a poet. Sōz, plainly, wasn't in the same class as the other three.

These judgements have more or less abided. But there were many other meritorious poets with fine contemporary reputations: ʿAbd al-Ḥayy

Tābān (1127–62/1715–49); In'ām al-Lāh Khān Yaqīn (1139?–68/1727?–55); Mīr Athar (1148–1208/1735f.–94); Mīr Ḥasan (1148–1200/1736f.–86); and Naẓīr Akbarābādī (1152–1245/1740–1830), whom S. W. Fallon compared to Chaucer and Shakespeare.[18] Shāh Ḥātim, Qā'im Chāndpūrī, Dīvāna and Muṣḥafī have already been mentioned. By 1168/1755 Ḥātim was claiming that he wrote in the language of the *mīrzās* (gentlemen) and *rinds* (liberal *bons vivants*) of Delhi. He is credited with launching the so-called Iṣlāḥ-i Zabān (language reform) movement. While there was in fact no such movement, a certain privileging of Persian (which term included Arabic) words and usages began to appear throughout the Urdu world in the second half of the century, and persists to a certain extent even today.

Muṣḥafī, Dīvāna, Qalandar Bakhsh Jur'at (1161–1224/1748–1809) and Inshā' al-Lāh Khān Inshā (1169–1232/1756–1817) settled in Lucknow. Sa'ādat Yār Khān Rangīn (1171–1249/1758–1834f.) spent long periods of time there. Rangīn is credited with inventing the *rēkhtī*, a genre of poetry expressing female sentiments and experience, using women's vocabulary. These poets helped establish Lucknow as a rival to Delhi. Centres of literary activity sprang up in many other places such as Allahabad, Banaras, Baroda, Calcutta, Murshidabad, Patna and Rampur. Hyderabad was already there, and had attracted Delhi's major poet Shāh Naṣīr (1168?–1253/1755?–1838), who left behind him numerous *shāgirds* in Delhi.

In 1800 the British established a college at Fort William in Calcutta for training British civil servants. The dynamism of John Gilchrist helped produce many Urdu works there which gained wide repute.The college also became famous as the virtual creator of modern Urdu prose. This is not quite true, but the works produced at the college, particularly *Bāgh o bahār* (Garden and spring, 1219/1805) by Mīr Amman (1163–1252/1750–1837), gained far wider currency than the work of Murād al-Lāh Sambhalī and others. The college printed Mīr's *Kulliyāt* (Collected verse) in 1811. Mīr had died in 1810 in Lucknow. A railway line passes through the area where his grave used to be.

18 S. W. Fallon, *A new Hindustani–English dictionary* (Lucknow, 1986 [1879] (repr.)), p. x.

17

History writing

LI GUO

The two Arabic words most commonly associated with 'history', *ta'rīkh* and *khabar* (pl. *akhbār*), reveal conflicting ideas regarding writing about the past. Derived from ancient Near Eastern roots, *ta'rīkh* conveys a sense of dating, whereas *khabar*, meaning 'story, anecdote', bears no notion of fixation of time at all. Earlier historical reports were known as *akhbār*, whereas *ta'rīkh* came later to acquire a wider definition of 'history' and 'historical interpretation'. By the end of the second/eighth century most of the works written on history bore the title *ta'rīkh*. It was later uniformly adopted into other Islamic languages: Persian, Turkish and Urdu.[1] A massive corpus under the rubric of *ta'rīkh* – chronicle, biographical dictionary, administrative geography – was produced over the period in question. Of these, only chronicles will be surveyed here.

The 'classical' period (*c*. 710–1150 CE)

The beginning: ḥadīth *scholars and* akhbārīs

In many ways Islamic history writing began with a 'clean slate'. While pre-Islamic Arabian inscriptions, poetry and the *ayyām al-ʿarab* folklore reflect a nostalgic curiosity about the past, the rise of Arabic-Islamic historiography stemmed from a more practical and immediate motivation. Its genesis lay in the early *akhbār*-reports, which were mostly short and introduced by an *isnād*, similar to that of the *ḥadīth*. The fact that the two pursuits went hand in hand in their development reveals the anxiety over control of the narrative in the early Islamic hermeneutic tradition, and places history squarely in the context of an auxiliary discipline vis-à-vis the Qur'ān, the collection of *ḥadīth* and legal studies.[2]

1 Franz Rosenthal, *A history of Muslim historiography* (Leiden, 1968), pp. 11–17.
2 On historiography of early Islam see *NCHI*, vol. I, part IV.

A historian, known as an *akhbārī*, is someone who wrote about remarkable events with a passion for chronology. An *akhbārī*, such as the Medinan ʿUrwa ibn al-Zubayr (d. 94/712), was usually a scholar of *ḥadīth*, who would keep his day-job as a jurist, but was also interested in the *maghāzī*, or the Prophet's military expeditions and various aspects of his life, as well as the Rāshidūn caliphs and the *ridda* wars. In addition to the mostly *ḥadīth* material, al-Zuhrī (d. 124/741) also dwelt on tales of the *qiṣaṣ al-anbiyāʾ* (poetry and genealogy). His contemporary Wahb ibn Munabbih (d. 110/728), of Yemen, used the Arabian folklore and the *isrāʾīlīyāt* (tales related to the Old Testament). Wahb's presentation of divine mission through historical narrative found a strong echo in the work of Ibn Isḥāq.

The *sīra* (biography of the Prophet Muḥammad) by Ibn Isḥāq (d. 150/767) will be discussed elsewhere. What should be noted here is its compositional structure that lays out a vision of 'universal history', which would have an everlasting impact on the later development of Islamic historiography. Consisting of three building-blocks – the *mubtadaʾ*, 'the beginning' (from creation to Muḥammad); the *mabʿath*, 'the mission' of the Prophet; and the *maghāzī* – it blended the methods of the *ḥadīth* scholars and the storytellers.[3]

While the *sīra* dominated early Muslim historical writing, the inquiry expanded to the activities of the Prophet's Companions and followers, as well as political, social and legal affairs of the Muslim community. A historian living in the Umayyad period, al-Wāqidī (d. 207/823), was also interested in his own time; in his *al-Taʾrīkh al-kabīr* a wide range of topics was addressed.

With the rise of garrison towns in Iraq, the Kūfan *akhbārīs*, Abū Mikhnaf (d. 157/774), ʿAwāna ibn al-Ḥakam (d. 147/764) and Sayf ibn ʿUmar (d. 180/796), emerged, as well as Naṣr ibn Muzāḥim (d. 212/827), the first Shīʿite *akhbārī*. However, it was in Baṣra that the activities of the *akhbārīs* blossomed, characterised by more extensive gathering and organisation of historical accounts. The *akhbārīs* also made use of government registers in Iraq and Syria, which served as sources for genealogy (*ansāb*) and administrative geography (*khiṭaṭ*). Among the *akhbārīs* who wrote on the *ansāb* were al-Madāʾinī (d. 225/839), Ibn al-Kalbī (d. 204/819) and al-Zubayrī (d. 233–6/847–50); attention should also be given to al-Haytham ibn ʿAdī (d. 206/821), whose *Kitāb al-taʾrīkh ʿalā al-sinīn* (History according to the years) was

3 A. A. Duri, *The rise of historical writing among the Arabs*, ed. and trans. Lawrence Conrad (Princeton, 1983), pp. 33–6.

probably the first in the annalistic form, which was to become the conventional format for chronicles. Besides the *akhbārīs*, philologists studied and wrote history. Their interest in Qurʾān-related philology led them to the *akhbār* and *ansāb* materials found in poetry. Abū ʿUbayda (d. 211/826) arranged these materials pertaining to particular events or subjects in book form. Little, however, is known about the process by which individual accounts were incorporated into books, since most of the aforementioned works are lost today. They only survive in later revised forms or quotations by a new generation of historians in the second half of the third/ninth century, who gave the classical tradition of Muslim history writing its definitive form.

Al-Ṭabarī and 'universal history'

The works of al-Balādhurī (d. 279/892), al-Yaʿqūbī (d. 284/897), Ibn Qutayba (d. 276/889), al-Dīnawarī (d. 282/895) and al-Ṭabarī (d. 310/923) exemplified the new trend towards producing 'universal histories'. Al-Balādhurī's *Futūḥ al-buldān* chronicled the Muslim conquests of the provinces. Despite his affiliations with the ʿAbbāsids al-Balādhurī made a serious effort to be 'objective' in presentation. The *Taʾrīkh* of al-Yaʿqūbī included a synopsis of universal history prior to Islam and of Islamic history up to his time. Al-Yaʿqūbī organised his history according to the reigns of the caliphs and then presented events in chronological order. Ibn Qutayba's *al-Maʿārif* offered an encyclopaedic compendium in which various narrative lines were blended together. It began with the creation and ended in the days of the ʿAbbāsid caliph al-Muʿtaṣim. Al-Dīnawarī's *al-Akhbār al-ṭiwāl* also adhered to chronological order, but was more selective in the presentations.

Al-Ṭabarī's *Taʾrīkh al-rusul wa-al-mulūk* (History of the prophets and kings) marks the high point of Muslim historical writing. The title reflects his view of history, expressed in two conceptions: the oneness of prophetic mission; and the experiences of the Muslim community through time. He was particularly keen to give variant accounts of an event or subject, and he kept a strict annalistic form, even at the expense of a coherent continuous narrative line. Al-Ṭabarī's prose is simple and straightforward, with little rhetorical embellishment. The 'Ṭabarī model' marked the end of the formative phase of Arabic-Islamic historiography, characterised by compilation of ancient *akhbār* introduced by their *isnāds*. It also marked a change of informants and writers, from early *akhbārīs* to the *kuttāb*-bureaucrats under whose stewardship other forms, such as biography and administrative geography (*masālik*, *kitāb al-kharāj*), also flourished.

Variations after al-Ṭabarī

Following in al-Ṭabarī's footsteps, annalistic chronicles centred on the affairs of the Muslim caliphate remained the mainstay of history writing. Many continuations of al-Ṭabarī were produced all over the Muslim empire; among these were the *Ṣilat Ta'rīkh al-Ṭabarī* by ʿArīb al-Qurṭubī (d. *c.* 365/975), of Spain, and those by the Sabian clan in Baghdad. The significance of the latter lies not only in the rich accounts they provided (being court physicians), but also in the fact that the patriarch Thābit ibn Qurra (d. 288/901) was commissioned by the caliph al-Muʿtaḍid to chronicle his reign, thus marking the beginning of court patronage of history writing.

It seems likely that the Persian Būyids were the dynasty that instigated the tradition of 'official history'. The long list of court historians began with Miskawayh (d. 421/1030), an Iranian-born *kātib* whose *Tajārib al-umam* is considered the most important source for the history of the ʿAbbāsids and Būyids. Miskawayh adopted an ethical and philosophical perspective, and was influential on Persian historiography. New types of historical writing emerged during the ʿAbbāsid period as well. The anonymous *Akhbār al-dawla al-ʿAbbāsīya* recounted the various stages of the ʿAbbāsid *daʿwa*. Al-Masʿūdī (d. 345/956), in *Murūj al-dhahab*, chronicled the early caliphate and covered a wide range of literary and intellectual topics. The *Kitāb al-awrāq* of Abū Bakr al-Ṣūlī (d. 335/946) offered a lyrical portrait, in prose and verse, of life at the court of the caliphs al-Rāḍī and al-Muttaqī. Al-Tanūkhī's (d. 384/995) *Nishwār al-muḥāḍara* is a collection of anecdotes on social life, reminiscent of Abū al-Faraj's masterpiece of *adab*, the *Kitāb al-aghānī*.[4]

Local histories developed in Iraq and Egypt. The Iraqīs tended to focus on the *ḥadīth* scholars associated with a place, such as Ṭayfūr's (d. 280/893) *Ta'rīkh Baghdād* and al-Azdī's (d. 334/945) *Ta'rīkh al-Mawṣil*, or on the topographical and geographical features of a place, such as Bahshal's (d. 288/900) *Ta'rīkh Wāsiṭ*. The works produced in Egypt, on the other hand, took different directions: Ibn ʿAbd al-Ḥakam's (d. 257/870) *Futūḥ Miṣr* chronicles the Muslim conquests of Egypt, and al-Kindī's (d. 350/961) *Kitāb al-wulāt* and *Kitāb al-quḍāt* dealt with administrative and legal affairs. Unfortunately, the study of the Fāṭimid dynasty in Egypt, by all indications a time of great history writing, is seriously hampered by the 'ghost' effect: that is, that so many lost Fāṭimid chronicles only survived in later compendiums. Among these, the works of

4 Hugh Kennedy, *The Prophet and the age of the caliphate: The Islamic Near East from the sixth to eleventh century* (London, 1986), pp. 350–97.

Ibn Zūlāq al-Laythī (d. 386/996) and Muḥammad al-Musabbiḥī (d. 420/1029) are frequently mentioned.

The 'post-classical' period (*c.* 1150–1500 CE)

'Islamic history' and dynastic chronicle

Despite its influence, al-Ṭabarī's paradigm of universal history with an Islamic perspective did not totally prevail. The centuries after al-Ṭabarī were a time of experimentation on the part of historians with diverse purposes and backgrounds. In this respect, ʿIzz al-Dīn Ibn al-Athīr (d. 630/1233) perhaps best exemplifies the 'post-Ṭabarī' phase that led up to the next efflorescence of history writing in the Ayyūbid and Mamlūk periods. Having witnessed Saladin's military campaigns and enjoyed the patronage of the Zangid rulers of Aleppo and Mosul, Ibn al-Athīr represented a line of provincial historians who chronicled Iraq, Syria and Egypt during a time of rapid transformation and upheaval within the Muslim community and on the international front.

The historiography of the Ayyūbid and Mamlūk periods is usually characterised as one of conservatism, in so far as the classical forms – chronicle, biography, administrative manual – were maintained and the activities of the political and military elites, along with the careers of the *ʿulamāʾ*, predominated.[5] Ibn al-Athīr is a fine example of this tradition. His *Kāmil fī al-taʾrīkh* (The complete work of history) presented a refined version of al-Ṭabarī's vision, but showed an inclination towards a topical approach that would break away from the rigid year-by-year format. The *Kāmil* also introduced the bipartite arrangement of *ḥawādith* (events) and *wafayāt* (obituaries); this, together with its judicious choice of sources (but usually without naming them), was to become the norm for centuries to come.[6]

Unlike Ibn al-Athīr, other contemporary historians were bureaucrats in the service of the Zangid dynasty and, later, the Ayyūbid princes, and they all wrote in a different genre: the dynastic chronicle-cum-royal biography. The courtier Ibn al-Qalānisī's (d. 555/1160) *Dhayl taʾrīkh Dimashq*, a sequel to an earlier chronicle, sheds light on the affairs in Syria as well as the Crusades. In Cairo, of Saladin's two 'official' historians, al-Kātib al-Iṣfahānī (d. 597/1201) wrote *al-Fatḥ al-qussī fī al-fatḥ al-Qudsī*, which gave an account of Saladin's

5 Donald Little, 'Historiography of the Ayyubid and Mamluk epochs', in Carl F. Petry (ed.), *The Cambridge history of Egypt*, 2 vols. (Cambridge, 1998), vol. I: *Islamic Egypt*; Li Guo, 'Mamluk historiographic studies: The state of the art', *Mamlūk Studies Review*, 1 (1997).

6 Ibn al-Athīr, *The annals of the Saljuq Turks: Selections from* al-Kāmil fī 'l-taʾrīkh *of ʿIzz al-Dīn Ibn al-Athīr*, trans. D. S. Richards (London, 2002), pp. 1–8.

career, and *al-Barq al-Shāmī*, which covered a wider range of Ayyūbid princes and events. His highly ornate Persianate style shows traits of the bilingualism popular at the time. Al-Qāḍī al-Fāḍil (d. 596/1200) was a Palestinian who had a successful career in the Fāṭimid chancery and then served at Saladin's court. His *Rasā'il* (Essays) and *Mutajaddidāt* (Diaries) are detailed records of his observations, showing a new attempt at thematic treatment of a particular subject or event. By and large, the approach of 'official historians', who combined dynastic chronicle and royal biography, laced with rhetoric embellishments, dominated the narratives of the period. This was the era of Muslim warrior-heroes. The literature reflected the zeitgeist.

While court-affiliated chroniclers wrote dynastic chronicles in Cairo, elsewhere, especially in Syria, the tradition of writing 'universal history' was carried on by the mostly Ḥanbalī *'ulamā'*/historians. Among these, Sibṭ Ibn al-Jawzī's (d. 654/1256) *Mir'āt al-zamān fī ta'rīkh al-a'yān* (The mirror of the ages with regard to the biographies of the notables) generated a series of sequels. From its title a new criterion for history may be discerned: a balanced presentation of remarkable events and biographies of the learned men.

The trend of dynastic chronicle-cum-royal biography, on the other hand, continued in Syria as well, with a tighter focus and new heroes. Abū Shāma (d. 665/1267) wrote *al-Rawḍatayn fī akhbār al-dawlatayn*, about the reigns of the Ayyūbid sultans Nūr al-Dīn and Saladin. Ibn Shaddād (d. 684/1285) wrote a history of his hometown Aleppo (*Ta'rīkh Ḥalab*) and a chronicle of the reign of the Mamlūk sultan Baybars. Ibn Wāṣil (d. 697/1298), born in Aleppo and later based in Cairo, wrote the *Mufarrij al-kurūb fī akhbār banī Ayyūb*, in which the house of Ayyūb was portrayed in an idealised light; he also covered the early Mamlūk period.

Tradition and diversity in Mamlūk historiography

The Mamlūk period is arguably the most documented era in Islamic history, in no small part due to the overwhelming quantity and extreme richness of the historical sources produced, of which only an outline account is possible here. An overview of Mamlūk historiography reveals the consolidation of the annalistic form. In the early ('Baḥrī') period, bureaucratic historians wrote both universal histories and dynastic annals. Abū al-Fidā' (d. 732/1331), an Ayyūbid prince of Ḥamā, wrote *al-Mukhtaṣar fī ta'rīkh al-bashar*, a chronicle supplemented by short obituaries. Baybars al-Manṣūrī (d. 725/1325) compiled the *Zubdat al-fikra fī ta'rīkh al-hijra*, a universal history, and *al-Tuḥfa al-mulūkīya fī al-dawla al-Turkīya*, an epitome, with special reference to the 'Turks' (Mamlūks), in rhymed prose. During the later ('Burjī') period independent and semi-official historians wrote mostly universal histories. Ibn al-Furāt's (d. 807/1405) *Ta'rīkh al-duwal wa-al-mulūk* was arranged on a day-by-day basis. Al-Maqrīzī's (d. 845/1442) *al-Sulūk li-ma'rifat duwal al-mulūk* and Ibn Ḥajar al-ʿAsqalānī's (d. 852/1449) *Inbāʾ al-ghumr fī abnāʾ al-ʿumr* are both annalistic histories of the Mamlūk state during the authors' lifetime, with a more focused approach. Badr al-Dīn al-ʿAynī's (d. 855/1451) *ʿIqd al-jumān fī taʾrīkh ahl al-zamān* stands out as accessible and judicious in identifying and quoting from sources. Ibn Taghrībirdī (d. 874/1470) wrote two major chronicles: *al-Nujūm al-zāhira fī mulūk Miṣr wa-al-Qāhira*, a history of Islamic Egypt, and the *Ḥawādith al-duhūr fī madā al-ayyām wa-al-shuhūr*, a continuation of al-Maqrīzī's *al-Sulūk*. Al-Sakhāwī (d. 902/1497) wrote continuations to al-Dhahabī's (d. 748/1348) *Taʾrīkh al-Islām* and al-Maqrīzī's *al-Sulūk*. The latter, titled *al-Tibr al-masbūk fī dhayl al-Sulūk*, was commissioned by the *amīr* Yashbak during the reigns of Khushqadam and Qāytbāy. By and large, later Mamlūk chroniclers maintained some distance from the regime.

All these works have a standard format: each year begins with a list of the rulers and general information (the Nile flood, market prices, natural disasters etc.). Events are narrated in month-by-month, or day-by-day, order, with some topical highlights. It became such a fixed procedure that we find, in an unfinished ninth/fifteenth-century autography, that numerous blanks were left so the data could be filled in when available.[7] The rigid annalistic format also dominated, or influenced, chancery manuals and biographical dictionaries. In al-Nuwayrī's (d. 733/1333) administrative handbook *Nihāyat al-arab fī funūn al-adab*, two-thirds consisted of annals arranged according to regions and dynasties. Al-ʿUmarī's (d. 749/1349) *Masālik al-abṣār fī mamālik al-amṣār*, an encyclopaedia of the lands and administration of the Mamlūk realm, contains a section of annals, dating from the *hijra* to the author's time. The entries of biographical dictionaries were mostly arranged according to year; on the other hand, obituaries became an integral part of a conventional chronicle. The renewed interest in such materials was an outgrowth of the regional studies in *ḥadīth*, especially as championed by the Ḥanbalīs in Syria.

This kind of regionalism, together with other factors, further fuelled competing versions in history writing. Despite the conservative conventions of mainstream history writing there were some noteworthy deviations in content, form and style.[8] Many factors contributed to the phenomenon, not least of

7 Ibrāhīm ibn ʿUmar al-Biqāʿī, *Taʿrīkh al-Biqāʿī*, MS Medina, Maktabat al-Shaykh ʿĀrif Ḥikmat 3789.

8 Ulrich Haarmann, 'Auflösung und Bewahrung der klassichen Formen arabischer Geschichtsschreibung in der Zeit der Mamluken', *ZDMG*, 121 (1971).

which is the broadening background of the historians: besides the *ʿulamāʾ* and the *kuttāb*-clerks, a third type emerged, that of the *awlād al-nās*, the offspring of the Mamlūks, whose connections enabled them to be prominent bureaucrats. All of these groups clustered in metropolitan centres and vied for prestige.

In Cairo, royal biographers / dynastic chroniclers continued their labour. Ibn ʿAbd al-Ẓāhir (d. 692 / 1292) was commissioned to write history on behalf of three sultans: Baybars, Qalāwūn and al-Ashraf Khalīl. Shāfiʿ al-Miṣrī (d. 730 / 1330) did the same for Baybars and Qalāwūn. In Syria, the *ḥadīth* scholars wrote annals chronicling political, military and religious affairs as well as obituaries of their fellow *ʿulamāʾ*. Ibn Kathīr (d. *c.* 774 / 1373) and al-Dhahabī penned 'popular' histories (*al-Bidāya wa-al-nihāya* and *Taʾrīkh al-Islām*, respectively). The lesser-known al-Jazarī (d. 739 / 1338), al-Birzālī (d. 739 / 1339) and al-Yūnīnī (d. 726 / 1326) wrote rigorously researched and original continuations of Ayyūbid works. Their compilations contain substantial *ḥadīth* materials and an excessive amount of space devoted to the Who's Who of the literati, with profuse quotations of poetry and *adab*.[9]

To be sure, the Syrian historians were by no means provincial in their coverage, in that their accounts about events in Egypt oftentimes proved to be more reliable than those of their Cairene counterparts.[10] The difference between the two camps lay in their concept of history writing, and in their selectiveness in coverage. The semi-official chroniclers in Cairo concentrated on the Mamlūk regime, whereas the Syrians were more concerned with preserving the religious and cultural heritage of the *umma*, especially at times of crisis. The dichotomy in the historical writings of the early Mamlūk period took an interesting turn later, with the increasing rivalry among the largely immigrant *ʿulamāʾ* populace in Cairo. The fierce competition produced winners, losers and eccentrics, in personality and writing style. For the last, the recording, and representation, of the past became increasingly autobiographical and opinionated, with unapologetically personal and deliberately subjective renderings of the events and persons.

This synergy between formal grandeur and individual eccentricity was evident in the trend of literarisation.[11] To popularise their works many

9 Al-Yūnīnī, *Early Mamluk Syrian historiography: al-Yūnīnī's* Dhayl mirʾāt al-zamān, ed. and trans. Li Guo (Leiden, 1998).

10 Little, 'Historiography', p. 429.

11 The phenomenon is not confined to the Mamlūk period (see Stefan Leder (ed.), *Storytelling in the framework of non-fictional Arabic literature* (Wiesbaden, 1998); Julie Meisami, 'History and literature', *Iranian Studies*, 33, 1–2 (2000)), but the Mamlūk time produced its most extensive documentation.

historians adopted literary devices. Ibn al-Dawādārī's (d. after 736/1335) *Kanz al-durar wa-jāmiʿ al-ghurar* revealed a return to pre-*ḥadīth*-era Arabian anecdotal narrative, peppered with poetry and storytelling. Mūsā al-Yūsufī's (d. 759/1358) *Nuzhat al-nāẓir fī sīrat al-malik al-Nāṣir* used street language to depict the looks and personalities of the people, and the atmosphere surrounding the dramatised events. Ibn Iyās's (d. 930/1524) *Badāʾiʿ al-zuhūr* is viewed by many as 'historicized folk romance'.[12]

In this regard, the marketability of history books was also important. History was useful. Works such as al-Nuwayrī's *Nihāyat al-arab* were composed to meet the need of the *kuttāb* and the career-oriented youth for historical information and narrative skills. Entertainment values also counted. Ibn al-Dawādārī's and Ibn Iyās's annals, spiced with *nawādir* and *ʿajāʾib* (witticism and mirabilia), were targeting a wide audience. The attempt to bring history closer to the reader is further seen in the new language cultivated by historians. Instead of the formal ʿArabīya that had dominated historical writings, the reader was now treated to a mixture of the classical Arabic and lightly stylised colloquial.

Ibn Khaldūn's legacy: the Maghrib and Ottoman experiences

The richness, and diversity, of post-classical Muslim historiography is also seen in yet another significant frontier: North Africa and Andalusia. In philosophical terms it was heralded by the 'new science' of history writing championed by Ibn Khaldūn. Centred around the notion of *ʿaṣabiyya*, or 'group consciousness', this took historical sequence, historical units and state structure as the guidelines for historical discourse. Both North African and Andalusian historians recognised a Berber identity within the Islamic framework, and made the history of the Berber dynasties the focus of historical interest. This Berber-centred historical thinking manifests itself in major works, such as the *Kitāb al-ansāb*, better known as the *Mafākhir al-barbar*, a narrative of the Berbers in chronological order attributed to Athīr al-Dīn Abū Ḥayyān (d. 745/1344), a Cairo-based Berber expatriate; Ibn Marzūq's (d. 781/1379) *Musnad*, a detailed account, in the form of memoir, of the Marīnids; and Ibn Khaldūn's *Kitāb al-ʿibar*, a history of the Maghrib, as part of his planned universal history of Arabs, Berbers and other people. With regard to composition, the new school also diverged from the Arabo-Islamic paradigm, in that

12 Ulrich Haarmann, *Quellenstudien zur frühen Mamlukenzeit* (Freiburg, 1969); Little, 'Historiography', pp. 424–5.

the thematic and encyclopaedic *majmūʿa*, or collections of essays, replaced the *taʾrīkh* annals.[13]

In the Mashriq this 'new science' never really took off until the tenth/sixteenth century, when Ibn Khaldūn was to be rediscovered by Ottoman historians.[14] Ibn Khaldūn, and especially his theory of the rise and decline of states, had a profound influence on the works of the major figures of Ottoman historiography; among them Weysī Effendi (d. 1628), whose *Khwāb-nāme* was a world history in the form of a conversation between Aḥmed I and Alexander the Great, with a comparison of the new and old orders and systems and a critique of the time; Ḥājjī Khalīfa (Kātib Çelebi, d. 1657), the most prolific Ottoman historian and bibliographer who wrote *Fadhlakat al-tawārīkh*, a universal history, in Arabic, and *Fedhleke*, a chronicle of the Ottoman empire, in Turkish; and Naʿīmā (d. 1716), the leading Ottoman historian whose *Taʾrīkh-i Naʿīmā* is considered to be the most important source on the Ottoman state ideology and history.[15]

Persian history writing (*c.* 1050–1600 CE)

Arab chroniclers' interest in Iran goes back to the beginning of Islamic historiography. Persian Islamic historical writing, however, came much later. The indigenous Iranian traditions – the pre-Islamic Sasanian works in Pahlavi (Middle Persian) and the Samanid *Shāhnāma* type – are collections of legends and myths. Devoid of chronological sequence and loose in factual accuracy, they were not considered serious histories among the cultural elite familiar with the Arabic model fashioned after al-Ṭabarī. Although Persian has long been the lingua franca in the Muslim east (Iran, Central Asia), major histories of Iran and Persianate dynasties, the Būyids and Saljūqs, were written

13 Maya Shatzmiller, *The Berbers and the Islamic state: The Marīnid experience in pre-protectorate Morocco* (Princeton, 2000), pp. 4–13, 71–81.

14 Modern scholars have long debated over the success and 'failure' of Ibn Khaldūn as a practising historian. A commonly held view is that the conventional narrative of the *Kitāb al-ʿibar* does not live up to the methodological boasts of the *Muqaddima*, or *Prolegomena*. This view has been challenged in recent publications; see Aziz al-Azmeh, *Ibn Khaldūn* (London, 1990); Little, 'Historiography', pp. 433–6; Tarif Khalidi, *Arabic historical thought in the classical period* (Cambridge, 1994), pp. 222–31; Chase Robinson, *Islamic historiography* (Cambridge, 2003), pp. 102, 185–6.

15 Ibn Khaldūn, *The* Muqaddimah*: An introduction to history*, trans. Franz Rosenthal, 3 vols. (London, 1986), vol. I, pp. lxvii–lxvii, xc–xcix; Cornell Fleischer, 'Royal authority, dynastic cyclism, and "Ibn Khaldunism" in sixteenth century Ottoman letters', *Journal of Asian and African Studies*, 17, 3–4 (1983), pp. 199–203.

in Arabic. Hence the long-standing Arabocentric overview which has recently been subjected to criticism.[16]

The pre-Mongol phase

The rise of Persian Islamic historical writing coincided with historical developments in the fourth/tenth century, when breakaway dynasties began to carve out territory. Maʿmarī's prose *Shāhnāma* was at the head of a tradition culminating in Firdawsī's verse *Shāhnāma*. Balʿamī translated al-Ṭabarī. During the ensuing period translations and imitations of histories written in Arabic, such as ʿUtbī's (d. 427 or 31/1036 or 40) *Taʾrīkh al-Yamīnī*, a history of the Ghaznavids, dominated the field. This coincided with the rise of a new Persian literary language, in which historians began writing original narratives. Abū al-Faḍl Bayhaqī (d. 470/1077) was a key figure and his *Mujalladāt* (Voluminous [history]) set a model for dynastic history. Bayhaqī's work showed the influence of his Arabic counterparts, such as Miskawayh, but also revealed Persian characteristics. From the surviving portion of the work, which covers the reign of Masʿūd, hence the title *Taʾrīkh-i Masʿūdī*, some marked features – the religio-moral dimension, the use of digressions (flashbacks and inserted anecdotes) and the indifference to the indigenous traditions – all reveal his Islamic project, with a strong Shīʿite undertone.[17] This Islamic perspective with a regional focus continued to be cultivated by other Ghaznavid historians, in Gardīzī's earlier *Zayn al-akhbār*, a history of Persia with special references to Khurāsān, and the anonymous *Tārīkh-i Sīstān*.

As for Saljūq history-writing, 'mirrors for princes' overshadowed the *taʾrīkh* genre. The *Siyāsatnāma* by Niẓām al-Mulk (d. 485/1092), who attempted to organise the Turko-Saljūq administration after the Persianate Ghaznavid manner, was one such 'mirror'. Essentially a handbook, it demonstrated the uses of history and the connection between historical, ethical and political thought. The idealised picture of the ruler was a recurrent theme in the dynastic histories of the Saljūq era. Among these were the *Fārsnāma* of Ibn al-Balkhī; the anonymous *Mujmal al-tavārīkh va-al-qiṣaṣ*, a textbook; Nīshāpūrī's (d. 582/1187) *Saljūqnāma*, which chronicled the twilight years of the regime; Rāvandī's lavish and encyclopaedic *Rāḥat al-ṣudūr wa-āyat al-surūr*, whose history section is replete with panegyrics of the Saljūq ruler. Jarbādhqānī's Persian treatment of ʿUtbī's *Taʾrīkh* was more telling. Like

16 Julie Meisami, *Persian historiography to the end of the twelfth century* (Edinburgh, 1999).
17 Marilyn Waldman, *Toward a theory of historical narrative: A case study in Perso-Islamicate historiography* (Columbus, 1980).

Balʿamī's translation of al-Ṭabarī, Jarbādhqānī's was more than a translation. By updating ʿUtbī and manipulating the wording, Jarbādhqānī's work is intricately intertextual: it is a history of the Ghaznavids, but one that alludes to the Saljūqs as ideal rulers. Ibn Funduq's (d. *c.* 565/1169) *Tārīkh-i Bayhaqī*, which focused on the learned men from Bayhaq, was something different. It also demonstrated a sophisticated bilingualism, with its eloquent and flowing Persian style together with heavy mixture of Arabic.

Features of Persian chronicle writing were already established in pre-Mongol works, chief among them the *dībāchah* (preface) and *khātima* (conclusion), that contained information about the purpose, method and sources. Other elements paralleled the development in Arabic counterparts: thematic presentation of a chronicle, supplemented by various interpolations. In terms of language and style, rhyming prose (*sajʿ*), inspired by chancery Arabic writing of the ʿAbbāsid era, was common.

The Mongol and post-Mongol phase

The wide horizons were explored under Mongol patronage in what was the golden age of Persian historiography. The importance of Persian sources for the history of the Mongol empire has long been acknowledged. The standard-bearers were Jūzjānī (*fl.* 1260), whose *Ṭabaqāt-i Nāṣirī* is a dynastic history of the Ghūrids of Afghanistan; Juwaynī (d. 681/1283), whose *Tārīkh-i Jahāngushāy* (The history of the world conqueror, i.e. Chinggis Khān) covered the history of the Mongol empire; Rashīd al-Dīn (d. 718/1318), whose *Jāmiʿ al-tawārīkh* was a wide-ranging 'world history'; and Waṣṣāf (*fl.* 698–723/1299–1323), whose *Taʾrīkh-i Waṣṣāf* was meant to be a continuation of Juwaynī's work, but ranged far and wide.[18]

The history of the Tīmūrid dynasty was extensively covered in Arabic, Persian and Ottoman Turkish. Numerous official histories were produced under the Tīmūrid princes. The conquests of Tīmūr provided the main subject of ʿAlī al-Shāmī (d. before 814/1411), Naṭanzī (*fl.* 818/1415), Ḥāfiẓ-i Abrū (d. 833/1430), ʿAlī Yazdī (d. 858/1454) and Ibn ʿArabshāh (d. 854/1450). Pretensions to Islamic universality were expressed in Ḥāfiẓ-i Abrū's *Zubdat al-tawārīkh*, Khwandamīr's (d. *c.* 941/1535) *Ḥabīb al-siyar fī akhbār afrād al-bashar* and ʿAbd al-Razzāq Samarqandī's (d. 887/1482) *Maṭlaʿ-i Saʿdayn*.[19]

18 David Morgan, 'Persian historians and the Mongols', in David Morgan (ed.), *Medieval historical writing in the Christian and Islamic worlds* (London, 1982).
19 John Woods, 'The rise of Timurid historiography', *JNES*, 46 (1987).

Under the Ṣafavids Persian historical writing continued to flourish, and included the method of 'imitative writings'. Ṣafavid historians based their histories on certain models, using certain conventional elements, while making changes over time to reflect current dynastic ideology. There was also a high literary tradition that followed the model of Mirkhvand (d. 903/1498), in his *Rawżat al-ṣafā*, which adopted the Tīmūrid trend of ornate prose. Later 'invented tradition' featured dramatisation, invented speech and deeds and predictive dreams. Iranian elements also stand out, such as the use of numerical symbolism (the *abjad* system) and the involvement of court astrologers in writing chronicles, in the case of Yazdī's *Ta'rīkh-i 'Abbāsī*.[20]

Indo-Muslim historical writing

Medieval Indian history writing effectively began with the Muslims. The early authors were all working with the didactic religious framework. Amīr Khusraw (d. 725/1325) was a court poet famous for his historical poems. The *Futūḥ al-salāṭīn* by 'Iṣāmī (completed in 750/1349) was modelled after the *Shāhnāma*. Rich in information and artistry, their value for historical inquiry has been disputed. Chronicles written in prose began to be produced soon after. The *Ta'rīkh-i-Fīrūz Shāhī* by Baranī (completed in 758/1357) and Sirāj 'Afīf (completed before 801/1399) respectively, and the *Ta'rīkh-i-Mubārak Shāhī* by Yaḥyā Sīrhindī (completed around 831/1428) are royal biographies-cum-dynastic chronicles of the Delhi sultanate.[21]

History writing was a cultural exercise at the Mughal court. Persian-speaking rulers were chroniclers of their own time, among them Bābur (r. 932–7/1526–30), the founder of the dynasty who wrote the *Bāburnāma* in Chaghatay Turkish, and his son Humāyūn (r. 937–47/1530–40 and 962–3/1555–6). The best known of the Mughal historians, Abū al-Fażl ibn Mubārak, flourished in the reign of Akbar ibn Humāyūn (r. 964–1014/1556–1605) and his *Akbarnāma* covered the later Mughal period.

History writing in the Islamic world, as it evolved, acquired distinctive purposes and narrative features. These determined the nature of chronicles – collections of human-interest stories purporting to contain some factual truth with fixed dates – which, in turn, goes a long way to explain why in most respects we know so little about past Islamic cultures. The limitations of the chronicle sources are obvious: little can be learned about economy; virtually

20 Sholeh A. Quinn, *Historical writing during the reign of Shah 'Abbas: Ideology, imitation, and legitimacy in Safavid chronicles* (Salt Lake City, 2000).

21 Peter Hardy, *Historians of Medieval India: Studies in Indo-Muslim historical writing* (London, 1997).

nothing about Everyman, women and children, let alone domestic life and community.[22] Moreover, problems arise when historians used literary, even fictional devices in their chronicles. Given the imperfect match between 'what really happened' and 'what was meant to be told', there is still much that needs to be investigated. The quality of chronicles may frustrate modern students; but in terms of their primary function – constructing meaningful narratives to educate, inspire and entertain – they worked quite well.

22 Stephen Humphreys, *Islamic history: A framework for inquiry* (Princeton, 1991).

18

Biographical literature

MICHAEL COOPERSON

Terms and definitions

Much of the so-called biographical literature in classical Arabic, Persian and Turkic has little in common with modern biography. Most of the pre-modern examples consist of short entries collected together in so-called biographical dictionaries. To modern readers such entries seem oddly uninformative. An entry on a poet, for example, may contain extensive citations of his or her verses, but practically nothing about his life. An entry on a jurist, similarly, will list his teachers and students, his works and his date of death; but it will not report his reasons for embarking upon the study of the law, or attempt to account for his professional successes and failures by referring to his quirks of personality. Because of these differences, some modern scholars refer to entries in collective works as 'prosopography', reserving the term 'biography' only for stand-alone works devoted to a single subject. Yet even the biographies proper display little interest in how the subject 'came to be who he was'.[1] His character is tacitly assumed to be fixed, and the succession of anecdotes merely displays it from different points of view.

Pre-modern authors do not use any term that corresponds exactly to 'biography'. Unlike such Greek terms as *musike* and *geografia*, *biografia* never found its way into the classical Islamic languages as the designation of an activity or a discipline. (The borrowed term does, however, exist in modern Arabic, Persian and Turkish – as *biyūghrāfiya*, *biyūgrāfī* and *biyoğrafi* respectively – where it is commonly used to designate works written on the now-naturalised Western model.) In classical Arabic, texts that foreground the human subject were called *tarjama* (entry) or *sīra* (stand-alone single-subject

1 Chase F. Robinson, *Islamic historiography* (Cambridge, 2003), p. 61.

biography), among another things.[2] In Persian, a text about a person was called *sharḥ-i aḥwāl* and in Ottoman Turkish *tarjame-ye ḥāl*, both terms meaning roughly 'account of circumstances'; or, in both languages, *tadhkira*, meaning 'document' or 'memoir', a term also applied to a collection of entries.[3] Generically, the texts that belong to all these categories were commonly understood as constituting a branch of *ta'rīkh*, 'writing about datable events' or, more broadly, 'history'.[4]

In applying the term 'biography' to the pre-modern corpus, twentieth-century Western scholars enabled themselves to complain that the texts in question fail to resemble the productions of Plutarch and Suetonius.[5] That pre-modern accounts of individuals in Arabic, Persian and Turkic differ from their Greek and Roman counterparts is indisputable. Whether this difference constitutes a failure is a question that has come to be addressed – and finally dismissed as a distraction – only in the last half-century of Western scholarship. Taking advantage of the documentary element of the corpus, historians now use it regularly as a source for social and intellectual history.[6] Meanwhile, literary critics have learned to analyse it in terms of its own conventions of production and reception.[7] In all these ways modern scholarship has dispelled some of the confusion created by applying the term 'biography' to

2 For surveys see M. J. L. Young, 'Arabic biographical writing', in M. J. L. Young, J. D. Latham and R. B. Sergeant (eds.), *The Cambridge history of Arabic literature*, vol. III: *Religion, learning, and science in the Abbasid period* (Cambridge, 1990); Robinson, *Islamic historiography*, pp. 61–74.

3 For surveys see Felix Tauer, 'History and biography', in Jan Rypka *et al.*, *History of Iranian literature* (Dordrecht, 1968), esp. pp. 449ff.; J. T. P. de Bruijn, 'Tadhkira (in Persian literature)', *EI2*, vol. X, pp. 53–4; J. Stewart-Robinson, 'The Ottoman biographies of poets', *JNES*, 24 (1965); J. Stewart-Robinson, 'Tadhkira (in Turkish literature)', *EI2*, vol. X, pp. 54–5.

4 Even here the terms are fluid: the so-called guidelines for writing history (*adab al-mu'arrikh*) attributed by al-Subkī (d. 771 / 1370) to his father are actually instructions for writing biographies. See Tāj al-Dīn al-Subkī, *Ṭabaqāt al-Shafiʿīya al-kubrā*, ed. Maḥmūd al-Ṭanāḥī and 'Abd al-Fattāḥ al-Ḥulw, 10 vols. (Cairo, 1964–76), vol. II, pp. 22–5; trans. in Franz Rosenthal, *A history of Muslim historiography*, 2nd rev. edn (Leiden, 1964), p. 372.

5 See, for example, Gustave E. von Grunebaum, *Medieval Islam* (Chicago, 1946), pp. 221ff.

6 For a survey see R. Stephen Humphreys, *Islamic history: A framework for inquiry* (Princeton, 1991), pp. 187–208.

7 For example, Fedwa Malti-Douglas, 'Controversy and its effects in the biographical tradition of al-Khaṭīb al-Baghdādī', *SI*, 46 (1977); Hartmut Fähndrich, 'The *Wafayāt al-aʿyān* of Ibn Khallikān: A new approach', *JAOS*, 93, 4 (1973); Reinhard Eisener, *Zwischen Faktum und Fiktion: Eine Studie zum Umayyedenkalifen Sulaimān b. 'Abdalmalik und seinem Bild in den Quellen* (Wiesbaden, 1987); T. Emil Homerin, *From Arab poet to Muslim saint: Ibn al-Fāriḍ, his verse, and his shrine* (Columbia, SC, 1994); Denise A. Spellberg, *Politics, gender, and the Islamic past: The Legacy of ʿĀisha bint Abī Bakr* (New York, 1994); Michael Cooperson, 'Classical Arabic biography', in Beatrice Gruendler and Verena Klemm (eds.), *Understanding Near Eastern literatures: A spectrum of interdisciplinary approaches* (Wiesbaden, 2000).

pre-modern Arabic, Persian and Turkic texts. Nevertheless, it should be remembered that the term is, at best, a convenience.

To better understand pre-modern biographical writing, it is helpful to recall that its primary purpose was often to place individuals within a genealogy of authority and a network of simultaneous relationships. This project certainly permitted an account of individual personality. However, it did not require one. Thus, it was possible to write a 'biographical dictionary' consisting of a list of names. The topic of the work and the ordering of the names – for example, Mālikī jurists active in a particular town, arranged in roughly chronological order – would supply enough context to allow the reader to appreciate what he was looking at: a list of persons who had participated in the transmission of vital knowledge in an unbroken sequence that reached back through the generations to Mālik ibn Anas (d. 179/796), and from him to the Prophet Muḥammad and ultimately to God. For living members of the fraternity, the biographical dictionary documented their claim to be able to tell their fellow Muslims the difference between right and wrong.

Arguably, then, biography served as a documentary archive and a token of authority rather than a literary genre. Nevertheless, Muslim scholars of the seventh/thirteenth century and afterwards speak of such texts as a source of readerly pleasure. The biographer Yāqūt al-Ḥamawī (d. 626/1229), for example, describes himself as seeking out 'accounts of scholars and men of letters ... like one enamored and impassioned, searching as a lover searches for his beloved'.[8] His successor Ibn Khallikān (d. 681/1282), similarly, admits to 'seeking out accounts about, and death dates of, worthy men of the past' with mounting ardour: 'The more material I collected, the more of it I sought.'[9] This self-awareness on the part of biographers culminates in the majestic peroration by al-Ṣafadī (d. 764/1362), who credits the genre with supplying a vision of the resurrected dead:

> The reader familiar with tales of people now dead, with the feats of those plunged into the cavern of extinction never to emerge, with the lore of those who scaled the heights of power, and with the virtues of those whom Providence delivered from the stranglehold of adversity, feels that he has known such men in their own time. He seems to join them on their pillowed thrones and lean companionably with them on their cushioned couches. He gazes into their faces – some framed in hoods, others lambent under helmets – seeing in the evil ones the demonic spark, and in the good ones the virtue that

8 Yāqūt, *Muʿjam al-udabāʾ*, 5 vols. (Beirut, 1991), vol. I, p. 27.

9 Ibn Khallikān, *Wafayāt al-aʿyān*, ed. Iḥsān ʿAbbās, 8 vols. (Beirut, 1968–72), vol. I, pp. 19–20.

> places them in the company of angels. He seems to share with them the best pressings of aged wine in an age where time no longer presses, and to behold them as in their battles they breathe the sweet scent of swordplay in the shadows of tall and bloodstained lances. It is as if all that company were of his own age and time; as if those who grieve him were his enemies, and those who give him pleasure, his friends. But they have ridden in the vanguard long before him, while he walks in the rear-guard far behind.[10]

Fortunately for the literary historian, al-Ṣafadī also provides a more prosaic definition of the genre. Chronicles, he says, narrate events year by year and thus convey information about persons only in a scattered and incidental fashion. Biographical entries, on the other hand, bring together all the information known about a particular person regardless of the year in which a particular event may have occurred.[11] This definition may be taken as the minimal formal characterisation of pre-modern biographical writing. Yet, as the comments of al-Ṣafadī and his colleagues suggest, the genre could achieve literary effects of the highest order.

Genealogies and charter myths

The minimal unit of biographical discourse is the name. In Arabic, names conventionally take the form 'so-and-so the son or daughter of so-and-so': that is, they contain a genealogical component. Commonly, too, they include a teknonym: 'father or mother of so-and-so'. Sometimes, they also include a cognomen: 'the wandering king', 'the one with the kitten', 'the pop-eyed'. Cited in full, a person's name is therefore a capsule biography. Many pre-modern Islamic biographical entries consist solely of names, and many others consist of names supplemented by a few words of commentary. Even standalone biographies begin with the citation of a full name that represents their subject as part of a group. The biographies of the Prophet Muḥammad, for example, begin with genealogies that trace his lineage through the ancient prophets all the way back to Adam. In a sense, genealogy is the essence of biography; all the rest is commentary.

Although tribal genealogies were often a matter of assertion and negotiation rather than biological fact, they did constitute a framework within which scribal culture could convey information about individuals. An even more

10 al-Ṣafadī, *al-Wāfī bi al-wafayāt*, ed. Helmut Ritter, Sven Dedering, Iḥsān 'Abbās *et al.*, 30 vols. (Leipzig, 1931–2004), vol. I, p. 4.
11 Ibid., p. 42.

powerful framework was that of figurative genealogy: that is, membership in an intellectual or spiritual line of descent. Among the earliest biographies in Arabic are those devoted to a single class (*ṭāʾifa*, pl. *ṭawāʾif*) of persons. According to the listings compiled by al-Dhahabī (d. 748/1348), al-Ṣafadī and al-Suyūṭī (d. 911/1505), the subjects of *siyar* and *tarājim* have included prophets, Companions of Muḥammad, readers and interpreters of the Qurʾān, transmitters of *ḥadīth*, legal theorists and jurisconsults, ascetics and mystics, calculators of inheritances, rhetoricians, judges, caliphs, viziers, preachers, physicians, astronomers, grammarians, theologians, poets, prose writers, lovers, gamblers and lunatics.[12] Admittedly, most of the surviving works are devoted to religious scholars, primarily *ḥadīth* transmitters and jurists. But entries on persons of all the classes mentioned can indeed be found somewhere, though not always in works devoted exclusively to persons of that class. Finally, it should be noted that a great many classes of people – for example, prayer callers, midwives and rubbish collectors – were never commemorated at all.

Commonly, works devoted to members of a scholarly *ṭāʾifa* begin with an entry on a foundational figure from whom knowledge 'has been transmitted from one generation to another'.[13] The entry on each subsequent figure lists his teachers and students and thus establishes his place in a lineage whose authority derives ultimately from that of the founder. Biographical collections dealing with grammarians, for example, credit ʿAlī ibn Abī Ṭālib with the discovery that language is susceptible to systematic description. ʿAlī is then represented as conveying this insight to Abū al-Aswad al-Duʾalī, who transmitted it to the first generation of grammarians.[14] The second generation is described as having studied with the first, and so on down to the time of the biographer, who is usually a grammarian himself.[15]

The most coveted founder was the Prophet, who stands – along with a transitional figure – at the head of several figurative lines of descent.

12 Al-Dhahabī in al-Sakhāwī, *al-Iʿlān bi-tawbīkh li-man dhamma ahl al-taʾrīkh*, ed. Franz Rosenthal (Baghdad, 1963), pp. 84–6, trans. in Rosenthal, *History*, pp. 388–91; al-Ṣafadī, *Wāfī*, vol. I, pp. 51–5; al-Suyūṭī, *Taʾrīkh al-khulafāʾ*, ed. Muḥyī al-Dīn ʿAbd al-Ḥamīd (Cairo, 1952), p. 1; and further Michael Cooperson, *Classical Arabic biography: The heirs of the prophets in the age of al-Maʾmūn* (Cambridge, 2000), pp. 13ff.

13 Al-Yaghmurī, *Nūr al-qabas al-mukhtaṣar min al-muqtabas fī akhbār al-nuḥāh wa al-udabāʾ wa al-shuʿarāʾ wa al-ʿulamāʾ*, ed. Rudolf Sellheim (Wiesbaden, 1964), p. 87.

14 Ibid., pp. 4–5; Ibn al-Anbārī, *Nuzhat al-alibbāʾ fī ṭabaqāt al-udabāʾ*, ed. ʿA. ʿĀmir (Stockholm, 1963), pp. 4–7.

15 See Cooperson, *Classical Arabic biography*, pp. 11–13; and further Monique Bernards, *Changing traditions: al-Mubarrad's refutation of Sībawayh and the subsequent reception of the* Kitāb (Leiden, 1997).

Biographers of *ḥadīth* scholars, for example, represent him as the source of *ḥadīth* reports and his Companions as the first to transmit them. Biographers of caliphs, similarly, present them as the successors of the Prophet through Abū Bakr. In biographies of the Shīʿite imams the transitional figure is ʿAlī, Muḥammad's cousin, son-in-law and appointed successor. In some cases, such as that of Sufi biography, the Prophet is invoked only to the extent that his *ḥadīths* are cited in defence of the group's characteristic activity. As the various intellectual traditions matured biographers often found it sufficient to trace the collective ancestry back to a more recent figure whose exemplification of the Prophet's *sunna* is taken for granted. Biographers of Sunnī jurists, for example, begin with an entry on the founder of the *madhhab* (legal school), whom they represent as the teacher of all the members of the first generation of jurists. A biography of the jurist Abū Ḥanīfa (d. 150/767) quotes one of his followers as saying: 'Knowledge has passed from God Almighty to Muḥammad, from him to his Companions, from them to the Successors, and from them to Abū Ḥanīfa and his disciples. If you accept this, be content with it; if you don't, too bad for you.'[16]

The authors of collective biographies present themselves as documenting historical fact. In reality they are constructing a history of their community, a process that necessarily involves revisionism and back-projection, if not outright fabrication. In the third/ninth century, for example, there were no schools of law; there were merely communities of like-minded jurists associated with particular teachers or regions. In the biographical collections devoted to jurists, however, we are given the impression that the Shāfiʿī school of law (for example) came into being with al-Shāfiʿī (d. 204/820), who transmitted its precepts to his faithful band of disciples. His teachings, moreover, are represented as including everything later taught by any member of his school. In reality, of course, the so-called *madhhab al-Shāfiʿī* developed over time and only later came to attribute all of its insights to a putative founder. The Shāfiʿī dictionaries do not simply record the results of this process of revisionism. Rather, they are among the interventions that enabled the process to take place. In the case of the legal schools, modern scholarship has only recently begun to correct for the distortions introduced by biographers.[17] In other cases the construction of a 'charter myth' is more

16 al-Khaṭīb al-Baghdādī, *Ta'rīkh Baghdād*, ed. ʿAbd al-Qādir ʿAṭā, 20 vols. (Beirut, 1997), vol. XIII, p. 336. On the dispute over the jurist's reputation see Eerick Dickinson, 'Aḥmad b. al-Ṣalt and his biography of Abū Ḥanīfa', *JAOS*, 116, 3 (1996).

17 See Christopher Melchert, *The formation of the Sunni schools of law, 9th–10th centuries CE* (Leiden, 1997).

obvious, as when, for example, a biographer of scientists traces the community's origins to the prophet Enoch, 'the first to teach mathematics, logic, physics and theology'.[18]

In later periods the structural role of the figurative genealogy fades or disappears altogether. In biographical dictionaries devoted to people of different *ṭawāʾif* who lived in a single town, the position normally occupied by the founder is occupied instead by a description of the town. For example, al-Khaṭīb's fifth/eleventh-century biographical dictionary *Taʾrīkh Baghdād* (History of Baghdad) begins with a detailed topography of the ʿAbbāsid capital.[19] The centennial dictionaries of the ninth/fifteenth century and afterwards, which are devoted to notables of all sorts who died during a particular hundred-year period, do not begin with a founder. They do, nevertheless, assume the generational scheme characteristic of the earlier collective works. Finally, the massive biographical dictionaries that include nearly everyone of importance often begin with a discussion of biography itself. It is in the introductions to such works that nearly all of the self-conscious statements about the genre are to be found.

The form and content of the entry

Given their intended purpose, individual entries in works of collective biography often have little meaning on their own. Rather, their significance derives from their place in a figurative genealogy. Here, for example, is an entry from a third/ninth-century Arabic work on *ḥadīth* transmitters:

> Hind bint al-Ḥārith al-Firāsiyya. She was old enough to have met the wives of the Prophet. She heard *ḥadīth* from Umm Salama and recited it on the authority of Ṣafiyya bint ʿAbd al-Muṭṭalib. Al-Zuhrī recited on her authority.[20]

For its original readers, this entry indicated that Hind had heard certain accounts of the Prophet's words and deeds from Umm Salama, presumably a reliable source. Hind then passed those accounts on to others, including al-Zuhrī (d. 124/742), who later came to be reckoned an exclusive authority for many reports. Before the compilation of comprehensive and authenticated collections of *ḥadīth* in written form this process of transmission was the community's only way of knowing what the Prophet had said and done. The transmitters were thus 'the only heirs of the prophets', as Muḥammad

18 Ibn al-Qifṭī, *Taʾrīkh al-ḥukamāʾ*, ed. Julius Lippert (Leipzig, 1903), p. 1.
19 al-Khaṭīb al-Baghdādī, *Taʾrīkh Baghdād*, vol. I, pp. 34–138.
20 Ibn Saʿd, *al-Ṭabaqāt al-kubrā*, ed. Riyāḍ ʿAbd al-Hādī, 8 parts in 4 (Beirut, 1996), no. 4658.

himself was supposed to have said.[21] For those who believed that the *sunna* had the power to 'guide the errant, warn against perdition' and 'save the ignorant and the damned'[22] the process of *ḥadīth* transmission was a matter of compelling interest. Even after the *ḥadīth* itself was committed to writing biographers continued to make lists of transmitters, often adding explicit assessments of each one's trustworthiness.[23]

As this account suggests, entries in biographical dictionaries could serve their intended purpose while containing relatively little information about the subject's life. Most biographers, however, were unable to resist characterising their subjects in some way, or supplementing the entry with historical accounts (*akhbār*) associated with them. One *ḥadīth* biographer, for example, lets it slip out that a certain transmitter was 'a harsh and ill-natured man, but he knew the *sunna*'.[24] Another biographer of *ḥadīth* transmitters occasionally produces entries that have nothing to do with transmission at all, like the following:

> Al-Walīd ibn ʿUqba ibn Muʿīṭ ibn Abī ʿAmr ibn Umayya ibn ʿAbd Shams. He was known as Abū Wahb. His mother was Arwā daughter of Kurayz ibn Ḥabīb ibn ʿAbd Shams. He was the half-brother of [the third caliph] ʿUthmān ibn ʿAffān on the mother's side. When ʿUthmān appointed him governor of Kūfa, he built a large residence next to the mosque. Then ʿUthmān recalled him, replacing him with Saʿīd ibn al-ʿĀṣ, so he returned to Medina and stayed there until ʿUthmān was assassinated. When the civil war between ʿAlī and Muʿāwiya broke out, al-Walīd refused to take sides; he went to al-Raqqa and secluded himself there until the conflict was over. He died in al-Raqqa, and some of his descendants still live there; he also has descendants in Kūfa. The house he built in Kūfa is the big one called the House of the Cloth-Fullers.[25]

Instead of describing *ḥadīth* activity this entry focuses on an issue of equal importance: how prominent believers of the first generations responded to the civil wars that divided the community. It also contains apparently trivial detail, such as the subject's home address. In other collections, such as those on grammarians, jurists and the like, we find similar digressions, often intended

21 A. J. A. Wensinck *et al.* (eds.), *Concordance et indices de la tradition musulmane*, 8 vols. (Leiden, 1933–88), vol. IV, p. 321.

22 Ibn Ḥanbal, cited in Ibn al-Jawzī, *Manāqib al-imām Aḥmad Ibn Ḥanbal* (Cairo, 1930), p. 167.

23 For more extended analyses of seemingly opaque entries see Humphreys, *Islamic history*, pp. 190–2, and Robinson, *Islamic historiography*, pp. 70–2.

24 al-ʿIjlī, cited in Miklos Muranyi, 'Zur Entwicklung der *ʿilm al-riǧāl*-Literatur im 3. Jahrhundert d. H. Qairawāner Miszellaneen IV', *ZDMG*, 142, 1 (1992), at p. 61.

25 Ibn Saʿd, *Ṭabaqāt*, no. 1848.

to illustrate the subject's excellence in a particular field, to clear him of accusations levelled against him by his detractors, or simply because – as one biographer of poets told his readers – the mere recitation of a name conveys little unless accompanied by 'a tale, a historical account, a genealogy, an anecdote or a verse deemed good or unusual'.[26]

Modification of the charter myth and expansion of entries

Like all constructed histories, the charter myths of the various *ṭawā'if* were subject to change over time. For example, the first biographer of the Sufi *ṭā'ifa*, al-Sulamī (d. 412/1021), divided the community's history into two parts. The first was that of the early pietists, the subject of his *Ṭabaqāt al-nussāk* (The generations of ascetics), and the second that of the later mystics, the subject of his *Ṭabaqāt al-ṣūfiyya* (The generations of Sufis). The titles of these works and the distribution of entries between them amount to an argument that mysticism had developed out of asceticism, as indeed seems plausible historically. But al-Sulamī's student Abū Nuʿaym (d. 430/1038) abandoned this carefully constructed history of Sufism, deciding instead that mystical impulse had existed since the time of the Prophet. His massive *Ḥilyat al-awliyā'* (Ornament of the saints) accordingly depicts men from all periods and walks of life as Sufis. He describes the literalist *ḥadīth* scholar Ibn Ḥanbal (d. 241/855), for example, as 'teaching the renunciants' and 'cultivating anxiety and preoccupation', both of which he did in fact do, but then adds that 'Sufism means polishing oneself with stains, and embellishing oneself with pains', the implication being that Ibn Ḥanbal was a Sufi whether he knew it or not.[27]

In this particular case, the expansion of the charter myth provoked an angry reaction and a new round of biography writing. Irritated by Abū Nuʿaym's loose and baggy definition of Sufism, the Ḥanbalī preacher and historian Ibn al-Jawzī (d. 597/1201) declared that the Prophet and a number of believers in every age were ascetics, and some of the latter may have been Sufis. But to speak of every ascetic Muslim as a Sufi is a gratuitous misrepresentation.

26 Ibn Qutayba, *al-Shiʿr wa-al-shuʿarā'*, ed. Aḥmad Muḥammad Shākir, 2 vols. (Cairo, 1966), vol. I, pp. 59–60. On the biographies of poets see further Stefan Leder, 'Frühe Erzählungen zu Mağūn. Mağūn als Figur ohne Lebensgeschichte', in W. Diem and A. Falaturi (eds.), *XXIV Deutscher Orientalistentag (1988)* (Stuttgart, 1990); and Hilary Kilpatrick, *Making the great Book of songs: Compilation and the author's craft in Abū l-Faraj al-Iṣbahānī's* Kitāb al-aghānī (London, 2003).

27 Abū Nuʿaym al-Iṣfahānī, *Ḥilyat al-awliyā'*, 10 vols. (Cairo, 1932–8; repr. Beirut, n.d.), vol. IX, p. 174.

Moreover, he says, Abū Nuʿaym was a bad biographer. A biographical entry should contain only reports about the subject, not reports about other people which the subject happened to have transmitted, but Abū Nuʿaym includes many reports of the second type. He also includes miracle stories, such as reports of levitation, which may lead impressionable readers to injure themselves by trying the same thing at home. Finally, no catalogue of saints should omit women. Al-Sulamī, the first Sufi biographer, had devoted a whole volume to them, but Abū Nuʿaym neglects them entirely.[28] To rectify these errors Ibn al-Jawzī compiled his own dictionary of saints, the *Ṣifat al-ṣafwa* (Description of the pure elite), which, despite adding numerous entries on women, is less than half the size of Abū Nuʿaym's.

Although many biographers were impressively scrupulous in transmitting older accounts, others preferred to expand and develop the material available to them. This expansion is nowhere more evident than in the transition from Arabic to Persian. The early Arabic biographies of the ascetic Bishr ibn al-Ḥārith (d. 227/842), for example, do not explain the source of his nickname al-Ḥāfī, 'the barefoot'. In the Persian *Kashf al-maḥjūb* (Revelation of the hidden) the biographer Hujwīrī (d. 465/1072) insists on a mystical interpretation of Bishr's behaviour, declaring that he was so intensely absorbed in the contemplation of God that he never put anything on his feet: 'A shoe seemed to him a veil between himself and God'.[29] A later Persian source, the *Tadhkirat al-awliyā*ʾ (Memorial of the saints) of ʿAṭṭār (d. 617/1220) goes even further. Bishr, we are told, was drinking in a tavern when a holy man came in bearing a message from God. Moved to repentance, Bishr fled the tavern without putting on his shoes, and remained barefoot for the rest of his life.[30] These elaborations, for which parallels exist in the biographies of many pious early Muslims, tell us nothing about the historical Bishr. Rather, they illustrate the ways in which the lives of past exemplars were made meaningful to new generations of readers. Eventually this process resulted in biographies that bore little or no relation to historical fact, but were nonetheless powerful affirmations of spiritual discipleship and collective identity.[31] Readers from

28 Ibn al-Jawzī, *Ṣifat al-ṣafwa*, 2 vols. (Hyderabad, 1936–8), vol. I, pp. 2ff. Al-Sulamī made women the subject of a separate work, *Dhikr al-niswa al-mutaʿabbidāt al-ṣūfiyāt*, ed. and trans. Rkia Elaroui Cornell as *Early Sufi women* (Louisville, 1999).

29 al-Hujwīrī, *The 'Kashf al-mahjūb', the oldest Persian treatise on Sufism*, trans. Reynold A. Nicholson, Gibb Memorial Series 17 (London, 1936 (repr.)), p. 105.

30 ʿAṭṭār, *Tadhkirat al-awliyā*ʾ, ed. R. A. Nicholson, 2 vols. (London, 1905), vol. I, p. 107; see further Maher Jarrār, 'Bišr und die Barfüssigkeit in Islam', *Der Islam*, 71 (1994); Cooperson, *Classical Arabic biography*, pp. 154–87.

31 See further J. A. Mojaddedi, *The biographical tradition in Sufism: The* ṭabaqāt *genre from al-Sulamī to Jāmī* (Richmond, 2001).

Konya, for example, could hardly fail to respond to the following passage from Aflākī's Persian biography of the mystic poet Jalāl al-Dīn Rūmī (d. 672/1273):

> After Jalāl's death, Kīgātū Khān, a Mogul general, came up against Konya, intending to sack the city and massacre its inhabitants. That night in a dream, he saw Jalāl, who seized him by the throat and nearly choked him, saying to him: 'Konya is mine. What seekest thou from its people?'[32]

Some biographers were reluctant to include stories involving supernatural events, in some cases denouncing their colleagues for including them. For the most part, however, authors and readers alike appear to have understood that biographical reports, like *ḥadīth*, came in different degrees of probability and served different purposes. Thus, dream-tales, which could not be confirmed by independent witnesses, were included not for their historical value but rather for their ability to 'cheer the heart of the believer'.[33]

Single-subject biographies

Two sub-genres of biography appear anomalous, at least from the perspective of the genealogical model. The first of these is the stand-alone, single-subject biography. This sub-genre owes its existence to the early appearance and widespread popularity of the Prophetic *sīra*, the first extant versions of which date to the second/eighth century. As we have seen, even Muḥammad does not entirely escape the genealogical model: the *sīra* begins by placing him in a line of prophetic succession that begins with Adam. Unusually, however, even the earliest biographies of the Prophet aim for complete coverage of his life from birth to death, with the relevant reports arranged in chronological order. In the following passage, al-Samawʾal al-Maghribī (d. *c*. 570/1175), a physician and mathematician, describes the experience of reading the *siyar*:

> In these history books there passed before me accounts of the Prophet – God's prayer and blessing be upon him – his conquests, the miracles God had performed for him, and the wonders he was given to work; the divine victory and help which were granted him in the battles of Badr, Khaybar, and others; the story of his beginnings in orphanhood and wretchedness; the animosity of his own people toward him while he stood up to his adversaries over a period

32 Aflākī, *Manāqib al-ʿārifīn*, trans. James W. Redhouse as *Legends of the Sufis*, 3rd edn (London, 1976), p. 88 (transliteration modified).

33 See M. Cooperson, 'Probability, plausibility, and "spiritual communication" in classical Arabic biography', in Philip F. Kennedy (ed.), *On fiction and* adab *in medieval Arabic literature* (Wiesbaden, 2005). The citation is from Shams al-Dīn al-Dhahabī, *Siyar aʿlām al-nubalāʾ*, vol. XI, ed. Ṣāliḥ al-Samr (Beirut, 1304/1982), p. 353.

> of many years, rejecting their faith openly and calling them to his own, until God permitted him to migrate to Medina; what calamities befell his enemies, who were slain before him by the swords of his supporters at Badr and elsewhere.[34]

After reading the *sīra* al-Samaw'al was visited by the Prophet in a dream, and soon after converted from Judaism to Islam. His description of his experience as a reader of biography is one of the few such accounts to be found in the pre-modern sources.

Modern scholarship has discerned at least three layers of narrative and other material in the *sīra*: memories, more or less well preserved, dating back to the time of the Prophet; legendary and polemical elaborations dating back to the first generations of Islam; and a final set of modifications reflecting the pro-ʿAbbāsid milieu of the compilers.[35] The legendary element, present even in the earliest versions, increased with the passage of time. For modern historians the later *siyar* are therefore useful only as a guide to the image of the Prophet in the minds of the faithful. For pre-modern Muslims, however, the composition of *siyar* seems to have been both an act of piety and a scholarly rite of passage. The tradition was trans-regional and multilingual: a list of the most popular versions includes both *al-Shifāʾ* (The remedy) by al-Qāḍī ʿIyāḍ (d. 544/1149), written in Arabic in al-Andalus, and the *Madārij al-nubuwwa* (The stages of prophethood) by ʿAbd al-Ḥaqq Dihlavī (d. 1052/1642), written in Persian in India.

Although the Prophet was the first and most popular subject of stand-alone biographies, he was not the only one. Prominent scholars such as Ibn Ḥanbal and al-Shāfiʿī, Shīʿite imams such as ʿAlī al-Riḍā and rulers such as Saladin and Baybars also inspired (or, in the case of rulers, sometimes merely paid for) independent works, called *sīra* or *manāqib* ('virtues') devoted to the commemoration of their careers. This treatment of character permits the occasional deployment of non-chronological forms of exposition, including thematic chapters on the subject's personal habits, for example, or his legal opinions. To the *sīra* writers' credit, their expositions sometimes contain enough detail to permit modern readers to discern a trajectory of character development. But such trajectories are never the point of the story. The point is rather to document a manifestation of an ideal type: the pious scholar, for example, or

34 Samaw'al al-Maghribī, *Ifḥām al-yahūd* ed. and trans. Moshe Perlmann as *Silencing the Jews*, in *Proceedings of the American Academy for Jewish Research*, 32 (1964), pp. 101–2 (Arabic) = 78–9 (English), translation slightly modified.

35 Rudolf Sellheim, 'Prophet, Calif, und Geschichte: Die Muhammed-Biographie des Ibn Isḥāq', *Oriens*, 18–19 (1967).

the just ruler. What makes these productions interesting is that the idealised subject must make his way through a non-idealised world. In Ibn al-Jawzī's *Manāqib* of Ibn Ḥanbal, for example, the hero is the perfect exemplar of *ḥadīth* scholarship. But he lives in a specific place and time – the Ḥarbiyya quarter of Baghdad in the first half of the third/ninth century – surrounded by a varied cast of contemporaries: devoted disciples, embittered relatives, troublesome neighbours, mischievous grandchildren and truculent caliphs. As he moves through this vividly detailed world we see saintliness manifested – or imagined – in specific historical circumstances.

Autobiography

Also problematic is autobiography, which some critics have characterised as a distinctively Western genre. These critics evidently believe that autobiography must be confessional: that is, it must be concerned with exposing the private reality that lies behind the author's public persona. But if we accept another definition, that of the Muslim authors who claimed to be 'speaking of the blessings of God' (an allusion to Q 93:11) in their lives, we find a great many texts that count as autobiographies: as many as 120 in Arabic alone, according to a recent survey that stops at the year 1900.[36] Many of these are merely *tarājim* written in the first person, and consist of a list of the author's teachers and students and a bibliography of his works. Others, however, contain accounts of the author's childhood, reports of his dreams, and selections from his poetry. Although not explicitly confessional, these scholarly self-*tarājim* use the coded language of dreams and poems to express a sense of self. In some cases the author's personality emerges quite clearly, as in the long and polemical thematic autobiography by the jurist al-Suyūṭī.[37]

Alongside the scholarly self-*tarjama* run several other strains of autobiographical writing. Inspired by the Persian and Greek traditions, many physicians and philosophers, including Ḥunayn ibn Isḥāq (d. 260/873?), al-Rāzī (d. 313/925) and Ibn Sīnā (d. 428/1037), wrote full or partial autobiographies. One such account, the autobiography of the physician Ibn Riḍwān (d. 453/1061),

36 Dwight F. Reynolds *et al.*, *Interpreting the self: Autobiography in the Arabic literary tradition* (Berkeley, 2001), which also contains references to Persian and Ottoman autobiographies.

37 Elizabeth Sartain, *Jalāl al-Dīn al-Suyūṭī*: vol. I: *Biography and background*, vol. II: *al-Taḥadduth bi niʿmat Allāh* (Cambridge, 1975); Kristen Brustad, 'Imposing order: Reading the conventions of representation in al-Suyūṭī's autobiography', *Edebiyât: Special Issue – Arabic Autobiography*, n.s. 7, 2 (1997); Reynolds *et al.*, *Interpreting the self*, pp. 202–7.

is notable for its discussion of his troubled domestic life. A second type of self-narrative is the spiritual autobiography, notably the conversion accounts of al-Muḥāsibī (d. 243/857), al-Ḥakīm al-Tirmidhī (d. between 295/905 and 300/910), al-Simnānī (d. 736/1336) and al-Shaʿrānī (d. 973/1565). The best-known example, the autobiography of al-Ghazālī (d. 505/1111), describes the author's disenchantment with philosophy, his search for truth among the representatives of various schools of thought, and his eventual decision to embrace the mystic path by virtue of a light that God cast into his heart. Finally, there is the memoir, composed by witnesses to – and sometimes participants in – noteworthy events. Examples include the works of Ibn Buluqqin (d. 488/1095), the last Zīrid ruler of Granada; Usāma ibn Munqidh (d. 584/1188), who provides a description of the European Crusaders; and ʿImād al-Dīn al-Iṣfahānī (d. 597/1201), whose account of Saladin's reign emphasises his own role in the events he describes. Works of this type are sometimes difficult to separate from the autobiographies of historians, such as those by Abū Shāma (d. 665/1267), a historian of Damascus; and Ibn Khaldūn (d. 808/1406), whose autobiography – originally an appendix to his work on history – records his meeting with Tīmūr Lang.[38] Memoirs are also difficult to separate from travel accounts, which in some cases cover substantial periods of the author's life and contain vivid reports of unusual experiences.

Outside the Arabic tradition, the most famous memoirs are those of Bābur (d. 937/1530), a Tīmūrid prince who founded what later became known as the Mughal dynasty of India. Written in Chaghatay (the spoken language of the Tīmūrids) rather than literary Persian, the partially preserved text follows Bābur's fortunes from his assumption of kingship at the age of twelve until the period shortly before his death. Much of the work is devoted to history and biography, and it includes keenly observed *tarājim* of princes, officers, finance ministers, viziers, scholars, poets, calligraphers, painters and musicians. Occasionally, however, Bābur turns his sharp eye on himself. He describes his marriage at the age of nineteen to a cousin, in whom he quickly lost interest and would have neglected entirely if not for his mother, who every month or so 'drove me to her with all the ferocity of a quartermaster'. Later he describes his struggle to give up wine, which he eventually does, although he continues to consume *maʿjūn*, a chewable narcotic. Making no effort to conceal his 'pretentions to rule' and 'desire for conquest', he speaks nonchalantly about flaying captives to death and constructing towers of enemy

38 A fuller account of all these texts, as well as translations of several of them, may be found in Reynolds *et al.*, *Interpreting the self.*

skulls. His straightforward accounts of his campaigns convey a sense of his charisma as a leader, as when he refuses to leave his troops and take shelter in a cave during a snowstorm: 'Whatever hardship and difficulty there was, I would suffer it too.' He is also honest about his errors in judgement, which he ascribes either to inexperience or to placing his trust in the wrong people. However, he insists that 'I have not written all this to complain: I have simply written the truth'.[39]

The end of the tradition

In a very literal sense, the classical Islamic biographical tradition was interrupted by the onset of modernity. The first Arabic account of Napoleon's invasion of Egypt in 1798 appears in a biographical chronicle, al-Jabartī's *ʿAjāʾib al-āthār* (The wonders of history), which turns abruptly from a list of recently deceased notables to a description of the French landing at Alexandria.[40] Of course, the conventions survived for a time, sometimes in unexpected places. In the early nineteenth century three African slaves were manumitted in the United States when it was discovered that they were literate Muslims who could write in Arabic; all three composed short autobiographies in that language.[41] 'It is indeed a powerful moment of *déjà vu* to read in the terse autobiographical writings of a person considered mere chattel in nineteenth-century America formulas and phraseology reminiscent of those used by medieval philosophers, religious scholars, and princes centuries earlier.'[42]

Since the early twentieth century literary biography and autobiography have been influenced by Western models, although spontaneous oral productions can still seem quite classical in form if not in content. In a recent study of tribal history in Jordan the anthropologist Andrew Shryock describes urging his informant Shaykh Khalaf to talk about himself. After some hesitation, the shaykh recites an account that begins not with his birth but rather with his genealogy. The persistence of classical forms should not, however, be taken to mean that their content is somehow exempt from history. In one case, Shryock reports that his efforts to elicit more than a bare genealogy failed

39 *The Baburnama: Memoirs of Babur, prince and emperor*, trans. Wheeler M. Thackston, Jr. (New York, 2002), pp. 89, 67, 234, 241.

40 al-Jabartī, *Taʾrīkh ʿajāʾib al-āthār fī al-tarājim wa al-akhbār*, 3 vols. (Beirut, *c.* 1970), vol. II, p. 179; al-Jabartī, *ʿAbd al-Raḥmān al-Jabartī's History of Egypt*, 5 vols. in 3, ed. Thomas Philipp and Moshe Perlmann (Stuttgart, 1994), vol. III (trans. Thomas Philipp), p. 1.

41 For discussion and references see Reynolds *et al.*, *Interpreting the self*, pp. 56–7.

42 Ibid., p. 8.

because his informants were unable 'to negotiate an acceptable version' of tribal history.[43] Classical biographies, whether in Arabic, Persian or Turkic, are doubtless the result of similar (albeit more successful) negotiations between competing impulses, among them the contradictory demands of documentary accuracy and literary delectation.

43 Andrew Shryock, *Nationalism and the genealogical imagination: Oral history and textual authority in tribal Jordan* (Berkeley, 1997), pp. 12, 108. For more examples of modern oral self-presentations in Arabic see Gary S. Gregg, *Culture and identity in Morocco* (Oxford, 2007).

19

Muslim accounts of the *dār al-ḥarb*

MICHAEL BONNER AND GOTTFRIED HAGEN

Muslim knowledge about the non-Muslim world, or the *dār al-ḥarb* (abode of war), was living knowledge. Its bearers – who included state officials, merchants, converts to Islam, Muslim captives in foreign lands, spies and adventurers – tended to circulate this knowledge informally and orally.[1] Since most of this material has now been lost, we are left with writings that have been preserved in literary texts, whether independently or incorporated into larger works. Most of these fall within the classical definition of *ta'rīkh*, and can be described in modern terms as geographical, cosmographical, historical, biographical, autobiographical or ethnographic.[2] This chapter will survey these writings in their social and intellectual contexts. It is structured according to the literary genres in which they appear. However, we must keep in mind that these accounts do not constitute one or several genres in and of themselves. They also show practically no limitation in their subject matter and themes: since the travellers and compilers were interested in nearly everything, from mundane observations to spectacular marvels, it is virtually impossible to link particular themes to specific formal categories of texts.[3]

Knowledge about the *dār al-ḥarb* was not part of the accepted canon of Islamic knowledge, and since information of this kind was usually obtained by individuals who lacked institutional backing or intellectual prestige, it was often contested, neglected or ignored.[4] Furthermore, the number of texts in question is small, both in comparison with Islamic literature in general, and

1 Suraiya Faroqhi, *The Ottoman empire and the world around it* (London, 2004), on the Ottoman case.

2 Ḥājjī Khalīfa (Kātib Çelebi), *Kashf al-ẓunūn ʿan asāmī l-kutub wal-funūn*, ed. K. R. Bilge and Ş. Yaltkaya, 2 vols. (Istanbul, 1941–3), p. 271; cf. Franz Rosenthal, *A history of Muslim historiography* (Leiden, 1968).

3 Daniel Newman, 'Arab travellers to Europe until the end of the eighteenth century and their accounts: Historical overview and themes', *Chronos*, 4 (2001).

4 Houari Touati, *Islam et voyage au moyen âge: Histoire et anthropologie d'une pratique lettrée* (Paris, 2000), p. 16.

with European travelogues.[5] All this has led some modern writers to characterise the Muslims as relatively uninterested in other cultures.[6] However, we need to account for the conditions of production and transmission of cultural knowledge within the Muslim world itself.

Cultural boundaries

The division of the world into an abode of Islam (*dār al-islām*) and abode of war (*dār al-ḥarb*) does not appear in the Qurʾān, and does not necessarily correspond to the conceptions of the earliest Muslim society.[7] We first find it in juridical texts of the late second/eighth century.[8] After being developed by al-Shāfiʿī (d. 204/820) and other jurists it became an accepted way of representing the world. Here, as the vocabulary indicates, the two abodes are in a permanent condition of war. Since the only legitimate sovereign is God, and the only legitimate political system is Islam, the various rulers within the *dār al-ḥarb* have no legitimacy, and their rule is mere oppression and tyranny. The Muslim state – in the classical theory, the imam – may conclude a truce with them for a limited period. Individuals from the *dār al-ḥarb* who wish to visit the *dār al-islām*, especially for purposes of trade or diplomacy, may be granted safe conduct (*amān*) for a time. Since, however, Muslim states did often live in peace with their non-Muslim neighbours for prolonged periods, some jurists recognised an intermediate abode of truce or treaty (*dār al-ṣulḥ, dār al-ʿahd*).[9] On the whole, however, the two-part distinction remained in force, especially regarding diplomatic relations with non-Muslim states, well into the twelfth/eighteenth century.[10]

This chapter will show that literature on the *dār al-ḥarb*, from the third/ninth century until the thirteenth/nineteenth, was shaped not only by the juridical distinction between the two abodes, but also by a variety of cultural, religious, political, linguistic, geographical–astronomical and historical boundaries. These intersected with the juridical boundary in multiple ways, but were mostly not coterminous with it. Other recent discussions have similarly

5 Muzaffar Alam and Sanjay Subrahmanyam, *Indo-Persian travels in the age of the discoveries, 1400–1800* (Cambridge, 2006), pp. 244, 358.
6 Bernard Lewis, *The Muslim discovery of Europe* (New York, 1982).
7 Michael Bonner, *Jihad in Islamic history* (Princeton, 2006).
8 Roy Mottahedeh and Ridwan al-Sayyid, 'The idea of *jihad* in Islam before the Crusades', in A. E. Laiou and R. P. Mottahedeh (eds.), *The Crusades from the perspective of Byzantium and the Muslim world* (Washington, DC, 2001).
9 Halil Inalcik, 'Dār al-ʿahd', *EI2*, vol. II, p. 116.
10 Virginia Aksan, *An Ottoman statesman in war and peace: Ahmed Resmi Efendi, 1700–1783* (Leiden, 1995), p. 45.

argued that the opposition of Islam / not-Islam was only one set within a larger system of 'nested polarities' which travellers and audiences deployed in the assertion of their identities.[11]

As a pragmatic starting-point we may visualise the mental map of Muslim travellers and geographers as a series of concentric circles. The innermost circle includes regions that are culturally and linguistically familiar. Then, moving out, we come to a second circle encompassing areas adjacent to the first, recognisable but significantly different. Then we arrive at the outer circle, the fringes of the world, a zone of monstrous creatures and bizarre phenomena, impossible to measure by any familiar standards.[12] Here we find what von Mžik defined as parageographical elements, deriving from speculation rather than empirical observation.[13] An example is the encyclopaedic *Nuzhat al-qulūb*, composed by Ḥamdallāh Mustawfī (d. after 740 / 1339f.). The geographical section of this work[14] focuses on the Islamic lands and provides first-hand information, on Ilkhānid Iran in particular. Other, separate chapters on marvels and wonders deal almost exclusively with the outer margins.

Accordingly, the frontier of the abode of Islam did not coincide with the frontier of the familiar and the domestic. After all, the production of knowledge about the 'other' could refer to regions and peoples located within the abode of Islam itself. Likewise, India, though at least partly under Muslim rule, belonged to the periphery (the middle circle). If we look at the *dār al-ḥarb* from an Islamic Middle Eastern perspective, we find that it includes parts of the periphery together with most of the outer fringe. From this point of view, three broad areas were objects of sustained interest: the east and north-east, including China and Inner Asia and extending to the land of Gog and Magog; the north-west, i.e. Christian Europe; and the south, i.e. sub-Saharan Africa and various islands in the southern regions of the Indian Ocean which came, at a late date, to include the Americas.

11 Roxanne Euben, *Journeys to the other shore: Muslim and Western travelers in search of knowledge* (Princeton, 2006), pp. 75–8 and *passim*.

12 Pınar Emiralioğlu, 'Cognizance of the Ottoman world: Visual and textual representations in the sixteenth-century Ottoman empire (1514–1596)', Ph.D. dissertation, University of Chicago (2006), pp. 16, 274, speaks of core, central and peripheral zones for the Ottoman classical age, a pattern which we may apply more generally.

13 Hans von Mžik, 'Parageographische Elemente in den Berichten der arabischen Geographen über Südostasien', in H. von Mžik (ed.), *Beiträge zur historischen Geographie, Kulturgeographie, Ethnographie, und Kartographie* (Leipzig and Vienna, 1929); Hans von Mžik, 'Mythische Geographie', *Wiener Zeitschrift für die Kunde des Morgenlandes*, 45 (1938).

14 Ḥamdallāh Mustawfī al-Qazwīnī, *The geographical part of the* Nuzhat-al-qulūb *composed by Ḥamd-allāh Mustawfī*, ed. and trans. G. Le Strange, 2 vols. (Leiden and London, 1915–19).

All these boundaries are dynamic. In the Middle Eastern heartlands, pre-Islamic monuments serve as reminders of an Egyptian, Iranian or Mesopotamian past. Over time the boundary between periphery and margin typically shifts outward, so that by the end of our period the margin (the outer circle) has all but disappeared. In the eleventh/seventeenth century Ilyās ibn Ḥannā al-Mawṣilī narrates his American journey as occurring in a distant land; however, this land appears far less exotic than it did less than two centuries previously in the Turkish *History of the West Indies*. At the same time, the border between the abodes of Islam and war sometimes contracted, as in the Spanish *reconquista*, so that what had formerly been part of the core became peripheral once again. In these ways the mental map shaped and reshaped the travel reports and other geographical literature, which also shaped the mental map in turn, by creating literary norms and expectations.

Ptolemy

Among the geographical traditions available to the early Muslims, that of the second-century Greek astronomer and geographer Ptolemy was the least concerned with political and cultural boundaries. Ptolemy's influence appears in his concept of clime (Gr. *klima*, Ar. *iqlīm*), which Muslim geographers deployed in a variety of ways.[15] Ptolemy used astronomical data and calculations to divide each half of the globe into seven parallel zones of equal latitude. Many Muslim geographers used this seven-part division, which extended over both the inhabited and uninhabited 'quarters' of the world. For the most part, however, texts in this tradition offered little by way of ethnographic information or portraits of cultural regions.

A smaller number of geographical writers used the Ptolemaic *iqlīm* as a near-synonym for the Persian *kishwar*. In this view, the world consists of seven circles, each corresponding to an empire (China, Rome etc.) with Iran in the central position. Here, of course, we are dealing with political rather than astronomical entities.[16] In any case, writers who divided the world according to *iqlīm* or *kishwar* did not make a fundamental distinction between Muslim

15 Wadie Jwaideh (ed. and trans.), *The introductory chapters of Yāqūt's* Muʿjam al-buldān (Leiden, 1959), pp. 26–52; Fuat Sezgin, *Mathematical geography and cartography in Islam*, trans. G. Moore and G. Sammon, 3 vols. (Frankfurt, 2000–7).

16 Ahmet Karamustafa, 'Military, administrative, and scholarly maps and plans', in J. B. Harley and D. Woodward (eds.), *The history of cartography*, vol. II/1 (Chicago, 1992), pp. 209–27.

and non-Muslim lands and cultures, since both of these could (and did) occur within the same clime.

A Ptolemaic grid forms the background for the geographical work of al-Idrīsī, composed during the 1150s at the court of Roger II of Sicily.[17] Like his successor Ibn Saʿīd al-Maghribī, al-Idrīsī follows Ptolemy in that he provides a commentary on a map or series of maps, though in fact al-Idrīsī did not have the skills or inclinations of an astronomical geographer. He used an array of written Arabic sources, but at the same time his coverage of non-Muslim regions, western and northern Europe in particular, stands out in Islamic literature for its volume and detail. Some have thought that al-Idrīsī actually travelled to such places as France and Britain,[18] but it seems more likely that he consulted informants, typically French speaking, who were available to him at the Norman court in Palermo.[19] The detail that al-Idrīsī devotes to the *dār al-ḥarb* results from the format of his work (proceeding from a Ptolemaic world map), but also from his unusual position as a Muslim beneficiary of the patronage of a Christian monarch. Al-Idrīsī did not have many imitators afterwards, although some Muslim authors (Ibn Khaldūn in particular) expressed admiration for him. Later works in the tradition of Ptolemaic geography, such as Abu al-Fidāʾ's *Taqwīm al-buldān*, tended to focus more on the *dār al-islām*.

Imperial administration and the 'atlas of Islam'

Bureaucrats in the service of the ʿAbbāsid caliphate and its successor states composed comprehensive geographical works. An early example is the *Book of routes and realms* by Ibn Khurradādhbih (d. *c.* 300/911).[20] While Ibn Khurradādhbih claims to have access to Ptolemy's work, in reality he has little use for it. His book is organised (loosely) according to the stages of the imperial post, following the great trunk routes. However, Ibn Khurradādhbih does not halt at the borders of Islam. He includes a section on the Byzantine empire, which modern historians have used for reconstructing the empire's

17 Muḥammad al-Idrīsī, *Nuzhat al-mushtāq fī ikhtirāq al-āfāq*, 9 fascicles (Naples, 1970–84), often known as the *Book of Roger*.

18 I. J. Krachkovskii, *Izbraniye sochineniya*, vol. IV: *Arabskaya geograficheskaya literatura* (Moscow and Leningrad, 1957), p. 182.

19 Al-Idrīsī calls England 'the island of Angleterre': A. F. L. Beeston, 'Idrisi's account of the British Isles', *BSOAS*, 13 (1950).

20 Ibn Khurradādhbih, *Kitāb al-masālik wa'l-mamālik*, ed. M. J. de Goeje, *BGA*, vol. VI (Leiden, 1889).

administrative structures. By contrast, his accounts of other parts of the non-Muslim world tend more towards the marvellous and the fantastical.

Another work in this tradition dates from the first half of the fourth/tenth century, the *Book of the land-tax and the secretary's art* by the Baghdad administrator Qudāma ibn Jaʿfar. Qudāma's seventh chapter provides a tour of the frontiers of Islam (*thughūr al-islām*).[21] Here Qudāma makes no mention of the juridical division of the world into abodes of Islam and war, but presents a hierarchical vision of the frontiers. 'Islam', he says, 'is surrounded on all sides and directions by nations and peoples who are hostile to it, some of them near to and others far away from its imperial capital (*dār mamlakatihi*).' Since the Romans (Byzantines) are the oldest and most dangerous of these, 'it behoves the Muslims to be most wary and on their guard against the Romans, from among all the ranks of their adversaries'. As in Ibn Khurradādhbih, the description of Byzantium and its frontier is relatively detailed and matter-of-fact; Qudāma inclines more towards the fantastical as he moves from the borders of the caliphate to the outer fringes of the world. In any case, all these regions appear as lands to be conquered. The near periphery – basically, Byzantium – is characterised by stubborn opposition, whereas the outer reaches – such as Tibet and China – are more amenable to conquest, especially since, in the past, Alexander the Great has already shown the way (see below).

Away from the chanceries and archives, we find a different approach in al-Jāḥiẓ (d. 255/868f.), who apparently wrote a geographical work which, however, has not survived. Al-Jāḥiẓ emphasised travel and personal observation, and was interested in researching relations among humans, their society and the surrounding environment. It is likely that this book did not deal much with the non-Muslim world.[22] Later writers who took up al-Jāḥiẓ's programme, however, did devote attention to the world beyond Islam. Prominent among these was al-Masʿūdī (d. 355 or 356/956f.), who travelled widely and relayed information on Africa, China and western Europe.

Also in the fourth/tenth century came the three authors sometimes known as the 'Balkhī school', after the first in the series, Abū Zayd al-Balkhī (d. *c.* 322/934).[23] These men devoted their lives to travel, observation and map making. They deployed the Ptolemaic *iqlīm*, but made no claim to astronomical

21 Qudāma ibn Jaʿfar, *al-Kharāj wa-ṣināʿat al-kitāba*, ed. H. al-Zubaydī (Baghdad, 1981), pp. 185–203.

22 André Miquel, *La géographie humaine du monde musulman jusqu'au milieu du 11e siècle*, 4 vols. (Paris and The Hague, 1967–88), vol. I, pp. 57–9.

23 The other two are authors of surviving books, al-Iṣṭakhrī (d. after 340/951), and Ibn Ḥawqal, who completed his work around 378/988.

precision. Instead they developed a programme, already anticipated by al-Jāḥiẓ, of what we may call human geography.[24] They deliberately limited themselves to observing and describing the Islamic world. At the same time they constructed their books around a set of beautifully drawn (though mathematically imprecise) maps, usually numbered at twenty-one. For this reason, their work is sometimes (perhaps misleadingly) known as 'the atlas of Islam'. At any rate, since Balkhī-school cartography covered all the known world, its maps – and, following them, its texts – had to account for the fact that many of the world's spaces, especially the seas, were shared between Muslims and non-Muslims. Accordingly, these authors make observations about non-Muslims, more or less in passing as they proceed. The same applies to their contemporary al-Muqaddasī,[25] who broadly shared their methods and concerns.

Writing in the service of Maḥmūd of Ghazna, but extending his interest far beyond administrative interests, to physical geography, language, religion and philosophy, was al-Bīrūnī (d. after 442/1050). His outlook as court astronomer and scientist proudly emphasises his first-hand knowledge, including fluency in Sanskrit, which he acquired during Ghaznavid military campaigns into northern India.[26]

Embassies

In Islamic legend Alexander the Great is the paradigmatic conqueror–explorer. He sent out ships to discover what lies beyond the oceans, he subdued the monarchs of India, Tibet and China, and he confined Gog and Magog behind an iron wall. This may explain why it happened that when the ʿAbbāsid caliph al-Wāthiq (r. 227–32/842–7) saw in a dream that this wall had been breached, he sent out an expedition to check on it.[27] In the account of this expedition, the delegation moves from princely court to princely court, until it finds itself in the wastelands of the world's outer margins. Even there,

24 Miquel, *La géographie humaine*, vol. I, pp. 35–6 and *passim*.

25 Muqaddasī's *Aḥsan al-taqāsīm li-maʿrifat al-aqālīm*, ed. M. J. de Goeje, *BGA*, vol. III (Leiden, 1877) was composed in the last decades of the fourth/tenth century. It has been translated by Basil Collins as *The best divisions for knowledge of the regions* (Reading, 2001).

26 D. J. Boilot, 'al-Bīrūnī (Bērūnī), Abu 'l-Rayḥān b. Aḥmad', *EI2* vol. I, p. 1236; Eduard Sachau (ed.), *al-Beruni's India: An account of the religion, philosophy, literature, chronology, astronomy, customs, laws and anthropology of India about AD 1030* (London, 1887; repr. Leipzig, 1925), English trans. Eduard Sachau under the same title, 2 vols. (London, 1888–1910).

27 Ibn Khurradādhbih, *Kitāb al-masālik*, pp. 162–70. For Alexander's exploits see also Qudāma ibn Jaʿfar, *al-Kharāj*, pp. 192–200.

however, they find people who are Muslims, speak Arabic and are delighted to hear of the existence of a caliph in Baghdad.

In 309/921 the caliph al-Muqtadir sent an embassy to the Bulghars of the Volga, far to the north. The account of this expedition follows a political paradigm rooted in narratives of *sīra* and *maghāzī*, namely, the linking of political alliances across the frontier with the conversion of people who live outside the *dār al-islām*. One of the participants, Ibn Faḍlān, left a travelogue which intertwines diplomacy together with the role of the missionary who instructs the foreign ruler in the principles of Islam. Ibn Faḍlān's ethnographic observations also privilege areas of interest to a legal scholar: the dispensation of justice, the performance of pagan rituals (including funerary rites) and the arrival of correct practice among the recent converts.[28] All the while, Ibn Faḍlān was aware of a steep cultural gradient between the highly civilised ʿAbbāsid caliphate and (as he portrays them) the uncouth peoples of the north.

Another embassy report, written centuries later in Persian, builds upon a similar notion. Muḥammad Rabīʿ's *Safīna-yi Sulaymānī*, describing a Ṣafavid embassy to Thailand in 1685–8, is imbued with the spirit of Iranian superiority. In its constructed dichotomy of Iranian culture versus local barbarism it goes so far as to state that the Siamese had only recently turned from the realm of bestiality to that of humankind.[29]

Such contacts were rare enough that an account of them could attract attention for its unusual, even exotic, contents. On the other hand, the Tīmūrid monarch Shāh Rukh exchanged no fewer than twenty embassies with Ming China between 1408 and 1428.[30] Only one of these, in 1420, left a literary trace, in a report by Ghiyāth al-Dīn Naqqāsh. This account became a classic, preserved in a long series of literary works in Persian and Turkic.[31] Ghiyāth al-Dīn had encountered a refined civilisation, and his interest in administrative and judicial practices set a precedent for future accounts of China.

Despite the number and intensity of these diplomatic contacts in the eastern Islamic world, they had surprisingly few reflections in literature. Much the

28 Richard Frye, *Ibn Fadlan's journey to Russia: A tenth-century traveler from Baghdad to the Volga River* (Princeton, 2006).

29 Alam and Subrahmanyan, *Indo-Persian travels*, pp. 159–71, esp. p. 167.

30 B. Forbes-Manz, 'Shāh Rukh', *EI2*, vol. IX, pp. 197–8.

31 C. A. Storey and Yuri Bregel', *Persidskaya literatura: Bio-bibliograficheskii obzor* (Moscow, 1972), p. 824; Ildikó Bellér-Hann, *A history of Cathay: A translation and linguistic analysis of a fifteenth-century Turkic manuscript* (Bloomington, 1995); Krachkovskii, *Arabskaya geograficheskaya literatura*, pp. 518–22.

same happened in the west, where dozens of embassies went from Tunisia and Morocco to European countries between 1600 and 1800.[32] Aḥmad ibn Qāsim al-Ḥajarī (d. after 1051/1641) served as a translator for the Spanish king, and afterwards as a diplomat for the dispossessed Moriscos. His travelogue, which includes many keen observations, is characterised by Islamic apologetics, summarised in its title and borne out in its accounts of religious disputations held with Christians and Jews along the way.[33]

Most of the accounts discussed so far had little or no official character. Returning embassies were expected to submit reports, especially regarding the respect they had been shown by foreign rulers. Hence, the official report is a part of the envoy's negotiation of his re-entry into his own society and order.[34] 'Xenology'[35] provides additional arguments: Muḥammad Rabīʿ's picture of cultural depravity in Thailand may have served to rationalise the failure of his diplomatic mission.

Ottoman agents went to Europe on various occasions, for instance to keep track of the pretender Jem Sulṭān, who found asylum with the Pope in his competition against his brother Bāyazīd II (r. 886–918/1481–1512).[36] Yet it was only in the eleventh/seventeenth century that regular diplomatic missions went out to European capitals, beginning in the aftermath of the Ottoman defeat at St Gotthard in 1665. The report of this mission, documented in two chronicles, focused entirely on its diplomatic aspect.[37] In the following generation the Ottoman–Habsburg Treaty of Karlowitz in 1699 put a de facto end to the conceptualisation of relations in the juridical terms of the abodes of

32 The focus shifted from ransoming captives to trade and peace agreements: see Newman, 'Arab travellers', p. 32.

33 Aḥmad ibn Qāsim al-Ḥajarī, *Kitāb nāṣir al-dīn ʿalā l-qawm al-kāfirīn*, ed. and trans. P. S. van Koningsveld, A. al-Samarrai and G. A. Wiegers (Madrid, 1997). See also Gerard Wiegers, 'A life between Europe and the Maghrib: The writings and travels of Aḥmad b. Qāsim ibn al-faqīh ibn al-shaykh al-Ḥajarī al-Andalusī', in G. J. van Gelder and E. de Moor (eds.), *The Middle East and Europe: Encounters and exchanges* (Amsterdam, 1992); Nabil Matar, *In the land of the Christians: Arabic travel writing in the seventeenth century* (New York and London, 2003).

34 Nicolas Vatin, 'Pourquoi un Turc racontait-il son voyage? Note sur les relations de voyage chez les Ottomans des *Vâkıʿât-ı Sulṭân Cem* au *Seyâhatnâme* d'Evliyâ Çelebi', in *Études turques et ottomanes: Document de travail no. 4 de l'URA du CNRS (décembre 1995)* (Paris, 1995).

35 Alam and Subrahmanyam, *Indo-Persian travels*, p. 12.

36 The report on Jem is edited by Nicolas Vatin in *Sultan Djem: Un prince ottoman dans l'Europe du XVe siècle d'après deux sources contemporaines: Vâḳıʿât-ı Sulṭān Cem, Œuvres de Guillaume Caoursin* (Ankara, 1997).

37 Faik Reşit Unat and Bekir Sıtkı Baykal, *Osmanlı sefirleri ve sefaretnameleri* (Ankara, 1968), pp. 47f.

Islam and of war, even though this rhetoric continued to shape Ottoman diplomatic discourse for at least another century.[38]

Meanwhile, embassy reports (*sefāretnāme*) developed into a literary genre which had a profound cultural impact, and despite its newness showed surprising maturity by the time of Yirmisekiz Çelebi Meḥmed's report on his embassy to Paris in 1721.[39] This work shows interest in a variety of cultural productions and scientific activities, including theatre and opera, the Paris observatory and various manufactures, all reported without any noticeable religious objections or concerns. Since the report circulated as a literary text rather than an official document, its diplomatic purpose became of secondary importance. Yirmisekiz Meḥmed seems aware of his position as an exotic object of interest for the Parisians. On the other hand, his work has been identified as a blueprint for transformations within the Ottoman empire, coinciding with the so-called Tulip Era and its innovations in the spirit of a 'new worldliness'.[40]

Subsequent embassy reports followed the pattern set by Yirmisekiz Meḥmed in privileging cultural exploration over diplomatic negotiation. In most cases, the diplomatic report provided the basis for a longer, descriptive account. These are read today as documents of perceptions of others or 'occidentalism', and indeed they offer many insights into cross-cultural encounters, from Aḥmed Resmī's Machiavellian characterisation of Frederick II of Prussia to the observations of Ebū Bekr Rāṭib on Austrian administration, to Muṣṭafā Rāsiḥ's critique of Russian serfdom. Embassy reports also suited an agenda for domestic reform.[41]

Travelogues similar to the Ottoman *sefāretnāme* were produced in India in the eighteenth and early nineteenth centuries, often by authors who, in the course of their official duties, accompanied Englishmen back to their homeland. Mīrzā Abū Ṭālib Khān's *Masīr*, a successful work which was

38 Berrak Burçak, 'The institution of the Ottoman embassy and eighteenth-century Ottoman history', *International Journal of Turkish Studies* 13, 1–2 (2007); Aksan, *An Ottoman statesman*, p. 45.

39 First printed as *Sefāret-nāme-i Fransa: Eser-i Meḥmed Efendi* (Istanbul, 1283/1866), with numerous reprints in Arabic and Latin characters.

40 Fatma Müge Göçek, *East encounters West: France and the Ottoman empire in the eighteenth century* (New York, 1987); Niyazi Berkes, *The development of secularism in Turkey* (Montreal, 1964).

41 Aksan, *An Ottoman statesman*; Stephan Conermann, 'Das Eigene und das Fremde: Der Bericht der Gesandtschaft Muṣṭafā Rāsiḫs nach St Petersburg im Jahre 1792–1794', *Archivum Ottomanicum*, 17 (1999); Carter Findley, 'Ebu Bekir Ratib's Vienna embassy narrative: Discovering Austria or propagandizing for reform in Istanbul?', *Wiener Zeitschrift für die Kunde des Morgenlandes*, 85 (1995).

immediately translated into English, became a prime example of how an additional, refracting layer could be added to the mutual perception of European colonialism and its 'oriental' subjects.[42]

By the nineteenth century diplomats no longer held a monopoly over travel to Europe. Trainees in the reformed administration of the Ottoman empire, as well as of its (nominal) province Egypt, were sent to study in France. One of these, the Egyptian cleric Rifāʿa Rāfiʿ al-Ṭahṭāwī, wrote a travelogue on his stay in Paris from 1826 to 1831.[43] In its combination of cultural exploration together with a search for models for social and political reform, al-Ṭahṭāwī's work had much in common with the Turkish *sefāretnāmes* of the eighteenth century. It included translations of French texts, including the constitution of 1830, and it played a crucial role in the formation of modern literary Arabic, as al-Ṭahṭāwī negotiated the tension between his own classical erudition and the need for expressions of new ideas. Afterwards al-Ṭahṭāwī became influential in Egyptian educational reform. Subsequently, reports on Europe by scholars, diplomats and journalists produced a variegated discourse on modernity, reform and the Islamic tradition.[44]

Individual travellers

Western travellers often ventured beyond their familiar world in pursuit of a 'hermeneutics of the other', in which they encountered themselves and translated their experiences into their own cultural terms. Islamic travellers, by contrast, generally preferred to seek knowledge from established scholars, in their constant movements across the abode of Islam.[45] However, this pattern did not prevent individuals from venturing across political, religious and cultural boundaries. Their motives included the pursuit of blessing (*baraka*) at remote sanctuaries, career goals, wanderlust (which Evliyā Çelebi described as divinely ordained) and simple happenstance.[46]

42 Krachkovskii, *Arabskaya geograficheskaya literatura*, p. 535; Alam and Subrahmanyan, *Indo-Persian travels*, pp. 245ff.; Juan Cole, 'Invisible occidentalism: Eighteenth-century Indo-Persian construction of the West', *Iranian Studies* 25 (1992).
43 Rifāʿa Rāfiʿ al-Ṭahṭāwī, *Takhlīṣ al-ibrīz fī talkhīṣ Bārīz* (Cairo, 1993), trans. Daniel Newman as *An imam in Paris: Account of a stay in Paris by an Egyptian cleric (1826–1831)* (London, 2004).
44 Baki Asiltürk, *Osmanlı seyyahlarının gözüyle Avrupa* (Istanbul, 2000).
45 Touati, *Islam et voyage*, p. 11.
46 Euben, *Journeys*, p. 66, on Ibn Baṭṭūṭa. The trade and missionary activity that are so compelling for Western travellers such as Marco Polo and William of Rubruck are virtually absent in the Muslim travel authors.

We have already noted a disparity between the number and intensity of the encounters, on the one hand, and the paucity of literary accounts describing them, on the other. Why, then, were certain experiences written about at all? Touati has argued that literary travelogues were justified by the marvels that one encountered along the way. If this is so, it must apply especially to travelogues from the outer periphery, the dwelling-place of the extraordinary and the abnormal. There, at the meeting-place of edification and entertainment, marvels (*ʿajāʾib*) are a basic concern, in conformance with the dictum of Abū Bakr al-ʿArabī (d. 543/1148) that the contemplation of the world should have knowledge of God as its goal.[47] Accordingly, Abū Ḥāmid al-Gharnāṭī collected not only the marvels of the Maghrib, but also various other marvels he had personally observed during his travels in Iran and the Eurasian steppes.[48]

In contrast to the thematically arranged work of Abū Ḥāmid, the chronologically arranged *riḥla* (travelogue) shifted its focus onto the persona of the traveller. First fully developed as a literary form by Ibn Jubayr (d. 614/1217), the *riḥla* reached far beyond the abode of Islam in the work of Ibn Baṭṭūṭa (d. 770 or 779/1368–77), who travelled throughout the Middle East, East and West Africa, Central Asia, China, India and South-East Asia, with long stays in Delhi and the Maldives, over almost thirty years. Modern researchers have scrutinised this text for historical and cultural details. However, Ibn Baṭṭūṭa's testimony, like that of many a geographer–traveller, was considered suspect.[49] To deflect such charges he used an array of rhetorical strategies, including emphasis on his piety, his status as a religious scholar, and the respect he was shown in various foreign societies. However, these efforts proved vain. By contrast, Abū Ḥāmid al-Gharnāṭī remained immune to such suspicions, as many later authors cited his natural and ethnographic observations.

More broadly, the travelogue defies authorisation by intellectual genealogy, a fundamental principle for valorisation of knowledge in medieval Islam.[50] Al-Muqaddasī was aware of this problem by the fourth/tenth century, and argues in favour of 'eyewitnessing' (lit. 'autopsy', *ʿiyān*) in the production of knowledge about the world's places. He proudly (and self-dramatisingly) lists all the roles he has assumed during his travels.[51] His predecessor

47 Touati, *Islam et voyage*, p. 293.

48 On *ʿajāʾib* (marvels) see below. On Abū Ḥāmid see César Emil Dubler, *Abū Ḥāmid el Granadino y su relación de viaje por tierras eurasiáticas: Texto árabe, traducción e interpretación* (Madrid, 1953).

49 Euben, *Journeys*, p. 46.

50 Touati, *Islam et voyage*, p. 14.

51 al-Muqaddasī, *Aḥsan al-taqāsīm*, pp. 43f.; trans. Collins, pp. 41f.

al-Masʿūdī makes a similar argument, pointing to his experiences in India, Zanzibar, the Caspian and al-Andalus. Both these writers (and al-Yaʿqūbī before them) developed systematic criteria for the selection of second-hand reports to use in their description of the world.[52]

The disregard for travel accounts lacking a respectable intellectual genealogy is exemplified by ʿAlī Akbar's description of China, the *Qānūnnāme-i Khiṭay*, submitted in Persian to Sultan Süleymān I (r. 926–74/1520–66) and subsequently translated into Turkish under Murād III (r. 982–1003/1574–95).[53] Despite this high patronage, later geographers such as Kātib Çelebi (Ḥājjī Khalīfa, 1017–67/1609–57) referred to ʿAlī Akbar only with reluctance, because other scholars had not validated his work.

It is Evliyā Çelebi (d. after 1095/1683) who is Ibn Baṭṭūṭa's only competitor for the title of 'greatest Muslim traveller'. In his ten-volume travelogue he gives a panorama of the Ottoman empire of his time, integrating administrative, historical and ethnographic data with personal anecdotes, in a delightful range of prose styles.[54] Where he ventures beyond the Islamic world, as in his participation in a mission to Vienna in 1665, Evliyā sometimes gives fanciful descriptions shaped by Ottoman imperial ideology, aiming at future conquest. Explaining his experiences entirely in Ottoman terms, he advances a domestic agenda, using the West as an example to criticise Ottoman faults.[55] At times Evliyā crosses over into fiction, as in his short narrative of a raid conducted by 40,000 Tatars through northern Europe, and his description of Sudan and Ethiopia.[56] Evliyā also takes pains to dispel his readers' doubts, offering precise observations and emphasis on eyewitnessing as evidence for his own veracity. Such rhetoric is often difficult to distinguish from irony, since Evliyā also includes thinly disguised hoaxes and obvious legends.[57] Nonetheless, he shared Ibn Baṭṭūṭa's fate, since his work, though incomparably rich in

52 Touati, *Islam et voyage*, pp. 143–53. Suspicions of al-Masʿūdī persisted nonetheless, see ibid., p. 151.

53 Emiralioğlu, 'Cognizance of the Ottoman world', pp. 181–221.

54 Robert Dankoff, *Evliya Çelebi: An Ottoman mentality* (Leiden and Boston, 2004).

55 Richard Kreutel and Erich Prokosch, *Im Reiche des goldenen Apfels: Des türkischen Weltenbummlers Evliyâ Çelebi denkwürdige Reise in das Giaurenland und in die Stadt und Festung Wien anno 1665* (Graz, Vienna and Cologne, 1985); Karl Teply, *Türkische Sagen und Legenden um die Kaiserstadt Wien* (Vienna, Cologne and Graz, 1980).

56 *Evliyā Çelebi Seyahatnamesi*, 10 vols. (Istanbul, 1896–1938), vol. X; Erich Prokosch, *Ins Land der geheimnisvollen Func: Des türkischen Weltenbummlers, Evliyā Çelebi, Reise durch Oberägypten und den Sudan nebst der osmanischen Provinz Habeš in den Jahren 1672/73* (Graz, 1994).

57 Dankoff, *Evliya Çelebi*.

information, was never used in later descriptions of the Ottoman empire until its 'rediscovery' by modern orientalists.

The Tīmūrid prince Bābur (r. 888–937/1483–1530), founder of the Mughal dynasty, left an autobiographical account which included a description of India through the eyes of its conqueror. Although India was technically not part of the *dār al-ḥarb*, Bābur perceived it as alien territory, to be ruled by Muslims in exemplary fashion.[58]

Captives

During the many centuries of conflict between Muslim and non-Muslim states, countless individuals were taken captive. Once they had escaped, or been ransomed, the former captives were theoretically well situated to provide information about their captors' lands. In early modern Europe, increasing literacy and the print revolution helped to make captivity narratives a much-disseminated source of knowledge about the Islamic lands. In the Islamic lands, however, captivity narratives were rarer. Even more than travelogues, they remained outside the authorised canon of knowledge. Accordingly, even as more first-person narratives come to light, we need to recall that these were not usually read as records of individual lives, in a culture that had an aversion to particularism.[59]

An early example is Hārūn ibn Yaḥyā, who was held prisoner in Constantinople some time around 900, and left a description of the city that gives valuable information on the city and its monuments.[60] Hārūn then went on to visit and describe Rome and Venice. The sixteenth-century Moroccan captive-turned-convert Leo Africanus provided Pope Leo with a description of Africa, written in an idiosyncratic Italian during his captivity in Rome, but he does not seem to have written an Arabic description of Italy after his return to his native land.[61]

Maʿjūncu-zāde Muṣṭafā Efendi, who spent time in Malta as a prisoner of the Knights before being ransomed, transformed his experience into moral

58 Trans. Wheeler Thackston as *The Baburnama: Memoirs of Babur, prince and emperor* (Washington, New York and Oxford, 1996).

59 Derin Terzioğlu, 'Autobiography in fragments: Reading Ottoman personal miscellanies in the early modern era', in O. Akyıldız, H. Kara and B. Sagaster (eds.), *Autobiographical themes in Turkish literature: Theoretical and comparative perspectives* (Würzburg, 2007).

60 Ibn Rustah, *al-Aʿlāq al-nafīsa*, ed. M. J. de Goeje, *BGA*, vol. VII (Leiden, 1892), pp. 119–30; M. Izzedin, 'Hārūn b. Yaḥyā', *EI2*, vol. III, p. 232.

61 Natalie Zemon Davis, *Trickster travels: A sixteenth-century Muslim between two worlds* (New York, 2006).

lessons. *Ser-güzesht-i Malṭa* (1010/1602) is woven around verses composed during the author's captivity, coping with surges of hope and despair, and invoking patience and trust in divine aid. There is little ethnographic information here beyond details that illustrate the suffering of the captives, who did not get to see much of Malta in any case.[62]

In an age of increasing individualism, ʿOsmān Ağa of Temesvar (d. after 1725) had more to tell about his captivity. Once he had risen to a position as servant in an aristocratic household in Vienna (not untypically for the period), ʿOsmān enjoyed aspects of his life, including an affair with a servant maid, training as a pastry maker and fights with servants of other households. He escaped to Ottoman territory after 1699. His work, in a distinctly unliterary Turkish, emphasises his merits as a translator and cultural mediator, and it has been suggested that he produced his autobiographical writings at the request of European diplomats in Istanbul, as a way of eking out a living.[63] Nothing is known about his fragmentary history of the Germans (*Nemçe tārīkhi*), beginning with Charlemagne and breaking off after 1662.[64]

Maritime handbooks and charts

Travellers acquired knowledge of the *dār al-ḥarb* in orbital movements, out from the *dār al-islām* and back again.[65] The Mediterranean in particular was a zone where knowledge and technology circulated among mariners of different origins. The portolan chart, produced and used by Christians, Jews and Muslims, is a good example.[66] The Turkish admiral Pīrī Reʾīs (d. 963/1554f.) composed a *Baḥriyye*, which he first submitted to the Sublime Porte in 1521, then in an expanded version in 1526. In addition to a set of maps, the *Baḥriyye* includes descriptions of the entire shoreline, mostly for the use of sailors

62 Maʿjūncuzāde Muṣṭafā Efendi, *Malta Esirleri*, ed. Cemil Çiftçi (Istanbul, 1996).

63 ʿOsmān Agha [Temeshvarlı], *Die Autobiographie des Dolmetschers ʿOsmān Āghā aus Temeschwar: Der Text des Londoner Autographen in normalisierter Rechtschreibung herausgegeben*, ed. R. Kreutel (Cambridge, 1980), ed. and trans. R. F. Kreutel and O. Spies as *Der Gefangene der Giauren: die abenteuerlichen Schicksale des Dolmetschers ʿOsman Ağa aus Temeschwar, von ihm selbst erzählt* (Graz, 1962); R. F. Kreutel (trans.), *Zwischen Paschas und Generälen: Bericht des ʿOsman Ağa aus Temeschwar über die Höhepunkte seines Wirkens als Diwansdolmetscher und Diplomat* (Graz, Vienna and Cologne, 1966).

64 Kreutel and Spies (ed. and trans.), *Der Gefangene der Giauren*, p. 13, refers to an unspecified manuscript in Istanbul.

65 John Wansbrough, *Lingua franca in the Mediterranean* (Richmond, 1996).

66 Tony Campbell, 'Portolan charts from the late thirteenth century to 1500', in Harley and Woodward (eds.), *The history of cartography*, vol. I (Chicago, 1987); Svatopluk Soucek, 'Islamic charting in the Mediterranean', in Harley and Woodward (eds.), *The history of cartography*, vol. II/1.

seeking information about shoals, reefs, harbours and access to fresh water. Some passages recall the author's exploits,[67] while others describe towns such as Venice or Naples, including legendary details.[68] While the first version claims to offer strategic information for future naval actions, the second is more literary, and includes a long introduction in verse on the seven seas and legendary cosmography.[69] Both versions treat Muslim and non-Muslim territories in the same fashion, showing no concern 'with boundaries other than those between navigable and unnavigable space'.[70] Pīrī Re'īs also produced two maps of America, in 1513 and 1528, for which he obtained information from Spanish sailors.[71]

In the Indian Ocean, pilots relied on celestial navigation rather than maps. Nautical manuals provided descriptions of routes and instructions about meteorological and astronomical phenomena, as well as some magical practices. Information about the shores and their population was mainly restricted to sailing instructions, with some references to local marvels.[72]

Synthetic descriptions of the world

Many accounts of the *dār al-ḥarb* that once circulated as independent works are known today through literary compilations that appeared from the fifth/eleventh century onwards. Fragments of Ibrāhīm ibn Ya'qūb al-Ṭurṭūshī's account of his sojourn in central and eastern Europe around 965 are preserved in the *Kitāb al-masālik wa'l-mamālik* (Book of routes and realms) of Abū 'Ubayd al-Bakrī (d. 487/1094). The work's title connects it to the genre of administrative

67 Svatopluk Soucek, 'Tunisia in the *Kitāb-ı baḥriyye* by Pīrī Re'īs', *Archivum Ottomanicum*, 5 (1973).

68 Elisabetta Serrao, 'La descrizione di Napoli nel *Kitāb-ı baḥrīye* di Pīrī Re'īs', in U. Marazzi (ed.), *Turcica et islamica: Studi in memoria di Aldo Gallotta* (Naples, 2003).

69 Svatopluk Soucek, *Piri Reis and Turkish mapmaking after Columbus: The Khalili portolan atlas* (London, 1996).

70 Palmira Brummett, 'Imagining the early modern Ottoman space, from world history to Pīrī Re'īs', in D. Goffman and V. Aksan (eds.), *The early modern Ottomans: Remapping the empire* (Cambridge, MA, 2007).

71 Giancarlo Casale, '"His Majesty's servant Lutfi": The career of a previously unknown sixteenth-century Ottoman envoy to Sumatra', *Turcica*, 37 (2005).

72 For Aḥmad ibn Mājid's *Kitāb al-fawā'id fī uṣūl al-baḥr* see Gerald Tibbetts, *Arab navigation in the Indian Ocean before the coming of the Portuguese: Being a translation of* Kitāb al-fawā'id fī uṣūl al-baḥr wa'l-qawā'id *of Aḥmad b. Mājid al-Najdī; together with an introduction on the history of Arab navigation, notes on the navigational techniques and on the topography of the Indian Ocean and a glossary of navigational terms* (London, 1972); for Seydī 'Alī Re'īs see M. Bittner and W. Tomaschek (ed. and trans.), *Die topographischen Kapitel des indischen Seespiegles Moḥît* (Vienna, 1897) and Jean-Louis Bacqué-Grammont (trans.), *Le miroir des pays* (Paris, 1999).

geography (going back to Ibn Khurradādhbih, see above), as does the literary character of its historical and ethnographic digressions.[73] Works by the fourth/tenth-century al-Warrāq (on Africa) and al-Jayhānī (on eastern Europe and Central Asia) have not survived, but al-Bakrī quotes them extensively. Al-Jayhānī is also quoted by many other geographers.[74]

Al-Bakrī also wrote a dictionary of toponyms, as did Yāqūt al-Ḥamawī (d. 626/1229), whose *Muʿjam al-buldān* (Dictionary of the countries) brings historical, ethnographic and philological information into alphabetically arranged articles. Yāqūt's sources include the travelogues of Ibn Faḍlān (see above) and a certain Tamīm ibn Baḥr al-Muṭṭawwiʿī, who visited China.[75] Yāqūt's own experience as a traveller plays a much smaller role. In another geographical work, *al-Mushtarik waḍʿan wal-muftarik suqʿan*, Yāqūt collects homonymous toponyms designating different places, a distinctly philological interest. A latecomer in this genre is Amīn Aḥmad Rāzī's dictionary of poets and places, *Haft iqlīm*.[76] The pattern of rewriting earlier works in a more literary fashion appears in Ibn Saʿīd al-Maghribī (610–85/1213–86), a prolific anthologist. His *al-Jughrāfiyā* follows al-Idrīsī in its structure and much of its content, especially regarding Europe and non-Muslim Africa.[77]

Another type of encyclopaedia brought together accounts of 'the marvels of creation', with the goal of recognising the omnipotence of the Creator. Situated at the margins of the world, these marvels did not have to meet strict standards of veracity, nor did they need to pertain to the present. Accordingly, literary sources were just as welcome as travelogues: al-Qazwīnī's (d. 682/1283) double-barrelled cosmographical encyclopaedia *ʿAjāʾib al-makhlūqāt* and *Āthār al-bilād* drew material from Yāqūt and similar sources. Works of this kind shaped a 'popular' world-view until the eve of modernity.[78] Attempts at

73 Krachkovskii, *Arabskaya geograficheskaya literatura*, pp. 275–9; E. Lévi-Provençal, 'Abū ʿUbayd al-Bakrī', *EI2*, vol. I, pp. 155–7.

74 Hansgerd Göckenjan and István Zimonyi, *Orientalische Berichte über die Völker Osteuropas und Zentralasiens im Mittelalter: Die Ǧayhānī-Tradition* (Wiesbaden, 2003).

75 Possibly dating to the second/eighth century: see Krachkovskii, *Arabskaya geograficheskaya literatura*, p. 137.

76 Aḥmad Rāzī, *Haft iqlīm*, ed. Jawād Fāḍil, 3 vols. (n.p., n.d. [Tehran, 1961]); E. Berthels, 'Rāzī, Amīn Aḥmad', *EI2*, vol. VIII, p. 478.

77 Al-Idrīsī has been identified as one of Ibn Saʿīd's sources: see Manfred Kropp, '*Kitāb ǧuǧrāfiyā* des Ibn Fāṭima: Eine unbekannte Quelle des Ibn Saʿīd oder "Neues" von al-Idrīsī?', in *Un ricordo che non si spegne: Scritti di docenti e collaboratori dell'Istituto Universitario Orientale di Napoli in memoria di Alessandro Bausani* (Naples, 1996).

78 Karin Rührdanz, 'Illustrated Persian *ʿAjāʾib al-makhlūqāt* manuscripts and their function in early modern times', in A. J. Newman (ed.), *Society and culture in the early modern Middle East: Studies on Iran in the Safavid period* (Leiden, 2003).

modernising the genre, such as the cosmography by Meḥmed ʿĀshiq (d. after 1005/1596), aimed more at the familiar world.[79]

The vast encyclopaedias compiled by state functionaries of the Mamlūk sultanate combined humanistic erudition (*adab*) with practical knowledge. Diplomatic relations required precise information about titles and ranks. An example is the description of the Ilkhānid empire in Ibn Faḍl Allāh al-ʿUmarī's *Masālik al-abṣār fī mamālik al-amṣār*. While al-ʿUmarī relied on literary sources, he also interviewed envoys and merchants who had experience of the Mongols.[80]

Integration of non-Muslim sources

For reasons we have already mentioned, non-Muslim sources regarding the *dār al-ḥarb* were mostly avoided or ignored during the classical and post-classical periods. The discipline of Islamic history tended to limit itself to the core Islamic lands, at least for the period beginning with the rise of Islam. This remained true even for such broad-ranging historians as Ibn Khaldūn (d. 808/1406).

However, there were exceptions. One of these was al-Masʿūdī (see above), an outstanding product of the intellectual milieu of fourth/tenth-century Baghdad.[81] For his world geography-cum-history, *Murūj al-dhahab*, al-Masʿūdī included a list of Frankish kings taken from a book by a Frankish bishop.[82] Another exception was Rashīd al-Dīn (d. 718/1318), a Jewish convert to Islam, who became one of the most influential politicians of the Ilkhānid empire under Ghāzān Khān. Rashīd al-Dīn composed a world history, *Jāmiʿ al-tawārīkh*, and sought to disseminate it widely in both Persian and Arabic. In order to situate the history of the Mongols and Ilkhānids within a universal framework he included an appendix on the Arabs, Franks, Israelites, Mongols and Chinese. For this purpose he engaged informants from the respective cultures. The chronicle of Martin of Troppau has been identified as his source for Frankish history, while his informant for China was a Mongol named Bolad, a former high functionary at the Yuan court. This collaboration

79 Meḥmed ʿĀshıq made additions to the work from his own travels in the Ottoman lands, but not from beyond: Gottfried Hagen, *Ein osmanischer Geograph bei der Arbeit: Entstehung und Gedankenwelt von Kātib Čelebis* ǧihānnümā (Berlin, 2003), pp. 111–18.

80 Klaus Lech, *Das mongolische Weltreich: al-ʿUmarī's Darstellung der mongolischen Reiche in seinem Werk* Masālik al-abṣār fī mamālik al-amṣār (Wiesbaden, 1968).

81 Bernd Radtke, *Weltgeschichte und Weltbeschreibung im mittelalterlichen Islam* (Stuttgart, 1992), pp. 169–83.

82 Lewis, *The Muslim discovery of Europe*, p. 183.

mirrors the position of the Ilkhānid empire as a conduit of cultural practices from east to west.[83]

Al-Mas'ūdī and Rashīd al-Dīn remained unusual in their use of non-Muslim sources. The Ottomans were not averse to using such sources, as we have seen in Pīrī Re'īs. However, as Ottoman horizons continued to broaden from the later tenth/sixteenth century onwards,[84] authors looked to older Islamic classics for information on the *dār al-ḥarb*. Muṣṭafā 'Ālī (d. 1008/1600) looked to al-Mas'ūdī for Frankish history and to 'Alī Akbar for China.[85] Münejjimbashı (d. 1113/1702) used al-Mas'ūdī's account of the Trojan War,[86] Kātib Çelebi (reluctantly) used 'Alī Akbar and Ghiyāth al-Dīn Naqqāsh for China, while Seyfī Çelebi's rather obscure history of India and China draws on (yet unidentified) Islamic sources.[87]

Meanwhile, with Venice furnishing maps to the Ottoman court,[88] European maps, atlases, historical and scientific works continued to trickle in. In an anonymous *History of the West Indies* (*c.* 1580) translations from Spanish and Italian historians about the Americas are integrated into a framework reminiscent of Islamic cosmography and *'ajā'ib* literature; illustrated copies also support the attribution of the work to this genre.[89] The Ottoman polymath Kātib Çelebi undertook a project on world geography, but did not feel satisfied with his work until he obtained European atlases by Mercator, Ortelius and others, to fill in the gaps in his Islamic sources. Basing his description of East and South-East Asia on these new sources, Kātib Çelebi switched back to Islamic sources for Central Asia, India and Iran, even as his method became increasingly informed by Mercator.[90]

This trend towards domination by Western sources and models continued, with the translation and abridgements of Willem Blaeu's *Atlas maior* by Ebū

83 Thomas Allsen, *Culture and conquest in Mongol Eurasia* (Cambridge, 2004), esp. pp. 63–102.

84 Jean-Louis Bacqué-Grammont, 'Remarques sur les chemins de la découverte du monde par les Ottomans', in J.-L. Bacqué-Grammont *et al.* (eds.), *D'un orient à l'autre: Actes des troisièmes journées de l'Orient, Bordeaux, 2–4 octobre 2002* (Paris and Louvain, 2005), p. 163.

85 Jan Schmidt, *Pure water for thirsty Muslims: A study of Muṣṭafā 'Ālī of Gallipoli's* Künhü l-aḫbār (Leiden, 1991), p. 30.

86 Jean-Louis Bacqué-Grammont, 'Remarques'.

87 Josef Matuz, *L'ouvrage de Seyfi Çelebi, historien ottoman du XVIe siècle: Édition critique, traduction et commentaires* (Paris, 1968).

88 Benjamin Arbel, 'Maps of the world for Ottoman princes? Further evidence and questions concerning "The mappamondo of Hajji Ahmed"', *Imago Mundi*, 54 (2004).

89 Thomas Goodrich, *The Ottoman Turks and the New World: A study of* Tarih-i Hind-i garbi *and sixteenth-century Ottoman Americana* (Wiesbaden, 1990).

90 Hagen, *Ein osmanischer Geograph*. The draft translation of Mercator's *Atlas minor*, originally made as a basis for Kātib Çelebi's *Jihānnümā*, also circulated separately. Yirmisekiz Çelebi Meḥmed consulted it in preparation for his trip to Vienna.

Bekr el-Dimeshqī (d. 1102/1691), and the dissemination of Kātib Çelebi's works in the official printing-press directed by İbrāhīm Müteferriqa (d. 1158/1745).[91] The latter also wrote treatises on European affairs, to provide Ottoman decision makers with information on their adversaries.[92] The Hungarian-born Müteferriqa's role is characteristic of the way in which learned individuals, both native Ottomans and converts, gained state patronage as cultural mediators and marshalled arguments in favour of political and military reforms.[93] Subsequently, this practice of translating geographical and political works blended with the accounts of embassies, when a former ambassador to Vienna and Berlin, Aḥmed Resmī, compiled a *Jughrāfyā-yi jedīd*.[94] The twelfth/eighteenth century saw the production of numerous other, smaller treatises on Europe, while other parts of the world went virtually unnoticed.

By the end of this period the literarisation of geography, still palpable in the *History of the West Indies* and the Ottoman reception of Pīrī Re'īs, had been reversed: knowledge about the *dār al-ḥarb* once again served clearly defined, practical purposes. This explains why Western sources could now be blended almost seamlessly with the Ottoman classics, although the share of the latter actually decreased to virtually nothing by the time of the *Jedīd atlas tercümesi*, a rendering of William Faden's *General atlas* printed together with a systematic introduction in 1803.[95] However, while geographical knowledge met a strategic need, this was not true for history, which still tended to be read moralistically, as a provider of examples. The numerous Ottoman world historians between Muṣṭafā ʿĀlī and Münejjimbashı took no notice of the translation into Turkish of a history of France, originally written in the sixteenth century.[96] Kātib Çelebi commissioned a translation of Johannes Carion's sixteenth-century Protestant chronicle, but it is not clear if he intended to use this

91 Orlin Sabev, *İbrahim Müteferrika ya da ilk Osmanlı matbaa serüveni (1726–1746): Yeniden değerlendirme*, (Istanbul, 2006).

92 Victor Ménage, 'Three Ottoman treatises on Europe', in C. E. Bosworth (ed.), *Iran and Islam: In memory of the late Vladimir Minorsky* (Edinburgh, 1971).

93 ʿOsmān ibn ʿAbdülmennān (d. *c.* 1786), a translator in Belgrade, wrote a world geography based largely on Varenius' *Geographia generalis*: see Konstantinos Thanasakis, 'The Ottoman geographer Osman b. Abdülmennan and his vision of the world in *Tercüme-i Kitāb-i coğrāfyā* (ca. 1749–1750)', MA thesis, Boğaziçi University (2006). We wish to thank Mr Thanasakis for making this work available to us.

94 Ekmeleddin İhsanoğlu (ed.), *Osmanlı coğrafya literatürü tarihi*, 2 vols. (Istanbul, 2000); Aksan, *An Ottoman statesman*, p. 38, refers to it as a translation of an unidentified text.

95 See Kemal Beydilli, *Türk bilim ve matbaacılık tarihinde Mühendishâne, Mühendishâne Matbaası ve kütüphanesi (1776–1826)* (Istanbul, 1995), pp. 169–72.

96 Jean-Louis Bacqué-Grammont (ed.), *La première histoire de France en turc ottoman: Chroniques des padichahs de France* (Paris, 1997).

work to revise his own world history.[97] Other translations of historical texts have been noted, but these also remained without further impact.[98]

Conclusion

From the beginnings of Islam until the early modern period, Muslims who crossed political and geographical boundaries into the *dār al-ḥarb* typically crossed social and literary boundaries as well. And when these Muslims wrote about what they had experienced, observed or imagined, their accounts could not be measured against the standard of what was considered to be secure knowledge, all the more so since these writers tended to lack scholarly pedigrees. Not surprisingly, therefore, Muslim accounts of the *dār al-ḥarb* usually ended up as fragments of knowledge situated at the margins of the accepted canon, or outside it altogether. All this did not prevent the circulation of practical information, but it was only in the early modern and colonial period, with its tendency towards the unification of knowledge, that 'xenology' – drawing on both eyewitness reports and older, written sources – found expression in a full-fledged, accepted set of literary genres. At that point, as literary and journalistic writing proliferated, the concept of *dār al-ḥarb* became more or less irrelevant, as cultural boundaries became blurred, and the exoticism of the periphery vanished altogether.

97 Hagen, *Ein osmanischer Geograph*, p. 67.

98 For another example, see Aksan, *An Ottoman statesman*, p. 41, n. 20. On Temeshvarlı 'Osmān Agha, see above.

PART IV

*

LEARNING, ARTS AND CULTURE

20

Education

FRANCIS ROBINSON

The English term 'knowledge', Franz Rosenthal reminds us, does not fully convey the 'factual and emotional' weight of the Arabic *'ilm*. *'Ilm*, he continues, 'is one of those concepts that have dominated Islam and given Muslim civilization its distinctive shape and complexion'.[1] The central role of knowledge, of course, flows from the importance of making Islamic civilisation's greatest treasures, the Qur'ān and the *ḥadīth* (the reported sayings and doings of the Prophet Muḥammad), live and work in each day, each year and each generation of Muslim life. There is no part of Muslim life, Rosenthal continues, 'that remained untouched by the all-pervasive attitude toward "knowledge" as something of supreme value for the Muslim being. *'Ilm* is Islam even if the theologians have been hesitant to accept the technical correctness of this equation.'[2] Without knowledge there could be no salvation.

It was for this reason that the famous treatise on teaching and learning by the seventh/thirteenth-century scholar al-Zarnūjī made the pursuit of learning a requirement for all Muslims, male and female.[3] They were to seek knowledge, moreover, as the oft-repeated tradition stated, 'even if it be in China'.[4] This was, furthermore, an activity that should consume them from the cradle to the grave, so al-Zarnūjī (d. 602/1223) tells the story of Muḥammad ibn al-Ḥasan (d. 179/795), who appeared to a believer in a dream to say that he had been so absorbed in thinking about the manumission of slaves that he had not noticed his own death.[5] Such was the emphasis on learning that traditions

1 Franz Rosenthal, *Knowledge triumphant: The concept of knowledge in medieval Islam* (Leiden, 1970) p. 2.
2 Ibid.
3 Burhān al-Dīn al-Zarnūjī, *Ta'līm al-muta'allim-ṭarīq at-ta'allum. Instruction of the student: The method of learning*, trans. G. E. Von Grunebaum and Theodora M. Abel (New York, 1947), p. 21.
4 Jonathan Berkey, *The transmission of knowledge in medieval Cairo: A social history of Islamic education* (Princeton, 1992), p. 1, n. 1.
5 Zarnūjī, *Ta'līm*, p. 57.

exalting the superiority of learning over prayer, or the ink of the scholar over the blood of the martyr, were frequently quoted. Such was the impact of learning, as well as the esteem in which it was held, that the thirteenth-century Baghdadi scholar ʿAbd al-Laṭīf (d. 629/1231) in his advice to students declared:

> Know that learning leaves a trail and a scent proclaiming its possessor: a ray of light and brightness shining on him, pointing him out, like the musk merchant whose location cannot be hidden, nor his wares unknown.[6]

This said, it was understood that a Muslim's learning should be in accordance with his status in the world. Every believer should know the requirements of the five pillars of Islam. Beyond this believers should know enough to conduct their occupations and professions lawfully in the sight of God.[7] Nevertheless, there was a predilection to place high value on achievement in learning, and unsurprisingly the learned gave it the highest value. Man, declared Ibn Khaldūn (d. 808/1406), 'reaches perfection of his form through knowledge'.[8]

By the same token Muslim societies accorded scholars great honour. They were, after all, the guardians in their time, and the transmitters to future generations, of the central messages that helped to mould Muslim societies. They were often referred to as the 'heirs to the Prophets'. 'Kings are the rulers of people', went one oft-quoted tradition, 'but scholars are the rulers of kings'.[9] In their role as teachers – and there were few scholars who did not teach – students were to esteem and venerate them as they were their own fathers:

> In venerating the teacher [among other things it is necessary to avoid] walking in front of him or sitting in his place. Also one should not begin speaking in his presence without his permission, and then one should not speak to any great extent before him. One should not ask him any [question] when he is weary. One should observe the correct time … In short one should seek his approval, avoid his resentment, and obey his commands in those things which are not sinful in the eyes of God.[10]

This respect for the teacher as the transmitter of the central messages of Islam was typical of Muslim societies down to the twentieth century.

6 George Makdisi, *The rise of colleges: Institutions of learning in Islam and the West* (Edinburgh, 1981), p. 91.
7 Zarnūjī, *Taʿlīm*, p. 21.
8 Ibn Khaldūn, *The* Muqaddimah*: An introduction to history*, trans. Franz Rosenthal, 2nd edn, 4 vols. (London, 1967), vol. II, p. 425.
9 Berkey, *Transmission of knowledge*, p. 4.
10 Zarnūjī, *Taʿlīm*, p. 33.

With this respect went an expectation of the highest standards of behaviour. In his *Iḥyāʾ* al-Ghazālī (d. 505/1111) sets out the 'signs of the learned man of the hereafter': he focuses on the next world rather than this; he practises what he preaches; he fosters piety; he avoids luxury in food and dress; he shuns the powerful; he is deliberate and careful in giving his opinion; he is sincere, humble, avoids innovation and so on.[11] But scholars, being no more than human, found it difficult to sustain these high ideals. There was a constant stream of criticism of those who fell short of the ideal. Al-Ghazālī himself was deeply critical of the scholars of his day who, out of self-interest, placed their weight behind government decrees, or who, as 'prattling wearers of flowing robes', became obsessed by the minutiae of law at the cost of the true meaning of the Qurʾān.[12] Indeed, al-Ghazālī's life itself, as depicted in his autobiography, *al-Munqidh min al-ḍalāl* (The deliverance from error), formed a journey in which he came to realise the worthlessness of worldly advancement as compared with growth in spiritual understanding.[13] Shaykh Saʿdī Shirāzī's (d. 691/1292) *Gulistān*, which was used in schools wherever Persian was spoken from Istanbul to Bengal, and from Central Asia to East Africa, reveals a sharp nose for the hypocrisy of the learned, whether it was the teacher who did not practise what he taught or the notorious *qāḍī* (judge of Islamic law) of Hamadhān, who was found, stupefied with drink, in bed with a boy.[14] Such was the sartorial splendour of the *ʿulamāʾ* (religious scholars) in Mamlūk Egypt, in particular their wearing of outsize turbans, that the streetplayers of Cairo would perform a satire called 'The manner of the judge' in which the scholarly interpreters of the *sharīʿa* (Islamic law) were lampooned, parading in outsize turbans, sleeves and long scarves.[15]

The fields of knowledge

Throughout the middle period of Islamic history knowledge tended to be divided into two broad fields: the *ʿulūm naqliyya*, the transmitted or traditional sciences, all of which owed their existence to God's revelation to man through Muḥammad; and the *ʿulūm ʿaqliyya*, the rational sciences, all of which were

11 Abū Ḥāmid Muḥammad al-Ghazālī, *Imam Gazzali's Ihya ulum-id-din*, trans. al-Haj Maulana Fazul-ul-Karim (Lahore, n.d.), book I, pp. 73–109.
12 Ebrahim Moosa, *Ghazālī and the poetics of imagination* (Karachi, 2005), pp. 8–10.
13 William Montgomery Watt (trans.), *The faith and practice of al-Ghazālī* (Oxford, 1994).
14 Shaykh Mushrifuddin Saʿdi of Shiraz, *The* Gulistan *of Saʿdi*, trans. W. M. Thackston (Bethesda, 2008), pp. 68, 119–23.
15 Berkey, *Transmission of knowledge*, pp. 182–3.

derived from man's capacity to think and in which he was guided by his human perceptions. These might equally be referred to as Greek, foreign or ancient sciences. This was how Khwārizmī (*fl.* 364–77/975–87) divided knowledge in the fourth/tenth century.[16] It is how Ibn Khaldūn described it in the eighth/fourteenth century.[17] It was, moreover, the classic division of knowledge in the academic curricula developed under the Ottomans, Ṣafavids and Mughals.[18] In these curricula the subjects associated with *adab*, the literary arts, were more often than not made supportive of the traditional sciences.[19] Nevertheless, in the fourth/tenth century Ibn al-Nadīm (d. 385/995) and in the fifth/eleventh Ibn Buṭlān (d. 485/1066) identified the literary arts as a separate field; and so, for expository purposes, shall we.[20]

In his *Muqaddima* Ibn Khaldūn lists the subjects that make up his two main fields of knowledge. In the traditional sciences the first, of course, was the Qur'ān; the seven established ways of reading it; and the forms of Qur'ān commentary (*tafsīr*). The second related to the *ḥadīth*, the systems for establishing 'sound' transmission and the great collections of traditions, of which al-Bukhārī's *Ṣaḥīḥ* held the highest rank. This was followed by jurisprudence (*fiqh*), the classification of the laws of God, as derived from the Qur'ān and the traditions, including especial attention to the laws of inheritance. There followed the principles of jurisprudence (*uṣūl al-fiqh*), the disciplines by which jurists and scholars reached decisions on matters of law plus the forms of disputation that lay at the core of legal studies. Speculative theology (*kalām*) was also included, in spite of the dangers to orthodoxy it might represent, because the skills the discipline developed were crucial to defending articles of faith and to refuting the claims of innovators.[21] The final major subject in this field was Sufism (*taṣawwuf*), the approach of which 'is based upon constant application to divine worship, complete devotion to God, aversion to the false splendor of the world, abstinence from the pleasure, property, and position to which the great mass aspires, and retirement from the world into solitude for divine worship'.[22] This had been the very particular experience of al-Ghazālī. It was also the personal achievement of al-Ghazālī to

16 George Makdisi, *The rise of humanism in classical Islam and the Christian West with special reference to scholasticism* (Edinburgh, 1990), p. 88.
17 Ibn Khaldūn, *The* Muqaddimah, vol. II, pp. 436–9.
18 Francis Robinson, *The 'ulama of Farangi Mahall and Islamic culture in South Asia* (Delhi, 2001), pp. 221–51.
19 Ibid.; Makdisi, *The rise of colleges*, p. 76.
20 Makdisi, *The rise of humanism*, p. 88.
21 Ibn Khaldūn, *The* Muqaddimah, vol. II, pp. 436–63, vol. III, pp. 1–75.
22 Ibid., vol. III, p. 76.

bring orthodoxy and Sufism into close enough contact for the two sides to respect each other's positions, for the most part, in word and deed. This said, by Ibn Khaldūn's time the emergence of the *wujūdī* doctrines of Ibn al-ʿArabī and the increasing manifestation of ecstatic practices was causing discomfort among jurists and *muftīs* (experts in Islamic law who deliver legal opinions (*fatāwā*)).[23] It was a discomfort felt throughout the middle period of Islamic history, and much more so in recent times.

The rational sciences, according to Ibn Khaldūn, were four in number. They were derived from the Greek works, the translation of which into Arabic began during the caliphate of Hārūn al-Rashīd (r. 170–93/786–809) and continued to the end of the tenth century, and the impact of which produced a major intellectual awakening. The first was logic (*manṭiq*), which protected 'the mind from error in the process of evolving unknown facts'.[24] Aristotle was the man who had systematised the subject and made it the first philosophical discipline. It was for this reason that he was called 'the First Teacher', and his book on logic 'The Text'.[25] Major commentaries and abridgements were written by al-Fārābī (d. 339/950), Ibn Sīnā (d. 428/1037) and Ibn Rushd (d. 595/1196). The second area was physics (*al-tabīʿiyyāt*), the elements perceived by the senses, minerals, plants and animals, plus the movements of the heavens. Two subsets of this subject were medicine, where Galen was the leading Greek authority and Ibn Khaldūn acknowledged a host of Muslim physicians of 'surpassing skill'; and agriculture, which involved the cultivation and growth of plants through irrigation, proper treatment, improvement of the soil and so on.[26] Metaphysics (*ʿilm al-ilāhiyyāt*), was the third major division, with all the dangers of uncontrolled philosophical speculation that went with it. Ibn Khaldūn was clear about where its boundaries should be drawn: 'When the Lawgiver (Muḥammad) guides us towards some perception, we must prefer that (perception) to our own perception.'[27] The fourth area was the mathematical sciences (*taʿālīm*), which included geometry, arithmetic, astronomy and music – the theory of tones and their definition by numbers. A series of further subdivisions were recognised – for instance, the craft of calculation, algebra, business arithmetic, the arithmetic of inheritance laws, spherical

23 Ibid., pp. 99–103.
24 Ibid., p. 111.
25 Ibid., p. 139.
26 Ibid., pp. 147–52.
27 Ibid., p. 154.

figures, conic sections, and mechanics, surveying, optics and astronomical tables.[28]

Scholars in the middle Islamic period differed over precisely what subjects constituted what has been termed *adab* humanism.[29] We shall follow the analysis of the leading scholar of the subject. Grammar was the most important part of *adab* studies. It was central to everything a scholar did in Arabic, from poetry through to the writing of formal documents and the making of speeches. But it was more than this; it was essential to maintaining the purity of the language of the Qurʾān, and of understanding it and interpreting it.[30] Of course, there were many maxims. 'Grammatical speech is the beauty of the lowly', went one, 'and solecism the blemish on the great'.[31] Poetry, with prose in close attendance, was the 'premier art of *adab*, as grammar is its premier instrument'.[32] It was the field of *adab*, moreover, in which literary production was more prolific than in almost all others combined. In a society in which command of language, and its public use, was particularly highly valued the capacity to fashion beautiful words was a central means of praise and persuasion no less than the command of a large stock of verse, and the capacity to deploy it in conversation to telling effect was the mark of a cultivated man. 'Poetry', declared Abu 'l-ʿAbbās al-Nāshiʾ (d. 293/906), 'is the bond of words, the rich ransom of humanism, the retaining wall of eloquence, the locus of skill, the range of the soul, the illustration of rhetoric'.[33] Eloquence, Makdisi tells us, was the most essential part of Arab humanism, 'the kernel and apex' of *adab* studies. The spur, of course, was the Qurʾān, which Muslims knew they could not emulate but which, nevertheless, made eloquence highly prized throughout the Muslim world. 'Learn how to speak eloquently', the caliph al-Maʾmūn's prime minister told his son, 'for it is through speech that man is superior to all other animals; and the more skilful you are in speaking, the more worthy you are of humanity.'[34] There was, moreover, the sense that eloquence was less about decorative language than about the effective match of language and meaning. 'Eloquence', declared a tenth-century poet, 'consists in words

28 Ibid., pp. 121–37. We should note that Ibn Khaldūn acknowledges other areas of knowledge: sorcery and the use of amulets, the evil eye, forms of letter magic and alchemy. He is profoundly aware both of their existence and of the damage that, along with metaphysics, they can do to religion. Ibid., pp. 156–246.

29 Makdisi, *The rise of humanism*, pp. 88–96.

30 Ibid., p. 129.

31 Ibid., p. 128.

32 Ibid., p. 131.

33 Ibid., pp. 137–8.

34 Ibid., p. 143.

reaching their meaning before travelling too long.'[35] Allied to eloquence was oratory, which might embrace all subjects and all occasions in Muslim public life, but which was always classically deployed in the *khuṭba*, or sermon, in Friday congregational prayers. 'A good part of the affairs of religion', declared the eleventh-century scholar Abū Hilāl al-ʿAskarī (d. after 400/1009), 'fall to the lot of oratory: for oratory is that part of ritual prayer which is the pillar of religion and feast days, Fridays, and gatherings of the Faithful.'[36]

Yet another form of *adab* in which eloquence had its place was the art of letter writing. This was an essential tool of government and diplomacy no less than the means by which personal relationships were sustained across distances. Manuals of good practice were produced, and the many collections of model letters have been an important source for historians down to the present. History as *akhbār*-history, literary history, as opposed to *ta'rīkh*, chronologically dated history, was a further dimension of *adab*, which reaches towards the historical novel and forms of biography.[37] Finally, there was the moral philosophy of *adab* which was 'an eclectic combination of foreign and Islamic traditions'. These might embrace Persian moral thought and Greek philosophical ethics as well as the Qur'ān and the *sunna* (the example of the Prophet Muḥammad).[38] Moral philosophy became a particular feature of *waʿẓ*, the academic sermon, which might be given by an independent scholar in a range of contexts from mosque or *madrasa* through to his own home. In the eleventh and twelfth centuries *waʿẓ* became an important vehicle for the assertion of traditionalist understandings against those of the rationalists.[39]

The relationship between the traditional sciences and the other two is worthy of comment. That with the rational sciences was never particularly smooth. Some scholars were always suspicious of an intellectual tradition whose sources lay outside Islamic history – which was not unreasonable, as few could forget the attempt of the rationalists in the third/ninth century to impose their understanding of revelation on the traditionalists. Endowments, moreover, establishing *madrasas* tended to exclude the teaching of rational subjects as inimical to Islam, although *madrasa* libraries might still contain their books.[40] On occasion hostility might go much further, as

35 Ibid., p. 145.
36 Ibid., p. 152.
37 Ibid., pp. 163–7.
38 Ibid., pp. 171–2.
39 Ibid., pp. 173–200. For comment on the art of the academic sermon, and its attendant dangers, see George Makdisi, *Ibn ʿAqil: Religion and culture in classical Islam* (Edinburgh, 1997), pp. 220–8.
40 Makdisi, *The rise of colleges*, pp. 77–8.

for instance when the Ayyūbid sultan al-Malik al-Kāmil (r. 615–35/1218–38), forbade the *ʿulamāʾ* of Damascus from teaching or studying any subject but the traditional sciences; students of the rational sciences were expelled.[41] This was an extreme action, but evidence of the tension between the fields of knowledge frequently cropped up. It lay behind the great rivalry at Tīmūr's court in Samarqand between Saʿd al-Dīn Taftāzānī (d. 792/1389), who favoured the traditional sciences, and Sayyid Sharīf al-Jurjānī (d. 816/1413), who favoured the rational sciences.[42] In Tīmūr's time it is generally thought that Jurjānī had the upper hand, but the patronage of Tīmūr's successor, Shāh Rukh, in establishing a *madrasa* at Herat a few years later shifted the advantage back to Taftāzānī's position.[43] This tension also lay behind the debate at the end of the fifteenth century between Muḥammad al-Maghīlī (d. 909/1503 or 910/1504) and al-Suyūṭī over the study of logic.[44] This said, teachers might give courses in both fields, while student patterns of learning would often include subjects from the two fields as well.[45] As time went on the areas in which the rational sciences flourished most vigorously were Tīmūrid Central Asia, Shīʿite Iran and Mughal northern India.

The relationship between the traditional sciences and *adab* studies was less fraught. The centrality of knowledge of Arabic, and how to use it well, to the traditional sciences sustained a strong link. 'Whoever seeks to learn *ḥadīth* without knowing grammar', went one tradition, 'is like a jackass whose feedbag has no oats.'[46] A second strong link was that the Qurʾān itself was the foundation and inspiration of many *adab* disciplines. This is not to suggest, however, that the relationship was completely harmonious. The masters of *ḥadīth* did not always value the presence of grammarians, while students of *ḥadīth* were not welcome among the humanists. 'Here come the bores', declared one poetry teacher as students of *ḥadīth* joined his teaching circle.[47] Nevertheless, we can conclude with Makdisi that 'the ideal education was to

41 Jonathan Berkey, *The formation of Islam: Religion and society in the Near East, 600–1800* (Cambridge, 2003), p. 230.

42 Maria Eva Subtelny and Anas B. Khalidov, 'The curriculum of Islamic higher learning in Timurid Iran in the light of the Sunni revival under Shah-Rukh', *JAOS*, 115, 2 (1995), p. 214.

43 Ibid., pp. 210–36.

44 Elias N. Saad, *The social history of Timbuktu: The role of Muslim scholars and notables 1400–1900* (Cambridge, 1983), p. 80.

45 Makdisi, *The rise of colleges*, pp. 78–9; Michael Chamberlain, *Knowledge and social practice in medieval Damascus, 1190–1350* (Cambridge, 1994), pp. 83–4.

46 Makdisi, *The rise of humanism*, p. 99.

47 Ibid., p. 105.

master both worlds of learning, to be a scholar and a humanist, to combine the critical scholarship of the *'ālim* [religious scholar] and the urbane elegance and refinement, *ẓarf*, of the humanist *adīb*'.[48]

The transmission of knowledge

The transmission of knowledge was not, for the most part, a matter of formal institutional arrangements: it was an informal and intensely personal process between teacher and pupil. Thus when Muslims talked of the bringing of learning to a particular region, or its revival, they talked of the impact of individual scholars, as Ibn Khaldūn did about the return of serious learning to north-west Africa in the thirteenth century,[49] and as the Kano Chronicle described the impact of al-Maghīlī on the city at the end of the fifteenth century[50] and the Muslims of Madras in 1941 described the impact of Baḥr al-'Ulūm Farangī Maḥallī (d. 1225/1810) on southern India at the end of the eighteenth.[51] Because the personal relationship was so important, it made the student's choice of teacher critical. He was urged to take time over the business and consider very carefully the man's learning, piety and age.[52] The personal element, moreover, was underlined by the great biographical dictionaries which recorded with whom a student studied and what he studied, but little if anything about where he studied. The quality of an education 'was judged', Berkey tells us, 'not on *loci* but on *personae*'.[53]

The personal nature of the transmission of knowledge was emphasised by the *ḥalqa*, or study circle, in which teaching took place, and the etiquette that governed its proceedings. Such circles might operate in a variety of environments, as the teacher found convenient: in a mosque, private house, shop or *madrasa*; or perhaps under a tree or on a river bank. The teacher decided who was to be admitted to the circle and when it met, as well as the sequence of subjects and the methods of instruction. Teaching began and ended with prayers. The teacher would sit on a cushion or a chair with his back to a wall or a pillar, and his students would sit cross-legged in a semi-circle before him. As the student succeeded in his studies he was invited to sit closer to the teacher, thus biographies might state of an able student: the teacher 'brought the

48 Ibid., p. 112.
49 Ibn Khaldūn, *The* Muqaddimah, vol. II, pp. 427–9.
50 H. J. Fisher, 'The eastern Maghrib and the central Sudan', in R. Oliver (ed.), *The Cambridge history of Africa*, vol. III: *From c. 1050 to c. 1600* (Cambridge, 1977), p. 295.
51 S. S. Pirzada, *Foundations of Pakistan: All India Muslim League documents 1906–1947*, 2 vols. (Karachi, 1970), vol. II, p. 351.
52 Berkey, *Transmission of knowledge*, pp. 22–3.
53 Ibid., p. 23.

student close to him'.[54] Biographical dictionaries used the term *ṣuḥba*, 'companionship' or 'discipleship', to describe the relationship between the teacher and his closest students. Derived from the days of the Prophet and his Companions, it implied, as Ephrat tells us, 'an extremely close personal and intellectual relationship between teacher and student, one fostered over the course of many years'.[55] The world of *ʿilm* from the Maghrib to South-East Asia was held together by tens of thousands of such relationships.

The personal nature of the teacher–student relationship was further expressed in the precise method of transmitting knowledge. Oral, person-to-person transmission was greatly preferred to private study. 'The Qurʾān', declared Ibn Khaldūn in discussing the art of teaching, 'has been the basis of instruction, the foundation of all habits that may be acquired later on.'[56] The Qurʾān, the recitation, was realised and received as divine, by being read out aloud. It was always transmitted orally. It was thus that the Prophet had transmitted the message he received from God to his followers. And when, a few years after the Prophet's death, these messages came to be written down, it was as an aid to memory and oral transmission. Learning the Qurʾān was the first task of young Muslim boys and girls, and in this context again it was orally transmitted. The usual method was that each day the teacher would dictate some verses, which the students would write on their slates, or have written for them. The student would then spend the rest of the day learning them. Those who were able to recite them successfully the next day, in addition to what had been recently transmitted, would have fresh verses dictated to them.

Oral transmission in the early Islamic centuries had a similar role to play in the publication of a book. Its writing down, like that of the Qurʾān, was merely an aid to oral publication. The author would dictate his first draft either from memory or from his own notes; the copyist would then read it back to him. Publication would then take place through the copyist reading the text to the author in public, usually in a mosque. During the process the author might make additions and emendations, and several readings might be required before it was given his authorisation. This was known as his *ijāza*, which

54 Daphna Ephrat, *A learned society in a period of transition: The Sunni ʿulamaʾ of eleventh-century Baghdad* (Albany, 2000), pp. 76–9; Christopher Melchert, 'The etiquette of learning in the early Islamic study circle', in Joseph E. Lowry, Devin J. Stewart and Shawkat M. Toorawa (eds.), *Law and education in medieval Islam: Studies in memory of Professor George Makdisi*, E. J. W. Gibb Memorial Trust (Chippenham, 2004), pp. 33–44.
55 Ephrat, *Learned society*, p. 81.
56 Ibn Khaldūn, *The* Muqaddimah, vol. III, p. 300.

meant 'to make lawful'. Thus the author gave permission for the work 'to be transmitted from him'. Further copies had real authority only when they had been read back to the author and approved.[57]

A teacher would transmit one of the great texts of Islamic education in a similar way. He would dictate the book to his students, who might write it down, but almost certainly would commit it to memory – in time such pedagogical texts came to be written in rhyme to help the memory. Subsequently there might be an explanation of the text, depending on its nature. The completion of the study of the book would involve a recitation of the text with an explanation. If this was done to the teacher's satisfaction, the student would be given an *ijāza*, a licence to transmit that text, which has been well described by Berkey as 'a personal authority' over the text.[58] On that *ijāza* would be the names of all those who had transmitted the text, going back to the original author. The pupil was left in no doubt that he was now the trustee of knowledge transmitted from person to person from the past.

It might be asked why person-to-person transmission of knowledge, involving recitation out aloud, should persist in a society where scholars were highly proficient in reading and writing, paper was plentiful and book production a major activity. The problem was that there was scepticism about the written word, the understandable scepticism of an oral society, in which an individual might be in the most literal sense *baḥr al-ʿulūm*, an ocean of knowledge. 'Language', declares Ibn Khaldūn, 'is merely the interpretation of ideas that are in the mind.' Oral expression was crucial to extracting the meaning from language. The study of books and written materials placed a veil between representation and meaning; it 'separates handwriting and the form of letters found in writing from the spoken words found in the imagination'.[59] To understand words properly the student had to read them out aloud. So as the Qurʾān gained full realisation only in being recited out aloud, so too did the academic book only give of its full meaning to the student by being read, or recited, aloud. Truth, it was felt, was more likely to be transmitted in speech than in writing. The *ḥalqa* could be a very noisy affair.

The emphasis on person-to-person transmission had at least two important consequences for the Muslim world. One was that most scholars travelled widely so that they could receive knowledge in person. The custom had begun with the early collection of *ḥadīth*. It was vigorously continued by

57 J. Pedersen, *The Arabic book*, ed. R. Hillenbrand, trans. G. French (Princeton, 1984), pp. 20–36.

58 Berkey, *Transmission of knowledge*, p. 34.

59 Ibn Khaldūn, *The* Muqaddimah, vol. III, pp. 316–17.

later scholars, spurred by a real desire for truth but not unaware of the increase in authority that such journeys might bring. Of course, the search for knowledge came in time to be combined with that for academic position. So ʿAbd al-Laṭīf moved from Baghdad to Mosul, from place to place in Anatolia, to Cairo twice, to Damascus twice, to Jerusalem twice and to Aleppo twice. The Spanish scholar-mystic Ibn al-ʿArabī (d. 638/1240) travelled from Murcia to Seville, Tunis, Fez, Cordoba, Almería, to Tunis again, twice each to Cairo, Jerusalem, Mecca and Baghdad, and to Mosul, Malatya, Sīvās, Konya and Damascus. So too, the remarkable writer of pedagogical texts, Sayyid Sharīf al-Jurjānī, travelled from Taju by the Caspian, to Herat, Karaman, Alexandria, Constantinople, Shīrāz and to Samarqand, where he was to become a great figure at Tīmūr's court. When a scholar could not get knowledge from an author in person, he strove to get it from a scholar whose *isnād*, or chain of transmission from the original author, was thought to be the most reliable.

The second consequence of person-to-person transmission, which flowed from the first, was that the Muslim world came to be covered by networks of teacher–student connections. From the eleventh century Baghdad found itself at the centre of such a network.[60] From the fifteenth century Timbuktu in West Africa was also such a centre.[61] Cairo was always a great centre, a role exemplified in the fifteenth century by the endowment deeds of several of its large *madrasa*s which enabled students to visit their families all over the world.[62] An *ijāza* given by the Egyptian polymath al-Sakhāwī (d. 902/1497) to Ibn al-Ḥīshī (b. 848/1444) in Mecca is equally revealing of a truly cosmopolitan world of scholarship.[63] It is thus that we can begin to see how *ʿilm*, and its person-to-person transmission across the Muslim world, was one of the key links that held this world together.

The deeply personal nature of this person-to-person transmission is brought home by the wording, and perhaps the underlying humour, of the following *ijāza* bestowed by ʿIzz al-Dīn ibn Jamāʿa (d. 819/1416):

> The student mentioned herein presented before me also in a good, precise, orderly, masterful, and excellent manner, a presentation of one whose memorization is perfect, whose pronunciation is adorned by excellent performance, and whose fortune has been bestowed abundantly by the spring of divine concern. He raced through the text like a fleet courser in a lion-infested

60 Ephrat, *Learned society*, pp. 33–74.
61 Saad, *Timbuktu*, pp. 58–93.
62 Berkey, *Transmission of knowledge*, p. 91.
63 A.J. Arberry, *Sakhawiana* (London, 1951).

> plain ... I hereby permit him to transmit from me the above-mentioned book, all that is permitted for me to transmit, and all that may be transmitted from me, of my own writings and those of others, in poetry and prose, in the transmitted, rational, and traditional sciences, according to the conditions recognized by the specialists in transmission.[64]

Among the aids to learning – and this went for all fields of knowledge – were memory, disputation and note taking. Memory, as the support merely of the transmission of knowledge, was the attribute of the ordinary scholar. Above this level, for the humanist and scholastic, it was the support for creativity and understanding, and finally at the forefront of knowledge it might be the basis of *ijtihād*, producing one's own ideas.[65] The biographical dictionaries are full of stories, doubtless some exaggerated, of prodigious feats of memory, of whole libraries restored from memory after a fire.[66] Moreover, men literally dipped into the memories of great scholars. 'When we needed knowledge', one wrote, 'we ladled from his ocean what was not to be had in books.'[67] The transmission of knowledge was only really valued from those who produced it from memory.[68] In consequence, the educational guides spoke of those things that helped memory: for instance, working early in the morning; avoiding heavy foods, and places where one might be distracted, and those things that hindered it, for instance, 'eating fresh coriander, acid apples and beholding a man crucified'.[69] For all its centrality memorisation was not an end in itself. Real learning also meant understanding, being able to use critically the materials memorised and apply them to academic problems. 'Memorizing two words is better than hearing two pages', went one aphorism, 'but understanding two words is better than memorizing two pages.'[70]

Forms of instructive conversation (*mudhākara*), and the notebook (*daftar*) were further aids to memory. At one level such conversations might involve students drilling or quizzing each other after a lesson. At another level this conversation might develop into a *munāẓara*, or formal disputation, over a point of grammar perhaps, or drawing on verse to debate a particular theme. At the apex of education, for a scholar about to emerge as a professor of law, mastery of disputation was the final stage. Great debates had all the thrills, in

64 D. Stewart, 'The doctorate of Islamic law in Mamluk Egypt and Syria', in Lowry *et al.* (eds.), *Law and education*, p. 74.
65 Makdisi, *The rise of humanism*, p. 202.
66 Makdisi, *The rise of colleges*, pp. 99–103.
67 Makdisi, *The rise of humanism*, p. 202.
68 Chamberlain, *Knowledge and social practice*, p. 145.
69 Zarnūjī, *Taʿlīm*, p. 69.
70 Berkey, *Transmission of knowledge*, p. 30.

performance and in recollection, of boxing matches.[71] Taking notes was crucial to prompt the memory and help preserve undistorted what had been transmitted. Scholars jealously guarded their notebooks; al-Ghazālī told a robber that he could take everything but his notebooks. 'My boon companion is my cat', declared the *adab* scholar Ibn Fāris (d. 395/1005), 'my notebook, the intimate of my soul.'[72]

The enormous emphasis on person-to-person transmission of knowledge should not lead us to think that self-teaching did not take place. It tended not to happen in the traditional sciences, where issues of authority were crucial and where teachers and students were often supported by institutional stipends and scholarships. But in the rational sciences and in *adab* studies self-teaching was not uncommon. This is evident from the numbers of books written specifically for the autodidact – for instance, Khwārizmī's *Miftāḥ al-'ulūm* (Keys to the sciences), which covered all the main fields of knowledge, or Ibn Hindū's (d. 410/1019) *Miftāḥ al-ṭibb* (The key to medicine). Some scholars admitted to teaching themselves, so Ibn Sīnā (d. 428/1037) taught himself medicine as a teenager and Fakhr al-Dīn al-Rāzī (d. 606/1209) taught himself the rational sciences while holding a position in a college of law. This said, the enduring preference was, whatever the subject, that the student should learn from a teacher. 'I command you not to learn your sciences from books unaided', 'Abd al-Laṭīf of Baghdad advised his students, 'even though you may trust your ability to understand.'[73]

The *ijāza* the student received after successfully completing the learning of a book at the feet of his teacher was a potent symbol of authority. As we have noted, it gave the student authority over a text – over part of the knowledge that helped to shape Islamic civilisation. In a specific social environment it was the symbol of the authority he derived from a close bond to a more senior scholar. It also enabled him to access some of the authority of those mentioned in the *ijāza*'s *isnād*, back to the original author of the book. It was also a form of authority that existed outside, and often opposed to, political power. Arguably in its supreme form it was not a licence to transmit knowledge but the *ijāzat al-tadrīs wa'l-iftā'*, the authorisation to teach law and issue legal opinions, that Makdisi has argued was the origin of the European *licentia docendi*.[74] The force of the *ijāza*, in whatever form, as a source of authority was evident in medieval Muslim society. So the great Egyptian scholar Ibn Suyūṭī

71 Makdisi, *The rise of humanism*, pp. 208–9; Makdisi, *The rise of colleges*, pp. 128–40.
72 Makdisi, *The rise of humanism*, p. 214.
73 Ibid., pp. 212–27.
74 Makdisi, *The rise of colleges*, pp. 140–52, 272–6; Stewart, 'The doctorate' .

refused to transmit books in a sphere in which he was an acknowledged expert because he had taught himself and therefore could not do so on the authority of a teacher.[75] Scholars went to great lengths to compile collective biographies indicating the authority that scholars in a family, a school of law or a place had gathered through their *ijāzas*. And so, too, in the ultimate accolade the prestige of the practice was underlined in its abuse as *ijāzas* came to be given without learning the text, or to children who were too young to understand what was going on, or they were just requested by letter.[76]

Madrasas and education

The informality and non-institutional nature of the transmission of knowledge raises the issue of the purpose and function of the *madrasa*, the foundation classically associated with Islamic secondary / higher education. The term itself was derived from the second form of the verb *darrasa*, which, used without a complement, means 'to teach law', giving rise to the term *dars*, a lecture on law, and *mudarris*, a professor of law: a *madrasa* was a school or college in which law was the main subject.[77] From the tenth century purpose-built *madrasas* began to be founded. In time they came to embrace a growing range of provision: stipends for staff; scholarships for students; cells for teachers and students; a residence, perhaps for the founder's family; a mosque; and a mausoleum where the founder's family might be buried. These foundations began in Khurāsān and from the eleventh century spread westward. In 1067 the Saljūq vizier Niẓām al-Mulk (d. 485/1092) founded his famed Niẓāmiyya *madrasa* in Baghdad, where al-Ghazālī was to hold a professorship. Down to the end of the twelfth century this was followed by the foundation of a further twenty-three *madrasas*.[78] By the 1090s the institution reached Damascus, where by 1261 there were fifty-three *madrasas*, and Cairo by the fifteenth century, where there were more than seventy-three. The first *madrasa* was founded in Mecca in 1175, in Delhi in the early thirteenth century, and in Tunis in 1252.[79] By this time, as Berkey suggests, the *madrasa* 'had become perhaps the most characteristic institution of the medieval Near Eastern urban landscape'.[80]

75 Berkey, *Transmission of knowledge*, p. 21.
76 Ibid., pp. 31–3; Ignaz Goldziher, 'Idjāza', *EI2*, vol. III, pp. 1020–2.
77 J. Pedersen and G. Makdisi, 'Madrasa', *EI2*, vol. V, pp. 1123–34.
78 Ephrat, *Learned society*, pp. 28–9.
79 Richard W. Bulliet, *Islam: The view from the edge* (New York, 1994), pp. 147–9.
80 Berkey, *Formation of Islam*, p. 137.

The evolution of the *madrasa* did not stop at this point. Indeed, from the thirteenth through to the fifteenth centuries *madrasa* foundations came to be just part of what has been termed an 'educational–charitable complex'. One of the first of these was completed in 1267–68 by Muḥammad Juwaynī (d. 681/1283), the vizier of the Ilkhān Hülegü. Built in Yazd, it comprised a mosque, a *madrasa*, a hospital, a pharmacy and a madhouse; it was established as one institution by its founding endowment.[81] This form, which might also embrace a library, a Sufi convent, an orphanage, an observatory and a hostel for travellers, spread across Iraq and Iran, reaching a peak in Tīmūrid Khurāsān and Transoxania. Notable examples were that of Ulugh Beg (r. 851–3/1447–9) in Samarqand, which it is said had 10,000 registered students, 500 of them in mathematics,[82] and that of Sultan Ḥusayn Bāyqarā's (r. 873–911/1469–1506) vizier Mīr ʿAlī Shīr Nawāʾī (d. 906/1500), the Ikhlāṣiyya in Herat, which embraced a wide range of functions and, according to Khwāndamīr (d. 940/1534 or 943/1537), fed 1,000 people a day.[83] The idea of the educational–charitable complex also spread to Mamlūk Syria and Egypt. Ten years after the inauguration of Juwaynī's complex in Yazd, the tomb of the Mamlūk sultan Baybars al-Malik al-Ẓāhir (r. 658–76/1260–77) was transformed in this fashion. Over fifty years later this was followed by the largest such development in Cairo, the mausoleum complex of Sultan al-Nāṣir al-Ḥasan (r. 748–52/1347–51), which had provision for among other things 120 Qurʾān readers and 506 students.[84] Such was the fashion for these complexes that earlier foundations began to transform themselves in their image.[85]

There was a view that the spread of *madrasas* was designed to fashion the ideological forces that made the eleventh-century 'Sunni revival' which ended a period of Shīʿite dominance in Iran and Egypt. This view was substantially undermined by George Makdisi, who argued instead that the spread of *madrasas* was part of a process of institutionalising the teaching of law. He saw *madrasas* 'as having an organized and differentiated student body, a specialized curriculum, a professoriate certified to teach, and an institutional

81 Saïd Amir Arjomand, 'The law, agency, and policy in medieval Islamic society: Development of the institutions of learning from the tenth to the fifteenth century', *Comparative Studies in Society and History*, 41, 2 (1999), p. 272.

82 Ibid., p. 275.

83 Ibid., p. 276; Maria Eva Subtelny, 'A Timurid educational and charitable foundation: The Ikhlasiyya complex of ʿAli Shir Navāʾī in 15th-century Herat and its endowment', *JAOS*, 111, 1 (1991).

84 Berkey, *Transmission of knowledge*, pp. 67–9.

85 Arjomand, 'The law', p. 275.

educational goal – the certification of teachers and jurists'.[86] More recent research – based admittedly on one city, Damascus, but supported by research elsewhere – suggests that there is little support for this argument: students had no collective sense of belonging to a group; they did not follow a particular curriculum in law, but put together their own programmes of study; they did not receive *ijāzas* from their *madrasas*, but from their teachers; indeed, *madrasas* seemed to have had no formal corporate existence.[87]

Madrasas were founded by sultans, administrators, soldiers, scholars and judges; they were also founded by the wives of such men. The law of *waqf*, which controlled the transfer of property for charitable purposes, enabled the founder to make whatever provisions he or she wished providing they did not contravene the tenets of Islam. Awareness of the social and political context in which *madrasas* came to be founded, plus a study of *waqfiyyas*, or founding documents, has enabled a more nuanced understanding of the reasons for their spread to emerge. In the context of Mamlūk Cairo, for instance, the building by sultans of great fortress-like *madrasas* was part of the politics of display and commemoration. Such foundations were also a way for the elite, who were not associated with learning, to annex the prestige of scholarship; and if a mausoleum was part of the foundation there was the added bonus of the material remains of the founder and his/her descendants being surrounded by the pursuit of knowledge, by worship. Such foundations also enabled great families to provide posts for all kinds of retainers in their urban milieu. We should not, however, discount genuine pious purposes – which were matters of no small concern, for instance, to Cairo's Mamlūks.[88] This said, there was a powerful material incentive to found *madrasas*: the process of endowment enabled the rich to hand on some of their wealth to their descendants. Once the charitable purposes of a *waqf* had been met, it was legitimate for the remaining resources to go to the descendants of the founder in whatever way had been stipulated.[89] Equally it was possible for the controllership of the endowment to be held by a family member – in one case in Mamlūk Cairo the controllership was worth more than three times the professorship of law.[90] Education, moreover, was not necessarily a high priority: in one *madrasa* foundation preachers, Qur'ān readers, porters and

86 Chamberlain, *Knowledge and social practice*, p. 70.
87 Chamberlain, *Knowledge and social practice*, pp. 69–90; Berkey, *Transmission of knowledge*, pp. 15–20.
88 Berkey, *Transmission of knowledge*, pp. 128–60.
89 Ibid., pp. 134–6.
90 Ibid., pp. 136–7.

cleaners had priority over teachers and students in payment; in another there was no mention of teachers and students at all.[91]

This does not mean that the spread of *madrasas* was insignificant in the development of Muslim education. Whereas it did not lead to the formalisation of educational processes which has been ascribed to it, it did enhance the great informal work of transmitting knowledge. The *madrasa* was one further forum in which person-to-person transmission of knowledge might take place. Furthermore, the generous provision of stipends and scholarships, for whatever purpose, greatly enhanced education, at the same time helping to contribute to the professionalisation of the *ʿulamāʾ* in general, and the study of the traditional sciences in particular. Arguably these developments contributed to a homogenisation of religious life,[92] a shaping of Sunnī identity[93] and what has been interpreted as a 'Sunni re-centering'.[94]

The spread of education beyond the central Islamic lands

This pattern for transmitting knowledge with the emphasis on person-to-person transmission and the involvement on occasion of *madrasas*, which had developed in Iran, Iraq and Egypt, spread through the rest of the Muslim world. One area of shared influences, though not exclusively so, was Mongol and post-Mongol Central Asia and Iran, plus the Ottoman and Mughal empires. One feature was the flourishing of the rational sciences in, for instance, circles around Naṣīr al-Dīn Ṭūsī (d. 672/1274) at Marāgha, Sayyid Sharīf al-Jurjānī in Samarqand, Ulugh Beg in Samarqand and Jalāl al-Dīn Dawānī (d. 908/1502) in Shīrāz. The rational sciences became more welcome in *madrasas*, with a consequent impact on theology and religious thought in general. Tīmūrid patronage made Samarqand and Herat into great teaching centres. It was in Samarqand that Sayyid Sharīf al-Jurjānī and Saʿd al-Dīn Taftāzānī wrote their many renowned commentaries, for instance, al-Jurjānī's *Mawāqif* and Taftāzānī's *Mukhtaṣar*, which became the staple of teaching from Istanbul to Calcutta down to the twentieth century.[95]

The Ottoman empire was the only part of the Islamic world to develop a rigidly hierarchical *madrasa* system. In the empire's early years scholars

91 Ibid., pp. 17–20.
92 Berkey, *Formation of Islam*, p. 189.
93 Ibid., p. 228.
94 Ibid., p. 189.
95 Robinson, *Farangi Mahall*, pp. 211–51.

travelled to Cairo or Damascus to complete their education; they had, moreover, a particular admiration for the scholarly and literary achievements of Tīmūrid Samarqand and Herat. By the late sixteenth century the Ottomans had established their full hierarchy of *madrasas*. At the bottom there were the 'exterior' *madrasas* which dealt with preparatory work in Arabic, the rational sciences and *adab* studies. These had three grades according to the salary of the teachers. Next there were the 'interior' *madrasas* which taught the traditional sciences. These too were graded. At the top of the system were the *semaniye madrasas* which Meḥmed II (r. 848–50/1444–6 and 855–86/1451–81) and Süleymān the Magnificent (r. 926–74/1520–66) established in their mosque complexes.[96] Strict control was exercised over the progress of both students and teachers through the hierarchy; students were not permitted to progress from one grade to the next until they had satisfactorily completed all that was required of the grade. Students and teachers progressed out of the *madrasas* into jobs in the judiciary, bureaucracy and noble households.[97] This was an imperial system in which the curriculum and appointments were controlled by the sultan and which retained this form until the nineteenth century. Nevertheless, the personal nature of the transmission of knowledge remained; it was normally only by the grant of an *ijāza* from his teacher that a student could progress from grade to grade.[98] As elsewhere, *adab* studies were also pursued beyond the *madrasa*; in the case of one distinguished Ottoman bureaucrat, in the tavern and the salon.[99] The rational sciences flourished in the early Ottoman centuries, especially under Meḥmed II, and this was reflected in a good balance in the curriculum between them and the traditional sciences.[100] But from the late sixteenth century they came under increasing pressure, their fate being symbolised by the destruction of Taqī al-Dīn's (d. 993/1585) observatory in Galata in 1580.[101]

The Mughal empire saw a rather different development in education. There was, for instance, a complete absence of hierarchy or system. Education was a matter for individual teachers; formal *madrasas* were a rarity. The rational sciences, moreover, came to play a larger role in scholarship than

96 Halil Inalcik, *The Ottoman empire: The classical age 1300–1600*, trans. N. Itzkowitz and C. Imber (London, 1973), pp. 165–71.
97 Colin Imber, *The Ottoman empire, 1300–1650: The structure of power* (Basingstoke, 2002), pp. 228–31.
98 Cornell H. Fleischer, *Bureaucrat and intellectual in the Ottoman empire: The historian Mustafa Ali (1541–1600)* (Princeton, 1986), pp. 27–9.
99 Ibid., pp. 22–4, 30–2.
100 Inalcik, *Ottoman empire*, pp. 175–8; Robinson, *Farangi Mahall*, pp. 240–3.
101 Inalcik, *Ottoman empire*, pp. 179–85.

elsewhere in the Sunnī world. Key to this was the translation of much of the scholarship in the field from Central Asia and Iran into northern India. One important moment was the arrival of Faḍl Allāh Shīrāzī (d. 997/1589) at the court of the emperor Akbar (r. 963–1014/1556–1605). He introduced the works in the field of Jalāl al-Dīn Dawānī, Ghiyāth al-Dīn Mansūr Shīrāzī (d. 949/1542) and Mīrzā Jān Shīrāzī, which led to the subsequent study of Mīr Bāqir Dāmād (d. 1040/1631 or 1041/1632) and his brilliant pupil Ṣadr al-Dīn Shīrāzī (d. 1050/1640). The next two centuries saw extraordinary developments in the field, in particular among scholars from the *qaṣbas* of Awadh.[102] The murder of one of the key figures in the movement, Quṭb al-Dīn Sihālī, in 1691 led to the formalisation of these developments in teaching. The Mughal emperor, Aurangzeb (r. 1068–1118/1658–1707), responded to the murder by granting the sequestered property of a European merchant in Lucknow, Farangī Maḥall, to his four sons. One son, Mullā Niẓām al-Dīn (d. 1161/1748) formulated the *Dars-i Niẓāmī*, a course which in Farangī Maḥallī hands made ample room for the advances in the rational sciences in Central Asia, Iran and Awadh, and which introduced a new style of teaching, focusing on the most difficult books. The Farangī Maḥallīs and their pupils spread the *Dars* throughout India. It was also adopted by the East India Company in its Calcutta *madrasa*. The *Dars* was popular because it enabled students to finish their education more quickly and because it prepared them well for bureaucratic posts.[103] From the nineteenth century, with the rise of Islamic reform under the leadership of the family of Shāh Walī Allāh (d. 1176/1762), the emphasis on the rational sciences in Indian education declined. This said, we should note that the *Dars-i Niẓamī*, however interpreted, has been maintained in the *madrasas* of the subcontinent down to the present. We should also note that from the Ottoman, through the Ṣafavid to the Mughal empire, there was a substantial overlap in the books and commentaries taught.[104]

The work of scholars and teachers was arguably more prominent in Africa than elsewhere, but that may be because they were the prime creators of sources. In West Africa great lineages transmitted knowledge: the Kunta in Mauritania and Senegambia; the Jakhanke in Senegambia, the Aqīt and And-Argh-Muḥammad in Timbuktu.[105] But we could talk equally of the Wangara

102 Robinson, *Farangi Mahall*, pp. 42–53.
103 Ibid., pp. 53–4.
104 Ibid., pp. 211–51.
105 Ira M. Lapidus, *A history of Islamic societies*, 2nd edn (Cambridge, 2002), pp. 409–10; Lamin O. Sanneh, *The Jakhanke: The history of an Islamic clerical people of the Senegambia* (London, 1979); Saad, *Timbuktu*, p. 82, 240–1.

communities of northern Ghana or the Nāṣirī Sufi brotherhood which spread through the northern Sahara.[106] In Timbuktu the sixteenth-century traveller Leo Africanus (*fl.* 895–933/1490–1527) noted that books were the most valuable items of trade.[107] The Shinqīṭ of Mauritania hunted books from Fez through to the Ḥijāz, bringing caravan-loads back to their lands. They were noted for their learning in West Africa and generally for their high levels of literacy.[108] The library which Maḥmūd Ka'ti (d. 1001/1593) began in Timbuktu in the sixteenth century, numbering nearly 3,000 volumes, has been described as 'the find of the century in terms of African history'.[109] It goes without saying that the African world of scholarship was international. To begin with, the scholars of Timbuktu looked northwards to Morocco, where the Aqīt Aḥmad Bāba (d. 1036/1627) was to acquire such a reputation. But increasingly they came to look eastwards to Egypt and the Ḥijāz. Al-Suyūṭī was engaged with Timbuktu for both political and scholarly reasons; his *Jalālayn* was widely studied. The records of that remarkable eighteenth-century Indian resident of Cairo, Murtaḍā al-Zabīdī (d. 1205/1790), reveal an astonishing network of scholarly connections across Africa from west to east.[110]

In this context Timbuktu emerged in the fifteenth and sixteenth centuries as a great 'university' city, assisted by its position at the crossroads of the north–south/east–west trade routes. It has been reckoned that there were up to 300 scholars in the city, who would have taught at the advanced level, plus 150 Qur'ān schools for the elementary level. The 300,000 manuscripts or more that exist in Timbuktu are a tribute to the scholarly effort of the era and its influence.[111] Scholars usually taught in their homes and, because the size of the body of scholars permitted specialisation, students would move from scholar to scholar. At a more advanced level students received individual tuition; it would appear that *ijāzas* were only given in this case.[112] There was an

106 Ivor Wilks, 'The transmission of Islamic learning in the western Sudan', in Jack Goody (ed.), *Literacy in traditional societies* (Cambridge, 1968); David Gutelius, 'Sufi networks and the social contexts for scholarship in Morocco and the northern Sahara, 1660–1830', in Scott Reese (ed.), *The transmission of learning in Islamic Africa* (Leiden, 2004).

107 Saad, *Timbuktu*, p. 79.

108 Ghislaine Lydon, 'Inkwells of the Sahara: Reflections on the production of Islamic knowledge in *Bilad Shinqīṭ*', in Reese (ed.), *Transmission*.

109 Albrecht Hofheinz, 'Goths in the lands of the blacks: A preliminary survey of the Ka'ti Library in Timbuktu', in Reese (ed.), *Transmission*; see also John O. Hunwick and Alida Jay Boye, *The hidden treasures of Timbuktu* (London, 2008).

110 Stefan Reichmuth, 'Murtaḍā al-Zabīdī (1732–1791) and the Africans: Islamic discourse and scholarly networks in the late eighteenth century', Reese (ed.), *Transmission*.

111 Hofheinz, 'Goths', p. 159.

112 Saad, *Timbuktu*, pp. 60–1.

emphasis on the traditional sciences, but the rational sciences were also taught, and there is no evidence of their being prohibited.[113] More generally, 'the curricula of study in Timbuktu', we are told, 'were designed to give the scholars as wide a humanistic training as was the vogue in the Middle East at the time'. Indeed, al-Suyūṭī was regarded as a model.[114]

Education was much less well developed in South-East Asia. Islam had been a much more recent arrival along the trade routes of the Indian Ocean. The sultanate of Aceh in the seventeenth century was the first major centre of Islamic learning. Scholars came from India and the Islamic heartland. ʿAbd al-Raʾūf al-Singkīlī (d. 1104/1693) was the dominant scholar of the period. In a stay of nineteen years in Mecca, Jiddah, Bayt al-Faqih, Zabīd and Medina he studied with fifteen teachers, among whom were Aḥmad al-Qushāshī (d. 1070/1660) and the great Ibrāhīm al-Kurānī (d. 1101/1690).[115] ʿAbd al-Raʾūf's writings in particular, and the emphasis of Malay scholarship in general, suggest that the prime concern was with the traditional sciences and with Sufism. If there was any serious tension it was not with the rational sciences, but Sufism and the appropriate interpretation of Ibn al-ʿArabī. This was a matter that Ibrāhīm al-Kurānī resolved in a magisterial work.[116] Among the more popular works studied were Bayḍāwī's (d. 685/1286) *Tanzīl* and Khāzin's (d. 740/1340) *Taʾwīl*. But by far the most popular work, as in many parts of the Muslim world, was al-Suyūṭī's *Jalālayn*.[117] There is no evidence for the transmission of knowledge being institutionalised into *pesantren*, the Indonesian version of the *madrasa* boarding-school, until the late eighteenth century. There is a close correspondence between the books taught in these *pesantren* and those at Cairo's al-Azhar and some Meccan *ḥalqas*, which suggests Middle Eastern influence over their development.[118]

Spiritual education

Mystical education, the process of learning how to know God in one's heart, which was called *taṣawwuf*, the process of becoming a Sufi, was another dimension of education. We treat these dimensions separately, but more

113 Ibid., pp. 74–81.
114 Ibid., pp. 78–9.
115 Peter Riddell, *Islam and the Malay-Indonesian world* (London, 2001), pp. 125–6.
116 Ibid., pp. 125–38.
117 Ibid., pp. 141–7.
118 Martin van Bruinessen, 'Continuity and change in a tradition of religious learning', in Wolfgang Marschall (ed.), *Texts from the islands: Oral and written traditions of Indonesia and the Malay world* (Berne, 1994), pp. 132–7.

often than not they were two sides of the same Islamic personality. It was widely accepted that the best scholars were those with spiritual understanding. Equally, it was widely understood that the starting-point for the Sufi was the faithful following of the injunctions of the *sharīʿa* as adumbrated by scholars. Sufis might discuss aspects of formal knowledge no less than *ʿulamāʾ* might discuss *taṣawwuf*.

To begin the process of spiritual education a man – although it could also be a woman – would have to be accepted by a master (Ar. *shaykh*; Pers. *pīr*). The process of being accepted was not easy. The aspirant might have to undergo humiliations to prepare for the hardships of the spiritual path – cleaning latrines was a favoured example. After three years of service, providing he had performed satisfactorily and his shaykh had developed an affinity with him, he would be permitted to enter his shaykh's circle. The relationship would be formalised by an initiation which would recall the oath of allegiance that Muḥammad's followers had sworn to him. Elements of the ceremony might vary from order to order, but the clasping of hands and the giving of a patched cloak, or *khirqa*, as a symbol of Sufi status, were common. The disciple would also receive a written *shajara* (tree), which would show how spiritual knowledge had come from the Prophet, through the founder of the order, down to his shaykh. One of his first tasks might be to write down his spiritual lineage and commit it to memory. We might note that whereas the pupil received his *ijāza* when he finished a book, the Sufi received his *shajara* at the beginning of his spiritual journey.[119]

If the teacher–pupil relationship was special, the master–disciple relationship was extra-special. All knowledge, all understanding, all progress flowed from the master. 'When the sincere disciple enters under obedience of the master, keeping his company and teaching his manners', wrote Shihāb al-Dīn Abū Ḥafṣ al-Suhrawardī (d. 632/1234), 'a spiritual state flows from within the master to within the disciple, like one lamp lighting another.' The disciple was called a *murīd*, one who desires, and the master, the *murād*, one who is desired.[120] The master oversaw the spiritual journey of the disciple as a father might a son. The reverence of a disciple for his master could go to extraordinary lengths. In fourteenth-century India one Chishtī Sufi rode the long distance from Dawlatabad to Delhi facing backwards on his horse out of respect for his master who remained in Dawlatabad.[121]

119 Annemarie Schimmel, *The mystical dimensions of Islam* (Chapel Hill, 1975), pp. 101–3; Carl Ernst, *The Shambhala guide to Sufism* (Boston, 1997), pp. 133–43.

120 Ernst, *Sufism*, p. 124.

121 Carl Ernst, *Eternal garden: Mysticism, history, and politics at a South Asian Sufi center*, 2nd edn (New Delhi, 2004), p. 124.

In his master's company the disciple would be taught the *dhikr* of his order, its way of remembering God and other rituals. Under his master's guidance he would follow the path or ladder to higher levels of mystical experience, a process often described as 'unveiling'. He might start with *tawba* (repentance), a turning away from sin and worldly concerns, and embrace the struggle against *nafs*, the body's sensual appetites. He might move through the stage of *tawakkul* (complete trust in God), to *maḥabba* (love) and *maʿrifa* (gnosis), achieving the state of *fanāʾ* and *baqāʾ*, the total annihilation of the self in the divine presence.[122] Once the disciple had achieved this level of understanding his master might make him a *khalīfa*, or successor, who was permitted to guide others along the path. At this point his master might bestow upon him another cloak, a cloak of succession. There were many disciples and few successors.

The powerful bonds of disciple–master allegiance were often closely intertwined with those of pupil and teacher. Often it was the connections of Sufi orders that played the central role in assisting the transmission of knowledge other than *taṣawwuf*, as the Naqshbandī Sufis did in Asia, or the Qādirī Sufis in Africa.[123] These two powerful educational bonds reinforced each other in transmitting knowledge across the Muslim world.

The early education of children

Approaches to the early education of children were for the most part driven by the need to save their souls. 'The child', declared al-Ghazālī, 'is by way of being "on loan" in the care of his parents … If he is made accustomed to good and is so taught, he will grow up in goodness, he will win happiness in this world and the next, and his parents and teachers will have a share of his reward.'[124] Parents were responsible before God for the education of their children; fathers were particularly responsible for protecting their sons from evil influences in their environment. The onset of the 'age of discernment' (*tamyīz*), when the child knew the difference between right and wrong and could begin to grasp abstract ideas, was the time for education to begin. This

122 Schimmel, *Mystical dimensions*, pp. 98–186.

123 Marc Gaborieau, Alexandre Popovic and Thierry Zarcone (eds.), *Naqshbandis: Cheminements et situation actuelle d'un ordre mystique musulman* (Paris, 1990); Lapidus, *Islamic societies*, p. 415; there is an excellent exposition of the intertwining of pupil–teacher and disciple–master links in Barbara D. Metcalf, *Islamic revival in British India: Deoband, 1860–1920* (Princeton, 1982), pp. 87–197.

124 Avner Gil'adi, *Children of Islam: Concepts of childhood in medieval Muslim society* (Basingstoke, 1992), p. 50.

development was thought to take place usually between age six and seven. Indeed, education at this age was a condition for success: 'At this age', al-Ghazālī said, 'learning is like engraving a stone.' Character training was part of the process; al-Ghazālī was concerned that the child 'get used to modesty, respect for others, and gentleness of speech'.[125] But the desire to play was not to be neglected, as it was seen as a means to attract the child towards more serious studies. Apart from those involving chance, there was a general approval of games. Indeed, tenth-century Baghdad was known to have a toyshop.[126]

Over much of the Muslim world the curriculum of the elementary school (known as *kuttāb* or *maktab*) was limited to the minimum that al-Ghazālī prescribed: the tenets of faith, learning the Qur'ān, traditions about the beginnings of Islam and its prominent figures.[127] Parents favoured the limitation, Ibn Khaldūn tells us, because they wished to exploit fully the opportunity of youth to instil the most essential knowledge.[128] There were, however, some areas where there was support for a broader curriculum. The Tunisians added some 'scientific problems', knowledge of different readings of the Qur'ān and laid much emphasis on handwriting. The Spanish went further, including poetry and composition, and making sure that children had a good knowledge of Arabic.[129]

An enduring feature of discussions of elementary education was the beating of pupils. That excessive corporal punishment was a problem is clear from the recollections of men from all parts of the Muslim world.[130] Moreover, one of the jobs of the *muḥtasib*, the market inspector, was to oversee elementary schoolteachers to make sure that they were not harming their charges.[131] In theory a teacher could only beat a pupil with the father's permission.[132] Al-Ghazālī took the line that moderate force might be used, but it should be seen as part of a package of measures designed to improve the conduct and

125 Ibid., p. 58.
126 Ibid., pp. 58–60.
127 Ibid., pp. 54–5.
128 Ibn Khaldūn, *The* Muqaddimah, vol. III, p. 305.
129 Ibid., pp. 301–4.
130 Fleischer, *Bureaucrat and intellectual*, p. 21; Lutfullah, *Autobiography of Lutfullah: An Indian's perceptions of the West*, introd. S. A. I. Tirmizi (New Delhi, 1985), pp. 14–21; L. O. Sanneh, 'The Islamic education of an African child: Stresses and tensions', in Godfrey N. Brown and Mervyn Hiskett (eds.), *Conflict and harmony in education in tropical Africa* (London, 1975).
131 Gil'adi, *Children of Islam*, p. 63.
132 Sherman A. Jackson, 'Discipline and duty in a medieval Muslim elementary school: Ibn Hajar al-Haytami's *Taqrir al-maqal*', in Lowry *et al.* (eds.), *Law and education*, pp. 25–8.

performance of the pupil.[133] Ibn Khaldūn was also opposed to the severe treatment of children, in part because it led them into deceitful ways; but in part, too, because it dehumanised them, with deleterious effects for society.[134] This said, it was to be expected that pupils would get their revenge on their teachers. Arguably, the most hilarious episode in that classic of the storyteller's repertoire, *The adventures of Amir Hamza*, which spread throughout the Asian Muslim world, described the revenge of Ḥamza and his sidekick, Amar, on their brutal *mullā* (teacher).[135]

The need to secure the child's salvation meant that *kuttābs*, often known as Qur'ān schools, were to be found throughout the Islamic world, from the great *sabīl-kuttābs* (fountain schools) of Mamlūk Cairo through to say Mauritania, where women would do the teaching in desert encampments. Indeed, elementary education provided the basis on which not just higher learning might flourish, but other activities, from trade to administration. In the sixteenth century Timbuktu supported between 150 and 180. In the late eighteenth Cairo had as many as 300.[136] There is an argument that their growth was, among other things, closely associated with that of trade.[137]

Slave education

A good number of Muslim regimes were either dependent on slaves or, indeed, ruled by them. Classic examples were the Ṣafavid and Ottoman empires and the Mamlūk regimes of Egypt and northern India. This meant that the education and training of slaves was a matter of no small importance. In the case of the Egyptian Mamlūks, they were usually imported as youths from the Eurasian steppe or the Caucasus. Converted to Islam, they learned Arabic and were trained for the most part as cavalry. Once their training was completed they were freed but had to serve either the Mamlūk ruler or in another Mamlūk household. Because the system was replenished not by birth but by the importation of fresh batches of slaves, training in the Mamlūk way had to be rigorous and intense. Mamlūks followed the dictates of *furūsiyya*, a code which valued courage and generosity as well as skills in horsemanship,

133 Gil'adi, *Children of Islam*, pp. 163–5.
134 Ibn Khaldūn, *The* Muqaddimah, vol. III, pp. 305–7.
135 Ghalib Lakhnavi and Abdullah Bilgrami, *The adventures of Amir Hamza*, introd. Hamid Dabashi (New York, 2007), pp. 70–83.
136 Nelly Hanna, *In praise of books: A cultural history of Cairo's middle class, sixteenth to the eighteenth century* (Syracuse, 2003), p. 51.
137 Ibid., pp. 57–64.

archery and cavalry tactics. Mamlūks lived together in garrisons. Skills were maintained by regular competitions, at least twice a week. Their first loyalty was to their Mamlūk master or *ustādh*.[138]

In the Ṣafavid empire slaves from the Caucasus were crucial both to asserting the power of central government and to success across a broad front. They were educated in the royal household alongside princes and the sons of noble families. They were taught both the traditional and rational sciences, horsemanship, polo and archery, as well as civility, humanity and painting. They progressed through the ranks by merit.[139]

The greatest achievement in the education of slaves, however, was that of the Palace School (Enderun), which was founded by Meḥmed II soon after his conquest of Constantinople, and which operated at the heart of the Ottoman state for nearly 400 years. The school, in fact, was at the apex of a cluster of schools in which slaves were trained. The *devşirme*, or levy of Christian subjects in lieu of taxes, was the main supplier of personnel – in the sixteenth century 10,000–12,000 slaves were supplied thus every three to four years. For most of its existence the school had 800–900 pupils. On arrival slaves were tested and divided into two classes: the comely and intelligent, who went into the sultan's service; and the remainder, who went into the Janissaries, the sultan's elite corps of household infantry. Of those in the sultan's service, the very able became student pages, and the remainder gardeners, gatekeepers etc. The student pages themselves were divided between the most able, who went into the Palace School, and the less able, who went into the auxiliary schools. The sultan normally took great interest in the school, watching sports, listening to debates and presiding over the admission and graduation of pupils.[140]

The curriculum was not dissimilar from that of the other slave systems, though perhaps rather more wide-ranging. The traditional sciences were studied, but of the rational sciences only arithmetic, at which the Turks excelled, and perhaps geometry. Turkish and Persian language and literature were also studied, along with Turkish history and music. A well-stocked library supported wider reading, while vocational subjects such as calligraphy were also available. Within the broad curriculum it appears that pages were

138 Robert Irwin, *The Middle East in the Middle Ages: The early Mamluk sultanate 1250–1382* (London, 1986), pp. 3–10; Berkey, *Transmission of knowledge*, pp. 9–11.

139 Sussan Babaie, Kathryn Babayan, Ina Baghdiantz-McCabe and Massumeh Farhad (eds.), *Slaves of the shah: New elites of Safavid Iran* (London, 2004), pp. 29–30, 129.

140 Barnette Miller, *The Palace School of Muhammad the Conqueror* (Cambridge, MA, 1941), pp. 70–94.

permitted to specialise according to inclination, only the Qur'ān and Turkish and Arabic languages being compulsory. Exercise was taken very seriously, embracing weightlifting, wrestling, archery, sword practice, dart throwing and horsemanship; there were many competitions. Progress was only by merit. Punishment for breaking rules or failing in performance was severe but controlled; a pupil could not be beaten more than once a day. The aim was to produce good Muslims who were warrior statesmen, cultivated and courteous. By the account of outsiders the Ottomans were most successful.[141]

It should be noted how far this system – and indeed the other slave systems – differed from the normal run of education in Muslim societies. Indeed, it has been suggested that, for instance, in the division of intellectuals and artisans, the training of the body and the freedom to specialise, it owed something to the inspiration of Plato's *Republic*.[142] We should also note that, while *ʿulamāʾ* and lay teachers taught the pages, they do not appear to have been offered the notable respect gained elsewhere in Muslim societies. That was reserved for the sultan,[143] as it was for the Ṣafavid shah and the Mamlūk *ustādh*.

Popular education

The transmission of knowledge was not just the particular work of *ʿulamāʾ* and their pupils, or that of specialist environments such as the Sufi *khānqāh* or the Palace School; it was an activity that could touch everyone in Muslim societies. There was the view that the *madrasa* should be open to the whole community. 'To lock the door of a madrasa', declared Ibn al-Ḥājj (d. 737/1336), 'is to shut out the masses and prevent them from hearing the [recitation] of knowledge … and being blessed by it and its people [i.e. the *ʿulamāʾ*].'[144] So *madrasas* in late medieval Cairo arranged the recitation of the Qur'ān so it might be heard by passers-by in the street.[145] They provided large numbers of lower-level posts – muezzins, gatekeepers etc. – for men in their localities who would not only be exposed themselves to the daily transmission of knowledge but might also attend some classes and become transmitters themselves.[146] *Madrasas* provided more direct educational services to the community: some

141 Ibid., pp. 94–125.
142 Ibid., p. 42.
143 Ibid., pp. 94–125.
144 Berkey, *Transmission of knowledge*, p. 202.
145 Ibid., pp. 192–3.
146 Ibid., pp. 193–200.

had employees to teach the Qurʾān or how to write; others, along with mosques or *khānqāhs*, might support men who would recite from memory, for popular consumption, basic books from the traditional sciences including Qurʾān commentaries and accounts of the early pious Muslims.[147] However, the activity in which the general public were most involved was the transmission of *ḥadīth*. They might be recited at moments of public anxiety or celebration. Some institutions held public sessions, distinct from normal classes, in the months of Rajab, Shaʿbān and Ramaḍān. There was also the practice of mass transmission when members of the public might receive *ijāzas* for *ḥadīth* they had heard. Such large-scale transmission of knowledge, though not necessarily with *ijāzas*, could be found in other urban environments, for instance, in eighteenth- and early nineteenth-century Lucknow, where the Shīʿa held *majlis* (assemblies for the remembrance of the imams) during Muḥarram and Sunnī *ʿulamāʾ* gave *mawlid* (birthday celebrations for the Prophet Muḥammad) lectures on the first twelve days of Rabīʿ al-Awwal.[148] At such points all could benefit from the transmission of knowledge.

One dimension of popular education was preaching and story telling. The popular preacher (*wāʿiẓ*), declared one experienced fourteenth-century teacher, 'had the responsibility of inspiring pious fear in his listeners and telling the stories of the early heroes of the Islamic faith'.[149] The storyteller, or *qāṣṣ*, on the other hand, 'would sit or stand in the streets, reciting from memory passages from the Qurʾān, *ḥadīth* and stories of the early Muslims and encouraging his audience to pray, fast, and fulfil their other cultic and legal obligation'.[150] These functionaries, whose roles clearly overlapped, could be found in many Muslim societies. Some preachers might be superstars, such as the visitor to eleventh-century Baghdad who drew audiences approaching 30,000.[151] Of course, the content might change according to time and context. From the thirteenth century it would appear that the themes embraced by storytellers in West Asia came increasingly to be infused by Sufi thought: the desirability of poverty and the renunciation of the world, suffering, death, judgement and salvation.[152] Scholars tended to have reservations, but were

147 Ibid., pp. 205–10.
148 Abdul Halim Sharar, *Lucknow: The last phase of an oriental culture*, ed. and trans. E. S. Harcourt and Fakhir Husain (London, 1975), pp. 215–17.
149 Jonathan P. Berkey, *Popular preaching and religious authority in the medieval Islamic Near East* (Seattle, 2001), p. 13.
150 Ibid.
151 Ibid., p. 25.
152 Ibid., pp. 45–7.

forced to acknowledge the value of the role they performed: 'The storytellers and preachers were also given a place in this order (*amr*) so as to exhort (*khiṭāb*) the common people', declared the Ḥanbalī jurist Ibn al-Jawzī (d. 597/1201) in the twelfth century; 'as a result the common people benefit from them in a way they do not from a great scholar.'[153]

That scholars had reservations about popular preachers and storytellers is worthy of note. They raised the issue of legitimate knowledge – that is, of authority – in at least two ways. First, storytellers and popular preachers tended to transmit spurious *ḥadīth* and use inappropriate emotionalism. But they also had great popular support. So, when al-Suyūṭī issued a *fatwā* (legal opinion) against a storyteller for transmitting spurious *ḥadīth*, the man's audience threatened to stone the scholar.[154] Second, they tended to transmit *ḥadīth* and other texts without having heard them from a scholar, and therefore without the authority of an *ijāza*. For all the good that these functionaries might do, they also threatened the very basis of authoritative knowledge.[155]

Women and education

It has been noted that copyists added to the well-known *ḥadīth* 'the seeking of knowledge is the duty of every Muslim' the words *wa muslima* to underline the point that this duty applied to every woman as well as man.[156] Throughout the Muslim world there were women who engaged with education as far as legal and social restrictions – and the latter could be very constraining – would permit. There certainly existed some prejudice against educating women. 'It is said that a woman who learns [how to] write', went a Mamlūk market inspector's manual, 'is like a snake given poison to drink'. This view tended not to be shared by *ʿulamāʾ*, who often played a leading role in educating their own daughters, nor is there much evidence that it was shared by ruling families. It was, after all, hard to gainsay the example of the women of the Prophet's family and those of his immediate followers.[157]

One female engagement with education was the patronage of learning. In Mamlūk Cairo women endowed a range of institutions in which education might take place, as well as five *madrasas*, most founded by royal women. A sixteenth-century history of *madrasas* in Damascus suggests that the city was

153 Ibid., pp. 23–4.
154 Ibid., p. 25.
155 Ibid., pp. 70–87.
156 Berkey, *Transmission of knowledge*, p. 161.
157 Ibid., pp. 161–2.

host to even more women's foundations.[158] Six of the thirteen major buildings endowed by women in Ṣafavid Iṣfahān were *madrasas*.[159] In Mamlūk Cairo the right to supervise the administration of a *madrasa* could go to the female descendants of a founder. But that was as far as their association might go. No woman held a post as a teacher or a student. Their presence, moreover, within the *madrasa* confines was deemed highly undesirable; they would put the students off their studies.[160]

Patronage of learning was a worthy act, but it was real learning for the individual that counted. Such learning might range from some engagement with the Qur'ān, *ḥadīth* and knowledge of basic religious obligations through to serious engagement with major books of advanced learning. Relatives played an important role in teaching women within the home. Thus Zaynab al-Ṭukhiyya (d. 894/1388), who in the fourteenth century was brought up in a small town in the Egyptian Delta, memorised the Qur'ān under her father, learned how to write, and studied several basic works of Shafiʿī jurisprudence. After she married she continued her education, studying *ḥadīth* under her husband's guidance.[161] Scholars encouraged their daughters to hear the transmission of *ḥadīth* and collect *ijāzas*.[162] Moreover, it was understood that with her husband's permission a woman might attend the *ḥalqa* of a scholar, at which men would be present, in a private house or a mosque.[163] Learned women could play an especially important role in enabling the learning of women. In Fāṭimid Cairo there were women who devoted themselves to teaching divorced and widowed women and young girls in their homes. There were, moreover, at least five Sufi *khānqāhs* where women taught women.[164] Nothing, perhaps, is quite as remarkable as the system of education for rural women created by Nana Asma'u (d. 1281/1865), daughter of ʿUsman dan Fodio, the creator of Nigeria's Sokoto caliphate. She sent groups of mature and intelligent women into the villages with her authority to bring girls under fourteen and women over forty-four to her. These women in groups led by the best choral singers would wend their way

158 Ibid., pp. 162–4.
159 Stephen P. Blake, 'Contributors to the urban landscape: Women builders in Safavid Isfahan and Mughal Shahjahanabad', in Gavin R. G. Hambly (ed.), *Women in the medieval Islamic world* (New York, 1998).
160 Berkey, *Transmission of knowledge*, pp. 165–7.
161 Ibid., pp. 169–70.
162 Ibid., pp. 170–1.
163 Ibid., pp. 170–2; Suraiya Faroqhi, *Subjects of the sultan: Culture and daily life in the Ottoman empire* (London, 2007), p. 115.
164 Berkey, *Transmission of knowledge*, pp. 173–5.

to Sokoto where during their stay with Asma'u they would be taught the essentials of the faith and how to apply the law. Asma'u's pupils would then return to their villages to teach others.[165]

The range of roles women had in transmitting knowledge is worthy of note. In the Tīmūrid and Mughal royal families the early education of young boys and girls was handed over to older women in the household. Senior women of the Ottoman harem taught young women how to speak and read, and the requirements of the law, in an institution that paralleled that of the Palace School. Doubtless, the improvement in the Turkish of the personal notes sent by Hürrem, Süleymān the Magnificent's favourite consort from Poland, to the sultan is testament to their success.[166] In the Sahara all the women in the family educated young boys and girls in the Arabic alphabet, grammar, reading and basic Qur'ānic knowledge.[167] In Ṣafavid Iran, in the cities where Shīʿism was particularly strong, women restricted their teaching to girls.[168] In Fāṭimid Cairo, and also in contemporary Damascus, women played a major and respected role in transmitting *ḥadīth*. So highly regarded were they in the role that leading scholars such as Ibn Ḥajar al-ʿAsqalānī (d. 852/1449) and Jalāl al-Dīn al-Suyūṭī relied on their authority in transmitting *ḥadīth*.[169]

A further outcome of women's engagement with education was seriously learned women. The restrictions of the harem mean that we shall never know their number as we do for men. Nevertheless, al-Sakhāwī's famed biographical dictionary tells of at least 411 women with some education, mentioning in particular the many learned women of Damascus's Bulqīnī family.[170] In the sixteenth century, Fakhrī of Herat produced a biographical dictionary entirely devoted to the poetesses and learned women of Tīmūrid and early Ṣafavid Iran. Focusing on women from noble and scholarly families, it points to active women's engagement in intellectual life, which in the Tīmūrid period was sometimes in mixed company. One notable figure was Bija Munajjima, an astrologer/astronomer renowned for her command of advanced

165 Jean Boyd, *The caliph's sister: Nana Asma'u 1793–1865, teacher, poet and Islamic leader* (London, 1989), pp. 42–53.
166 Leslie P. Peirce, *The imperial harem: Women and sovereignty in the Ottoman empire* (New York, 1993), pp. 63–5, 139–41.
167 Lydon, 'Inkwells of the Sahara', p. 48.
168 Maria Szuppe, 'The "jewels of wonder": Learned ladies and princess politicians in the provinces of early Safavid Iran', in Hambly (ed.), *Women in the medieval Islamic world*, p. 330.
169 Berkey, *Transmission of knowledge*, pp. 175–81.
170 Ibid., pp. 167–71.

mathematics. A mystic, too, she was also known for her rivalry with the Sufi thinker and poet ʿAbd al-Raḥmān Jāmī (d. 898/1492).[171] The Mughal royal household was remarkable for its literary and learned women, produced in every generation from the emperor Bābur's (r. 932–7/1526–30) daughter, Gulbadan Begum (d. 1011/1603), to the emperor Aurangzeb's daughter Zēb al-Nisāʾ (d. 1114/1702).[172] Few, however, were likely to match the range of Nana Asma'u, who wrote in Arabic, Fulfulde and Hausa on: health, women's education, *sharīʿa* law as it applied to women, women and *bori* (spirit possession), women as sustainers, the family, history, eschatology, politics, theology and her father's caliphate.[173]

Conclusion

It is worth stepping back to consider the impact on the development of Muslim societies from about 1000 to about 1800 of the high value placed on the pursuit of *ʿilm*. Certainly it meant that by the end of the period, despite the continuing emphasis on the oral transmission of knowledge, forms of literacy were spreading. Admittedly, 'literacy' is a slippery concept. We take it to embrace all forms from the skills of the great scholar to the techniques learned by a boy in a *kuttāb* which were later put to use in his business in the bazaar. But the search for *ʿilm* was just one of the driving-forces behind literacy. It intertwined with the growth of trade; there is a correlation between the intensification of international trade from the sixteenth century and literacy in the regions involved. It also intertwines with the expansion of bureaucratic and legal cultures over the same period. Arguably it is also expressed in the growing practice of letter-writing among middling folk and the keeping of diaries.[174]

Focusing on *ʿilm* as knowledge transmitted by *ʿulamāʾ* and Sufis, we must acknowledge their role in deepening the Islamic presence in different environments. They might do so in great urban centres ruled by Muslim potentates such as Fāṭimid Cairo or Nawabi Lucknow. They might do so on the Islamic frontier in South and South-East Asia, where, working, perhaps, with the expansion of arable cultivation or more frequently with the long-distance

171 Szuppe, 'The "jewels of wonder"', pp. 325–48.

172 Ruby Lal, *Domesticity and power in the early Mughal world* (Cambridge, 2005); Annie Krieger Krynicki, *Captive princess: Zebunissa, daughter of Aurangzeb* (Karachi, 2005).

173 Boyd, *The caliph's sister*, pp. 121–35.

174 Nelly Hanna, 'Literacy and the "great divide" in the Islamic world, 1300–1800', *Journal of Global History*, 2, 2 (2007).

trade, they brought the high Islamic tradition into new environments, linked them into great centres of Islamic scholarship and stimulated them with their continuing discourse on how best to be a Muslim. Nowhere, however, does their role seem to have been more prominent than in Africa.

It has been argued that the Muslim world in this period represented the world system that preceded the Wallerstinian one based on the emergence of capitalism in Europe. If the long-distance trade across land and sea was one dimension of this world system, the second was the pursuit of *ʿilm*. From Africa to South-East Asia Arabic was the language of Islamic scholarship; Muslims learned the Qurʾān, transmitted *ḥadīth* and absorbed the tenets of their faith. Some of the same textbooks were used both in Timbuktu and in Sumatra. *ʿUlamāʾ* and Sufis travelled freely across this world in search of *ʿilm*. The connections of teachers and pupils, masters and disciples, represented powerful linkages; indeed, they were the veins and arteries along which the life-giving blood of *ʿilm* flowed.

One important point flows from the oral transmission of authoritative knowledge and the non-institutional nature of the teacher–pupil relationship. It gave the process of transmission a flexibility which enabled it to be remarkably inclusive. Foreign elites such as Mamlūks could be included, so could women, so could the urban masses. Storytellers could entertain whomever came their way, and a princess could reach out to rural villagers. *ʿIlm* was not locked behind the doors of institutions. It was not the sole possession of a caste of scholars, even though there was always the danger that, in fear of inaccuracy and innovation, the *ʿulamāʾ* would rather that this was so.[175]

Marshall Hodgson characterised the classic systems of Islamic learning as essentially conservationist.[176] We have noted its central concern to pass down the priceless heritage of *ʿilm*, the Qurʾān, *ḥadīth* and the skills to make them socially useful, which were adumbrated in the books of great scholars of the past, in pristine form, a task that seemed more difficult with each passing generation. This did not mean that changing times were completely ignored; they were addressed in fresh commentaries on, and sometimes introductions to, the great books. More generally they might be addressed in preaching. We have noted, furthermore, the enduring suspicion of the rational sciences, which meant that by the eighteenth century their study in any substantial sense had come to be confined to Iran and northern India. On its own terms

175 Berkey, *Transmission of knowledge*, pp. 216–18.

176 Marshall G. S. Hodgson, *The venture of Islam: Conscience and history in a world civilisation*, 3 vols. (Chicago, 1974), vol. II, pp. 437–44.

the system was remarkably successful in reproducing itself and in sustaining Islamic societies. Again, on its own terms it was able to produce creative responses to the challenges of Europe, as it did in nineteenth and twentieth-century South Asia.[177] Some have thought that, had the rational sciences been allowed to flourish, education and learning might have been able to produce a more creative response to Europe. But apart from the odd will-o'-the-wisp, such as the translation into Persian in the early nineteenth century of Newton's *Principia* by a scholar in the Farangī Maḥall tradition, the areas where the rational sciences flourished seemed to offer little hope. Their study was in its way as conservationist as that of the traditional sciences.

This said, we should note the system's capacity, when transmitting knowledge construed in its broadest sense, to produce levels of intellectual development and human understanding able to support great bureaucratic empires, administer vast armies, design some of the world's most beautiful buildings, create some of the world's most-loved poetry, bring a highly respected law to many human societies and, most important of all, provide large numbers of human beings with the guidance in life that offered them hope of salvation in the hereafter.

177 Francis Robinson, *Islam, South Asia and the West* (New Delhi, 2007), pp. 59–98.

21

Philosophy

RICHARD C. TAYLOR

Although the original meaning of the Greek term 'philosophy' (*falsafa* in Arabic) is 'love of wisdom', philosophy encompasses a wide variety of methods and subjects, including the structure of reality, the character of human actions, the nature of the divine and much more. Philosophical method certainly includes human rational argumentative discourse and investigation (*al-naẓar*) by the use of intellect (*bi-l-ʿaql*) in the search for what is true or right in the realms of nature, metaphysics and ethics. If understood in this sense, philosophy – or something much like it, employing many of the methods found in philosophy – can be seen in Islam among the *mutakallimūn* or practitioners of *kalām* (Islamic argumentative theology) well before the advent of the *falāsifa*, or philosophers working in the framework of Platonic and Aristotelian thought. The Arabic term *kalām* has many senses, including speech, word, account and more, depending on context, including Divine Speech. Some later well-known philosophers of the classical rationalist period, such as al-Fārābī, Ibn Sīnā/Avicenna and Ibn Rushd/Averroes, commonly regarded *kalām* as unscientific dialectical argumentation in defence of basic tenets of the Islamic faith. However, some of the proponents of *ʿilm al-kalām*, the science of *kalām*, regarded themselves as engaged in expounding issues which today would commonly be considered within the purview of philosophy, even if 'the primary function of *kalām* – its end and its activity – is to rationalise the basic beliefs of the Muslims as they are given in the Koran and the Sunna and are present in the way these are read and understood by orthodox believers'.[1] To this extent it seems appropriate to call *kalām* a distinctly philosophical theology. From the advent in the Islamic milieu of *falsafa* as a widely recognised intellectual

1 R. M. Frank, 'The science of *kalām*', *Arabic Sciences and Philosophy*, 2 (1992) p. 22. Also see Harry A. Wolfson, *The philosophy of the kalam* (Cambridge, MA, and London, 1976); and the authoritative and comprehensive work of Josef van Ess, *Theologie und Gesellschaft im 2. und 3. Jahrhundert Hidschra: eine Geschichte des religiösen Denkens im frühen Islam*, 6 vols. (Berlin and New York, 1991–7).

discipline in the third/ninth century, *kalām* and *falsafa* existed as parallel discourses on issues of physics, metaphysics and ethics. They involved distinct principles and analyses, with *kalām* having a place inside religious institutions such as schools and mosques, while *falsafa* was taught separately as a secular science espoused by Muslims, Christians, Jews and others outside the confines of their religious confessions. These disciplines certainly eyed each other with considerable suspicion, and at times with outright hostility. There were some instances of methodological conciliation and many others of conflict, as is clear in the philosophers and also in well-known theologians such as al-Ghazālī, Fakhr al-Dīn al-Rāzī and al-Ījī. While the present chapter focuses for the most part on *falsafa*, some remarks on *kalām* are in order.

ʿIlm al-kalām, or Islamic philosophical theology

The *mutakallimūn* are generally divided into two camps, the Muʿtazilites and the Ashʿarīs, although reasoned theological disputes antedate these groupings. The major centres of *kalām* were Baṣra and Baghdad, although it was practised widely with great diversity of doctrine and reasoning. Muʿtazilism is traced to Wāṣil ibn ʿAṭāʾ (d. 131/748f.), who in the matter of grave violation of religious law is said to have separated himself (*iʿtazala*) from the extreme positions of the Khārijite charge of *kufr* (unbelief), entailing ostracism from the Muslim community, and the Murjiʾite view of the offender as remaining a believer within the community. The term may also denote a middle position in the dispute over ʿAlī's succession as leader of the Muslim community. Muʿtazilites are often characterised as holding for rational criteria in theological issues, as is evident in the five principles found in ʿAbd al-Jabbār (d. *c.* 415/1025): *tawḥīd* (divine unity and uniqueness); *ʿadl* (justice); *al-waʿd wa-l-waʿīd* (promise and threat, reward and punishment in the afterlife); *al-manzila bayna al-manzilatayn* (the intermediate position mentioned); and *al-amr bi-l-maʿrūf wal-nahy ʿan al-munkar* (the commanding of good and prohibition of evil).[2] There is an insistence on the value and efficacy of human rationality present in all these issues. As Frank remarks, 'The earlier Muʿtazilite masters held that the mind's autonomous judgment, based on purely rational principles and axioms, is the sole arbiter of what must be or what may be true in theology

2 For a translation of the 'Book of the five principles' by ʿAbd al-Jabbār and a discussion of classical and modern Muʿtazilism see Richard C. Martin and Mark R. Woodward, with Dwi S. Atmaja, *Defenders of reason in Islam: Muʿtazilism from medieval school to modern symbol* (Oxford, 1997). Also see D. Gimaret, 'Muʿtazila', *EI2*, vol. VII, pp. 782–93, available at www.brillonline.nl/subscriber/entry?entry=islam_COM-0822'.

and their theology is, in this and in other respects, rationalistic in the proper sense of the term.'[3] This is particularly evident in regard to divine justice, which Muʿtazilites famously held necessarily to entail a strong assertion of human free will for the sake of moral responsibility and justly deserved divine reward and punishment. There also followed from the negative theology of their conception of *tawḥīd* that the Qur'ān is created, not eternal, a doctrine that was a key point of contention during the infamous *miḥna* of third / ninth-century Baghdad. The basis for this teaching was their ontological atomism, which held that all created things are composed of atoms and accidents,[4] while God alone is eternal absolute unity without attributes distinct from his essence.[5]

Sophisticated opposition to this rationalist approach and the limitation of divine will and power it appears to entail was set forth vehemently by Abu 'l-Ḥasan al-Ashʿarī, who was born in Baṣra in 260 / 873 and died in Baghdad in 324 / 935f. First a student of the Muʿtazilite Abū ʿAlī al-Jubbā'ī in Baṣra, al-Ashʿarī held for a more literal approach to the statements of the Qur'ān following the views of the Baghdad jurist Ibn Ḥanbal (d. 241 / 855) who was imprisoned during the *miḥna* for refusing to accept the created nature of the Qur'ān. While Ibn Ḥanbal rejected anthropomorphism, as did the Muʿtazilites, he famously refused to accept extensive allegorical interpretation of scripture, and instead asserted that divine attributes and other assertions about God must be accepted in their transcendent mystery *bi-lā-kayf*, that is, without asking precisely how they can characterise the Divine in a way acceptable to human reasoning. Al-Ashʿarī followed Ibn Ḥanbal in this and held the Qur'ān to be the uncreated speech of God, by whose will and action alone all things exist.[6] His doctrine of occasionalism, which ascribes all agency to God who acts without restriction on his will, even in the case of acts

3 R. M. Frank, 'Elements in the development of the teaching of Ashʿari', *Le Muséon*, 104 (1991), p. 144; repr. in Dimitri Gutas (ed.), *Richard M. Frank: Early Islamic theology: The Muʿtazilites and al-Ashʿarī: Texts and studies on the development and history of kalām*, vol. II (Aldershot, 2005).

4 For brief accounts see M. Rashed, 'Natural philosophy', in P. Adamson and R. C. Taylor (eds.), *The Cambridge companion to Arabic philosophy* (Cambridge, 2005); and Jon McGinnis, 'Arabic and Islamic natural philosophy and natural science', in Edward N. Zalta (ed.), *The Stanford Encyclopedia of Philosophy*, available at http://plato.stanford.edu/entries/arabic-islamic-natural/, first published 19 December 2006. A more comprehensive account is found in A. Dhanani, *The physical theory of* kalām: *Atoms, space, and void in Basrian Muʿtazili cosmology* (Leiden, 1994).

5 See Peter Adamson, 'al-Kindī and the Muʿtazila: Divine attributes, creation and freedom', *Arabic Sciences and Philosophy*, 13 (2003); and Catarina Bello, 'Muʿtazilites, al-Ashʿarī and Maimonides on divine attributes', *Veritas* (Porto Alegre), 52 (2007).

6 'One must grant, in brief, that between the traditionalist fundamentalism of ibn Ḥanbal [on the one hand] and the leading masters of the Muʿtazila on the other, there may be some third and it is, in fact, this third "intermediate way" to which the Ashʿarites lay claim': Frank, 'Elements in the development of the teaching of Ashʿari', p. 144.

attributed to human beings, was developed in response to the perceived limitations of divine will and power set forth by the Muʿtazilites. Espousing a form of theological voluntarism or divine command theory,[7] al-Ashʿarī held that 'God determines our works and creates them as determined [and] belonging to us'[8] for 'God creates it as the motion of another' such that 'our acquisition (*kasba-nā*) is a creation by another'[9] (sc. God). That is, the actions of human beings are created in human beings as acquisitions from God, in whom all power for all actions, events and things solely resides. In this way divine justice is faithfully held and defended by the notion that 'He creates injustice for another, not for Himself, and is not thereby unjust Himself.'[10] These and related views provided foundations for the development of a flourishing Ashʿarite school in Islam in which followed a long list of theologians, many knowledgeable and sophisticated in *falsafa*, such as Fakhr al-Dīn al-Rāzī (d. 606/1209) and al-Ījī (d. *c.* 756/1355).

Falsafa, or the foreign science of philosophy

Translations

Philosophy in the Islamic milieu followed upon the availability of texts of the Aristotelian and Platonic traditions. An enormous number of translations came from Greek or Greek via Syriac during the reign of the ʿAbbāsid dynasty at the newly created city of Baghdad designed by order of the second caliph, al-Manṣūr (r. 136–58/754–75). His support of the intensive translation movement of more than 200 years brought to Muslims, Christians, Jews and other thinkers in Islamic lands the scientific and intellectual wealth of a Greek tradition stretching back to Galen, Aristotle, Plato, the Pre-Socratics and Homer.[11] While there is no easily identifiable single motivating factor for this movement, it has been suggested that a 'culture of translation' present in a 'Zoroastrian imperial ideology' was inherited, adopted and furthered by al-Manṣūr and his successors, who had strong familial and cultural links to Persian influences.[12] Most well known are the two

7 On theological voluntarism see Mark Murphy, 'Theological voluntarism', in Edward N. Zalta (ed.), *The Stanford encyclopedia of philosophy*, available at http://plato.stanford.edu/entries/voluntarism-theological/, first published 8 January 2008.

8 al-Ashʿarī, *Kitāb al-lumaʿ*, in Richard J. McCarthy, SJ (ed. and trans.), *The theology of al-Ashʿarī* (Beirut, 1953), Arabic, p. 35, English, p. 74 (translation modified).

9 Ibid., Arabic, p. 44, English, p. 62.

10 Ibid,. Arabic, p. 44, English, p. 64.

11 See Dimitri Gutas, *Greek thought, Arabic culture: The Graeco-Arabic translation movement in Baghdad and early ʿAbbāsid society (2nd–4th/8th–10th centuries)* (New York and London, 1998).

12 Ibid., pp. 40–5.

distinct early translation movements at Baghdad in both of which Christians played key roles: the movement associated with the circle of al-Kindī (d. 252/866) – though some of these translations preceded al-Kindī – and the movement initiated by the famous Ḥunayn ibn Isḥāq al-ʿIbādī, a Christian Arab.[13]

Works concerning issues of metaphysics, Platonic and Aristotelian, are strongly represented in the translations associated with al-Kindī's circle. These include Aristotle's *Metaphysics* by Usṭāth (Eustathios) and the *Meteorology*, *On the heavens*, as well as works of zoology by Ibn Baṭrīq, who is mentioned in the *Fihrist* of Ibn al-Nadīm[14] as having been commissioned to translate by al-Manṣūr. A much modified version of the *Parva naturalia* bears internal resemblance to these, as does a treatise on the *De anima* probably by Ibn Baṭrīq, who also translated the *Timaeus* of Plato, which in the Neoplatonic tradition was read as an important work of metaphysics. One of the most important and influential translations of this period consisted of thoughtfully selected texts on Soul, Intellect, the One and more from *Enneads* IV–VI by Plotinus in three collections constituting the *Plotiniana Arabica*: the *Theology of Aristotle*; a *Treatise on divine science* falsely attributed to al-Fārābī; and a group of *dicta* attributed to the 'Greek Sage'. Other works of Neoplatonism such as the *Introduction to arithmetic* by Nicomachus and propositions from the *Elements of theology* by Proclus also display the common characteristics of this group: foreign terms, transliterations, phraseology from Greek, Persian or Syriac, neologisms and abstract nouns such as *māhiyya* (which became 'quiddity' in later medieval Latin translation) and more.[15] The preface of the largest portion of *Plotiniana Arabica*, the *Theology of Aristotle*,[16] mentions the Syrian Christian Ibn Nāʿima al-Ḥimṣī as translator and describes this work as an exposition by Porphyry (the original editor of the Greek *Enneads*) edited by al-Kindī for Aḥmad ibn al-Muʿtaṣim, son of the caliph al-Muʿtaṣim (r. 218–27/833–42). There the work is also characterised as 'the

13 On the importance of Christians in the development of intellectual culture in Islam with particular reference to philosophy see Sidney H. Griffith, 'Christian philosophy in Baghdad and beyond: A major partner in the development of classical Islamic intellectual culture', in *The church in the shadow of the mosque: Christians and Muslims in the world of Islam* (Princeton and Oxford, 2008).

14 This catalogue contains a wealth of information on translations. See Ibn al-Nadīm, *Kitāb al-fihrist*, ed. G. Flügel, 2 vols. (Leipzig, 1871–2); also in *Kitāb al-fihrist*, ed. Rida Tajaddud (Tehran, 1971); trans. Bayard Dodge as *The* Fihrist *of al-Nadim*, 2 vols. (New York, 1970).

15 See Gerhard Endress, 'The circle of al-Kindī: Early Arabic translations from the Greek and the rise of Islamic philosophy', in Gerhard Endress and Remke Kruk (eds.), *The ancient tradition in Christian and Islamic Hellenism* (Leiden, 1997), esp. pp. 58–62.

16 See Peter Adamson, *The Arabic Plotinus: A philosophical study of the 'Theology of Aristotle'* (London, 2002).

totality of our philosophy' in accord with what has already been spelled out in the *Metaphysics*.[17] More than a mere translation, this work contains significant omissions, interpolations and also translations of an Aristotelian flavour that produced a deliberately crafted hybrid metaphysics in which the Neoplatonic One beyond being and naming is restyled in Aristotelian fashion as being and actuality, albeit now understood in a thoroughly non-Aristotelian way as pure being and actuality without the delimitations of form. This philosophical transformation gave rise to an early form of the distinction of essence and existence in medieval philosophy and was reflected in chapter 8 of another work of the circle of al-Kindī, the *Kitāb al-īḍāḥ fī al-khayr al-maḥḍ* (Exposition on the pure good) (which powerfully influenced metaphysical thought in the Latin West under the title *Liber de causis* (Book of causes)).[18] In this work the First Cause is said to be *anniyya faqaṭ* ('only being', *esse tantum*), while all created things are form and being.[19] This hybrid metaphysics also set forth an influential account of divine analogical predication which negated any comprehensive natural knowledge of God and set out a negative theology by denying of God the names of created things. At the same time it permitted affirmative predication of attributes with the proviso that they be understood in a higher, more transcendent way in God, the cause of all things. The Plotinian doctrine of soul as both universal and transcendent was also harmonised with the Aristotelian hylomorphic doctrine to some degree by the translator/adaptor in a way that preserved the transcendent origin and nature of the individual rational soul while retaining the Aristotelian view of it as form, actuality and perfection in relation to the body.[20] The *Theology* also contains Plotinus' famous account of the soul's mystical ascent to the One, an ascent in which the soul '*is able to recognize the glory, light and splendour of the intellect and to recognize the power of that thing which is above the intellect*, being the light of lights, the beauty of all beauty and the splendour of all splendour'.[21] The

17 'Jumlata falsafati-nā': *Plotinus apud Arabes*, ed. A. Badawi (Cairo, 1947), p. 6; English trans. of most of the *Plotiniana Arabica* by G. Lewis in *Plotini opera*, vol. II: *Enneades IV–V*, ed. P. Henry and H.-R. Schwyzer (Paris and Brussels, 1959).

18 See Cristina D'Ancona and Richard C. Taylor, 'Le *Liber de causis*', in Richard Goulet *et al.* (eds.), *Dictionnaire de philosophes antiques: Supplément* (Paris, 2003).

19 See Richard C. Taylor, 'Aquinas, the *Plotiniana Arabica*, and the metaphysics of being and actuality', *Journal of the History of Ideas*, 59 (1998).

20 See the detailed account of this in Adamson, *The Arabic Plotinus*, pp. 49–68.

21 See *Plotinus apud Arabes*, p. 56; English trans., *Plotini opera*, p. 375 (translation slightly modified). In his translation Lewis uses italics to indicate corresponding Greek text and normal script to indicate additions and interpolations not found in the original Greek. On 'the splendour of all splendour' see C. Bucur and B. G. Bucur, '"The place of splendor and light": Observations on the paraphrasing of *Enn* 4.8.1 in the *Theology of Aristotle*', *Le Muséon*, 119 (2006).

much-read *Plotiniana Arabica*, and these views in particular, exercised a significant influence on later philosophical thinkers.[22]

A more sophisticated and enduring tradition of translation was initiated by the Nestorian Christian Ḥunayn ibn Isḥāq al-ʿIbādī (d. 260/873), who was expelled from medical studies by Yūḥannā ibn Māsawayh only to reappear a few years later reciting Homer in Greek.[23] His deep interest in medicine coincided with strong demand for translations of medical works. He is said to have translated over 100 works by Galen as well as works by Hippocrates and the pharmaceutical *Material medica* by Dioscorides. Although learned in Syriac, Greek and Arabic, Ḥunayn himself often translated from Greek into Syriac, with others of his group translating from Syriac into Arabic. Working with his son, Isḥāq, and many others, Ḥunayn followed a much more sophisticated understanding and scientific methodology. Translations by this group are much more precise, especially in contrast to the paraphrasing and modifying tendencies found in works studied in the circle of al-Kindī. They made a deliberate effort to form a technical vocabulary for science and philosophy in Arabic, and at the same time to capture the sense of the texts without a slavish literalness following the original. Both a prime motivation for this and also its value to the philosophical tradition in Arabic are aptly described by Dimitri Gutas:

> The high level of translation technique and philological accuracy achieved by Hunayn, his associates, and other translators early in the fourth/tenth century was due to the incentive provided by the munificence of their sponsors, a munificence which in turn was due to the prestige that Baghdadi society attached to the translated works and the knowledge of their contents. Better long-term investment was perhaps never made, for the result was spectacular for the Arabic language and Arabic letters. The translators developed an Arabic vocabulary and style for scientific discourse that remained standard well into the present century.[24]

They also produced translations of a much wider variety, among them summaries or complete translations of works such as the *Timaeus*, *Sophist*, *Politics* and *Laws* by Plato and most of the *Organon* as well as the *Rhetoric*, *Physics*, *On generation and corruption*, *On the soul*, *Metaphysics*, *Nicomachean ethics* and *Magna moralia* of Aristotle. Ḥunayn himself is said to have provided

22 See Peter Adamson, 'The *Theology* of Aristotle', section 5, in Edward N. Zalta (ed.), *The Stanford encyclopedia of philosophy*, available at //plato.stanford.edu/entries/theology-aristotle/, first published 5 June 2008.

23 See G. Strohmaier, 'Homer in Bagdad', *Byzantinoslavica*, 41 (1980); G. Strohmaier, 'Ḥunayn b. Isḥāḳ al-ʿIbādī,' *EI2*, vol. III, 578–9, available at www.brillonline.nl/subscriber/entry?entry=islam_COM-0300, Marquette University, 27 February 2009.

24 Gutas, *Greek thought, Arabic culture*, p. 141.

an explanatory account of the *Republic* of Plato. Isḥāq translated the *De anima* and the *Paraphrase* of it by Themistius and also worked with the Sabian Thābit ibn Qurra from Ḥarrān, where Neopythagorean interest in astrology and mathematics was strong. Thābit commented on Aristotle's *Physics*, and corrected Isḥāq's version of the *Elements of Euclid* and the *Almagest* of Ptolemy. Many other translators were active in this period, among them: Qusṭā ibn Lūqā, a Christian and expert in medicine who translated works of Galen and Hippocrates as well as the *Metaphysics* of Theophrastus, the *Mechanica* of Hero, the *Arithmetica* of Diophantus, and a *Placita philosophorum* (*Opinions of the philosophers*) and also works of astronomy, and who was probably involved in translations of Aristotle's *Physics* and works of Alexander of Aphrodisias and John Philoponus; and Abū ʿUthmān al-Dimashqī, a Muslim who translated works of medicine and mathematics as well as Aristotle's *Topics*, Porphyry's *Isagoge* and works by Alexander. Other translations of texts of Alexander, Porphyry, Proclus, Themistius, Nemesius and others were also made available in this period when works might be translated twice or more. This tradition of translation continued at Baghdad well into the fourth/tenth century, when al-Fārābī set out the philosophical foundations for the classical rationalist tradition. New translations, revisions of earlier versions and commentaries and explications of Greek philosophy abounded in a continuation of cooperation of philosophers and translators to bring this secular learning to prominence alongside the ongoing development of religious thought in their diverse Abrahamic traditions. Abū Bishr Mattā ibn Yūnus (d. 328/940) led a second wave of translations from Syriac, rendering Aristotle's account of Divinity in book 12 of the *Metaphysics* together with a commentary by Alexander, in addition to translations of Aristotle's *Posterior analytics*, *Meteorology*, *On sense*, *Poetics* and *On the heavens*. He is also credited with being the teacher of the philosopher al-Fārābī. The Christian logician Yaḥyā ibn ʿĀdī (d. 363/974), a student of al-Fārābī, engaged in philosophical and theological debates and also was involved in the translations of Aristotle's *Categories*, *Topics*, *Sophistics*, *Physics*, *On the soul*, *Metaphysics* and *Poetics*, as well as the *Metaphysics* of Theophrastus and commentaries on Aristotle from the Greek tradition.[25] As the era of translation was coming to an end, Ibn

25 Many of the commentaries made available were of works from the dominant Neoplatonic tradition. For details see Cristina D'Ancona, 'Greek into Arabic: Neoplatonism in translation', in Adamson and Taylor (eds.), *The Cambridge companion to Arabic philosophy*; Cristina D'Ancona, 'Greek sources in Arabic and Islamic philosophy', in Edward N. Zalta (ed.), *The Stanford encyclopedia of philosophy*, available at http://plato.stanford.edu/entries/arabic-islamic-greek/, first published 23 February 2009.

al-Khammār (d. 408/1017) and Ibn Zurʿa (d. 399/1008) translated works of Aristotle including *On the generation of animals*, *History of animals* and *Meteorology*. However, scientific achievements advancing beyond translated sources were well under way, as was the formation of new philosophical syntheses which developed into philosophical approaches native to the Islamic milieu. With the conclusion of the translation movement the cultural assimilation of Greek philosophical thought begun in earnest with al-Kindī, furthered by al-Fārābī and the Baghdad Aristotelians, as well as the Humanists of Abū Sulaymān al-Sijistānī's circle, came to fruition in the brilliant mind of Avicenna, who crafted a genuinely new philosophical account that proved to be profoundly influential among many later philosophers and *mutakallimūn*.

al-Kindī (d. 252/866)

Known as 'the philosopher of the Arabs', al-Kindī played the roles of philosopher, adaptor, text editor, organiser and leader for a group of translators and thinkers versed in the philosophical works of Aristotle and at the same time much attached to the philosophical teachings of the Neoplatonic tradition. With the support of members of the caliphal family, al-Kindī was the first major philosopher of the Arabic tradition to promulgate the ideas of the Greek tradition in a concerted effort to establish a firm place in the Islamic milieu for the secular and foreign science of philosophy. For nearly thirty years of al-Kindī's adult life the *miḥna*, or imposition of religious views by al-Maʾmūn and his successors, was in effect, with its distinctive insistence upon the created nature of the Qurʾān, a doctrine characteristic of Muʿtazilite teachings whose position on divine attributes may be consonant with that espoused by al-Kindī on the basis of philosophical argumentation from the Neoplatonic tradition. Author of perhaps as many as 250 works, al-Kindī wrote on cosmology, mathematics, optics, music and medicine, as well as metaphysics, philosophical psychology and ethics. All but a small selection of his works are lost, though what remains extant provides valuable information on his philosophical thought.

Perhaps the most valuable of the surviving works of al-Kindī is a portion of his *On first philosophy* in which we find him both advocating insistently for the study of Greek philosophy in his day as a sound and valuable approach to the true understanding of the nature of Divinity religiously revealed in the Qurʾān and also demonstrating the powerful argumentation of the Neoplatonists in behalf of divine unity (*tawḥīd*). In his thoughtfully structured argument in the preface, he establishes that philosophy at its highest level is consonant with Islam in that 'the noblest part of philosophy and the highest in rank is the First Philosophy, i.e., knowledge of the First Truth Who is the cause of all truth'.[26] Logic and Aristotle's account of the four causes – material, efficient, formal and final – reveal the definitions essential to the attainment of knowledge and truth under the methods of the ancient philosophers, to whom thanks are owed. He then proceeds to attack as devoid of religion those theologians of his day who, with their weak methods, little knowledge, poor interpretations and undeserved positions of leadership, label as unbelief (*kufr*) the philosophical understanding of the real natures of things (*ʿilm al-ashyāʾ bi-ḥaqāʾiqi-hā*). Yet they do not understand that what they condemn encompasses the knowledge of divinity, unity and virtue brought by true messengers (*al-rusul al-ṣādiqa*) in confirmation of the divinity of God with truth which even these who oppose philosophy are required to acknowledge as necessary. He then closes the preface with an appeal to God for support and defence in this work which will argue for God's divinity, explain His unity, and defend God against unbelievers with arguments (*bi-l-ḥujaj*) squelching their unbelief.[27] In this way al-Kindī understands philosophy, as found in Aristotelian metaphysics, the Neoplatonism of the *Plotiniana Arabica* and Arabic texts from the *Elements of theology* of Proclus, to constitute a single philosophical investigation that has divine unity (*tawḥīd*) as its object, just as Islamic theology has as its object *tawḥīd* and what it entails. That is, he determines that metaphysics has God as its object and he asserts that this philosophical study of divinity with its method of definition and demonstration is an equal to the methods of Islamic revelation and theology in the attainment of the knowledge of the divinity and unity of God. While the determination of God as object of this science has important ramifications for the study of metaphysics, the assertion of an equality of philosophy and religion marks the initiation of argumentation that would be used to assert the primacy of philosophy over theology in the thought of a number of major philosophers in Islam. The terms in which al-Kindī framed the debate set the stage for the classical rationalist accounts of al-Fārābī, Avicenna and Averroes which find the necessity of philosophical methods, particularly the ideals of demonstration, to yield a certain primacy for philosophy in the interpretation of revelation.

In what remains of the incomplete version of *On first philosophy* extant today, al-Kindī argues for the physical and temporal finitude of body and,

26 al-Kindī, *Oeuvres philosophiques et scientifiques d'al-Kindī*, ed. Roshdi Roshed and Jean Jolivet, 2 vols. (Leiden, 1997–8), vol. II, p. 9. English translation in al-Kindī, *al-Kindi's metaphysics: A translation of Yaʿqūb ibn Isḥāq al-Kindī's Treatise 'On first philosophy'* (Fī al-falsafah al-ūlā), trans. Alfred Ivry, Studies in Islamic Philosophy and Science (Albany, 1974), p. 58.

27 al-Kindī, *Oeuvres philosophiques*, vol. II, pp. 11–17; al-Kindī, *al-Kindī's metaphysics*, pp. 56–60.

under the influence of arguments from Philoponus, rejects the common view of Aristotle and the Neoplatonic tradition that the world is eternal, instead insisting upon its creation. He further supports this conclusion by reasoning that unity in individual things is accidental, not true unity, and that it must have as an agent cause the One for creation in unity and existence, for conservation in being, for motion, and for all the various forms of unity. In the True One itself there is a unity of oneness and being requiring the denial of attributes, though in all other things there must be caused unity as a necessary condition for being. 'The cause of unity in unified things is accordingly the True One, the First, and everything which receives unity is caused, every one other than the One in truth being one metaphorically and not in truth' (fa-kullu wāḥidin ghayra al-wāḥid bi-l-ḥaqīqati fa-huwa bi-l-majāzi lā bi-l-ḥaqīqati).[28] A similar account of metaphorical predication and the derivative reality of creatures is found in his *Treatise on the one true [and] perfect agent and the deficient agent which is [so] by metaphor*. There al-Kindī reasons that act (*fiʿl*) is an equivocal term only properly predicated of God whose act of creation (*ibdāʿ*) presupposes nothing in his true act of 'making existents to exist from non-existence' (ta'yīs al-aysāt ʿan laysa).[29] Secondary and metaphorical is the agency of an intermediary which acts upon something else and yet is itself dependent upon the agency of the Creator for the power by which it acts. But only the Creator is an agent in the proper sense, presupposing no other agency, and providing agency immediately and mediately to creatures acting in virtue of the Creator's true agency. This account of primary and secondary causality was a commonplace of the Neoplatonic tradition and is similar to that found in the *Kitāb al-īḍāḥ fī al-khayr al-maḥḍ* mentioned earlier, another work associated with the circle of al-Kindī.

In his philosophical psychology al-Kindī writes of four intellects: three are characteristics of the immortal human soul and the fourth is the transcendent agent intellect in an interpretation of Aristotle's underdetermined account in *De anima* 3.5. Yet while he speaks of what is sensible in act being acquired by the soul, knowledge comes not through abstraction but in the apprehension of immaterial forms by intellect. The Platonist meaning of this is confirmed in *On recollection*, where al-Kindī argues explicitly that sense perception cannot provide knowledge of intelligible forms, which it instead apprehends through its own essence in recollection.[30] Though the remote source is Plato, rather

28 al-Kindī, *Oeuvres philosophiques*, vol. II, p. 95.

29 Ibid., p. 169.

30 Gerhard Endress, 'al-Kindī's theory of anamnesis: A new text and its implications', in *Islão e arabismo na Península Ibérica: Actas do XI Congreso da União Europaeia de Arabistas e Islamólogos* (Évora, 1986).

than reaching back to his *Phaedo* for this doctrine, it seems likely that al-Kindī's view results from late Neoplatonic debates over whether predicated universals founded on the experience of sensibles of the world can be the source of an intellectual understanding of the transcendent forms themselves; instead, they may merely be promptings for the soul to recollect or otherwise apprehend transcendent eternal forms in the First Intellect.[31]

Although it was eventually eclipsed in the tradition by the powerful and creative philosophical synthesis of Avicenna, the tradition of al-Kindī continued well into the fourth/tenth century. A follower in that tradition, al-ʿĀmirī (d. 381/992) used philosophical texts in the interpretation of the Qurʾān and religious teachings of Islam. In his native Khurāsān al-ʿĀmirī studied with Abū Zayd al-Balkhī (d. 322/934), the well-known geographer and polymath, who apparently conveyed from al-Kindī to his student the value of both philosophy and religion in understanding God and creation. Of al-ʿĀmirī's works there survive treatises on optics, predestination, the defence of Islam using philosophical argumentation, a work on the afterlife and an interesting metaphysical text, but none of his commentaries on the works of Aristotle. His familiarity with works and arguments from the tradition of al-Kindī is particularly evident in his *Kitāb al-amad ʿalā l-abad* (On the afterlife)[32] in which al-ʿĀmirī draws on Plato's *Phaedo* to argue for the reward or punishment of the immortal soul and in his *Fuṣūl fī al-maʿālim al-ilāhiyya* (Chapters on metaphysical topics) where he draws on the *Kitāb al-īḍāḥ fī al-khayr al-maḥḍ* (*Liber de causis*) in its adaptation of portions of the *Elements of theology* of Proclus.[33] Religion seems to play a more prominent role in the works of al-ʿĀmirī than in those of al-Kindī, as indicated by the former's use of Qurʾānic terms and phrases to label philosophical teachings. Generally al-ʿĀmirī held that philosophy plays a valuable complementary role to that of religion in the immortal rational soul's quest for knowledge of the Creator and His creatures. As Wakelnig puts it, al-ʿĀmirī 'wants to relate the concepts of Neoplatonic philosophy closely to the Koran and the Islamic tradition, in order to show that philosophy and religion are in accordance

31 For the account of Porphyry, who may have been among the first to prompt debate of this issue, see H. Tarrant, *Thrasyllan Platonism* (Ithaca and London, 1993), pp. 108–47.

32 For the text with English translation and study see Everett K. Rowson (ed. and trans.), *A Muslim philosopher on the soul and its fate: al-ʿĀmirī's* Kitāb al-abad ʿalà l-abad (New Haven, 1988).

33 For a valuable study of this work and al-ʿĀmirī's extensive knowledge of metaphysical texts of the Neoplatonic tradition see Elvira Wakelnig (ed. and trans.), *Feder, Tafel, Mensch: Al-ʿĀmirī's* Kitāb al-fuṣūl fī l-maʿālim al-ilāhīya *und die arabische Proklos-Rezeption im 10. Jh* (Leiden, 2006).

with each other with regard to their objectives'.[34] It should also be noted that his metaphysical reflections gave rise to his use of the term *wājib al-wujūd* ('necessary existent') in characterising divine existence, a notion that would be developed extensively by Avicenna.[35]

The rise of philosophy in the fourth/tenth century

While al-Fārābī is the most well-known philosopher of fourth/tenth-century Baghdad, his era was one of a broad diversity of intellectual flourishing in philosophy, *kalām*, literature and much more, with ongoing translation, lively philosophical and theological debate and methodologically multiple approaches and teachings by a wide array of thinkers. It was in this period that the iconoclastic philosopher and famous physician Abū Bakr al-Rāzī (d. *c.* 313–23/925–35) taught clinical medicine at Rayy and Baghdad, wrote detailed works of medicine widely known in Islam (and translated into Latin) and infamously held that prophecy and revelation are not necessary. Little of the philosophical work of al-Rāzī survives, but from reports and what is available it is clear he was much influenced by the *Timaeus* as well as other works by Plato, and held a Platonic conception of the soul,[36] together with a powerful aversion to revealed religion. In a well-known debate in 320/932 the logician and Aristotelian commentator Mattā ibn Yūnus, mentioned earlier as a translator, famously defended logic as a universal tool transcending the grammar of a particular language against Abū Saʿīd al-Sīrāfī, who rejected that idea, insisting that logic is merely a form of Greek grammar. Al-Fārābī had the Christian Yūḥannā ibn Ḥaylān as a teacher for portions of the *Organon* and apparently knew Mattā. Yaḥyā ibn ʿAdī, another Syriac Christian, was a student of al-Fārābī and became a leading figure as translator, philosopher and theologian in the developing school of Baghdad Aristotelians.[37] Abū Sulaymān al-Sijistānī al-Manṭiqī (the logician) (d. *c.* 375/985), whose companion

34 Elvira Wakelnig, 'Metaphysics in al-ʿĀmirī: The hierarchy of being and the concept of creation', *Medioevo*, 32 (2007), esp. p. 46.

35 See Robert Wisnovsky, *Avicenna's metaphysics in context* (Ithaca, 2003), pp. 239–40.

36 Two of his important philosophical treatises are extant and available in English translation, 'Spiritual medicine' and 'The philosopher's way of life'. See respectively, al-Rāzī, *The spiritual physick of Rhazes*, trans. A. J. Arberry (London, 1950); and Jon McGinnis and David C. Reisman (ed. and trans.), *Classical Arabic philosophy. An anthology of sources* (Indianapolis, 2007), pp. 36–44. For a general account of al-Rāzī see L. E. Goodman, 'al-Rāzī, Abū Bakr Muḥammad b. Zakariyyā', *EI2*, vol. VIII, pp. 474–5, available at www.brillonline.nl/subscriber/entry?entry=islam_SIM-6267, Marquette University, 28 February 2009.

37 For a list of his writings see Gerhard Endress, *The works of Yaḥyā Ibn ʿAdī: An analytical inventory* (Wiesbaden, 1977). Also see Griffith, *The church in the shadow of the mosque*, pp. 122–7.

Abū Ḥayyān al-Tawḥīdī recorded sessions of the circle of al-Sijistānī at Baghdad, led an intellectually rich group of thinkers, and himself held philosophy and religion as two distinct methods, philosophy concerned with the created realm and able to know only the fact of the existence of God, not the divine nature itself. The original version of Abū Sulaymān al-Sijistānī's *Ṣiwān al-Ḥikmah,* a historical account of philosophy, survives only in various abbreviated versions.[38] As for the group's view of the role of philosophy in relation to religion, Kraemer writes, 'The objective of the Falasifa was to enable society to depart safely and gradually from the old beaten paths of inherited belief.'[39] For the Ismāʿīlī branch of Shīʿism the key to the proper guidance of the community in all matters depends upon a divinely inspired prophet. In their theological descriptions the Ismāʿīlīs drew deeply on Neoplatonic thought to express their doctrines. In this tradition Abū Yaʿqūb al-Sijistānī (d. *c.* 361/971) stressed the complete transcendence of God beyond all intelligibility, even insisting that there be not a single but rather a double negation said of God. As Walker puts it, 'One states that God is *not* not a thing, *not* not limited, *not* not describable, *not* not in a place, *not* not in time.'[40] During this period there was also under way the assembling of the *Rasāʾil Ikhwān al-Ṣafāʾ*, a religiously inspired collection of treatises drawing on philosophical translations, Sufism, Ismāʿīlī thought, Qurʾānic revelation, religious teachings, politics and science, with the aim of the purification and salvation of the soul.[41] While by no means the sole concern of those studying philosophy, the issue of philosophy and its relation to religion was one of universal interest with a considerable variety of conclusions reached.

al-Fārābī (d. 339/950f.)

Although Abū Naṣr al-Fārābī is often said to have been of Turkish ethnic origin, the historical sources vary considerably. He probably came from the eastern part of the empire to Baghdad, where he did most of his work, for philosophical studies, though he spent time in Damascus, Aleppo and Egypt before his death in Baghdad. Al-Fārābī understood himself and his associates to be reconstructing philosophy as practised in the Alexandrian tradition, according to his own account

38 See Joel L. Kraemer, *Philosophy in the renaissance of Islam: Abū Sulaymān al-Sijistānī and his circle* (Leiden, 1986), pp. 119ff.

39 Ibid., p. xii.

40 Paul E. Walker, 'The Ismāʿīlīs', in Adamson and Taylor (eds.), *The Cambridge companion to Arabic philosophy*, p. 82.

41 For a recent brief account with a valuable bibliography and web links see Carmela Baffioni, 'Ikhwan al-Safa', in Edward N. Zalta (ed.), *The Stanford encyclopedia of philosophy*, available at plato.stanford.edu/entries/ikhwan-al-safa/, first published 22 April 2008.

in his *Fī ẓuhūr al-falsafa* (The appearance of philosophy), which – significantly – makes no reference at all to the work of al-Kindī or al-Rāzī.[42] There al-Fārābī relates that upon the arrival of Islam philosophical studies moved from Alexandria to Antioch and finally, on the initiative of a few individuals, made its way to Baghdad, where religious restrictions by Christians were dismissed and al-Fārābī himself studied the entire *Prior* and *Posterior analytics* with Yūḥannā ibn Ḥaylān. Focus was now on the proper curriculum and order of study, and in particular the need to begin with logical studies, in which al-Fārābī himself was a master, writing commentaries and paraphrases of the *Organon* and the *Isagoge* or *Introduction* to the *Categories* of Aristotle by Porphyry. For al-Fārābī logic was understood also to include rhetoric and poetics – and itself to be a sort of universal grammar of thought and reason, in contrast to the grammars of particular languages. And demonstration is understood as that form of syllogistic that yields absolute certainty, while other forms of syllogistic yield lesser states of assent by the soul.[43] These logical notions played an important role in al-Fārābī's understanding of the roles of citizens and leaders in the state where non-demonstrative affirmations based on dialectical argumentation and rhetorical suasion are seen to have important value for the formation of a societal community aspiring for the full attainment of happiness. Following the hierarchical account found in Plato's *Republic*, al-Fārābī argues in several works that the perfect state is that in which the legislator, philosopher and imam are found in a single person, while in less perfect cities these may be found in a plurality of individuals, or perhaps not be found at all in those cities lacking proper hierarchy and unity. This doctrine or political philosophy as philosophy of state involves a special coincidence of logical teachings with those of cosmology, metaphysics and philosophical psychology in al-Fārābī.[44]

The cosmological and metaphysical scheme crafted by al-Fārābī situates the First Cause as the First Being (*al-mawjūd al-awwal*) and the eternal creative emanative source for the existence (*wujūd*) of all other beings and as itself free

42 This is noted by Dimitri Gutas in 'The "Alexandria to Baghdad" complex of narratives: A contribution to the study of philosophical and medical historiography among the Arabs', *Documenti e Studi sulla Tradizione Filosofica Medievale*, 10 (1999), p. 155.

43 See Deborah L. Black, 'Knowledge (*ʿilm*) and certitude (*yaqīn*) in al-Fārābī's epistemology', *Arabic Sciences and Philosophy*, 16 (2006). On logic in al-Fārābī in its historical context see the introduction by F. W. Zimmermann to his translation of *al-Farabi's commentary and short treatise on Aristotle's* De interpretatione (London, 1981).

44 For a recent synthetic account of the thought of al-Fārābī on these matters see Philippe Vallat, *Farabi et l'École d'Alexandrie: Des prémisses de la connaissance à la philosophie politique* (Paris, 2004).

of every sort of deficiency.[45] The science that treats of the First Cause is metaphysics, but it does so in so far as it treats of all being under the rubric of being qua being.[46] Under the influence of another hybrid of Neoplatonism and Aristotelianism, in this case traced to Ammonius at Alexandria, al-Fārābī characterises the First Cause as the One in the most deserving sense (since divisibility, corporeality, materiality, subject and beginning are all denied of it) and also as at once intellect, understood, and understanding (fa-anna-hu ʿaqlun wa-anna-hu maʿqūlun wa-anna-hu ʿāqilun).[47] Positive predication or naming of the First Cause is permitted, albeit with the important restriction that these names cannot have the meaning and level of perfection of created beings, but instead must be predicated in accord with its ultimate and transcendent perfection.[48] From the First Cause there emanates an intellect which thinks (*yaʿqilu*) its own essence and that of the First, and from the latter another intellect results as well as the outermost heavens. This begins a series of mediated emanations of celestial bodies and intellects extending to the eleventh intellect in the hierarchy which is the Agent Intellect (*al-ʿaql al-faʿʿāl*) associated with the sphere of the moon and the sub-lunar world.

The Agent Intellect, charged with governance of the sublunary realm in some works but called the emanative cause of it in others, plays an essential role in human reason and in the guidance of humanity through prophecy. Following Alexander of Aphrodisias and most of the Greek tradition, al-Fārābī understands the Agent Intellect to be both an eternal immaterial entity existing in actuality separate from the world and also as intimately involved in human epistemology. In an account of intellect only superficially similar to that of al-Kindī, al-Fārābī explains that the intellectual apprehension necessary for the formation of universals takes place thanks to the Agent Intellect which 'provides something like light to the material intellect', that is, provides soul with a power by which it transfers (*yanqulu*) intelligibles that 'come to be from the sensibles which are preserved in the imaginative power'.[49] In this way it abstracts or extracts

45 al-Fārābī, *On the perfect state (*Mabādiʾ ārāʾ ahl al-madīna al-fāḍila*)*, ed. and trans. Richard Walzer (Oxford, 1985), p. 57.

46 This is significant because it entails a rejection of the approach of al-Kindī, who described Divinity as the object of both metaphysical and religious investigation. In contrast, al-Fārābī holds the consideration of the First Cause as a special part of metaphysics and assigns religion to a position subordinate to political governance.

47 al-Fārābī, *On the perfect state*, pp. 68 and 70 respectively.

48 al-Fārābī, *al-Fārābī's* The political regime *(*al-Siyāsa al-madaniyya *also known as the* Treatise on the principles of beings*)*, ed. Fauzi Najjar (Beirut, 1964), p. 49.

49 al-Fārābī, *On the perfect state*, p. 202. The term *material intellect* derives from Alexander of Aphrodisias. While immaterial in itself, the material intellect derives its name from its receptivity, which also exists, though in a different sense, in matter. Marc Geoffroy

(*tantaziʿa*) forms of material things in the mimetic power of imagination and receives them as actualised intelligibles in the material intellect.[50] With this power now existing as intellect in act, the separated and immaterial intelligibles themselves can be the objects of human intellection at a new level al-Fārābī calls acquired intellect. No longer requiring a body for its activity, the human soul can then rise in a transformation or realisation into its immaterial substance as intellect at the level of the Agent Intellect. For al-Fārābī the attainment of the human end to which the Agent Intellect directs the soul is happiness in the perfection of intellect by voluntary action and individual effort in the context of human society. The conditions for this achievement must be provided by society, even though the majority are brought to truth not by demonstration and the high intellectual methods of the philosopher but rather by rhetorical or dialectical persuasion. For this reason the mimetic power of imagination is needed by the prophet to represent the intelligibles received from the Agent Intellect for the guidance of humanity in persuasive images for the formation of society in the way most suitable for the attainment of happiness.[51] Religious teachings here function as mimetic representations of true philosophy made suitable in a particular culture and at a level appropriate to those incapable of the fullness of philosophical understanding.[52]

Avicenna (d. 428/1037)

It is especially fortunate that the most influential philosopher in the history of Islamic thought, Ibn Sīnā or Avicenna, wrote an autobiography which is extant with a continuation by Abū ʿUbayd al-Jūzjānī.[53] There he relates that his father

argues that al-Fārābī may never have read Aristotle's *De anima* but instead relies on Alexander. See his 'La tradition arabe du *Peri nou* d'Alexandre d'Aphrodise et les origines de la théorie farabienne des quatre degrés de l'intellect', in Cristina D'Ancona and Giuseppe Serra (eds.), *Aristotele e Alessandro di Afrodisia nella tradizione Araba*, Subsidia Mediaevalia Patavina 3 (Padua, 2002).

50 Al-Fārābī, *Alfarabi: Risalat fi 'l-ʿaql*, ed. Maurice Bouyges, SJ, 2nd edn (Beirut, 1983), p. 12. On this issue see Richard C. Taylor, 'Abstraction in al-Fārābī', *Proceedings of the American Catholic Philosophical Association*, 80 (2006).

51 On this understanding, the thought of al-Fārābī is a continuing development of the philosophical tradition in the societal context of Islam rather than a break and an advancement of a new science of politics. Regarding the former see Dominic O'Meara, *Platonopolis: Platonic political philosophy in Late Antiquity* (Oxford, 2005); regarding the latter approach see Christopher A. Colmo, *Breaking with Athens: Alfarabi as founder* (Lanham, MD, 2005).

52 Thérèse-Anne Druart observes that al-Fārābī seems to have held that ethics necessarily involves religion for all with the exception of the true philosopher. See her 'al-Fārābī (870–958): Une éthique universelle fondée sur les intelligibles premiers', in Louis-Léon Christians *et al.* (eds.), *Droit naturel: Relancer l'histoire?* (Brussels, 2008), p. 231.

53 For this and other sources on the life of Avicenna see William E. Gohlman, *The life of Ibn Sina: A critical edition and annotated translation* (Albany, 1974). The most comprehensive

was a government administrator and Ismāʿīlī follower who, after moving to Bukhārā, arranged for teachers for Avicenna, who proved to have extraordinary intellectual talents. His study of the Qurʾān completed by the age of ten, Avicenna was provided with teachers in jurisprudence and then, beginning with the *Isagoge* of Porphyry, in philosophy, in which he quickly excelled his teachers. By sixteen he was distinguished in law and medicine, and proceeded deeper into philosophy, creating a collection of notes and proofs for himself as he proceeded through all the branches of the discipline. His only bump in the road was frustration with the *Metaphysics* of Aristotle – which he claims to have read forty times, and even memorised, without grasping its purpose. But thanks to the chance purchase of al-Fārābī's *Fī aghrāḍ kitāb Mā baʿd al-ṭabīʿa* (On the aims of Aristotle's *Metaphysics*), Avicenna was able to come to a clear vision of Aristotle's end, one very different from al-Kindī's identification of religious theology and metaphysics.[54] Noteworthy for the understanding of the philosophical thought of Avicenna is the absence of reference to studies in a particular school of thought or circle of teachers in which he learned the ways of philosophical analysis and argumentation in a particular tradition. Rather, aside from some modest guidance in his pre-teen and early teen years, he relied on his own remarkable powers of intellect and approached texts of philosophy with a genuine openness that led to new philosophical doctrines that have had powerful and continuing influence on the development of philosophy in Islam, and also in the West through Latin translations. His most influential teachings are in metaphysics, and in particular concerning the nature of God.

According to Avicenna God must be conceived as the Necessary Being, the sole being necessary in itself, and as the sole entity in which existence (*wujūd*) and essence (*māhiyya*) are in complete unity. This is most clearly expressed in his latest major work, his *Ishārāt wa-tanbīhāt* (Pointers and reminders), where in the section on 'Existence and its causes' he distinguishes essence from existence, argues for the need of an efficient cause of existence, and sets forth his account of necessity and possibility in essences. Dismissing what is impossible in itself, he reasons that every chain of caused beings must be finite or infinite and must be founded on a being which is the Subsistent and is itself the Necessary Being (*wājib al-wujūd*). Since every being is either necessary in its own right or possible in its own right, and even an infinite causal chain of possible beings cannot bring about the realised necessity of a possible being,

guide to the development of the philosophical thought of Avicenna is Dimitri Gutas's invaluable *Avicenna and the Aristotelian tradition: Introduction to reading Avicenna's philosophical works* (Leiden, 1988).

54 Gutas, *Avicenna and the Aristotelian tradition*, pp. 238ff.

then there must be a being necessary in itself as an uncaused cause extrinsic to the chain as its term and foundation. This is the unique Necessary Being, which is without definition and can be indicated by no one but he who possesses intellectual knowledge in purity, although its existence can be established by consideration of being itself.[55] The compact late account in *Ishārāt wa-tanbīhāt* combines distinct arguments set forth elsewhere in Avicenna, some of which have sources in early Islamic *kalām*. As Wisnovsky has shown,[56] Avicenna's famous distinction of existence and essence is rooted in theological issues concerning the ontological status of 'thing' (*shay*ʾ) as requiring a divine determinative cause for its existence, and also in al-Fārābī's metaphysical analysis of existent and thing. That distinction appears in his earlier *Metaphysics* of the *Shifā*ʾ where in book 1, chapter 5, Avicenna considers the notions or meanings of the existent (*al-mawjūd*), the thing (*al-shay*ʾ) and the necessary (*al-ḍarūrī*), and proceeds to argue that the first conceived is the necessary (*al-wājib*). His famous analysis of necessity and possibility is then found in chapter 6, where he dismisses the impossible and argues that 'whatever is possible in existence (*mumkin al-wujūd*) when considered in itself, its existence and nonexistence are both due to a cause'.[57] On the basis of an analysis which has its roots in his careful consideration of Aristotle on necessity,[58] Avicenna then reasons with a new and widely influential argument that all that exists owes its instantiation to a necessitating that can be traced to God as the Necessary Being. In book 8 of the same work he goes on to offer argument for the finitude of essential causes and to conclude for the Necessary Being as uncaused and itself a first cause (ʿillatun ghayra maʿlūlatin wa-ʿillatun ūlā),[59] from whom eternally emanates the celestial hierarchy of intellects, bodies and soul (book 9), which come to an end in the Agent Intellect functioning as emanative cause of the world of generation and corruption and all its forms. For the great majority of philosophers and many theologians who followed, Avicenna's metaphysical teachings were

55 Avicenna, *al-Ishārāt wa-l-tanbīhāt*, ed. S. Dunyā, 4 vols. (Cairo, 1960–6), see vol. IV, pp. 7ff.; trans A.-M. Goichon in *Ibn Sīnā, livre des directives et remarques* (Beirut and Paris, 1951), pp. 350ff.

56 See Wisnovsky, *Avicenna's metaphysics in context*, pp. 145 ff. For a short account see Robert Wisnovsky, 'Avicenna and the Avicennian tradition', in Adamson and Taylor (eds.), *The Cambridge companion to Arabic philosophy*, pp. 92–136.

57 Avicenna, *Avicenna: The metaphysics of the healing*, trans. Michael E. Marmura (Provo, UT, 2005), p. 31.

58 See Wisnovsky, *Avicenna's metaphysics in context*, pp. 197–217; and Wisnovsky, 'Avicenna and the Avicennian tradition', pp. 115–19.

59 Avicenna, *The metaphysics of the healing*, p. 258.

simply accepted as providing the terminology and agenda for later philosophical and theological discussions of God and creatures.[60]

While Avicenna was the dominant influence in metaphysics for centuries, his philosophical psychology contained some teachings that hampered its widespread acceptance. For, while Islam and Christianity both held for the resurrection of the body in the afterlife, Avicenna's philosophical argumentation, under the influence of the late Neoplatonic school of Ammonius at Alexandria,[61] held that the rational soul alone survives the death of the body. Created by emanation in a suitably disposed material preparation in the womb and individuated by its initial relationship with body, the rational soul for Avicenna remains separate from the body, functioning as its final cause and existing immaterially, as Avicenna repeatedly reminds his readers with his famous 'flying man' in which the soul recognises its own existence even in the absence of sensation.[62] The body and its senses also serve the rational soul in the formation of knowledge on the part of the soul. Sense-perception of the world is conveyed through abstraction (*tajrīd*) to the common sense, then to the retentive imagination, and then to the active compositive imagination. Avicenna also asserted the existence of an intuitive power (*ḥads*), responsible for quick – or even immediate and certain – insight into the middle term of a syllogism, or prophetic intuitive knowledge. These internal powers are responsible for prenoetic bodily stages of abstraction, and it is at this level that the estimative power (*wahm*) present in all animals apprehends non-sensible characteristics (intentions, *maʿānin*) such as those involved in the sheep's fear in the presence of a wolf. Memory and recollection complete his account of the internal powers related to sense. Abstractions are formed by use of these powers in the brain, although for Avicenna intelligibles in act are not realised in human understanding without the involvement of the Agent Intellect which is said to provide an emanation (*fayḍ*) of intelligible forms to the soul or to realise a conjoining (*ittiṣāl*) with the Agent Intellect. The human receptive (i) material intellect comes to be (ii) possible intellect (or dispositional intellect (*ʿaql bi-l-malaka*)) when it has the primary principles of thought whereby it can become

60 On the development and influence of Avicenna's metaphysical thought see Jules Janssens, 'Bahmanyār ibn Marzubān: A faithful disciple of Ibn Sīnā?', in David C. Reisman (ed.), *Before and after Avicenna: Proceedings of the First Conference of the Avicenna Study Group* (Leiden and Boston, 2003); and Jules Janssens, 'Bahmanyār, and his revision of Ibn Sīnā's metaphysical project', *Medioevo*, 32 (2007). Also see Heidrun Eichner, 'Dissolving the unity of metaphysics: From Fakhr al-Dīn al-Rāzī to Mullā Ṣadra al-Shīrāzī', *Medioevo*, 32 (2007); and the articles by Mayer, Al-Rahim, Rizvi and Takahashi in the bibliography to this chapter.

61 See Wisnovsky, *Avicenna's metaphysics in context*, pp. 21–141; Wisnovsky, 'Avicenna and the Avicennian tradition', pp. 96–104.

62 Michael Marmura, 'Avicenna's "Flying Man" in context', *Monist*, 69 (1986).

(iii) the perfection of this power as intellect in act (*ʿaql bi-l-fiʿl*) as able to know at will previously attained intelligible forms. This latter is intellect in potency in comparison to (iv) acquired intellect (*ʿaql mustafād*) which is the immediate state of actual conjoining with the Agent Intellect and apprehending intelligible forms. Those intelligibles in act exist as such only in the Agent Intellect with the result that for the actuality of knowledge the rational soul, which is without intellectual memory, reverts to conjoining with the Agent Intellect which provides the forms for human intellection as well as those constituting the world when the receptive subject is suitably disposed.[63] Prophecy also occurs intuitively in a select few through a natural emanation from the Agent Intellect or Holy Spirit.

al-Ghazālī (d. 505/1111)

The philosophical accounts of al-Fārābī and Avicenna conveyed an intellectually powerful understanding of the world, human nature and the Creator; but significant parts of their views conflicted with common Islamic religious tenets, and prompted the Ashʿarite theologian and teacher al-Ghazālī to attain a mastery of parts of philosophy in order to craft a detailed response. Based on philosophical studies reflected in his summary of Avicennian thought in the *Maqāṣid al-falāsifa* (Intentions of the philosophers),[64] al-Ghazālī authored his incisive *Tahāfut al-falāsifa* (Incoherence of the philosophers)[65] as a revelation of the philosophers' dissimulations and as a detailed refutation indicating the inadequacy of the arguments of the philosophers for key positions. In particular he held that they and their followers should be condemned as unbelievers for three metaphysical doctrines: (1) denial of resurrection of the human body on the last day; (2) denial of God's knowledge of particulars; and (3) assertion of the past and future eternity of the world. Particularly interesting are his accounts of agency and causality. In the third discussion al-Ghazālī argues that the very notion of agency must include that of will such that the philosophers' assertion that the world emanates necessarily by divine agency is incoherent. Rather, God as agent of the world acts by a will free of all determination other than that of the will itself. In the seventeenth discussion al-Ghazālī famously denies that

63 This account is based on *Avicenna's* De anima *(Arabic text) being the psychological part of* Kitāb al-shifāʾ, ed. F. Rahman (London, 1959), pp. 48 ff. The often-used term *wāhib al-ṣuwar*, 'the giver of forms', appears at Avicenna, *The metaphysics of the healing*, p. 337.

64 The *Maqāṣid al-falāsifa* is based on Avicenna's Persian *Dānish nāma-i alāʾī*. Regarding an untitled work by al-Ghazālī on the metaphysical thought of the philosophers, see Frank Griffel, 'MS London, British Library Or. 3126: An unknown work by al-Ghazālī on metaphysics and philosophical theology', *Journal of Islamic Studies*, 17 (2006).

65 See al-Ghazālī, *The incoherence of the philosophers/Tahāfut al-falāsifa, a parallel English–Arabic text*, ed. and trans. M. E. Marmura (Provo, UT, 1997).

there is a necessary connection between cause and effect, asserting a doctrine of occasionalism which places all causal agency immediately with God. There al-Ghazālī also provides a second account closer to the philosophical account of primary and secondary causality which also finds in God the causality for all events. Whether al-Ghazālī in fact prefers this second philosophical account is a matter of controversy among scholars today.[66] While the *Tahāfut* was written to combat the ways of the philosophers, al-Ghazālī's strong approval of the value of philosophical logic and natural philosophy in his *Tahāfut*, his *al-Munqidh min al-ḍalāl* (Deliverance from error), and some other works contributed influentially to the introduction of methods of logic and natural philosophy into *kalām*. Even some doctrines of metaphysics, which al-Ghazālī specifically condemns, were eventually adopted from Avicenna by the *kalām* tradition in a way that allowed the introduction of methods from the foreign science of philosophy into traditional discussions of *kalām*. Though he taught the value of religious faith and tradition, al-Ghazālī's analysis in the *Munqidh* comes to the conclusion that the most certain and fulfilling method is that of the Sufi way of life in the immediacy of the mystical experience (*dhawq*).[67]

Falsafa in Andalusia

In the western lands of Islam philosophy rose to prominence in the twelfth century, though texts from the east were available earlier. This is clear in the Jewish poet Solomon Ibn Gabirol (d. *c.* 1058), who wrote the philosophical dialogue *Mekor hayyim* (known as *Fons vitae* in its highly influential Latin translation) which espoused a doctrine of universal hylomorphism crafted under the influence of the *Plotiniana Arabica*, among other works.[68]

The first major Muslim philosopher was Ibn Bājja/Avempace (d. 533/1139), who was a poet and philosopher as well as a person of political engagement serving different times as vizer, emissary or judge (*qāḍī*), with these involvements perhaps contributing to his death in Fez – reportedly by poisoning. He was deeply interested in Aristotelian natural philosophy, to which he applied a

66 An analysis with reference to the issues and literature is available in Frank Griffel, 'al-Ghazālī', in Edward N. Zalta (ed.), *The Stanford encyclopedia of philosophy*, available at http://plato.stanford.edu/entries/al-ghazali/, first published 14 September 2007.

67 Al-Ghazālī, *al-Munqidh min al-ḍalāl/Erreur et délivrance*, ed. and trans. F. Jabre (Beirut, 1959), Arabic p. 44; English trans. Richard Joseph McCarthy SJ in *Freedom and fulfillment: An annotated translation of al-Ghazālī's* al-Munqidh min al-ḍalāl *and other relevant works by al-Ghazālī* (Boston, 1980), p. 100; repr. as *al-Ghazali's path to Sufism* (Louisville, 2000).

68 See Sarah Pessin, 'Jewish Neoplatonism: Being above being and divine emanation in Solomon ibn Gabirol and Isaac Israeli', in Daniel H. Frank and Oliver Leaman (eds.) *The Cambridge companion to medieval Jewish philosophy* (Cambridge, 2003).

new conception of the dynamics of motion and argued against Aristotle's rejection of motion in a void, possibly under some influence of the writings of John Philoponus. In philosophical psychology Ibn Bājja wrote a *De anima* after Aristotle; but in that and also in his *Risāla ittiṣāl al-ʿaql bi-l-insān* (On the conjoining of the intellect with human beings) and his *Risāla al-wadāʿ* (Letter of farewell) the influence of al-Fārābī and critical arguments from the Neoplatonic tradition are evident. Following al-Fārābī in part, Ibn Bājja presented an account of the formation of abstractions from sense in which imagination plays a double role of spiritualising (or de-materialising) forms or intentions and of being the subject for abstractions in so far as it functions as the personal material intellect belonging to each human being individually.[69] But under the influence of Neoplatonism Ibn Bājja rejected Aristotle's Third Man Argument in critique of the Platonic Theory of Forms and insisted that true intelligibles are not intentions abstracted from experience of imperfect particulars, but rather are those found united in the transcendent Agent Intellect. Efforts at abstraction from sensory experience can never yield more than the imperfect content of the objects experienced. Hence, human epistemological advancement through the stages of abstraction is merely preparatory for the soul's gradual ascent from ideas through ideas to ideas found in the Agent Intellect. Science and the attainment of knowledge in all their levels are in this way the means to the end of ultimate human happiness in an immaterial uniting and conjoining with the Agent Intellect.[70] In his *Tadbīr al-mutawaḥḥid* (Rule of the solitary) he speaks of the happy in an imperfect city, explaining that the life of the body must be renounced since it is without happiness, while the spiritual is to be embraced for its nobility. But it is the life of the wise person or philosopher that is virtuous and divine, for it is through intellectual understanding of transcendent intellects that he comes himself to be intellect and attain a kind of divinity and perfect happiness. This can come to pass only if one declines association with those devoted to the body and pursues association with those who are spiritual, and ultimately with those who are at the highest level of intellect.[71]

69 Ibn Bājja, *Risālat ittiṣāl al-ʿaql bi-l-insān*, ed. and trans. Miguel Asín Palacios in 'Tratado de Avempace sobre la union del intelecto con el hombre', *al-Andalus*, 7 (1942), pp. 1–47, Arabic pp. 13–16; English trans. in McGillis and Reisman (ed. and trans.), *Classical Arabic philosophy*.

70 See Alexander Altmann, 'Ibn Bajja on man's ultimate felicity', in *Harry Austryn Wolfson jubilee volume*, 3 vols. (Jerusalem, 1965) vol. I.

71 For a recent and very valuable short account of Ibn Bājja and his works see Josep Puig Montada, 'Ibn Bajja', in Edward N. Zalta (ed.), *The Stanford encyclopedia of philosophy*, available at http://plato.stanford.edu/entries/ibn-bajja/, first published 28 September 2007.

A very different approach to the imperfection of human cities and the goal of the philosopher is found in the philosophical novel *Ḥayy ibn Yaqẓān* by the physician Ibn Ṭufayl (d. 581/1185f.) who also served as vizier to the caliph Abū Yaʿqūb Yūsuf (d. 580/1184). Under inspiration from Avicenna's allegorical *Epistle of Ḥayy ibn Yaqẓān*, Ibn Ṭufayl crafted the story of Ḥayy with two possible beginnings. The first is that he was born to the king's sister, who sought to save this child of a secret marriage by setting him to sea in a small boat which reached a deserted isle where the child was discovered and raised by a gazelle. The second account has it that a mixture of material constituents advanced to the point of being a preparation sufficient for the reception of a human soul from God (after Avicenna). Passing through several stages of development, Ḥayy learns natural science and even the nature of the soul, advancing to reason the necessary existence of a First Cause for the world and the heavens. Displaying obvious Sufi influence, Ḥayy realises that his fulfilment is to be found in imitating the ways of the Necessary Being and in exercises leading to the mystical vision of the Divine. But the life of Ḥayy changes through a meeting with a visitor, Absāl, who pursues the deeper inner meanings of religion and had left behind his contemporary, Salāmān, who prefers the literal and surface interpretation of religious law. Ḥayy eventually learns language and Absāl explains to him the ways of organised religion that guides the mass of humanity in their weakness of mind and will. At the opportunity of a passing boat, the two travel to the island city ruled by Salāmān. There Ḥayy views the ignorance and preference for passions and sensory pleasures of the people of that society in their inability or unwillingness to know and to follow the true ways of God. He and Absāl then retreat from the island of Salāmān and return together to their contemplative ways on Ḥayy's island. With this story Ibn Ṭufayl expressed despair for the masses in imperfect societies and endorsed the need for the individual through Sufism to find happiness and transcendent mystical fulfilment in the inner reaches of the human rational soul independent of the strictures of traditional religion.[72]

Averroes (d. 595/1198)

Ibn Rushd / Averroes was trained in law (*fiqh*), as were his father and his famous grandfather, for whom he was named, and put skills of careful textual scholarship and of persuasive argumentation to work both in his professional career as lawyer and judge and also in his philosophical studies. He was known in the

72 See Josep Puig Montada, 'Philosophy in Andalusia: Ibn Bājja and Ibn Ṭufayl', in Adamson and Taylor (eds.), *The Cambridge companion to Arabic philosophy*.

philosophical tradition in Islam though no school based on his thought was established and no great prominence was given to his writings. In the Latin west he was a figure of enormous influence through his purportedly demonstrative commentaries on the works of Aristotle, which taught theologians and philosophers of medieval Europe how to understand Aristotle's difficult texts. There his work soon engendered condemnation for its support of the genuinely Aristotelian doctrines of the eternity of the world and of happiness attainable in the earthly life, and for his own novel doctrine of the unique separately existing material intellect shared by all human knowers. In the initial wave of Latin translations in the early thirteenth century there were included none of his dialectical writings written for a less expert audience: his legal treatise *Faṣl al-maqāl*, his short explanatory *al-Masāʾil allati dhakara-hā al-shaykh Abū al-Walīd fī 'Faṣl al-maqāl'* (Treatise on what Averroes mentioned in the 'Decisive treatise'), his theological *al-Kashf ʿan manāhij al-adilla fī ʿaqāʾid al-milla* (Explanation of the sorts of proofs in the doctrines of religion) and his detailed response to al-Ghazālī in the *Tahāfut at-tahāfut* (Incoherence of the incoherence).

Today he is perhaps best known in the Muslim world for his *Faṣl al-maqāl* (Book of the distinction of discourse and the establishment of the relation of religious law and philosophy),[73] a much-misunderstood work sometimes superficially thought to provide a harmonious account of the conciliation of reason and philosophy with revelation and religious tradition in a way respecting each fully and equally as sources of truth and knowledge of God and his creation. Written as a sort of *fatwā* or legal determination regarding whether philosophy and logic should be permitted, prohibited or commanded either as recommended or required, the *Faṣl al-maqāl* is a carefully crafted dialectical treatise arguing for the priority of philosophy with its method of demonstrative reason over all other methods in the determination of the meanings and import of religious revelation and tradition. Key to its argument are the equivocal meanings of *al-naẓar* as religious reflection or Aristotelian theoretical science; *qiyās* as religious analogical reasoning or Aristotelian syllogistic; and *iʿtibār* as religious consideration or scientific inference explained at the very beginning of Aristotle's *Posterior analytics*. These equivocations allow Averroes to substitute philosophical meanings for the theological and to assert that 'this method of reflection (*al-naẓar*) which religious Law has called for is the most perfect of the kinds of reflection by the most

73 With this translation I follow A. El Ghannouchi, 'Distinction et relation des discours philosophique et religieux chez Ibn Rushd: *Fasl al maqal* ou la double verité', in R. G. Khoury (ed.), *Averroes (1126–1198) oder der Triumph des Rationalismus: Internationales Symposium anlässlich des 800: Todestages des islamischen Philosophen* (Heidelberg, 2002).

perfect kind of *qiyās* which is called demonstration (*burhān*)', that is, the most perfect and certain method of philosophy. With this reasoning and the principle, 'Truth does not contradict truth but rather is consistent with it and bears witness to it', which is taken directly from the *Prior analytics* (1.32) without mention of its source in Aristotle,[74] Averroes declares the unity of truth in a way that permits philosophy with its certain (*al-yaqīn*) method of demonstration a place of priority in the judgement of what is true in all matters, including religion. This is simply because philosophical demonstration by definition itself contains truth with necessity per se, while assent (*taṣdīq*) through rhetorical persuasion or on the basis of dialectical assumptions does not contain truth per se but only *per accidens*. With this methodological approach established, Averroes goes on in the *Faṣl al-maqāl* to reinterpret the three issues for which al-Ghazālī charged the philosophers with unbelief and to affirm precisely what al-Ghazālī had claimed as unbelief in two matters: (1) scripture itself supports a sense of eternality for the world since the Qur'ān mentions God's throne and also water as prior to creation, a view reconcilable with the eternality of matter and the efficacy of God in Aristotle; (2) God's knowledge is neither of universals nor of particulars since both of those are posterior to sensation; rather, God's knowledge is distinct from both since it is causative of particulars and universals. As for (3) resurrection of the body, in the *Faṣl al-maqāl* he declares it obligatory for unscientific people (*min ghayr ahl al-ʿilm*) and says it is unbelief to deny it.[75] But in *al-Kashf ʿan manāhij al-adilla fī ʿaqā'id al-milla* he explains that its true purpose is to help the majority of humanity who live by their imaginations to reflect upon immateriality and perhaps attain something of a proper understanding of the invisible God.[76] This is significant because in his demonstrative Aristotelian commentaries and other strictly philosophical works Averroes finds no room for a teaching on the immortality of the soul.[77]

74 See Richard C. Taylor, '"Truth does not contradict truth": Averroes and the unity of truth', *Topoi*, 19 (2000).

75 Averroes, *Ibn Rushd (Averroes): Kitāb faṣl al-maqāl*, ed. George F. Hourani (Leiden, 1959), pp. 16–17. trans. Charles E. Butterworth with facing-page Arabic text as *Averroës: The book of the decisive treatise determining the connection between the law and wisdom & epistle dedicatory* (Provo, UT, 2001).

76 Ibn Rushd, *al-Kashf ʿan manāhij al-adilla fī ʿaqāʿid al-milla*, ed. Muḥammad ʿĀbid al-Jābrī, 2nd edn (Beirut, 2001) pp. 147ff., trans. Ibrahim Najjar in *Averroes' exposition of religious arguments* (Oxford, 2001) pp. 64ff.

77 The distinction between dialectical and demonstrative works is indicated at Averroes, *Averroës: Tahafot at-tahafot*, ed. Maurice Bouyges, SJ (Beirut, 1930), pp. 427–8; trans. Simon Van Den Bergh as *Averroes'* Tahafut al-tahafut *(The incoherence of the incoherence)*, 2 vols. (London, 1969), vol. I, pp. 257–8.

In philosophy Averroes composed early short commentaries (*Mukhtaṣarāt* or *Jawāmīʿ*) often concerned with key issues, paraphrasing middle commentaries (sing. *talkhīṣ*), detailed long commentaries (sing. *sharḥ* or *sharḥ kabīr*) containing the complete text of Aristotle, a very Aristotelian *Commentary on the* Republic *of Plato*, and a brief *Commentary on the* De intellectu *of Alexander of Aphrodisias*, as well as shorter works on various topics, including a valuable collection of essays under the title *De substantia orbis*. The *Long commentaries* on Aristotle's *De anima*, *Physics*, *De caelo*, *Posterior analytics* and *Metaphysics* are generally thought to contain his most sophisticated and mature teachings. In his mature physics he follows Aristotle's account of the eternity of the world, and reasons that God is the unmoved mover of the outermost heavens. In metaphysics he argues for God as pure act and thought thinking thought with knowledge of the universe only in so far as He knows Himself as the cause of all being through a final causality that refers all other beings to the ultimate perfection of the First. In the early pages of his *Tafsīr mā baʿd al-ṭabīʿa* (Long commentary on the *Metaphysics*) he even goes so far as to assert that the study of metaphysics constitutes the most complete worship of God: 'The *sharīʿa* specific to the philosophers is the investigation of all beings, since the Creator is not worshipped by a worship more noble than the knowledge of those things that He produced which lead to the knowledge in truth of His essence – may He be exalted!'[78]

Averroes' most controversial and perhaps least well understood teachings concerned the nature of human intellect, a doctrine that developed through various stages in his short, middle and long commentaries on Aristotle's *De anima*, as well as in five other works. Throughout his works Averroes followed the common tradition holding for a transcendent Agent Intellect involved in human intellection. The point of most contention in his thought was the nature of the receptive material intellect. In the short commentary he holds for a plurality of individual intellects, and follows Ibn Bājja in holding that the human material intellect is a disposition of the forms of the imagination. In the later middle commentary he retains the plurality of intellects and eschews his earlier view of the material intellect as too closely associated with a power of the body truly to be intellect. He then argues that the human material intellect must be a disposition separate from matter yet belonging to the human being from whom it derives its individuation. In his final position in the *Long commentary on the* De anima Averroes spells out a doctrine of the transference of intentions in the abstraction of intelligibles from the

78 Averroes, *Averroès Tafsīr mā baʿd aṭ-ṭabīʿat*, ed. Maurice Bouyges, SJ, 4 vols. (Beirut, 1938–52), vol. I, pp. 10.11–16. This particular text was not available in the Latin translation.

experience of the world through the internal powers of the soul and the abstractive 'light' of the Agent Intellect which comes to be 'form for us'. He goes on further to insist on the unity of intelligibles for the sake of common discourse and science (relying on reasoning from the *Paraphrase of the* De anima by Themistius) and concludes to the existence of a second transcendentally existing intellect, the unique Material Intellect shared by all human beings. In this new doctrine of intellect Averroes finds that both these transcendent Intellects must be 'in the soul' to be used by the individual knower at will. For Averroes this very activity of intellectual understanding through use of these two transcendent Intellects constitutes the end for human beings and ultimate human happiness. Here and also in his other two commentaries on the *De anima* there is no argument or provision for the Islamic religious doctrine of resurrection or for personal immortality.[79]

In 591/1195, just three years before his death, Averroes and his writings were condemned, he was exiled from Cordoba for a time, and philosophy was banned. Although the reasons for this may have been political, there is little doubt that his philosophical rationalism pushed at the limits of Islamic tolerance at a time when philosophy in the east had already been moving away from Aristotelian rationalism towards becoming a truly Islamic philosophy with the integration of key religious doctrines of Islam. While his sons are reported to have carried his books to the court of Frederick II Hohenstaufen at Sicily,[80] Averroes and his students formed no school to continue his methodological approach in the lands of Islam. Instead, his thought proved to be powerfully influential in Jewish circles, where his authority displaced that of Aristotle,[81] and in Christian Europe, where his teachings were variously embraced, challenged, condemned and revivified through the period of the Renaissance.

Sufi mysticism and a very distinctive philosophy of mystical unity and experience was already present in Andalusia in the person of Ibn al-ʿArabī

79 For a detailed discussion of the development of his doctrine of intellect see the introduction to Averroes, *Averroes (Ibn Rushd) of Cordoba: Long commentary on the* De anima *of Aristotle*, trans. Richard C. Taylor, with Thérèse-Anne Druart (New Haven and London, 2009).

80 See Charles Burnett, 'The "Sons of Averroes with the emperor Frederick" and the transmission of the philosophical works by Ibn Rushd', in Gerhard Endress and Jan A. Aertsen (eds.), *Averroes and the Aristotelian tradition: Sources, constitution and reception of the philosophy of Ibn Rushd (1126–1198): Proceedings of the Fourth Symposium Averroicum, Cologne, 1996* (Leiden, 1999).

81 See Steven Harvey, 'Arabic into Hebrew: The Hebrew translation movement and the influence of Averroes upon Jewish thought', in Daniel H. Frank and Oliver Leaman (eds.), *The Cambridge companion to medieval Jewish philosophy* (Cambridge, 2003).

(d. 638/1240) who when very young is said to have met Averroes. Islamic philosophy was soon also to appear in many thinkers such as the widely travelled Andalusian philosopher Ibn Sabʿīn (d. 669/1270), who reflected this movement with a philosophical approach learned in Aristotelianism and Neoplatonism but constituted as Sufi mystical wisdom.

al-Suhrawardī (d. c. 587/1191)

In the tumultuous era of the Crusades, the warrior ruler of Egypt, Syria and Mesopotamia, Saladin (d. 589/1193), recaptured Jerusalem in 1187 from the Christians, who had held it for nearly a century. The Christian response in the form of the Third Crusade four years later initiated a debilitating military struggle which came to an end in 1192 with a truce with Richard the Lionhearted. In 1183 the mystic and philosopher Shihāb al-Dīn Yaḥyā al-Suhrawardī had come to recently captured Aleppo, now governed by Saladin's young son, who came under the influence of this unorthodox and popular philosopher. In 1191 Saladin, already fully engaged with the Christians, apparently became concerned over the stability of his hold on Aleppo and the sway al-Suhrawardī wielded over his son. In that year Saladin ordered the execution of al-Suhrawardī, who may well have suffered death in connection with his philosophical views. While those views were perhaps Platonic in political matters, the philosophy set forth by al-Suhrawardī was a novel construction of his own making. Well versed in the history of philosophy and in the Peripatetic tradition of al-Fārābī and Avicenna, al-Suhrawardī attacked the distinction of essence and existence in things set out by Avicenna as merely a conceptual distinction in the mind, not in the reality of things.

Al-Suhrawardī also rejected that tradition's epistemological foundations for the apprehension of intelligibles and essential definitions purportedly grasped through abstraction or emanation. Rather, true apprehension of real essences is not mediated, but rather found in the unmediated presence (*ḥuḍūr*) of the known to the knower. Al-Suhrawardī expounds this new teaching in his *Ḥikmat al-ishrāq* (The philosophy of illumination), where he explains his Platonism with an implicit reference to the mystical account of Plotinus found in the *Theology of Aristotle*. He writes:

> Plato and his companions showed plainly that they believed the Maker of the universe and the world of intellect to be light (*nūr*) when they said that the pure light is the world of intellect. Of himself, Plato said that in certain of his spiritual conditions he would shed his body and become free from matter. Then he would see light and splendor within his essence. He would ascend to

> that all-encompassing divine cause and would seem to be located and suspended in it, beholding a mighty light in that lofty and divine place.[82]

For al-Suhrawardī the Platonic forms and the transcendent intellects of the tradition as well as human knowers are essentially lights, for light requires no mediation but only its own presence to make itself known. From the creative Light of Lights (God) come all the other lights, varying in intensity as well as other things, including time, which is without beginning or end. In this metaphysics it is the task of human beings to transcend the shadows of corporeality and realise themselves as lights. Fully integrating into his philosophical account passages of the Qur'ān and urging his readers to the ways of prayer and religious observance, al-Suhrawardī crafted both from a critical epistemology and from his own mystical experiences a distinctive illuminationist metaphysics of light as a *ḥikma* (wisdom) encompassing in a unitary way religion and philosophy.

Rejection and integration of *falsafa*

The prolific and influential theologian Fakhr al-Dīn al-Rāzī (d. 606/1209) in his early years became well versed in philosophy and read Avicenna broadly. He furthered al-Ghazālī's openness to the value of philosophical logic and argumentation by use in his own reasoning, but he was a deeply committed Ashʿarī. He rejected Avicenna's metaphysical teachings on emanationism and the restriction of divine knowledge to universals and instead embraced the atomism and occasionalism characteristic of the Ashʿarite tradition's emphasis on divine power, though with some significant modifications. While he frequently wrote in favour of a thoroughgoing determinism, he found the issue of determinism and freedom without a satisfactory resolution. He wrote: 'There is a mystery (*sirr*) in [this issue]; viz. that proving the existence of God compels one to uphold determinism (*jabr*) … while proving prophecy compels one to uphold [human] autonomy (*qudra*). For if man does not act autonomously, what use is there in sending prophets and in revealing scriptures?'[83] However, Avicenna had a lasting impact on the discussion of metaphysical matters in both *kalām* and *falsafa*, as thinkers from both traditions used and developed his thinking and influenced one another.[84] The

82 al-Suhrawardī, *The philosophy of illumination*, ed. and trans. John Walbridge and Hossein Ziai (Provo, UT, 1999), p. 110. Also see John Walbridge, 'Suhrawardī and illuminationism', in Adamson and Taylor (eds.), *The Cambridge companion to Arabic philosophy*.

83 Ayman Shihadeh, *The teleological ethics of Fakhr al-Dīn al-Rāzī* (Leiden, 2006), p. 39.

84 See, for example, the discussion of the metaphysical issue of *al-umūr al-ʿāmma* and the subject of metaphysical science as developed in those traditions through the centuries with various interactions from Fakhr al-Dīn al-Rāzī to Mullā Ṣadra in Eichner, 'Dissolving the unity of metaphysics'.

Kitāb al-mawāqif fī ʿilm al-kalām (Book of stations on the science of *kalām*) by the Ashʿarite theologian ʿAḍud al-Dīn al-Ījī (d. 756/1355) also displays a powerful proficiency in philosophical argumentation, both in its critical assessments of the reasoning of the *falsafa* tradition and in its philosophical theology in the *kalām* tradition. In six parts, this work deals with theory of knowledge and syllogistic proof, issues of ontology, unity and causality, atoms, substance, accidents and astronomy, God and divine attributes, actions etc. (*ilāhiyyāt*), faith, prophecy and more. There he rejects the notion of knowledge by presence and prefers to understand knowledge as a created attribute.[85] Sabra rightly cites the work of al-Ījī as an example of 'the overcoming of *falsafa* by *kalām*' and as an example of what the philosopher of history Ibn Khaldūn (d. 808/1406) considered a mixing of *falsafa* and *kalām*, which generally 'resulted in making "the one discipline ... no longer distinguishable from the other"'.[86]

Efforts to integrate *falsafa* into Islam, found in the followers of al-Kindī, most notably in al-ʿĀmirī, and also in al-Suhrawardī, were continued in connection with interpretation of Avicenna's late *al-Ishārāt wa-l-tanbīhāt* (Pointers and reminders), the last section of which was read in accord with developing mystical and illuminationist philosophical accounts. Naṣīr al-Dīn al-Ṭūsī (d. 672/1274), a Shīʿī well known for his influential *Akhlāq-i nāṣirī* (Nasirian ethics), responded to Fakhr al-Dīn al-Rāzī in his own commentary on *al-Ishārāt wa-l-tanbīhāt*.[87] He embraced Avicenna's account of possible and necessary being leading to the assertion of the Necessary Being and furthered the mystical reading of Avicenna with his commentary on Avicenna's *Epistle of Ḥayy ibn Yaqẓān*. Quṭb al-Dīn al-Shīrāzī (d. 710/1311) studied Avicenna's *al-Ishārāt wa-l-tanbīhāt* with al-Ṭūsī and wrote his own commentary on *Ḥikmat al-ishrāq* (The philosophy of illumination) by al-Suhrawardī. These were the beginnings of a philosophical tradition of thinkers united by their interest in the integration of philosophy, religion, mysticism (under the influence of Ibn al-ʿArabī and his followers) and illuminationism, culminating in the founding of the 'School of Iṣfahān' by Mīr Dāmād (d. 1041/1631) and Ṣadr

85 ʿAḍud al-Dīn al-Ījī, *Kitāb al-mawāqif fī ʿilm al-kalām*, ed. ʿAbd al-Raḥman ʿUmayrah, 3 vols. (Beirut, 1997), vol. I, pp. 582ff. This text and others are cited by A. I. Sabra in 'Science and philosophy in medieval Islamic theology: The evidence of the fourteenth century', *ZGAIW*, 9 (1994), pp. 18 ff. Also see Josef van Ess, *Die Erkennetnislehre des ʿAḍudaddīn al-Īcī: Übersetzung und Kommentar des esten Buches seiner Mawāqif* (Wiesbaden, 1966).

86 Sabra, 'Science and philosophy', p. 13.

87 See Toby Mayer, 'Fakhr ad-Dīn ar-Rāzī's critique of Ibn Sīnā's argument for the unity of God in the *Ishārāt*, and Naṣīr ad-Dīn aṭ-Ṭūsī's defence', in David C. Reisman (ed.), *Before and after Avicenna: Proceedings of the First Conference of the Avicenna Study Group* (Leiden and Boston, 2003).

al-Dīn al-Shīrāzī or Mullā Ṣadrā (d. 1050/1640),[88] whose thought continues as foundational to modern philosophy in contemporary Iran. This can be seen in *The principles of epistemology in Islamic philosophy: Knowledge by presence*[89] by the late Iranian Shīʿite philosopher Mehdi Ha'iri (d. 1999), who received a doctorate at the University of Toronto and followed in that tradition but also integrated aspects of Western philosophy into his work.[90]

88 On 'first philosophy' and 'divine science' in the metaphysical thought of Mullā Ṣadrā see Rüdiger Arnzen, 'The structure of Mullā Ṣadra's *al-Ḥikma al-mutta'āliya fī l-asfār al-'aqilyaa al-arba'a* and his concepts of first philosophy and divine science: An essay', *Medioevo*, 32 (2007).

89 Mehdi Ha'iri Yazdi, *The principles of epistemology in Islamic philosophy: Knowledge by presence* (New York, 1992).

90 Also see Hossein Ziai, 'Recent trends in Arabic and Persian philosophy', in Adamson and Taylor (eds.), *The Cambridge companion to Arabic philosophy*.

22

The sciences in Islamic societies (750–1800)

SONJA BRENTJES WITH ROBERT G. MORRISON[1]

Introduction

The study of the non-religious scholarly disciplines in Islamic societies has mostly focused on elite writings, instruments and, occasionally, images. A vertical historical approach that compares texts, tables or instruments produced at different places and times has prevailed over a horizontal approach that situates a scholar within the complex environment of his time and space. The vertical approach favoured the comparison between ancient Greek achievements and those of scientists in Islamic societies. During recent decades a minority of historians of mathematics have focused on the comparison of achievements by scientists in Islamic societies with those of later Western scholars.

A corollary of the vertical approach is its preference for the study of outstanding achievements over more ordinary ones, the correct over the erroneous and the realistic over the symbolic. Historical questions such as whether mathematicians and astronomers in Islamic societies preferred Greek theories, models and methods over their Indian and Persian counterparts, and if so, why, have been answered primarily by pointing to cognitive superiority (better models, exact methods, more difficult subjects, axiomatic and deductive structure) to the neglect of other possible factors involved in such decisions. In contrast, the overarching theme of this chapter is the complex relationships between the work of scientists and physicians and the societies that they lived in.

The expressions *scholarly disciplines* and *science(s)* used in this chapter render the Arabic *ʿilm* (pl. *ʿulūm*). Although there is a strong religious connotation to *ʿilm* in particular, the reader of this chapter should note

1 The section entitled The Islamic aspects of cosmology, astronomy and astrology is written by Robert Morrison.

that this word and its plural were also used to denote other fields of knowledge such as mathematics or astronomy. It is hoped that using its modern equivalents as well as the less value-laden term *scholarly disciplines* is a tolerable compromise.

The translation movement

The translation movement was the court-sponsored process of massive translations of Pahlavi, Sanskrit, Syriac and Greek texts – on philosophy, astronomy, astrology, mathematics, theoretical music, alchemy, magic, divination, human and veterinary medicine, gnomology, princely ethics, agriculture, military science and some history – that took place between the second half of the second/eighth and the late fourth/tenth centuries, primarily in Baghdad. Many historians consider this process either exclusively or primarily as the translation of Greek books from the late eighth to the late ninth or early tenth centuries. They see this process as focused upon writings by leading Greek and Hellenistic scholars such as Hippocrates, Plato, Aristotle, Archimedes, Euclid, Apollonius, Diophantus, Ptolemy, Galen and Dioscorides. The motives and objectives that caused this massive cross-cultural transfer of knowledge under the first ʿAbbāsid caliphs and their courtiers are seen as answering the practical needs of the new dynasty, among them astrological and medical concerns. Ritual duties of the Muslim community such as praying at particular times and in specific directions are thought to have inspired an interest in various mathematical disciplines. Religious debates that brought together members of various Christian Churches, Manichaean dualists, Mazdakites, Jews and adherents of various Muslim factions left Muslim disputants in an uncomfortable position, as they were unfamiliar with the various tools of pre-Islamic philosophical and theological debates. It has been argued that a handful of ʿAbbāsid caliphs promoted enlightened, tolerant and rational values in a politics that was opposed to obscurantism and literalism. Professional and cultural aspirations and the needs of mostly Christian physicians are often seen as the most important single factor that stimulated the translation of Greek texts into Syriac and Arabic.

This concept of continuity, utilitarianism and enlightenment focuses primarily on the scholarly aspects of the movement and exaggerates the importance of some of its contributors. It leaves unexplored the social and cultural factors that sustained two hundred years of heavily financed and highly visible efforts to acquire and transform knowledge of pre-Islamic provenance. In 1998 Gutas offered a new perspective that tried to explain the translation movement as a social and cultural phenomenon.[2] The major points he raised seem to be well founded. The survival of Hellenic and Hellenistic philosophy, science and medicine was affected by the rupture between Orthodox Byzantium and Hellenism and by the schisms within the Christian Church.[3] As a result, Nestorian and Monophysite communities in Sasanian Iraq and Iran pursued a substantially truncated practice of Hellenism. Certain Coptic communities outside Alexandria continued to cultivate hermetic medical and alchemical teachings. The so-called Sabian communities of northern Iraq resisted pressures to abolish their adoration of the planets and taught a mixture of hermetic gnosticism and mathematical astrology. All these communities were freed from Byzantine Orthodox control after the Arab Muslim armies conquered Syria, Palestine, Egypt, Iraq and Iran. The abolition of Byzantium's oppressive control was a major factor behind the cultural possibilities open to the Umayyads and the ʿAbbāsids.

The second major factor was the material improvements that followed the conquests. A new Pax Islamica united territories formerly divided by crown, Church and war. Trade, crafts and agriculture profited from increased security, stability, the repair of irrigation, new crops and the migration of people and husbandry.[4] But the end of Orthodox oppression and the material betterment of life did not bring about a substantial Umayyad translation movement. The locus of the Umayyad caliphate (41–132/661–750) in Byzantine Syria and Palestine with its Greek-speaking Orthodox majority among the population did not encourage such a cultural transformation. The few translations into Arabic that occurred under Umayyad rule were undertaken on the initiative of *mawālī* of possibly Persian descent, that is, newly converted clients of Arab tribes, who served as secretaries in the administration, as well as by Arabic-speaking Nestorians in Iraq and by unidentified astrologers in the north-west of the Indian subcontinent.[5] Some of these translations were already part of the cultural environment of the ʿAbbāsid revolt, which started around 102–3/719–20.[6]

2 Dimitri Gutas, *Greek thought, Arabic culture: The Graeco-Arabic translation movement in Baghdad and early ʿAbbāsid society (2nd–4th/8th–10th centuries)* (New York and London, 1998).
3 Ibid., pp. 176–86.
4 Ibid., pp. 11–14, 17–20.
5 Ibid., pp. 25–7; David Pingree, 'Astronomy and astrology in India and Iran', *Isis*, 54 (1963); Mario Grignaschi, 'Un roman épistolaire gréco-arabe: La correspondence entre Aristote et Alexandre', in M. Bridges and J. C. Bürgel (eds.), *The problematics of power: Eastern and Western representations of Alexander the Great*, Schweizer Asiatische Studien, Monograph 22 (Bern, Berlin, Frankfurt am Main etc., 1996).
6 See also Gutas, *Greek thought, Arabic culture*, p. 27.

The translation movement was primarily caused by forces that opposed the Umayyad dynasty and sought to restore pre-Islamic Iranian rule and splendour. Iranian groups in Khurāsān were among those who fought for this. As part of these efforts and as a result of the slowly changing linguistic patterns in Iran, Iranian members of the anti-Umayyad movement, including those who fought for a Sasanian and Zoroastrian revival and hence against any kind of Arab Islamic rule, established translating as one of their political and cultural tools, and drew on Sasanian precedent and anti-Macedonian cultural and religious rhetoric.[7]

It has been argued that the Sasanian propaganda of re-collecting Zoroastrian scripture, the Avesta, and re-translating wisdom shattered by Alexander of Macedonia (d. 323 BCE) and his marauding troops after the defeat of Dara (Darius III, r. 336–331 BCE) did not lead to a broad and sustained cultural process of translating Greek works on philosophy and the sciences. While it is undisputed that such translations took place, their limited number and thematic scope has been seen as an argument against Gutas's view of the importance of the Sasanian model. This argument overlooks that the emphasis of the Sasanian propaganda was first and foremost on religious knowledge. Wisdom and practical secular knowledge came second. Although the disciplinary breadth was substantially smaller than in the later translation movement sponsored by the ʿAbbāsids, Sasanian pro-translation propaganda was more than mere propaganda. It reflected historical events and managed to create a cultural climate favourable to translating scholarly writing. The importance of this sort of translation was accepted by Iranian scholars, nobles and priests for several centuries after the fall of the empire itself, including those who already had converted to Islam, as references to the Sasanian politics of translation in the *Denkard* and Abū Sahl ibn Nawbakht's (*fl.* second/eighth century) report in his *Kitāb al-nahmūṭān fī l-mawālīd* indicate.[8]

It is possible that the historical memory as described in eighth- and ninth-century Zoroastrian sources such as the *Denkard* might be a construction based on what happened during the ʿAbbāsid rebellion and under the two ʿAbbāsid caliphs, al-Manṣūr (r. 136–58/754–75) and al-Maʾmūn (r. 198–218/813–33), who were responsible for adopting and implementing the politics of patronising and commissioning translations of Middle and New Persian, Sanskrit, Syriac and Greek books into Arabic. Nevertheless, the fact that

7 Ibid., pp. 47–50.
8 Ibid., pp. 36–7, 39–40. See also Ibn al-Nadīm, *The Fihrist of al-Nadim*, trans. Bayard Dodge, 2 vols. (New York, 1970), vol. II, p. 651, note 67.

translating was represented as a major cultural tool of the anti-Umayyad movement both by its ʿAbbāsid beneficiaries and their Iranian clients is indubitable. In this sense the translation movement owes its origins and cultural force to Zoroastrian imperial ideology. This imperial ideology saw all knowledge as ultimately derived from the Avesta. Knowledge was lost for the Iranians through Alexander's material destruction of the Holy Book. It was transferred to the Greeks because Alexander had ordered the translation into Greek of those parts of the Avesta that he saw fit. From this event, the story concludes, Greek philosophy, science and medicine had their beginnings. Rulers of the two subsequent Iranian dynasties, the Arsacids (284 BCE–226 CE) and the Sasanians (226–642 CE), are remembered with declarations, prescriptions and testaments that call for re-collecting the scattered remnants of Zoroastrian wisdom including those parts that had in the mean time been translated into foreign languages.[9] By drawing on this complex pre-Islamic propaganda, translating was legitimised and justified as an imperial cultural activity for the ʿAbbāsid movement and dynasty. It is only when the process of courtly sponsored and encouraged translations was well under way at the end of the eighth and the beginning of the ninth centuries that translations from Greek became important. It took at least several decades before Islamic scholars considered Greek philosophy and science as superior and neglected the other cultural components of the translation movement.

The decision by the caliph al-Mahdī (r. 158–69/775–85) around 166/782 to order the Nestorian patriarch and caliphal counsellor Timothy I to translate Aristotle's *Topics* was an important step in extending the scope of translations and integrating the local Aramaic elite in that activity. Al-Mahdī chose the book because it taught dialectics, the art of argumentation. It gave support to the use of demonstrative proofs and dialectic disputations as major tools among the early practitioners of *kalām*.[10] Al-Mahdī's decision was part of a political strategy to maintain and consolidate ʿAbbāsid power against the resurgence of pre-Islamic Iranian doctrinal debates and the emergence of strong non-Islamic tendencies among members of the ʿAbbāsid administrative personnel. The memory of these conceptual clashes is preserved in later Arabic books on *uṣūl al-dīn* with their standard references to the arguments raised by dualists, naturalists, natural philosophers, astrologers and geometers against positions held by Muʿtazilites, Qadarites and other religious factions of the first ʿAbbāsid century. It is also reflected in reports by Muslim historians

9 Ibid., pp. 41–5.
10 Ibid., p. 65.

such as al-Masʿūdī (d. 345/956), who described al-Mahdī's politics as directed against followers of religious doctrines by Marcion (*c.* 140 CE), Bardesanes (154–222 CE) and Mani (216–77 CE). Al-Mahdakhbārī ordered the *mutakallimūn* to write books against these doctrines.

Al-Mahdī's turn to Aristotle was not, however, the beginning of a process that would lead directly to his dream of Aristotle. (Al-Maʾmūn is reported to have had a dream in which Aristotle appeared and the caliph interrogated him about what was good.) The following of Iranian cultural patterns continued under Hārūn al-Rashīd (r. 170–93/786–809), who is credited with the establishment of the Bayt al-Ḥikma, often hailed as a scientific academy and the centre of the Graeco-Arabic translation movement. The data about this institution as reported in Arabic historical sources such as Abū Jaʿfar Muḥammad ibn Jarīr al-Ṭabarī's (d. 311/923) *Taʾrīkh* (Annals), Ibn al-Nadīm's *Kitāb al-fihrist* (Catalogue) and later books does not, however, support such an interpretation.[11] These sources, enriched by poetry, suggest that the Bayt al-Ḥikma was a library where rare books on history, poetry and strange alphabets were collected and which was established when al-Manṣūr structured the administration of his court and empire along the lines of Sasanian tradition.[12]

A second institution little mentioned in the context of the ʿAbbāsid translation movement was the hospital funded by Hārūn al-Rashīd's vizier, Yaḥyā ibn Khālid al-Barmakī (d. 189/805). According to Ibn al-Nadīm, Yaḥyā ibn Khālid paid several physicians from India to run the hospital, to translate books on medical subjects from Sanskrit into Arabic and to collect pharmaceutical plants and drugs in India and bring them to Baghdad.[13] As well as this transfer of mainly medical knowledge Yaḥyā ibn Khālid ordered that a book should be written about the doctrines various peoples in India believed in. Ibn al-Nadīm claims to have had access to the Arabic report to Yaḥyā ibn Khālid in a manuscript owned and annotated by Abū Yūsuf Yaʿqūb ibn Isḥāq al-Kindī (d. *c.* 256/870), the major philosopher of the third/ninth century.[14] These activities confirm that the influx of Indian scholarly knowledge in the later decades of the second/eighth century into Baghdad also was directly connected with the ʿAbbāsid court and its cultural politics. The descent of the Barmakid family from Zoroastrian and Buddhist clergy apparently contributed to the vizier's specific interest in and attention to knowledge and

11 Marie-Génèvieve Balty-Guesdon, 'Le Bayt al-Ḥikma de Baghdad', *Arabica*, 39 (1992); Gutas, *Greek thought, Arabic culture*, pp. 54–60.

12 Gutas, *Greek thought, Arabic culture*, pp. 54–9.

13 Ibn al-Nadīm, *Fihrist*, trans. Dodge, vol. II, pp. 590, 710, 826–7.

14 Ibid., pp. 826, 831–2.

goods from India. The larger relevance of such knowledge consisted in its contribution to 'an atmosphere of culture' – as Ibn al-Nadīm wrote about the entrance of the Jewish secretary, physician and convert to Islam ʿAlī ibn Sahl al-Ṭabarī (d. 247/861) into the circle of boon companions of the caliph al-Mutawakkil (r. 232–47/847–61).[15]

Adherence to Sasanian-style imperial politics and the preference for political astrology and translations continued until the second half of the 810s. Things changed when al-Maʾmūn decided to return to Baghdad. In 203/818 he left Marw after executing his mentor, general and vizier al-Faḍl ibn Sahl (d. 203/818). Arriving in Baghdad, al-Maʾmūn had to pacify the ravaged city, convince the local elites of his capability to effectively quell all opposition and gain loyalty from at least some of their factions. According to later Islamic historians he achieved these goals by turning to Muʿtazilite doctrines and by allegedly introducing Greek philosophy and science.[16] This representation of the caliph's politics reflects the success of al-Maʾmūn's legitimising propaganda. He did not introduce Greek philosophy and science into ʿAbbāsid society; he merely showed favour to the translation movement that was already under way. The application of Muʿtazilite concepts as state doctrines also occurred relatively late in his life, after he had tested other possibilities – in particular, cooperation with the Shīʿa. What unified al-Maʾmūn's various efforts to solve his manifold problems was the adoption of an absolutist interpretation of Islam which defined the caliph as the sole arbiter of orthodoxy and the reinforcement of the politics of centralisation adopted by his great-grandfather al-Manṣūr. Coinage, military and fiscal reforms were part of this new politics, as was his new foreign policy. The major factor behind the enormous growth of the translation movement was al-Maʾmūn's introduction of a philhellenic anti-Byzantinism.[17]

As in the case of the earlier application of Zoroastrian imperial ideology, al-Maʾmūn's new philhellenic imperial ideology brought with it new translations, new social elements and specific practices. Universalists such as al-Kindī emerged. He was one of the most radical and comprehensive practitioners of the new intellectual programme. It was through his personal patronage, teaching and writing that many Aristotelian and pseudo-Aristotelian as well as Neopythagorean and Neoplatonic writings on philosophy were translated into Arabic, commented upon and recast as a philosophy in a Muslim

15 Ibid., p. 697.
16 Gutas, *Greek thought, Arabic culture*, pp. 77–8.
17 Ibid., pp. 83–95.

community.[18] Professionally defined specialists such as Yūḥannā ibn Māsawayh (d. 243/857), a Nestorian physician from Gondeshapur and court physician to Hārūn al-Rashīd and subsequent ʿAbbāsid caliphs, engaged in systematic translations of Greek medical works as translators and patrons. While most historians consider the translation of Greek medical books to be the result of professional exigencies rather than as a part of courtly patronage, the fact that before al-Maʾmūn's new politics developed most medical translations apparently were made from languages other than Greek suggests that Ibn Māsawayh's activities as well as those of his students and collaborators were also closely connected to ʿAbbāsid cultural politics, rather than being merely an effort to bring ʿAbbāsid medical teaching in line with the late Alexandrian curriculum.[19] The stories of the translocation of Alexandrian medical and philosophical teaching via intermediary stops in Syria and northern Iraq to Baghdad should also be placed in the context of the stress on ʿAbbāsid superiority as the result of Muslim acceptance of ancient Greek knowledge. One of the most outspoken formulations of this connection is given by Ibn Jumayʿ (d. 594/1198), court physician of the first Ayyūbid sultan, Saladin (Ṣalāḥ al-Dīn, r. 564–89/1169–93). He claims that if it had not been for al-Maʾmūn, 'medicine and other disciplines of the Ancients would have been effaced and obliterated just as medicine is obliterated now from the lands of the Greeks, which had been most distinguished in this field'.[20] When compared to the variant told by the Christian scholar Job of Edessa (second–third/eighth–ninth centuries), it becomes obvious that the account of al-Maʾmūn's involvement in the transfer of Greek and Hellenistic knowledge is an embellishment that does not describe simple, straightforward historical facts, but reflects values attached to al-Maʾmūn's politics.[21]

When weighing the merits of these new views on the social history of the translation movement, it has to be taken into account that previous accounts overstressed the importance of ancient Greek, Byzantine and Christian components. Well into the first half of the third/ninth century ʿAbbāsid scholars

18 Gerhard Endress, 'al-Kindī über die Wiedererkennung der Seele: Arabischer Platonismus und die Legitimation der Wissenschaften im Islam', *Oriens*, 34 (1994), pp. 179–84.

19 Manfred Ullmann, *Handbuch der Orientalistik*, division I, supplementary vol. VI, section 1 (Leiden, 1970); Felix Klein-Franke, *Vorlesungen über die Medizin im Islam*, Sudhoff Archiv, supplement 23 (Wiesbaden, 1982).

20 Hartmut Fähndrich (ed.), *Ibn Jumayʿ: Treatise to Ṣalāḥ ad-Dīn on the revival of the art of medicine*, Abhandlungen für die Kunde des Morgenlandes XLVI, 3 (Wiesbaden, 1983), p. 19.

21 Gutas, *Greek thought, Arabic culture*, pp. 92–4.

worked with concepts and methods from different pre-Islamic cultures. Even with the preponderance of Greek and Hellenistic concepts and methods from the late third/ninth century onwards, scientific knowledge from other cultures was never completely eradicated. Problems, methods, parameters, techniques and instruments of Indian, Iranian, Mesopotamian and Chinese origin either remained available as alternatives to Greek and Hellenistic knowledge or were merged with this knowledge. Moreover, the scholarly world of ʿAbbāsid Iraq and Iran was by no means homogeneous, for some of the scholars who worked on religious, historical and philological themes looked at the translations of Greek philosophical books and Indian arithmetic with scorn, disdain or condescension. Scholars who were primarily engaged in the sciences took different positions on such questions as whether algebra was inferior and number theory superior to geometry, whether astrology was the queen of all sciences or not a science at all and whether divination from the cooked shoulder blades of sheep was part of Greek philosophy.

Patronage and education

Court patronage was the major element that provided the necessary means to carry out the translations. Most of the ʿAbbāsid caliphs of the second/eighth and third/ninth centuries were involved in this patronage in various forms (receiving dedications; employing professionals as tutors and healers; including Muslim and non-Muslim scholars in their cultural entourage; paying stipends and giving gifts). The caliphs alone, however, could not have maintained the depth and breadth of this process. Numerous viziers, starting in the second/eighth century with the Barmakids al-Khālid and Yaḥyā and continuing in the third/ninth century with al-Faḍl ibn Sahl or Abū Ṣaqr Ismāʿīl ibn Bulbul, generals such as Ṭāhir ibn Ḥusayn (d. 207/822), administrators such as the Banū Nawbakht and courtiers such as al-Kindī, the three Banū Mūsā – Muḥammad, Aḥmad and al-Ḥasan – and the Banū al-Munajjim contributed their own funds to the enterprise. In addition to the money they spent, the courtiers and administrators invested cultural capital. They shaped the translation movement and the kind of knowledge and practices that sustained it by composing scholarly works and by installing circles for teaching and discussion. Such *majālis* were also held by caliphs. They were an important courtly institution that elicited the necessary interest for further patronage and sponsorship.

One major result of courtly patronage for the ancient sciences of the third/ninth century was the formulation of scientific programmes that were linked to different religious and political outlooks. Al-Kindī, for instance, worked to create a scientific philosophy in Arabic for Muslims that harmonised pre-Islamic Arabic, Neoplatonic, Aristotelian and hermetic knowledge as well as belief about all parts of the universe (the heavens, nature, the human body, fate, society and the afterlife) in the form of a systematic exposition, deductive structuring and demonstrative proofs.[22] The Banū Mūsā followed a different course by focusing primarily on the mathematical sciences such as geometry, astronomy, optics and mechanics. Al-Kindī mainly worked with high-ranking Christian clergy such as Ḥabīb ibn Bahrīz, the Nestorian metropolitan of Mosul, and descendants of Byzantine nobility such as Yaḥyā ibn Baṭrīq. The Banū Mūsā sided with leaders of the Shuʿūbiyya such as the Banū al-Munajjim, funded Christian professionals such as Ḥunayn ibn Isḥāq (d. 260 or 264/870 or 873) and Isḥāq ibn Ḥunayn (d. 298/911) and trained gifted Sabians such as the money-lender Thābit ibn Qurra (d. 288/901). The different religious, political and scientific goals of al-Kindī and the Banū Mūsā turned them into bitter enemies.

A second important result of courtly patronage for the ancient sciences was the reliance on cross-denominational cooperation. This included Nestorians, Jacobites, Sabians, Greek Orthodox, Sunnīs, Shīʿa, Zoroastrians and Jews. Only members of the medical profession expressed rivalries, tensions and enmities as religious difference. Religious difference was, however, only one factor that shaped the fortunes of a discipline at the ʿAbbāsid court. Galenism, for instance, emerged as the leading medical theory and practice during the third/ninth and fourth/tenth centuries because of the higher number of its practitioners compared to competing practitioners, their better local availability, more extensive networks, better literary skills and the greater political power of their patrons.[23]

In the fourth/tenth century the diversification of the ʿAbbāsid empire into a number of vassal as well as independent dynasties such as the Ṭāhirids (205–59/820–72), the Sāmānids (261–389/874–999) and the Ḥamdānids

22 al-Kindī, *al-Kindī's* Metaphysics*: A translation of Yaʿqūb ibn Isḥāq al-Kindī's treatise 'On first philosophy' (*Fī al-falsafah al-ūlā*)*, trans. with introd. and commentary Alfred L. Ivry, Studies in Islamic Philosophy and Science (Albany, 1974); al-Kindī, 'Kitāb fī ʿilm al-katif: Textvs arabicvs et translatio anglica. Cvra et stvdio Gerrit Bos et Charles Burnett', in Gerrit Bos, Charles Burnett, Thérèse Charmasson, Paul Kunitzsch, Fabrizio Lelli and Paolo Lucentini (eds.), *Hermetis trismegisti astrologica et divinatoria* (Turnhout, 2001), pp. 290–3; Endress, 'al-Kindī über die Wiedererkennung der Seele', p. 179.

23 Keren Abbou, 'Medicine and physicians in the ʿAbbāsid court, from the reign of al-Manṣūr until al-Mutawakkil', MA thesis, Ben-Gurion University (2000), pp. 69–91; al-Jāḥiẓ, *The book of misers*, trans. R. B. Sergeant (London, 1996), pp. 86–7.

(317–94/929–1003) and the emergence of rivals such as the Andalusian Umayyads (138–422/756–1031) and the North African and Egyptian Fāṭimids (297–567/909–1171) broadened the opportunities for scholars as new courts, cultural centres and intellectual policies appeared. Decentralisation as well as anti-ʿAbbāsid policies inside and outside the caliphate shaped the funding and sponsoring of philosophy, astronomy, medicine, geometry, optics, botany and alchemy. The Umayyads in Cordoba sought to emulate ʿAbbāsid cultural splendour, while at the same time cooperating with Byzantium and the Fāṭimids.[24] The Fāṭimids turned to Neoplatonic philosophy as a helpful tool for formulating their theory of the imamate and to back up their claims to genealogical legitimacy. The Būyids drew upon three major strands of cultural politics: pre-Islamic Sasanian heritage; Arab culture; and Shīʿite belief. The ancient sciences constituted one aspect of Būyid princely education in Arab court culture. Their patronage flourished at the courts in Baghdad, Rayy, Shīrāz, Iṣfahān and Hamadhān. Competition with the ʿAbbāsid court probably provided an additional impetus. Similar motives led rulers in Central Asia, eastern Iran, Syria and northern Iraq to attract astrologers, philosophers, physicians and 'engineers' to their courts and to pay for the copying of treatises by ancient and Muslim authors.

The strong cultural role of Būyid viziers as tutors of princes, together with their own splendid sponsoring of the arts and sciences, suggests that the support for these two cultural domains at courts in subsequent Islamic societies, in particular in Iran and Central Asia, was partly the result of the cultural identity of the vizierate.[25] Family networks created by intermarriage diversified the patronage of the sciences below the level of rulers and princes. Several generations of physicians, geometers, astronomers and historians came from families linked with the ʿAbbāsid and Būyid courts such as the Bukhtīshūʿs, the Ibn Qurras and the al-Ṣābi's. In later centuries such family networks formed around the *madrasa*, where they brought together jurists, *ḥadīth* scholars, astronomers and physicians.

Court patronage for the sciences continued to flourish after the end of the Būyid and Fāṭimid dynasties.[26] Several courts included physicians and

24 Marie-Geneviève Balty-Guesdon, 'Médecins et hommes de sciences en Espagne musulmane (IIe/VIIIe–Ve/XIe)', Ph.D. thesis, Sorbonne (1988), pp. 106–25.

25 See R. N. Frye, 'The Samanids', in R. N. Frye (ed.), *The Cambridge history of Iran*, vol. IV: *From the Arab invasion to the Saljuqs* (Cambridge, New York, Melbourne and Madrid, 1975), pp. 142–3.

26 Heinz Halm, *The Fatimids and their traditions of learning* (London, 1997), p. 71, Yahya Michot, 'Variétés intellectuelles … L'impasse des rationalismes selon le Rejet de la Contradiction d'Ibn Taymiyyah', in Carmela Baffioni (ed.), *Religion versus science in Islam: A medieval and modern debate, Oriente Moderno* 19, 3 (2000), p. 602.

astrologers among those who had to be addressed by special honorific titles according to courtly protocol, and these professionals were treated as being of equal reputation and standing as the judges and the students of the Qurʾān and *ḥadīth*. The best-known examples are the courts of the Ottomans, Ṣafavids and Mughals.[27] The Mamlūks (648–922/1250–1517) in Egypt are a rare exception. They acknowledged only physicians as worthy of such treatment.[28] This does not mean, however, that the Mamlūks did not seek astrological counselling. Their approach to this discipline took a different course. They regarded it as a minor element of the practice of a new class of astronomical professionals, which they sponsored through religious donations and by appointments to *madrasas* and mosques. *Muwaqqits*, as these new professional astronomers were called, came to be regarded as full members of the class of *ʿulamāʾ*, and hence received the same honorific titles as the judges and *imāms*. The change is illustrated in the shift of emphasis between Ibn Khallikān (d. 681/1282), who does not mention a single *muwaqqit* in his biographies, and Shams al-Dīn al-Sakhāwī (d. 902/1496) almost two centuries later, who included a good number of *muwaqqits* in his dictionary.[29]

The courtly salon culture continued to be promoted by later dynasties too. Administrators, boon companions, jurists, poets, musicians, Sufis, grammarians, transmitters of *ḥadīth*, astrologers, physicians and people with an interest in metaphysics as well as natural philosophy populated its sessions and dominated its atmosphere. A specific kind of scientific literature emerged within this salon culture – the genre of questions and answers.[30] Several later encyclopaedias such as the *Nawādir al-tabādur* (Rarities of spontaneity) of Shams al-Dīn al-Dunayṣirī, compiled in 669/1270, and the *Nafāʾis al-funūn fī ʿarāʾis al-ʿuyūn* (The precious arts of the choice brides) by Shams al-Dīn al-Āmulī (d. 752/1352), dated around 741/1340, were created in this framework. Both literary genres indicate that courts played a major role for the dissemination and preservation of scientific knowledge and its underlying philosophical concepts both after 500/1107 and outside the sphere of Arabic.

A major field of courtly patronage was the copying and illustrating of scientific treatises in courtly *kitābkhānes* or *kārkhānes*, workshops for the arts

27 See MS Paris, BNF, Supplement Persan 1838, Appendix.
28 Abu ʾl-ʿAbbās Aḥmad ibn ʿAlī al-Qalqashandī, *Ṣubḥ al-aʿshā fī ṣināʿat al-inshāʾ*, 14 vols. (Cairo, 1331–8/1913–20), vol. VI, pp. 168–70.
29 Ibn Khallikān, *Wafāyāt al-aʿyān wa-anbāʾ abnāʾ al-zamān*, 8 vols. (Beirut, n.d.); Shams al-Dīn al-Sakhāwī, *al-Ḍawʾ al-lāmiʿ li-ahl al-qarn al-tāsiʿ*, 10 vols. (Beirut, n.d.).
30 Živa Vesel, 'La science à la cour: Les questions et les réponses', in C. Balaÿ, C. Kappler and Ž. Vesel (eds.), *Pand-o Sokhan: Mélanges offerts à Charles-Henri de Fouchcour* (Tehran, 1995).

of the book. Almost no illustrated scientific manuscripts in Arabic or Persian survive from earlier than the sixth/twelfth century. But there is evidence that this process started in the fourth/tenth century, if not earlier. The iconography of the extant illustrated scientific manuscripts points to cross-cultural artistic exchange with Byzantium, Egypt, Khurāsān, Sogdiana, Balkh, China, non-Muslim India and the nomadic steppes of Eurasia. With the exception of later courts in North Africa, dynasties in apparently all major cultural areas of the core Islamic territories contributed in this way to the spread and maintenance of scientific literature.

The connection between the arts and the sciences was not limited to the occult and the popular such as magical bowls or illustrations of the miraculous. Neither was it stereotypical and conventional. Scientific works profited from the innovative changes in the arts that took place under various Islamic and non-Islamic dynasties, from new views about which scholarly disciplines should be sponsored by princely and other courtly patrons and from an opening of disciplines to artistic illustration that previously had pursued rather austere modes of the visual. Examples include translations of Chinese medical and agricultural writings at the Ilkhānid court under the patronage of the vizier Rashīd al-Dawla (d. 718/1318) and the Mongol military and diplomatic counsellor at the Ilkhānid court, Bolad Ch'eng-Hsiang (d. 713/1313), or the illustration of Quṭb al-Dīn al-Shīrāzī's (d. 710/1311) theoretical work on planetary movements *al-Tuḥfa al-shāhiyya* (The royal gift) in the style of one of the leading painters of the Ṣafavid court, Rezā ʿAbbāsī (d. 1045/1635).[31] The literary, religious and scientific anthologies of the Tīmūrid prince of Shīrāz and Iṣfahān Iskandar Sulṭān (r. 812–17/1409–14) represent another example of the relationship between science and art. The scientific texts in these anthologies are illustrated by carefully constructed diagrams, colourful images of zodiacal signs, planetary houses and related subjects as well as a beautifully drawn map. A number of them are inscribed on the margins, thus serving themselves

31 Thomas T. Allsen, 'Biography of a cultural broker: Bolad Ch'eng-Hsiang in China and Iran', in Julian Raby and Teresa Fitzherbert (eds.), *The court of the Il-Khans 1290–1340* (Oxford, New York and Toronto, 1994); Nasrollah Pourjavady (gen. ed.), *The splendour of Iran*, 3 vols. (London, 2001), vol. III: C. Parham (ed.), *Islamic period*, pp. 282–7; Thomas W. Lentz and Glenn D. Lowry (eds.), *Timur and the princely vision: Persian art and culture in the fifteenth century* (Los Angeles, 1989), pp. 57–8, 79–103, 108–39; Zeren Akalay [Tanindi], 'An illustrated astrological work of the period of Iskandar Sultan', in *Akten des VII. Internationalen Kongresses für Iranische Kunst und Archäologie (Munich, 1976)*, Archäologische Mitteilungen aus Iran, n.s., supplementary vol. (Berlin, 1979), pp. 418–25; Priscilla P. Soucek, 'The manuscripts of Iskandar Sultan', in Lisa Golombek and Maria Subtelny (eds.), *Timurid art and culture: Iran and Central Asia in the fifteenth century* (Leiden, New York and Cologne, 1992).

as decorations. The only known miniature of astronomers studying and observing the sky in a domed building, dated before the late tenth/sixteenth century, comes from one of these manuscripts.

The evolution of the Sunnī *madrasa* in Iran, Anatolia, Syria, Iraq, Egypt and North Africa created a new outlet for court patronage. Caliphs, sultans, *atabegs*, royal wives and daughters, officers, merchants and scholars engaged in funding *madrasas*, Sufi convents, hospitals, houses for the study of *ḥadīth* and the Qur'ān and tombs. The ancient sciences also benefited from these donations. ʿAbbāsid caliphs funded chairs for medicine in prominent *madrasas*. Ilkhānid Buddhist and Muslim rulers sponsored the observatories of Marāgha and Tabrīz. They kept a travelling *madrasa* in their camps, where scholars taught literature, religion, philosophy and mathematical sciences. Mamlūk sultans sponsored a chair for *ʿilm al-mīqāt* (science of timekeeping), appointed *muwaqqits* as professors of *fiqh* and heads of Sufi convents, opened medical *madrasas* and donated chairs for medicine at central mosques in Cairo. Ottoman, Ṣafavid and Mughal rulers likewise provided for other than religious and legal teaching at the *madrasas* they gifted with funds. The impact of rulers, wives and court officials remained mostly limited to funding, the creation of positions, the appointment of professors and the settling of power struggles among the *ʿulamāʾ*. They rarely interfered in the subjects taught at the *madrasas*, mosques and other teaching institutes. Neither did they set up administrative bodies that unified the teaching and controlled its results, with the exception of medicine. The Mamlūks, for instance, entrusted the control of medical qualification to the head physician, who was attached to the court. The Manṣūriyya *madrasa* in Cairo and its affiliated hospital was governed by a *dīwān* specifically created for this purpose.[32]

A third strand of patronage came from individuals who invested their own funds and labour. Marginalia and colophons in numerous extant manuscripts testify that they were copied and even illuminated by practitioners of one of the sciences or scientific professions. Physicians and students of medicine not only copied medical textbooks and astrological treatises, but were responsible for attractively illustrated copies of Zakariyyāʾ al-Qazwīnī's work, Euclid's *Elements* and astronomical texts. Such activities indicate that Ibn Jumayʿ's demand that physicians should study *ʿilm al-hayʾa* (mathematical cosmology), not *ʿilm al-nujūm* (astrology) in order to become truly scientific experts of the art of medicine was not a mere topos of complaint, but was derived from

32 al-Qalqashandī, *Ṣubḥ*, vol. VI, pp. 34, 38–9.

competing scientific practices.[33] Students of astronomical and astrological knowledge also copied treatises from related mathematical sciences such as arithmetic or algebra. The contribution of private sponsorship to the production, reproduction and distribution of scientific manuscripts and objects has not yet received much attention.

Innovation in the mathematical sciences

The concepts of what the mathematical sciences were, the tools with which they should work, the purposes they should fulfil and the names that were thought appropriate for them differed substantially over time, space and culture. In part, divergent pre-Islamic traditions lay behind the differences. Not only did Indian perceptions differ from those of classical Greece, those of classical Greece differed from those of Byzantine Late Antiquity, those of ancient Mesopotamia from those of ancient Egypt and those of Seleucid Iraq from those of Sasanian Iran, but there was more than one school of mathematics taught in Byzantine Late Antiquity. There was also more than one local tradition by which tax-collectors, merchants and constructors calculated their gains, the labourers' wages and the necessary hours of work and measured or weighed the harvest, the commodities, the building-blocks and the fields. Hence, in the first centuries of Islam not only did a multitude of peoples, religions and lifestyles come together under a new central government with a different creed and concept of leadership, but the empire did not and could not operate with uniform standards of calculating, measuring, weighing, solving mathematical problems and proofs.

Our knowledge about the local mathematical practices during these early centuries is not very good. Egyptian papyri of the second / eighth century were long believed to contain the first record of Indian numerals in an Arabic document. But this reading has been contested.[34] The Qur'ān indicates that inheritance shares were determined before Muḥammad recited the verses with the new quota, but we don't know which mathematical rules were used for calculating the shares in a concrete case.[35] When Muḥammad ibn Mūsā al-Khwārizmī wrote the first surviving Arabic handbook on algebra, which

33 Fähndrich (ed.), *Ibn Jumay'*, pp. 2, 16.

34 Paul Kunitzsch, 'The transmission of Hindu-Arabic numerals reconsidered', in Jan P. Hogendijk and Abdelhamid I. Sabra (eds.), *The enterprise of science in Islam: New perspectives* (Cambridge, MA, and London, 2003).

35 *The Koran Interpreted: A translation*, trans. A. J. Arberry, 2 vols. (New York, 1996), vol. I, sura 4: Women, pp. 100–2.

also contained chapters on surveying, commercial transactions and inheritance mathematics (*farāʾiḍ*), he presented the rules according to Abū Ḥanīfa (d. 150/767) in a fairly formalised manner. By doing so he may even have contributed to the process of standardising Abū Ḥanīfa's teaching. Moreover, Muḥammad al-Khwārizmī used pre-Islamic methods of geometrical arguing as well as proofs that were developed by Babylonian and Seleucid scribes.[36] Another Arabic text on algebra written by Ayyūb al-Baṣrī may contain even earlier Islamic mathematical knowledge and techniques than al-Khwārizmī's work.[37]

While we know very little about mathematics until the fall of the Umayyads, it is clear that a new level of mathematical interest and sophistication was reached under the early ʿAbbāsids. Arabic historical sources reported that the second ʿAbbāsid caliph, al-Manṣūr, sent to Byzantium for a manuscript of Euclid's *Elements*. The manuscripts acquired as booty or tribute during the many clashes with Byzantine armies probably contained other texts by Euclid such as the *Data* and by other Greek scholars. A small but steady stream of translations of mathematical texts was produced during the first fifty years of ʿAbbāsid rule, sponsored by the caliphs, their viziers, commanders and administrators. Yaḥyā ibn Khālid al-Barmakī, for instance, was patron of the translation of Euclid's *Elements* and Ptolemy's *Almagest*. The Nestorian metropolitan Ḥabīb ibn Bahrīz translated the *Introduction to arithmetic*, written by the Neopythagorean philosopher Nicomachus of Gerasa (second century CE), for the caliph al-Maʾmūn's general Ṭāhir ibn Ḥusayn. Al-Kindī gave seminars on this newly translated text.[38] The political, philosophical, religious and cultural differences between al-Kindī and the Banū Mūsā included divergent views on mathematics. While al-Kindī favoured Neoplatonic, Neopythagorean and hermetic texts and themes, the use of mathematical concepts and tools for proving major philosophical and religious tenets (the existence of God; *creatio ex nihilo*; the finiteness of the universe) as well as the application of Greek number theory to recreational mathematics of mixed origins (Mesopotamia, India, China), the Banū Mūsā supported the translation

36 Jens Høyrup, 'al-Khwārizmī, Ibn Turk, and the *Liber mensurationum*: On the origins of Islamic algebra', *Erdem*, 5 (1986).

37 Barnabas Hughes, 'Problem-solving by Ajjūb al-Basrī, an early algebraist', *Journal for the History of Arabic Science*, 10 (1992–4).

38 Gad Freudenthal and Tony Lévy, 'De Gérase à Bagdad: Ibn Bahrīz, al-Kindī, et leur recension arabe de *l'Introduction arithmétique* de Nicomaque, d'après la version hébraïque de Qalonymos ben Qalonymos d'Arles', in Régis Morelon and Ahmad Hasnawi (eds.), *De Zénon d'Élée à Poincaré: Recueil d'études en homage à Roshdi Rashed* (Louvain and Paris, 2004).

of Apollonius' *Conics*, favoured the creation of new mathematical results over the memorising of mathematical textbooks and recommended the study of Archimedean books and tools.[39] They agreed, on the other hand, in applying Greek theoretical mathematics to practical problems; and they studied not only Greek mathematical theory, but practice too, as much as it was codified in textual form. The fields of application comprised surveying, sundials, optics, burning mirrors, mechanics and medicine. The contribution of these groups of courtly patrons, scholars and translators to the development of a mathematical terminology in Arabic, the pursuit of different approaches to mathematics, the emergence of highly skilled and innovative mathematicians in the later third/ninth and throughout the fourth/tenth centuries and the spread of acceptance of mathematics as a well-reputed set of disciplines and methods for finding truth among different groups of educated Muslims and members of the religious minorities cannot be overrated.

The relationship between algebra and arithmetic was shaped by the impact of the translations of Nicomachus' *Introduction to arithmetic*, books VII–IX of Euclid's *Elements* and Diophantus' *Arithmetic*, on the one hand, and of the various local traditions of calculation for purposes of business, inheritance and surveying, on the other. The Neoplatonic and Neopythagorean classifications of the mathematical sciences identified arithmetic as number theory, ignored calculation, interpreted numbers and their properties as carriers of philosophical and religious meaning and ranked arithmetic above geometry, astronomy and theoretical music (theory of proportions). This approach was propagated by al-Kindī in the first half of the third/ninth century and by Thābit ibn Qurra in the second. Fragments of an Arabic edition of Euclid's *Elements* indicate that it was also applied to interpreting book II and certain theorems in books I, III and VI of the *Elements*, which did not belong to number theory as taught in the framework of this work. It became the position taken by the author(s) of the *Rasāʾil Ikhwān al-Ṣafāʾ*, Ibn Sīnā in his *Kitāb al-shifāʾ* (The book of healing) and other writers of encyclopaedic works of the fourth/tenth and fifth/eleventh centuries. While the philosophical attitudes of such writers may explain their preferences in number theory certain parts of Nicomachus' teaching were also privileged by writers who came from a different milieu – *fuqahāʾ* and *mutakallimūn* such as Abū Manṣūr ʿAbd al-Qāhir ibn Ṭāhir al-Nīsābūrī al-Baghdādī (d. 428/1037). Numerous later writers from this milieu such as Ismāʿīl ibn Ibrāhīm ibn al-Fallūs (d. 637/1239), Abu ʾl-ʿAbbās Aḥmad ibn Muḥammad ibn al-Bannāʾ al-Marrākushī (d. 721/1321) or Shihāb al-Dīn ibn

39 Ibn al-Nadīm, *Fihrist*, trans. Dodge, vol. II, pp. 637–8.

al-Majdī (d. 851/1447) continued along this line and taught this kind of number theory in their classes at *madrasas*, mosques and *khānqāhs*. In contrast to Greek traditions, algebra, number theory and calculation became classified in Arabic, Persian and Turkish treatises as parts of a comprehensive *ʿilm al-ḥisāb* (the science of calculation), in which number theoretical knowledge in the Nicomachean tradition kept its position at the highest rank.

Muḥammad al-Khwārizmī's books on algebra and Indian arithmetic had a significant impact on several scholarly milieus. When Qusṭā ibn Lūqā (d. *c.* 297/910) translated Diophantus' *Arithmetic* in the second half of the third/ninth century, he interpreted its contents according to the technical terminology of al-Khwārizmī's algebra.[40] Diophantine problems came to be seen as belonging to both algebra and arithmetic. The extension and reshaping of algebra by Abū Bakr al-Karajī (d. *c.* 420/1029) and al-Samaw'al ibn Yaḥyā al-Maghribī (d. 570/1175) is shown by their treatment of algebraic themes with arithmetical concepts and methods. They extended the earlier limited concept of unknowns of higher than second order ($x^3 \ldots x^9$) to unknowns of finite but unlimited order, and applied this new view also to 'parts', i.e. fractions of the type $1/x^n$. These new objects became the focus of the new approach to algebra, above all the solution of polynomial equations of second and higher degree, as well as the development of a calculus for such equations.[41] As a result of these developments algebraic methods came to be seen as tools that also could be used in other mathematical areas. Several scholars such as Ibn Munʿim (sixth–seventh/twelfth–thirteenth centuries) or Kamāl al-Dīn al-Fārisī (d. 718/1318?) applied them to problems of combinatorics and found new methods or proofs for a number of theoretical problems such as the calculation of perfect or amicable numbers. A perfect number is a number the sum of whose parts equals the number such as $6 = 1 + 2 + 3$. Amicable numbers are a pair of numbers where the sum of the parts of one number equals the other number such as $220 = 1 + 2 + 4 + 5 + 10 + 11 + 20 + 22 + 44 + 55 + 110 = 284$, $284 = 1 + 2 + 4 + 72 + 142 = 220$.[42]

40 Jacques Sesiano, *Books IV to VII of Diophantus'* Arithmetica: *In the Arabic translation attributed to Qusṭā ibn Lūqā* (New York and Berlin, 1982).

41 Roshdi Rashed, *Entre arithmétique et algèbre: Recherches sur l'histoire des mathématiques arabes* (Paris, 1984); Roshdi Rashed, *The development of Arabic mathematics: Between arithmetic and algebra* (London, 1994).

42 Ahmed Djebbar, *L'analyse combinatoire au Maghreb: l'Exemple d'Ibn Munʿim (XIIe–XIIIe siècles)*, Publications Mathématiques d'Orsay 85-01 (Paris, 1985); Roshdi Rashed, 'Materials for the study of the history of amicable numbers and combinatorial analysis', *Journal for the History of Arabic Science*, 6, 1–2 (1982); Roshdi Rashed, 'Nombres amiables, parties aliquotes et nombres figurés aux XIIIème et XIVème siècles', *Archive for History of Exact Sciences*, 28, 2 (1983).

The relationships between these two disciplines and geometry were similarly complex. Scholars such as Thābit ibn Qurra, Abū ʿAbd Allāh Muḥammad ibn ʿĪsā al-Māhānī (d. *c.* 246/860), Thābit's grandson Ibrāhīm ibn Sinān (d. 335/946) and Abū ʿAlī al-Ḥasan Ibn al-Haytham (d. *c.* 432/1041) used number theory or algebra when dealing with geometrical problems such as the determination of the surface of a parabola and the volume of bodies of rotation or the discussion of an unproven lemma by Archimedes.[43] Thābit ibn Qurra also demonstrated that two theorems of book II of Euclid's *Elements* were a more rigorous tool for proofs than al-Khwārizmī's own geometrical reasoning.[44] Despite his major contribution to the new algebra, Abū Bakr al-Karajī believed that geometry was of a higher scientific value because of its demonstrative rigour and axiomatic structure.

Other scholars such as Abū Jaʿfar al-Khāzin (d. between 349 and 360/961 and 971), Abu 'l-Jūd ibn Layth (fourth/tenth century), Aḥmad ibn Muḥammad al-Sijzī (d. *c.* 410/1020) and ʿUmar al-Khayyām (d. 517/1123) pursued an opposite approach and used Apollonius' *Conics* for tackling problems that led to cubic and bi-quadratic equations. Several of these problems originated in a geometrical context, such as the debate about how to inscribe a regular heptagon into a circle. This and related problems came from discussions of works of Archimedes and classical mathematical problems such as the trisection of an angle, as well as certain mathematical tools that had already caused lively debates among ancient geometers such as the use of movements in geometrical constructions, for instance the device called *neusis* (verging construction).[45]

Due to the diversification of courts, patronage and cultural centres the fourth/tenth century saw a particularly productive and widespread discussion carried on by mathematicians, mainly in greater Iran, through the exchange of personal letters, evening discussions, competitive questioning and proud – occasionally even boastful – reports about apparently or truly successful new ideas and solutions. As a result, several treatises on constructing the side of

43 Aḥmad Salīm Saʿidān, *Rasāʾil Ibn Sinān* (Kuwait, 1983).

44 Paul Luckey, 'Thabit b. Qurra über den geometrischen Richtigkeitsnachweis der Auflösung der quadratischen Gleichungen', in *Berichte über die Verhandlungen der Sächsischen Akademie der Wissenschaften zu Leipzig*, Mathematisch-physikalische Klasse 93 (Heidelberg, 1941).

45 Ahmet Djebbar and Roshdi Rashed (eds., trans. and comm.), *L'oeuvre algébrique d'al-Khayyām* (Aleppo, 1981), p. 11; Jan P. Hogendijk, 'How trisections of the angle were transmitted from Greek to Islamic geometry', *Historia Mathematica*, 8 (1981); Jan P. Hogendijk, 'Greek and Arabic constructions of the regular heptagon', *Archive for History of Exact Sciences*, 30 (1984); Jan P. Hogendijk, 'The geometrical works of Abū Saʿīd al-Ḍarīr al-Jurjānī', *SCIAMVS*, 2 (2001).

a regular heptagon, trisecting the angle and related problems were written and a systematic geometrical theory for solving cubic equations was established.[46]

Besides these cross-disciplinary works and debates, much innovative work was done within the classical disciplines. The ancient methods of analysis and synthesis were at the centre of mathematical research and discussion. Several scholars of the third/ninth, fourth/tenth and fifth/eleventh centuries wrote manuals about these two methods, among them Ibrāhīm ibn Sinān and Ibn al-Haytham. Others, such as al-Sijzī and Abū Sahl Wījān ibn Rustam al-Kūhī (fourth/tenth century), compiled collections of problems for which they proposed various kinds of synthesis and analysis. Their texts make clear that different opinions were held about how to work with these two methods, and disputes arose over violations of mathematical rigour.[47] The problems treated in these and related works were either derived from texts of ancient Greek authors or devised in a similar way. The works used in this context were in particular Euclid's *Data*, *Division of figures* and *Porisms*, Apollonius' *Conics*, *Cutting off a ratio*, *Plane loci* and *Determinate section*, Menelaus' *Introduction to geometry* and Archimedes' *Sphere and cylinder*, *Measuring the circle* and the spurious work on the heptagon.[48] The extant writings by al-Sijzī, Abu 'l-Jūd and others indicate that these problems, the two methods (analysis and synthesis) and their results were studied, debated and challenged in the milieu of the private evening *majlis*, publicly shared letters and publicly held disputes – as is documented, for instance, in the treatise *Jawāb Aḥmad b. Muḥammad b. ʿAbd al-Jalīl li-asʾila handasiyya suʾila ʿanhā bi-'l-nās min Khurāsān* (Reply by Aḥmad ibn Muḥammad ibn ʿAbd al-Jalīl to geometrical questions asked by people from Khurāsān).[49] Al-Sijzī placed the art of finding new results in geometry in an epistemological context. He opposed the claim that 'discovery

46 Jan P. Hogendijk, 'Abū l-Jūd's answer to a question of al-Bīrūnī concerning the regular heptagon', in D. A. King and G. Saliba (eds.), *From deferent to equant: A volume of studies in the ancient and medieval Near East in honor of E. S. Kennedy* (New York, 1987).

47 J. Lennart Berggren and Glen van Brummelen, 'The role and development of geometric analysis and synthesis in ancient Greece and medieval Islam', in Patrick Suppes, Julius M. Moravcsik and Henry Mendell (eds.), *Ancient and medieval traditions in the exact sciences: Essays in memory of Wilbur Knorr* (Stanford, 2001).

48 See, for instance, Jan P. Hogendijk, 'Arabic traces of lost works of Apollonius', *Archive for History of Exact Sciences*, 35 (1986); Jan P. Hogendijk, 'On Euclid's lost *Porisms* and its Arabic traces', *Bolletino di Storia delle Science Matematiche*, 7 (1988); Jan P. Hogendijk, 'The Arabic version of Euclid's *On division*', in M. Folkerts and J. P. Hogendijk (eds.), *Vestigia Mathematica: Studies in medieval and early modern mathematics in honour of H. L. L. Busard* (Amsterdam, 1993); J. L. Berggren, J. P. Hogendijk, *The fragments of Abu Sahl al-Kuhi's lost geometrical works in the writings of al-Sijzī* (University of Utrecht, Department of Mathematics, Preprint no. 1226, February 2002), pp. 4–18.

49 See Fuat Sezgin, *Geschichte des arabischen Schrifttums*, 12 vols. (Leiden, 1974), vol. V, p. 333, no. 22.

in geometry proceeds only by means of innate ability and not by study'.[50] He then proceeded to enlist and discuss seven rules to find new results, mostly constructions. These rules included knowledge of the conditions of a problem; knowledge of common features and differences of a set of problems; mastery of the relevant theorems and preliminaries; familiarity with tricks used by experienced mathematicians; and specific mathematical methods (analysis, transformation).[51]

In a similar way, the branches of optics and mechanics, which ancient Greek scholars had mostly seen as parts of geometry, were modified, enlarged and in some of their parts revolutionised. Optics, for instance, merged the various strands of ancient mathematical, philosophical and medical theories about vision into a coherent whole that added the study of light to that of sight and also included parts of astronomy and surveying. On the methodological side, it abandoned the ancient preference for geometrical demonstrative theory and made room for experiments, practical concerns and technical constructions.[52] During the third/ninth and fourth/tenth centuries, optical themes were discussed in four main intellectual contexts: geometry (vision through air, vision through mediums other than air, burning mirrors and lenses); philosophy (theories of light and perception, meteorology); astronomy (shadows, perception, visual errors); and medicine (anatomy and physiology of the eye). A decisive step towards a new disciplinary understanding took place in the fifth/eleventh century with the work of Ibn al-Haytham, who aimed at combining the mathematical and physical aspects of vision, moved the focus of the discipline towards light and integrated into his approach topics from Ptolemy's *Optics* such as refraction. Ibn al-Haytham's most important work on optics is his *Kitāb al-manāẓir* (Book of optics), which gives an experimental and mathematical treatment of the properties of light and colour in relationship to vision.[53] A summary of its arguments and a fuller presentation of his experimental results is the *Maqāla fī l-ḍaw'* (Treatise on light).[54] He differentiated

50 Al-Sijzī, *Treatise on geometrical problem solving:* Kitāb fī tashīl al-subul li-istikhrāj al-ashkāl al-handasīya, ed., trans. and comm. Jan P. Hogendijk, Arabic text and a Persian trans. Mohammad Bagheri (Tehran, 1996), p. 2.

51 Ibid., pp. x–xiii.

52 Elaheh Kheirandish, 'Optics: Highlights from Islamic lands', in Ahmad Y. al-Hassan, Maqbul Ahmed and Ahmad Z. Iskandar (eds.), *The different aspects of Islamic culture*, vol. IV: *Science and technology in Islam*, part 1, *The exact and natural sciences* ([Paris], 2001), pp. 337–8, 345; Abdelhamid I. Sabra, *The optics of Ibn al-Haytham*, books 1–3, book 2: *On direct vision* (with introduction, commentary, glossaries, concordance, indices) (London, 1989).

53 Sabra, *On direct vision*, p. lv.

54 Ibid., p. li, fn 73.

between the approach of the natural philosopher, who studies the *māhiyya* (quiddity) of light, transparency or the ray, and that of the mathematician, who deals with the *kayfiyya* ('howness') of the ray's extension in transparent bodies and the shapes of rays.

Natural philosophers and mathematicians also differed in their basic belief about what light is. Ibn al-Haytham set out to synthesise the two different disciplinary programmes, and did so by experimenting with 'dark chambers' and by criticising theories, methods and concepts of previous scholars of both approaches. Through experiments he discovered that the Euclidean theory of vision (visual rays extend from the eye to the object) was wrong. Through his critical analysis of previous writings he observed that the natural philosophers and physicians, who correctly believed that vision took place by a *form* (light) that emerged from a shining object and was received by the eye, had no precise doctrine of the ray.[55] Following on from this, he applied the methods of the mathematicians to the doctrines of the natural philosophers and physicians.[56] He introduced new categories such as 'primary light' and 'secondary light', and posed new questions. Primary light is light that issues from self-luminous bodies. Secondary light is light that emanates from accidental light, i.e. light existing in bodies illuminated from the outside. One of Ibn al-Haytham's new questions was: if vision resulted from the imprint of a form onto the eye, why does one see the object outside the eye?[57]

But while revolutionising the science of optics in many ways, Ibn al-Haytham's *Kitāb al-manāẓir* did not discuss all optical themes he had treated in previous writings and other disciplinary settings.[58] The major breakthrough in respect to a new disciplinary understanding of optics came with Kamāl al-Dīn al-Fārisī's *Tanqīḥ al-manāẓir li-dhawī al-abṣār wa 'l-baṣā'ir* (Revision of [The book of] optics for the possessors of insight and discernment), a commentary on Ibn al-Haytham's opus. He added three further treatises by Ibn al-Haytham on shadows, perception and light together with his own analysis and exposition of the subjects. Kamāl al-Dīn justified this collection by claiming these subjects as part of the science of optics. Except for burning mirrors, Kamāl al-Dīn considered all other previously disconnected strands that dealt with themes related to light and vision as constituting optics.[59]

55 Ibid., p. liii.
56 Ibid., pp. liv–lv.
57 Ibid., pp. lii, liv.
58 Ibid., p. liii.
59 Kheirandish, 'Optics', p. 349.

A similar process took place with regard to the ancient domains of statics, hydrostatics, dynamics and weights discussed in the contexts of geometry, medicine, natural philosophy and technology. Various works by or ascribed to Aristotle, Euclid, Apollonius, Archimedes, Heron, Pappus and Galen were translated into Arabic during the third/ninth century and taken up in a process that reshaped the various disciplines. The major figures who contributed to this process were the Banū Mūsā, Qusṭā ibn Lūqā, Thābit ibn Qurra, Abū Naṣr al-Fārābī (d. 340/950), Wījān al-Kūhī, Ibn al-Haytham, Ibn Sīnā, al-Karajī, Abū Ḥātim al-Muẓaffar ibn Ismāʿīl al-Isfizārī (d. *c.* 504/1110), ʿUmar al-Khayyām, ʿAbd al-Raḥmān al-Khāzinī (d. after 515/1121) and Ibn Ismāʿīl ibn al-Razzāz al-Jazarī (*fl. c.* 603/1206). The result of this process was twofold. On one hand, al-Fārābī, in his *Iḥṣāʾ al-ʿulūm* (Enumeration of the sciences), testified to and justified philosophically the evolution of two separate mathematical disciplines of mechanics: *ʿilm al-athqāl* (the science of weights) and *ʿilm al-ḥiyal* (the science of machines). Neither of the two new disciplines unified all relevant ancient strands. The first focused on a relatively small range of subjects (the theory of the balance and practical problems of weighing).[60] Its conceptual core is the investigation and explanation of mechanical questions through motion and force. The inspiration for this approach stems from the Pseudo-Aristotelian *Problemata mechanica*. As a result, the new discipline was closely linked to natural philosophy, on the one hand, and to medical and commercial practices of weighing, on the other. The study of the centres of gravity of surfaces and solids was seen by al-Kūhī, al-Isfizārī and al-Khāzinī as the theoretical nucleus of this new discipline, which is a new point of view when compared to Thābit ibn Qurra's *Kitāb al-qarasṭūn*, which mainly dealt with the law of the lever for material beams and balances. The second new discipline also may be considered as formed by two different domains. One domain was part of natural philosophy and dealt with the so-called five simple machines of Antiquity (the windlass, the lever, the pulley, the wedge and the screw). It studied, as al-Fārābī explained, the ways in which mathematical knowledge could be brought from *quwwa* (potentiality) to *fiʿl* (actuality) by applying it to natural bodies by means of machines.[61] The other shared the mathematical methodology, but dealt with practical machines for time measuring, water lifting, entertainment, healing and other purposes.

60 Mohammed Abattouy, *The Arabic tradition of the science of weights and balances: A report on an ongoing research project* (Max Planck Institute for the History of Science, Preprint 227, 2002), pp. 7–11, 13.

61 Al-Fārābī, *Iḥṣāʾ al-ʿulūm*, ed. ʿUthmān Amīn, 2nd edn (Cairo, 1949), pp. 88–9.

The enormous attraction exercised by the axiomatic, deductive structure of geometry can be seen in al-Karajī's treatise on water lifting, which is written in the style of Euclid's *Elements*. Al-Jazarī, in his monumental book on machines, which he composed at the Artuqid court of Diyarbakr, also considered what he did as an application of geometry to machines, which he understood as a philosophical act.[62] In the title of his book *al-Jāmiʿ bayna l-ʿilm wa'l-ʿamal al-nāfiʿ fī ṣināʿat al-ḥiyal* (The combination of theory and practice in the mechanical arts) al-Jazarī formulated a second purpose, namely to bring together *ʿilm* (knowledge) and *ʿamal nāfiʿ* (useful practice).[63] This aim refers on one level to theory and practice in a scientific context. On another level the chosen title has a religious subtext. Every Muslim was called to acquire *ʿilm* and exercise it through *ʿamal* in order to do things useful for the community. Al-Ghazālī made this point repeatedly in his influential writings when he discussed the sciences as well as the duties of a Muslim. The praise for the usefulness of books written by scholars of all disciplines, expressed time and again in the biographical dictionaries, underlines the social relevance of these terms for the scholarly world in medieval Islamic societies.

Innovations were not restricted to those disciplines that were already established before the advent of Islam. From the third/ninth century onwards mathematicians and astronomers created new mathematical branches by either building upon certain components inherited from Greek and Indian predecessors or by inventing completely new fields of mathematical knowledge. Such new branches often did not receive a specific name, or if they did the names do not fit into modern divisions of mathematics. Examples are trigonometry, magic squares, combinatorics, multi-entry astronomical tables with auxiliary functions and the use of mathematics in philosophy and *kalām*. While many of the above-mentioned innovations developed within the context of the appropriated ancient sciences, the newly emerging fields of knowledge also had strong connections with particular needs and interests of Islamic societies, their religions, languages and everyday life. Combinatorics first appeared in the work of the Arabic grammarian Khalīl ibn Aḥmad (d. 170/786?) as he tried to arrange the three and four consonants of Arabic roots for a

62 al-Jazarī, *The book of knowledge of ingenious mechanical devices:* Kitāb fī maʿrifat al-ḥiyal al-handasiyya, trans. Donald R. Hill with annotations (Dordrecht, London and New York, 1973). For a critique of Hill's interpretation of al-Jazarī's work and title see George Saliba, 'The function of mechanical devices in medieval Islamic society', in P. Long (ed.), *Science and technology in medieval society*, Annals of the New York Academy of Sciences 441 (New York, 1985).

63 al-Jazarī, *al-Jāmiʿ bayna l-ʿilm wa'l-ʿamal al-nāfiʿ fī ṣināʿat al-ḥiyal*, ed. Ahmad Y. al-Hassan (Aleppo, 1979).

dictionary. Magic squares and their development were part of the search for licit methods of protecting oneself from misfortune, disease and death and determining the best approaches to travelling, marriage, house building and other undertakings.[64] Mathematical themes and methods as applied in philosophy and *kalām* were used for arguing about what separated *tawḥīd*, the specific Muslim notion of the oneness of God, from other forms of oneness as well as from multitude, for proving God's existence and for discussion about the material structure of the universe and its regularities, i.e. about atomism, continuity, infinity and causality. The most frequently borrowed mathematical themes in such contexts came from Euclid's *Elements* and from Nicomachus's *Introduction to arithmetic*, for instance the definition of *one* as the beginning and the root of integers, but no number itself; the question of whether the area between an arc and a tangent to one of its points was a geometrical quantity, i.e. a plane angle in the Euclidean sense; whether the ratio between the circumference and the diagonal of a circle was a rational number; and whether motion was a permissible geometrical concept.

From the beginning algebra and Indian arithmetic were deeply linked to the needs and interests of an Islamic society. Muḥammad al-Khwārizmī had argued for the relevance of these two fields by pointing in clear terms to merchants, surveyors and jurists as the three major groups in society who were in need of them. By applying his methods to positions and prescriptions taken from the not yet fully codified teachings of Abū Ḥanīfa rather than from the Qurʾān, or in general from all legal schools that were emerging during the second/eighth and early third/ninth centuries, al-Khwārizmī made a clear point about the truly practical orientation of the two new fields in contrast to a merely illustrative function of potential fields of application for mathematical knowledge. When comparing the impact different treatises on algebra and Indian arithmetic had in later Arabic, Persian and Ottoman Turkish writings about commercial and legal calculations as composed and taught in the context of the *madrasa*, al-Khwārizmī's *al-Kitāb al-mukhtaṣar fī ḥisāb al-jabr wa 'l-muqābala* (Abbreviated book on algebra) without doubt was the most successful one. Its elementary mathematical content, the visual accessibility

64 See Jacques Sesiano, *Un traité médiéval sur les carrés magiques: De l'arrangement harmonieux des nombres* (Lausanne, 1996); Jacques Sesiano, 'Herstellungsverfahren magischer Quadrate aus islamischer Zeit', (I, II, II', III) *Sudhoffs Archiv*, 64 (1980), 65 (1981), 71 (1987), 79 (1995); Jacques Sesiano, 'Une compilation arabe du XIIe siècle sur quelques propriétés des nombres naturels', *SCIAMVS*, 4 (2003); Francis Maddison and Emilie Savage-Smith, *Science, tools and magic*, part 1: *Body and spirit: Mapping the universe*, Nasser D. Khalili Collection of Islamic Art 12 (London, 1997).

of its arguments and its practical relevance may all have contributed to this preference given to al-Khwārizmī's work over those by Abū Kāmil al-Miṣrī (d. *c.* 235/850), al-Karajī or al-Samaw'al.

The Islamic aspects of cosmology, astronomy and astrology

Throughout the history of Islamic civilisation, as had been the case in the ancient world, astronomy was a sophisticated science that enjoyed much prestige. Astronomy, though at first closely connected to astrology, became, by the fourth/tenth century (or possibly the third/ninth), a more purely theoretical science of the heavens.[65] This increased distance between astronomy and astrology affected both fields, so this chapter places important developments in astronomy within the context of its relationship to astrology and to other applications and areas of religious scholarship.

The decision about whether to describe the astronomy and astrology of this chapter as 'Islamic' or as 'Arabic' deserves explanation. The appellation 'Arabic science' calls attention to the language in which many, but not all, important scientific texts were written. Arabic, too, remains the most important (but not the only) language of Islamic scholarship. The term 'Islamic science' recalls the dominant religion of the science's broader context, but the participation of non-Muslims in this science begs the question of the centrality of Islam to Islamic science. One leading journal in the field, *Zeitschrift für Geschichte der Arabisch-Islamischen Wissenschaften*, acknowledges both terms.[66] Because users of this book are more likely to be students of Islamic civilisation than historians of science I have emphasised the intellectual and social contexts of astronomy and astrology in Islamic civilisation over the technical details.

Origins

The pre-Islamic Arabs had a folk astronomy based on omens, but not lunar mansions, and perhaps a lunar calendar that they intercalated to keep pace with the solar year.[67] Isolated translations of scientific texts from Greek into

65 George Saliba, 'Astronomy and astrology in medieval Arabic thought', in Roshdi Rashed and Joël Biard (eds.), *Les doctrines de la science de l'antiquité à l'âge classique* (Leuven, 1999), pp. 137, 163.

66 Ahmad Dallal, 'Science, medicine, and technology', in John L. Esposito (ed.), *The Oxford history of Islam* (Oxford and New York, 1999), p. 158.

67 Daniel M. Varisco, 'The origin of the *anwā'* in Arab tradition', *SI*, 64 (1991).

Syriac and Pahlavi occurred in more settled regions of the pre-Islamic Near East. But the explosion of scientific activity during the ʿAbbāsid caliphate was neither coincidental nor simply a continuation of translation activities in the pre-Islamic Near East.[68] Social, economic and political conditions in the ʿAbbāsid caliphate, and in the earlier Umayyad caliphate, created a demand for top-notch scholars and translators. The Umayyads had initially preserved the pre-existing administrative apparatus of the lands they conquered. Then the caliph ʿAbd al-Malik (d. 86/705), or perhaps Hishām (d. 125/743), decided to translate the administrative records of the caliphate into Arabic, which led to an influx of Arab administrators, ministers who were not proficient in Greek or Persian.[69] Information about administrative activities, such as surveying and calendar calculation, would also have to be in Arabic for the benefit of these Arab ministers and scribes. Such practical considerations are one of the reasons why the Islamic empire would pay attention to the heritage of the civilisations that it vanquished. The ʿAbbāsid caliphs, after coming to power in 132/750, saw an additional value in the translation of scientific texts. One factor that brought the ʿAbbāsids to power was solidarity among Iranian converts to Islam. Translation, then, lent political prestige to the ʿAbbāsids by fostering a link to the Sasanian empire and thus to its real and mythical contacts with the rest of the ancient world. The acquisition of paper-making technology in 132/751 from Chinese prisoners of war helped the translation movement flourish, and scientific knowledge became an asset in the socio-economic competition among viziers for the caliph's favour. Literature about the education of scribes and ministers enjoined a rudimentary knowledge of scientific and technical subjects.

The earliest translations that we know of were of handbooks of astronomy with tables (Ar. *zīj*, pl. *azyāj*) in Sanskrit and Pahlavi.[70] Though the astronomers of Islamic civilisation have attained great renown for their responses to Hellenistic astronomy, Sanskrit and Pahlavi texts attracted their attention initially. The types of tables included varied slightly from *zīj* to *zīj*, but one

68 Gutas, *Greek thought, Arabic culture*, pp. 28–60.

69 Ibn al-Nadīm, *Kitāb al-fihrist*, ed. Gustav Flügel, 2 vols. (Cairo, 1929–30), p. 242; trans. in Franz Rosenthal, *The classical heritage in Islam*, trans. Emile and Jenny Marmorstein (Berkeley and Los Angeles, 1975), p. 48. See now George Saliba, *Islamic science and the making of the European Renaissance* (Cambridge and London, 2007), pp. 15–19 and 45–72. My account of the translation movement draws on both Saliba and Gutas's accounts.

70 The classic work on these handbooks with tables is E. S. Kennedy, 'A survey of Islamic astronomical tables', *Transactions of the American Philosophical Society*, n.s., 46, 2 (1956), p. 151. See now David King (with Julio Samsó), 'Astronomical handbook and tables from the Islamic world (750–1900), an interim report', *Suhayl*, 2 (2001).

would expect to find chronological tables, tables of trigonometric functions, the equation of time (which accounts for variations in the Sun's speed), planetary positions and positions of the fixed stars. Stars other than the Sun, Moon and five known planets (Venus, Mercury, Mars, Jupiter and Saturn) were the fixed stars.

The earliest Arabic *zīj* was *Zīj al-Arkand*, composed in 117/734f. but no longer extant, based on the seventh-century Sanskrit *Khaṇḍakhadyaka* of Brahmagupta.[71] In the early 150s/770s, at the court of the caliph al-Manṣūr (d. 158/775), Ibrāhīm al-Fazārī and Yaʿqūb ibn Ṭāriq (*fl. c.* 143/760) produced translations that resulted in the *Zīj al-Sindhind*.[72] This *zīj* would prove to be quite influential in al-Andalus. Al-Khwārizmī's (*fl.* 215/830) *Zīj al-Sindhind* (no relation to the first) was the first complete, original text of astronomy from the Islamic period to survive, although not in Arabic.[73] Contemporary scholars have worked hard to determine the origin of the contents of *zījes*. While most of the parameters in *Zīj al-Sindhind* were of Indian origin, for example, some of the *zīj*'s contents derived from Ptolemy's (*fl.* 125–50) *Handy tables*. Yaḥyā ibn Abī Manṣūr's (d. 215/830) *al-Zīj al-Mumtaḥan* (Verified astronomical handbook with tables) contained more Ptolemaic parameters,[74] and then al-Battānī's (d. 317/929) *al-Zīj al-Ṣābi*' (Sabian astronomical handbook with tables) indicated the ascendance of Ptolemaic planetary theory in the astronomy of Islamic civilisation.[75]

Another application to which the *zījes* were well suited was astrological forecasting. Al-Khwārizmī's *zīj* included tables with explicitly astrological applications such as the 'Table of the projections of the rays', and al-Manṣūr consulted astrologers to great public effect when he commenced the construction of the new ʿAbbāsid capital at Baghdad in 145/762.[76] Astronomy's contributions to astrological forecasts were an interest of those connected with the rise of astronomy in al-Andalus. The caliphs of al-Andalus would eventually declare their independence from the ʿAbbāsids; when the *amīr*

71 David Pingree, 'The Greek influence on early Islamic mathematical astronomy', *JAOS*, 103 (1973), p. 37.

72 Ibid, p. 38.

73 ʿAlī ibn Sulaymān Hāshimī, *The book of the reasons behind astronomical tables:* Kitāb fī ʿilal al-zījāt, trans. Fu'ād Ḥaddād and E. S. Kennedy with commentary by David Pingree and E. S. Kennedy (Delmar, NY, 1981), p. 224.

74 Ibid., p. 225.

75 Willy Hartner, 'al-Battānī', in Charles Gillispie (ed.), *Complete dictionary of scientific biography*, 28 vols. (New York, 2008), vol. I.

76 Bernard Goldstein, *Ibn al-Muthannā's commentary on the astronomical tables of al-Khwārizmī* (New Haven, 1967); and Otto Neugebauer, *The astronomical tables of al-Khwārizmī* (Copenhagen, 1962). On al-Manṣūr see Gutas, *Greek thought, Arabic culture*.

Hishām (d. 180/796) gained the throne he summoned the astrologer al-Ḍabbī (d. *c.* 184/800), who predicted the length of his reign.[77] Al-Ḍabbī's writings, however, have no trace of the influence of the Indian, Persian or Greek texts that spurred the translation and development of astronomy and astrology under the ʿAbbāsids. After the Islamic conquest of al-Andalus in 92/711 the earliest literature on astrology and astronomy in al-Andalus, such as the *Libro de las cruces*, was of a Latin and Visigothic cast.[78] But during the reign of ʿAbd al-Raḥmān II (r. 206–38/822–52) handbooks of astronomy with tables from the ʿAbbāsids began to appear. For example, ʿAbbās ibn Firnās (d. 274/887) or ʿAbbās ibn Nāṣiḥ (d. after 230/844) introduced al-Khwārizmī's *Zīj* to al-Andalus.[79] Astrology was entrenched at the royal court.[80] The late fourth/tenth-century *Calendar of Córdoba* reflected not just the astronomy of the Muslim east but also the application of astronomy to religious timekeeping (*mīqāt*).[81]

Applications: astrology

A key theme of the rise of astronomy in the Islamic world was astrology's place as astronomy's most significant application. Some details about several types of forecasts in astrology are in order. Omens – for example, shooting stars or conjunctions of major planets such as Jupiter and Saturn – were the basis for predictions about nature and nations. With horoscopic astrology the astrologer used celestial positions at the moment of a child's conception or birth to determine, for example, financial success in life. An interrogation was a type of prediction where an astrologer would be consulted to determine the optimal time for a battle or another major undertaking. Technical precision in astrology depended on accurate tables of planetary positions and some understanding of theories of planetary motion so as to predict future planetary positions. Astrology's lofty goals led its foremost defender in Islamic civilisation, Abū Maʿshar (d. 272/886), to present astrology as the highest natural science and to legitimise astrology with Aristotelian philosophy.[82] Astrology's

77 Julio Samsó, 'La primitiva version árabe del Libro de las Cruces', in Juan Vernet (ed.), *Nuevos estudios sobre astronomía española en el siglo de Alfonso X* (Barcelona, 1983).

78 Roser Puig, 'La astronomía en al-Andalus: Aproximacíon historiográfica', *Arbor*, 142 (1992), pp. 170–1.

79 Juan Vernet and Julio Samsó, 'Development of Arabic science in Andalusia', in Roshdi Rashed and Régis Morelon (eds.), *Encyclopedia of the history of Arabic science*, 3 vols. (London and New York, 1996), vol. I, p. 248.

80 Monica Rius, 'La Actitud de los emires hacia los astrólogos: Entre la adicción y el rechazo', *Identidades marginales (Serie Estudios Onomástico-Bibliográficos de al-Andalus)*, 13 (2003).

81 Puig, 'La astronomía', p. 171.

82 Abū Maʿshar, *al-Madkhal al-kabīr ilā ʿilm al-nujūm*, ed. Richard Lemay (Naples, 1995).

inability to live up to its ambitious claims elicited critiques that would widen the gap between astrology and astronomy.

Applications: service of Islam

Astronomy's ability to provide answers to practical problems in Islam was an excellent justification for pursuit of that science.[83] Such religious applications justified astronomy in the face of its most dogged sceptics. After the revelation of verse Q 2:144 ('Turn your face towards the sacred mosque') the sacred direction of prayer, the *qibla*, became the direction of Mecca, specifically the Kaʿba.[84] Outside Mecca, *qibla* determination was more difficult and very important, both for marking the *qibla* in mosque construction and for individuals praying away from a mosque. Inexact methods of *qibla* determination pre-dated the technical. Islamic literature mentions methods of approximating the *qibla* based on wind directions and the rising and setting of certain stars (*anwāʾ*). The Kaʿba itself, a structure that antedates Islam, was oriented with respect to certain astronomical phenomena and to wind directions. Because Muḥammad's sayings were a source of revealed knowledge, a saying of Muḥammad to the effect that the *qibla* was to the south was sufficiently influential so that mosques constructed through the early second/eighth century in locales to the north-west of Mecca nevertheless faced due south. The research of David King has shown that even after mathematical solutions of the *qibla* problem appeared, there endured a parallel popular literature that answered the same questions in a less exacting manner. How, when and where different techniques of *qibla* computation were employed remain open questions.

Technical solutions to the *qibla* problem appeared perhaps by the end of the second/eighth century and certainly by the third/ninth.[85] The *qibla* problem was akin to the construction of a great circle arc, measured on the local meridian either from the north or from the south, between the given locale and Mecca. The angle between that great circle arc and the local meridian, measured from the south, is the *qibla* angle. Because this arc is on the surface of a sphere, and not a plane, one's intuition of the *qibla* direction is imprecise. A precise solution requires knowledge of the differences in

83 David King, 'The sacred direction in Islam: A study of the interaction of religion and science in the Middle Ages', *Interdisciplinary Science Reviews*, 10 (1985), p. 319.

84 David King, 'Astronomy and Islamic society: Qibla, gnomonics, and timekeeping', in Rashed and Morelon (eds.), *Encyclopedia of the history of Arabic science*, vol. I. I draw on this article for the rest of the paragraph.

85 David King, 'Ḳibla', *EI2*, vol. V, pp. 83–8.

longitude and latitude between Mecca and the given locale. Although rudimentary spherical trigonometry, in the form of the Menelaus theorem, was available from Hellenistic texts, other solutions to the *qibla* problem elicited the most elegant formulae of spherical trigonometry that scientists had ever developed.

Of importance too were analemmas, solutions in which one projects the celestial sphere and its arcs onto a plane. The simplest analemmas were serviceable approximations: the Earth was at the centre of a circle and diameters passed from the cardinal points through the centre of the circle. Then, the difference in longitude was an arc on the circumference from the north–south diameter; the difference in latitude was an arc on the circumference from the east–west diameter. The endpoint of the arc of the difference in longitude became the endpoint for a chord parallel to the north–south diameter, and the same for the difference in latitude and the east–west diameter. The approximate *qibla* was the line from the circle's centre through the intersection of the chords. Other analemmas, such as Ḥabash al-Ḥāsib's (*fl. c.* 236/850), were more complex, but accurate because they transformed a spherical problem, through fully accurate geometrical constructions, into a planar problem.[86] Ibn al-Haytham (d. *c.* 432/1041) devised a universal solution to the *qibla* problem.[87] Ultimately, al-Khalīlī (*fl.* 767/1365) computed *qibla* tables for all longitudes and latitudes. David King has uncovered two world maps for determining the *qibla*.[88] The efforts necessary to develop the precise solutions served double duty because the *qibla* problem was analogous to other problems in timekeeping.

ʿIlm al-mīqāt (religious timekeeping) computed times for the five daily prayers (daybreak, midday, afternoon, sunset and nightfall).[89] Of the five, the timing of the afternoon prayer was in especial need of analysis.[90] Early Islamic sources had defined the time of that prayer to be when the length of a shadow was equal to the height of a gnomon casting a shadow. This phenomenon could not occur at certain latitudes at certain times of the year. So, by the

86 Yūsuf ʿĪd and E. S. Kennedy, 'Ḥabash al-Ḥāsib's analemma for the qibla', *Historia Mathematica*, 1 (1974).

87 Ahmad S. Dallal, 'Ibn al-Haytham's universal solution for finding the direction of the *qibla* by calculation', *Arabic Sciences and Philosophy*, 5 (1995).

88 David King, *World-maps for finding the direction and distance to Mecca: Innovation and tradition in Islamic science* (London, Leiden, Boston and Cologne, 1999), p. xiii.

89 David King, 'Mīḳāt', *EI2*, vol. VII, pp. 27–32. See now David King, *In synchrony with the heavens: Studies in astronomical timekeeping and instrumentation in medieval Islamic civilization*, 2 vols. (Leiden, 2004–5).

90 E. S. Kennedy, 'al-Bīrūnī on the Muslim times of prayer', in Peter Chelkowski (ed.), *The scholar and the saint* (New York, 1975).

third/ninth century, legal scholars had to redefine the time of the afternoon prayer to be when the shadow was equal to the length of the shadow at midday plus the length of the gnomon. The definition of midday was when the Sun was at its highest altitude for the day, and at that time the shadow was at its shortest. Al-Khwārizmī's development of prayer tables served the causes of both convenience and accuracy.[91] *Mīqāt* served astronomers by providing an institutional foothold in the seventh/thirteenth century with the development of the office of *muwaqqit*.[92]

A final example of a religious application of astronomy is lunar crescent observation. The Islamic calendar is lunar, and the beginning of a new month depends on the observation of the new crescent Moon on the evening of the twenty-ninth day of the old month; the precise length of a lunar month is 29.54 days. The visibility of the lunar crescent, a problem which astronomers of Islamic civilisation treated with greater energy than Hellenistic astronomers, was especially complex because multiple variables were involved. Yaʿqūb ibn Ṭāriq was one of the early scientists to work on this problem, and Ḥabash al-Ḥāsib's *zīj* included a table of lunar crescent visibilities.[93] Another solution, one that considered four variables, comes from Thābit ibn Qurra (d. 288/901).[94] Thābit calculated the four variables for the evening of the twenty-ninth day of a month: the angular distance between the Sun and the Moon; the arc of the Sun's depression under the horizon; the Moon's angular distance on the horizon from the horizon's brightest spot; and the Moon's motion on its epicycle. Then he computed the crescent's arc of visibility from all but the second. If the arc of depression was greater than the arc of visibility, then the Moon was visible. Thābit's contributions are notable not only for their sophistication, but also for how they show that a non-Muslim could participate fully in science in Islamic civilisation. Though scholars disagree over the contribution of astronomy's applications to the rise of that science in Islamic civilisation, certain applications did pose interesting theoretical questions.

91 E. S. Kennedy and Mardiros Janjanian, 'The crescent visibility table in al-Khwārizmī's Zīj', *Centaurus*, 20 (1965–7).

92 David King, 'On the role of the muezzin and *muwaqqit* in medieval Islamic society', in F. Jamil Ragep and Sally P. Ragep (eds.), with Steven Livesey, *Tradition, transmission, transformation: Proceedings of two conferences on pre-modern science held at the University of Oklahoma* (Leiden, 1996).

93 Kennedy, 'A survey', p. 152; Marie-Thérèse Debarnot, 'The zīj of Ḥabash al-Ḥāsib: A survey of MS Istanbul Yeni Cami 784/2', in David King and George Saliba (eds.), *From deferent to equant* (New York, 1987).

94 Régis Morelon, 'Tābit b. Qurra and Arabic astronomy in the ninth century', *Arabic Sciences and Philosophy*, 4 (1994), pp. 118–22.

The astrolabe

All of these applications, whether religious or astrological, involved timekeeping in some way. The best *zīj* would be of no use without knowledge of one's location and the time of day or night. Among the instruments available to Islamic astronomers were sundials, armillary spheres and magnetic compasses (by the seventh/thirteenth century); the most popular and versatile instrument was the astrolabe (see plate 22.1).[95] The astrolabe was an analogue computer perfect for timekeeping, a variety of mathematical computations, astrological predictions and even sighting stars. The plate of an astrolabe is a projection onto the plane of the equator of the celestial longitude (azimuth) lines for a given latitude. Over this plate rested a see-through grid, known as the spider (Ar. *al-ʿankabūt*) or rete, which was a planar map of chosen constellations. One would use the alidade, similar to a rotating ruler with sights on it, to sight an object in the heavens. One then rotated the rete so that the sighted object, and thus all other objects, was in its appropriate location on the map of the heavens engraved on the astrolabe plate. While specific features of astrolabes might differ, material frequently engraved on astrolabes would often include curves to determine trigonometric functions, sundials and astrological diagrams.

Significant developments in astrolabe design occurred in al-Andalus. In the fifth/eleventh century ʿAlī ibn Khalaf and Ibn al-Zarqālluh designed a universal plate that could solve problems of spherical astronomy for all latitudes, although universal astrolabes could not provide a picture of the heavens on the plate.[96] Emilia Calvo's research has brought to light the improved universal plate of Ibn Bāṣo (d. 716/1316), who became chief *muwaqqit* in Granada.[97] Ibn Bāṣo's plate was reproduced throughout Europe.[98]

The significance of Ptolemy's Almagest

Further developments in astronomy and its applications, astrological and religious, cannot be understood outside the context of the implications of

95 Willy Hartner, 'Aṣṭurlāb', *EI2*, vol. I, pp. 722–8.

96 These scientists were aware of research in the Islamic east (al-Mashriq). See Roser Puig, 'On the eastern sources of Ibn al-Zarqālluh's orthographic projection', in Josep Casulleras and Julio Samsó (eds.), *From Baghdad to Barcelona: Studies in the Islamic exact sciences in honour of Prof. Juan Vernet* (Barcelona, 1996). See also Ibn al-Zarqālluh, *al-Shakkāziyya*, ed., trans. and comm. Roser Puig (Barcelona, 1986).

97 Emilia Calvo, 'Ibn Bāṣo's astrolabe in the Maghrib and the east', in Casulleras and Samsó (eds.), *From Baghdad to Barcelona*.

98 Emilia Calvo, 'Ibn Bāṣo's universal plate and its influence on European astronomy', *Scientiarum Historia*, 18 (1992).

22.1 Astrolabe. Courtesy of the Whipple Museum, Cambridge.

the reception of Ptolemy's planetary theory. Ptolemy was the single most influential astronomer, Hellenistic or otherwise, for Islamic astronomy and astrology. Islamic astronomers' introduction to him came, as I have mentioned, via the growing presence of Ptolemaic parameters in the *zījes*. Little time elapsed before the surviving third/ninth-century translations of Ptolemy's *magnum opus*, the *Almagest*.[99] The *Almagest*'s significance was that

99 Paul Kunitzsch, *Der* Almagest: *Die Syntaxis mathematica des Claudius Ptolemäus in arab.-latein. Überlieferung* (Wiesbaden, 1974), pp. 60–71.

it used a wealth of observational data to derive geometrical abstractions of a physical model of the heavens. The *Almagest* allows one to compute, on the basis of the geometrical models, tables of planetary positions. A popular (judging by the number of surviving manuscripts) recension of the *Almagest* translations by Naṣīr al-Dīn al-Ṭūsī (d. 672/1273f.) appeared in the seventh/thirteenth century. Al-Ṭūsī's recension spawned, through the tenth/sixteenth century, the composition of a host of commentaries. Even the commentators' complaints about astronomers' unfamiliarity with the original *Almagest* evince its enduring relevance.

Astronomers must have reassessed important parameters as the translations of the *Almagest* were occurring, because the later translations of the *Almagest* have parameters different from those in the original. Indeed, astronomers under the caliph al-Maʾmūn (d. 218/833) started a programme of observation, mostly in the vicinities of Baghdad and Damascus, that addressed observational questions raised by the early *Almagest* translations.[100] These astronomers produced new values for important parameters such as the length of a solar year and the dimensions of the solar model. These observations resulted in *al-Zīj al-Mumtaḥan*.[101] Just as translations created more possibilities for research, research (which could include translation) sparked more translations because a surviving *Almagest* translation was produced after al-Maʾmūn's death. Massive instruments were involved, such as a mural quadrant with a radius of five metres. Through these observations Islamic astronomers found, notably, that the solar apogee (the point of the Sun's greatest distance from the Earth) moved independently (see fig. 22.1).[102] Mathematical analyses of the solar apogee's motion ensued.

Astronomers took an interest in Ptolemy's other texts, and by the end of the third/ninth century Thābit ibn Qurra and others produced a translation of the *Planetary hypotheses*.[103] In that text Ptolemy summarised his model of the heavens in wholly physical terms. Ptolemy's physical principles, which he sometimes compromised for the purpose of predictive

100 Aydin Sayılı, *The observatory in Islam and its place in the general history of the observatory* (Ankara, 1960), pp. 56–63.

101 Benno van Dalen, 'A second manuscript of the *Mumtaḥan Zīj*', *Suhayl*, 4 (2004), pp. 28–30.

102 Régis Morelon, 'Eastern Arabic astronomy', in Rashed and Morelon (eds.), *Encyclopedia of the history of Arabic science*, vol. I, p. 26.

103 Bernard R. Goldstein, *The Arabic version of Ptolemy's* Planetary hypotheses (Philadelphia, 1967). For an edition and French translation of the first book see Régis Morelon, 'La version arabe du *Livre des hypothèses* de Ptolémée', *Mélanges de l'Institut Dominicain des Études Orientales du Caire*, 21 (1993).

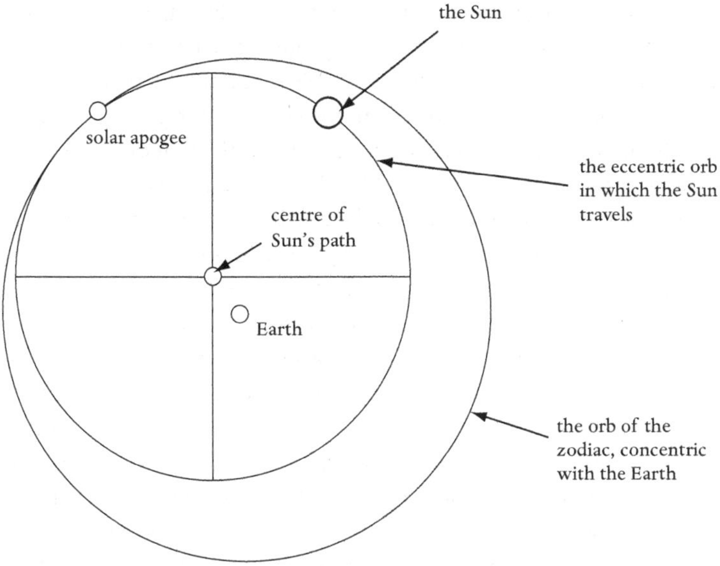

22.1 The solar apogee, the Sun's greatest distance from the Earth

accuracy, assumed, supposedly, that the motions of the heavens resulted from combinations of orbs that rotated uniformly in place about an axis passing through their centre. And just as al-Maʾmūn's astronomers revised Ptolemy's parameters, Ptolemy's views about how concentric orbs could move each other came into question.[104] The attention to the physical consistency of astronomical theories that would lead to the outstanding innovations of the seventh/thirteenth century and beyond had already emerged.

The astronomy of the ninth, tenth and eleventh centuries

The general impression scholarship has provided of the astronomy of the third/ninth, fourth/tenth and fifth/eleventh centuries is that topics of mathematical and observational astronomy were paramount. ʿAbd al-Raḥmān al-Ṣūfī (d. 376/986) focused on observations and instrumentation and produced a book on fixed stars that was best known in al-Andalus, Iran and

104 George Saliba, 'Early Arabic critique of Ptolemaic cosmology: A ninth-century text on the motion of the celestial spheres', *Journal for the History of Astronomy*, 25 (1994).

Europe.[105] Thābit ibn Qurra's involvement with the translation of the *Almagest* led to mathematical studies of important problems from the *Almagest*. Thābit was the first to ask the question of a mobile's speed at a particular point.[106] A host of theoretical questions arose from the construction of instruments such as sundials, an instrument necessary for the determination of prayer times.[107] Most sundials have to be recalibrated for different latitudes. Thābit produced mathematical analyses of a sundial valid for all latitudes, and his interest in that instrument led him to purely theoretical examinations of conic sections. Thābit's grandson Ibrāhīm ibn Sīnān (d. 335/946) extended Thābit's analysis of sundials and conic sections. Ibrāhīm was particularly interested in the application of the geometry of conic sections to lenses and burning mirrors.

While much of al-Bīrūnī's (d. *c.* 442/1050) output is probably lost, what has survived is prodigious by any standard. He too was a gifted ethnographer (to wit his *India*) and historian of insatiable curiosity, upon whom we rely for much of our history of observations in Islamic civilisation. A native speaker of Khwārazmian, al-Bīrūnī had to depend on the study of foreign languages, and composed works in Arabic and Persian. He also translated several texts from Sanskrit into Arabic, and knew something of Greek, Hebrew and Syriac. In astronomy, his most important work was an enormous *zīj* entitled *al-Qānūn al-Masʿūdī*.[108] His study of Greek, Hebrew and particularly Sanskrit, among other languages, meant that the section of *al-Qānūn al-Masʿūdī* on calendars was a few hundred pages long. He treated topics of descriptive and mathematical geography in exhaustive detail, too. Al-Bīrūnī's knowledge of the history of his subject allowed him to present the range of available approaches to solving a problem, from the common to the elegant and refined. His mathematical analysis of the motion of the solar apogee stands out.[109] Al-Bīrūnī's *Kitāb maqālīd ʿilm al-hayʾa* (Book of the keys of astronomy) was an important work on spherical trigonometry that also had a section on *hayʾa*'s astrological applications.[110] Abū al-Wafāʾ al-Būzajānī (d. *c.* 387/997f.), whose

105 Julio Samsó and Mercè Comes, 'al-Ṣūfī and Alfonso X', *Archives Internationales d'Histoire des Sciences*, 38 (1988).

106 Morelon, 'Tābit b. Qurra'.

107 Roshdi Rashed and Hélène Bellosta, *Ibrāhīm ibn Sīnān: Logique et géométrie au Xe siècle* (Leiden, Boston and Cologne, 2000).

108 al-Bīrūnī, *Kitāb al-qānūn al-masʿūdī*, 3 vols. (Hyderabad, 1954–6).

109 W. Hartner and M. Schramm, 'al-Biruni and the theory of the solar apogee: An example of originality in Arabic science', in A. C. Crombie (ed.), *Scientific change* (London, 1963).

110 al-Bīrūnī, *Kitāb maqālīd ʿilm al-hayʾa: La trigonométrie sphérique chez les Arabes de l'est à la fin du Xe siècle*, ed. and trans. Marie-Thérèse Debarnot (Damascus, 1985), pp. 276–90.

work was a foundation for al-Bīrūnī's research, co-operated with him on simultaneous lunar eclipse observations in two different cities.[111] By comparing local time at the time of the eclipse they could obtain the difference in longitude between the cities. In addition to his observational work, Abū al-Wafā' al-Būzajānī wrote a book, entitled *al-Majisṭī* (The almagest), on spherical trigonometry.

Finally, recent research has shown that theoretical questions did not escape the attention of these astronomers. For example, when Thābit critiqued the assumptions underlying the physical operation of Ptolemy's lunar model, he did not assume a qualitative difference between celestial and terrestrial physics; when Ptolemy spoke of the heavens as unchanging, he had implied such a distinction. There are seeds of an important transformation of astronomy from a branch of natural philosophy in the Hellenistic tradition to a science that could and should stand on its own. For instance, al-Bīrūnī rejected the necessity of any relationship between astronomy and physics, specifically Ptolemy's recourse to the findings of physics to prove the sphericity of the heavens.[112] By doing so, Ptolemy, in al-Bīrūnī's view, added nothing to astronomy's prestige. Conversely, when Ptolemy insinuated that observations could prove that the Earth was at rest, i.e. not rotating in place, al-Bīrūnī agreed. Later, in the ninth/fifteenth century, al-Qūshjī (d. 879/1474) would argue that since observations could not prove that the Earth was not rotating, there was no impediment to considering the Earth's rotation.[113] We have seen that critiques of Ptolemy's attention to physical principles emerged relatively early in the history of astronomy in Islamic civilisation. These critiques broadly resembled attacks on astrology's claims about physical causes.

The eleventh and twelfth centuries in Andalusia

Abu 'l-Qāsim Maslama al-Majrīṭī's (d. *c.* 398/1007) adaptation of al-Khwārizmī's *Zīj* to al-Andalus was a harbinger of a productive period of astronomy in al-Andalus.[114] The best-known figure of the period was Ibn al-Zarqālluh (d. 493/1100). A contributor to the *Toledan tables* of Ṣā'id al-Andalusī, Ibn al-Zarqālluh was also the first known Islamic astronomer to write that the

111 al-Bīrūnī, *Kitāb taḥdīd nihāyāt al-amākin li-taṣḥīḥ masāfāt al-masākin*, ed. P. Bulgakov (Cairo, 1964), p. 250.
112 F. Jamil Ragep, 'Ṭūsī and Copernicus: The Earth's motion in context', *Science in Context*, 14 (2001).
113 F. Jamil Ragep, 'Freeing astronomy from philosophy: An aspect of Islamic influence on science', *Osiris*, n.s. 16 (2001).
114 Juan Vernet, 'al-Madjrīṭī', *EI2*, vol. V, pp. 1109–10.

motion of the solar apogee was not equal to the motion in precession, and thus not equal to the motion of the ecliptic.[115] Ibn al-Kammād's (*fl.* sixth/twelfth century) *zīj* tells us about Ibn al-Zarqālluh's solar theory, and Ibn al-Hāʾim (*fl.* 602/1205) relied on Ibn al-Zarqālluh's solar theory.[116] Connected to Ibn al-Zarqālluh's work on the universal astrolabe was his instrument that determined the Earth–Moon distance graphically.[117]

During the fifth/eleventh and sixth/twelfth centuries astronomers in al-Andalus devoted more attention than their counterparts in the Islamic east to the development of theories to explain trepidation and variations in the obliquity of the ecliptic. The obliquity of the ecliptic is the angle, in the vicinity of 23.5°, between the celestial equator and the zodiac. Astronomers had also believed that they detected trepidation, variations in the Sun's position in the zodiac at the time of the equinoxes. Theories to explain one or both of these phenomena depended on accurate measurements of these parameters. Observations throughout the history of astronomy in Islamic civilisation, at the seventh/thirteenth-century observatory at Marāgha for example, produced new values for the rate of precession. Although the existence of both trepidation and variations in the obliquity was always open to question, astronomers nevertheless did develop models first for trepidation, and then for both phenomena in combination. Such models had originated in the work of eastern astronomers such as Thābit ibn Qurra and al-Battānī.[118]

The first combined theories showed only how one model could account for both phenomena. Andalusians such as Ibn al-Zarqālluh and Ibn al-Hāʾim proposed more sophisticated models that considered the precise parameters of both the changes in the obliquity and trepidation, and acknowledged that the ranges of their variation were different.[119] The models that explain both phenomena in combination are of historical importance due to their structural similarities with the models that Andalusian astronomers would develop to try to reform Ptolemy. Astrologers, for their part, were quite interested in

115 G.J. Toomer, 'The solar theory of al-Zarqāl: A history of errors', *Centaurus*, 14 (1969).

116 José Chabás and Bernard Goldstein, 'Andalusian astronomy: *al-Zīj al-muqtabis* of Ibn al-Kammād', *Archive for the History of the Exact Sciences*, 48 (1994); see also Emilia Calvo, 'Astronomical theories related to the Sun in Ibn al-Hāʾim's *al-Zīj al-kāmil fīʾl-taʿālīm*', *ZGAIW*, 12 (1998).

117 Roser Puig, 'al-Zarqālluh's graphical method for finding lunar distances', *Centaurus*, 32 (1989).

118 F. Jamil Ragep, 'al-Battānī, cosmology, and the early history of trepidation in Islam', in Casulleras and Samsó (eds.), *From Baghdad to Barcelona*, pp. 353–4.

119 Mercè Comes, 'Ibn al-Hāʾim's trepidation model', *Suhayl*, 2 (2001).

the impact of trepidation and variations in the obliquity of the ecliptic on forecasts.

Changes in the discipline of astronomy

By the fourth/tenth century critiques of astrology had come to a head in the Islamic east. These critiques would force astronomy to become more independent not only of astrology but also of the natural philosophy upon which astrology depended. Al-Bīrūnī wrote against astrology in his *al-Qānūn al-Masʿūdī*; and his handbook of astrology, *Kitāb al-tafhīm* (Book of instruction), was composed for a royal patron and adopted a distanced position. Astrology's prestige relative to astronomy's other applications had declined. Why did astrology's position decline? Writers in the ancient world such as Cicero, in *De divinatione*, and Augustine, in *City of God*, formulated cogent critiques of astrology that resurfaced after the rise of Islam. Astrology threatened God's absolute unity and omnipotence. Astrologers were also often wrong, and had difficulty explaining why, for example, identical twins could lead lives that were not at all identical. More important, as even Hellenistic texts had distinguished between astronomy and astrology, the most serious arguments against astrology attacked its foundations in Hellenistic philosophy.[120] Astronomy shared with astrology many of those foundations.

Ibn Sīnā (d. 428/1037), who refuted many of astrology's claims himself, produced a text on the classification of the sciences in which astrology (*ʿilm aḥkām al-nujūm*) and astronomy (*ʿilm al-hay'a*) were no longer grouped together in the same category.[121] Ibn al-Akfānī's (d. 749/1348) classification of the sciences presented an *ʿilm al-hay'a* that concentrated on holistic qualitative and quantitative descriptions of the orbs.[122] This new type of *ʿilm al-hay'a* had become the locus for most of Islamic astronomy's outstanding achievements.

Considerations of physical consistency

ʿIlm al-hay'a texts maintained an overt distance from questions of metaphysics. Instead, writers on *ʿilm al-hay'a* asked descriptive questions. Ibn al-Haytham

120 Saliba, 'Astronomy and astrology', p. 152.

121 Ibn Sīnā, 'Fī aqsām al-ʿulūm al-ʿaqliyya', in *Tisʿ rasā'il fī al-ḥikma wa-'l-ṭabīʿiyyāt* (Constantinople, 1880), pp. 71–81.

122 Ibn al-Akfānī, *Irshād al-qāṣid ilā asnā al-maqāṣid*, ed. ʿAbd al-Laṭīf Muḥammad al-ʿAbd (Cairo, 1978), p. 144.

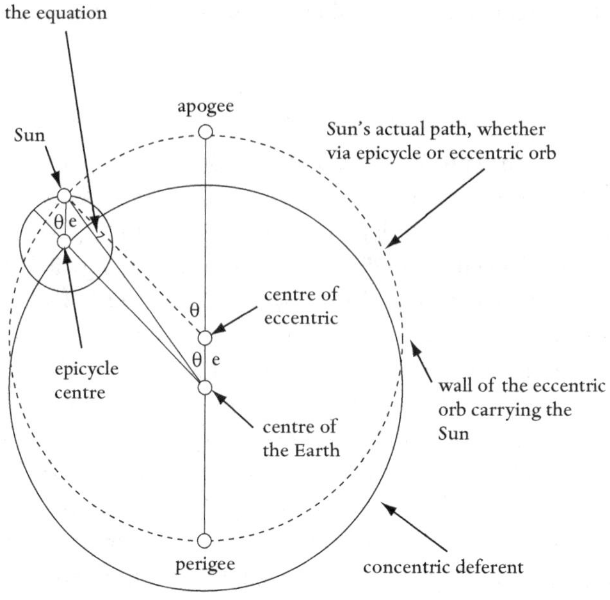

22.2 Eccentric and epicyclic orbs, two hypotheses for celestial motions

(d. *c.* 432/1041) asked whether Ptolemy's configurations of orbs could move as described, and found that they could not. Ibn al-Haytham's *al-Shukūk ʿalā Baṭlamyūs* (Doubts against Ptolemy) catalogued the physical inconsistencies of Ptolemy's *Almagest* and *Planetary hypotheses.*[123] On one level Ptolemy transgressed Aristotle's principle that the observed celestial motions result from combinations of uniformly rotating orbs; on another, Ibn al-Haytham's critiques arose from a consideration of how orbs must rotate. An orb could not rotate uniformly about an axis that did not pass through the orb's centre.[124] The model for the Sun's motions is an excellent introduction to the foundation of all Ptolemaic (and Islamic) planetary theory. The simplest model would be to suppose that the Sun moves embedded in the wall of an orb (see fig. 22.2); the Earth would be at the centre of that orb. Babylonian astronomers, however, had observed variations in the Sun's motion, and Ptolemy used,

123 Ibn al-Haytham, *al-Shukūk ʿalā Baṭlamyūs*, ed. A. I. Sabra and Nabil Shehaby (Cairo, 1971).
124 See A. I. Sabra, 'Configuring the universe: Aporetic, problem solving, and kinematic modeling as themes of Arabic astronomy', *Perspectives in Science*, 6 (1998); George Saliba, 'Arabic versus Greek astronomy: A debate over the foundations of science', *Perspectives in Science*, 8 (2000); A. I. Sabra, 'Reply to Saliba', *Perspectives in Science*, 8 (2000).

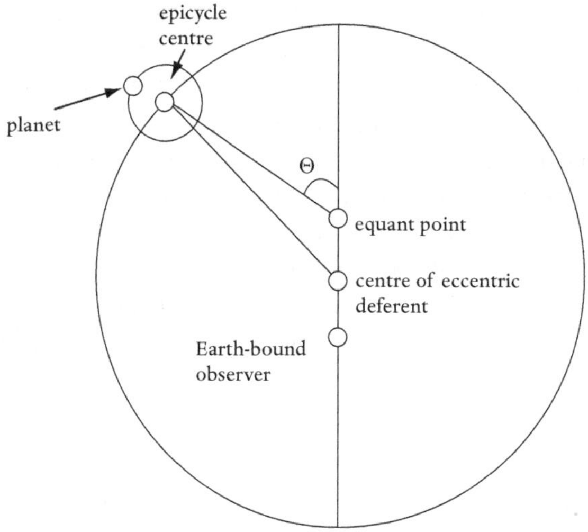

22.3 The equant point, the centre of the planet's mean motion, but not the centre of any orb

as Hipparchus had, these variations to refine a solar model.[125] If the centre of the Sun's orb were removed from the centre of the Earth, the resulting model would account for the observed anomalies. In addition, Ptolemy noted that if the Sun were moving on a small circle known as an epicycle, which was carried in turn on a large circle at whose centre was the Earth, an equivalent motion would result.

In the models for the outer planets (Mars, Jupiter and Saturn) Ptolemy employed the principle of an orb eccentric to the centre of the Earth to account for the planet's mean motion in longitude. An analogy with the solar model would suggest that the centre of the planet's motion on the eccentric orb is at the centre of that orb, from which the centre of the Earth was removed by a given amount. Ptolemy's careful analysis found that the centre of the planet's mean motion in longitude was not the centre of the eccentric deferent orb. Nor was that motion uniform about the centre of the Earth. The motion was uniform about another point called the equant (see fig. 22.3), which was removed from the centre of the orb on the opposite side from the Earth. Indeed, the fact that the eccentric orb, according to Ptolemy, would have to rotate uniformly about a point other than its centre

125 Otto Neugebauer, *History of ancient mathematical astronomy*, 3 vols. (New York, Heidelberg and Berlin, 1975), vol. I, p. 56.

contradicted the Aristotelian principle of the heavens' uniform circular motion. Moreover, one could not conceive of an orb moving in place about an axis that did not pass through its centre. So Ptolemy's innovative mathematical approach to determining the centre of the planet's motion on the eccentric orb led to the problem of the equant that Ibn al-Haytham noted.

Related to the problem of the equant were other cases where Ptolemy had failed to propose a conceivable physical mover for observed motions of the celestial bodies. Ibn al-Haytham's doubts were not restricted to matters of physical consistency; he noted the discrepancy between the apparent and predicted size of the Sun. Indeed, the ensuing programme to reform Ptolemy was comprehensive.

The reforms of the Marāgha astronomers

Beginning in the mid-seventh/thirteenth century, Islamic astronomers proposed new models that preserved, and in some cases improved, Ptolemy's models' correspondence with observations. These models did not suffer from the physical inconsistencies arising from the equant point. In other words, these new, non-Ptolemaic models no longer posited that the axis of any orb's uniform motion should pass through the equant. Many figures in that line of research who wrote *ʿilm al-hayʾa* texts with these new models, such as Muʾayyad al-Dīn al-ʿUrḍī (d. 664/1266), Naṣīr al-Dīn al-Ṭūsī (d. 672/1273f.), and Quṭb al-Dīn al-Shīrāzī (d. 711/1311), were associated with the Marāgha Observatory in Azerbaijan.[126] Later figures, such as Ṣadr al-Dīn al-Sharīʿa (d. 747/1347) and Ibn al-Shāṭir (d. 777/1375), composed works in the intellectual tradition of the astronomers at Marāgha.[127] Al-ʿUrḍī was, in addition, responsible for the engineering of the Marāgha Observatory's instruments that were a part of the observational programme there. These instruments' design was influential, and would later be mirrored, for example, by the instruments at the Jai Singh Observatory in Jaipur, India. Though Ibn al-Shāṭir's theories

126 On al-ʿUrḍī's astronomy see George Saliba, *The astronomical work of Muʾayyad al-Dīn al-ʿUrḍī (*Kitāb al-hayʾa*): A thirteenth-century reform of Ptolemaic astronomy* (Beirut, 1990). On al-Ṭūsī's astronomy see F. J. Ragep (ed., trans. and comm.), *Naṣīr al-Dīn al-Ṭūsī's memoir on astronomy (*al-Tadhkira fī ʿilm al-hayʾa*)*, 2 vols. (New York and Berlin, 1993). On al-Shīrāzī's astronomy see George Saliba, 'Arabic planetary theories after the eleventh century AD', in Rashed and Morelon (eds.), *Encyclopedia of the history of Arabic science*. See now Robert Morrison, 'Quṭb al-Dīn al-Shīrāzī's hypotheses for celestial motions', *Journal for the History of Arabic Science*, 13 (2005).

127 Ahmad Dallal, *An Islamic response to Greek astronomy:* Kitāb taʿdīl al-aflāk *of Ṣadr al-Sharīʿa* (Leiden, Cologne and Boston, 1995). See also George Saliba, 'Theory and observation in Islamic astronomy: The work of Ibn al-Shatir of Damascus (d. 1375)', *Journal for the History of Astronomy*, 18 (1987).

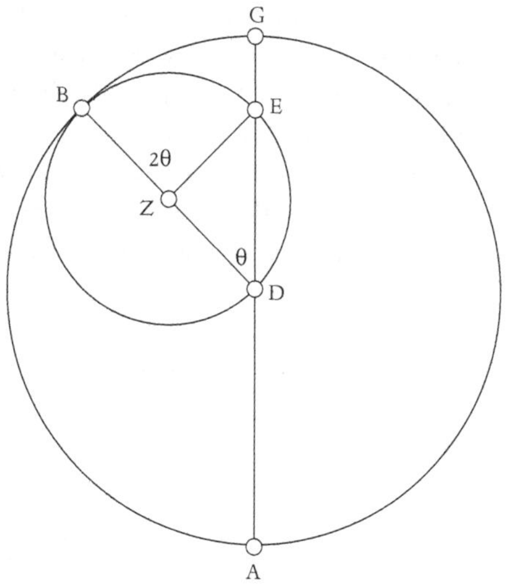

22.4 The Ṭūsī Couple, the basis of a model that solved the equant problem

improved on those of the astronomers at Marāgha, his revised solar model relied on observational considerations. The Marāgha Observatory was notable, too, because it drew its financial support from the revenues of a *waqf*, an endowment to serve religious purposes. The construction of non-Ptolemaic models continued at least into the tenth/sixteenth century, as Shams al-Dīn al-Khafrī (d. 957/1550) proposed multiple mathematically equivalent models for the complicated motions of the planet Mercury.[128] In addition, a circumstantial link has appeared between the Marāgha astronomers and Renaissance astronomers such as Copernicus.[129]

Al-Shīrāzī, al-Ṭūsī's student, enumerated in his writings four hypotheses or principles (*uṣūl*) common to these post-Ptolemaic models. One of these hypotheses was the Ṭūsī Couple, so named by contemporary scholars because it first appeared in the work of al-Ṭūsī. It was based on the following lemma: we assume a small circle inside a large circle, with the radius of one the diameter of the other, and their circumferences are tangent at a given point (see fig. 22.4).

128 George Saliba, 'A redeployment of mathematics in a sixteenth-century Arabic critique of Ptolemaic astronomy', in A. Hasnawi, A. Elamrani-Jamal and M. Aouad (eds.), *Perspectives arabes et médiévales sur la tradition scientifique et philosophique grecque* (Leuven and Paris, 1997).

129 Saliba, *Islamic science*, pp. 193–232 and F. Jamil Ragep, ''Alī Qushjī and Regiomontanus: Eccentric transformations and Copernican revolutions', *Journal for the History of Astronomy*, 36 (2005).

If the large circle moves in one direction with a given angular velocity, and the small circle moves in the opposite direction at twice that angular velocity, then a given point oscillates on the diameter of the large circle. If these circles become the belts of orbs, one has the foundation of a physically consistent model in which the planet's mean motion is uniform about the equant point. Al-Shīrāzī used the Ṭūsī Couple to rebut Aristotle's statement in the *Physics* (262a) that there must be rest between two contradictory motions; al-Shīrāzī in addition mentioned an experiment one could perform to disprove Aristotle's contention that there must be rest between two contradictory motions.[130] Al-Shīrāzī's challenge to Aristotle demonstrates that the astronomers of Islamic civilisation, perhaps because of criticisms of astrology and Hellenistic philosophy, came to be less interested in defending particular principles of Aristotle than in physically coherent models.

A second important hypothesis or principle of the post-Ptolemaic models drew on the equivalence between the eccentric and epicyclic hypotheses present in the two versions of Ptolemy's solar model. If we think of the distance between the equant point and the centre of the deferent orb as an additional eccentricity, then one could attempt to account for the equant point with an additional epicycle to carry the original epicycle centre. That solution, however, proposed by Ibn Sīnā's student Abū ʿUbayd al-Jūzjānī, distorted planetary distances.[131] Al-ʿUrḍī made the theory conform with observations by proposing a second epicycle (see fig. 22.5) whose radius was half the distance between the centre of the Ptolemaic deferent and the equant centre.[132] That new epicycle would rotate in the same direction and with the same angular velocity as the new deferent, whose centre was halfway between the centre of the old deferent and the equant point. The result was that the motion of a point on the new epicycle would be uniform about the equant point and would almost (but not quite) trace the path of the epicycle centre in the Ptolemaic model. Rather than explain away that remaining discrepancy with the Ptolemaic model, al-ʿUrḍī contested Ptolemy's assumption of a perfectly circular path for the epicycle centre.[133] After all, conclusive observational proof to support a circular path for the epicycle centre did not exist.

130 The experiment that al-Shīrāzī proposed might be due, originally, to Ibn Buṭlān. See Roshdi Rashed, 'al-Qūhī versus Aristotle on motion', *Arabic Sciences and Philosophy*, 9 (1999), pp. 17–18.

131 George Saliba, 'Ibn Sīnā and Abū ʿUbayd al-Jūzjānī: The problem of the Ptolemaic equant', *Journal for the History of Arabic Science*, 4 (1980).

132 George Saliba, 'The original source of Quṭb al-Dīn al-Shīrāzī's planetary model', *Journal for the History of Arabic Science*, 3 (1979).

133 Saliba, *Astronomical work*, p. 223.

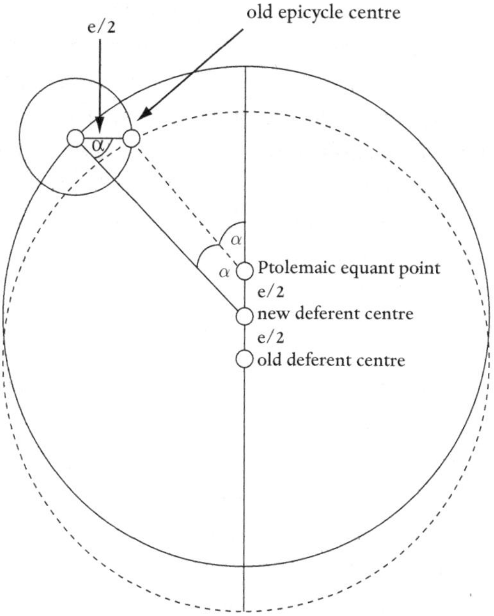

22.5 al-ʿUrḍī's model for planetary motions, based on the equivalence of angles at the base of a parallelogram

Philosophers and earlier astronomers had posited such a circular path based on empirical evidence.

Reforms of Ptolemaic astronomy in al-Andalus

In al-Andalus the critique of Ptolemy began at a different starting-point. In the sixth/twelfth century philosophers such as Ibn Bājja (d. 533/1138) and Ibn Rushd (d. 594/1198) advocated a reading of Aristotle's *Physics* that precluded epicyclic and eccentric orbs.[134] Neither an epicycle nor an eccentric rotated uniformly about the centre of the Earth. Drawing on these Andalusian philosophers, one astronomer, al-Biṭrūjī (*fl. c.* 600/1200), proposed models incorporating only homocentric orbs.[135] This elimination of epicyclic and eccentric orbs meant that al-Biṭrūjī's models could not approach the predictive

134 A. I. Sabra, 'The Andalusian revolt against Ptolemaic astronomy: Averroes and al-Biṭrūjī', in Everett Mendelsohn (ed.), *Transformation and tradition in the sciences* (Cambridge and New York, 1984; repr. 2003).

135 Al-Biṭrūjī, *On the principles of astronomy*, ed., trans. and comm. Bernard R. Goldstein, 2 vols. (New Haven and London, 1971).

accuracy of the Marāgha astronomers' models or of those of Ptolemy. In al-Biṭrūjī's model for the Sun's motion, the Sun ventured from its observed path through the signs of the zodiac by as much as 1.5°! Only at four points, the equinoxes and the solstices, did the Sun's predicted position in al-Biṭrūjī's model match observations. Still, al-Biṭrūjī's work, besides being interesting in its own right, provides a useful contrast to understand better the essence of the work of the Marāgha astronomers. Whereas al-Biṭrūjī privileged a certain reading of Aristotle, the work of the Marāgha astronomers valued consistency, conceivability and fidelity to observations.

An attempt to improve on al-Biṭrūjī has come to light. Ibn Naḥmias' (*fl. c.* 800/1400) *Nūr al-ʿālam* (The light of the world) noted al-Biṭrūjī's theories' lack of agreement with observations.[136] Ibn Naḥmias devised improvements that addressed such discrepancies to some extent. In order to do so he had to introduce epicycles that rotated on the equator of the orb, but which were not moved by a pole rotating about the pole of the orb. Ibn Naḥmias' solar model included a double-circle hypothesis similar, but not identical, to the Ṭūsī Couple. Ibn Naḥmias' increased attention to predictive accuracy and decreased obsession with Aristotle's philosophy, along with his models' greater resemblance to the astronomy of the East, distinguished him from the figures of the sixth/twelfth-century Andalusian response to Ptolemy that Sabra noted.[137] Diverse regional research agendas coexisted with connections between astronomers and astronomies from different parts of the Islamic world.

Relations between astronomy and religious scholarship

This sketch of the history of astronomy in Islamic civilisation so far has chronicled astronomy's increasing independence from its applications in astrology, and from its foundations in Hellenistic philosophy. For religious scholars astronomy was transformed from a science within the Aristotelian scheme of natural philosophy into an independent science that could demonstrate God's glory. Famous statements of al-Ghazālī (d. 505/1111) encapsulated the relationship of astronomy, and to a lesser extent astrology, to traditions of religious scholarship. In a work entitled *al-Munqidh min al-ḍalāl* (Deliverance from error) al-Ghazālī noted that most of the errors of the philosophers were in the areas of metaphysics and philosophical theology.[138]

136 Robert Morrison, 'The solar model in Joseph ibn Naḥmias' *Light of the world*', *Arabic Sciences and Philosophy*, 15 (2005).

137 Sabra, 'The Andalusian revolt'.

138 W. Montgomery Watt, *The faith and practice of al-Ghazālī* (London, 1953), pp. 37–8.

Astronomy did not depend directly on the three questionable positions of the philosophers that he singled out in *al-Munqidh min al-ḍalāl* (denial of resurrection, the eternity of the world and God's inability to know particulars). Al-Ghazālī's criticisms of Hellenistic philosophy, inasmuch as it pertained to astronomy, were more acute in his famous *Tahāfut al-falāsifa* (Incoherence of the philosophers). In Discussion Seventeen of the *Tahāfut* he disagreed with the philosophers' position that fire causes burning in cotton: 'Observation, however, [only] shows the occurrence [of burning] at [the time of the contact with the fire] but does not show the occurrence [of burning] by [the fire] and [the fact] that there is no other cause for it.'[139] This statement questioned whether astronomers could in fact view the orbs as the proximate movers of the planets, or whether the orbs' causal role was only apparent. If astronomy distanced itself from Hellenistic philosophy, then could astronomers make any statement about the structure of the universe that was not purely contingent? Though authors of *ʿilm al-hayʾa* texts would eventually take subtle positions in favour of the reality of their models, they would do so without explicit recourse to Hellenistic philosophy.

Al-Shīrāzī, in his *al-Tuḥfa al-shāhiyya* (The royal gift), made an effort to establish the principles of *ʿilm al-hayʾa* directly from observation.[140] ʿAlāʾ al-Dīn al-Qūshjī (d. 879/1474), who produced an innovative model for Mercury's motions, argued in a *kalām* (rational speculation about God) text that *ʿilm al-hayʾa* could stand on its own without relying on philosophical metaphysics. Such awareness of critiques of Hellenistic philosophy explains reports of astronomy being studied as late as the nineteenth and early twentieth centuries within a *madrasa*, a foundation for the study of Islamic subjects, most notably Islamic law.[141] Texts of astronomy abounded in the libraries attached to *madrasas*.

At the beginning of the *Tahāfut* al-Ghazālī made another statement that limited the implications of his own critique of causality. He mentioned a scientific explanation of a lunar eclipse which 'consists in the obliteration of the Moon's light due to the interposition of the Earth between it and the Sun, the Earth being a sphere surrounded by the sky on all sides. Thus, when the

139 al-Ghazālī, *The incoherence of the philosophers*/Tahāfut al-falāsifa, *a parallel English–Arabic text*, ed., trans. and intro. Michael E. Marmura (Provo, UT, 1997), p. 167.

140 See Ragep, 'Freeing astronomy' on al-Shīrāzī and al-Qūshjī. See also Robert Morrison, *Islam and science: The intellectual career of Niẓām al-Dīn al-Nīsābūrī* (London and New York, 2007), chap. 5.

141 Robert Morrison, 'The response of Ottoman religious scholars to European science', *Archivum Ottomanicum*, 21 (2003).

Moon falls in the Earth's shadow, the Sun's light is severed from it.'[142] Al-Ghazālī rebuked those who would dispute, out of a sense of religious duty, such indubitable arithmetical and geometrical demonstrations. *ʿIlm al-hayʾa*'s success within a tradition of religious scholarship was due in part to the fact that criticisms of astronomy emphasised the weaknesses of its foundations in Hellenistic philosophy and not the value of its findings. Inasmuch as *ʿilm al-hayʾa* texts ceased to situate themselves within a Hellenistic taxonomy of the sciences, in which astronomy was connected to Hellenistic philosophy, *ʿilm al-hayʾa* became an Islamic science.

The oeuvres of some of Islamic civilisation's outstanding astronomers attest to the coexistence of scientific and religious scholarship. Al-Ṭūsī, al-Shīrāzī, Ṣadr al-Sharīʿa and al-Khafrī were all religious scholars of note. In addition, Ibn al-Shāṭir served as the timekeeper in the Grand Mosque in Damascus. Scientific and religious arguments coincided in certain texts. Fakhr al-Dīn al-Rāzī's (d. 606/1209) Qurʾān commentary brought a great deal of astronomy and natural philosophy to bear on the Qurʾān's portrayal of nature.[143] To be sure, there were debates over the reality and validity of certain explanations for celestial phenomena, but the existence of those debates along with their religious subtexts is proof of the relevance of astronomy to themes of *kalām* and Qurʾān commentary. A famous statement of ʿAḍud al-Dīn al-Ījī (d. 756/1355) asserted the fictionality and contingency of the astronomers' theories and sparked debate in super-commentaries for centuries.[144]

Most of the religious scholar/astronomers whom I have just cited were not Arab, and while some of them did write on astrology, they did not write such texts in Arabic, the pre-eminent language of Islamic scholarship. Despite astrology's loss of intellectual prestige, it endured in Islamic societies as a craft for which there was always a steady demand. Astrology retained some support among physicians as a foundation of disease aetiology. Even al-Ghazālī had pointed out in his *Iḥyāʾ ʿulūm al-dīn* (Revival of the religious sciences) that astrology was similar to medicine in that both sciences depended on induction.[145] Niẓām al-Dīn al-Nīsābūrī (d. *c.* 730/1329–30), an astronomer and Qurʾān commentator, wrote in his Persian commentary on al-Ṭūsī's *Zīj-i Īlkhānī*, and in his Qurʾān commentary, that quotes in the Qurʾān could be interpreted to mean that the heavens were an instrument for God's control

142 al-Ghazālī, *Incoherence of the philosophers*, p. 6.
143 Morrison, *Islam and science*, chap. 6.
144 A. I. Sabra, 'Science and philosophy in medieval Islamic theology: The evidence of the fourteenth century', *ZGAIW*, 9 (1994).
145 al-Ghazālī, *Iḥyāʾ ʿulūm al-dīn*, 5 vols. (Cairo, 1955), vol. I, p. 29.

over terrestrial events.[146] So while an author such as al-Shīrāzī wrote on astronomy, astrology and philosophy, these fields no longer depended directly on each other.

To be sure, each astronomer was but a point on a broad spectrum of opinions about astronomy's value, its applications and its relation to astrology. Nevertheless, astronomers' sensitivity to such questions and their achievement in relating a theoretically sophisticated astronomy to religious scholarship are key characteristics of Islamic astronomy. The development of astronomy within Islamic civilisation can be fully understood only with attention to astronomy's applications and its connection to religious scholarship.

The cultures of cartography

Cartography in Islamic societies shares common ground with geography without being part of it. Many texts on geography do not contain a single map. Numerous maps are not connected to a text. The world of those that are intimately linked to a verbal narrative covers a broad range of disciplines, among them political history, creational history, pilgrimage and mathematical cosmography. Maps were drawn or painted on paper, papier mâché or cotton, embroidered on precious silks, woven into carpets or incised into metal. They were illustrations of manuscripts, single-sheet pictures or parts of atlases, elements of mural decoration, instruments or parts thereof and symbolic components of miniature paintings. One set of items that could be considered maps was tables and diagrams.[147] The other set consists of landscape paintings and town views in miniatures adorning texts on history, military campaigns or romances.[148] Maps served as mnemonic devices, objects of art and entertainment, symbols of authority and power, diplomatic gifts, instruments of war and faith as well as organisers of order and knowledge. Maps depicted the Earth, the stars or the universe.[149] The most vivacious and multifaceted map culture evolved in the Ottoman empire from the ninth/fifteenth century.

146 Morrison, *Islam and science*, chaps 4 and 6.

147 A tabular world map can be found in Ibn Faḍl Allāh al-ʿUmarī's encyclopaedic work *Masālik al-abṣār*. A tabular map for determining the *qibla* for Bursa and a number of other towns in Anatolia, Egypt, Syria and Azerbaijan is enclosed in an eighteenth-century Ottoman Egyptian manuscript. See King, *World-maps*, pp. 92–3.

148 Examples are maps of Mecca in Niẓāmī's *Iskandarnāme*, Mughal town views and landscape paintings with routes passed through by Ottoman sultans and their armies.

149 This section discusses only terrestrial maps.

It started apparently as a component of the dynasty's ambitions for recognition by and superiority over other Muslim dynasties in Anatolia. In this context Ottoman rulers, their relatives and their advisers engaged in a sustained support of *madrasas*, hospitals and other educational institutes as well as in sponsoring the translation of Arabic and Persian works, including geography, cartography and other sciences. While other dynasties such as the ʿAbbāsids, the Fāṭimids, the Būyids or the Tīmūrids were apparently lending most of their patronage to world maps and regional maps of Islamic territories, maps of sacred spaces and architectural plans, the Ottoman court's attention also embraced maps for navigation, regulating border disputes and the administration of water supplies.[150] Its substantial involvement in Europe led to the integration and adaptation of a variety of Italian, Spanish, Dutch and French maps and the emergence of a distinctive mix in the visual and conceptual languages of Ottoman maps.

Terrestrial maps in Islamic societies cover at least five broad categories. The first category contains maps based on astronomical observations, calculations and geometrical constructions. Their languages were Arabic and Persian. The institutional realm was formed by courts, which were joined by *madrasas* from the seventh/thirteenth century, if not earlier. From the second/eighth to the seventh/thirteenth centuries maps based on astronomy and mathematics were either part of the scientific written cultures or were produced as self-contained material objects on sheets of precious metal or on spherical solids made from paper and cloth. They were created in various regions of the Islamic world such as Iraq, Central Asia, Egypt, Sicily, al-Andalus and North Africa. From the seventh/thirteenth to the ninth/fifteenth centuries such maps were mostly part of one of the last chapters of treatises on *ʿilm al-hayʾa*. The regional spread of such mapmaking activities seems to have been more limited than in the previous centuries. They are mainly known from Iran and Central Asia.[151] Reports about cartographic research and the mapping of coastal lines in Anatolia as well as specific Iranian territories testify to the

150 Ahmet Karamustafa, 'Introduction to Ottoman geography', in J. B. Harley and David Woodward (eds.), *The history of cartography*, vol. II, book 1: *Cartography in the traditional Islamic and South Asian societies* (Chicago and London, 1992); Ahmet Karamustafa, 'Military, administrative, and scholarly maps and plans', in Harley and Woodward (eds.), *Cartography in the traditional Islamic and South Asian societies*; J. M. Rogers, 'Itineraries and town views in Ottoman histories', in Harley and Woodward (eds.), *Cartography in the traditional Islamic and South Asian societies*.

151 The work on *ʿilm al-hayʾa* of Niẓām al-Dīn al-Nīsābūrī (sixth–seventh/thirteenth–fourteenth centuries), for instance, contains such a map. I thank Jamil Ragep for providing me with a copy of it.

continued existence of interest among scholars and courtly patrons for more than a merely literary and illustrative cartography.[152]

Maps of the second category work with a geometrical symbolism representing physical and political units such as lakes (circular), rivers (combinations of straight lines or arcs) or provinces (rectangles, squares or combinations thereof), emphasise routes linking towns, cities and ports and prefer simplicity and minimalism with respect to details and naming.[153] They originated as an independent collection of world and regional maps. Their main commentators and transmitters were the philosopher Abū Zayd al-Balkhī (d. 322/934), al-Iṣṭakhrī (*fl.* 318–40/930–51), a member of the ʿAbbāsid administration, and the travellers Ibn Ḥawqal (d. after 378/988) and Shams al-Dīn Muḥammad ibn Aḥmad al-Muqaddasī (d. *c.* 390/1000). It is only with al-Muqaddasī that the text took on the primary position.[154] Savage-Smith argues that the features perceived by other historians as deficits (an absence of mathematical tools and neglect of reality) should be seen as what both the creator(s) of and later commentators on these maps wished to achieve, and hence should be considered as conceptual properties, not deviations or failures.[155] She also suggests that the apparent increase in realism achieved by Ibn Ḥawqal and al-Muqaddasī reflects a decrease in understanding of the original purpose of the maps, and perhaps even a substantial conceptual shift.[156]

Terrestrial maps of a similar nature can also be found in works on natural history, the wonders of creation and the strange things on Earth and at sea as well as in treatises describing the whole universe. These texts proved very popular in various parts of the Islamic world. They are known in Arabic, Persian and Ottoman Turkish versions. Courts and occasionally urban commercial centres provided the financial and material basis. Authors, copyists, illustrators and patrons chose different types of maps to illustrate the books. The Damascene writer Shams al-Dīn Muḥammad ibn Abī Ṭālib (d. 728/1327)

152 Muḥammad ibn Najīb Bakrān, *Jahānnāmeh: Matn-i jughrāfī'i tālīf shodeh dar 605 hijrī az Muḥammad b. Najīb Bakrān*, ed. Muḥammad Amīn Riyāhī (Tehran, 1342), p. 7; Fuat Sezgin, *Geschichte des Arabischen Schrifttums*, 12 vols., vol. X, part 1: *Mathematische Geographie und Kartographie im Islam und ihr Fortleben im Abendland: Historische Darstellung* (Frankfurt am Main, 2000), pp. 310–14.

153 Emilie Savage-Smith, 'Memory and maps', in Farhad Daftari and Josef W. Meri (eds.), *Culture and memory in medieval Islam: Essays in honour of Wilferd Madelung* (London and New York, 2003), p. 120, figs. 1–4.

154 Ibid., pp. 115–16; E. Edson and E. Savage-Smith, *Medieval views of the cosmos with a foreword by Terry Jones: Picturing the universe in the Christian and Islamic Middle Ages* (Oxford, 2004), p. 76, fig. 38.

155 Savage-Smith, 'Memory and maps', pp. 110, 113, 116–17.

156 Ibid., p. 116.

of the cosmography *Nukhbat al-dahr fī ʿajāʾib al-birr wa-ʾl-baḥr* (Eternal selection on the wonders of the land and the sea) apparently wished to provide his readers with different types of images of the Earth such as birds, or sets of circles or rectangles divided into smaller rectilinear units connecting them with pre-Islamic cultures.[157] The illustrator of *Kharīdat al-ʿajāʾib wa-farīdat al-gharāʾib* (Pearl of wonders and the uniqueness of strange [things]), a text ascribed to Sirāj al-Dīn ʿUmar ibn Muẓaffar ibn al-Wardī (d. 850/1456), but more likely the work of another author, chose merely one world map in the style of Ibn Ḥawqal to which he added a diagrammatic representation of various prayer directions towards Mecca.[158] Muḥammad ibn Maḥmūd ibn Aḥmad Ṭūsī Salmānī (sixth/twelfth century) included highly stylised variants of world and regional maps from the tradition of al-Balkhī and his successors.[159] Zakariyyāʾ ibn Muḥammad al-Qazwīnī (d. 682/1283), in contrast, chose Abū Rayḥān al-Bīrūnī's map of the oceans and a diagrammatic map of the seven climes of the ancient Greek tradition for his work. Tīmūrid and Ottoman translations replaced al-Bīrūnī's map by complex symbolic images of the entire universe with (Ottoman) and without (Tīmūrid) terrestrial maps. The Ottoman illustrator chose a map of a completely different type acknowledging the new geographical knowledge about Africa and South Asia available in the tenth/sixteenth century within the older frame of Islamic world maps surrounded by Mount Qāf.[160]

A third category of maps presents images of sacred spaces and rituals. Visualisation of the prayer direction started, according to King, in the late second/eighth or early third/ninth century.[161] Often very simple arrangements were made, such as taking the Kaʿba as the central point and dividing a concentric circle or a polygon into sections that represented major customs of praying attached to chosen cities or regions.[162] Such maps can also be interpreted as diagrams. Other specimens are arranged in a tabular form. Such an arrangement implies that it was not absolute position but relational position that mattered to the creator of the map, both in respect to the Holy

157 A. Mehren, *Cosmographie de Chems-ed-Din Abou Abdallah Mohammed ed-Dimichque* (St Petersburg, 1866).
158 MS Paris, BNF, Arabe 2188, ff. 2b–3a, 25b, dated 883/1479.
159 MS Paris, BNF, Supplément Persan 332, ff. 45a, 46a, 49b, 56a, 57a, 58a. This copy was produced in Baghdad in 790/1388.
160 See www.loc.gov/rr/amed/guide/nes-turkey.html.
161 King, *World-maps*, pp. 51–4.
162 David A. King and Richard P. Lorch, 'Qibla charts, qibla maps, and related instruments', in Harley and Woodward (eds.), *Cartography in the traditional Islamic and South Asian societies*; King, *World-maps*, pp. 50–5, 92, 94, 113, 117.

Places and the localities from which one wished to pray.[163] Such maps reflect some familiarity with tables of geographical coordinates, which they seem to use in an approximate manner. A profound and intimate knowledge of mathematics, geography and astronomy is embodied in a Mecca-centred map known today as engraved onto three Ṣafavid astrolabes. The rectazimuthal projection invented by the map's creator works with arcs of ellipses rather than arcs of circles. The Ṣafavid astrolabe-makers, however, followed the standard usage of arcs of circles for engraving astronomical and astrological curves on instruments.[164] While King argued that a scholar of the ʿAbbāsid period, possibly Ḥabash al-Ḥāsib, invented the projection, Hogendijk suggests that the inventor lived a century later, and possibly in Iran.[165]

Other maps of this category provide the traveller with a pictorial guide for either visiting the pilgrimage sites or remembering their visit. They appear in various intellectual and material settings. They can adorn texts on the advantages of Mecca and Medina and related matters or decorate colourful tiles.[166] They can be part of portolan chart atlases or be painted on single sheets of paper or rolls of paper-reinforced cloth.[167] In the latter form they are a certificate either for an executed pilgrimage or a pilgrimage by proxy.[168] These maps come primarily from commercial urban centres where they were sold to a wider public. The maps certifying a pilgrimage were produced by local artisans and signed by major notables of the holy sites. Most of the extant specimens are linked to Mecca and Medina. A few maps also include Jerusalem or represent Shīʿite sites such as Karbalāʾ.[169]

163 King, *World-maps*, p. 92.

164 David A. King, 'Safavid world-maps centred on Mecca: A third example and some new insights on their original inspiration', in David A. King, *In synchrony with the heavens: Studies in astronomical timekeeping and instrumentation in Islamic civilization*, 2 vols. (Boston and Leiden, 2004–5), vol. I: *The call of the Muezzin*, studies I–IX, study VIIc, p. 843.

165 See King, *World-maps*, pp. 197–364; King, *In synchrony with the heavens*, vol. I, p. 842.

166 Sheila S. Blair and Jonathan M. Bloom, *The art and architecture of Islam 1250–1800* (New Haven, 1995), figs. 307, 332; Mikhail B. Piotrovsky and John Vrieze (gen. ed.), *Heavenly art, earthly beauty: Art of Islam*, exhibition, De Nieuwe Kerk, Amsterdam (16 December 1999–24 April 2000), pp. 78–83, nos. 15–17c; Ahmet Ertug and Oleg Grabar, *In pursuit of excellence: Works of art from the Museum of Turkish and Islamic Arts, Istanbul* (Istanbul, 1993), plates 103A-C, 103D.

167 See the *qibla* diagram in the atlas made by ʿAlī al-Sharafī al-Ṣafāqusī in 979/1571: MS Oxford, Bodleian Library, Marsh 294, fo. 4b; Mónica Herrera Casais, 'The nautical atlases of ʿAlī al-Sharafī', *Suhayl*, 8 (2008) pp. 236, 246; King, *World-maps*, p. 55.

168 Rogers, 'Itineraries and town views in Ottoman histories', p. 244; Ertug and Grabar, *In pursuit of excellence*, plate 7.

169 Rogers, 'Itineraries and town views in Ottoman histories', p. 244.

The fourth category of maps focuses on the representation of oceans, lakes, rivers and water-supply channels. Maps of individual seas, lakes and rivers such as the Mediterranean Sea, the Indian Ocean, the Caspian Sea, the Nile, the Euphrates or the Indus were part of cartographic or geographical works such as Muḥammad al-Khwārizmī's *Ṣūrat al-arḍ* (Image of the Earth), the collection of maps of the Balkhī tradition and the recently discovered copy of a book on trade, travel, geography and wonders most probably compiled by an fifth / eleventh-century Fāṭimid administrator at Ṭinnīs in Egypt.[170] They do not seem to be directly connected to Ptolemy's *Geography*. They are probably an independent outcome of mapmaking in Islamic societies.

A new group of maps of the Mediterranean Sea emerged in the eighth / fourteenth century. Their portrait of the coastal lines comes close to natural conditions. Its nomenclature was at first a mixture of Arabic, Catalan, Venetian and other Italian place names. Later, other languages spoken in the Mediterranean basin can be found too. In addition to the physical space, these charts picture political, economic and cultural knowledge and beliefs in form of rulers, tents, clothing, cushions, flags and inscriptions. The Arabic and later Ottoman Turkish portolan charts share many geographical, visual and verbal elements with their contemporary pendants made at Majorca, in Italy, Portugal, Spain or France. It is often claimed that Arabic and Ottoman Turkish portolan charts are mere copies of Catalan or Italian specimens or vice versa.[171] A closer inspection both of the nomenclature and the rich symbolism suggests, however, that multiple ways of exchange of knowledge and iconography linked the different centres of portolan chart-making across the Mediterranean Sea.[172]

A special group within this category is formed by maritime handbooks that picture islands in the Mediterranean Sea as well as fortresses and ports along its coasts. In the early tenth / sixteenth century the sailor and later admiral of the Ottoman fleet Pīrī Reʾīs (d. 963 / 1554f.) compiled his highly successful *Kitab-i bahriye* (Book of the sea). He dedicated the book in two variants to the

170 MS Paris, BNF, Arabe 2214, ff. 52b–53a. Jeremy Johns and Emilie Savage-Smith, '*The book of curiosities*: A newly discovered series of Islamic maps', *Imago Mundi*, 55 (2003); Edson and Savage-Smith, *Medieval views of the cosmos*, p. 92, fig. 46, p. 94, fig. 47, p. 96, fig. 48, p. 98, fig. 49.

171 Sezgin, *Mathematische Geographie und Kartographie*, vol. X, pp. 300–15, vol. XI, pp. 13–26; Svat Soucek, 'Islamic charting in the Mediterranean', in Harley and Woodward (eds.), *Cartography in the traditional Islamic and South Asian societies*, pp. 263–5.

172 Sonja Brentjes, 'Revisiting Catalan portolan charts: Do they contain elements of Asian provenance?', in Philippe Forêt and Andreas Kaplony (eds.), *The journey of maps and images on the Silk Road*, Brill's Inner Asian Library 21 (Leiden and Boston, 2008), pp. 186–98.

Ottoman sultans Selīm I (r. 918–26/1512–20) and Süleymān (926–74/1520–66).[173] A few other, partly anonymous, Ottoman maritime handbooks and collections of maps of the Mediterranean, the Aegean and the Black Sea are extant from the tenth/sixteenth or eleventh/seventeenth century. The names of their authors, such as Ali Macar Reis (d. 980/1571?) or Mehmet Reis (*fl. c.* 999/1590f.), confirm that they too were linked to the Ottoman naval forces.[174]

The last category consists of maps that visualise towns or parts of towns such as buildings or gardens. Maps of towns can be found occasionally in early manuscripts such as the map of al-Mahdiyya in the anonymous Fāṭimid manuscript.[175] Most maps of towns known from Islamic societies, however, illustrate Ottoman and Mughal books on military campaigns and dynastic histories or are visual expressions of planned or ongoing sieges and battles.[176] Maps of buildings and gardens are mostly architectural plans. They had been sketched in the ʿAbbāsid period. They appear to have been used as a regular architects' tool from the Tīmūrid dynasty.[177]

The boundaries between these broad classes of maps made were fairly flexible. Numerous global, regional and local maps show traces from other mapping cultures. The formation of hybrids was a lively cross-cultural practice in a number of Islamic societies. The Fāṭimid maps combine Ptolemaic features with the symbolism of the Balkhī tradition, al-Khwārizmī's map of the Nile and the rectangular subdivisions in al-Dimashqī's book.[178] The world map for Iskandar Sulṭān merges the symbolism of the Balkhī tradition with a displaced symbolic line of longitude degrees, Chinese mountains and a focus on the Tīmūrid world. The world map in a non-mathematical treatise on timekeeping (dated 697/1210f.) ascribed to a certain Sirāj al-Dīn wa'l-Dunyā, identified by King with the well-known legal scholar Sirāj al-Dīn Muḥammad ibn Muḥammad al-Sajāwandī (*fl. c.* 597/1200), appears to position its cities and towns in a rectangular coordinate system. Due to its errors and deviations from scientific astronomy, King considers the map a distorted copy of an

173 Svat Soucek, *Piri Reis and Turkish mapmaking after Columbus: The Khalili portolan atlas* (London, 1995); Soucek, 'Islamic charting in the Mediterranean', pp. 265–79.

174 Soucek, *Piri Reis and Turkish mapmaking*, pp. 10–33; Svat Soucek, 'The 'Ali Macar Reis atlas' and the Deniz kitabı: Their place in the genre of portolan charts and atlases', *Imago Mundi*, 25 (1971); Soucek, 'Islamic charting in the Mediterranean', pp. 279–87.

175 Edson and Savage-Smith, *Medieval views of the cosmos*, p. 91, fig. 45.

176 Blair and Bloom, *The art and architecture of Islam*, figs. 3, 268, 306.

177 Lisa Golombek and Donald Wilber, *The Timurid architecture of Iran and Turan*, 2 vols. (Princeton, 1988), vol. I, pp. 138–9, 211.

178 Edson and Savage-Smith, *Medieval views of the cosmos*, pp. 79–80, fig. 39, p. 82, fig. 40.

original world map of the first category to which Sirāj al-Dīn wa'l-Dunyā added elements of traditional non-mathematical astronomy.[179] As Ottoman versions of translated Latin maps from Gerhard Mercator's *Atlas minor* (edition by Henricus Hondius, Arnheim 1622) indicate, men of different origin and background often collaborated in the production of cartographic hybrids. The scholar and scribe of the Ottoman army Ḥājjī Khalīfa (Kātib Çelebi, d. 1069/1658) worked together with Mehmed Ikhlāṣī, a convert, possibly of French origin, in this translation. But it was members of Istanbul workshops – calligraphers and painters – who produced fully Ottomanised and occasionally even modernised editions of the copies of Mercator's maps, badly transliterated and executed without much care by the two scholars. The maps attached to Ḥājjī Khalīfa's *Cihānnumā* (Version 2) as produced in the first half of the twelfth/eighteenth century in an Istanbul workshop replaced all transliterations with local names, privileged manual precision over the application of instruments and treated maps as part of the text, analogous with miniatures.[180]

The sciences and the arts

Art historians have argued for several decades that illustrated Hellenistic and Byzantine scientific works are one of the most important roots of painting as practised in the ʿAbbāsid and Fāṭimid empires, although Hoffmann underlined that the beginnings of illustrations in Arabic manuscripts in general remain rather uncertain.[181] Additionally, Coptic and Syriac church painting offered important artistic styles and techniques that were used by Christian artists

179 David A. King, 'A world-map in the tradition of al-Bīrūnī (ca. 1040) and al-Khāzinī (ca. 1120) presented by Sirāj al-Dīn al-Sajāwandī (1210)', in Frank Daelemans, Jean-Marie Duvosquel, Robert Halleux and David Juste (eds.), *Mélanges offerts à Hossam Elkhadem par ses amis et ses élèves*, Archives et bibliothèques de Belgique/Archief- en bibliotheekwezen in België, Numéro spécial/Extranummer 83 (Brussels, 2007), pp. 136–42, 155.

180 Sonja Brentjes, 'Multilingualism in early modern maps', in Daelemans *et al.* (eds.), *Mélanges offerts à Hossam Elkhadem*, pp. 320–2.

181 See, for instance, Kurt Weitzmann, 'The Greek sources of Islamic scientific illustrations', in George C. Miles (ed.), *Archaeologia orientalia: In memoriam Ernst Herzfeld* (Locust Valley, NY, 1952); D. S. Rice, 'The oldest illustrated Arabic manuscript', *BSOAS*, 22, 1/3 (1959), p. 207. The assumptions that inform the thesis, however, seem to be outdated, to say the least, in the sense that they reserve most, if not all, aspects of active and innovative work to ancient Greek and medieval Byzantine authors, copyists and patrons, while putting Arabic, Iranian, Turkic and other writers, painters and sponsors from Islamic societies on the lesser level of imitators. See, for instance, Weitzmann, 'The Greek sources', pp. 249, 251–2; Eva Rose F. Hoffman, 'The emergence of illustration in Arabic manuscripts: Classical legacy and Islamic

working for a Muslim ruler and his court, and were imitated by their Muslim colleagues.[182] The translation of illustrated Greek or Syriac scientific texts was not limited merely to the text, but included the illustrations.[183] An example where the history of the textual transmission and the extant Greek codices seem to support such a claim is Dioscorides' *Materia medica*. According to Grube all extant Greek manuscripts contain Arabic marginalia that comment on both the text and the illustrations.[184] According to Ibn Juljul (fl. 372/982) the Umayyad caliph of al-Andalus ʿAbd al-Raḥmān III (r. 300–50/912–61) received a lavishly illustrated copy of Dioscorides' book that was used to correct and supplement the earlier Arabic translation of Stephanos (second/ninth century).[185] And Ibn Abī Uṣaybiʿa claims that his compatriot Rashīd al-Dīn ibn al-Manṣūr (d. *c*. 640/1243), inspired by an illustrated Arabic manuscript of the *Materia medica*, invited a painter to join him when he travelled to observe and collect medicinal plants. The painter's task was to produce coloured images of the observed plants for a later illustrated book on drugs.[186]

At the same time, art historians also suggest that scientific manuscripts produced in Islamic societies constitute at best a minor and less vigorous part of the art of the book in Turkic languages, Arabic and Persian.[187] The

transformation', Ph.D. thesis, Harvard University (1982), p. 14; Eva R. Hoffman, 'The beginnings of the illustrated Arabic book: An intersection between art and scholarship', *Muqarnas*, 17 (2000).

182 Hoffman, 'The emergence of illustration', p. 29. A different view has been offered by Ward, who rather sees contemporary Syriac manuscript art influenced by innovation in Artuqid court art: Rachel Ward, 'Evidence for a school of painting at the Artuqid court', in Julian Raby (ed.), *The art of Syria and the Jazīra 1100–1250* (Oxford, 1985), p. 80. Nassar, moreover, points to the concurrent presence of stylistic elements of Byzantine and Saljūq origin in most of the illustrated manuscripts extant from the sixth/twelfth and seventh/thirteenth centuries, whether Arabic or Syriac: Nahla Nassar, 'Saljuq or Byzantine: Two related styles of Jazīran miniature painting', in Raby (ed.), *The art of Syria and the Jazīra 1100–1250*, pp. 86–8, 92–3, 96–7. She concludes that this interchangeable use of motifs of diverse provenance and the appearance of the same motifs in Jazīran metalwork implies the emergence of 'a single school of painting, albeit of a markedly eclectic character … The artists were inspired by Byzantine and Saljuq art, no doubt, but they changed, mixed and added to these borrowed elements to create a new style of their own' (p. 97).

183 Hoffman, 'The emergence of illustration', pp. 98, 100, 111–14.

184 Ernst J. Grube, 'Materialien zum Dioskurides Arabicus', in Richard Ettinghausen (ed.), *Aus der Welt der islamischen Kunst: Festschrift für Ernst Kühnel zum 75. Geburtstag am 26.10.1957* (Berlin, 1959), p. 166.

185 Ibid., p. 168.

186 Ibid., p. 169.

187 See, for instance, Rice, 'The oldest illustrated Arabic manuscript', p. 207. A very similar point of view was expressed by Anna Contadini in her paper at the Arab Painting: Text and Image in Illustrated Arabic Manuscripts conference, SOAS, London, 17 and 18 September 2004.

relationship between the arts and the sciences in Islamic societies was, however, more complex than these views suggest. Mediterranean pre-Islamic arts and sciences were not the only sources of inspiration. Pre-Islamic Iranian and Central Asian arts brought their own share, as did, after the Sāmānid and Qarakhānid dynasties, Chinese and Turkic artists.[188] The sciences showed a great variability in their involvement in the process of illustration. The kind of illustrations added to a scientific text also differed substantially. Mathematical, astronomical and magical texts often contain only diagrams, which were not perceived as art. Exceptions are ʿAbd al-Raḥmān al-Ṣūfī's star catalogue *Kitāb ṣuwar al-kawākib al-thābita* (The book of constellations) and a Ṣafavid copy of Quṭb al-Dīn al-Shīrāzī's work on planetary theory, *al-Tuḥfa al-shāhiyya*. They share their spheres of production and readership with works that contain only very few diagrams, such as works on natural history, agriculture and mechanics. Such texts are often adorned by series of images of individual animals, plants, astrological signs, marvels, monsters or machines. The various pictorial sequences that illustrate Arabic, Persian, and Turkic copies and translations, for instance of Abū Zakariyyaʾ al-Qazwīnī's *ʿAjāʾib al-makhlūqāt wa-gharāʾib al-mawjūdāt* (The wonders of creation and strange things in existence) indicate the vivacious processes of adapting the text and its images to the taste, interest and scientific outlook of a particular court and its surrounding culture.[189] Books on medicine, pharmacy and astrology could be even more lavishly illustrated. Those from the seventh/thirteenth century often carry frontispieces and so-called portraits of authors that are comparable to those adorning books on literature. Examples are the well-known images of the Pseudo-Galenic *Kitāb al-diryāq* or Dioscorides' *Materia medica* produced for rulers of local dynasties in Central Asia

188 Chinese paintings and painters are said to have been present at the Sāmānid court in the form of maps, royal portraits and images adorning Rūdakī's versification of the fables of *Kalīla wa-Dimna*. See, for instance, Vladimir Minorsky, 'The older preface to the Shāh-nāma', in *Studi orientalistici in onore di Giorgio Levi della Vida*, 2 vols. (Rome, 1956), vol. II, p. 168. Manichaean and shamanist elements are discussed in Emel Esin, 'An angel figure in the miscellany album H.2152 of Topkapi', in Oktay Aslanapa (ed.), *Beiträge zur Kunstgeschichte Asiens: In memoriam Ernst Diez*, Istanbul Üniversitesi Edebiyat Fakültesi, Sanat Tarihi Enstitüsü 1 (Istanbul, 1963).

189 Karin Rührdanz, 'Populäre Naturkunde illustriert: Text und Bild in persischen *ʿAjāʾib*-Handschriften spätjala'iridischer und frühtimuridischer Zeit', *Studia Iranica*, 34 (2005); Karin Rührdanz, 'Illustrated Persian *ʿajāʾib al-makhlūqāt* manuscripts and their function in early modern times', in A. J. Newman (ed.), *Society and culture in the early modern Middle East* (Leiden, 2003); Karin Rührdanz, 'Qazwīnī's *ʿajāʾib al-makhlūqāt* in illustrated Timurid manuscripts', in M. Szuppe (ed.), *Iran: Questions et connaissances, Actes du IVe Congrès Européen des Études Iraniennes, Paris 1999*, vol. II: *Périodes médiévale et modern*, *Studia Iranica*, Cahiers 26 (Paris, 2002).

and Iraq.[190] In the following centuries producers of illustrated medical, pharmaceutical and astrological manuscripts applied calligraphy, geometrical ornaments and other forms of artful divisions of space to give for instance Abu 'l-Ḥasan Ibn Buṭlān's (d. 458/1066) *Taqwīm al-siḥḥa* (The regime of health) the same artistic appearance as texts on religion, the occult arts and wisdom sayings.[191] Mamlūk society encouraged illustrations of botanical and other texts, while painting animals seems to have been discouraged in some scholarly circles, as implied by an act of self-censorship by Ibn Faḍl Allāh al-ʿUmarī (d. 749/1349) in Damascus.[192] In Ilkhānid, Tīmūrid and Ṣafavid Iran elaborate decorations of cover pages, titles and margins were applied indiscriminately to works on religion, literature, medicine and science. Copies of Ibn Sīnā's magisterial work *al-Qānūn fī l-ṭibb* (The law of medicine) produced in this mode show the same style of artistic decoration as manuscripts of the Qurʾān.[193] The Ottoman art of the book applied such decorative style also to mathematical works as Euclid's *Elements*. An example is the Ottoman manuscript Valide Turhan 217 in the Süleymaniye Library, which is dated 893/1487. It was in the possession of a physician before it came into Turhan's library.[194] Books on geography and cartography are mostly illustrated by world maps, regional maps, town plans and diagrams for the determination of the *qibla*. The maps' integration into different disciplinary contexts shaped their appearance and artistic quality. Maps in works on *ʿilm al-hayʾa* are often drawn freehand with little attention to exactitude in either form or content. Their attention is on geographical coordinates, the size of the Earth's circumference and the seven climates. Often it appears to have been of a symbolic nature rather than an exercise of practised science. In contrast, maps in works linked with trade, travel, postal routes, marvels and cultural contest show a broad range of pictorial styles, although their main geographical language, as a rule, does not alter very much. The Persian

190 Grube, 'Materialien zum Dioskurides Arabicus', pp. 169–80; Eva R. Hoffman, 'The author portrait in thirteenth-century Arabic manuscripts: A new Islamic context for a Late-Antique tradition', *Muqarnas*, 10 (1993).

191 *À l'ombre d'Avicenne: La médecine au temps des califes* (Paris, 1996), pp. 194, 236. Three magnificent copies illustrated one or two hundred years after the author's death are MSS London, BL, Or 1347, 2793 and 5590. A Persian translation was made probably in the middle of the seventh/thirteenth century and illustrated at the end of Ilkhānid rule in 732/1332: A.J. Arberry, M. Minovi, E. Blochet and J.V.S. Wilkinson (eds.), *The Chester Beatty Library. A catalogue of the Persian manuscripts and miniatures*, 3 vols., vol. I: *MSS 101–150* (Dublin, 1959), p. 20, no. 108.

192 Bishr Farès, 'Un herbier arabe illustré du XIVe siècle', in Miles (ed.), *Archaeologia orientalia*, p. 86.

193 *À l'ombre d'Avicenne*, pp. 72, 120.

194 MS Istanbul, Süleymaniye Library, Valide Turhan 217, frontispiece.

geography *Kitāb al-aqālīm* (The book of climates) ascribed to Naṣīr al-Dīn al-Ṭūsī, but identified as a translation of al-Iṣṭakhrī's *Kitāb al-mamālik wa'l-masālik* (Book of principalities and roads), for instance, integrates famous prophets and religious stories.[195] The world map attached to one of Iskandar Sulṭān's anthologies takes up an element of Chinese landscape painting.[196] Maps to an Ottoman translation of Ibn Ḥawqal's *Kitāb ṣūrat al-arḍ* (Book of the image of the Earth) resemble miniatures in Ottoman histories and literary works more closely than Arabic versions of the work.[197]

Through the material, artistic and intellectual affiliation to the courts and their cultures, scientific manuscripts and their disciplinary knowledge became part of the courts' artistic, ideological and educational programmes. Art historians have shown that the illustrations of scientific texts patronised by three Tīmūrid rulers – Shāh Rukh (r. 807–50/1404–47), Iskandar Sulṭān and Ulugh Beg (r. 812–53/1409–49) – differed in style and breadth as a result of differences in personal taste, religious outlook, literary preference and political orientation.[198] The cultures of the courts also created new outlets for scientific and sub-scientific narrative and illustrative themes. After portraits of rulers and patrons became fashionable in Ilkhānid and Tīmūrid times, portraits of painters and scholars followed suit in Mughal and Ṣafavid arts. Naṣīr al-Dīn al-Ṭūsī drew the most attention of this kind of personified representation of the sciences.[199] Works of literature such as those by Abū Muḥammad Niẓāmī (d. *c.* 600/1202f?) not only expressed their authors' vast erudition in literature, religious sciences, philosophy, mathematics, astronomy, astrology or alchemy and their personal beliefs in an astrologically organised universe;[200] they also served as major carriers of illustrative forms such as miniatures, bordures or medallions. In the broad spectrum of themes that were covered in these illustrations, philosophy, medicine, alchemy, astronomy/astrology,

195 H. Mzik, 'al-Iṣṭaḫrī und seine Landkarten im Buch "Ṣuwar al-Akālīm" nach der persischen Handschrift Cod. Mixt. 344 der Österreichischen Nationalbibliothek', in R. Kinauer and S. Balic (eds.), *Veröffentlichung der Reihe Museion*, 6. Reihe, 1. Bd., Österreichische Nationalbibliothek (Vienna, 1965).

196 Lentz and Lowry (eds.), *Timur and the princely vision*, fig. 50; King, *World-maps*, p. 144.

197 MS Bologna, UB 3611, ff. 120a, 159a, 333a, 367a.

198 For a substantial discussion of these different orientations and their respective links to the sponsored arts and science see Lentz and Lowry (eds.), *Timur and the princely vision*, pp. 78, 84, 90, 94–5, 119.

199 Francis Richard, 'Les "portraits" de Naṣīr al-Dīn Ṭūsī', in N. Pourjavady and Ž. Vesel (eds.), *Naṣīr al-Dīn Ṭūsī: Philosophe et savant du XIIIe siècle* (Tehran, 2000), pp. 199–201, figs. 1–4.

200 Živa Vesel, 'Réminiscences de la magie astrale dans les *Haft Peykar* de Neẓāmī', *Studia Iranica*, 24 (1995).

the linkage of these sciences with Plato, Aristotle, Alexander and Mary and the supernatural power of sages over nature and her beasts were depicted time and again.[201]

The relationship between the arts and the sciences did not stop with manuscript and miniature production. Other materials such as silk, metal, pottery and stone were also used to produce objects of art that displayed scientific themes. Examples are maps, magic squares, medicinal cups, zodiacal signs, planets, the animals of the Turco-Chinese duodecimal calendar, the human representation of the micro- and macro-cosmos and naturalistic images of plants and animals. Maps produced on silk or metal were to be hung at palace walls of various dynasties ruling in Egypt, Sicily, Iran, Central Asia and Anatolia.[202] Some of them, such as the well-known work of Abū ʿAbd Allāh Muḥammad ibn Muḥammad al-Sharīf al-Idrīsī (d. 562/1166) and the little-known work of Muḥammad ibn Najīb Bakrān, were accompanied by textual descriptions and explanations that have survived to our time.[203] Tiles were used for mapping the *qibla*, Mecca and Medina. They were integrated into walls of libraries, palaces and private houses. The best-known exemplars are those produced in Iznik in the tenth/sixteenth and eleventh/seventeenth centuries.[204] Zodiacal signs, planets and the animals of the Turco-Chinese duodecimal calendar illustrated metal plates, coins, mirrors, pottery, bridges, citadels, churches and *madrasas* in greater Iran, northern Iraq, Anatolia and India during the Saljūq, Artuqid, Muẓaffarid, Ṣafavid and Mughal dynasties between the sixth/twelfth and eleventh/seventeenth centuries.[205] They were means of expressing loyalties, establishing legitimacy, declaring the

201 See, for instance, Norah M. Titley, *Miniatures from Persian manuscripts: A catalogue and subject index of paintings from Persia, India and Turkey in the British Library and the British Museum* (London, 1977).

202 Examples are the anonymous silk maps for the Fāṭimid caliph al-Muʿizz (r. 341–65/52–975) and his successors; al-Idrīsī's map on silver for the Norman king of Sicily, Roger II (d. 1154); Muḥammad ibn Najīb Bakrān's map on silk made for the *khwārazmshāh* ʿAlāʾ al-Dīn Muḥammad (r. 596–617/1199–1220); Aḥmad ibn Muḥammad al-Sijzī's globe of the universe, including the heavens and the Earth, possibly made before 359/969 in Sīstān (MS Dublin, Chester Beatty 3562, fo. 17b; see al-Sijzī, *Treatise on geometrical problem solving*, p. viii); and anonymous Ottoman silk maps (twelfth/eighteenth century) in the Topkapı Palace and the Archaeological Museum, Istanbul.

203 Carsten Drecoll, *Idrísí aus Sizilien: Der Einfluß eines arabischen Wissenschaftlers auf die Entwicklung der europäischen Geographie* (Egelsbach, Frankfurt am Main, Munich and New York, 2000).

204 J. P. Roux (ed.), *L'Islam dans les collections nationales* (Paris, 1977), p. 116, nos. 210–21.

205 Katharina Otto-Dorn, 'Darstellungen des Turco-Chinesischen Tierzyklus in der islamischen Kunst', in O. Aslanapa (ed.), *Beiträge zur Kunstgeschichte Asiens*, pp. 131–65; Nicholas Lowick, 'The religious, the royal and the popular in the figural coinage of the Jazīra', in J. Raby (ed.), *The art of Syria and the Jazīra 1100–1250*, pp. 159–74.

independent status of an individual ruler, influencing fate, honouring courtiers and eternalising private feelings, mostly love to a wife.[206] The use of the human body to express the intimate relationship between the sub- and supralunar worlds according to ancient Greek philosophical cosmology was not widespread in the iconographic repertoire of the arts in Islamic societies. It is found in a miniature preserved at the Wellcome Institute for the History of Medicine in London and on a single plate preserved in the Victoria and Albert Museum in London, which is thought to have belonged originally to an astronomical instrument produced in eleventh/seventeenth-century Ṣafavid Iran. The iconography of the two images differs substantially. The first strongly resembles the anatomical illustrations of Manṣūr ibn Ilyā's (*fl. c.* 782–93/1380–90) *Tashrīḥ-i badan-i insān* (The anatomy of the human body) as far as the human body is concerned.[207] Its zodiacal signs show all important features of the Near and Middle Eastern iconography of these signs, such as the Sun rising on the back of the lion or Sagittarius shooting backwards on a lion's body at a dragon's head at the end of the lion's tail.[208] The zodiacal man on the Ṣafavid copper plate resembles a Renaissance drawing and is flanked by naked women. It is a sign of the local integration of knowledge elements from Christian cultures in Europe by Ṣafavid artisans, artists, merchants and scholars during the eleventh/seventeenth century.[209] Naturalistic images of plants and animals can be found in miniature paintings within manuscripts and albums of individual leaves produced in the Ottoman, Ṣafavid, Mughal and Qājār dynasties between the tenth/sixteenth and thirteenth/nineteenth centuries.[210] Mughal fortresses and tombs integrated this taste for the naturalistic in their ornamentation.[211] There is, however, no study that investigates the kind of knowledge about plants and animals that the

206 For an autograph copy of this work see Sotheby's *Oriental manuscripts and miniatures* (London, Wednesday 18 October 1995), p. 43, no. 51.

207 See www.nlm.nih.gov/hmd/arabic/bioM.html; Andrew Newman, 'Tashrīḥ-i Manṣūrī: Human anatomy between the Galenic and prophetical medical traditions', in Ž. Vesel, H. Beikbaghan and B. Thierry de Crussol des Epesse (eds.), *La science dans le monde iranien à l'époche islamique* (Tehran, 1998).

208 *À l'ombre d'Avicenne*, p. 188; A. U. Pope and P. Ackerman, *A survey of Persian art*, 6 vols. (London and New York, 1939), vol. V, plates 511–908, also plates 712, 713, 1301, 1312, 1314, 1317, 1328, 1336.

209 Victoria and Albert Museum, London, Ex. No. 209.

210 Amina Okada, *Indian miniatures of the Mughal court* (New York, n.d.), pp. 216–25; Dorothea Duda, *Islamische Handschriften I: Persische Handschriften Tafelband* (Vienna, 1983), pp. 193–4; Stuart Cary Welch and the Metropolitan Museum of Art, *The Islamic world* (New York, 1987), p. 111, no. 82.

211 Blair and Bloom, *The art and architecture of Islam*, figs. 346, 351.

painters acquired in their training and how it related to written compendia of botanical and zoological knowledge.

A third major locus where the arts and the sciences met was architecture. Although some historians of art and architecture deny that there was any substantial exchange of knowledge and skills between architects and mathematicians due to social barriers in training and practice, many others, as well as historians of mathematics, believe otherwise.[212] However, ideas vary considerably about where the exchange of knowledge and skills took place and what kind of knowledge and skills were discussed and passed on. Özdurgal, for instance, argues on the basis of remarks in mathematical treatises that individual mathematicians in the fourth/tenth, sixth/twelfth, ninth/fifteenth and eleventh/seventeenth centuries in Baghdad, Nīshāpūr, Samarqand and Istanbul met at least once, if not more frequently, with artisans. While the artisans who met with Abu 'l-Wafā' and ʿUmar al-Khayyām worked on ornaments and serial patterns and the scientists met with them to discuss the soundness of their methods, to teach them correct geometrical knowledge by cut-and-paste and to find solutions for problems raised by the artisans, Ghiyāth al-Dīn Jamshīd al-Kāshī (d. 833/1429) visited the actual building site of the new observatory in Samarqand and lent a hand when a problem arose regarding a levelling instrument. Caʿfer Efendi (eleventh/seventeenth century), in contrast, seems to have participated in such meetings over a period of twenty years, and compiled a treatise based on notes he took during these meetings.[213] Obviously, the quantity and quality of the exchange as well the subject matter differed quite remarkably. Golombek and Wilber, following previous Soviet scholarship on Central Asian architectural remains from the Tīmūrid period, see the relationship between mathematics and architecture in this period as one that took place mainly in the youth and early adulthood of those who aspired to become successful architects of princes – they studied all the sciences offered in their society. The exemplar, praised in Tīmūrid literature as excelling in engineering/geometry, design and architecture, but also skilled in composing calendars, is Qavvām al-Dīn Shīrāzī (d. 842/1438 or 844/1440).[214] Hence, the leading architect of a building project himself seems to have applied geometrical, technical and artistic knowledge in the process of designing and erecting the building, the systemic components of which Golombek

212 Jonathan Bloom expressed this view in a paper given in Zurich in April 2004.

213 Alpay Özdural, 'Mathematics and arts: Connections between theory and practice in the medieval Islamic world', *Historia Mathematica*, 27 (2000), pp. 171–2ff.

214 Golombek and Wilber, *Timurid architecture*, vol. I, pp. 189–90.

and Wilber describe as analytic and geometric.[215] The content of the first component is to determine modules from which the individual rooms and their various elements will be constructed. The content of the second is to choose 'a single generative unit according to a set of rules derived from geometry' and to ensure the application of correct geometrical proportions.[216] As for works that also treat architectural problems by scholars specialised in the mathematical sciences such as Ghiyāth al-Dīn al-Kāshī, a comparison of preserved Tīmūrid architecture and its elements with al-Kāshī's discussion of various arches, vaults, domes and *muqarnas* led Golombek and Wilber to the conclusion that this treatise is not a comprehensive mirror of actual architectural practice, but rather a kind of idealising summary.[217] Dold-Samplonius, in contrast, argues that the calculations taught in Arabic and Persian manuals of practical mathematics in regard to architecture served primarily to appraise the needed labour and building materials.[218] She considers al-Kāshī to be the mathematician who achieved the most accomplished explanations and calculations of basic elements of Islamic architecture. She sees his solutions as reflecting a well-developed skill in finding approximations suitable for practical purposes.[219] In reply to Golombek and Wilber, Dold-Samplonius emphasises that their comparative question is at odds with al-Kāshī's self-expressed purpose of calculating volumes and surfaces. According to her interpretation, al-Kāshī did not mean to assist architects in their daily business. He rather aimed to ease the life of a professional calculator by providing him with elegant approximations that simplified the calculations.[220] A third view was pronounced by Necipoğlu. In her book on a set of architectural drawings (the so-called Topkapi scroll), made, as she argues, by Tīmūrid–Turcoman architects in the ninth/fifteenth or tenth/sixteenth century, she sees the tasks of the head architect as consisting primarily in working out designs on paper that describe the geometrical patterns for surfaces, the arrangement of architectural elements and ground plans based on geometrical modules.[221] These drawings and plans lack scale and numerical values. Their translation into

215 Ibid., pp. 138–9, 211.
216 Ibid., p. 211.
217 Ibid., p. 156.
218 Yvonne Dold-Samplonius, 'Calculating surface areas and volumes in Islamic architecture', in Jan P. Hogendijk and Abdelhamid I. Sabra (eds.), *The enterprise of science in Islam: New perspectives* (Cambridge, MA, and London, 2003), p. 237.
219 Ibid., p. 246.
220 Ibid.
221 Gülru Necipoğlu, *The Topkapı Scroll: Geometry and ornament in Islamic architecture: Topkapı Palace Museum Library MS H 1956*, with an essay on the geometry of the *muqarnas* by Mohammad al-Asad (Santa Monica, 1995), p. 50.

concrete buildings did not take place through calculations and precise geometrical constructions, but rather followed procedures of adjustment according to rules of thumb.[222] The calculation of cost estimates and the final financial evaluation Necipoğlu sees as in the hands of an overseer.[223]

Magic, medicine and mathematics

Magic, often regarded as either an occult science or a base art, as either evil or false, and while fought against by the Prophet Muḥammad and Sunnī mainstream scholars, never disappeared from Islamic societies. Rather, it was one of the spheres where beliefs and practices from various Asian and African tribal and urban cultures entered the realm of Islam as a religion. Several writers, such as Maslama ibn Qāsim al-Qurṭubī (d. 353/964), Aḥmad al-Būnī (d. 622/1225) or ʿAbd al-Raḥmān al-Bisṭāmī (d. 858/1454), saw magic as the all-encompassing fundamental knowledge of the open and secret worlds that drew from rational as well as spiritual sources. Sufis in the ʿAbbāsid period such as al-Ḥallāj (d. 309/922) developed the art of *karāmāt*, special wonders performed by an individual friend of God through divine grace. Battles in al-Andalus were fought under the leadership of men who performed *karāmāt*.[224] Legal scholars and *mutakallimūn* such as Ibn Abī Zayd al-Qayrawānī (d. 386/996), writing against these non-prophetic wonders, rejected them as mere magic, as the work of sorcerers and soothsayers.[225] Others taught that a magician is an apostate and thus needed to be punished by death. A third group accepted magic as an acceptable practice for Muslims as long as it did not lead to death for a client and was carried out with true belief in God Almighty.[226] The permeation of *kalām* by philosophy led to a stable linkage between miracles, magic, the theory of prophecy and the theory of the rational soul.[227] Astrological and magical practices were regarded as

222 Ibid., p. 44.

223 She does not clarify, however, whether she means the head architect or another person involved in the process: ibid.

224 Maribel Fierro, 'The polemic about the karāmāt al-awliyāʾ and the development of Sufism in al-Andalus (fourth/tenth–fifth/eleventh centuries)', *BSOAS*, 55, 2 (1992), pp. 246–7; Maribel Fierro, 'Opposition to Sufism in al-Andalus', in Frederick de Jong and Bernd Radtke (eds.), *Islamic mysticism contested: Thirteen centuries of controversies and polemics* (Leiden, Boston and Cologne, 1999), p. 177.

225 Fierro, 'The polemic about the karāmāt al-awliyāʾ', p. 238.

226 See, for instance, Kātib Çelebī, *Keşf-el-ẓunūn*, 2 vols. (Istanbul, 1943), vol. II, cols. 1137–8: *ʿilm al-ʿazāʾim*.

227 See, for instance, Ibn Khaldūn's (d. 808/1406) discussion of prophecy, soothsaying, sorcery and magic: Ibn Khaldūn, *al-Muqaddimah: An introduction to history*, trans. Franz Rosenthal, 3 vols., 2nd edn (Princeton, 1980), vol. I, pp. 184–226, vol. III, pp. 156–70.

threatening in Mamlūk Syria. *Muwaqqits* were seen by orthodox scholars such as Ibn Qayyim al-Jawziyya (d. 751/1350) or Tāj al-Dīn al-Subkī (d. 771/1369) as practitioners of these illicit arts who violated the standards of good religion and good science at the same time.[228] Adherence to magic and astrology was not confined to popular culture and some stray *muwaqqits*. Several dynasties such as the Almohads (524–667/1130–1269), the Artuqids (495–811/1101–1408), the Muẓaffarids (713–95/1313–93), the Tīmūrids, the Ottomans and the Ṣafavids were deeply committed to belief in horoscopes and the magical properties of letters, numbers and signs. After the Almohads had conquered al-Andalus they coined quadratic money carrying magical signs and meaning.[229] Muẓaffarid and Artuqid rulers paid for magical mirrors and magical tablets made from precious metal.[230] Iskandar Sulṭān and other Tīmūrid princes ordered artfully designed horoscopes at important moments in their careers.[231] Ottoman sultans wore magic shirts in battle or when performing courtly rituals.[232] The Ṣafavid shah Ṭahmāsp (r. 930–84/1524–76) sponsored the lavish illustration of a *fālnāme*, a book on a branch of divination.[233] The Mughal ruler Jahāngīr (r. 1014–37/1605–28) asked his ambassador to Shāh ʿAbbās I (r. 995–1038/1587–1629) to bring the shah's horoscope in order to determine his political outlook and military strength.[234]

Besides the contributions of philosophy and *kalām* to the debates on miracles and magic, two other sciences, mathematics and medicine, delivered theories, methods and tools for creating magical objects, and used magical devices and invocations in their dealings with patients. Divinatory techniques served for determining the kind of disease a patient was afflicted by and the kind of therapy that would heal her. Bowls and amulets adorned by Qurʾānic verses, magic squares, the seal of Solomon and mysterious letters served for

228 John W. Livingston, 'Science and the occult in the thinking of Ibn Qayyim al-Jawziyya', *JAOS*, 112, 4 (1992).

229 Maribel Fierro, 'La magia en al-Andalus', in A. Pérez Jiménez and G. Cruz Andreotti (eds.), *Daímon Páredros: Magos y prácticas mágicas en el mundo mediterráneo* (Madrid and Málaga, 2002), pp. 270–3.

230 Douglas Barnett, *Islamic metalwork in the British Museum* (London, 1949), plates 16 and 17; A. Mazaharie, *Der Iran und seine Kunstschätze: Albert Skira, Die Kunstschätze der Welt* (Geneva, 1970), p. 207; Abolala Soudavar, *Art of the Persian courts: Selections from the Art and History Trust Collection* (New York, 1992), p. 46, no. 17.

231 Lentz and Lowry (eds.), *Timur and the princely vision.*

232 Maddison and Savage-Smith, *Body and spirit*, pp. 117–18.

233 See www.parstimes.com/events/hunt_paradise.html.

234 Sanjay Subrahmanyam, 'An infernal triangle: Portuguese, Mughals and Safavids in the first decade of the reign of Shah Abbas I', *Iran and the World in the Safavid Age* (London, 4–7 September 2002), available at www.iranheritage.com/safavidconference/soas/abstract45.htm.

preparing and administering drugs for the sick. Magic healing was very influential in Egypt and Syria in the sixth/twelfth century under the rule of the Zangids (521–631/1127–1234) and Ayyūbids. It is from this time that the earliest magic-medicinal bowls are preserved and occasionally ascribed to princes of the ruling dynasties such as Nūr al-Dīn ibn Zangī (541–69/1146–73) and Saladin.[235] Several inscriptions on such bowls to an ʿAbbāsid caliph in Baghdad as well as to Ayyūbid, Mamlūk and Rasūlid rulers in Egypt, Syria and Yemen are obvious fakes. They were probably added to lend the bowls greater authority. While the first extant magic-medicinal bowls were produced for and in Sunnī communities, later centuries saw a special interest among Shīʿite communities in Iran, India and perhaps also South-East Asia for such bowls. There were even workshops in China, with artisans whose knowledge of Arabic letters and numbers was at best mediocre, but who produced magic-medicinal bowls for export to Muslim lands.[236]

The mathematical sciences contributed theories and methods of constructing magic squares and determining amicable numbers to the arsenal of the magicians from the third/ninth century. Major mathematicians such as Thābit ibn Qurra, Abu ʾl-Wafāʾ, Ibn al-Haytham or Kamāl al-Dīn al-Fārisī contributed to the evolution of sophisticated mathematical theories of amicable numbers and magic squares. The latter was called *ʿilm wafq al-ʿadad* (knowledge of the harmonious arrangement of numbers). Both theories have their origins in definitions, theorems and rules formulated, proven or explained through examples in Euclid's *Elements* and Nicomachus' *Introduction to arithmetic*.[237] On this basis, Thābit ibn Qurra established the first proven theorem for finding a pair of even amicable numbers, which was taken up by a multitude of later writers across different disciplines and creeds.[238] Many of them only repeated Thābit's rule and gave a few examples. Some legal scholars teaching mathematical sciences and medicine at *madrasas*, such as Ibn Fallūs (d. 637/1239) in Ayyūbid Damascus, searched for amicable numbers in each decimal power and calculated many correct, but also wrong, pairs.[239] Others, such as Kamāl al-Dīn al-Fārisī, carried out profound theoretical research, developing new

235 Maddison and Savage-Smith, *Body and spirit*, p. 61.

236 Ibid., pp. 76–8, 88–102.

237 See Sesiano, *Un traité médiéval*, pp. 23–6.

238 Thābit proved a theorem equivalent to the following modern notation: For $n > 1$, let $p_n = 3.2^n - 1$ and $q_n = 9.2^{2n-1} - 1$. If p_{n-1}, p_n, and q_n are prime numbers, then $a = 2^n p_{n-1} p_n$ and $b = 2^n q_n$ are amicable numbers: Thābit ibn Qurra, *Kitāb al-aʿdād al-mutaḥābba*, ed. Aḥmad Saʿīdān (n.p., 1977), pp. 50–3.

239 Sonja Brentjes, 'The first seven perfect numbers and three types of amicable numbers in a manuscript on elementary number theory by Ibn Fallus', *Erdem*, 4 (1988).

concepts and applying tools from other mathematical fields such as algebra to find a new and shorter proof for Thābit's theorem.[240]

ʿIlm wafq al-ʿadād sorts magic squares into two main classes: magic squares filled with consecutive numbers; and those filled with non-consecutive numbers. The first class differentiates between squares of uneven, even, even times uneven and even times even times uneven order. Further subcategories include squares with borders or squares where even and uneven numbers are placed in compartments.[241] The second class reduces numbers in arithmetic progression to the first class and turns then to numbers in irregular progression. Here the issue is to finish filling a square of given size after a subset of its cells has been inscribed by such numbers.[242] Diverse methods to construct magic squares of arbitrary size in each of these classes as developed by known and anonymous scholars are analysed by Sesiano.[243] The close mathematical as well as cultural relationship between the two types of theories led to their sharing common textual spaces. Treatises were written that combined chapters on properties of amicable, perfect and other numbers with subsequent sections on magic squares.[244] Authors of encyclopaedias and texts classifying the disciplines available or recommended for study included sections on or references to the two branches in close proximity.[245]

In the ninth/fifteenth and tenth/sixteenth centuries the cultural interest in these mathematical theories and methods was so widespread that the section on the harmonious arrangement of numbers from Shams al-Dīn al-Āmulī's encyclopaedia was included in one of the Persian translations of Zakariyyāʾ al-Qazwīnī's work, which had originally excluded all mathematical sciences except astronomy, astrology and optics. In the eleventh/seventeenth century Ḥājjī Khalīfa reported that all spheres of nature and many disciplines, including mathematics, astronomy and geography, contributed to the science of

240 Kamāl al-Dīn al-Fārisī, *Tadhkirat al-aḥbāb fī bayān al-taḥābb*, discussed in Roshdi Rashed, 'Nombres amiables, parties aliquotes et nombres figurés aux XIIIème et XIVème siècles', *Archive for History of Exact Sciences*, 28, 2 (1983); A. G. Agargün and Colin R. Fletcher, 'al-Farisi and the fundamental theorem of arithmetic', *Historia Mathematica*, 21, 2 (1994). The authors of these papers reach different conclusions in respect to what al-Fārisī did in his work and what the relationship may be between his theorems and theorems established in later centuries in Europe.

241 Sesiano, *Un traité médiéval*, pp. 27–83.

242 Ibid., pp. 84–125.

243 Sesiano, 'Herstellungsverfahren magischer Quadrate'; Sesiano, 'Une compilation arabe'.

244 Sesiano, 'Une compilation arabe'.

245 Examples are Fakhr al-Dīn al-Rāzī's (d. 606/1209) *Jāmiʿ al-ʿulūm*; Shams al-Dīn al-Akfānī's (d. 749/1348) *Irshād al-qāṣid*; Shams al-Dīn al-Āmulī's *Nafāʾis al-funūn*; and Shams al-Dīn al-Fanarī's (d. 839/1435) *Kitāb unmūdhaj al-ʿulūm*.

virtues and (special) properties. He named Kamāl al-Dīn al-Fārisī's purely mathematical treatise *Tadhkirat al-aḥbāb fī bayān al-taḥābb* (Memoir of lovers on the declaration of mutual love) as falling into this category and teaching the properties of amicable and inimical numbers.[246] Although the smallest pair of even amicable numbers 220, 284 was used on amulets, the magical application of larger pairs such as 17296, 18416 has not been attested yet. In contrast, the largest known calculated magic squares are part of three magic charts made during the Qājār dynasty in Iran. These squares consist of 100 rows and columns, i.e. 10,000 cells. Their magic number, i.e. the sum of each row, column and diagonal, is 500,050.[247] Other objects with magic squares were plaques, mirrors, shirts and amulets. Amulets and mirrors are extant from the seventh/thirteenth century. It is believed that the production and usage of magic mirrors started in Ilkhānid Iran among Sufis who venerated the twelve imams.[248] Talismanic shirts were in use among the Ottomans, Ṣafavids, Mughals, in West Africa among Hausas and Yorubas as well as on Java and other Indonesian islands. Ottoman sultans such as Selīm, princes such as Bāyazīd and grand viziers such as Qara Muṣṭafā Paşa wore them in war and ritual. Their shirts carry numerous magic squares of up to 20 rows and columns. Ṣafavid talismanic shirts are mostly anonymous and undated. They carry magic squares of even larger size (40 times 40). The shirts were considered to be bullet-proof vests, as Hürrem Sultan wrote to her husband Süleymān Qanuni in the 940s/1530s.[249] They also could serve medical purposes, provided one took a sweaty one previously worn by a sick person or by a woman in childbirth.[250] Protection against evil forces (demons, spirits, the evil eye) and the power to obtain love or gain political and social favour were also linked to shirts and undergarments decorated with magic squares, Qur'ānic verses, the 100 beautiful names of God, magic alphabets and other symbols.

Science and reform

For almost five hundred years Islamic scholarly cultures have mostly been downplayed, or their existence has been flatly denied. Most travellers from Italy, France, England, Germany, the United Provinces and the Habsburg

246 Kātib Çelebī, *Keşf-el-ẓunūn*, vol. II, cols. 725–6: *ʿilm al-khawāṣṣ*, col. 726.
247 Maddison and Savage-Smith, *Body and spirit*, p. 106.
248 Ibid., p. 125.
249 Ibid., p. 117.
250 Ibid., p. 118.

empire reported that no sciences or liberal arts existed in the Ottoman empire. The same travellers, however, acknowledged the existence of a lively scholarly culture in the Ṣafavid empire in Iran.[251] With regard to the Mughal empire and other Muslim or Hindu states in India the reports oscillated between condescending acknowledgement of some scholarly life, total silence and praise for medical and pharmaceutical knowledge.[252] The various stories told by these visitors from Catholic, Protestant and, later, secular European countries continue to influence the analysis of the historical evolution of different scientific cultures in Islamic societies in Asia and Africa. Only slowly, during the last two decades, have new methodological approaches with new questions started to emerge that allow for a more nuanced picture, one that does not see the main issue as being the fact that no scientific nor industrial revolutions took place in these societies.[253]

The relationship between science and reform in the Ottoman empire reflected the centralised as well as military nature of Ottoman rule, administration and institutions. Although substantial components of Ottoman society were decentralised and local, the efforts to reform certain of its aspects concentrated mainly on the capital, the army, the fleet and military institutions. Some disciplines, in particular medicine, mathematics, astronomy and cartography, were included in these efforts because they had been part of the education of the *devşirme* boys in the Palace School (Enderun). These disciplines also became part of the reform efforts because the Ottoman court included two scientific officials among its personnel – the *ḥekīm başı* (head physician) and the *münejjim başı* (head astrologer). These scientific officials and their subordinate colleagues had contributed since the tenth/sixteenth century, if not earlier, to the acquisition and appropriation of new medical knowledge from Jewish, Catholic and Protestant communities and institutions. The mixed composition of the body of Ottoman court physicians created favourable conditions for such cross-cultural activities. Several head physicians were Jewish refugees from Spain, Portugal or Italy. Christian physicians from Ottoman Greek and Armenian communities as well as from France, Italy and other Catholic or Protestant countries in Europe also served

251 Sonja Brentjes, 'Pride and prejudice: Some factors that shaped early modern (scholarly) encounters between "Western Europe" and the "Middle East"', in John Brooke and Ekmeleddin İhsanoğlu (eds.), *Religious values and the rise of science in Europe* (Istanbul, 2005).

252 Kate Teltscher, *India inscribed: European and British writing on India 1600–1800* (Delhi, 1997).

253 S. Irfan Habib and Dhruv Raina (eds.), *Situating the history of science: Dialogues with Joseph Needham* (Delhi, 1999).

at the Ottoman court. Most of the Jewish and Ottoman Christian physicians had studied medicine at Italian or Spanish and Portuguese universities. In the eleventh/seventeenth and twelfth/eighteenth centuries Muslim court physicians became actively involved in the transfer of medical knowledge. New diseases, treatments, drugs and anatomical illustrations were introduced. Before the reforms started in the early twelfth/eighteenth century this transfer of new medical knowledge was characterised by its immediate integration into newly composed texts without intermediary translations. Muṣṭafā Feyḍī's (d. 1084/1692) *Khamsa-yi ḥayātī* (Quintet of living beings), for instance, incorporates descriptions of new diseases and their treatments by physicians from Italy, France, Spain and Germany. It also gives information about research on medicinal plants imported from the Americas.[254]

Oral transmission of new knowledge also took place in astronomy and astrology. Reports by travellers such as John Greaves (1602–52) from Oxford or Ismaël Boulliau (1605–94) from Paris confirm that Arab and Turkish astronomers in Aleppo as well as educated Sufis in Istanbul were familiar with Nicolaus Copernicus' (1473–1543) and Tycho Brahe's (1546–1601) astronomical theories and books before the first Arabic and then Ottoman Turkish translation of a Latin astronomical and astrological handbook printed in Paris in 1635 was produced in the 1660s.[255] Manuscripts of the head astrologer Müneccimek Meḥmed Efendi (d. 1078/1667) as well as other texts show that astrological works from Catholic and Protestant Europe also circulated among Ottoman scholars in the capital.[256]

A similar practice characterised Ottoman use of geographical books and maps from Spain and Italy during the tenth/sixteenth and the first half of the eleventh/seventeenth centuries. It is in this disciplinary context that arguments were made to explain or justify the borrowing and assimilating of foreign knowledge from inimical cultures and countries. The arguments focused on the intensifying threat of Portuguese naval power in the Red Sea

254 Feza Günergun, 'Science in the Ottoman world', in G. N. Vlahakis, I. M. Malaquias, N. M. Brooks, F. Regourd, F. Günergun and D. Wright (eds.), *Imperialism and science: Social impact and interaction* (Santa Barbara, 2006).

255 Thomas Hyde, *Geographiae veteris scriptores Graeci minores: Accedunt geographica Arabica etc.*, 3 vols. (Oxford, 1712), vol. III, pp. 86–7. Sonja Brentjes, 'On the relationship between the Ottoman empire and the west European Republic of Letters (17th–18th centuries)', in Ali Çaksu (ed.), *International Congress on Learning and Education in the Ottoman World, Istanbul, 12–15 April 1999: Proceedings* (Istanbul, 2001), p. 139; Ekmeleddin İhsanoğlu, 'Introduction of Western science to the Ottoman world: A case study of modern astronomy (1660–1860)', in Ekmeleddin İhsanoğlu (ed.), *Transfer of modern science and technology to the Muslim world* (Istanbul, 1992).

256 MS Princeton, University Library, Yahuda 373.

and the Indian Ocean to the detriment of Ottoman interests and the well-being of the Muslim world at large. The study of geography was presented as one important means to protect these interests.[257] Translating Latin atlases into Ottoman Turkish became a major element in this process of cross-cultural learning in the eleventh/seventeenth and twelfth/eighteenth centuries. Ḥājjī Khalīfa and Abū Bakr ibn Bahrām al-Dimashqī (d. 1102/1691) cooperated with converts, Jesuits and Ottoman Greek scholars when translating Gerhard Mercator's (1512–94) *Atlas minor* and Willem Janszoon Blaeu's (1571–1638) and Joan Blaeu's (d. 1673) *Atlas maior*. Petros Baronian's (*fl.* 1151/1738) and ʿUthmān ibn ʿAbd al-Mannān al-Muhtadī's (d. 1200/1786) translations of French and Latin geographies confirm that members of minorities and converts continued to participate in the acquisition of foreign knowledge during the twelfth/eighteenth century.[258] This cross-cultural collaboration ensured that the more informal oral ways of accessing foreign knowledge remained a relevant practice. Geographical and philosophical books available in Istanbul's numerous libraries were perused for valuable information without being formally translated.[259] The results were included in new Ottoman Turkish compositions.

While Ḥājjī Khalīfa's geographical opus *Cihānnumā* (Version 2) is seen in current research as primarily a work of disinterested literary scholarship, there can be no doubt that his numerous writings were seen by himself, his friends and his successors as a contribution to the reform of Ottoman thought, if not politics.[260] Reform ideas were found within a circle of high-ranking Ottoman religious office-holders who challenged court behaviour on various levels. This circle wished to return to what had worked in the past without abandoning every novelty. They felt that such a restoration would bring order, stability and welfare for the whole.[261] İbrāhīm Müteferriqa (d. 1157/1744), who in 1145/1732 printed a revised and slightly augmented version of the *Cihānnumā*, went a step further. He declared Ottoman participation in the allegedly universally valid field of contemporary geography and cartography as one of

257 Thomas D. Goodrich, *The Ottoman Turks and the New World: A study of* Tarih-i Hind-i Garbi *and sixteenth-century Ottoman Americana* (Wiesbaden, 1990), pp. 351, 354.

258 Ekmeleddin İhsanoğlu (ed.), *Osmanlı coğrafya literatürü tarihi: History of geographical literature during the Ottoman period*, 2 vols. (Istanbul, 2000), vol. I, pp. 132–3; Ramazan Şeşen, 'The translator of the Belgrade Council Osman b. Abdulmannan', in İhsanoğlu (ed.), *Transfer of modern science and technology to the Muslim world*.

259 Gottfried Hagen, *Ein osmanischer Geograph bei der Arbeit: Entstehung und Gedankenwelt von Kātib Čelebis* Ǧihānnumā, Studien zur Sprache, Geschichte und Kultur der Turkvölker 4 (Berlin, 2003), pp. 190–6, 218, 228–31.

260 Ibid., pp. 248–51, 254–6.

261 Ibid., pp. 255–6.

his motives for printing the book. Likewise, the unfinished status of Ḥājjī Khalīfa's *Cihānnumā* furnished the pretext for Abū Bakr al-Dimashqī's translation of the *Atlas maior*. He meant his own works to supersede and replace it.[262] Abū Bakr's works, prompted by a diplomatic gift of Justinus Colyaer (Colyer, Collier; 1596–?), the new Dutch ambassador (1668–82) to the Ottoman court, in 1668 and placed under the supervision and patronage of the grand vizier Köprülü Fāzil Aḥmed Paşa (1072–87/1661–76) and his successor Merzifonlu Qara Muṣṭafā Paşa, can be seen as an element in the efforts to address the grievances of Ḥājjī Khalīfa's circle and to alleviate tensions. While the textual history of the translation and its subsequent editions and abbreviations is highly complex and not well studied, its connection with politico-military purposes seems highly likely. Travellers from Catholic Europe reported that Köprülü Fāzil Aḥmed Paşa invited readings of the work while he waged war against Venice. In 1683 Qara Muṣṭafā Paşa ordered a description of Hungary and Germany as part of the preparation of the campaign against Vienna. The extant text shows strong resemblance to Abū Bakr's works.[263]

The link between Ottoman scholarly works based on foreign knowledge and Ottoman efforts to reform the army, the fleet, the administration and parts of the education system became more explicit during the so-called Tulip Period (1131–42/1718–30). Müteferriqa, an important voice in this period and of substantial influence upon later Islamic reformist writings and movements, created a set of arguments for reform that were situated entirely in an Islamic perspective. He referred to the will and work of the divine creator, the glorious rule of the just caliph and sultan, the exemplarity of Muslim religious history as compared to those of Judaism and Christianity, the loss of territory and culture due to superior enemies (Mongols, Castilians), the need for *tajdīd* (religious renewal) and *iḥyā'* (revival) and the appeal of Ottoman 'pan-Islamism' serving the religious, cultural and social needs of the entire Muslim world.[264] Reichmuth proposes seeing this rhetoric as a call for a bureaucratic state with a strong ruler and a modernised army that resonated positively among parts of the educated elite.[265] Hagen takes a slightly different stance,

262 Ibid., pp. 259–61.
263 Ibid., p. 258.
264 Stefan Reichmuth, 'Islamic reformist discourse in the Tulip Period (1718–1730): Ibrahim Müteferriqa and his arguments for printing', in Çaksu (ed.) *International Congress on Learning and Education in the Ottoman World*, pp. 153–8.
265 Ibid., p. 160.

and emphasises that Müteferriqa, in addition to his use of categories of the Ottoman reform and decline discourse of the eleventh/seventeenth century, unmistakably demanded a turn to modern sciences, technologies and forms of institutions.[266]

The numerous efforts to reform parts of the Ottoman army, navy and military education undertaken during the twelfth/eighteenth century took place within this complex framework that combined the traditional with the modern, the practical with the scientific.[267] The new schools for engineering, medicine and naval training were either linked to new military corps or attached to older institutions such as the navy or those that provided the army with weapons and gunpowder, such as the Arsenal.[268] The only other sphere of academic reform was the Enderun. Its educational programme incorporated elements such as geography, cartography and geometry that were taught at the new military schools. Ágoston believes that the limitations of these reforms in size, scope and social sector do not reflect the traditionally propounded scientific, technological or political inferiority, but rather restraint out of fear of grave social repercussions.[269]

The vast sphere of civil education provided in the *madrasas* remained largely untouched, although individual scholars collected, annotated and excerpted foreign books and maps or their translations. Although the majority of books and maps printed abroad are stored in libraries linked to the court or state institutions such as the Topkapi Palace, the Naval Museum or Köprülü Library, several *madrasa* libraries founded in twelfth/eighteenth-century Istanbul by scholars such as ʿAṭif Efendi or ʿIṣat Efendi contain at least Ottoman Turkish translations of the latest new maps and geographical books. Istanbul and several other Ottoman towns linked to foreign trade had small, stable foreign communities where books, maps, drugs, instruments and toys such as spectacles, watches, telescopes or microscopes could be bought and botanical gardens were founded. The availability of mechanical clocks and watches in eleventh/seventeenth- and twelfth/eighteenth-century

266 Hagen, *Ein osmanischer Geograph bei der Arbeit*, pp. 262–3.

267 Ibid., pp. 264–5.

268 See Frédéric Hitzel, 'Les écoles de mathématiques turques et l'aide française (1775–1798)', in *Actes du sixième congrès international d'histoire économique et sociale de l'Empire ottoman et de la Turquie (1326–1960), Aix-en-Provence, du 1er au 4e juillet 1992, Collection Turcica*, 8 (1995); Frédéric Hitzel, 'François Kauffer (1751?–1801): Ingénieur-cartographe français au service de Selim III', in Ekmeleddin İhsanoğlu and Feza Günergun (eds.), *Science in Islamic civilisation* (Istanbul, 2000).

269 Gábor Ágoston, 'Ottoman warfare in Europe 1453–1826', in Jeremy Black (ed.), *European warfare 1453–1815* (London, 2002), pp. 143–4.

Istanbul is well established.[270] Other scientific instruments were less easily available. There are, nonetheless, a number of sources confirming that they were sold in the Ottoman empire. Balthasar de Monconys reported for instance from mid-eleventh/seventeenth-century Cairo that he bought long-distance sighting tubes to replace his telescopes bought in France and lost in a shipwreck.[271] Paul Lucas, an itinerant trader and royal emissary at the turn of the twelfth/eighteenth century, listed more than a dozen microscopes among his wares.[272] Instrument-makers in Augsburg produced at least one telescope for the Ottoman market. Physicians, merchants, diplomats and other travellers participated in this form of exchanging new as well as old knowledge, largely free from state interference.

This sphere of civil education was seriously challenged only after the period discussed here. The reforms of the nineteenth century led to the reform of education in all its major aspects, i.e. contents, institutional forms and career opportunities, in the Ottoman empire as well as in Qājār Iran by imports from France, Great Britain, Austria, Germany and occasionally Russia. The colonisation of India, Central Asia and North Africa presented another, severe challenge to local Muslim traditions of scientific knowledge. The colonial powers brought their own institutions, personnel, goals and forms of repression that either deliberately destroyed the local traditions or forced them to adapt in various ways to the new types of foreign knowledge. The ability of various previous Islamic societies to incorporate, integrate and transform foreign scientific knowledge into local traditions broke apart.

270 Otto Kurz, *European clocks and watches in the Near East*, Studies of the Warburg Institute 34 (London and Leiden, 1975).

271 Brentjes, 'On the relationship', p. 139.

272 *Voyage du Sieur Paul Lucas au Levant*, 2 vols. (Paris, 1704); Henri Omont, *Missions archéologiques françaises en Orient aux XVIIème et XVIIIème siècles*, 2 vols. (Paris, 1902).

23

Occult sciences and medicine

S. NOMANUL HAQ

In his *Muqaddima* (Prolegomena) the well-known sage Ibn Khaldūn (d. 808 / 1406) reported a diversity of opinion among Muslim jurists concerning the grounds for the imposition of the death penalty upon practitioners of magic.[1] The term he employed here is *siḥr*, an appellation which denotes a very wide range of occult phenomena; it is generally rendered by scholars as 'magic' or 'sorcery' in the generic sense, the two words often used interchangeably. Ibn Khaldūn's account constitutes one of the two classic discourses on occult sciences in medieval Islam, and his report is, typically, of a very high historical and sociological value. For example, one notes that it throws into relief what are the two fundamental features of the approach to *siḥr* in the Islamic milieu. One is the sustained belief in the reality of *siḥr* – that it is *ḥaqq* (true / real); the second, a legal determination of its reprehensibility – that the practice of *siḥr* is a contravention of the articulated body of divine law. But all of this needs to be qualified and elaborated.

In the chapter 'On the sciences of *siḥr* and *ṭilasmāt*'[2] Ibn Khaldūn wrote of three degrees of the souls that have magical ability (*al-nufūs al-sāḥira*). To the first degree belong those that carry out their influence upon the world of corporeal elements, or upon other souls, through their own endeavour (*himma*) alone, without any external instrument or aid. In the second degree are placed those souls that exercise such influence with the aid of the celestial spheres or of the elements, or with the aid of the hidden properties (*khawāṣṣ*) of numbers. Finally, the third degree is assigned to those that work their influence upon the powers of imagination, planting in the mind of the subject 'different sorts of phantasms, images, and pictures … and bring[ing] them down to the level of [the subject's] sensual perception'.[3]

1 Ibn Khaldūn, *Muqaddima* (Cairo, n.d.), p. 498; trans. F. Rosenthal as *The* Muqaddimah*: An introduction to history*, 3 vols. (London, 1967), vol. III, p. 159.

2 Ibn Khaldūn, *Muqaddima*, pp. 496–503; Ibn Khaldūn, *Muqaddima*, trans. Rosenthal,vol. III, pp. 156–70.

3 Ibn Khaldūn, *Muqaddima*, trans. Rosenthal, vol. III, p. 158.

We are then told that the practices belonging to the first degree are denoted by the term *siḥr*; those that are in the second degree by *ṭilasm* (from the Greek *telesma*, talisman; pl. *ṭilasmāt*), and that this is a subdivision of *siḥr*; the ones occupying the third degrees are called *shaʿwadha* or *shaʿbadha*.[4] Ibn Khaldūn also tells us that the second degree is weaker than the first; and that while the third one is indeed without real being, the first two constitute a robust reality (*ḥaqīqa*). He speaks emphatically: 'Know that no intelligent person doubts the existence of *siḥr*!'[5]

Analogous, though not identical, is the case with the fourth/tenth century esoteric *Rasāʾil* (Epistles) of the anonymous Ikhwān al-Ṣafāʾ (Brethren of Purity), the other of the two classic expositions of occult sciences in the Islamic tradition.[6] The Ikhwān devote their entire final and fifty-second epistle to 'magic (*siḥr*), incantations (*ʿazāʾim*), and the evil eye (*ʿayn*)'.[7] We find here a detailed discourse on magic, including its typology and subdivisions. Thus, there is theoretical magic and practical magic; and there is true/real magic (*ḥaqq*) and false/non-existent magic (*bāṭil*).[8] To argue for that magic which is *ḥaqq* the anonymous writers invoke *inter alia* the entire Neoplatonic emanationist causal chain of being – given this, true/real magic, brought into being in the sensible world by means of the soul's knowledge of astrology and celestial determinations, is as true/real as the natural processes of the cosmos itself.[9] Again, magic (of the right kind) had a compelling reality: and this in its general thrust is standard in the culture.

Turning to the second fundamental feature of the approach to magic that Ibn Khaldūn brings into relief, namely the juristic condemnation of *siḥr*, the matter is simple in its broad outlines but rather complex in its details, both substantively and sociologically. The word *siḥr* appears expressly and specifically in the Qurʾān twenty-eight times – not favourably, to be sure, for it is severely denounced. The magician (*sāḥir*) is always depicted on the other side of the believer–unbeliever divide.[10] And yet the Qurʾān presents a complex

4 Ibn Khaldūn, *Muqaddima*, p. 498; Ibn Khaldūn, *Muqaddima*, trans. Rosenthal, vol. III, pp. 158–9.

5 Ibn Khaldūn, *Muqaddima*, p. 498; Ibn Khaldūn, *Muqaddima*, trans. Rosenthal, vol. III, p. 159.

6 See P. Lory, 'La magie chez les Ikhwān al-Ṣafāʾ', *Bulletin d'Études Orientales de l'Institut Français de Damas*, 44 (1992); Y. Marquet, 'La détermination astrale de l'évolution selon Frères de la Pureté, *Bulletin d'Études Orientales de l'Institut Français de Damas*, 44 (1992).

7 Ikhwān al-Ṣafāʾ, *Rasāʾil Ikhwān al-Ṣafāʾ wa khullān al-wafāʾ*, 4 vols. (Beirut, 1957), vol. IV, pp. 283–463.

8 Ibid., pp. 312–13.

9 Ibid., pp. 407–14.

10 Q 2:102; 5:110; 6:7; 7:116; 10:76, 77, 81; 11:7; 20:57, 58, 63, 66, 71, 73; 21:3; 26:35, 49; 27:13; 28:36, 48; 34:43; 37:15; 43:30; 46:7; 52:15; 54:2; 61:6; 74:24.

picture. One notes, for example, that it does not explicitly pronounce prohibition on magic, nor does it explicitly speak of any penalty for its practice; as, for example, it does, and repeatedly so, in the case of the ascription of partners to God (*shirk*) or polytheism. At the same time, it admits the reality of magic and its efficacy and, by the same token, the reality of occult beings whose aid magicians are understood to summon, such as devils (*shayāṭīn*, sing. *shayṭān*), fallen angels and *jinn*.[11]

While Ibn Khaldūn does not really distinguish between good/real and evil/false magic, condemning all magicians to death in blanket terms, jurists in general did separate permitted magic from that which is prohibited.[12] Thus, for example, the position of Abū Ḥāmid al-Ghazālī (d. 505/1111), the architect of latter-day normative Islam, is that the acquisition of esoteric knowledge which provides magical powers is not culpable in itself; only the actual exercise of these powers is culpable.[13]

So, in one way or another, in one form or another, magic is legally and theologically accommodated in the Islamic culture after all. The position of the Ikhwān al-Ṣafāʾ was strongly favourable: while they dismissed the 'false/non-existent magic' of charlatans, they did not speak in legal terms about these corrupt practitioners at all.[14] But then they harshly censured those who do not consider magic worthy of attention and call it utter nonsense and a falsehood; we are told that this was the case with the majority of people of the day (*akthar al-nās*) who were accustomed to accusing the wise seeker of magical sciences with the capital sin of unbelief. Little do these people know, mourn the Ikhwan, that magic 'is an integral part of wisdom; nay, it is the culmination of all the sciences of wisdom'.[15] It is difficult to imagine stronger support.

The backdrop

Magic should be placed in its context. That magic and magical practices were never altogether suppressed in the Islamic world is hardly surprising, given that the cultural streams that fed into the ocean of Islam were all preoccupied with magic, whether Babylonian, Greek, Ḥarrānian, Indian, Iranian or other. But more: magic of certain peculiar kinds and occult practices of a characteristic nature were actually cultivated further in Islam, especially in three

11 See T. Fahd, *Anges, demons et djinns en Islam*: *Sources orientales*, vol. VIII (Paris, 1971).
12 See T. Fahd, 'Siḥr', EI2, vol. IX, pp. 567–71; T. Fahd, *La divination arabe* (Paris, 1987).
13 al-Ghazālī, *Iḥyāʾ ʿulūm al-dīn*, 2 vols. (Damascus, 1939), vol. I, pp. 49–50.
14 Ikhwān al-Ṣafāʾ, *Rasāʾil*, vol. IV, pp. 314–15.
15 Ibid., p. 284.

specific domains: in Sufi–mystical circles; in the alchemical tradition; and in popular piety. In fact, by the time of Ibn Khaldūn letter magic (*ʿilm al-ḥurūf*) and geomancy (*raml*) had been incorporated into the standard *madrasa* curricula.

What is the Qurʾān's stance on magic? Given the circumstantial variations and the use of rhetorical devices that are so typical of the holy text, it is small wonder that one finds in it a recognition of the reality of magic, mixed with contrasting assertions of its illusory character. This tension is particularly evident in the Qurʾānic versions of the familiar story of Moses being pitted against Pharaoh's magicians.[16] But what is particularly revealing, and here is an instance of an unbroken consistency in the Qurʾān, is that any efficacy of magical acts, we are told, derived ultimately from God Himself.[17] God, then, is the very subject of the reality of magic.

Then there is the tale of King Solomon. Under his command, as we read in the Qurʾān, were not only the winds, but also birds and *jinn* and demons (*ʿifrīt*, pl. *ʿafārīt*); devils assisted him.[18] And, of course, there were those occult beings, the many angels of God; indeed, to reject these angels was no less than *kufr* (Q 2:97). The Qurʾān also speaks of the Spirit (*al-rūḥ*) (Q 97:4); and of God's own Spirit that he infused into Adam (Q 15:29), of the Holy Spirit (*rūḥ al-qudus*) that supported Jesus (Q 2:87, 253) and which was the agent of revelation (Q 16:102), and of the Spirit of Trust (*al-rūḥ al-amīn*) (Q 26:193), identified by Muslims with Gabriel, who brought the Qurʾān to the Prophet Muḥammad. Satan too, the Qurʾān's Iblīs, who had refused to prostrate himself before Adam, was at large in this world, hidden from sight, but all the time planting evil desires into the hearts of both prophets and ordinary folk.[19] And there were demons who thievishly attempted to break into celestial assemblies, eavesdropping on angels and being chased away by shooting stars.[20]

Sociological factors also had a role. Given the pre-Islamic Arab's proverbial preoccupation with poetry, those who rejected Muḥammad accused him of being a magician (*sāḥir*) (Q 10:2, 21:3 etc.) This accusation, we read, was made against earlier prophets too (Q 10:76). But what is distinctive is that Muḥammad alone, of all the prophets in the Qurʾān, is reported by the revealed text to have been disparagingly called a mere *kāhin*, a soothsayer

16 Q 7:116; 10:81; 20:66; 20:69.

17 Q 2:102. Cf. Aḥmad ibn Muḥammad ibn Ibrāhīm al-Thaʿālabī, *Qiṣaṣ al-anbiyāʾ* (Beirut, 1980), pp. 43–7.

18 Q 21:81–3; 27:15–17; 34:12–15; 38:34–40.

19 Qurʾān, *passim*. See F. Rahman, *Major themes of the Qurʾān* (Minneapolis, 1989), pp. 121–31.

20 Q 15:16–18; 37:6–10; 67:5; 72:8–9.

known in Semitic cultures to pronounce oracles in rhymed prose (Q 52:29, 69:42). Mentioned more frequently in the text, however, is another charge *uniquely* levelled against Muḥammad: that he is a *shāʿir*, a poet, himself under the spell of magic (*masḥūr*).[21] Also, he is the only apostle besides Moses who is portrayed as one accused of being a *majnūn* (Q 44:14), possessed by that irrational spirit which was believed in ancient Arabia to deliver poetic inspiration to the afflicted. Note that 'magic' here denotes something that bewitches or beguiles or charms or seduces or dazzles by its sheer aesthetic qualities, this indeed being one of the meanings of *siḥr* that the Ikhwān had noted.[22] Effectively what we have here, then, is an admission of the sublime language of the Qurʾān, a fact happily recognised and fully exploited by Muslims.

All of this appears to embody the larger part of that intricate backdrop which provides a context to the occult sciences in Islam: their cultivation; their practice; and their legal and social status. The depiction of *siḥr* always linked with prophecy; the images of prophets pitted against magicians; the dramatic competition between God's clear signs and magical trickery; the contrast between *siḥr* and Divine Guidance (*al-hudā*); the vehement denials that Muḥammad is not a soothsayer, nor is he a magician; and, above all, the impassioned announcements that he is not a *majnūn*, not a poet; the portrayal of magic in an environment of deceits and falsehoods; the admission, on the other hand, of the reality and efficacy of magic, and the declarations of the real existence of occult beings such as *jinn*, devils and angels; the descent of the Spirit into the flow of history; the contact, even if mediated, between the transcendental–hidden and the real–manifest: reflected in the vicissitudes of *siḥr* in Islam are all these Qurʾānic motifs, with all of their inner challenges, contrasts and tensions.

The reality of magic is confirmed and reinforced in the Muslim tradition, particularly in the *ḥadīth*, with the stories emerging that the Prophet himself had fallen victim to magic. In one account, an adversary is reported to have cast a spell on him by taking a lock of his hair from a comb and depositing it in the well.[23] Citing a widely believed variation on this story, Ibn Khaldūn reported that it was this event that occasioned the revelation of the Qurʾānic verse 'Say: And I take refuge in God from the evil of the women who blow into knots.' He also twice quoted the Prophet's wife ʿĀʾisha as saying, 'As soon as the Prophet recited the Qurʾān over one of those knots into which a spell

21 Q 36:69; 21:5; 37:36; 52:30; 69:41.
22 Ikhwān al-Ṣafāʾ, *Rasāʾil*, vol. IV, pp. 312–13.
23 Abū ʿAbd Allāh al-Bukhārī, *al-Jāmiʿ al-ṣaḥīḥ*, ed. L. Krehl and T. W. Juynboll, 9 vols. (Cairo, 1958), 'Book of medicine'; also elsewhere.

against him had been placed, that particular knot became untied.'[24] So the implication here is that the magical spell was effected through tying of knots and blowing evil breath over them. One also finds *ḥadīth* reports in which the Prophet speaks of the devil tying knots at the back of people's necks.[25]

The cited verse appears in *sūra* 113 of the Qurʾān; it bears the title 'The crack of dawn', and together with the following and last one, 'The humankind', it forms the unit called *Muʿawwidhatān* – 'The Two Seekers of Refuge (in God)' of the standard Muslim hermeneutic tradition.[26] With their rich undulating imagery of enveloping darkness and evil, contrasted with pure dawn and its divine Lord, and of human beings who are manifest, juxtaposed with occult beings who remain hidden, these Two Seekers are generally believed in the Islamic culture, especially at the popular level, to be efficacious in warding off evil and voiding magic spells.[27] But upon the authority of none other than the Prophet himself, the Two Seekers are reported in numerous *ḥadīth* to have curative powers.

Given all this, it is small wonder that even the most committed Muslim rationalist could not possibly deny the true existence of magic: Qurʾānic doctrine asserted this, and there were numerous *ḥadīth* reports historicising it; and there were the ghosts of the magical traditions of pre-Islamic milieus lurking about. This gave rise to a characteristically Islamic phenomenon: explaining magic in naturalistic-rationalist terms as opposed to transcendental–symbolic ones. In this way, many Muslim sages effectively bestowed upon magic the status of a genuine science, a science that followed rules of logic, as well as natural laws: psychological, physical and epistemological. We have already noted that the Ikhwān argued for the ontology of magic in terms of the Neoplatonic causal hierarchy of emanations from intelligible hypostases, thereby giving magic as robust a reality as that of the corporeal elements of this world. Al-Ghazālī's approach too was rationalistic: he analysed magical knowledge in terms of two forms of knowledge, both considered genuine sciences: the science of physical elements and that of astrology.[28]

24 Ibn Khaldūn, *Muqaddima*, pp. 498, 502; Ibn Khaldūn, *Muqaddima*, trans. Rosenthal, vol. III, pp. 160, 168.
25 Muslim ibn al-Ḥajjāj, *Ṣaḥīḥ*, ed. M. ʿAbd al-Bāqī, 5 vols. (Cairo, 1955–6), 'Book of prayer of travellers and shortening it'.
26 See C. E. Bosworth, E. van Donzel, W. P. Heinrichs and C. Pellat (eds.) 'Muʿawwidhatān', *EI2* vol. VII, pp. 269–70.
27 See W. A. Graham, *Beyond the written word* (Cambridge, 1989), p. 109.
28 al-Ghazālī, *Iḥyāʾ*, vol. I, pp. 49–50.

Magic, prophecy and the secret of letters

But more complex and revealing is the case of Ibn Khaldūn. Reflecting a Qur'ānic motif, he discusses magical powers in the context of prophecy. His argument is discursive: human souls, he says, are one in species, but they differ in their particular qualities, which come to constitute a unique natural disposition. The souls of the prophets have a particular quality by means of which they are disposed to receiving divine knowledge, to be addressed by angels and to exercise an influence upon created beings. The souls of magicians share the last of these three prophetic attributes – influencing created beings – but do so by attracting the spirituality of stars (*ṭilasm*) or through their own psychic or satanic powers (*siḥr*). Ibn Khaldūn then develops a thoroughly rational psychological explanation. A soul, he observes, exercises an influence upon its own body without corporeal means; this may result from psychic perceptions – for example, someone walking upon the ledge of a wall will certainly fall down if the idea of falling is strongly present in his imagination. Thus it was legitimate to suppose that if a soul can influence its own body, it can influence other bodies too. Being at pains to provide a naturalistic explanation of magic, Ibn Khaldūn makes it analogous to contagion: he tells us that a harmful breath issues forth from the mouth of the magician, attaches itself to his spittle, and comes in contact with the victim.[29] This theory of harmful breath is reminiscent of the Qur'ānic 'blowing evil breath over knots', here receiving a naturalistic treatment.

Ibn Khaldūn could ultimately differentiate a prophet from a magician only on sociological and empirical – as opposed to inherent and essentialist – grounds, 'differentiating the two merely from obvious signs (*al-ʿalāmāt al-ẓāhira*)': prophets are found to be good people, entirely given to good deeds, who work miracles (*muʿjiza*) for good purposes; magicians, on the other hand, happen to be evil persons, entirely devoted to evil deeds, who work *siḥr* for evil purposes.[30] The difference between prophecy and magic, then, was not a matter of essence, but happened to be a contingency.

Then, under the shadow of the prophets, an exception is made for the Sufis – they too, we are told, can exercise an influence upon the world without the mediation of corporeal causes, and involve themselves in magical practices, especially in the 'science of the secrets of letters', but what they do cannot

29 Ibn Khaldūn, *Muqaddima*, pp. 497–502 ; Ibn Khaldūn, *Muqaddima*, trans. Rosenthal, vol. III, pp. 160–1.

30 Ibn Khaldūn, *Muqaddima*, p. 502; Ibn Khaldūn, *Muqaddima*, trans. Rosenthal, vol. III, p. 167. The expression here is *al-ʿalāmāt al-ẓāhira*.

be counted as *siḥr*. The reason was that the occult activities of the Sufis were effected by divine support; this was so – and here again we ultimately have a social–historical explanation – because the attitude and approach of these men result from prophecy and are a consequence of it.[31] The germs of this explicit exception and the consequent opening of prospects for magic in the culture are to be found in the *ḥadīth* tradition, where the tenor and context of reports keep shifting and where it was possible to find favour for magic, at least in some form.

Magic is certainly condemned in the *ḥadīth*, and explicitly counted among the seven most grievous sins, with the death penalty (*ḥadd*) categorically pronounced over the magician.[32] Furthermore, magicians are placed in an environment of fraud and trickery – those who were friends of evil occult beings.[33] But then, in contrast, the *ḥadīth* does speak of good magicians too, those who recognised that it was God who made their spells work,[34] and the Ikhwān confidently cite 'famous *ḥadīth* reports' of the Prophet himself magically reversing the spells of the evil eye.[35] And there are numerous supportive *ḥadīth* references to *ruqya* (sympathetic magic / charm / incantation) – but with one fundamental proviso: *ruqya* was always to be performed by the unique procedure of invoking God, and none other, most often by reciting the opening chapter of the Qurʾān (*al-Fātiḥa*).[36]

As noted, the *ḥadīth* tradition also establishes Qurʾānic verses as having healing powers, particularly the Two Seekers: it is frequently narrated that the Prophet would recite them and then blow his breath over the ailing body as a cure. But, most noteworthy here, by far the largest single collection of reports about the occult powers of the Qurʾān are to be found in the section on medicine (*ṭibb*) in the *ḥadīth* collections: these reports appear in a context of naturalistic drug recipes and medically accepted surgical modes of treatment – that is, in a scientific environment. This explains another unique peculiarity of the milieu: in Islamic sources we find that the therapeutic use of medicines proper and of medicinal plants is also classified among magical practices – that is, as a kind of *siḥr*. Thus, 'seeking help from the specific properties of medicines' is one of the several types of magic listed in the standard

31 Ibn Khaldūn, *Muqaddima*, p. 502; Ibn Khaldūn, *Muqaddima*, trans. Rosenthal, vol. III, p. 167.
32 Specific *ḥadīth* references in Fahd, 'Siḥr', p. 569.
33 Bukhārī, *Ṣaḥīḥ*, 'Beginning of creation'.
34 Ibid., 'Book of the virtues of the Prophet and his Companions'.
35 Ikhwān al-Ṣafāʾ, *Rasāʾil*, vol. IV, pp. 310–11.
36 Bukhārī, *Ṣaḥīḥ*, 'Book of medicine'.

eleventh/seventeenth-century bio-bibliographic source of Ḥājjī Khalīfa (Kātib Çelebi, d. 1069/1658), the indispensable *Kashf al-ẓunūn*.[37]

We have now reached the threshold of a profound irony of Islamic culture: throughout the history of Islam we hear loud Muslim voices denying that the Qur'ān is a work of poetry; and yet, on the other hand, from the very formative years of Islam we see the literary qualities of the highly stylised language of the Qur'ān being jealously celebrated by Muslims, a celebration that fed into the Arabic poetic tradition. Indeed, the cadence and sweep, the rhythms and rhymes, the imagery and rhetorical flourishes, the metaphors and symbolism; all of this could not but arouse at the humanistic level a sense of aesthetic wonder, a sense of 'magic'. So with Sufism all of this was raised from the analytical domain of literary criticism into the metaphysical domain of the occult: soon Sufis developed elaborate theories about mysterious magical powers of the words and letters of the Qur'ān. It is only in this context that we can make a 'local', historical sense of the growth in Islam of a particularly mature tradition of letter magic, and of the widely cultivated science of the secrets of letters; no other culture seems to show this degree of speculative preoccupation with the letters of the alphabet.

In particular, Sufis spoke of the occult powers of two kinds of linguistic units: first, those letters of the Qur'ān that are known as 'the spelled out' ones (*al-muqaṭṭaʿāt*) – fourteen of the twenty-eight (twenty-nine on some counts) letters of the Arabic alphabet, occurring in rhythmic-rhyming modes, singly or in combination, at the beginning of 29 of the 114 of *sūras* of the Qur'ān; and second, appellative words of the Qur'ān that denote divine attributes, words known by the Qur'ānic phrase 'the Most Beautiful Names' of God (*al-asmā' al-ḥusnā*), and fixed at ninety-nine in number by the tradition. The ontological basis is a correspondence between natures and letters: natures living in letters and letters embodied in natures. One finds a strong metaphysical Sufi expression of this in the quasi-pantheistic thinking of Ibn al-ʿArabī (d. 638/1240), who considered the created world as so many manifestations or epiphanies of the Most Beautiful Names.[38]

Over the years we see grafted upon this, and often variously integrated into the speculations on the occult mysteries of the letters of the Arabic alphabet, a range of indigenous disciplines, and much of the Aristotelian and Neoplatonic cosmology as well as the hermetic and Pythagorean lore – from the theory of four Empedoclean elements, Aristotle's system of potency and act, and the

37 Ḥājjī Khalīfa, *Kashf al-ẓunūn*, ed. G. Flügel, 7 vols. (London, 1835–58).
38 See H. Corbin, *Creative imagination in the Sufism of Ibn ʿArabī* (Princeton, 1969).

Plotinian metaphysics of hypostases and emanation, to the cosmology of the four natures (*ṭabāʾiʿ*, sing. *ṭabʿ/ṭabīʿa*), and the hermetic doctrine of occult specific properties of things (*khawāṣṣ*); and from numerology and phonetics to philology, musical theory and prosody. Of course, the most elaborate and complex embodiment of the fullness of this phenomenon is the Balance of Letters (*mīzān al-ḥurūf*) doctrine attributed to Jābir ibn Ḥayyān, the enigmatic alchemist of Islam.[39] We shall meet him in detail later on. However, it is important at this point to note that the field crucial to magic – a field with which magic is found to be intimately and indispensably connected, both by its practitioners and its primary historians, and upon which magic has been considered by the tradition to be ultimately based – is astrology.[40]

By the end of the Middle Ages Islamic culture had accumulated a fairly large body of magical literature, though much of it consisted of tantalising pseudo-tracts. As sources of magical knowledge Ibn Khaldūn cites the familiar *Nabataean agriculture* attributed to Ibn Waḥshiyya (b. second half of the third/ninth century), but most probably written by the later Abū al-Qāsim al-Zahrāwī (d. *c.* 400/1009);[41] he also cites another well-known work, the *Ghāyat al-ḥakīm* (Aim of the sage, Lat. *Picatrix*) of Maslama ibn Qāsim al-Qurṭubī (d. 353/964), incorrectly attributed to the mathematician Maslama ibn Aḥmad al-Majrīṭī (d. *c.* 398/1007).[42] Also mentioned by Ibn Khaldūn is an obscure magical treatise of one Ṭumṭum the Indian, its subject matter being astrological magic.[43]

But missing from the *Muqaddima* is an important early work relevant to the history both of alchemy and magic, the *Kitāb sirr al-asrār* (The book of secret of secrets; Lat. *Secretum secretorum*) of Pseudo-Aristotle, a book of advice to kings written around the end of second/eighth century: this work is important to scholars in that it is the bearer of that enigmatic but immensely influential string of a dozen cryptic aphorisms, the hermetic *Tabula smaragdina* or 'Emerald tablet', *al-Lawḥ al-zumurrudī* in Arabic, purporting to reveal to the

39 For a critical edition and annotated translation of a Jabirian Balance of Letters discourse see S. Nomanul Haq, *Names, natures and things: The alchemist Jābir ibn Ḥayyān and his* Kitāb al-aḥjār (Dordrecht, Boston and London, 1994).

40 See, for example, Ikhwān al-Ṣafāʾ, *Rasāʾil*, vol. IV, pp. 286–7.

41 Fahd, 'Ṣihr', p. 569.

42 For a history of modern scholarly treatments of the text see D. Pingree, 'al-Ṭabarī on the prayers to the planets', *Bulletin d'Études Orientales de l'Institut Français de Damas*, 44 (1992). For the authorship question see F. Sezgin, *Geschichte der arabischen Schrifttums*, 9 vols. (Leiden, 1967–84), vol. IV, pp. 294–8; M. Fierro, 'Bāṭinism in al-Andalus: Maslama b. Qāsim al-Qurṭubī (d. 353/964), author of the *Rutbat al-ḥakīm* and the *Ghāyat al-ḥakīm* (*Picatrix*)', *SI*, 84 (1996), 87–112; Fahd, 'Ṣihr', p. 568.

43 Ibn Khaldūn, *Muqaddima*, trans. Rosenthal, vol. III, p. 156, n. 748.

seeker the whole secret of occult sciences.[44] This 'Tablet', which was even read by Isaac Newton,[45] is also found in the *Sirr al-khalīqa* (Secret of creation), another hermetic text falsely attributed to the first century CE Neopythagorean sage Apollonius of Tyana (Ar. Balīnās),[46] and this may well be earlier than the *Sirr al-asrār*.[47] Another early work in this Arabic hermetic cluster, still not dated by scholars, is the treatise on astrological magic the *Isṭimāṭis*.[48]

There are two early texts whose fortunes are easier to trace, both of them of seminal importance in the history of occult sciences: the *Kitāb al-madkhal al-kabīr ilā ʿilm aḥkām al-nujūm* (Comprehensive introduction to the science of astrology) of the hermetic sage Abū Maʿshar al-Balkhī (d. 272/886), the Albumasar of the Latins; the treatise is a compilation embodying a complex mixture of Persian, Indian and Greek ideas and methodologies.[49] Second, the *Kitāb al-thamara* (Book of the fruit), a collection of one hundred astrological propositions attributed to the second-century CE Greek astronomer Ptolemy, but actually put together around 310/922 by one Abū Jaʿfar Aḥmad ibn Yūsuf, a mathematician, physician and astrologer. This second tract, the celebrated *Centiloquium* in its twelfth-century Latin translation, remained indispensable reading for European physicians until the end of the seventeenth century.[50] Abū Jaʿfar explained occult sciences in naturalistic terms, without invoking transcendental beings or symbolic causes.

44 J. Ruska, 'Tabula smaragdina': *Ein Beitrag zur Geschichte der hermetischen Literatur* (Heidelberg, 1926). Cf. J. Needham, *Science and civilisation in China*, vol. V, part 4 (Cambridge, 1980), p. 368.

45 For Newton's obsessive involvement in alchemy see B. J. Dobbs, *The Janus faces of genius: The role of alchemy in Newton's thought* (Cambridge, 1991), pp. 66–73.

46 Pseudo-Apollonius of Tyana, *Kitāb sirr al-khalīqa wa-ṣanʿat al-ṭabīʿa*, ed. U. Weisser (Aleppo, 1979).

47 For the question of dating and the Arabic Balīnās tradition see Haq, *Names, natures and things*, pp. 29–39, 203–5.

48 C. S. F. Burnett, 'Arabic, Greek and Latin works on astrological magic attributed to Aristotle', in J. Kraye, W. F. Ryan and C. B. Schmitt (eds.), *Pseudo-Aristotle in the Middle Ages* (London, 1986).

49 Abū Maʿshar, *The abbreviations of the introduction to astrology, together with the medieval translation of Adelard of Bath*, ed. and trans. C. S. F. Burnett and K. Yamamoto (Leiden, 1994); D. Pingree, 'Abū Maʿshar', in C. D. Gillispie (ed.-in-chief), *Dictionary of scientific biography*, 18 vols. (New York, 1970–80), vol. I, pp. 32–9. See also R. Lemay, 'L'Islam historique et les sciences occultes', *Bulletin d'Études Orientales de l'Institut Français de Damas*, 44 (1992).

50 Ptolemy, *Ptolemy's Tetrabiblos, or Quadripartite: Being four books of the influence of the stars. Newly translated from the Greek paraphrase of Proclus. With a preface, explanatory notes, and an appendix, containing extracts from the* Almagest *of Ptolemy, and the whole of his* Centiloquy*; together with a short notice of Mr Ranger's Zodiacal planisphere, and an explanatory plate* (London, 1822); Lemay, 'L'Islam historique', pp. 27–9.

By the time Ḥājjī Khalīfa wrote his *Kashf al-ẓunūn* around the second half of the eleventh/seventeenth century – well into the Ottoman–Ṣafavid–Mughal period – he could name as many as fourteen developed techniques and concepts that are denoted by the term *siḥr*, each having its own esoteric vocabulary. Included among these were divination (*kihāna*) and invocation of the planets (*daʿwat al-kawākib al-sayyāra*);[51] occult specific properties (*khawāṣṣ*) of letters and numbers, and of the Most Beautiful Names; conjuration and incantation (*ʿazāʾim*); summoning of spirits (*istiḥḍār*); natural magic (*nīranjāt*); phylacteries; disappearance from sight (*khafāʾ*); and *ruqya* and sympathetic spells and charms (*taʿalluq al-qalb*, lit. 'attachment to the heart'). But, most significantly, also listed here are techniques of working artifice and fraud (*ḥiyal*), and the counter-discipline of exposing and reversing them (*kashf al-dakk*); and, as we have noted, dispensation of the specific properties of medicines. Characteristically, our early modern compiler considers *siḥr* as one of the naturalistic physical sciences.

Revisiting alchemy

When we turn to alchemy in Islamic tradition, something that was most important for the history of science, we are in a confused field: obscure here, pellucid there, now esoteric, now open, at times unmistakably Aristotelian, at times utterly wrapped in hermeticism – a field that still awaits fuller attention from modern scholars, especially in view of the fact that Isaac Newton's extensive involvement in alchemy, and hence its relevance to the Scientific Revolution, has now been brought into focus. To say anything definitive about Islamic alchemy, then, is hardly possible at this stage of our research, and any generalisation made must remain tentative.[52]

Jābir ibn Ḥayyān and Abū Bakr al-Rāzī (d. 313/925) are the greatest names in the history of Arab alchemy, though for very different reasons.[53] But numerous personages figure in this story, some genuine alchemists, others falsely reputed to be so, yet others entirely legendary. Traditional accounts begin

51 See D. Pingree, 'al-Ṭabarī on the prayers'.

52 For a comprehensive survey of the Islamic alchemical tradition see Needham, *Science and civilisation*.

53 See Paul Kraus's still unsurpassed *Jābir ibn Ḥayyān*, vol. I: *Le corpus des écrits Jābiriens* (Cairo, 1943), vol. II: *Jābir et la science Grecque* (Cairo, 1942). See also Haq, *Names, natures and things*. For al-Rāzī's alchemy see the works of J. Ruska (fuller bibliography in Needham, *Science and civilisation*), esp. al-Rāzī, *Kitāb sirr al-asrār*, trans. J. Ruska as *Übersetzung und Bearbeitungen von al-Rāzī's* Buch Geheimnis der Geheimnisse (Berlin, 1935); and J. Ruska, 'Die Alchemie al-Rāzī's', *Der Islam*, 22 (1935), pp. 281ff.

with two people, the Umayyad prince Khālid ibn Yazīd (d. 85/704), and the alleged master of Jābir ibn Ḥayyān, the sixth Shīʿite imam, Jaʿfar al-Ṣādiq (d. 148/765). Associated with the disgruntled prince in the colourful tales are two Byzantine figures: Stephanus, a monk who is supposed to have taught him alchemy; and Morienus, a hermit with whom, so the tradition has it, he exchanged letters. Indeed, both Khālid and Jaʿfar were historical figures, but their involvement in alchemy is a pious fiction; the Khālid–Morienus correspondence, though it had a great vogue in Europe after its Latin translation in *De compositione alchimiae*, is also apocryphal.[54] As for Jābir, a massive alchemical corpus has been attributed to him, but he himself may never have existed. There is a similar case regarding the enigmatic Arabic text known only in its Latin translation, the *Turba philosophorum*, a symposium of ancient alchemists and pre-Socratic Greek philosophers probably compiled around the end of the second/ninth century; the compiler is unknown.[55]

Then, in the standard histories we encounter Dhu ʾl-Nūn al-Miṣrī (d. 245/860), the famous Sufi who is known for his mystical involvement in alchemy; and Ibn Umayl (d. *c.* 349/960), who loomed large in the Latin west as Zadith Senior filius Hamuel, the author of the *Tabula chemica*, a widely disseminated alchemical poem in some ninety strophes derived directly from his authentic *al-Māʾ al-waraqī waʾl-arḍ al-nujūmiyya* (Silvery water and starry earth) and *Risālat al-shams ilaʾl-hilāl* (Epistle of the sun to the crescent moon).[56] As late as the second half of the seventh/thirteenth century the alchemist Abu ʾl-Qāsim al-ʿIrāqī in his *al-ʿIlm al-muktasab fī zirāʿat al-dhahab* (Acquired knowledge concerning the cultivation of gold), studied and edited by Holmyard,[57] could still draw inspiration from Ibn Umayl, and this shows continuity in the tradition. The thread runs to Aydamur al-Jildakī (*fl.* 743/1342), who commented upon al-ʿIrāqī and whose *Nihāyat al-ṭalab* (End of the search) shows, in contrast to Ibn Umayl, a genuine spirit of experimental science.[58]

54 See Ibn Khallikān, *Kitāb wafayāt al-aʿyān*, trans. Baron de Slant, 4 vols. (Paris, 1842–71), vol. I, p. 481.

55 *Turba Philosophorum*, trans. A. E. Waite as *The 'Turba philosophorum', or 'Assembly of the sages'* (London, 1896); J. Ruska, 'Turba philosophorum, ein Beitrag zur Geschichte der Alchimie', *Quellen und Studien zur Geschichte der Naturwissenschaft und der Medizin*, 1 (1932).

56 For an extensive bibliography see Needham, *Science and civilisation*, pp. 373, 401.

57 Abu ʾl Qāsim Muḥammad ibn Aḥmad al-ʿIrāqī, *Kitāb al-ʿilm al-muktasab fī zirāʿat al-dhahab*, trans. E. J. Holmyard (Paris, 1923).

58 M. Taslimi, 'An examination of the *Nihāyat al-ṭalab* and the determination of its place and value in the history of Islamic chemistry', inaugural dissertation, University of London (1954).

In this cluster we also have Maslama ibn Qāsim al-Qurṭubī's *Rutbat al-ḥakīm* (The sage's step), an outstanding work from the standpoint of chemical technology.[59] In the fifth/eleventh century came the *'Ayn al-ṣan'a wa 'awn al-ṣana'a* (Essence of the art and aid to the artisans) of al-Ṣāliḥī al-Khwārizmī al-Kaṭī: basically concerned with metallurgical chemistry, this treatise also figures in the standard accounts of Islamic alchemy.[60] From the following century, the time when the translation of Arabic works into Latin saw its heyday, two writers of alchemical poems appear in traditional histories: Abū Ismā'īl al-Ṭughrā'ī, who produced the *al-Jawhar al-naḍīr fī ṣinā'at al-iksīr* (Brilliant stone in the manufacture of elixir);[61] and Ibn Arfa' Ra's al-Andalusī, the poet who called his verse collection (*dīwān*) *Shudhūr al-dhahab* (Particles of gold).[62] A little later, the Damascene 'Abd al-Raḥīm al-Jawbarī (early seventh/thirteenth century) is also recognised by historians of alchemy.[63]

Within this massive corpus there is a wildly diverse body of texts. Indeed, it is sometimes difficult to see why all these writings are lumped together and classified as 'alchemical', given the fundamental differences – sometimes even contradictory views and approaches – found among them. A fresh taxonomy is needed, especially if we are to move beyond mere descriptions in order to provide fuller historical explanations. While this has yet to be done, a few taxonomic principles suggest themselves. For example, there are some authors in this corpus who wrote in terms that are allegorical, symbolic, esoteric, cryptic, and more speculative than practical (for instance, Ibn Umayl, al-Ṭughrā'ī and al-Irāqī); and this group is distinguishable from another that happens to be clear in its expressions, rationalistic, open, naturalistic, free of symbolism, espousing an approach we would call scientific (e.g. Abū Bakr al-Rāzī and the author(s) of much of the *corpus Jabirianum*); yet there are some others who represent an ecstatic–visionary–mystical trend, far removed from the furnace and crucible (e.g. Dhu 'l-Nūn).

Then there exists a sizeable body of texts in this alchemical literature that are unmistakably Aristotelian, working as they do within the tradition of Greek alchemy (e.g. the *Turba*); and an equally massive body far removed from Aristotle (e.g. most Jabirian writings) and overwhelmingly hermetic (e.g.

59 E. J. Holmyard, 'Maslama al-Majrīṭī and the *Rutbat al-ḥakīm*', *Isis*, 6 (1924), p. 293.

60 H. E. Stapleton and R. F. Azo, 'Alchemical equipment in the 11th century', *Memoirs of the Asiatic Society of Bengal*, 1 (1905).

61 F. R. Razuq, 'Studies on the works of al-Ṭughrāī', inaugural dissertation, University of London (1963).

62 E. J. Holmyard, *Alchemy* (London, 1957), p. 100.

63 A. Mieli, *La science arabe et son rôle dans l'evolution scientifique mondiale* (Leiden, 1966), p. 156.

the *Sirr* of Pseudo-Balīnās). Also, there are some Arabic 'alchemical' writings belonging, rather, to chemical craft and metallurgy – that is, works of proto-chemistry and not of alchemy, strictly speaking (e.g. the *ʿAyn al-ṣanʿa*); and there are even those texts that deny the possibility of the transmutation of base metals into gold – denying, that is, what is considered the hallmark of alchemy (for example, the *Mukhtār* of al-Jawbarī).

As it stands, this classification is crude and its categories are not mutually exclusive, but even this kind of rough sorting is very helpful. To begin with, the question arises as to why someone who teaches that turning base metals into gold is an impossibility should be called an 'alchemist'. And why is someone such as al-Rāzī, whose theories, procedures and explanations are all naturalistic, not a physicist or chemist, but rather an alchemist? This leads to the fundamental question about alchemy itself: what is it?

As far as alchemy in Islam is concerned – and by virtue of its transmission to medieval Europe, this applies to Latin alchemy too – one thing becomes clear at the outset of this pursuit: that turning base metals into gold is neither a necessary nor a fundamental concern of this alchemical tradition, as we know this tradition from those who identified themselves as alchemists and whose doctrines were substantively distinct from other discernible intellectual and scientific currents of the culture. This is even more strongly true of Chinese alchemy.[64]

This is an appropriate point to turn to that huge body of writings that go under the name of Jābir ibn Ḥayyān. 'Jābir', as it turns out, is the name not of an individual but of a fraternity or fraternities of several generations of Shīʿite-oriented authors who in all probability lived between the third/ninth and fourth/tenth centuries. While the question of Jābir's historicity has remained controversial, it seems more and more likely that there did exist some small authentic core of texts written by a historically real Jābir living in the second/eighth century, and from this core grew the extensive apocryphal *corpus Jabirianum* which has come down to us. Indeed, the Jabirian corpus is so diverse that it constitutes one of the most urgent cases requiring a taxonomic treatment. And yet it does possess certain consistent features that define a system and an alchemical school – indeed, *the* alchemical school of Islam. This is the school in which we find all of Islam's major contributions to chemistry: the theory that all metals are composed of sulphur and mercury, a chemical belief that led to the phlogiston theory of modern science; the introduction of

64 N. Sivin, 'Research on the history of Chinese alchemy', in Z. R. W. M. von Martels (ed.), *Alchemy revisited* (Leiden, 1990).

sal ammoniac in the repertoire of chemistry; and the use of plant and animal substances in chemical procedures, something not found among the Greek alchemists.[65] But more important, some of the metaphysical features of the Jabirian system became a central part of the doctrines of Latin alchemists, still influencing Robert Boyle in the seventeenth century.

Considering the Jabirian school as the epitome of Islamic alchemy, this much can be said, albeit tentatively: the wide canvas of the ideas of both Arabic and Latin alchemists shows an identifiable set of particulars that gives them a distinctive identity in the respective histories of the two cultures. These particulars have three fundamental elements: a cosmological doctrine of the *occultum* and the *manifestum* (*al-bāṭin* and *al-ẓāhir*); a non-Aristotelian mechanistic physical theory of primary elements of bodies, namely natures (*ṭabāʾiʿ*); and a hermetic epistemology. Alchemists in both traditions shared these defining doctrines, which stood in contrast with other intellectual–scientific currents, in particular the Aristotelian–Galenic current.[66] One implication of all this is that sheer chemical technology or metallurgical craft cannot be considered alchemy; nor can alchemy be naively viewed as the prehistory of our science of chemistry.

It is the Jabirian system wherein seem to lie the roots of both the alchemical theory of the occult and the manifest, and the related cosmological system of the natures. What is most interesting here is that all of this is intimately connected to and operates within the framework of Shīʿite sectarian politics and theology. Indeed, the Jabirian corpus is as much part of the religio-political history of early Shīʿism as it is that of the history of Arabic science. The metaphysics of the occultation of the imam and his messianic apparition; the Ismāʿīlī hiero-history of the Prophet and the imam – the Prophet being the manifest (*al-ẓāhir*) speaking one (*al-nāṭiq*) who taught the outer meaning of the Qurʾān, and the imam the hidden (*ghāʾib*), silent one (*ṣāmit*) who knew the revealed text's occult meaning (*bāṭin*); the chiliastic Shīʿite propaganda of imminent apocalyptic events that would usher in a new era of just political leaders and the related astrological predictions; all of this is closely interconnected with Jābir's cosmology and scientific theories.

Note the parallelism here: just as the imam is hidden from the eyes of the common lot, so is one substance hidden (*bāṭin*, occult) in another, which is

65 See note 52 above. See also Jābir ibn Ḥayyān, *L'élaboration de l'élixir suprême: Quartorze traités de Ǧābir ibn Hayyān sur le grand œuvre alchimique*, ed. P. Lory (Damascus, 1988).

66 P. M. Rattansi, 'The social interpretation of science in the seventeenth century', in P. Mathias (ed.), *Science and society, 1600–1900* (Cambridge, 1972), p. 132; A.-J. Festugière, *La révélation d'Hermés Trismegiste*, 4 vols. (Paris, 1944–54).

manifest (*ẓāhir*); and just as it requires privileged knowledge to recognise the imam, esoteric alchemical knowledge is needed to recognise the hidden substance. This privileged, esoteric epistemology is reinforced by the basic hermetic principle that knowledge does not arise out of a process of logical reasoning whereby innumerable particulars are subsumed under a few general principles, as Aristotelians would have it, but that it is somehow 'given' or 'delivered': knowledge is handed on by some supreme prophet or sage ('by my Master' is the invocative formula found practically throughout the Jabirian corpus), or brought through some kind of revelation, emerging in the mind as a clear idea, or coming to pass by virtue of some intimate experience, or divulged to the adept in the form of inscriptions on cave walls. As noted, this epistemological principle is one of the identifying traits of Latin alchemy too, an essential characteristic of Late Antique magic and the leitmotiv of Paracelsian doctrine.[67]

It is important to note the sharp contrast between Aristotle's famous four qualities – hot, cold, moist and dry – and the Jabirian four natures (*ṭabāʾiʿ*) referred to by the same appellations. Aristotle's qualities *distinguished* in four pairs the four primary Empedoclean elements of physical bodies, Air (hot–moist), Water (cold–moist), Earth (cold–dry) and Fire (hot–dry). Jābir's natures *were* the primary elements. The alchemist's natures, practically never called by the Aristotelian terms *dynameis* (Ar. *quwā*, sing. *quwwa*) or *poiotêtes* (Ar. *kayfiyya*, sing. *kayfiyyāt*), were independently existing corporeal entities, occupying space, having weight, quantifiable, lending themselves to being extracted out in isolation, and were found in mechanical and geometric arrangements in different bodies. The qualities of the Greek philosopher, which he never called natures (*physeis*), were 'forms'; they did not have an independent corporeal existence; they were conceptual entities not to be found in actual isolation from the four elements in which they inhered. The case with the *physeies* of Greek alchemists is similar: these too were incorporeal entities, conceived in terms of Aristotle's theory of potency and act, and cannot be identified with Jābir's *ṭabāʾiʿ*.

According to Jabirian doctrine all material bodies arose out of the combination of the four natures occurring in innumerably different numerical relationships. Two of these natures were manifest (*ẓāhir*) and two were occult (*bāṭin*); alchemical transmutation essentially consisted in changing the arithmetic proportions existing between them, but more particularly in extracting the occult natures out (*istikhrāj*). Thus, hidden in one metal was another – such as gold hidden in lead – and the adept reverses this, making manifest what was occult.

67 Festugière, *La révélation*, *passim*; Rattansi, 'Social interpretation', p. 11.

In fact, this was effectively a mechanical process: transmutation was a kind of 'movement' (*naql*) of the natures.

It is this Jabirian *ẓāhir–bāṭin* doctrine with its attendant mechanical system of *reified* natures that was transmitted to the Latin alchemists.[68] Indeed, the *occultum* and the *manifestum* of these alchemists merged with their corpuscular thinking over the centuries, eventually fusing with Paracelsian vitalism to yield the theory that matter is composed of complex, layered corpuscles; Van Helmont was a major exponent of this theory in the seventeenth century, influencing the redoubtable scientist Robert Boyle.[69] It must give the historian a pause that an alchemist, identified by Ibn Khaldūn as 'the chief magician of Islam',[70] would play such a sustained and direct role in the history of science proper; and that the roots of our modern science would lie in some manner also in Shīʿite sectarian metaphysics and politics.

Medicine: pluralism and the irony of incompatibilities

Abū Bakr al-Rāzī (the Rhazes of the Latins) is one of the outstanding figures of the history of medicine in Islam. But al-Rāzī is equally as important as an alchemist, and his case throws into sharp relief the question of the relationship between medicine and occult sciences in Islamic culture. In general, Islamic medicine has been identified with that predominantly Hippocratic tradition elaborated and systematised by Galen and harmonised with Aristotelianism. This became a powerful cultural and political institution in the world of Islam, receiving patronage from rulers and nobles, operating in a secular–humanistic mode, establishing grand hospitals, and determining the course of medical science and practice in Europe.[71] This picture is certainly legitimate, but it remains oversimplified in that it obscures a number of complexities, for example the fact that strains of medicine other than the Aristotelian–Galenic also existed in the Islamic milieu, and that these strains influenced the mainstream medical system in ways that are important.

68 For a detailed discussion see S. Nomanul Haq, 'Greek alchemy or Shīʿī metaphysics? A preliminary statement concerning Jābir ibn Ḥayyān's *ẓahir* and *bāṭin*', *Bulletin of the Royal Institute for Inter-Faith Studies*, 4 (Autumn/Winter 2002). See also S. Nomanul Haq, 'Ṭabīʿa', *EI2*, vol. X, pp. 25–8.

69 W. R. Newman, 'The occult and the manifest among the alchemists', in F. J. Ragep and S. P. Ragep (eds.), *Tradition, transmission, transformation* (Leiden, 1996).

70 'Kabīr al-saḥra': Ibn Khaldūn, *Muqaddima*, p. 497.

71 For a rigorous general survey of Islamic medicine as constituting the pre-history of the modern science and practice of medicine see, for example, M. Ullmann, *Islamic medicine* (Edinburgh, 1978).

To begin with, Galen's own system was itself eclectic: in general physiology and pathology he elaborated the famous Hippocratic doctrine of four humours; his anatomy came from the Alexandrians; pharmacology from Dioscorides; and in special physiology he drew upon Platonic, Stoic and Aristotelian ideas. This was all transmitted to the Arabs along with other Greek ideas; and then Syrian, Persian and Indian ideas were absorbed in Islam's medical culture, bringing with them some magical tendencies too, as well as additional pharmacological data.[72] But the medical system into which this complex was incorporated remained that of Galen – a rational system with its Aristotelian epistemological commitments whereby the specific and particular was to be derived deductively by the general and the universal.

Two parallel traditions of medical thought and practice also existed in the Islamic milieu, distinguished by their contrasting epistemological grounds that can generically be described as hermetic. These were, first, the traditions of occultism, and, second, that which became known as Prophetic medicine. It ought to be noted that neither of these was in its main thrust superstitious or non-naturalistic, or based on the invocation of mysterious transcendental entities such as devils or spirits. But despite their influence on the dominant Islamic Galenic medicine, these two strains remained distinct, incompatible with the system of Galenism, since they never affected its theoretical foundations and so never became integral to it. There were important sociological and cultural–historical aspects to this. While al-Rāzī was an exception for his times, until around the seventh/thirteenth century those who studied and practised Galenic medicine constituted by and large a social group different from the alchemists and magicians, while those who were involved in Prophetic medicine were largely theologians and religious traditionists who formed yet another separate community. But this grouping had its own peculiar dynamics, and in later centuries both social and intellectual boundaries began shifting, readjusting and blurring.

As an alchemist al-Rāzī did not degenerate into irrationalism. Rather, he paid attention to the specifics (*khawāṣṣ*) rather than to the general; the former being a defining hermetic feature of alchemy. This fed into the methodology of al-Rāzī the Galenic physician, and explains his intense preoccupation with individual clinical cases, thousands of them, that led to his historical compilation, the *Kitāb al-ḥāwī* (Lat. *Continens*), an immense body of anatomically arranged medical notes capped by his own clinical observations in a very large number of cases.[73] Again, it was from his study of specific instances empirically generalised that, for

72 Ibid., pp. 20–4.
73 Abū Bakr al-Rāzī, *Kitāb al-ḥawī fi'l-ṭibb*, (Hyderabad, 1955–71), parts 1–23.

example, al-Rāzī was able to describe, for the first time in the history of world civilisation, the disease of smallpox, as distinguished from measles; and to make the discovery that the scent of roses can produce allergic cold or catarrh.[74] Indeed, the *Continens* quotes Balīnās and his *Kitāb al-ṭabīʿiyyāt* (The book of physics) as well as a similar work attributed to Hermes.[75]

It should be reiterated that when al-Rāzī speaks of what have been called 'magical' cures, he does not deem symbols to be causes; rather, he still remains thoroughly naturalistic in his explanations. Such cures are 'magical' only in the sense that no general principles are offered to explain them, and that they sound far-fetched, such as prescribing the application of a squashed scorpion to heal scorpion-sting wounds, or applying the burnt hair of a woman to control bleeding. But mystery is not an irrational principle of explanation for al-Rāzī, and he espouses the idea that unexplained phenomena and wonders exist in nature that cannot be rejected merely because no theoretical generalisations are at hand to account for them. Therefore his work is an example of how Galenic medicine and occultism, while remaining epistemologically incompatible, have nevertheless fruitfully mingled.

Before examining the similar case of Prophetic medicine, one important observation must be made here. Al-Rāzī's alchemical attitude takes him to the point where he exposes the theoretical foundations of Galenism to the danger of empirical destruction. The notion that the body is warmed or cooled only by warmer or cooler bodies is central to the system of humours; al-Rāzī rejects this on grounds of specific clinically observed cases. A warm drink, he points out, sometimes heats the body to a degree hotter than itself; and this means that the drink triggers a response in the body rather than mechanically communicating its own warmth or cold. This kind of criticism threatens to bring down – and over time it did – the whole theory of humours and the four elements on which it was based.[76] But al-Rāzī did not go quite so far – in Islamic culture, the alchemical approach did not make *theoretical* inroads into the Galenic medical system.

Prophetic medicine (*al-ṭibb al-nabawī*), the other parallel tradition in this culture of what has appropriately been described as medical pluralism,[77] is also an eclectic system, incorporating traditional Arabian folk medicine,

74 Ullmann, *Islamic medicine*, pp. 82–5.
75 Ibid., pp. 108–9.
76 See particularly Rāzī's *Shukūk ʿalā Jalīnūs* (Doubts concerning Galen); the observation is made by L. E. Goodman, 'al-Rāzī', *EI2*, vol. VIII, pp. 474–7.
77 Cf. L. Conrad, 'Medicine', in J. L. Esposito (ed.), *The Oxford encyclopedia of the modern Islamic world* (New York, 1995); L. Conrad, 'Arab-Islamic Medicine', in W. F. Bynum and R. Porter (eds.), *Companion encyclopedia of the history of medicine* (London, 1993).

including an extensive *materia medica*, naturalistic Qur'ānic teachings and, later on, all kinds of borrowings from Galenic medicine: all of this centred around the figure of the Prophet. A large number of medically relevant statements and actions attributed to him became part of the large compendia of *ḥadīths* that typically contain a separate book on medicine, and then these medical sections began to be compiled independently. After admitting a good deal of diverse additions the genre reached its maturity in the eighth/fourteenth century, when two classic works appeared in the field, both with the title *al-Ṭibb al-nabawī* (Prophetic medicine) – one by the Shāfiʿite theologian and historian Abū ʿAbd Allāh Muḥammad al-Dhahabī (d. 748/1348), the other by Ibn Qayyim al-Jawziyya (d. 751/1350), a Ḥanbalī jurist and student of the famous theologian Ibn Taymiyya.[78]

This tradition, which has hardly been studied, did not exist in a combative relationship with Galenic medicine; nor was it, in its general thrust, a 'magical' or animistic system of rites involving invocations of transcendental beings. What we find is largely a formulary of naturalistic traditional remedies, along with rules of hygiene, disease prevention and dietetics. In general, all of this was presented without any theories, and the small number of 'magical' remedies that do exist in this tradition seem, by and large, to be such only in the sense that some of al-Rāzī's remedies are 'magical' – far-fetched and ad hoc, but not non-naturalistic.

Prophetic medicine showed a great predilection for simple medicines (*mufradāt*) as against compound ones (*aqrābādhīn*, from the Greek *graphidion*) and this provided a tremendous impetus to the scientific discipline of pharmacology or *materia medica*, a field much more developed in Islam than among the Greeks and regarded by many modern historians as the main contribution of the Islamic civilisation to medicine.[79] The tradition does invoke the curative powers of Qur'ānic verses and of the efficacy of prayers and invocation of God; but again this is explained in rational psychological terms as providing strength and a vehicle to the will of the patient for recovery.[80] Ibn Khaldūn,

78 al-Dhahabī, *al-Ṭibb al-nabawī* (Cairo, 1961); Ibn Qayyim al-Jawziyya, *al-Ṭibb al-nabawī* (Cairo, 1978). For seminal work in the field see L. Conrad, *The Western medical tradition, 800 BC–1800 AD* (Cambridge, 1995); F. Rahman, *Health and medicine in the Islamic tradition* (New York, 1987); and A. Newman, '*Tašrīḥ-i Manṣūrī*: Human anatomy between the Galenic and Prophetic traditions', in Ž. Vesel *et al.* (eds.), *La science dans le moderne Iranien* (Tehran, 1998).

79 Rahman, *Health and medicine*, p. 52.

80 See Rahman, 'The Prophetic medicine' in ibid., pp. 41–58, where he gives extensive primary-source citations.

too, rationalist as he was, admitted the psychological benefits of all this, despite his lack of enthusiasm for this whole tradition.[81]

Nor does Prophetic medicine embody a retrogressive or reactionary religious movement; and this is an observation that has far-reaching consequences for the social and political history of Islam. Thus, it would appear to us daringly progressive and most surprising, for example, that al-Dhahabī, a protégé of the notoriously strict theologian Ibn Taymiyya, considered it legitimate for women not only to treat men and vice versa, but also for them to examine each other's sexual organs. The same liberal view is reported of the most 'orthodox' of all founders of Islamic legal schools, Aḥmad ibn Ḥanbal (d. 241/855). But further, we see a similar relaxed attitude with regard to music not only on the part of al-Dhahabī but also on that of one of the earliest compilers of Prophetic medicine, the fourth/tenth century theologian Abū Nuʿaym. Music repels diseases and beautifies the body, they say without trepidation.[82]

The difference between the mainstream Galenic medical tradition and Prophetic medicine lies in their incompatible philosophical commitments and their differing motives and social contexts. While Galenism espoused a Hellenistic Aristotelian epistemology, those theologians who laid the foundations of Prophetic medicine were committed to what I have called a hermetic principle of knowledge – more specifically, the principle that knowledge is something that is 'delivered' by a prophet, to whom it is 'revealed' by God; and this is grounded on the theological doctrine that ultimate causation lies with God. The motives were different too: Hellenised Galenic physicians were in fact practitioners of medicine, quite often in metropolitan hospitals (*bīmāristāns*) that competed for prestige and royal patronage, and they had scientific and career ambitions. Compilers in the Prophetic medicine genre, on the other hand, were theologians and religious leaders, not practising physicians. What motivated them was a sense of religious duty *pro bono publico*; they were trying to claim medicine for Islam, emphasising the integrity of the human person – who not only had a body (*jism*) but also spirit (*rūḥ*) and soul (*nafs*) – and they aimed at providing the general populace with easy access to curative and preventive measures given a general shortage of physicians in Islamic societies. A good example of this spirit is the *Tashīl al-manāfiʿ* (Medical

81 Ibn Khaldūn, *Muqaddima*, pp. 493–4; Ibn Khaldūn, *Muqaddima*, trans. Rosenthal, vol. III, pp. 148–51.
82 Rahman, *Health and medicine*, pp. 55–8.

benefits made easy) of the ninth/fifteenth-century writer ʿAbd al-Raḥmān al-Azraq, who also complains of the shortage of physicians.[83]

Again, and this might strike one as ironic, Prophetic medicine created a highly progressive religious attitude to medicine in general, and this proved favourable to scientific medicine. For example, one finds quoted all over the place sayings of the Prophet to the effect that there is no science nobler than medicine after the science of sacred law. Then al-Ghazālī, who has been portrayed as the opponent of the scientific spirit in Islam due to his criticism of the metaphysical underpinnings of certain of the Greek sciences, considered anatomy and medicine praiseworthy (*maḥmūd*) sciences, and he lamented that Muslims were neglecting them, and wrote on anatomy himself; his writings were in fact a source of powerful encouragement to the medical sciences.[84] It is important to note that the writers of manuals of Prophetic medicine were not thereby involved in any commercial enterprise; nor, for about 500 years after Greek medicine took root in Islamic societies, did they receive any court patronage for this work.

But patronage was crucial to Galenic medicine, which remained the overpowering and official medical tradition in Islam. The ʿAbbāsid caliphs, in emulation of their Sasanid predecessors, considered it a source of imperial glory and prestige to build and patronise through endowments (*waqf*s) increasingly elaborate hospitals, and to have prominent physicians among their courtiers and royal personnel, such as the Christian physician Jabrāʾīl ibn Bakhtīshūʿ who was attached to the caliphal court of al-Manṣūr (r. 136–58/754–75) and Hārūn al-Rashīd (r. 170–93/786–809). Michael Dols has written of a number of interest groups in early ʿAbbāsid times struggling for medical authority and domination. Eastern Christian doctors promoted Greek medicine and did win in the end, with the Syriac set of mainly Galenic works *Summaria Alexandrinorum* (*Jawāmiʿ al-Iskandarāniyyīn*) becoming the foundation of the Islamic curriculum.[85] According to the standard accounts that certainly need further investigation, the following picture emerges: the first hospital in Baghdad was set up by Ibn Bakhtīshūʿ, and in quick succession hospitals were founded by other Christians. Thus, Abū ʿUthmān al-Dimashqī

83 ʿAbd al-Raḥmān al-Azraq, *Tashīl al-manāfiʿ* (Cairo, 1963), pp. 3–4. For the question of this shortage see R. Murphy, 'Ottoman medicine and transculturalism from the sixteenth through the eighteenth century', *Bulletin of the History of Medicine*, 66 (1992).

84 For al-Ghazālī in particular see E. Savage-Smith, 'Attitudes toward dissection in medieval Islam', *Journal of the History of Medicine and Allied Sciences*, 50 (1995), pp. 94–7.

85 M. W. Dols, 'The origins of the Islamic hospital: Myth and reality', *Bulletin of the History of Medicine*, 61 (1987).

headed a *bīmāristān* founded in 302/914 by a vizier of the caliph al-Muqtadir (r. 295–320/908–32); then, the caliph's medical advisor Sinān ibn Thābit, a Sabian Galenic physician, succeeded al-Dimashqī, himself establishing a new hospital for the ruler. Ibn Bakhtīshūʿ's hospital was later directed by the Persian Christian physician Yūḥannā ibn Māsawayh (d. 243/857).

Later on, while we hear of fewer Christian names, largely due to conversions, hospitals continued to be founded, standing as monuments of royal patronage, and even sometimes of dynastic opulence. Performing both patient treatment and teaching functions, they remained secular public welfare institutions in which the state had a direct role, and they produced a large number of very important trained doctors. Indeed, the hospital stands out as one of the greatest contributions of Islam to the medical sciences and health care. But not all great figures in the history of official Islamic medicine, which seems to have been state regulated by a licensing procedure, were trained in hospitals. And yet almost all of them were dependent on the patronage of a local or grand ruler.

Rabban al-Ṭabarī, whose *Firdaws al-ḥikma* (Paradise of wisdom) is one of the first Arabic compendia of medicine, was a secretary of a prince in Ṭabaristān, and dedicated his well-known work to the ʿAbbāsid caliph al-Mutawakkil (r. 232–47/847–61); Ibn Māsawayh was a personal physician to the caliphs al-Maʾmūn (r. 198–218/813–33), al-Muʿtaṣim (r. 218–27/833–42), al-Wāthiq (r. 227–32/842–7) and al-Mutawakkil; Ibn Māsawayh's pupil Ḥunayn ibn Isḥāq, the leading translator of Greek and Syriac works into Arabic and a medical writer whose own work on ophthalmology was ground-breaking, also served the ʿAbbāsid caliphs; Abū Bakr al-Rāzī was formally involved in ʿAbbāsid *bīmāristāns* and served the Sāmānid prince Manṣūr ibn Isḥāq, to whom he dedicated his *Kitāb al-Manṣūrī*; a part of this work was translated as *Liber nonus* and later worked on by a figure no less than Andreas Vesalius.

In the western Islamic lands the outstanding surgeon of Cordoba Abū al-Qāsim al-Zahrāwī served at the court of the caliph ʿAbd al-Raḥmān III (r. 300–50/912–61). In Transoxania and the Central Asian regions we have the example of the supreme figure of Ibn Sīnā (Lat. Avicenna) whose *al-Qānūn* (The canon) remained one of the basic reference works in the European medical world well into the sixteenth century: not only did he serve the ruler of Bukhārā, he also became directly involved in court politics, moving from place to place, and eventually in Hamadhān he became vizier of the Būyid ruler Shams al-Dawla Abū Ṭāhir (r. 387–412/997–1021).

In comparative history, it has been proposed that the European Renaissance arose in part as a reaction to scholasticism; but in Islam events followed a reverse order – a 'renaissance' came first and a kind of 'scholasticism' followed.[86] We see this clearly in the history of medicine in Islam. Until around the seventh/thirteenth century medical education was largely the prerogative of individual Hellenised philosopher–physician teachers, who sometimes taught in hospitals under state sponsorship, sometimes privately; also, medical study was sometimes carried out within the family, whereby a physician's father taught his own sons and daughters; while some physicians, such as Ibn Sīnā, were self-taught. All of this went on in a secular framework outside the *madrasas*, the well-known private prototypical religious institutions.[87] But in the fifth/eleventh century Niẓām al-Mulk, the 'wise' minister of Turk Saljūq rulers, began to establish state-sponsored *madrasas*. They multiplied, and the teaching of medical sciences gradually became a part of their curricula.

The famous Mustanṣiriyya *madrasa*, surviving until our own times, was founded in the seventh/thirteenth century by the ʿAbbāsid caliph Mustanṣir Bi'llāh. In about 632/1234 it opened a medical section with its own separate building. In Central Asia *madrasas* flourished under Tīmūrid patronage during the late eighth/fourteenth and early ninth/fifteenth centuries; many of them taught natural and mathematical sciences, including medicine. In the seventh/thirteenth century at the Ilkhānid court a new and happy relationship developed between, on the one hand, the religious sciences, the disciplines of *kalām* and *fiqh* being typically most prominent among them, and, on the other, what were known as the 'ancient sciences', those traditionally studied by the Hellenised philosophers, including Galenic medicine.[88] Moreover, in the ninth/fifteenth century the Ottoman sultan Meḥmed the Conqueror built in Istanbul a *madrasa* that specialised in both the religious and the natural sciences; scientific medicine was an integral part of the latter. Two leading figures both worked in hospitals and taught in *madrasas*: Ibn Abī Uṣaybiʿa (d. 668/1270), whose *Ṭabaqāt al-aṭibbāʾ* (Classes of physicians) has served us as one of the fundamental primary sources for Islam's medical history; and his teacher Ibn Bayṭār (d. 646/1248), considered to be the greatest Muslim botanist.[89]

86 A. I. Sabra, 'Situating Arabic science: Locality versus essence', *Isis*, 87 (1996), p. 662.

87 See G. Leiser's somewhat dated but comprehensive 'Medical education in Islamic lands from the seventh to the fourteenth century', *Journal of the History of Medicine and Allied Sciences*, 38 (1983).

88 See S. Carboni and L. Komaroff (eds.), *The legacy of Genghis Khan: Courtly art and culture in western Asia 1256–1353* (New Haven, 2002).

89 Here drawing heavily upon Sonja Brentjes' both published and unpublished recent works on *madrasas*, including 'The location of ancient or "rational" sciences in Muslim educational landscapes', *Bulletin of the Royal Institute for Inter-Faith Studies*, 4 (2002).

In fact, the seventh/thirteenth century was the time when the jurist–physician replaced the traditional philosopher–physician, and there was a productive interaction between the religious sciences and their alleged adversary, the ancient sciences. The interaction is complex in the sense that it becomes more and more difficult from this time to tell which discipline includes what subjects: thus Euclid's *Elements* are sometimes found to be part of *kalām*, and logic and arithmetic included in *uṣūl al-dīn* (principles of religion). This was also the time when boundaries between Galenic and Prophetic medicine become blurred, and it is no longer clear which tradition medical writers were working in. The interaction was productive: sciences made great strides during this period. It is at this time that the some of the ground-breaking scientific work in Islam was accomplished.

In the medical sciences we have the case of Ibn Nafīs (d. 687/1288), a Shāfiʿī jurist–theologian, but also a prominent figure in the history of scientific medicine. Historians know that, in the course of his commentary on Ibn Sīnā's *Qānūn*, Ibn Nafīs had announced his important discovery of the pulmonary circulation of blood. This ushered in a new era in the science of human anatomy and physiology, and marked a fundamental and fateful break with Galenism. In Galenic physiology blood was thought to be perpetually generated in the liver, moving from the right ventricle of the heart to the left through a passage in the septum – this passage was problematic. It haunted the great William Harvey, and was not settled until 1661, when Marcello Malpighi saw through the microscope the capillaries in the lungs and bladder of frogs. 'There is no passage between the two,' Ibn Nafīs had said categorically, 'dissection (*tashrīḥ*) refutes [this], for the septum between the two ventricles is much thicker than elsewhere.'[90] Did Ibn Nafīs, the Shāfiʿī jurist, perform human dissection? The possibility cannot be ruled out.[91]

Somewhat later we have another example of the fruitful blending of the two traditions and attitudes of Prophetic and Galenic medicines. This is the case of the *Tashrīḥ-i Manṣūrī* of Ibn Ilyās, a Persian-language treatise on anatomy which presents for the first time in the Islamic world a full-page scientific anatomical illustration of a pregnant woman. This text, completed in 798/1396 and dedicated to Tīmūr's grandson and ruler of Fārs, Muḥammad Bahādur Khān, is based as much on Prophetic medicine as it is on the Galenic

90 Ibn Nafīs, *Kitāb sharḥ tashrīḥ al-qānūn*, ed. S. Qaṭāyah and B. Ghaliyūnjī (Cairo, 1988), p. 388.

91 For a learned work on the question of dissection in Islam see Savage-Smith, 'Attitudes toward dissection'.

tradition. In fact, in his discussion of conception and foetal development – a question of legal value in connection with the issue of foeticide – Ibn Ilyās shows a preference for the evidence from the *ḥadīth*, as well as a heavy dependence on the Prophetic medicine compilers such as al-Dhahabī and Ibn Qayyim al-Jawziyya; he completely ignores the arguments offered by Galen and Ibn Sīnā. Both al-Dhahabī and Ibn Qayyim had discussed anatomy, citing the Qurʾān and *ḥadīth* as well as the scientific theories of Aristotle, Galen, Hippocrates, Ibn Sīnā and al-Rāzī. Again, in support of his view that the shortest possible period of human pregnancy is six months, Ibn Ilyās first cites the Qurʾān – Q 46:15; 2:233 – and only then the conclusion of Ibn Sīnā.[92]

In India a third element entered Islamic medicine, where it still survives today as *yūnānī ṭibb*, with its practitioners referred to as *ḥakīms* (sages). It derived from local Indian medical systems. The bulk of the Islamic medicine literature produced in India is in Persian, which became the chief vehicle for these writings from the late eighth/fourteenth century onwards. In the history of this sort of medicine we find many names and titles from Persianate regions – from Rayy the *Khulāṣat al-tajrīb* (Quintessence of experiment) of Ibn Nūr Baksh al-Rāzī, completed in 907/1501f.,[93] and *Risāla-i mujarrabāt* (Treatise on tested curatives) of Ibn Masʿūd of Shīrāz (tenth/sixteenth century)[94] are among them; *mujarrabāt* compilations were then established as a new genre. But from the second half of the tenth/sixteenth century one has to look to Mughal India.

It is reported that one Bhūva Khavāṣṣkhān complained to the Lodhī sultan Sikandār that Greek medicine was not suitable for Indians, and sought royal blessings for a medical compilation in Persian based on Sanskrit sources. Blessings were granted, and the result was the *Maʿdan al-shifāʾ* (Treasure of healing) completed in 918/1512. This book has enjoyed tremendous authority in Indian Muslim medicine ever since. We have numerous instances of the incorporation, in fact almost complete absorption, of Indian material into a mélange in which the determining element was the Galenic–Prophetic tradition. Thus, Qāsim Hindūshāh in the eleventh/seventeenth century wrote his highly influential work on therapeutics, the *Dastūr al-aṭibbāʾ* (Memorandum for physicians), which combined Islamic and Indian elements. The same was true of the many works of Muḥammad Akbar Arzānī who wrote several works

92 See Newman, '*Tašrīḥ-i Manṣūrī*', pp. 262–71.

93 A. Fonahn, *Zur Quellenkunde der persischen Medizin* (Leipzig, 1910), no. 28; F. Tauer, 'Persian learned literature from its beginning to the end of the eighteenth century', in K. Jahn (ed.), *History of Iranian literature* (Dordrecht, 1968), p. 474.

94 Fonahn, *Quellenkunde*, no. 167; Tauer, 'Persian learned literature', p. 474.

for Aurangzeb, including a *mujarrabāt* treatise.[95] In the Mughal period medicine was in general taught in the *madrasas*. Given this, almost all religious scholars were also well versed in medicine.

But a fundamental shift was under way. In the eleventh/seventeenth century Ṣāliḥ ibn Naṣr Allāh, the physician to the Ottoman sultan Meḥmed IV, produced his *Ghāyat al-itqān fī tadbīr badan al-insān* (Aim of the greatest perfection in the treatment of the human body): this work not only described hitherto unidentified illnesses, but also introduced a new system of medicine – the chemical medicine of Paracelsus. The Galenic humoral pathology was abandoned in favour of the theory of three basic substances – sulphur, mercury and salt – and therapy was carried out by means of the philosopher's stone.[96] Ironically, the Paracelsian system, as noted, was itself directly influenced by the Arabic alchemical tradition. So in a complex manner Ibn Naṣr Allāh was in part reconnecting the Islamic world to its own scientific roots, but reaching it through the intermediary of European learning, which had transformed it, and in many cases transcended it.

In the eleventh/seventeenth and twelfth/eighteenth centuries a whole body of Paracelsian-oriented medical work appeared in the Ottoman empire, referred to as *ṭibb-i jadīd* (new medicine): this included a highly elaborate work by one Shifāʾī (d. *c.* 1155/1742), as well as translations of the Dutch medical figure Herman Boerhaave's (d. 1738) writings; discussions on the merits of the 'old' and 'new' were also feverishly conducted during this period. Concerned about the toxic effects of some of the new medications administered, the sultan, Aḥmed III (r. 1115–43/1703–30) issued a decree to prevent this practice. The decree opens with the following announcement:

> Some charlatan European doctors left the school of the old medicine, and administering some drugs under the name of new medicine harmed some patients. Mehmet, the convert, and his partner, a European doctor, who had started an office at Adrianople were expelled from the city![97]

We are now entering a time in which Islam finds itself in a world both intellectually and politically controlled and constructed by a rapidly ascending modern Europe; but that is another story.[98]

95 Tauer, 'Persian learned literature', pp. 474–5.
96 Ullmann, *Islamic medicine*, p. 50.
97 N. Sari and B. Zulfikar, 'The Paracelsusian [*sic*] influence on Ottoman medicine in the seventeenth and eighteenth centuries', in E. Ihsanoğlu (ed.), *Transfer of modern science and technology to the Muslim world* (Istanbul, 1992).
98 Murphy, 'Ottoman medicine', p. 379; Ullmann, *Islamic medicine*, p. 51.

24

Literary and oral cultures

JONATHAN BLOOM

A most distinctive feature of Arabic is the coexistence of a relatively uniform written language, read by a great number of people from Morocco to Malaysia and by literate Muslims throughout the world, alongside several divergent and mutually unintelligible dialects, spoken in significant but smaller regions between the Atlantic coast of northern Africa and the Arabian Sea. Many individuals may speak a dialect at home while learning at school to read, write, speak and understand Modern Standard Arabic (Ar. *fuṣḥā*), an elevated language used for speeches, lectures, newspapers, literature and radio and television broadcasts throughout the Arab world.[1] The coexistence of written and spoken forms of the language appears to be as old as Arabic itself, and has led to the emergence and perpetuation of distinct literary and oral cultures.

Like other Semitic languages Arabic relies on verbal roots, usually composed of three (sometimes four) phonemes. While some words are shared between the elevated language and the various colloquials, many differences in vocabulary and grammar distinguish them. The most important is syntax: the elevated language normally uses verb/subject/object word order, with grammatical function indicated by conjugated verbs and inflected nouns, whereas the colloquials normally use subject/verb/object word order and reduce conjugations and inflections to a minimum. In actual practice the regional dialects may blend into the literary language, yet *fuṣḥā* still remains virtually the only acceptable vehicle for written communication throughout the Arabic-speaking world. This elevated and highly inflected language is virtually identical in structure with the language of the Qurʾān, revealed some fourteen centuries ago. This fact underscores not only the long and deep relationship between the Arabic language and Islam, but also the

1 Teri DeYoung, 'Arabic language and Middle East/North African language studies', available at www.indiana.edu/~arabic/arabic_history.htm, accessed September 2004.

fundamental role of the Qur'ān for understanding the relationship between literary and oral cultures in Islamic civilisations.

The pre-Islamic period

Oral culture is, by its very nature, transient, and hence the story of the relationship between orality and writing has to be constructed largely from secondary sources, many of which were committed to writing long after the period to which they refer. Scattered evidence shows that different oral and written forms of discourse have characterised the Arabic language since its emergence in central and northern Arabia during the early centuries of the Common Era. Speakers surely had poems and stories, but their literature appears to have been composed, transmitted and preserved by oral means alone.

Of the several forms of oral literature thought to have existed in pre-Islamic Arabia, only some poems and stories have survived.[2] The most famous is a corpus of poems probably composed by the late sixth century CE but only transcribed in the second/eighth century or later. The poems show that a distinct poetic idiom had emerged in the Arabian Peninsula by the coming of Islam. Despite some differences in vocabulary and pronunciation, this poetic language was practically uniform throughout Arabia. Poems were usually short and were composed to be recited in public, either by the poet or by a professional reciter, who might add his own details and background. Because transmitters constantly reworked and embellished poems, no single 'authentic' version of a particular work existed. Poetry was composed mentally, without the aid of writing, and the professional reciter relied on his prodigious memory when performing.

The earliest Arabic writings are simple graffiti, funerary inscriptions and the like. Later sources indicate that writing was also used in pre-Islamic Arabic for contracts, treaties, letters etc., although none has survived. By the fourth century CE some writers of Arabic used the Nabataean script, to judge from the Namāra inscription of 328 CE, which records the burial place of the second Lakhmid king, Imru' al-Qays.[3] Although the language is virtually identical to that known from the Qur'ān, the script has not yet assumed its later form, which was deeply indebted to Syriac script. The rhetoric and layout of the Namāra inscription indicate that it was neither a transcription of everyday

2 Alan Jones, 'Orality and writing in Arabia', in Jane Dammen McAuliffe (ed.), *Encyclopaedia of the Qur'ān*, 5 vols. (Leiden, 2001–6), vol. III, pp. 587–93.

3 James A. Bellamy, 'A new reading of the Namārah inscription', *JAOS*, 105, 1 (1985).

speech nor a mere graffito. Although no earlier examples have yet been found, it cannot have been a first effort.

Arabic, like most Semitic scripts, is written from right to left and based on an *abjad* (consonantary) rather than a true alphabet, for it uses one symbol per consonantal phoneme. Since Arabic had more phonemes than Nabataean, some of the letters had to represent more than one consonant. By the seventh century CE diacritical marks over or under the letters distinguished those with a similar shape, such as *bāʾ*, *tāʾ* and *thāʾ* or *ḥāʾ*, *jīm* and *khāʾ*. Arabic also lacks symbols for vowels because the morphemic structure of the language makes them redundant. Eventually, however, it came to use 'helping' consonants to represent the long vowels and other signs for short vowels in fully vocalised texts. Arabic script, furthermore, has no separate monumental and cursive forms: it requires that some letters always be joined to or separated from others. Each of the twenty-eight letters, therefore, has the potential to have a slightly different shape depending on where it stands in a word or fragment: independent, initial, medial or final.

These complexities indicate that Arabic writing must have had a limited audience: although some individuals might have used writing for personal ends, in general only special texts were committed to writing in order to confer authenticity, a special status that would have been particularly important for such documents as treaties and contracts.[4] Arabic writing was meant to be read only by readers who already had a good idea of what a given text would say; conversely, writing was not intended to convey new information to the uninitiated.

Orality and writing in early Islam

Islam dramatically propelled Arabic to new roles in world affairs. According to Muslim tradition the Prophet Muḥammad received God's revelations in the early seventh century CE. They were initially understood to be oral texts meant to be meticulously rehearsed and recited as God's revealed word, for Qurʾān (or Koran, from the Arabic *qurʾān*), the name by which they are known in Arabic, literally means 'recitation'. The first verses revealed (Q 96, 'The embryo') begin with the command to 'Recite in the name of your lord who created/Created the human from an embryo./Recite.' Other revelations beginning with the command to 'Say!' further underscore its verbal nature. Muḥammad initially repeated the revelations to his followers, who rehearsed

4 Gregor Schoeler, *Écrire et transmettre dans le début de l'islam* (Paris, 2002), p. 17.

and recited them in turn, thereby disseminating the divinely inspired text by the same long-established traditions used for reciting and memorising Arabic poetry. The Qur'ān, however, established a new standard of oral and literary excellence for the Arabic language.

Muslims conceive of the Qur'ān not as a physical book like the Torah or the Gospels but as a recitation in Arabic (*qur'ān ʿarabiy*; see Q 12:2; 20:113); this concept has provided powerful impetus to the widespread memorisation of the Arabic text and its artful and reverent recitation.[5] Recitation became the backbone of Muslim education, and innumerable anecdotes recount how Muslims learned the Qur'ān orally. For example, the ʿAbbāsid caliph Hārūn al-Rashīd (r. 170–93/786–809) made his son al-Ma'mūn recite for the great scholar al-Kisā'ī. While al-Ma'mūn recited, al-Kisā'ī sat listening until al-Ma'mūn made a mistake, whereupon the scholar raised his head and the young man corrected himself.[6] In the 1940s the Moroccan sociologist Fatima Mernissi learned the Qur'ān from her aunt in much the same way.[7]

The language of the Qur'ān appears to lie somewhere between the standard poetical idiom of pre-Islamic poetry and the spoken dialect of the Ḥijāz.[8] When Arab grammarians began work in the second/eighth century they intended to create only a descriptive grammar, but they actually developed a prescriptive one in which all conflicting variants were deemed substandard. The principles they established were taken to be normative and correct for the formal language, and remain the basis of language teaching throughout the Arabic-speaking world. In short, classical Arabic is the only classical language still in current use. As Muslims carried Islam from Arabia, Arabic became the language of religion and administration everywhere. Every believer came to learn part or all of the Qur'ān by heart and to develop some competence in Arabic, for it allowed one not only to practise one's religion but also to negotiate within the society framed by that religion. The Qur'ān's incomparable prestige crystallised the written and elevated form of Arabic as a literary model.

Memorisation of the Qur'ān has always been an accomplishment of great pride and status among Muslims. The *ḥāfiẓ* (f. *ḥāfiẓa*; one who 'knows by heart') might be young or old, male or female, a layperson or a scholar. The great Persian poet Shams al-Dīn Muḥammad Shīrāzī (726–91/1326–89), for

5 Jones, 'Orality'.

6 Johannes Pedersen, *The Arabic book: With an introduction by Robert Hillenbrand*, trans. Geoffrey French (Princeton, 1984), p. 28.

7 Fatima Mernissi, *Dreams of trespass: Tales of a harem girlhood* (Reading, MA, 1995), p. 96.

8 C. Rabin *et al.* 'ʿArabiyya', *EI2*, vol. I, p. 565.

example, received a classical Islamic education and had memorised the Qur'ān by an early age. This feat earned him the sobriquet Ḥāfiẓ by which he is universally known and revered. In all Islamic societies memorising the Qur'ān was assumed to be a prerequisite for higher learning.[9] Memorisation of the Qur'ān also created an environment in which orality and memorisation played a critical role in the creation and transmission of knowledge. Consequently the training of memory was a constant feature of medieval Islamic education.

Human memory, however, is not always infallible, so already in Muḥammad's lifetime some of the revelations were transcribed on whatever writing materials were available at that time in western Arabia. Muslim tradition generally accepts that Muḥammad was illiterate, although his early career as a long-distance merchant would have made some knowledge of writing and reading useful, if not essential. Nevertheless, it is unlikely that Muḥammad would himself have transcribed the revelations; he is said to have dictated some of them, particularly as they grew longer and more numerous, but these writings were considered only memory aids for the believers, not scripture.[10]

The need to guarantee and preserve an unequivocal text of the revelations soon led to their codification, and this in turn led to the codification of written Arabic, a system that has remained remarkably consistent over the ensuing fourteen centuries. Justification was found in the pivotal role writing played in the revelation, transmission and experience of the Qur'ān. Although the first verses revealed to Muḥammad begin with the command to recite, the same verses continue with the observation that 'Your lord is all-giving/Who taught by the pen (*qalam*)/Taught the human what he did not know before.' One of several Qur'ānic metaphors involving writing and written texts (e.g. the word *lawḥ*, 'tablet', occurs five times), this verse underscores the primacy of writing as that which distinguishes man from God's other creations.[11] Although theologians and others may debate the exact meaning of this and other verses, from the start writing was accorded unusually high prestige in the Islamic scheme of things.

The first caliph, Abū Bakr, ordered all the revelations to be collected and transcribed on sheets; this collection is said to have passed to his successor ʿUmar and then to his daughter Ḥafṣa, underscoring the essentially private nature of this initial compilation. The third caliph, ʿUthmān (r. 23–35/644–56),

9 William A. Graham, *Beyond the written word: Oral aspects of scripture in the history of religion* (New York, 1993), pp. 105–6.
10 Schoeler, *Écrire et transmettre*, p. 31.
11 A. J. Wensinck and C. E. Bosworth, 'Lawḥ', *EI2*, vol. V, p. 698.

ordered an official recension and sent copies to the provincial capitals, where they served as exemplars of reference.[12] The earliest evidence for the consonantal text of the Qur'ān is the inscription inside the Dome of the Rock in Jerusalem (72/692). Diacritical points distinguish some words with similar forms (e.g. *ʿabd* from *ʿinda*), yet despite these aids to legibility, the ability to decode a written text remained a very specialised skill.[13] Of course, those who had memorised the Qur'ān or parts of it might need only recognise one group of letters to 'read' the text of an entire inscription.

A fully vocalised text of the Qur'ān was only established in the early fourth/tenth century.[14] Because ʿUthmān's recension lacked diacritical marks and short vowels, manuscripts provided only guidance to readers, who learned by oral transmission.[15] From the second/eighth century seven traditions of 'readers' (Ar. *qāri'*, actually *reciter*) developed slightly different vocalisations of the text. By the fourth/tenth century these had been codified as canonical 'readings' (*qirā'āt*).[16] Thenceforth 'readers' had to keep to the canonical 'readings', and manuscripts increasingly indicated the 'correct' vocalisation of the text according to one of these systems.

Qur'ān recitation thereby became a distinct theological discipline with many practitioners. Teachers would recite the text, indicating correct pronunciation and explaining difficult passages, while students memorised verses and their interpretation. By the mid-second/eighth century they had probably begun to take notes for personal use, but passed on their knowledge only verbally.[17] Preferring to transmit their specialised knowledge through audition, few reciters wrote treatises. To facilitate memorisation, the Qur'ān is normally chanted or recited using a technique between stylised speech and song. The technique has always been transmitted orally from master to pupil, leading to the evolution of innumerable personal and regional variants. Even

12 Schoeler, *Écrire et transmettre*, pp. 31–4.
13 Christel Kessler, ''Abd al-Malik's inscription in the Dome of the Rock: A reconsideration', *JRAS*, 3 (1970). Diacritical marks had already been used on the earliest complete Arabic papyrus to survive from Egypt, a bilingual requisition of sheep written on 29 Jumādā I 22/25 April 643, to distinguish important or potentially unfamiliar words, such as names. See Beatrice Gruendler, *The development of the Arabic scripts: From the Nabatean era to the first Islamic century according to dated texts*, Harvard Semitic Series (Atlanta, 1993), p. 157; Alan Jones, 'The dotting of a script and the dating of an era: The strange neglect of PERF 558', *Islamic Culture*, 72, 4 (October 1998).
14 A. T. Welch, 'al-Ḳur'ān', *EI2*, vol. V, p. 408.
15 A. Jones, 'The Qur'ān-II', in A. F. L. Beeston *et al.* (eds.), *The Cambridge history of Arabic literature*, vol. I: *Arabic literature to the end of the Umayyad period* (Cambridge, 1984), p. 242.
16 Schoeler, *Écrire et transmettre*, p. 37.
17 Ibid., p. 38.

in the twentieth century the pre-eminent theologians of al-Azhar remained opposed to notating it.[18]

Revelation made scripture central in the new Islamic society, but Muslims understood and diffused it in two very different ways.[19] They continued to consider the text God's spoken word and transmitted it by audition. At the same time, representatives of the state had established and 'published' a written text by depositing reference copies throughout the realm. As the people involved in the two modes of transmission differed both in motive and practice, they eventually came into conflict. Audition won out: 'readers' relying on what they had heard checked manuscripts for accuracy.[20] Even the 1343/1924 'official' Egyptian edition of the Qur'ān was based not on a comparison of extant manuscripts but on information gleaned from audition as well as the literature of 'readings'.[21]

Early graffiti and documents confirm the essentially oral nature by which the Qur'ānic text was learned and transmitted. Although the majority of these writings adhere to the canonical text, others sometimes introduce slight variations either purposefully to personalise the quotation or inadvertently because of imperfect recollection.[22] The continuity of this oral tradition to the present day is a distinctive feature of Islamic societies, and the oral recitation of the Qur'ān remains an essential element of daily worship.

Oral and written literature

Soon after the Prophet's death in 10/632 his associates and contemporaries began to collect reports (*ḥadīth*) of what he had said and done during his lifetime in order to better understand the Qur'ānic revelation and lead the correct Muslim life. The typical report consists of two parts: the chain of transmission and the text itself. Being somewhat colloquial in tone, the language often deviates from classical Arabic norms, but these stylistic

18 Eckard Neubauer, 'Islamic religious music', in Stanley Sadie (ed.), *The new Grove dictionary of music and musicians*, 20 vols. (London, 1980).

19 For an eloquent discussion of orality and scripture in the Islamic world see Graham, *Beyond the written word*.

20 Schoeler, *Écrire et transmettre*, p. 41.

21 R. Paret, 'Kirā'a', *EI2*, vol. V, pp. 127–9.

22 Thus, not only the inscription on the Dome of the Rock but also a graffito from the environs of Mecca slightly adjusts the wording of Qur'ānic verses; an Egyptian marriage contract of the Fāṭimid period strings together snippets from several different but similar verses. See Yusuf Rāġib, 'Un contrat de mariage sur Soie d'Egypt Fatimide', *AI*, 16 (1980); Robert Hoyland and Venetia Porter, 'Epigraphy', in McAuliffe (ed.), *Encyclopaedia of the Qur'ān*, vol. II, pp. 25–43.

peculiarities may either represent contemporary speech or artifices introduced subsequently to give 'atmosphere'.[23]

For some centuries Muslims had remained a minority and indigenous populations continued to speak other languages, whether Berber dialects in North Africa or Persian in Iran, albeit with an increasing admixture of Arabic vocabulary. Many regions developed their own distinctive colloquial languages. These dialects incorporated local vocabulary, simplified pronunciation, abandoned inflection, and increased the importance of word order and other features of analytical languages. Known collectively as Middle Arabic, these colloquials were widely spoken but rarely written. As writers – who were always educated – never wrote the spoken language, colloquials are known from either literary quotations that represent contemporary speech or informal documents, such as lists, contracts and letters.[24]

At first *ḥadīths* were transmitted orally.[25] Students memorised them (and the accompanying chains of transmission) by repetition, regularly repeating texts fifty, seventy or even one hundred times. The famous preacher and encyclopaedist al-Khaṭīb al-Baghdādī (392–463/1002–71) advised students to repeat to each other what they had learned and quiz each other on it. Once learned, the lesson should be written down from memory; the written record should serve only as a reference when the student's memory failed.[26] Individuals with prodigious memories were often the subjects of popular anecdotes. The philologist and lexicographer Ibn Durayd (223–321/837–933) would himself transcribe *ḥadīths* from memory before giving his notes to his students to copy. Afterwards, he would tear up his notes. The young poet al-Mutanabbī (303–54/915–65) won a thirty-folio book written by al-Aṣmaʿī (d. 213/828) by memorising its contents after a single reading. When al-Ghazālī (d. 505/1111) was robbed, he told the robber to take everything but his books, to which the robber retorted, 'How can you claim to *know* these books when by taking them, I deprive you of their contents?' The theologian took the theft as a warning from God, and spent the next three years memorising his notes. Such great masters of

23 Rabin *et al.*, ''Arabiyya'.

24 Perhaps the largest such collection is the Geniza Documents, a trove of some 300,000 writings in Judaeo-Arabic (Middle Arabic written in Hebrew characters), which were discovered in a Cairo synagogue in the nineteenth century. See S. D. Goitein, *A Mediterranean society: The Jewish communities of the Arab world as portrayed in the documents of the Cairo Geniza*, 6 vols. (Berkeley and Los Angeles, 1967–93).

25 Michael Cook, 'The opponents of the writing of tradition in early Islam', *Arabica*, 44 (1997).

26 For *ḥadīth* see Beeston *et al.* (eds.), *Arabic literature to the end of the Umayyad period*, chap. 10; George Makdisi, *The rise of colleges: Institutions of learning in Islam and the West* (Edinburgh, 1981), pp. 99–105.

ḥadīth as Aḥmad ibn Ḥanbal (164–241/780–855), al-Bukhārī (194–256/810–70) and Muslim (202–61/821–75) memorised hundreds of thousands of traditions along with their chains of transmission. Abū Ḥanīfa the Younger (d. 511/1118) quoted *ḥadīths* without reference to any book, and jurisconsults based their opinions on what he said. Reports of great trustworthiness were transmitted on his authority alone.[27] Zayn al-Dīn al-ʿIrāqī, a prominent member of the late eighth/fourteenth-century *ʿulamāʾ*, memorised up to four hundred lines of text per day while holding several jobs in Cairo's leading academic institutions.[28]

The earliest transmitters may have taken notes, but they did not systematically collect and arrange them in the first century of Islam. Writers were probably hampered by the widespread belief that the Qurʾān should be the Muslims' only book, and that knowledge about the Qurʾān, the traditions of the Prophet, Arabic language, literature, law etc. should be transmitted from master to pupil only by audition. Muḥammad is reported to have said, 'Do not write anything about me except the Qurʾān, and if anybody has written anything, he is to erase it.'[29] Nevertheless, scholars began to keep notes and even systematically organised notebooks for their personal use; occasionally a caliph or other official might also commission a collection of *ḥadīths* or other knowledge, but these were intended for private libraries, not general circulation.[30]

After some two centuries writing became increasingly important as a means of transmitting religious and secular knowledge, although audition retained its great prestige as the most reliable means of transmitting Prophetic traditions, Qurʾānic exegesis, history, grammar, literature and even medicine. Scholars travelled to hear others recite their works and receive permission to transmit them. Audition became closely tied to manuscript culture: since copying a book was always considered the weakest form of transmission, to be avoided whenever possible, permission to transmit knowledge was granted on the basis not of actually owning a particular manuscript but of having heard it read aloud.[31] Indeed, some objected to popular teachers and storytellers transmitting knowledge because they had not learned through personal contact with a licensed authority.[32] Although some of this criticism conceals an

27 Makdisi, *The rise of colleges*, pp. 99–105, 'Memory and its aids'.
28 Jonathan P. Berkey, *Popular preaching and religious authority in the medieval Islamic Near East* (Seattle and London, 2001), p. 33.
29 See Ignaz Goldziher, 'The writing down of the hadith', in *Muslim studies (Muhammedanische Studien)*, ed. S. M. Stern, trans. C. R. Barber and S. M. Stern, 2 vols. (Chicago, 1971), vol. II, pp. 181–8.
30 Schoeler, *Écrire et transmettre*, pp. 54–5.
31 Ibid., p. 130.
32 Berkey, *Popular preaching*, p. 75.

establishment disdain for non-traditional modes of transmission, even some noted scholars believed that truth was not the exclusive privilege of the elite: the prolific scholar ʿAbd al-Wahhāb al-Shaʿrānī (d. 973/1565) sold all his books to take up study with an illiterate shaykh.[33]

Although audition always retained its pre-eminence, three independent developments coalesced by the late second/eighth century to encourage writing. First, scribes (*kuttāb*; sing. *kātib*) began to play increased roles in the administrative bureaux as the Islamic empire expanded. This trend burgeoned as many Persians came to be employed in state offices, slowly transforming political and social values with their deep knowledge of Sasanian institutions and practice.[34]

Second, patrons such as al-Maʾmūn commissioned books for the royal library, including translations of Greek and Persian literature and systematic compilations of law, exegesis, tradition, history, philology and administration.[35] Although authors composed only single copies, the climate of authorship slowly but eventually spread to other fields, particularly the religious sciences.

Finally, the Arab conquest of Central Asia in the late first/seventh and early second/eighth centuries brought knowledge of paper and papermaking to the Islamic lands. Paper afforded a cheaper, durable and widely available alternative to papyrus rolls or codices made from parchment sheets. Invented in China in the centuries before Christ, paper was carried by Muslims from Central Asia throughout the Islamic lands. Paper-mills were established at Baghdad in the late second/eighth century, Syria and Egypt in the third/ninth, and reached North Africa, Sicily and Spain in the fourth/tenth. Simultaneously in Iran, the Qurʾān, which had been copied exclusively on parchment sheets, began to be transcribed on paper using new, more legible and more fully vocalised scripts derived from the 'cursive' scripts formerly used by scribes for ordinary writing.[36]

The explosion of book-learning in the medieval Islamic world is truly astonishing. The ready availability of paper made it possible not only to write books, but also to write on virtually any subject.[37] Few other cultures

33 Ibid., p. 92.
34 Schoeler, *Écrire et transmettre*, p. 60.
35 Ibid., pp. 64–6.
36 Jonathan M. Bloom, *Paper before print: The history and impact of paper in the Islamic world* (New Haven, 2001).
37 For a tenth-century list of books and authors see al-Nadīm, *The* Fihrist *of al-Nadīm: A tenth-century survey of Muslim culture*, ed. and trans. Bayard Dodge (New York and London, 1970).

possessed as vast a literature, although it remains impossible to catalogue it with any degree of accuracy. Some individuals were able to amass enormous libraries: the neo-Umayyad caliphs of Cordoba are said to have had 400,000 books, and comparable numbers are given for the libraries of Fāṭimid Egypt, ʿAbbāsid Baghdad and Būyid Shīrāz.[38] In 383/993f. the Fāṭimid library contained thirty copies of al-Khalīl ibn Aḥmad's lexicographical masterpiece *Kitāb al-ʿayn*, twenty copies of al-Ṭabarī's multi-volume *Taʾrīkh* (History) and one hundred copies of Ibn Durayd's dictionary, the *Jamhara*.[39] These numbers, even if exaggerated, testify to the effectiveness of publication by audition before the era of printing.

Written and oral culture

The prevalence of writing is yet another remarkable feature of medieval Islamic culture, for words were routinely inscribed on buildings, textiles and objects of daily use.[40] This presupposes either an elevated level of literacy or widespread familiarity with writing. From the late first/seventh century virtually all coins issued by Muslim rulers were exclusively decorated in Arabic with religious sayings and the name of the ruler issuing the coin, the place and the date. One had to be literate to visually distinguish a coin issued by one ruler from another. From an almost equally early date ceramics were decorated with signatures and expressions of good wishes. By the fourth/tenth century potters in Nīshāpūr and Samarqand inscribed wares with Arabic aphorisms in decorative scripts that indicate the high level of competence in Arabic in this Persian-speaking region. Public buildings were routinely inscribed with historical and Qurʾānic texts.[41]

The extraordinary pervasiveness of writing in medieval Islamic visual culture does not mean that Islamic culture became exclusively a culture of writing. For modern literates reading is a silent, wholly mental process, but until recently reading was always a distinctly vocal and physical activity.

38 Youssef Eche, *Les bibliothèques arabes publiques et semi-publiques en Mésopotamie, en Syrie et en Égypte au moyen âge* (Damascus, 1967).

39 Paul E. Walker, 'Fatimid institutions of learning', *Journal of the American Research Center in Egypt*, 34 (1997), p. 195.

40 Sheila S. Blair, *Islamic inscriptions* (Edinburgh, 1998).

41 Ibid. The high degree of literacy in fifth/eleventh-century Cairo is attested by plaques (*alwāḥ*) and graffiti cursing the Companions of the Prophet that were briefly placed around the city. See Devin J. Stewart, 'Popular Shiism in medieval Egypt: Vestiges of Islamic sectarian polemics in Egyptian Arabic', *SI*, 84, 2 (November 1996), p. 55.

Reading aloud also gave non-literates access to writing, and most literates preferred listening to something rather than scrutinising it written. Islamic law developed an ambivalent attitude towards written documents. Legal theorists considered written documents merely aids to memory and evidence only in so far as the verbal testimony of witnesses confirmed them. Jurists tended to view them with suspicion, primarily because they could be manipulated in a manner impossible with the oral testimony of trustworthy persons.[42] The effective legal instrument remained the verbal agreement made in the presence of witnesses. Nevertheless judges kept records, and commercial law relied on documents. Despite their theoretical neglect, they proved indispensable in practice and were constantly used, becoming a normal accompaniment of every important transaction and engendering a highly developed branch of practical law.[43]

Some medieval Arabic documents even confirm the persistence of orality. For example, four fourth/tenth-century Egyptian contracts state that they had been 'read to the seller in Arabic and explained to him' in Coptic, the language of the Egyptian peasantry.[44] The contract may have been written, but its power was activated only by reading aloud. In late medieval Cairo popular literature was recited publicly.[45] The English traveller Edward Brown wrote in 1673–4 that reading aloud was commonplace, with people listening in their leisure.[46] Even in the mid-twentieth century the few literates in an Egyptian village were responsible for communicating cultural and religious information requiring literacy; they served as mediators between the written and the oral.[47]

42 See David S. Powers, 'The Maliki family endowment: Legal norms and social practices', *IJMES*, 25, 3 (1993), p. 390. On written documents in Islamic law see Emile Tyan, *Le notariat et le régime de la preuve par écrit dans la pratique du droit musulman* (Beirut, 1959); Jeanette A. Wakin, *The function of documents in Islamic law* (Albany, 1972); and Cook, 'Opponents of the writing'.

43 Joseph Schacht, *An introduction to Islamic law* (Oxford, 1966 [1964]), pp. 82, 193.

44 The fact that even oral Arabic had to be 'explained' to the parties to these contracts indicates a lack of Arabisation after more than three hundred years of Arabic linguistic dominance. It also confirms the lack of Arabisation and conversion in Egypt suggested by both contemporaries and modern researchers. See, for example, Abu 'l-Qāsim Ibn Ḥawqal, *Kitāb ṣūrat al-arḍ*, ed. J. H. Kramers, Bibliotheca Geographorum Arabicorum (Leiden, 1967 [1938]), p. 161; and Gladys Frantz-Murphy, 'Arabic papyrology and Middle Eastern studies', *Middle East Studies Association Bulletin*, 19, 1 (July 1985), p. 37.

45 Boaz Shoshan, 'On popular literature in medieval Cairo', *Poetics Today*, 14, 2 (Summer 1993), p. 350.

46 Nelly Hanna, *In praise of books: A cultural history of Cairo's middle class, sixteenth to the eighteenth century*, Middle East Studies Beyond Dominant Paradigms (Syracuse, 2003), p. 96.

47 Shoshan, 'Popular literature', p. 351.

Preachers and storytellers would sit or stand in the streets, reciting from memory passages from the Qurʾān, traditions of the Prophet and stories of the heroic exploits of early Muslims and others.[48] Some traditionists and jurists worried that the stories were misleading or false, and that the common people would transmit these 'unsound' or 'weak' sayings and stories.[49] Nevertheless preachers attracted huge crowds: Abū ʿAbd Allāh al-Shīrāzī al-Wāʾiẓ ('the preacher'; d. 439/1047f.) had 30,000 people in one Baghdad audience alone.[50]

Storytellers played an important social role. The main season for storytelling was winter or evenings during Ramaḍān, after the fast is broken. In the Maghrib long summer evenings are a time for storytelling, while in Iran festivals such as the New Year, weddings and birthdays provide the occasion. Surviving texts are inadequate records of what exactly took place during an actual reading or performance.[51] The oldest Arabic popular text known is a damaged bifolio bearing the beginning of the text of the *Thousand nights*. The sheet once formed the first pages of a manuscript, copied in early third/ninth-century Syria, before a certain Aḥmad ibn Maḥfūẓ used it as scratch paper in Ṣafar 266/October 879.[52]

Other popular tales concerned real and mythic heroes. The romance of Battal, who died in battle against the Byzantines in 122/740, seems to have emerged by the fourth/tenth century, and a full-length version probably existed by the sixth/twelfth century, although no copies are known to survive. The written version of the *Sīrat ʿAntar* (Adventures of ʿAntar) is known as early as the sixth/twelfth century, and it remained popular for centuries. In mid-ninth/fifteenth-century Cairo a miller named Khalīl owned copies of it and the *Sīrat dhāt al-himma* (Romance of [the woman of] noble purpose) which he gave to a preacher to recite for paying audiences. Perhaps the most popular romance in Egypt was *Sīrat Baybars*, first attested by the Egyptian chronicler Ibn Iyās (852–*c.* 930/1448–*c.* 1524).[53] The colloquial text is interrupted and enlivened by sections of rhymed prose and poems in classical metres. It has remained popular, with frequent public recitals in Cairo and Damascus.

48 Berkey, *Popular preaching*, p. 13.
49 Ibid., p. 28.
50 Ibid., p. 25.
51 Shoshan, 'Popular literature', p. 351.
52 Nabia Abbott, 'A ninth-century fragment of the "Thousand Nights": New light on the early history of the *Arabian Nights*', *JNES*, 8, 3 (1949); Gulnar Bosch, John Carswell and Guy Petherbridge, *Islamic bindings and bookmaking* (Chicago, 1981) (exhibition catalogue), no. 97.
53 Shoshan, 'Popular literature', pp. 350–4.

The relationship between literary and oral cultures is therefore long and complex, and oral culture, whether storytelling or popular preaching, continues to play an important role in modern life. Any attempt to reconstruct the oral culture of the past necessarily relies on written evidence, most of which was produced by and for an important but narrower segment of society than that which participated in the oral culture. One should, therefore, remember that the rich written record represents only one facet of a richer and even more varied culture of words.

25

Islamic art and architecture

MARCUS MILWRIGHT

This chapter presents an introduction to the art and architecture of the Islamic world from the first/seventh century through to the end of the twelfth/eighteenth.[1] This is an exceptionally rich visual culture that encompasses the portable artefacts and buildings produced in a region comprising Spain, North and sub-Saharan Africa, Sicily, Eastern and Central Europe, the Middle East, Central Asia, the Indian subcontinent and South-East Asia. Islamic art is renowned for its achievements in calligraphy and complex forms of geometric and vegetal ornament, but it also boasts a vigorous and inventive tradition of figurative painting. It is important to recognise from the outset that the distinctions made in traditional scholarship of Western European visual culture between 'high art' (usually defined as architecture, painting and sculpture) and 'craft' cannot be applied to an Islamic context. In order to evaluate the main lines of development in Islamic art it is necessary to consider media including pottery, metalwork, glass, textiles, mosaics, stucco, stone, ivory and wood. Nor is it simply a matter of the sheer variety of media and techniques; frequently the craftsmen involved in the manufacture of seemingly humble media such as glazed ceramics, carved and moulded stucco or base metal vessels worked at the forefront of significant phases of artistic creativity. Islamic architecture is equally diverse in character; masons and allied craftsmen adapted to local building traditions, and made innovative use of brick, stone, wood, glazed tile, plaster and other materials in the construction and decoration of both religious and secular structures.

Forming a concise definition of Islamic art is not a straightforward task. In the context of this discussion, artefacts and buildings are considered 'Islamic' if they were made in regions under the control of rulers who professed the faith

1 I would like to thank Ruba Kanaʿan, Astri Wright, Hussein Keshani, Barry Flood, James Allan, Andrew Marsham and Luke Treadwell for their assistance in obtaining images used in this chapter.

of Islam. Some scholars extend the definition to include art and architecture produced within non-Muslim polities that were strongly influenced by the cultural practices of Muslim regions. While this secondary definition is not employed in this chapter, a clear distinction should be made between the adjectives 'Muslim' and 'Islamic' as they are applied to art and architecture. The term 'Islamic' encompasses the art and architecture associated with Muslim religious practice (places of worship, manuscripts of the Holy Qur'ān, liturgical furniture and so on), but includes artefacts designed to perform secular functions as well as those made for the ritual practices of other religious communities living under Muslim rule. Furthermore, it should not be assumed that the artisans responsible for the buildings and artefacts discussed in this chapter were, necessarily, Muslims.

This chapter does not attempt an arrangement of significant artefacts and monuments according to chronological or geographical criteria. This approach has been adopted in a number of survey books, and these works are the best place to start a deeper study of the art and architecture of the Umayyad, 'Abbāsid, Fāṭimid, Saljūq, Ilkhānid, Ayyūbid, Mamlūk, Naṣrid, Tīmūrid, Ottoman, Ṣafavid, Mughal and other dynasties.[2] The principal aim of this chapter is to isolate consistent preoccupations found in the art and architecture produced in the Islamic regions of Europe, Africa and Asia. After considering the cultural background of the Ḥijāz (western Arabia) in the first/seventh century and the formative phase of Islamic art, the main body of the chapter looks at the varied ways in which key issues – sacred space, the role of writing, ornamental traditions, commemorative art and architecture, and modes of artistic interaction with other cultures – are interpreted in different regions and cultural contexts. The remainder of the chapter is concerned with the creation of art and architecture in different types of human environment: urban life, palatial culture and rural areas.

Background to the genesis of Islamic art

Islam had its origins in the Ḥijāz, but this arid region on the western side of the Arabian Peninsula plays a less significant role in the history of Islamic art and architecture. In the absence of reliable data from archaeological research it is difficult to assess the character of the arts in towns such as Mecca and Yathrib

2 See the general works listed in the chapter bibliography. Many of the buildings and artefacts discussed in this chapter are illustrated in these survey texts. The following footnotes concentrate upon more recent publications in the study of Islamic art and architecture.

(later renamed Medina) in the sixth and early first/seventh centuries. These settlements contained active trading communities maintaining contacts with southern Arabia and Ethiopia in the south and Palestine, Syria and Iraq in the north. The economic links must have led to the importation of luxury goods, and perhaps craftsmen from other regions. Some idea of the diversity of the material culture of the towns of pre-Islamic Ḥijāz is provided by the artefacts excavated from an ancient mercantile settlement of Qaryat al-Faw in the south of Saudi Arabia. Nevertheless, it is clear that the visual arts of the Ḥijāz were far less developed than those of the south of Arabia or of other regions of the Middle East and eastern Mediterranean.[3] This is best demonstrated by considering the chief ritual sanctuary of the pre-Islamic Ḥijāz, the Kaʿba in Mecca.

The Quraysh, the chief tribe of Mecca, ordered the reconstruction of the Kaʿba in around 608. This structure comprised walls of alternating courses of stone and wood (a style of building probably deriving from Ethiopian architecture) with a flat roof supported by six wooden columns.[4] The Kaʿba, and the area around it, have undergone numerous phases of reconstruction over the intervening centuries, but the essential elements – a small cuboid building surrounded by an open space for the circumambulation of pilgrims – remain from this early period. The visual impact of the pre-Islamic Kaʿba would, however, have differed considerably from its appearance today. According to the descriptions provided by early Muslim historians, the structure was draped in brightly coloured, striped silks (sing. *ʿaṣb*) from Yemen, while the plastered walls of the interior were decorated with pictures (sing. *ṣūra*) of prophets, trees and angels. These painted motifs, and the 'idols' (sing. *nuṣb* or *ṣanam*; probably referring to both figural sculptures and uncarved blocks of stone) stored within the Kaʿba, were destroyed following Muḥammad's conquest of Mecca in 7/629.

We have no evidence concerning the precise appearance of paintings or sculptures in the Kaʿba, but it is unlikely that they exhibited any great artistic pretensions. Yemen was the only region of the Arabian Peninsula to possess a major tradition of monumental art and architecture in the centuries before Islam. The magnificent palaces, such as the semi-mythical Ghumdān, lived long in the imagination of Arab Muslim poets, though it is more difficult to establish the tangible ways in which these structures may have affected the design or ornamentation of later palatial or religious architecture in the

3 D. T. Potts, 'Arabia: Pre-Islamic', in *The Grove dictionary of art*, ed. Jane Turner, 34 vols. (New York, 1996), vol. II; Robert Hoyland, *Arabia and the Arabs from the Bronze Age to the coming of Islam* (London and New York, 2001), pp. 167–97.

4 K. Creswell, *Early Muslim architecture*, rev. edn, 2 vols. (Oxford, 1969), vol. I.1, pp. 1–4.

Islamic world. Likewise, the contributions made by other pre-Islamic Arab dynasties, such as the Lakhmids of south-western Iraq and the Ghassānids of northern and eastern Syria, to the early development of Islamic art and architecture remain uncertain. Other influences came from the visual cultures of the Christian communities of the region, most notably those in Egypt and Syria.

While the nature and extent of the influences continue to be the subject of debate, there can be no doubt as to the overwhelming impact of the two dominant cultures of the Mediterranean in the sixth and early first/seventh centuries: the Byzantine empire and the Sasanian dynasty of Iran. The Byzantine empire lost her eastern provinces – including the great cities of Alexandria, Damascus and Antioch – to the Arab Muslim armies. This conquest not only brought the areas strongly influenced by Graeco-Roman culture into the domain of the Islamic world, but also was to have far-reaching consequences both in the visual arts and in numerous fields of Islamic scholarship. Though the capital, Constantinople, stayed beyond the reach of the caliphs, Byzantine culture retained an elevated status in the Islamic world.[5] The Sasanian empire was to have an equally enduring legacy in the decades and centuries after the death of the last shah, Yazdegerd III, in 30/651. The ruins of the great palace of Ctesiphon and the rock reliefs of Naqsh-i Rustam and Ṭāq-i Bustān stand today as impressive monuments of the Sasanian dynasty, but they exerted an even more powerful presence in the decades following the Arab conquest. Sasanian culture bequeathed to the rulers of the early Islamic world an iconography of absolute kingship as well as a cycle of images devoted to the theme of princely pleasure.[6]

The formative period of Islamic art

This section explores the period from the migration (*hijra*) to Medina in 1/622 through to 84/703. These chronological boundaries are, of course, a matter of convenience, but they are designed to illustrate the fundamental and enduring importance of concepts developed during these decades. It is during this period that the words of the Holy Qur'ān were committed to writing, most

5 Richard Ettinghausen, *From Byzantium to Sasanian Iran and the Islamic world: Three modes of artistic influence* (Leiden, 1972); Nadia El Cheikh, *Byzantium viewed by the Arabs* (Cambridge, MA, and London, 2004).

6 Guitty Azarpay, 'Sasanian art beyond the Persian world', in John Curtis (ed.), *Mesopotamia and Iran in the Parthian and Sasanian periods: Rejection and revival, c. 238 BC–AD 642* (London, 2000).

of the component parts of the mosque were codified and many of the significant attitudes towards the content and production of art were first expressed. The political elite also began to exploit art and architecture as a means to communicate the ideology of the Islamic state.

The Qurʾān is the only significant text of the first/seventh century that provides first-hand evidence for the ways in which Muslims defined their religious spaces and for the attitudes they expressed concerning the arts. It should be noted that manufactured goods appear only peripherally in the Qurʾān. For instance, discussions of paradise (*janna*) in Q 18:31, 22:23, 43:70–3, 76:15–22 and 88:10–16 promise that the faithful will be robed in garments of brocaded green silk and bracelets of gold and pearls, recline upon cushions and rich carpets and drink from goblets of gold, silver and rock crystal. It may be assumed that such luxuries were beyond the means of many Muslims in early first/seventh-century Mecca and Medina, but the choice of media – and particularly the silk textiles, carpets and cushions – give some indications about what was valued in the society of the time.

Surprisingly, the Qurʾān does not contain the sorts of explicit condemnation of figural painting and sculpture found in the Old Testament (e.g. Exod. 20:4 and Lev. 19:4). Those references to figural art that do appear (particularly Q 3:43 and 34:12–13) lack the coherence of meaning that would lead one to assume that the visual arts were the focus of extensive debate within the Muslim community. The worship of idols – whether representational or not – is, however, the subject of unambiguous condemnation in the Qurʾān because those who venerate idols commit the sin of *shirk* (i.e. associating gods with the One God, Allāh). While a much harder line on the representation of humans and animals can be detected in the *ḥadīth* (the collections of sayings attributed to the Prophet Muḥammad), scholars have demonstrated that few of the relevant texts can be traced earlier than the beginning of the second/eighth century. As a result, many of the attitudes expressed in the *ḥadīth* – and particularly those bearing on the prohibition of figural representation – reflect the conservative standpoints of jurists in the second/eighth and third/ninth centuries rather than the concerns of the Muslim community during the lifetime of the Prophet.[7]

One of the five 'pillars' (sing. *rukn*) of Islam is the obligation to join in communal prayer (*ṣalāt*). In order to fulfil its primary functional requirement a mosque – whether it is a congregational mosque (often known as a Great Mosque, Friday mosque, and in Arabic as *masjid al-jāmiʿ*, or in Persian as *masjid-i*

7 Oleg Grabar, *The formation of Islamic art*, rev. edn (New Haven and London, 1987), pp. 73–98; Dan Van Reenan, 'The *Bilderverbot*, a new survey', *Der Islam*, 67 (1990).

jāmiʿ) used for Friday prayer or a local mosque used at other times (*masjid*) – needs only to comprise a flat area for the worshippers and a wall, or other barrier, oriented toward the *qibla* (i.e. the Black Stone set into the corner of the Kaʿba in Mecca). This remarkably simple stipulation allowed the mosque to develop into a wide range of formal categories (see pp. 693–710), but the most important point in the present context is that, within a few decades after 1/622, the Muslim community managed to fix upon a distinct arrangement of architectural components that would remain fundamental through to the present day. The earliest mosque to survive in its original plan was found during excavations in the Iraqi town of Wāsiṭ, and has been attributed to the governor al-Ḥajjāj ibn Yūsuf in the year 84/703. The mosque is square in plan and enclosed by a wall pierced by gateways on all sides except the south (*qibla*) wall. The interior space is dominated by an open courtyard (*ṣaḥn*) surrounded by arcades (sing. *riwāq*) on three sides, while the area in front of the *qibla* wall is made up of a roofed prayer hall (*ẓulla*) five bays deep.[8]

Built of brick and carved sandstone, the hypostyle (i.e. with a roof supported on columns) mosque at Wāsiṭ follows a basic design that, according to the written descriptions provided by Arab historians, was already employed in the more rudimentary mosque in the Iraqi town of Kūfa in the 50s/670s. Going back still further, there are descriptions of earlier Iraqi mosques in Baṣra (14/635) and Kūfa (17/638). The former consisted simply of an area of land demarcated by a fence, and the latter a compound defined by an encircling ditch with a colonnade in front of the *qibla*. Not all early mosques followed this arrangement, but a general pattern can be discerned: structures commonly contain a rectangular courtyard distinguished from the surrounding area by some form of barrier punctuated by regular openings or gateways. The most important feature of each mosque was the wall orienting the faithful to the *qibla*, and, in most cases, this area was marked by a single-storey covered area supported by columns. The inclusion of arcades around the courtyard occurs in the second mosque at Kūfa.[9]

Most modern scholars have identified the house of the Prophet in Medina as the prototype of the courtyard mosque. In this interpretation, the component parts of the mosque came about through the functional adaptation of the house of the Prophet as it accommodated the needs of the growing Muslim population. Recently, the historical veracity of this 'organic' model has been questioned.

8 Creswell, *Early Muslim architecture*, vol. I.1, pp. 132–8.

9 Ibid., pp. 6–64; Jeremy Johns, 'The "House of the Prophet" and the concept of the mosque', in Jeremy Johns (ed.), *Bayt al-Maqdis: Jerusalem and early Islam*, Oxford Studies in Islamic Art 9.2 (Oxford, 1999), pp. 59–69.

Without entering into detail on this issue, it now seems unlikely that Muḥammad and his family had their dwelling-places (sing. *bayt*) in the compound where the Muslim community worshipped (i.e. the *masjid* of the Prophet) around 1–11/622–32. In the absence of reliable evidence concerning the evolution of the Prophet's mosque in Medina during the first decade, it cannot be demonstrated with certainty that the specific combination of elements making up the hypostyle mosque came into being prior to the late 10s/630s or 20s/640s.[10]

Though the early mosques are unlikely to have been impressive examples of architectural design, they did provide a visible sign of the presence of the Muslim community. Another important area in which a Muslim identity (and political authority) was given a public form from an early date was in the minting of coinage. The first phase of Islamic coin production starts in around 30/651 and consists primarily of undistinguished imitations of silver Sasanian coins (*drachm*, Ar. *dirham*) and Byzantine copper coins (*folles*, Ar. *fals*). The most significant change is the addition of Arabic phrases such as *bism allāh* ('in the name of God') and *lillāh al-ḥamd* ('praise to God'). The imitation of gold coins (*solidus*, Ar. *dīnār*) of the rule of Byzantine emperor Heraclius (r. 610–41), took this process further in around 74/694 with the removal of the crossbars from all the crosses and the addition of the Muslim profession of faith (*shahāda*) around the reverse.

In the 60s/680s and 70s/690s there was an increasing awareness of the potential role of coinage as a means to propagate the values of the new state. Three coins from the crucial phase 72–9/692–9 are illustrated on plate 25.1. The obverse of the first type (pl. 25.1 (a)), dating 73–5/692–5, has the profile bust of the Sasanian shah Khusrau II (r. 590–628) on the obverse, but the reverse abandons the traditional fire altar in favour of a central praying figure flanked by attendants. Most striking is that this represents a very public commemoration of a caliph or governor engaged in Muslim ritual practice (either the act of prayer or the giving of the Friday sermon (*khuṭba*)). This desire to find visual means to express central aspects of the Islamic state is also exhibited in the second example (pl. 25.1 (b)), dated 77/696f., and often known as the 'standing caliph' *dīnār*. The caliph's Arab cultural identity is signalled by his long robe and head-covering while his authority is indicated by the sword he holds.[11] It is not certain why these, and other, experimental motifs were abandoned, but final resolution of the question of coin design is more radical

10 Johns, '"House of the Prophet"', pp. 109–12.
11 Steve Album and Tony Goodwin, *The pre-reform coinage of the early Islamic period*, Sylloge of Islamic Coins in the Ashmolean 1 (London, 2002), pp. 28, 91–3, cat. nos. 5, 705.

25.1 (a) 'Orans' type *dirham* (73–5/692–5), SIC no. 107; (b) 'Standing caliph' *dīnār* (77/696–7), SIC no. 705; (c) epigraphic *dīnār* (78/697–8), Shamma no. 11 (not to scale). By permission of the Visitors of the Ashmolean Museum.

and confident in tone (pl. 25.1 (c)). In 77/696f. ʿAbd al-Malik (r. 65–86/685–705) issued a *dīnār* devoid of imagery, comprising instead Arabic inscriptions: the *shahāda* and Q 9:33 on the obverse and Q 112 on the reverse. *Dirhams* carrying the same formulae appeared in 79/698f. and, with remarkably few exceptions, coins minted in the Islamic world remained restricted to epigraphy through to the modern period.[12]

The confidence exhibited in the choice of Qurʾānic verses and the bold visual quality of the script on the epigraphic *dīnār* of 77/696f. was the result of considerable activity in two areas: first, the writing and dispersal of a canonical recension of the Qurʾān during the caliphate of ʿUthmān (r. 23–35/644–55); and second, the development of scripts suitable for the writing of Arabic. Though the first issue is beyond the scope of the present chapter, the second is of considerable importance to the subsequent development of Islamic art. The words of the Qurʾān occupy a pre-eminent position in Islamic culture, and calligraphy remained the most respected of all the artistic disciplines. Furthermore, the decision to emphasise the role of text as the primary bearer of meaning in the ornamentation of religious architecture and artefacts associated with the practice of Islam inevitably focused attention on the aesthetic qualities of the scripts themselves.

The lack of uniformity in cursive scripts used in everyday transactions and much official documentation is illustrated by the first/seventh- and second/eighth-century papyri excavated in the Middle East. This may be contrasted with the more formal scripts that appear on the earliest surviving pages from manuscripts of the Qurʾān, the monumental inscriptions from the Dome of the Rock, the milestones erected along the major roads by caliph ʿAbd al-Malik and the coins issued in the 70s/690s. The earliest Qurʾān fragments are written in an angular, slightly right-sloping script known as Ḥijāzī. In the coins and monumental inscriptions commissioned by ʿAbd al-Malik the proportions of the individual letters were regularised and the vertical components of the script straightened.

The greatest artistic achievement of the first/seventh century is the Dome of the Rock in Jerusalem (pl. 25.2). Dated by an inscription to 72/691f., and constructed during the rule of ʿAbd al-Malik, the Dome of the Rock forms part of a complex of structures on the Temple Mount (Ar. Ḥaram al-Sharīf) that includes the Aqṣā mosque, completed by his son, caliph al-Walīd I (r. 86–96/

12 Sheila Blair, 'What is the date of the Dome of the Rock', in Julian Raby and Jeremy Johns (eds.), *Bayt al-Maqdis: ʿAbd al-Malik's Jerusalem*, Oxford Studies in Islamic Art 9.1 (Oxford and New York, 1992), pp. 63–7.

25.2 Dome of the Rock, Jerusalem (72/691–2). Creswell archive no. 180, Ashmolean Museum.

705–15). The Dome of the Rock (Qubbat al-Ṣakhra) has an octagonal plan with two ambulatories running around the area containing the Rock, the summit of Mount Moriah. The building has a wooden dome supported on a circular drum and a combination of piers and columns. Centrally planned domed structures had long been employed as martyria in the Middle East and Mediterranean regions, and the influence of Byzantine architecture can be seen in the plan and the proportional systems of the Dome of the Rock. The surviving internal decoration makes use of both Byzantine and Sasanian themes. This list of influences fails to account either for the innovative nature of the Dome of the Rock or for the visual impact the lavish decoration has on the viewer. ʿAbd al-Malik's building was conceived on an imperial scale and ornamented in the finest materials – gold-leaf mosaic, quarter-sawn marble and gilded bronze – available in the first/seventh century.

The tiles that now adorn the exterior were added to the building by the Ottoman sultan Süleymān I in 951–8/1545–51, but much of the interior mosaic decoration survives intact. The mosaics are taken up with a wide variety of abstract motifs and stylised vegetal designs including vinescrolls, acanthus leaves, palm trees and fruit. There are also representations of cornucopiae and jewelled vases, as well as Sasanian winged crowns and Byzantine imperial regalia. In addition, the mosaics contain bands of Arabic inscriptions written in a bold Kūfic script. Measuring some 240 metres, the longest inscription runs around the internal and external faces of the inner octagonal arcade. The precise selection of Qurʾānic *sūras* (chapters) reveals a proselytising message; passages take issue with the Christian interpretation of Christ and of the Trinity, and exhort other 'Peoples of the Book' (i.e. Christians and Jews) to submit to the new faith of Islam. Despite the presence of so many inscriptions, the precise function and meaning of the Dome of the Rock remain obscure. Associations between the Dome of the Rock and the miraculous Night Journey (*isrāʾ*; see Q 17:1) and Ascension (*miʿrāj*) of the Prophet cannot be traced back to the time of the construction of the building, though the centralised plan might lend credence to the idea that it was designed as a focus for pilgrimage. It is possible that the structure was intended to be a monument to the victory of Islam. Many of the vegetal themes in the mosaics also bring to mind visions of paradise, and perhaps the role of Jerusalem during the judgement of souls at the end of time.[13]

A number of important points can be drawn from the buildings and artefacts of this formative period. Within two decades of the death of Muḥammad in 10/632 the Qurʾān had been recorded in codex form. The writing and decorating of the Qurʾān would become one of the most

13 For different interpretations see Grabar, *Formation*, pp. 46–71; Miriam Rosen-Ayalon, *The early Islamic monuments of the Ḥaram al-Sharīf: An iconographic study*, Qedem 28 (Jerusalem, 1989).

important artistic achievements of Islamic culture. By the end of the first/seventh century inscriptions – both religious and secular – became a key mode of artistic creativity in architecture and the portable arts. The first/seventh century also witnessed the evolution of the mosque as a distinctive architectural form. The Kaʿba and the Dome of the Rock point to another important direction in Islamic architecture: the commemorative monument. In later centuries this area of artistic activity was dominated by funerary structures built over the burial places of holy men and women, Muslim martyrs, or members of political elites.

The Dome of the Rock and the experimental designs on early Islamic coinage both illustrate the willingness of Muslim patrons to adapt motifs and conventions appropriated from other artistic traditions. In the first century after 1/622 there was an urgent need to construct a visual vocabulary that would express the religious and political values of the state. Historical circumstances changed in later periods, but it is striking how craftsmen and patrons in the Islamic world remained open to cultural influences from beyond the borders of the Islamic world. While the prohibition on human and animal representations in religious art and architecture was firmly established by the end of the first/seventh century, figural painting and sculpture continued to thrive in secular contexts. Phases of state-sponsored iconoclasm are notable in Islamic history precisely because they are so rare. Likewise, disapproval expressed in *ḥadīth* and the writings of later Muslim jurists for such issues as consuming food and drink from precious metal vessels or the wearing of silk by men did not seem to affect the demand for such luxury commodities by those wealthy enough to afford them. High-quality silks, and other types of dyed and patterned textiles, enjoy an important place in Islamic culture. It has been suggested that the aesthetic values associated with richly patterned cloth permeated other aspects of the decorative arts such as the cladding of architecture with mosaics, glazed tiles, painted stucco and *opus sectile*.[14]

Sacred spaces

Though the mosque in Wāsiṭ (84/703) has a relatively simple plan, it exhibits a degree of elaboration not found in the earliest mosques in Iraq. The mosque has arcades around three sides of the courtyard and, possibly, a

14 Lisa Golombek, 'The draped universe of Islam', in Priscilla Soucek (ed.), *Content and context of the visual arts in the Islamic world* (University Park, PA, and London, 1988).

royal enclosure (*maqṣūra*) in front of the central zone of the *qibla* wall. The excavations did not reveal a *minbar* (a pulpit that, according to Muslim tradition, had its origins in the throne-chair used by the Prophet), but this may have been a portable feature in the mosque. That said, the structure at Wāsiṭ lacks two features that were to become characteristic in later mosque design: a concave niche (*miḥrāb*) located near the centre of the *qibla* wall and a minaret (a tower from which the call to prayer is made). Other important, though not universally encountered, features include monumental domes and the introduction of axiality into the planning of the mosque. This section traces how Muslim sacred spaces came to be defined in architectural terms, and considers the variant interpretations of two key features associated with the mosque – the minaret and the *miḥrāb* – in different regions of the Islamic world.

During the reign of the Umayyad caliph al-Walīd I monumental mosques were constructed in Medina (on the site of the Prophet's mosque), Jerusalem (the Aqṣā mosque), Ṣanʿāʾ in Yemen and Damascus in Syria. The ambitious and innovative character of this phase is most easily appreciated in the best-preserved example, the Great Mosque of Damascus (constructed 87–97/706–16). The mosque occupies the site of the ancient pagan *temenos* in the centre of the old city, and the exterior walls and corner towers retain elements of the original Hellenistic and Roman masonry. Like the mosque of Wāsiṭ, the Damascus mosque comprises a central courtyard with arcades on three sides and a prayer hall in front of the *qibla* wall (pl. 25.3), but there are also very significant differences. The Great Mosque of Damascus is much larger, with the ground plan measuring 157 by 100 metres. The mosque was constructed of limestone and faced with the finest materials: marble for the floors, revetments and grille windows and, in the upper parts of the walls in the arcades and the prayer hall, gold-leaf mosaics. These mosaics comprised stylised landscapes and, on the *qibla* wall, a long panel of Qurʾānic inscriptions. Only a few sections of the original mosaic decoration survive around the courtyard.[15]

The prayer hall of the mosque is composed of three aisles running parallel to the *qibla*. The aisles are bisected by a perpendicular nave, and the central crossing is marked by a monumental dome. The Great Mosque

15 For aspects of the structure and decoration of the building see Klaus Brisch, 'Observations on the iconography of the mosaics in the Great Mosque of Damascus', in Soucek (ed.), *Content and context*; Finbarr B. Flood, *The Great Mosque of Damascus: On the makings of an Umayyad visual culture* (Leiden, 2001).

25.3 Great Mosque of Damascus, Syria (87–97/706–16). Façade of the prayer hall. Photo: Marcus Milwright.

of Damascus contains the first surviving *miḥrāb* (an earlier *miḥrāb* placed in the Mosque of the Prophet between 88/707 and 90/709 no longer exists) located on the same axis as the perpendicular nave and the northern entrance to the courtyard. The *miḥrāb* – an architectural feature that admits no obvious teleological interpretation – has been interpreted as a symbolic commemoration of the place on the *qibla* wall in the mosque in Medina occupied by the Prophet during prayers.[16] The Umayyad caliphs perhaps employed the *miḥrāb* and the monumental *minbar* in their mosques as symbols of their authority.

Though the Great Mosque of Damascus has undergone many changes through its history, the plan of the building has remained largely unchanged. One of the remarkable features of the courtyard plan, however, is its capacity to expand through the repetition of specific building units. Often, phases of expansion were necessitated by the growth in the Muslim community in a given locality, though rebuilding also provided an opportunity for Muslim rulers to make conspicuous displays of piety through the elaboration of specific components of the mosque or the use of expensive decorative materials. Different aspects of this process can be seen in three major mosques of the early Islamic period: Qayrawān in Tunisia, Cordoba in Spain and Iṣfahān in Iran. It would be possible to isolate many issues from these examples, but I will concentrate upon the treatment of three crucial architectural features – the minaret, the dome and the *miḥrāb*.

The first mosque at Qayrawān was constructed in 50/670 by the general ʿUqba ibn Nāfiʿ, but no trace of this structure survives. The present plan of the mosque can be attributed to three phases of building ordered by the Aghlabid governors of the region in the third/ninth century (221/836, 248/863 and 261/875). Another restoration was ordered by the Ḥafṣid dynasty in the seventh/thirteenth century. The mosque constructed by the Aghlabid governors is a hypostyle structure with a large courtyard surrounded by arcades on three sides and a prayer hall on the south-east side. The adaptations of this basic courtyard mosque plan are significant, however. The prayer hall is elaborated through the widening of the central aisle and the creation of a perpendicular aisle running parallel to the *qibla* wall. The central aisle has domes at the point of convergence with the *qibla* aisle (i.e. in front of the *miḥrāb*) and where it meets the courtyard. This creates a main axis through the building that is picked up by the monumental minaret (pl. 25.4 (a)) located near the centre of the north-western arcade. This axial arrangement of *miḥrāb*, widened central aisle and monumental minaret was probably first formulated in the ʿAbbāsid imperial mosques of Iraq. The influence of the arts of the ʿAbbāsid heartland is also seen in the

16 George Miles, '*Miḥrāb* and ʿ*anazah*: A study of early Islamic iconography', in G. Miles (ed.), *Archaeologica orientalia in memoriam Ernst Herzfeld* (Locust Valley, NY, 1952); Estelle Whelan, 'On the origins of the *miḥrāb mujawwaf*: A reinterpretation', *IJMES*, 18 (1986).

(a)

25.4 (a) Minaret of the Great Mosque in Qayrawān. Creswell archive no. 6725, Ashmolean Museum; (b) Quṭb minār, Quwwāt al-Islām mosque, Delhi (592/1195). Photo: Hussein Keshani.

lustre-painted glazed ceramic tiles, imported from Iraq, that ornament the *miḥrāb*.[17]

While the Iraqi influences reflect the fact that the Aghlabid governors continued to acknowledge the authority of the ʿAbbāsid caliphs, it would be a mistake to underestimate the importance of local factors in the structure and decoration of the Great Mosque of Qayrawān. For instance, the two ruined third/ninth-century mosques of the city of Sāmarrāʾ (which functioned as the ʿAbbāsid capital between 221/836 and 279/892) have giant helicoidal minarets located just outside the main walled area of the mosque. It has been suggested

17 George Marçais, *Les faiences à reflets métalliques de la grande moschée de Kairouan* (Paris, 1928).

(b)

25.4 (cont.)

that these dramatic features owe their origins to ancient Mesopotamian ziggurats.[18] By contrast, the square-planned minaret at Qayrawān, with its arrangement of three diminishing stages and a dome crowning the uppermost section, can be traced back to the antique lighthouses and towers found in North African sites such as Salakta and Leptis Magna. In other words, architectural concepts might be transferred around the Islamic world, but the precise manner in which they were manifested was conditioned by factors including local building traditions, the availability of building materials and the political concerns of the ruling dynasty.

The Great Mosque of Cordoba provides another example of the adaptation of the basic courtyard mosque design. The mosque underwent a series of

18 Jonathan Bloom, *Minaret: Symbol of Islam*, Oxford Studies in Islamic Art 7 (Oxford and New York, 1989), p. 102.

major expansions and renovations from the time of its first construction in the second/eighth century, but the most magnificent phase is attributed to the rule of the Umayyad caliph al-Ḥakam II between 350/961 and 366/976. His extension of the prayer hall to the south involved the creation of a royal enclosure, or *maqṣūra*, composed of three domed bays in front of the *miḥrāb*. The *miḥrāb* itself is not simply a concave niche, but an elaborate horseshoe-shaped arch leading into a small octagonal chamber surmounted by a shell-shaped dome. This *maqṣūra* was distinguished from the remainder of the prayer hall by the use of polylobed and interlocking arches carrying delicately carved bands of ornament (an elaboration of the bichromatic voussoirs used for the arches in the remainder of the prayer hall). The grandeur of this zone was further emphasised by the elaborate domes. Marble veneer, carved marble panels and mosaic form the main components of the decoration of the *miḥrāb* arch. The arch is framed by an impressive rectangular band containing a Qurʾānic inscription in golden Kūfic on a dark-blue mosaic ground.[19]

The Great Mosque of Iṣfahān points towards another variant on the courtyard mosque design. The structural history of this building is particularly complex, but archaeological work has identified the important phases of activity starting from the second/eighth century. Most important in the present context is the transformation of the conventional courtyard mosque during the fifth/eleventh and sixth/twelfth centuries. The first significant change was the construction of a monumental domed chamber in front of the *miḥrāb* in around 478/1086. Commissioned by Niẓām al-Mulk, the chief minister (*wazīr*) of the Saljūq sultan Malikshāh (r. 465–85/1072–92), the domed chamber radically altered the visual impact of the prayer hall. In 480/1088 Niẓām al-Mulk's rival Tāj al-Mulk ordered the building of another domed chamber (Gunbad-i Khākī) just outside the north-eastern boundaries of the mosque (as the mosque has expanded, this chamber has been incorporated into the main structure). The last major change from this phase occurred over the following decades and involved the insertion of four large vaulted chambers (*īwāns*) into the façades of the courtyard.[20]

While the *īwān* is a common feature of pre-Islamic Persian architecture – employed, most famously, in the façade of the Sasanian palace at Ctesiphon – the reasons behind the adoption of the four-*īwān* plan in Iranian mosques and

19 Jerrilyn Dodds, 'The Great Mosque of Cordoba', in Jerrilyn Dodds (ed.), *al-Andalus: The art of Islamic Spain* (New York, 1992).
20 Oleg Grabar, *The Great Mosque of Isfahan* (New York, 1990), pp. 43–60.

25.5 Zone of transition in the dome chamber, Great Mosque of Ardistān, Iran (early sixth/twelfth century). Photo: Marcus Milwright.

madrasas (religious schools) remain obscure.[21] These imposing chambers facing onto the courtyard have no liturgical function but, at Iṣfahān, they have the effect of creating a major axis from the dome in front of the *miḥrāb* through to the north dome, and a secondary axis from the north-west to the south-east. The domed chamber in front of the *miḥrāb* and the four *īwāns* around the courtyard were soon picked up in provincial mosques. The mosque at Ardistān was given the four-*īwān* plan in the early sixth/twelfth century. The most impressive section of the mosque is the domed chamber, which contains a monumental carved stucco *miḥrāb*. The elaborate squinches in the zone of transition (pl. 25.5) follow the design of those in the north dome at Iṣfahān. The four-*īwān* plan was to become standard for mosques, and other types of religious structure, in Iran and the Islamic east for the following centuries. Outstanding later examples include the Bībī Khānum mosque in Samarqand (801–8/1398–1405), the Ghiyāthiyya *madrasa* in Khargird (846–9/1442–5) and the Masjid-i Shāh in Iṣfahān (1021–40/1612–30).

21 Robert Hillenbrand, *Islamic architecture: Form, function and meaning* (Edinburgh and New York, 1994), pp. 173–86.

25.6 Entrance portal of *bīmāristān* of Nūr al-Dīn, Damascus, Syria (549/1154). Photo: Marcus Milwright.

This architectural concept became popular in other regions, and numerous examples of four-*īwān* mosques, *madrasas* and *bīmāristāns* (hospitals) can be identified from the sixth/twelfth century onward. The *bīmāristān* of the Zangid ruler Nūr al-Dīn in the Syrian city of Damascus (549/1154) illustrates the transposition of this eastern building plan, and other innovations such as the *muqarnas* vault, into Syrian architecture (pl. 25.6). More monumental in character is the complex constructed in the Egyptian capital, Cairo, by the Mamlūk sultan al-Nāṣir al-Ḥasan in 757–64/1356–63. Standing beneath the citadel, and originally located next to a large parade ground, this vast complex comprises a mosque, four *madrasas* (one for each orthodox school of Muslim law), a mausoleum for the founder, an orphanage, a hospital and shops.[22] The four *īwāns* dominate the façades of the central courtyard and tower above the viewer in a manner that contrasts markedly with the more spacious impression found in the Great Mosque of Iṣfahān. While this imposing sense of verticality is maintained throughout the interior and exterior of the Sultan Ḥasan complex, the decoration finds a balance between monumentality and fineness of detail. Striking features include the use of alternating bands of white and coloured marble veneer (a style known as *ablaq*) and the wealth of carved ornament.

Both the dome and the minaret were put to use with dramatic effect in the mosques constructed during the Ottoman period (680–1342/1281–1924). One of the most impressive in the Ottoman capital, Istanbul, is the Süleymaniye mosque (958–64/1550–57), built for sultan Süleymān I (r. 926–74/1520–66) by the famous architect Sinān (d. 996/1588). The precinct containing the mosque and the founder's tomb is surrounded by a bathhouse (*ḥammām*), five *madrasas* and several other teaching institutions and ancillary structures. While the mosque retains the courtyard as part of the plan, the emphasis of the design is firmly located with the prayer hall. The dominant feature of the prayer hall is the large central dome, though the architect employs two semi-domes to introduce a processional axis from the main entrance to the *miḥrāb* (and, beyond that, to the tomb of Süleymān behind the *qibla* wall). The design of the prayer hall alludes to the sixth-century Hagia Sophia, though it is clear that Sinān's structure was meant to be a reinterpretation of this theme and not merely a pastiche. Where the ancient church was dark and sombre in character, the walls of the Süleymaniye mosque are punctured by numerous windows flooding the interior with light. Another conspicuous feature of this, and all other Ottoman mosques, is the use of the thin, pencil-like minarets.[23]

The basic model established in the imperial mosques of Istanbul proved to be highly influential upon the regions of the Ottoman empire. Architects and engineers were sent from the Ottoman capital to undertake specific

22 Howyda al-Harithy, 'The complex of Sultan Hasan in Cairo: Reading between the lines', *Muqarnas*, 13 (1996).
23 Godfrey Goodwin, *A history of Ottoman architecture* (London, 1971), pp. 215–239.

25.7 Tzisdaraki mosque in Athens (*c.* 1170/1757). Photo: Marcus Milwright.

commissions in the provinces. State control over the central aspects of design ensured a remarkable degree of continuity in the appearance of Ottoman religious architecture from regions as dispersed as Syria, Palestine, Egypt, Cyprus and the Balkan countries.[24] An example of this type of provincial Ottoman structure is the Tzisdaraki mosque in Athens, dating from around 1170/1757 (pl. 25.7). The lower storey is given over to shops with the mosque occupying the area above. Now missing its minaret, the mosque is composed of a portico covered by three domes and a square-planned prayer hall surmounted by an octagonal zone of transition and a dome.

Other solutions were found for the design of the mosque. Some, such as the third/ninth-century Masjid-i Ta'rīkh in Balkh in Afghanistan and the Bāb Mardūm in Toledo, Spain (390/1000) dispensed with the courtyard and arranged the square-planned prayer hall into nine bays, each surmounted by a vault.[25] This type of nine-bay mosque is known in a few examples spread

24 For Greece and the Balkans see essays in Machiel Kiel, *Studies on the Ottoman architecture of the Balkans* (Aldershot, 1990).

25 Geoffrey King, 'The mosque of Bab Mardum', *Art and Archaeology Research Papers*, 2 (1972).

across the Islamic world, but other developments were more localised in character and reflected the building traditions and cultural values of a specific region. A few examples can be given to illustrate the considerable degree of diversity. The Great Mosque of Xian in central China (founded in 176/792f., and constructed in its present form in 794/1392f.) adopts Chinese modes of construction and arranges the structure along the east–west axis into a series of courtyards and pavilions. The minaret takes the form of an octagonal pagoda three storeys high, decorated at each corner with sculptures of traditional Chinese dragons.[26] Traditional mosques in Indonesia, such as the Masjid Agung in Demak in Java (from *c.* 879/1474), are based around a square-planned prayer hall covered by a tall, three-tiered hipped roof.[27] The Sankore mosque in Mali (constructed between the eighth/fourteenth and the thirteenth/nineteenth centuries), and most other traditional mosques in western sub-Saharan Africa employ the conventional courtyard plan, though the repeated buttresses on the exterior and the practice of inserting groups of logs at regular intervals into the walls are unique in the religious architecture of the Islamic world.[28]

The minaret became a standard feature of mosque design in areas under the control of Sunnī rulers in the third/ninth century, and in later periods it was also adopted by most other Muslim groups. One Muslim sect, the Ibāḍīs, remains doctrinally opposed to the use of minarets, regarding them as an innovation unknown during the life of the Prophet.[29] The association between the minaret and the call to prayer (*adhān*) may seem so obvious as to need little explanation, but it is worth pointing out that the *adhān* could just as easily be made from the roof of the mosque (and, according to Muslim tradition, the Prophet instructed Bilāl to call the faithful to prayer in just such a manner). Furthermore, many minarets are so tall as to obstruct what appears to be their primary function. Indeed, it is only with the advent of modern sound amplification that *mu'adhdhins* atop lofty minarets are able to make themselves audible in the town below. The implication to be drawn from these observations is that minarets might be designed with other purposes than simply the call to prayer.[30]

26 Luo Xiaowei, 'China', in Martin Frishman and Hasan-uddin Khan (eds.), *The mosque: History, architectural development and regional diversity* (London, 1994).
27 Hugh O'Neill, 'South-east Asia', in Frishman and Khan (eds.), *Mosque*, pp. 225–40. See also Zakaria Ali, *Islamic art in Southeast Asia, 830 AD–1570 AD* (Kuala Lumpur, 1994), pp. 279–93.
28 Labelle Prussin, 'Sub-Saharan West Africa', in Frishman and Khan (eds.), *Mosque*, pp. 181–93.
29 Paolo Costa, *Historic mosques and shrines of Oman*, BAR International Series 938 (Oxford, 2001), p. 35.
30 Bloom, *Minaret*; Hillenbrand, *Islamic architecture*, pp. 129–71.

The divergent characteristics of the minarets in the mosques of Sāmarrāʾ, Qayrawān, Istanbul and Xian illustrate the ways in which local building traditions may affect this most conspicuous feature of mosque architecture. For instance, the brick-and-stone minaret (dated 474/1081) attached to the mosque of the southern Egyptian town of Isna appears to owe little to the contemporary architecture of the capital, Cairo. Rather, the influences seem to derive from the rural traditions of the area and the building styles of the Ḥijāz.[31] Iranian minarets are usually tall with a circular plan on a square base, and most have bands of decoration and inscriptions either within the brick-work or picked out in glazed tile. The virtuosity displayed in the use of brick patterns (*bannāʾī*) can be seen in the minaret added to the Tārī khāna at Dāmghān in 417–20/1026–29 (pl. 25.8 (a)) and continues into the Saljūq period (429–590/1038–1194). The Iranian mode of minaret building seems to have affected architectural styles to both the west and the east. Persianate minarets were constructed in sites in northern Syria during the sixth/twelfth and early seventh/thirteenth centuries. Looking east, the brick minaret of the Amīn mosque (1197/1778) in the western Chinese city of Turfān is ornamented with bands of repeated geometric designs that recall earlier Iranian structures. The unusual tapered profile seems, however, to owe more to local building traditions (pl. 25.8 (b)).[32]

A further function for the minaret is suggested by the giant Quṭb Minār within the Quwwāt al-Islām mosque in Delhi in India (pl. 25.4 (b)). Constructed in several phases from 592/1195, the 72-metre minaret originally stood to the south-east of the mosque (it is now incorporated into the larger complex). This impressive construction, consisting of five tapering shafts with balconies supported on *muqarnas* corbels, was commissioned by Quṭb al-Dīn Aybak, the governor of Ghūrid territories in India. The mosque stood upon the site of a demolished temple and made extensive use of spolia from Hindu and Jain religious sites. It is likely that the Quṭb Minār was meant to be read as a symbol of the victory of Islam over the existing faiths of the region. This triumphal theme is also seen in the 62-metre tower of Jām in Afghanistan, constructed by the Ghūrid ruler Ghiyāth al-Dīn Abū al-Fatḥ Muḥammad (completed in 590/1194). Like the Quṭb Minār, the notion of victory is suggested through the use of scale and the choice of Qurʾānic inscriptions encircling the tower. These same architectural and epigraphic themes are

31 Bloom, *Minaret*, pp. 136–40.
32 Bernard O'Kane, 'Iran and Central Asia', in Frishman and Khan (eds.), *Mosque*, p. 136.

(a)

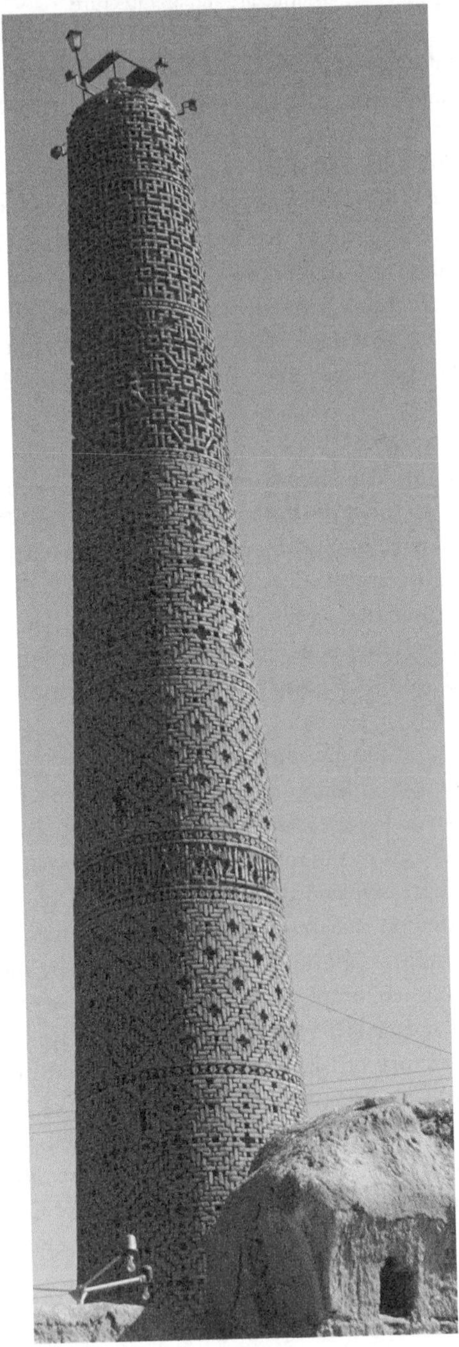

25.8 (a) Minaret attached to the Tārī khāna mosque in Dāmghān, Iran (*c.* 417–20/1026–29). Photo: Barry Flood; (b) Minaret of the Amīn mosque, Turfān (1197/1778). Photo: Astri Wright.

(b)

25.8 (cont.)

evident in towers erected by the earlier Ghaznavid rulers in Ghazna (Afghanistan) in the first half of the sixth/twelfth century.[33]

The *miḥrāb* became an important feature in major mosques in locations such as Qayrawān and Cordoba, but it could also form the main focus of artistic activity in much smaller structures. In regions such as Iran and Oman it is not uncommon to find elaborately carved stucco *miḥrāb*s up to five metres tall within small mosques and mausolea. Stucco is a relatively cheap material, and it has the advantage of being easy to mould and carve into complex designs. An early example of an elaborately carved stucco *miḥrāb* can be found in the mosque of the Iranian town of Nā'in, dating to the fourth/tenth century, although a much larger number of extant examples come from the Saljūq and Ilkhānid (654–754/1256–1363) periods. The *miḥrāb*s in sixth/twelfth-century Iran may have been produced by teams of itinerant craftsmen, and it seems likely that the proliferation of stucco prayer niches (it is not unusual for an Iranian mosque to have several along the length of the *qibla* wall) can, in part, be attributed to individual commissions by pious Muslims who wished to beautify their local mosque or shrine.[34] Iranian *miḥrāb*s of the Saljūq and Ilkhānid periods usually comprise a series of elaborate frames around a small concave niche with a shallow arched recess above. Typically these features combine bands of inscriptions with panels of stylised vegetation and geometric patterns carved in high relief.

A group of monumental *miḥrāb*s dating from the seventh/thirteenth to the eleventh/seventeenth centuries survives in the Ibāḍī mosques of Oman. One of the most impressive is to be found in the al-Shawādhina mosque in al-ʿAqr (Nizwā) (pl. 25.9). The inscription above the central arched recess gives the date of Ramaḍān 936/April–May 1530, and provides the names of those who funded the work as well as the craftsman, ʿĪsā ibn ʿAbdallāh ibn Yūsuf. The imposing inscription at the top of the *miḥrāb* comprises the profession of faith (*shahāda*). The entire surface is made up of dense vegetal interlace patterns and repeated abstract designs that appear to echo the motifs found on printed and embroidered textiles. A further decorative aspect is provided by the inclusion of Chinese blue-and-white porcelain bowls embedded into the stucco surface.[35]

*Miḥrāb*s could also be constructed using other media. The wooden *miḥrāb*s made for the mosque of Sayyida Ruqayya in Cairo (533–40/1138–45) and the

33 Ralph Pinder-Wilson, 'Ghaznavid and Ghūrid minarets', *Iran*, 39 (2001).
34 Raya Shani, 'On the stylistic idiosyncracies of a Saljūq stucco workshop from the region of Kāshān', *Iran*, 27 (1989), pp. 73–4.
35 Costa, *Mosques*, pp. 53–7, 242.

25.9 *Miḥrāb* in al-Shawādhina mosque, al-ʿAqr, Oman (936/1530). Photo: Ruba Kanaʿan.

shrine (*maqām*) of Ibrāhīm in the Aleppo citadel, Syria (563/1168f.) are constructed of small interlocking sections that combine to form complex geometric interlace patterns (the same technique was commonly employed in the construction of *minbars* at this time).[36] Glazed tile also became a popular

36 Anna Contadini, *Fatimid art at the Victoria and Albert Museum* (London, 1998), p. 112, fig. 36; Yasser Tabbaa, *The transformation of Islamic art during the Sunni revival* (London, 2001), pp. 88–91, fig. 39.

medium for *miḥrābs* in the eastern Islamic world. This type of glazed ceramic *miḥrāb* is exemplified by one made in the Iranian town of Kāshān in 623/1226 by Ḥasan ibn ʿArabshāh Naqqāsh.[37] Like the stucco prayer niches of Iran, the composition relies upon an upper and a lower arch (each supported by attached columns) framed by rectangular bands containing script, but the ornamentation on the Kāshān *miḥrāb* is provided by underglaze painting in cobalt blue and overglaze lustre decoration. Finally, the *miḥrāb* could be translated into a two-dimensional image on portable artefacts such as the carpets used by Muslims during prayer.

The written word

Arabic written in Kūfic script is encountered in the mosaic inscriptions of the Dome of the Rock and portable artefacts such as coins from the 70s/690s. From the second/eighth to the end of the fourth/tenth centuries there exist numerous examples of Qurʾāns written in Kūfic script on parchment. Typically, the format of the page is horizontal with wide margins left around three sides. Some Kūfic Qurʾāns have as few as three lines on each page with the complete text contained within as many as thirty separately bound parts (sing. *juzʾ*). While each *juzʾ* would usually have decorated frontispieces and finis-pieces, the main body of the text is striking for the absence of ornament. The script is usually laid out in thick strokes of black with the vocalisation sometimes marked with red dots.[38] One of the most dramatic of the Kūfic Qurʾāns has been attributed to North Africa (perhaps Qayrawān) in the early fourth/tenth century. Possibly produced for the Fāṭimid caliphs, the parchment leaves are stained blue and the Kūfic script is written in gold.[39] Variant forms of Kūfic script can be found in different regions of the Islamic world. Maghribī (i.e. western Islamic) styles often introduce an oblique emphasis and long, sloping tails into the letter forms as a means to create a rhythmic quality on the page. Complex forms of Kūfic also appear in architecture. For instance, the Duvāzda Imām in the Iranian town of Yazd (429/1037) contains a series of Qurʾānic and foundation inscriptions painted on the interior (pl. 25.10). The plaiting of the vertical characters and the elaboration of the terminals are

37 Arthur Lane, *Early Islamic pottery* (London, 1947), pl. 66; Oliver Watson, *Persian lustre ware* (London and Boston, 1985), pp. 130–1, 190.

38 François Déroche, *The Abbasid tradition: Qurʾāns of the 8th to the 10th centuries AD*, Nasser D. Khalili Collection of Islamic Art 1 (London, 1992).

39 Ibid., pp. 92–5, no. 42.

25.10 Inscription from the Duvāzda Imām, Yazd (429/1037). Photo: Barry Flood.

features also encountered in carved stucco *miḥrābs* and glazed ceramics in eastern Iran during this period.[40]

Many other types of script existed – the Iraqi bookseller and scholar Ibn al-Nadīm (d. 385/995 or 388/998) lists twenty-six separate styles – but, until the end of the fourth/tenth century, they were employed for secular purposes. The proportional systems governing these variant scripts had been regularised by Ibn Muqla (d. 328/940), the *wazīr* (chief minister) to the ʿAbbāsid caliph in Baghdad, but the most significant change can be traced several decades later with the production of a small, single-volume Qurʾān by the scribe ʿAlī ibn Hilāl ibn al-Bawwāb (d. 413/1022).[41] Written on pale-brown paper, Ibn al-Bawwāb's Qurʾān (dated 391/1000f.) is the first to make use of two forms of cursive script – *naskh* for the main text and *thuluth* for the *sūra* headings – and has all of the diacritical points and vowels marked into the main text. The unpretentious quality of the manuscript disguises its significance to the history of Islamic art. The change from the austere and monumental Kūfic to the more flowing *naskh* and *thuluth* scripts greatly enhanced the legibility of the Qurʾān and paved the way for the development of other scripts in later

40 Lisa Volov (Golombek), 'Plaited Kufic on Samanid epigraphic pottery', *Ars Orientalis*, 6 (1966).
41 Tabbaa, *Transformation*, pp. 25–52.

centuries. Cursive scripts also became standard for monumental inscriptions on architecture from the sixth/twelfth century. The domed chamber of the Great Mosque of Ardistān contains an inscription in *thuluth* script carved in a stucco band beneath the zone of transition (pl. 25.5).

Some of the finest Qurʾāns of the later Islamic period were produced in Egypt and Syria during the Mamlūk sultanate (548–922/1250–1517). Often the work of several skilled craftsmen, these multi-volume works were commissioned for religious institutions built by Mamlūk sultans and *amīrs*. Qurʾāns such as the seven-volume version commissioned by Baybars al-Jāshnikīr (r. 704–5/1304–6) are notable both for the quality of the scripts and the elaborately painted and gilded pages that form the frontispieces of each volume (pl. 25.11). As with the Ibn al-Bawwāb Qurʾān, the calligraphers of the Mamlūk period often employed different scripts for the main text and the *sūra* headings.[42] This combination of more than one script is also seen in inscriptions applied onto architecture. For instance, Iranian stucco *miḥrābs* often have *naskh* script for the Qurʾānic verses in the framing band and Kūfic for secondary inscriptions around the inner arches.

Inscriptions are a common feature of the portable arts, though their content is not exclusively religious in character. The glazed ceramics produced in north-eastern Iran and Transoxania in the Sāmānid period (204–395/819–1005) sometimes carry elegant Kūfic script painted in black pigment over a white slip. These inscriptions may wish blessings to the owner of the vessel, but the most elaborate contain improving aphorisms such as 'patience is the key to felicity' and 'generosity is the quality of the people of paradise'.[43] The interior and exterior decoration of the Egyptian inlaid brass basin made for the Mamlūk sultan al-Nāṣir Muḥammad ibn Qalāwūn (*c.* 730/1330) is dominated by bands of Arabic inscriptions written in *thuluth* script similar to that employed in Mamlūk Qurʾāns of the eighth/fourteenth century (pl. 25.12).[44] The grandiose inscriptions have no religious content, but rather celebrate the sultan for whom it was made. The smaller, secondary inscriptions in the roundels magnify this message with the words 'Glory to our master, the sultan'. Similar themes are picked up on textiles. For instance, in the early centuries, robes bestowed upon an official by the caliph would be decorated with embroidered inscriptions (*ṭirāz*) carrying the latter's regnal name and titles. Embroidered *ṭirāz* bands are also often seen on the clothing of

42 David James, *Qurʾāns of the Mamluks* (London, 1988).
43 Sheila Blair, *Islamic inscriptions* (New York, 1998), pp. 151–2.
44 Esin Atil, *Renaissance of Islam: Art of the Mamluks* (Washington, DC, 1981), pp. 50–116.

25.11 Frontispiece of volume seven of the Qur'ān of Baybars al-Jāshnikīr, Egypt (704–5/1304–6), Add. 22406–13, fos. 1v–2r. By permission of the British Library.

25.12 Inlaid brass basin made for Sultan al-Nāṣir Muḥammad, Egypt (c. 730/1330), OA 1851.1–4.1. By permission of the British Museum.

characters in manuscript illustrations painted in Syria and Iraq during the seventh/thirteenth century (pl. 25.18).

Ornamental traditions

Complex geometric interlace, repeated patterns and stylised vegetal themes are often seen as defining characteristics of Islamic art and architectural decoration – and, indeed, there are countless examples of these phenomena in the visual cultures of the Islamic world. That said, this is far from being the only culture to exhibit such an interest in forms of non-representational and vegetal ornament. Furthermore, the ornamental designs we possess from the first two centuries of Islam show clear relationships to pre-existing modes of ornament in the Late Antique Mediterranean and Middle East. Comparing the continuous knot patterns in the mosaic floors of Byzantine churches in Jordan with the famous bathhouse in the Umayyad palace complex of Khirbat al-Mafjar (dating to the 120s/740s) near Jericho, it is apparent that the latter represents an expansion of scale rather than an elaboration in terms of the structural complexity in the designs themselves. This reliance upon earlier traditions is also seen in classicising vinescroll ornaments in other Umayyad architectural ornament such as the carved limestone façade of the palace of Mshattā in Jordan, probably dating to the late 120s/740s.[45]

A decisive shift away from the systems of repeated ornament of the Late Antique Mediterranean occurred in Iraq during the third/ninth century. This change is seen best in the stucco decoration applied to the palaces and houses of the ʿAbbāsid capital, Sāmarrāʾ. Three main styles of stucco were isolated in the excavations at Sāmarrāʾ. The first style (also seen in the earlier ʿAbbāsid palaces at Raqqa in Syria) is a debased form of Late Antique vegetal scroll which exhibits a tendency to standardise and repeat the forms of the leaves, tendrils and fruit. This process is intensified in the second style where the naturalistic forms are entirely subordinated to the larger geometric forms arranged symmetrically in each panel. In both styles the foreground details are clearly distinguished from the deeply carved and drilled background. In the last style (often known as the 'bevelled style') this distinction between foreground and background is dissolved by cutting the stucco at a shallow angle.[46]

This radical change may be attributed in part to the use of carved wooden moulds that were pressed into the surface of the wet stucco – a development that greatly reduced the labour involved in ornamenting large spaces – but its significance is not merely technical in nature. The spatial ambiguity created by the bevelled edges liberated craftsmen from the necessity to employ naturalistic motifs in their designs. One is no longer sure whether the sinuous shapes derive from natural forms, and it also becomes difficult to establish where one form ends and the new one begins. Most important is that these patterns have the capacity for infinite repetition both along the horizontal and vertical planes. The origins of the bevelled style remain obscure – it may have come from another medium such as leatherwork – but there can be no doubt about the popularity of the style in later centuries. Examples of bevelled-style ornament can be found on architectural decoration and portable artefacts from North Africa to Central Asia.[47]

New forms of two- and three-dimensional geometric ornament also developed in Islamic art and architecture. The most important types are geometric interlace patterns (often known by the Persian word *girih*, meaning 'knot') and

45 Grabar, *Formation*, pp. 178–87, pl. 71, 119–3.

46 Maurice Dimand, 'Studies in Islamic ornament, II: The origin of the second style of Samarra decoration', in Miles (ed.), *Archaeologica orientalia*; Creswell, *Early Muslim architecture*, vol. II, pp. 286–8; Gülru Neçipoğlu, *The Topkapi scroll: Geometry and ornament in Islamic architecture* (Santa Monica, 1995), pp. 93–7.

47 Richard Ettinghausen, 'The "beveled style" in the post-Samarra period', in Miles (ed.), *Archaeologica orientalia*.

the *muqarnas*. Geometric strapwork patterns can be identified in the marble window grilles of the Great Mosque of Damascus and the palace of Khirbat al-Mafjar, but these designs employ relatively simple threefold rotational symmetry that is already found in ornamental panels on surviving Roman–Byzantine buildings in Syria. In the fifth/eleventh century in Iraq there appears a new group of interlace designs based on much more sophisticated geometric principles. *Girih* designs are first found on the frontispieces of Qurʾān manuscripts produced in Baghdad in the early fifth/eleventh century. Panels of complex geometric interlace are found later in the century on the two mausolea at Kharraqān (460/1067f. and 486/1093) in Iran (pl. 25.13). Comparable designs have been located at excavations of fifth/eleventh- and sixth/twelfth-century domestic and palace structures in Sīrāf, Nīshāpūr, Rayy (Iran), Tirmidh (Uzbekistan) and Lashkār-i Bāzār (Afghanistan).[48]

Girih usually comprises star polygons combined with a range of convex polygons in symmetrical arrangements. These shapes are separated from one another by straps – which often appear to be weaving under and over one another. Like the bevelled style, these patterns possess the potential for endless expansion. This expansion is governed by a strict geometric grid based around two-, three-, four-, or sixfold rotational symmetry around a set of regularly spaced points. The imposition of a geometric grid does not preclude the inclusion of curvilinear or vegetal components. A few examples may be mentioned here to demonstrate the diverse application of these principles. The frontispiece – often known as 'carpet pages' – of the seven-volume Qurʾān of Baybars al-Jāshnikīr (pl. 25.11) shows how *girih* was employed in the religious art of eighth/fourteenth-century Egypt (strapwork designs also appear on *minbars*, Qurʾān boxes and other mosque furnishings). Another variant on the *girih* is found in the elegant pierced marble screens of the tomb of Salīm Chishtī in the Indian city of Fatehpur Sikri (after 979/1571). In this example the geometric designs carved in white marble are animated by changing effects of the light. In the case of the Ben Yūsuf *madrasa* (972/1564f.) in the Moroccan town of Marrakesh, the colour and texture of this lower band of decoration contrasts with the delicately carved stucco ornament above.

Muqarnas is perhaps the most original and distinctive component of Islamic architecture, though it remains difficult to provide the word with a single definition. A *muqarnas* may be a self-supporting vault made of stone or wood, a stucco structure hanging from a vault built of a more durable material, a decorative addition onto a capital or a shallow niche in a façade. The

48 Neçipoğlu, *The Topkapi scroll*, pp. 97–109; Tabbaa, *Transformation*, pp. 73–102.

25.13 Detail of the earlier tomb at Kharraqān (460/1067f.). Photo: Andrew Marsham.

fundamental principle governing the composition of a *muqarnas* is the repetition in rows of concave elements and other three-dimensional geometric shapes in order to create a larger concave form.[49] The precursor of the *muqarnas* is the structural feature known as the squinch employed in the zones of transition within square-planned domed buildings. Squinches are first

49 Tabbaa, *Transformation*, pp. 103–36.

found in Sasanian buildings, but it was in the Islamic period that masons learned to elaborate this structural feature by breaking it down into a series of smaller concave and convex units. This process of spatial experimentation is seen in the tomb of ʿArab Aṭāʾ at Tīm (367/977f.) and the sixth/twelfth-century domed chamber in the Great Mosque of Ardistān (pl. 25.5).

The earliest surviving *muqarnas* dome is to be found over the shrine of Imām Dūr, at the Iraqi town of Dūr near Sāmarrāʾ (478/1085f.). The dome surmounts a square brick base. The dramatic sculptural quality of the exterior belies the delicacy and complexity of the *muqarnas* dome within. The confidence of the execution of the *muqarnas* on this provincial monument indicates that the experimental phase of the *muqarnas* occurred elsewhere in earlier decades. The vogue for *muqarnas* vaulting soon spread around the Islamic world and beyond its borders. For instance, the palace chapel of the Norman king Roger II in Palermo still possesses its painted wooden stalactite vault (completed *c.* 534/1140).

The entrance portal of the *bīmāristān* (hospital) built by Nūr al-Dīn in Damascus (549/1154f.) is a good illustration of the varied application of *muqarnas* in this period (pl. 25.6). Above the gate is a shallow vault constructed of stucco. The lowest register is composed of a row of niches with cusped arches alternating with the colonettes that support the undulating honeycomb structure above. The portal leads to a vestibule that, itself, is covered by a tall wood and stucco *muqarnas* dome. *Girih* is also represented on the portal of the *bīmāristān* on the bronze doors of the entranceway. Probably the most sophisticated of all the later *muqarnas* vaults are to be found in the Alhambra palace in Granada, Spain. The Hall of the Two Sisters constructed by the Naṣrid ruler Yūsuf I (r. 733–55/1333–54) comprises a square base with an octagonal zone of transition and a dome above. Carved and painted stucco *muqarnas* vaulting is employed to dazzling effect both in the dome and in the squinches and arches of the zone of transition.

It seems likely that the evolutionary leap represented by *girih* and *muqarnas* was a product of developments in geometry, and other areas of mathematics, in the fourth/tenth and fifth/eleventh centuries. Manuals of practical geometry designed for craftsmen also appear in this period. Masons, tile-cutters and stucco workers also compiled 'pattern books' with the different geometric designs they employed in their crafts, though few survive today. The most impressive manuscript of this type is a ninth/fifteenth-century scroll now in the Topkapı Saray Museum, Istanbul. Probably produced for a Tīmūrid patron in Central Asia, and never intended for practical use, this elegant work contains examples of inscription panels and two-dimensional rectilinear brick patterns and geometric interlace designs as well as diagrammatic representations of *muqarnas* vaulting.[50]

Other modes of repeated decoration can be found in Islamic art. The introduction of the bevelled style did not spell the end of the classicising modes of vegetal ornament. Vinescrolls, acanthus leaf and other vegetal patterns continued to be employed in Islamic lands. For instance, examples of intricate inhabited vinescroll designs – containing both human and animal representations – are found in the carved ivory panels made in Fāṭimid Egypt (358–567/969–1171) and the ivory pyxides produced for the Spanish Umayyad court (138–422/756–1031).[51] Vegetal forms are often employed as a means to subdivide the decorated space into a series of roundels, but individual leaves are usually distorted in order to fill spaces in the compositions. This tendency to subordinate vegetal ornament to the requirements of the larger pattern remains a common theme in later Islamic decoration. The frontispieces of the multi-volume Mamlūk and Ilkhānid Qurʾāns are dominated by the epigraphic component and the *girih* in the central panels, but closer examination often reveals stylised leaves, tendrils and flowers in the polygonal panels created by the geometric interlace.[52] The inscriptions on the inlaid brass basin made for the Mamlūk sultan al-Nāṣir Muḥammad in around 730/1330 (pl. 25.12) have been discussed above, but attention may also be drawn to the supporting role performed by the dense foliage that fills much of the remaining space on the interior and exterior. In addition, the craftsmen recognised visual ambiguities inherent in the leaf forms and transformed some into ducks and geese.

Commemorative art and architecture

Commemoration has played an important role in Islamic art and architecture from the earliest periods. The spear (*ʿanaza*) that was driven into the ground where the Prophet Muḥammad stood in the mosque in Medina remained in the prayer hall of the building in the decades following his death, and is even represented on a coin minted in 76/695f.[53] The Dome of the Rock illustrates the adoption of the centrally planned Roman–Byzantine martyrium into Islamic architecture. Moving to the present, Muslim families in the Middle East sometimes commission paintings of Mecca and Medina for the exterior

50 Neçipoğlu, *The Topkapi scroll*, pp. 231–347.
51 Contadini, *Fatimid art*, pp. 109–11; Francisco Prado-Vilar, 'Circular visions of fertility and punishment: Caliphal ivory caskets from al-Andalus', *Muqarnas*, 14 (1997).
52 James, *Qurʾāns*; Atil, *Renaissance of Islam*, pp. 24–48.
53 Miles, '*Miḥrāb*'.

walls of their houses after a member of the household has performed the *ḥajj*, and it is still common practice for Muslims visiting the Shīʿite shrines of al-Ḥusayn ibn ʿAlī at Karbalāʾ and Imām Riḍā at Mashhad to purchase decorated clay tablets (sing. *muhr*) in commemoration of their pilgrimage.

Citing the authority of the Prophet, the four schools (sing. *madhhab*) of Sunnī Muslim law generally opposed the veneration of tombs and the construction of edifices over places of burial. The austerity of Muslim practices of interment seems, therefore, at odds with the growth of funerary architecture around the Islamic world. The domed structure known as Qubbat al-Sulaybiyya in the Iraqi city of Sāmarrāʾ (*c*. 248/862) is perhaps the earliest mausoleum to survive, and may be the resting-place of three of the ʿAbbāsid caliphs. The octagonal plan of the structure brings to mind the Dome of the Rock. The early fourth/tenth-century tomb of Ismāʿīl the Sāmānid in Bukhārā (Uzbekistan) is a key example in the subsequent evolution of the Islamic mausoleum. Constructed of baked brick, the domed building is square in plan with slightly tapering walls, each pierced by an arched entrance. The interior and exterior surfaces are animated by decorative brick courses and cut-brick patterns. Later mausolea to adopt the square plan with the dome include the undated Fāṭimid tombs in the southern Egyptian town of Aswān, the Ghaznavid structure at Sangbast in Iran (possibly for Arslān Jādhib: early fifth/eleventh century) and those dedicated to Sultan Sanjar in Marw in Turkmenistan (*c*. 444/1152) and Imām Shāfiʿī in Cairo (614/1217).

Other solutions were found to the design of the mausoleum, though most retained the concepts of the centralised plan with a dome or conical roof. Perhaps the most dramatic of all the early Islamic mausolea is Gunbad-i Qābūs (397/1006f.) near to the Iranian town of Jurjān. Located on a slight rise in the land, the tower has a circular shaft surrounded by ten angular projections and a tall, conical roof. The two brick mausolea at Kharraqān (460/1067f. and 486/1093) have octagonal plans with rounded corner buttresses and double shell domes (pl. 25.13).[54] Variants of the polygonal plan tower seen in later Iranian mausolea include Gunbad-i Qabud in Marāgha (593/1196f) and Bastām (708/1308f.).

Monumental tombs could become a major focus of imperial patronage. This phenomenon can be illustrated by two famous examples. Constructed with an octagonal domed chamber with a smaller rectangular chamber to the south, the mausoleum of the Ilkhānid ruler Öljaytū in Sulṭāniyya (*c*. 710–16/1310–16) picks up on the themes noted in the previous examples but lends

54 David Stronach and T. Cuyler Young, 'Three Seljuq tomb towers', *Iran*, 4 (1966).

them a greater scale and magnificence. The interior appears to have been decorated twice, with the earlier layer of ornamental brickwork, glazed tile and carved stucco and terracotta largely obliterated by a second skin of plaster painted with inscriptions and geometric designs. It has been suggested that the first phase of decoration, containing the repeated pairing of the names of Muḥammad and ʿAlī, was covered up because the ruler switched his allegiance from Shīʿite to Sunnī Islam in the last years of his life.[55] Another imperially sponsored mausoleum, the Tāj Maḥal in Āgrā (completed 1057/1647), has a very different history. Commissioned by the Mughal ruler Shāhjahān in honour of his favourite wife, Mumtāz-i Maḥal, the domed mausoleum is located at the north end of a large formal garden. The visual impact of the monument is enhanced by the white marble cladding of the structure and the delicate carved and inlaid decoration. The Qur'ānic verses pick up on themes of paradise and the Day of Judgement. Paradisaical themes are perhaps also to be seen in the carvings of flowers (copied from European botanical illustrations) in the dadoes.[56]

The life and actions of the Prophet Muḥammad were matters of profound interest to the Muslim community in the decades and centuries after his death. His deeds and pronouncements (*ḥadīth*) were assembled into written form in the second/eighth and third/ninth centuries, while authors such as Ibn Isḥāq (d. 150/767) provided Muslim readers with biographies of the Prophet. Despite the proliferation of this branch of Muslim literature, there appears to have been no demand among the authors or the patrons of manuscripts to complement the texts with illustrations. The first surviving images of the Prophet occur in a series of manuscripts made for the Mongol (Ilkhānid) rulers of Iran; their presence at this time is perhaps explained by the fact that the Mongols were new converts to Islam. Significantly, the illustrations are not found in collections of *ḥadīth* or biographies, but in historical works such as the *Jāmiʿ al-tawārīkh* (Compendium of histories), written in the Iranian city of Tabrīz by the powerful vizier Rashīd al-Dīn (d. 718/1318). Another group of images is contained in a manuscript of al-Bīrūnī's (d. 439/1048) *Āthār al-bāqiya* (Chronologies of ancient nations) dating to 707/1307f.[57] The painting of the

55 Eleanor Sims, 'The "iconography" of the internal decoration of the mausoleum of Ūljāytū at Sultaniyya', in Soucek (ed.), *Content and context*.
56 Catherine Asher, *The Cambridge history of India*, vol. I.4: *Architecture of Mughal India*, (Cambridge, 1992), pp. 209–15.
57 Robert Hillenbrand, 'Images of Muhammad in al-Biruni's "Chronology of ancient nations"', in Robert Hillenbrand (ed.), *Persian painting from the Mongols to the Qajars: Studies in honour of B. W. Robinson* (London and New York, 2000).

25.14 Investiture of ʿAlī, Ghadīr Khumm, from al-Bīrūnī, *Āthār al-bāqiya* (707/1307f.), Arab 161 f. 162r. By permission of Edinburgh University Library.

investiture of ʿAlī at Ghadīr Khumm (pl. 25.14) creates a symmetrical composition of figures in the foreground with a landscape behind. Though the poses of the figures are rather static, the raised arm of the Prophet as he grasps ʿAlī's shoulder and the direct exchange of glances between the two introduces a sense of drama to the scene. Depictions of Muḥammad, often accompanied by angels and other heavenly figures, also appear in the painted manuscripts of the Tīmūrid (771–912/1370–1506) and Ṣafavid (907–1145/1501–1732) periods detailing the Prophet's mystical journey (*miʿrāj*). *Miʿrāj* literature evidently stimulated the imaginations of the illustrators, and resulted in some of the most vibrant compositions in the tradition of Persian painting.[58]

Cultural interaction

The Islamic world continued to be influenced by Graeco-Roman art and intellectual culture from the first contacts with the Byzantine empire in the first/seventh century through to the fall of Constantinople in 857/1453. Byzantine mosaicists were sent by the Byzantine emperor to work on the decoration of caliph al-Walīd's mosques in Damascus and Medina, and Muslim writers also claim that in the fourth/tenth century the emperor Nikephoros Phokas acquiesced to a request sent by the Spanish caliph al-Ḥakam II for mosaicists to work on the Great Mosque of Cordoba.[59] In 337/948f. another diplomatic exchange resulted in the dispatch to Cordoba of an illustrated manuscript of the herbal (commonly known as *De materia medica*, and in Arabic as *Kitāb al-ḥashā'ish*) of the first-century botanist and physician Pedanius Dioscorides. Translations of this famous Antique Greek text were made in the Middle East, and lavishly illustrated versions survive from the seventh/thirteenth to the tenth/sixteenth centuries.[60] Other Greek medical and scientific texts were translated and illustrated in the Middle East during this period, while some authors also assembled compilations of improving anecdotes drawn from the Classical past. An early seventh/thirteenth-century copy of al-Mubashshir ibn Fātik's *Mukhtār al-ḥikam* (Selection of wise sayings, 445/1048f.) contains a frontispiece with depictions of six Antique scholars.[61] While this convention of representing a scholarly debate can be traced back to Late Antique manuscripts such as the herbal made for the sixth-century Byzantine princess Juliana Anicia, the Islamic artist gives the genre a new twist by arranging the scholars symmetrically within a simple *girih* pattern.

58 Marie-Rose Séguy, *The miraculous journey of Mahomet*/Mirâj nâmeh (New York, 1977); Oleg Grabar, *Mostly miniatures: An introduction to Persian painting* (Princeton, 2000), pp. 91–6; Eleanor Sims, Boris Marshak and Ernst Grube, *Peerless images: Persian painting and its sources* (New Haven and London, 2002), pp. 147–52.

59 El Cheikh, *Byzantium*, pp. 56–60.

60 Minta Collins, *Medieval herbals: The illustrative traditions* (London and Toronto, 2000), pp. 31–147.

61 Richard Ettinghausen, *Arab painting* (Geneva, 1962), pp. 75–7; Eva Hoffman, 'The author portrait in thirteenth-century Arabic manuscripts: A new Islamic context for a Late Antique tradition', *Muqarnas*, 10 (1993), pp. 6–8.

The exchange of paintings and other forms of visual imagery also had an impact on Islamic art in later periods. The Ottoman sultans Meḥmed II (r. 849/1444f. and 855–86/1451–81) and Süleymān I both commissioned art works from Europe, while the Persian painter Muḥammad Zamān (*fl.* 1059–1116/1649–1704) produced paintings of Old Testament scenes that drew inspiration from imported Flemish and Italian prints.[62] The interaction between different cultures was not always benign in character, however. For instance, the Quwwāt al-Islām mosque in Delhi, and other Ghūrid religious monuments in India and Pakistan, made conspicuous use of spolia from destroyed Hindu and Jain temples as trophies of victory. These complex issues cannot be addressed in detail here, but one important area of cultural interaction will be discussed: the relationship between the Islamic world and China.

The inclusion of Chinese porcelain bowls into the tenth/sixteenth-century *miḥrāb* of the al-Shawādhina mosque (pl. 25.9) provides a revealing insight into the value accorded to this type of imported commodity in the medieval Islamic world. Chinese ceramics have been found in other stucco *miḥrābs* in Oman, but the practice does not appear to be known elsewhere. It is clear that the conspicuous presence of these imported items in a *miḥrāb* reflects the economic and cultural importance of international maritime trade to the coastal populations around the Persian Gulf. Excavations in the Gulf have shown that Chinese ceramics, as well as a wide range of other commodities from India and South-East Asia, were being imported into the Middle East throughout the Islamic period.

Economic contact with China was to have a far-reaching influence upon the development of the arts in the Islamic world. For instance, paper was manufactured in China long before the appearance of the first paper mills in Samarqand and Baghdad in the second half of the second/eighth century.[63] As important as specific technological borrowings was the elevated status accorded in Islamic literature to the craftsmen of China; imported Chinese objects set standards of manufacture and decoration against which Islamic craftsmen could measure themselves. This was particularly true in the case of pottery production. Those with sufficient wealth often chose to amass collections of Chinese celadons and porcelains – one of the world's greatest

62 Topkapi Museum, *The sultan's portrait: Picturing the house of Osman* (Istanbul, 2000), pp. 64–109; Eleanor Sims, 'Towards a monograph on the 17th-century Iranian painter Muḥammad Zamān ibn Ḥāji Yūsuf', *Islamic Art*, 5 (2001).

63 Jonathan Bloom, *Paper before print: The history and impact of paper in the Islamic world* (New Haven and London, 2001), pp. 42–5.

collections of Chinese pottery was assembled by the Ottoman sultans and remains in the Topkapı Saray in Istanbul – but there was always a ready market for cheaper local copies. Literary sources and archaeological research attest to the import of T'ang dynasty (618–906) *sancai* (three colour) and white wares in the second/eighth century, though this trade intensified from the third/ninth century. By the last quarter of the second/eighth century potters in Iraq were not only imitating aspects of the vessel shape and glaze colours of the Chinese vessels but also incorporating new features such as slip-incised (sgraffito) decoration and Arabic inscriptions painted in cobalt on opaque white glaze.[64]

Perhaps the most influential of all the types of Chinese pottery was blue-and-white porcelain. Cobalt had been used to create blue glazes in the T'ang period, but it was not until the Yuan dynasty (*c.* 678–770/1279–1368) that the technique of painting this pigment under the glaze was perfected.[65] Chinese blue-and-white wares of the eighth/fourteenth and ninth/fifteenth centuries are painted with delicate wave and cloud designs and lotus, prunus and chrysanthemum blossoms, as well as birds and animals. In response to the aesthetic challenge posed by the porcelain body Islamic potters developed a new type of white ceramic, known as stonepaste or frit ware, composed of pale clay mixed with finely ground quartz and glass (or glass frit).[66] This technological development allowed the skilled potters of the Middle East to paint in cobalt (sometimes with other colours such as turquoise, green and black) beneath a colourless glaze. The underglaze-painted stonepaste wares of the Ilkhānid, Mamlūk (648–922/1250–1517) and Tīmūrid (771–912/1370–1506) domains illustrate the range of artistic responses.[67] Some surviving examples are almost exact replicas of Chinese prototypes but, more commonly, one encounters the introduction of Islamic themes such as epigraphy and geometric patterns. Perhaps the finest of all such stonepaste wares were produced in the Turkish town of Iznik during the late ninth/fifteenth and tenth/sixteenth centuries. Though the potters of Iznik produced glazed wares with

64 Lane, *Early Islamic pottery*, pp. 10–16; Alastair Northedge and Derek Kennet, 'The Samarra horizon', in Ernst Grube (ed.), *Cobalt and lustre: The first centuries of Islamic pottery*, Nasser D. Khalili Collection of Islamic Art 9 (London, 1994); Anne-Marie Bernsted, *Early Islamic pottery: Materials and techniques* (London, 2003), pp. 2–7.

65 John Carswell, *Blue and white: Chinese porcelain around the world* (London, 2000), pp. 79–105.

66 Bernsted, *Early Islamic pottery*, pp. 23–8.

67 Arthur Lane, *Later Islamic pottery* (London, 1957), pp. 1–67; Atil, *Renaissance of Islam*, pp. 146–92; Lisa Golombek, Robert Mason and Gauvin Bailey, *Tamerlane's tableware: A new approach to chinoiserie ceramics of fifteenth- and sixteenth-century Iran* (Costa Mesa, 1996).

polychromatic painting, they also exploited the visual possibilities of the more restricted palette of cobalt blue and white (sometimes with the addition of turquoise).[68] The same techniques were also employed in the production of tiles. Among the most magnificent are the tenth/sixteenth-century pair of tiles (each over a metre high) made for the circumcision room (Sünnet Odasi) in the Topkapı Saray in Istanbul (pl. 25.15).[69]

The influence of Chinese scroll painting can be found in the early eighth/fourteenth-century Ilkhānid manuscripts produced in Iran and Iraq.[70] The illustration from al-Bīrūnī's *Āthār al-bāqiya* (pl. 25.14) provides an example of the way in which Persian painters sought to combine aspects of Middle Eastern and Chinese aesthetic conventions. The figures in the foreground are defined in sharp lines and solid areas of pigment, but the landscape – including the gnarled trees and gold-edged clouds – is painted using more diffuse washes of colour in a more Chinese manner. Imported Chinese ceramics, silk and carved lacquer also had an impact upon arts further west during the eighth/fourteenth century.[71] Chinoiserie designs have been noted on the decoration of the Egyptian inlaid brass basin made in around 730/1330 (pl. 25.12) and the carving of the mausoleum complex of sultan al-Nāṣir al-Ḥasan in Cairo (757–64/1356–63), but they can also be found in the decorated pages of the lavish Qurʾāns produced for wealthy patrons in Egypt, Syria, Iraq and Iran at this time.

Urban life

It was in the towns and cities of the Islamic world that the finest craftsmen congregated. Craftsmen were often organised into workshops, either directly under the control of a royal court or, more typically, as commercial enterprises undertaking a wide range of commissions for the open market. These urban workshops were almost exclusively populated by men. This is not to suggest, of course, that women were not involved in craft activities; the roles

68 Nurhan Atasoy and Julian Raby, *Iznik: The pottery of Ottoman Turkey* (London, 1989), pp. 121–8.

69 Gülru Neçipoğlu, 'From international Timurid to Ottoman: A change in taste in sixteenth-century ceramic tiles', *Muqarnas*, 7 (1990), pp. 148–53.

70 Basil Gray, *Persian painting* (Cleveland, 1961), pp. 19–55; Sims, Marshak and Grube, *Peerless images*, pp. 41–50; Robert Hillenbrand, 'The arts of the illustrated book in Ilkhanid Iran', in Linda Komaroff and Stefano Carboni (eds.), *The legacy of Genghis Khan: Courtly art and culture in Western Asia, 1256–1353* (New Haven and London, 2002).

71 Linda Komaroff, 'The transmission and dissemination of a new visual language', in Komaroff and Carboni (eds.), *Legacy*.

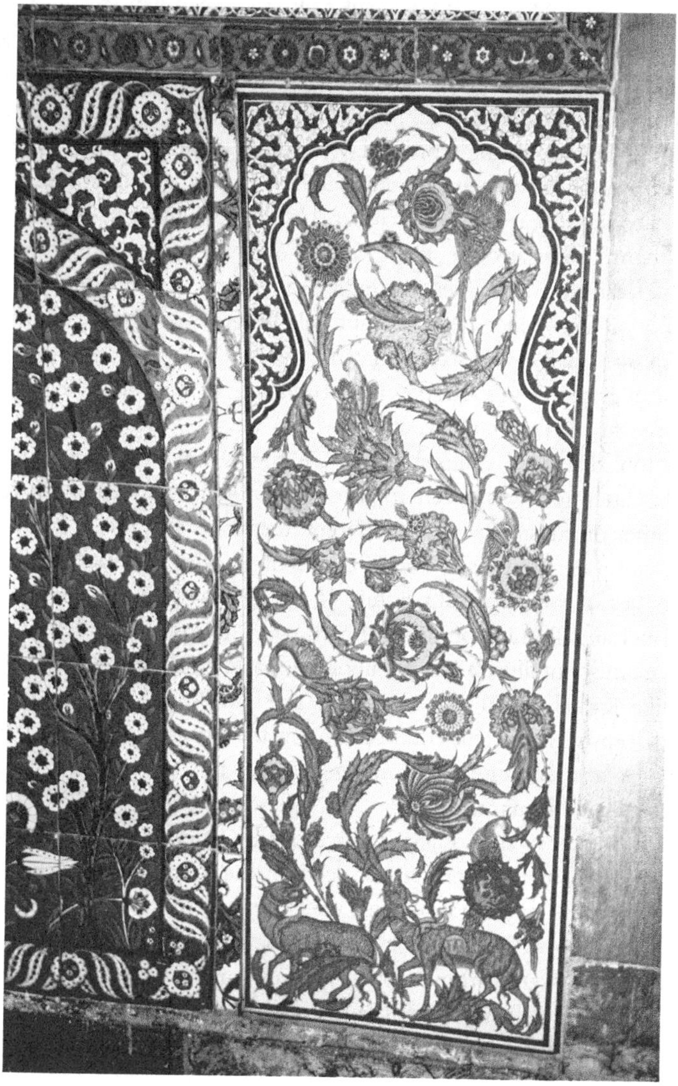

25.15 Glazed tiles from the circumcision room, Topkapı Saray, Istanbul (tenth/sixteenth century). Photo: Marcus Milwright.

performed by women in urban areas tended to be those that could be done within the domestic environment, such as dyeing and weaving.

In the famous *Muqaddima* (the prolegomenon to his universal history), the North African polymath Ibn Khaldūn (d. 808/1406) provides a list of the 'crafts' (sing. *ṣināʿa*) that are either 'noble' (*sharīf*) or simply 'necessary' (*ḍarūrī*) to the functioning of a town or city. Interestingly, his definition of 'craft' – comprising activities ranging from tailoring, book production, writing and architecture to agriculture and midwifery – is much wider than would normally be applied to the word today. Though he acknowledges the crafts as a fundamental component of urban life, it is clear that neither Ibn Khaldūn nor other contemporary Muslim scholars held the practitioners of the crafts in high esteem.[72] Perhaps the most telling evidence concerning the socio-economic status of craftsmen in traditional Islamic society is their virtual invisibility in the historical, geographical, biographical and poetic works written prior to the tenth/sixteenth century.

The calligraphers responsible for producing copies of the Qur'ān are among the few skilled artisans about whom we possess much biographical information. The best calligraphers were highly paid for their skills, and particular attention was given to those individuals who either developed new scripts or mastered many different forms of script.[73] It is from the Persian cultural milieu that we have one of the first attempts to describe the activities of the principal painters of the age, written in 951/1544 by the calligrapher and illuminator Dūst Muḥammad.[74] It is not possible to attribute specific manuscript illustrations to all of the masters that appear in his list, but some, like Kamāl al-Dīn Bihzād (d. 942/1536) and Mīr Musavvir (*fl.* tenth/sixteenth century), are still counted among the finest exponents of Persian painting. A further example of this genre was penned by a Persian, Qāḍī Aḥmad, in around 1015/1606.

The greater survival of official archives from Ottoman Turkey and Ṣafavid Iran also allows us to reconstruct aspects of the organisation of guilds and individual workshops responsible for the production of luxury goods for the court.[75] Our knowledge of the status and activities of craftsmen in earlier periods comes largely from another source: inscriptions on objects. The names of master craftsmen start to appear on Islamic metalwork and glazed pottery from the latter part of the second/eighth century,[76] though it should

72 ʿAbd al-Raḥmān ibn Muḥammad ibn Khaldūn, *The* Muqaddimah*: An introduction to history*, trans. Franz Rosenthal, 3 vols. (New York, 1958), vol. II, pp. 346ff.

73 James, *Qur'āns*; Robert Irwin, *Islamic art* (London, 1997), pp. 177–81; Tabbaa, *Transformation*, pp. 34–52.

74 David Roxburgh, *Prefacing the image: The writing of art history in sixteenth-century Iran*, Studies and Sources in Islamic Art and Architecture 9 (Leiden and Boston, 2001), pp. 160–208.

75 Irwin, *Islamic art*, pp. 133–41.

76 Blair, *Islamic inscriptions*, pp. 117–19, 150–2.

be recognised that they are never a common feature on the objects produced in any period. Occasionally further details about the organisation of workshops and familial links may be inferred from these 'signatures'. For instance, the names of both Ghaybī al-Ṭawrizī and his son, Ibn Ghaybī, have been found on pottery vessels (sometimes even on the same object) and glazed tiles of the ninth / fifteenth century in Egypt and Syria. In some cases we can also trace the movement of skilled craftsmen through the distinctive final component (*nisba*) of their personal names that identifies the place of birth. Signatures of potters working in eighth / fourteenth and ninth / fifteenth-century Cairo include the *nisbas* 'Ajamī ('the Persian') and Shāmī ('of Damascus') as well as titles such as Ustād al-Miṣrī ('Egyptian master').[77] Rarely, craftsmen, or the workshops they controlled, diversified into different materials and techniques. The metal-worker Muḥammad ibn al-Zayn placed his name no fewer than six times on his masterpiece, the late seventh / thirteenth-century inlaid brass basin known as the Baptistère de Saint Louis. His signature has been found on other inlaid vessels, but it has also been identified on a set of steel gates from a religious institution in Jerusalem.[78]

Cities and towns often became centres specialising in the production of a specific medium. The study of glazed ceramics – one of the most creative aspects of Islamic visual culture – has revealed numerous distinctive styles of glazed pottery production. One of the most challenging techniques was lustre painting. This difficult and costly process was designed to leave an extremely thin metallic deposit (composed of silver and copper) on the surface of a glazed vessel.[79] Lustre decoration was first employed on pottery in southern Iraq in the early third / ninth century, and was later promoted in Cairo during the period of Fāṭimid rule. While lustre-painted glazed pottery only comprised a small proportion of the ceramics manufactured in Cairo at this time, they do appear to have been the most highly valued, and have been recovered from excavations all around the Mediterranean basin.[80] Dating to the fifth / eleventh century, this elegant storage jar (pl. 25.16) is painted with golden lustre over an opaque white glaze. The decorative scheme combines bands of knotwork, geometric motifs, stylised vegetation and fish.

77 Marilyn Jenkins, 'Mamluk underglaze painted pottery: Foundations for further study', *Muqarnas*, 2 (1984), pp. 104–12.
78 James Allan, 'Muhammad ibn al-Zain: Craftsman in cups, thrones and window grilles?', *Levant*, 28 (1996).
79 Alan Caiger-Smith, *Lustre pottery: Technique, tradition and innovation in Islam and the Western world* (London, 1985), pp. 197–220; Bernsted, *Early Islamic pottery*, pp. 7–11.
80 Marilyn Jenkins, '*Sa'd*: content and context', in Soucek (ed.), *Content and context*; Contadini, *Fatimid art*, pp. 71–89.

25.16 Lustre painted and glazed ceramic jar, Egypt (fifth/eleventh century), C.48–1952. By permission of the Board of Trustees of the Victoria and Albert Museum.

In the sixth/twelfth century other centres for lustre production sprang up in Syria, southern Anatolia and Iran. The delicate style of lustre painting on the *miḥrāb* signed by Ḥasan ibn ʿArabshāh Naqqāsh is also found on the glazed ceramic bowls, platters and ewers produced in Kāshān during the late sixth/twelfth and early seventh/thirteenth centuries. The names of several painters have been identified on surviving examples. The potters of Kāshān also perfected another decorative style (*minā'ī*) involving the use of enamel pigments that were fired onto the surface of a white-bodied ceramic covered with a transparent glaze. This technique allowed the potters to combine fine detail with a polychromatic palette (pl. 25.17). This delicate beaker comprises three

25.17 Overglaze-painted glazed ceramic beaker, Kāshān, Iran (late sixth/twelfth or early seventh/thirteenth century), Purchase F1928.2. By permission of the Freer Gallery of Art, Smithsonian Institution, Washington, DC.

friezes running around the exterior, each containing narrative scenes. The style of painting found on *mināʾī* ware exhibits strong similarities to modes of representation found in manuscript painting, and in the case of the beaker it is possible to identify the source of the narrative as Firdawsī's epic poem, the *Shāhnāma* (Book of kings, composed *c.* 400/1010).[81]

This process of regional specialisation can also be seen in metalwork. The late sixth/twelfth and early seventh/thirteenth centuries were a period of great creativity in the field of inlaid metalwork. Numerous manufacturing centres have been identified in Afghanistan, north-east Iran, Iraq, Syria and south-east Turkey. The *nisba* al-Mawṣilī ('of Mosul', the city in north-west

81 Lane, *Early Islamic pottery*, pp. 41–3; Marianna Simpson, 'The narrative structure of a medieval Iranian beaker', *Ars Orientalis* (1981).

Iraq) has been identified on the inscriptions on twenty-eight surviving metal objects. Interestingly, the *nisba* refers to the craftsman and does not signify the place where the object was actually made. In fact, only one of these vessels – an inlaid copper alloy vessel (known as the Blacas ewer) by the craftsman Shujāʿ ibn Manʿa, and dated 629/1232 – specifies Mosul as the place of manufacture.[82] The repeat patterns and geometric interlace on the Blacas ewer provide a visual contrast to the elegant inscription bands and the scenes in the main roundels. Craftsmen might choose to move to another locality in search of wealthier clients, but their movement could also be dictated by external factors such as impending military threat or natural disaster.[83] These skilled craftsmen adapted themselves to the different tastes of new patrons; some inlaid metal vessels produced in Syria during this period even contain images of Christian saints and scenes from the life of Christ.[84]

Those who operated their own workshops might undertake commissions for members of the political elite, but it is also clear that they served a more diverse urban clientele, including groups such as administrators, scholars and merchants. An inlaid bronze vessel made in the Afghan city of Herat in 559/1163 carries an inscription that names the recipient as 'the brilliant *khwāja*, Rukn al-Dīn, pride of the merchants, the most trustworthy of the faithful, grace of the pilgrimage and the two shrines, Rashīd al-Dīn ʿAzīzī Abū al-Ḥusayn al-Zanjanī, may his glory last'. Known as the Bobrinski bucket, this vessel is significant because it carries the earliest example of the name (and grandiose titles) of a merchant to survive on an Islamic artefact. From this time it is possible to detect the ways in which paintings and portable artefacts sought to address the concerns of this affluent, and increasingly self-confident, merchant class.[85]

This new direction in Islamic art can be seen in the illustrated manuscripts of the *Maqāmāt* (Assemblies) of al-Ḥarīrī (d. 516/1122) produced in Syria and Iraq during the seventh/thirteenth and eighth/fourteenth centuries.[86] The fifty stories contained in the *Maqāmāt* are narrated by a trader, al-Ḥārith, and focus upon the activities of a scoundrel named Abū Zayd al-Sarūjī. Many of the stories take place in environments – marketplace, mosque, caravanserai,

82 Rachel Ward, *Islamic metalwork* (London, 1993), pp. 80–4.

83 James Allan, *Islamic metalwork: The Nuhad es-Said collection* (London, 1982), pp. 58–73, nos. 7–10.

84 Eva Baer, *Ayyubid metalwork with Christian images* (Leiden, 1989).

85 Ward, *Islamic metalwork*, pp. 74–5.

86 Oleg Grabar, *The illustrations of the* Maqamat (Chicago, 1984); Shirley Guthrie, *Arab social life in the Middle Ages: An illustrated study* (London, 1995).

countryside, aboard ship and so on – that would have been familiar to merchants. One of the finest of the *Maqāmāt* manuscripts was illustrated by Yaḥyā ibn Maḥmūd al-Wāsiṭī in 634/1237. His paintings are full of detailed observation of everyday life and perceptive insights into human nature. The illustration of Abū Zayd and al-Ḥārith approaching a village (pl. 25.18) exemplifies his ability to encapsulate an environment with a few carefully chosen details. In the foreground al-Wāsiṭī places the chief protagonists riding their camels. Significantly, the illustrator pays considerable attention to the depiction of the different textiles. Cloth was one of the staples of Middle Eastern trade, and the painter provides a visual feast of coloured and patterned textiles. His desire to cater for the textile sensibility of his wealthy urban audience leads al-Wāsiṭī, with some humour, to clothe even the villager holding a shovel in a bright red caftan ornamented with golden *ṭirāz* bands on the sleeves.

Palace life

The extant palaces of the Umayyad caliphs in Jordan, Syria and Palestine set the tone for later developments in Islamic palace architecture. While some, like the fresco-painted bathhouse of Quṣayr ʿAmra in Jordan (*c.* 92–6/711–15), are modest structures, there is a marked increase in scale and opulence in the last decade of Umayyad rule. Most important are the palatial complex of Khirbat al-Mafjar near Jericho, with its elaborately decorated bathhouse, and the enigmatic palace of Mshattā in northern Jordan. The latter palace is most famous for its carved limestone frieze that runs the length of the 144-metre entrance façade.[87] Scale, internal complexity and axiality are also key features of the vast palaces built by the ʿAbbāsid caliphs in Sāmarrāʾ in Iraq between 221/836 and 279/892. The cheap building materials employed at Sāmarrāʾ – largely mud brick with stucco facing – have contributed to the poor preservation of these once imposing structures.[88] The same compromise between the patron's desire for scale and the cost of building materials can also be seen in the fifth/eleventh-century palaces of Lashkār-i Bāzār in Afghanistan.[89]

87 Robert Hillenbrand, 'La *dolce vita* in early Islamic Syria', *Art History*, 5 (1982); Oleg Grabar, 'Umayyad palaces reconsidered', in Gülru Neçipoğlu (ed.), *Pre-modern Islamic palaces*, *Ars Orientalis*, 23 (special issue) (1993).

88 See contributions by Alastair Northedge, Derek Kennet and Marcus Milwright in Chase Robinson (ed.), *A medieval Islamic city reconsidered: Interdisciplinary approaches to Samarra*, Oxford Studies in Islamic Art 14 (Oxford and New York, 2001).

89 Daniel Schlumberger, *Lashkari Bazar: Une résidence royale ghaznévide et ghoride* (Paris, 1978).

25.18 Village scene, *Maqāmāt* of al-Ḥarīrī (634/1237), Arabe 5847, fol. 138r. Bibliothèque Nationale de France.

While it takes a considerable effort to imagine the original magnificence of most palaces of the earlier Islamic centuries, some complexes of later periods survive largely intact, including the Alhambra in Spain, the Ṣafavid palaces in Iṣfāhān and the Topkapı palace of the Ottoman sultans in Istanbul (from 863/1459). The concept of the Islamic palace is exemplified by the Alhambra, located on top of a hill south of Granada. Built in numerous phases from the fifth/eleventh century, it was brought to its present form by the Naṣrid dynasty (r. 627–897/1230–1492). The forbidding exterior fortifications contrast with the grace and delicacy of the architecture of the palace and the formal gardens. Carved stucco patterns of great sophistication adorn many of the walls, and the same medium is used to dazzling effect in the *muqarnas* vaulting. The palace also contains lavish decoration made from cut tile, wood, marble and painted leather.[90] Though many other media are also employed, glazed tiles constitute the most conspicuous part of the decorative programme within the many structures of the Topkapı.[91] Those that adorn the circumcision room are a demonstration of technical virtuosity, and contain birds, deer and flowing vegetal and floral designs painted in a palette of blue and turquoise (pl. 25.15).

Royal patronage not only attracted the most skilled craftsmen, but also encouraged the use of the most expensive materials. Throughout the Islamic period extravagant objects were made from precious metals and encrusted with gemstones, though only a tiny proportion of these artefacts from before the tenth/sixteenth century survives. The opulence, and sometimes rather gaudy taste, of Islamic palace life in later centuries can be seen in the embroidered silks, velvets, weapons and jewellery produced for the Ottomans in Istanbul, the Ṣafavids and Qājārs (1193–1342/1779–1924) in Iran and the Mughals (932–1274/1526–1858) in India.[92] For earlier dynasties it is often necessary to turn to the written record to gain a picture of the luxury arts and entertainments in the royal courts.[93] Historical sources relate that the palaces of the ʿAbbāsids in third/ninth- and early fourth/tenth-century Iraq

90 See contributions by Darío Cabanelas Rodríguez, James Dickie, Jesús Bermúz Lopez and Dede Fairchild Ruggles in Dodds (ed.), *al-Andalus*; Oleg Grabar, *The Alhambra* (Cambridge, MA, 1978).

91 Gülru Neçipoğlu, *Architecture, ceremonial and power: The Topkapi palace in the fifteenth and sixteenth centuries* (New York and Cambridge, MA, 1991).

92 For instance, see examples illustrated in Michael Piotrovsky and J. Michael Rogers (eds.), *Heaven on earth: Art from Islamic lands: Works from the State Hermitage Museum and the Khalili Collection* (Munich and Berlin, 2004), nos. 52–9, 111–13, pp. 103–9, 162–83.

93 Ghāda al-Hijjāwī Qaddūmī (trans.), *The book of gifts and rarities:* Kitāb al-hadāyā wa al-tuḥaf (Cambridge, MA, 1996), pp. 146–65.

were famed for their automata, and this tradition was also picked up by the Umayyad caliphs in the palace complex of Madīnat al-Zahrāʾ near Cordoba in Spain (from 324/936). Sadly, no vestiges of these magnificent contraptions survive, but comparable automata are illustrated in seventh/thirteenth and eighth/fourteenth-century copies of Abū al-ʿIzz ibn Ismāʿīl ibn al-Razzāz al-Jazarī's *Kitāb fī maʿrifat al-ḥiyal al-handasiyya* (Book of knowledge of ingenious mechanical devices), composed before 602/1206.[94]

The workshops attached to royal courts sometimes became centres of excellence for specific media. For instance, Muslim dynasties often established large textile workshops (sing. *dār al-ṭirāz*) for the production of the high-quality cloth needed by the royal wardrobe. In the case of Fāṭimid Egypt this industry can be reconstructed on the basis of written records and the embroidered inscriptions on the surviving textiles.[95] The Umayyad court in Spain is particularly famous for its ivory containers. Ivory pyxides were employed for the storage of perfumed substances such as musk and camphor, but their carved decoration and inscription bands might also contain explicit or coded messages for the recipient. One was commissioned in 353/964 as a gift for Ṣubḥ, the concubine of the caliph al-Ḥakam II, to mark the birth of their son, ʿAbd al-Raḥmān. The decoration of the pyxis made for al-Ḥakam's brother, al-Mughīra, is more complex in character, and the original meaning attached to the designs is uncertain. It has been suggested that the figural scenes within the three large roundels on the body of the vessel may be read as a warning to al-Mughīra not to interfere with the caliphal succession.[96]

Some of the finest artefacts carved from rock crystal (the purest form of quartz) were produced for the Fāṭimid court in Cairo. A few, such as the ewer made for caliph al-ʿAzīz (r. 365–86/975–96) that is now in the treasury of San Marco in Venice, carry the names of members of the court though, strangely, many of the finest examples lack dedicatory inscriptions. Probably dated to the early fifth/eleventh century, the ewer illustrated in plate 25.19 exemplifies the quality of Fāṭimid rock-crystal carving. Notable features are the high degree of stylisation in the drawing of the animals and plant forms and the subtle balance maintained between the positive and negative spaces. The carving

94 Ettinghausen, *Arab painting*, pp. 93–6; Rachel Ward, 'Evidence for a school of painting at the Artuqid court', in Julian Raby (ed.), *The art of Syria and the Jazīra, 1100–1250*, Oxford Studies in Islamic Art 1 (Oxford, 1985), pp. 69–76.

95 Contadini, *Fatimid art*, pp. 39–48.

96 Prado-Vilar, 'Circular visions', pp. 21–9; Renata Holod, 'Pyxis of al-Mughira', in Dodds (ed.), *al-Andalus*, pp. 192–7.

25.19 Rock-crystal ewer, Egypt (early fifth/eleventh century), 7904–1862. By permission of the Board of Trustees of the Victoria and Albert Museum.

of the form and relief decoration of this vessel required immense skill and relies upon the great resilience of the material; the body of the vessel is only 1.7–2 millimetres thick.[97] The same carving technique was employed in the manufacture of glass beakers and ewers in this period.[98]

97 Avinoam Shalem, *Islam Christianized: Islamic portable objects in medieval church treasuries of the Latin West*, Ars Faciendi 7 (Frankfurt am Main, 1996), pp. 56–63; Contadini, *Fatimid art*, pp. 16–38.

98 Shalem, *Islam Christianized*, pp. 113–15; David Whitehouse, 'Cut and engraved glass', in Stefano Carboni and David Whitehouse (eds.), *Glass of the sultans* (New York, 2002), pp. 155–97.

Muslim rulers were also great patrons of illustrated manuscripts, and numerous court workshops have been identified. In some cases royal patronage was announced in the form of a painted frontispiece depicting the patron. The frontispieces of a multi-volume copy of Abū al-Faraj al-Iṣfahānī's (d. 356/967) *Kitāb al-aghānī* (Book of songs) dating to 615/1218f. each contain representations of the prince of Mosul, Badr al-Dīn Lu'lu', attended by members of his court. Enthroned rulers can be found on the frontispieces of copies of the *Kitāb al-diryāq* (Book of antidotes) of Pseudo-Galen and the *Maqāmāt* of al-Ḥarīrī produced in Iraq, Egypt and Syria during the seventh/thirteenth and eighth/fourteenth centuries.[99] Other texts, most notably the manuscripts of Firdawsī's *Shāhnāma* produced during the Ilkhānid, Tīmūrid and Ṣafavid periods,[100] dealt directly with royal themes and provided illustrators with the opportunity to examine different aspects of the representation of authority. This epic poem details the lives of the rulers of Iran from the dawn of time to the death of the last Sasanian shah in 30/651 and, predictably, many of the paintings found in the extant manuscripts are enthronement scenes. One of the most elegant examples of this genre is the depiction of the court of the mythical first king of Iran, Gayumars, in the *Shāhnāma* produced for the Ṣafavid shah Ṭahmāsp dating to around 931–42/1525–35.[101] Evoking an age before the invention of architecture, the fur-clad king and his court sit within a rocky amphitheatre set against a golden sky dotted with ornate chinoiserie clouds.

The illustrations of the *Shāhnāma* are not limited to enthronements, however; other themes relating to royalty – courtly love, battles and succession – were also approached. For instance, death is a particularly conspicuous theme within the so-called Great Mongol *Shāhnāma* (c. 735–6/1335–6), and images such as 'the mourning of Alexander the Great' and 'the bier of Isfandiyār' possess a degree of emotionalism seldom seen in Persian painting.[102]

99 Ettinghausen, *Arab painting*, pp. 83–6, 90–2, 147–9; Atil, *Renaissance of Islam*, pp. 258–9, fig. 5.

100 Marie Swietochowski, 'The Metropolitan Museum of Art's *Small Shāhnāma*', in Marie Swietochowski and Stefano Carboni (eds.), *Illustrated poetry and epic images: Persian painting of the 1330s and 1340s* (New York, 1994); Grabar, *Mostly miniatures*, pp. 99–104; Sims, Marshak and Grube, *Peerless images*, pp. 302–15.

101 Stuart Cary Welch, *A king's book of kings: The* Shah-nameh *of Shah Tahmasp* (New York, 1972), pp. 88–91, no. 20; Sims, Marshak and Grube, *Peerless images*, pp. 63–4.

102 Oleg Grabar and Sheila Blair, *Epic images and contemporary history: The illustrations of the Great Mongol* Shah-nama (Chicago, 1980), pp. 18–19, 22–3; Sims, Marshak and Grube, *Peerless images*, pp. 45–6.

Conventions of depicting royalty could be subverted both in the illustrations of the *Shāhnāma* and other works. The Persian painter Bihzād provides a surprising image of the ʿAbbāsid caliph Hārūn al-Rashīd (r. 170–93/786–809) in the bathhouse in the copy of the *Khamsa* (Five poems) of Niẓāmī (d. 605/1209) completed in 899/1494 (pl. 25.20).[103] The caliph is stripped of all the trappings of authority (his robes and crown are unceremoniously piled on a bench in the changing-room to the right) and depicted naked to the waist and sitting cross-legged on the floor. In perhaps the most audacious touch, the artist allows a humble detail, the patterned towels in the upper part of the painting, to become one of the dominant visual elements of the composition.

Villagers and nomads

The artistic achievements of the sedentary and nomadic groups in rural regions of the Islamic world have tended to be the domain of archaeological study, supplemented by the ethnographic observations of traditional craft activities. Rural areas tend to support craft activities that do not need large amounts of costly equipment and can be performed in, or near, the home. For instance, al-Wāsiṭī's illustration of an Iraqi village from the *Maqāmāt* manuscript of 634/1237 shows a woman using a spindle (pl. 25.18). She makes use of a simple and effective technology still employed by Bedouin women in the Middle East. Pottery vessels, textiles, flat-weave rugs, knotted carpets, tents, basketry, reed mats and leather were all types of portable artefacts that could be produced by villagers and pastoral nomads around the Islamic world. Two examples are chosen here to illustrate some of the major themes.

Excavations of villages in the Middle East often bring to light small numbers of shards of decorated and glazed ceramic vessels imported from urban centres, but it is clear that other types of pottery were also produced in the villages themselves. A particularly important development occurred in the south of Jordan in the fifth/eleventh century. In this region the potters abandoned the use of the kick-wheel – the standard tool used for forming pottery in urban workshops – in favour of constructing vessels out of coils of clay that were smoothed into shape by hand. Within a few decades this rudimentary technology had spread all over Jordan, Palestine and Syria.[104]

103 For the works of Bihzād see Ebadollah Bahari, *Behzad: Master of Persian painting* (London, 1996); Gray, *Persian painting*, pp. 109–25.

104 Jeremy Johns, 'The rise of Middle Islamic hand-made geometrically-painted ware in Bilâd al-Shâm (11th–13th centuries AD)', in Roland-Pierre Gayraud (ed.), *Colloque international d'archéologie islamique* (Cairo, 1988), pp. 65–8, 88–9.

25.20 Hārūn al-Rashīd in the bathhouse from the *Khamsa* of Niẓāmī painted by Bihzād (899/1494), Or. 6810, fol. 27v. By permission of the British Library.

We possess very little information concerning the makers of this type of pottery between the fifth/eleventh and twelfth/eighteenth centuries, though it is perhaps significant that in most of the available anthropological studies from the Middle East and North Africa handmade pottery is made by village

25.21 Handmade slip-painted ceramic jar (seventh–eighth / thirteenth–fourteenth century), Amman Citadel Museum, Jordan. Photo: Marcus Milwright.

women for use in the home. The complete and fragmentary vessels from Jordan dating from the sixth–eighth / twelfth–fourteenth centuries often carry complex patterns painted onto the surface with coloured slip clays (pl. 25.21). These attractive designs appear to be very localised in character, and it has been suggested that the dense, geometric patterns may be related to the motifs on basketry, weaving and embroidery. The archaeological evidence indicates that, unlike urban pottery production, vessel forms and decorative modes evolved very slowly in villages. Our evidence from archaeological research is more fragmentary in other parts of the Islamic world, but it is evident that similar processes of hand forming pottery were employed in rural areas ranging from Central Asia to the Persian Gulf, North Africa and sub-Saharan Africa.

Perhaps the most famous art forms associated with the nomadic populations of the Islamic world are carpets, felts, and woven and embroidered textiles. The flocks of sheep and goats tended by nomads provided the wool needed for these items, while the caustic agents and dyes could be gathered from plant and mineral sources. Woollen textiles may perform a wide range of functions, including clothing, tent fabrics, floor coverings, storage bags and saddle cloths. Numerous traditions of nomadic textile work can be identified around the Islamic world, though some of the most sophisticated are found in Turkey, Iran and Central Asia. For instance, the Qashqāʾi tribal confederation in the Persian province of Fārs produces a wide range of patterned textiles.[105] The traditional loom (*charkh*) – which can be used for the manufacture of woven textiles, tapestry rugs (sing. *gilim* or *kilim*) and knotted pile carpets – is horizontal and held in place with wooden pegs driven directly into the ground. Other equipment includes the heddle rods (for alternating the warp threads when weaving) attached onto a triangular wooden frame and, for making knotted pile carpets, a metal carpet comb (*āhanja*) and pair of scissors. Carpet making is often a communal activity among the women. Like other tribal carpet traditions in the Islamic world, the designs found on Qashqāʾi carpets are subject to considerable variation. Common features are a polychromatic palette of reds, blues, greens and yellows and a composition based round large lozenges enclosed within a series of rectangular bands of repeated ornament. The vocabulary of motifs is extensive, comprising simple geometric shapes, stylised plant forms, birds, fish and other animals. This vibrant visual tradition is one of many still to be found in the rural areas of the Islamic world.

105 Hans Wulff, *The traditional crafts of Persia: Their development, technology and influence on Eastern and Western civilizations* (Cambridge, MA, 1966), pp. 212–17; Whitworth Art Gallery, *The Qashqāʾi of Iran* (Manchester, 1976).

26

Music

AMNON SHILOAH

From instinctive chanting to sophisticated singing

Reflecting on the question of the origin of music, al-Fārābī argues in his *Kitāb al-mūsīqī al-kabīr* (The great book of music) that, like other animals, man is instinctively motivated to express a range of emotions via sound. From this initial phase, through observation and experience, man attained a sophisticated vocal art. This discovery led to the gradual development of musical instruments with which he enhanced the art of singing. The musical theorist appears in the final stage of development, which coincides with the achievements in the realm of Islamic civilisation.[1]

Four hundred years later Ibn Khaldūn (d. 808/1406), in his *Muqaddima* (Prolegomenon), describes another progressive development, from the primary, simple tunes of pre-Islamic society to the sophisticated forms of music created in the prosperous urban centres of Muslim society in its golden age. He also argues that unlike the forms of folk music and the cantillation of sacred texts, which are grasped by nature without instruction, professional musicians in urban centres base their art on codified norms.[2]

The systematic crystallisation of such a newly sophisticated art after the advent of Islam may be described as the forging of a great musical tradition, which provided a vehicle and a standard for those who shared it to identify with others in a common civilisation. It refers to the skilful fusion of selected elements from the previous great traditions of conquered peoples with elements from the homogenous Arab 'little tradition'. This synthesis, achieved in a spirit of compromise, resulted in successful 'new arrangements' so conceived as to appear to both conquerors and conquered as an outgrowth of the old. Indeed, scattered evidence shows the borrowing of elements from

1 R. D. Erlanger (trans.), *La musique arabe*, 6 vols. (Paris 1930–9), vol. I, pp. 18–19.
2 Ibn Khaldūn, *The* Muqaddimah *of Ibn Khaldūn: An introduction to history*, trans. F. Rosenthal, 3 vols. (London, 1958; repr. Princeton, 1967), vol. II, pp. 399–402.

conquered cultures which were grafted upon an Arabic tradition that had a character of its own. Arabisation, whose most prominent manifestations are the quest for and use of linguistic purity, was considered as a general unifying factor, including the musical domain.[3]

Following the subsequent decentralisation, one witnesses the rise of local styles, particularly in Iran, Central Asia and the Ottoman empire. Nevertheless, they continued to draw upon structural and aesthetic elements of the great tradition.

In dealing with the development of this art, the observer is hampered by the total lack of musical documents, and must therefore fall back on the abundant surviving literature about music. However, some extant rudimentary notational systems deserve mention. They include al-Kindī's exercise in two parts for lutenists using the 'solfegio' system, referring to the name of the strings and the fingers used to shorten them;[4] the use by many theorists of an alphabetical notation to indicate the pitches of scales; and al-Dhahabī's (eighth/fourteenth-century) notational system using an eight-lined stave in different colours.[5] Yet all were used only for pedagogical purposes.

Religion and music

The long debate on the permissibility of music emerged during the first centuries of Islam. At first the protagonists founded their arguments on scattered verses of the Qur'ān, hardly touching upon music as such. Later the theologians and juridical disputants were led to base their argumentation on the *ḥadīth* and the interpretations of the leaders of the schools of law. Their method of reasoning by analogy often led the antagonists to draw opposite, and arbitrary, conclusions from the same tradition.

In the first full-scale treatise based on the *ḥadīth*, Ibn Abi 'l-Dunyā (d. 281/894), used the term *malāhī* in a broad sense implying all kinds of amusements, forbidden pleasure and moral misbehaviour, from which music and its practice were considered inseparable.[6] While *malāhī* continued to signify musical instruments in particular, the prominent term used in the writings on the

3 A. Shiloah, *Music in the world of Islam* (Aldershot and Detroit, 1995; repr. 2000), pp. 19–22.

4 A. Shiloah (ed. and trans.), *The dimension of music in Islamic and Jewish culture*, Variorum Collected Studies Series CS393 (London, 1993), section 1, pp. 203–5 and facsimile of the Manisa MS 1705.

5 A. Shiloah and A. Berthier, 'A propos d'un petit livre arabe sur la musique', *Revue de Musicologie*, 71 (1986).

6 J. Robson (ed. and trans.), *Tracts on listening to music: Being* Dhamm al-malāhī *by Ibn Abī 'l-Dunyā and* Bawāriq al-ilmā' *by Majd al-Dīn al-Ṭūsī al-Ghazālī* (London, 1938).

lawfulness of music is *samāʿ*. It literally means listening, and, by extension, the music listened to. The concept of *samāʿ* is usually contrasted with *ghināʾ* (*cantus*) which designates secular music. The theologians and religious authorities regarded the latter's influence as a depraving and debasing agent. Many authors ascribe its origin and effects to Satan's evil forces, or they transfer the biblical invention of music from Jubal to his father Lamek, emphasising his affiliation to the legacy of the sinful Cain. They were also concerned with respect for the holy texts and their appropriate rendition; formally composed melodies were considered distractions preventing the faithful from concentrating on the message of the text.

The mystical movement developed a different approach to music. The earliest Sufis' simple piety and gospel of love were gradually transformed into an elaborate mystical doctrine, in which music and dance occupied a prominent role. The mystics developed complex congregational rituals and spiritual exercises designed to create religious ecstasy (*wajd*) in the participants and to realise a union with the Godhead. The most remarkable ritual was the *dhikr* (lit. 'remembrance'), which referred to the Qurʾānic injunction 'to remember God as often as possible'. The Sufis' *dhikr* usually included singing, and occasionally dancing, which were considered a manifestation of their infinite, ecstatic love of God. The most spectacular and sophisticated music and dance associated with mystical practices are those of the Mevlevīs' *ʿayn sharīf* (hymns composed specifically to lead worshippers to a state of union with God).

Literary writings on music

The encyclopaedic and literary works are primarily conceived along the lines of the *adab* literature. Thus one finds discussions in works by al-Jāḥiẓ (d. 255/869) on the characteristics of sounds, the class of singing-girls (*qaynāt*), rules of performance established by the Sasanians, classification of professional musicians etc. The grammarian Mufaḍḍal ibn Salāma (d. *c.* 290/903) and the geographer Ibn Khurradādhbih (d. 300/911) both wrote books on the *malāhī* (as musical instruments), including a great variety of topics: the origin and virtues of music, sayings of Greek philosophers concerning the benefit of music, the Persian modal system etc. The historian al-Masʿūdī (d. 345/956) reports, in his *Murūj al-dhahab*, two extensive orations by specialists on music and dance.

This type of writing culminated in the monumental work *Kitāb al-aghānī* (Book of songs) of Abū al-Faraj al-Iṣfahānī (d. 356/967). It contains a collection of poems set to music from the pre-Islamic period to the third/ninth century.

He indicated the origin and melodic and rhythmic mode of each song. In addition to biographical details about more than ninety famous male and female singers, instrumentalists and writers on music, the work includes a mine of information on the history of music, musical life and musical aesthetics.

The science of music and the Greek legacy

In the framework of the ideal of learning during the golden age of Muslim civilisation the study of music acquired a prominent place among the areas of knowledge, and committed itself to a systematic definition of its scope and object, while establishing appropriate methods for the analysis of its various norms. This development reached its culmination with the translation into Arabic of Greek treatises on music in the framework of the Bayt al-Ḥikma. In his *Kitāb al-fihrist* (Index [to Arabic books]), Abu 'l-Faraj ibn al-Nadīm (d. 385/995) lists thirty-three titles of such translated treatises.[7]

Thenceforth *ʿilm al-mūsīqī* (the science of music) became part of the branches of learning often opposed to the Arabic *ghināʾ*, usually applied to the practice of sophisticated music.

In writings of this type familiar Greek topics and ideas are repeated, refined, improved, expanded or conceived in a new light. This concerns the broad philosophical–metaphoric approach, analyses of music in terms of numbers, the definition of the different melodic and rhythmical parameters, the moral and therapeutic effects of music and the linking of cosmological and astral phenomena.

The philosophical–metaphoric approach

Abū Yūsuf Yaʿqūb ibn Isḥāq al-Kindī (d. 260/870) is the first author in the field of the science of music whose achievements are known to us. He is said to have composed thirteen treatises on the art and science of music, of which only six have come down to us. Most of his writings on music are centred on the doctrine of ethos, the Pythagorean speculations concerning the relationship of music with the universal scheme of things, of human life, character and emotions. The guiding idea behind this approach is that the primary aim of a philosopher studying music should be the necessary link to broad theoretical knowledge. Al-Kindī refers to the Persian and Byzantine modes and to the

7 H. G. Farmer, 'Greek theorists of music in Arabic translation', *Isis* (1929–30).

eight rhythmical modes of the Arabs. He also made the first attempt at notation.

The fourth epistle in the Ikhwān al-Ṣafā'’s encyclopaedia, the *Rasā'il*, is devoted to music. In its range, purpose, and the interweaving of metaphoric ideas and practical subjects, this treatise is unique in Arabic musical literature.

According to their theory the wonders of creation, the phenomena of nature and matters within the domain of human creation are all subordinate to the ideal laws of music and harmony, of which the music made by man is only a pale reflection. Since the harmony is expounded by means of numbers, the epistle is full of arithmetical speculations that expand into many and varied domains such as calligraphy, language, poetic metre, human corporeal structure, the system of stars etc. It also claims that music is a force exerting ethical and therapeutic influence on humanity and a factor in establishing the spiritual, physical and philosophical equilibrium of man.

Among the practical issues the Ikhwān deal with are the sciences of sounds, of rhythm and prosody and of instruments. Of particular interest is the chapter on the science of sounds, which exemplifies everything written up to that period. It provides a systematic classification of all the sounds that exist in nature and mankind.[8]

The speculative trend

The treatment of Arabic music as a subject of significant intellectual value per se began with Thābit ibn Qurra (d. 288/901), a Sabian astrologer, mathematician and translator from Greek and Syriac into Arabic. He wrote treatises on music in Arabic and an extensive, important one in Syriac. All are lost except *Mas'ala fi'l-mūsīqī* (The problem of music) in Arabic. This work deals with a question concerning occasional singing in octaves as well as the appropriate accompaniment of a vocal piece. A similar problem occurs in Pseudo-Aristotle's *Problemata*.

Al-Fārābī (d. *c.* 339/950), known in Europe as Alpharabius, has written several treatises on music. His *Iḥṣā' al-ʿulūm* (Enumeration[/Classification] of the sciences), in which he enumerates all the known sciences, including music, was accorded the highest respect by Arab, Christian and Jewish medieval authors, as proved by its various translations into Latin and Hebrew. The chapter on music provides a definition of the science of music, its principles, methodology, musical parameters and instruments, rules of rhythm and

8 Shiloah (ed. and trans.), *The dimension*, section 3.

composition. Besides two treatises on the science of rhythms, his major and foremost among Arabic treatises on music is *Kitāb al-mūsīqī al-kabīr*. In this work al-Fārābī considers musical theory as the supreme intellectual enterprise contributing to the body of human knowledge. It is true that as a trained musical performer he based much of his study on the living music of his time, but he emphasised, in the spirit of Greek and Latin theorists, that the perfect theorist should reason on the basis of his knowledge of all the rudiments of his art, and be able to deduce the principles governing musical science.[9]

Ibn Sīnā (d. 428/1037), known in Europe as Avicenna, followed the encyclopaedic conception of the sciences in uniting philosophy with the study of nature and in seeing man's perfection as lying in both knowledge and action. He refers to music in his monumental *Qānūn fi'l-ṭibb* (Canon on medicine) in dealing with the pulse, arguing that a well-ordered pulse is comparable to the most perfect consonances: the octave, fifth and fourth.

Ibn Sīnā's most comprehensive discussion on the science of music appears in chapter twelve of the third part of his major work, *Kitāb al-shifā'* (The book of healing).[10] In the introduction to this chapter he describes sound as a physiological sensation, as a device of communication from a distance among humans and animals, and as a means of communication between men and animals. However, he adds that meaningful sound used in the animal and human kingdoms does not achieve musical sense unless it has defined pitch and duration. Noteworthy are the passage on ornaments and embellishment as used both in melody and rhythm, and the chapters dealing with genres and systems that foreshadow the systematic modal presentation of Ṣafī al-Dīn.

The Andalusian and Maghribī tradition

After the Arab conquest (92/711) the Iberian Peninsula became the scene of one of the most fascinating examples of intercultural contacts; members of a highly diversified society took part in crystallising a social and cultural symbiosis, wherein music occupied a prominent place.

Al-Maqqarī, in his *Nafḥ al-ṭīb* (Breath of perfumes), depicted the Baghdadī musician Ziryāb, who became the chief minstrel at the Cordoban court, as a cultural hero and the innovator of Andalusian music *in toto*. However, a manuscript of the Tunisian Aḥmad al-Tīfāshī (d. 651/1253), discovered in the 1950s, offers us a new outlook on the development of this style. He describes it

9 Erlanger, *La musique arabe*, vols. I and II.
10 Ibid., vol. II.

as a dynamic process supported by several renowned figures, the most prominent of whom was the philosopher Ibn Bājja (d. 533/1139). Al-Tīfāshī writes about him: 'After having secluded himself for a few years to work with skilled singing-girl slaves he improved musical forms by mixing the songs of the Christians and those of the East.'[11] At all events, the most remarkable local innovation is related to the new poetic genres: the *muwashshaḥ* in classical Arabic and the *zajal* in the vernacular. The intimate association of these strophic genres with music gave them considerable popularity, and they became instrumental in the development of another important innovation concerning the sophisticated compound form: the *nūba*.[12]

It is assumed that musicians among the Hispano-Arab exiles brought the art of the *nūba* with them, and cultivated it in the major North African centres. Old styles are still extant in Fez, Tlemcen, Algiers and Tunis. Their *nūba* repertories are called respectively *āla*, *gharnāṭī*, *ṣanʿa* and *maʾlūf*. Some differences notwithstanding, they are very similar in spirit and structure. There are numerous anthologies containing poems arranged according to the *nūba* to which they belong and according to its characteristic parts, along with added indications pertaining to the musical components. One also finds an obvious interpenetration of the art of the *nūba* and prominent religious forms, namely the mystic rituals.[13]

A change in musical theory

Ṣafī al-Dīn al-Urmawī (d. 693/1294), who, after the fall of Baghdad (656/1258), became the official musician of the Mongol conquerors, is the first great theorist to base his entire work on his observations and experience as a performing musician. In his two major treatises, *Kitāb al-adwār* (The book of cycles[/modes]) and the *Risāla al-sharafiyya fi'l-nisab al-taʾlīfiyya* (The Sharafian treatise on musical proportions),[14] he achieved a systematisation of the general scale and the whole modal system. He based his theory mainly on the music in vogue, while at the same time taking advantage of earlier

11 See A. Shiloah, *The theory of music in Arabic writings (ca 900 to 1900)*, RISM Bx, vol. II (Munich, 2003), pp. 184–6.

12 O. Wright, 'Music in Muslim Spain', in Salma Khadra Jayyusi (ed.), *The legacy of Muslim Spain* (Leiden, 1992).

13 C. Poché, *La musique arabo-andalouse* (Paris, 1995).

14 Erlanger, *La musique arabe*, vol. III; Ṣafī al-Dīn al-Urmawī, *Kitāb al-adwār*, ed. E. Neubauer, facsimile of MS 3449, Topkapi, Istanbul; Ṣafī al-Dīn al-Urmawī, *al-Risāla al-sharafiyya*, ed. E. Neubauer, facsimile of MS 3460, Topkapi, Istanbul, Series C, vol. XXVI, (Frankfurt am Main, 1984).

theoretical achievements. Thus he became an ideal junction of the Persian modal tradition and all the other elements incorporated in the framework of the art of music in Muslim civilisation. His works became the model for subsequent generations throughout the whole Middle Eastern region and Central Asia. However, the majority of treatises written after him differed from their model by singling out local particularities and stylistic features that reflect the practice of each author's milieu.

ʿAbd al-Qādir al-Marāghī ibn Ghaybī (d. 839/1435) was a famous Iranian theorist and a distinguished lute player, poet and painter. He was Tīmūr's chief minstrel in Samarqand, and served as a musician in other courts. He wrote several works, some of which are in Persian; they are of the highest importance because of the information they contain about the practical art of music. He is usually placed with Ṣafī al-Dīn in the front rank of the theorists.

Shortly after Ṣafī al-Dīn's death a new theoretical trend seems to have emerged in the Ottoman empire and the Near East. Evidence that such a trend came into being is indicated in the encyclopaedia of Ibn al-Akfānī (d. 749/1348), *Irshād al-qāṣid* (The guiding seeker), by the popular and didactic versified treatise the *Risāla fī'l-mūsīqī* of Shams al-Dīn al-Ṣaydāwī al-Dhahabī (fourteenth century), which includes an important system of notation, and in the work of the distinguished Ottoman theorist Muḥammad al-Lādhiqī (d. 901/1495). The last was a favourite of the sultan Bāyazīd II (r. 886–918/1481–1512), to whom he dedicated his major work, the *Risāla al-fatḥiyya fī'l-mūsīqī* (The epistle of victory), probably a kind of homage commemorating the sultan's victory.[15]

Musical instruments are described in a variety of ways. Sometimes they are simply listed with minimal information, while at others they are treated in a systematic, classificatory manner.

The sources mention a bewildering array of instruments, designated by names and specific characteristics. They number 138, featuring drums, aerophones and chordophones. Many of those instruments have fallen into disuse. The list includes a few Greek and Byzantine instruments: *urghan* (organ), *armunikī* (panpipes), *salbak* (*sambyke* or *sambuka*); *lūr* (lyre), *kithāra*, the Persian *jank* (harp) and the Chinese *mushtak* (mouth organ).

One should add to this list the Greek and original treatises devoted to pneumatic and hydraulic apparatuses and organs.[16]

15 Erlanger, *La musique arabe*, vol. IV.

16 H. G. Farmer, *Studies in oriental musical instruments* (first series London 1931; second series Glasgow, 1939).

27

Cookery

DAVID WAINES

Introduction: the inheritors

The fourth/tenth-century traveller and geographer al-Muqaddasī (d. c. 390/1000) observed laconically that the inhabitants of central Arabia were both 'frugal and emaciated, so little nourished are they by food'.[1] In the account of his travels through nineteenth-century Arabia Deserta, Doughty noted that the 'Arab can live for long months so slenderly nourished that it seems to us they endure without food'.[2] While one cautions against assuming that conditions remained static over the intervening millennium, both comments strikingly reflect a mood found in Muslim 'recollections' of their early community. This introduction, impressionistic as it must be, attempts to capture basic features of the Arab food culture before the rise to prominence of the major urban centres of the emerging Islamic tradition in the provinces of Iraq, Syria, Egypt, Persia and beyond.

First, central Arabia in the Prophet's lifetime experienced a relative scarcity of food resources, and hence its fellow traveller, hunger. The Prophet Muḥammad was once asked, 'We live in a land where we are afflicted by hunger, so when may we eat animals which have died a natural death?'[3] The tradition (*ḥadīth*) is making a legal point concerning meat not ritually slaughtered. Implicitly it also touches on a familiar problem of scarcity and necessity. The Prophet answered, 'As long as you have neither a morning or evening drink [presumably milk] or gather vegetables you may eat them.' The situation is alluded to in the Qurʾān (5:3), where the term for severe hunger is

1 Muḥammad ibn Aḥmad al-Muqaddasī, *Descriptio imperii moslemici*, ed. M. J. de Goeje (Leiden, 1906), p. 254.
2 C. M. Doughty, *Travels in Arabia Deserta*, 2 vols. (London, 1964), vol. I, p. 446.
3 All the *ḥadīth* citations are taken from Muḥammad ibn ʿAbd Allāh al-Khaṭīb al-Tabrīzī, *Mishkāt al-maṣābīḥ*, trans. James Robson, 2 vols. (Lahore, 1990), vol. II, pp. 886–911.

makhmasa, and it echoes the expression 'a day of hunger/famine' (90:14, *fī yawm dhī masghaba*). Other *ḥadīths* point to the same underlying reality. The Prophet's wife 'Ā'isha is reported as saying that 'sometimes a month would come in which they did not kindle a fire [for cooking] having only dates and water', the two so-called 'black things'. Scarcity made a virtue of moderation, in eating as in the goal of the moral life. 'Two people's food is enough for three' is repeated in *ḥadīth* sources. Nonetheless, as Doughty stressed, for the Bedouin 'it is seldom in their lives they must make a shift to endure with a squalid diet of locusts'[4] – a sober reminder that in times of food crises the poor may just cope better than the more comfortably off.

Following from this was the absence of a 'differentiated cuisine' in the Prophet's Arabia. Town, village or oasis and desert dwellers alike lived on a margin, albeit flexible, where hunger – if seldom abject malnutrition – was never a distant memory. In various *ḥadīths* Muḥammad, himself a town dweller, is said to have rarely or never seen white bread in his lifetime. It is reported, too, that the Prophet never saw a sieve. When asked how unsifted barley (a lesser grain, despised in Europe at the same period) could be eaten he replied that 'they ground it and blew it and when some of it had blown away they moistened and ate what was left'. Doubtless this was a type of gruel that Doughty had frequently tasted, declaring that 'the Arab housewives can make savoury messes of any grain, seething it and putting thereto only a little salt and samn'.[5] Salt, a key ingredient of the pot, was called by the Prophet's contemporary Isidore of Seville 'as useful as the sun' and labelled by Muḥammad himself as 'the Lord of condiments'.

Simple fare required simple cooking methods. A pot for boiling grain-based gruel sufficed also for steeping vegetables or occasional portions of meat. After water skins, a pair of millstones would be the most essential implement in a town or village household. For preparing their own grain nomads borrowed the stones owned by their tribal leaders. Grinding everywhere was women's work. In settled areas the hearth fire served to heat the pot as well as a round, shield-like iron pan called *tannūr* (also known as *sāj*) upon which flat bread was baked. Desert dwellers dug a fire pit filled with whatever tinder was at hand and baked barley cakes under the ashes (called *malla*) or roasted small desert fauna in their skins. Meat, cut into strips, was sun dried and kept for future consumption, generally in stews.

4 Doughty, *Arabia Deserta*, vol. I, p. 520.
5 Ibid., vol. II, p. 220.

The inheritance

With the rise and expansion of Muslim rule beyond the confines of the Ḥijāz from the first/seventh through the fourth/tenth centuries came the inheritance of the food cultures of the conquered lands. Here Muslims encountered in abundance the famous triad of the classical world: wheat, the grape and the olive. This contrasted with the basic dual source of Arab nourishment, the date palm and the camel. Muḥammad's fondness for dates is clear from *ḥadīths* on food. ʿĀʾisha reported him as saying that 'a family which has dates will not be hungry'. He also remarked that no food or drink satisfies like milk. The importance of the date palm is signalled in the Qurʾān and, in a *ḥadīth*, it is called the most blessed of trees. Milk (*laban*) is one of God's earthly bounties (Q 16:66) and forms one of the heavenly rivers 'forever fresh' (Q 47:15). Both dates and milk were eaten fresh or sun-dried and stored until required. In the medieval lexicon, *marisa* referred to a preparation of dates, macerated by hand and mixed in milk (or water).

Also in contrast to the classical distinction between cultivated and uncultivated lands, the Arab drew sustenance from both. In his study of early Islamic dietary law Michael Cook describes both liberal and restrictive tendencies in the law.[6] The more inclusive and permissive trend was notable in the Ḥijāz centres of Mecca and Medina where the Mālikī legal school originated. Iraq was the home of the restrictive tendency, particularly among the scholars of Kūfa. Islamic law developed and was consolidated chiefly outside the Ḥijāz, in regions within the historical ambit of richly cultivated spaces, urban trade and political power. The camel was, unsurprisingly, accepted by all Muslim legal schools (but rejected in Jewish law) as emblematic of the Arab culture from which Islam emerged. In broader terms of contrasting food cultures, Iraqi or Egyptian legal scholars were less pressed with a nagging reality of scarcity and hunger than were their Ḥijāzī counterparts. Scholars of the Ḥijāz lived on in a milieu where the lizard and the hare were unequivocally accepted as food while being rejected elsewhere. Traditions attributed to the Prophet concerning the consumption of birds and beasts of prey may reflect this broad distinction: of all the legal schools, both Sunnī and Shīʿite, only Mālikīs permitted the eating of birds while merely disapproving beasts of prey. They were prohibited by all other scholars. Finally, it is perhaps owing to a lingering memory of famine that both Muslim and Jewish legal traditions permitted as edible that most dreaded famine food of all, the locust.

6 Michael Cook, 'Early Islamic dietary law', *JSAI*, 7 (1986).

The formation of new cultural frontiers is a process involving multiple contributors and commodities. Describing the process, like all historical enquiry, is subject to the nature of the sources available. In his *Fihrist*, Ibn al-Nadīm (d. 380/990) notes that in ʿAbbāsid Iraq, during the first half of the third/ninth century, there appeared an informal group of gastronomes associated with court circles. To each person, whether poet, musician, astrologer, physician or indeed member of the ruling caliphal family, Ibn al-Nadīm attributed a cookbook.[7] These are no longer extant. Traces of them survive, along with recipes from other collections, in the first surviving culinary manual in Arabic compiled by one Ibn Sayyār al-Warrāq, probably a contemporary of Ibn al-Nadīm. Ibn Sayyār's *Kitāb al-ṭabīkh*[8] provides clues required for piecing together the component elements of a 'new' haute cuisine, now cast in its Arabic/Muslim fashion characterised by cosmopolitanism, complexity of preparation of dishes and the use of costly ingredients.

Briefly stated, the main strands are, first, Sasanian Persian, the names of dishes, such as *sikbāj* and *zirbāj*, and of numerous ingredients such as *isfānākh* (spinach) indicating their Persian origin. Ibn al-Sayyār preserves a story of how *sikbāj* came to be created by the cooks in the court of Khusrau Anūshīrwān. The small triangle-shaped meat-filled pastry called *sanbūsak*, known in India as *samosa*, is also Persian. Second, the Arab tradition is represented by dishes modified to meet the tastes of the new urban leisured class. A traditional Arab preparation, such as *tharīd*, was compared by the Prophet to his wife ʿĀʾisha, the most excellent of women; another dish, *maḍīra*, was said to be a favourite of Muʿāwiya, founder of the Umayyad dynasty. Both these preparations in the Prophet's time were simple and unpretentious. *Tharīd*, for example, was prepared by breaking up bread with the hands and moistening it in broth, often with some meat added; it could also be made with crumbled bread, broth, marrow and eggs. The recipes for *tharīd* in the *Kitāb al-ṭabīkh*, however, are far more elaborate and costly. One contains both meat and poultry cooked in a pot with truffles, caramelised honey, chick peas, leeks and rue, and seasoned with salt, pepper, cumin, caraway and coriander; then fine baked bread was broken, moistened with the stock and the contents of the pot poured on top. Third, regional dishes, often of indeterminate origin, are found. Yet another dish bearing a Persian name, *isfīdhbāja*, is associated with the region of Sughd (Sogdia), while a version of *tharīd* is called Syrian.

7 Ibn al-Nadīm, *The* Fihrist *of al-Nadim: A tenth century survey of Muslim culture*, ed. and trans. Bayard Dodge, 2 vols. (New York, 1970), vol. II, p. 742.

8 Ibn Sayyār al-Warrāq, *Kitāb al-ṭabīkh*, ed. K. Ohrnberg and S. Mroueh (Helsinki, 1987).

Fourth, new plants from India were incorporated into many tempting dishes. The eggplant, *bādhinjān*, recently introduced to the Middle East from India (Sanskrit *vatingana*), was a favourite of the most famous of the early gourmands, the erstwhile caliph Ibrāhīm ibn al-Mahdī (d. 224/839), whose cookbook contained several recipes for dishes using the vegetable. Finally, the Hellenistic medical/dietetic tradition is reflected in several chapters in the *Kitāb al-ṭabīkh* on a wide variety of foodstuffs, describing their 'natures' in terms of the Galenic humoral system: lettuce, for example, is 'cold, calming the flame of a hot stomach, cutting sexual desire and inducing sleep'.[9]

It is probable, although more research will be required, that the Arabs' culinary inheritance may ultimately be traced further back than the Sasanians. The French scholar Jean Bottero has examined Babylonian cuneiform texts dating from the seventeenth century BCE containing, he claims, the 'most ancient recipes of all'. Some of the recipes relate in precise detail a dish's preparation, with the aim, says Bottero, 'of creating a plate with a taste intelligently achieved and a presentation both recherche and nutritionally rich'.[10] This closely fits the style and purpose of the vast majority of recipes both in Ibn Sayyār al-Warrāq and in the handful of later culinary manuals of the Arabic corpus.

In these later manuals[11] evidence of other culinary legacies is also found. In a cookbook of Maghribī provenance there are Berber preparations for couscous, an Andalusī manual contains recipes for chicken dishes made in the Jewish community, and another manual's Egyptian provenance is suggested in part by the inclusion of dishes employing species of Nile fish, and also by recipes using mallow leaves (*mulukhiyya*). Collectively, the compilers of the Arabic cookbooks had captured, by selection and organisation, portions of manifold Middle Eastern cooking traditions, both high and low, which hitherto had been orally transmitted over the generations. The significance of the corpus is that it represents historically the earliest recorded, extensive culinary

9 Ibid., p. 39.

10 Jean Bottero, 'The most ancient recipes of all', in J. Wilkins, D. Harvey and M. Dobson (eds.), *Food in Antiquity* (Exeter, 1996), p. 253.

11 The contents of these manuals will be treated collectively to save space in the discussion. See chapter bibliography for full details. They are: al-Warrāq, *Kitāb al-ṭabīkh*, fourth/tenth century; al-Baghdādī, *Kitāb al-ṭabīkh*, written in 622/1226; Ibn Razīn al-Tujībī, *Faḍālat al-khiwān*, written around 640/1266; Ibn al-ʿAdīm, *al-Wuṣla ila 'l-ḥabīb*, seventh/thirteenth century; Anonymous, *La cocina hispano-magrebi*, seventh/thirteenth century; Anonymous, *Kanz al-fawāʾid*, compiled *c.* eighth/fourteenth century.

tradition of any pre-modern civilisation, including that of the southern Sung Chinese (1127–1279).[12]

The classical Arabic/Islamic culinary heritage, 184–803/800–1400

Luxury may be said to be an activity or commodity that is expensive, pleasurable and unnecessary. Luxury foods are no exception.[13] The historian al-Masʿūdī (d. 345/956) provides an example from the reign of the ʿAbbāsid caliph Hārūn al-Rashīd (d. 194/809). Invited to dinner by his half-brother, Ibrāhīm ibn al-Mahdī, the caliph was presented with a dish in the shape of a fish made from hundreds of fish tongues. It was said to have cost 1,000 *dirhams*. Even the caliph deemed this extravagant, and ordered an equivalent amount of money distributed to the poor in expiation. Overall, the recipes in the Arabic corpus do not reflect such a degree of luxury. This, despite Ibn Sayyār al-Warrāq's introductory remark that he had gathered together for his anonymous patron dishes from the tables of kings, caliphs, notables and chiefs. In general the dishes contained in the culinary manuals were intended for a comfortable urban class of bureaucrats, scholars, merchants and military personnel. Another anecdote from al-Masʿūdī is instructive. The caliph al-Mutawakkil (d. 247/861) was relaxing one day with his courtiers and singers beside one of the canals traversing Baghdad. The aroma of cooking being prepared by a sailor on his boat drifted towards the group. The caliph ordered the pot brought to him. It was a sweet-and-sour beef stew of *sikbāj*, which the party completely devoured. The caliph paid 2,000 *dirhams* for the pleasure, saying it was the best *sikbāj* he had ever tasted. The luxury element in the story, if authentic, is the amount the caliph was prepared to reward the cook. Recalling the story, also if authentic, that *sikbāj* was the creation of the court of the Sasanian ruler Khusrau Anūshīrwān, by early ʿAbbāsid times the dish's popularity had 'trickled down' to the lower social strata in undoubtedly a different, affordable preparation. The key characteristic of the dish was a sweet–sour taste created by cooking meat in a stock containing vinegar and honey/sugar. This example illustrates the reverse process, already mentioned, of simple, traditional Arab fare transformed by more and costly ingredients. Knowledge of matters culinary and dietetic was available through both oral

12 Michael Freeman, 'Sung', in K. C. Chang (ed.), *Food in Chinese culture* (New Haven, 1977), p. 144.

13 See David Waines, '"Luxury foods" in medieval Islamic societies', in Marijke van der Veen (ed.), *World Archaeology: Luxury Foods*, 34, 3 (2003), special issue.

and written channels. Written works included two encyclopaedias, each of which contained sections on food and drink: one by Ibn Qutayba (d. 276/889), the other by Ibn ʿAbd Rabbih (d. 329/940). During this same period (257–308/870–920) the standard collections of *ḥadīth* (traditions) of the Prophet Muḥammad were compiled, in which food and drink were also treated. The earliest Arabic work on agronomy, written in the early fourth/tenth century and attributed to one Ibn Waḥshiyya, contains information on the culinary and medical uses of the many plants covered in it.

The kitchen

Food preparation took place in areas ranging from greater to lesser specialisation, depending upon their social location. In palaces there were separate public and private kitchens, and the cookhouses (*maṭābikh*) were separate from the bakeries (*makhābiz*). In modest urban and rural homes the cooking area shared the space in which other domestic functions such as sleeping or eating took place. In prosperous urban households the kitchen occupied its own special space with or without ancillary areas for storage, a latrine or cook's room. The following discussion will focus on this last example as the one best reflected in the extant cookbooks.

Complex food preparation called for a full *batterie de cuisine*. One of the major appliances in the kitchen was the oven or *tannūr*, not to be confused with the round, shield-shaped instrument mentioned above. The oven resembled a large earthenware beehive or inverted pot. Charcoal or other fuel was inserted through a low side opening and ignited. Baking could begin when the fuel had burned down to ashes and the oven was sufficiently hot. To some extent, temperature could be controlled by adjusting the lower aperture, or a larger one in the top. Bread was baked by slapping the flat-rolled dough on the curved inner surface near the top opening, and leaving it for a few moments until cooked. Nearly a dozen implements are known to have been used in bread making, from a dough board and rolling-pins to a poker used to extract a loaf that had fallen onto the ashes. A clear distinction between social classes was in bread consumption. The well-to-do had access to the finest wheat flour, while the daily loaf of the poor was made of inferior quality wheat or barley; in times of hardship 'secondary grains' such as pulses, acorns or chestnuts had to suffice.[14]

The *tannūr* was used also for baking other dishes. A kind of chicken pie prepared in a pan was lowered into the oven to bake; sometimes oven dishes

14 See David Waines, 'Cereals, bread and society', *JESHO*, 30 (1980).

(called *tannūriyya*) were left to stew overnight in a slowly cooling oven and served the following day. In another recipe, the prepared carcass of a whole animal was placed on a spit and inserted through the top of the oven with a pan placed at the bottom to catch the dripping fat. Of Mesopotamian origin (Akaddian *tinūru*), the *tannūr* probably made its way westwards under Muslim rule, examples having been uncovered by archaeologists in the Iberian Peninsula.[15]

Another contrivance, less frequently mentioned in the sources, was the *mustawqid*, or 'fireplace'. This was constructed along a wall to about half a person's height and provided with vents for air intake and the expulsion of smoke. It was designed chiefly to accommodate several pans/pots side by side at a time. The smaller *kānūn* was a brazier-like metal appliance, moveable or stationary, which supported a pot over the heat; the term *al-nār*, common in the North African and Andalusī cookbooks, was probably short for *kānūn al-nār*.

The communal oven (*furn*) was used for baking its owner's bread for sale or the dough for those households who prepared it in their own kitchens. The *furn* was further employed in cooking dishes initially prepared in the domestic kitchen and then returned to be garnished and served in the home. It could also be used for festive occasions when a household might require additional cooking space and labour.

The range of implements and utensils, containers and vessels mentioned in the culinary sources suggest a prosperous household's degree of self-sufficiency and independence from commercial cooked-food establishments described in the market inspectors' handbooks (*ḥisba*). Ibn al-Ukhuwwa (d. 729/1329) lists a number of these: the sellers of roast meat, liver preparations and relishes, sausage makers, butchers, cooked and pickled meat vendors, fish fryers and sweetmeat makers.[16] All these perhaps catered more specifically to the needs of other sections of the populace. Two reasons may be adduced for this. First, the culinary manuals contain recipes for home-made versions of most if not all of the commercial market preparations. Second, the inspectors' manuals convey the impression that market-cooked food could be regarded with some suspicion. Quality was best controlled in the domestic kitchen itself. Advice and instructions found in certain cookbooks further indicate a concern for kitchen hygiene. Meat must be thoroughly cleaned of blood and washed in cold water; a knife used to cut up vegetables should not

15 See Armas Salonen, 'Die Ofen der alten Mesopotamier', *Baghdader Mitteilungen*, 3 (1964).
16 Ibn al-Ukhuwwa, *Maʿālim al-qurba fī aḥkām al-ḥisba*, ed. Reuben Levy (London, 1938).

be used at the same time to cut up meat; old spices which had lost their essential flavour and become bitter could corrupt the pot. Utensils and pots should be carefully cleaned by rubbing with brick dust, then with dry powdered potash and saffron, and finally with fresh citron leaf. To ensure cleanliness, one advice was to change earthenware pots every day, and glazed pots every five days. Even humoral theory may have informed cooking practices. It was said that fish should be fried in a metal pan, as both the fish and the pan were 'cold' while fire and the oil were 'hot' and thus the desired equilibrium between elemental opposites was achieved in the cooking process.

Food preparation involved labour-intensive and time-consuming activities regardless of household size. The culinary manuals yield no data on the kitchen personnel or who was directly in charge of the supervision and organisation of the daily routine. It is possible, in the larger households, that a baker's (*khabbāz*) initial function evolved into the role of a kitchen steward or household major-domo. The number of persons to be fed on any given day could vary considerably, from immediate family occupants to meals including other relations and/or other dependants and guests.

Food preparation: ingredients and processes

As contemporary recipe collections indicate, meat stews or casseroles represented the single most common type of preparation. Whether goat, mutton or chicken was used, the animal was slaughtered just prior to cooking, suggesting that the meat was 'kept fresh' in the courtyard of the house or purchased live from the market on the day of preparation. The non-fowl meat recipes often only mention the word *laḥm* (meat), which should be assumed to mean mutton as this was the meat of preference mentioned by physicians in their accounts of diet. Lamb and kid were also enjoyed. Physicians recommended kid as suitable for the leisured class because of the meat's natural balance between the four elements. Similarly beef, only rarely mentioned, was judged more appropriate for those who toiled and laboured, owing to its natural coarseness. The cookbooks also contain recipes for game meat such as rabbit (which might also have been raised 'fresh' in the courtyard), hare, wild cow, wild ass and gazelle; the horse, mountain goat, oryx and stag were considered edible as well. One recipe for *sikbāj* called for beef, mutton and chicken. Fish dishes were popular as well, fresh rather than salted being the more common, and generally prepared in a frying-pan.

Typically, meat dishes were prepared together with vegetables, or fruit, milk or cheese and seasonings. At times the preparation was simplicity itself. 'Take chicken breasts, sliced, cut up into small pieces and fry in oil until cooked. Add pepper, fresh coriander and sprinkle over vinegar and [the condiment] *murri* over it, then spread ground almonds on top. God willing.'[17] In other recipes, in addition to the characteristic step-by-step description of the process, precise quantities of ingredients are provided, even to the spices, the proper proportion and combination of which usually being left to the cook. A spice combination in common use throughout the Middle East was cinnamon and (dried) coriander – often combined with cumin – with pepper and saffron widely employed as well. It was this 'spice spectrum' that Europe inherited from the Middle East from the fourteenth century onward. The essential oils of cinnamon and pepper were known for their antiseptic, preservative properties, but their use was probably as much a matter of aesthetics as anything, their preservative function being useful when left-over food could be served the following day with the flavour enhanced. The traditional cooking mediums, the rendered fat of the fat-tailed sheep and clarified butter, are mentioned in the cookbooks but so too is the frequently used olive oil, and occasionally sesame oil, while almond and walnut oil appear in some preparations.

Meat dishes with vegetables or fruit were often known by the name of the ingredient highlighted in them: *isfānākhiyya* was a spinach dish, *tuffāḥiyya* an apple dish. Vegetables frequently used included leeks, onions, turnip and cabbage, but also plants which today we would classify as herbs such as mint, rue, fresh coriander and thyme. Fruits used were fresh and dried. A common fresh fruit was the date, which was found in several hundred varieties; apricot, plum and quince featured as well. Dried fruits could mean both soft fruit, such as pears and peaches, and nuts, such as almonds, pistachios and pine seeds. Plants classified as 'seeds' included chick peas and lentils and the grasses wheat, barley and rice.

Dishes prepared with vegetables alone belonged to a category of cold (*bawārid*) side dishes to accompany others at the table, although they could be made with meat, fowl or fish as well. Vinegar was a common ingredient, and the resulting flavour of these dishes would range from sharp and piquant, through sweet and sour with the addition of sugar or honey to a delicately balanced taste by adding chopped almonds or oil. Vinegar in the medieval Middle Eastern cuisine was genuine *vin aigre* (*khall khamr*). It was the preserving agent in dishes called *mukhallalāt*, which referred to, among others, pickled onions, capers, cucumber, turnip and eggplant. These were said to cleanse a

17 Anonymous, *Kanz al-fawāʾid fī tanwīʿ al-mawāʾid*, ed. Manuela Marín and David Waines (Beirut, 1993), p. 26.

greasy palate and to assist digestion. Other pickle preparations were relishes or condiments called *kawāmikh* which required almost daily attention for six to twelve weeks. They appear to have been served in several small bowls into which bread or other morsels of food could be dipped. Another preparation requiring many weeks' elaboration was *murrī*, made from wheat and barley and resembling in its bitter flavour the classical Roman fish-based substance *garum* or *liquamen* or the modern Vietnamese *nuoc mam*. It was used as one seasoning among others in a wide variety of dishes.[18]

The later Middle Ages, 803–1112/1400–1700

The above account has covered in some detail the culinary features shared throughout the medieval Arab world as they appear in the extensive treasury of recipes preserved in the cookbooks. The latest of these is most likely of Egyptian provenance of the eighth/fourteenth or ninth/fifteenth century. The manuals reflect values of Islamic societies in the sense that there are no recipes explicitly for pork, prohibited by dietary law. Meat dishes found in the cookbooks nonetheless belonged to all irrespective of religious faith by the simple expedient of meat substitution, a Christian replacing mutton with pork if desired. Also prohibited is wine, broadly defined. However, certain preparations for beverages could produce a forbidden brew, the liquid fermenting by remaining several weeks in its container in the sun. However, for pious Muslims everywhere, alcohol, like pork, would be strictly avoided.

The three centuries down to 1700 witnessed the further expansion of Muslim rule, with the rise of the three great empires of the Ottoman Turks, the Persian Ṣafavids and the Mughals in India. So far as is known, extensive primary evidence of the kind described in the foregoing sections is not extant for these regions. True, there are, for example, the Turkish–Arabic dictionary of the fifth/eleventh century compiled by Maḥmūd al-Kāshgharī and a ninth/fifteenth-century Ottoman Turkish translation of Baghdādī's work. Several printed cookbooks in Turkish have been identified for the period between 1840 and 1930.[19] In Persian, two works describing Indian cookery of the sultan's court belong to the tenth/sixteenth and eleventh/seventeenth centuries.[20] However, we shall approach these later centuries with broad brush strokes only, leaving it to future research to fill in the detail.

18 See David Waines, '*Murrī*: The tale of a condiment', *al-Qanṭara*, 12, 2 (1991).
19 Turgut Kut, 'A bibliography of Turkish cookery books up to 1927', *Petits Propos Culinaires*, 36 (1990).
20 See C. A. Storey, *Persian literature*, 2 vols. (Leiden, 1977), vol. II/3, p. 389.

First, the single overwhelming influence on culinary vocabulary and practice throughout the Arab Islamic world and beyond was Persian. In Britain today the names of many popular cooked products are recognisably Persian in origin: kebab, biriani, nan, tikka. Pilaf (pilau, polow) is a three-stage method of cooking rice by washing/soaking, boiling and steaming that ensures light, dry, plump, separate grains. This was distinct from more traditional methods which produced thicker kinds of rice porridge or pudding. Pilaf rice may then be mixed with various ingredients from herbs, pulses, vegetables or fruits to meat or poultry, grilled, stuffed or roasted. Plain white rice made in this fashion is called *chelow*. The basic method is described in two medieval Arabic cookbooks, and the more elaborate preparations, already widely used in Persia, found their way into Turkish and Mughal cooking as well.

With the rise of the Ottoman power, first in Anatolia and then from the capture of Constantinople in 857/1453, another fusion of cultural frontiers was realised. One the one hand, the Turks inherited the culinary delights of the Persians, Arabs and other peoples, as well as bringing certain of their own traditional practices with them. As a result of cultural mixing there emerged in the cosmopolitan capital's vast imperial kitchens of Topkapı an astonishing number of specialists, such that by the tenth/sixteenth century there were nearly 1,600 cooks at work providing subsidised food for as many as 10,000 people: an act of charity on a grandiose scale. The system was replicated, albeit on a smaller scale, in cities and larger towns in the empire, as an extensive network of social aid in the form of public soup kitchens for the benefit of widows, orphans, the poor, the destitute and travellers. A parallel network was founded in the Sufi *zāwiyas*. On the other hand, one of the Turks' own contribution to the culinary map was bulghur wheat or *burghul*, parboiled wheat dried in the sun and then coarsely ground. Possessing a distinctive nutty flavour, it was and is used in making pilaf, and mixed together with meat to produce *küfte* and *kubba*. This was an innovation equal to the Berber development of couscous. Another contribution is the stew known as *güveç*, popular all over the Balkans and made in a vessel of the same name, a round or oval, wide, shallow, glazed or unglazed casserole.

The Mughal empire was a Muslim enclave in a Hindu continent; no matter how great the extent of Muslim rule, Muslims always constituted a minority religious community within the total Indian population. Mughal cuisine might refer, therefore, to the court culture of the emperors where the major influence was once again the refined tastes and dishes of Persia. Yet certain emperors, particularly Akbar (964–1014/1556–1605), owing to his policy of religious syncretism, became influenced by Hindu customs, and he forswore beef and declared a number of days, called *ṣūfiyāna* days, in which he ate no meat and slaughtering animals for meat was prohibited. Cooking and eating habits among the populace under Mughal rule is a different matter and more difficult to describe. The ordinary Muslims and Hindus were divided on the question of meat. The Muslim had no problem with any meat other than pork. The vegetarian Hindu might have found the Muslim's fondness for meat an obstacle even to social intercourse, let alone to the prospect of conversion. One Indian preparation that both communities could share was the spiced sauce or paste called curry, readily adopted into Mughal cooking. Curry (Tamil *kari*) employed a more complex spice spectrum than that used in the Persian tradition. As a sauce prepared separately and then added to rice, vegetables or meat and poultry, its function also differed from the Middle Eastern traditions, where seasonings were added to the pot during cooking.

Left to themselves, peoples' food habits are conservative if not immutable. Left to the forces of history, peoples' tastes change and are changed so that 'he who sets out on the path of acceptance soon forgets how to refuse'.[21] This is a fitting summation of over a millennium-long series of culinary transformations that accompanied the rise and spread of a new religious tradition.

21 Jean-Anthelme Brillat-Savarin, *The philosopher in the kitchen* (Harmondsworth, 1970 [1825]), p. 170.

Glossary

ʿAbbāsids	major Islamic dynasty (132–656/750–1258), based in Baghdad and, later, Cairo (659–923/1261–1517)
adab	(pl. *ādāb*) manners; belles-lettres
ʿahd	covenant
ahl	people: *ahl al-bayt*, the Prophet's family; *ahl al-dhimma*, people with a contract of protection; *ahl al-kitāb*, People of the Book; *ahl al-sunna*, (lit. 'the people of the *sunna*', Sunnī Muslims
akhbār	(sing. *khabar*) traditions; stories, anecdotes: *akhbār*-history, literary history
Almohads	(al-Muwaḥḥidūn) Berber reformist dynasty (524–667/1130–1269) based in North Africa and al-Andalus
Almoravids	(al-Murābiṭūn) Berber dynasty (448–541/1056–1147) that flourished in North Africa and al-Andalus before being overthrown by the Almohads
amīr	leader; military leader: *amīr al-muʾminīn*, commander of the faithful
amṣār	(sing. *miṣr*) garrison cities established by the Muslim conquerors in Iraq and elsewhere
ʿaql	reason, intellect
Ashʿarism	school of theology named after Abu ʾl-Ḥasan al-Ashʿarī, which emphasised a rationalist defence of traditional Islam and came to represent the mainstream of Sunnī theology
atabeg	(also *atābak*) tutor to a young prince
Ayyūbids	dynasty of Kurdish origin which ruled Egypt (564–650/1169–1252) before the Mamlūks, and also had branches in Damascus, Aleppo and elsewhere
bāb	(lit. 'gate') agent of the twelfth imam

baraka	blessing, spiritual power (of an individual holy man)
bāṭin	inward, esoteric (aspect of the divine revelation)
bayʿa	oath of allegiance, public proclamation of fealty
bayt	house, dwelling-place: Bayt al-Ḥikma, institution of higher learning in Baghdad
bidʿa	innovation
Būyids	Shīʿite dynasty of Daylamite origin that flourished in Iran and Iraq (320–454/932–1062), and coexisted with the ʿAbbāsid caliphs in Baghdad
Companions	(*ṣaḥāba*) the Prophet's associates
dāʿī	missionary, preacher; in Ismāʿīlism *dāʿī muṭlaq* (*dāʿī* with absolute authority)
dār	realm, abode: *dār al-ʿadl*, court of justice; *dār al-ʿahd*, territory governed by a treaty (with non-Muslims); *dār al-ḥarb*, (lit. 'the abode of war', the non-Muslim world); *dār al-imāra*, government house; *dār al-islām*, territories brought by conquest under Muslim rule; *dār al-ṣulḥ*, territory governed by a truce (with non-Muslims)
daʿwa	missionary movement
dawla	(Pers. *dawlat*) a change in power; state, government
devşirme	levy of young males imposed on Christian villages in the Ottoman empire
dhikr	(lit. 'remembrance') 'recollection' of God; in Sufism, ritualistic repetition of a prayer or formula
dhimma	agreement of protection
dhimmī	non-Muslim living in a Muslim country and guaranteed security and freedom of worship in exchange for the payment of tribute (*jizya*)
dīn	religion, faith
dīnār	gold coin
dirham	silver coin
dīwān	administrative bureau; collection of a poet's works
falsafa	philosophy
fanāʾ	(lit. 'annihilation') absorption of the self into the divine
faqīh	(pl. *fuqahāʾ*) jurist
Fāṭimids	Ismāʿīlī dynasty that flourished in North Africa (from 297/909) and Egypt (358–567/969–1171) until overthrown by Saladin

fatwā	(pl. *fatāwā*) legal opinion, issued by a legal scholar in response to a question
fiqh	(lit. 'understanding') Islamic jurisprudence, the substantive law of the *sharīʿa*
ghayba	the absence or occultation of an imam: *al-ghayba al-kubrā*, greater occultation; *al-ghayba al-ṣughrā*, lesser occultation
ghazal	love poem
ghulām	(pl. *ghilmān*) lad; slave; slave-soldier
ghulāt, ghāliya	(sing. *ghālī*) follower of extreme Shīʿite heterodox doctrines such as the transmigration of souls and the divinity of the imams
ḥadīth	orally transmitted report of a saying of the Prophet and his Companions; such reports in general
ḥājib	chamberlain
ḥajj	pilgrimage to Mecca
ḥalqa	(pl. *ḥalaqāt*) circle; study-circle
ḥammām	bathhouse, public bath
Ḥanafism	one of the four main schools of law (*madhhabs*) of Sunnī Islam, named after Abū Ḥanīfa, most popular in Turkey, Central Asia and the Indian subcontinent
Ḥanbalism	one of the four main schools of law (*madhhabs*) of Sunnī Islam, named after Aḥmad ibn Ḥanbal, it is the *madhhab* to which the founder of Wahhabism belonged
ḥaqīqa	(pl. *ḥaqāʾiq*) hidden spiritual truth; reality
ḥaqq	truth, right, reality
hijra	the Prophet's flight/emigration from Mecca to Medina; the obligation to emigrate from countries dominated by infidel or unjust rulers
ḥikma	wisdom: *ḥikmat-i ʿamali*, practical philosophy; *al-ḥikma al-ilāhiyya* (Pers. *ḥikmat-i ilāhī*), divine wisdom or theosophy; *al-ḥikma al-ishrāqiyya*, illuminationist philosophy; *al-ḥikma al-mashshāʾiyya*, Peripatetic philosophy
ḥiyal	'tricks' or legal devices to circumvent prohibitions such as that on usury; artifice, fraud
ḥudūd	(sing. *ḥadd*) punishments laid down by the Qurʾān
ijāza	a 'licence' to teach or transmit a particular text issued by the master with whom one had studied; in Sufism, to

	instruct one's own disciples in accordance with the master's spiritual 'method': *ijāzat al-tadrīs wa'l-iftā'*, the authorisation to teach law and issue legal opinions
ijmāʿ	consensus
ijtihād	independent reasoning: *ijtihād al-ra'y*, the exertion of mental energy for the sake of arriving, through reasoning, at a considered opinion
ikhtilāf	difference of opinions among *mujtahids*
Ikhwān al-Ṣafā'	(Brethren of Purity) group of Ismāʿīlī-influenced Neoplatonist philosophers and intellectuals that compiled the *Rasā'il*, an encyclopaedia of all the sciences in the form of fifty-two epistles
ʿilm	(pl. *ʿulūm*) knowledge
imam	Shīʿite spiritual and political leader; founder of a *madhhab*; major scholar
imām	prayer leader
iqṭāʿ	land whose revenue is allocated to a soldier; fief
islām	submission
Ismāʿīlīs	also Seveners; members of a branch of Shīʿite Islam emphasising an esoteric interpretation of the Qur'ān, influenced by Neoplatonism and with a belief in a cyclical theory of history centred on the number seven
isnād	(pl. *asānīd*) chain of transmitters
Ithnā ʿAsharīs	also Twelvers or Imāmīs; majority branch of the Shīʿites, who acknowledge twelve imams after the death of the Prophet, and believe that the twelfth imam went into occultation and will return
jihād	(lit. 'struggle') holy war; also spiritual discipline ('greater *jihād*')
jizya	(Tur. *jizye*) poll-tax paid by *dhimmīs* living in Islamic lands
kalām	(lit. 'speech') scholastic theology, dialectic
karāmāt	miracles, special wonders performed by a saint through divine grace
kātib	(pl. *kuttāb*) scribe, secretary
khalīfa	(lit. 'successor' or 'deputy') caliph, leader of the Islamic community: *khalīfat allāh*, deputy of God; *khalīfat rasūl Allāh*, deputy of the messenger of God; deputy of a Sufi master

khalwa	retreat, seclusion
khānqāh	Sufi convent
Khārijites	also Khawārij; members of an early schismatic movement that rejected ʿAlī and subsequent caliphs and inspired numerous rebellions; often known as fanatical
khāṣṣa	(pl. *khawāṣṣ*) elite; initiates; crown land; occult property of an object
khaṭīb	orator; one who delivers the sermon at the Friday prayer
khilāfa/khilāfat	caliphate
khuṭba	Friday sermon
kitāb	(pl. *kutub*) book
kufr	unbelief
kuttāb	elementary school
madhhab	(pl. *madhāhib*) school of law
madrasa	religious college
mahdī	(lit. 'the rightly guided one') expected messianic leader
majlis	(pl. *majālis*) meeting, assembly; music/literary salon
Mālikism	one of the four main schools of law (*madhhabs*) of Sunnī Islam, named after Mālik ibn Anas
mamlūk	slave-soldier
Mamlūks	Egyptian dynasty (648–922/1250–1517) founded by *mamlūks*, who presided over a flowering of Egyptian art and architecture until overthrown by the Ottomans
maʿrifa	gnosis
masjid	(lit. 'place of prostration') mosque: *masjid jāmiʿ*, congregational mosque where the Friday prayer is performed
mathnawī	(Urdu *mathnavī*) religious poem composed of rhyming couplets
mawlā	(pl. *mawālī*) relative; client; non-Arab convert to Islam
maẓālim	(lit. 'wrongful acts') ruler's court where grievances would be heard
miḥna	inquisition; an attempt by the caliph al-Maʾmūn to impose adherence to the doctrine of a created Qurʾān
miḥrāb	niche within a mosque indicating the *qibla*
miʿrāj	heavenly journey of the Prophet
muftī	(in India *mulavi*) legal scholar qualified to deliver a *fatwā*

Mughals	Islamic dynasty that flourished in India (932–1274/1526–1858) and presided over a cultural and artistic golden age
mujtahid	jurist, scholar entitled to deliver an independent judgment
muqarnas	stalactite-like architectural ornamentation
murīd	(pl. *murīdūn*) Sufi novice/disciple
mutakallim	(pl. *mutakallimūn*) practitioner of *kalām*, dialectical theologian
Muʿtazilism	early theological school characterised by belief in human free will and the createdness of the Qurʾān
nabī	(pl. *anbiyāʾ*) prophet
nafs	the human soul or spirit; the body's sensual appetites
naṣṣ	designation (of a successor)
nisba	final component of a personal name that identifies place of birth, tribal affiliation, occupation etc.
qāḍī	judge
qāʾim	awaited messianic leader, *mahdī*
qānūn	regulation, law; Ottoman state law: *qānūn-nāme*, law code
qaṣīda	multi-thematic poem, ode
qibla	the direction (towards the Kaʿba) faced by worshippers in prayer
qiyās	analogy, analogical reasoning (in law)
rasūl	messenger
raʾy	reason; individual opinion (in law)
ribāṭ	Sufi convent
riḥla	journey, travelogue
rūḥ	soul, spirit: *rūḥ al-qudus*, holy spirit
Ṣafavids	Persian dynasty (907–1145/1501–1732) that made Ithnā ʿAsharī Shīʿism the official branch of Islam in Iran
ṣalāt	prayer
Saljūqs	Turkish dynasty (429–590/1038–1194) that established itself in Iran in the fifth/eleventh century and extended its rule westward to Iraq, Syria and Anatolia
samāʿ	(lit. 'listening') ritualised 'listening' to music and mystical poetry; music
Shāfiʿism	one of the four main schools of law (*madhhabs*) of Sunnī Islam, named after Muḥammad ibn Idrīs al-Shāfiʿī,

	which became popular in Lower Egypt, Syria, East Africa, southern Arabia and South-East Asia
shahāda	profession of faith
sharīʿa	Islamic law
shaykh	(pl. *shuyūkh*; f. *shaykha*) elder; spiritual master
shaykh al-islām	(Tur. *şeyhülislam*) chief religious authority; head of the *ʿulamāʾ*
Shīʿism	branch of Islam that originated with the belief that ʿAlī should have succeeded the Prophet as *khalīfa*; the majority of Muslims in Iran and Iraq are Shīʿites
sīra	(pl. *siyar*) exemplary conduct of a ruler; biography of the Prophet; heroic romance; stand-alone single-subject biography
siyāsa(t)	statecraft; Ottoman penal system; execution
Sufism	Islamic mysticism; there are many Sufi orders all over the Muslim world, with a variety of beliefs and practices
sulṭān	authority, sovereignty; government; ruler
sunna	(pl. *sunan*) exemplary mode of conduct; the practice of Muḥammad and his Companions
Sunnism	branch of Islam adhered to by the majority of Muslims in most non-Shīʿite countries
sūra	chapter of the Qurʾān
tafsīr	Qurʾānic exegesis
tanāsukh	transmigration of souls (metempsychosis)
taqiyya	precautionary dissimulation of one's true religious belief and practice
taqlīd	(lit. 'imitation') dependence on the views of earlier legal authorities
taʾrīkh	chronologically dated history
ṭarīqa	(pl. *ṭuruq*) Sufi order; mystical way or path
tarjama	(pl. *tarājim*; lit. entry) biographical entry; biography
taṣawwuf	Sufism; the wearing of a woollen robe
tawakkul	complete trust in, and total reliance on, God
tawḥīd	divine unity
Tīmūrids	Turco-Mongol dynasty founded by Tīmūr Lang in the late eighth/fourteenth century which ruled Iran and Central Asia and presided over a flowering of culture
ʿulamāʾ	religious scholars

Umayyads	first major Islamic dynasty (41–132/661–750), established after the death of ʿAlī, which ruled until the ʿAbbāsid revolution; a branch of the family also ruled in al-Andalus (138–422/756–1031)
umma	community (of believers); nation
uṣūl	foundations, principles: *uṣūl al-dīn*, principles of theology; *uṣūl al-fiqh*, foundations/principles of jurisprudence
waḥdat al-wujūd	doctrine of the 'oneness of being'
wājib	that which is obligatory under Islamic law; necessary: *wājib al-wujūd*, 'necessary existent'
walāya	friendship with God; sainthood
walī	(pl. *awliyāʾ*) saint; authority: *walī Allāh*, friend of God
waqf	(pl. *awqāf*) pious foundation; endowment, charitable trust
wilāya	authority
wujūd	existence
ẓāhir	outward, manifest, exoteric (aspect of the divine revelation)
zakāt	alms-tax
zāwiya	Sufi convent
Zaydīs	branch of Shīʿism, following imams of ʿAlid descent, based mainly in northern Iran and Yemen, characterised by Muʿtazilite beliefs and a willingness to participate in armed rebellions

Bibliography

Chapter 1: Islam

Practical suggestions for further reading

Berkey, Jonathan, *The formation of Islam: Religion and society in the Near East, 600–1800*, Cambridge, 2003.

Bulliet, Richard, *Islam: The view from the edge*, New York, 1994.

Endress, Gerhard, *Islam: An historical introduction*, New York, 2002.

Esposito, John (ed.), *The Oxford history of Islam*, New York, 1999.

Hodgson, Marshall G. S., *The venture of Islam: Conscience and history in a world civilization*, 3 vols., Chicago, 1974.

Kennedy, Hugh, *The Prophet and the age of the caliphates*, London, 1986.

Nasr, Seyyid Hossein, *Islam: Religion, history, and civilization*, San Francisco, 2003.

Primary sources

Ibn Isḥāq, *Ṣīrat rasūl allāh*, trans. Alfred Guillaume as *The life of Muḥammad*, Oxford, 1955.

Ibn Khaldūn, *The* Muqaddimah*: An introduction to history*, trans. Franz Rosenthal, 2nd edn, 3 vols., Princeton, 1967.

al-Māwardī, ʿAlī ibn Muḥammad, *al-Aḥkām al-sulṭāniyya*, trans. Wafaa H. Wahba as *The ordinances of government*, Reading, 1996.

al-Shāfiʿī, Muḥammad ibn Idrīs, *al-Risāla fī uṣūl al-fiqh*, trans. Majid Khadduri, 2nd edn, Cambridge, 1987.

al-Shahrastānī, Muḥammad ibn ʿAbd al-Karīm, *Muslim sects and divisions: The section on Muslim sects in* Kitāb al-milal wa ʾl-niḥal, trans. A. K. Kazi and J. G. Flynn, London, 1984.

al-Ṭabarī, Muḥammad ibn Jarīr, *Tārīkh al-rusul wa'l-mulūk* (*The history of al-Ṭabarī*), 40 vols., Albany, 1987–2007.

Secondary sources

Ayoub, Mahmoud, *The crisis of Muslim history: Religion and politics in early Islam*, Oxford, 2003.

Berkey, Jonathan, *Popular preaching and religious authority in the medieval Islamic Near East*, Seattle, 2001.

The transmission of knowledge in medieval Cairo: A social history of Islamic education, Princeton, 1992.

Bulliet, Richard, *Conversion to Islam in the medieval period*, Cambridge, MA, 1979.
The patricians of Nishapur: A study in medieval Islamic social history, Cambridge, MA, 1972.
Chamberlain, Michael, *Knowledge and social practice in medieval Damascus, 1190–1350*, Cambridge, 1994.
Cook, David, *Understanding jihad*, Berkeley, 2005.
Cook, Michael, *Commanding right and forbidding wrong in Islamic thought*, Cambridge, 2000.
Cook, Michael, and Patricia Crone, *Hagarism: The making of the Islamic world*, Cambridge, 1977.
Cooperson, Michael, *Classical Arabic biography: The heirs of the prophets in the age of al-Maʾmūn*, Cambridge, 2000.
Crone, Patricia, *God's rule: Government and Islam*, New York, 2004.
Crone, Patricia, and Martin Hinds, *God's caliph: Religious authority in the first centuries of Islam*, Cambridge, 1986.
Donner, Fred, *The early Islamic conquests*, Princeton, 1981.
Narratives of Islamic origins: The beginnings of Islamic historical writing, Princeton, 1998.
Ephrat, Daphna, *A learned society in transition: The Sunnī ʿulamāʾ of eleventh-century Baghdad*, Albany, 2000.
Hallaq, Wael B., *Authority, continuity, and change in Islamic law*, Cambridge, 2001.
A history of Islamic legal theories, Cambridge, 1997.
The origins and evolution of Islamic law, Cambridge, 2005.
Hawting, G. R., *The idea of idolatry and the emergence of Islam: From polemic to history*, Cambridge, 1999.
Hillenbrand, Carole, *The Crusades: Islamic perspectives*, Chicago, 1999.
Holt, P. M., *The age of the Crusades: The Near East from the eleventh century to 1517*, London, 1986.
Humphreys, R. Stephen, *Islamic history: A framework for inquiry*, Princeton, 1991.
Imber, Colin, *Ebu's-suʿud: The Islamic legal tradition*, Stanford, 1997.
Itzkowitz, Norman, *Ottoman empire and Islamic tradition*, Chicago, 1980.
Karamustafa, Ahmet, *God's unruly friends: Dervish groups in the later Islamic middle period, 1200–1500*, Salt Lake City, 1994.
Lambton, A. K. S., *State and government in medieval Islam: An introduction to the study of Islamic political theory: The jurists*, Oxford, 1981.
Lapidus, Ira, *Muslim cities in the later Middle Ages*, Cambridge, MA, 1967.
Madelung, Wilferd, *Religious trends in early Islamic Iran*, Albany, 1988.
The succession to Muḥammad: A study of the early caliphate, Cambridge, 1997.
Makdisi, George, *Ibn ʿAqīl: Religion and culture in classical Islam*, Edinburgh, 1997.
The rise of colleges: Institutions of learning in Islam and the West, Edinburgh, 1981.
Melchert, Christopher, *The formation of the Sunni schools of law, 9th and 10th centuries CE*, Leiden, 1997.
Menocal, Maria Rosa, *The ornament of the world: How Muslims, Jews, and Christians created a culture of tolerance in medieval Spain*, New York, 2002.
Nagel, Tilman, *The history of Islamic theology from Muhammad to the present*, Princeton, 2000.
Petry, Carl, *The civilian elite of Cairo in the later Middle Ages*, Princeton, 1981.
Repp, R. C., *The müfti of Istanbul: A study in the development of the Ottoman learned hierarchy*, London, 1986.
Trimingham, J. S., *The Sufi orders in Islam*, Oxford, 1971.

Watt, W. Montgomery, *The formative period of Islamic thought*, Edinburgh, 1973.
Muhammad at Mecca, Oxford, 1953.
Muhammad at Medina, Oxford, 1953.
Zaman, Muhammad Qasim, *Religion and politics under the early ʿAbbasids: The emergence of the proto-Sunni elite*, Leiden, 1997.
Zilfi, Madeleine, *The politics of piety: The Ottoman ulema in the postclassical age (1600–1800)*, Minneapolis, 1988.

Chapter 2: Sufism

Practical suggestions for further reading

Baldick, Julian, *Mystical Islam: An introduction to Sufism*, London, 1989.
Chittick, William, *Sufism: A short introduction*, Oxford, 2000.
Ernst, Carl, *The Shambhala guide to Sufism*, Boston and London, 1997.
Karamustafa, Ahmet, *Sufism: The formative period*, Berkeley, 2007.
Lewisohn, Leonard (ed.), *The heritage of Sufism*, 3 vols., Oxford, 1999.
Sedgwick, Mark, *Sufism: The essentials*, Cairo, 2000.
Sirriyeh, Elizabeth, *Sufis and anti-Sufis*, Richmond, 1999.

Primary sources

ʿAṭṭār, Farīd al-Dīn, *Muslim saints and mystics: Episodes from the Tadhkirat al-awliyāʾ by Farīd al-Dīn ʿAṭṭār*, trans. Arthur Arberry, London and New York, 1990 (repr.).
Böwering, Gerhard (ed.), *The minor Qurʾān commentary of Abū ʿAbd al-Raḥmān ... al-Sulamī (d. 412/1021)*, Beirut, 1995.
Heer, Nicholas (ed.), *The precious pearl: al-Jāmī's* al-Durrah al-fākhirah, Albany, 1979.
al-Kalābādhī, Muḥammad ibn Ibrāhīm, *The doctrine of the Sufis: Kitāb al-taʿarruf li-madhhab ahl al-taṣawwuf by Muḥammad ibn Ibrāhīm al-Kalābādhī*, trans. Arthur Arberry, Cambridge and New York, 1977 (repr.).
Nicholson, Reynold (ed.), *The Kitāb al-lumaʿ fi ʾl-taṣawwuf of Abū Naṣr ... al-Sarrāj*, Leiden and London, 1914.
al-Qushayrī, Abu ʾl-Qāsim, *Al-Qushzyri's epistle on Sufism*, trans. Alexander Knysh, Reading, 2007.
Wakīʿ ibn al-Jarrāḥ, *Kitāb al-zuhd*, ed. ʿAbd al-Raḥmān al-Faryawānī, 2nd edn, 2 vols., Riyadh, 1994.

Secondary sources

Abun-Nasr, Jamil, *The Tijāniyya: A Sufi order in the modern world*, Oxford, 1965.
Alikberov, Alikber, *Epokha klassicheskogo islama na Kavkaze*, Moscow, 2003.
Arberry, Arthur, *Sufism: An account of the mystics of Islam*, London, 1950.
Baldick, Julian, 'Les Qalenderis', in A. Popovic and G. Veinstein (eds.), *Les voies d'Allah: Les ordres soufis dans le monde musulman*, Paris, 1996, 500–3.
Bannerth, Ernst, 'La Khalwatiyya en Égypte', *Mélanges de l'Institut Dominicain d'Études Orientales*, 8 (1964–6), 1–74.
Bashir, Shahzad, *Messianic hopes and mystical visions: The Nūrbakhshīya between medieval and modern Islam*, Columbia, SC, 2003.

Birge, John, *The Bektashi order of dervishes*, London, 1937.
van den Bos, Matthijs, *Mystic regimes: Sufism and state in Iran*, Leiden, 2002.
Böwering, Gerhard, *The mystical vision of existence in classical Islam*, Berlin, 1980.
Brown, John, *The darvishes or oriental mysticism*, ed. H. A. Rose, London, 1968.
Chabbi, Jacqueline, 'Réflexions sur le soufisme iranien primitif', *Journal Asiatique*, 266, 1–2 (1978), 37–55.
Chittick, William, 'Ibn ʿArabī and his school', in S. H. Nasr (ed.), *Islamic spirituality: Manifestations*, New York, 1991, 49–79.
'Rūmī and waḥdat al-wujūd', in A. Banani, R. Hovannisian *et al.* (eds.), *Poetry and mysticism in Islam*, Cambridge, 1994, 77–9.
Clayer, Natalie, 'La Bektachiyya', in A. Popovic and G. Veinstein (eds.), *Les voies d'Allah: Les ordres soufis dans le monde musulman*, Paris, 1996, 469–74.
Corbin, Henry, *Creative imagination in the Sufism of Ibn ʿArabī*, Princeton, 1969.
Cornell, Vincent, *Realm of the saint*, Austin, 1998.
DeWeese, Devin, *Islamization and native religion of the Golden Horde: Baba Tükles and conversion to Islam in historical and epic tradition*, University Park, PA, 1994.
Ernst, Carl, *Eternal garden: Mysticism, history, and politics at a South Asian Sufi center*, Albany, 1992.
van Ess, Josef, *Theologie und Gesellschaft im 2. und 3. Jahrhundert Hidschra*, 6 vols., Berlin and New York, 1991–5.
Faroqhi, Suraiya, *Der Bektaschi-Orden in Anatolien*, Vienna, 1981.
'The Bektashis: A report on current research', in A. Popovic and G. Veinstein (eds.), *Bektachiyya: Études sur l'ordre mystique des Bektachis et les groupes relevant de Hadji Bektach*, Istanbul, 1995, 9–28.
Heath, Peter, *Allegory and philosophy in Avicenna (Ibn Sina)*, Philadelphia, 1992.
Hodgson, Marshall, *The venture of Islam*, 3 vols., Chicago, 1974.
de Jong, Frederick, 'Muṣṭafā Kamāl al-Bakrī (1688–1749): Revival and reform of the Khalwatiyya tradition', in N. Levtzion and J. O. Voll (eds.), *Eighteenth-century renewal and reform in Islam*, Syracuse, 1987, 117–32.
Ṭuruq and ṭuruq-linked institutions in nineteenth-century Egypt, Leiden, 1978.
Karamustafa, Ahmet, *God's unruly friends*, Salt Lake City, 1994.
Knysh, Alexander, *Ibn ʿArabī in the later Islamic tradition: The making of a polemical image in medieval Islam*, Albany, 1999.
Islamic mysticism: A short history, Leiden, 2000.
'The *tariqa* on a Landcruiser: The resurgence of Sufism in Yemen', *Middle East Journal*, 55, 3 (2001), 399–411.
Landolt, Herman, 'al-Ghazali and Religionswissenschaft', *Asiatische Studien*, 55, 1 (1991), 19–72.
Martin, Bradford, *Muslim brotherhoods in nineteenth-century Africa*, Cambridge, 1976.
Mélikoff, Irène, 'L'ordre des Bektachis et les groupes relevant de Hadji Bektach', in A. Popovic and G. Veinstein (eds.), *Bektachiyya: Études sur l'ordre mystique des Bektachis et les groupes relevant de Hadji Bektach*, Istanbul, 1995, 3–7.
Morris, James, 'How to study the Futūḥāt', in S. Hirtenstein and M. Tiernan (eds.), *Muḥyiddīn ibn ʿArabī: A commemorative volume*, Brisbane, 1993, 73–89.
Nwyia, Paul, *Exégèse coranique et langage mystique*, Paris, 1970.
O'Fahey, Rex, *The enigmatic saint: Aḥmad ibn Idrīs and the Idrīsī tradition*, Evanston, IL, 1990.

Radtke, Bernd, 'Theologen und Mystiker in Hurasan und Transoxanien', *ZDMG*, 136, 1 (1986), 536–69.
Reinert, Benedikt, *Die Lehre vom tawakkul in der klassischen Sufik*, Berlin, 1968.
Schimmel, Annemarie, *Mystical dimensions of Islam*, Chapel Hill, NC, 1975.
Smith, Margaret, *Studies in early mysticism in the Near and Middle East*, 2nd edn, Oxford, 1995.
Trimingham, John, *Sufi orders in Islam*, 2nd edn, Oxford, 1998.
Vööbus, Arthur, *Syriac and Arabic documents regarding legislation relevant to Syrian asceticism*, Stockholm, 1960.
Watt, William Montgomery, *Faith and practice of al-Ghazali*, London, 1953.
Yahia, Osman, *Histoire et classification de l'oeuvre d'Ibn ʿArabī*, 2 vols., Damascus, 1964.
Zarcone, Thierry, 'Muḥammad Nūr al-ʿArabī et la confrérie Malāmiyya', in A. Popovic and G. Veinstein (eds.), *Les voies d'Allah: Les ordres soufis dans le monde musulman*, Paris, 1996, 479–83.
'Le Turkestan chinois', in A. Popovic and G. Veinstein (eds.), *Les voies d'Allah: Les ordres soufis dans le monde musulman*, Paris, 1996, 268–73.

Chapter 3: Varieties of Islam

Practical suggestions for further reading

Crone, Patricia, *Medieval Islamic political thought*, Edinburgh, 2004.
Halm, Heinz, *Shiism*, 2nd edn, trans. J. Watson and M. Hill, Edinburgh, 2004.
Kohlberg, Etan (ed.), *Shīʿism*, Aldershot, 2003.
Madelung, Wilferd, *Religious trends in early Islamic Iran*, Albany, 1988.

Primary sources

al-Ashʿarī, Abu'l-Ḥasan ʿAlī ibn Ismāʿīl, *Kitāb maqālāt al-Islāmiyyīn*, ed. H. Ritter, 2 vols., Istanbul, 1929–30.
al-Baghdādī, Abū Manṣūr ʿAbd al-Qāhir ibn Ṭāhir, *al-Farq bayn al-firaq*, ed. M. Badr, Cairo, 1328/1910, trans. as *Moslem schisms and sects*: part I trans. K. C. Seelye, New York, 1919; part II trans. A. S. Halkin, Tel Aviv, 1935.
Ibn al-Athīr, ʿIzz al-Dīn ʿAlī ibn Muḥammad, *al-Kāmil fi'l-ta'rīkh*, ed. C. J. Tornberg, 12 vols., Leiden, 1851–76.
Ibn Bābawayh, Abū Jaʿfar Muḥammad, *Man lā yaḥḍuruhu'l-faqīh*, ed. Ḥ. M. al-Kharsān, Najaf, 1957.
Ibn Ḥazm, Abū Muḥammad ʿAlī ibn Aḥmad, *Kitāb al-faṣl fi'l-milal wa'l-ahwā' wa'l-niḥal*, 5 vols., Cairo, 1317–21/1899–1903.
Ibn Shahrāshūb, Abū Jaʿfar Muḥammad ibn ʿAlī, *Manāqib āl Abī Ṭālib*, Bombay, 1313/1896; Najaf, 1376/1956.
al-Kashshī, Abū ʿAmr Muḥammad ibn ʿUmar, *Ikhtiyār maʿrifat al-rijāl*, as abridged by Muḥammad ibn al-Ḥasan al-Ṭūsī, ed. Ḥ. al-Muṣṭafawī, Mashhad, 1348/1969.
al-Kulaynī, Abū Jaʿfar Muḥammad ibn Yaʿqūb, *al-Uṣūl min al-kāfī*, ed. ʿAlī Akbar al-Ghaffārī, 2 vols., Tehran, 1388/1968.
al-Nawbakhtī, Abū Muḥammad al-Ḥasan ibn Mūsā, *Kitāb firaq al-Shīʿa*, ed. H. Ritter, Istanbul, 1931.

al-Nuʿmān ibn Muḥammad, al-Qāḍī Abū Ḥanīfa, *Daʿāʾim al-Islām*, ed. A. A. A. Fyzee, 2 vols., Cairo., 1951–61; trans. A. A. A. Fyzee as *The pillars of Islam*, rev. I. K. Poonawala, 2 vols., New Delhi, 2002–4.

al-Qummī, Saʿd ibn ʿAbd Allāh al-Ashʿarī, *Kitāb al-maqālāt wa'l-firaq*, ed. M. J. Mashkūr, Tehran, 1963.

al-Shahrastānī, Abu'l-Fatḥ Muḥammad ibn ʿAbd al-Karīm, *Kitāb al-milal wa'l-niḥal*, ed. W. Cureton, 2 vols., London, 1842–6; partial trans. A. K. Kazi and J. G. Flynn as *Muslim sects and divisions*, London, 1984; French trans. D. Gimaret *et al.* as *Livre des religions et des sectes*, 2 vols., Paris, 1986–93.

al-Sijistānī, Abū Yaʿqūb Isḥāq ibn Aḥmad, *Kitāb al-yanābīʿ*, ed. and French trans. H. Corbin, in his *Trilogie Ismaélienne*, Tehran and Paris, 1961, text pp. 1–97, trans. pp. 1–127; English trans. P. E. Walker 25 'The Book of wellsprings', in P. E. Walker, *The wellsprings of wisdom*, Salt Lake City, 1994, pp. 37–111.

al-Ṭabarī, Abū Jaʿfar Muḥammad ibn Jarīr, *Taʾrīkh al-rusul wa'l-mulūk*, ed. M. J. de Goeje *et al.*, 15 vols. in 3 series, London, 1879–1901; English trans. by various scholars as *The history of al-Ṭabarī*, 40 vols., Albany, 1985–99.

al-Ṭūsī, Abū Jaʿfar Muḥammad ibn al-Ḥasan, *Tahdhīb al-aḥkām*, ed. Ḥ. M. al-Kharsān, 10 vols., Najaf, 1958–62.

al-Ṭūsī, Naṣīr al-Dīn Muḥammad ibn Muḥammad, *Rawḍat al-taslīm*, ed. and trans. W. Ivanow, Leiden, 1950; ed. and trans. J. Badakhchani as *Paradise of submission*, London, 2005.

Secondary sources

Abu-Izzeddin, Nejla M., *The Druzes: A new study of their history, faith and society*, Leiden, 1993.

Amir-Moezzi, Mohammad Ali, *The divine guide in early Shiʿism*, trans. D. Streight, Albany, 1994.

van Arendonk, Cornelis, *Les débuts de l'imāmat zaidite au Yémen*, trans. J. Ryckmans, Leiden, 1960.

Arjomand, Said Amir, *The shadow of God and the hidden imam: Religion, political organization and societal change in Shiʿite Iran from the beginning to 1890*, Chicago, 1984.

Babayan, Kathryn, *Mystics, monarchs, and messiahs*, Cambridge, MA, 2002.

Bar-Asher, Meir M. and A. Kofsky, *The Nuṣayrī–ʿAlawī religion*, Leiden, 2002.

Calder, Norman, 'Doubt and prerogative: The emergence of an Imami Shiʿi theology of *ijtihād*', *SI*, 70 (1989), 57–78.

Cole, Juan, *Roots of North Indian Shīʿism in Iraq and India*, Berkeley, 1988.

Corbin, Henry, *Cyclical time and Ismaili Gnosis*, London, 1983.

En Islam iranien, 4 vols., Paris, 1971–2.

Crone, Patricia, and M. Hinds, *God's caliph: Religious authority in the first centuries of Islam*, Cambridge, 1986.

Daftary, Farhad, *Ismaili literature*, London, 2004.

The Ismāʿīlīs: Their history and doctrines, 2nd edn, Cambridge, 2007.

A short history of the Ismailis, Edinburgh, 1998.

(ed.), *Mediaeval Ismaʿili history and thought*, Cambridge, 1996.

Dussaud, René, *Histoire et religion des Noṣairîs*, Paris, 1900.

Halm, Heinz, *The empire of the Mahdi: The rise of the Fatimids*, trans. M. Bonner, Leiden, 1996.

Die islamische Gnosis, Zurich and Munich, 1982.

The Fatimids and their traditions of learning, London, 1997.
'Nuṣayriyya', *EI2*, vol. VIII, 145–8.
Hodgson, Marshall G. S., *The order of Assassins: The struggle of the early Nizārī Ismāʿīlīs against the Islamic world*, The Hague, 1955.
Jafri, S. Husain M., *Origins and early development of Shīʿa Islam*, London, 1979.
Kohlberg, Etan, *Belief and law in Imāmī Shīʿism*, Aldershot, 1991.
Lewicki, Tadeusz, 'al-Ibāḍiyya', *EI2*, vol. III, 648–60.
Madelung, Wilferd, 'Imamism and Muʿtazilite theology', in T. Fahd (ed.), *Le Shîʿisme imâmite*, Paris, 1970, 13–29, repr. in Wilferd Madelung, *Religious schools*, article VII.
Der Imam al-Qāsim ibn Ibrāhīm und die Glaubenslehre der Zaiditen, Berlin, 1965.
'Ismāʿīliyya', *EI2*, vol. IV, 198–206.
Religious schools and sects in medieval Islam, London, 1985.
'Shīʿa', *EI2*, vol. IX, 420–4.
'Zaydiyya', *EI2*, vol. XI, 477–81.
Momen, Moojan, *An introduction to Shiʿi Islam: The history and doctrines of Twelver Shiʿism*, New Haven, 1985.
Rubinacci, Roberto, 'The Ibāḍīs', in A. J. Arberry (ed.), *Religion in the Middle East*, 2 vols., Cambridge, 1969, vol. II, 302–17.
Sachedina, Abdulaziz A., *Islamic messianism: The idea of the Mahdi in Twelver Shiʿism*, Albany, 1981.
Sobhani, Jaʿfar. *Doctrines of Shiʿi Islam*, ed. and trans. R. Shah-Kazemi, London, 2001.
Tabataba'i, S. Muḥammad Ḥusayn, *Shiʿite Islam*, ed. and trans. S. H. Nasr, London, 1975.
Walker, Paul E., *Early philosophical Shiism*, Cambridge, 1993.
Watt, W. Montgomery, *The formative period of Islamic thought*, Edinburgh, 1973.
Wellhausen, Julius, *The religio-political factions in early Islam*, trans. R. C. Ostle and S. M. Walzer, Amsterdam, 1975.

Chapter 4: Islamic law

Practical suggestions for further reading

Anderson, Michael, 'Legal scholarship and the politics of Islam in British India', in R. S. Khare (ed.), *Perspectives on Islamic law, justice, and society*, Lanham, MD, 1999, 65–91.
An-Na'im, Abdullahi, *Islamic family law in a changing world*, London, 2002.
Asad, Talal, 'Conscripts of Western civilization', in Christine W. Gailey (ed.), *Civilization in crisis: Anthropological perspectives*, Gainesville, 1992, 333–51.
Formations of the secular, Stanford, 2003.
Bravmann, M. M., *The spiritual background of early Islam*, Leiden, 1972.
Cohn, Bernard, *Colonialism and its forms of knowledge: The British in India*, Princeton, 1996.
Feener, Michael, 'Indonesian movements for the creation of a "national madhhab"', *ILS*, 9, 1 (2002), 83–115.
Hallaq, Wael B., *Authority, continuity and change in Islamic law*, Cambridge, 2001.
'Model *shurūṭ* works and the dialectic of doctrine and practice', *ILS*, 2, 2 (1995), 109–34.
The origins and evolution of Islamic law, Cambridge, 2005.
'*Qāḍīs* communicating: Legal change and the law of documentary evidence', *al-Qanṭara*, 20, 2 (1999), 437–66.
Sharia: Theory, practice, transformations, Cambridge, forthcoming.

'What is sharia?' *Yearbook of Islamic and Middle Eastern Law, 2005–2006*, vol. XII, Leiden, 2007, 151–80.

Hélie-Lucas, Marie-Aimée, 'The preferential symbol for Islamic identity: Women in Muslim personal laws', in Valentine Moghadam (ed.), *Identity politics and women: Cultural reassertions and feminisms in international perspective*, Boulder, 1994, 188–96.

Hurvitz, Nimrod, *The formation of Ḥanbalism: Piety into power*, London, 2002.

Johansen, B., *The Islamic law on land tax and rent*, London, 1988.

'Legal literature and the problem of change: The case of the land rent', in Chibli Mallat (ed.), *Islam and public law*, London, 1993, 29–47.

Kugle, Scott A., 'Framed, blamed and renamed: The recasting of Islamic jurisprudence in colonial South Asia,' *Modern Asian Studies*, 35, 2 (2001), 257–313.

Makdisi, G., 'The significance of the schools of law in Islamic religious history', *IJMES*, 10 (1979), 1–8.

Melchert, Christopher, *The formation of the Sunni schools of law*, Leiden, 1997.

'The formation of the Sunni schools of law', in W. B. Hallaq (ed.), *The Formation of Islamic Law*, The Formation of the Classical Islamic World 27 (gen. ed. L. Conrad), Aldershot, 2003, XIII.

Moors, Annelies, 'Debating Islamic family law: Legal texts and social practices', in M. L. Meriwether and Judith E. Tucker (eds.), *Social history of women and gender in the modern Middle East*, Boulder, 1999, 141–75.

Motzki, H., 'The role of non-Arab converts in the development of early Islamic law', *ILS*, 6, 3 (1999), 293–317.

Nielsen, J., *Secular justice in an Islamic state*, Leiden, 1985.

Peirce, Leslie, *Morality tales: Law and gender in the Ottoman court of Aintab*, Berkeley and Los Angeles, 2003.

Peters, F. E. (ed.), *The Arabs and Arabia on the eve of Islam*, The Formation of the Classical Islamic World 3 (gen. ed. L. Conrad), Aldershot, 1999.

Powers, D., *Law, society, and culture in the Maghrib, 1300–1500*, Cambridge, 2002.

'Orientalism, colonialism and legal history: The attack on Muslim family endowments in Algeria and India', *Comparative Studies in Society and History*, 31, 3 (July 1989), 535–71.

Rubin, U. (ed.), *The Life of Muhammad*, The Formation of the Classical Islamic World 4 (gen. ed. L. Conrad), Aldershot, 1998.

Spectorsky, Susan, '*Sunnah* in the responses of Isḥāq B. Rāhawayh', in B. Weiss (ed.), *Studies in Islamic legal theory*, Leiden, 2002, 51–74.

Strawson, John, 'Islamic law and English texts', *Law and Critique*, 6, 1 (1995), 21–38.

Tsafrir, N., *The history of an Islamic school of law: The early spread of Hanafism*, Cambridge, MA, 2004.

Tyan, E., *Histoire de l'organisation judiciare en pays d'Islam*, 2nd edn, Leiden, 1960.

'Judicial organization', in M. Khadduri and H. Liebesny (eds.), *Law in the Middle East*, Washington, DC, 1955, 236–78.

Weiss, B., *The search for God's law*, Salt Lake City, 1992.

Zaman, M. Q., *Religion and politics under the early ʿAbbāsids: The emergence of the proto-Sunni elite*, Leiden, 1997.

The ulama in contemporary Islam: Custodians of change, Princeton, 2002.

Primary sources

Bājī, Abū al-Walīd, *Iḥkām al-fuṣūl fī aḥkām al-uṣūl*, ed. ʿAbd al-Majīd Turkī, Beirut, 1986.

Dimashqī, Abū Zurʿa, *Tārīkh*, ed. Shukr Allāh al-Qawjānī, 2 vols., n.p., 1970.

Ḥusām al-Shahīd, Ibn Māza, *Sharḥ Adab al-qāḍī lil-Khaṣṣāf*, Beirut, 1994.

Ibn ʿAbd al-Barr, Abū ʿUmar Yūsuf, *Jāmiʿ bayān al-ʿilm wa-faḍlihi*, 2 vols., Beirut, n.d.

Ibn Abī Shayba, M., *al-Muṣannaf*, 9 vols., Beirut, 1995.

Ibn al-Ḥājib, Jamāl al-Dīn ibn ʿUmar, *Jāmiʿ al-ummahāt*, ed. Abū ʿAbd al-Raḥmān al-Akhḍarī, Damascus and Beirut, 1421/2000.

Ibn Ḥibbān, M., *Kitāb al-thiqāt*, Hyderabad, 1968.

Ibn al-Najjār, Taqī al-Dīn, *Muntahā al-irādāt*, ed. ʿAbd al-Mughnī ʿAbd al-Khāliq, 2 vols., Cairo, 1381/1962.

Ibn Qāḍī Shuhba, Taqī al-Dīn, *Ṭabaqāt al-Shāfiʿiyya*, 4 vols., Hyderabad, 1978.

Ibn Taymīya, Taqī al-Dīn, *Istiḥsān*, in G. Makdisi, 'Ibn Taymīya's autograph manuscript on *istiḥsān*: Materials for the study of Islamic legal thought', in G. Makdisi (ed.), *Arabic and Islamic studies in honor of H. A. R. Gibb*, Cambridge, MA, 1965, 446–79.

Jammāʿīlī, ʿAbd al-Ghanī ibn ʿAbd al-Wāḥid, *al-ʿUmda fī al-aḥkām*, ed. M. ʿAṭāʾ, Beirut, 1986.

Kindī, M. ibn Yūsuf, *Akhbār quḍāt Miṣr*, ed. R. Guest, Cairo, n.d.

Mālik ibn Anas, *al-Muwaṭṭaʾ*, Beirut, 1414/1993.

Marghīnānī, Burhān al-Dīn ʿAlī ibn Abī Bakr, *al-Hidāya: Sharḥ bidāyat al-mubtadī*, 4 vols., Cairo, 1980 (repr).

Qalqashandī, Aḥmad ibn ʿAlī, *Ṣubḥ al-aʿshā fī ṣināʿat al-inshā*, 14 vols., Beirut, 1987.

Samarqandī, Abū Naṣr, *Rusūm al-quḍāt*, ed. M. Jāsim al-Ḥadīthī, Baghdad, 1985.

Shīrāzī, Abū Isḥāq Ibrāhīm, *Ṭabaqāt al-fuqahāʾ*, ed. I. ʿAbbās, Beirut, 1970.

Wakīʿ, M. ibn Khalaf, *Akhbār al-quḍāt*, 3 vols., Beirut, n.d.

Secondary sources

Alon, Y., 'The tribal system in the face of the state-formation process: Mandatory Transjordan, 1921–46', *IJMES*, 37 (2005), 213–40.

Anderson, B. *Imagined communities: Reflections on the origin and spread of nationalism*, 2nd edn, London and New York, 2006.

Anderson, J. N. D., 'Law reform in Egypt: 1850–1950', in P. M. Holt (ed.), *Political and social change in modern Egypt*, London, 1968, 209–30.

Anderson, Michael R., 'Legal scholarship and the politics of Islam in British India', in R. S. Khare (ed.), *Perspectives on Islamic law, justice, and society*, Lanham, MD, 1999, 65–91.

Asad, T., *Formations of the secular*, Stanford, 2003.

Calder, N., 'Law', in S. H. Nasr and O. Leaman (eds.), *History of Islamic philosophy*, London, 1996, 979–98.

'al-Nawawī's typology of *muftīs* and its significance for a general theory of Islamic law', *ILS*, 3, 3 (1996), 137–64.

Chatterjee, Partha, 'Colonialism, nationalism, and colonized women: The contest in India', *American Ethnologist*, 16, 4 (1989), 622–33.

Cohn, B., *Colonialism and its forms of knowledge: The British in India*, Princeton, 1996.

Coulson, N. J., *A history of Islamic law*, Edinburgh, 1964.

van Creveld, M., *The rise and decline of the state*, Cambridge, 2000.

Dirks, Nicholas B., *The scandal of empire: India and the creation of imperial Britain*, Cambridge, MA, 2006.
El-Nahal, G. H., *The judicial administration of Ottoman Egypt in the seventeenth century*, Minneapolis and Chicago, 1979.
Fadel, M., 'The social logic of *taqlīd* and the rise of the *mukhtaṣar*', *ILS*, 3, 2 (1996), 193–233.
Glenn, P., *Legal traditions of the world*, Oxford, 2000.
Hallaq, Wael B., 'Fashioning the moral subject: Sharia's technologies of the self', unpublished MS, 35 pp.
'Groundwork of the moral law: A new look at the Qur'ān and the genesis of sharī'a', *ILS*, 17, 1 (forthcoming, 2010).
A history of Islamic legal theories: An introduction to Sunnī uṣūl al-fiqh, Cambridge, 1997.
'The *qāḍī's dīwān (sijill)* before the Ottomans', *BSOAS*, 61, 3 (1998), 415–36.
'The quest for origins or doctrine? Islamic legal studies as colonialist discourse', *UCLA Journal of Islamic and Near Eastern Law*, 2, 1 (2002–3), 1–31.
'Was al-Shafi'i the master architect of Islamic jurisprudence?', *IJMES*, 25 (1993), 587–605.
'Was the gate of ijtihad closed?', *IJMES*, 16 (1984), 3–41.
(ed.), *The formation of Islamic law*, The Formation of the Classical Islamic World 27 (gen. ed. L. Conrad), Aldershot, 2003.
Hooker, M. B., *Legal pluralism: An introduction to colonial and neo-colonial laws*, Oxford, 1975.
Hoyland, R. G., *Seeing Islam as others saw it: A survey and evaluation of Christian, Jewish and Zoroastrian writings on early Islam*, Princeton, 1997.
Johansen, B., *The Islamic law on land tax and rent*, London, 1988.
'Legal literature and the problem of change: The case of the land rent', in Chibli Mallat (ed.), *Islam and public law*, London, 1993, 29–47.
Jones, William, *al-Sirajiyah or the Mahomedan law of inheritance*, Calcutta, 1861.
Kolff, D. H. A., 'The Indian and the British law machines: Some remarks on law and society in British India', in W. J. Mommsen and J. A. De Moor (eds.), *European expansion and law: The encounter of European and indigenous law in 19th- and 20th-century Africa and Asia*, Oxford, 1992, 201–35.
Liebesny, H., *Law of the Near and Middle East*, Albany, 1975.
Makdisi, G., 'Ibn Taymīya's autograph manuscript on *istiḥsān*: Materials for the study of Islamic legal thought', in G. Makdisi (ed.), *Arabic and Islamic studies in honor of H. A. R. Gibb*, Cambridge, MA, 1965, 446–79.
Menski, Werner, *Hindu law: Beyond tradition and modernity*, Oxford, 2003.
Motzki, H., 'The role of non-Arab converts in the development of early Islamic law', *ILS*, 6, 3 (1999), 293–317.
Powers, D., '*Kadijustiz* or qāḍī-justice? A paternity dispute from fourteenth-century Morocco', *ILS*, 1, 3 (1994), 332–66; repr. in D. Powers, *Law, society, and culture in the Maghrib, 1300–1500*, Cambridge, 2002, 23–52.
'On judicial review in Islamic law,' *Law and Society Review*, 26 (1992), 315–41.
Singha, Radhika, *A despotism of law: Crime and justice in early colonial India*, Delhi, 1998.
Strawson, John, 'Islamic law and English texts,' *Law and Critique*, 6, 1 (1995), 21–38.
Thung, M., 'Written obligations from the 2nd/8th to the 4th century', *ILS*, 3, 1 (1996), 1–12.
Udovitch, A. L., *Partnership and profit in medieval Islam*, Princeton, 1970.
Weiss, B., *The search for God's law*, Salt Lake City, 1992.
Zaman, M. Q., *Religion and politics under the early 'Abbāsids*, Leiden, 1997.

Chapter 5: Conversion and the *ahl al-dhimma*

Practical suggestions for further reading

Amitai-Preiss, Reuven, 'Ghazan, Islam and Mongol tradition: A view from the Mamlūk sultanate', *BSOAS*, 59 (1996), 1–10.

Brett, Michael, *The rise of the Fatimids: The world of the Mediterranean and the Middle East in the fourth century of the hijra, tenth century CE*, The Medieval Mediterranean: Peoples, Economies and Cultures, 400–1453 30, Leiden, 2001.

'The spread of Islam in Egypt and North Africa', in Michael Brett (ed.), *Northern Africa: Islam and modernization*, London, 1973, 1–12.

Cohen, Mark R., *Under crescent and cross: The Jews in the Middle Ages*, Princeton, 1994.

Coope, Jessica, 'Religious and cultural conversion to Islam in ninth-century Umayyad Córdoba', *Journal of World History*, 4 (1993), 47–68.

Cuoq, Joseph, *L'église d'Afrique du Nord, du deuxième au treizième siècle*, Paris, 1984.

DeWeese, Devin, *Islamization and native religion in the Golden Horde: Baba Tükles and conversion to Islam in historical and epic tradition*, University Park, PA, 1994.

Fargues, Philippe, 'Demographic Islamization: non-Muslims in Muslim countries', *SAIS Review*, 21 (2001), 103–16.

Florida, Nancy K., *Writing the past, inscribing the future: History as prophecy in colonial Java*, Durham, NC, and London, 1995.

Goitein, S. D., *A Mediterranean society: The Jewish communities of the Arab world as portrayed in the documents of the Cairo Geniza*, 6 vols., Berkeley and Los Angeles, 1967–93.

Hooker, M. B., 'Introduction: The translation of Islam into South-East Asia', in M. B. Hooker (ed.), *Islam in South-East Asia*, Leiden, 1983, 1–22.

Ricklefs, M. C., *A history of modern Indonesia since c. 1200*, 3rd edn, Basingstoke, 2001.

The seen and unseen worlds in Java, 1726–1749: History, literature and Islam in the court of Pakubuwana II, St Leonards, 1998.

Primary sources

'Abd al-Ḥaqq al-Islâmî, *al-Sayf al-mamdûd fî al-radd 'alà aḥbâr al-yahûd (Espada extendida para refutar a los sabios judíos)*, ed., trans. and with notes and introd. Esperanza Alfonso, Madrid, 1998.

Abumalham, Monserrat, 'La conversión según formularios notariales andalusíes: valoración de la legalidad de la conversión de Maimonídes', *Miscelánea de Estudios Arabes y Hebraicos*, 34 (1985), 71–84.

Beihammer, Alexander Daniel, *Quellenkritische Untersuchungen zu den ägyptischen Kapitulationsverträgen der Jahre 640–646*, Österreichische Akademie der Wissenschaften, philosophisch-historische Klasse, Sitzungsberichte 671, Vienna, 2000.

Chalmeta, Pedro, 'Le passage à l'Islam dans al-Andalus au Xe siècle', in *Actas del XII Congreso de la UEAI (Malaga 1984)*, Madrid, 1986, 161–83.

Ibn Isḥāq, *The life of Muhammad (Sīrat Rasūl Allāh)*, trans. with introd. and notes Alfred Guillaume, Oxford, 1955.

Marín, Manuela and Rachid El Hour, 'Captives, children and conversion: A case from late Naṣrid Granada', *JESHO*, 41 (1998), 453–73.

Noth, Albrecht, 'Abgrenzungsprobleme zwischen Muslimen und Nicht-Muslimen: Die "Bedingungen 'Umars (*aš-šurūṭ al-'umariyya*)" unter einem anderen Aspekt gelesen', *JSAI*, 9 (1987), 290–315.

van Ronkel, P. S., 'Malay tales about conversion of Jews and Christians to Muhammedanism', *Acta Orientalia*, 10 (1932), 56–66.

al-Samaw'al al-Maghribī, *Ifḥām al-Yahūd*, ed. and trans. Moshe Perlmann, *Proceedings of the American Academy for Jewish Research*, 32 (1964).

Yavari, Neguin, 'The conversion stories of Shaykh Abū Isḥāq Kāzarūnī', in Guyda Armstrong and Ian N. Wood (eds.), *Christianizing peoples and converting individuals*, International Medieval Research 7, Turnhout, 2000, 225–46.

Secondary sources

Amitai, Reuven, 'The conversion of Tegüder Ilkhan to Islam', *JSAI*, 25 (2001), 15–43.

Amitai-Preiss, Reuven, 'Sufis and shamans: Some remarks on the Islamization of the Mongols in the Ilkhanate', *JESHO*, 42 (1999), 27–46.

Balivet, Michel, 'Aux origines de l'islamisation des Balkans ottomans', *Revue du monde musulman et de la Méditerranée*, 66 (1993), 11–20.

Banani, Amin, 'Conversion and conformity in a self-conscious elite', in *Individualism and conformity in classical Islam (5th Giorgio Levi Della Vida Biennial Conference, May 23–25, 1975, Gustave E. von Grunebaum Center)*, Los Angeles, 1977, 19–31.

Biran, Michal, 'The Chaghadaids and Islam: The conversion of Tarmashirin Khan (1331–34)', *JAOS*, 122 (2002), 742–52.

Blachère, Regis, 'Regards sur l'"acculturation" des arabo-musulmans jusque vers 40/661', *Arabica*, 3 (1957), 247–65.

Bulliet, Richard W., *Conversion to Islam in the medieval period: An essay in quantitative history*, Cambridge, MA, 1979.

Cohen, Mark R., 'What was the Pact of 'Umar? A literary-historical study', *JSAI*, 23 (1999), 100–57.

Cuoq, Joseph, *Islamisation de la Nubie chrétienne VIIe–XVIe siècle*, Bibliothèque d'études islamiques 9, Paris, 1986.

Décobert, Christian, 'Sur l'arabisation et l'islamisation de l'Egypte médiévale', in C. Décobert (ed.), *Itinéraires d'Egypte, mélanges offerts au père Maurice Martin sj*, Cairo, 1992, 273–300.

Dennet, D. C., *Conversion and the poll tax in early Islam*, Cambridge, MA, 1950.

Deringil, Selim, '"There is no compulsion in religion": On conversion and apostasy in the late Ottoman empire: 1839–1856', *Comparative Studies in Society and History*, 42 (2000), 547–75.

Eaton, Richard, *Essays on Islam and Indian history*, New Delhi, 2000.

Fattal, Antoine, *Le statut légal des non-musulmans en pays d'Islam*, Beirut, 1958.

Frantz-Murphy, Gladys, 'Conversion in early Islamic Egypt: The economic factor', in *Documents de l'Islam médiéval: Nouvelles perspectives de recherche, actes de la table ronde, Paris, 3–5 mars 1988*, Paris, 1991, 11–17.

Friedmann, Yohanan, *Tolerance and coercion in Islam: Interfaith relations in the Muslim tradition*, Cambridge, 2003.

Guessous, Azeddine, 'Le rescrit fiscal de 'Umar b. 'Abd al-'Azīz: Une nouvelle appréciation', *Der Islam*, 73 (1996), 113–37.

Hadziiossif, Jacqueline, 'Les conversions des juifs à l'islam et au christianisme en Méditerranée, XIe-XVe siècles', in Henri Bresc and Christiane Veauvy (eds.), *Mutations d'identités en Méditerranée: Moyen âge et époque contemporaine*, [Saint Denis], 2000, 159–73.

Hangloo, R. L., 'Accepting Islam and abandoning Hinduism: A study of proselytization process in medieval Kashmir', *Islamic Culture*, 71 (1997), 91–110.

Kiel, Machiel, 'La diffusion de l'Islam dans les campagnes bulgares à l'époque ottomane (XVe–XIXe siècles): Colonisation et conversion', *Revue du monde musulman et de la Méditerranée*, 66 (1993), 39–53.

Lal, K. S., *Growth of Muslim population in medieval India (AD 1000–1800)*, Delhi, 1973.

Lazarus-Yafeh, Hava, *Intertwined worlds: Medieval Islam and Bible criticism*, Princeton, 1992.

el-Leithy, Tamer, 'Coptic culture and conversion in medieval Cairo, 1293–1524 AD', Ph.D. dissertation, Princeton University, 2005.

Levtzion, Nehemia, 'Conversion to Islam: Some notes towards a comparative study', in *Études arabes et islamiques (Actes du XXIXe Congrès international des orientalistes)*, I-Histoire et Civilisation 3, Paris, 1975, 125–9.

'Conversion under Muslim domination: A comparative study', in David N. Lorenzen (ed.), *Religious change and cultural domination: XXX International Congress of Human Sciences in Asia and North Africa*, Mexico, 1981, 19–38.

'Patterns of Islamization in West Africa', in Daniel F. McCall and Norman R. Bennett (eds.), *Aspects of West African Islam*, Boston University Papers on Africa 5, Boston, 1971, 31–9.

(ed.), *Conversion to Islam*, New York and London, 1979.

Levtzion, Nehemia, and Randall L. Pouwels (eds.), *The history of Islam in Africa*, Athens, OH, Oxford and Cape Town, 2000.

Levy-Rubin, Milka, 'New evidence relating to the process of Islamization in Palestine in the early Muslim period: The case of Samaria', *JESHO*, 43 (2000), 257–76.

Lichtenstadter, Ilse, 'The distinctive dress of non-Muslims in Islamic countries', *Historia Judaica*, 5, 1 (April 1943), 35–52.

Little, Donald P., 'Coptic conversion to Islam under the Baḥrī Mamlūks, 692–755/1293–1354', *BSOAS*, 39 (1976), 552–69.

'Coptic converts to Islam during the Baḥrī Mamlūk period', in Michael Gervers and Ramzi Jibran Bikhazi (eds.), *Conversion and continuity: Indigenous Christian communities in Islamic lands, eighth to eighteenth centuries*, Papers in Medieval Studies 9, Toronto, 1990, 263–88.

Melville, Charles, '*Pādshāh-i Islām*: The conversion of Sultan Maḥmūd Ghāzān Khān', *Pembroke Papers*, 1 (1990), 159–77.

Miran, Marie, *Islam, histoire et modernité en Côte-d'Ivoire*, Paris, 2006.

Morony, Michael G., *Iraq after the Muslim conquest*, Princeton, 1984.

Pouwels, Randall L., 'The East African coast, *c.* 780 to 1900 CE', in Nehemia Levtzion and Randall L. Pouwels (eds.), *The history of Islam in Africa*, Athens, OH, Oxford and Cape Town, 2000, 251–71.

Pritsak, Omeljan, 'The Khazar kingdom's conversion to Judaism', *Harvard Ukrainian Studies*, 2 (1978), 261–81.

Richard, Jean, 'La conversion de Berke et les débuts de l'islamisation de la Horde d'Or', *Revue des Études Islamiques*, 35 (1967), 173–84.

Rizvi, S. A. A., 'Islamic proselytisation (seventh to sixteenth centuries)', in G. A. Oddie (ed.), *Religion in South Asia: Religious conversion and revival movements in South Asia in medieval and modern times*, New Delhi, 1977, 13–33.

Saad, Elias N., *Social history of Timbuktu: The role of Muslim scholars and notables, 1400–1900*, Cambridge, 1983.

Savage, Elizabeth, 'Conversion or metamorphosis: The Christian population after the Islamic conquest', in Mark Horton and Thomas Wiedemann (eds.), *North Africa from Antiquity to Islam: Papers of a conference held at Bristol, October 1994*, Bristol, 1994, 45–7.

Shatzmiller, Maya, 'Marriage, family, and the faith: Women's conversion to Islam', *Journal of Family History*, 21 (1996), 235–66.

Stewart, Angus, 'The assassination of King Het'um II: The conversion of the Ilkhans and the Armenians', *JRAS* (2005), 45–61.

Stillman, Norman A., *The Jews of Arab lands: A history and source book*, Philadelphia, 1979.

Teissier, Henri, 'La desaparición de la antigua iglesia de África', in H. Teissier and R. Lourido Díaz (eds.), *El Cristianismo en el norte de Africa*, n.p., 1993, 37–54.

Vásáry, István, '"History and legend" in Berke Khan's conversion to Islam', in D. Sinor (ed.), *Aspects of Altaic civilization, III: Proceedings of the thirtieth meeting of the permanent International Altaistic Conference, Bloomington, 1987*, Uralic and Altaic series 145, Bloomington, 1990, 230–52.

Vryonis, Speros, *The decline of medieval Hellenism in Asia Minor and the process of Islamization from the eleventh through the fifteenth century*, Berkeley, Los Angeles and London, 1971.

Wake, Christopher, 'Malacca's early kings and the reception of Islam', *Journal of Southeast Asian History*, 5 (1964), 104–28.

Chapter 6: Muslims and the natural world

Practical suggestions for further reading

Foltz, Richard C., *Animals in Islamic tradition and Muslim cultures*, Oxford, 2006.

Foltz, Richard, Frederick M. Denny and Azizan Baharuddin (eds.), *Islam and ecology: A bestowed trust*, Center for the Study of World Religions, Cambridge, MA, 2003.

Huff, Toby E., *The rise of early modern science: Islam, China and the West*, 2nd edn, Cambridge, 2003.

Nasr, Seyyed Hossein, *Islamic science: An illustrated study*, London, 1976.

Religion and the order of nature, New York, 1996.

Saliba, George, *Islamic science and the making of the European Renaissance*, Cambridge, MA, 2007.

Primary sources

al-Bīrūnī, Muḥammad ibn Aḥmad, *al-Biruni's book on pharmacy and materia medica*, ed. and trans. Hakim Mohammed Said, Pakistan Series on Central Asian Studies 1–2, Karachi, 1973.

Exhaustive treatise on shadows, trans. E. S. Kennedy, Aleppo, 1976.

The case of the animals versus man before the king of the Jinn: A tenth-century ecological fable of the Pure Brethren of Basra, trans. Lenn Evan Goodman, Woodbridge, CT, 1978.

al-Damīrī, Muḥammad ibn Mūsā, *ad-Damīrī's* Ḥayāt al-ḥayawān*: A zoological lexicon*, trans. Atmaram Sadashiv G. Jayakar, 2 vols., Frankfurt am Main, 2001.
The hanged poems, trans. F. E. Johnson, in Charles F. Horne (ed.), *Ancient Arabia*, Sacred Books of the East 5, New York, 1917.
The message of the Qur'ān, trans. Muḥammad Asad, Gibraltar, 1980.
al-Muqaddasī, Muḥammad ibn Aḥmad, *The best divisions for knowledge of the regions: A translation of* Ahsan al-taqasim fi ma'rifat al-aqalim, trans. Basil Anthony Collins, n.p., 2001.
al-Qazwīnī, Ḥamdullāh Mustawfī, *The geographical part of the Nuzhat al-qulub*, trans. Guy Le Strange, n.p., 2006 (repr.) [1919].
The zoological section of the Nuzhatu-l-qulub, ed. and trans. J. Stephenson, Oriental Translation Fund, n.s. 30, London, 1928.

Secondary sources

Bowen, John R., *Muslims through discourse*, Princeton, 1993.
Harley, J. B., and David Woodward, *The history of cartography*, vol. II, book 1: *Cartography in the traditional Islamic and South Asian societies*, Chicago, 1992.
Manjhan, *Madhumalati: An Indian Sufi romance*, trans. Aditya Behl and Simon Weightman, Oxford, 2000.
Masrī, al-Ḥāfiẓ ibn A., *The Islamic code of animal–human relationships*, Horsham, n.d.
Miquel, André, *La géographie humaine du monde musulman jusqu'au milieu du 11e siècle*, 4 vols., Paris, 1967–88.

Chapter 7: Caliphs, kings and regimes

Practical suggestions for further reading

Arjomand, S. A., *The shadow of God and the hidden imam: Religion, political organization and societal change in Shi'ite Iran from the beginning to 1890*, Chicago, 1984.
Crone, Patricia, *God's rule: Government and Islam*, New York, 2004.
Crone, Patricia, and Martin Hinds, *God's caliph: Religious authority in the first centuries of Islam*, Cambridge, 1986.
Fleischer, Cornell H., *Bureaucrat and intellectual in the Ottoman empire: The historian Mustafa Âli (1541–1600)*, Princeton, 1986.
de Fouchécour, Charles-Henri, *Moralia: Les notions morales dans la littérature persane du 3e/9e au 7e/13e siècle*, Paris, 1986.
Gibb, H. A. R., 'Constitutional organization', in M. Khadduri and H. J. Liebesney (eds.), *Law in the Middle East*, Washington, DC, 1955, 3–27.
Inalcik, H., *The Ottoman empire: The classical age, 1300–1600*, trans. N. Itzkowitz and C. Imber, New York, 1973.
'Suleiman the Lawgiver and Ottoman law', *Archivum Ottomanicum*, 1 (1969), 105–38.
Lambton, Ann K. S., *Continuity and change in medieval Persia: Aspects of administrative, economic and social history: 11th–14th century*, New York, 1988.
State and government in medieval Islam, Oxford, 1981.
Lewis, Bernard (ed. and trans.), *Islam from the Prophet to the capture of Constantinople*, 2 vols. New York, 1974, vol. I, chapters 9–11.

Madelung, Wilferd, 'Authority in Twelver Shiʿism in the absence of the imam', in G. Makdisi, D. Sourdel and J. Sourdel-Thomine (eds.), *La notion d'autorité au moyen âge: Islam, Byzance, Occident*, Paris, 1982, 163–73.
'Imama', *EI2*, vol. III, 1163–9.
Mikhail, Hanna, *Politics and revelation: Māwardī and after*, Edinburgh, 1995.
Milner, A. C., 'Islam and Malay kingship', *JRAS*, 1 (1981), 46–70.
Richards, J. F., 'The formation of imperial authority under Akbar and Jahangir', in Muzaffar Alam and Sanjay Subrahmanyam (eds.), *The Mughal state 1526–1750*, Delhi, 1998, 126–67; repr. from J. F. Richards (ed.), *Kingship and authority in South Asia*, Madison, 1978.
Tyan, Émile, *Institutions du droit public musulman*, 2 vols., Paris, 1954, 1957.

Primary sources

ʿAbbās, Iḥsān (ed.), *ʿAhd Ardashīr*, Beirut, 1967.
Abu'l-Faḍl ibn Mubārak, *The* Ā'īn-i Akbarī/*Abul Fazl*, 3 vols., trans. H. Blochmann, Calcutta, 1927.
Abū Yūsuf Yaʿqūb, *Abū Yūsuf's* Kitāb al-kharāj, ed. and trans. A. Ben Shemesh, Leiden and London, 1969.
Barani, Zia-ud-Din, *Fatāwā-i jahāndārī (Rulings on temporal government)*, ed. A. S. Khan, Lahore, 1972.
Bosworth, C. E., 'An early Arabic mirror for princes: Ṭāhir Dhū'l-Yamīnain's Epistle to his son, ʿAbdallāh (206/821)', *Journal of Near Eastern Studies*, 29, 1 (1970), 25–41.
al-Dinawarī, Ibn Qutayba, 'Kitāb al-sulṭān', in *ʿUyūn al-akhbār*, ed. Y. ʿA. Tawil, 4 vols., Beirut, 1986, vol. I, 53–183; trans. Josef Horovitz as 'The book of government', *Islamic Culture*, 4 (1930), 171–98, 331–62, 487–530; 5 (1931), 1–27.
Eberhard, E., *Osmanische Polemik gegen die Safawiden im 16. Jahrhundert nach arabischen Handschriften*, Freiburg im Breisgau, 1970.
Faḍlallāh Rūzbihān Khunjī, *Sulūk al-mulūk*, Hyderabad, 1966.
Fang, Liaw Yock (ed.), *Undang undang Melaka: The laws of Melaka*, The Hague, 1976.
Farā'id al-sulūk, ed. N. Wiṣālī and G. Afrāsiyābī, Tehran, 1368/1989.
al-Ghazālī, Abū Ḥāmid Muḥammad, *Makātīb-i Fārsī-yi Ghazālī*, ed. ʿAbbās Iqbāl-Āshtiyānī, Tehran, 1333/1954.
Naṣīḥat al-mulūk, ed. J. Humā'ī, 4th edn, Tehran, 1367/1988.
Grignaschi, M., 'Quelques spécimens de la littérature sassanide conservés dans les bibliothèques d'Istanbul', *Journal Asiatique*, 254 (1956), 25–142.
Ḥājib, Yūsuf Khāṣṣ, *Wisdom of royal glory: A Turko-Islamic mirror for princes*, ed. and trans. Robert Dankoff, Chicago, 1983.
Ibn Jamāʿa, Badr al-Dīn, 'Handbuch des islamischen Staats- und Verwaltungsrechtes von Badr-ad-dīn Ibn Ǧamāʿa', ed. Hans Kofler, *Islamica*, 6, 4 (1934), 349–414; 7, 1 (1934), 1–64.
Ibn al-Muqaffaʿ, ʿAbdallāh, *Rasā'il al-bulaghā'*, ed. M. Kurd ʿAlī, Cairo, 1331/1913.
Ibn al-Muṭahhar al-Ḥillī, 'The ʿAllāma al-Ḥillī on the imamate and *ijtihād*', ed. and trans. John Cooper in S. A. Arjomand (ed.), *Authority and political culture in Shiʿism*, Albany, 1988, 240–9.
Ibn Taymiyya, Aḥmad ibn ʿAbd al-Ḥalīm, *al-Siyāsa al-sharʿiyah fī iṣlāḥ al-rāʿī wa-al-raʿīyah*, Beirut, 1966; trans. H. Laoust as *Le traité de droit publique d'Ibn Taimiya*, Beirut, 1948.

Iṣfahānī, ʿAlī ibn Abī Ḥafṣ, *Tuḥfat al-mulūk*, ed. ʿA.-A. Ahmadī Dārānī, Tehran, 1382/2003.

Iṣfahānī, Muḥammad ibn Muḥammad ibn Ḥasan, *Dastūr al-wizāra*, ed. R. Anzābi-nizhād, Tehran, 1364/1985.

Kaykāwūs ibn Iskandar, ʿUnṣur al-Maʿālī, *Qābūs-nāma*, ed. G.-H. Yūsufī, Tehran, 1345/1966, trans. Reuben Levy as *A mirror for princes: The Qābūs nāma, by Kai-Kāvūs ibn Iskandar, Prince of Gurgān*, London, 1951.

Khwānd-Amīr, *Qānūn-i Humāyūnī*, included in *Maʿāthir al-mulūk*, ed. Mīr Hāshim Muḥaddith, Tehran, 1372/1993, 257–307.

al-Māwardī, ʿAlī ibn Muḥammad, *al-Aḥkām al-sulṭānīyah wa-al-wilāyāt al-dīnīyah*, Cairo, 1978.

Najm-i Sānī [Thānī], Muḥammad Bāqir, *Advice on the art of governance: An Indo-Islamic mirror for princes: Mauʿiẓah-i Jahāngīrī*, Persian text with introd., trans. and notes Sajida Sultana Alvi, Albany, 1989.

Niẓām al-Mulk, *Siyar al-mulūk (Siyāsatnāma)*, ed. Hubert Darke, Tehran, 1355/1976.

Pseudo-Māwardī, *Naṣīḥat al-mulūk*, Baghdad, 1986.

Sabzawārī, Muḥammad Bāqir, *Rawḍat al-anwār-i ʿabbāsī*, Tehran, 1377/1998.

Sĕjarah Mĕlayu or Malay annals, trans. and annotated C. C. Brown, new introd. R. Roolvink, Kuala Lumpur, 1970.

Tāj us-Salāṭīn, ed. Khalid Hussain, Kuala Lumpur, 1966.

Tietze, Andreas (ed. and trans.), *Muṣṭafā ʿĀlī's counsel for sultans of 1581*, 2 vols., Vienna, 1979.

Ṭūsī, Naṣīr al-Dīn, *Akhlāq-i Nāṣirī*, ed. M. Mīnuwī and ʿA.-R. Ḥaydarī, Tehran, 1356/1976; trans. G. M. Wickens as *The Nasirean ethics*, London, 1964.

Winstedt, R. O., 'Kedah laws', *Journal of the Malayan Branch of the Royal Asiatic Society*, 6 (1928), 1–44.

Secondary sources

Ahmad, Aziz, 'Delhi sultanate and the universal caliphate', in Aziz Ahmad, *Studies in Islamic culture in the Indian environment*, Oxford, 1964, 3–11.

Alam, Muzaffar, *The languages of political Islam: India, 1200–1800*, London and Chicago, 2004.

Alam, Muzaffar, and Sanjay Subrahmanyam (eds.), *The Mughal state 1526–1750*, Delhi, 1998.

Alvi, Sajida S., 'Religion and state during the reign of Mughal emperor Jahāngīr (1605–27): Nonjuristic perspectives', *SI*, 69 (1989), 95–119.

Andaya, Barbara Watson, *To live as brothers: Southeast Sumatra in the 17th and 18th centuries*, Honolulu, 1993.

Andaya, Barbara Watson, and Leonard Y. Andaya, 'Melaka and its heirs', in *A history of Malaysia*, 2nd edn, Honolulu, 2001, 39–76.

Andaya, Leonard Y., *The world of Maluku: Eastern Indonesia in the early modern period*, Honolulu, 1993.

Arjomand, S. A., 'Coffeehouses, guilds and Oriental despotism: Government and civil society in late-17th–early 18th century Istanbul and Isfahan, and as seen from Paris and London', *Archives européennes de sociologie/European Journal of Sociology*, 45, 1 (2004), 23–42.

'Conceptions of authority and the transition of Shiʿism from sectarian to national religion in Iran', in F. Daftary and J. W. Meri (eds.), *Culture and memory in medieval Islam*, London, 2003, 388–409.

'The Constitution of Medina: A socio-legal interpretation of Muhammad's acts of foundation of the umma', *IJMES*, 41, 4 (August 2009), 555–75.

'The law, agency and policy in medieval Islamic society: Development of the institutions of learning from the tenth to the fifteenth century', *Comparative Studies in Society and History*, 41, 2 (1999), 263–93.

'Medieval Persianate political thought', *Studies on Persianate Societies*, 1 (2003), 5–34.

'Political ethic and public law in the early Qajar period', in Robert M. Gleave (ed.), *Religion and society in Qajar Iran*, London, 2005, 21–40.

al-Azmeh, Aziz, *Muslim kingship: Power and the sacred in Muslim, Christian and pagan polities*, London, 1997.

Bartol'd, V. V., 'Kalif i sultan', *Mir Islama*, 1 (1912), 202–26, 345–400; partial trans. N. S. Doniach, published as 'Caliph and sultan', *Islamic Quarterly*, 7 (1963), 117–35.

Becker, Carl H., 'Barthold's studien über Kalif und Sultan', *Islam*, 6 (1916), 350–412.

Blake, Stephen P., 'The patrimonial-bureaucratic empire of the Mughals', *Journal of Asian Studies*, 39, 1 (1979), 77–94.

Darling, Linda, 'Islamic empires, the Ottoman empire and the circle of justice', in S. A. Arjomand (ed.), *Constitutional politics in the Middle East*, Oxford, 2008, 11–32.

Gibb, H. A. R., 'Theory of the caliphate in al-Māwardī', in S. J. Shaw and W. R. Polk (eds.), *Studies on the civilization of Islam*, Boston, 1968, 151–65.

Hardy, Peter, 'The authority of Muslim kings in medieval South Asia', in M. Gaboriaux (ed.), *Islam et société en Asie du Sud*, Paris, 1986, 37–55.

'The growth of authority over a conquered political elite: The early Delhi sultanate as a possible case study', in J. F. Richards (ed.), *Kingship and authority in South Asia*, Madison, 1978, 192–214.

Hodgson, Marshall G. S., *The venture of Islam*, 3 vols., Chicago, 1974.

Holt, P. M., 'The position and power of the Mamluk sultan', *BSOAS*, 38, 2 (1975), 237–49.

'The structure of government in the early Mamluk sultanate', in P. M. Holt (ed.), *The eastern Mediterranean lands in the period of the Crusades*, Warminster, 1977, 44–61.

Imber, Colin, 'Ideals and legitimation in early Ottoman history', in M. Kunt and C. Woodhead (eds.), *Süleyman the Magnificent and his age*, London, 1995, 138–53.

Inalcik, H., 'Kanun iii – Financial and public administration' and 'Kanun-nama', *EI2*, vol. IV, 558–66.

'State, sovereignty and law during the reign of Süleymân', in H. Inalcik and C. Kafadar (eds.), *Süleymân the Second and his time*, Istanbul, 1993, 49–92.

'Suleiman the Lawgiver and Ottoman law', *Archivum Ottomanicum*, 1 (1969), 105–38.

Iskandar, T., 'Three Malay historical writings in the first half of the 17th century', *Journal of the Malayan Branch of the Royal Asiatic Society*, 40, 2 (1967), 38–53.

Jackson, Peter, *The Delhi sultanate: A political and military history*, Cambridge, 1999.

Kunt, Metin, *The sultan's servants: The transformation of Ottoman provincial government, 1550–1650*, New York, 1983.

Lombard, Denys, 'Le sultanat malais comme modèle socio-économique', in D. Lombard and J. Aubin (eds.), *Marchands et hommes d'affaires asiatiques dans l'Océan Indien et la Mer de Chine 13e–20e siècles*, Paris, 1988, 117–24.

Madelung, Wilferd, 'Shiʿite discussions on the legality of the *kharāj*', in R. Peters (ed.), *Proceedings of the Ninth Congress of the Union européenne des arabisants et islamisants*, Leiden, 1981, 193–202.

The succession to Muḥammad: A study of the early caliphate, Cambridge, 1997.

'A treatise on the imamate dedicated to Sultan Baybars', in *Proceedings of the Fourteenth Congress of the Union européenne des arabisants et islamisants*, Budapest, 1988, 91–102.
Marlow, L., *Hierarchy and egalitarianism in Islamic thought*, Cambridge, 1997.
McKenna, Thomas, *Muslim rulers and rebels: Everyday politics and armed separation in the southern Philippines*, Berkeley and Los Angeles, 1998.
Melville, Charles, '*Pādshāh-i Islām*: The conversion of Sultan Mahmūd Ghāzān Khān', *Pembroke Papers*, 1 (1990), 159–77.
Milner, A. C., 'Islam and Malay kingship', *JRAS*, 1 (1981), 46–70.
KERAJAAN: Malay political culture on the eve of colonial rule, Tucson, 1982.
Pellat, Charles, 'Imamat dans la doctrine de Jāḥiẓ', *SI*, 15 (1961), 23–52.
Reid, Anthony, 'Trade and state power in the 16th and 17th century Southeast Asia', in *Proceedings of the Seventh IAHA Conference*, Bangkok, 1977, 391–419.
Reid, Anthony, and Lance Castles (eds.), *Pre-colonial state systems in Southeast Asia*, Kuala Lumpur, 1975.
Rosenthal, E. I. J., *Political thought in medieval Islam*, Cambridge, 1958.
Subrahmanyam, Sanjay, 'Iranians abroad: Intra-Asian elite migration and early modern state formation', *Journal of Asian Studies*, 51, 2 (1992), 340–63.
'State formation and transformation in early modern India and Southeast Asia', *Itinerario*, 12, 1 (1988), 91–109.
Wake, C. H., 'Melaka in the fifteenth century: Malay historical traditions and the politics of Islamization', in Kernial Singh Sandhu and Paul Wheatley (eds.), *Melaka: The transformation of a Malay capital c.1400–1980*, 2 vols., Kuala Lumpur, 1983, vol. I, 121–69.
Wellhausen, Julius, *The Arab kingdom and its fall*, trans. M. G. Weir, Beirut, 1963 [1927].

Chapter 8: The city and the nomad

Practical suggestions for further reading

Blair, S., and J. Bloom, *The art and architecture of Islam 1250–1800*, New Haven, 1994.
Eickelman, D. F., *The Middle East: An anthropological approach*, Englewood Cliffs, 1989.
Jabbur, J. S., *The Bedouins and the desert*, trans. L. Conrad, Albany, 1995.
Jayyusi, S. K. (ed.), *The city in the Islamic world*, 2 vols., Leiden, 2008.
Lapidus, I., *Muslim cities in the later Middle Ages*, Cambridge, 1984.
Wheatley, P., *The places where men pray together*, Chicago, 2001.

Secondary sources

Behrens-Abouseif, D., *Cairo of the Mamluks*, London, 2007.
Bennison, A. K., and A. L. Gascoigne (eds.), *Cities in the pre-modern Islamic world*, London, 2007.
Bulliet, R. W., *The camel and the wheel*, Cambridge, MA, 1975.
Islam: The view from the edge, New York, 1994.
Burgoyne, M., *Mamluk Jerusalem*, London, 1984.
Cole, D. P., *Nomads of the nomads: The Āl Murrah Bedouin of the Empty Quarter*, Chicago, 1975.
Crone, P., *Meccan trade and the rise of Islam*, Princeton, 1986.
Djait, H., *al-Kufa: Naissance de la ville islamique*, Paris, 1986.
Gellner, E., *Saints of the Atlas*, Chicago, 1969.

Goitein, S. D., 'The rise of the Near Eastern bourgeoisie', *Cahiers d'histoire mondiale*, 3 (1956–7), 583–604.
Heck, G. W., 'Gold mining in Arabia and the rise of the Islamic state', *JESHO*, 42 (1999), 364–95.
Herrmann, G., *The monuments of Merv*, London, 1999.
Hourani, A. and S. M. Stern, *The Islamic city: A colloquium*, Oxford, 1970.
Kennedy, H., *An historical atlas of Islam*, Leiden, 2002.
'From *polis* to *madina*: Urban change in Late Antique and early Islamic Syria', *Past and Present*, 106 (1985), 3–27.
'From Shahristan to Medina', *SI*, 101–2 (2006), 1–30.
Kubiak, W., *al-Fustat: Its foundation and early urban development*, Cairo, 1987.
Lancaster, W., *The Rwala Bedouin today*, Cambridge, 1981.
Lassner, J., *The topography of Baghdad in the early Middle Ages*, Detroit, 1970.
Leisten, T., *Excavation of Samarra, volume I: Architecture*, Mainz, 2003.
Nelson, C. (ed.), *The desert and the sown: Nomads in the wider society*, Berkeley, 1973.
Northedge, A., *The historical topography of Samarra*, London, 2007.
Petruccioli, A., *Bukhara: The myth and the architecture*, Cambridge, MA, 1999.
Robinson, C. F. (ed.), *A medieval Islamic city reconsidered: An interdisciplinary approach to Samarra*, Oxford, 2001.
Sack, D., *Damaskus: Entwicklung und Struktur einer orientalisch-islamischen Stadt*, Mainz, 1989.
Sanders, P., *Ritual, politics and the city in Fatimid Cairo*, Albany, 1994.
Sauvaget, J., *Alep*, Paris, 1941.
Serjeant, R. B., and R. Lewcock (eds.), *Ṣanʿāʾ: An Arabian Islamic city*, London, 1983.
Staffa, S. J., *Conquest and fusion: The social evolution of Cairo AD 642–1850*, Leiden, 1977.
Warner, N., *The monuments of historic Cairo*, Cairo, 2005.

Chapter 9: Rural life and economy

Practical suggestions for further reading

Chaudhuri, K. N., *Asia before Europe: Economy and civilisation of the Indian Ocean from the rise of Islam to 1750*, Cambridge, 1990.
de Planhol, Xavier, *Les fondements géographiques de l'histoire de l'Islam*, Paris, 1968.
Watson, Andrew M., *Agricultural innovation in the early Islamic world: The diffusion of crops and farming techniques, 700–1100*, Cambridge, 1983 (repr. 2008 with new foreword and bibliographical update; also published in Spanish by the University of Granada Press and in Arabic by the Institute for the History of Arabic Science of the University of Aleppo).

Primary sources

Abū al-Fidā (1273–1331), *Géographie d'Aboulfeda*, ed. and trans. M. Renaud, 3 vols., Paris, 1840–83.
Abū al-Khayr al-Ishbīlī (*fl.* twelfth century), *Kitāb al-filāḥa: Tratado de agricultura*, ed. J. Carabaza, Madrid, 1991.
Abū Yūsuf, (?731–98) *Taxation in Islam II: Abū Yūsuf's* Kitāb al-kharāj, ed. and trans. A. Ben Shemesh, Leiden and London, 1969.

al-Bakrī (d. 1094), *Description de l'Afrique septentrionale*, ed. and trans. MacGuckin de Slane, Algiers, 1913.

Description de l'Egypte: Ou recueil des observations et des recherches qui ont été faites en Egypte pendant l'expédition de l'armée française, 22 vols., Paris, 1802–29.

al-Ghazzī (wrote 1529), 'Jāmiʿ fawā'id al-malāḥa fi'l filāḥa', Agric. MS 134, Dār al-Kutub, Cairo.

al-Hamdānī (?893–?945), *The antiquities of South Arabia*, trans. N. A. Faris, Princeton, 1938.

Ibn al-ʿAwwām, (*fl.* twelfth century), *Kitāb al-filāḥa*, ed. and trans. J. A. Banqueri, 2 vols., Madrid, 1802; trans. J.-J. Clément-Mullet as *Le livre de l'agriculture d'Ibn al-Awam*, 2 vols. in 3, Paris, 1864–7.

Ibn Baṣṣāl(?) (d. 1105), *Kitāb al-filāḥa*, ed. and trans. J. M. Millás Vallicrosa and M. Aziman, Tetuan, 1955.

Ibn Ḥawqal (wrote 988), *Configuration de la terre*, trans. J. H. Kramers and G. Wiet, 2 vols., Paris, 1964.

Ibn Luyūn (1282–1349), *Tratado de agricultura*, ed. J. Iguaras Ibáñez, Granada, 1975.

Ibn Mammātī (d.1209), *Kitāb qawānīn al-dawāwīn*, ed. A. S. ʿAtiya, Cairo, 1943.

Ibn Waḥshīya (*fl.* tenth century), *al-Filāḥa al-Nabaṭīya*, ed. T. Fahd, 3 vols., Frankfurt, 2003.

al-Idrīsī (*fl.* 12th c.), *Description de l'Afrique et de l'Espagne*, ed. and trans. R. Dozy and M. J. de Goeje, Leiden, 1866.

Varisco, D. (ed.), 'An anonymous 14th century almanac from Rasulid Yemen', *ZGAIW*, 9 (1994), 195–228.

(trans.), 'A royal crop register from Rasulid Yemen', *JESHO*, 34 (1991), 1–22.

Varisco, D. and G. R. Smith (eds.), *The manuscript of al-Malik al-Afḍal al-ʿAbbās b. ʿAlī ibn Rasūl: A medieval anthology from the Yemen*, London, 1998.

Secondary sources

Berthier, Sophie, *et al.*, *Peuplement rural et aménagements hydroagricoles dans la moyenne vallée de l'Euphrate, fin VIIe–XIXe siècle*, Damascus, 2001.

Bolens, Lucie, *Les méthodes culturales au moyen-âge d'après les traités d'agronomie andalous: Traditions et techniques*, Geneva, 1974.

Agronomes andalous du moyen âge, Geneva, 1981.

Butzer, K. 'The Islamic tradition of agroeconomy: Cross-cultural experience, ideas and innovations', *Ecumene*, 1 (1994), 7–50.

Frantz-Murphy, G., *The Agrarian administration of Egypt from the Arabs to the Ottomans: Supplément aux Annales islamologiques*, vol. IX, Cairo, 1986.

Garcin, Jean-Claude, *et al.*, *Etats, sociétés et cultures du monde musulman médiéval: Xe–XVe siècle*, Paris, 1995.

Glick, T., *Irrigation and Islamic technology: Medieval Spain and its legacy*, Aldershot, 1996.

al-Hasan, A., and D. Hill, *Islamic technology: An illustrated history*, Cambridge and Paris, 1986.

Hehmeyer, I., 'Irrigation farming in the ancient oasis of Mārib', *Proceedings of the Seminar for Arabian Studies*, 19 (1989), 33–44.

Inalcik, Halil, and Donald Quataert (eds.), *An economic and social history of the Ottoman empire, 1300–1914*, Cambridge, 1994.

Lagardère, Vincent, *Campagnes et paysans d'al-Andalus, VIIe–XVe siècles*, Paris, 1993.

Lambton, A. K. S., *Landlord and peasant in Persia*, Oxford, 1953.

Malpica Cuello, A., 'Mundo urbana y mundo rurale en al-Andalus: El ejemplo de Madinat Ilbira', in Brian Catlos (ed.), *Worlds of history and economics: Essays in honour of Andrew M. Watson*, Valencia, 2009.

(ed.), *Paisajes del azúcar*, Granada, 1995.

Spooner, B., 'Abyārī', *Encyclopedia Iranica*, London, 1982–, vol. I, 405–11.

Subtelny, Maria, 'A medieval Persian agricultural manual in context: The *Irshād al-zirā'a* in late Timurid and early Safavid Khorasan', *Studia Iranica*, 22 (1993), 167–217.

Trillo, Carmen (ed.), *Asentamientos rurales y territorio en el Mediterráneo medieval*, Granada, 2002.

Agua, tierra y hombres en al-Andalus: La dimensión agrícola del mundo Nazarí, Granada, 2004.

Vanacker, Claudette, 'Géographie économique de l'Afrique du Nord selon les auteurs arabes, du XIe siècle au milieu de XIIe siècle', *Annales: Économies, Sociétés, Civilisations*, 28 (1973), 659–80.

Varisco, Daniel, *Medieval folk astronomy and agriculture in Arabia and the Yemen*, Ashgate, 1997.

Medieval agriculture and Islamic science: The almanac of a Yemeni sultan, Seattle, 1994.

Wagstaff, J. M., *The evolution of the Middle Eastern landscapes*, London, 1985.

Chapter 10: Demography and migration

Practical suggestions for further reading

Dols, Michael, *The Black Death in the Middle East*, Princeton, 1977.

Lowry, Heath, 'The Ottoman Tahrir Defterleri as a source for social and economic history: Pitfalls and limitations', in Heath Lowry, *Studies in defterology: Ottoman society in the fifteenth and sixteenth centuries*, Istanbul, 1992, 3–18.

Musallam, Bassim, *Sex and society in Islam*, Cambridge, 1983.

Öz, Mehmet, 'Population fall in seventeenth century Anatolia: Some findings for the districts of Canik and Bozok', *Archivum Ottomanicum*, 22 (2004), 159–71.

Özel, Oktay, 'Population changes in Anatolia during the 16th and 17th centuries', *IJMES*, 36 (2004), 183–205.

Panzac, Daniel, *La peste dans l'empire ottoman, 1700–1850*, Louvain, 1985.

Petrushevsky, I. P., 'The socio-economic condition of Iran under the Īl-khāns', in J. A. Boyle (ed.), *The Cambridge history of Iran*, vol. V: *The Saljuq and Mongol periods*, Cambridge, 1968, 483–537.

Raymond, André, *Grandes villes arabes à l'époque ottomane*, Paris, 1985.

Vryonis, Speros, *The decline of medieval Hellenism in Asia Minor and the process of Islamization from the eleventh through the fifteenth century*, Berkeley, Los Angeles and London, 1971.

Primary sources

Barkan, Ömer Lütfi, 'XVI. Asrın Başında Rumeli'de Nüfusun Yayılış Tarzını Gösterir Harita', *İstanbul Üniversitesi İktisat Fakültesi Mecmuası*, 11 (1949–50), map glued into volume, no pagination.

Binark, İsmet *et al.* (eds.), *166 Numaralı Muhâsebe-i Vilâyet-i Anadolu Defteri (937/1530)*, 2 vols., Ankara, 1995.

387 Numaralı Muhâsebe-i Vilâyet-i Karaman ve Rum Defteri (937/1530), 2 vols., Ankara, 1996.
438 Numaralı Muhâsebe-i Vilâyet-i Anadolu Defteri (937/1530), 2 vols., Ankara, 1994.
Hütteroth, Wolf Dieter, and Kamal Abdulfattah, *Historical geography of Palestine, Transjordan and southern Syria in the late 16th century*, Erlangen, 1977.
Özkılınç, Ahmet *et al.* (eds.), *998 Numaralı Muhâsebe-i Vilâyet-i Diyâr-i Bekr ve 'Arab ve Zü'l-kadriyye Defteri (937/1530)*, 2 vols., Ankara, 1999.
Tietze, Andreas (ed.), *Mustafâ 'Âlî's counsel for sultans of 1581*, 2 vols., Vienna, 1979–82.

Secondary sources

Abdel Nour, Antoine, *Introduction à l'histoire urbaine de la Syrie ottomane (XVIe–XVIIIe siècle)*, Beirut, 1982.
Akdağ, Mustafa, *Celâlî İsyanları (1550–1603)*, Ankara, 1963.
Arenal, Mercedes Garcia, *La diaspora des Andalousiens*, Paris, 2003.
Ateş, Ahmed, 'Ibn al 'Arabī', *EI2*, vol. III, 707.
Ayalon, David, 'Studies in al-Jabarti I: Notes on the transformation of Mamluk society in Egypt under the Ottomans', *JESHO*, 3 (1960), 148–74.
Barkan, Ömer Lütfi, 'Essai sur les données statistiques des registres de recensement dans l'Empire ottoman aux XVe et XVIe siècles', *Journal of the Economic and Social History of the Levant*, 1 (1958), 9–36 and 331–3.
'Osmanlı İmparatorluğunda bir iskân ve kolonizasyon metodu olarak sürgünler', *İstanbul Üniversitesi İktisat Fakültesi Mecmuası*, 11, 1–4 (1949–50), 524–69; 13, 1–4 (1951–2), 56–78; 15, 1–4 (1953–4), 209–37.
Süleymaniye Cami ve İmareti inşaatı, 2 vols., Ankara, 1972–9.
Barkey, Karen, *Bandits and bureaucrats: The Ottoman route to state centralization*, Ithaca and London, 1994.
Beldiceanu, Nicoară, 'La conquête des cités marchandes de Kilia et de Cetatea Albă par Bāyezīd II'; repr. in Nicoară Beldiceanu, *Le monde ottoman des Balkans (1402–1566): Institutions, société, économie*, London, 1976.
Bishko, Charles Julian, 'The Spanish and Portuguese reconquest', in Kenneth Setton (gen. ed.), *A history of the Crusades*, Madison, 1969–89, vol. III: Harry Hazard (ed.), *The fourteenth and fifteenth centuries*, Madison, 1989, 397–456.
Bosworth, C. E., 'Barbarian incursions: The coming of the Turks into the Islamic world', in D. S. Richards (ed.), *Islamic civilisation 950–1150: A colloquium published under the auspices of the Near Eastern History Group Oxford*, Oxford, 1973, 1–16.
Bulliet, Richard, *The patricians of Nishapur*, Cambridge, MA, 1972.
Çelik, Şenol, 'Türk fethi sonrasında Kıbrıs Adasına yönelik iskân çalışmaları', in Zehra Toska (ed.), *Kaf Dağının ötesine varmak: Festschrift in honor of Günay Kut: Essays presented by her colleagues and students, 3 vols.*, Cambridge, MA, 2003, vol. I, 263–304/*Journal of Turkish Studies* 27, 1–3 (2003).
Cook, Michael A., *Population pressure in rural Anatolia 1450–1600*, London and New York, 1972.
Dominguez Ortiz, Antonio, and Bernard Vincent, *Historia de los Moriscos: Vida y tragedia de una minoría*, Madrid, 1978.
Donner, Fred McGraw, *The early Islamic conquests*, Princeton, 1981.
Dunn, Ross, *The adventures of Ibn Battuta: A Muslim traveler of the 14th century*, Berkeley and Los Angeles, 1986.

Erder, Leila, 'The measurement of pre-industrial population changes: The Ottoman empire from the 15th to the 17th century', *Middle Eastern Studies*, 11 (1975), 322–45.

Faroqhi, Suraiya, 'Political tensions in the Anatolian countryside around 1600: An attempt at interpretation', in J. L. Bacqué-Grammont, Barbara Flemming, Macit Gökberk and İlber Ortaylı (eds.), *Türkische Miszellen: Robert Anhegger Festschrift, Armağanı, Mélanges*, Istanbul, 1987, 117–30.

'Under state control: Sixteenth and seventeenth-century Ottoman craftsmen on their way to Istanbul', in Suraiya Faroqhi, *Stories of Ottoman men and women: Establishing status, establishing control*, Istanbul, 2002, 267–88.

Foss, Clive, 'The defenses of Asia Minor against the Turks', in Clive Foss, *Cities, fortresses and villages of Asia Minor*, Aldershot, 1996.

Goitein, S. D., 'The beginnings of the Karim merchants and the nature of their organization', in S. D. Goitein, *Studies in Islamic history and institutions*, Leiden, 1966, 351–60.

'Letters and documents on the India trade in medieval times', in S. D. Goitein, *Studies in Islamic history and institutions*, Leiden, 1966, 329–50.

A Mediterranean society: The Jewish communities of the Arab world as portrayed in the documents of the Cairo Geniza, 6 vols., Berkeley and Los Angeles, 1967–93, vol. I: *Economic foundations*, Berkeley, 1967.

Halaçoğlu, Yusuf, *XVIII. Yüzyılda Osmanlı İmparatorluğunun iskân siyaseti ve aşiretlerin yerleştirilmesi*, Ankara, 1988.

Hanna, Nelly, *Making big money in 1600: The life and times of Isma'il Abu Taqiyya, Egyptian merchant*, Syracuse, 1998.

Hathaway, Jane, *The politics of households in Ottoman Egypt: The rise of the Qazdağlıs*, Cambridge, 1997.

Idris, H. R., 'Banū Hilāl', *EI2*, vol. III, 385.

Inalcik, Halil, 'Military and fiscal transformation in the Ottoman empire, 1600–1700', *Archivum Ottomanicum*, 6 (1980), 283–337.

'The policy of Mehmed II toward the Greek population of Istanbul and the Byzantine buildings of the city', *Dumbarton Oaks Papers*, 23 (1969–70), 213–49.

İslamoğlu-İnan, Huri, *State and peasant in the Ottoman empire: Agrarian power relations and regional economic development in Ottoman Anatolia during the sixteenth century*, Leiden, 1994.

Jennings, Ronald, *Christians and Muslims in Ottoman Cyprus and the Mediterranean world*, New York, 1993.

Kissling, Hans Joachim, 'Badr al-Dīn b. Ḳāḍī Samāwnā', *EI2*, vol. I, 869.

Kuniholm, Peter I., 'Archaeological evidence and non-evidence for climatic change', *Philosophical Transactions of the Royal Society*, A330 (1990), 645–55.

Lévi-Provençal, E., 'al-Andalus', *EI2*, vol. I, 486.

Lowry, Heath, 'Pushing the stone uphill: The impact of bubonic plague on Ottoman urban society in the fifteenth and sixteenth centuries', *Osmanlı Araştırmaları: The Journal of Ottoman Studies*, 23 (2004), 93–132.

Manz, Beatrice, *The rise and rule of Tamerlane*, Cambridge, 1989.

Moačanin, Nenad, *Town and country on the Middle Danube, 1526–1690*, Leiden, 2005.

Necipoğlu, Gülru, *The age of Sinan: Architectural culture in the Ottoman empire*, London, 2005.

Architecture, ceremonial and power: The Topkapı Palace in the fifteenth and sixteenth centuries, Cambridge, MA, and London, 1991.

Orhonlu, Cengiz, *Osmanlı İmparatorluğunda aşiretleri iskân teşebbüsü (1691–1696)*, Istanbul, 1963.

Petry, Carl F., *The civilian elite of Cairo in the later Middle Ages*, Princeton, 1981.

de Planhol, Xavier, *Les fondements géographiques de l'histoire de l'Islam*, Paris, 1968.

Raymond, André, 'The Ottoman conquest and the development of the great Arab towns', *International Journal of Turkish Studies*, 1 (1979–80), 84–101.

'The population of Aleppo in the sixteenth and seventeenth centuries according to Ottoman census documents', *IJMES*, 16 (1984), 447–60.

Titley, Norah M., *Persian miniature painting and its influence on the art of Turkey and India: The British Library collections*, Austin, 1983–4.

Uzunçarşılı, İsmail Hakkı, 'Osmanlı sarayında Ehl-i Hiref (Sanatkârlar) Defteri', *Belgeler*, 11, 15 (1986), 23–76.

Yerasimos, Stefan, '15. yüzyılın sonunda Haslar Kazası', in Tülay Artan (ed.), *18. yüzyıl kadı sicilleri ısığında Eyüp'te sosyal yaşam*, Istanbul, 1998, 82–102.

Chapter 11: The mechanisms of commerce

Primary sources

Coin corpora, catalogues, and sylloges

Album, S., *A checklist of popular Islamic coins*, 2nd edn, Santa Rosa, CA. 1998 [1993].

Arabia and East Africa, Sylloge of Islamic Coins in the Ashmolean 10, Oxford, 1999.

Iran after the Mongol invasions, Sylloge of Islamic Coins in the Ashmolean 9, Oxford, 2001.

Album, S., and T. Goodwin, *The pre-reform coinage of the early Islamic period*, Sylloge of Islamic Coins in the Ashmolean 1, Oxford, 2002.

Bacharach, J. L. 'Coins', in *Fusṭāṭ finds: Beads, coins, medical instruments, textiles, and other artifacts from the Awad Collection*, Cairo and New York, 2002, 44–87.

Islamic history through coins: An analysis and catalogue of tenth-century Ikshidid coinage, Cairo, 2006.

Bacharach, J. L. , R. al-Nabarawy, S. Anwar and A. Yousef, *A complete catalog (sylloge) of the glass weights, vessel stamps, and ring weights in the Gayer-Anderson Museum, Cairo (Matḥaf Bayt al-Kritliyya)*, available at www.numismatics.org/dpubs/islamic/ga/.

Balog, P., *The coinage of the Ayyūbids*, London, 1980.

'The coinage of the Mamlūk sultans: Additions and corrections', *American Numismatic Society Museum Notes*, 16 (1970), 113–71.

The coinage of the Mamlūk sultans of Egypt and Syria, Numismatic Studies 12, New York, 1964.

al-Barahīm, A. I. S., *al-Maskūkāt al-Ayyūbiyya wa-al-Mamlūkiyya fī 'l-Matḥaf al-Waṭanī li'l-Āthār wa-al-Turāth al-Sha'bī bi'l-Riyāḍ: Dirāsa āthāriyya muqārana*, Riyadh, 2005.

Fedorov, M., B. Kocnev (†), G. Kurbanov and M. Voegeli, *Buḫara/Samarqand XVa Mittelasien I, Sylloge Numorum Arabicorum Tübingen*, Tübingen, 2008.

Goodwin, T. *Arab-Byzantine coinage, Studies* in the Khalili Collection 4, London, 2005.

Goron, S., and J. P. Goenka, *The coins of the Indian sultanates*, New Delhi, 2001.

Ilisch, L. *Palästina IVa: Bilād aš-Šām I*, Sylloge Numorum Arabicorum Tübingen, Tübingen, 1993.

Korn, L., *Hamah IVc: Bilād aš-Šām III*, Sylloge Numorum Arabicorum Tübingen, Tübingen, 1998.

Meyer, T., *Sylloge der Münzen des Kaukus und Osteuropas im Orientalischen Münzkabinett Jena*, Wiesbaden, 2005.

Nord- und Ostzentralasien XVb: Mittelasien II, Sylloge Numorum Arabicorum Tübingen, Tübingen, 1998.

Nicol, N. D., *A corpus of Fāṭimid coins*, Trieste, 2006.

'Paul Balog's *The Coinage of the Ayyūbids:* Additions and corrections', *Numismatic Chronicle*, 146 (1986), 119–154.

The Egyptian dynasties, Sylloge of Islamic Coins in the Ashmolean 6, Oxford, 2007.

Nicol, N. D., R. M. al-Nabarawi and J. L. Bacharach, *Catalog of the Islamic coins, glass weights, dies and medals in the Egyptian National Library*, Cairo and Malibu, 1982.

Schwarz, F., *XIVd Ḫurāsān IV: Ġaznā/Kābul*, Sylloge Numorum Arabicorum Tübingen, Tübingen, 1995.

XIV Ḫurāsān III: Balḫ und Landschaften am oberen Oxus, Sylloge Numorum Arabicorum Tübingen, Tübingen, 2001.

Shamma, S., *A catalogue of 'Abbasid copper coins*, London, 1998.

Spengler, W. F., and W. G. Sayles, *Turkoman figural bronze coins and their iconography*, vol. I: *The Artuqids*, Lodi, WI, 1992.

Turkoman figural bronze coins and their iconography, vol. II: *The Zengids*, Lodi, WI, 1996.

Sreckovic, S., *Akçes*, vol. I: *Orhan Gazi–Murad II, 699–848 AH*, Belgrade, 1999.

Akçes, vol. II: *Mehmed II Fatih–Selim I Yavuz, 848–926 AH*, Belgrade, 2000.

Akçes, vol. III: *Suleyman I Kanuni, 926–974 AH*, Belgrade, 2003.

Akçes, vol. IV: *Selim II Sarı–Murad III, 974–1003 AH*, Belgrade, 2005.

Akçes, vol. V: *Mehmed III–Mustafa I, 1003–1032 AH*, Belgrade, 2007.

Ottoman mints and coins, Belgrade, 2002.

Treadwell, L., *Buyid coins: A corpus*, Oxford, 2001.

Literary sources

Ibn Mammātī, *Kitāb qawāwīn al-dawāwīn*, ed. A. S. Atiya, Cairo, 1943.

Ibn al-Nābulusī, *Ta'rīkh al-fayyūm wa-bilādih*, ed. B. Moritz, Cairo, 1898.

Ibn al-Ukhuwwa, *The Ma'ālim al-qurba fī aḥkām al-ḥisba*, ed. R. Levy, London, 1938.

al-Maqrīzī, *Ighāthat al-umma*, ed. M. M. Ziyāda and J. M. al-Shayyāl, Cairo, 1940.

Secondary sources

al-'Asalī, K. J., *Wathā'iq maqdasiyya ta'rīkhiyya*, 2 vols., Beirut, 1985.

Ashtor, E., *Histoire de prix et des salaires dans l'orient médiéval*, Paris, 1969.

Levant trade in the later Middle Ages, Princeton, 1983.

'Makāyīl and mawāzīn', *EI2*, vol. VI, 117–21.

The medieval Near East: Social and economic history, London, 1978.

Les métaux precieux et la balance des payements du proche-orient à la basse époque, Paris, 1971.

A social and economic history of the Near East in the Middle Ages, Berkeley, 1976.

Studies on the Levantine trade in the Middle Ages, London, 1978.

Balog, P., 'The Ayyūbid glass jetons and their use', *JESHO*, 9 (1966), 242–56.

'The Fāṭimid glass jetons: Token currency or coin weights', *JESHO*, 24 (1981), 93–109.

'Islamic bronze weights from Egypt', *JESHO*, 13 (1970), 233–56.

Umayyad, 'Abbāsid, and Ṭūlūnid glass weights and vessel stamps, New York, 1976.

Bass, G. F., S. Matthews, J. R. Steffy and F. H. van Doorninck, Jr (eds.), *Serçe Limanı, an eleventh-century shipwreck*, vol. I: *The ship and its anchorage, crew, and passengers*, Ed Rachal Foundation Nautical Archaeology Series, College Station, TX, 2004.

Bates, M. L., 'Coins and money in the Arabic papyri', in Yousef Ragheb (ed.), *Documents de l'Islam médiéval: Nouvelles perspectives de recherche*, Cairo, 1991, 43–64.

'The function of Fāṭimid and Ayyūbid glass weights', *JESHO*, 24 (1981), 63–92.

Islamic coins: ANS handbook no. 2, New York, 1982.

'Islamic numismatics', *MESA Bulletin*, 12, 2 (1978), 1–16; 12, 3 (1978), 2–18; 13, 1 (1979), 3–21; 13, 2 (1979), 1–9.

Borsch, S. J., *The Black Death in Egypt and England: A comparative study*, Austin, 2005.

'Thirty years after Lopez, Miskimin, and Udovitch', *Mamluk Studies Review*, 8, 2 (2004), 191–201.

Brunschvig, R., 'Conceptions monétaires chez les juristes musulmans (VIIIe–XIIIe siècles)', *Arabica*, 14 (1967), 113–43.

Buckley, R. P., 'The book of the Islamic market inspector', *Journal of Semitic Studies Supplement*, 9 (1999).

Chaudhuri, K. N., *Trade and civilization in the Indian Ocean: An economic history from the rise of Islam to 1750*, Cambridge, 1985.

Cook, M. A. (ed.), *Studies in the economic history of the Middle East from the rise of Islam to the present day*, London, 1970.

Cooper, R. C., 'Ibn Mammātī's rules for the ministries: Translation with commentary of the *Qawāwīn al-dawāwīn*', Ph.D. thesis, University of California, Berkeley, 1973.

Dunlap, D. M. 'Sources of gold and silver in Islam according to al-Hamdānī', *SI*, 8 (1952), 29–49.

Ehrenkreutz, A. S., 'The standard of fineness of gold coins circulating in Egypt at the time of the Crusades', *JAOS*, 74 (1954), 162–6.

'Studies in the monetary history of the Near East in the Middle Ages: (I) The standard of fineness of some dīnārs', *JESHO*, 2 (1959), 128–61.

'Studies in the monetary history of the Near East in the Middle Ages: (II) The standard of fineness of western and eastern dīnārs', *JESHO*, 6 (1963), 243–77.

'Contributions to the knowledge of the standard of fineness of silver coinage struck in Egypt and Syria during the period of the Crusades', *JESHO*, 31 (1988), 301–3.

Frantz-Murphy, G., *The agrarian administration of Egypt from the Arabs to the Ottomans*, Cairo, 1986.

Arabic agricultural leases and tax receipts from Egypt, 148–427 AH/765–1035 AD, Vienna, 1991.

Goitein. S. D., *Letters of medieval Jewish traders*, Princeton, 1973.

A Mediterranean society: The Jewish communities of the Arab world as portrayed in the documents of the Cairo Geniza, 6 vols., Berkeley and Los Angeles, 1967–93, vol. I: *Economic foundations*, Berkeley, 1967.

Goitein, S. D., and M. A. Friedman, *India traders of the Middle Ages: Documents from the Cairo Geniza*, Leiden, 2008.

Guo, L., *Commerce, culture, and community in a Red Sea port in the thirteenth century: The Arabic documents from Quseir*, Leiden, 2004.

Hanna, N., *Making big money in 1600: The life and times of Isma'il Abū Taqiyya, Egyptian merchant*, Syracuse, 1998.

Hennequin, G. P., 'Problèmes théoriques et pratiques de la monnaie antique et médiévale', *AI*, 10 (1972), 1–57.

'*Waqf* et monnaie dans l'Égypte mamluke', *JESHO*, 38 (1995), 305–12.

Hinds, M., and H. Sakkout, *Arabic documents from the Ottoman period from Qasr Ibrīm*, London, 1986.

Hinds, M., and Victor Menage, *Qasr Ibrīm in the Ottoman period: Turkish and further Arabic documents*, London, 1991.

Holland, L., 'Islamic bronze weights from Caesarea Maritima', American Numismatic Society Museum Notes, 31 (1986), 171–201.

Weights and weight-like objects from Caesarea Maritima, Hadera, 2009.

Holt, P. M., *et al.* (eds.), *The Cambridge history of Islam*, 2 vols., Cambridge, 1970.

Inalcik, H., and Donald Quataert, *An economic and social history of the Ottoman empire*, 2 vols., Cambridge, 1994, vol. I: *1300–1600* and vol. II: *1600–1914*.

Jaouiche, K., 'al-Ḳarasṭūn', *EI2*, vol. IV, 629.

Kolbas, J., 'Mongol money: The role of Tabriz from Chingiz Khan to Uljaytu: 616 to 709 H/ 1220 to 1309 AD', Ph.D. thesis, New York University, 1992.

Lewis, B., 'Sources for the economic history of the Middle East', in M. A. Cook (ed.), *Studies in the economic history of the Middle East from the rise of Islam to the present day*, London, 1970, 78–92.

Little, D. P., *A catalogue of the Islamic documents from al-Ḥaram aš-Šarīf in Jerusalem*, Beirut, 1984.

Lopez, R., H. Miskimin and A. L. Udovitch., 'England to Egypt, 1350–1500: Long-term trends and long-distance trade', in M. A. Cook (ed.), *Studies in the economic history of the Middle East*, Oxford, 1970, 91–128.

Margariti, R. E., *Aden and the Indian Ocean trade: 150 years in the life of a medieval Arabian port*, Chapel Hill, 2007.

Miles, G. C., '*Dīnār*', *EI2*, vol. II, 297–9.

'*Dirham*', *EI2*, vol. II, 319–20.

'On the varieties and accuracy of eighth century Arab coin weights', *Eretz Israel*, 7 (1963), 79–87.

Pamuk, Ş., *A monetary history of the Ottoman empire*, Cambridge, 2000.

Popper, W., *Egypt and Syria under the Circassian sultans 1382–1468 AD: Systematic notes to Ibn Taghri Birdi's chronicles of Egypt*, University of California Publications in Semitic Philology 15–16, Berkeley, 1955–7.

Rabie, H., *The financial system of Egypt AH 564–741/AD 1169–1341*, London, 1972.

Rapoport, Y., *Marriage, money and divorce in medieval Islamic society*, Cambridge, 2005.

Raymond, A., *Artisans et commerçants au Caire au XVIIIe siècle*, Damascus, 1973.

Richards, D. S. (ed.), *Islam and the trade of Asia: A colloquium*, Oxford, 1970.

Richards, J. F. (ed.), *The imperial monetary system of Mughal India*, Oxford, 1987.

Sato, T., *State and rural society in medieval Islam: Sulṭāns, muqṭaʿas and fallāḥūn*, Leiden, 1997.

Schultz, W. C., 'Mamlūk metrology and the numismatic evidence', *al-Masāq*, 15, 1 (2003), 59–75.

'The monetary history of Egypt, 642–1517', in C. F. Petry (ed.), *The Cambridge history of Egypt*, vol. I: *Islamic Egypt, 640–1517*, Cambridge, 1998, 318–38.

Sellwood, D., 'Medieval minting techniques', *British Numismatic Journal*, 31 (1982), 57–65.

Spufford, P., 'Appendix: Coinage and currency', in *The Cambridge economic history of Europe*, vol. III: M. M. Postan, E. F. Rich and Edward Miller (eds.), *Economic organization and policies in the Middle Ages*, Cambridge, 1963, 576–602.

Udovitch, A. L., *Partnership and profit in medieval Islam*, Princeton, 1970.

Varisco, D. M., *Medieval agriculture and Islamic science: The almanac of a Yemeni sultan*, Seattle, 1994.

Vernet, J., 'al-Khāzinī', *EI2*, vol. IV, 1186.

Wakin, J. A., *The function of documents in Islamic law: The chapter on sales from Ṭaḥāwī's* Kitāb al-shurūṭ al-kabīr, Albany, 1972.

Walker, J., and D. R. Hill, 'Sanadjāt', *EI2*, vol. IX, 3.

Wiedemann, E., 'al-Mīzān', *EI2*, vol. VII, 195–204.

von Zambaur, E., 'Ḳirāṭ', *EI*, vol. IV, 1023–4.

Chapter 12: Women, gender and sexuality

Practical suggestions for further reading

Adang, Camilla, 'Ibn Ḥazm on homosexuality: A case-study of Ẓāhirī legal methodology', *al-Qanṭara*, 24 (2003), 5–31.

'Love between men in *Ṭawq al-ḥamāma*', in Cristina de la Puente (ed.), *Identidades marginales (EOBA, XIII)*, Madrid, 2003, 111–45.

'Women's access to public space according to *al-Muḥallā bi-l-āthār*', in Manuela Marín and Randi Deguilhem (eds.), *Writing the feminine: Women in Arab sources*, London, 2002, 75–94.

Aḥmad, N., *al-Mar'a fī Miṣr fī l-ʿaṣr al-fāṭimī*, Cairo, 1993.

Ahmed, L., *Women and gender in Islam: Historical roots of a modern debate*, New Haven, 1992.

Ait Sabbah, Fatna, *La femme dans l'inconscient musulman*, Paris, 1986.

Amri, Nelly and L., *Les femmes soufies ou la passion de Dieu*, St-Jean-de-Braye, 1992.

Baer, Gabriel, 'Women and waqf: An analysis of the Istanbul *Tahrîr* of 1546', *Asian and African Studies*, 17 (1983), 9–27.

Basrūr, Rashīda, 'Nafaqat al-zawja wa-umm al-walad min khilāl fatāwī al-Burzulī', in Dalenda Larguèche (ed.), *Historie des femmes au Maghreb: Culture matérielle et vie quotidienne*, Tunis, 2000, 89–114.

Behrens-Abousseif, Doris, 'The maḥmal legend and the pilgrimage of the ladies of the Mamluk court', *Mamluk Studies Review*, 1 (1997), 87–96.

Benmiled, Emna, 'Vie des femmes à travers la rihla d'Ibn Battutah (8e s/14e s.)', *Revue Tunisienne de Sciences Sociales*, 28 (1991), 109–62.

Benslama, Fethi, and Nadia Tazi (eds.), *La virilité en Islam*, Paris, 2004.

Bos, Gerrit, 'Ibn al-Jazzār on sexuality and sexual dysfunction and the mystery of 'Ubaid ibn 'Alī bn Jurāja ibn Ḥillauf solved', *JSAI*, 19 (1995), 250–66.

Chapoutot-Ramadi, Mounira, 'Chagar al-durr esclave mamluke et sultane d'Egypte', in *Les Africains*, vol. IV, Paris, 1977, 101–27.

Crompton, Louis, 'Male love and Islamic law in Arab Spain', in Stephen O. Murray and Will Roscoe (eds.), *Islamic homosexualities: Culture, history, and literature*, New York, 1997, 142–57.

Déjeux, Jean, *Femmes d'Algérie: Légendes, traditions, histoire, littérature*, Paris, 1987.

Di Giacomo, L., 'Une poétesse grenadine du temps des Almohades: Ḥafṣa bint al-Ḥājj ar-Rukūnīya', *Hespéris*, 34 (1947), 9–101.

Doumani, Beshara (ed.), *Family history in the Middle East: Household, property, and gender*, Albany, 2003.

Esposito, J. L., *Women in Muslim family law*, Syracuse, 1982.

Fadel, Mohammad, 'Two women, one man: Knowledge, power and gender in medieval Sunni legal thought', *IJMES*, 29 (1997), 185–204.

Fay, Mary Ann, 'Women and waqf: Toward a reconsideration of women's place in the Mamluk household', *IJMES*, 29 (1997), 33–51.

Giladi, Avner, 'Breast-feeding in medieval Islamic thought: A preliminary study of legal and medical writings', *Journal of Family History*, 23 (1998), 107–23.

'Normative Islam versus local tradition: Some observations on female circumcision with special reference to Egypt', *Arabica*, 44 (1997), 254–67.

Goitein, S. D., *A Mediterranean society: The Jewish communities of the Arab world as portrayed in the documents of the Cairo Geniza*, 6 vols., Berkeley and Los Angeles, 1967–93, vol. III: *The family*, Berkeley, 1978.

'The sexual mores of the common people', in A. L. al-Sayyid-Marsot (ed.), *Society and the sexes in medieval Islam*, Malibu, 1979, 43–61.

Hambly, G. R. G., 'Becoming visible: Medieval Islamic women in historiography and history', in G. R. G. Hambly (ed.), *Women in the medieval Islamic world: Power, patronage, and piety*, Basingstoke and New York, 1998, 3–28.

Hathaway, Jane, 'Marriage alliances among the military households of Ottoman Egypt', *AI*, 29 (1995), 133–49.

Hoffman, Valerie J., 'Le soufisme, la femme et la sexualité', in Alexandre Popovic and Gilles Veinstein (eds.), *Les voies d'Allah: Les ordres mystiques dans l'islam des origines à aujourd'hui*, 2 vols., Algiers, 1996, vol. I, 253–7.

al-Imad, L., 'Women and religion in the Fatimid caliphate: The case of al-Sayyida al-Hurrah, queen of Yemen', in M. Mazzaoui and V. B. Moreen (eds.), *Intellectual studies on Islam: Essays written in honor of Martin B. Dickson*, Salt Lake City, 1991, 137–44.

Ivanova, Svetlana, 'Muslim and Christian women before the Kadi Court in eighteenth century Rumeli: Marriage problems', *Oriente Moderno*, 18 (1999), 161–76.

Johnson, K., 'Royal pilgrims: Mamluk accounts of the pilgrimages to Mecca of the khawand al-kubra (senior wife of the sultan)', *SI*, 91 (2000), 107–29.

Kahle, Paul, 'A Gypsy woman in Egypt in the thirteenth century AD', *Journal of the Gypsy Lore Society*, 29 (1950), 11–15.

Kruk, Remke, 'Ibn Baṭṭūṭa: Travel, family life, and chronology: How seriously do we take a father?', *al-Qanṭara*, 16 (1995), 369–84.

'Pregnancy and its social consequences in mediaeval and traditional Arab society', *Quaderni di Studi Arabi*, 5–6 (1987–8), 418–30.

Larguèche, Abdelhamid, *Les ombres de Tunis: Pauvres, marginaux et minorités aux XVIIIe et XIXe siècles*, Paris, 1999.

Larguèche, Dalenda (ed.), *Historie des femmes au Maghreb: Culture matérielle et vie quotidienne*, Tunis, 2000.

Lutfi, Huda, 'A study of six fourteenth century iqrārs from al-Quds relating to Muslim women', *JESHO*, 26 (1983), 246–94.

Malti-Douglas, F., *Woman's body, woman's word: Gender and discourse in Arabo-Islamic writing*, Princeton, 1991.

Marín, Manuela, 'Marriage and sexuality in al-Andalus', in Eukene Lacarra Lanz (ed.), *Marriage and sexuality in medieval and early modern Iberia*, New York, 2002, 3–20.

Martinez-Gros, Gabriel, 'Femmes et pouvoir dans les mémoires d''Abd Allāh b. Zīrī', in *La condición de la mujer en la Edad Media: Actas del Coloquio celebrado en la Casa de Velázquez, del 5 al 7 de noviembre de 1984*, Madrid, 1986, 371–8.

Mediano, Fernando R., 'Una sociabilidad oblicua: Mujeres en el Marruecos moderno', *al-Qanṭara*, 16 (1995), 385–402.

Mernissi, Fatima, *Sultanes oubliées: Femmes chefs d'état en Islam*, Paris, 1990.

Munajjid, Salah al-din, 'Women's roles in the art of Arabic calligraphy', in G. N. Atiyeh (ed.), *The book in the Islamic world: The written word and communication in the Middle East*, New York, 1995, 141–8.

Murray, Stephen O., 'Male homosexuality, inheritance rules, and the status of women in medieval Egypt', in Stephen O. Murray and Will Roscoe (eds.), *Islamic homosexualities: Culture, history, and literature*, New York, 1997, 162–73.

'Woman–woman love in Islamic societies', in Stephen O. Murray and Will Roscoe (eds.), *Islamic homosexualities: Culture, history, and literature*, New York, 1997, 97–104.

Nichols, J. M., 'Arabic women poets in al-Andalus', *The Maghreb Review*, 4 (1979), 114–17.

Peirce, Leslie, '"She is trouble ... and I will divorce her": Orality, honor, and representation in the Ottoman court of 'Aintab', in G. R. G. Hambly (ed.), *Women in the medieval Islamic world: Power, patronage, and piety*, Basingstoke and New York, 1998, 269–300.

Petry, Carl, 'Conjugal rights versus class prerogatives: A divorce case in Mamlūk Cairo', in G. R. G. Hambly (ed.), *Women in the medieval Islamic world: Power, patronage, and piety*, Basingstoke and New York, 1998, 227–40.

Powers, David, 'Women and divorce in the Islamic west: Three cases', *Hawwa*, 1 (2003), 29–45.

Rispler-Chaim, V., '*Nushūz* between medieval and contemporary Islamic law: The human rights aspect', *Arabica*, 39 (1992), 315–27.

Schmidtke, Sabine, 'Homoeroticism and homosexuality in Islam: A review article', *BSOAS*, 62 (1999), 260–6.

Schmitt, Arno, '*Liwāṭ* im *fiqh*: Männliche Homosexualität?', *Journal of Arabic and Islamic Studies*, 4 (2001–2), 49–110.

Schregle, Götz, *Die Sultanin von Ägypten, Šağarat ad-Durr*, Wiesbaden, 1961.

Semerdjian, Elyse, 'Sinful professions: Illegal occupations of women in Ottoman Aleppo, Syria', *Hawwa*, 1 (2003), 60–85.

Seng, Yvonne, 'Standing at the gates of justice: Women in the law courts of early sixteenth-century Üsküdar, Istanbul', in Midie Lazarus-Black and Susan F. Hirsch (eds.), *Contested states: Law, hegemony and resistance*, New York, 1994, 184–206.

Shatzmiller, Maya, 'Aspects of women's participation in the economic life of later medieval Islam: Occupations and mentalities', *Arabica*, 35 (1988), 36–58.

'Women and property rights in al-Andalus and the Maghrib: Social patterns and legal discourse', *ILS*, 2 (1995), 219–57.

Singer, Amy, *Constructing Ottoman beneficence: An imperial soup kitchen in Jerusalem*, New York, 2002.

Sonbol, Amira, 'Rape and law in Ottoman and modern Egypt', in Madeline C. Zilfi (ed.), *Women in the Ottoman empire: Middle Eastern women in the early modern era*, Leiden, 1997, 214–31.

Spellberg, D., 'Writing the unwritten life of the Islamic Eve: Menstruation and the demonization of motherhood', *IJMES*, 28 (1996), 305–24.

Tolmacheva, Marina, 'Female piety and patronage in the medieval "ḥajj"', in G. R. G. Hambly (ed.), *Women in the medieval Islamic world: Power, patronage, and piety*, Basingstoke and New York, 1998, 161–79.

Tucker, Judith, *In the house of the law: Gender and Islamic law in Ottoman Syria and Palestine*, Berkeley, 1998.

Viguera, María Jesús, '*Aṣluḥu li-l-maʿālī*: On the social status of Andalusi women', in S. K. Jayyusi (ed.), *The legacy of Muslim Spain*, Leiden, 1992, 709–24.

Walther, W., *Die Frau im Islam*, Stuttgart, 1980.

(ed.), *Women in Islam: From medieval to modern times*, Princeton, 1993.

Zayyāt, Ḥabīb, 'al-Marʾa al-ghulāmīya fī l-islām', *al-Mashriq*, 50 (1956), 153–92.

Zomeño, Amalia, 'Abandoned wives and their possibilities for divorce in al-Andalus: The evidence of the *wathāʾiq* works', in Manuela Marín and Randi Deguilhem (eds.), *Writing the feminine: Women in Arab sources*, London, 2002, 111–26.

Secondary sources

Abdal-Rehim, Abdal-Rehim Abdal-Rahman, 'The family and gender laws in Egypt during the Ottoman period', in Amira El Azhary Sonbol (ed.), *Women, the family, and divorce laws in Islamic history*, Syracuse, 1996, 96–111.

'Abd ar-Rāziq, A., *La femme au temps des mamlouks en Egypte*, Cairo, 1973.

Abou El Fadl, Khaled, *Speaking in God's name: Islamic law, authority and women*, Oxford, 2001.

Addas, Claude, *Ibn ʿArabī ou la quête du soufre rouge*, Paris, 1989.

Aguilar, Victoria, and Manuela Marín, 'Las mujeres en el espacio urbano de al-Andalus', in Julio Navarro Palazón (ed.), *Casas y palacios de al-Andalus*, Barcelona, 1995, 39–44.

Amri, Nelly, 'Les *ṣāliḥāt* du Ve au IXe siècle/XIe–XVe siècle dans la mémoire maghrébine de la sainteté à travers quatre documents hagiographiques', *al-Qanṭara*, 21 (2000), 481–509.

Ávila, María Luisa, 'Las "mujeres sabias" en al-Andalus', in María Jesús Viguera (ed.), *La mujer en al-Andalus: Reflejos históricos de su actividad y categorías sociales*, Madrid and Seville, 1989, 139–84.

'Women in Andalusi biographical sources', in Manuela Marín and Randi Deguilhem (eds.), *Writing the feminine: Women in Arab sources*, London, 2002, 149–63.

Bellamy, James A., 'Sex and society in Islamic popular literature', in A. L. al-Sayyid-Marsot (ed.), *Society and the sexes in medieval Islam*, Malibu, 1979, 23–42.

Berkey, Jonathan P., 'Circumcision circumscribed: Female excision and cultural accommodation in the medieval Near East', *IJMES*, 28 (1996), 19–38.

'Women and Islamic education in the Mamluk period', in N. R. Keddie and B. Baron (eds.), *Women in Middle Eastern history: Shifting boundaries in sex and gender*, New Haven, 1991, 143–57.

Bouhdiba, Abdelwahhab, *La sexualité en Islam*, Paris, 1975.

Bousquet, G. H., *L'Éthique sexuelle de l'Islam*, Paris, 1966.

Bürgel, J. C., 'Love, lust, and longing: Eroticism in early Islam as reflected in literary sources', in A. L. al-Sayyid-Marsot (ed.), *Society and the sexes in medieval Islam*, Malibu, 1979, 81–117.

Chapoutot-Ramadi, Mounira, 'Femmes dans la ville mamlūke', *JESHO*, 38 (1995), 145–64.

Chodkiewicz, M., 'La sainteté féminine dans l'hagiographie islamique', in Denise Aigle (ed.), *Saints orientaux*, Paris, 1995, 99–115.

Coulson, Noel J., 'Regulation of sexual behavior under traditional Islamic law', in A. L. al-Sayyid-Marsot (ed.), *Society and the sexes in medieval Islam*, Malibu, 1979, 63–8.

Daftary, F., 'Sayyida Ḥurra: The Ismāʿīlī Ṣulayḥid queen of Yemen', in G. R. G. Hambly (ed.), *Women in the medieval Islamic world: Power, patronage, and piety*, Basingstoke and New York, 1998, 117–30.

Declich, Lorenzo, 'L'erotologia arabe: Profilo bibliografico', *Rivista degli Studi Orientali*, 68 (1994), 249–65.

Eddé, Anne-Marie, 'Images de femmes en Syrie à l'époque ayyoubide', in Patrick Henriet and Anne-Marie Legras (eds.), *Au cloître et dans le monde: Femmes, hommes et sociétés (Ixe–XVe siècle): Mélanges en l'honneur de Paulette L'Hermite-Leclercq*, Paris, 2000, 65–77.

El Cheikh, Nadia Maria, 'In search of the ideal spouse', *JESHO*, 45 (2002), 179–96.

'Mourning and the role of the *nāʾiḥa*', in Cristina de la Puente (ed.), *Identidades marginales*, Estudios Onomástico-Biográficos de al-Andalus 13, Madrid, 2003, 395–412.

Establet, Colette, and Jean-Paul Pascual, 'Women in Damascene families around 1700', *JESHO*, 45 (2002), 301–19.

Faroqhi, Suraiya, *Stories of Ottoman men and women: Establishing status, establishing control*, Istanbul, 2002.

Fay, Mary Ann, 'The ties that bound: Women and households in eighteenth-century Egypt', in Amira El Azhary Sonbol (ed.), *Women, the family, and divorce laws in Islamic history*, Syracuse, 1996, 155–72.

Garulo, Teresa, *Dīwān de las poetisas de al-Andalus*, Madrid, 1986.

Gerber, Haim, 'Social and economic position of women in an Ottoman city, Bursa, 1600–1700', *IJMES*, 12 (1980), 231–44.

Ghaṭṭās, ʿĀʾisha, 'Mumtalakāt al-marʾa fī mujtamaʿ madīnat al-Jazāʾir khilāl al-ʿahd al-ʿuthmānī', in Dalenda Larguèche (ed.), *Historie des femmes au Maghreb: Culture matérielle et vie quotidienne*, Tunis, 2000, 149–59.

Gibert, Soledad, 'Abū l-Barakāt al-Balafīqī, qāḍī, historiador y poeta', *al-Andalus*, 28 (1963), 381–424.

Giffen, Lois Anita, *Theory of profane love among the Arabs*, London and New York, 1972.

Giladi, Avner, 'Gender differences in child rearing and education: Some preliminary observations with reference to medieval Muslim thought', *al-Qanṭara*, 16 (1995), 291–308.

Hanna, Nelly, 'Marriage among merchant families in seventeenth-century Cairo', in Amira El Azhary Sonbol (ed.), *Women, the family, and divorce laws in Islamic history*, Syracuse, 1996, 143–54.

Humphreys, R. Stephen, 'Women as patrons of religious architecture in Ayyubid Damascus', *Muqarnas*, 11 (1994), 35–54.

Irwin, Robert, 'ʿAlī al-Baghdādī and the joy of Mamluk sex', in Hugh Kennedy (ed.), *The historiography of Islamic Egypt (c. 950–1800)*, Leiden, 2001, 45–57.

Jennings, Ronald, 'Women in early 17th century Ottoman judicial records: The sharia court of Anatolian Kayseri', *JESHO*, 18 (1975), 53–114.

Juynboll, G. H. A., 'Siḥāḳ', *EI2*, vol. IX, 565–7.

al-Kīkī, Muḥammad ibn ʿAbd Allāh, *Mawāhib dhī l-jalāl fī nawāzil al-bilād al-sāʾiba min al-jibāl*, ed. Aḥmad Tawfīq, Beirut, 1997.

Lamdan, Ruth, *A separate people: Jewish women in Palestine, Syria and Egypt in the sixteenth century*, Leiden, 2000.

Larguèche, Dalenda and Abdelhamid Larguèche, *Marginales en terre d'Islam*, Tunis, 1992.

de La Véronne, Chantal, 'Sida el-Ḥorra, la noble dame', *Hespéris*, 48 (1956), 222–5.

Lev, Y., 'Aspects of the Egyptian society in the Fatimid period', in U. Vermeulen and J. Van Steenbergen (eds.), *Egypt and Syria in the Fatimid, Ayyubid and Mamluk eras*, 5 vols., Leuven, 2001, vol. III, 1–31.

López-Baralt, Luce, *Un Kāma-sūtra español*, Madrid, 1992.

Lutfi, Huda, 'Manners and customs of fourteenth-century Cairene women: Female anarchy versus male *sharʿī* order in Muslim prescriptive treatises', in N. R. Keddie and B. Baron (eds.), *Women in Middle Eastern history: Shifting boundaries in sex and gender*, New Haven, 1991, 99–121.

'al-Sakhāwī's *Kitāb al-nisāʾ* as a source for the social and economic history of Muslim women during the fifteenth century AD', *The Muslim World*, 21 (1981), 104–24.

Marín, Manuela, *Mujeres en al-Ándalus*, Madrid, 2000.

'Parentesco simbólico y matrimonio entre los ulemas andalusíes', *al-Qanṭara*, 16 (1995), 335–56.

Monroe, James T., 'The striptease that was blamed on Abū Bakr's naughty son: Was Father being shamed, or was the poet having fun? (Ibn Quzmān's *zajal* no. 133)', in J. W. Wright and Everett K. Rowson (eds.), *Homoeroticism in classical Arabic literature*, New York, 1997, 94–139.

Musallam, B. F., *Sex and society in Islam: Birth control before the nineteenth century*, Cambridge, 1983.

Oberhelman, Steven H., 'Hierarchies of gender, ideology, and power, in ancient and medieval Greek and Arabic dream literature', in J. W. Wright and Everett K. Rowson (eds.), *Homoeroticism in classical Arabic literature*, New York, 1997, 55–93.

Peirce, Leslie, 'Gender and sexual propriety in Ottoman royal women's patronage', in D. Fairchild Ruggles (ed.), *Women, patronage and self-representation in Islamic societies*, Albany, 2000, 53–68.

The imperial harem: Women and sovereignty in the Ottoman empire, Oxford and New York, 1993.

Morality tales: Law and gender in the Ottoman court of Aintab, Berkeley and Los Angeles, 2003.

'Seniority, sexuality, and social order: The vocabulary of gender in early modern Ottoman society', in Madeline C. Zilfi (ed.), *Women in the Ottoman empire: Middle Eastern women in the early modern era*, Leiden, 1997, 169–96.

Petry, Carl F., 'Class solidarity versus gender gain: Women as custodians of property in later medieval Egypt', in N. R. Keddie and B. Baron (eds.), *Women in Middle Eastern history: Shifting boundaries in sex and gender*, New Haven, 1991, 122–42.

'Royal justice in Mamlūk Cairo: Contrasting motives of two sulṭāns', in *Saber religioso y poder político en el Islam*, Madrid, 1994, 197–211.

Pouzet, Louis, *Damas au VIIe/VIIIe siècle: Vie et structures religeuses dans une métropole islamique*, Beirut, 1991.

Roded, Ruth, *Women in Islamic biographical collections: from Ibn Saʿd to Who's who*, London, 1994.

Rosenthal, Franz, 'Fiction and reality: Sources for the role of sex in medieval Muslim society', in A. L. al-Sayyid-Marsot (ed.), *Society and the sexes in medieval Islam*, Malibu, 1979, 3–22.

'Male and female: Described and compared', in J. W. Wright and Everett K. Rowson (eds.), *Homoeroticism in classical Arabic literature*, New York, 1997, 24–54.

Rowson, Everett K., 'The categorization of gender and sexual irregularity in medieval Arabic vice lists', in Julia Epstein and Kristina Straub (eds.), *Body guards: The cultural politics of gender ambiguity*, New York, 1991, 50–79.

'Two homoerotic narratives from Mamlūk literature: al-Ṣafadī's *Lawʿat al-shākī* and Ibn Dāniyāl's *al-Mutayyam*', in J. W. Wright and Everett K. Rowson (eds.), *Homoeroticism in classical Arabic literature*, New York, 1997, 158–91.

Ruggles, D. Fairchild (ed.), *Women, patronage and self-representation in Islamic societies*, Albany, 2000.

Saleh, Walid, 'The woman as a locus of apocalyptic anxiety in medieval Sunnī Islam', in Angelika Neuwirth, Birgit Embaló, Sebastian Gunther and Maher Jarrar (eds.), *Myths, historical archetypes and symbolic figures in Arabic literature*, Beirut, 1999, 123–45.

Sanders, Paula, 'Gendering the ungendered body: Hermaphrodites in medieval Islamic law', in N. R. Keddie and B. Baron (eds.), *Women in Middle Eastern history: Shifting boundaries in sex and gender*, New Haven, 1991, 74–95.

al-Sayyid Marsot, Afaf Lutfi, 'Entrepreneurial women in Egypt', in Mai Yamani (ed.), *Feminism and Islam: Legal and literary perspectives*, Reading, 1996, 33–47.

Schimmel, Annemarie, 'Eros – heavenly and not so heavenly – in Sufi literature and life', in A. L. al-Sayyid-Marsot (ed.), *Society and the sexes in medieval Islam*, Malibu, 1979, 119–41.

My soul is a woman: The feminine in Islam, trans. Susan H. Ray, New York, 1999.

Seng, Yvonne J., 'Invisible women: Residents of early sixteenth-century Istanbul', in G. R. G. Hambly (ed.), *Women in the medieval Islamic world: Power, patronage, and piety*, Basingstoke and New York, 1998, 241–68.

Shatzmiller, Maya, 'Women and wage labour in the medieval Islamic west: Legal issues in an economic context', *JESHO*, 40 (1997), 174–206.

Sonbol, Amira (ed.), *Women, the family, and divorce laws in Islamic history*, Syracuse, 1996.

Tabbaa, Yasser, 'Ḍayfa Khātūn, regent queen and architectural patron', in D. Fairchild Ruggles (ed.), *Women, patronage and self-representation in Islamic societies*, Albany, 2000, 17–34.

Viguera, María Jesús, 'A borrowed space: Andalusi and Maghribi women in chronicles', in Manuela Marín and Randi Deguilhem (eds.), *Writing the feminine: Women in Arab sources*, London, 2002, 165–80.

Zarinebaf-Shahr, Fariba, 'Women, law, and imperial justice in Ottoman Istanbul in the late seventeenth century', in Amira El Azhary Sonbol (ed.), *Women, the family, and divorce laws in Islamic history*, Syracuse, 1996, 81–95.

Ze'evi, Dror, 'Women in 17th-century Jerusalem: Western and indigenous perspectives', *IJMES*, 27 (1995), 157–73.

Zilfi, Madeline C., 'Elite circulation in the Ottoman empire: Great mollas of the eighteenth century', *JESHO*, 26 (1983), 318–64.

'Servants, slaves, and the domestic order in the Ottoman Middle East', *Hawwa*, 2 (2004), 1–33.

'"We don't get along": Women and hul divorce in the eighteenth century', in Madeline C. Zilfi (ed.), *Women in the Ottoman empire: Middle Eastern women in the early modern era*, Leiden, 1997, 264–96.

Zomeño, Amalia, *Dote y matrimonio en al-Andalus y el norte de África: Estudios sobre la jurisprudencia islámica medieval*, Madrid, 2000.

Chapter 13: Arabic literature

Practical suggestions for further reading

Allen, R., and D. S. Richards (eds.), *The Cambridge history of Arabic literature*, vol. VI: *Arabic literature in the post-classical period*, Cambridge, 2006.

Bauer, T., 'Mamluk literature: Misunderstandings and new approaches', *Mamluk Studies Review*, 9 (2005), 105–32.

Frolov, D., *Classical Arabic verse: History and theory of* ʿarūḍ, Leiden, 2000.

Goodman, L. E., *Islamic humanism*, Oxford, 2003.

Hamori, A., *The composition of Mutanabbī's panegyrics to Sayf al-Dawla*, Leiden, 1992.

Heijkoop, H., and O. Zwartjes, Muwaššaḥ, zajal, kharja*: Bibliography of strophic poetry and music from al-Andalus and their influence in East and West*, Leiden and Boston, 2004.

Irwin, R. (ed.), *Night and horses and the desert: An anthology of classical Arabic literature*, Harmondsworth, 1999.

Lowry, J., and D. Stewart (eds.), *Essays in Arabic literary biography 1350–1850*, Wiesbaden, 2009.

Lyons, M. C., *Identification and identity in classical Arabic poetry*, Warminster, 1999.

Marzolph, U., and R. van Leeuwen, with the collaboration of Hassan Wassouf, *The Arabian Nights encyclopedia*, 2 vols., Santa Barbara, 2004.

Ouyang, Wen-chin, *Literary criticism in medieval Arabic-Islamic culture: The making of a tradition*, Edinburgh, 1997.

Reynolds, D. F. (ed.), *Interpreting the self: Autobiography in the Arabic literary tradition*, Berkeley, 2001.

Stetkevych, J., *The zephyrs of Najd: The poetics of nostalgia in the classical Arabic* nasīb, Chicago, 1993.

Toorawa, S. M., *Ibn Abī Ṭāhir Ṭayfūr and Arabic writerly culture: A ninth-century bookman in Baghdad*, London and New York, 2005.

Wright, J. W. Jr, and E. K. Rowson (eds.), *Homoeroticism in classical Arabic literature*, New York, 1997.

Primary sources

al-Āmidī, *al-Muwāzana bayna shiʿr Abī Tammām wa-al-Buḥturī*, vols. I and II ed. A. Ṣaqr, Cairo, 1961, 1965; vols. III (i) and (ii) ed. ʿA. A. Ḥ. Muḥārib, Cairo, 1990.

Beeston, A. F. L. (ed. and trans.), *The epistle on singing-girls of Jāḥiẓ*, Warminster, 1980.

Selections from the poetry of Baššar, Cambridge, 1977.

Bosworth, C. E., *Bahāʾ al-Dīn al-ʿĀmilī and his literary anthologies*, *Journal of Semitic Studies* Monograph 10, Manchester, 1989.

Dagher, J. and G. Troupeau (trans.), *Ibn Buṭlān: Le banquet des médecins*, Paris, 2007.

Ibn Buṭlān: Le banquet des prêtres, Paris, 2004.

Ibn ʿAbd al-Barr al-Namarī, *Bahjat al-majālis wa-uns al-mujālis*, ed. M. M. al-Khūlī, 3 vols., Beirut, n.d.

Ibn Abī Uṣaybiʿa, *ʿUyūn al-anbāʾ fī ṭabaqāt al-aṭibbāʾ*, ed. N. Riḍā, Beirut, n. d. [1965].

Ibn Ḥazm, *The ring of the dove*, trans. A. J. Arberry, London, 1953.

Ibn al-Muqaffaʿ, *Risāla fī al-ṣaḥāba*, ed. and trans. C. Pellat in *Ibn al-Muqaffaʿ, mort vers 140/757, 'conseilleur' du calife*, Paris, 1976.

al-Ibshīhī, *al-Mustaṭraf fī kull fann mustaẓraf*, ed. I. Ṣāliḥ, 2 vols., Beirut, 1999; trans. G. Rat as *al-Mostatraf: Recueil de morceaux choisis ... dans toutes les branches ... de connaissances reputées attrayantes ... ouvrage philologique, anecdotique, littéraire et philosophique*, 2 vols., Paris and Toulon, 1899–1902.

al-Masʿūdī, *Murūj al-dhahab wa maʿādin al-jawhar*, ed. and trans. C. Barbier de Meynard and Pavet de Courteille, Paris, 1861–77; rev. C. Pellat: text, 7 vols., Beirut, 1966–79, trans., 5 vols., Paris, 1962–89; partial English trans. E. P. Lunde and C. Stone as *Meadows of gold: The Abbasids*, London, 1989.

Miquel, A. (trans.), *Majnûn: Le fou de Laylâ*, Arles, 2003.

Miskawayh, *The eclipse of the ʿAbbasid caliphate*, ed. and trans. H. F. Amedroz and D. S. Margoliouth, 7 vols., Oxford, 1920–1.

Monroe, J. T. (trans.), *The Shuʿūbiyya in al-Andalus: The* Risāla *of Ibn García and five refutations*, Berkeley, 1970.

al-Nīsābūrī, *ʿUqalāʾ al-majānīn*, ed. ʿU. al-Asʿad, Beirut, 1407/1987.

al-Nuwayrī, *Nihāyat al-arab fī funūn al-adab*, ed. M. ʿA. H. Shuʿayra and M. M. Ziyāda *et al.*, 33 vols., Cairo, 1346–1417/1923–97.

Petit, O., and W. Voisin (trans.), *Poèmes d'amour de ʿOmar ibn Abî Rabîʿa*, Paris, 1993.

al-Qalyūbī, *al-Nawādir*, trans. R. Khawam as *Le fantastique et le quotidien*, Paris, 1981.

al-Qifṭī, *Inbāh al-ruwāt ʿalā anbāh al-nuḥāt*, ed. M. A. F. Ibrāhīm, 4 vols., Cairo, 1950–74.

al-Ṣābiʾ, Hilāl ibn al-Muḥassin, *Rusūm dār al-khilāfa*, ed. M. ʿAwwād, Baghdad, 1383/1964; trans. E. Salem as *The rules and regulations of the ʿAbbasid court*, Beirut, 1977.

Ṣafwat, A. Z. (ed.), *Jamharat rasāʾil al-ʿArab fī ʿuṣūr al-ʿarabiyya al-zāhira*, 4 vols., Cairo, 1937.

al-Sarrāj, *Maṣāriʿ al-ʿushshāq*, ed. A. R. Shaḥḥāta, 2 vols., Beirut, 1419/1998.

Serjeant, R. B. (trans.), *Abū ʿUthmān ibn Baḥr al-Jāḥiz: The book of misers: A translation of al-Bukhalāʾ*, Reading, 1997.

al-Shābushtī, *Kitāb al-diyārāt*, ed. G. ʿAwwād, 3rd edn, Beirut, 1986.

al-Ṣūlī, *Akhbār al-Rāḍī wa-al-Muttaqī*, ed. J. Heyworth-Dunne, Cairo, 1935; trans. M. Canard as *Histoire de la dynastie abbaside de 322 à 333/933 à 944*, published in *Publications de l'Institut d'Études Orientales*, Faculté des lettres et sciences humaines d'Alger 10 (1946) and 12 (1950).

al-Ṭāluwī, *Sāniḥāt Dumā al-qaṣr fī muṭāraḥāt banī al-ʿaṣr*, ed. M. M. al-Khūlī, 2 vols., Beirut, 1403/1983.

al-Tanūkhī, *al-Faraj baʿd al-shidda*, ed. ʿA. al-Shāljī, 5 vols., Beirut, 1398/1978.

Nishwār al-muḥāḍara, ed. ʿA. al-Shāljī, 8 vols., Beirut, 1391–3/1971–3; trans. D. S. Margoliouth as *The table-talk of a Mesopotamian judge*, London, 1922, and in *Islamic Culture*, 3–6 (1929–32).

al-Tawḥīdī, *Akhlāq al-wazīrayn*, partial trans. F. Lagrange as *La satire des deux vizirs*, Paris, 2004.

al-Imtāʿ wa-al-muʾānasa, ed. A. Amīn and A. al-Zayn, 2nd edn, 3 vols. in 1, Cairo, 1953.

(attrib.), *al-Risāla al-Baghdādiyya*, ed. ʿA. al-Shāljī, Beirut, 1400/1980.

al-Ṭurṭūshī, *Sirāj al-mulūk*, ed. M. F. Abū Bakr, 2 vols., Cairo, 1414/1994.

al-Washshāʾ, *Kitāb al-Muwashshāʾ*, partial trans. S. Bouhlal as *Le livre de brocart*, Paris, 2004.

Yāqūt, *Irshād al-arīb ilā maʿrifat al-adīb*, ed. I. ʿAbbās, 7 vols., Beirut, 1993.

Secondary sources

al-Asad, N. D., *al-Qiyān wa-al-ghinā' fī al-'aṣr al-jāhilī*, 3rd edn, Beirut, 1988 [1960].

Bauer, T., *Liebe und Liebesdichtung in der arabischen Welt des 9. und 10. Jahrhunderts*, Wiesbaden, 1998.

de Blois, F., 'Ibn al-Muqaffa'', *EAL*, vol. I, 352–3.

Bray, J., ''Abbasid myth and the human act: Ibn 'Abd Rabbih and others', in P. F. Kennedy (ed.), *On fiction and adab in medieval Arabic literature*, Wiesbaden, 2005, 1–54.

'Men, women and slaves in Abbasid society', in L. Brubaker and J. M. H. Smith (eds.), *Gender in the early medieval world: East and West, 300–900*, Cambridge, 2004, 121–46.

'al-Mu'taṣim's "bridge of toil" and Abū Tammām's Amorium *qaṣīda*', in G. R. Hawting *et al.* (eds.), *Studies in Islamic and Middle Eastern texts and traditions in memory of Norman Calder, Journal of Semitic Studies* Supplement 12, Oxford, 2000, 31–73.

'The physical world and the writer's eye: al-Tanūkhī and medicine', in J. Bray (ed.), *Writing and representation in medieval Islam: Muslim horizons*, London and New York, 2006, 215–49.

'Yāqūt's interviewing technique: "Sniffy"', in C. F. Robinson (ed.), *Texts, documents and artefacts: Islamic studies in honour of D. S. Richards*, Leiden and Boston, 2003, 191–209.

(ed.), *Writing and representation in medieval Islam: Muslim horizons*, London and New York, 2006.

Carter, M. G., ''Abd al-Qādir ibn 'Umar al-Baghdādī', *EAL*, vol. I, 15–16.

'al-Astarābādhī', *EAL*, vol. I, 110–11.

'Ibn al-Ḥājib', *EAL*, vol. I, 328.

Chraïbi, A.,'Classification des traditions narratives arabes par "conte-type": Application à l'étude de quelques rôles de poète', *Bulletin d'Études Orientales*, 50 (1998), 29–59.

El-Rouayheb, K., 'The love of boys in Arabic poetry of the early Ottoman period, 1500–1800', *Middle Eastern Literatures*, 8 (2005), 3–22.

Enderwitz, S., 'al-Shu'ūbiyya', *EI2*, vol. IX, 513–16.

van Gelder, G. J. H., 'Abū al-'Alā' al-Ma'arrī', *EAL*, vol. I, 24–5.

'Ibn Ma'ṣūm', *EAL*, vol. I, 349.

'*The nodding noddles* or *Jolting the yokels*: A composition for marginal voices by al-Shirbīnī (fl. 1687)', in R. Ostle (ed.), *Marginal voices in literature and society: Individual and society in the Mediterranean Muslim world*, Strasbourg, 2000, 49–67.

Giffen, L. A., 'al-Anṭākī, Dā'ūd ibn 'Umar', *EAL*, vol. I, 92.

'al-Biqā'ī, Ibrāhīm ibn 'Umar, al-Shāfi'ī', *EAL*, vol. I, 152.

Hämeen-Anttila, J., *Maqāma: A history of a genre*, Wiesbaden, 2002.

Hanna, N., *In praise of books: A cultural history of Cairo's middle class, sixteenth to the eighteenth century*, Cairo, 2004.

Hillenbrand, C., ''Imād al-Dīn al-Iṣfahānī', *EAL*, vol. I, 392–3.

Kennedy, H., *The court of the caliphs: The rise and fall of Islam's greatest dynasty*, London, 2004.

Kennedy, P. F., 'The *maqāmāt* as a nexus of interests: Reflections on Abdelfattah Kilito's *Les séances*', in J. Bray (ed.), *Writing and representation in medieval Islam: Muslim horizons*, London and New York, 2006, 153–214.

The wine song in classical Arabic poetry: Abū Nuwās and the literary tradition, Oxford, 1997.

Kilpatrick, H., *Making the great book of songs: Compilation and the author's craft in Abū l-Faraj al-Iṣbahānī's* Kitāb al-aghānī, London and New York, 2003.

'Monasteries through Muslim eyes: The *diyārāt* books', in D. Thomas (ed.), *Christians at the heart of Islamic rule: Church life and scholarship in 'Abbasid Iraq*, Leiden and Boston, 2003, 19–37.

Kraemer, J. L., *Humanism in the renaissance of Islam: The cultural revival during the Buyid age*, Leiden, 1986.

Le Coz, R., *Les médecins nestoriens au moyen âge: Les maîtres des Arabes*, Paris, 2004.

Lowry, J. E., 'Ibn Qutaybah', *DLB:ALC*, 172–83.

Meisami, J. S., 'Abū Tammām', *EAL*, vol. I, 47–9.

'al-Buḥturī', *EAL*, vol. I, 161–2.

'*Madīḥ, madḥ*', *EAL*, vol. II, 482–4.

'al-Mutanabbī', *EAL*, vol. II, 558–60.

Montgomery, J. E., 'al-Jāḥiẓ', *DLB:ALC*, 231–42.

The vagaries of the qaṣīdah: *The tradition and practice of early Arabic poetry*, E. J. W. Gibb Memorial Trust, n.p., 1997.

Ostle, R. (ed.), *Marginal voices in literature and society: Individual and society in the Mediterranean Muslim world*, Strasbourg, 2000.

Pellat, C., 'Ḳayna', *EI2*, vol. IV, 820–4.

al-Qāḍī, W., ''Abd al-Ḥamīd ibn Yaḥyā al-Kātib', *EAL*, vol. I, 13–14.

'Sālim Abū al-'Alā'', *EAL*, vol. II, 681–2.

Reynolds, D., 'Music', in M. R. Menocal *et al.* (eds.), *The Cambridge history of Arabic literature*, vol. V: *The literature of al-Andalus*, Cambridge, 2000, 60–82.

Rowson, E. K., 'al-Bākharzī, 'Alī ibn al-Ḥasan', *EAL*, vol. I, 129.

'al-Tha'ālibī', *EAL*, vol. II, 764–5.

'The effeminates of early Medina', *JAOS*, 111 (1991), 671–93.

Rowson, E. K., and S. Bonebakker, *Notes on two poetic anthologies: Ṯa'ālibī's* Tatimma *and Bākharzī's* Dumya, Los Angeles, 1984.

Smoor, P., ''Umāra's poetical views of Shāwar, Ḍirgham, Shīrkūh and Ṣalāḥ al-Dīn as viziers of the Fatimid caliphs', in F. Daftary and J. W. Meri (eds.), *Culture and memory in medieval Islam: Essays in honour of Wilferd Madelung*, London and New York, 2003, 411–32.

Stetkevych, S. P., *Abū Tammām and the poetics of the 'Abbāsid age*, Leiden, 1991.

Toelle, H., and K. Zakharia, *À la découverte de la littérature arabe du VIe siècle à nos jours*, Paris, 2003.

Vrolijk, A., 'The better self of a dirty old man: Personal sentiments in the poetry of 'Alī ibn Sūdūn (1407–1464)', in R. Ostle (ed.), *Marginal voices in literature and society: Individual and society in the Mediterranean Muslim world*, Strasbourg, 2000, 39–47.

Chapter 14: Persian literature

Practical suggestions for further reading

Bausani, A., *Storia della letteratura persiana*, Milan, 1960.

Khāliqī Muṭlagh, Djalāl, *Gul-i ranjhāyi kuhan*, Tehran, 1372/1993.

Losensky, Paul, *Welcoming Fighānī*, Costa Mesa, 1998.

Meisami, Julie Scott, *Medieval Persian court poetry*, Princeton, 1987.

Persian historiography, Edinburgh, 1999.

Rypka, Jan, *History of Iranian literature*, Dordrecht, 1968.

Primary sources

Amīr Khusraw, *Dīwān-i kāmil-i Amīr Khusraw Dihlawī*, ed. Saīd Nafīsī, Tehran, 1361/1982.
Anṣārī, *Ṭabaqāt al-ṣūfīya*, ed. Mawlā'ī, Tehran, 1362/1983.
ʿAṭṭār, Farīd al-Dīn, *Manṭiq al-ṭayr*, ed. A. Ranjbar, Tehran, 1366/1987.
ʿAyyuqī, *Warqa wa gulshāh*, ed. Ẓ. Ṣafā, Tehran, 1343/1964.
Bayhaqī, *Tārīkh-i Bayhaqī*, ed. ʿAlī Fayyāḍ, Mashhad, 1356/1977.
Firdausi, Abolqāsim, *Shāhnāma*, ed. Y. Bertels *et al.*, 9 vols., Moscow, 1966–71.
Gurgānī, Fakhr al-Dīn, *Wīs wa Rāmīn*, ed. Muḥammad Rawshan, Tehran, 1381/2002.
Ḥāfiẓ, *Dīwān-i Khwāja Ḥāfiẓ Shīrāzī*, ed. Parwīz Khānlarī, Tehran, 1359/1980.
Hujwīrī, *Kashf al-maḥjūb*, ed. V. Zhukufski, Tehran, 1358/1979.
Jahān Malik Khātūn, *Dīwān-i Kāmel-i Djahān Malik Khātūn*, ed. Purāndokht Kāshānīrād *et al.*, Tehran, 1374/1995.
Jāmī, Nūr al-Dīn ʿAbd al-Raḥmān, *Mathnawī-yi haft awrang*, ed. M. Mudarris Gīlānī, Tehran, 1361/1982.
al-Juwaynī, Muḥammad, *Tārīkh-i jahān gushā*, ed. Muḥammad Ramaḍānī, Tehran, 1337/1958.
Kay Kāwūs ibn Iskandar, *Qābūsnāma*, ed. G. H. Yūsufī, Tehran, 1364/1985.
Nāṣir-i Khusraw, *Safarnāma*, ed. Vazīnpūr, Tehran, 1363/1984.
Naṣr Allāh, *Kalīla wa dimna*, ed. Mujtaba Minovi, Tehran, 1362/1983.
Niẓām al-Mulk, *Siyāsatnāma*, ed. ʿAbbās Iqbāl, Tehran, 1369/1990.
Niẓāmī, *Kulliyāt-i khamsa-yi Ḥakīm Niẓāmī Ganja-ī*, Tehran, 1366/1987.
Qaīrān-i Tabrīzī, *Dīwān-i Ḥakṭm Qaṭrān Tabrīzī*, ed. Foruzanfar *et al.*, Tehran, 1362/1983.
Rūdakī, *Dīwān-i Rudakī*, ed. Jahāngīr Manṣur, Tehran, 1373/1994.
Rūmī, Djalāl al-dīn, *Mathnawī-yi maʿnawī*, ed. R. Nicholson, London, 1925–40.
Ṣā'ib Tabrīzī, *Dīwān-i Ṣā'ib Tabrīzī*, ed. Muḥammad Qahramān, Tehran, 1364/1985.
Saʿdī, *Kulliyāt-i Shaykh Saʿdi*, ed. M. A. Furūghī, Tehran, 1373/1994.
Samak-i ʿayyār, ed. Parwīz Khānlarī, Tehran, 1362–3/1983–4.
Sanā'ī, *Ḥadīqat al-Ḥaqiqa Sanā'ī*, ed. Mudarris Razavī, Tehran, 1359/1980.
Tārīkh-i Sīstān, ed. Jaʿfar Mudarris Sādiqī, Tehran, 1373/1994.
Ṭarsūsī, *Dārābnāma*, ed. Z. Ṣafā, Tehran, 1374/1995.
ʿUbayd-i Zākānī, *Kuliyyāt-i ʿUbayd-i Zākānī*, ed. Muḥammad Maḥjūb, New York, 1999.
ʿUmar Khayyām, *Rubāʿīyyāt-i Ḥakīm Khayyām*, ed. M. A. Furūghī, Tehran, 1362/1983.

Secondary sources

Bahār, Muḥammad Taqī, *Sabkshenīsī*, Tehran, 1355/1976 (repr.).
Browne, Edward G., *Literary history of Persia*, 4 vols., Cambridge, 1969 (repr.).
De Bruijn, J. T. P., *Persian Sufi poetry: An introduction to the mystical use of classical poems*, London, 1997.
Qazwīnī, Muḥammad, *Bīst Maqāla-yi Qazwīnī*, ed. ʿAbbās Iqbāl *et al.*, Tehran, 1363/1984.
Ṣafā, Ḍabīḥulla, *Ḥimāsa sarāī dar Īrān*, Tehran, 1369/1990.
Tārīkh-i adabiyāt dar Īrān, 5 vols., Tehran, 1366/1987 (seventh printing).
Yārshāṭir, Iḥsān, *Persian literature*, New York, 1988.

Chapter 15: Turkish literature

Practical suggestions for further reading

Andrews, Walter G., Najaat Black and Mehmet Kalpaklı, *Ottoman lyric poetry: An anthology*, Austin, 1997.

The book of Dede Korkut, trans. Geoffrey Lewis, London, 1988.

Sılay, Kemal (ed.), *An anthology of Turkish literature*, Bloomington, 1996.

Primary sources

The Baburnama: Memoirs of Babur, prince and emperor, Zahir-ud-din Mohammad Babur, ed., trans. and annot. Wheeler M. Thackston, New York, 2002.

al-Kashgari, Mahmud, *Compendium of the Turkic dialects (*Diwan *lugat at-Turk)*, trans. Robert Dankoff and J. Kelly, 3 vols., Sources of Oriental Languages and Literatures 7, Turkish Sources 7, Cambridge, MA, 1982–5.

Mīr ʿAlī Şīr Nawāʾī, *Muḥākamat al-lughatain*, trans. Robert Devereux, Leiden, 1966.

Şeyh Galip, *Hüsn-ü aşk: Beauty and love*, trans. with introd. and key by Victoria Rowe Holbrook, New York, 2005.

The thiefless city and the contest between food and throat: Four Eastern Turki texts, ed. and trans. Gunnar Jarring, Stockholm, 1989.

Yusuf Khass Hajib, *Wisdom of royal glory (*Kutadgu bilig*): A Turko-Islamic mirror for princes*, trans. Robert Dankoff, Chicago, 1983.

Secondary sources

Andrews, Walter G., *Poetry's voice, society's song: Ottoman lyric poetry*, Seattle, 1985.

Andrews, Walter G., and Mehmet Kalpaklı, *The age of beloveds: Love and beloved in early-modern Ottoman and European culture and society*, Durham, NC, 2005.

Bodgrodligeti, Andras, 'A collection of Turkish poems from the 14th century', *Acta Orientalia Academica Scientarum Hungarica*, 16 (1963), 244–311.

Dankoff, Robert, *An Ottoman mentality: The world of Evliya Çelebi*, Leiden, 2004.

DeWeese, Devin A., *Islamization and native religion in the Golden Horde: Baba Tükleş and conversion to Islam in historical and epic tradition*, University Park, PA, 1994.

Eckmann, Janos, 'The Mamluk Kipchak literature', *Central Asiatic Journal*, 8 (1983), 303–6.

Golden, Peter B., *Nomads and their neighbours in the Russian steppe: Turks, Khazars and Qipchaqs*, Variorum Collected Studies series, Aldershot, 2003.

Holbrook, Victoria R., *The unreadable shores of love: Turkish modernity and mystic romance*, Austin, 1994.

Levi, Scott C., and Ron Sela, *Islamic Central Asia: An anthology of historic sources*, Bloomington, 2009.

Chapter 16: Urdu literature

Practical suggestions for further reading

Ahmad, Aziz, *An intellectual history of Islam in India*, Islamic Surveys 7, Edinburgh, 1969.

Bailey, T. Grahame, *Studies in North Indian languages*, London, 1938.

Barker, M. A. R., *et al.* (eds.), *Classical Urdu poetry (*Naqsh-e Dilpizir*)*, 3 vols., Ithaca, 1977.
Chand, Tara, *The problem of Hindustani*, Allahabad, 1944.
Chatterji, Suniti Kumar, *Languages and literatures of modern India*, Calcutta, 1963.
Faruqi, Shamsur Rahman, 'A stranger in the city: The poetics of Sabk-i Hindi', in Naqi Husain Jafri (ed.), *Critical theory: Perspectives from Asia*, New Delhi, 2004, 180–285.
Grierson, Sir George Abraham, *Linguistic survey of India, vol. I, part I*, Calcutta, 1927.
Linguistic survey of India, vol. IX, part I, Calcutta, 1916.
Hansen, Kathryn, and David Lelyveld (eds.), *A wilderness of possibilities: Essays presented to C. M. Naim*, New Delhi, 2005.
Kelkar, Ashok R., *Studies in Hindi–Urdu I: Introduction and word phonology*, Poona, 1968.
Kidwai, S. R., *Gilchrist and the 'language of Hindoostan'*, New Delhi, 1972.
Matthews, D. J., C. Shackle and S. Husain, *Urdu literature*, London, n.d.
Muhamed, Sayed, *The value of Dakhni language and literature*, Mysore, 1968.
Orsini, Francesca (ed.), *Before the divide: Hindi and Urdu literary culture*, New Delhi, 2010.
Petievich, Carla R., *Assembly of rivals: Delhi, Lucknow and the Urdu ghazal*, New Delhi, 1992.
Shackle, C. (ed.), *Urdu and Muslim South Asia: Essays in honour of Ralph Russell*, London, 1989.

Primary sources in English

Ali, Ahmed (ed.), *The golden tradition: An anthology of Urdu poetry*, New York and London, 1973.
Azad, Muhammad Husain, *Ab-e Hayat*, trans. Frances W. Pritchett in association with Shamsur Rahman Faruqi, New Delhi and Oxford, 2001.
Faruqi, Shamsur Rahman, *Early Urdu literary culture and history*, New Delhi and Oxford, 2001.
Matthews, D. J., and C. Shackle, *An anthology of classical Urdu love lyrics: Text and translations*, London and Oxford, 1972.
Naim, C. M., *Urdu texts and contexts*, New Delhi, 2004.
Russell, Ralph, *The pursuit of Urdu literature: A select history*, London, 1992.
Russell, Ralph, and Khurshidul Islam, *Three Mughal poets: Mir, Sauda, Mir Hasan*, Cambridge, MA, 1968.
Sadiq, Muhammad, *A history of Urdu literature*, New Delhi, 1984 [1964].
Schimmel, Annemarie, *Classical Urdu literature from the beginning to Iqbal*, fasc. 3 of Jan Gonda (ed.), *A history of Indian literature*, vol. VIII, Wiesbaden, 1975.
Zaidi, Ali Jawad, *A history of Urdu literature*, New Delhi, 1993.

Secondary sources

Bailey, T. Grahame, *A history of Urdu literature*, Delhi, 1979 (repr.) [1928].
Farooqi, Mehr Afshan, 'The secret of letters: Chronogram in Urdu literary culture', *Edebiyat*, 13, 2 (November 2003), 147–58.
Faruqi, Shamsur Rahman, *The flower-lit road: Essays in Urdu literary theory and criticism*, Allahabad, 2005.
How to read Iqbal: Essays on Iqbal, Urdu poetry and literary theory, Lahore, 2007.
'A long history of Urdu literary culture, part 1: Naming and placing a literary culture', in Sheldon Pollock (ed.), *Literary cultures in history: Perspectives from South Asia*, Berkeley, 2003, New Delhi and Oxford, 2004, 805–63.
Petievich, Carla, *When men speak as women: Vocal masquerade in Indo-Muslim poetry*, New Delhi, 2007.

Pritchett, Frances W., 'A long history of Urdu literary culture, part 2: Histories, performances and masters', in Sheldon Pollock (ed.), *Literary cultures in history: perspectives from South Asia*, Berkeley, 2003; New Delhi and Oxford, 2004, 864–911.

Nets of awareness: Urdu poetry and its critics, Berkeley, 1994.

'The world turned upside down: Shahr Ashob as a genre', *Annual of Urdu Studies*, 4 (Madison 1984), 37–41.

Rai, Alok, *Hindi nationalism*, New Delhi, 2002.

Russell, Ralph, *Hidden in the lute: An anthology of two centuries of Urdu literature*, New Delhi, 1995.

'How not to write the history of Urdu literature', *Annual of Urdu Studies*, 6 (Madison, 1987), 1–10.

Saksena, Ram Babu, *A history of Urdu literature*, New Delhi, 2002 (repr.) [1927].

Chapter 17: History writing

Practical suggestions for further reading

Khalidi, Tarif, *Arabic historical thought in the classical period*, Cambridge, 1994.

al-Munajjid, Ṣalāḥ al-Dīn, *al-Mu'arrikhūn al-Dimashqīyūn wa-āthāruhum min al-qarn al-thālith al-hijrī ilā nihāyat al-qarn al-ʿāshir*, Cairo, 1956.

Muʿjam al-mu'arrikhīn al-Dimashqīyīn wa-āthārihim al-makhṭūṭa wa-al-maṭbūʿa, Beirut, 1978.

Robinson, Chase, *Islamic historiography*, Cambridge, 2003.

Rosenthal, Franz, *A history of Muslim historiography*, Leiden, 1968.

Safran, Janina, *The second Umayyad caliphate: The articulation of legitimacy in al-Andalus*, Cambridge, MA, 2000.

Sayyid, Ayman Fu'ād, *Maṣādir ta'rīkh al-Yaman fī al-ʿaṣr al-Islāmī*, Cairo, 1974.

Primary sources

al-Biqāʿī, Ibrāhīm ibn ʿUmar, Ta'rīkh al-Biqāʿī, MS Medina, Maktabat al-Shaykh ʿĀrif Ḥikmat 3789.

Ibn al-Athīr, *The annals of the Saljuq Turks: Selections from* al-Kāmil fī 'l-ta'rīkh *of ʿIzz al-Dīn Ibn al-Athīr*, trans. D. S. Richards, London, 2002.

Ibn Khaldūn, *The* Muqaddimah*: An introduction to history*, trans. Franz Rosenthal, 3 vols., London, 1986.

al-Yūnīnī, *Early Mamluk Syrian historiography: al-Yūnīnī's* Dhayl mir'āt al-zamān, ed. and trans. Li Guo, Leiden, 1998.

Secondary sources

Donner, Fred, *Narratives of Islamic origins: The beginnings of Islamic historical writing*, Princeton, 1998.

Duri, A. A., *The rise of historical writing among the Arabs*, ed. and trans. Lawrence Conrad, Princeton, 1983.

Guo, Li, 'al-Biqāʿī's chronicle: A fifteenth century learned man's reflection on his time and world', in Hugh Kennedy (ed.), *The historiography of Islamic Egypt (c. 950–1800)*, Leiden, 2001, 121–48.

'Mamluk historiographic studies: The state of the art', *Mamlūk Studies Review*, 1 (1997), 15–44.

Haarmann, Ulrich, 'Auflösung und Bewahrung der klassichen Formen arabischer Geschichtsschreibung in der Zeit der Mamluken', *ZDMG*, 121 (1971), 46–60.

'al-Maqrīzī, the master, and Abū Ḥāmid al-Qudsī, the disciple: Whose historical writing can claim more topicality and modernity?', in Hugh Kennedy (ed.), *The historiography of Islamic Egypt (c. 950–1800)*, Leiden, 2001, 149–65.

Quellenstudien zur frühen Mamlukenzeit, Freiburg, 1969.

Hardy, Peter, *Historians of medieval India: Studies in Indo-Muslim historical writing*, London, 1997.

Humphreys, Stephen, *Islamic history: A framework for inquiry*, Princeton, 1991.

Kennedy, Hugh, *The Prophet and the age of the caliphates: The Islamic Near East from the sixth to eleventh century*, London, 1986.

Lassner, Jacob, *Islamic revolution and historical memory: An inquiry into the art of 'Abbasid apologetics*, New Haven, 1986.

Leder, Stefan (ed.), *Story-telling in the framework of non-fictional Arabic literature*, Wiesbaden, 1998.

Little, Donald, 'Historiography of the Ayyubid and Mamluk epochs', in Carl F. Petry (ed.), *The Cambridge history of Egypt*, 2 vols., Cambridge, 1998, vol. I: *Islamic Egypt, 640–1517*, 412–44.

Meisami, Julie, *Persian historiography: To the end of the twelfth century*, Edinburgh, 1999.

'History and literature', *Iranian Studies*, 33, 1–2 (2000), 15–30.

Morgan, David, 'Persian historians and the Mongols', in David Morgan (ed.), *Medieval historical writing in the Christian and Islamic worlds*, London, 1982, 109–24.

Noth, Albrecht, in collaboration with Lawrence Conrad, *The early Arabic historical tradition: A source-critical study*, trans. Michael Bonner, Princeton, 1994.

Quinn, Sholeh A., *Historical writing during the reign of Shah 'Abbas: Ideology, imitation, and legitimacy in Safavid chronicles*, Salt Lake City, 2000.

'Problems in the study of Safavid historiography', *al-'Uṣūr al-Wusṭā*, 16, 1 (2004), 8–10.

Rabbat, Nasser, 'Representing the Mamluks in Mamluk historical writing', in Hugh Kennedy (ed.), *The historiography of Islamic Egypt (c. 950–1800)*, Leiden, 2001, 59–75.

Rosenthal, Franz, *A history of Muslim historiography*, Leiden, 1968.

Waldman, Marilyn, *Toward a theory of historical narrative: A case study in Perso-Islamicate historiography*, Columbus, 1980.

Woods, John, 'The rise of Timurid historiography', *JNES*, 46 (1987), 81–107.

Chapter 18: Biographical literature

Practical suggestions for further reading

Cooperson, Michael, *Classical Arabic biography: The heirs of the prophets in the age of al-Ma'mūn*, Cambridge, 2000.

'Classical Arabic biography', in Beatrice Gruendler and Verena Klemm (eds.), *Understanding Near Eastern literatures: A spectrum of interdisciplinary approaches*, Wiesbaden, 2000, 177–87.

Humphreys, R. Stephen, *Islamic history: A framework for inquiry*, Princeton, 1991.
Makdisi, George, 'Ṭabaqāt-biography: Law and orthodoxy in classical Islam', *Islamic Studies*, 32 (1993), 371–96.
al-Qadi, Wadad, 'Biographical dictionaries: Inner structure and cultural significance', in George N. Atiyeh (ed.), *The book in the Islamic world: The written word and communication in the Middle East*, Albany, 1995, 93–122.
Reynolds, Dwight F., *et al.*, *Interpreting the self: Autobiography in the Arabic literary tradition*, Berkeley, 2001.
Robinson, Chase F., *Islamic historiography*, Cambridge, 2003.
Roded, Ruth, *Women in Islamic biographical collections: From Ibn Saʿd to* Who's who, Boulder, 1994.
Tauer, Felix, 'History and biography', in Jan Rypka *et al.*, *History of Iranian literature*, Dordrecht, 1968, 438–59.
Young, M. J. L., 'Arabic biographical writing', in M. J. L. Young, J. D. Latham and R. B. Sergeant (eds.), *The Cambridge history of Arabic literature*, vol. III: *Religion, learning, and science in the Abbasid period*, Cambridge, 1990, 168–87.

Primary sources

Aflākī, *Manāqib al-ʿārifīn*, trans. James W. Redhouse as *Legends of the Sufis*, 3rd edn, London, 1976.
ʿAṭṭār, *Tadhkirat al-awliyāʾ*, ed. R. A. Nicholson, 2 vols., London, 1905.
The Baburnama: Memoirs of Babur, prince and emperor, trans. Wheeler M. Thackston, Jr., New York, 2002.
al-Dhahabī, Shams al-Dīn, *Siyar aʿlām al-nubalāʾ*, vol. XI, ed. Ṣāliḥ al-Samr, Beirut, 1304/1982.
al-Hujwīrī, *The 'Kashf al-maḥjūb', the oldest Persian treatise on Sufism*, trans. Reynold A. Nicholson, Gibb Memorial Series 17, London, 1936 (repr.).
Ibn al-Anbārī, *Nuzhat al-alibbāʾ fī ṭabaqāt al-udabāʾ*, ed. ʿA. ʿĀmir, Stockholm, 1963.
Ibn al-Jawzī, *Manāqib al-imām Aḥmad Ibn Ḥanbal*, Cairo, 1930.
Ṣifat al-ṣafwa, 2 vols., Hyderabad, 1936–8.
Ibn Khallikān, *Wafayāt al-aʿyān*, ed. Iḥsān ʿAbbās, 8 vols., Beirut, 1968–72.
Ibn al-Qifṭī, *Taʾrīkh al-ḥukamāʾ*, ed. Julius Lippert, Leipzig, 1903.
Ibn Qutayba, *al-Shiʿr wa al-shuʿarāʾ*, ed. Aḥmad Muḥammad Shākir, 2 vols., Cairo, 1966.
Ibn Saʿd, *al-Ṭabaqāt al-kubrā*, ed. Riyāḍ ʿAbd al-Hādī, 8 parts in 4, Beirut, 1996.
al-Iṣfahānī, Abū Nuʿaym, *Ḥilyat al-awliyāʾ*, Cairo, 1932–8; repr. Beirut, n. d.
al-Khaṭīb al-Baghdādī, *Taʾrīkh Baghdād*, ed. ʿAbd al-Qādir ʿAṭā, 20 vols., Beirut, 1997.
al-Ṣafadī, *al-Wāfī bi al-wafayāt*, ed. Helmut Ritter, Sven Dedering, Iḥsān ʿAbbās *et al.*, 30 vols., Leipzig, 1931–2004.
al-Sakhāwī, *al-Iʿlān bi-tawbīkh li-man dhamma ahl al-taʾrīkh*, ed. Franz Rosenthal, Baghdad, 1963.
Samawʾal al-Maghribī, *Ifḥām al-yahūd*, ed. and trans. Moshe Perlmann as *Silencing the Jews* in *Proceedings of the American Academy for Jewish Research*, 32 (1964).
al-Subkī, Tāj al-Dīn, *Ṭabaqāt al-Shafiʿīya al-kubrā*, ed. Maḥmūd al-Ṭanāḥī and ʿAbd al-Fattāḥ al-Ḥulw, 10 vols., Cairo, 1964–76.
al-Sulamī, *Dhikr al-niswa al-mutaʿabbidāt al-ṣūfīyat*, ed. and trans. Rkia Elaroui Cornell, as *Early Sufi women*, Louisville, 1999.
Ṭabaqāt al-ṣūfiyyah, ed. Nūr al-Dīn Sharība, 2nd edn, Cairo, 1969.

al-Suyūṭī, *Ta'rīkh al-khulafā'*, ed. Muḥyī al-Dīn 'Abd al-Ḥamīd, Cairo, 1952.

al-Yaghmurī, *Nūr al-qabas al-mukhtaṣar min al-muqtabas fī akhbār al-nuḥāh wa al-udabā' wa al-shu'arā' wa al-'ulamā'*, ed. Rudolf Sellheim, Wiesbaden, 1964.

Yāqūt al-Ḥamawī, *Mu'jam al-udabā'*, 5 vols., Beirut, 1991.

Secondary sources

Auchterlonie, Paul, *Arabic biographical dictionaries: A summary guide and bibliography*, Durham, 1987.

Bernards, Monique, *Changing traditions: al-Mubarrad's refutation of Sībawayh and the subsequent reception of the* Kitāb, Leiden, 1997.

de Bruijn, J. T. P., 'Tadhkira (in Persian literature)', *EI2*, vol. X, 53–4.

Brustad, Kristen, 'Imposing order: Reading the conventions of representation in al-Suyūṭī's autobiography', *Edebiyât: Special Issue – Arabic Autobiography*, n.s. 7, 2 (1997), 327–44.

Cooperson, Michael, 'Probability, plausibility, and "spiritual communication" in classical Arabic biography', in Philip F. Kennedy (ed.), *On fiction and* adab *in medieval Arabic literature*, Wiesbaden, 2005, 69–83.

Dickinson, Eerick, 'Aḥmad b. al-Ṣalt and his biography of Abū Ḥanīfa', *JAOS*, 116, 3 (1996), 406–17.

Eisener, Reinhard, *Zwischen Faktum und Fiktion: Eine Studie zum Umayyedenkalifen Sulaimān b. 'Abdalmalik und seinem Bild in den Quellen*, Wiesbaden, 1987.

Fähndrich, Hartmut, 'The *Wafayāt al-a'yān* of Ibn Khallikān: A new approach', *JAOS*, 93, 4 (1973), 432–45.

Gregg, Gary S., *Culture and identity in Morocco*, Oxford, 2007.

von Grunebaum, Gustave E., *Medieval Islam*, Chicago, 1946.

Homerin, T. Emil, *From Arab poet to Muslim saint: Ibn al-Fāriḍ, his verse, and his shrine*, Columbia, SC, 1994.

Jarrār, Maher, 'Bišr und die Barfüssigkeit in Islam', *Der Islam*, 71 (1994), 191–240.

Kilpatrick, Hilary, *Making the Great book of songs: Compilation and the author's craft in Abū l-Faraj al-Iṣbahānī's* Kitāb al-aghānī, London, 2003.

Leder, Stefan, 'Frühe Erzählungen zu Mağūn: Mağūn als Figur ohne Lebensgeschichte', in W. Diem and A. Falaturi (eds.), *XXIV Deutscher Orientalistentag (1988)*, Stuttgart, 1990, 150–61.

Malti-Douglas, Fedwa, 'Controversy and its effects in the biographical tradition of al-Khaṭīb al-Baghdādī', *SI*, 46 (1977), 115–31.

Melchert, Christopher, *The formation of the Sunni schools of law, 9th–10th centuries CE*, Leiden, 1997.

Mojaddedi, J. A., *The biographical tradition in Sufism: The* ṭabaqāt *genre from al-Sulamī to Jāmī*, Richmond, 2001.

Muranyi, Miklos, 'Zur Entwicklung der *'ilm al-riğāl*-Literatur im 3. Jahrhundert d. H. Qairawāner Miszellaneen IV', *ZDMG*, 142, 1 (1992), 57–71.

Rosenthal, Franz, *A history of Muslim historiography*, 2nd rev. edn, Leiden, 1964.

Sartain, Elizabeth, *Jalāl al-Dīn al-Suyuṭī*, vol. I: *Biography and background*; vol. II: *al-Taḥadduth bi ni'mat Allāh*, Cambridge, 1975.

Sellheim, Rudolf, 'Prophet, Calif, und Geschichte: Die Muhammed-Biographie des Ibn Isḥāq', *Oriens*, 18–19 (1967), 33–91.

Shryock, Andrew, *Nationalism and the genealogical imagination: Oral history and textual authority in tribal Jordan*, Berkeley, 1997.

Spellberg, Denise A., *Politics, gender, and the Islamic past: The legacy of ʿĀisha bint Abī Bakr*, New York, 1994.

Stewart-Robinson, J., 'The Ottoman biographies of poets', *JNES*, 24 (1965), 57–74.

'Tadhkira (in Turkish literature)', *EI2*, vol. X, 54–5.

Wensinck, A. J. A. *et al.* (eds.), *Concordance et indices de la tradition musulmane*, 8 vols., Leiden, 1933–88.

Chapter 19: Muslim accounts of the *dār al-ḥarb*

Practical suggestions for further reading

Alam, Muzaffar, and Sanjay Subrahmanyam, *Indo-Persian travels in the age of the discoveries, 1400–1800*, Cambridge, 2006.

Dunn, Ross E., *The adventures of Ibn Battuta, a Muslim traveler of the fourteenth century*, Berkeley and Los Angeles, 1989.

Euben, Roxanne L., *Journeys to the other shore: Muslim and Western travelers in search of knowledge*, Princeton, 2006.

Faroqhi, Suraiya, *The Ottoman empire and the world around it*, London, 2004.

Fisher, Michael H., *Counterflows to colonialism: Indian travellers and settlers in Britain 1600–1857*, New Delhi, 2004.

İhsanoğlu, Ekmeleddin (ed.), *Osmanlı coğrafya literatürü tarihi*, 2 vols., Istanbul, 2000.

Levtzion, N., and J. F. P. Hopkins (eds.), *Corpus of early Arabic sources on West African history*, Princeton, 2000.

Lewis, Bernard, *The Muslim discovery of Europe*, New York, 1982.

Matar, Nabil, *In the land of the Christians: Arabic travel writing in the seventeenth century*, New York and London, 2003.

Miquel, André, *La géographie humaine du monde musulman jusqu'au milieu du 11e siècle*, 4 vols., Paris and The Hague, 1967–88.

Netton, Ian Richard (ed.), *Golden roads: Migration, pilgrimage and travel in medieval and modern Islam*, Richmond, 1993.

Seek knowledge: Thought and travel in the house of Islam, Richmond, 1993.

Newman, Daniel, 'Arab travellers to Europe until the end of the eighteenth century and their accounts: Historical overview and themes', *Chronos*, 4 (2001), 7–61.

Tibbetts, Gerald Randall, *A study of the Arabic texts containing material on South-east Asia*, Leiden, 1979.

Touati, Houari, *Islam et voyage au moyen âge: Histoire et anthropologie d'une pratique lettrée*, Paris, 2000.

Primary sources

Abū Ḥāmid al-Gharnāṭī: see under Ferrand, G.

Aḥmad ibn Mājid: see under Tibbetts, Gerald.

al-Bīrūnī: see under Sachau, Eduard.

Babur, Zahiruddin Muhammad Mirza, *Bâburnâma: Chaghatay Turkish text with Abdul-Rahim Khankhanan's Persian translation*, Turkish transcription, Persian edn and English trans.

W. M. Thackston, Jr, 3 vols., Cambridge, MA, 1993; trans. W. M. Thackston as *The Baburnama: Memoirs of Babur, prince and emperor*, Washington, New York and Oxford, 1996.

Bacqué-Grammont, Jean-Louis (ed.), *La première histoire de France en turc ottoman: Chroniques des padichahs de France*, Paris, 1997.

Bellér-Hann, Ildikó, *A history of Cathay: A translation and linguistic analysis of a fifteenth-century Turkic manuscript*, Bloomington, 1995.

Bittner, M., and W. Tomaschek (ed. and trans.), *Die topographischen Kapitel des indischen Seespiegels Moḥîṭ*, Vienna, 1897.

Buzurg ibn Shahriyār of Ramhurmuz, *The book of the wonders of India: Mainland, sea and islands*, ed. and trans. G. S. P. Freeman-Grenville, London, 1980.

[Ebū Bekr Rāṭib], *Ebubekir Ratib Efendi'nin Nemçe Sefaretnamesi*, ed. Abdullah Uçman, Istanbul, 1999.

Evliyā Çelebi, *Evliya Çelebi Seyahatnâmesi: Topkapı Sarayı Bağdat 304 Yazmasının Transkripsiyonu, Dizini, Seyahatnâme*, ed. Orhan Şaik Gökyay, Istanbul, 1996–; partial trans. Richard F. Kreutel and Erich Prokosch as *Im Reiche des Goldenen Apfels: Des türkischen Weltenbummlers Evliyâ Çelebi denkwürdige Reise in das Giaurenland und in die Stadt und Festung Wien anno 1665*, Graz, Vienna and Cologne, 1985; partial trans. Erich Prokosch as *Ins Land der geheimnisvollen Func: Des türkischen Weltenbummlers, Evliyā Çelebi, Reise durch Oberägypten und den Sudan nebst der osmanischen Provinz Habeš in den Jahren 1672/73*, Graz, 1994.

Ferrand, Gabriel, 'Le *Tuḥfat al-albāb* de Abū Ḥāmid al-Andalusī al-Gharnāṭī édité d'après les Mss. 2167, 2168, 2170 de la Bibliothèque Nationale et le Ms. d'Alger', *Journal Asiatique*, 205 (1925), 1–148, 193–304; trans. Ana Ramos as *Tuḥfat al-Albāb = El Regalo de los Espíritus/Abū Ḥāmid al-Garnāṭī (m. 565/1169)*, Madrid, 1990.

Frye, Richard N., *Ibn Fadlan's journey to Russia: A tenth-century traveler from Baghdad to the Volga River*, Princeton, 2006.

Goodrich, Thomas D., *The Ottoman Turks and the new world: A study of* Tarih-i Hind-i garbi *and sixteenth-century Ottoman Americana*, Wiesbaden, 1990.

al-Ḥajarī, Aḥmad ibn Qāsim, *Kitāb nāṣir al-dīn ʿalā l-qawm al-kāfirīn*, ed. and trans. P. S. van Koningsveld, A. al-Samarrai and G. A. Wiegers, Madrid, 1997.

Ḥājjī Khalīfa: see under Kātib Çelebi.

Ibn Baṭṭūṭa, *The travels of Ibn Battuta*, trans. H. A. R. Gibb, 4 vols., Cambridge, 1958–94.

Ibn Faḍlān: see under Frye, Richard N.

Ibn Ḥawqal, Abū al-Qāsim, *Ṣūrat al-arḍ*, ed. J. H. Kramers, *BGA*, vol. II; trans. J. H. Kramers and G. Wiet as *Configuration de la terre (*Kitab surat al-ard*)*, 2 vols., Beirut, 1964.

Ibn Khurradādhbih, Abū al-Qāsim, *Kitāb al-masālik wa'l-mamālik*, ed. M. J. de Goeje, *BGA*, vol. VI, Leiden, 1889 (Arabic text and French translation).

Ibn Rustah, Aḥmad ibn ʿUmar, *al-Aʿlāq al-nafīsa*, ed. M. J. de Goeje, *BGA*, vol. VII, Leiden, 1892; trans. G. Wiet as *Les atours précieux*, Cairo, 1955.

Ibn Saʿīd al-Maghribī, ʿAlī ibn Mūsā, *Kitāb al-Jughrāfiyā*, Beirut, 1970.

al-Idrīsī, Abū ʿAbdallāh Muḥammad, *Nuzhat al-mushtāq fī ikhtirāq al-āfāq*, 9 fascicles, Naples, 1970–84.

Iṣfahānī, Mīrzā Abū Ṭālib, *Travels of Mirza Abu Taleb Khan*, trans. C. Stewart, New Delhi, 1972.

al-Iṣṭakhrī, Abū Isḥāq, *al-Masālik wal-mamālik*, ed. M. J. de Goeje, *BGA*, vol. I, Leiden, 1870.

I'tesamuddin, Mirza Sheikh (I'tiṣām al-dīn, Mīrzā Shaykh), *The wonders of Vilayet: Being the memoir, originally in Persian, of a visit to France, and Britain in 1765*, trans. Kaiser Haq, Leeds, 2001.

Itzkowitz, Norman, and Max E. Mote (ed. and trans.), *Mubadele: An Ottoman–Russian exchange of ambassadors*, Chicago, 1970.

Jwaideh, Wadie (ed. and trans.), *The introductory chapters of Yāqūt's* Muʿjam al-buldān, Leiden, 1959.

Kātib Çelebi (also known as Ḥājjī Khalīfa), *Jihān-nümā*, Istanbul, 1732.

Kashf al-ẓunūn ʿan asāmī l-kutub wal-funūn, ed. K. R. Bilge and Ş. Yaltkaya, 2 vols., Istanbul, 1941–3.

Khaṭāʾī, ʿAlī Akbar, *Khatāynāma: Sharḥ-e Mushāhadāt-e Sayyid ʿAlī Akbar Khaṭāʾī dar sarzamīn-e Chīn*, ed. Īrāj Afshār, 2nd edn, Tehran, 1993/4.

Kreutel, Richard F. (trans.), *Zwischen Paschas und Generälen: Bericht des ʿOsman Ağa aus Temeschwar über die Höhepunkte seines Wirkens als Diwansdolmetscher und Diplomat*, Graz, Vienna and Cologne, 1966.

Lech, Klaus, *Das Mongolische Weltreich: al-ʿUmarī's Darstellung der mongolischen Reiche in seinem Werk* Masālik al-abṣār fī mamālik al-amṣār, Wiesbaden, 1968.

Maʿjūncuzāde, Muṣṭafā Efendi, *Malta Esirleri*, ed. C. Çiftçi, Istanbul, 1996; also İz, Fahir, 'Macuncuzade Mustafa'nın Malta Anıları', *Türk Dili Araştırmaları Yıllığı Belleten* (1970), 69–122.

al-Masʿūdī, ʿAlī ibn al-Ḥusayn, *Murūj al-dhahab wa-maʿādin al-jawhar*, 5 vols., Beirut, 1962–97; trans. Barbier de Meynard and Pavet de Courteille, rev. Charles Pellat, *Les prairies d'or*, 3 vols., Paris, 1962–71.

Matuz, Josef, *L'ouvrage de Seyfi Çelebi, historien ottoman du XVIe siècle: Édition critique, traduction et commentaires*, Paris, 1968.

Mehmed Āşık, *Menāzirü 'l-avālim*, ed. M. Ak, 3 vols., Ankara, 2007.

Muḥammad Rabīʿ ibn Muḥammad Ibrāhīm, *Safīna-i Sulaymānī (Safarnāma-i safīr-i Īrān bi Sīyām) 1094–1098*, ed. ʿAbbās Fārūqī, Tehran, 1977; trans. John O'Kane as *The ship of Sulaimān*, New York and London, 1972.

al-Muqaddasī, Muḥammad ibn Aḥmad, *Aḥsan al-taqāsīm li-maʿrifat al-aqālīm*, ed. M. J. de Goeje, *BGA*, vol. III, Leiden, 1877; trans. Basil Collins as *The best divisions for knowledge of the regions*, Reading, 2001.

ʿOsmān Āghā, *Die Autobiographie des Dolmetschers ʿOsmān Āghā aus Temeschwar: Der Text des Londoner Autographen in normalisierter Rechtschreibung herausgegeben*, ed. R. F. Kreutel, Cambridge, 1980; ed. and trans. R. F. Kreutel and O. Spies as *Der Gefangene der Giauren: Die abenteuerlichen Schicksale des Dolmetschers 'Osman Ağa aus Temeschwar, von ihm selbst erzählt*, Graz, 1962; trans. Frédéric Hitzel as *Prisonnier des infidèles: Un soldat ottoman dans l'empire des Habsbourg*, Paris, 1998.

ʿOsmān Āghā: see also under Kreutel.

Piri Reis, *Kitabi bahriye*, ed. Fevzi Kurdoğlu and Haydar Alpagot, Istanbul, 1935; facsimile edn E. Z. Ökte with Turkish and English trans. as *Kitab-ı bahriye*, 4 vols., Istanbul, 1988.

al-Qazwīnī, Ḥamdallāh Mustawfī, *The geographical part of the* Nuzhat-al-qulūb *composed by Ḥamd-allāh Mustawfī*, ed. and trans. G. Le Strange, 2 vols., London and Leiden, 1915–19.

al-Qazwīnī, Zakarīyā ibn Muḥammad, *Zakarija Ben Muhammed Ben Mahmud el-Cazwini's Kosmographie* (ʿAjāʾib al-makhlūqāt and Āthār al-bilād), ed. F. Wüstenfeld, Göttingen, 1848–9.

Qudāma ibn Jaʿfar, *al-Kharāj wa-ṣināʿat al-kitāba*, ed. H. al-Zubaydī, Baghdad, 1981.

Rashīduddīn: see under Thackston, Wheeler M.

Sachau, Eduard (ed.), *al-Beruni's India: An account of the religion, philosophy, literature, chronology, astronomy, customs, laws and anthropology of India about AD 1030*, London, 1887, repr. Leipzig, 1925; English trans. Eduard Sachau under the same title, 2 vols., London, 1888–1910.

Sauvaget, Jean (ed. and trans.), *Relation de la Chine et de l'Inde (*Ahbār al-Sind wa l-Hind*)*, Paris, 1948.

Seydī ʿAlī Reʾīs (Kātib-i Rūmī), *Mir'at ül-memâlik*, Istanbul, 1896; new edn M. Kiremit as *Mir'âtü'l-memâlik*, Ankara, 1999; trans. J.-L., Bacqué-Grammont as *Le miroir des pays de Seyyidî Ali Re'is*, Paris, 1999.

Seydī ʿAlī Reʾīs: see also Bittner and Tomaschek; Vambéry

Seyfi Çelebi: see under Matuz, Josef.

Ṭahṭāwī, Rifāʿa Rāfiʿ, *Takhlīṣ al-ibrīz fī talkhīṣ Bārīz*, Cairo, 1993; trans. Daniel L. Newman as *An imam in Paris: Account of a stay in France by an Egyptian cleric (1826–1831)*, London, 2004.

Thackston, Wheeler M. (trans.), *Rashiduddin Fazlullah's Jamiʿu't-tawarikh = Compendium of chronicles: A history of the Mongols*, 3 vols., Cambridge, MA, 1998–9.

Tibbetts, Gerald Randall, *Arab navigation in the Indian Ocean before the coming of the Portuguese: Being a translation of* Kitāb al-fawāʾid fī uṣūl al-baḥr wa'l-qawāʿid *of Aḥmad b. Mājid al-Najdī; together with an introduction on the history of Arab navigation, notes on the navigational techniques and on the topography of the Indian Ocean and a glossary of navigational terms*, London, 1972.

al-ʿUmarī: see Lech, Klaus.

Vámbéry, Ármin, *The travels and adventures of the Turkish Admiral Sidi Ali Reïs in India, Afghanistan, Central Asia, and Persia, during the years 1553–1556: Translated from the Turkish, with notes*, Lahore, 1975.

Vatin, Nicolas, *Sultan Djem: Un prince ottoman dans l'Europe du XVe siècle d'après deux sources contemporaines: Vâḳıʿât-ı Sulṭān Cem, Œuvres de Guillaume Caoursin*, Ankara, 1997.

Yāqūt ibn ʿAbdallāh al-Ḥamawī, *Muʿjam al-buldān*, 5 vols., n.p. [Beirut?], 1955; see also under Jwaideh Wadie.

Jacut's Moschtarik [al-Mushtarik waḍʿan wal-muftarik ṣuqʿan], das ist, Lexicon geographischer Homonyme, ed. F. Wüstenfeld, Göttingen, 1846.

[Yirmisekiz Meḥmed Chelebi], *Yirmisekiz Çelebi Mehmed Efendi'nin Fransa sefâretnâmesi*, ed. B. Akyavas, Ankara, 1993; trans. Şevket Rado as *Yirmisekiz Mehmet Çelebi 'nin Fransa seyahatnamesi*, Istanbul, 1970; trans. A. Galland as *Le paradis des infidèles: Relation de Yirmisekiz Çelebi Mehmed efendi, ambassadeur ottoman en France sous la Régence*, ed. Gilles Veinstein, Paris, 1981.

Secondary sources

Aksan, Virginia, *An Ottoman statesman in war and peace: Ahmed Resmi Efendi, 1700–1783*, Leiden, 1995.

Allsen, Thomas T., *Culture and conquest in Mongol Eurasia*, Cambridge, 2004.

Arbel, Benjamin, 'Maps of the world for Ottoman princes? Further evidence and questions concerning "The Mappamondo of Hajji Ahmed"', *Imago Mundi*, 54 (2002), 19–29.

Asiltürk, Baki, *Osmanlı seyyahlarının gözüyle Avrupa*, Istanbul, 2000.

Bacqué-Grammont, Jean-Louis, 'Remarques sur les chemins de la découverte du monde par les Ottomans', in J.-L. Bacqué-Grammont *et al.* (eds.) *D'un orient l'autre: Actes des troisièmes journées de l'Orient, Bordeaux, 2–4 octobre 2002*, Paris and Louvain, 2005, 163–70.

Beeston, A. F. L., 'Idrīsī's account of the British Isles', *BSOAS*, 13 (1950), 265–80.

Berkes, Niyazi, *The development of secularism in Turkey*, Montreal, 1964.

Bonner, Michael, *Jihad in Islamic history*, Princeton, 2006.

Brummett, Palmira, 'Imagining the early modern Ottoman space, from world history to Pīrī Re'īs', in D. Goffman and V. Aksan (eds.), *The early modern Ottomans: Remapping the empire*, Cambridge, MA, 2007, 15–58.

Burçak, Berrak, 'The institution of the Ottoman embassy and eighteenth-century Ottoman history: An alternative view to Göçek', *International Journal of Turkish Studies* 13, 1–2 (2007), 147–51.

Casale, Giancarlo, '"His Majesty's servant Lutfi": The career of a previously unknown sixteenth-century Ottoman envoy to Sumatra', *Turcica*, 37 (2005), 43–82.

Cole, Juan R., 'Invisible occidentalism: Eighteenth-century Indo-Persian construction of the West', *Iranian Studies*, 25, 3–4 (1992), 3–16.

Conermann, Stephan, 'Das Eigene und das Fremde: Der Bericht der Gesandtschaft Mustafa Rasihs nach St Petersburg im Jahre 1792–1794', *Archivum Ottomanicum*, 17 (1999), 249–70.

Dankoff, Robert, *Evliya Çelebi: An Ottoman mentality*, Leiden and Boston, 2004.

Davis, Natalie Zemon, *Trickster travels: A sixteenth-century Muslim between worlds*, New York, 2006.

Dubler, César Emil, *Abū Ḥāmid el Granadino y su relación de viaje por tierras eurasiáticas: Texto árabe, traducción e interpretación*, Madrid, 1953.

Emiralioğlu, Pınar, 'Cognizance of the Ottoman world: Visual and textual representations in the sixteenth-century Ottoman empire (1514–1596)', Ph.D. thesis, University of Chicago, 2006.

Findley, Carter V., 'Ebu Bekir Ratib's Vienna embassy narrative: Discovering Austria or propagandizing for reform in Istanbul?', *Wiener Zeitschrift für die Kunde des Morgenlandes*, 85 (1995), 41–80.

Göçek, Fatma Müge, *East encounters West: France and the Ottoman empire in the eighteenth century*, New York, 1987.

Hagen, Gottfried, *Ein osmanischer Geograph bei der Arbeit: Entstehung und Gedankenwelt von Kātib Čelebis* Ǧihānnümā, Berlin, 2003.

Krachkovskii, I. J., *Izbraniye sochineniya*, vol. IV: *Arabskaya geograficheskaya literatura*, Moscow and Leningrad, 1957.

Kropp, Manfred, '*Kitāb ǧuġrāfiyā* des Ibn Fāṭima: Eine unbekannte Quelle des Ibn Saʿīd oder "Neues" von al-Idrīsī?', in *Un ricordo che non si spegne: Scritti di docenti e collaboratori dell'Istituto Universitario Orientale di Napoli in memoria di Alessandro Bausani*, Naples, 1996, 163–79.

Ménage, Victor L., 'Three Ottoman treatises on Europe', in C. E. Bosworth (ed.), *Iran and Islam: In memory of the late Victor Minorsky*, Edinburgh, 1971, 421–33.

Mottahedeh, Roy, and Ridwan al-Sayyid, 'The idea of *jihad* in Islam before the Crusades', in A. E. Laiou and R. P. Mottahedeh (eds.), *The Crusades from the perspective of Byzantium and the Muslim world*, Washington, DC, 2001, 23–9.

von Mžik, Hans, 'Mythische Geographie', *Wiener Zeitschrift für die Kunde des Morgenlandes*, 45 (1938), 85–108.

'*Parageographische Elemente in den Berichten der arabischen Geographen über Südostasien*', in H. von Mžik (ed.), *Beiträge zur historischen Geographie, Kulturgeographie, Ethnographie, und Kartographie (Festschrift Eugen Oberhummer)*, Leipzig and Vienna, 1929, 172–202.

Özdemir, Kemal, *Ottoman nautical charts and the Atlas of Ali Macar Reis*, Istanbul, 1992.

Prokosch, Erich, *Ins Land der geheimnisvollen Func: Des türkischen Weltenbummlers, Evliyā Çelebi, Reise durch Oberägypten und den Sudan nebst der osmanischen Provinz Habeš in den Jahren 1672/73*, Graz, 1994.

Radtke, Bernd, *Weltgeschichte und Weltbeschreibung im mittelalterlichen Islam*, Stuttgart, 1992.

Rosenthal, Franz, *A history of Muslim historiography*, Leiden, 1968.

Rührdanz, Karin, 'Illustrated Persian *'Ajā'ib al-makhlūqāt* manuscripts and their function in early modern times', in A. J. Newman (ed.), *Society and culture in the early modern Middle East: Studies on Iran in the Safavid period*, Leiden, 2003, 33–47.

Sabev, Orlin, *İbrahim Müteferrika ya da ilk Osmanlı matbaa serüveni (1726–1746): Yeniden değerlendirme*, Istanbul, 2006.

Schmidt, Jan, *Pure water for thirsty Muslims: A study of Muṣṭafā 'Ālī of Gallipoli's* Künhü l-ahbār, Leiden, 1991.

Şehsuvaroğlu, Bedi N., 'Kânûnî devrinde yazılmış ve şimdiye kadar bilinmeyen bir coğrafya kitabı', in *Kanunî Armağanı*, Ankara, 1970, 207–25.

Serrao, Elisabetta, 'La descrizione di Napoli nel *Kitāb-ı baḥriyye* di Pīrī Re'īs', in U. Marazzi (ed.), *Turcica et islamica: Studi in memoria di Aldo Gallotta*, Naples, 2003, 909–40.

Sezgin, Fuat, *Mathematical geography and cartography in Islam*, trans. G. Moore and G. Sammon, 3 vols., Frankfurt, 2000–7.

Soucek, Svatopluk, *Piri Reis and Turkish mapmaking after Columbus: The Khalili portolan atlas*, London, 1996.

'Tunisia in the *Kitāb-ı baḥrīye* by Pīrī Re'īs', *Archivum Ottomanicum*, 5 (1973), 129–296.

Storey, C. A., and Y. E. Bregel, *Persidskaia literatura: Bio-bibliograficheskii obzor*, Moscow, 1972.

Teply, Karl, *Türkische Sagen und Legenden um die Kaiserstadt Wien*, Vienna, Cologne and Graz, 1980.

Terzioğlu, Derin, 'Autobiography in fragments: Reading Ottoman personal miscellanies in the early modern era', in O. Akyıldız, H. Kara and B. Sagaster (eds.), *Autobiographical themes in Turkish literature: Theoretical and comparative perspectives*, Würzburg, 2007, 83–99.

Thanasakis, Konstantinos, 'The Ottoman geographer Osman b. Abdülmennan and his vision of the world in *Tercüme-i Kitāb-i coğrāfyā* (ca. 1749–1750)', MA thesis, Boğaziçi University, 2006.

Unat, Faik Reşit, and Bekir Sıtkı Baykal, *Osmanlı sefirleri ve sefaretnameleri*, Ankara, 1968.

Vatin, Nicolas, 'Pourquoi un Turc ottoman racontait-il son voyage? Note sur les relations de voyage chez les Ottomans des *Vâkı'ât-ı Sulṭân Cem* au *Seyâhatnâme* d'Evliyâ Çelebi', in *Études turques et ottomanes: Document de travail no. 4 de l'URA du CNRS (décembre 1995)*, Paris, 1995, 3–15.

Wansbrough, John, *Lingua franca in the Mediterranean*, Richmond, 1996.

Wiegers, Gerard, 'A life between Europe and the Maghrib: The writings and travels of Aḥmad b. Qāsim ibn al-faqīh ibn al-shaykh al-Ḥajarī al-Andalusī (born c. 977/1569–70)', in G.J. van Gelder and E. Moor (eds.), *The Middle East and Europe: Encounters and exchanges*, Amsterdam and Atlanta, 1992, 87–115.

Chapter 20: Education

Practical suggestions for further reading

Berkey, Jonathan, *The transmission of knowledge in medieval Cairo: A social history of Islamic education*, Princeton, 1992.

Makdisi, George, *The rise of colleges: Institutions of learning in Islam and the West*, Edinburgh, 1981.

Robinson, Francis, *The ʿulama of Farangi Mahall and Islamic culture in South Asia*, Delhi, 2001.

Primary sources

al-Ghazālī, Abū Ḥāmid Muḥammad, *Imam Gazzali's Ihya ulum-id-din*, trans. al-Haj Maulana Fazul-ul-Karim, Lahore, n.d.

Ibn Jamāʿa, Badr al-Dīn Muḥammad, *Tadhkirat al-sāmiʿ wa'l mutakallim fī adab al-ʿālim wa'l-mutaʿallim*, Hyderabad, AH 1353.

Ibn Khaldūn, *The* Muqaddimah*: An introduction to history*, trans. Franz Rosenthal, 2nd edn, 4 vols., London, 1967.

al-Sakhāwī, Shams al-Dīn Muḥammad, *al-Ḍawʾ al-lāmiʿ li-ahl al-qarn al-tāsiʿ*, Cairo, 1934.

az-Zarnūjī, Burhān al-Dīn, *Taʿlīm al-mutaʿallim, ṭarīq at-taʿallum. Instruction of the student: The method of learning*, trans. G. E. Von Grunebaum and Theodora M. Abel, New York, 1947.

Secondary sources

Arberry, A. J., *Sakhawiana*, London, 1951.

Arjomand, Saïd Amir, 'The law, agency, and policy in medieval Islamic society: Development of the institutions of learning from the tenth to the fifteenth century', *Comparative Studies in Society and History*, 41, 2 (1999), 263–93.

Azra, Asyumadi, *The origins of Islamic reform in Southeast Asia: Networks of Malay-Indonesian and Middle Eastern ʿulama in the seventeenth and eighteenth centuries*, Honolulu, 2004.

Berkey, Jonathan P., *Popular preaching and religious authority in the medieval Islamic Near East*, Seattle, 2001.

Boyd, Jean, *The caliph's sister: Nana Asmaʾu 1793–1865, teacher, poet and Islamic leader*, London, 1989.

Chamberlain, Michael, *Knowledge and social practice in medieval Damascus*, Cambridge, 1994.

Ephrat, Daphna, *A learned society in a period of transition: The Sunni 'ulama' of eleventh-century Baghdad*, Albany, 2000.

Ernst, Carl, *The Shambhala guide to Sufism*, Boston, 1997.

Gil'adi, Avner, *Children of Islam: Concepts of childhood in medieval Muslim society*, Basingstoke, 1992.

Hanna, Nelly, *In praise of books: A cultural history of Cairo's middle class, sixteenth to the eighteenth century*, Syracuse, 2003.

'Literacy and the "great divide" in the Islamic world, 1300–1800', *Journal of Global History*, 2, 2 (2007), 175–93.
Hunwick, John O., and Alida Jay Boye, *The hidden treasures of Timbuktu*, London, 2008.
Inalcik, Halil, *The Ottoman empire: The classical age 1300–1600*, trans. N. Itzkowitz and C. Imber, London, 1973.
Lowry, Joseph E., Devin J. Stewart and Shawkat M. Toorawa (eds.), *Law and education in medieval Islam: Studies in memory of Professor George Makdisi*, E. J. W. Gibb Memorial Trust, Chippenham, 2004.
Makdisi, George, *Ibn ʿAqil: Religion and culture in classical Islam*, Edinburgh, 1997.
The rise of humanism in classical Islam and the Christian West with special reference to scholasticism, Edinburgh, 1990.
Miller, Barnette, *The Palace School of Muhammad the Conqueror*, Cambridge, MA, 1941.
Pedersen, J., *The Arabic book*, ed. R. Hillenbrand, trans. G. French, Princeton, 1984.
Pedersen, J., and G. Makdisi, 'Madrasa', *EI2*, vol. V, 1123–34.
Reese, Scott (ed.), *The transmission of learning in Islamic Africa*, Leiden, 2004.
Riddell, Peter, *Islam and the Malay-Indonesian world*, London, 2001.
Rosenthal, Franz, *Knowledge triumphant: The concept of knowledge in medieval Islam*, Leiden, 1970.
Saad, Elias, N., *The social history of Timbuktu: The role of Muslim scholars and notables 1400–1900*, Cambridge, 1983.
Sanneh, Lamin O., 'The Islamic education of an African child: Stresses and tensions', in Godfrey N. Brown and Mervyn Hiskett (eds.), *Conflict and harmony in education in tropical Africa*, London, 1975, 168–86.
The Jakhanke: The history of an Islamic clerical people of the Senegambia, London, 1979.
Sartain, Elizabeth, *Jalāl al-Dīn al-Suyūṭī: Biography and background*, Cambridge, 1975.
Schimmel, Annemarie, *The mystical dimensions of Islam*, Chapel Hill, 1975.
Subtelny, Maria Eva, 'A Timurid educational and charitable foundation: The Ikhlāṣiyya complex of ʿAlī Shīr Navāʾī in 15th-century Herat and its endowment', *JAOS*, 111, 1 (1991), 38–61.
Subtelny, Maria Eva, and Anas B. Khalidov, 'The curriculum of Islamic higher learning in Timurid Iran in the light of the Sunni revival under Shah-Rukh', *JAOS*, 115, 2 (1995), 210–36.
Wilks, Ivor, 'The transmission of Islamic learning in the western Sudan', in Jack Goody (ed.), *Literacy in traditional societies*, Cambridge, 1968, 162–97.

Chapter 21: Philosophy

Practical suggestions for further reading

Adamson, Peter, and R. C. Taylor (eds.), *The Cambridge companion to Arabic philosophy*, Cambridge, 2005.
van Ess, Josef, *Theologie und Gesellschaft im 2. und 3. Jahrhundert Hidschra: Eine Geschichte des religiösen Denkens im frühen Islam*, 6 vols., Berlin and New York, 1991–7.
Fakhry, Majid, *A history of Islamic philosophy*, 2nd edn, London and New York, 1983.
McGinnis, Jon, and D. C. Reisman (ed. and trans.), *Classical Arabic philosophy. An anthology of sources*, Indianapolis, 2007.

Nasr, Seyyed Hossein, and O. Leaman (eds.), *History of Islamic philosophy*, London and New York, 1996, 2001.

Winter, Tim (ed.), *The Cambridge companion to classical Islamic theology*, Cambridge, 2008.

Zalta, Edward N. (ed.), *The Stanford encyclopedia of philosophy*, available at http://plato.stanford.edu.

Primary sources

al-ʿĀmirī, *Kitāb al-amad ʿalā al-abad*, in Everett K. Rowson (ed. and trans.), *A Muslim philosopher on the soul and its fate: al-ʿĀmirī's Kitāb al-amad ʿalā l-abad*, New Haven, 1988.

Kitāb al-fuṣūl fī l-maʿālim al-ilāhīya, in Elvira Wakelnig (ed. and trans.), *Feder, Tafel, Mensch: al-ʿĀmirī's Kitāb al-fuṣūl fī l-maʿālim al-ilāhīya und die arabische Proklos-Rezeption im 10. Jh*, Leiden, 2006.

al-Ashʿarī, *Kitāb al-lumaʿ*, in Richard J. McCarthy, SJ, (ed. and trans.), *The theology of al-Ashʿarī*, Beirut, 1953.

Averroes, *Averroes (Ibn Rushd) of Cordoba: Long commentary on the* De anima *of Aristotle*, trans. Richard C. Taylor, with Therese-Anne Druart, New Haven and London, 2009.

Averroès Tafsīr mā baʿd aṭ-ṭabīʿat, ed. Maurice Bouyges, S J, 4 vols., Beirut, 1938–52.

Averroës: Tahafot at-tahafot, ed. Maurice Bouyges, SJ, Beirut, 1930; trans. Simon Van Den Bergh as *Averroes' Tahafut al-tahafut (The incoherence of the incoherence)*, 2 vols., London, 1969.

Ibn Rushd (Averroes): Kitāb faṣl al-maqāl, ed. George F. Hourani, Leiden, 1959; trans. Charles E. Butterworth as *Averroës: The book of the decisive treatise determining the connection between the law and wisdom & epistle dedicatory*, Provo, UT, 2001.

al-Kashf ʿan manāhij al-adillah fī ʿaqāʾid al-milla, ed. Muhammad ʿĀbid al-Jābrī, 2nd edn, Beirut, 2001, trans. Ibrahim Najjar in *Averroes' exposition of religious arguments*, Oxford, 2001.

Avicenna, *Avicenna's* De anima *(Arabic text) being the psychological part of* Kitāb al-shifāʾ, ed. F. Rahman, London, 1959.

Avicenna: The metaphysics of the healing, trans. Michael E. Marmura, Provo, UT, 2005.

al-Ishārāt wa-l-tanbīhāt, ed. S. Dunyā, 4 vols., Cairo, 1960–6, trans. A.-M. Goichon in *Ibn Sīnā, livre des directives et remarques*, Beirut and Paris, 1951.

al-Fārābī, *Alfarabi: Risalat fi 'l-ʿaql*, ed. Maurice Bouyges, S J, 2nd edn, Beirut, 1983.

al-Farabi's commentary and short treatise on Aristotle's De interpretatione, trans. F. W. Zimmermann, London, 1981.

al-Fārābī's The political regime (al-Siyāsa al-madaniyya *also known as the* Treatise on the principles of beings), ed. Fauzi Najjar, Beirut, 1964.

On the perfect state (Mabādiʾ ārāʾ ahl al-madīna al-fāḍila), ed. and trans. Richard Walzer, Oxford, 1985.

al-Ghazālī, *The incoherence of the philosophers/Tahāfut al-falāsifa, a parallel English–Arabic text*, ed. and trans. M. E. Marmura, Provo, UT, 1997.

al-Munqidh min al-ḍalāl/Erreur et délivrance, ed. and trans. F. Jabre, Beirut, 1959; trans. Richard Joseph McCarthy, SJ in *Freedom and fulfillment: An annotated translation of al-Ghazālī's al-Munqidh min al-ḍalāl and other relevant works by al-Ghazālī*, Boston, 1980; repr. as *al-Ghazali's path to Sufism*, Louisville, 2000.

Ibn al-Nadīm, *Kitāb al-fihrist*, ed. G. Flügel, 2 vols., Leipzig, 1871–2; also in *Kitāb al-fihrist*, ed. M. Riḍā Tajaddud, Tehran, 1971; trans. Bayard Dodge in *The* Fihrist *of al-Nadim*, 2 vols., New York, 1970.

Ibn Bājja, *Risālat ittiṣāl al-ʿaql bi-l-insān*, ed. and trans. Miguel Asín Palacios in 'Tratado de Avempace sobre la union del intelecto con el hombre', *al-Andalus*, 7 (1942), 1–47; English trans. in Jon McGinnis and D. C. Reisman (ed. and trans.), *Classical Arabic philosophy: An anthology of sources*, Indianapolis, 2007, 269–83.

al-Ījī, ʿAḍud al-Dīn, *Kitāb al-mawāqif fī ʿilm al-kalām*, ed. ʿAbd al-Raḥmān ʿUmayrah, 3 vols., Beirut, 1997; partial German trans. Josef van Ess in *Die Erkenntnislehre des ʿAḍudaddīn al-Īcī: Übersetzung und Kommentar des ersten Buches seiner Mawāqif*, Wiesbaden, 1966.

al-Kindī, *al-Kindī's metaphysics: A translation of Yaʿqūb ibn Isḥāq al-Kindī's treatise 'On first philosophy'* (*Fī al-falsafah al-ūlā*), trans. Alfred L. Ivry, Studies in Islamic Philosophy and Science, Albany, 1974.

Oeuvres philosophiques et scientifiques d'al-Kindī, 2 vols., ed. Roshdi Roshed and Jean Jolivet, Leiden, 1997–8.

Plotinus apud Arabes, ed. A. Badawi, Cairo, 1947; English trans. of most of the *Plotiniana Arabica* by G. Lewis is available in *Plotini opera*, vol. II: *Enneades IV–V*, ed. P. Henry and H.-R. Schwyzer, Paris and Brussels, 1959.

al-Rāzī, Abū Bakr, *The spiritual physick of Rhazes*, trans. A. J. Arberry, London, 1950.

al-Suhrawardī, *The philosophy of illumination*, ed. and trans. John Walbridge and Hossein Ziai, Provo, UT, 1999.

Secondary sources

Adamson, Peter, *The Arabic Plotinus: A philosophical study of the 'Theology of Aristotle'*, London, 2002.

'al-Kindī and the Muʿtazila: Divine attributes, creation and freedom', *Arabic Sciences and Philosophy*, 13 (2003), 45–77.

'The *Theology* of Aristotle', in Edward N. Zalta (ed.), *The Stanford encyclopedia of philosophy*, available at http://plato.stanford.edu/entries/theology-aristotle/, first published 5 June 2008.

Al-Rahim, Ahmed H., 'The Twelver-Shīʿī reception of Avicenna in the Mongol period', in David C. Reisman (ed.), *Before and after Avicenna: Proceedings of the First Conference of the Avicenna Study Group*, Leiden and Boston, 2003, 219–31.

Altmann, Alexander, 'Ibn Bajja on man's ultimate felicity', in *Harry Austryn Wolfson jubilee volume*, 3 vols., Jerusalem, 1965, vol. I, 47–87.

Arnzen, Rüdiger, 'The structure of Mullā Ṣadra's *al-Ḥikma al-mutaʿāliya fī l-asfār al-ʿaqliyya al-arbaʿa* and his concepts of first philosophy and divine science: An essay', *Medioevo*, 32 (2007), 199–239.

Baffioni, Carmela, 'Ikhwan al-Safa', in Edward N. Zalta (ed.), *The Stanford encyclopedia of philosophy*, available at http://plato.stanford.edu/entries/ikhwan-al-safa/, first published 22 April 2008.

Bello, Catarina, 'Muʿtazilites, al-Ashʿarī and Maimonides on divine attributes', *Veritas* (Porto Alegre), 52 (2007), 117–31.

Black, Deborah L., 'Knowledge (*ʿilm*) and certitude (*yaqīn*) in al-Fārābī's epistemology', *Arabic Sciences and Philosophy*, 16 (2006), 11–45.

Bucur, C., and B. G. Bucur, '"The place of splendor and light": Observations on the paraphrasing of *Enn.* 4.8.1 in the *Theology of Aristotle*', *Le Muséon*, 119 (2006), 271–92.

Burnett, Charles, 'The "Sons of Averroes with the emperor Frederick" and the transmission of the philosophical works by Ibn Rushd', in Gerhard Endress and Jan A. Aertsen (eds.), *Averroes and the Aristotelian tradition: Sources, constitution and reception of the philosophy of Ibn Rushd (1126–1198): Proceedings of the Fourth Symposium Averroicum, Cologne, 1996*, Leiden, 1999, 259–99.

Colmo, Christopher A., *Breaking with Athens: Alfarabi as founder*, Lanham, MD, 2005.

Conrad, Lawrence I. (ed.), *The world of Ibn Ṭufayl: Interdisciplinary perspectives on Ḥayy ibn Yaqẓān*, Leiden and New York, 1996.

D'Ancona, Cristina, 'Greek into Arabic: Neoplatonism in translation', in Peter Adamson and R. C. Taylor (eds.), *The Cambridge companion to Arabic philosophy*, Cambridge, 2005, 10–31.

'Greek sources in Arabic and Islamic philosophy', in Edward N. Zalta, (ed.), *The Stanford encyclopedia of philosophy*, available at http://plato.stanford.edu/entries/arabic-islamic-greek/, first published 23 February 2009.

D'Ancona, Cristina, and Richard C. Taylor, 'Le *Liber de causis*', in Richard Goulet *et al.* (eds.), *Dictionnaire de philosophes antiques: Supplément*, Paris, 2003, 599–647.

Davidson, Herbert A., *Alfarabi, Avicenna, and Averroes on intellect: Their cosmologies, theories of active intellect and theories of human intellect*, New York, 1992.

Proofs for eternity, creation, and the existence of God in medieval Islamic and Jewish philosophy, New York and Oxford, 1987.

Dhanani, A., *The physical theory of kalām: Atoms, space, and void in Basrian Muʿtazili cosmology*, Leiden, 1994.

Druart, Thérèse-Anne, 'al-Fārābī (870–958): Une éthique universelle fondée sur les intelligibles premiers', in Louis-Léon Christians *et al.* (eds.), *Droit naturel: Relancer l'histoire?*, Brussels, 2008, 215–32.

Eichner, Heidrun, 'Dissolving the unity of metaphysics: From Fakhr al-Dīn al-Rāzī to Mullā Ṣadra al-Shīrāzī', *Medioevo*, 32 (2007), 139–97.

El Ghannouchi, A., 'Distinction et relation des discours philosophiques et religieux chez Ibn Rushd: *Fasl al maqal* ou la double verité', in R. G. Khoury (ed.), *Averroes (1126–1198) oder der Triumph des Rationalisimus: Internationales Symposium anlässlich des 800: Todestages des islamischen Philosophen*, Heidelberg, 2002, 139–45.

Endress, Gerhard, 'The circle of al-Kindī: Early Arabic translations from the Greek and the rise of Islamic philosophy', in Gerhard Endress and Remke Kruk (eds.), *The ancient tradition in Christian and Islamic Hellenism*, Leiden, 1997, 43–76.

'al-Kindī's theory of anamnesis: A new text and its implications', in *Islão e arabismo na Península Ibérica: Actas do XI Congreso da União Europaeia de Arabistas e Islamólogos*, Évora, 1986, 393–402.

The works of Yaḥyā Ibn ʿAdī: An analytical inventory, Wiesbaden, 1977.

Frank, R. M., 'Elements in the development of the teaching of Ashʿari', *Le Muséon*, 104 (1991), 141–90; repr. in Dimitri Gutas (ed.), *Richard M. Frank: Early Islamic theology: The Muʿtazilites and al-Ashʿarī: Texts and studies on the development and history of kalām*, vol. II, Aldershot, 2005.

'The science of *kalām*', *Arabic Sciences and Philosophy*, 2 (1992), 7–37.

Geoffroy, Marc, 'La tradition arabe du *Peri nou* d'Alexandre d'Aphrodise et les origines de la théorie farabienne des quatre degrés de l'intellect', in Cristina D'Ancona and

Giuseppe Serra (eds.), *Aristotele e Alessandro di Afrodisia nella tradizione Araba*, Subsidia Mediaevalia Patavina 3, Padua, 2002, 191–231.

Gimaret, D., 'Mu'tazila', *EI2*, vol. VII, 782–93, available at www.brillonline.nl/subscriber/entry?entry=islam_COM-0822, Marquette University, 1 February 2009.

Goodman, L. E., 'al-Rāzī, Abū Bakr Muḥammad b. Zakariyyā', *EI2*, vol. VIII, 474–5, available at http://www.brillonline.nl/subscriber/entry?entry=islam_SIM-6267, Marquette University, 28 February 2009.

Griffel, Frank, 'al-Ghazālī', in Edward N. Zalta (ed.), *The Stanford encyclopedia of philosophy*, available at http://plato.stanford.edu/entries/al-ghazali/, first published 14 September 2007.

'MS London, British Library Or. 3126: An unknown work by al-Ghazālī on metaphysics and philosophical theology', *Journal of Islamic Studies*, 17 (2006), 1–42.

Griffith, Sidney H., *The church in the shadow of the mosque: Christians and Muslims in the world of Islam*, Princeton and Oxford, 2008.

Gutas, Dimitri, 'The "Alexandria to Baghdad" complex of narratives. A contribution to the study of philosophical and medical historiography among the Arabs', *Documenti e Studi sulla Tradizione Filosofica Medievale*, 10 (1999), 155–93.

Avicenna and the Aristotelian tradition: Introduction to reading Avicenna's philosophical works, Leiden, 1988.

Greek thought, Arabic culture: The Graeco-Arabic translation movement in Baghdad and early 'Abbāsid society (2nd–4th/8th–10th centuries), New York and London, 1998.

Harvey, Steven, 'Arabic into Hebrew: The Hebrew translation movement and the influence of Averroes upon Jewish thought', in Daniel H. Frank and Oliver Leaman (eds.), *The Cambridge companion to medieval Jewish philosophy*, Cambridge, 2003, 258–80.

Janssens, Jules, 'Bahmanyār ibn Marzubān: A faithful disciple of Ibn Sīnā?', in David C. Reisman (ed.), *Before and after Avicenna: Proceedings of the First Conference of the Avicenna Study Group*, Leiden and Boston, 2003, 177–97.

'Bahmanyār and his revision of Ibn Sīnā's metaphysical project', *Medioevo*, 32 (2007), 99–117.

Kraemer, Joel L., *Philosophy in the renaissance of Islam: Abū Sulaymān al-Sijistānī and his circle*, Leiden, 1986.

Kukkonen, Taneli, 'Nature and Neo-Platonic Ethics in *Ḥayy Ibn Yaqẓān*', *Journal of the History of Philosophy*, 46 (2008), 187–204.

Marmura, Michael, 'Avicenna's "Flying Man" in context', *Monist*, 69 (1986), 383–95.

Martin, Richard C., and Mark R. Woodward, with Dwi S. Atmaja, *Defenders of reason in Islam: Mu'tazilism from medieval school to modern symbol*, Oxford, 1997.

Mayer, Toby, 'Fakhr ad-Dīn ar-Rāzī's critique of Ibn Sīnā's argument for the unity of God in the *Ishārāt*, and Naṣīr ad-Dīn aṭ-Ṭūsī's defence', in David C. Reisman (ed.), *Before and after Avicenna: Proceedings of the First Conference of the Avicenna Study Group*, Leiden and Boston, 2003, 199–218.

McGinnis, Jon, 'Arabic and Islamic natural philosophy and natural science', in Edward N. Zalta (ed.), *The Stanford encyclopedia of philosophy*, available at http://plato.stanford.edu/entries/arabic-islamic-natural/, first published 19 December 2006.

Murphy, Mark, 'Theological voluntarism', in Edward N. Zalta (ed.), *The Stanford encyclopedia of philosophy*, available at http://plato.stanford.edu/entries/voluntarism-theological/, first published 8 January 2008.

O'Meara, Dominic, *Platonopolis: Platonic political philosophy in Late Antiquity*, Oxford, 2005.

Pessin, Sarah, 'Jewish Neoplatonism: Being above being and divine emanation in Solomon ibn Gabirol and Isaac Israeli', in Daniel H. Frank and Oliver Leaman (eds.), *The Cambridge companion to medieval Jewish philosophy*, Cambridge, 2003, 91–110.

Puig Montada, Josep, 'Ibn Bajja', in Edward N. Zalta (ed.), *The Stanford encyclopedia of philosophy*, available at http://plato.stanford.edu/entries/ibn-bajja/, first published 28 September 2007.

'Philosophy in Andalusia: Ibn Bājja and Ibn Ṭufayl', in Peter Adamson and R. C. Taylor (eds.), *The Cambridge companion to Arabic philosophy*, Cambridge, 2005, 153–79.

Rashed, M., 'Natural philosophy', in Peter Adamson and R. C. Taylor (eds.), *The Cambridge companion to Arabic philosophy*, Cambridge, 2005, 287–307.

Rizvi, Sajjad, 'Process metaphysics in Islam? Avicenna and Mullā Ṣadra on intensification in being', in David C. Reisman (ed.), *Before and after Avicenna: Proceedings of the First Conference of the Avicenna Study Group*, Leiden and Boston, 2003, 233–47.

Sabra, A. I., 'Science and philosophy in medieval Islamic theology: The evidence of the fourteenth century', *ZGAIW*, 9 (1994), 1–42.

Shihadeh, Ayman, *The teleological ethics of Fakhr al-Dīn al-Rāzī*, Leiden, 2006.

Strohmaier, G., 'Homer in Bagdad', *Byzantinoslavica*, 41 (1980), 196–200.

'Ḥunayn b. Isḥāḳ al-ʿIbādī', *EI2*, vol. III, 578–9, available at 'www.brillonline.nl/subscriber/entry?entry=islam_COM-0300', Marquette University, 27 February 2009.

Takahashi, Hidemi, 'The reception of Ibn Sīnā in Syriac: The case of Gregory Barhebraeus', in David C. Reisman (ed.), *Before and after Avicenna: Proceedings of the First Conference of the Avicenna Study Group*, Leiden and Boston, 2003, 249–81.

Tarrant, H., *Thrasyllan Platonism*, Ithaca and London, 1993.

Taylor, Richard C., 'Abstraction in al-Fārābī', *Proceedings of the American Catholic Philosophical Association*, 80 (2006), 151–68.

'Aquinas, the *Plotiniana Arabica*, and the metaphysics of being and actuality', *Journal of the History of Ideas*, 59 (1998), 217–39.

'"Truth does not contradict truth": Averroes and the unity of truth', *Topoi*, 19 (2000), 3–16.

Vallat, Philippe, *Farabi et l'École d'Alexandrie: Des prémisses de la connaissance à la philosophie politique*, Paris, 2004.

Walbridge, John, 'Suhrawardī and illuminationism', in Peter Adamson and R. C. Taylor (eds.), *The Cambridge companion to Arabic philosophy*, Cambridge, 2005, 201–23.

Walker, Paul E., 'The Ismāʿīlīs', in Peter Adamson and R. C. Taylor (eds.), *The Cambridge companion to Arabic philosophy*, Cambridge, 2005, 72–91.

Wisnovsky, Robert, 'Avicenna and the Avicennian tradition', in Peter Adamson and R. C. Taylor (eds.), *The Cambridge companion to Arabic philosophy*, Cambridge, 2005, 92–136.

Avicenna's metaphysics in context, Ithaca, 2003.

Wolfson, Harry A. , *The philosophy of the kalam*, Cambridge, MA, and London, 1976.

Ziai, Hossein, 'Recent trends in Arabic and Persian philosophy', in Peter Adamson and R. C. Taylor (eds.), *The Cambridge companion to Arabic philosophy*, Cambridge, 2005, 405–25.

Chapter 22: Sciences in Islamic societies

Practical suggestions for further reading

Gutas, Dimitri, *Greek thought, Arabic culture: The Graeco-Arabic translation movement in Baghdad and early ʿAbbāsid society (2nd–4th/8th–10th centuries)*, New York and London, 1998.

Harley, J. B., and David Woodward (eds.), *The history of cartography*, vol. II, book 1: *Cartography in the traditional Islamic and South Asian societies*, Chicago and London, 1992.

Ibn Khaldūn, *The* Muqaddimah*: An introduction to history*, trans. Franz Rosenthal, 3 vols., 2nd edn, Princeton, 1980.

Kennedy, Edward S., *et al.*, *Studies in the Islamic exact sciences*, ed. David A. King and Mary Helen Kennedy, Beirut, 1983.

Ragep, F. Jamil (ed., trans. and comm.), *Naṣīr al-Dīn al-Ṭūsī's memoir on astronomy (*al-Tadhkira fī ʿilm al-hay'a*)*, 2 vols., Berlin, 1993.

Rashed, Roshdi and Régis Morelon (eds.), *Encyclopedia of the history of Arabic science*, 3 vols., New York and London, 1996.

Saliba, George, *A history of Arabic astronomy: Planetary theories during the golden age of Islam*, New York, 1994.

Islamic science and the making of the European Renaissance, Cambridge, MA, 2007.

Sayılı, Aydın, *The observatory in Islam and its place in the general history of the observatory*, Ankara, 1960.

Primary sources

al-Bīrūnī, *Kitāb maqālīd ʿilm al-hay'a: La trigonométrie sphérique chez les Arabes de l'est à la fin du Xe siècle*, ed. and trans. Marie-Thérèse Debarnot, Damascus, 1985.

Kitāb al-qānūn al-masʿūdī, 3 vols., Hyderabad, 1954–6.

Kitāb taḥdīd nihāyāt al-amākin li-taṣḥīḥ masāfāt al-masākin, ed. P. G. Bulgakov, Cairo, 1964.

al-Biṭrūjī, *On the principles of astronomy*, ed., trans. and comm. Bernard R. Goldstein, 2 vols., New Haven and London, 1971.

Dallal, Ahmad, *An Islamic response to Greek astronomy:* Kitāb taʿdīl al-aflāk *of Ṣadr al-Sharīʿa*, Leiden, Cologne and Boston, 1995.

Djebbar, Ahmed, and Roshdi Rashed (eds., trans. and comm.), *L'oeuvre algébrique d'al-Khayyām*, Aleppo, 1981.

al-Fārābī, *Iḥṣā' al-ʿulūm*, ed. ʿUthmān Amīn, 2nd edn, Cairo, 1949.

Ibn al-Haytham, *al-Shukūk ʿalā Baṭlamyūs*, ed. A. I. Sabra and Nabil Shehaby, Cairo, 1971.

Ibn al-Nadīm, *Kitāb al-fihrist*, ed. Gustav Flügel, 2 vols., Cairo, 1929–30; trans. Bayard Dodge as *The* Fihrist *of al-Nadim*, 2 vols., New York, 1970.

Ibn al-Zarqālluh, *al-Shakkāziyya*, ed., trans. and comm. Roser Puig, Barcelona, 1986.

al-Jazarī, *The book of knowledge of ingenious mechanical devices: Kitāb fī maʿrifat al-ḥiyal al-handasiyya*, trans. Donald R. Hill, Dordrecht, London and New York, 1973.

al-Kindī, *al-Kindī's* Metaphysics*: A translation of Yaʿqūb ibn Isḥāq al-Kindī's treatise 'On first philosophy' (*Fī al-falsafah al-ūlā*)*, trans. with introd. and comm. Alfred L. Ivry, Studies in Islamic Philosophy and Science, Albany, 1974.

Luckey, Paul, 'Thabit b. Qurra über den geometrischen Richtigkeitsnachweis der Auflösung der quadratischen Gleichungen', in *Berichte über die Verhandlungen der Sächsischen Akademie der Wissenschaften zu Leipzig*, Mathematisch-physikalische Klasse 93, Heidelberg, 1941, 93–114.

Sabra, Abdelhamid I., *The optics of Ibn al-Haytham*, books I–III, book 2: *On direct vision* (with introduction, commentary, glossaries, concordance, indices), 2 vols., London, 1989.

Sesiano, Jacques, *Un traité médiéval sur les carrés magiques: De l'arrangement harmonieux des nombres*, Lausanne, 1996.

al-Sijzī, *Treatise on geometrical problem solving: Kitāb fī tashīl al-subul li-istikhrāj al-ashkāl al-handasiyya*, ed., trans. and comm. Jan P. Hogendijk, and Persian trans. Mohammad Bagheri, Tehran, 1996.

Witkam, Jan Just, *De Egyptische Arts Ibn al-Akfānī*, Leiden, 1989.

Secondary sources

Abattouy, Mohammed, *The Arabic tradition of the science of weights and balances: A report on an ongoing research project*, Max Planck Institute for the History of Science, 2002, Preprint 227.

Allsen, Thomas T., 'Biography of a cultural broker: Bolad Ch'eng-Hsiang in China and Iran', in Julian Raby and Teresa Fitzherbert (eds.), *The court of the Il-Khans 1290–1340*, Oxford, 1994, 7–22.

Balty-Guesdon, Marie-Génèvieve, 'Le Bayt al-Ḥikma de Baghdad', *Arabica*, 39 (1992), 131–50.

Berggren, J. Lennart, and Glen van Brummelen, 'The role and development of geometric analysis and synthesis in ancient Greece and medieval Islam', in Patrick Suppes, Julius M. Moravcsik and Henry Mendell (eds.), *Ancient and medieval traditions in the exact sciences: Essays in memory of Wilbur Knorr*, Stanford, 2001, 1–31.

Brentjes, Sonja, 'Pride and prejudice: Some factors that shaped early modern (scholarly) encounters between "Western Europe" and the "Middle East"', in John Brooke and Ekmeleddin İhsanoğlu (eds.), *Religious values and the rise of science in Europe*, Istanbul, 2005, 229–54.

Charette, François, *Mathematical instrumentation in fourteenth-century Egypt and Syria: The illustrated treatise of Najm al-Dīn al-Miṣrī*, Leiden, 2003.

Comes, Mercè, 'Ibn al-Hā'im's trepidation model', *Suhayl*, 2 (2001), 291–408.

Dold-Samplonius, Yvonne, 'Calculating surface areas and volumes in Islamic architecture', in Jan P. Hogendijk and Abdelhamid I. Sabra (eds.), *The enterprise of science in Islam: New perspectives*, Cambridge, MA, and London, 2003, 237–65.

Goodrich, Thomas D., *The Ottoman Turks and the New World. A study of Tarih-i Hind-i Garbi and sixteenth-century Ottoman Americana*, Wiesbaden, 1990.

Günergun, Feza, 'Science in the Ottoman world', in G. N. Vlahakis, I. M. Malaquias, N. M. Brooks, F. Regourd, F. Günergun and D. Wright (eds.), *Imperialism and science: Social impact and interaction*, Santa Barbara, 2006, 71–118, 264–78, 350–6.

Habib, S. Irfan and Dhruv Raina (eds.), *Situating the history of science: Dialogues with Joseph Needham*, Delhi, 1999.

Hagen, Gottfried, *Ein osmanischer Geograph bei der Arbeit: Entstehung und Gedankenwelt von Kātib Čelebis Gihānnumā*, Studien zur Sprache, Geschichte und Kultur der Turkvölker 4, Berlin, 2003.

Halm, Heinz, *The Fatimids and their traditions of learning*, London, 1997.

Hogendijk, Jan P., 'Greek and Arabic constructions of the regular heptagon', *Archive for History of Exact Sciences*, 30 (1984), 197–330.

'How trisections of the angle were transmitted from Greek to Islamic geometry', *Historia Mathematica*, 8 (1981), 417–38.

Høyrup, Jens, 'al-Khwārizmī, Ibn Turk, and the *Liber mensurationum*: On the origins of Islamic algebra', *Erdem*, 5 (1986), 445–84.

Kennedy, E. S., 'A survey of Islamic astronomical tables', *Transactions of the American Philosophical Society*, n.s. 46, 2 (1956).

King, David A., *In synchrony with the heavens: Studies in astronomical timekeeping and instrumentation in Islamic civilization*, 2 vols., Boston and Leiden, 2004–5.

Lentz, Thomas W., and Glenn D. Lowry (eds.), *Timur and the princely vision: Persian art and culture in the fifteenth century*, Los Angeles, 1989.

Morrison, Robert, *Islam and science: The intellectual career of Niẓām al-Dīn al-Nīsābūrī*, London and New York, 2007.

Pingree, David, 'The Greek influence on early Islamic mathematical astronomy', *JAOS*, 103 (1973), 32–43.

Ragep, F. Jamil, 'Freeing astronomy from philosophy: An aspect of Islamic influence on science', *Osiris*, n.s. 16 (2001), 49–71.

'Ṭūsī and Copernicus: The Earth's motion in context', *Science in Context*, 14 (2001), 145–63.

Rashed, Roshdi, *The development of Arabic mathematics: Between arithmetic and algebra*, London, 1994.

Rashed, Roshdi, and Hélène Bellosta, *Ibrāhīm ibn Sīnān: Logique et géométrie au Xe siècle*, Leiden, Boston and Cologne, 2000.

Reichmuth, Stefan, 'Islamic reformist discourse in the Tulip Period (1718–1730): Ibrahim Müteferriqa and his arguments for printing', in Ali Çaksu (ed.), *International Congress on Learning and Education in the Ottoman World, Istanbul, 12–15 April 1999: Proceedings*, Istanbul, 2001, 149–61.

Sabra, Abdelhamid I., 'Science and philosophy in medieval Islamic theology: The evidence of the fourteenth century', *ZGAIW*, 9 (1994), 1–42.

Saliba, George, 'Astronomy and astrology in medieval Arabic thought', in Roshdi Rashed and Joël Biard (eds.), *Les doctrines de la science de l'antiquité à l'âge classique*, Leuven, 1999, 131–64.

'Early Arabic critique of Ptolemaic cosmology: A ninth-century text on the motion of the celestial spheres', *Journal for the History of Astronomy*, 25 (1994), 115–43.

Sezgin, Fuat, *Geschichte des Arabischen Schrifttums*, vols. X–XII: *Mathematische Geographie und Kartographie im Islam und ihr Fortleben im Abendland*, Frankfurt am Main, 2000.

Chapter 23: Occult sciences and medicine

Practical suggestions for further reading

Brockopp, J., and T. Rich, *Muslim medical ethics: From theory to practice*, Columbia, SC, 2008.

Bürgel, J. Christoph, *Feathers of simurgh: The 'licit magic' of the arts in medieval Islam*, New York, 1988.

Burnett, C. S. F., 'Arabic, Greek and Latin works on astrological magic attributed to Aristotle', in J. Kraye, W. F. Ryan and C. B. Schmitt (eds.), *Pseudo-Aristotle in the Middle Ages*, London, 1986, 84–96.

Farooqi, M. I. H., *Medicinal plants in the traditions of Prophet Muhammad: Medicinal, aromatic and food plants mentioned in the traditions of Prophet Muhammad (SAAS)*, Lucknow, 1998.

Haq, S. Nomanul, *Names, natures and things: The alchemist Jābir ibn Ḥayyān and his* Kitāb al-aḥjār, Dordrecht, Boston and London, 1994.

Ibn Qayyim al-Jauziyya, *Medicine of the Prophet*, trans. P. Johnstone, Cambridge, 1988.

Ispahany, B. (trans.), *Islamic medical wisdom: The* Ṭibb al-a'imma, ed. A. Newman, London, 1991.

Khan, M. S., *Islamic medicine*, London, 1986.

Lory, P. (trans.), *Dix traits d'alchimie: Les dix premiers traités du* Livre des soixante-dix *Jābir ibn Ḥayyān*, Paris, 1996.

Needham, J., 'Arabic alchemy in rise and fall', in J. Needham, *Science and civilisation in China*, vol. V, part 4, Cambridge, 1980, 389–408.

O'Connor, K., 'The alchemical creation of life (takwin) and other concepts of Genesis in medieval Islam', Ph.D. thesis, University of Pennsylvania, 1994.

Pormann, E., and E. Savage-Smith, *Medieval Islamic medicine*, Edinburgh, 2007.

Rosenthal, F., *Science and medicine in Islam: A collection of essays*, Aldershot, 1990.

Savage-Smith, E., *Science, tools and magic*, London, 1997.

(ed.), *Magic and divination in early Islam*, Aldershot, 2004.

Savage-Smith, E., and M. Smith, *Islamic geomancy and a thirteenth-century divinatory device*, Malibu, 1980.

Ullmann, M., *Islamic medicine*, Edinburgh, 1978.

Weisser, U., *Das 'Buch über das Geheimnis der Schöpfung' von pseudo-Apollonios von Tyana*, Berlin, 1980.

Primary sources

'Abd al-Raḥmān al-Azraq, *Tashīl al-manāfi'*, Cairo, 1963.

Abū Ma'shar al-Balkhī, *The abbreviations of the introduction to astrology, together with the medieval translation of Adelard of Bath*, ed. and trans. C. S. F. Burnett and K. Yamamoto, Leiden, 1994.

al-Bukhārī, Abū 'Abd Allāh, *al-Jāmi' al-ṣaḥīḥ*, ed. L. Krehl and T. W. Juynboll, 9 vols., Cairo, 1958.

al-Dhahabī, Abū 'Abd Allāh Muḥammad, *al-Ṭibb al-nabawī*, Cairo, 1961.

al-Ghazālī, Abū Ḥāmid, *Iḥyā' 'ulūm al-dīn*, 2 vols., Damascus, 1939.

Ḥājjī Khalīfa, *Kashf al-ẓunūn*, ed. G. Flügel, 7 vols., London, 1835–58.

Ibn Khaldūn, *Muqaddima* Cairo, n.d.

The Muqaddimah*: An introduction to history*, trans. F. Rosenthal, 3 vols., London, 1967.

Ibn Khallikān, *Kitāb wafayāt al-a'yān*, trans. Baron de Slant, 4 vols., Paris, 1842–71.

Ibn Nafīs, *Kitāb sharḥ tashrīḥ al-qānūn*, ed. S. Qaṭāyah and B. Ghaliyūnjī, Cairo, 1988.

Ibn Qayyim al-Jawziyya, *al-Ṭibb al-nabawī*, Cairo, 1978.

Ikhwān al-Ṣafā', *Rasā'il Ikhwān al-Ṣafā' wa khullān al-wafā'*, 4 vols., Beirut, 1957.

al-'Irāqī, Abu 'l-Qāsim Muḥammad ibn Aḥmad, *Kitāb al-'ilm al-muktasab fī zirā'at al-dhahab*, trans. E. J. Holmyard, Paris, 1923.

Jābir ibn Ḥayyān, *Kitāb al-aḥjār 'alā ra'y Balīnās*, ed. and trans. S. N. Haq in *Names, natures and things*, Dordrecht, Boston and London, 1994.

L'élaboration de l'élixir suprême: Quatorze traités de Ǧābir ibn Hayyān sur le grand œuvre alchimique, ed. P. Lory, Damascus, 1988.

Muslim ibn al-Ḥajjāj, *Ṣaḥīḥ*, ed. M. ʿAbd al-Bāqī, 5 vols., Cairo, 1955–6.

Pseudo-Apollonius of Tyana, *Kitāb sirr al-khalīqa wa-ṣanʿat al-ṭabīʿa*, ed. U. Weisser, Aleppo, 1979.

Ptolemy, *Ptolemy's Tetrabiblos, or Quadripartite: Being four books of the influence of the stars. Newly translated from the Greek paraphrase of Proclus. With a preface, explanatory notes, and an appendix, containing extracts from the Almagest of Ptolemy, and the whole of his Centiloquy; together with a short notice of Mr Ranger's Zodiacal planisphere, and an explanatory plate*, London, 1822.

al-Rāzī, Abū Bakr ibn Zakariyyāʾ, *Kitāb al-ḥāwī fi'l-ṭibb*, parts 1–23, Hyderabad, 1955–71.

Kitāb sirr al-asrār, trans. J. Ruska as *Übersetzung und Bearbeitungen von al-Rāzī's* Buch Geheimnis der Geheminisse, Berlin, 1935.

Thaʿālabī, Aḥmad ibn Muḥammad ibn Ibrāhīm, *Qiṣaṣ al-anbiyāʾ*, Beirut, 1980.

Turba philosophorum (author unknown), trans. A. E. Waite as *The 'Turba philosophorum', or 'Assembly of the sages'*, London, 1896.

Secondary sources

Bosworth, C. E., E. van Donzel, W. P. Heinrichs and C. Pellat (eds.), 'Muʿawwidhatān', *EI2*, vol. VII, 269–70.

Brentjes, S., 'The location of ancient or "rational" sciences in Muslim educational landscapes', *Bulletin of the Royal Institute for Inter-Faith Studies*, 4 (2002), 47–71.

Carboni, S., and L. Komaroff (eds.), *The legacy of Genghis Khan: Courtly art and culture in western Asia 1256–1353*, New Haven, 2002.

Conrad, L., 'Arab-Islamic medicine', in W. F. Bynum and R. Porter (eds.), *Companion encyclopedia of the history of medicine*, London, 1993, 676–727.

'Medicine', in J. L. Esposito (ed.), *The Oxford encyclopedia of the modern Islamic world*, 4 vols., New York, 1995, vol. III, 84–9.

The Western medical tradition, 800 BC–1800 AD, Cambridge, 1995.

Corbin, H., *Creative imagination in the Sufism of Ibn ʿArabī*, Princeton, 1969.

Dobbs, B. J., *The Janus faces of genius: The role of alchemy in Newton's thought*, Cambridge, 1991.

Dols, M. W., 'The origins of the Islamic hospital: Myth and reality', *Bulletin of the History of Medicine*, 61 (1987), 367–90.

Fahd, T., *Anges, demons et djinns en Islam: Sources orientales*, vol. VIII, Paris, 1971.

La divination arabe, Paris, 1987.

'Siḥr', *EI2*, vol. IX, 567–71.

Festugière, A.-J., *La révélation d'Hermès Trismégiste*, 4 vols., Paris, 1944–54.

Fierro, M., 'Bāṭinism in al-Andalus: Maslama b. Qāsim al-Qurṭubī (d. 353/964), author of the Rutbat al-ḥakīm and the Ghāyat al-ḥakīm (Picatrix)', *SI*, 84 (1996), 87–112.

Fonahn, A., *Zur Quellenkunde der persischen Medizin*, Leipzig, 1910.

Goodman, L. E., 'al-Rāzī', *EI2*, vol. VIII, 474–7.

Graham, W. A., *Beyond the written word*, Cambridge, 1989.

Haq, S. Nomanul, 'Ṭabīʿa', *EI2*, vol. X, 25–8.

'Greek alchemy or Shīʿī metaphysics? A preliminary statement concerning Jābir ibn Ḥayyān's *ẓahir* and *bāṭin*', *Bulletin of the Royal Institute for Inter-Faith Studies*, 4 (Autumn/Winter 2002), 19–32.

Holmyard, E. J., *Alchemy*, London, 1957.

'Maslama al-Majrīṭī and the *Rutbat al-ḥakīm*', *Isis*, 6 (1924), 293–305.

Kraus, P., *Jābir ibn Ḥayyān, vol. I: Le corpus des écrits Jābiriens*, Cairo, 1943.

Jābir ibn Ḥayyān, vol. II: *Jābir et la science grecque*, Cairo, 1942.

Leiser, G., 'Medical education in Islamic lands from the seventh to the fourteenth century', *Journal of the History of Medicine and Allied Sciences*, 38 (1983), 48–75.

Lemay, R., 'L'Islam historique et les sciences occultes', *Bulletin d'Études Orientales de l'Institut Français de Damas*, 44 (1992), 19–32.

Lory, P., 'La magie chez les Ikhwān al-Ṣafāʾ', *Bulletin d'Études Orientales de l'Institut Français de Damas*, 44 (1992), 147–59.

Marquet, Y., 'La détermination astrale de l'évolution selon Frères de la Pureté', *Bulletin d'Études Orientales de l'Institut Français de Damas*, 44 (1992), 127–46.

Mieli, A., *La science arabe et son rôle dans l'évolution scientifique mondiale*, Leiden, 1966.

Murphy, R., 'Ottoman medicine and transculturalism from the sixteenth through the eighteenth century', *Bulletin of the History of Medicine*, 66 (1992), 376–403.

Newman, A., '*Tašrīḥ-i Manṣūrī*: Human anatomy between the Galenic and Prophetic traditions', in Ž. Vesel *et al.* (eds.), *La science dans le monde Iranien à l'époque islamique*, Tehran, 1998, 253–72.

Newman, W. R., 'The occult and the manifest among the alchemists', in F. J. Ragep and S. P. Ragep (eds.), *Tradition, transmission, transformation*, Leiden, 1996, 173–98.

Pingree, D., 'Abū Maʿshar', in C. D. Gillispie (ed.-in-chief), *Dictionary of scientific biography*, 18 vols., New York, 1970–80, vol. I, 32–9.

'al-Ṭabarī on the prayers to the planets', *Bulletin d'Études Orientales de l'Institut Français de Damas*, 44 (1992), 105–17.

Rahman, F., *Health and medicine in the Islamic tradition*, New York, 1987.

Major themes of the Qurʾān, Minneapolis, 1989.

Rattansi, P. M., 'The social interpretation of science in the seventeenth century', in P. Mathias (ed.), *Science and society, 1600–1900*, Cambridge, 1972, 1–32.

Razuq, F. R., 'Studies on the works of al-Ṭughrāʾī', inaugural dissertation, University of London, 1963.

Ruska, J., 'Die Alchemie al-Rāzī's', *Der Islam*, 22, 4 (1935), 281–319.

'Tabula smaragdina': Ein Beitrag zur Geschichte der hermetischen Literatur, Heidelberg, 1926.

'Turba philosophorum, ein Beitrag zur Geschichte der Alchimie', *Quellen und Studien zur Geschichte der Naturwissenschaft und der Medizin*, 1 (1932), 1–368.

Übersetzung und Bearbeitungen von al-Rāzī's Buch Geheimnis der Geheminisse, Berlin, 1935.

Sabra, A. I., 'Situating Arabic science: Locality versus essence', *Isis*, 87 (1996), 654–70.

Sari, N., and B. Zulfikar, 'The Paracelsusian [*sic*] influence on Ottoman medicine in the seventeenth and eighteenth centuries', in E. Ishanoğlu (ed.), *Transfer of modern science and technology to the Muslim world*, Istanbul, 1992, 168–9.

Savage-Smith, E., 'Attitudes toward dissection in medieval Islam', *Journal of the History of Medicine and Allied Sciences*, 50 (1995), 67–110.

Sezgin, F., *Geschichte der arabischen Schrifttums*, 9 vols., Leiden, 1967–84.

Sivin, N., 'Research on the history of Chinese alchemy', in Z. R. W. M. von Martels (ed.), *Alchemy revisited*, Leiden, 1990, 3–20.

Stapleton, H. E., and R. F. Azo, 'Alchemical equipment in the 11th century', *Memoirs of the Asiatic Society of Bengal*, 1 (1905), 47–93.

Taslimi, M., 'An examination of the *Nihāyat al-ṭalab* and the determination of its place and value in the history of Islamic chemistry', inaugural dissertation, University of London, 1954.

Tauer, F., 'Persian learned literature from its beginning to the end of the eighteenth century', in K. Jahn (ed.), *History of Iranian literature*, Dordrecht, 1968, 419–82.

Chapter 24: Literary and oral cultures

Practical suggestions for further reading

Beeston, A. F. L., T. M. Johnstone, R. B. Serjeant and G. R. Smith (eds.), *The Cambridge history of Arabic literature*, vol. I: *Arabic literature to the end of the Umayyad period*, Cambridge, 1984.

Berkey, Jonathan P., *Popular preaching and religious authority in the medieval Islamic Near East*, Seattle and London, 2001.

Blair, Sheila S., *Islamic calligraphy*, Edinburgh, 2006.

Islamic inscriptions, Edinburgh, 1998.

Bloom, Jonathan M., *Paper before print: The history and impact of paper in the Islamic world*, New Haven, 2001.

Cook, Michael A., 'The opponents of the writing of tradition in early Islam', *Arabica*, 44 (1997), 437–530.

DeYoung, Teri, 'Arabic language and Middle East / North African language studies', available at www.indiana.edu/~arabic/arabic_history.htm, accessed September 2004.

Eche, Youssef, *Les bibliothèques arabes publiques et semi-publiques en Mésopotamie, en Syrie et en Égypte au moyen âge*, Damascus, 1967.

Graham, William A., *Beyond the written word: Oral aspects of scripture in the history of religion*, New York, 1993.

Gruendler, Beatrice, *The development of the Arabic scripts: From the Nabatean era to the first Islamic century according to dated texts*, Harvard Semitic Series, Atlanta, 1993.

Hanna, Nelly, *In praise of books: A cultural history of Cairo's middle class, sixteenth to the eighteenth century*, Middle East Studies Beyond Dominant Paradigms, Syracuse, 2003.

Makdisi, George, *The rise of colleges: Institutions of learning in Islam and the West*, Edinburgh, 1981.

Schoeler, Gregor, *Écrire et transmettre dans le début de l'islam*, Paris, 2002.

Shoshan, Boaz, 'On popular literature in medieval Cairo', *Poetics Today*, 14, 2 (Summer 1993), 349–65.

Tyan, Emile, *Le notariat et le régime de la preuve par écrit dans la pratique du droit musulman*, Beirut, 1959.

Wakin, Jeanette A., *The function of documents in Islamic law*, Albany, 1972.

Secondary sources

Abbott, Nabia, 'A ninth-century fragment of the "Thousand Nights": New light on the early history of the *Arabian Nights*', *JNES*, 8, 3 (1949), 129–64.

Bellamy, James A., 'A new reading of the Namārah inscription', *JAOS*, 105, 1 (1985), 31–48.

Bosch, Gulnar, John Carswell and Guy Petherbridge, *Islamic bindings and bookmaking*, Chicago, 1981 (exhibition catalogue).

Encyclopaedia of the Qu'rān, gen. ed. Jane Dammen McAuliffe, Leiden, 2001.

Frantz-Murphy, Gladys, 'Arabic papyrology and Middle Eastern studies', *Middle East Studies Association Bulletin*, 19, 1 (July 1985), 34–48.

Goitein, S. D., *A Mediterranean society: The Jewish communities of the Arab world as portrayed in the documents of the Cairo Geniza*, 6 vols., Berkeley and Los Angeles, 1967–93.

Goldziher, Ignaz, *Muslim studies (Muhammedanische Studien)*, ed. S. M. Stern, trans. C. R. Barber and S. M. Stern, 2 vols., Chicago and London, 1971.

Ibn Ḥawqal, Abu 'l-Qāsim, *Kitāb ṣūrat al-arḍ*, ed. J. H. Kramers, Bibliotheca Geographorum Arabicorum, Leiden, 1967 [1938].

Jones, A. 'The Qur'ān-II', in A. F. L. Beeston, T. M. Johnstone, R. B. Serjeant and G. R. Smith (eds.), *The Cambridge history of Arabic literature*, vol. I: *Arabic literature to the end of the Umayyad period*, Cambridge, 1984, 228–45.

'The dotting of a script and the dating of an era: The strange neglect of PERF 558', *Islamic Culture*, 72, 4 (October 1998), 95–103.

Kessler, Christel, ''Abd al-Malik's inscription in the Dome of the Rock: A reconsideration', *JRAS*, 3 (1970), 2–14.

Mernissi, Fatima, *Dreams of trespass: Tales of a harem girlhood*, Reading, MA, 1995.

al-Nadim, *The Fihrist of al-Nadīm: A tenth-century survey of Muslim culture*, ed. and trans. Bayard Dodge, New York and London, 1970.

Pedersen, Johannes, *The Arabic book: With an introduction by Robert Hillenbrand*, trans. Geoffrey French, Princeton, 1984 [1946].

Powers, David S., 'The Maliki family endowment: Legal norms and social practices', *IJMES*, 25, 3 (1993), 379–406.

Rāġib, Yusuf, 'Un contrat de mariage sur soie d'Egypte fatimide', *AI*, 16 (1980), 31–7.

Sadie, Stanley (ed.), *The new Grove dictionary of music and musicians*, 20 vols., London, 1980.

Schacht, Joseph, *An introduction to Islamic law*, Oxford, 1966 [1964].

Stewart, Devin J., 'Popular Shiism in medieval Egypt: Vestiges of Islamic sectarian polemics in Egyptian Arabic', *SI*, 84, 2 (November 1996), 35–66.

Walker, Paul E., 'Fatimid institutions of learning', *Journal of the American Research Center in Egypt*, 34 (1997), 179–200.

Chapter 25: Art and architecture

Practical suggestions for further reading

Blair, Sheila, and Jonathan Bloom, *The art and architecture of Islam, 1250–1800*, New Haven and London, 1994.

Ettinghausen, Richard, Oleg Grabar and Marilyn Jenkins-Madina, *Islamic art and architecture, 650–1250*, New Haven and London, 2001.

Frishman, Martin, and Hasan-uddin Khan (eds.), *The mosque: History, architectural development and regional diversity*, London, 1994.

Hillenbrand, Robert, *Islamic architecture: Form, function and meaning*, Edinburgh and New York, 1994.

Islamic art and architecture, London, 1999.

Irwin, Robert, *Islamic art*, London, 1997.

Michell, George (ed.), *Architecture of the Islamic world: Its history and social meaning*, New York, 1978.

Primary sources

Ibn Khaldūn, ʿAbd al-Raḥmān ibn Muḥammad, *The* Muqaddimah*: An introduction to history*, trans. Franz Rosenthal, 3 vols., New York, 1958.

Secondary sources

Album, Steve, and Tony Goodwin, *The pre-reform coinage of the early Islamic period*, Sylloge of Islamic Coins in the Ashmolean 1, London, 2002.

Ali, Zakaria, *Islamic art in Southeast Asia, 830 AD–1570 AD*, Kuala Lumpur, 1994.

Allan, James, *Islamic metalwork: The Nuhad es-Said collection*, London, 1982.

'Muhammad ibn al-Zain: Craftsman in cups, thrones and window grilles?', *Levant*, 28 (1996), 199–208.

Asher, Catherine, *The Cambridge history of India, vol. I.4: Architecture of Mughal India*, Cambridge, 1992.

Atasoy, Nurhan, and Julian Raby, *Iznik: The pottery of Ottoman Turkey*, London, 1989.

Atil, Esin, *Renaissance of Islam: Art of the Mamluks*, Washington, DC, 1981.

Baer, Eva, *Ayyubid metalwork with Christian images*, Leiden, 1989.

Bahari, Ebadollah, *Behzad: Master of Persian painting*, London, 1996.

Bernsted, Anne-Marie, *Early Islamic pottery: Materials and techniques*, London, 2003.

Blair, Sheila, *Islamic inscriptions*, New York, 1998.

Bloom, Jonathan, *Minaret: Symbol of Islam*, Oxford Studies in Islamic Art 7, Oxford and New York, 1989.

Paper before print: The history and impact of paper in the Islamic world, New Haven and London, 2001.

Caiger-Smith, Alan, *Lustre pottery: Technique, tradition and innovation in Islam and the Western world*, London, 1985.

Carboni, Stefano, and David Whitehouse (eds.), *Glass of the sultans*, New York, 2002.

Carswell, John, *Blue and white: Chinese porcelain around the world*, London, 2000.

Collins, Minta, *Medieval herbals: The illustrative traditions*, London and Toronto, 2000.

Contadini, Anna, *Fatimid art at the Victoria and Albert Museum*, London, 1998.

Costa, Paolo, *Historic mosques and shrines of Oman*, BAR International Series 938, Oxford, 2001.

Creswell, K., *Early Muslim architecture*, rev. edn, 2 vols., Oxford, 1969.

A short account of early Muslim architecture, rev. James Allan, Aldershot, 1989.

Curtis, John (ed.), *Mesopotamia and Iran in the Parthian and Sasanian periods: Rejection and revival, c.238 BC–AD 642*, London, 2000.

Déroche, François, *The Abbasid tradition: Qurʾāns of the 8th to the 10th centuries AD*, Nasser D. Khalili Collection of Islamic Art 1, London, 1992.

Dodds, Jerrilyn (ed.), *al-Andalus: The art of Islamic Spain*, New York, 1992.

El Cheikh, Nadia, *Byzantium viewed by the Arabs*, Cambridge, MA, and London, 2004.
Ettinghausen, Richard, *Arab painting*, Geneva, 1962.
From Byzantium to Sasanian Iran and the Islamic world: Three modes of artistic influence, Leiden, 1972.
Flood, Finbarr B., *The Great Mosque of Damascus: On the makings of an Umayyad visual culture*, Leiden, 2001.
Golombek, Lisa, Robert Mason and Gauvin Bailey, *Tamerlane's tableware: A new approach to chinoiserie ceramics of fifteenth- and sixteenth-century Iran*, Costa Mesa, 1996.
Goodwin, Godfrey, *A history of Ottoman architecture*, London, 1971.
Grabar, Oleg, *The Alhambra*, Cambridge, MA, 1978.
The formation of Islamic art, rev. edn, New Haven and London, 1987.
The Great Mosque of Isfahan, New York, 1990.
The illustrations of the Maqamat, Chicago, 1984.
Mostly miniatures: An introduction to Persian painting, Princeton, 2000.
Grabar, Oleg, and Sheila Blair, *Epic images and contemporary history: The illustrations of the Great Mongol Shah-nama*, Chicago, 1980.
Gray, Basil, *Persian painting*, Cleveland, 1961.
Grube, Ernst (ed.), *Cobalt and lustre: The first centuries of Islamic pottery*, Nasser D. Khalili Collection of Islamic Art 9, London, 1994.
Guthrie, Shirley, *Arab social life in the Middle Ages: An illustrated study*, London, 1995.
al-Harithy, Howyda, 'The complex of sultan Hasan in Cairo: Reading between the lines', *Muqarnas*, 13 (1996), 68–79.
Hillenbrand, Robert, 'La *dolce vita* in early Islamic Syria', *Art History*, 5 (1982), 1–35.
(ed.), *Persian painting from the Mongols to the Qajars: Studies in honour of B. W. Robinson*, London and New York, 2000.
Hoffman, Eva, 'The author portrait in thirteenth-century Arabic manuscripts: A new Islamic context for a Late Antique tradition', *Muqarnas*, 10 (1993), 6–20.
Hoyland, Robert, *Arabia and the Arabs from the Bronze Age to the coming of Islam*, London and New York, 2001.
James, David, *Qur'āns of the Mamluks*, London, 1988.
Jenkins, Marilyn, 'Mamluk underglaze painted pottery: Foundations for further study', *Muqarnas*, 2 (1984), 95–114.
Johns, Jeremy, 'The rise of Middle Islamic hand-made geometrically-painted ware in Bilâd al-Shâm (11th–13th centuries AD)', in Roland-Pierre Gayraud (ed.), *Colloque international d'archéologie islamique*, Cairo, 1988, 65–93.
(ed.), *Bayt al-Maqdis: Jerusalem and early Islam*, Oxford Studies in Islamic Art 9.2, Oxford, 1999.
Kiel, Machiel, *Studies on the Ottoman architecture of the Balkans*, Aldershot, 1990.
King, Geoffrey, 'The mosque of Bab Mardum', *Art and Archaeology Research Papers*, 2 (1972), 29–40.
Komaroff, Linda, and Stefano Carboni (eds.), *The legacy of Genghis Khan: Courtly art and culture in Western Asia, 1256–1353*, New Haven and London, 2002.
Lane, Arthur, *Early Islamic pottery*, London, 1947.
Later Islamic pottery, London, 1957.
Marçais, George, *Les faiences à reflets métalliques de la grande moschée de Kairouan*, Paris, 1928.
Miles, George (ed.), *Archaeologica orientalia in memoriam Ernst Herzfeld*, Locust Valley, NY, 1952.

Neçipoğlu, Gülru, *Architecture, ceremonial and power: The Topkapi palace in the fifteenth and sixteenth centuries*, New York and Cambridge, MA, 1991.
'From international Timurid to Ottoman: A change in taste in sixteenth-century ceramic tiles', *Muqarnas*, 7 (1990), 136–70.
The Topkapi scroll: Geometry and ornament in Islamic architecture, Santa Monica, 1995.
(ed.), *Pre-modern Islamic Palaces, Ars Orientalis*, 23 (special issue) (1993).
Pinder-Wilson, Ralph, 'Ghaznavid and Ghūrid minarets', *Iran*, 39 (2001), 155–86.
Piotrovsky, Michael, and J. Michael Rogers (eds.), *Heaven on earth: Art from Islamic lands: Works from the State Hermitage Museum and the Khalili Collection*, Munich and Berlin, 2004.
Pope, Arthur U. (ed.), *Survey of Persian art from prehistoric times to the present*, 12 vols., London and New York, 1938–9.
Potts, D. T., 'Arabia: Pre-Islamic', in Jane Turner (ed.), *The Grove dictionary of art*, 34 vols., New York, 1996, vol. II, 246–75.
Prado-Vilar, Francisco, 'Circular visions of fertility and punishment: Caliphal ivory caskets from al-Andalus', *Muqarnas*, 14 (1997), 19–42.
Qaddūmī, Ghāda al-Hijjāwī (trans.), *The book of gifts and rarities: Kitāb al-hadāyā wa al-tuḥaf*, Cambridge, MA, 1996.
Raby, Julian (ed.), *The art of Syria and the Jazīra, 1100–1250*, Oxford Studies in Islamic Art 1, Oxford, 1985.
Raby, Julian, and Jeremy Johns (eds.), *Bayt al-Maqdis: 'Abd al-Malik's Jerusalem*, Oxford Studies in Islamic Art 9.1, Oxford and New York, 1992.
Robinson, Chase (ed.), *A medieval Islamic city reconsidered: Interdisciplinary approaches to Samarra*, Oxford Studies in Islamic Art 14, Oxford and New York, 2001.
Rosen-Ayalon, Miriam, *The early Islamic monuments of the Ḥaram al-Sharīf: An iconographic study*, Qedem 28, Jerusalem, 1989.
Roxburgh, David, *Prefacing the image: The writing of art history in sixteenth-century Iran*, Studies and Sources in Islamic Art and Architecture 9, Leiden and Boston, 2001.
Schlumberger, Daniel, *Lashkari Bazar: Une résidence royale ghaznévide et ghoride*, Paris, 1978.
Séguy, Marie-Rose, *The miraculous journey of Mahomet/Mirâj nâmeh*, New York, 1977.
Shalem, Avinoam, *Islam Christianized: Islamic portable objects in medieval church treasuries of the Latin West*, Ars Faciendi 7, Frankfurt am Main, 1996.
Shani, Raya, 'On the stylistic idiosyncracies of a Saljūq stucco workshop from the region of Kāshān', *Iran*, 27 (1989), 67–74.
Simpson, Marianna, 'The narrative structure of a medieval Iranian beaker', *Ars Orientalis*, 12 (1981), 15–24.
Sims, Eleanor, 'Towards a monograph on the 17th-century Iranian painter Muḥammad Zamān ibn Ḥājjī Yūsuf', *Islamic Art*, 5 (2001), 183–99.
Sims, Eleanor, Boris Marshak and Ernst Grube, *Peerless images: Persian painting and its sources*, New Haven and London, 2002.
Soucek, Priscilla (ed.), *Content and context of the visual arts in the Islamic world*, University Park, PA, and London, 1988.
Stronach, David, and T. Cuyler Young, 'Three Seljuq tomb towers', *Iran*, 4 (1966), 1–20.
Swietochowski, Marie, and Stefano Carboni (eds.), *Illustrated poetry and epic images: Persian painting of the 1330s and 1340s*, New York, 1994.
Tabbaa, Yasser, *The transformation of Islamic art during the Sunni revival*, London, 2001.
Topkapi Museum, *The sultan's portrait: Picturing the house of Osman*, Istanbul, 2000.

Van Reenan, D.,'The *Bilderverbot*, a new survey', *Der Islam*, 67 (1990), 27–77.

Volov (Golombek), Lisa, 'Plaited Kufic on Samanid epigraphic pottery', *Ars Orientalis*, 6 (1966), 107–34.

Ward, Rachel, *Islamic metalwork*, London, 1993.

Watson, Oliver, *Persian lustre ware*, London and Boston, 1985.

Welch, Stuart C., *A king's book of kings: The Shah-nameh of Shah Tahmasp*, New York, 1972.

Whelan, Estelle, 'On the origins of the *miḥrāb mujawwaf*: A reinterpretation', *IJMES*, 18 (1986), 205–23.

Whitworth Art Gallery, *The Qashqā'i of Iran*, Manchester, 1976.

Wulff, Hans, *The traditional crafts of Persia: Their development, technology and influence on Eastern and Western civilizations*, Cambridge, MA, 1966.

Chapter 26: Music

Practical suggestions for further reading

Bencheikh, J. E., 'Les musiciens et la poésie: Les écoles d'Isḥāq al-Mawṣilī et d'Ibrāhīm ibn al-Mahdī, *Arabica*, 22 (1975), 114–52.

Farmer, H. G., *Historical facts for the Arabian musical influence*, London, 1970 (repr.) [1930].

Faruqi, L. I., *An annotated glossary of Arabic musical terms*, Westport, 1981.

Godwin, J., *Music, mysticism and magic: A source book*, London and New York, 1986.

Poché, C., *La musique arabo-andalouse*, Paris, 1995.

Shiloah, A., *Music and its virtues in Islamic and Judaic writings*, Variorum Collected Studies Series CS 875, Aldershot, 2007.

Music in the world of Islam, Aldershot and Detroit, 1995; repr. 2000.

Wright, O., 'Music in Muslim Spain', in Salma Khadra Jayyusi (ed.), *The legacy of Muslim Spain*, Leiden, 1992, 555–79.

Primary sources

Cowl, Carl, and Sheila M. Craik, *Henry George Farmer: A bibliography*, Glasgow, 1999.

Erlanger, R. D. (trans.), *La musique arabe*, 6 vols., Paris, 1930–9: see esp. vol. I: al-Fārābī, *Kitāb al-mūsīqī al-kabīr*, books I–II, 1930; vol. II: *al-Fārābī ... livre III et Avicenne ... Kitāb al-shifā'*; vol. III: Ṣafī al-dīn al-Urmawī: part 1, *ash-Sharafiyya*, part 2, *Kitāb al-adwār*; vol. IV: part 1, *Traité anonyme dédié au sultan Osmanli Muḥammad II* (XV s.), part 2, al-Lādhiqī, *Traité* al-fatḥiyya (XVI s.), 1939.

al-Fārābī, Abū Naṣr, *Kitāb al-mūsīqī al-kabīr*, ed. E. Neubauer, Frankfurt am Main, 1998.

Farmer, H. G., 'Greek theorists of music in Arabic translation', *Isis* (1929–30), 325–33.

(ed. and trans.), *The organ of the ancients from eastern sources*, London, 1931.

al-Hujwīrī, 'Alī, *The Kashf al-maḥjūb, the oldest treatise on Sufism by al-Hujwīrī*, trans. R. A. Nicholson, Gibb Memorial Series 17, London, 1970 (repr.) [1911].

Ibn Khaldūn, 'The craft of singing', in *The* Muqaddimah *of Ibn Khaldūn*, trans. F. Rosenthal, vol. II, London, 1958, 399–405.

The Muqaddimah *of Ibn Khaldūn: An introduction to history*, trans. F. Rosenthal, 3 vols., London, 1958; repr. Princeton, 1967.

Ibn al-Ṭaḥḥān, *Ḥāwī al-funūn wa-salwat al-maḥzūn*, ed. E. I. Neubauer, Frankfurt, 1990.

Macdonald, D. B., 'Emotional religion in Islam as affected by music and singing: Being a translation of a book of the *Iḥyā' 'ulūm al-dīn* of al-Ghazzālī, with analysis, annotation and appendices', *JRAS* (1901), 195–252 and 705–48; (1902), 1–28.

Poché, C., and Jean Lambert, *Musiques du monde Arabe et Musulman: Bibliographie et discographie*, Paris, 2000.

Robson, J., (ed. and trans.), *Tracts on listening to music: Being* Dhamm al-malāhī *by Ibn Abī'l-Dunyā and* Bawāriq al-ilmā' *by Majd al-Dīn al-Ṭusī al-Ghazālī*, London, 1938.

Shiloah, A., (ed. and trans.), *The dimension of music in Islamic and Jewish culture*, Variorum Collected Studies Series CS 393, London, 1993.

The theory of music in Arabic writings (ca 900 to 1900), RISM Bx, vol. I, Munich, 1979; vol. II, Munich, 2003.

al-Shirwānī, Fatḥ Allāh, *Majalla fī'l-mūsīqī*, ed. E. I. Neubauer, facsimile of MS 3449, Topkapi, Istanbul, Series C, v. 26., Frankfurt am Main, 1984.

al-Urmawī, Ṣafī al-Dīn, *Kitāb al-adwār*, ed. E. I. Neubauer, facsimile of MS 3449, Topkapi, Istanbul, 1984.

al-Risala al-sharafiyya, ed. E. I. Neubauer, facsimile of MS 3460, Topkapi, Istanbul, 1984.

Wright, O., *The modal system of Arab and Persian music AD 1250–1300*, London, 1978.

Secondary sources

Barkeshli, M., *L'art sassanide base de la musique arabe*, Tehran, 1947.

Burnett, C., 'Teoria e pratica musicale arabe in Sicilia e nell'Italia meridionale in eta normanna e sveva', *Nuove effmeridi*, 11, 3 (1990), 79–89.

Chottin, A., *Tableau de la musique marocain*, Paris, 1999 (repr.) [1939].

During, Jean, *Musique et mystique dans les traditions de l'Iran*, Paris and Tehran, 1989.

El-Kholy, S., *The function of music in Islamic culture in the period up to 1100 AD*, Cairo, 1984.

El-Mellah, L., *Arabische Musik und Notenschrift*, Münchner Veröflentlichungen zur Musikgeschichte 53, Tutsig, 1996.

Elsner, J. (ed.), *Maqam-Raga-Zeilenmelodik: Materialen der 1. Arbeistagung der Study group 'maqam' beim International Council for Traditional Music, vom 28 Juni bis 2 Juli 1988 in Berlin*, Berlin, 1989.

Farhat, H., *The traditional music of Iran*, Tehran, 1973.

Farmer, H. G., *A history of Arabian music to the thirteenth century*, London, 1967 (repr.) [1929].

Faruqi, L. I., 'The cantillation of the Qur'ān', *Asian Music*, 19, 1 (1987), 2–25.

Hickmann, H., 'Die Musik des arabisch-islamischen Bereichs', in H. Hickmann and W. Stauder (eds.), *Orientalische Musik*, Leiden and Cologne, 1970, 1–134.

Qureshi-Burckhardt, R., *Sufi music of India and Pakistan: Sound, context and meaning in Qawwali*, New York, 1986.

Rajabi, V., and F. Karamatov, *Shashmakom*, Tashkent, 1966.

Rouanet, J., 'La musique arabe', in A. Lavignac (ed.), *Encyclopédie de la musique et dictionnaire du conservatoire*, Paris, 1922, part 1, vol. V, 2676–812.

'La musique arabe dans le Maghreb', in A. Lavignac (ed.), *Encyclopédie de la musique et dictionnaire du conservatoire*, Paris, 1922, part 1, vol. V, 2813–944.

Shehadi, F., *Philosophies of music in medieval Islam*, Leiden, 1995.

Yekta Bey, R., 'La musique Turque', in A. Lavignac (ed.), *Encyclopédie de la musique et dictionnaire du conservatoire*, Paris, 1922, part 1, vol. V, 2945–3064.

Chapter 27: Cookery

Practical suggestions for further reading

Davidson, Alan (ed.), *The Penguin companion to food*, London, 2002.
Halici, Nevin, *From 'sini' to the tray: Classical Turkish cuisine*, Istanbul, 1999.
Batmanglij, Najmieh, *New food for life*, Washington, DC, 1999.
Reejhsinghani, Aroona, *The great art of Mughlai cooking*, Ghaziabad, 1982.
Roden, Claudia, *A book of Middle Eastern food*, Harmondsworth, 1978.
Scott, Tom, *Traditional Arab cookery*, London, 1983.
Stobart, Tom, *The cook's encyclopaedia: Ingredients and processes*, London, 1980.

Primary sources

Anonymous, *La cocina hispano-magrebi en la epoca almohade segun un manuscrito anonimo*, ed. A. Huici Miranda, Madrid, 1965.
Kanz al-fawāʾid fī tanwīʿ al-mawāʾid, ed. Manuela Marín and David Waines, Beirut, 1993.
al-Baghdādī, Muḥammad ibn Ḥasan al-Kātib, *Kitāb al-ṭabīkh*, ed. Daoud Chelebi, Mosul, 1934; trans. A. J. Arberry as 'A Baghdad cookery book', *Islamic Culture*, 13 (1939), 21–47, 189–214.
Ibn ʿAbd Rabbihi, *al-ʿIqd al-farīd*, ed. Aḥmad Amīn *et al.*, 6 vols., Cairo, 1940.
Ibn al-ʿAdīm, *al-Wuṣla ila 'l-ḥabīb fī wasf al-ṭayyibāt wa 'l-ṭīb*, ed. S. Maḥjūb and D. al-Khaṭīb, Aleppo, 1988.
Ibn Qutayba, *ʿUyūn al-akhbār*, ed. Aḥmad Amīn, 2 vols., Cairo, 1925–30.
Ibn Razīn al-Tujībī, *Faḍālat al-khiwān fī ṭayyibāt al-ṭaʿām wa'l-alwān*, ed. Muḥammad b. Shaqrūn, Beirut, 1984.
Ibn al-Ukhuwwa, *Maʿālim al-qurba fī aḥkām al-ḥisba*, ed. Reuben Levy, London, 1938.
al-Warrāq, Ibn al-Sayyār, *Kitāb al-ṭabīkh*, ed. Kaj Ohrnberg and Sahban Mroueh, Helsinki, 1987.

Secondary sources

Marín, Manuela, and David Waines (eds.), *La alimentacion e las culturas islamicas*, Madrid, 1994.
Pellat, C., 'Khubz', *EI2*, vol. V, 41–3.
Rodinson, M., 'Ghidhāʾ', *EI2*, vol. II, 1057–72.
'Recherches sur les documents arabes relatifs à la cuisine', *Revue des études islamiques* (1949), 95–165.
Waines, David, 'Agriculture and vegetation', *Encyclopaedia of the Qur'ān*, vol. I, 40–50.
'Food and drink', *Encyclopaedia of the Qur'ān*, vol. II, 216–23.
'Maṭbakh', *EI2*, vol. VI, 807–9.
'Ṭabkh', *EI2*, vol. X, 30–2.
(ed), *Patterns of everyday life*, Aldershot, 2002.
Zubaida, Sami, and Richard Tapper (eds.), *Culinary cultures in the Middle East*, London, 1994.

Index

NOTES

1. The Arabic definite article (*al-*), the transliteration symbols for the Arabic letters *hamza* (ʾ) and *ʿayn* (ʿ), and distinctions between different letters transliterated by the same Latin character (e.g. *d* and *ḍ*) are ignored for purposes of alphabetisation.
2. In the case of personal names sharing the same first element, rulers are listed first, then individuals with patronymics, then any others.
3. Locators in italics denote illustrations.